Borgo Family Histories
ISSN 0733-6764
Number One

The House of the Burgesses

BEING A GENEALOGICAL HISTORY OF

William Burgess of Richmond (later King George) County, Virginia,
His Son, Edward Burgess of Stafford (later King George) County, Virginia,

WITH THE DESCENDANTS IN THE MALE LINE OF EDWARD'S SONS:

Garner Burgess of Fauquier County, Virginia
William Burgess of Stafford County, Virginia
Edward Burgess, Jr. of Fauquier County, Virginia
Moses Burgess of Orange County, Virginia
Reuben Burgess of Rowan (later Davie) County, North Carolina

Second Edition
Revised and Expanded

BY

Michael Burgess

WITH Mary Wickizer Burgess

1994
BURGESS AND WICKIZER
San Bernardino, California
DISTRIBUTED BY THE BORGO PRESS

THE BORGO PRESS
Publishers Since 1975
Post Office Box 2845
San Bernardino, CA 92406
United States of America

* * * * * * * *

 Printed in the United States of America by Van Volumes, Ltd. Cover design by Highpoint Type & Graphics.

Library of Congress Cataloging-in-Publication Data

Burgess, Michael, 1948-
The house of the Burgesses / by Michael Burgess with Mary Wickizer Burgess. — 2nd ed., rev. and expanded.
p. cm. — (Borgo family histories, ISSN 0733-6764 ; no. 1)
"Being a genealogical history of William Burgess of Richmond (later King George) County, Virginia, his son, Edward Burgess of Stafford (later King George) County, Virginia, with the descendants in the male line of Edward's sons: Garner Burgess of Fauquier County, Virginia, William Burgess of Stafford County, Virginia, Edward Burgess Jr. of Fauquier County, Virginia, Moses Burgess of Orange County, Virginia, Reuben Burgess of Rowan (later Davie) County, North Carolina.
Includes bibliographical references and index.
ISBN 0-89370-379-6 (cloth). — ISBN 0-89370-479-2 (pbk.)
1. Burgess family. I. Burgess, Mary Wickizer, 1938- . II. Title. III. Series.
CS71.B955 1994 87-6316
929'.2'0973—dc19 CIP

SECOND EDITION

CONTENTS

EDWARD BURGESS, JR.—THE THIRD BRANCH

MOSES BURGESS—THE FOURTH BRANCH

REUBEN BURGESS—THE FIFTH BRANCH

INTRODUCTION

This book is a guide to the descendants of one man: William Burges of Richmond (later King George) County, Virginia, who died in April of 1712 on his farm in northeastern Virginia. Eleven years ago, when the first edition of this genealogy was published, I naively believed that it was the last word on the subject, that very little should or could be added to my basic work. No one could have been more surprised than I to find the book taking on a life of its own. This second edition of the Burgess genealogy is ten times larger than the original, and better organized and presented, with the number of direct, name-line descendants of William Burges doubling from 2,400 individuals in the earlier book to 4,690 here, and the total number of descendants now exceeding 25,100. One major new branch of the family, the line of Edward Burgess Jr., has been added, and I have refined, corrected, and updated the original data to strengthen the roots from which all of our families sprout.

The origins of this volume can be traced to the summer of my sixteenth year, in 1964, when I first started asking my grandparents questions about our family. I found an antique Underwood in my grandmother's cellar, and meticulously typed out four sheets of data, two on my mother's family and two on my father's, all that they then knew about our past. I still have those original notes. Three years later I found my great-uncle, George O. Burgess, and the hunt was on. For three decades I have pursued this endless detective story with whatever time I could spare from my career. I was fortunate to locate other cousins who helped along the way, and was blessed to find my wife, Mary, who has shared my interest in genealogy and in so many other things.

The challenge is a deceptively simple one: to find every Burgess who has ever lived who is related to us. In recent years I have also become more concerned with the preservation of Burgess family heritage, having become acutely aware of how much has been lost over the past three centuries to indifference and the accidents of time. At one time *all* of the questions about the origins of the Burgess family could easily have been answered contemporaneously by any members of those families. No one thought such things were important enough to write down, or if they did put them on paper the documents have not survived to the present day. My primary intent with this genealogy is to recover whatever of our heritage still remains, and to preserve it by publishing it and disseminating it as widely as possible.

Of course, the further back one goes the less one finds, until finally the well runs completely dry. Some of the material in this book remains sketchy, particularly with generations prior to 1900, displaying very little of the real personalities of the men and women who were our ancestors; in most cases, nothing survives of these individuals beyond their names and dates. Whenever I've found some illuminating document or story, I've always tried to include them.

For present-day generations I have relied very heavily on the memories and records of living members of the family, supplemented by research in courthouses, archives, libraries, and cemeteries. I've been pleased by the almost universal cooperation I've received from distant cousins who couldn't possibly have known who I was; without their help, this book could never have been published. Much work remains to be done, of course, and more families need to be found or contacted. Some lines are incomplete because I've been unable to locate living descendants of these branches, others because I could not confirm that a specific individual died without heirs, or because I was unable to get a response from current descendants.

Additions and corrections can be sent to me at P.O. Box 2845, San Bernardino, CA 92406, or by fax to 909-888-4942, or via E-mail to "mburgess@wiley.csusb.edu".

HOW TO USE THIS BOOK

To find a specific family member, please look in the indexes at the end of this book. The first index lists those born with the name Burgess in alphabetical order by their full given names, with the page numbers where they appear in the text; the second index records unrelated Burgesses, the third lists slaves by their given names, the fourth lists the first names of Burgess spouses whose maiden names are unknown, and the fifth records all other individuals mentioned in the book in alphabetical order by surname. The contents pages also provide a thumbnail sketch of the family through its first six generations, and the seven genealogical charts similarly display in graphic form the relationships of those early generations.

This book is a guide to those born with the name Burgess, to those individuals adopted into or out of the family, and to their Burgess-named descendants; female members of the family are listed in more compact form with their children and grandchildren normally embedded entirely within their own entries, or expanded as necessary through a series of paragraphs that are progressively indented for each generation. The genealogy is arranged in descending order by branch and family from the most senior to the most junior lines. Complete families are grouped together, with the grandfather or father and each of his children listed in order of birth; those sons or grandsons who carried on the line may sometimes be mentioned briefly with a reference to a more complete entry later in the book if their own descendants exceed three or four generations. The numbers in front of each name indicate both the generation level of each individual and his or her order of birth in each family; for example, the number in front of my name, "*10a*," shows that I'm a tenth-generation descendant of William Burges (our original ancestor), and that I'm the oldest of my father's four children. These numbers are not unique, but repeat over and over again, and have usually been used only with name-line descendants born with the name Burgess.

A typical entry tries to provide the full names of persons and the full dates and places of vital events, plus a mention of the census years, tax lists, city directories, military service, and other records in which an individual appears (particularly for those living before 1920), and something about the individual's career or accomplishments. The details included in a particular entry may vary due to lack of knowledge or response.

SOME COMMON QUESTIONS I'VE BEEN ASKED

People want to know what kind of heritage we have, so they tend to ask the same questions over and over again. Here are the responses I would have given if I'd had time to consider each one carefully.

1. Where in Europe does our family come from?

The trail for our Burgess line ends in Virginia in 1712, and there's absolutely no hard evidence to indicate where we lived before then. Oral traditions in separate branches of the family have contributed many different stories about our origins, but all are too far removed from the actual arrival of our family in North America to be taken with more than a grain of salt. These stories variously claim that the Burgess family derives from England, Scotland, Wales, France, Ireland, Germany, or even Switzerland. My own guess would be the British Isles generally, although France would run a strong second.

2. What does the name "Burgess" mean?

A "burgess" was a free citizen of an English borough. A borough was a town or region in England that had the right to elect representatives to the British Parliament. In Scotland, the word had a slightly different meaning, a borough being any large incorporated town (Edinburgh, for example). Later, representatives to the Parliament, having been elected from boroughs, began calling themselves "burgesses." In colonial Maryland and Virginia, the legislature was called the House of Burgesses, and their elected representatives burgesses; the use of the word "burgess" for this purpose went out of fashion in America in the 1780s, and in England by the 1840s.

The word derives originally from the Latin word *burgus*, meaning town, and the related word *burgensis*, meaning citizen; with various foreign-language cognates, such as the French *bourgeois/burgeis/bourges*, the Spanish *borjes*, and the German *burger*, and so on. The Norman invasion of England in 1066 brought French words such as *burgeis* into the English language, often in corrupted form. By the thirteenth century, Burges(s) or Burgeis was being used as a surname in England, and by Elizabethan times, the name had become common in certain British counties. It was also fairly common in colonial America, more so proportionately than it is today. Also, many foreign immigrants to the United States in the nineteenth century changed similar-sounding names (such as Burgeis, Bourgeois, Borjes, Bourges, or Burger) to the more acceptable, anglicized form of Burgess.

Prior to the Revolutionary War, when spellings were not fixed, the name often appears in records as Burges or sometimes even as Burge, and with many other variations (Burgis, Berges, Barguss, Burghess, etc.); these gradually became standardized to Burgess in most of our families after the year 1800, although one or two branches used "Burges" into modern times.

3. Are there any famous Burgesses?

None that we're related to. There aren't many scoundrels either. I'm afraid we're a pretty dull bunch. We do have several members who were rich by the standards of their day, some who killed or were killed in the heat of passion, a few who died in rather interesting ways, and a great many who were just modest successes in their own communities. Most of our family members were fairly ordinary, middle-class citizens. I've included a number of the more exotic stories that I've found, but have deliberately omitted events or scandals in which currently living individuals were involved, with a cut-off date of roughly seventy years ago.

4. Are all the Burgesses related?

No. Our family constitutes about 3.7% (one out of 27) of all those named Burgess residing in the United States. I reached that conclusion by matching the number of family members recorded in the Social Security death index (13,666) against the total number of deaths recorded (46,000,000) to generate an estimated percentage of .000297 for Burgess-named individuals in the general population of the United States. Multiplying that percentage times the estimated number of persons living in the U.S. (250,000,000) gives some 74,250 Burgesses resident in America. Roughly 59% of all the Burgesses in our family who ever lived are alive today, or 2,768 individuals, which, if divided by 74250, yields a final percentage of .0372794 of the total. There are at least twenty or thirty apparently unrelated Burgess families living in the American colonies prior to the Revolutionary War.

5. Why doesn't your book include all of the descendants in the female lines of William Burges?

I recently tried to project the number of descendants in all lines of our ancestor, William Burges of King George Co., Virginia, based upon the 4,690 known descendants in the male line. Figuring that males and females divide about equally for each generation, and counting the actual numbers for the first five generations, I "guestimated" that William has between 1.2 to 2.4 million descendants, give or take a half a million.

6. Why didn't you include more pictures?

Two reasons: running a lot of pictures would cost so much that the price of the book would have to increase drastically; also, many of the pictures that I have wouldn't reproduce very well, either because they're faint or a copy of a copy.

7. Where's our coat of arms?

Unfortunately, there's none we're legally entitled to. A "coat of arms" was always granted to an individual, not a family, and normally inherited by that individual's eldest son, and so on down the line. Only proven descendants in the male line of the individual in question are legally entitled to display a particular coat of arms. There may be many different coats of arms for the same surname, or even for the same family, particularly if it's a common name; but since we're unable to establish any connection with a European ancestor, we're out of luck. The coats of arms offered for sale by commercial firms are, I'm sorry to say, just a bunch of hokum.

8. What kind of work did our ancestors do?

Most of the Burgesses (and just about everyone else) prior to the Civil War were farmers. There were also a few ministers (who usually farmed as well), tradesmen (blacksmiths, for example), and soldiers (but only on a temporary basis). Very few members of the family before the Civil War had more than minimal schooling, although the majority of men could at least read and write. By the mid-1800s a few of the wealthier families began sending some of their brighter sons to academies or colleges. Girls became housewives or old maids—in the "good old days" there just weren't many other choices available. Most women were not educated beyond the most basic level, and often were not literate, particularly in colonial times.

Life in those days was hard and simple, with few of the amenities we're accustomed to. Infant and child mortality was high, medical care was primitive, and it wasn't uncommon to have whole families wiped out within a few days by epidemics of, say, typhoid or cholera. Country life was far more communal than it is now, centered very closely around church and neighbor. The Burgesses were protestant from the beginning, originally belonging to the Church of England prior to the American Revolution, and then adhering to whatever protestant denomination was available as family branches moved west. In the late nineteenth century, we begin to see many more railroad and factory workers, as the young men begin moving off their farms into the big cities. This trend continues to accelerate into the 1920s and '30s.

9. How do I know our ancestry is correct?

For those who want to check my sources, I've tried to provide enough information for any competent researcher to follow my trail, family by family, branch by branch. This is particularly true with the older generations, where I've gone into much greater detail in citing evidence. The underlying logic of the family structure is detailed more fully in the section on evidence, and I've also provided transcriptions of key documents. Since the vast majority of my readers won't be interested in redoing the work, I suggest that a good measure of the book's reliability is your own family. Is it complete? Is it accurate? If so, then probably the rest of the book is, too. (And if it isn't, please tell me!)

10. What do the Roman numerals after some names mean?

I inserted these numbers to indicate that there's more than one person born with the surname Burgess who has exactly the same given names. Identical names are numbered in order by date of birth. The numbers aren't fixed—they change as persons with those names are added or deleted from the genealogy. Because of this, I've put them in parentheses to indicate that they don't really exist except in the context of this book.

11. Why did you write this book?

I've always enjoyed history, and genealogy is history in its most personal form. I also appreciate the "puzzle" element, the piecing together of little bits of information to form a coherent whole; solving mysteries and making sense of disparate pieces of information are things I enjoy doing. I like talking to people and traveling, and this is a relatively harmless way of accomplishing both—and having something more to show for it than a tan. Finally, I discovered, after marrying my wife in 1976, that we shared the same interest in genealogy, and that *she* had been working on *her* family history for many years. Now it's something we can do together. Over the years, we gradually began spending most of our free time digging around in libraries, courthouses, and cemeteries. Since the work never can be finished, we find it eternally fascinating.

ABOUT THE FORMAT

The following sections provide technical information on how this book is structured and why, and the underlying evidence for the family structure as presented:

I have used in this book an adaptation of the Burke's Peerage format, which features a descending, hierarchical structure keyed to the paternal line, each successive generation being indented one "m" space further than the previous. In the Burke's system, different styles of non-unique identification numbers are used to designate each generation, beginning with the *stammvater*, who is unnumbered, and continuing with boldface numbers, regular face numbers, numbers in parentheses, and then numbers followed by italicized "a's," "b's," "c's," etc. These levels are not fixed, but start over again with the continuing head of a particular family branch (each succeeding monarch or peer, for example). Boldface dots in front of each name indicate currently living descendants.

I have maintained Burke's basic generational structure, each successive level being partially identified through set paragraph indentations, and I have also used a variation of their non-unique identification numbers. However, I assign each individual a generation number equal to the actual generation of descent from the person's most distant ancestor (William Burges of Richmond [later King George] Co., Virginia, being the first), followed by a letter which indicates order of birth within each person's family, beginning with "a." Generation level in some formats is indicated by a superscripted number following the given name of the individual; I have used a modified version of this scheme in headings to show immediate descent through the first five generations, but have eschewed such numbers in the main text, where they look too much like footnotes.

In other genealogical formats, all persons of a particular generation are grouped together into one section, and listed with their children, whose entries appear in turn in the next generation's chapter, and so on; with this type of arrangement, understanding immediate family relationships is virtually impossible without plotting the structure on a separate piece of paper. In still other formats, birth order in a family is indicated with lower case Roman numerals; however, these cause problems when one is trying to create standard indentation levels with word processing programs, since Roman numerals vary widely in width. In my book, the number "*9c*" tells us immediately that this individual belongs to the ninth generation, and is the third in order of birth in his or her family. All members of the ninth generation have their entries indented to the same level, a level unique to that generation. I have not used unique sequential identification numbers for each individual because they are confusing to the uninitiated, and must be changed with each new addition to the family.

With the Burke's format, one can see immediately at a glance the structure of a particular branch, *except* when a member of an early generation has a significant number of interpolated descendants. The Burgess family now stretches twelve generations at its greatest extent, and will reach the thirteenth during the 1990s. This creates problems of continuity and structure that defy the best possible genealogical formats ever devised. The 25,000 individuals included herein cannot be readily comprehended in a family structure even by the genealogist who has constructed this book. Therefore, certain compromises have had to be made.

As with the Burke's volumes, I have elected to "carry over" certain key individuals (those with numerous descendants) in the male line; unlike the Burke's format, however, I have maintained generation-level indentation and entry numbering as before. In practical terms, this usually means that a male progenitor with at least three or four generations of descendants will be listed under his father together with his brothers and sisters in a "bare bones" record that gives only his name and date and place of birth, so that one can see how he fits into his immediate family structure; and then will be repeated with a more complete entry and a full list of his descendants at some later point in the volume.

This format tends to preserve "family clusters," particularly those living in the same area, together with their immediate cousins, and makes possible immediate comprehension of at least one's closest family members. I have provided "see references" back to each of these individuals' progenitors, so that the average user can, through the index, immediately "hop" up or down the family tree. In every case my choices have been dictated by an effort to make the material readily accessible, comprehensible, and understandable by the most unsophisticated of readers. Descendants of Burgess daughters have been compacted into a single entry under the progenitor's name, but even here I have spread the data as far as necessary to make them comprehensible, sometimes over several pages.

I have also chosen not to use footnotes, which I find intrusive in a book destined primarily for popular consumption, but instead have cited key evidence as part of each individual entry. For those born after 1900 (exactly two-thirds of the family), I have relied heavily on personal testimony from family members in those branches, both by mail and through telephone interrogation, supplemented with on-site investigation into whatever vital, court, and land records are available, or through research at the Family History Library in Salt Lake City, Utah and its local branches in Southern California, and in other library and archival collections. These entries include very few citations of evidence, since the sources in most cases have been immediate relatives; individuals who have been particularly helpful in supplying information for their respective branches have been noted in the text. I have attempted to identify cities of residence for all family members, living or dead, without supplying exact addresses.

For persons born prior to 1900, I have tried to provide, at the minimum, a listing of every census in which the individual appears, keyed to year, state, and county (and those censuses in which the person has *not* been found); dates of birth, death, and marriages keyed to state and county, where they are extracted from official records, or specific citations to other sources, where appropriate; a list of reference tools in which the person's biography has appeared (with full bibliographical data); known military service with exact names and numbers of units; career details (most male individuals from this period were farmers, and most women were housewives); known movements and resettlements; appearances in tax lists; burial places; and any key evidence of descent, including wills, probates, land, and other records, with full citations to county, book number, date, and page number.

I have also tried to show how this evidence was interpreted. From such signposts along the way, I believe that any knowledgeable researcher can follow my reasoning, and can confirm any specific piece of evidence easily and independently, and why I thought it important enough to record. A summation of the logic underlying the entire family structure, with its strengths and weaknesses, is also included in the section, "Evaluating the Evidence." Key documents have been transcribed verbatim in the text.

Finally, a note concerning my own qualifications. I've been a librarian at California State University, San Bernardino since 1970, from 1984 with the rank of full professor. This book is my seventieth published monograph. My works include bibliographies, indexes, chronologies, and similar reference guides, among them the standard subject bibliographies of fantastic literature and the mass market paperback, the standard chronological history of Eastern Orthodoxy and Eastern Church patriarchs, a history of the Falkland Islands War, a dictionary of arms control terms, an annotated guide to reference works, a guide to vital records, etc. My bibliographies use a format designed by me to present the writer's primary and secondary works in an attractive and efficient layout, one that simultaneously forces the answering of certain bibliographical questions, with the intent of using the responses to create a comprehensive, readily intelligible display of the author's creative and personal life.

Similarly, the design of this genealogy represents a deliberate attempt on my part to devise a new, more attractive, more usable format for very long and complex genealogies. The formats currently accepted by the National Genealogical Society and the major genealogical journals certainly have merit, particularly for the presentation of shorter genealogical structures in a scholarly milieu; but they display significant structural weaknesses when employed with larger families. The basic difficulty, as always, is to find a format that is both unobtrusive and simultaneously instructive, to discover a structure that can present complicated and intricate masses of data without having the average, uninitiated member of the public constantly stumbling over them. Mine is not the only solution, of course, or even the best possible answer to the problem, but it is the one that I have found most satisfying for this particular book.

Inevitably, those portions of this book dealing with earlier generations are based not just on fact, but on personal judgments extrapolated from sometimes scarce or even contradictory data. Sometimes other conclusions could have been drawn from the same information. I've been careful to label my claims clearly, stating where I am sure and where I am not so sure, and where I'm somewhere in between. What is here is as good as I could make it, given the inevitable pressures of time and money. In the end, I am reasonably certain that a middle-aged, middle-class farmer named William Burges who died in northeastern Virginia in 1712 is the common ancester of most of those listed in this book (except for the John Meredith Burgess line). I welcome corrections and updates for a third edition five or ten years hence.

EVALUATING THE EVIDENCE

This book was begun in 1964 by questioning immediate relatives, and working outwards and backwards through successive family layers. I proceeded on this basis for about ten years, until I had pushed the line as far back as I could go; I then began running each male line down to modern times. I've had reasonably good success in identifying and finding current descendants of these lines, and in locating cooperative individuals in each branch to help complete them.

William Burges was ultimately pinned to a place and time certain: the Northern Neck of Virginia in late April of 1712 (when he presumably died). I was left with a series of key questions which I will now address:

Where did the Burgess family originate?

More specifically, where did William Burges live prior to his arrival in Richmond/King George Co.? I have no answer to this, and I personally doubt that the question can or ever will be answered, or that the line can be extended past the 1712 barrier. It is conceivable that, should all surviving seventeenth- and eighteenth-century records ever be made directly accessible in some master computer data base, that a verifiable reference to William Burges will emerge from the shadows (certain family lines can only be traced in one direction); but the chances of this actually happening are, I think, slim. One realizes very quickly in looking at this man's estate inventory that he possessed few goods or other real property, and this lack of estate, personal or otherwise, does not bode well for successful searching elsewhere. Also, the name William Burges is relatively common in English and Scottish records, appearing in many surviving parish registers from this period; and one must presume that many such records are lost or unindexed. There were also Burgess families at this time in Barbados, in other parts of Virginia, Maryland, and the colonies, and in Ireland, as well as cognate names that could have been altered to Burgess in France, Germany, Spain, Portugal, etc. So, barring a genealogical miracle, the line ends with William.

Of William himself, the only records that survive are his will and inventory. The former was dictated to friends or acquaintances from his deathbed, presumably at his home (one of the bequests is the bed on which he died), and recorded several months later in the far-distant Richmond County courthouse. Since he left little property and certainly no land, the primary rationale for the will seems to be that his wife (who is unmentioned) had predeceased him, and that his four underaged and/or unmarried children were about to be left orphans, and therefore needed to be provided for. The will mentions three daughters who cannot (and perhaps will never) be traced, and one son, Edward Burges.

Were these William's only children?

The question is unanswerable; on the one hand, the primary *raison d'être* for William's will was the provision of a guardian for William's unattached children, and there was no need to mention any other siblings who could already have been provided for; on the other side, two of the daughters were of age (though unmarried), and the ages of the children suggest a family terminated ten or more years earlier by the premature death of the wife, and perhaps complete as stated. The only other male Burgess who appears anywhere close to William's location during this period is Joseph Burgess, and it is apparent from later records that he was living in the section of King George Co. that was given to Westmoreland Co. during the Revolutionary War. William's will suggests that he had no close relatives nearby (including older married children) who would otherwise have normally adopted and/or raised his four children; that William, his wife, and his family derived from some other comparatively distant location; and that William was a relatively recent immigrant at the time of his death.

Where did William live?

The only location specified in his will is St. Marie's (i.e., Mary's) Parish in Richmond Co., which at that time encompassed the south (Rappahannock) side of the rise between the Rappahannock and Potomac Rivers, from Richmond County to the Blue Ridge Mountains, including what is now Richmond Co., part of Westmoreland Co. (the section that now crosses the ridge to the Rappahannock River), and what are now the southern halves of King George, Stafford, and Fauquier Cos. This is a very broad area, potentially encompassing many hundreds of square miles.

One must therefore examine the other persons mentioned in William's will, including Jeremiah Bronaugh (the guardian), the Copleys (witnesses), and the three men who inventoried William's estate. The most important of these is the guardian, who can only be Jeremiah Bronaugh I (1670-1749), a major plantation owner on Lambs Creek in what is now King George Co. (the other two men of this name in northern Virginia during the early-to-mid-eighteenth century were Jeremiah Jr. [1702-1747], and his first cousin who lived in Prince William Co.; both of these were too young to have been the guardian mentioned in William Burges's will). The Bronaughs are believed to have emigrated from Scotland in the 1670s, but their exact origin remains unknown; David Bronaugh, Jeremiah's father, is recorded as having bought his 350-acre estate on Willow Creek in Old Rappahannock County on 24 Apr. 1671 (*Deed Book 1668-1672*, p. 219-220). Old Rappahannock County then encompassed both sides of the Rappahannock River to the ridges separating the watershed lines from the flanking river valleys. There is no doubt that Jeremiah Bronaugh Sr. later inherited part of this plantation.

The Bronaughs were middling-level landed gentry, prosperous enough to be recorded in numerous county transactions throughout the changing jurisdictions of the Northern Neck. The Bronaugh plantation undoubtedly used numerous slaves, indentured servants, and other white employees to work the farm, some as overseers, and others as tradesmen (smiths, carpenters, etc.). Probably William Burges was one of these laborers, or he may have leased fifty or a hundred acres of land from Bronaugh or one of his neighbors. Certainly he thought highly enough of Jeremiah Bronaugh to make him the guardian of his children (lest we make too much of William's will, however, it should be noted that Jeremiah Bronaugh is recorded several times in county records with similar "adoptions").

The Copleys may also have lived in the Lambs Creek area; they appear several times in Richmond and King George County records, but never as land owners, and never in sufficient detail to pin them to a specific location. Nonetheless, it seems reasonable to infer that William Burges knew Jeremiah Bronaugh and lived somewhere nearby. He probably extracted a promise from Bronaugh that William's daughters would be honorably married off and that his son would be trained in the art and science of farming, and given a chance to buy his own plot at some future date—in exchange, of course, for their free labor over a certain number of years. It was a common bargain, and a fair one, for the times. Since such duties would normally be assumed by surviving relatives on either side of the family, one may also presume that none were close at hand, or (less likely) that they were too poor to assume financial responsibility for the children.

Where was Edward Burgess's land located?

The presumed son, Edward (I say "presumed" because we cannot be absolutely certain that the Edward mentioned in William's will as his son is the same Edward that appears in later records), bought land in 1731 in King George Co., at which time we know he was of age (one had to be twenty-one to conduct legal transactions). Judging from the ages mentioned in his father's will, he was probably closer to thirty at the time, born in the late 1690s or early 1700s. His land, unlike that of the Bronaughs, was not even close to prime, being located somewhere up on the dividing line between the counties, where water was scarcer, and where growing tobacco, the primary cash crop, and transporting it to the rivers for export, would be more difficult. He owned a couple of slaves and some livestock, grew a variety of crops, and raised cattle, sheep, and horses, mostly to feed his own family, selling off surpluses. We know from the original deed that Edward's land was in the "never-never" land that straddled the unsurveyed county lines, and that his farm switched back and forth between King George and Stafford Cos. at least twice without having actually moved. Attempts to pinpoint the *exact* location of Edward's land have thus far proved futile; the possibilities are greater than one might think, given the fact that the watershed lines are about a half-mile apart in places at some points on the ridge. The land was on or near what is now State Route 3, about two miles northwest of the current county courthouse.

Why was Edward's land not sold until 1797?

After Edward's death his fourth son, Moses Burgess, remained on the original homestead to take care of Margaret Burgess, Edward's widow. She died about 1783. Within a year of her death, Moses left King George Co. and moved to Orange Co., VA, leaving his oldest son, Lunsford Burgess (and presumably Lunsford's family), to tend the Burgess farm. Lunsford apparently died about 1789 (he last appears in the personal property tax lists in 1788). Thereafter the farm is recorded on the land tax records as belonging to the "Burgess heirs." Moses Burgess died in Orange Co. at the end of 1796. His widow may have assumed that he owned the King George Co. farm on which he had lived for so many years (indeed, he may have been told by his siblings that he could have the farm if he would take care of their mother), and may have attempted to sell it as part of the settlement of his estate, only to discover when attempting to record the sale that the title had not been cleared, and that the last legal owner of record was Edward Burgess Sr. To clear the title, the County Clerk of King George Co. may have required that Edward's heirs-at-law be traced to sign the deed of sale. This is the most plausible explanation for the timing of the transfer.

Who was Edward's wife?

Previous researchers have assumed that Edward's wife, Margaret Burgess, was a Garner, because their oldest son was named Garner (the Garners were a prominent family on the Northern Neck, particularly in Westmoreland Co.). However, a 1725 estate record for Henry Fewell mentions legacies to two daughters, including "Margaret Burge," and I believe this Margaret was Edward's (probably very recent) wife. The Fewells lived in the same part of King George Co. as the Burgesses and Bronaughs, and there is no other Burge or Burgess family mentioned in county records as living anywhere closer to these families than Joseph Burgess, about eight miles distant. This is not proof, merely presumption, but it seems a reasonable one to make. It also might explain where the name Henry Burgess came from, two generations later.

Why, then, did Edward and Margaret name their oldest son Garner? Judging from eighteenth-century naming patterns common in this region, the connection could have been either familial or personal, and is as likely to have come from either the father's or mother's side of the family—or perhaps their parents. When Edward's son, Moses Burgess, named his daughter Catharine Ellis Burgess, after her prominent great-grandmother and step-great-aunt on her mother's and stepmother's side of the family, respectively, it was a clear indication that names often skipped generations before being used again. Perhaps if Catharine Burgess had been male, she would have been named for her great-great-grandfather, Charles Ellis, whose name was given to her uncle, Charles Ellis Bennett.

Who were Edward's children?

We are fortunate that one of the few documents surviving from the pre-Civil War period in Stafford Co., Virginia is *Liber O*, which contains the will of Edward Burgess. That document mentions six children: five sons—Gardener [sic], William, Edward, Moses, and Rubin—and one unmarried daughter, Mary. The latter is probably the Mary Burgess recorded in the *St. Paul's Parish Register* as having been born in 1736, and is very likely the Mary Burgess who married Nathan Skipweth White in 1759, a few months after her father's will was written, and about the time he died. Another potential daughter, Margaret Burgess, married John French, a son of Catherine Ellis and Mason French, in 1750. Neither of these relationshps can definitely be proven, but both are probable. The Anne Burgess who married Joseph Rogers in 1749 is less certainly a third daughter.

The First Generations

Establishing a relationship between the William Burges who died in Richmond County in 1712 and the Edward Burge(ss) who bought land in King George County in 1731 depends both upon William's noncupative will, which mentions an Edward Burges as a male heir, and a demonstration of proximity in time and space between the two. If Margaret Fewell "Burge" is Edward's wife, then he was married and living in King George Co. in 1725, thirteen years after his presumed father's death, and thirteen years after he was put into the care of Jeremiah Bronaugh. If William lived near Jeremiah Bronaugh, as seems likely (but which cannot be conclusively established), the chances of a coincidental occurrence of these names lessens considerably, given the scarcity of Burgess family names (and cognates) in this region at this time. There was another Burgess family living on the Northern Neck in the late 1600s and 1700s, but the members of this group are generally recorded in counties closer to the end of the peninsula (except for Joseph and Lettice Burgess, who both appear in *St. Paul's Parish Register*). At present, there remains enough doubt about Edward's relation to William to regard the connection as unproven, although this scenario seems the most probable and reasonable explanation of the known facts.

Edward Burgess's relationship to the five sons mentioned in his will is much more certain. Reuben Burgess, the youngest of his sons, can be tracked to his final resting place in North Carolina through a combination of personal property tax lists and land records, all of which mesh exactly, moving from Stafford Co. to Albemarle Co. to Rowan Co.; when one adds his uncommon given name to the mix, the result is conclusive. Similarly, Moses Burgess, Edward's fourth son, is stated in his initial Orange Co. deed to be a resident of King George Co.; his subsequent records are complete through his early death.

The movements of Edward Burgess Jr., the middle son, are less easily measured. From 1764, when Edward Jr. is mentioned as a witness to a Stafford Co. deed, to his first appearance in the Prince William Co. personal property tax lists in 1782, Edward is absent from the records for almost two decades. In fact, the relation between the Edward Burgess of King George and Stafford Cos. and the Edward Burgess of Prince William and Fauquier Cos. can only be demonstrated by the fact that several of the Fauquier County Burgess's descendants were given the middle name "Price" (derived from Edward's wife's family), including a set of twins, Edward and Sarah Price Burgess, who were clearly named for their grandparents. This cannot be coincidental.

The relation to their father of the two older sons of Edward Burgess Sr., Garner and William, can be legally demonstrated through the sale of the original Burgess land in King George Co. in 1797, sixty-six years after its purchase by Edward. Under terms of Edward's will, his executors were his wife, Margaret (who died in

1783), and Garner and William. By 1797 both of these sons had themselves died, but their own legal heirs sold the land in their stead. Garner left a will naming his oldest son, Edward Burgess, and oldest son-in-law, Matthew Neale, as executors, and these two men represented his estate in the sale; William Burgess died intestate in Stafford Co. in 1780, leaving two or three sons, one of whom (another Edward Burgess) was selected to represent his interest.

The Fourth Generation

Of Edward Burgess Sr.'s five sons, four left detailed wills and probates; only William died intestate. Garner Burgess mentions three sons in his will: Edward, John, and James; the subsequent probate indicates that James died unmarried and intestate in 1798. Edward Burgess III is easily tracked to Culpeper (later Rappahannock) Co. through personal property and land tax records, and through the fact that he acted as the legal representative of his late father in the sale of the original Burgess land. He left no will, but his widow, Francis (who died in 1851), did, and his descendants are firmly established through tax, census, and legal documents. Garner's second son, John Burgess, left Fauquier Co. after the death of his mother in 1802, moving to Bourbon Co., Kentucky by 1804, then to Harrison Co., Kentucky five years later, and finally to Putnam Co., Indiana. The relation between the Fauquier County John Burgess and his counterpart in Harrison County can only be proven through comparison of two matching signatures on documents signed thirty years apart, one in Virginia, one in Kentucky. He left no will, but several 1846 settlement deeds and other tax, marriage, and land documents in Kentucky and Indiana tie together his children in a web of paper that leaves possible few other conclusions regarding the relationships of these individuals. Nonetheless, the absence of a comprehensive settlement of his estate makes this family the least firm of the lines deriving from Garner Burgess.

Edward Sr.'s second son, William Burgess, died intestate, leaving two known sons, Henry and Edward Burgess, who moved with their stepfather to Kentucky in the 1780s, and a possible third son, William Jr., whose potential existence and relationship is tenuously supported by family tradition and by a surviving 1779 Stafford Co. petition to the Virginia Legislature, which includes the signature of one "William Burgess Jr." No further record has been found for this line, and its inclusion should be regarded as speculative. William Sr.'s son, Edward Burgess of Bourbon and Scott Cos., Kentucky, acted as the legal representative of his father's estate in 1797 when he cosigned a deed selling the original Burgess lands in King George Co., Virginia. His descendants are well established through a wide variety of interlocking legal, census, tax, and personal records. Henry Burgess of Bourbon and Fleming Cos., Kentucky, is tied to the Scott Co. Burgesses through two documents in Bourbon Co. linking him to Ralph Hughes, his stepfather, and to James Hughes, his step-brother and brother-in-law; and through the marriage of his grandson, George Washington Burgess, to his brother's granddaughter, Marietta Dungan. Since the Scott Co. line was more prosperous than its Fleming Co. counterpart, and since Henry's son, John Henry, was living in Indiana at the time the couple met, it is extremely unlikely that their courtship could have been accidental. Henry's descendants are enumerated in a series of Fleming County lawsuits filed in the 1840s and '50s between and among the Burgess family and their Mauzy in-laws, leaving all other relationships in this line solid and well documented.

The family of Edward Burgess Jr. of Fauquier Co., Virginia, included three sons enumerated in his 1819 will: William, John, and Mason. John remained in Fauquier Co., and his will, subsequent probate records, family Bible record, and tax and census records tie together his children in a comprehensive package, leaving no doubt as to their exact relationships. William Burgess is recorded in the personal property and land tax records of Fauquier Co., originally with his father, until he left the area in 1804. He settled in Shenandoah Co. with several related families, and then moved to Muskingum Co., Ohio by 1817, again with relatives of his wife's Redman family; personal property tax records for Fauquier and Shenandoah Cos. exactly match these comings and goings, and a nineteenth-century biography of his grandson, George Washington Burgess, specifically names the latter's grandparents as William Burgess and Susan Redman, providing the final proof. William's 1839 will delineates his children, and all have been successfully traced with the exception of his daughter Lucinda. The odd given name of Bedy for his oldest son further cements this family to the Redman line, since his wife's uncle was Bedy Redman. However, the family of a Bede D. Burgess born about 1820 in Muskingum Co., whose line has been added at the end of William's section, can neither be established nor disestablished at this time, and its listing here should be regarded as speculative.

Mason Burgess also left Fauquier Co. in the earlier 1800s, moving to Jefferson Co., Kentucky, where he is recorded for several years in the early tax and census records as Peyton Burgess, and then again as Mason, the dates of departure and arrival in the personal property tax rolls again matching those of Fauquier Co. He settled in Orange Co., Indiana, about 1817, the related Cornwall families moving at about the same time to nearby Vigo Co., Indiana, and just across the state line in Edgar Co., Illinois. The tracing of this family depends partially on Mason's unusual given name, and also on his connection to the Cornwall line, whose movements match those of the Burgess family (Mason's sister Sarah, who married Jeremiah Cornwall, died in Edgar Co.). Mason's 1845 will delineates all of his children, and all later relationships in this family are clearly established through a confluence of legal, tax, census, and land records.

Moses Burgess's will identifies two surviving sons—John P. B. and Edward—a third son, Lunsford, having apparently died before his father. Lunsford is identified in the *St. Paul's Parish Register* as Moses's son, and is recorded in the personal property tax lists of King George Co. through 1788, when he apparently died (he has not been found in any subsequent records); he may have left two underaged sons, Garner and William, mentioned as being apprenticed in 1792 in neighboring Spotsylvania County, but of whom there is no further record. John Burgess moved to Halifax Co., Virginia, near the North Carolina border. In the 1830s he sold his remaining property under court order, in settlement of a lawsuit brought against him by his in-laws, the Deshazers; included in the sale was a slave named Bumberry or Bunbury, a name identical to that of a slave he received in the division of his father's estate in 1816. His children are associated with him in the personal property tax lists of Halifax Co., and in a financial note that formed the basis of the above-mentioned lawsuit; and one of his sons, Williamson Burgess, married one of the Jacksons, several of whom also intermarried with the Deshazers, many members of both families moving west with the Burgesses in the 1820s and '30s to Robertson Co., Tennessee. Edward Burgess of Kanawha Co., Virginia (later West Virginia) is tied to his father through several deeds recorded in Orange Co. in which he sells his share of his father's estate, and is noted as being a resident of Kanawha. Although Edward did not leave a will, his two sons, Garland and John, are continually associated with him in the personal property tax lists of Kanawha Co. through 1845, when they move to Missouri as a group; and it is clear that these sons are listed with their father in the 1820-40 censuses. Included at the end of this section is the family of John Meredith Burgess, whose descendants intermarried at several points with those of Edward, and whose daughter, Caroline Burgess McCown, went west with the Burgesses, but who does not otherwise appear to be connected to the direct line. John Meredith Burgess's origin is unknown.

Reuben Burgess left a will which mentions three sons: William, Reuben Jr., and Thomas. These children moved with their father and their own families to Albemarle Co., Virginia in 1789, and thence to Rowan (later Davie) Co., North Carolina in 1799. William and Reuben's five or six sons can be identified by proximity (they appear either to have lived together or very close to each other), but only one, Samuel, can be firmly attached to the proper parent, and he probably died without heirs. The lines of James and Moses Burgess are probably extinct; John Burgess either died or moved away about 1831, leaving no further record, and Edward Burgess died in 1840, leaving two sons whose names and fates are unknown. Thomas Burgess moved to White (later Putnam) Co., Tennessee in 1815; his relation to his father is confirmed through his son Anderson Burgess's personal biography, published a century ago in a Warren Co., Missouri history. Anderson's account also lists all of Thomas's children, whose subsequent fates have been traced through a combination of probate, census, tax, and legal records.

Correcting a Genealogical Error

The most prominent Burgess family in colonial America was that of Colonel William Burgess of Anne Arundel, Maryland, whose wealth, influence, and progeny have been chronicled in several sources, especially *Anne Arundel Gentry*, which details and documents his numerous descendants for a number of generations, and upon which I have partially relied for the argument given below. Many genealogists have tried to tie their Burgess lines to Col. William's offspring. About forty years ago a researcher hired by descendants of the Rappahannock Co. line proclaimed that the original Edward Burgess, who died in 1759 in King George Co., was the same as the Edward Burgess mentioned as a son of Samuel Burgess (a grandson of Col. William Burgess of Maryland). This "same name" theory was rediscovered in the 1950s by an amateur genealogist from another branch who had located descendants of the Rappahannock Co. family, and who wholeheartedly embraced the earlier researcher's solution to the problem of the Burgess family's origins, but made no effort to confirm it. Other cousins then spread the theory without vetting it further; it was then published in *Virginia Settlers, Volume II*, by A. Maxim Coppage III (Utica, KY: McDowell Publications, 1988, p. 103-105).

Unfortunately for the proponents of this notion, the true facts are these: Edward Burgess, the oldest son of Samuel Burgess of Anne Arundel Co., Maryland (who was a grandson of Col. William Burgess), was christened on 14 Apr. 1717. The christening of a child in those days did not necessarily occur immediately after birth, but usually the event was not long delayed, occurring at the first convenient visit by the family to the church after the birth, and in any case within six to eighteen months. It is highly unlikely that Edward Burgess son of Samuel Burgess was born earlier than 1715. However, Edward Burgess of King George Co., Virginia purchased one hundred acres of land in King George Co. in 1731, and it is indisputable that this farm is the same land later sold by his Burgess heirs in 1797; he also was married by 1725, and had children born in the late 1720s and early 1730s. Under the law prevailing at the time, minors had few legal rights, and those rights could only be exercised in their name by their parents or legal guardians until they reached their majority. Males attained legal majority at the age of twenty-one. If Edward Burgess of King George Co., VA was indeed the same person as Edward Burgess of Anne Arundel Co., MD, then how could he have bought a farm at age fourteen? It simply would not have been allowed: any such sale would have been highly irregular, and probably considered null and void, since a minor would not have had the legal power to enter into such an agreement.

There is a further difficulty overlooked by these earlier researchers. Samuel Burgess of Anne Arundel County had three sons mentioned in the christening records: Edward, Benjamin, and Richard, in that birth order. Yet in Samuel's later will, which was probated during the lifetime of Edward Burgess of King George Co., Richard Burgess, known to be the *third* son of Samuel, is specifically mentioned as Samuel's *oldest* son. The only way this document can be interpreted is that Richard is Samuel's oldest *surviving* son, and that his two brothers are dead. But if his brother Edward is dead, he cannot be Edward Burgess of King George Co., who is very much alive during this period.

Finally, there is the problem of names. Naming patterns are very pronounced during this period, and while not themselves a final indication of relation or non-relation, can constitute a powerful prohibitive argument against one family being related to another. The naming pattern of Col. William Burgess's line does indeed favor the names Edward, William, and John, as does the family of Edward Burgess of King George Co., VA. However, Col. William's immediate descendants also frequently employ such names as Basil, Michael, Mordecai, Samuel, and Richard for their males, while Edward's line uses such pet names as Garner, Moses, Reuben, Lunsford, James, Thomas, Joel, and Anderson. There is not one Basil, Michael, Mordecai, Richard, or *Samuel* in the Edward Burgess family until a much later period; at the least, one would expect a profusion of Samuels if Edward was the son of Sam. But he isn't, and all the wishing in the world that one might be connected to a prominent family won't make it so.

Correcting Another Genealogical Error

In the late 1970s a history of the descendants of Thomas Burgess of Putnam and Cumberland Cos., Tennessee was published. Although basically sound in its presumptions, the book made two unfortunate conclusions based upon a coincidence of similar names occurring in the local region. The author identified his ancestor, Thomas Burgess of White (later Putnam) Co., TN, with another Thomas Burgess of White (later Warren) Co., TN who received a Revolutionary War bounty grant. But the earlier Thomas Burgess was resident in White Co. by the year 1800, while the ancestor of the Putnam and Cumberland Cos. line did not leave North Carolina until 1815, his movements being clearly delineated in surviving tax and deed records, and his connection to his father being stated in a county history biography later published by his son, Anderson Burgess. The Warren Co. family can similarly be followed down the generations without difficulty. In fact, the families do not appear to be connected.

A second error was made by the Tennessee researcher in identifying the children of Thomas Burgess's son, Joel Burgess, who was also called Joseph in some records and "Joe" by his descendants. Another apparently unrelated Burgess line in neighboring Jackson Co. had as its progenitor one Josiah Burgess, also called Joseph or Joe, and his possible grandson Joe Burgess (son of James Burgess), who died in 1911 in Jackson Co., leaving hundreds of contemporary descendants. The latter was mislabeled in the Tennessee book as the oldest son of Joel Burgess. The problem is compounded by the fact that many of the members of this line drifted down into the Cookeville, Putnam Co. area in the early twentieth century, apparently intermingling with the original Putnam lines, who moved north from the White-Putnam Co. border region at about the same time.

Joel Burgess left no will or settlement deed, and neither did Josiah Burgess, but Joel's place of residence *is* known to have been southern Putnam Co., nowhere near the Jackson Co. Burgess families, who stayed during this period well north of the Jackson-Putnam county boundary. Here again, naming patterns are very different in the two families. Also, the 1840 census conforms exactly in numbers to the names and ages we have for Joel's family. Joe Burgess of Jackson Co. was born in 1833, and is listed with James Burgess of Jackson Co. in 1850. Joe clearly and consistently indicates in the 1880, 1890 (a sliver of which survives and has been published for Jackson Co.), 1900, and 1910 censuses that both of his parents were born in *South* Carolina, and this attribution corresponds with that of his presumed father, James Burgess, in the 1850 census for Jackson Co.; the older members of the Putnam Co. families just as clearly state that they and their ancestors were all born in *North* Carolina or Virginia. The two families are not the same, and Joe Burgess's descendants have consequently not been included in this book.

A WORD OF APPRECIATION

This book could never have been produced without the willing assistance of hundreds of other researchers, family members, librarians, and courthouse officials. My great-uncle, George O. Burgess, was the key to making my first contacts outside of my immediate family. Paul D. Burgess, Raymond O. Burgess, and Forrest P. Burgess formed (with me) the first group of dedicated amateurs seeking to investigate the truth of our origins, and their memories and correspondence and our one meeting will always remain with me. They're all gone now, all except George. I also owe very special thanks to Susan Mortensen, whose efforts to organize and record the history of all Burgess lines, and to publish the results in her *Burgess Bulletin*, have been extraordinary. Finally, my wife, Mary Wickizer Burgess, has been a constant source of assistance and good advice, and this book would have been much poorer without her.

Over the past thirty years I've met hundreds of Burgess cousins, have talked to hundreds of others on the phone, and have corresponded with still more hundreds by mail. Without *your* help, without *your* willingness to give me family group sheets, photographs, documents, Bible records, without *your* recollections, this book would be far less complete. Some have contributed more than others, of course, and it's appropriate that they be mentioned below. Please accept my apologies if I've missed anyone.

Margaret Bates Amundson, Sandra Fitzwater Andersen, C. O. "Andy" Anderson, Beulah Burgess Baber, Travis F. Baldwin, Effie Burgess Ball, Hilda Burgess Beall, Barbara Prather Beede, Eugenia Johnson Bell, Clifford P. Bendau, Sally Blessing, Evelyn Ashworth Bodine, Joan C. Bohm, Margie Pennel Bradley, Betty Burgess Branson, Holly Horton Breidenbach, Jean Crawford Breidenbach, Diana Burgess Brown, Betty J. Kapel Burgess, Brenda Brown Burgess, C. Benjamin Burgess, Bessie Frank Burgess, Charles E. "Carl" Burgess, Clarence P. Burgess, Dorothy Sandifer Burgess, Ethel Burgess, Forrest P. Burgess, George O. Burgess, Hattie Neely Burgess, J. Carl Burgess, James A. Burgess (Arizona), James A. Burgess (Florida), James W. Burgess, James Z. Burgess, Jerry D. Burgess, Joachim Burgess, June Burgess-Nicholas, Kathleen Christian Burgess, Lyle W. Burgess, Mark E. Burgess, Mary Wickizer Burgess, Milford L. Burgess, Paul D. Burgess (Tennessee), Paul D. Burgess (Washington), Pauline Wyatt Burgess, Pearl Davis Burgess, Phyllis Hayward Burgess, Raymond O. Burgess, Robert T. Burgess, Roy Walter Burgess, Scott Alan Burgess, Semp D. Burgess, Vaughn A. Burgess, William G. Burgess, Jeanne Duclos Bussell, Cora Burgess Campbell, Lola Burgess Campbell, Peggy Foster Carlston, Betty Dean Burgess Carroll, John L. Chandler, Mary Burgess Cleland, Mona Stephens Looper Cloud, Noble F. Connor Jr., James W. Courtney, Dora Burgess Davis, Marie Wood Lomen DeFrees, Susan Burgess Demuth, Cornelia Andrews DuBois, Daryl L. Duncan, Jacob S. Eggborn, Jeffrey M. Elliot, Sandra Burgess Faulkner, Holly Burgess Fenton, Harlene Ferreira, Theo Prather Finch, Dorothy Burgess Finn, Della P. "Pat" Franklin, Alice Trowbridge Gardner, Myrtle Burgess Garrison, Christine Burgess Glass, Phillip A. Gowan, Goldena Burgess Green, Sande Burgess Grose, J. Kirk Hardy, Ethel Burgess Harlan, Beulah Burgess Hedges, Nora Burgess Helton, Linda Mooneyham Hill, Bradley Burgess Hinz, Brenda Edwards Howland, Oma Burgess Hubbard, Donald L. Huber, Veronica A. "Roni" Bolin Huber, Cleo Burgess Hutchinson, Sue Burgess James, Audrey Nelson Jones, Louis F. Jones, Karen Wolfinbarger Kees, Zona Burgess Kerley, Ruth Drane King, Fern Burgess Knight, Martha Johnson Marshall, Helen J. McClung, Kathleen Burgess McClung, Burgie Roberts McComas, Harold E. McCormick, Margueritte Cropp Millen, Nancy Shumate Miller, Mary Burgess Moon, Maggie Howard Morgan, Susan Williams Mortensen, John T. Myers Jr., Leona "Onie" Burgess Odle, Frances Harlan Odor, Bessie Burgess Orme, Betty Vice Orme, Kay Hall Pacheco, Phillip L. Pacheco, Johnia Burgess Parker, Leona Wheeler Parnell, Phyllis Burgess Payne, Delbert M. Poole, Diane Summers Poole, Judith Burgess Potter, Leona Mintz Presley, Mae Fields Price, Mary Burgess Redmann, Sarah Burgess Renaker, M. Louise Rogers Reynnells, Christine Robar, Mary Hussong Rodney, Faye Burgess Ross, Reva Burgess Rudasill, Mary Burgess Saunders, J. Fred Scarbrough, J. J. "Buck" Schaible Jr., Reah Burgess Sessions, Mary A. Shields, Ella Wyatt Sowers, Lola Cate Starbuck, Mandy Burgess Swafford, Ella Burgess Thomson, Margaret Gray Thomson, Francis Blackwell Trenary, Mable Burgess Trimble, Cora Burgess Tucker, Duane Burgess Turner, Barbara Gilbert Urban, Ronald T. Vance, Natheleen Murphy Vaughan, John A. Vice, Doris Burgess Wagner, Frances Holmes Wagoner, Margaret Burgess Waiting, Allen E. Wells, Ernest H. Wells, James A. Wheeler, Laurine Burgess White, Dee Wick, Ronald S. Wick, Floreine Sinclair Wickizer, Azilee Patton Wilkerson, Irene Burgess Worten, Margie Burgess Wyatt, Grace Lytle Young.

ABBREVIATIONS

NOTE: The two-letter ZIP Code abbreviations for U.S. states and Canadian provinces and their precursors have been used throughout to save space:

AB=Alberta
ad.=adopted
AK=Alaska
AL=Alabama
Apr.=April
AR=Arkansas
Aug.=August
AZ=Arizona
BC=British Columbia
CA=California
CO=Colorado
Co.=County
Co.=Company (businesses)
Corp.=Corporation
CT=Connecticut
CZ=Canal Zone
dau.=daughter
DC=District of Columbia
DE=Delaware
dec.=deceased
Dec.=December
Dept.=Department
DF=Distrito Federal
div.=divorced
DT=Dakota Territory
Feb.=February
FL=Florida
GA=Georgia
GU=Guam
HI=Hawaii
IA=Iowa
ID=Idaho
IL=Illinois
IN=Indiana
Inc.=Incorporated
I.O.O.F.=International Order of Odd Fellows
IT=Indian Territory
Jan.=January
KS=Kansas
KY=Kentucky
LA=Louisiana
MA=Massachusetts
Mar.=March
MB=Manitoba
MD=Maryland
ME=Maine
MI=Michigan
MN=Minnesota
MO=Missouri
MS=Mississippi
MT=Montana
NB=New Brunswick
NC=North Carolina
ND=North Dakota
NE=Nebraska
NF=Newfoundland
NH=New Hampshire
NJ=New Jersey
NM=New Mexico
nmn=no middle name
Nov.=November
NS=Nova Scotia
NV=Nevada
NW=Northwest Territories
NY=New York
Oct.=October
OH=Ohio
OK=Oklahoma
ON=Ontario
OR=Oregon
O.S.=Old Style*
p.=page(s)
PA=Pennsylvania
PE=Prince Edward Island
PR=Puerto Rico
PQ=Québec
RI=Rhode Island
SC=South Carolina
SD=South Dakota
Sept.=September
SK=Saskatchewan
TN=Tennessee
TX=Texas
UT=Utah
VA=Virginia
VI=Virgin Islands
VT=Vermont
WA=Washington
WI=Wisconsin
WV=West Virginia
WY=Wyoming
YU=Yukon

*"Old Style" is used to designate a Julian calendar date prior to 14 September 1752. To convert a Julian calendar date to the present-day Gregorian calendar, add eleven days to dates between 1700-2 Sept. 1752, or ten days to dates in the 1600s. The adjustment was made when the British government decreed that the day following 2 Sept. 1752 would be 14 Sept. 1752, thereby adding eleven days to the calendar. Prior to this time New Year's day officially occurred on 25 March, although ordinary custom had already begun to use 1 January as a demarcation point. Hence, dates between 1 January-25 March usually show two years (for example, 1751/52), indicating that the legal year was 1751, although we would now regard that period as 1752. The year 1752 officially ran from 25 March-31 December 1752, at which point 1 January was adopted as the legal New Year. Hence, George Washington was born on 11 February 1731/32; he adjusted his birthday to 22 February 1732 following the adoption of the new calendar (but some of his fellow Americans retained their original dates).

For my Father,
WALT BURGESS,
A tower of strength,
A fortress of intelligence

And in memory of my Grandfather,
ROY P. BURGESS,
Whom I wish I had known better

Roy P. Burgess and Family
(from left) Peggy, Walt, Jo, Eva, Roy, Ozzie, Mary

THE FIRST GENERATIONS

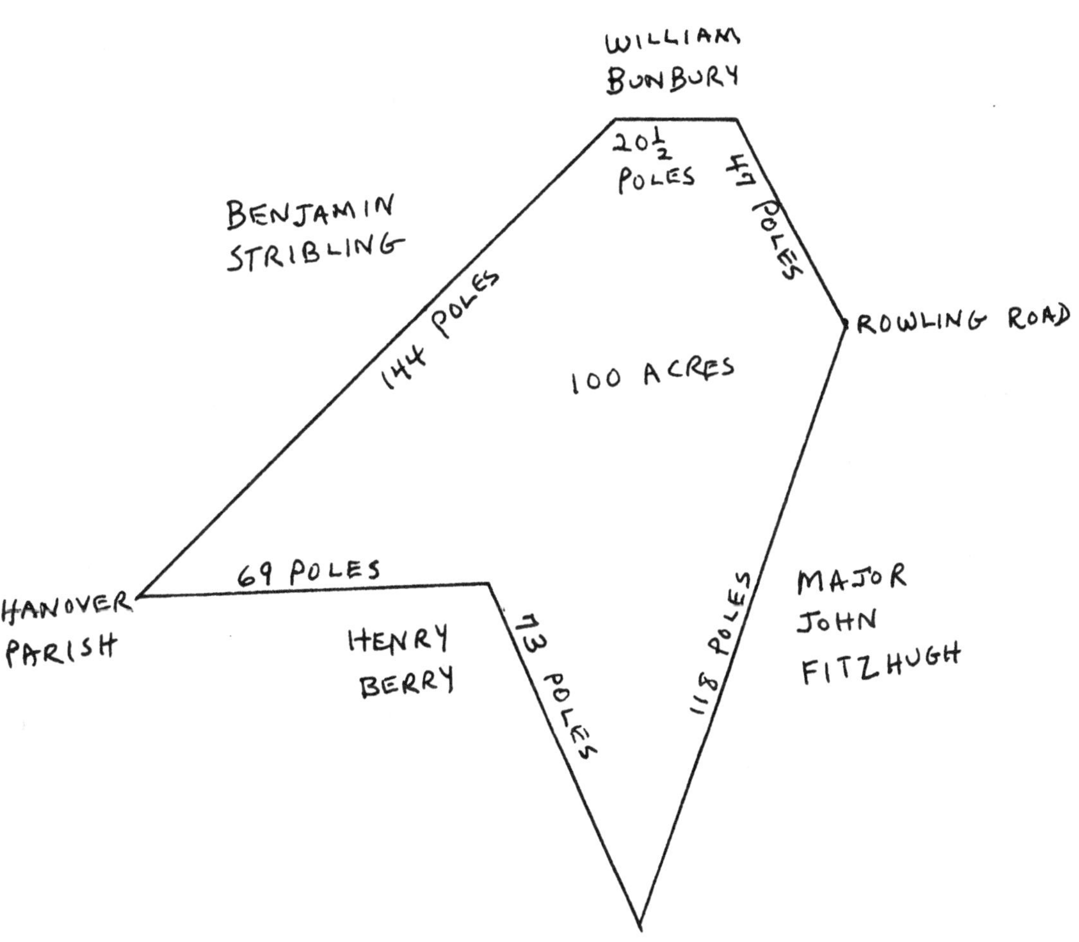

The Original Burgess Farm Drawn to Scale

THREE BURGESS SISTERS
*Miranda J. Pickle*Sarah I. Simonds*Martha A. Cate*

THE BURGESSES IN COLONIAL AMERICA

The Northern Neck slides determinedly into the cold waters of Chesapeake Bay, flanked on one side by the huge snake of the Potomac River and on the southern bank by the smaller, more placid Rappahannock River. To the early settlers it must have seemed a green oasis floating amidst the waters. This long peninsula was settled in the 1640s and '50s by predominantly English farmers, who within a generation had driven away, conquered, or overwhelmed the indigenous native populations with superior firepower and disease. The flanks of this fertile strip of land were quickly cleared of brush and trees, and a variety of crops planted. In the 1680s tobacco was king, being the one product that could be grown and exported to Europe for hard cash, or traded for the metals, goods, and other implements so badly needed by the first pioneers.

By the time William Burges arrived, in the late 1600s or early 1700s, the Indians were only a memory, the best lands long since settled and cleared, the tobacco boom somewhat waning, and the opportunities for a bright young man somewhat less than they would have been a generation before. Yet, for whatever reason—poverty, religious persecution, politics—William and family felt compelled to make the difficult trek across the Atlantic and start over again in a new land. The world that he found was a microcosm of English country life, complete with counties, country squires, an established Anglican Church system that was supported by and in turn supported the government, and a colonial parliament (the House of the Burgesses). There were significant differences, too, including the absence of nobility, the fact that the large plantation owners were mostly self-made men, and the vast expanse of the land itself, promising, if the Indians could be pushed back, endless opportunities for those willing to work. William and his wife never lived to see those possibilities, but his son Edward did.

For the Burgess family, the one key event of these early years was Edward Burgess's purchase of a 100-acre farm in King George Co. in 1731. He must have scrimped for years to make the payments on the land, which was located in the "back woods" on the ridge between the rivers. But the fact that he owned land made him self-sufficient, and it also gave him the right to vote. Suddenly his sons could advance themselves, and each made the most of their opportunities. At a time when only a third of the adult males of Virginia had the right to vote, when even less of the population found it necessary to make wills disposing of their property, four of Edward's five sons bought farms larger than their father's, and all four left wills; only the second son, William (who died relatively young), did not leave an estate.

The portrait of the Burgess clan prior to the Revolutionary War is one of a close family group clustered around two centers: the old family farm in King George Co., and the somewhat more bustling world of Stafford Co. ten miles to the northwest, where the port of New Marlborough provided an eye to the outside world and its attractions. And it was to the Accokeek Creek area of Stafford (not far from the port, courthouse, and church) that the two older sons, Garner and William Burgess, were attracted in the 1750s. King George Co. provided a comfortable haven from the world, a backwater little touched over the centuries by outside events (even the Civil War scarcely caused a rumble). But Stafford and its port were a center of activity during the seventeenth and eighteenth centuries, with a constant stream of travelers and goods and activities flowing through its borders. They must have beckoned to the Burgess boys like lights attracting moths. They married local girls and worked as farmhands for the established landowners of the region. By the 1760s Garner Burges had pushed on into the frontier, leasing 200 acres on the Manor of Leeds, a huge tract personally owned by the Proprietor of the Northern Neck, Lord Fairfax, in the back woods of Fauquier Co.

When the Revolutionary War broke out in 1776, Garner was in Fauquier Co., William and Reuben in Stafford, Edward Jr. either in Stafford or Prince William Co., and Moses with his mother on the family farm in King George. There is no evidence of any of these men serving in the Revolutionary War, although such service may well have not been recorded. Most were too old and too well established; even the youngest, Reuben, was thirty-one, and all had families to support. Only William Burgess may have had a son old enough to join the army, and family traditions state that William Burgess Jr. and Reuben Burgess did both serve. William Sr. was the first of the brothers to die, in 1780, leaving a widow and several married or underaged children. It was left to his and his brothers's descendants to begin the long trek West.

Chart I: The First Generations

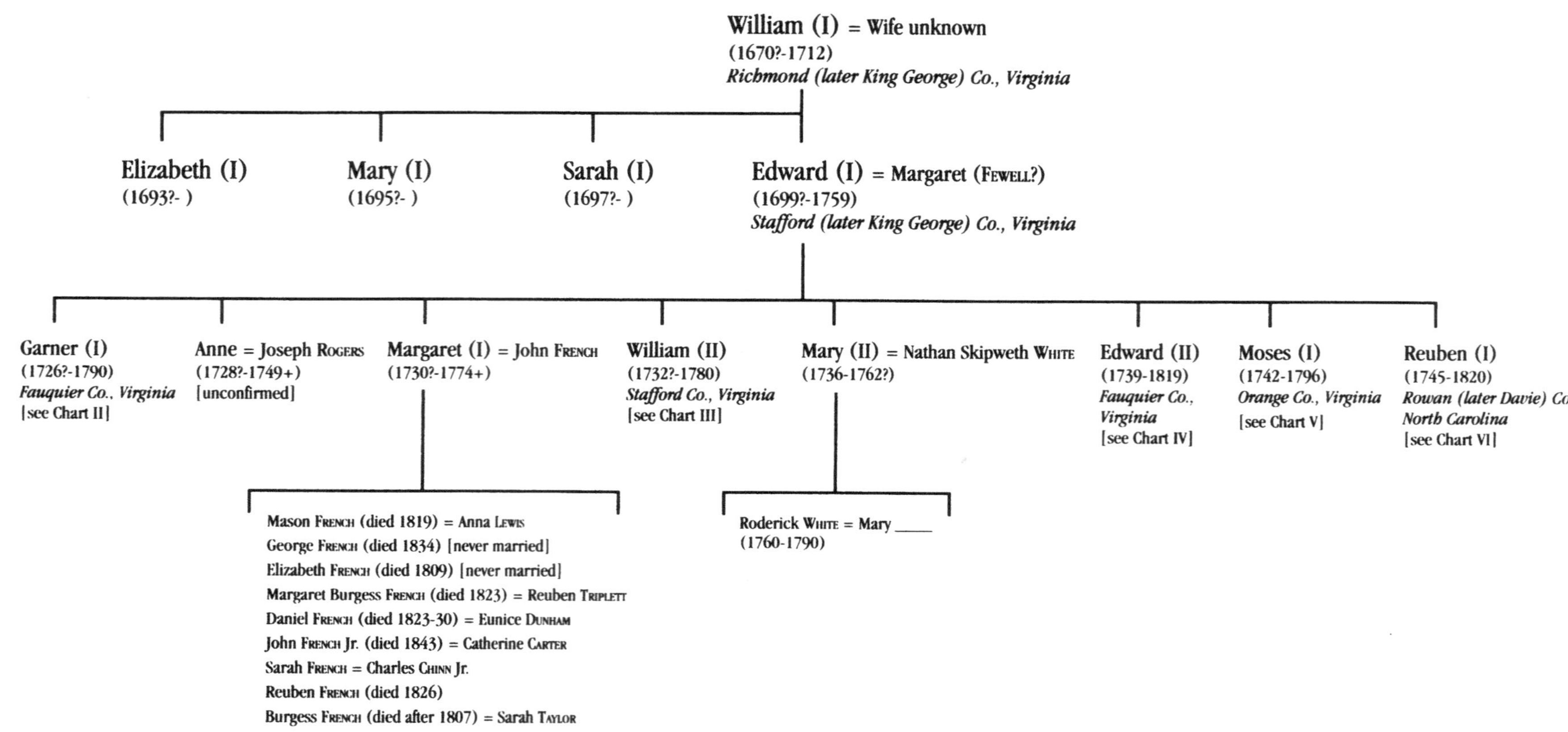

William (I) = Wife unknown
(1670?-1712)
Richmond (later King George) Co., Virginia
Elizabeth (I)
(1693?-)
Mary (I)
(1695?-)
Sarah (I)
(1697?-)
Edward (I) = Margaret (Fewell?)
(1699?-1759)
Stafford (later King George) Co., Virginia
Garner (I)
(1726?-1790)
Fauquier Co., Virginia
[see Chart II]
Anne = Joseph Rogers
(1728?-1749+)
[unconfirmed]
Margaret (I) = John French
(1730?-1774+)
William (II)
(1732?-1780)
Stafford Co., Virginia
[see Chart III]
Mary (II) = Nathan Skipweth White
(1736-1762?)
Edward (II)
(1739-1819)
Fauquier Co., Virginia
[see Chart IV]
Moses (I)
(1742-1796)
Orange Co., Virginia
[see Chart V]
Reuben (I)
(1745-1820)
Rowan (later Davie) Co., North Carolina
[see Chart VI]
Mason French (died 1819) = Anna Lewis
George French (died 1834) [never married]
Elizabeth French (died 1809) [never married]
Margaret Burgess French (died 1823) = Reuben Triplett
Daniel French (died 1823-30) = Eunice Dunham
John French Jr. (died 1843) = Catherine Carter
Sarah French = Charles Chinn Jr.
Reuben French (died 1826)
Burgess French (died after 1807) = Sarah Taylor
Roderick White = Mary ____
(1760-1790)

THE FIRST GENERATION

WILLIAM BURGES
(1670?-1712)

OF RICHMOND (LATER KING GEORGE) COUNTY, VIRGINIA

1a. **William (I).** He was probably born between 1650-1670 (perhaps closer to the latter date), if he is contemporary with his friend (or employer?), Jeremiah Bronaugh Sr. (1670-1749). William Burges appears in one known legal record: his noncupative (deathbed verbal) will is recorded on page 89 of *Richmond Co. Will Book #3*, dated 23 Apr. 1712 O.S., proven on 4 June 1712 O.S. In it he identified four surviving children (there may have been others who had already left home): Edward, a son under the age of 21; Elizabeth and Mary, two unmarried daughters over the age of 16; and Sarah, an unmarried daughter under the age of 16. His accounting mentioned no land, only beds, furniture, a mare, an "old sword," unspecified books, and various stock and farm implements. William lived in St. Marie's [sic] Parish, which covered a large part of Richmond County. His two underaged children were left to the care of Bronaugh, who was named administrator of William's estate. The document was witnessed by Richard and Rebekah Copley, husband and wife. One may infer from this brief record that William Burges was a farm laborer or overseer or craftsman (unlikely), that his wife had predeceased him, that he was literate, that he or someone else in his family had been a soldier (possibly a professional), and that no surviving close relatives lived anywhere nearby. From the names mentioned in his will, we may also deduce that he was living somewhere near the Lambs Creek area of present-day King George Co., and may well have been employed by Bronaugh, whose plantation was located near the Rappahannock River at about the point where State Highway 3 (if followed from Fredericksburg) bends inland from the River toward the peninsular ridge. His wife's name is unknown, as are the exact order and dates of birth of his children.

This family was located about thirty miles directly south of present-day Washington, D.C. The Northern Neck of Virginia, the long peninsula of land stretching between the Potomac and Rappahannock Rivers, experienced a boom in the tobacco trade during the mid-1680s that resulted in a large influx of farmhands, both white and slave, to work the plantations which had grown up along the fertile river plains. Land ownership was concentrated in the hands of a relatively small number of country gentlemen, who had built up their holdings cheaply through the "headright" system, by financing the importation of labor into the colonies. For each settler whose passage was paid, the sponsor received fifty free acres of land, plus (usually) a contract binding the immigrant to seven years of indentured service. Settlers who managed to pay their own way to the British colonies, or those who paid off their servitude after seven years, worked as overseers, tradesmen, and farmers, buying small plots of land in less favorable areas, or leasing plots from the larger plantations. William Burges was probably one of the laborers who flooded into the Northern Neck region between 1685-1710. We know nothing of his origins.

However, it is conceivable that he is the same person as the William Burges mentioned in *The Complete Book of Emigrants, 1661-1699*, by Peter Wilson Coldham (Baltimore, MD: Genealogical Publishing Co., 1990, p. 682) as shipping goods (or himself and his possessions) from Bristol, England to Virginia between 4 Dec. 1697 and 2 Feb. 1697/98 O.S., on the same vessel (the *Mountjoy*) as goods shipped by William French and George Mason. The later Burgess connection with the French and Mason families is at least suggestive, although it must again be emphasized that there is no hard evidence to link our Burgess family with any other family or specific location in Europe.

The Children of William Burgess:

2a. **Elizabeth (I).** Born about 1693. No further record.
2b. **Mary (I).** Born about 1695. No further record.
2c. **Sarah (I).** Born about 1697. She or a sister may have married ___ Swillivan(t) or Sullivan(t), and had children: ***Burgess*** (born about 1725, married Anne Carver on 3 Feb. 1747/48 O.S. [*St. Paul's Parish Register*], listed in the King George Co. tax lists in the 1780s, and had children: *Sallie* [born 24 Oct. 1748 O.S.]; *William* [born 8 Oct. 1750 O.S.]; *Harry* [born 6 July 1758]).
2d. **Edward (I).** Born about 1699. See below for full entry.

THE WILL OF WILLIAM BURGES

The noncupative will of William Burges late of the parish of Saint Maries in the County of Richmond deced. who published and declared the same before us on Thursday the 23th [sic] day of Aprill in the yeare of our Lord 1712, in manner and forme ffollowing Sart. (?)

Imp he did give and bequeath unto his son Edward Burges one gray mare

Item he gave unto his Daughter Elizabeth Burges one catt teule [i.e., cattail] bed wh the appurtenances

Item he did give the bed whereon he dyed to his Daughter Sarah and also to his Daughter Mary one fflock bed.

Item he left his son Edward Burges to Jeremiah Bronaugh untill he came of the age of one and twenty yeares, and also his daughter Sarah untill she came to be sixteene yeares of age.

Item the rest of his Estate he gave to and amongst his children to be equally divided betweene them.

Evidence to the above Will
Richard Copeley
Rebekah Copley

Att a Court held for Richmond County ye fourth day of June 1712 presented to the Court by Jeremiah Bronaugh and proved by Richard Copley and Rebekah his wife, who upon oath declare that the words or the same in effect in the aforesaid will or writing expressed were declared and publiquely spoken by the said William Burges in their presence and hearing the 23d day of Aprill 1712, and that he was att the same time of perfect mind and memory, to the best of their judgments whereupon on the motion of the said Jeremiah Bronaugh it is ordered to be recorded and administration with ye said will annexed granted him on the said estate

Test. Jno Tayloe Dll (?)

NOTE: A cattail bed was stuffed with the fluffed heads of cattail plants; a flock bed was stuffed with bits and pieces of rags and scrap cloth.

THE INVENTORY OF WILLIAM BURGES

(*Richmond Co. Will Book #3*, p. 105-106)

A true inventory of the estate of William Burges [measured in pounds of tobacco]

To cow and calfe	500
To a cow and calfe and one brown cow	1100
To 2 steers and a heefer	750
To 1 steer	350
To a parcell of hoggs	550
To a parcell of old iron	200
To a small gun and a old sword	100
To a parcell of old lumber	100
To 2 old woolen wheeles and & 3 pr wool-cards	220
To a parcell of old pewter	112
To an old looking-glass	020
To a parcell of books and other things	110
To 2 iron potts, an earthen pott & fflesh ffork* & ffrying pan	130
To old chest	100
To 9 hundred nailes [or "a" hundred]	050
To a parcell of cotton	079

James Grant, Henry Golley, William Proctor

Darby Sullivant wh delivered the above & had the estate in possession sworne before me as also the above appraisers sworne before me. Allexr Doniphan

Recorded amongst the records of Richmond County the third day of Septt. 1712 and ordered to be recorded—Test. M. Beckwith CCur

*NOTE: A flesh fork was a large prong used to lift meat from a pot.

[William (I)[1]]

EDWARD BURGE(SS)
(1699?-1759)

OF KING GEORGE COUNTY, VIRGINIA

2d. **Edward (I).** Born between 1691-1712, but probably about 1699; his place of birth is unknown. He is believed to have married Margaret Fewell about 1725 (see below). Edward Burgess is mentioned in William Burges's will (*Richmond Co. Will Book #3*, page 89, dated 23 Apr. 1712 O.S., proven 4 June 1712 O.S.), which put him under the guardianship of a prominent planter, Jeremiah Bronaugh Sr. He purchased a 100-acre farm in King George Co. from John Seamans of Farnham Parish, Richmond Co. on 1 Apr. 1731 O.S. (*King George Co. Deed Book #1-A*, p. 126-129). This deed directly follows one cosigned by Jeremiah Bronaugh Sr. (p. 121-125), his former guardian, the deeds and bonds having been executed on the same days, in the same legal style, and recorded by the same hand (a different hand than preceding entries) consecutively in the *Deed Book* (although the recording dates are a month apart). Edward's land is described as having straddled the King George/Stafford Co. boundary line, which then followed the watershed "ridge" line between the two rivers, a very uncertain region which in places widened to a quarter mile or more. At the right edge of his farm is the "Rowling" or Rolling Road (used to roll tobacco to the river), which may be what later became Virginia State Route 3, or one of the connecting county roads which run off it to the south; later descriptions place the location of the farm two miles northwest of the present courthouse. Neighbors mentioned in the deed include: Benjamin Stribling, Henry Berry, Maj. John Fitzhugh, and "the late" William Bunbury. Payment is noted as five shillings, bonded by six thousand pounds of tobacco.

Edward's land was originally part of a 375-acre parcel granted by Lord Fairfax, Proprietor of the Northern Neck, to Sim (or Simon or Lem) Cox on 7 Mar. 1694/95 O.S. in Stafford and Richmond Cos., adjoining George King, Henry Berrie (Berry), Hale's Cart Path (i.e., the Rowling Road), Owmen Creek (now Kays Run), James Key Jr., [no first name given] Owen, Lewis Griffin, Bunburry's Corner, on the so-called Machotak Dams (or Upper Machodoc Creek); the grant was witnessed by Thos. Catlett, William Strother, and Joseph Berry (*Northern Neck Grant Book #2*, p. 128). Sim or Lem Cox (his name appears both ways) later sold the land off piecemeal, the 100-acre section which became Edward's farm going originally to John Seamans's father. The Burgess land was peculiarly shaped, its top part looking like the cut-off half of a hexagon, with the bottom section coming to two very sharp points, as if perched on a single stilt, with one projection to the left. His land may fall within an area on Route 3 halfway between Comorn and Arnolds Corner (the junction of Route 3 with County Route 208), about two miles northwest of the present-day courthouse of King George village, and just a few miles northeast of the Bronaugh plantation on Lambs Creek.

Edward witnessed the will of Robert Strother in King George Co. on 14 May 1735 (*Will Book #A-1*, p. 114-115), but is not mentioned in county records again. Commissioners were appointed by King George and Stafford Co. in the early 1750s to adjudicate the often confusing, meandering boundary line between the two elongated county jurisdictions; one result of this realignment appears to have been the placement of Edward's land, for tax and voting purposes, in Stafford Co., perhaps because Edward's house was located on the north side of the property. Voting qualifications were also changed at about this time to limit voting to those who owned at least 100 acres of land. Edward is listed as voting in the Burgess Poll (legislators' election) of 1758 in Stafford Co., the only such record surviving from this period. At this time, the Stafford Co. courthouse was located on Aquia Creek, while the King George courthouse was near present-day Port Conway; the church used by the Burgess family, St. Paul's Parish (of the Anglican Church, the official, state-supported religious body both in England and the colonies), was located eight miles northeast of the Burgess plot (down what is presently County Route 208 toward the Potomac River). Most of the early record books of Stafford Co. were lost during the Civil War, leaving only a half dozen deed and will books surviving prior to 1800, plus an incomplete index to the remaining volumes. The two counties were reoriented along present-day boundaries on 1 Jan. 1777.

Edward's will, recorded in *Stafford Co. Liber #O* (p. 359, dated 9 Jan. 1759, probated 8 May 1759), mentions his wife and four youngest children as legatees, naming as executors his wife and sons

Garner and William; his wife is to live on his land until her death, which is then to be sold and distributed equally among his heirs. The will is recorded under the name "Burge," but the later inventory record (p. 366-367, dated 12 June 1759) gives his name as "Burgess." This curious spelling variation also occurs in 1725, when a Margaret "Burge" is mentioned in the accounting of Henry Fewell's estate, again in Prince William Co. in 1785 with Edward Burgess Jr., in 1787 with the personal property tax record of Lunsford Burges in King George Co., with his two possible orphans in Spotsylvania Co. in 1792, and with two records (11 Sept. 1744 and 31 July 1747) in the Edward Dixon merchant accounts.

Edward's wife Margaret is believed to have been a daughter of Henry Fewell and Sarah Whiteman (who was the sister of John Whiteman), and the granddaughter of Stephen and Katherine Fewell. A Margaret "Burge" is mentioned in *King George Co. Inventory Book #1* (p. 47) on 7 May 1725 O.S. as a co-legatee with her sister, Frances Smith, in the accounting of Henry Fewell's estate; at this time, there is no other known Burge(s) family living within fifteen miles of the immediate area. Stephen Fewell, Henry's father, was probably born in London in 1653 (christened on 7 Nov. 1653 O.S. at St. Olave's Parish, Southwark), the son of William Fewell, was transported to the colonies in 1674, and witnessed the will of John Waight in Old Rappahannock Co., VA on 3 Mar. 1679 (*Will Book #2*, p. 151, mentioned as then being 26 years of age). Fewell bought fifty-eight acres of land in Richmond (later King George) Co., VA on 20 Feb. 1692/93 O.S., bounded by Hugh Williams, John Owens, and James Lamb, believed to be within a mile of Bronaugh's land, near the intersection of Lambs Creek and the Rowling Road (see *King George Co. Deed Book #5*, p. 5); the only known Fewells in this part of Virginia all appear to be his descendants. Although the connection of Margaret "Burge" with Edward Burges is not certain, it is the most probable interpretation of the known facts. Margaret Burges is listed in surviving land tax lists of Stafford Co. in 1768, 1773, and 1776 as the owner of 100 acres, and on the personal property tax list of 1782 for King George Co. (as Edward "Burge"). She probably died about 1783, when a second inventory of Edward's estate is recorded in the index book for *Stafford Co. Liber #N* (p. 535; the record itself failed to survive the Civil War).

Edward's fourth son, Moses Burges, probably lived with his mother until her death, at which point he remarried and moved to Orange Co., VA; Moses's oldest son, Lunsford Burges, is listed on the King George Co. personal property tax rolls from 1785-1788, when he presumably died or moved away. Thereafter, the King George Co. tax lists designate the land as belonging to the "Burgess heirs." By the time the Burgess land was sold on 10 Oct. 1797 (*King George Co. Deed Book #8*, p. 145-147), Edward's executors were all dead; therefore, the deed *had* to be executed by the legal representatives of the deceased executors. Garner Burges's two executors, his oldest son, Edward Burgess of Culpeper Co., VA, and his oldest son-in-law, Matthew Neale of Fauquier Co., VA, represented his portion of the estate. William Burges had died young and intestate without a will, so his representative could be any heir male; his youngest son, Edward Burgess (called "Jr." on the deed to distinguish him from his older cousin) of Bourbon Co., KY, signed on William's behalf. The importance of this deed cannot be understated: it proves beyond any reasonable doubt that Garner Burges of Fauquier Co. is Edward's son, that Edward Burgess of Culpeper (later Rappahannock Co.), VA is Garner's son, and that Matthew Neale is Garner's son-in-law; and that the Edward Burgess of Bourbon Co., KY, who later settled in Scott Co., KY, is a direct descendant in the male line of William Burges of Stafford Co., VA, thereby cementing all later relationships in these branches.

The Burgess farm was acquired on 10 Oct. 1797 by Humphrey Steward or Stewart (*Deed Book #8*, p. 145-147), merged with his adjoining 240-acre lot, and then sold on 26 May 1810 to Dr. William Wishart (*Deed Book #9*, p. 394, which mentions an earlier, unrecorded deed of 1 Apr. 1806 witnessed by Charles E. Bennett). In the later sale of Wishart's estate by his son-in-law, Lawrence Taliaferro (see *Deed Book #15*, p. 189), two separate parcels are named, of which "Pudding Hill" seems likeliest to have been the Burgess property (this name is not mentioned again), the other being called "Stewarts." The Wishart lands were acquired by John Arnold on 10 Jan. 1838, but to this day the hills behind Comorn, Virginia, are still called "Wisharts." Until recent years, this area consisted of undeveloped and heavily wooded rolling hills, with occasional farm houses or single-family dwellings, probably very similar in appearance to what it was when the Burgesses owned it 260 years ago; but now many of the trees are being cut to build housing tracts, as the population pushes south from Washington, DC. By the end of the century, this picturesque piece of Virginia countryside will undoubtedly have almost completely vanished.

The Children of Edward Burgess:

3a. **Garner (I).** Born about 1726 in King George Co., VA. See below for full entry.

3b. **Anne.** Born about 1728 in King George Co., VA. Married Joseph Rogers on 24 Oct. 1749 O.S. (*St. Paul's Parish Register*) in Stafford Co., VA. A Joseph Rodgers is listed on the 1782 land tax roll of King George Co., VA, and an Ann Rogers is listed in 1787 in Stafford Co., but both names are too common in the general population to be positively identified with either person. He is *not*, however, the Joseph Rogers of

Culpeper Co., VA who died there in 1762, leaving a son, Burgess Rogers. There is also a Joseph Ro(d)-gers recorded in the 1787 tax lists of Orange Co., VA, and a Joseph and an Ann Rogers are recorded in the Stafford Co. tax lists during the 1780s. However, it should be noted that nothing specific has been found that would definitely tie Anne Rogers and her husband into the Edward Burges family, save for date and proximity. Her inclusion here should therefore be regarded as speculative.

3c. **Margaret (I).** Born about 1730 in King George Co., VA. Married John French on 15 Jan. 1749/50 O.S. (*St. Paul's Parish Register*) in Stafford Co., VA (he was born about 1725, son of Mason French and Catherine [Ellis] Bennett [who was the daughter of Capt. Charles Ellis and the widow of Cossum Bennett Sr.], and died on 24 Oct. 1806 in Fauquier Co.; his will [*Fauquier Co. Will Book #4*, p. 286, dated 1 Nov. 1805, probated 26 Oct. 1806], mentions as survivors the children listed below). Margaret and John French had children (listed in the same order as the final payment record of John's estate):

Mason FRENCH. Born about 1751, served as an officer in the Revolutionary War from 1777-78, married Anna Lewis on 20 Jan. 1783 in Loudoun Co., VA (she was born 1761, daughter of Thomas Lewis and Ann Hickman, and died 1831). He purchased "Creek View" on Goose Creek in Loudoun Co., VA in 1808, and died there on 6 June 1819, leaving children:

Sarah FRENCH (born about 1784, married Alexander Bowen on 24 Feb. 1803).

Mary FRENCH (born about 1786, married John Rutter).

James Burgess FRENCH (born 9 July 1789, married Ann "Nancy" Triplett on 21 Aug. 1817 [she was born 11 Apr. 1795, daughter of Thomas Triplett and Phoebe Lunsford, and died 13 Oct. 1870], moved to Ohio in 1820, and died 6 Oct. 1858, having had children: Sarah [born 27 May 1818, married Aquilla Harrop on 13 Dec. 1836, and died about 1878]; Anna Maria [born 24 Nov. 1821, died 27 Mar. 1893]; Grafton [born 15 June 1822, married Amanda Cartel on 18 Nov. 1846, and died 15 Feb. 1900]; Margaret Jane [born 18 Apr. 1824, married Tobias Thomas on 9 May 1852, and died 29 Jan. 1899]; Thomas [born 3 July 1826, married Lovisa Wheeler on 6 Nov. 1851, and died 16 May 1894]; Delilah [born 29 Oct. 1828, died 1829]; Mary [born 18 June 1830, married John Beard, died 17 Apr. 1900]; Mason [born 6 Aug. 1832, married Caroline Wheeler on 1 Jan. 1855, and died 10 Apr. 1903 at Zanesville, OH]; Reuben [born 30 Sept. 1834, died 16 May 1866]; Lewis [born 9 June 1837, died 28 Nov. 1919]; Hugh Rutter [born 27 Sept. 1839, died 16 July 1841]).

Jane FRENCH (born about 1791, married William Henderson in 1811 [he was the son of Bennett Henderson and Elizabeth Lewis], moved to Kentucky, and had children: Frances Ann [married Hiram Duncan French, and had children: Frances]).

Frances Ann FRENCH (born 1798, married William Triplett, son of Thomas Triplett, on 1 Feb. 1820, and died in 1878).

Lewis FRENCH (born about 1800, married his first cousin, Sarah White, on 27 Nov. 1822 in Fauquier Co. [she was born about 1800, the daughter of George White and Ann "Nancy" Burgess, and died 1833; John Burgess provided the bond], and had children: James Burgess (II) [born about 1823, married Amanda Dant]; Emily Elizabeth (married Andrew Taylor on 9 Feb. 1850); Matilda; Sarah Moore [twin; born 1833]; Sarah Frances [twin; born 1833]; *Lewis FRENCH* married secondly Elizabeth Marshall on 15 Feb. 1836 in Loudoun Co., VA, moved to Lincoln, VA, and died there in the 1860s).

Reuben FRENCH (born about 1802, married Catherine Watkins on 3 Jan. 1833 in Loudoun Co., VA, and moved to Ohio).

Margaret Burgess FRENCH (born 9 Oct. 1807 in Loudoun Co., VA, married Sydnor Garrett in 1834 in Fauquier Co. [he was born 8 Apr. 1808 in Loudoun Co., the son of Henry Garrett and Caroline Matilda Moffett, and died 22 Apr. 1861 in Clarke Co., VA], and died 8 July 1880 at Orleans, Fauquier Co., having had children):

Albert Franklin GARRETT (born 10 Aug. 1832 in Fauquier Co., VA, married Sarah Jane Latham on 30 June 1853 at Washington, DC [she was born about 1835 in Fauquier Co., and died 12 Nov. 1921 at Marshall, VA], and died about 1862 at City Points, VA, having had children: James Franklin [born about 1857]; Cornelia Alice [born 8 May 1859 in Fauquier Co., married Frankford Cullen Sparshott on 17 Jan. 1883 at Georgetown, DC {he was born 30 Aug. 1858 at Camden, NJ, son of Samuel Sparshott and Emma Bullock, and died 3 Apr. 1946 at Montgomery, MD}, and died 9 Feb. 1933 at Washington, DC, having had children: Morris; Margaret May {born 21 Oct. 1884 at Washington, DC, married John Dolan King on 7 Aug. 1902 at Washington, DC <he was born 7 Oct. 1881 at Tennallytown, DC, son of Benjamin F. King and Mary Elizabeth Peverill, and died 18 Jan. 1959 at Washington, DC>, and died 22 Nov. 1911 at Washington, DC, having had children: Ruth Cornelia <born 10 Apr. 1903 at Tennallytown, DC, married Alvaro Robert Bates on 23 Oct. 1922 at Washington, DC |he was born 27 Mar. 1901 at Defiance, OH, son of Alvaro Bates and Sarah Ann Agnes Blue, and died 12 Aug. 1966 at Washington, DC|, and died 26 Mar. 1958 at Washington, DC>; John Russell <born 16 Aug. 1904 at Tennallytown, DC, married Helen Elizabeth Stanley on 15 Dec. 1928, and died 3 Aug. 1970>; Horace Leon <born 1 May 1907 at Tennallytown, DC, married Mildred Ideal White, and died 11 Apr. 1980 at Lanham, MD>}; Alice Elizabeth {born 24 Apr. 1891 at Washington, DC, married Gordon Elice Taylor, and died 1976 at Los Angeles, CA}; Lily Virginia {born 10 Dec. 1893 at Washington, DC, married Sanford Erman Brooks}; Nannie {born about 1897}, died May 1982 at Falls Church, VA]; Sarah M. [born about 1862]; Lula [born 1868, relationship unconfirmed]).

Ruth Cornelia KING and Alvaro Robert BATES had children: Alvaro Robert Jr. (born 2 Dec. 1923, and died 5 Dec. 1923 at Washington, DC); Frederick LeRoy (born 2 Dec. 1924 at Washington, DC, married Hettie Dowtin on 13 July 1946 at Troy, SC); Elizabeth Ann (born 6 Jan. 1926 at Washington, DC, married John Elliot Bandu on 24 Feb. 1950 at Washington, DC); Margaret Ruth (born 24 Nov. 1935 at Washington, DC, married Charles Augustine Carroll Jr. on 26 May 1956 at Washington, DC [he was born 5 Mar. 1927 at Brooklyn, NY, son of Charles Augustine Carroll and Anna Rosa Conrad, and died 19 Apr. 1980 in Prince Georges Co., MD], and had children: Daniel Charles [born 2 Jan. 1957 at Honolulu, HI, married Mary Ann Ferguson on 21 Nov. 1986 at Baltimore, MD, and had children: Michael Conrad Ferguson {born 13 Aug. 1990 at Frederick, MD}]; Ann Elizabeth [born 19 Mar. 1958 at Ewa, HI, married Lawrence Glenn Barstow on 26 Nov. 1977 at Lexington Park, MD, and had children: Ryan Glenn {ad.; born 7 May 1989 in South Korea}; Ann lives at Kent, WA]; Charles Alvaro [born 15 Jan. 1961 at Lexington Park, MD, married Kathaleen Anne Feeney on 5 Oct. 1986 at Little Falls, NY, and had children: James Andrew {born 3 Mar. 1988}]; Margaret Ruth married secondly her childhood sweetheart, Clarence Edward Amundson, on 18 Feb. 1983 at Lexington Park, MD [he was born 8 Dec. 1934 at Mandan, ND, and died 7 Mar. 1989 at Oakton, MD]); Audrey Louise (born 26 Sept. 1937 at Washington, DC, married John Phillip Schwartz on 20 Sept. 1955 at Silver Spring, MD).

Joseph Edward GARRETT (born 30 July 1835 in Fauquier Co., VA, married Anne ___).

John Randolph GARRETT (born 22 Apr. 1837 in Fauquier Co., VA, married his cousin, Virginia A. Burgess, daughter of Moses Burgess, on 12 Aug. 1858; see her entry for their children).

James Eulises GARRETT (born 23 Aug. 1840 in Fauquier Co., VA, died there on 5 Jan. 1861).

Ann Lewis GARRETT (born 27 Oct. 1844 [or 27 Sept. 1846] in Fauquier Co., died there on 28 Aug. 1864).

Lewis Henry GARRETT (born 8 May 1848 in Fauquier Co., married Ella M. Fletcher on 21 Dec. 1871 in Fauquier Co., and died 20 Feb. 1879).

George FRENCH. He bought the old home place in Fauquier Co. after his father's death, dying there unmarried in 1834.

Elizabeth "Eliza" FRENCH. She lived with her brother, George, and died unmarried in Dec. 1809 in Fauquier Co.

Margaret Burgess FRENCH. Married Reuben Triplett on 8 July 1790 in Loudoun Co., VA (he was born 8 June 1750, the son of Francis Triplett and Mildred Edrington, and died about 1823), and died 1 Feb. 1823, having had children: *Delilah* (married James Church on 21 Sept. 1813, and died before 1834); *William* (married Rachel Smith, and moved to Baltimore, MD); *Roderick* (married Mary Jacobs, and moved to Ohio); *Elizabeth* (married Joseph Eidson); *Melinda* (married Adam Bowers on 26 June 1816, and secondly John Anderson); *Frances* (married Thornton Walker); *Harriett* (married John N. T. G. E. Keene on 8 Apr. 1821); *Reuben* (married Eleanor Williams on 16 Mar. 1833); *John* (retarded; never married). This family is delineated from the lawsuit *Triplett vs. French* (*Fauquier Co., VA Chancery Case #81*), which was brought to settle the estates of George and Reuben French, brothers of Margaret Burgess French; since she had predeceased her brothers, her children then alive are listed as her heirs.

Daniel FRENCH. Mentioned in his father's will (1805). Married, and had children: *Daniel Jr.* (born about 1798). Married secondly Eunice Dunham on 14 Jan. 1800 (she was the daughter of Amos Dunham), and died before 1830, having had children: *Lorenzo Dow*; *Reuben*; *Lebbeus*; *Alpheus* (married Juliet Byrne on 23 Jan. 1832); *Mary*; *Margaret*; *Sidney* (born about 1823, died 1857).

John FRENCH Jr. Married Catherine Carter on 13 Mar. 1794 in Loudoun Co., VA (she was born about 1766 in Loudoun Co., the daughter of Richard and Agnes Carter, and died after 1836), moved to Mason Co., KY by 1800, and died there in Nov. 1843, having had children: *Burgess P.* (died before July 1836); *Elizabeth A.*; *John E.* (married Elizabeth Dobbins on 17 Dec. 1834 in Mason Co., KY); *Matilda* (married William Russell before 1836); *Agnes* (married T. Martin on 17 Dec. 1827 in Mason Co.); *Richard Carter* (married Maira Collins on 24 June 1823 in Mason Co.); *Hiram Duncan* (born before 1800, married his cousin, Frances Ann Henderson). This family is delineated through John French Sr.'s will, which was probated in 1843 in Mason Co., KY.

Sarah FRENCH. Born about 1770. Married Charles Chinn Jr. on 14 Feb. 1794 in Loudoun Co. (he was the son of Charles Chinn and Sythia Davis), and had children: *Pamela* (married Burr Triplett in 1816); *Charles E.* (married Rebecca Elgin on 6 June 1839); *Elijah* (married Tamer Moore on 2 Sept. 1829); *John French* (born 27 July 1810 in Fauquier Co., married Lydia Elizabeth Byrne on 23 Jan. 1832, and died 7 Oct. 1875 in Independence Co., AR); *Sarah* (married Samuel Powell Triplett, and secondly

Samuel Puller on 30 Dec. 1820 in Fauquier Co.); *Lucinda*; *Margaret Burgess* (married Alexander J. McMullin in 1829).

Reuben FRENCH. He died childless in Jan. 1826.

Burgess FRENCH. Married Sarah "Sallie" Taylor on 30 Apr. 1807 in Fauquier Co. (she was born 9 June 1787, daughter of William Tarlton Taylor and Elizabeth Hampton).

John FRENCH is mentioned as a voter in the Stafford Co. election of 1758, and Margaret may be mentioned in the will of Henry Bussy in Stafford Co. on 16 Apr. 1764 (a will which is witnessed by Edward Burgess Jr.). By 1760 the Frenches had moved to Loudoun Co., VA, when John French is listed on the tax rolls; John bought 180 acres in Fauquier Co., VA in 1768 from William and Martha Pearle (*Deed Book #3*, p. 338-39), and is listed there on the tax rolls from 1782. Margaret is alive by inference as late as 1774, the approximate date of the birth of her last child, but died before her husband.

Although there is no specific evidence tying Margaret French to her presumed father, there are so many interconnections between the Burgess, Bennett, French, and Ellis families (through Catherine Ellis) that I discount the possibility of any other relationship. See also the section on "The Ellis Connection" (p. 14). Much of the material on the French family has been supplied by Margaret Amundson, who has contributed greatly to this book.

3d. **William (II).** Born about 1732 in King George Co., VA. See below for full entry.

3e. **Mary (II).** Born 3 Nov. 1736 O.S. in King George Co., VA (*St. Paul's Parish Register*), listed as the daughter of *Richard Burges* (no mother given). The handwritten version of the *Register* shows curious gaps in the listings. Many mothers' names are missing from the birth records, but few fathers' names; and many marriage records lack the maiden names (but not the given names) of the brides. This can only be explained if the records were transcribed sometime after the events took place, with the minister filling in details from his memory and from jotted notes. Perhaps this is why Mary's father is recorded as Richard (this is the first Burgess name in the book, probably not long after the family joined the church; an abbreviated Rich.[d] and Edw.[d] would look very much alike if scrawled); or it may be that there were simply two unrelated persons of the name. There is no other record of a Richard Burges in this part of Virginia during this time.

Mary BURGESS is mentioned as unmarried in her presumed father's will on 9 Jan. 1759. She married Nathan(iel) Skipweth White on 15 Apr. 1759 in Stafford Co., VA (*St. Paul's Parish Register*), and had at least the following children: *Roderick* (born 3 Oct. 1760 in Stafford Co. [*St. Paul's Parish Register*], may have married Mary ___, had children: Elizabeth Grant "Betsy" and Mary Pannel "Polly," and died 1790 in Spotsylvania Co., VA [*Will Book #E*, p. 1012-1014, dated 23 Sept. 1790, probated 7 Dec. 1790]).

Nathan S. White was a clock and watch maker. He is mentioned as receiving a £100 bond from George Long on 7 July 1761 (*Spotsylvania Co. Will Book #B*, p. 535, dated 3 Aug. 1761) pending resolution of a lawsuit, as witnessing a bond between William Elliott of Prince William Co. and Thomas Chilton of Westmoreland Co. (*Fauquier Co. Deed Book #2*, p. 164-165, dated 25 June 1764), as being owed money by the estate of Nimrod Ashby (*Fauquier Co. Will Book #1*, p. 243; Ashby died in 1764, the estate was probated 20 Apr. 1774). They are not the same Nathan and Mary White who moved to Frederick Co., VA by 5 Nov. 1770 (evidently from Pennsylvania), when they were admitted to the Hopewell Friends Church, leaving children: *Ann* (married Goldsmith Chandlee); *Sarah* (married Abraham Branson); *Lydia*; *Nathaniel Jr.*; *Nancy*; *Dinah*. A possible grandson of Nathan, Nathan S. White (1817-1888), lived in Jefferson Co., WV. Mary White died by 21 July 1763, when her husband is mentioned with a new wife, Sharlotte (*Prince William Co. Deed Book #Q*, p. 5-6). Relationship not verified, but likely.

3f. **Edward (II).** Born 27 Nov. 1739 O.S. in King George Co., VA. See below for full entry.

3g. **Moses (I).** Born 2 Dec. 1742 O.S. in King George Co., VA. See below for full entry.

3h. **Reuben (I).** Born 12 Feb. 1744/45 O.S. in King George Co., VA. See below for full entry.

THE WILL OF EDWARD BURGE(SS)

January the ninth day in the year of our Lord one thousand seven hundred & fifty nine I Edward Burge being sick & weak of body but of perfect mind & memory thanks be to God therefore & calling to mind the mortality of my body knowing it is appointed for all men once to die do make & ordain this my last will & testament. And as it has pleased God to bless me in this life I give & dispose of the same in the following manner & form—

Imprinis [sic] I give & to my Margit Burge the hole & sole execute of all my estate during her natural life & after my wife decease—

Item I give & bequeath to my daughter Mary Burge one feather bed & furniture & one cow & calf. Item I give & bequeath to my sons Edward Moses & Rubin—eight pounds each to be raised out of my estate. & after my wifes decease my land Negroes goods & chattles to be sold & equally to be divided among all my children & I also appoint my sons Gardener & William Burge to be executor of this my last will & testament in WITNESS hereof I put my hand & seal—

Signed in the presence of

Joel Anchorom
Anne Amerson

Edward Burge

At court held for Stafford County 8th May 1759
The within last will & testament of Edward Burge dec^d was presented into court by Margritt Burge Exec^re therein named who made oath thereto according to law & being proved by the oaths of Joel Anchorom & Anne Ammerson the two witnesses thereto subscribed is admitted to record & on motion of the s^d Ex^r & she performing what is usual in such cases certificate is granted her for obtaining a probat thereopon due form

Test, Henry Tyler Cte

THE INVENTORY OF EDWARD BURGESS

(*Stafford County Liber #O*, p. 366-367)

An Inventory of the estate Mr Edwd Burgess Deced.
[many abbreviations, some unclear; d.^o =ditto]
[*values in Virginia pounds (£), shillings (/), and pence (d), in that order*]

To cash 7£-10/. To an orphan girl bound p.^s indenture 1£ 8-10-0
To 1 negro man 50£. To 2 negro woman @ 50£ 150-0-0
To mare & colt 12£. To 1 mare 4£. To 1 old horse 3£.
1 young d^o 8£ 27-0-0
To 22 head of cattle at 25£-6/. To 21 sheep @ 6/.
To 8 lambs @ 3/ 32-16-0
To 48 head of hogs 9£-18-6^d. To 4 hives of bees at 10/.
To 18 geese at 1/3^d 13-0-6
To 1 bed & furniture 6£ 10/. To 2 d^o at 5£. To 4 beds
& furniture at 3£ 15/ 31-10-0
To 8 3/4 ^lb thread @ 1/6. To 12½ yd.
chock linnen @ 1/3^d 6-17-1½
To 4 yd. white linn. @ 2/. To 19 yd.
of Virginia cloath @ 2/ 2-6-0
To 8½ yds. of horns @ 9^d. To 1 jarr & 2 juggs 5/.
To 3 yds. cloth @ 2/. To 1 bop 6^d 0-13-12½
To 1 fine felt hatt 3/. To 4½ foot of iron chain 4/ 0-7-0
To 1 chest 6/. To 1 walnut cubberd 1£-5/ 1-11-0
To 1 ovil table 1£-5/. To 1 square d^o & some lumber 12/6 1-17-6
To 1 pair styliards* 7/6. To 1 spice
morter & pestle 7/6^d 0-15-0
To 1 table chest 1 piggin* & mug 15/. To 1 old table
chan* & piggin* 5/ 1-0-0
To 1 padlock & some other trifles 1/6^d.
To 1 looking glass & towels 5/ 0-6-6
To 1 gun 2 pistles 1 cop* & other lumber 3-10-0
To 14 ^lb of spun cotton @ 3/6^d.
To 2 ^lb spun wool @ 1/9^d 2-12-6
To 3 mens saddles & 1 womans ditto 5-0-0
To 40 ^lb of wool @ 1/. 20 ^lb of pick^d cotton @ 2/.
2 chests & 1 bop at 1£-10/ 5-10-0
To a pair of trucks & a parcel of hoes & plowes 1-10-0
To a pracel [sic] of wooden ware 15/.
To a parcel of pewter 3£-10/ 4-13-0
To parcel of old lumber 3£-10/. 6 i^n pots 2 d^o frying pans
1 iron skillett .... [carried over]
To 2 sadles & a pair of flesh forks
To a parcel of carpenter stools 8-10-0
To 1 crosscut saw & 1 whipsaw 1-10-0
To 2 looms & harness 3£. To 3 spin^d wheals
& a quill wheal 1£.5 4-5-0
To 1 grindstone 2/6^d. A parcel of old cyder cask 2£ 2-2-6
To a parcel of raw hides 17/. A parcel of flax & flax seed 2-2-0
To a parcel of knives & forks 5/. To 6 flag chairs* 10/ 0-15-0
The am.^t 315-3-6

We the subscribers being by order of court dated May Court 1759 appointed appraisers of the estate of Edward Burgess decead & being foresworn have in obediance to the s[d] order appraised y[e] s[d] estate according to the above inventory witness our hands this 12th of June 1759—Tho.[s] Bunbury Jn.[r], Howson Hooe, Harris Hooe.

At a court held for Stafford County 10th July 1759
This inventory & appraisment of the estate of Edw[d] Burgess being returned & sworn to by the administrators is admitted to record—

Test
Henry Tyler Cte

*NOTE: A steelyard (styliard) is a type of scale with a short arm to take the thing being weighed, and a long, calibrated arm along which a smaller weight is moved until it balances; a piggin is a small wooden pail with one stave extending upward as a handle; "chan" might be a misrendering of "chair"; "cop" may be short for "copper," sometimes used to refer to a copper kettle; the term "flag chair" has so far escaped discovery.

THE PURCHASE OF THE ORIGINAL BURGESS LAND
(*King George Co. Deed Book #1-A*, p. 126-129)

This indenture made the first Day of April in the year of our Lord Christ one Thousand seven Hundred & Thirty one **between** John Seamans of the parish of Farnham in the county Richmond Planter of the one part and Edward Burges of the Parish of Hanover in the county of King George Planter of the other part **Witnesseth** that the s[d] John Seamans for & in consideration of the sum of five shillings to him in hand paid by the sd the Receipt whereof he doth hereby acknowledge **hath** bargained & sold & by these Presents **doth** bargain & Sell unto the s[d] Edward Burges one Hundred acres of Land Lying on the main Ridge between the Rivers of Rappahanock & Pertomack part in King George & part in Stafford County & Bounded as followeth (viz.) Begining in Hanover Parish in King George County at a Locust Post standing in the Line of the Land of Benjamin Sribling [sic] & Runing N81 E69 poles to a Red Oak Corner tree of Henry Berryes land Then S68 E73 poles along the s[d] Berryes Line to an old Red Oak Corner tree of the Land of Maj[r] John Fitzhughs then along the s[d] Fitzhughs line N20 E118 poles to a Red Oak standing by the Rowling Road, then N26½ W47 poles to a small Black Oak sapling standing in the Line of the Land formerly belong to M[r]. William Bunbury, then along then s[d] Bunbury's Line West 90½ poles S26 W144 poles to the Beginning, which s[d] Land above bounded is part of a Tract of Land formerly granted to M[r]. Sim Cox by Patent from the Proprietors of the Northern Neck of Virginia Bareing Date the first Day of March in the year of our Lord one Thousand six Hundred & ninty four or five and sold by the s[d] Sim Cox to Joseph Seamans of Lancaster County as by Deed Bearing Date the Twentieth Sixth of October in the year of our Lord one Thousand seven Hundred & Nine, Doth appear & after demised to the above s[d] John Seamans by the Last will & Testament of the afores[d] Joseph Seamans Father to the s[d] John Seamans Bearing Date the Twentieth Day of November one Thousand seven Hundred & Twenty nine Recourse being had to the Records above Mentioned may more fully appear and the Reversion & Reversions Remander & Remanders & other Rents & Prophits of the Premises of every Part & Paid thereof **to have and to hold** the said one Hundred Acres of Land above Bounded & all & singular other the premises intended to be hereby granted with the appertenences unto the said Edward Burges his Exe[rs] & assigns from the Day before the Date hereof for Dureing the term of one whole year from thence Next ensuing & fully to be Compleated & ended **yeilding and paying** therefore the yearly Rent of one year of Indian Corn at the feast of S[t] Michael the arch Angel only if the same be Demanded to the Intent that by Virtue of these Presents & of the statute for Transfering Uses into Possessions the s[d] Edward Burges May be in actual Possession of the Premises & be Enabled to accept of a grant of the Reversion and Inheritance thereof to him & his Heirs for ever. **In testimony** of which the Parties of these presents their hand & seals Interchangably have sett & affixed the Date above Written.

Signed, Sealed & Delivered in the Presence of us, John Seamans
Tho[s] Catlett
W[m] Strother
Jo[s] Berry T. Turner, CC

Following the above lease is an almost identical "release" dated 2 Apr. 1731 in which Edward Burges pays John Seamans "six thousand pounds of good sound merchantable tobacco in cask" to obtain final title to the land. Elizabeth Seamans is examined and relinquishes her rite of dower and shares.

THE SALE OF THE ORIGINAL BURGESS LAND
(*King George Co. Deed Book #8*, p. 145-147)

This indenture made this tenth day of october in the year of our Lord one thousand seven hundred & ninety seven Betwen Matthew Neale of Fauq[r] County, Edward Burgess of Culpeper County, Exors. of Garner Burgess late of Fauq[r]. County & Edward Burgess of the County of Bourboun in the state of Kentucky of the one part & Humphrey Steward of the County of King George of the other part, witnesseth that the s[d] Matthew Neale, Edward Burgess, Edward Burgess J[r]. for & in consideration of the sum of fifty five pounds to them in hand paid by the said Humphrey Steward, the receipt whereof they do hereby Acknowledge, hath granted bargained & sold aliend & Confirmed and doth by these presents grant bargain & sell alien & confirm unto the said Humphrey Steward & his heirs all that tract or dividend of land formerly belonging to Edward Burgess containing one hundred Acres lying & being in the County of King George & bound as followeth Begining at a locust post standing in the line of the [land] of Benj[a] Stripling & runs N81 E69 poles to a red oak Corner tree of Henry Berrys land then S68 E73 pole along the said Berrys line to an old red oak corner tree to the land of Maj[r]. John Fitzhugh then along the Fitzhughs line N20 E118 poles to red corner oak tree standing by the Rowling road, then N26½ W47 poles to a small black oak saplin standing in the line of the land formerly belong to M[r] William Bunbury, then along the said Bunburys line W90½ poles S26 W144 poles to the begining with said land above bounded is part of a tract of Land formerly granted to Sim Cox by Patent from the proprietors of the Northern neck of Virginia dated the first day of March 1694/5 & sold by the s[d] Sim Cox to

Jo[s] Seamans of Lancaster County by Deeds bearing date the twenty sixth of october 1709 doth appear and after demised to the above said John Seamans by the last will and testament of Jo[s] Seamans Father of the aforesaid John Seamans bearing date of 20th day of November 1729—& since devised to be sold to Edward Burgess who purchased of John Seamans for the benefit of his children To have and to hold all & singular the premises [with] the appurtenances unto the said Humphrey Steward & his heirs & assigns forever together with all houses buildings ways, woods, weaters, hereditaments & appurtenances to the same belonging & the reversion, Remainders, Rents, issues, profits thereof & all the estate right title Interest claim & demand of them the s[d] Matthew Neale & Edward Burgess Exr[s] of Garner Burgess who was the Exor[s] of Edward Burgess afores[d] & Edward Burgess Jun[r] aforesaid & the said Matthew Neale, Edward Burgess Sen[r] & Edward Burgess J[r] for themselves and their heirs doth covenant & grant to and with the said Humphrey Steward & assigns that he and they shall & may at all times hereafter pesably & quietly have hold & possess the premises without the hindrance or molestation of the said Matthew Neale, Edward Burgess, and Edward Burgess J[r]. or either of their heirs or any other person claiming under them & that freed & discharged from all incumbrances & further that the said Matthew Neale, Edward Burgess, and Edward Burges J[r] shall & will at any time hereafter upon the request & at the cost and charges of the said Humphrey Steward his heirs & assigns—make and execute all such further and other reasonable acts and conveyances for the better & more perfect conveying & assureing the s[d] land & premises with the appurtenances thereunto belonging unto the said Humphrey Steward his heirs & assigns as by him or them or by his or their councel learned in the law shall be advised or required..And, lastly, that the said Matthew Neale Edward Burgess & Edward Burgess J[r] & their heirs the foregoing bargained and sold land and premises unto the said Humphrey Steward his heirs & assigns from the claim & demand of the said Matthew Neale, Edward Burgess, Edward Burgess J[r] & their heirs and from the claim & demand of every other person shall & will warrant & forever defend by these presents In Witness whereof the said Matthew Neale, Edward Burgess & Edward Burgess J[r] hath hereuntil set their hnd[s] and seals the day and year first mentioned.

W. Hooe
Nathaniel Hooe
(witnesses)

Matthew Neale
Edward Burgess
Edward Burgess J[r].

THE ELLIS CONNECTION

Although the earliest members of the Burgess family never rose above the lowest levels of the *bourgeoisie*, barely qualifying for the vote with the ownership of 100 acres of land, the third generation of the family married into a much wealthier and more influential class of planters and local politicians. The link that connects these disparate relationships is Captain Charles Ellis, who died in 1708. Ellis had four daughters, two of whom, Catherine and Sarah, had offspring who are known to have been directly connected to the Burgess family. Catherine Ellis married (as her first husband) Cossomb Bennett Sr. (who died 1718), by whom she had (among others) a son, Cossomb Jr. (who died about 1766), who married Katherine Bunbury in 1743. The latter couple had, among seven known children, a daughter, Margaret Bennett, who married about 1784 (as his second wife) Moses Burgess, fourth son of Edward Burgess Sr.

After her first husband's early death, Catherine Ellis Bennett remarried Mason French (who died 1746), and by him had a son, John French, who married Margaret Burgess in 1750. Catherine's sister, Sarah, married Anthony Buckner (who died about 1734), and by him had a son, John Buckner, and a daughter, Sarah Jr., who married Thomas Price in 1734. Among the latter couple's children were Elizabeth Price (born 1741), who was Moses Burgess's first wife; Sarah Price (born 1743), who married Edward Burgess Jr.; and Anthony Price (born 1736), who married Elizabeth Stribling, sister of Margaret Stribling, who married Reuben Burgess. It should also be noted that Moses Burgess had a son by his first wife named John Buckner Burgess, after his great-uncle, and a daughter by his second wife named Catherine Ellis Burgess, after her great-grandmother. Thus, four later children of Edward Burgess Sr. married very close relatives, who were at least cousins by marriage. Only the two older sons, Garner and William, who appear to have left the area entirely, settling on or near Accokeek Creek in what is now Stafford Co., broke the pattern by marrying into other families in Overwharton Parish; Mary's husband may or may not have been related, and Anne's relationship to our Burgess family remains uncertain in any event.

More work remains to be done in cementing these and other family connections to the earliest known Burgess family, but that such multiple relationships exist should not be surprising, given the rural nature of the area, the difficulty of travel in those days, and the rather sparse population. The marital choices available in the ten-mile radius that one could expect to frequent were necessarily limited; and similar cousin marriages can be observed in later Burgess branches that remained for long periods in one small farming region. The naming patterns of the time and locale strongly suggest that most (if not all) family members were named for relatives and/or close friends (who often served as godparents), and that if one only knew more about the close Burgess neighbors and cousins, much would become clear that is now obscured.

THE FIRST BRANCH

GARNER BURGESS
OF FAUQUIER COUNTY, VIRGINIA

The Home of Isaac Franklin Burgess and Family, Tilton, Kentucky, Circa 1901
I. F. & Mary Burgess (left of porch), W. T. & Bertha Burgess (next right), E. T. & Minnie Burgess (right of porch), Harry & Emma (in carriage) [see pages 149-153]

John Garner Burgess (1805-1883)
(see page 57)

THE BURGESSES BETWEEN THE REVOLUTIONARY WAR AND THE WAR OF 1812

In the aftermath of the unrest caused by the Revolutionary War, the settlers on the eastern seaboard began moving inland, rapidly displacing the Indian populations and opening up the vast lands to the west. The Burgess family soon followed suit, for after the death of Margaret Burgess about 1783, there was no reason for any family members to stay on or near the old home place. Garner Burges had already settled in western Fauquier Co. in the 1760s, and his brother, Edward Burgess Jr., had moved to Prince William Co. sometime in the next decade. Now further emigrations took place. William Burgess died about 1780 in Stafford Co.; his widow, Bathsheba Courtney Burgess, remarried a prosperous widower, Ralph Hughes, and by 1786 the Hughes had settled in Bourbon Co., Kentucky with William's sons, Henry and Edward Burgess. Moses Burgess remarried in the 1780s, and bought land in Orange Co. in 1784, leaving his oldest son, Lunsford, on the original Burgess plot (the latter died or moved away in 1788, leaving the land vacant). The youngest son, Reuben Burgess, was the last to leave the area near the Potomac River; he took his family south and west to Albemarle Co. in 1789. Edward Burgess Jr. shifted across the county line into eastern Fauquier Co. in the late 1780s. Finally, Reuben Burgess moved again in 1799, south to Rowan (later Davie) Co., North Carolina.

These migrations were symptomatic of a new nation on the move. Opportunities were available to anyone with a little money and a large willingness to work, and the Burgesses were caught up in the frontier fever. The distances traveled might seem slight by present-day standards, but in fact these families were cutting all or most of their ties with their immediate relatives (other than those actually joining their expeditions), except for occasional correspondence and very infrequent visits. Thus was established the pattern that would be followed during the ensuing century, of families pushing steadily westward with whatever small collection of belongings that could be carried along—and with very little else. Roads were poor, travel hard: most of these trips were one-way journeys. Once the land had been converted to cash and the family's possessions reduced to what one or two wagons could carry, there was no going back. The original Burgess farm was finally sold in 1797, and with it were cut the last ties to King George Co.

There were other journeys being made as well. The Anglican Church had been disestablished with the American Revolution, and many of its physical structures fell into ruin or disrepair. Suddenly, religious freedom everywhere became a reality, and new churches and groups of churches sprung up to displace older and less favored denominations. The Burgesses had been protestant from the beginning; many family members now began joining the Methodist, Baptist, and Christian denominations as these were formed and locally organized.

By the early 1800s the Burgess grandchildren were themselves moving on, spreading out to Kanawha Co., Virginia (later West Virginia), Halifax Co., Virginia, the Shenandoah Valley, Jefferson Co., Kentucky, Culpeper (later Rappahannock) Co., Virginia, Scott Co., Kentucky, Fleming Co., Kentucky, Harrison Co., Kentucky, all located at this time in the central southern states, south of the Mason-Dixon line. No one had yet ventured very far either north or south: the trend was ever west, over the Blue Ridge and Cumberland Moutains into the newly opened virgin lands in the interior. The risks were great, but most were willing to take them. Only two Burgess branches stayed permanently in Virginia: one in Culpeper and Rappahannock Cos. and the other in Fauquier Co.

Almost all of the Burgess families of this period owned slaves to help work their 100-to-200-acre farms. Life during this period was centered around farm, family, community, and church. Except for major moves to other locations, most individuals spent their lives within ten miles of home. None of these families were wealthy by the standards of their day, but none were poor, either, and most were almost entirely self-sufficient except for the few commodities and manufactured goods which needed to be imported from overseas or from the northern states. Life was simple but hard, formal education minimal, life expectancy short, families large, medicine primitive, and virtually every adult male in the family farmed for a living.

Then came the War of 1812.

Chart II: Garner Burgess of Fauquier Co., Virginia

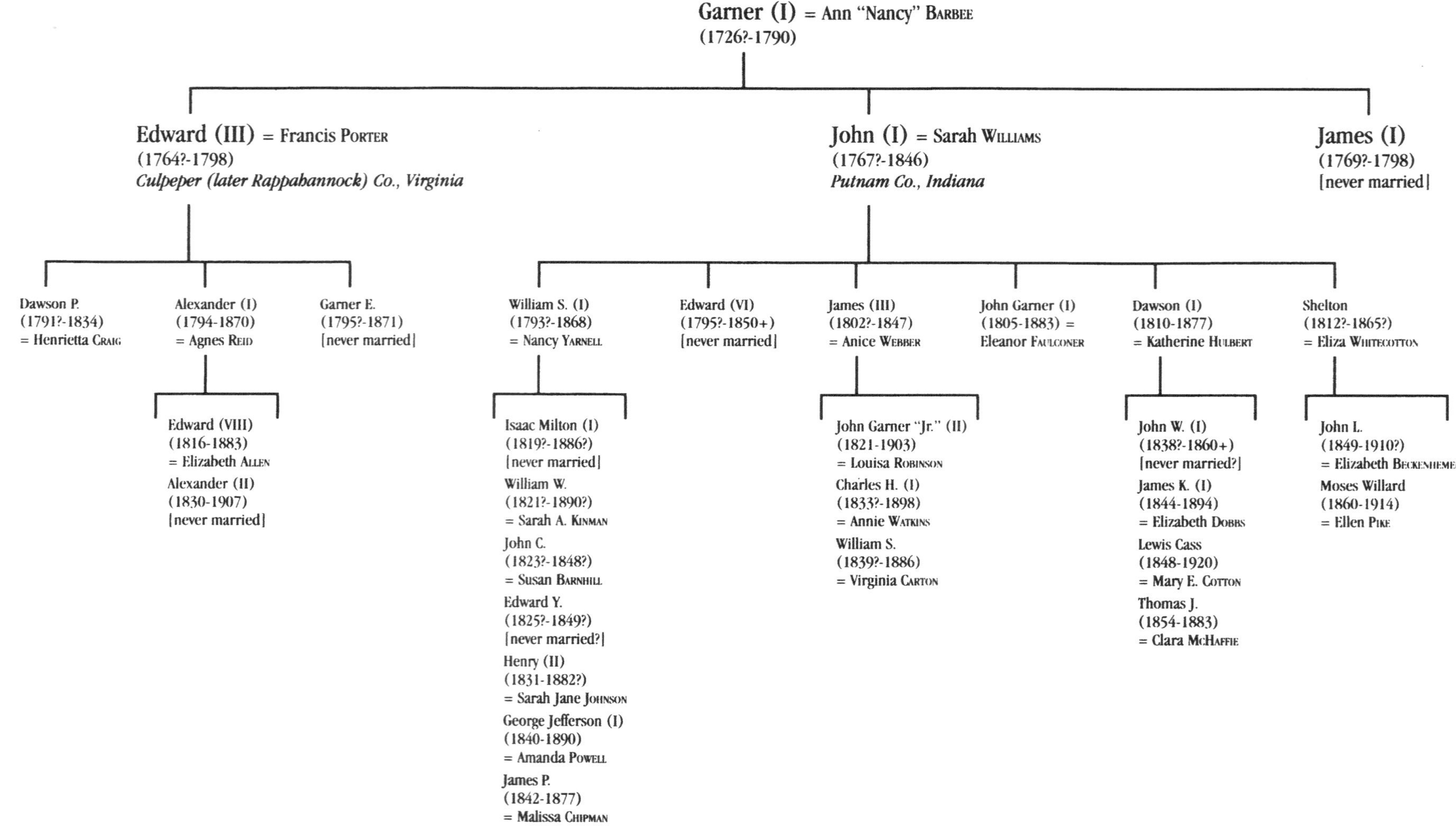
Garner (I) = Ann "Nancy" Barbee
(1726?-1790)
Edward (III) = Francis Porter
(1764?-1798)
Culpeper (later Rappahannock) Co., Virginia
John (I) = Sarah Williams
(1767?-1846)
Putnam Co., Indiana
James (I)
(1769?-1798)
[never married]
Dawson P.
(1791?-1834)
= Henrietta Craig
Alexander (I)
(1794-1870)
= Agnes Reid
Garner E.
(1795?-1871)
[never married]
William S. (I)
(1793?-1868)
= Nancy Yarnell
Edward (VI)
(1795?-1850+)
[never married]
James (III)
(1802?-1847)
= Anice Webber
John Garner (I)
(1805-1883) =
Eleanor Faulconer
Dawson (I)
(1810-1877)
= Katherine Hulbert
Shelton
(1812?-1865?)
= Eliza Whitecotton
Edward (VIII)
(1816-1883)
= Elizabeth Allen
Alexander (II)
(1830-1907)
[never married]
Isaac Milton (I)
(1819?-1886?)
[never married]
William W.
(1821?-1890?)
= Sarah A. Kinman
John C.
(1823?-1848?)
= Susan Barnhill
Edward Y.
(1825?-1849?)
[never married?]
Henry (II)
(1831-1882?)
= Sarah Jane Johnson
George Jefferson (I)
(1840-1890)
= Amanda Powell
James P.
(1842-1877)
= Malissa Chipman
John Garner "Jr." (II)
(1821-1903)
= Louisa Robinson
Charles H. (I)
(1833?-1898)
= Annie Watkins
William S.
(1839?-1886)
= Virginia Carton
John W. (I)
(1838?-1860+)
[never married?]
James K. (I)
(1844-1894)
= Elizabeth Dobbs
Lewis Cass
(1848-1920)
= Mary E. Cotton
Thomas J.
(1854-1883)
= Clara McHaffie
John L.
(1849-1910?)
= Elizabeth Beckenhemer
Moses Willard
(1860-1914)
= Ellen Pike

[William (I)[1], Edward (I)[2]]

GARNER BURGES
(1726-1790)
OF FAUQUIER COUNTY, VIRGINIA

3a. **Garner (I)** *[son of Edward (I)].* He may have been named for his maternal grandmother, or for some other unknown relative on either side of the family; his surname is consistently spelled "Burges." Born about 1726 in King George Co., VA. Married Ann(e) "Nancy" Barbee on 19 Feb. 1750/51 O.S. (*Overwharton Parish Register*) in Stafford Co., VA. Garn Burges had moved to Stafford Co. (probably near Accokeek Creek) by 21 Feb. 1749/50 O.S., when he witnessed the will of Charles Hinson (*Liber #O*, p. 86) and appraised the estate of William Welch on 12 July 1750 O.S. (*Ibid.*, p. 107); he is mentioned in his father's will (1759), and inventoried the estate of Thomas Monk on 14 Dec. 1762 (*Ibid.*, p. 432). By 1 Nov. 1770 Garn Burges had purchased a 200-acre farm in the Manor of Leeds, Leeds Parish, western Fauquier Co. (*Deed Book #4*, p. 370), adjoining the land of Charles Waller. He is noted on the 1783 Fauquier land tax record as having a twenty-year mortgage; if he is dropped from the register in 1784 because the mortgage has been paid, then he moved there about 1763. On 28 February 1777 he appraised the estate of his brother-in-law, Thomas Barbee Jr., assisted by his son-in-law, Matthew Neale, Samuel Luttrel, James Foley, and C. Duleny (*Will Book #1*, p. 307-308). He also appeared on the list of tenants for the Manor in 1777, on the land tax rolls of Fauquier Co. in 1783, and on the personal property tax lists from 1782-1790; Anne Burgess continued to be listed there from 1791-1801. He died in Fauquier Co. in the fall of 1790; his will (*Fauquier Co. Will Book #2*, p. 180, dated 19 Apr. 1790, probated 25 Oct. 1790) names his wife and the nine children given below, in the same order as listed in his will (except for "Peggy," who appears fourth on the list). His original will with signature attached still survives in the Fauquier County Courthouse. The settlement (*Will Book #5*, p. 63-65) was rendered to the court of Fauquier Co. by executor Matthew Neale on 22 June 1809, and approved four days later.

"Nancy" Burges was born about 1731, the daughter of Thomas Barbee Sr. (he died in Stafford Co. in 1752; his will [*Stafford Co. Liber #O*, p. 216, dated 8 Nov. 1748 O.S., probated 10 Mar. 1752 O.S.], mentions the following children: Sarah O'Connon; Andrew; Thomas Jr. [married Mary Rogers in Stafford Co. on 1 Feb. 1737 O.S., and died in 1777 in Fauquier Co.]; John; Catherine Withers; Mary Coalmay; Sylvia Grant; Ann(e); Betty [i.e., Elizabeth?]; and Joseph). Ann "Nancy" Burges died between June 1801 and 2 June 1802, when she is noted on the Fauquier Co. tax list as "dc."

The Children of Garner Burges:

4a. **Margaret (II) "Peggy."** Born 27 July 1751 O.S. in Stafford Co., VA (*Overwharton Parish Register*). She is listed fourth (rather than first) on her father's record of children in his will, perhaps indicating that the Margaret Burgess who was born in 1751 had died young, and been supplanted with a second of that name born about 1759/60. She apparently never married. On 20 June 1804 she deeded her personal property, including "one Negro girl named Art," and her share of her brother James Burgess's estate to her sister, Nancy Hitch (*Fauquier Co. Deed Book #15*, p. 615, recorded 23 July 1804, witnessed by George Page, Frances Hillery, and John Grant), apparently in return for lifelong sustenance. She may well be the second older woman living with Nancy Hitch in the 1820-1830 censuses for Fauquier Co. (born in the 1760s), in which case she may have died there between 1830-1840.

4b. **Mary (III) "Molly."** Born 9 Dec. 1753 in Stafford Co., VA (*Overwharton Parish Register*). Married Matthew Neale about 1770 (he was born 1750, and died 1824). The Neales moved to Fauquier Co., possibly at the same time as Garner Burges. Mentioned in 1802 in the second accounting of her father's estate, but apparently died between 1810-20 (not listed in the latter census record). Matthew Neale was an appraiser (with Garner Burges) of Thomas Barbee Jr.'s estate in 1777, and one of his father-in-law's two executors. Thus, he became one of the three co-signers of the 1797 deed of sale of the original Burgess farm in King George Co. No probate record has been found for the Neales; however, from Fauquier Co. marriage records they had at least the following children: *Lettice* (born about 1770, married Henry Miller on 10 Feb. 1791); *Elizabeth* (born about 1772, married Hugh Kerrick, bond date 17 Mar. 1791; John

Burgess provided the bond); *John* (born about 1776, married his cousin, Margaret Burgess, bond date 20 Jan. 1801, bonded by Edward Burgess, Margaret's father); *Nancy* (born about 1779, married John Priest; bond date 4 Jan. 1800); *Hannah* (born about 1781, married Elisha Dearing, bond date 28 Dec. 1802); *Molly* (born about 1783, married Samuel Evans, bond date 14 May 1804); *Sally* (born about 1785, married William Dearing on 15 Aug. 1805); *Martha* (born about 1789, married George Dearing, bond date 8 Jan. 1811); *Fanny* (born about 1792, married John Ellis, bond date 2 Nov. 1812); *Peggy* (born about 1796, married James Turner, bond date 4 Nov. 1816); *Lucy* (born about 1798, married John Dowell, bond date 3 Feb. 1819); and possibly *Thomas* and *James*.

4c. **Susanna (I).** Her name is also written Susannah and Susana. Born about 1755 in Stafford Co., VA. Although she apparently never married, Susanna inherited half of her father's estate. In 1802 she deeded her personal property (including her slave, Wine) and her half interest in her father's estate to her brother-in-law, Matthew Neale (*Fauquier Co. Deed Book #15*, p. 187, dated 21 May 1802, recorded 26 July 1802, with witnesses John Neale, Francis Payne, and Clement Hitch), evidently for lifelong care. She may be listed with the Neales in the 1810 census for Fauquier Co., but is not there in 1820.

4d. **Sarah (II).** Born about 1757 in Stafford Co., VA. Married Joel Settle about 1773 (he was born about 1752, son of Francis Settle), and had at least the following children: *Thornton* (born about 1773, died about 1840 in Barren Co., KY); *Sarah "Sally"* (born about 1775, married William Pickett in 1807); *Willis* (born 12 Jan. 1783, married Mary Pickett on 14 Aug 1804 in Culpeper Co., VA, and died after 1850 in Barren Co., KY); *Leroy B.* (born about 1790, and died in 1881 at Lebanon, TN, aged 91 years); *Lucy* (born about 1792, married Charles Perkins in 1811); *Joel L.* (born 10 Mar. 1796, and died on 28 Feb. 1839 in Jackson Co., TN); *Isaac W.* (born about 1798, and died in 1886 in Barren Co., TN); *Ann* (born about 1800, married Jeremiah Wilson in 1820 in Barren Co., KY). The Settle family had lived in King George Co., possibly very close to the Burgess family, prior to moving to Fauquier Co.; a Verlinda Settle married Joel Ancrum/Anchorom, a witness to the will of Edward Burgess Sr., on 12 Sept. 1745 O.S. (*St. Paul's Parish Register*) in Stafford Co. Sarah Settle died between 1800 and 1803, when her husband remarried Elizabeth Pickett. The Settles then moved to Barren Co., KY, where Joel Settle was killed by a falling tree in 1807.

4e. **Elizabeth (III).** Born about 1762 in Stafford Co., VA. Married John Austin Jr. on 20 Jan. 1783 in Fauquier Co., VA (bond date, Garner Burges giving his consent on 18 Jan.), and had children: *George* (born about 1784, mentioned as being alive in 1809 in the accounting of his grandfather's estate). Elizabeth died between 1784-86; John Austin remarried Elizabeth Browning on 23 Oct. 1786 in Fauquier Co., Matthew Neale providing the bond.

4f. **Edward (III) "Edwin."** Born about 1764 in Stafford or Fauquier Co., VA. See below for full entry.

4g. **John (I).** Born about 1767 in Stafford or Fauquier Co., VA. See below for full entry.

4h. **James (I).** Born about 1769 in Stafford or Fauquier Co., VA. He inherited half of his father's farm. Recorded on the personal property tax lists of Fauquier Co. between 1791-1798 living with his mother. James Burgess was a farmer in Fauquier Co. He died there unmarried in late 1798; his estate was ordered appraised on 24 Dec. 1798, and inventoried on 25 Feb. 1799 (*Will Book #3*, p. 326). His lands and goods were then divided in 1802 as part of the second accounting of his father's estate.

4i. **Anna (I) "Nancy."** Born about 1771 in Fauquier Co., VA. Unmarried at the time of her father's death, she wed Nathan(iel) Hitch Sr. on 27 Jan. 1791 in Fauquier Co. (her mother gave her consent, John Burgess provided the bond [dated 14 Jan.]). Nathan and Nancy Hitch had at least the following children:

Maria(h) HITCH. Born about 1792 in Fauquier Co., VA, married Samuel Russell Grant, grandson of John Grant and Lydia Barbee, on 30 Apr. 1811 in Fauquier Co., and had children: *John Addison* (born 15 Jan. 1828 in Fauquier Co.; a great-great-grandson is Paul Addison Grant of Eugene, OR). Living in Perry Co., OH in 1847, when Samuel Grant and James Hitch deeded off their rights to their mother's estate (*Fauquier Co. Deed Book #46*, p. 180-181, 20 Apr. 1847).

Garner Burgess HITCH. Born about 1794 in Fauquier Co., VA, married Mary Barbee on 8 Dec. 1815 in Fauquier Co. (his cousin?; she was a daughter of John Barbee and Mary Dyson, and granddaughter of Andrew Barbee and Jane Delaney).

Nathaniel HITCH Jr. Born about 1796 in Fauquier Co., VA, married Fanny Drummond on 26 Sept. 1817 in Fauquier Co.; Matthew Neale warranted that he was over the age of 21.

James HITCH. Born about 1798 in Fauquier Co., VA. Living in Perry Co., OH in 1847.

John A(ddison?) HITCH. Born about 1800 in Fauquier Co., VA, married Dinah Stephens on 12 Aug. 1834 in Fauquier Co.

Alexander HITCH. Born about 1802 in Fauquier Co., VA, married Rebecca Smoot on 15 Nov. 1827 in Fauquier Co. (she died in 1854 in Marion Co., MO), and hung himself on 15 Oct. 1849 in Marion Co., MO, having had children: *Susan Ann* (or Susanna) (born 25 May 1829 in Fauquier Co., married John Wiley Day on 28 Mar. 1848 in Marion Co., MO, died 16 Feb. 1861 of tuberculosis at Upton, Marion Co., MO or Van Buren Co., IA, and had children: Catherine [born about 1849 in Marion Co.]; John Tesso [born 2 Nov. 1856 in Marion Co., died 18 Feb. 1932 at Bickleton, Klickitat Co., WA]; Ellenor [born 1859 in Marion Co.]; Cordelia Belle [born 13 Feb. 1861 in Marion Co., married William Wisehart on 27 June 1878 in Rooks Co., KS, and died 31 Jan. 1950 in Phillips Co., KS, leaving children: Mattie Ann; Edith Lillian; Helena; James Edward; Eva Belle; Fannie Fern; Alice Irene; James's descendant, Harlene Ferreira, lives at Carmichael, CA]; *Harriet* (born about 1831); *Josephine* (born about 1833 in Fauquier Co., died before 1855); *Mariah* (born about 1838); *John Christopher* (born 1839 in Marion Co., MO, married Hester McCloud on 20 Mar. 1866 in Marion Co., MO); *Eleven S.* (born 1842 in Marion Co., MO, married Paulina Taylor on 17 Sept. 1862 in Marion Co., and secondly Mattie McCullough on 14 Sept. 1874 in Marion Co.). Harlene Ferreira has contributed greatly to this book.

Anna B(urgess?) Hitch. Born 13 Aug. 1805 in Fauquier Co., VA, married Josiah Graston (or John P. Ball) on 28 Dec. 1829 in Fauquier Co.

Nathan Hitch was born 10 Apr. 1768 (christening date, *St. John's Parish Register*) in Prince Georges Co., MD, son of Christopher Hitch (who bought 50 acres of land in the Manor of Leeds in 1787), and died between 30 Jan. 1809 and June of 1810 (before the census was taken); his wife is listed as head of the family in the 1810-30 censuses for Fauquier Co. Nancy Hitch was granted guardianship for her under-aged children (Alexander, John, James, and Anna, "orphans of Nathan Hitch, deceased") on 22 June 1818 in Fauquier Co. (*Fauquier Co. Guardian Book #1*, unpaginated); guardianship for Maria Hitch was granted on 23 Apr. 1811 (a week before her marriage) to William Keys (*Fauquier Co. Minute Book 1809-14*, unpaginated). Nancy Hitch died in Fauquier Co. between the tax lists of 25 Mar. 1839 and 17 Apr. 1840, before the 1840 census was taken.

THE WILL OF GARNER BURGES

In the name of God Amen I Garner Burges of the County of Fauquier & Parish of Leeds being mindfull of the uncertainty of life & certainty of death do make this my last will & testament in manner & form following, after recommending my soul to Almighty God trusting to the merits of my Blessed redeemer Jesus Christ, do dispose of my worldly estate as follows,

Imprimis I give unto my beloved wife Anne Burges during her life or widowhood all my whole estate and after her death I give & bequeath unto my daughter Susanna Burges & James Burges the plantation whereon I live, likewise one cow & calf & one bed & furniture to each of them & their heirs forever

Item I give & bequeath unto my s^d^ daughter Susanna one Dutch oven & one pewter dish & two plates forever

Item I give & bequeath unto my daughter Peggy Burges one bed & furniture & one cow & calf & two pewter plates to her & her heirs forever

Item I give & bequeath unto my son John [written over a partially erased Edwd] Burges one bed & furniture & one cow & calf to him & his heirs forever

Item I give & bequeath unto my daughter Nancy Burges one bed & furniture & one cow & calf & two pewter plates and one iron skillet to her & her heirs forever

Now my will & desire is that the ^all^ rest of my Estate be equally divided among my children, to wit, Mary Neal, Susanna Burges, Sarah Settle, Peggy Burges, Edwd Burges, Jno Burges, James Burges, & Nancy Burges. Lastly I recommend constitute and appoint my beloved wife Anne Burges Executrix and my son Edwd Burges & Matthew Neal Executors to this my last Will & Testament revoking all former Will or Wills by me made

In witness whereof I have hereunto set my hand & seal this nineteenth day of April 1790.

Sealed signed & acknowledged in presence of—

B. Shackelford
Matthew Neale
Isaac Arnold

Garner Burges

At a court held for Fauquier County the 25. day of October 1790
This will was proved by the oaths of Matthew Neale and Isaac Arnold witnesses thereto and ordered to be recorded and on the motion of Ann Burgess, Edward Burgess and Matthew Neale the executors therein named who made oath and together with Dickenson Wood and Isaac Arnold their securities entered into and acknowledged bond in the penalty of one thousand pounds conditioned as the law directs certificate is granted them for obtaining a probate thereof in due form.

Test H. Brooke CC

AN INVENTORY OF THE ESTATE OF GARNER BURGES
(*Will Book #2*, p. 200)

1 old Negro woman named Dinah .... £20—
1 young woman Milly £55. 1 boy Harry £35 .... 90—
1 woman Lucy & child Betty £60. 1 girl Hannah £25 .... 85—

1 girl Ell £23. 1 girl Wine £18. 1 do Artay £15	56—
1 man Sam £60. 1 girl Winny £40	100—
1 old horse 30/. 1 ditto 20/. 1 ditto £15	17.10
14 head sheep @ 8/	5.12
2 sows & 11 piggs 40/. 15 hogs £4/10. 1 sow 12/	7.2
5 cows & calves £17.10. 1 cow £3. 2 stears £5	25.10
3 heifers £3. 1 do 30/	4.10
1 bed & furniture £6. 1 do £7. 1 do £5	18—
3 flax & wheels 45/. 1 do 6/. 1 woolen wheel 6/	2.7
a parcell feathers 24/. 1 rug & blankett 10/	1.14
3 chest 32/ 1 pine table 3/. 1 small chest 3/	1.18
8 chairs 16/. 3 pewter basons 18/. 7 plates 10/6	2.4.6
1 pewter dish 4/. 7 spoons 1/6. 1 bason 3/. 1 dish 2/	0.10.6
knives & forks 2/. 2 butter potts 4/	0.6
earthen ware 8/. 1 spire [?] mortar & coffee pott 18/	1.6
1 p^{r} stilards 8/. 1 buffet 13/. 1 shot gun 18/	2.1
1 rifle gun 40/. 1 looking glass 1/6. 1 slate 1/6	2.3
1 cart £3. 4 pott 18/. 1 cain [?] & 1 skellett 15/	4.13
1 pan 3/. 1 loomb & geer 20/. wooden ware 6/	1.9
pantation utensals 50/. coopers tools & [?] 20/	3.10
books 9/. 1 gimblet 6^{d}. Cask tubb p^{r} 38/	2.7.6
Total:	£456.3.6

Given under our hands this 31 day of Jan. 1791. B. Shackleford, Henry Clarkson, Aquila Davis, James Foley.

Two Letters from Francis Burgess to Edward Burgess Jacobs

"August 28, 1847. Dear Edward, I will be glad if you and your family will come down. I want something done with the Negroes, as they are here doing nothing. Come down. I would like to see you, so we could make some arrangements about it. Garner has never been home since he went to Goony Camp Meeting. I am very poorly sometimes, and sometimes better. William, I don't know why you and Betty Ragan don't come down. All of our relatives are enjoying good health at this time, and I hope these few lines will find you all well. Our loves to you and family and to Mrs. Shumate. Yrs., & Frances Burgess."

"Pleasant Valley, November 9th, 1847. Dear Edward, We have been anxiously expecting you over for some time in order to complete (with your assistance) the arrangement of my affairs suggested to you in my last letter, and hope that you will not disappoint me in coming over, time enough before you leave for Richmond to attend to it. Some disposition must be made of the servants, either by hire or sale, as I find it very unprofitable to keep them. It will also be to my advantage to sell the stock immediately to save the expense of wintering them and to yours to attend the sale, so you must not fail to come. We heard from Ann the other day, her health and spirits are good, she does not intend visiting us before next spring. She sends her love to all relatives and friends. Garner has been absent to Clark County or Frederick for about fifteen days, and since I commenced writing the last paragraph has just walked in. My best love with that of Kitty to yourself and family. Your affectionate Grandma, Frances Burgess."

Goony was on Goony Run in Warren Co., Virginia, and named for one of Lord Fairfax's hounds. These letters were preserved in the family of Edward Burgess Jacobs, and descended to Francis Trenary.

[see page 90]
Kitty P. GEBLER BURGESS
Ralph Clyde BURGESS Sr.
Arthur Clay BURGESS

[William (I)[1], Edward (I)[2], Garner (I)[3]]

EDWARD "EDWIN" BURGESS
(1764?-1798)

OF CULPEPER (LATER RAPPAHANNOCK) COUNTY, VIRGINIA

4f. **Edward (III) "Edwin"** *[son of Garner (I)].* He was evidently nicknamed "Edwin" to distinguish him from his many cousins named Edward. Born about 1764 in Stafford or Fauquier Co., VA. Married Francis Porter (the odd spelling of her given name was carried down by her descendants) on 29 Nov. 1787 in Fauquier Co., VA (bond date; the marriage bond is signed "Edwin"). Listed on the 1785 and 1787 tax rolls for Fauquier Co., VA, and from 1789-1798 in Culpeper Co. (the section that later became Rappahannock Co.). On 26 Apr. 1795 Samuel Porter gave his son-in-law a 200-acre farm, "Pleasant Valley," in Culpeper (later Rappahannock) Co., VA, two miles northeast of the present-day village of Washington, VA (the county seat of Rappahannock Co.), encompassing Wolf Mountain, and now located at the back of the late Sally Ward's farm, "Echo Hill" (*Culpeper Co. Deed Book #S*, p. 194). Edwin had probably already been living on this estate since 1789, clearing and developing raw farmland. His relationship to his grandfather, Edward Burgess Sr., is proven through his participation (acting as co-executor of Garner Burges's estate) in the 1797 sale of the original Burgess lands in King George Co. Edwin was a farmer in Culpeper Co.; he died there between 19 Mar. 1798, when he last appeared on the personal property tax rolls, and 26 Oct. 1798, when his estate was inventoried (*Culpeper Co. Will Book #D*, p. 300).

Francis Burgess was born about 1765 in VA, daughter of Samuel Porter and Eve Weaver; she never remarried, but continued to farm at Pleasant Valley for more than a half century after her husband's untimely death. She is listed in the 1810-30 censuses for Culpeper Co., VA, in the tax lists there from 1799, and in the 1840-50 censuses of Rappahannock Co., VA (Rappahannock Co. having been split off from Culpeper Co. in Feb. 1833). A Fauquier Co. guardian bond dated 24 Feb. 1806 (*Minute Book 1805-06*, unpaginated) mentions the six children of Edwin Burgess in the following order: Elizabeth, Dawson, Caty, Alexander, Garner, and Nancy. Francis Burgess died on her farm in Sept./Oct. 1851; her will (*Rappahannock Co. Will Book #C*, p. 195-200, inventories on p. 203, 213, and 215, sales on p. 369) was dated May 1847 with codicil dated Sept. 1851, was recorded on 13 Oct. 1851, and was probated on 22 Nov. 1851; a settlement deed was recorded on 1 Apr. 1853 (*Deed Book #I*, p. 387-388). Six of her letters to various relatives survive in the possession of her descendant, Mrs. Francis Trenary of Front Royal, VA.

THE SETTLEMENT DEED OF FRANCIS BURGESS'S ESTATE

This deed, made the first day of April in the year 1853, between Alexander Burgess and Lucy, his wife, Garner E. Burgess, Edward B. Jacobs and Mary Ann, his wife, William Jacobs, Elizabeth B. Ragan, and Thomas A. Jacobs by the said Edward B. Jacobs his attorney in fact, of the one part, and Ann Camp and Catharine Burgess of the other part, witnesseth, that in consideration of one dollar, the said Alexander Burgess and Lucy, his wife, Garner E. Burgess, Edward B. Jacobs and Mary Ann, his wife, William Jacobs, Elizabeth B. Ragan, and Thomas A. Jacobs by the said Edward B. Jacobs his attorney in fact, do grant unto the said Ann Camp and Catharine Burgess, all their Estate, right, title, and interest of in and to the tract of land upon which Frances Burgess resided at the date of her last will and Testament, which said tract of land was conveyed by the father of the said Frances Burgess to her deceased husband, and is situate in the County of Rappahannock, adjoining the lands of Willis Browning, James Jett, John Jett, and H. G. Moffett.

The Children of Edwin Burgess:

5a. **Elizabeth (IV).** Born 21 Feb. 1789 in Culpeper (later Rappahannock) Co., VA. Married Thomas Jacobs on 3 Apr. 1806 in Culpeper Co. (he was born 26 July 1784, and died 8 Sept. 1831 at Front Royal, VA), and had children: *Edward Burgess* (see below); *Selonnary W.* (born 17 June 1808, married Jonathan Hager Ragan, and died 26 Oct. 1828, having had children: Elizabeth B(urgess?) [born about 1828, living with her uncle Edward in Warren Co., VA in 1850-53]); *James L.* (born 22 July 1810, died unmarried 2 Sept. 1831); *William Henry* (born 19 Apr. 1814, listed with his brother in the 1860 census, died 9 Jan. 1871); *Elizabeth Francesca* (born 22 Dec. 1815, died in infancy); *Thomas Alexander* (born 4 Dec. 1816, married

Elizabeth [or Caroline] Quarles, and was living in Warren Co., VA in 1853, but died in Missouri); *Charles Newton* (born 14 Feb. 1820, died unmarried before 1853).

Col. Edward Burgess JACOBS was born 10 Feb. 1807, married Mary Ann Shumate on 2 Sept. 1834 (she was born 3 Nov. 1811, daughter of Bailey Shumate and Ann Elizabeth Weaver [who was a first cousin of Francis Burgess], and died 16 Mar. 1891 at Front Royal, VA). Listed in the 1850-70 censuses of Warren Co., VA. He died 15 Dec. 1873 at Front Royal, VA, having had at least the following children: *Bailey Shumate* (born 1835); *Elizabeth S.* (born 1837); *Mary A.* (born 1840, married ___ Brown, and had children: Eliza [born 1864]; Lou [born 1867], listed with her father in the 1870 census); *Edward* (born 1846, died by 1860); *William Henry (II)* (born 1849); *Sidney S.* (twin; born 19 Sept. 1851); *Catherine Burgess* (twin; born 19 Sept. 1851, married Dr. Manly Littleton Garrison on 15 Sept. 1874 [he was born 17 Mar. 1835 in Frederick Co., VA, and died Apr. 1920 at Front Royal, VA), and died 16 Dec. 1916 at Front Royal, having had at least the following children: Nannie Littleton [born 23 July 1875 at Front Royal, VA, married John Francis Blackwell on 15 June 1897 {he was born 4 Jan. 1868 in Lunenburg Co., VA, son of Robert Augustus Blackwell and Martha "Pattie" Dance, and died 22 Apr. 1906 at Front Royal, VA}, and had children: Francis Garrison {born 31 May 1902 at Front Royal, VA, married William Colin Trenary Jr. on 28 Jan. 1933 <he was born 13 Jan. 1900, and died July 1987 at Front Royal, VA>, and had children: William Colin III}; Nannie married secondly Manley Olin Simpson Sr. {a great-nephew of Dr. Manly L. Garrison}, and died on 16 Oct. 1951 at St. Petersburg, FL]); *James Charles* (born 1856). Francis Trenary has contributed greatly to this book, and currently lives in the old family house at Front Royal, VA.

The JACOBSES settled on a farm near Front Royal, Warren Co., VA, where **Elizabeth JACOBS** died on 6 July 1821.

5b. **Dawson P(orter?).** He was apparently named for Sgt. Dawson Burgess of Fauquier and Frederick Cos., VA, bachelor son of Mr. Francis Burgess of Fauquier Co., VA (there is no known relationship between the two families), and a Revolutionary War soldier. Born about 1791 in Culpeper (later Rappahannock) Co., VA. Married Henrietta Craig on 25 May 1815 at Washington, D.C., and is listed there with his wife in the 1820 census. By 1830 he had returned to Culpeper Co., where he is listed with his mother in the 1830 census (his wife is listed by herself in the D.C. census of the same year). Also listed in the personal property tax lists of Culpeper and Rappahannock Cos. between 1811/14 and 1833. Dawson P. Burgess, a prominent farmer in Rappahannock Co., VA, was one of about a dozen commissioners appointed to establish the new Rappahannock County government in Feb. 1833. He died childless in 1834 while on a trip to Louisiana, according to the probate of his estate (*Rappahannock Co. Will Book #A*, p. 104 and 178-179).

5c. **Catharine "Kitty" or "Caty."** Born about 1792 in Culpeper (later Rappahannock) Co., VA. Listed with her mother in the 1850 census (age 50). Mentioned in her mother's will. Kitty Burgess was a farmer and housekeeper on her mother's estate. She died unmarried on 7 Aug. 1859 in Rappahannock Co., VA (county death records); her estate was appraised in *Rappahannock Co. Will Book #D* (p. 192, 194).

5d. **Alexander (I).** Born 14 July 1794 in Culpeper (later Rappahannock) Co., VA. See below for full entry.

5e. **Garner E(dward?).** Born about 1795 in Culpeper (later Rappahannock) Co., VA. Listed in the tax records of Culpeper Co. and Rappahannock Co., VA from 1816(?)-1850+, in the 1810-50 censuses with his mother (age 45), and in 1860-70 with his sister, Ann. A farmer all his life in Rappahannock Co. VA, Garner E. Burgess died there childless on 12 Jan. 1871, aged 75 years (county death records); his estate was inventoried in Rappahannock Co. on 13 Feb. 1882 (*Rappahannock Co. Will Book #F*, p. 149).

5f. **Ann (II) "Nancy."** Born about 1797 in Culpeper (later Rappahannock) Co., VA. Married James M. Camp of Lewis Co., VA (later WV) on 2 Mar. 1847 in Rappahannock Co. (a prenuptial agreement is recorded in *Lewis Co. Deed Book #M*, dated 1 Mar. 1847, p. 375-378; he apparently died before 1850). Listed with her mother in the 1850 census for Rappahannock Co. (age 43). Married secondly her cousin, John Porter, on 9 Dec. 1862 in Rappahannock Co. (he was born 1 Apr. 1802 in VA, son of Martin and Agnes Porter, and died in 1871 [his estate is appraised on June 12th]). Listed with her brother, Garner, in the 1860 census for Rappahannock Co., and with her husband in 1870. Ann Porter died childless, probably on her mother's farm, in the Spring of 1875, her estate being inventoried on 28 Apr. 1875 (*Rappahannock Co. Will Book #E*, p. 338-341, with sales on p. 346-353).

[William (I)[1], Edward (I)[2], Garner (I)[3], Edward (III)[4]]

ALEXANDER BURGESS, SR.
(1794-1870)

OF RAPPAHANNOCK COUNTY, VIRGINIA

5d. **Alexander (I)** *[son of Edward (III)]*. Born 14 July 1794 in Culpeper (later Rappahannock) Co., VA. Married Agnes Reid on 9 Jan. 1815 in Culpeper Co. (she was the daughter of Joseph and Polly Reid, and died between 1830-1834); married secondly Lucy Elgin on 25 Feb. 1834 in Fauquier Co. (she was born about 1790 in VA, and died on 30 Aug. 1874, aged 84, at Salem, Fauquier Co., VA, the informant being her nephew, Bennett Sanders). Listed on the tax rolls of Culpeper Co. through 1832, and in Rappahannock Co. from 1833-50+; listed in the 1820-30 censuses for Culpeper Co., VA, and from 1840-70 in Rappahannock Co. (in 1850 age 56). Alexander Burgess was a farmer on his mother's farm, Pleasant Valley, near Washington, Rappahannock Co., VA. His inheritance of Francis Burgess's estate resulted in a complicated series of lawsuits, the first of which was filed against him by Ann Burgess Porter in the 1860s, the action being carried on by both their heirs well into the 1880s (*Porter vs. Burgess [Case #160], Burgess vs. Burgess [Case #851]*). He died on 14 Sept. 1870 in Rappahannock Co. (county death records); his heirs immediately filed a settlement on 16 Sept. 1870 (*Rappahannock Co. Deed Book #M*, 359-361).

The Children of Alexander Burgess:

6a. **Edward (VIII) "Edwin."** Born 5 Jan. 1816 in Culpeper (later Rappahannock) Co., VA. See below for full entry.

6b. **Julia Ann (II).** Born about 1819 in Culpeper (later Rappahannock) Co., VA. Married as his second wife Dr. John Bushrod Rust, a physician, on 9 Mar. 1847 in Rappahannock Co. (he was born 21 Aug. 1811, and died 20 Mar. 1867), and had children: *(Edward) Scott* (born 1848); *Alexander Burgess* (born 1850); *Marshall* (born 1852); *(Agnes) Elizabeth* (born 1854, married Robert Miller); *(Lewis?) Cass* (born 1856, married Gertrude Weaver); Dr. Rust also had five known children by his first marriage (wife unknown): *John M.* (born 1836); *Charles W.* (born 1838); *Oliver O.* (born 1840); *(Henry?) Clay* (born 1842); *(John?) Bushrod* (born 1844). Listed in the 1850 census in Warren Co., VA; John Rust is recorded there in 1860 with his third wife, Angelina. Julia Ann Rust died on 7 May 1859 in Rappahannock Co. (county death records).

6c. **Henrietta (I).** Born about 1821 in Culpeper (later Rappahannock) Co., VA. Married B(enjamin) James Shumate of Warren Co. on 28 Mar. 1843 in Rappahannock Co. (he apparently died before 1850), and had children: *Julia Mary* (born 1844, married Delaware Weaver); *Nancy Worth "Nannie"* (born 1846, married Pawhatan Ellis Jones); *Zackary Taylor* (born 1848). Listed with her father in the 1850-60 censuses, and with her family in the 1870 census for Rappahannock Co., but has not been found in 1880. She deeded away her Rappahannock Co. property and interest in her father's and sister Agnes's estate on 21 Feb. 1887 to her daughter, Julia M. Weaver (*Deed Book #R*, p. 179-180), and died before 1900.

6d. **Agnes.** Born about 1823 in Culpeper (later Rappahannock) Co., VA. Listed with her father in the 1850-70 censuses for Rappahannock Co.; she later moved just over the county line into Culpeper Co., not far from Alexander Burgess Jr. She died there unmarried by 21 Feb. 1887 (as noted in her sister Henrietta's deed); her estate was probated in *Culpeper Co. Will Book #Y*, p. 254-255, 326-327, 450.

6e. **Francis (II) "Fanny."** Her name is also spelled "Frances." Born 25 July 1825 in Culpeper (later Rappahannock) Co., VA. Married Richard F. S. Carr on 22 May 1851 in Rappahannock Co. (he was born 6 Apr. 1832, and died 11 June 1910), and had children: *Alexander T.* (born June 1852, married L. M. ___ [born Mar. 1851 in IL], listed in the 1900 census for Algona, Kossuth Co., IA); *Edward* (born Dec. 1854, married Anna E. ___ [she was born Mar. 1862, and died 1920], and died 1919, having had children: Dorothy [born June 1899 in IA]); *Richard* (born Oct. 1855, married Martha N. "Mattie" ___ [she was born Mar. 1861, and died 1955], and died 1933, having had children: Elsa B. [born Dec. 1883 in IA]; Roscoe J. [born Apr. 1888 in IA]); *Julia* (born 13 Oct. 1857, married Phillip Neals [he was born 3 Jan. 1848, and died 13 Apr. 1912], and died 9 July 1936); *Burgess* (born May 1860, married Ida M. Hemphill [she was born Dec. 1858 in IL, and died 1932], and died 1943); *William W.* (born 1861, married Josephine E. ___ [she was born 1870, and died 1958], and died 1942, having had children: Virginia Francis [born 2 Aug. 1900, died 2 Feb. 1902]); *Joseph H.* (born June 1863, married May C. ___ [she was born Mar. 1870, and died 1958], and died 1939, having had children: Lucile [born May 1898 in IA]); *Elizabeth "Bessie"* (born 22 Nov. 1865, married John T. Jenkins [he was born 11 May 1855, and died 14 May 1921], and died 2 Oct. 1926). Listed in the 1860-70 censuses for Rappahannock Co., VA. The Carrs then moved to Swaledale, Cerro Gordo Co., IA, and are listed there in the 1900 census. Fanny died there on 4 Nov. 1911, and is buried with her husband, sons, daughters, and sister, Bettie Whitescarver, in the Pleasant Valley Cemetery, Swaledale, IA.

6f. **Elizabeth (X) "Bettie."** Born 29 Sept. 1827 (1825 on her tombstone) in Culpeper (later Rappahannock) Co., VA. Married Robert A. "Wayne" Whitescarver on 26 Dec. 1871 in Rappahannock Co. (he was born 1819 in Culpeper Co., VA, son of Fredrick and Frances Whitescarver). Listed in the 1860 census for Rappahannock Co. with John Rowles, in 1870 with her father, and in 1880 with her husband. She later moved to Cerro Gordo Co., IA to live with her sister, Fanny Carr; she died there (apparently childless) on 29 Sept. 1895 (or 28 Sept., according to her probate), and is buried in the Pleasant Valley Cemetery. In her will (*Rappahannock Co. Will Book #G*, p. 175-180, dated 30 Dec. 1893, probated 11 Nov. 1895), she left her entire estate to her nephews, Alexander T. Carr and Burgess Carr, with the latter named her executor.

6g. **Alexander (II).** Born May 1830 in Culpeper (later Rappahannock) Co., VA. Listed in the 1850-70 censuses for Rappahannock Co., VA with his father, in 1880 with his sister, Bettie Whitescarver, and in 1900 in Culpeper Co. with his nephew-in-law, William Hugh Eggborn Sr. In 1876 he was appointed by the Rappahannock Co. court to act as executor for his aunt Ann Porter's estate, and to continue the lawsuit against Alexander Burgess Sr. (and Alexander Sr.'s executor, Edward Burgess) that Ann had filed in the 1860s. Alexander Burgess Jr. was a farmer all his life in Rappahannock Co., VA, dying there unmarried and childless on 31 May 1907. He was buried in an unmarked grave in the Gourdwine Church Cemetery, near the Eggborn farm.

THE SETTLEMENT DEED OF THE ESTATE OF ALEXANDER BURGESS

(*Rappahannock Co. Deed Book #M*, 359-361)

This deed made and entered into this sixteenth day of September 1870 between Lucy Burgess (widow of Alexander Burgess deceased) of the one part and Edward Burgess, Alexander Burgess Jr., Henrietta Shumate, Agnes Burgess, Bettie Burgess, Richard F. S. Carr and Frances his wife, E. Scott Rust, Alexander B. Rust, Marshall Rust, A. Elizabeth Rust, and Cass Rust (heirs at law of the said Alexander Burgess deceased) of the second part. The said Alexander Burgess departed this life on the 14th day of September 1870, leaving the said Lucy Burgess his widow and leaving also the parties of the second part heirs at law and whereas by operation of law the said Lucy Burgess is entitled to dower of the real and personal estate of which the said Alexander Burgess died seized and possessed; And whereas the said Lucy Burgess prefers and desires to receive an annuity [___] in place of her dower interest in the said estate, now witnesseth that the said Lucy Burges for the consideration hereinafter mentioned doth grant bargain and sell and by these presents doth convey and release under the said parties of the other part all her right title and interest in the real and personal estate of which the said Alexander Burgess died seized and possessed, and the said parties of the other part in consideration of the promises covenant agree to pay to the said Lucy Burgess the sum of one hundred dollars during her natural life the first year to commence on the first day of January 1871, and the parties agree to pay the said sum of one hundred dollars in semiannual payments fifty dollars on the first day of July 1871 and fifty dollars on the first day of January 1872, paying fifty dollars on the expiration of each six months during her life, and they further covenant to assign and transfer all their interest in an agreement made on the twelfth day of November 1841 between Alexander Burgess and Bennett Sanders agreed by and with the said parties that the said transfer and assignment is without recourse to the said parties whatever and the said parties of the other part further agree to return to the said Lucy Burgess the household furniture which she brought to her last marriage and to move the said Lucy Burgess together with her furniture [__] of Fauquier. Said Lucy Burgess further agrees to give possession of the manor house the appurtenances thereto in which she now resides by the first day of January 1871 to said parties of the other part in order to secure to the said Lucy Burgess the annuity mentioned grant to the Lucy Burgess a lien upon all the real estate the said Alexander Burgess died seized.

[William (I)[1], Edward (I)[2], Garner (I)[3], Edward (III)[4], Alexander (I)[5]]

EDWIN BURGESS
(1816-1883)

OF CULPEPER COUNTY, VIRGINIA

6a. **Edward (VIII) "Edwin"** *[son of Alexander (I)].* Born 5 Jan. 1816 in Culpeper (later Rappahannock) Co., VA. Married Elizabeth Frances Allen on 2 Nov. 1841 in Culpeper Co. (she was born 20 Nov. 1823, daughter of Newman Allen and Mary Ann Brown, and died 12 Oct. 1872; Baptist minister Silas M. Bruce conducted the ceremony). Edwin Burgess was a farmer and merchant (as "Porter and Burgess") in Rappahannock Co., VA. Listed on the tax rolls there from 1837-1848. He moved to Culpeper Co. about 1849, appearing there on the 1860-80 censuses (but has not been found in 1850). He built a house called "Alta Vista" one-half mile north of the Hope Hill School on Route 626; the structure was abandoned in the 1930s. According to *Historical Culpeper* [1974], "during a Civil War skirmish, Gen. Lee told Mrs. Burgess to go in the house; before she could comply, a bullet took off a lock of her hair". He died on his farm on 4 Aug. 1883, and is buried with his wife in unmarked graves under a grove of trees to the left of their ruined house, near the old site of Reva, VA. His family Bible record survives in the possession of his great-granddaughter, Mary Bayol.

The Children of Edwin Burgess:

7a. **Ann Newman.** Born 20 Nov. 1842 in Rappahannock Co., VA; died there on 21 Dec. 1842.

7b. **(Alexander) Armistead.** Listed as Armistead Alexander in the VMI *Memorial* record. Born 22 Nov. 1843 in Rappahannock Co., VA (or in Culpeper Co., according to his biography). Armistead Burgess attended V.M.I., and later enlisted in Co. I, 1st Virginia Infantry, Confederate Army. He was killed charging a Federal battery on 31 May 1862 at the Battle of Seven Pines, east of Richmond, Virginia, and is buried in the Memorial Gardens, Richmond. His biography appears in the *Memorial, Virginia Military Institute*, edited by Charles D. Walker (Philadelphia: J. B. Lippincott Co., 1875, p. 72-73):

"Armistead Alexander Burgess, a son of Edward and Elizabeth F. Burgess, was born in Culpeper County on the 22 of November 1843. After a previous training of some years, young Burgess was sent to the Virginia Military Institute, entering in July, 1860, being at the time in his seventeenth year. His attainments enabled him to become a member of the Second Class, and in the semi-annual Report of the Institute for January, 1861, we find he had made excellent progress in his studies, having been specially successful in mathematics, standing fifth in a class of forty members. But the exigencies of the War, which at this time came upon us, prevented the completion of his education. The State of Virginia felt the need of expert drillmasters to train her volunteers gathering at Richmond. Governor Letcher assigned this duty to the Corps of Cadets. How well they performed that duty has been told. Cadet Burgess, as a member of that Corps, executed the duties of his position satisfactorily and well. When the Cadets were disbanded, he returned to his home in Culpeper, and remained there until the following Spring, when he left home for the purpose of joining the Army. In the Spring campaign of 1862, he attached himself to the Ist Regiment, Virginia Infantry, composed of troops from Richmond and vicinity. With this command he served until the Battle of Seven Pines, May 31, 1862, where he was killed in charging a Federal battery. Cadet Burgess' youth, his age, just nineteen at his death, and short service, preclude any suppositions as to what his success, as a soldier or as an officer might have been, yet his duty had been well done, and he fell with his face to the foe."

7c. **Sarah Julia.** Born 28 Dec. 1845 in Rappahannock Co., VA; died there on 12 Nov. 1848.

7d. **Mary Catharine.** Born 12 Mar. 1848 in Rappahannock Co., VA. Married William Hugh Eggborn Sr. on 13 June 1867 in Culpeper Co. (he was born Feb. 1844 in VA, son of Perry Jackson Eggborn, grandson of George Eggborn, and the nephew of Jacob Samuel Eggborn [who married Mary's sister, Ida Burgess]), and had children: *(Edward) Jackson* (born Feb. 1870, married Robbie S. ___ [she was born Oct. 1877], and had children: (Sarah) Catherine [born Oct. 1894, married Cornelius E. Bruce];

Edward Jackson Jr. [born 1 June 1903 in Culpeper Co., listed in the 1900-20 censuses for Culpeper Co., served as Mayor of Culpeper town, and died Mar. 1976]); *(Jacob) Armistead* (born 1872 in VA, married Anita Robbins [she was born 1875], listed in the 1920 census for Alexandria, VA, and had children: Margaret E. [born 1912]); *(Martha) Elizabeth "Bessie"* (born 1876, married T. Q. Thomson, and had children: Mary; Burgess [a physician]). Listed in the 1870-80 censuses for Culpeper Co., VA. Mary Eggborn died between 1 Nov. 1892 (when she received her share of Agnes Burgess's estate) and 1900, possibly on 15 Oct. 1895 (date unconfirmed); she was dismissed from the rolls of the Gourdvine Baptist Church on 20 June 1896. She was buried in the Eggborn family cemetery, but was later reinterred with her husband in the Masonic Cemetery, Culpeper, VA.

William Hugh EGGBORN Sr. married secondly Blanche Aylor about 1899 (she was born Mar. 1862, and died 1946), and had children: *William Hugh Jr.* (born 16 Aug. 1900, and died 15 Feb. 1952, buried Masonic Cemetery, Culpeper, VA, having had children: William Hugh III [married Pauline Inskeep {she was born 15 Sept. 1925, died 27 June 1974}; he lives at the old Eggborn home built by Perry Jackson Eggborn in 1852 at Rixeyville, VA]; Margaret [married ___ Kite, and lives near Culpeper, VA]). William Eggborn Sr. is listed in the 1900-20 censuses for Culpeper Co. He died there on 20 Feb. 1923, and is buried with his two wives and third son in the Masonic Cemetery, Culpeper, VA.

7e. **Walter W.** Born 5 Jan. 1850 in Culpeper Co., VA. See below for full entry.

7f. **(Edward) Edwin.** Born 26 Aug. 1853 in Culpeper Co., VA. See below for full entry.

7g. **Jane Lee "Jennie."** Born 8 (or 5, according to her tombstone) Apr. 1855 in Culpeper Co., VA. Married Albert Samuel Roberts (later Adjutant General of the Texas State Militia) on 15 Jan. 1885 in Culpeper Co. (he died in Jan. 1927), and had children: *Burgess* (died at age one); *Allen* (attended Virginia Military Institute, had children: Frank Allen, and died about 1934, buried St. Louis, MO). The Roberts family settled at Austin, Travis Co., TX. Jennie Roberts died there on 5 Dec. 1925, but is buried with her husband in the Fairview Cemetery, Culpeper, VA. Jennie's grandson, Frank Roberts, currently lives at Baltimore, MD.

7h. **Ida May (I).** Born 22 Aug. 1857 in Culpeper Co., VA. Married Jacob Samuel Eggborn on 11 Dec. 1884 in Culpeper Co. (he was born Dec. 1824, son of George and Amy Ann Eggborn and uncle of William Hugh Eggborn [who married Ida's sister, Mary Burgess], and died 5 Jan. 1905), and had children: *George M.* (born 23 Nov. 1885, successively married his first cousins, Mary Newman Burgess and Reva Burgess, and died 5 Jan. 1941, buried Fairview Cemetery); *(Amy) Elizabeth* (born 29 Aug. 1892, married Emmett Gleason, and died 4 Jan. 1919). Listed in the 1900 census for Culpeper Co., VA. Ida Eggborn belonged to the Gourdvine Baptist Church in Culpeper Co. She died there on 14 Oct. 1903, and is buried with her husband in a private cemetery in the garden back of the house on the old George Eggborn farm, in rural Culpeper Co., VA. Jacob Eggborn served as Sheriff of Culpeper Co. and then as a member of the Virginia Legislature.

WALTER W. BURGESS OF CULPEPER CO., VIRGINIA

[Edward (VIII)[6]]

7e. **Walter W.** *[son of Edward (VIII)].* His middle initial is also listed as "B." (for Brown?); he was named for Walter A. Brown, husband of his mother's sister, (Sarah) Jane Allen. Born 5 Jan. 1850 in Culpeper Co., VA. Married Carrie Lee Quaintance on 22 Dec. 1879 in Rappahannock Co. (she was born 26 July 1862, daughter of Henry Harford "Harry" and Frances A. Quaintance, and died 22 June 1946 while talking on the phone to her daughter Bessie). Listed in the 1880-1920 censuses for Culpeper Co. After inheriting his father's lands, W. W. Burgess (as he usually signed his name) worked as a cattle rancher, merchant, and miller in Culpeper Co. A lifelong member of the Novum Baptist Church, Walter Burgess died on 25 Oct. 1925 near Culpeper, VA, three days after his grandson, and is buried there in the Fairview Cemetery.

8a. **Carroll Vivian (I).** Born 8 Oct. 1880 in Culpeper Co., VA. Married Rebecca Miller Smith on 18 Dec. 1907 in Culpeper Co. (div.; she was the daughter of Hugh Smith and Mary Elizabeth O'Bannon, and died on 5 Mar. 1941). Listed in the 1910-20 censuses for Culpeper Co., VA. Carroll Burgess was a farmer and stock buyer in Culpeper Co. He died there on 6 Oct. 1936 of heart disease, and is buried in the Fairview Cemetery, Culpeper, VA; Rebecca Burgess is buried in a separate section of the same cemetery.

9a. **Elizabeth Lee.** Born 31 July 1909 in Culpeper Co., VA. Married Edward Dudley Turner Jr. on 14 July 1928, and had children: *Edward Dudley III.* Elizabeth Turner died on 5 Mar. 1981 at Richmond, VA, and is buried in the Fairview Cemetery, Culpeper, VA with her mother and brother.

9b. **Carroll Vivian (II).** Born 2 Apr. 1913 in Culpeper Co., VA. He died of blood poisoning and pneumonia on 22 Oct. 1925 at the University Hospital, Charlottesville, VA, and is buried with his mother and sister in the Fairview Cemetery.

THE OBITUARY OF CARROLL V. BURGESS

"Carroll V. Burgess, member of a well-known Culpeper family, and prominently identified with the cattle business in this section, died of an acute heart attack about one o'clock, Tuesday, October 6th. Mr. Burgess, who had experienced a slight attack about a week ago, had seemed to have entirely recovered, and on Monday accompanied a truckload of cattle to the Baltimore market, making the journey on Hoffman's truck of Brightwood. He returned on Monday to his home at Reva, where he spent the night, and on Tuesday morning, in company with Reynolds Fraser, an employee, came to Culpeper in his car, stopping for a conversation with Russell Yowell, near Gaines Run. While talking with Mr. Yowell, he complained of feeling very badly, and came on to Culpeper, going at once to his room at the home of Mr. and Mrs. J. J. Davies, on East Street. Reynolds Fraser, who was with him, states that he did not realize that Mr. Burgess was in such a serious condition, but at his request sent at once for a doctor. Drs. J. L. Stringfellow and Grandville Eastham answered the call, finding Mr. Burgess conscious when they entered the room, but he died within a few minutes. This sudden death has been a shock to the entire community, where he was well-known since his boyhood, and where he has a large circle of relatives and friends. He was the only son of Mrs. Carrie Burgess and the late Walter Burgess of Reva, and is survived by his mother and sisters, Mrs. Bessie Spilman and Mrs. Peter Booth Pullman of Alexandria, and Mrs. George Eggborn of Eggbornsville. He is survived by a daughter, Mrs. Edward Turner of Richmond. The funeral will be held today, Thursday, at two o'clock, at the graveside at Fairview Cemetery."—*The Virginian*, 8 Oct. 1936.

8b. **Elizabeth Frances "Bessie."** Born 3 Sept. 1883 in Culpeper Co., VA. Married Coleman Brown Spilman on 23 Sept. 1904 in Culpeper Co. (he was born on 11 Nov. 1874, and died on 8 Aug. 1922), and had children: *Mary Lee* (born 3 May 1906 in Culpeper Co., married Edgar Bayol [a newspaperman], and had children: Permelia Burgess [born about 1930, married Albert S. Eggerton, and lives at North Springfield, VA]). Bessie Spilman died on 4 Feb. 1956 in Culpeper Co., and is buried with her husband in the Fairview Cemetery. Mary Lee Bayol inherited the family Bible record of her great-grandfather, Edward Burgess; she lives with her daughter, Permelia.

8c. **Mary Newman "May."** Born 31 Jan. 1886 in Culpeper Co., VA. Married her first cousin, George M. Eggborn, on 6 Apr. 1906 in Culpeper Co. (he was born 23 Nov. 1885, son of Jacob Samuel Eggborn and Ida May Burgess, remarried her sister, Reva Tesora Burgess, and died on 5 Jan. 1941 in Culpeper Co.), and had children:

Jacob Samuel "Jake" EGGBORN II. Born 13 June 1907 at Eggbornsville, VA, married Hazel Frye on 25 Jan. 1933 at Harpers Ferry, WV, and had children: *Dolores Ann* (born 25 Jan. 1936, died 6 Sept. 1945, buried St. Peters Cemetery); *Jacob Samuel III* (born 13 Aug. 1946, died 27 Jan. 1960, buried St. Peters Cemetery). Jake Eggborn retired in 1971 after 44 years with Potomac Edison Co. He lives at Harpers Ferry, WV, and has contributed greatly to this book.

(Walter) Burgess EGGBORN. Born 8 May 1910, married Mary Jane Crafton at Orange, VA, and had children: *Mary George II* (born 22 Jan. 1942, currently owns the Eggborn family Bible, works as a commercial artist, and lives at Los Angeles, CA). Burgess died of heart disease in Apr. 1953 in Connecticut, and is buried in the Fairview Cemetery (interred 11 Apr. 1953).

Mary George EGGBORN. Born 19 July 1914, died 15 Sept. 1914, buried on farm.

May Burgess EGGBORN was a school teacher in Culpeper Co., and a member of Gourdvine Baptist Church. Listed in the 1920 census for Culpeper Co., VA. May died there on 25 Dec. 1924, and is buried with her husband in the Fairview Cemetery, Culpeper, VA. George Eggborn was a farmer.

8d. **Reva Tesora "Ree."** Born 15 Dec. 1888 in Culpeper Co., VA. Married her first cousin and brother-in-law, George M. Eggborn, on 14 Dec. 1929 in Culpeper Co. (he was born 23 Nov. 1885, son of Jacob Samuel Eggborn and Ida May Burgess, married first her sister, Mary Newman Burgess, and died 5 Jan. 1941); married secondly William Priest Rudasill on 30 Apr. 1942 in Culpeper Co. (he died in June 1949). Listed in the 1920 census living with her father. The post office and community of Reva, VA were named for her, the only such honor recorded in the history of the Burgess family. Reva Rudasill attended Powhatan College at Charles Town, WV, and later taught school for three years. She moved to the Newport News Baptist Retirement Community in the late 1960s. This remarkable lady died childless on 17 Aug. 1992 at Newport News, VA, aged 103 years, then the oldest living member of the Burgess family and the most senior representative of the most senior Burgess line—and thus of the entire family. Up to the day she died she was a repository of stories and knowledge about the Burgess family. She is buried with her first husband and sister, May Eggborn, in the Fairview Cemetery.

"**Reva** was the first name of miller Walter Burgess's daughter. We like to think of Reva as his first choice for a post office name, but someone did suggest Burgess, since the post was to be on his property. However, Burgess was the county seat of Northumberland [*not true*; however, there is a post office called "Burgess" {originally Burgess Store} there], and Reva the village became, on March 24, 1893. James Mason was first postmaster. The mill and Alex H. Spilman's store were the businesses until the post closed, January 4, 1907.

"But soon Ashby R. Rosson and his father, M. B. 'Mon' Rosson, built a store atop the hill a half mile east, and that August 30 a second Reva post office opened with Ashby Rosson, postmaster. He also ran a gasoline-powered grist mill across from the store. Down by 'Old Reva,' as the first Reva community was called, Charlie Hall and John Bruce ran a second store. In 1940, E. Page Carpenter became the postmaster and storekeeper at 'New Reva,' and he kept both duties until 1976. A year later the post office moved to a third site, on the Madison Road, where the voting precinct Brown's Store stood three-quarters of a century before."—Eugene M. Scheel, writing in *Culpeper: A Virginia County's History Through 1920* (Culpeper: Culpeper Historical Society, 1982). The present site of Reva on U.S. Highway 29, southwest of the town of Culpeper, lies in an area where new developments are rapidly being built.

8e. **Carolyn** (nmn). Born 14 Feb. 1900 in Culpeper Co., VA. Married Dr. Peter Booth Pulman on 28 June 1928 at Alexandria, VA (he was born 20 Mar. 1899, worked as a physician, and died June 1986 at Boca Raton, FL), having had children: *Peter Booth Jr.* (born 1936, married Mary Ann Potterfield [div.], and had children: Sean Allen [married, and lives at Leesburg, VA]; John Donnaldson Potterfield [married, and lives at Leesburg, VA]; married secondly Patricia "Patsy" Bragg, and had children: Charles Oliver; Kate Laura); *John Allen* (born 2 Aug. 1939, died 12 Apr. 1946, buried Fairview Cemetery). Listed with her father in the 1920 census. Carolyn Pulman attended Farmville College. She died on 17 Nov. 1987 at Berryville, VA, and is buried with her husband in the Arlington National Cemetery. Peter B. Pulman Jr. lives at Purcellville, VA.

Reva Rudasill wrote in 1983: "Papa loved to see farming going on, and we fed a lot of working hands, and they had to be cooked for. He had five tennant houses on the farm, and in Spring, Summer, and Fall we had four or five working men to feed at our home, and company nearly all the Summer. Mama was the main cook, with some woman or girl to help almost all the time. My mother was the best cook. We Southerns are noted for being good cooks. Papa during his life had a good-sized farm, a country store, and post office at the store, Reva, Virginia, Culpeper County. He was also in the sawmill business at one time. They fed themselves, thank goodness! And when my father died, I looked after the farm. I had to learn what to do and when, and I kept busy."

EDWIN BURGESS OF BALTIMORE CO., MARYLAND

[Edward (VIII)[6]]

7f. **(Edward) Edwin "Eddy"** *[son of Edward (VIII)].* Listed as Edward Burgess, E. E. Burgess, or E. Burgess Jr., in various deeds and newspaper accounts through the 1880s, but only as Edwin after his marriage. Born 26 (or 24) Aug. 1853 in Culpeper Co., VA. Married Louisa Lenette "Lulu" Butler on 9 Apr. 1891 at Baltimore, MD, the marriage being conducted by the well-known Roman Catholic prelate, James Cardinal Gibbons (she was born 28 Jan. 1862, daughter of Thomas Cronmiller Butler and Louisa Jane Tucker, and died 26 July 1925 at Baltimore). Edwin Burgess graduated from Richmond College, then worked as a mill operator in Culpeper. He was elected Democratic Mayor of Culpeper, the county seat of Culpeper Co., in May 1881, serving a two-year term from July 1881-June 1883. He moved to Baltimore by 1886, and then to Prescott, Arizona in 1887, where he accepted a position as Registrar of Public Lands, and became the first person to pass the then newly-instituted bar examination for the state of Arizona (he was sworn in by the Chief Justice of the Arizona Supreme Court). He returned East by 1891, when he appeared in the 1891 Baltimore city directory as President of Tiger Mining and Milling Co.; at this time he still apparently entertained the idea of returning to Arizona, and with the inauguration of Democratic President Grover Cleveland in 1893, saw his opportunity, beginning an unsuccessful campaign to have himself appointed Territorial Governor (for a brief account, see *Arizona Territory, 1863-1912: A Political History*, by Jay J. Wagoner [Tucson: University of Arizona Press, 1970], p. 313, which mentions that Morris Goldwater, among others, signed a petition supporting his candidacy). Not long thereafter, he set up practice as an attorney in Baltimore, and became a prominent figure there. Listed in the 1900-20 censuses for Baltimore, MD, and in the 1906-1925 city directories as an attorney and agent. He died there of liver cancer on 13 May 1925, and is buried with his wife in Greenmount Cemetery. Lulu Burgess was sometime Registrar of the Baltimore Chapter of the Daughters of the American Revolution (DAR).

Reva Rudasill wrote in 1983: "About the only [Burgess] man that I know now is my Uncle Edward Burgess Jr.'s grandson, whose father was James Burgess. James was the youngest of three boys of Uncle Edward (we always called him Uncle Eddy). Uncle Eddy did live in Arizona and practiced law in Baltimore. The oldest boy was Thomas Butler Burgess, who was in the Second World War and got to be Colonel Thomas Burgess. He lived in Florida. The second boy is dead. Thomas was about a year younger than myself.

"When I visited Uncle Eddy after an operation at Johns Hopkins, James was five or six years old, and I was twenty-one [about 1909]. Both Thomas and Edwin visited us at Reva, Virginia, in 1921 and 1922. I wrote to Edwin for a long time, we thought we were in love. Edwin was two years younger than I, and handsome like his dad. In Culpeper County some families thought to marry a first cousin was all right. My father thought that way, but since I am older I do not advise it. But my first marriage was to a first cousin."

8a. **Thomas Butler.** Born 8 Jan. 1892 at Baltimore, MD. Married Anna Thomasina McAuliffe (dec.; div.); married secondly Peggy Meyer (dec.; sister of Charles Robert "Monk" Meyer). Listed in the 1913-1921 Baltimore city directories as a clerk working for his father, and sporadically in the *Baltimore Blue Book* through the late 1940s. Has not been found in the 1920 census. He enlisted in the U.S. Army during World War I, and by 1942 had achieved the rank of full Colonel. He lived at Richmond, VA in the 1930s. He was stationed at Scofield Barracks, Oahu, HI at the time of the Pearl Harbor attack in 1941; after World War II he was stationed at Fort Missoula, MT. He retired from the Army in 1951, and is listed as a retired officer in the *Official Army Directory* through 1968. He then settled at Bradenton, Manatee Co., FL, just south of St. Petersburg, where he died in Dec. 1968. He attained the highest rank of any military officer in the Burgess family to date.

9a. **Anne Therese.** Born 2 Oct. 1918 at Baltimore, MD. Married Capt. Charles Robert "Monk" Meyer in 1941 in Hawaii (he was born 1 May 1913 in NY, graduated from the U.S. Military Academy in 1937, and was also a nationally famous football star for Army under his nickname, Monk Meyer; he served in the U.S. Army during World War II, was decorated for gallantry [distinguished service cross, two silver stars, two legions of merit, and two bronze service medals], served in Vietnam [receiving two distinguished service medals and an air medal], and retired in 1967 with the rank of Brigadier General; he later became became managing director of Cannery Row Development Corp., Monterey, CA), and had children: *Charles Robert II* (born 29 July 1944 in FL, attended the U.S. Military Academy, graduating in 1967, served in Vietnam [being awarded a bronze service medal, air medal, and purple heart], and retired in 1987 with the rank of Lieut. Colonel; he earned his M.B.A. from Golden Gate University in 1989, and lives at Salinas, CA; he was married, and had children: Karen); *Christine Anne* (born 15 June 1946, married ___ Tracey, had children: Sean, and lives at Arlington, TX). Anne Meyer currently lives at Pacific Grove, CA.

8b. **Edwin Armistead.** Born 27 Feb. 1893 in Baltimore, MD. Married Lucile O. Alvord in 1932 (she was born 19 June 1900 at Harton, MI, daughter of Prince and Ivy Alvord, worked as a registered nurse, and died 29 Sept. 1967 at Baltimore). Listed in the 1917 draft register for Baltimore, Baltimore Co., MD, in the 1900-20 censuses living with his parents, in the 1918-1926 Baltimore city directories working as a clerk, and in the *Baltimore Blue Books* through 1932. Served as a private in the U.S. Army in 1917. He later worked as a civil service clerk for the City of Baltimore. Edwin Burgess died of a heart attack on 17 Jan. 1935 at Baltimore, MD, and is buried in the Greenmount Cemetery. Lucile is listed in the Baltimore city directories from 1936-65.

9a. **Louise Butler**. Born 13 June 1933 at Baltimore, MD. Married James Eugene Huebler on 14 Mar. 1953 at Baltimore, MD, and had children: *James Eugene Jr.* (born 8 Feb. 1954 at Baltimore, MD, married JoAnn Dannaman on 7 Aug. 1976, and had children: Ryan Michael [born 16 May 1978 at Baltimore, MD]; Lauren Michele [born 25 July 1981 at Baltimore, MD]; James Huebler Jr. is comptroller of the Baltimore Museum of Art); *Ann Louise* (born 6 Apr. 1957 at Baltimore, MD, married Christopher William Furst on 24 Nov. 1979, and had children: Christopher William Jr. [born 20 Sept. 1981 at Baltimore, MD]; Steven Francis [born 21 Sept. 1985 at Baltimore, MD]; Ann Furst is a teacher for the Catholic Archdiocese of Baltimore; they live at Severna Park, MD); *Jeanne Burgess* (born 2 Sept. 1959 at Baltimore, MD, married Charles Scott Brannan on 19 Apr. 1980, and had children: Katie Burgess [born 31 Dec. 1982 at Baltimore, MD]; Stacey Jeanne [born

26 Sept. 1985 at Baltimore, MD]; Jeanne Brannan is the social director for the Meridian Nursing Home; they currently live at Columbia, MD). Louise and James Huebler currently live at Lewes, DE.

8c. **James Butler.** Born 28 Dec. 1902 at Baltimore, MD. Married Annie Laurie Sexton on 9 Mar. 1929 at Baltimore, MD (she was born 7 Feb. 1902 at Decatur, GA, daughter of Dr. Joshua Glenn Sexton, and is currently living near Orlando, FL). Jim Burgess is listed in the Baltimore City Directories from 1920-1965, originally working as a clerk for his father, and later (from 1925) as an inspector for the Baltimore City Bureau of Sewers; listed in the 1920 census with his father. He retired from Baltimore City employment after forty years in 1965, died there of heart complications on 9 July 1966, and is buried in the Woodlawn Cemetery, Baltimore.

9a. **James Alan.** Born 31 Aug. 1930 in Baltimore, MD. Married Ruby Wallace on 8 May 1954 at Washington, DC. Attended Loyola College from 1948-49. Jim Burgess entered the U.S. Naval Academy through competitive examination from the U.S. Naval Reserve, and graduated on 6 June 1953. He served aboard the *U.S.S. Adirondack* (AGC-15), the Navy submarine school, and aboard the following submarines: *U.S.S. Quillback*, *U.S.S. Archerfish*, *U.S.S. Croaker*. He attended post-graduate school at Monterey, CA, where he received his degree in electrical engineering in 1961, and served aboard the guided missile submarine *U.S.S. Tunny* as navigator and executive officer. He was executive officer and administrator during the building of the Fleet Ballistic Training Center on Ford Island, HI, and commanded the attack submarine *U.S.S. Sterlet* (SS-392) between 1965-67, operating out of Pearl Harbor. Subsequent tours included: Office of Naval Research, Washington, DC; the U.S. Naval Torpedo Station, Keyport, WA; and the Underwater System Center, Newport, RI. He retired with the rank of Commander on 1 July 1974.

The following day he was employed by the Northrop Corp. as a torpedo engineer specialist, moving to Camarillo, CA, with extended assignments to Washington State, Peru, Scotland, and Canada. In 1979 he transferred to Orlando, FL to work on the Saudi Navy Training School equipment being installed in Jubail, Saudi Arabia. In 1986 he retired from Northrop on the closing of the Orlando operation. From 1987-93 he was employed by Science Applications International Corp. as a systems engineer on new Army training device developments. He now lives retired at Winter Springs, FL. Jim Burgess and his family represent the last descendants with the name Burgess from the line of Garner Burges's older son, Edward, the most senior branch of the entire Burgess family. He has contributed greatly to this book.

10a. **Constance Ann** (twin). Born 4 Feb. 1955 at the U.S. Naval Submarine Base, New London, CT. Married Barry Allen Wood in 1979 at Middletown, RI (div. 1985), and had children: *Garrett Randall* (born 23 Apr. 1980 at Newport, RI); *Carlee Elizabeth* (born 28 Feb. 1984 at Newport, RI); Constance Ann married secondly Lt. Michael Barrow in 1987 (div. 1989). Constance Wood attended the University of Rhode Island in 1973, and California Lutheran College from 1974-76; she later graduated from the Florida Hospital Licensed Practical Nurse School, and received her R.N. in 1991 from Seminole Community College School of Nursing. Constance Wood currently works as a primary care nurse for Florida Hospital, and she and her children reside at Winter Springs, FL.

10b. **Karen Lee (I)** (twin). Born 4 Feb. 1955 at the U.S. Naval Submarine Base, New London, CT. Married Curtis Wert in 1981 at Newport, RI (div. 1982); married secondly Lance Kelley in 1983 at Middletown, RI (div. 1986); married thirdly Jesse Williams in 1992 at Winter Springs, FL. Karen Williams attended the Bauder School of Fashion and Merchandising between 1973-74, and later raised and trained horses at Middletown, RI during the mid-1980s. Since 1987 she has worked as a veterinary technician, and currently lives at Winter Springs, FL.

11a. **Ryan Alan.** He uses the name Burgess. Born 29 Aug. 1985 at Newport, RI.

10c. **Stephen Alan.** Born 4 Dec. 1956 at Key West, FL. Steve Burgess attended Georgia Tech University from 1974-75, and later graduated from California Lutheran College with a B.A. in education in 1978; he also took education courses at the University of Central Florida between 1982-84. He currently owns and operates a mobile preschool gymnastics business at Boca Raton, FL.

THE OBITUARY OF EDWIN BURGESS

"Yesterday morning, at his home in Baltimore, Mr. Edwin B. Burgess died after a brief illness. Deceased, who was born in Culpeper County, was a brother of Mr. Walter W. Burgess of Reva, in this county. He was about 72 years of age. When a young man, Mr. Burgess was engaged in business in Culpeper, occupying a building at the corner of David and Main Streets, now the site of the Second National Bank Building. Shortly after leaving Culpeper in 1884, Mr. Burgess was appointed Governor of Arizona Territory [sic] by President Grover Cleveland. Deceased is survived by his wife and three children. The interment will be in Baltimore. One of his sons is a Major in the U.S. Army."—*Culpeper Exponent*, 14 May 1925.

Eleanor Faulconer Burgess (1805-1868?) *(see page 57)*

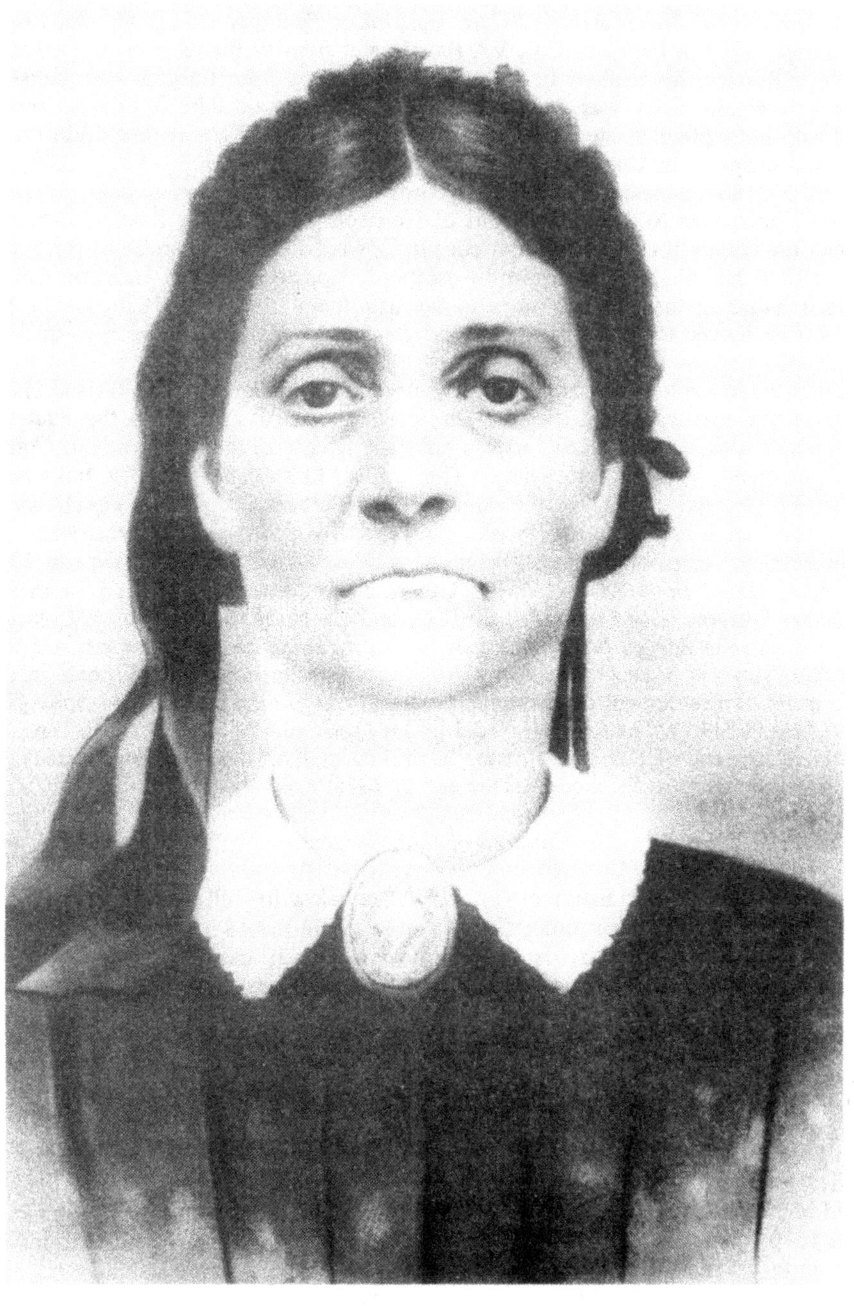

[William (I)[1], Edward (I)[2], Garner (I)[3]]

JOHN BURGESS
(1767?-1846)

OF PUTNAM COUNTY, INDIANA

4g. **John (I)** *[son of Garner (I)].* Born about 1767 in Stafford or Fauquier Co., VA. Married Sarah "Sally" Williams on 13 Sept. 1792 in Fauquier Co., VA (bond date, John Williams gave his permission; the bond is signed by Hugh Kerrick, his nephew-in-law, and witnessed by John Burgess's brothers-in-law, Nathan Hitch and Matthew Neale; Sally was born about 1772, daughter of John Williams, and was living in 1843). Listed with his mother in the Fauquier Co. tax lists from 1789 until her death in 1802; he mortgaged his personal property in Culpeper Co. on 20 Aug. 1803 (*Deed Book #Y*, p. 208), and moved to Bourbon Co., KY by 1804, appearing on the tax records there with the same number of horses as he had in Virginia. In 1809 he moved to the western part of Harrison Co., KY (the Rutland Precinct, on Raven's Creek), just over the county line from his first cousin, Edward Burgess, founder of the Scott Co. Burgess families. About 1810 he bought goods from the estate of Thomas Naylor in Harrison County (*Will Book #I*, p. 79), and is listed on the personal property tax lists there from 1809-1826, and in the censuses of 1810-20. In 1827 he moved to Putnam Co., IN with his son, William, and two sons-in-law, and is listed there in the 1830-40 censuses.

A key piece of evidence linking the John Burgesses of Fauquier Co., VA and Harrison Co., KY is his signature on the marriage bond of 1792 (the original record survives in the Fauquier Co. Courthouse), and on a note attached to his son James's marriage license in the Harrison Co. Courthouse, giving James (who is underaged) permission to marry. They appear to be the same. The links between the John Burgess of Harrison Co. and the man of the same name in Putnam Co., IN are equally persuasive: John and three of his children disappear from Harrison Co. records virtually simultaneously and reappear almost immediately in Putnam Co. (John Burgess "Seignor" is deeded land in Putnam Co. on 17 Mar. 1827 by Samuel L. Rodgers [*Deed Book #A*, p. 165]). Others deeds mention John "and Sarah/Sally his wife," William and Nancy Burgess (*Deed Book #B*, p. 271), and (in *Deed Book #B*, p. 472, for the same exact plot as the preceding) John Burges *Junior* (the only record in which he is so referred) and Ellen his wife *of the County of Harrison and State of Kentucky*. Although John left no will or probate in Putnam or Harrison Cos., he made two settlement deeds to his younger sons (*Putnam Co. Deed Book #L*, p. 658 [both deeds], dated 8 Sept. 1843 [to Shelton; witnessed by Dawson] and 28 Oct. 1837 [to Dawson]; these were recorded together at the end of Dec. 1846 or the beginning of Jan. 1847 (no dates stated). This undoubtedly indicates that John Burgess Sr. died near the end of 1846, aged about 79 years.

The Children of John Burgess:

5a. **William S. (I).** Born about 1793 in Fauquier Co., VA. See below for full entry.

5b. **Edward (VI).** Born about 1795 in Fauquier Co., VA. Listed in the 1850 census for Harrison Co., KY as an "idiot" living with Benson Roberts. Apparently never married, and died between 1850-1860. His inclusion here is speculative, since he is unmentioned in any other source, but probable.

5c. **Cynthia (I).** Born about 1798 in Fauquier Co., VA. Married Thomas Chadd (variously Shadd) on 22 Apr. 1816 in Harrison Co., KY (he was born about 1799 in KY), and had children: *Daniel* (or David; he was born about 1817, married Mary ___ [she was born 1818 in VA], and had children: John T. [born 1841 in IN]; Cynthia [born 1843 in IN]; Mary E. [born 1845 in IN]; Leannah [born 1847 in IN]; David [born 1850 in IN]; George [born 1852 in IN]; Susan [born 1854 in IN]; James B. [born 1855 in IN]; Samuel [born 1857 in IN]; Ruth [born 1859 in IN]); *Daughter* (born about 1819); *Samuel* (born about 1825, relation not verified). Listed in the 1820 census for Harrison Co., KY, but died between 1825-30; by 1830 Thomas Chadd had moved with his sons, brothers-in-law, and father-in-law to Putnam Co., IN, where he is listed in the 1830 census; listed in the 1840 census in Hendricks Co., IN, and with his son, Daniel (or David) Chadd, in the 1850-60 censuses for Marian Township, Hendricks Co., IN.

5d. **James (III).** Born about 1802 in Fauquier Co., VA. See below for full entry.

5e. **John Garner (I) "Jack."** Born 26 May 1805 in Bourbon Co., KY. See below for full entry.

5f. **Elizabeth (VIII).** Born about 1807 in Bourbon Co., KY. Married William Hampton on 30 Sept. 1826 in Harrison Co., KY (he was born about 1800 in Kentucky), and had at least the following children: *Son* (born about 1828); *Mary* (born about 1830); *Sarah E.* (born about 1832); *John L.* (born about 1834); *George W.* (born about 1837); *William F.* (born about 1840); *Elizabeth* (born about 1842, married Alexander Cox on 21 Oct. 1866 in Putnam Co.); *Martha A.* (born about 1844, married Columbus Kesterton on 20 Oct. 1865 in Putnam Co.); *Tillman H.* (born about 1848); *Jesse P.* (born about 1852, married Lutisha McCammack on 20 Apr. 1870 in Putnam Co., and secondly Laura L. Purcell on 22 Feb. 1886 in Putnam Co., and thirdly Hattie N. Keen on 5 Jan. 1895 in Putnam Co., and died on 17 Sept. 1914 in Greencastle Township, Putnam Co.); *Matilda* (granddaughter?; born about 1858). Listed in the 1830 census for Putnam Co., in 1840-1860 in Marian Township, Hendricks Co., IN, and in 1870 in Marion Township, Putnam Co., IN. A descendant, Beverly Ann Dickinson, was living in 1984 at Hobbs, NM.

5g. **Dawson (I).** Born 1 July 1810 in Harrison Co., KY. See below for full entry.

5h. **Shelton.** Born about 1812 in Harrison Co., KY. See below for full entry.

5i. **Daughter.** Born about 1814 in Harrison Co., KY. No further record.

A SETTLEMENT DEED OF JOHN BURGESS

(*Putnam County Deed Book #L*, p. 658)

Know all men by these presents that I John Burgess of the County of Putnam and State of Indiana am held and firmly bound unto Shelton Burgess in the penal sum of one thousand dollars the payment whereof well and truly to be made I bind myself and my heirs firmly by these presents sealed with my seal this 8th day of September A.D. 1843. The condition of this bond is such that that [sic] whereas the said John Burgess has this day sold unto the said Shelton Burgess the following tract of Land, to wit, the north half of the east half of the South East quarter of Section twelve in Township Fourteen North of Range four West for the sum of $200 dollars the express understanding between the parties in this bond is that this bond is not to force a conveyance from the said John Burgess to the said Shelton Burgess for said tract of land during the lifetime of the said John Burgess but on the contrary is only to be binding on the heirs at law of the [said] John Burgess to make a conveyance by warranty deed to the said Shelton Burgess after the natural death of said John Burgess. Now if the said conveyance shall be made to the said Shelton Burgess as aforesaid and according to the agreement of the parties to this bond as above stated then this obligation to be void else to remain in full force in law.

Attest: Samuel Reves Jr. — John Burgess [his mark]
Attest: Dawson Burgess [his mark] — Sally Burges [her mark]

Carolyn Burgess Pulman (1900-1987)
(see page 30)

[William (I)[1], Edward (I)[2], Garner (I)[3], John (I)[4]]

WILLIAM S. BURGESS
(1793?-1868?)

OF GRANT COUNTY, KENTUCKY

5b. **William S. (I)** *[son of John (I)].* Born about 1793 in Fauquier Co., VA. Married Nancy Yarnell on 12 Mar. 1817 in Harrison Co. (she was the daughter of Isaac Yarnell and Jane McDonald, and died between 1832-38; her siblings included: Sarah Brown, James, Columbus, Jane Fishback, David, Milton, and Thomas); married secondly Quintilla LaForce on 26 Dec. 1838 in Harrison Co. (she was born about 1814 in KY, and died about 1872). Listed in the Harrison Co. tax records from 1818-24, and again from 1837-53, and in Grant Co. from 1854-68. Listed in the 1820 census of Harrison Co. with his father, in 1830 in Putnam Co., IN, in 1840 again in Harrison Co., in 1850 in Scott Co., KY, and in 1860 in the Downingsville Precinct, Grant Co., KY; Quintilla is listed with her son James in 1870. William Burgess moved to Putnam Co., IN about 1825, being soon followed by his father and sisters and their families; he and Nancy sold their land in 1832, and he returned to Kentucky after her death.

In the absence of a probate record or will, the relationship of William S. Burgess to his children can only be demonstrated circumstantially. His son, George J. Burgess, is deeded land by George's uncle, John Burgess of Harrison Co., on 5 Nov. 1871 (*Deed Book #Q*, p. 524). William S.'s son, William W. Burgess, moved to Grant Co. at the same time as his father; in some early tax records, he is called William Burgess "Jr." Henry Burgess named his second son Isaac Milton, evidently after his older brother, the names clearly deriving from the Yarnell side of the family; Isaac Jr. is listed with his uncle, George, in the 1880 census. A grandson of James P. Burgess, Johney H. Burgess Sr., recalled hearing the family talk about a cousin, Esau Burgess, who is undoubtedly the same person as Albert Esau Burgess, son of William W. William S. Burgess died in Grant Co. about 1868, when he disappeared from the tax lists; his widow is living with her son, James P. Burgess, in the 1870 census for Grant Co., KY. Many members of this family are missing, having evidently moved away to other locales. The order and dates of some of the children listed below are based upon their appearances in the personal property tax lists of Harrison Co.

The Children of William S. Burgess:

6a. **Isaac M(ilton?) (I).** Born about 1819 in Harrison Co., KY. Has not been found in the 1850 census; listed in the 1860 census of Harrison Co. living with Hannah Coonrad, in 1870 with his uncle, John Burgess, and in 1880 with his uncle, Milton Yarnell. Listed in the tax records for Harrison Co. from 1841-42, 1844-45, and 1847, when he apparently moved to Scott Co., and again in Harrison Co. from at least 1870-85. Isaac M. Burgess was a carpenter and farmer in Harrison Co.; he apparently died there unmarried about 1886, when he is dropped from the tax lists.

6b. **William W(ebber?).** Born about 1821 in Harrison Co., KY. See below for full entry.

6c. **John C.** Born about 1823 in Harrison Co., KY. Married Susan Sarah C. Barnhill on 2 May 1844 in Scott Co., KY. Listed in the Harrison Co. tax lists between 1845-46, and in the Scott Co. lists between 1847-48, when he apparently died childless. His widow remarried Benjamin N. McDaniel on 4 Sept. 1851 in Scott Co.

6d. **Edward Y(arnell?).** Born about 1825 in Kentucky or Indiana. Listed in the tax records of Harrison Co. in 1847 and 1849. No further record has been found.

6e. **Henry (II).** Born about 1831 in Virginia or Kentucky or Indiana (variously cited). See below for full entry.

6f. **George J(efferson?) (I).** Born 1840 in Greene Co., IL. See below for full entry.

6g. **James P.** Born 1 Jan. 1842 in Greene Co., IL. See below for full entry.

6h. **Martha J(ane?) (I).** Born about 1844 in Greene Co., IL. Listed with her father in the 1860 census. Married Randolph Cramer on 20 Feb. 1861 in Grant Co., KY, and had children: *James P.* (born 1862 in Grant Co., KY). Martha Cramer died about 1862; her husband remarried Mary E. ___ about 1867, and is listed with her in the 1870 census for Grant Co.

6i. **(Sarah) Ann (II).** Born Oct. 1846 in Greene Co., IL. Listed with her father in the 1860 census. Married Edker A. McGlasson about 1862 (he was born about 1820, and died between 1880-1900), and had children: *Georgia Ann* (born Mar. 1863 in KY, married Samuel J. Martin in 1891 [he was born May 1863], and had children: Sarah A. [born June 1898 in OH]); *Doctor* (born 22 Aug. 1874 in Grant Co.); *Clarence* (born 1879 in KY). Listed in the 1870-80 censuses for Grant Co., KY; Ann is listed in the 1900 census for Covington, Kenton Co., KY living with her daughter Georgia. A James "Glason" is listed with George J. Burgess in the 1880 census for Grant Co. as his "brother."

6j. **(Mary) Ellen (II) "Ella."** Born 1850 in Scott Co., KY. Married as his second wife Alfred E. (or Alford) Powell on 23 Nov. 1869 in Grant Co., KY (he was born about 1833 in KY, probably a brother of Amanda Powell, wife of George J. Burgess; by his first wife, he had children: Lyon [born 1853]; Arthur [born 1863]; Eli [born 1865]; Angeline [born 1867]), and had at least the following children: *Effie* (born 26 Aug. 1871, married Daniel Bruner, and died 19 Apr. 1962, aged 90 years, at Cincinnati, OH, and is buried in the Flag Spring Cemetery, Newtown, Hamilton Co., OH); *Jefferson Davis* (born 1873 in KY); *Hallie* (son; born 1875 in KY). Listed in the 1870 census for Grant Co., KY. She and her husband received and conveyed a 640-acre tract in Clay Co., TX (in northern Texas near the border with Oklahoma) to and from George J. and Amanda Burgess in 1877 (*Grant Co. Deed Book #U*, p. 48 and *Clay Co. Deed Book #D*, p. 404), but apparently never moved there. Listed in the 1880 census for Scott Co., KY, but has not been found in 1900.

6k. **Nancy M.** Born about 1852 in Scott Co., KY. Listed with her brother, James P. Burgess, in the 1870 census. No further record.

6l. **Elizabeth (XVI).** Born about 1854 in Scott Co., KY. Listed with her father in the 1860 census, but either died or married by 1870.

PETER B. PULMAN JR. & REVA BURGESS RUDASILL (1888-1992) *(see pages 29-30)*

[William (I)[1], Edward (I)[2], Garner (I)[3], John (I)[4], William S. (I)[5]]

WILLIAM W. BURGESS
(1821?-1880?)

OF GRANT COUNTY, KENTUCKY

6b. **William W(ebber?)** *[son of William S. (I).].* He is also called William Burgess Jr. Born about 1821 in Harrison Co., KY. Married Mrs. Sarah Ann "Sallie" (Crosswhite?) Kinman on 9 Nov. 1857 in Grant Co. (she was born about 1831 in KY, and died there on 1 Feb. 1894). Listed in the Harrison Co. tax records in 1843, 1846-49, 1851-53, 1855, in Grant Co. from 1854-80, in the 1850 census for Harrison Co., KY with William A. Webber, and in the 1860-80 censuses for Stewartsville, Downingsville Precinct, Grant Co., KY. William Burgess was a farmer in Grant Co. He died there between 1880-1890 (his wife is listed as head of the family on the 1890 personal property tax list, the only one surviving from this period). Sarah Burgess's estate is recorded in *Grant Co. Inventory and Appraisal Book #C*, p. 204-205, dated 12 Mar. 1894, but since it had more debts than assets, no settlement was recorded.

The Children of William W. Burgess:

7a. **William T.** Born about 1858 in Grant Co., KY. Listed with his father in the 1870 census, but died by 1880, and is mentioned in his mother's obituary in the *Williamstown Courier* (1894).
7b. **(Albert) Esau.** Born 25 Mar. 1859 in Grant Co., KY. See below for full entry.
7c. **John N. (II) "Jack."** Born Apr. 1860 in Grant Co., KY. See below for full entry.
7d. **Daughter.** Born and died about 1863 in Grant Co., KY. Her niece, Betty Branson, remembers Esau Burgess talking about her. Mentioned in her mother's obituary as having died before her.
7e. **George W.** Born about 1866 in Grant Co., KY; apparently died there by 1880.

ESAU BURGESS OF GRANT CO., KENTUCKY
[William W.[6]]

7b. **(Albert) Esau** *[son of William W.].* Born 25 Mar. 1859 in Grant Co., KY. Married Tina Bell Piercefield on 9 Nov. 1908 in Grant Co. (she was born 1892, and died 13 Oct. 1949). Listed in the 1900 census for Kenton Co., KY with Robert S. Hampton, and in 1910-20 in Grant Co., KY. Esau Burgess was a farmer near Holbrook, Grant Co., KY. He died there on 2 Apr. 1943.

8a. **Golda Mae "Goldie."** Born 6 Jan. 1910 in Grant Co., KY. Married George Edwards on 3 Jan. 1927 in Fayette Co. (he was born 24 Jan. 1910, and died 5 May 1978), and had children: *LeRoy* (born 6 Aug. 1927, married Geraldine Lay in Sept. 1952, and died 31 July 1990 at Covington, KY, buried Williamstown Cemetery, having had children: Bobby Lee [born June 1957]; Peggy Ray [married Nick Morrison, and died at 21]; David Franklin; Karen [married ___ Forgue, and lives near Covington, KY]; Mary Elizabeth; Carol); *Charles Franklin* (born 17 Nov. 1931, married Delores ___, and had children: Peggy Ann [married Dale Shaw]; Charles Franklin Jr. [married Tracy ___, and had children: David; Victoria]; Sandra Kay [twin]; Sharon Fay [twin]; Mark; Valerie); *Harold G.* (born 4 Dec. 1933, married Lorene Beck, and had children: Terry Lynn; Pamela Kay; Tina Marie; Michael [had children: Missy; Samantha]); *Clifford* (died at age one); *Martha* (born May 1938, died 13 Aug. 1938, buried Williamstown Cemetery); *Marshall* (born 5 June 1941, married and had children: Gary; Marsha; Billy [had children: Eric {twin}; Erica {twin}]); *Shirley* (born 5 Sept. 1944, married ___ Jacobs, and had children: Ronald Keith [had children: Skyla; Lauren]; married secondly Wayne Pennington); *Brenda Kay* (born 20 Aug. 1947 at Crittenden, KY, married Gary Craig Searcy on 7 June 1967 at Louisville, KY [div.], and secondly Gregory Kane Howland on 9 May 1987 at Louisville, KY; Brenda works as a paralegal assistant, and lives at Louisville, KY; she contributed greatly to this book). Goldie Edwards died on 14 Dec. 1964, and is buried with her husband in the Williamstown Cemetery.

8b. **Kenneth Mason.** Listed as Clifford in the KY birth records. Born 30 July 1911 in Grant Co., KY. Married Iva Fisk. Kenneth was a trucker at Clarksville, IN. He died there childless on 2 Dec. 1976.

8c. **Anna Bell.** Born 24 Aug. 1913 in Grant Co., KY. Married (George) Russell Purnell on 21 Mar. 1929 in Grant Co., KY, and had two daughters. Anna Purnell died 1 May 1975 at Cincinnati, OH.

8d. **Betty Lee.** Born 12 Aug. 1915 in Grant Co., KY. Married William Shirley Page, and had children: *William Shirley Jr.* (born 6 Jan. 1944 at Louisville, KY, married Inge Brigitte Friersbord on 3 July 1964, and had children: Susanne [born 12 Aug. 1964, married Bernard Joseph Higgins on 2 Sept. 1988, and had children: Julie Lynn {born 14 Oct. 1985}; Jeffrey Bernard {born 1 July 1988}]; Patricia [born 6 Sept. 1965, married Allen Henderson on 16 Jan. 1982, and had children: Craig {born 25 Feb. 1983}; Linda Renee {born 18 July 1984}]; Debbie [born 29 Jan. 1968, married Mark Delatorre, and had children: Adam Page {born 12 Apr. 1986}; Justin {born 22 Mar. 1991}]; Nicole Elizabeth [born 18 Nov. 1983]; Stephanie [born 11 June 1985]; William Shirley III [born 16 May 1991]; married secondly Evie Wilson on 9 Oct. 1993); *Judith Kaye* (born 26 May 1945 at Louisville, married Timothy Foster on 28 May 1971, and had children: Angie [born 31 July 1967, married Scott Joseph Flint on 28 Feb. 1987, and had children: Jessie {born 27 July 1987}]; Rodney [born 9 July 1969, married Tonja ___ on 16 Apr. 1988, and had children: Coty {born 2 Feb. 1989}; Kelsey {born 2 Mar. 1993}]; married secondly Donald McDaniel, and had children: Danny [twin; born 9 Nov. 1981]; David [twin; born 9 Nov. 1981]; she lives at New Albany, IN). Betty married secondly Darrell Branson, and contributed greatly to this book; she died on 3 Jan. 1992 at Louisville, KY.

8e. **Corrine** (nmn). Born 10 Nov. 1916 in Grant Co., KY. Married Elzie Romans on 10 July 1937 in Grant Co., and had children: *Betty Jean*; *Frances*; *Bartis*; married secondly Benjamin Bishop.

9a. **Anna Grace.** Born 6 June 1935 in Grant Co., KY.

8f. **Katherine Juanita.** Her name was originally Kelsie Juanita. Born 24 Mar. 1918 in Grant Co., KY. Married secondly Woodrow Wilson. Katherine Wilson died in July 1980 at Covington, KY.

8g. **Albert Herbert "Allie."** Born 18 May 1921 (or 29 Aug. 1920) in Grant Co., KY. Married. Served in World War II (discharged 19 Oct. 1945 in Grant Co., KY). Allie Burgess was the manager of a service station at Covington, KY. He died on 28 June 1981 at Independence, KY.

9a. **Peggy.**
9b. **Daughter.**
9c. **Daughter.**
9d. **Daughter.**

8h. **William Earl (I).** Born 11 Aug. 1925 in Grant Co., KY. Bill Burgess was a security guard at Louisville, KY. He died there unmarried on 25 Mar. 1984.

JOHN N. BURGESS OF HAMILTON CO., OHIO

[William W.[6]]

7c. **John N. (II) "Jack"** *[son of William W.]*. Listed as John M. in the 1860 census. Born Apr. 1860 in Grant Co., KY. Married Nannie Fortner about 1890 (she was born June 1869 in KY, daughter of William F. Fortner). Listed with his father in the 1880 census, and in the 1900 census for Grant Co., but has not been found in 1910; Nannie Burgess is listed alone in the 1920 census for Cincinnati, OH. Listed in the 1903-13 city directories of Cincinnati, OH working as a carpenter. Jack Burgess is said to have died at Cincinnati about 1930 (possibly on 11 Sept. 1933 or in 1913). Both he and his wife are buried in the Williamstown Cemetery (no dates appear on their stone).

8a. **Stella (II).** Born Mar. 1891 in Grant Co., KY. Listed with her father in the 1900 census. Apparently died young, and is buried with her parents.

8b. **Evelyn L. "Eva."** Born June 1892 in Grant Co., KY. Listed with her father in the 1900 census. Apparently died young, and is buried with her parents.

8c. **(Charles) Porter.** Born 20 May 1895 in Grant Co., KY. Married Gertrude Hausman about 1916 (she was born 25 Mar. 1899, and died 30 Apr. 1990 at Cincinnati, OH). Listed in the 1913 city directory of Cincinnati, in the 1917 draft list, in the 1920 census at Elmwood Place, Hamilton Co., OH (but has not been found in 1910), and in the 1948-51 directories as a resident of Mt. Healthy, working for Tresler Oil Co. Porter Burgess died in Nov. 1984 at Cincinnati, OH.

9a. **Eleanore.** Born Sept. 1917 in Ohio.
9b. **Child.**

[William (I)[1], Edward (I)[2], Garner (I)[3], John (I)[4], William S. (I)[5]]

HENRY BURGESS
(1831?-1882?)

OF HARRISON COUNTY, KENTUCKY

6e. **Henry (II)** *[son of William S. (I)].* Born about 1831 in Virginia or Kentucky or Iowa or (probably) Putnam Co., IN (variously cited). Married Mrs. (Sarah) Jane (Johnson) Stump on 24 Jan. 1854 in Harrison Co. (she was born 28 July 1832, daughter of Daniel and Syrene Johnson, and died on 8 Jan. 1867); married secondly Mary "Mollie" Jones on 30 Sept. 1867 in Harrison Co. (she was born about 1842 in KY). An 1839 guardianship proceeding in Harrison Co. stated that Henry was the son of William and Nancy Burgess, and made him the ward of his grandfather, Isaac Yarnell (*Minute Book #H*, p. 389); this was confirmed by Yarnell's will (*Will Book #F*, p. 595, dated 20 Sept. 1849). Listed in the 1850 census with Yarnell, in the 1860 census for Pendleton Co., KY, with his family in the 1870-80 censuses for the Casons District (#2), Harrison Co., and in the 1854-82 tax records for Harrison Co. Henry Burgess was a farmer in Harrison Co., KY; he either died or moved away about 1882.

The Children of Henry Burgess:

7a. **James L. (I).** Born Mar. 1855 (or 1856) in Harrison Co., KY. Married Ida B. Cummin(g)s on 28 Oct. 1875 in Harrison Co. (she was born May 1854 in KY, and died 12 Dec. 1938 in Bourbon Co., KY). Listed in the 1870-1900 censuses for Harrison Co.; Ida is listed there alone in 1910-20. James L. Burgess was a saloon keeper at Cynthiana, Harrison Co., KY. He apparently died childless in 1908, and was buried with his wife in the Georgetown Cemetery, Scott Co.

7b. **Isaac Milton (II).** Born 20 Nov. 1856 in Harrison Co., KY. See below for full entry.

7c. **Susan E.** Born about 1859 in Harrison Co., KY. Living with her father in 1870. By inference she died before 1916.

7d. **Mary E. (III) "Mollie."** Born May 1862 in Harrison Co., KY. She may have married Lewis T. Day on 25 Nov. 1880 in Harrison Co. (he was born May 1855 in KY). She is *not* the Mollie Day (born Mettie Richardson) who married Louis Day about 1895, died on 17 July 1913 at White Oak, Harrison Co., KY, and is buried in Battle Grove Cemetery, Cynthiana. By inference she died before 1916.

7e. **Sarah W(illiams?) (II) "Sallie."** Born Feb. 1866 (or 1865) in Harrison Co., KY. Married Robert Coleman on 21 Mar. 1883 in Harrison Co. (he was born Apr. 1846), and had at least the following children: *James* (born Mar. 1884); *George* (born May 1886); *Mathew* (born June 1887); *Charles* (born Feb. 1889); *Clay* (born Aug. 1892); *Sidney* (born June 1893); *Sarda* (born July 1895); *Lucy* (born Aug. 1896). Listed in the 1900 census for Harrison Co., but has not been found in 1910. By inference she died before 1916.

7f. **Charles H. (II).** Born 7 Jan. 1867 in Harrison Co., KY. See below for full entry.

7g. **Margaret (VIII) "Maggie."** Born about 1868 in Harrison Co., KY. Living with her father in 1880. She or one of her sisters married R. H. Hughes, and was living in Utah in 1939 (but is not listed there in the 1920 Soundex). The Rulon H. Hughes listed in the Salt Lake City directories during the 1930s (with wife Emily J.) is unrelated.

7h. **Richard E. (?).** Born about 1870 in Harrison Co., KY. Two Richard Burgesses born in Kentucky about 1870 appear in the 1900 soundexes: the Richard E. Burgess (whose wife, Sadie ___, was born Mar. 1876 in PA), who is living in Kansas City, MO working as a fireman; and the Richard A. Burgess who is living in Madison Co., KY in 1900, and Tazewell Co., IL in 1910, with wife Linda (his second wife), and children: *Edward* (born May 1891 in KY); *Grace* (born Jan. 1893 in KY); *Jesse* (born May 1895 in KY); *Ada* (born May 1900 in KY); *Christina* (born 1902 in KY); *Robert* (born 1904 in KY); *Ray* (born 1906 in KY); *Lloyd* (born 1910 in KY). One of these is probably Henry's son Richard, and the other is probably the Richard Burgess of Estill Co., KY who is listed with his father in the 1880 census. By inference he died before 1916.

7i. **Nancy (VI) "Nannie."** Born about 1873 in Harrison Co., KY. Married ___ Needles, and is living in Florida in 1939. She has not been found in the 1900-10 KY, the 1910 TN, OH, FL, GA, PA, IL, or the 1900 IN and MO Soundexes; has not been found in the 1920 Soundex for any state. There were several Needles families living at Orlando, Orange Co., FL during the period 1920-60, and a Homer N. Needles died in 1931 in St. Lucie Co., FL.

7j. **Ida (II).** Born about 1875 in Harrison Co., KY. By inference she died before 1916.

7k. **Benjamin.** Born 1 Dec. 1877 in Harrison Co., KY; died there before 1880.

ISAAC MILTON BURGESS OF BUTLER CO., OHIO

[Henry (II)[6]]

7b. **Isaac Milton (II)** *[son of Henry (II)].* Born 20 Nov. 1856 (or 1857, according to his death certificate) in Harrison Co., KY. Married Alice M. ___ (she was born 2 June 1868 at Chicago, IL, remarried John B. Yerigan, and died 17 Oct. 1941 at Hamilton, OH, buried St. Stephen's Cemetery [or Greenwood]). Listed in the 1870 census for Harrison Co., in 1880 in Grant Co. (as "Milton Burgess") living with his uncle, George J. Burgess, and in the 1900 census for Wood Co., OH, but has not been found in 1910; listed in the 1883/84-1886, 1903, and 1906/07-1908 city directories for Columbus, OH, and in the 1915 directory for Hamilton, Butler Co., OH. Isaac M. Burgess was a laborer in Kentucky and Ohio. He died of pneumonia on 11 July 1916 at Hamilton, Ohio, and is buried in the Greenwood Cemetery. His widow is listed with John B. Yerigan in the 1919/20 directory of Hamilton; the next directory (1921/22) lists her as Yerigan's wife, and she continues to be listed through the 1940/41 directories. Isaac's brief obituary indicates that two children, two sisters, and a brother survive (the number of siblings corresponds with his brother Charles's 1939 obituary).

8a. **Anna W.** Born Oct. 1886 in Ohio. By inference she survived the death of her father (1916).

8b. **Elmer M.** His name is spelled Elmur in the 1900 census. Born 10 Jan. 1890 (or 1889, according to his marriage record) in Ohio. Married Della McCain on 18 Jan. 1910 at Columbus, OH (she was born 25 Oct. 1891, daughter of Charles M. McCain and Lucinda "Lucy" Palmer, remarried Jasper W. Dildine on 14 Sept. 1918 at Columbus, OH [div.; the marriage certificate states that Della is a widow], and thirdly (Jessie) Arthur Robertson on 27 June 1925, and died May 1985 at Logan, Hocking Co., OH, aged 93 years). Listed in the 1908-15 city directories of Columbus, OH; Della is listed there alone from 1916-29, and from 1930 with Robertson, and in the 1920 census for Columbus, Franklin Co., OH living with her parents (as a divorcée). Elmer Burgess was a railroad brakeman in Ohio; he apparently died there about 1915.

9a. **Gerald.** Born 28 Jan. 1911 at Columbus, OH. He may have married Wanda ___. Gerald Burgess died on 24 Sept. 1988 at Logan, Hocking Co., OH.

8c. **James L. (II).** Born Jan. 1893 in Ohio. Listed variously in the early city directories of Columbus, OH; however, he is *not* the James Burgess (no middle initial) who was listed working as a bartender in Columbus during the late teens. By inference he is living in 1916.

CHARLES H. BURGESS OF HARRISON CO., KENTUCKY

[Henry (II)[6]]

7f. **Charles H. (II)** *[son of Henry (II)].* His name is given as Charles S. Burgess in the 1920 census. Born 7 Jan. 1867 in Harrison Co., KY. Married Susan Mary McKinley on 23 Nov. 1894 in Harrison Co. (she was born Dec. 1877 in KY). Listed in the 1900-20 censuses for Harrison Co. (in 1920 with Jem S. Chandler). Charlie Burgess was a farmer at Poindexter, KY, four miles north of Cynthiana, in Harrison Co. He died there on 28 Feb. 1939, and is buried with his wife in the Battle Grove Cemetery, Cynthiana, KY. His obituary mentions two surviving siblings, Nannie Needles and Mrs. R. H. Hughes (an unidentified sister) of Utah.

8a. **(Mary) Lucinda "Lula."** Born Oct. 1895 at Poindexter, KY. Living in 1910 with her father, but is said to have died there young of tuberculosis, and is buried in the Battle Grove Cemetery. She was engaged at the time of her death.

8b. **Charles Everett "Judge."** Born 10 Oct. 1897 (or 1898, according to his draft record) at Poindexter, KY. Married Mary Katherine Casey on 14 Mar. 1923 in Harrison Co. (she was born 9 Sept. 1898, daughter of Thomas Casey and Katherine Wolfe, and died 26 Mar. 1983 at Berry, KY). Listed in the 1917 draft list for Harrison Co., KY, and in the 1920 census there living alone (as Charles M.

Burgess Jr.). Judge Burgess was a farmer all of his life near Berry, Harrison Co., KY. He died there on 9 Oct. 1979, and is buried with his wife in the Battle Grove Cemetery.

9a. **Wanda Lois.** Born 9 Sept. 1927 in Harrison Co. Married (Maurice) Dempsey Earle on 8 Aug. 1946 in Harrison Co., KY, and had children: *Ronald Dempsey* (born 17 Aug. 1948 at Lexington, KY, married Cindy Scott); *Kenneth Lynn* (born 30 Mar. 1955 at Lexington, KY). Wanda Earle currently lives at Berry, KY.

9b. **Charles Bryant.** Born 7 Jan. 1942 in Harrison Co., KY. Married Jane Ann Cason on 19 Dec. 1965 in Harrison Co., KY. Charles Burgess currently works as a farmer near Berry, KY.

10a. **Bryant Keith.** Born 22 Dec. 1977 at Berry, KY.

Thomas Fleming BURGESS
(1833-1911)
Sarah Jane HARRIS
(1832-1902)
(see page 120)

[William (I)[1], Edward (I)[2], Garner (I)[3], John (I)[4], William S. (I)[5]]

GEORGE J. BURGESS
(1840-1890)

OF GRANT COUNTY, KENTUCKY

6f. **George J(efferson?) (I)** *[son of William S. (I)].* Born 1840 in Greene Co., IL. Married Amanda Powell on 10 June 1861 in Scott Co., KY (div. 7 Dec. 1883; she was born Jan. 1838, and died 1908); married secondly Elizabeth Brown on 1 May 1884 at Cincinnati, OH. Listed in the 1860 census with his father, and in 1870-80 in Grant Co., KY (in 1880 his nephew, Isaac Milton Burgess, is living with him, and is called his "brother"). Served as a 2nd Lieut. in the Union Army during the Civil War (Co. B, 11th Kentucky Cavalry). He was deeded land by his uncle, John Burgess "Sr." of Harrison Co., KY, on 15 Nov. 1871 (*Deed Book #Q*, p. 524), thereby confirming the relationship of Quintilla Burgess's children to the rest of the family. George J. Burgess owned a tavern and livery stable at Williamstown, Grant Co., KY, as well as land in Clay Co., TX, Jasper and Smith Cos., MS, and Washington Co., KS. On 2 Dec. 1890 he was killed at his saloon at Williamstown. After his death, Amanda Burgess and her children moved to Hollenberg, Washington Co., KS in 1897, but returned to Kentucky by 1900, when Amanda is listed in the census with her daughter, Anna Carnes. Both are buried in separate plots in the Williamstown Cemetery.

The Children of George J. Burgess:

7a. **(Nancy) Ella.** Born Jan. 1865 in Grant Co., KY. Married Frank O. Menaugh on 10 Sept. 1885 in Grant Co. (he was born May 1864 in OH, and died 17 Nov. 1923 in Mason Co., KY), and had children: *Edith* (born June 1887 in KY). Listed in the 1900 census for Williamstown, Grant Co., KY. Ella Menaugh was living in Williamstown at her sister's death in 1932, but has not been found in the Kentucky death indexes.

7b. **(Lorena) Anna.** Born Sept. 1867 in Grant Co., KY. Married William Carnes on 27 Aug. 1881 (he was born 15 July 1849, began practicing law in 1876, was elected County Attorney of Grant Co. in 1895, and died 20 Apr. 1912 at Williamstown, KY), and had children: *Mabel* (born Aug. 1885 in KY, married D. E. Ernst, lived at Russell, KY, and had children: W. G. [son]); *Marie* (born May 1899 in KY, died before 1932); *Cecilia* (married Leo Tysar or Kysar, lived at Detroit, and had children: George Burgess); *Crystal* (living unmarried at Detroit in 1932). Listed in the 1900-10 censuses for Grant Co., KY. Anna Carnes died on 20 Nov. 1932 at Detroit, MI, but is buried with her husband in the Williamstown Cemetery.

7c. **James W.** Born 11 Mar. 1870 in Grant Co., KY. Listed with his mother in the 1900 census. James W. Burgess inherited his father's tavern and livery stable in Williamstown, but was forced to sell his goods and property on 25 Feb. 1892, and moved with his mother and brother to Hollenberg, Washington Co., KS in 1897. A James W. "Burgers" who died 1908 is buried in the Hollenberg Cemetery with his wife Fannie Jones (she was born 1876, and died 1912, but has not been found in the 1910 Soundex); he is *not* the James W. Burgess who is listed in the 1922 city directory of Columbus, OH. By inference he died before 1932.

7d. **Cora A.** Born 27 Dec. 1873 in Grant Co., KY; died there on 23 Sept. 1874, and is buried with her mother.

7e. **Daisy.** Born 22 Mar. 1875 in Grant Co., KY; died there on 3 Sept. 1875, and is buried with her mother.

7f. **William C.** Born 9 Mar. 1876 in Grant Co., KY; died there on 21 Feb. 1878, and is buried with his mother.

7g. **George P.** Born 9 Dec. 1878 in Grant Co., KY. He was taken by his mother to Kansas in 1897 for his health. George Burgess died unmarried on 15 Aug. 1898 at Hollenberg, KS, but was returned to Kentucky for burial, and was interred next to his mother in the Williamstown Cemetery.

SHOT DOWN BY DETERMINED OFFICERS OF THE LAW

"About seven o'clock Tuesday evening the denizens of Mill Street were startled by the report of a pistol. Hastening to their doors, they heard the screams of a woman at the residence of Mrs. McKinley, and saw a man with a smoking pistol in his hand, bareheaded, and apparently under the influence of liquor, fleeting [sic] through the darkness as though pursued by all of the demons of Hell. The man was G. J. Burgess. A short time before, he had entered the residence of the McKinley's to see his friend, Alice McKinley. He and the McKinley woman have been on very intimate terms for many months past. Shortly after Burgess entered the house, there was a war of words between the two, which Burgess quickly ended by drawing his pistol and shooting the woman, the ball striking just below the left breast and passing through the lungs, coming out at the back. As soon as the shot was fired, Burgess bolted from the room, and it was his form the denizens of Mill Street saw fleeting through the darkness like a specter.

"Dr. J. D. Viollett lives across the street from the McKinley house, and in less than five minutes he had been summoned to the woman's side, and was examining the wound. He found her in a very danger's [sic] condition, the wound being almost necessarily fatal. In a very few minutes, Chas. and John McKinley, brothers of the wounded woman, came in vowing vengeance against Burgess, and attempted to arm themselves, but, prevented by their Mother and Dr. Viollett, who persuaded them to go to Judge C. C. Cram, and swear out a warrant for Burgess' arrest. This the boys, acting on their better judgment, did. Judge Cram was found at home in bed. He quickly dressed himself and came up town to D. J. Charbonneau's grocery, prepared the warrant of arrest, and delivered it to James Cates, deputy marshal, who happened to be present. About this time deputy sheriff Jack Webb came into town, and was summoned by Cates to assist him in making the arrest. Together the two officers sought the fugitive, little dreaming he would resist to the death.

"They found Burgess in his saloon on Main Street, with the doors barred and bolted. They tried to gain admittance, but were refused. Seizing a beer keg, they hurled it against the door and smashed it in. The keg rebounded, striking Webb and knocking him down to his knees. That fall was very fortunate for deputy Webb, it probably saved his life. When the door swung open, Burgess was standing directly in the passage, armed with a self acting revolver, and opened a murderous fire upon the officers of the law. His first shot passed through deputy Webb's clothes near the hips, the second shot grazed the skin on Webb's pistol hand and knocked the pistol to the ground. The officers were not idle, and were not to be deterred from making the arrest. When Burgess opened fire, they immediately followed suit, and with terrible execution. Burgess was shot four times in the body before dropping his pistol, having emptied every chamber. He staggered out at the door, and sunk to the ground unconscious. His body was carried into the residence of his daughter, Mrs. F. C. Menaugh. Dr. J. M. Wilson was hastily summoned to his side, but his surgical skill was useless, work had been well done, and at ten o'clock George Burgess was a corpse, and one of the bloodiest tragedies ever enacted in the town of Williamstown was ended."—*Williamstown Courier*, 4 Dec. 1890.

ROY P. BURGESS (1890-1954)
EDNA JOSEPHINE MATHEWS BURGESS (1899-1985)
[see page 132]

[William (I)[1], Edward (I)[2], Garner (I)[3], John (I)[4], William S. (I)[5]]

JAMES P. BURGESS
(1842-1877)

OF GRANT COUNTY, KENTUCKY

6g. **James P.** *[son of William S. (I)].* Born 1 Jan. 1842 in Greene Co., IL (so stated on his marriage license application). Married Malissa Catherine "Millie" Chipman on 3 Dec. 1868 in Grant Co., KY (she was born 26 Mar. 1846, daughter of William Chipman and Rilly Ann Jouett, and died 16 Apr. 1921 at Stewartsville, KY). James P. Burgess served in Co. B, 18th Kentucky Infantry, Union Army, during the Civil War, and in Co. A of the Veterans Reserve Corps. Listed in the 1860 census with his father, and in 1870 in Grant Co., KY; Millie is listed there as head of the family in 1880-1910 (two of five children survive in 1910), and by herself in 1920. James P. Burgess was a farmer in Grant Co., KY. He died on 29 Sept. 1877 (or 1878) at Stewartsville, KY; both he and his wife are buried in the Williamstown Cemetery. The road on which his property was once situated is now called the Burgess Road.

The Children of James P. Burgess:

7a. **William Jefferson.** Born 30 Apr. 1871 in Grant Co., KY; he died there on 13 Feb. 1888, and is buried with his parents.

7b. **(Mary) Ann (V) "Anna."** Born 15 July 1873 (or 1872, according to her tombstone) in Grant Co., KY. Married Charles L. Harrison on 10 Nov. 1891 in Grant Co. (he was born 1867, son of P. J. Harrison, and died 1948), and had one child who died in infancy on 27 Aug. 1893. Ann Harrison died on 1 Sept. 1893, and is buried with her parents in the Williamstown Cemetery.

7c. **Elizabeth E. (III) "Lizzie."** Born 10 Dec. 1874 in Grant Co., KY. Married J. F. Crouch about 1894 in Grant Co. (he was born 7 Mar. 1869, and died 4 Mar. 1904), and had children: *William Moody* (born 4 Mar. 1896, married Mabel Clara ___ [she was born 1894, and died 1961], and died 22 Aug. 1968, buried Williamstown Cemetery). Listed in the 1910 census for Grant Co. Lizzie Crouch died on 28 Nov. 1946 in Kenton Co., KY, and is buried with her husband in the Williamstown Cemetery. A Mrs. Forrest Crouch, second daughter of Mrs. Millie Burgess, is mentioned in the *Williamstown Courier* as having been buried in the Williamstown Cemetery on 1 Oct. 1891; she remains unidentified.

7d. **James Lester.** Born 22 July 1876 in Grant Co., KY. See below for full entry.

JAMES L. BURGESS OF GRANT CO., KENTUCKY
[James P.[6]]

7d. **James Lester** *[son of James P.].* Born 22 July 1876 in Grant Co., KY. Married Bertha Williams on 28 Mar. 1895 in Grant Co. (she was born 11 Dec. 1873, daughter of W. C. Williams, and died 3 Dec. 1945). Listed in the census with his mother in 1900, and in 1910-20 in Grant Co., KY; he also appears there on the 1917 draft list. James L. Burgess was a farmer near Stewartsville, KY. He died there on 7 Apr. 1943, and is buried in the Williamstown Cemetery.

8a. **Willie.** Born 5 Mar. 1896 at Covington, KY. See below for full entry.

8b. **Zelmer** (son). His name is listed as Zemba in the county death records. Born 4 Dec. 1897 in Grant Co., KY; died there on 12 Apr. 1898, and is buried with his parents.

8c. **Nannie Catherine.** Born 2 Feb. 1899 in Grant Co., KY. See below for full entry.

8d. **Vernon Eshil.** Born 31 Oct. 1901 in Grant Co., KY. See below for full entry.

8e. **Lizzie Viola.** Her name is listed in the 1920 census as Elizabeth V. Burgess. Born 23 Dec. 1903 in Grant Co., KY. Married Willie W. Souder on 23 Feb. 1921 in Grant Co. (he was born 4 Oct. 1899, and died 21 Nov. 1982 at Williamstown, KY), and had children: *Catherine* (or Kathryn; married ___ Moore); *William J.* (who lives at Williamstown, KY); *James* (born 26 May 1926, and died Mar. 1978 at Williamstown, KY); *Sanford*; *David E.* Lizzie Souder died Dec. 1987 at Williamstown, KY, and is buried in the Williamstown Cemetery.

8f. **George Jefferson (II).** Born 22 Sept. 1905 in Grant Co., KY. Married Florence Wainscott on 1 Mar. 1930 in Grant Co. (she died 25 Nov. 1969). George Burgess was a farmer all of his life in Grant Co., KY. He died there childless on 28 Sept. 1986.

8g. **Millie.** Born 22 Sept. 1906 in Grant Co., KY; died there before 1910.

8h. **James Russell.** Born 1 Nov. 1908 in Grant Co., KY. See below for full entry.

8i. **Johney Holden (I).** Born 17 Nov. 1911 in Grant Co., KY. See below for full entry.

WILLIE BURGESS OF GRANT CO., KENTUCKY

[James P.[6], James Lester[7]]

8a. **Willie** (nmn) *[son of James Lester].* Born 5 Mar. 1896 at Covington, Kenton Co., KY. Married Jennie Katherine Evans (she was born 1 Nov. 1898, daughter of Edward Evans and Lizzie Brewer, and died 28 Apr. 1975 at Lexington, KY). Living with his grandmother in the 1910 census (as "William"). Listed in the 1917 draft list for Grant Co., KY, and served in World War I. Willie Burgess was a farmer in Grant Co. He died there on 3 Oct. 1974, and is buried with his wife in the Williamstown Cemetery.

9a. **(Mary) Lucille.** Born 15 Feb. 1920 in Grant Co., KY. Married Willie Fritz on 7 Oct. 1937 in Grant Co. (he was born 4 Feb. 1910), and had children: *Judy Anita* (born 23 Sept. 1942 at Williamstown, KY, married (Howard) Gary Beach on 17 Dec. 1960 at Dry Ridge, KY, and had adopted children: Anita Marie; Howard Shelby; Gary Beach is an assistant fire marshal for the University of Kentucky, Lexington, KY; Judy Beach is a hair stylist); *(Rose) Darlene* (born 3 Oct. 1947 at Williamstown, KY, married James Howard Souder on 24 July 1964 at Dry Ridge, KY [div.], and had children: Sean Robert [born 21 Mar. 1971; by Jackie Elliott he had children: Garret James {born 6 Sept. 1989 at Cincinnati, OH}]; *Darlene* married secondly (Marvin) Gayle West on 11 Jan. 1985 at Williamstown, KY, and works for Sprite Flite Jets at the Blue Grass Airport, Lexington, KY). Willie Fritz worked for the Williamstown School, retiring in 1975. Lucille Fritz worked at the Williamstown Cafeteria for 24 years, retiring in 1989. They currently live at Williamstown, KY.

9b. **Beulah Mae (III).** Born 3 Mar. 1925 in Grant Co., KY. Married Kline Eldred Hedges on 20 Feb. 1951 in Grant Co. (he was born 10 Jan. 1918). Beulah Hedges farms near Williamstown, KY; she has contributed greatly to this book.

9c. **James Edward (VII) "Jake."** Born 29 Apr. 1929 in Grant Co., KY. Married Betty Jo Clemens on 10 Sept. 1958 in Grant Co. (div.; she was born 29 Sept. 1939). Jake is a truck driver at Williamstown, KY.

10a. **Tanda Louise.** Born 18 Apr. 1959 at Williamstown, KY. Married (William) Daryl Yates on 29 June 1984 in Grant Co. Tanda Yates lives at Dry Ridge, KY.

10b. **Sally Jo.** Born 5 July 1965 at Williamstown, KY. Married Keith A. McMain, an attorney, on 19 July 1986 in Grant Co. Sally McMain lives at Elsmere, KY.

9d. **Jewel Rose "Jo."** Born 9 Apr. 1934 in Grant Co., KY. Married Robert Martin Schulte on 22 Aug. 1964 at Kenton, KY (he was born 3 Mar. 1926). Jo Schulte is an insurance adjuster for Continental Insurance Co. at Cincinnati, OH.

9e. **Barbara June** (twin). Born 8 Aug. 1937 in Grant Co., KY. Married Wendell L. Owen on 22 Nov. 1961 in Grant Co. (div.), and had children: *Staci Darlene* (born 29 June 1963, married Gary Barber on 17 Oct. 1992); *Stephanie Sue* (born 20 Aug. 1965, married Gary Rose on 17 Nov. 1990, and had children: Joshua Christian [twin; born 9 Feb. 1993]; Jennie Christine [twin; born 9 Feb. 1993]; *Stephanie* is a social worker for the State of Kentucky); *Steven Kline* (born 20 Aug. 1967, married Jeannine Bays on 8 Sept. 1990 [div.]; *Steve OWEN* is a Kentucky State Police trooper). Barbara Owen is Executive Director of the Housing Authority of Dry Ridge, KY.

9f. **Bobby Junior** (twin). Born 8 Aug. 1937 in Grant Co., KY. Married Linda Lou Rosenstiel on 19 June 1963 in Grant Co. (div.); married secondly Lou Ellen Barnett on 25 Feb. 1984 in Grant Co. (she was born 31 Mar. 1954). Bobby Burgess is a surveyor for the Kentucky State Highway Dept. at Williamstown, KY.

10a. **Sherry Lynn (II).** Born on 3 June 1964 in Kenton Co., KY. Married Glenn R. Hearn on 20 Sept. 1980 in Boone Co., KY, and had children: *Melinda* (born 29 Jan. 1981); *Amberly* (born Jan. 1986). Sherry Hearn works in a rest home at Florence, KY.

10b. **Jeffrey Allen (II).** Born 10 May 1966 in Kenton Co., KY. Married Kimberly E. Rudd on 23 Nov. 1985 in Gallatin Co., KY. Jeff Burgess works for a lumber company at Erlanger, KY.

11a. **Melissa "Lisa."** Born Dec. 1986 in KY.
11b. **Melisha Allena.** Born 7 Feb. 1990 at Erlanger, KY.

10c. **(Betty) Suzanne "Suzie."** Born 11 Sept. 1971 in Grant Co., KY. Married Tony Epperson in 1990.
10d. **(Robert) Scott.** Born 5 May 1978 in Grant Co., KY.

NANNIE BURGESS OF GRANT CO., KENTUCKY
[James P.[6], James Lester[7]]

8c. **Nannie Catherine** *[daughter of James Lester].* Born 2 Feb. 1899 in Grant Co., KY, according to a contemporaneous newspaper announcement, or 1900, according to her tombstone. Listed in the 1920 census living with her parents. Nannie Burgess was a cook in Williamstown all of her life; she died there unmarried on 25 June 1980, and is buried in the Williamstown Cemetery.

9a. **Noah (II)** (nmn). Born 14 Dec. 1921 in Grant Co., KY. Married Lucille Charlene Elliott on 3 Jan. 1945 in Grant Co. Served in World War II. Noah Burgess was a farmer in rural Grant Co. He died there on 19 July 1971, and is buried in the Williamstown Cemetery.

10a. **Bonnie Lou (I).** Born 6 Dec. 1945 in Grant Co., KY. Married Marshall Scroggins on 2 July 1965 in Grant Co. Bonnie Scroggins lives at Dry Ridge, KY.
10b. **Charles Edward (III).** Born 8 June 1947 in Grant Co., KY. Married Lois Mulberry on 9 May 1969 in Grant Co. (div.). Charles Burgess is a machinist at Williamstown, KY.

11a. **Timothy Allen (II).** Born 29 Apr. 1970 at Covington, KY.
11b. **Vickie Lee.** Born 3 Apr. 1972 at Covington, KY.
11c. **Chrystal Dawn.** Born 5 Dec. 1974 (?) at Covington, KY.

10c. **Larry Wayne (I).** Born 26 Nov. 1950 in Grant Co., KY. Married Benita Anderson on 5 Aug. 1978 in Grant Co. Larry Burgess works for a paper supply company at Independence, KY.

11a. **Erica Lee.** Born 28 Sept. 1981 at Covington, KY.

10d. **Dennis Ray (I).** Born 1 Feb. 1954 in Owen Co., KY. Married Marilyn Turner on 17 Feb. 1972 in Grant Co.; married secondly Judith A. "Judy" Burkett on 12 Feb. 1983 in Boone Co., KY. Dennis Burgess works as a concrete loader at Independence, KY.

11a. **Dennis Lee (IV).** Born 28 Jan. 1973 at Covington, KY.
11b. **Ray Allen.** Born Aug. 1979 at Covington, KY.
11c. **Dennis Ray (II).** Born 1982 at Covington, KY.

VERNON E. BURGESS OF PINELLAS CO., FLORIDA
[James P.[6], James Lester[7]]

8d. **Vernon Eshil** *[son of James Lester].* Born 31 Oct. 1901 in Grant Co., KY. Married Jean Beighle on 17 Apr. 1934 (she lives at St. Petersburg, FL). Listed in the 1920 census with his father. Vernon Burgess was a bus driver for Greyhound Lines at Lexington, KY. He died on 20 Nov. 1973 at St. Petersburg, FL, and is buried in the Memorial Park Gardens.

9a. **Norma Mae** (ad.). Born 1 Jan. 1924 at Logan, WV. Married ___ Wineland.

JIMMIE BURGESS OF GRANT CO., KENTUCKY
[James P.[6], James Lester[7]]

8h. **James Russell "Jimmie"** *[son of James Lester].* Born 1 Nov. 1908 in Grant Co., KY. Married Jewell E. Wainscott (she was born 25 Sept. 1920). Jimmie Burgess was a farmer and school bus driver in Grant Co. He died there on 24 Oct. 1972, and is buried in the Williamstown Cemetery.

9a. **Geraldine** (nmn). Born 21 Oct. 1935 in Grant Co., KY. Married Ray Marksberry. Geraldine Marksberry works as a motel maid at Williamstown, and lives at Dry Ridge, KY.

9b. **Katherine Louise (I).** Born 25 June 1937 in Grant Co., KY. Married Bill Evans. Katherine Evans is a waitress in Grant Co.

9c. **Jimmie Larry.** Born 31 Mar. 1945 in Grant Co., KY. Married Patricia "Patty" Webster. Jimmie Burgess works for General Motors at Stewartsville, KY.

10a. **Kimberly Renee.** Born 19 Apr. 1968 in Campbell Co., KY.

10b. **Trena Michelle.** Born 25 Feb. 1969 in Campbell Co., KY. Married Jeffrey A. Riggs on 15 Feb. 1990 in Owen Co., KY.

JOHNEY H. BURGESS, Sr. OF GRANT CO., KENTUCKY

[James P.[6], James Lester[7]]

8i. **Johney Holden (I)** *[son of James Lester].* Listed in the official birth records of Kentucky as John Holton Burgess, and in the 1920 census as John H. Burgess. Born 17 Nov. 1911 in Grant Co., KY. Married Mayme Jump about 1936. Johney Burgess was a farmer in Grant Co., KY. He died on 16 June 1990 at Williamstown, KY, and is buried in the Williamstown Cemetery. His memories helped greatly in establishing the background of the Burgess family of Harrison and Grant Cos., Kentucky.

9a. **Betty Jean (II).** Born 26 Apr. 1937 in Grant Co., KY. Married Marvin Marshall, had two children, and lives in Grant Co.

9b. **John(ey) Holden (II).** Born 9 Jan. 1939 in Grant Co., KY. Married Martha Harris about 1959; married secondly Gloria Maddox. John Burgess is a foreman for a construction company at Florence, KY.

10a. **Johnny Thomas.** Born 26 Jan. 1960 at Covington, KY. Married Beverly J. Sanford on 25 May 1979 and again on 22 July 1982 in Warren Co., KY (div.). John Burgess lives at Bowling Green, KY.

11a. **Michael Thomas.** Born 11 Dec. 1979 at Bowling Green, KY.

11b. **Brian Scott (II).** Born 11 Sept. 1981 at Bowling Green, KY.

10b. **Lisa Rena.** Born 13 June 1963 at Covington, KY. Currently attending law school in New York.

Working on the railroad west of Biggar, SK, Canada, 1915; G. Walter Burgess (2nd from left); Roy Burgess (4th from left)

[William (I)[1], Edward (I)[2], Garner (I)[3], John (I)[4]]

CAPT. JAMES BURGESS
(1802?-1847)

OF HARRISON COUNTY, KENTUCKY

5d. **James (III) "Capt."** *[son of John (I)].* Born about 1802 in Fauquier Co., VA. Married Anice "Ann" Webber on 18 Sept. 1821 in Harrison Co. (she was the daughter of Sarah [and William?] Anderson, and died 1834; by her first marriage to ___ Webber, she had children: *William Anderson*); married secondly Mary Hings(t)on on 17 Aug. 1837 in Harrison Co. (she was born 1810 in DE, and died by 2 Oct. 1865, when her share of her husband's estate is apportioned among her children). Listed in the 1830-40 censuses and 1823-46 tax records for Harrison Co., KY; Mary is listed in 1850 with Leonard Barker, and in the tax records as guardian for William and Mary through 1864. After her death, her children deeded their share of her widow's dower to the Scotts (*Deed Book #30*, p. 448, 2 Oct. 1865). A Harrison Co. lawsuit names James as a brother of John Burgess (*Lail vs. Burgess, Case #6065*, 8 June 1832). His military service is unknown. A farmer in the Rutland Precinct of Harrison Co., Capt. James Burgess died intestate by 8 Mar. 1847, when he is mentioned as deceased in a Harrison Co. guardian record. His children are proven through subsequent probate divisions (*Record Book #F*, p. 483); Charles and Cynthiana were placed under the guardianship of John Burgess Jr., and William and Mary under their mother.

The Children of James Burgess:

6a. **John G(arner?) (II) "Jr."** Born 21 Nov. 1821 in Harrison Co., KY. See below for full entry.

6b. **Sarah Jane (I).** Born about 1823 in Harrison Co., KY. Married (as his second wife) John S. Scott on 7 Mar. 1844 in Harrison Co. (he was born 8 May 1821 in Sussex Co., DE, and was living in 1882 in the Rutland Precinct, Harrison Co.). John Scott's biography appears in the *History of Bourbon, Scott, Harrison, and Nicholas Counties, Kentucky*, edited by William Henry Perrin (Chicago: O. L. Baskin & Co., 1882, p. 713). They had children: *James T.* (born 25 Dec. 1844; he was a doctor); *William W.* (born 8 June 1846); *John B.* (born 10 Apr. 1848); *Sarah* (born 10 Mar. 1854); *Louisa* (born 9 Apr. 1856); *Effie J.* (born 24 Sept. 1860); *Henry* (born 17 May 1863); *Charles* (born 15 June 1865). The profile also states that Sarah is the daughter of James Burgess and Ann Webber. Listed in the 1850-60 censuses for Harrison Co., KY. From 1854-58 Scott served as Magistrate of the Rutland District, and was Deputy County Clerk of Harrison Co. from 1858-1882+. He also owned 320 acres of land on Raven Creek. The Scotts belonged to the Methodist Church at Mt. Zion, KY. An article on the Scott family appeared in the 7 May 1891 issue of the *Williamstown Courier*. Some of the children in this family settled in Baxter Springs, Cherokee Co., KS (near the border with Missouri and Oklahoma), and Montgomery, AL. Sarah Scott apparently died between 1882-1900.

6c. **Cynthiana.** Her name is listed in her guardianship record as Cynthia Anna Burgess. Born Mar. 1830 in Harrison Co., KY. She was made a ward of her brother, John Burgess "Jr.," on 8 Mar. 1847. Married James C. Ruddell on 14 Jan. 1850 in Harrison Co. (he was born 18 Sept. 1819 in Grant Co., KY, and was living in 1887), and had children: *(Dorothy) Ann* (born 1850); *(William) Burgess* (born 1853); *Lenora* (born 1858); *Thomas J.* (born 1866); *Martha "Mattie"* (born Oct. 1870 in KY, married ___ Kirby); *Effie*; *Sallie*; *Etta*; *Lucy*. The Ruddells moved to Crawford Co., IL before the Civil War, but had returned to Glencoe, Gallatin Co., KY by 1859. Listed in the 1850-60 censuses for Harrison Co., KY, and in 1870-1900 in Gallatin Co., KY (in 1870 with her daughter, Mattie). James Ruddell's biography appears in *Kentucky: A History of the State, Seventh Edition*, by W. H. Perrin (Louisville: F. A. Battey & Co., 1887, p. 877-878). Cynthiana Ruddell died after 1900, probably in Gallatin Co., KY.

6d. **Charles H. (I).** Born about 1833 in Harrison Co., KY. See below for full entry.

6e. **William S(helton?).** Born about 1839 in Harrison Co., KY. See below for full entry.

6f. **Mary Ellen (I).** Born about 1841 in Harrison Co., KY. She was made a ward of her mother on 10 May 1847 in Harrison Co. Married James R. Shingleton (he was born 1832), and had children: *Jerusha* (born 1861, living with the Scotts in 1870); *William* (born 1863, living with John Shingleton in 1870). Listed in the 1860 census for Harrison Co., KY. She died between 1865-70.

[William (I)[1], Edward (I)[2], Garner (I)[3], John (I)[4], James (III)[5]]

JOHN BURGESS, "JR." (1821-1903)

OF HARRISON COUNTY, KENTUCKY

6a. **John G(arner?) (II) "Jr."** *[son of James (III)].* Born 26 Nov. 1821 in Harrison Co., KY. Married (Mariah) Louisa Robinson on 29 June 1843 in Harrison Co. (she was born 24 Sept. 1822, daughter of Benjamin and Caltha E. Robinson, and died 20 May 1866); married secondly Manerva Baxter on 2 Oct. 1866 in Grant Co. (she was born 26 Aug. 1846 in KY, and died 1871); married thirdly Mrs. Nancy Frances "Nannie" (Rash) Parker on 16 Jan. 1872 in Fleming Co. (she was born 10 June 1834, and died 12 Jan. 1912). John "Jr.," so called to distinguish him from his uncle, Jack Burgess, is listed in the census records for Harrison Co. between 1850-1900, and in the tax records from 1843. A farmer all of his life, John died on 14 Sept. 1903 in Harrison Co., and is buried with his first and third wives and many of his children in the Robinson Cemetery, Stringtown, KY. His widow is living with her daughter, Lillie, in 1910.

The Children of John Burgess, Jr.:

7a. **Benjamin Franklin (I).** Born 1 Aug. 1844 in Harrison Co., KY. See below for full entry.

7b. **Mary Ann (I).** Born 11 Nov. 1846 in Harrison Co., KY. Married (William) Thomas Caldwell on 20 Mar. 1866 in Harrison Co. (he was born Dec. 1842 [or 1844], and died 1911). Listed in the 1900-20 censuses for Harrison Co., KY. Mary Caldwell died on 18 Nov. 1934 in Harrison Co., and is buried with her husband in the Robinson Cemetery.

7c. **Alice (I).** Born 26 Feb. 1849 in Harrison Co., KY. Living with her father in the 1880 census, and in 1900 in Harrison Co. Married James T. Baird on 12 Apr. 1886 in Harrison Co. (he was born 17 June 1842, and died 22 Jan. 1927), and had at least the following children: *Emma L.* (born Feb. 1887 in KY, married Brent M. Meeks [he was born 1885, and died 1964], had children: Audra [born 23 Apr. 1911, died 9 Oct. 1973], and died 1970, buried Robinson Cemetery). Alice Baird died on 15 Jan. 1941, aged 91 years, and is buried with her husband in the Robinson Cemetery.

7d. **Jane "Jennie"** (nmn). Born 31 July 1853 (or 26 Mar. 1851) in Harrison Co, KY. Married William Matthews on 16 Sept. 1873 in Harrison Co. (he was born 24 June 1849, and died 29 Dec. 1917), and had at least the following children: *John H.* (born 23 Oct. 1874, died 5 Dec. 1874, buried with his parents); *William Jr.* (born Nov. 1877, living with his aunt, Mary Caldwell, in 1900); *Charley T.* (born 8 Dec. 1879, died 3 Feb. 1881, buried with his parents); *Willard P.* (born 19 Jan. 1893, died 2 July 1894, buried with his parents); *Benjamin Franklin* (born 1 Apr. 1895, died 21 May 1896, buried with his parents). Jennie Matthews died on 27 Aug. 1934 in Harrison Co., and is buried with her husband in the Robinson Cemetery.

7e. **William Anderson (II).** Born 27 July 1856 in Harrison Co., KY. See below for fu'l entry.

7f. **Elizabeth (XVII) "Lizzie."** Born 25 Mar. 1861 in Harrison Co., KY. Listed with her father in the 1880 census. Married A. Ross Brooks on 23 Dec. 1884 in Harrison Co. (he was born 1858, and died 1924), and had at least the following children: *Child* (born and died 27 Nov. 1885, buried with its parents); *Elmer* (relation not verified; born 12 Nov. 1886, married Effie ___ on 22 Dec. 1909 [she was born 1887, and died 1964], and died Aug. 1968 at Corinth, KY, buried Robinson Cemetery); *Thomas* (born 9 Mar. 1889, died 28 June 1918, buried with his parents); *Herman* (born 3 Aug. 1897, died 8 Mar. 1914, buried with his parents); *Hattie* (born 8 July 1899, died 9 Nov. 1900, buried with her parents). Lizzie Brooks died on 8 Nov. 1939 in Harrison Co., and is buried with her husband in the Robinson Cemetery.

7g. **Louisa (II) "Lula."** Born 16 July 1867 in Harrison Co., KY. Married John Strathers Redd on 23 July 1891 at Covington, KY, and had at least the following children: *Raymond* (born and died 11 July 1891, buried with his parents); *Mary* (born 29 May 1893, died 13 July 1894, buried with her parents); *Willie* (born and died 25 Oct. 1895, buried with his parents); *Lillie Elizabeth* (born 7 Dec. 1896, married James Darraugh in 1919 [he died July 1953, buried Pythian Grove Cemetery], and secondly Paul

Brooks on 26 July 1967 [he was born 29 Sept. 1905, and died on 5 Feb. 1975, buried in the Robinson Cemetery], and was living at Berry, KY in 1982). Lula Redd died on 2 Sept. 1902 in Harrison Co., and is buried in the Robinson Cemetery.

7h. **James Thomas (I).** Born 23 Feb. 1869 in Harrison Co., KY. See below for full entry.

7i. **Lillie May.** Her middle name was originally Maurice. Born 15 Apr. 1874 in Harrison Co., KY. Married Sinnett R. Barnes on 4 Jan. 1905 in Harrison Co. (he was born 1861, and died 1910, buried Robinson Cemetery), and had children: *Robert* (who lives at Williamstown, KY); married secondly Robert Elliott. Lillie Elliott died on 24 Sept. 1942 in Grant Co., KY, and is buried in the Robinson Cemetery.

BENJAMIN F. BURGESS, Sr. OF HARRISON CO., KENTUCKY

[John Garner (II)[6]]

7a. **Benjamin Franklin (I)** *[son of John Garner (II)].* Born 1 Aug. 1844 in Harrison Co., KY. Married Maria Guenveur on 25 Nov. 1880 in Harrison Co. (she was born May 1859 in LA, and died 30 Sept. 1905 [age 46] at Montgomery, AL, buried Scott's Free Ground). Listed in the 1870 census for Harrison Co. with his grandfather, Benjamin Robinson, in 1880 with his father, in 1900 in Grant Co., and in 1920 in Harrison Co. with his sister, Mary Caldwell. A farmer and stockman in Harrison Co., KY, Ben Burgess moved to Salina, KS two years before he died on 8 June 1932. He was returned for burial in the Robinson Cemetery, Harrison Co., KY.

8a. **John Guenveur.** Born 12 Mar. 1882 in Harrison Co., KY. Married (Mary) Josephine Reynolds. Listed in the 1918 draft list of Salina, KS, and in the 1921 city directory there. John Burgess was a conductor for the Union Pacific Railroad, operating out of Salina, KS. He died in Sept. 1931 at Denver, CO, but both he and his wife are buried in the Mt. Calvary Cemetery, Salina, KS.

9a. **Lucille Adele.** Born 6 June 1908 at Montgomery, AL. Married James Glasscock, and had children: *Jayne* (married Gerry F. Mikan). Lucille Glasscock lives in Florida.

9b. **(Margaret) Leone "Lee."** Born 14 Oct. 1910 at Salina, KS. Married Donald Walker. Lee Walker lives at Arlington, VA.

9c. **(Mary) Jane (V).** Born 26 July 1912 at Salina, KS. Married Paul Reitz; married secondly Bill Cook. Jane Cook lives at Dallas, TX.

9d. **Frances Anne.** Born 21 Sept. 1918 at Montgomery, AL. Married James McKinney, and lives at Port St. Lucie, Florida.

8b. **Lucille C.** Born July 1884 in Harrison Co., KY. Married Lyman Hall. Not found in the Social Security Death Index. She may be the Lucile Hall who died on 9 July 1936 in Harrison Co.

8c. **Frank P.** Born 14 Nov. 1886 in Harrison Co., KY.; he died there on 16 Sept. 1907, and is buried in the Robinson Cemetery.

8d. **Bernard W. S.** Born 20 Feb. 1889 in Grant Co., KY. Bernard Burgess was a bookkeeper in Harrison Co. He died there unmarried of consumption on 5 Nov. 1914, and is buried in the Robinson Cemetery.

8e. **Benjamin Franklin (III).** Born 23 Nov. 1892 in Harrison Co., KY. See below for full entry.

8f. **Amelia.** Born 12 June 1895 in Grant Co., KY; died on 22 Jan. 1897 in Harrison Co., and is buried in the Robinson Cemetery. However, she also appears to be listed with her father in the 1900 census.

BENJAMIN F. BURGESS, Jr. OF SALINE CO., KANSAS

[John Garner (II)[6], Benjamin Franklin (I)[7]]

8e. **Benjamin Franklin (III)** *[son of Benjamin Franklin (I)].* Born 23 Nov. 1892 in Harrison Co., KY. Married Anna Mary McMillin on 21 Sept. 1914 (she was born 22 Dec. 1893, and died Feb. 1973 at Salina, KS). Listed in the 1918 draft list of Salina, KS, and in the city directory there in 1921. Ben Burgess settled at Salina, KS in 1912, where he owned a motorcycle and bicycle shop. He died in 1957 at Salina, and is buried in the Mt. Calvary Cemetery.

9a. **Benjamin Louis (I).** Born 2 Mar. 1920 at Salina, KS. Married Evalena Eleanor Lohman; married secondly Marva Lee Edwards. Ben Burgess is a retired postal worker at Salina, KS.

10a. **Michael Patrick (I).** Born 9 Jan. 1942 at Salina, KS. Married Debra Sue Dunnett (div.). Michael P. Burgess works for the U.S. Postal Service at Chicago, IL.

11a. **Michael Patrick (II).** Born 3 Aug. 1965 at Chicago, IL.
11b. **Bryon David.** Born 5 Nov. 1967 at Chicago, IL.

10b. **Marilyn Sue.** Born 16 Jan. 1943 at Salina, KS. Married John Edward Liljestrand. Marilyn Liljestrand currently lives at Oklahoma City, OK.
10c. **Benjamin Louis (II).** Born 20 July 1943 at Salina, KS. Married Jolene K. Bellerive on 20 Aug. 1966. Benjamin L. Burgess received his B.A. from Kansas Wesleyan University, and his J.D. degree from Washburn University in 1971. He served as Assistant County Attorney for Reno Co., KS in 1972, as Assistant U.S. Attorney for the U.S. Dept. of Justice, Wichita, KS from 1973-78 and 1980-84, and as U.S. Attorney from 1984-90. He had his own law partnership (Rock, Smith & Burgess) at Arkansas City, KS from 1978-80, and since 1990 has been Senior Attorney, Litigation, for Koch Industries, Inc., Wichita, KS. He has also served on the Board of Directors of the Wichita Crime Commission, Crime Stoppers of Wichita/Sedgwick Co. His biography has appeared in *Who's Who in American Law*, *Who's Who of Emerging Leaders in America*, and *Who's Who in America*.

11a. **Matisha Lynn.** Born 12 Aug. 1968 at Lawton, OK.
11b. **(Benjamin) Bret.** Born 21 Apr. 1974 at Wichita, KS.

10d. **Jennifer Jean.** Born 5 Mar. 1960 at Salina, KS.

9b. **John Francis.** Born 7 Sept. 1925 at Salina, KS. Married Marie Elizabeth McGettigan on 22 Sept. 1945 (she was born 2 Nov. 1922, and died 5 May 1980); married secondly Ann D. Hodge on 2 May 1981. John F. Burgess inherited his father's bicycle shop, Burgess Schwinn Cyclery, which he continues to operate out of the same building where it has been located for the past forty years.

10a. **Mary Ann (XI).** Born 17 May 1947 at Salina, KS. Married Don Thomas. Lives at Salina, KS.
10b. **Joan Frances.** Born 23 Apr. 1949 at Salina, KS. Married Charles Mann, and lives at Salina.
10c. **Linda Kay (II).** Born 27 Oct. 1951 at Salina, KS. Married Bruce Sikora.
10d. **Debra Louise "Debbie."** Born 2 Feb. 1957 at Salina, KS. Married Rick Yerke.

WILLIAM A. BURGESS OF HARRISON CO., KENTUCKY
[John Garner (II)[6]]

7e. **William Anderson (II)** *[son of John Garner (II)].* Born 27 July 1856 in Harrison Co., KY. Living with his father in the 1880 census; has not been found in 1910; living with his sister, Mary Caldwell, in Harrison Co. in 1920. Married Candace E. Robinson on 1 Apr. 1902 in Scott Co. (she was born 31 Dec. 1874, and died 22 May 1908, buried Skinner Cemetery). William Burgess was a farmer in Harrison Co., KY. He died there on 11 Mar. 1935, and is buried in the Robinson Cemetery.

8a. **Elizabeth Mae "Lizzie."** Born 14 Oct. 1903 in Harrison Co., KY. Married Ralph Angel, brother of George R. Angel, in Fayette Co., KY. Listed in the 1910 census for Scott Co., KY living with Elizabeth F. Robinson. Lizzie Angel died childless on 12 Mar. 1993 at Lexington, KY.
8b. **Alice F.** Born 28 Apr. 1908 in Harrison Co., KY. Married George R. Angel on 10 Nov. 1928 in Harrison Co. (he was born 1907, brother of Ralph Angel, and died 22 July 1946 in Harrison Co.), and had at least the following children: *Billy Douglas* (born 20 Apr. 1932, died 26 Sept. 1933, buried with his parents); *Bobby C.* (born and died 10 Dec. 1937, buried with his parents); *Brenda* (married ___ Dawson, and lives at Cynthiana, KY). Listed in the 1910 census with Jimmie Matthews. Alice died on 18 Apr. 1979 at Cynthiana, KY, and is buried in the Robinson Cemetery.

JAMES T. BURGESS OF HARRISON CO., KENTUCKY
[John Garner (II)[6]]

7h. **James Thomas (I)** *[son of John Garner (II)].* Born 23 Feb. 1869 in Harrison Co., KY. Married Mattie J. Matthews on 20 Jan. 1892 in Harrison Co. (she was born 1874, and died on 25 Oct. 1903). James Burgess was a farmer in Harrison Co. He, his wife, and his father all died there within weeks of each other in the Fall of 1903. He died on 15 Oct. 1903, and is buried in the Pythian Grove Cemetery, Berry, KY.

8a. **Everett Brown.** Born 8 Apr. 1894 in Harrison Co., KY. Married Mary Ellen Layton on 17 Aug. 1916 in Harrison Co. (she was born 1895, daughter of W. H. Layton, and died 14 Oct. 1958); married secondly Maud Helen Lowe on 10 Oct. 1959 in Harrison Co. Listed with Louis Matthews in the 1910 census for Harrison Co., in the 1917 draft register there, and in 1920 in Harrison Co. Everett Burgess was a farmer in Harrison Co. He died there on 16 May 1976, and is buried with his first wife in the Battle Grove Cemetery, Cynthiana, KY.

9a. **Mattie Marie.** Born 19 Jan. 1918 in Harrison Co., KY. Married Silvis Crosthwait on 6 May 1939 in Harrison Co. (he died 9 Mar. 1948, buried Battle Grove Cemetery, Cynthiana); married secondly (Robert) Curtis Tarter on 15 Nov. 1950 (he was born 16 Dec. 1902, and died 20 Sept. 1975 at Cincinnati, OH), and had children: *Pamela* (born 22 July 1953); *Patricia* (born 30 Oct. 1958, married Joe Elvington on 25 May 1985, and had children: Jessica [born 5 July 1989]; Ashleigh [twin; born 20 Aug. 1993]; Andrew [twin; born 20 Aug. 1993]; *Patricia ELVINGTON* lives at Cheraw, SC). Mattie Tarter lives at Cincinnati, OH.

9b. **Marjorie Allen.** Born 27 Sept. 1920 in Harrison Co., KY. Married Marvin G. Morgan on 30 Aug. 1941 in Harrison Co. (he died 15 Feb. 1991 at Cynthiana, KY), and had children: *Jane Carol* (born 8 July 1942, married Dudley Paynter in 1963, and had children: Allen [born 3 Nov. 1964, married Robin Creech on 1 Nov. 1986, and had children: Samantha {born 1 Aug. 1987}; Allen married secondly Tammy Fye on 4 July 1992, and had children: Kasey {born 20 Dec. 1992}]; Beth [born 30 Sept. 1967, married Robert Rice on 20 Dec. 1989, and had children: Brittany {born 28 Aug. 1990}; Beth lives at Lexington, KY]; *Jane Carol* married secondly Strother Mahorney on 27 Feb. 1983, and lives at Belleair, FL). Marjorie Morgan currently lives near Cynthiana, KY.

9c. **Olena Elizabeth.** Born 9 June 1926 in Harrison Co., KY. Married Ernest W. Ramey on 1 Sept. 1946 in Harrison Co. (he was born 10 Apr. 1924, and died 24 May 1979 at Covington, KY), and had children: *Anita* (twin; born 7 Oct. 1947, married ___ Smith, and had children: Darrell; *Anita* lives at Covington, KY]; *Rita* (twin; born Oct. 7 1947, married ___ Comer, and had children: Monique; Danny; *Rita* lives at Cincinnati, OH). Olena Ramey lives at Covington, KY.

James Thomas BURGESS (1869-1903)
Everett Brown BURGESS (1894-1976)
Mattie J. MATTHEWS BURGESS (1874-1903)

[William (I)[1], Edward (I)[2], Garner (I)[3], John (I)[4], James (III)[5]]

CHARLES H. BURGESS
(1833?-1898)

OF MONTGOMERY COUNTY, ALABAMA

6d. **Charles H. (I)** *[son of James (III)].* Born about 1833 in Harrison Co., KY. After his father's death, he was made on 8 Mar. 1847 a ward of his brother, John Burgess "Jr.," at which point he was under fourteen years of age (*Harrison Co. Minute Book #K*, p. 61). Listed in the 1850-60 censuses for Harrison Co. with John Burgess, his brother, and in the tax records as underaged between 1848-53, and as an adult 1854-67. He may have served in Co. D, 4th Kentucky Cavalry, Confederate Army. He moved to Montgomery, AL after the Civil War, where he married Annie Watkins on 20 Feb. 1871 in Montgomery Co. (she was born about 1846 in New York, and died 10 Oct. 1905 at Montgomery, AL, aged 59 years). Charles Burgess is listed as a stock dealer in the 1878 city directory of Montgomery, and is also listed there in the 1880 census; Annie is recorded as head of the family in 1900. He died of tuberculosis on 13 Feb. 1898 at Montgomery, AL, and is buried with his wife and several children in Scott's Free Ground Cemetery.

The Children of Charles H. Burgess:

7a. **Child.** Born and died about 1871 at Montgomery, AL.
7b. **Ida Mae (I).** Born 1873 at Montgomery, AL; died there unmarried on 22 Oct. 1887, and is buried with her parents.
7c. **Child.** Born and died about 1875 at Montgomery, AL.
7d. **Child.** Born Mar. 1877 at Montgomery, AL; died there on 8 Aug. 1877, and is buried with its parents.
7e. **William Anderson (III).** Born 3 Sept. 1878 at Montgomery, AL. See below for full entry.

WILLIAM A. BURGESS OF JEFFERSON CO., ALABAMA
[Charles H. (I)[6]]

7e. **William Anderson (III)** *[son of Charles H. (I)].* Born 3 Sept. 1878 at Montgomery, AL. Married Dorothea Patrick on 3 Sept. 1901 in Montgomery Co., AL (she was born 11 Nov. 1880, daughter of George H. Patrick and Malissa Todd, and died 1 Dec. 1940 at Ensley, AL). Listed with his mother in the 1900 census, and in 1910 at Selma, Dallas Co., AL. William A. Burgess was a railroad clerk in Alabama, eventually settling in Jefferson Co. He died on 30 July 1950 at Montgomery, Montgomery Co., AL.

8a. **Dorothy Van Cortland.** Born 23 Aug. 1902 at Ensley, Jefferson Co., AL. Married as his second wife Anthony John Steinworth in June 1919 in Jefferson Co., AL (he was born 30 May 1893 at St. Cloud, MN, son of Johann Ludwig Steinworth and Maria Cropp, married firstly Mamie Brandstetter [who was buried at Holdingford, MN], and died 31 Mar. 1978 at St. Paul, MN). Their children included:

(Anthony) John "Jack" STEINWORTH Jr. Born 16 Apr. 1920 at Montgomery, AL. Never married.

Dorothy Virginia STEINWORTH. Born 25 Dec. 1922 at St. Paul, MN, married William Homer Fitzwater on 20 Nov. 1943 at Fort Smith, AR (he was born 30 Apr. 1916 in Duchesne Co., UT, son of William Henry Fitzwater and Lucretia B. Buckalew), and had children: *Sandra Lee* (born 22 Aug. 1945 at St. Paul, MN, married Vertis Martin Andersen on 2 Aug. 1968 at Logan, UT [he was born 11 Nov. 1941 at Brigham City, UT, son of Alonzo Andersen and Margaret Bassett], and had children: Ginger [born 19 Apr. 1969 at Bountiful, UT, married John Andrew Johnson on 20 July 1990 at Salt Lake City, UT]; Jay Patrick [born 17 Sept. 1970 at Bountiful, UT]; Rachelle [born 5 Nov. 1974 at Bountiful, UT]; Joan [born 18 Sept. 1977 at Bountiful, UT]; Russell Vance [born 14 Feb. 1979 at Bountiful, UT]; Benjamin Vertis [born 11 Dec. 1980 at Bountiful, UT]); *Patrick Eu-*

gene (born 24 June 1949 at Roosevelt, UT, married Kathryn Bennett on 8 Aug. __ at Springville, UT [div.; born 19 Aug. __], and had children: Sarah Ann [born 5 Feb. 1982 at Provo, UT]; Steven [born 7 July 1983 at Provo, UT]).

William Eugene STEINWORTH. Born 29 Nov. 1923 at St. Paul, MN, married Lois Carolyn Horton on 4 Sept. 1948 at St. Paul, MN (she was born 27 Sept. 1924 at St. Paul, MN), and had children: *William Eugene Jr. "Skip"* (born 2 May 1950 at St. Paul, MN, married Linda Marie Witzman on 19 July 1974 at St. Paul, MN, and had children: Bailey [dau.]); *Carolyn Jean "Carie"* (born 15 Nov. 1951 at St. Paul, MN); *Susan Lois* (born 25 Feb. 1956 at St. Paul, MN, married Noel Norton, and had children: Bo; Eric).

(John) Joseph "Joe" STEINWORTH. Born 23 Mar. 1926 at St. Paul, MN, married Jeanetta Alice Borsch on 23 Oct. 1948 at St. Paul, MN (she was born 28 Aug. 1927 at St. Paul, MN, daughter of Joseph Mathew Borsch and Erna Caroline Gross), and had children: *John Joseph Jr.* (born 7 July 1950 at St. Paul, MN, married Patricia Ann Terry on 19 Feb. 1977 at White Bear Lake, MN [she was born 26 June 1955, daughter of James Terry and Virginia Zullner], and had children: Jessamine Mary Ann [born 17 July 1977 at St. Paul, MN]; John Joseph III [born 17 Feb. 1983 at St. Paul, MN]; Elizabeth Virginia [born 14 Jan. 1989 at St. Paul, MN]); *James Richard* (born 11 Nov. 1952 at St. Paul, married Patricia Clare Schultz on 20 Dec. 1980 at St. Louis Park, MN [she was born 8 May __], and had children: Jane Elizabeth [born 7 Feb. 1982]); *Jerome Thomas* (born 28 July 1954 at St. Paul, married Kathy Guiser Gowen on 12 Nov. 1988 at Baldwin, WI [she was born 22 July __ at Baldwin, WI]); *Jeffrey William* (born 4 July 1957 at St. Paul, MN, married Deborah Howe Ryan on 5 Nov. 1983 at White Bear Lake, MN [she was born 29 Mar. 1957], and had children: Kimberly Ryan [born 14 July 1976]); *Jill Patricia* (born 6 Sept. 1959 at St. Paul, MN, married Rudy Santino Pitera on 2 Oct. 1981 [he was born 1 Nov. 1954 in Italy], and had children: Nicholas Joseph [born 7 Mar. 1986 at St. Paul, MN]; Dominic Mario [born 8 Sept. 1988 at St. Paul, MN]; Rudy Luigi [born 12 Oct. 1990 at Brussels, Belgium]; Jill Pitera currently lives at Waterloo, Belgium); *Jay Anthony* (born 22 June 1961 at St. Paul, MN).

Mary Ann STEINWORTH. Born 6 July 1938 at St. Paul, MN, married William Eugene Blake on 20 July 1957 at St. Paul (he was born 13 Sept. 1936 at Backus, MN, son of Lowell Blake), and had children: *Douglas Eugene* (born 14 Apr. 1959 at St. Paul, married, and had children: Kevin D. [born 27 June 1988 at St. Paul, MN]; Ryan Joseph [born 17 Sept. 1991 at St. Paul, MN]); *Brian Joseph* (born 19 Mar. 1960 at St. Paul, married Lorri __); *Scott William* (born 4 Sept. 1963 at St. Paul, married, and had children: Jonathan J. [born 22 Feb. 1989 at St. Paul, MN]; Jay S. [born 27 Mar. 1991 at St. Paul, MN]). Mary Ann and William Blake own and operate Blake Specialties, Inc., an advertising agency, at St. Paul, MN.

Dorothy STEINWORTH died on 8 Aug. 1975 at St. Paul, MN. Sandra Andersen has contributed greatly to this book; she currently lives at Farmington, UT.

8b. **(Jocelyn) Virginia "Jennie."** Born 28 Aug. 1907 at Ensley, AL. Married Troy Hargrove. Jennie Hargrove currently lives in Minnesota.

James Franklin BURGESS I (1835-1928)

Bert Bowers BURGESS (1907)-

Beulah Grace BURGESS BOWERS (1909-)

(see page 79)

[William (I)[1], Edward (I)[2], Garner (I)[3], John (I)[4], James (III)[5]]

WILLIAM S. BURGESS
(1839?-1886)

OF APPANOOSE COUNTY, IOWA

6e. **William S(helton?)** *[son of James (III)].* Born about 1839 in Harrison Co., KY. After his father's death, he was made a ward of his mother on 10 May 1847 in Harrison Co. (*Minute Book #K*, p. 83). Married Virginia C. Carter on 5 Dec. 1871 in Scotland Co., MO (she was born 1849 in VA, and has not been found in the 1900 census). Listed as underaged in the Harrison Co. tax records between 1848-66 or 1868. Listed in the 1850 census for Harrison Co. in the household of John Scott, his brother-in-law. William S. Burgess enlisted in Co. A, 1st Kentucky Cavalry, Confederate Army, in 1862, and later in Co. F, 7th Kentucky Cavalry. He was captured by federal troops and tried as a spy. Sentenced to be hung, he was reprieved at the last moment, sent to prison, and then released in Jan. 1865. After the Civil War, he lived in Missouri, Indiana, and Iowa, settling in Appanoose Co. about 1876, where he worked as a miner. Listed in the 1880-85 censuses for Center Township, Appanoose Co., IA. He died of an overdose of morphine on 11 Nov. 1886 at Brazil, IA, his death record confirming an "old wound received in the late war" (dating back 23 years), and was buried in the Centerville Cemetery.

The Children of William S. Burgess:

7a. **(William) Walter.** Born 10 Apr. 1874 (or 1872) in Indiana. See below for full entry.
7b. **Charles S(helton?).** Born about 1876 (or 1874) in Appanoose Co., IA. Listed twice in the 1895 state census for Appanoose Co., IA, once in the county jail (since 1894), and again with his brother, but has not been found in the 1900 or 1915 Iowa censuses, or in the 1917 draft list.

WALTER BURGESS OF APPANOOSE CO., IOWA
[William Shelton[6]]

7a. **(William) Walter** *[son of William Shelton].* Born 10 Apr. 1874 (or 1872) in Indiana. Married Maggie M. ___ (she was born Oct. 1878 in IA); married secondly Lucy E. Buck on 22 May 1902 at Appanoose Co., IA (she was born about 1882 in Morris Co., KS, daughter of Edward Buck). Listed in the 1895 state census for Appanoose Co. (a Georgia R. Burgess, aged 5, is listed between Charles and Walter in this census), in 1900 in Chouteau Co., MT, in 1910 in Putnam Co., MO, and in 1915-20 in Cincinnati Township, Appanoose Co., IA (having returned to Iowa in 1911); has not been found in the 1925 state census of Cincinnati Township; also listed in the 1918 draft register for Appanoose Co. Walter Burgess was part owner of a store in Cincinnati Township, Appanoose Co., IA. He died there after 1920. He should not be confused with the William Burgess of Appanoose Co. who was born about 1860 and married Cora Benge.

8a. **Ernest B.** Born Jan. 1894 in Scotland Co., MO. Not with his father in the 1910 census, but is listed in the 1915 state census for Appanoose Co., IA.
8b. **Milo William**. Listed as "M. B." in some records. Born 24 June 1898 at Havre, Chouteau Co., MT. Married Irene M. ___ (she was born 1898, and died 1981 in FL). Not listed with his father in the 1900 or 1920 censuses. Listed in the 1917 draft register of Appanoose Co., IA, with his place of work given as Canton, OH and his residence as Maywood, IL. Milo Burgess was a pipefitter for United Steel Co., Canton. He died in 1979 at Winter Park, Orange Co., FL, and is buried with his wife in Glen Haven Memorial Park.
8c. **(Uliss) Lina G.** Born about 1910 at Ulindota, MO.
8d. **Vivian E.** Born about 1912 at Cincinnati, IA.

[William (I)[1], Edward (I)[2], Garner (I)[3], John (I)[4]]

JACK BURGESS
(1805-1883)

OF HARRISON COUNTY, KENTUCKY

5e. **John Garner (I) "Jack"** *[son of John (I)].* He was frequently called John Burgess "Sr." to distinguish him from his nephew of the same name. Born 26 May 1805 in Bourbon Co., KY. Witnessed the will of Richard Faulconer, his cousin, on 2 Sept. 1826 in Harrison Co. (*Will Book #B*, p. 535). Married Eleanor "Ellen" Faulconer on 11 Oct. 1827 in Harrison Co. (she was born July 1805 in VA, daughter of Reuben Faulconer [he was the son of Samuel Faulconer Sr. and Elizabeth Moseley Newman, and brother of Samuel Faulconer Jr., who married John Burgess's cousin, Sarah Burgess of Orange Co., VA], and died 17 Dec. 1867 [or 1868]); married secondly Mrs. Nancy E. "Nannie" Penn on 2 May 1871 in Harrison Co. (she was born about 1827 in Harrison Co.). Mentioned as a brother of James Burgess in an 1831 lawsuit in Harrison Co., KY (*Lail vs. Burgess, Case #6065*, 8 June 1832). Sold his land in Putnam Co., IN on 31 Oct. 1832 (*Putnam Co. Deed Book #B*, p. 472; this is the only record in which he is called John Burgess, *Junior*, in deference to his father, a resident of Putnam Co.; the physical description of the land exactly matches that of a deed made by his brother, William S. Burgess [*Deed Book #B*, p. 271]). Listed in the 1850-80 censuses for the Rutland (10th) District, Harrison Co., KY (in 1870 with William A. Webber), and in the tax lists from 1826-83; in 1880 he is aged 75 years, born in Kentucky, with both parents listed as having been born in Virginia. Jack Burgess was a farmer in Harrison Co. He (or possibly his nephew, John) was elected Democratic magistrate of the Rutland Precinct in Harrison Co. in 1865 for a two-year term. Jack Burgess died on 20 Nov. 1883 in Harrison Co., KY (his will was probated on 27 Nov. 1883).

The Children of Jack Burgess:

6a. **Elizabeth Jane (I).** Born 3 Sept. 1828 in Harrison Co., KY. Married (Andrew) Jackson Matthews on 3 June 1845 in Harrison Co. (he was born 30 Apr. 1818, a cousin of Ambrose Collins, who married Elizabeth's sister, and died 17 July 1899), and had at least five children: *John* (born about 1846); *William* (born about 1849); *Thomas* (born about 1850); *James* (born about 1854); *Sarah Williams "Sallie"* (born about 1856, married ___ McDonald, and had children: (Sarah) Ellie). Listed in the 1850-80 censuses for Harrison Co. Elizabeth Matthews died on 6 Apr. 1897 in Harrison Co., and is buried in the Robinson Cemetery. Elizabeth and her sister are listed in *History and Genealogy of the Collins Family, 1740-50-1940*, by Nora L. Collins (Crawfordsville, IN: Howell-Goodwin Printing Co., 1940, p. 27 and 36), the information on these two families being supplied by Sallie's daughter, Ellie McDonald, with whom Sallie lived in her old age.

6b. **Sarah Williams (I) "Sallie."** Born 14 Sept. 1840 in Harrison Co., KY. Married as his second wife Ambrose Dudley Collins on 5 Oct. 1857 in Harrison Co. (he was born 4 June 1823 at Keene, Jessamine Co., KY, a cousin of his brother-in-law, Jackson Matthews, and died there on 18 June 1895). Their children included:

Elizabeth Jane COLLINS. Born 3 Aug. 1858 at Keene, KY, married Lewis Richard Woods on 16 May 1877 (he was born 24 Mar. 1849 at Keene, and died 23 Sept. 1923), had seven children, and died 22 Oct. 1922; both are buried Lexington Cemetery, Lexington, KY. Her daughter was: *Sarah Eleanor "Sallie" Woods* (born 2 Mar. 1892, married Maurice Derby LEACH, and died on 28 May 1993, aged 101 years), having had children:

Maurice Derby LEACH Jr. (born 23 June 1923 at Lexington, KY, married Virginia Stuart Baskett on 16 Mar. 1953 at Lexington, KY, and had children: Sarah Stuart [born 10 Dec. 1956 at Naples, Italy, became a physician, married Dr. James Peter Davis {he was born 12 Jan. 1957 at Lebanon, PA}, and had children: Margaret Stuart "Mollie" {born 21 Dec. 1990 at Fairfax, VA}; Matthew Cowan {born 23 Aug. 1993 at Fairfax, VA}]). Maurice Leach obtained his B.L.S. from the University of Chicago in 1946. He served as a bibliographer for the U.S. Department of State from 1947-50, as a vice consul and attaché for the Dept. of State from 1950-59 in Egypt and Lebanon, as Professor and Chairman of the Department of Library Science, University of Kentucky, 1959-66, as regional program officer for the Ford Foundation at Beirut, Lebanon from 1967-68, as University Librarian (with the rank of Professor) at Washington and Lee University, Lexington, VA from 1968-85, and as Assistant to the President there from 1985-88. His biography has appeared in numerous editions of *Who's Who in America*. He currently lives at Lexington, VA.

Kenneth Woods LEACH (born 18 July 1924 at Keene, KY, married Maxine Metcalf on 16 Jan. 1948 at Rosebud, IL [she was born 22 July 1927 at Rosebud, IL]).

Lewis Cowan LEACH (born 30 May 1926 at Keene, KY, married Juanita Fox on 9 June 1947 at Lexington, KY [she was born 12 July 1925, and died 27 Oct. 1989], and had children: Maurice Fox [born 8 May 1954, married secondly Carla Lee Smith on 1 Sept. 1984 in Fayette Co., KY {she was born 19 Nov. 1954}, and had children: Aaron Fox {born 30 Dec. 1987 at Lexington, KY}; Meredith Ann {born 1 Mar. 1990}]; Kenneth Lewis [born 2 Mar. 1958, married and divorced]; Daniel Cowan [born 13 Mar. 1961, married Sharon Flynn on 15 Feb. 1986 at Midway, KY {she was born 29 Mar. 1964}, and had children: Tiffany Nicole {born 17 Feb. 1987 at Lexington, KY}; Tara Danielle {born 13 Jan. 1989 at Lexington, KY}]. *Lewis LEACH* married secondly Mrs. Barbara Eaves Mullens on 9 Aug. 1991 at Lexington, KY [she was born 15 Mar. 1941]).

John Basil LEACH (born 21 Sept. 1928 at Lexington, KY, married Naomi Riggs on 19 Sept. 1961 at Lexington, KY).

Bettie Eleanor LEACH (born 27 Aug. 1933, married Albert Porter McCubbins on 14 July 1951 in West Virginia [he was born 24 Jan. 1933], and had children: Sandra Eleanor [born 4 Feb. 1953 at Lexington, KY, married secondly David Dale Kellenberger on 19 Jan. 1976 in Fayette Co., KY {he was born 15 Dec. 1950 in KS}, and had children: Kevin Dale {born 17 Feb. 1983 at Sherman, TX}]; Gina Carol [born 24 Jan. 1956 at Lexington, KY, married Gregory Kent Fightmaster on 5 July 1974, and had children: Cari Beth {born 28 Oct. 1977 at Lexington, KY}; Gina Carol married secondly Joseph Daniel Hill {he was born 29 Oct. 1943}, and had children: Daniel Porter {born 2 Aug. 1982 in FL}; Joseph Patrick {born 12 Feb. 1987 in FL}]).

John Burgess COLLINS. Born 16 May 1860 at Keene, married Nettie Jones on 13 Jan. 1887 (she was born 8 Dec. 1861 in Mercer Co. (?), and died 22 June 1959 at Lexington, aged 97 years), had three children, and died 24 Nov. 1890 at Lexington, both being buried in the Lexington Cemetery.

George Lewis COLLINS. Born 4 May 1862 at Keene, married Carrie Barkley Young on 16 Oct. 1890 (she was born 15 July 1870 at Keene, KY, and died 4 Jan. 1947 at Nicholasville, KY), had six children, and died 30 Mar. 1942 at Nicholasville, both being buried in the Lexington Cemetery. His daughter, *Elizabeth Bell*, married Emory Jones Wesley, and had children: Louis C. (who lives at Arlington, VA).

(Sarah) Eleanor "Ellie" COLLINS. Born 2 Apr. 1866 at Keene, married Joe T. McDonald on 6 Nov. 1894 (he was born 30 Apr. 1866 in Woodford Co., KY, and died 17 Feb. 1947 at Versailles, KY), and died childless in 1958 at Versailles, both being buried in the Versailles Cemetery. She supplied much of the information on her branch in the book, *History and Genealogy of the Collins Family*.

Frances S. "Fannie" COLLINS. Born 13 Nov. 1869 at Keene, married Lawrence "Larry" Judge on 27 Jan. 1887, had one daughter, died May 1947 at Versailles, KY, and was probably buried Lexington Cemetery; a descendant, Michael Glaros, lives at Norfolk, VA.

James Beck COLLINS. Born 17 Apr. 1871 at Keene, married Louella E. Howard on 25 June 1902 (she was born 1875 in Woodford Co., and died 1957 at Versailles), had one adopted daughter, and died 15 June 1967 at Versailles, aged 96 years, both being buried in the Versailles Cemetery.

Hettie Celeste COLLINS. Born 19 Sept. 1876 at Keene, married Samuel Owen Sublett on 4 Nov. 1896, and died 28 July 1911 in Woodford Co., both being buried in the Versailles Cemetery.

Ambrose Dudley "A. D." COLLINS Jr. Born 24 Mar. 1878 at Keene, married Betty Sublett on 4 Nov. 1896 (she was born 1881 in Woodford Co., and died 14 Feb. 1934 at Lexington), had two children, and died 11 Dec. 1957 at Lexington, both being buried in the Lexington Cemetery.

Ambrose COLLINS'S biography appears in *Kentucky: A History of the State*, by W. H. Perrin (Louisville: F. A. Battey & Co., 1887, p. 776-777); his farm, located near Keene, KY, was called Rose Hill. Ambrose Collins is listed in the 1860 census for Keene, Jessamine Co., KY. **Sallie COLLINS** died on 20 Dec. 1925 at Versailles, Woodford Co., KY, and is buried with her husband in the Lexington Cemetery, Lexington, KY.

[William (I)[1], Edward (I)[2], Garner (I)[3], John (I)[4]]

DAWSON BURGESS
(1810-1877)

OF HENDRICKS COUNTY, INDIANA

5g. **Dawson (I)** *[son of John (I)].* Born 1 July 1810 in Harrison Co., KY. Married Katherine Hulbert (or Catherine Holbert) on 29 Aug. 1832 in Putnam Co., IN (she was born 12 June 1818, and died 13 June 1889). Mentioned as an heir in a settlement deed of his father (*Putnam Co. Deed Book #L*, p. 658, dated 28 Oct. 1837). Listed in the 1840-60 censuses for Marion Township, Putnam Co., IN, and in 1870 in Franklin Township, Hendricks Co., IN; Katherine is listed as head of the family in the 1880 census for Stilesville, Hendricks Co. Dawson Burgess was a farmer in Putnam Co., and later worked as a hotel keeper in Hendricks Co. He died there on 27 Aug. 1877, and is buried with his wife in the Stilesville Cemetery.

The Children of Dawson Burgess:

6a. **John W. (I).** Born about 1838 in Putnam Co., IN. Listed with his father in the 1860 census, working as a farmer, but has not been found thereafter. He may have died in the Civil War.

6b. **Elizabeth F. "Lizzie."** She should not be confused with her cousin, Elizabeth P. Burgess of Putnam Co. Born about 1841 in Putnam Co., IN. Married Jesse Hurst on 6 Mar. 1860 in Putnam Co. (he was born Jan. 1836 in IN), and had at least the following children: *Lydia A.* (born 1865, married Henry C. Nichols on 1 Feb. 1893 in Putnam Co.); *Albert D.* (born 1869, married Tinie E. Prichard on 18 Nov. 1896 in Putnam Co.); *Hester V.* (born Dec. 1874); *Laura D.* (born 1875); *Roenna F.* (born 1879, married Golden Cummins on 26 Dec. 1899 in Putnam Co.); *Doris* (born 4 Jan. 1882, married Pearl Dorset on 16 Sept. 1908 in Putnam Co.); *Clara M.* (born 26 June 1886, married Andy McCammack on 13 Mar. 1904 in Putnam Co.). Listed in the 1860-80 censuses for Putnam Co., IN; Jesse is listed there alone in 1900. Elizabeth Hurst died on 25 Apr. 1890 in Putnam Co. Her descendant, Woodrow F. Hurst, lives at Kingman, AZ.

6c. **James K(nox?) (I).** Born 12 Oct. 1844 in Putnam Co., IN. See below for full entry.

6d. **Lewis C(ass?).** Born 3 July 1848 in Putnam Co., IN. See below for full entry.

6e. **Deborah.** Born about 1852 in Putnam Co., IN. Listed with her father in the 1860 census, but has not been found thereafter.

6f. **Thomas J.** Born 31 Oct. 1854 in Putnam Co., IN. He may have married Clara V. McHaffie about 1872 (she was born 5 May 1854, and died on 5 Dec. 1872, daughter of Melville McHaffie and Mary A. Thomas, and is buried with her parents in the Stilesville Cemetery, her name being written "Borggess"). Listed with his father in the 1870 census working as a "mail boy," and with his mother in 1880. Tom Burgess died on 26 Jan. 1883 in Hendricks Co., IN, and is buried with his parents.

6g. **Mary (XII) "Mollie."** Born Dec. 1858 in Putnam Co., IN. Listed with her father in the 1870 census, and with her mother in 1880. Married Rufus M. Wallace on 18 Sept. 1890 in Hendricks Co. (he was born Nov. 1849 in TN, and died 1926), and had children: *Claude M.* (born Oct. 1895 in IN); *Hester B.* (born Nov. 1899 in IN). Listed in the 1900 census for Hendricks Co., IN. Mollie Wallace died in 1925, and is buried with her husband in the Stilesville Cemetery.

[William (I)[1], Edward (I)[2], Garner (I)[3], John (I)[4], Dawson (I)[5]]

JAMES K. BURGESS
(1844-1894)

OF MORGAN COUNTY, INDIANA

6c. **James K(nox?) (I)** *[son of Dawson (I)].* Born 12 Oct. 1844 in Putnam Co., IN. Married Elizabeth Dobbs on 16 Oct. 1869 in Putnam Co. (she was born 4 Apr. 1849, daughter of H. H. Dobbs and Lucy Hurst, and died 27 Feb. 1929). Served in Co. H, 43rd Indiana Infantry, Union Army, during the Civil War. Listed in the 1870 census for Marion Township, Putnam Co., IN, and in 1880 in Morgan Co., IN; Elizabeth is listed with her daughter, Claudia, in 1900-20. James K. Burgess was a druggist at Eminence, Morgan Co., IN. His biography appears in *Counties of Morgan, Monroe & Brown, Indiana: Historical and Biographical*, edited by Charles Blanchard (Chicago: F. A. Battey & Co., Publishers, 1884, p. 298-299). He died on 25 July 1894 at Greencastle, Putnam Co., IN, and is buried with his wife in the Stilesville Cemetery, Stilesville, Hendricks Co., IN.

The Children of James K. Burgess:

7a. **Dora (I).** Born June 1870 in Morgan Co., IN. Married Curtis S. Watson on 25 Dec. 1890 in Morgan Co. (he was born July 1869 in IN, possibly the brother of Oscar Watson, and worked as a teacher), and had at least the following children: *Paul* (born Oct. 1891); *Eugene* (born 24 Jan. 1893, and died Mar. 1984 at Franklin, IN, aged 91 years); *Dennis* (born 1 Mar. 1896, married Marcia E. Dixon on 15 May 1920 in Morgan Co., and died Apr. 1970 at Martinsville, IN); *Clara* (born 10 Feb. 1900); *Gladys S. "Giddy"* (born 13 Mar. 1910). Listed in the 1900-10 censuses for Adams Township, Morgan Co., IN. Curtis Watson's biography appears in *One Hundred Years: A Masonic History of Eminence, Indiana*, by Noble Kieth Littell (Eminence, IN: [N. K. Littell], 1972, p. 146).

7b. **Claudia.** Born Dec. 1875 in Morgan Co., IN. Married Oscar E. Watson on 20 Aug. 1896 in Morgan Co. (he was born Aug. 1872, possibly the brother of Curtis Watson, worked as a carpenter, and died 1949), and had at least the following children: *Ruth* (born 24 June 1897, married Maurice McCracken on 28 Oct. 1916 in Morgan Co.); *Georgia* (born May 1900); *Mary E.* (born 1903, died 1904, buried with her parents). Listed in the 1900-10 censuses for Adams Township, Morgan Co., IN, and in 1920 in Marion Co., IN. Claudia Watson died in 1955, probably in Morgan Co., and is buried with her husband in the Stilesville Cemetery, Stilesville, Hendricks Co., IN.

THE BIOGRAPHY OF JAMES K. BURGESS

James K. Burgess, druggist, was born in Putnam County, Ind., October 12, 1844, and is the third child in a family of seven children born to Dawson and Catherine (Holbert) Burgess, natives of Kentucky, the former of German and the latter of Irish descent [sic]. Dawson Burgess received his early education in his native state. While yet a young man, he removed to Putnam County, Ind. Here he bought 100 acres of wild land, and improved a farm, upon which he resided until December, 1868, when he removed to Stilesville, Hendricks Co., Ind., where his death occurred August 12, 1878, in his sixty-fourth year. James K. Burgess, the subject of our sketch, received a fair common school education, and was employed on the home farm until he was twenty years old. In October, 1864, he enlisted in Company H, Forty-third Indiana Volunteer Infantry, and served with that regiment in all its marches and engagements until the close of the war, being mustered out at Indianapolis in June, 1865. After his return from the army, he farmed the home place on shares, and ran a threshing machine for three years. He then removed to Hendricks County, Ind., near Stilesville, where he remained one year, then returned to Putnam County, and engaged in agricultural pursuits until March, 1880. He then came to Eminence, Morgan Co., Ind., where he has since been engaged in the drug trade. He was married, October 14, 1869, to Elizabeth Dobbs, a native of Putnam County, Ind. Two daughters have blessed their union, viz., Dora and Claudia. In politics, Mr. Burgess is a Democrat.

[William (I)[1], Edward (I)[2], Garner (I)[3], John (I)[4], Dawson (I)[5]]

LEWIS C. BURGESS
(1848-1920)

OF CLAY COUNTY, INDIANA

6d. **Lewis C(ass?)** *[son of Dawson (I)].* Born 3 July 1848 in Putnam Co., IN. Married Mary E. Cotton on 25 Mar. 1868 in Putnam Co. (she was born 1 Apr. 1850 in IN, and died 18 Mar. 1923). Listed in the 1870-80 censuses for Marion Township, Putnam Co., IN, and in 1900-20 at Brazil, Brazil Township, Clay Co., IN. Lewis C. Burgess was a farmer in Putnam Co., and later a watchman in a clay factory at Brazil, IN. He died there on 28 Feb. 1920, and is buried with his wife in the Deer Creek Cemetery, Warren, Putnam Co., IN.

The Children of Lewis C. Burgess:

7a. **Charles (I).** Born May 1869 in Putnam Co., IN. See below for full entry.
7b. **Ida L.** Born about 1873 in Putnam Co., IN. Listed with her father in the 1880 census.
7c. **Mattie M.** Born Feb. 1876 in Putnam Co., IN. Married Frank E. McKamey (or McCaney) on 6 Nov. 1892 in Putnam Co. (he was born Mar. 1870 in IN), and had at least the following children: *Elna M.* (born 23 Nov. 1893 in Putnam Co.); *Pauline* (born 25 Oct. 1895 in Putnam Co.). Listed in the 1900 census for Cloverdale Township, Putnam Co., IN.
7d. **Homer (I).** Born 8 Sept. 1878 in Putnam Co., IN; died there on 10 Aug. 1884, and is buried with his parents.
7e. **Ernest.** Born 17 Oct. 1882 in Putnam Co., IN. Married Frances Gifford by 1920 (born about 1882 in IN). Listed in the 1918 draft record and 1920 census for Brazil, Clay Co., IN. Ernest Burgess worked in a clay factory. He died in 1925 in Clay Co., and is buried in the Deer Creek Cemetery at Warren, Putnam Co., IN.
7f. **Covie P.** Born Dec. 1887 in Indiana. Listed with her father in the 1910-20 censuses working in an electrical plant. She may be the Covie Huffman born 14 Dec. 1886 who died Nov. 1979 at Paris, TN.

CHARLES BURGESS OF CLAY CO., INDIANA
[Lewis Cass[6]]

7a. **Charles (I)** *[son of Lewis Cass].* Born May 1869 in Putnam Co., IN. Married Ruth Bowman on 12 Aug. 1897 in Vigo Co., IN. (div.; she was born July 1876 in IN, remarried John F. Hoffa on 6 July 1902 [he remarried Viola ___ by 1920]). Listed in the 1900 census for Brazil, Clay Co., IN with his family, and in 1910-20 living with his father (listed as "single" with no family); his two known children have not been found in the 1910-20 censuses; another possible child, Ruth Burgess, was born Sept. 1896 and died 27 Nov. 1896 at Brazil, IN. Charles Burgess worked in a clay factory at Brazil, IN. He died there in 1948, and is buried in the Deer Creek Cemetery.

8a. **Emily M.** Born 11 June 1896 in Clay Co., IN. She may be the child of another mother.
8b. **James K(nox?) (II).** Born 26 Apr. 1898 in Clay Co., IN.

[William (I)[1], Edward (I)[2], Garner (I)[3], John (I)[4]]

SHELTON BURGESS
(1812?-1860?)

OF HANCOCK COUNTY, INDIANA

5h. **Shelton** *[son of John (I)].* Born about 1812 in Harrison Co., KY. Mentioned as an heir in a settlement deed of his father (*Putnam Co. Deed Book #L*, p. 658, dated 8 Sept. 1843). He obtained a marriage license on 18 Sept. 1847 in Hendricks Co., IN to marry Celia Ayres, but "the above couple was not married on account of the lady's not being found on the day set for marriage." This did not stop him, however, as he promptly married Betsy Hill Lister on 30 Nov. 1847 in Putnam Co. (she appears to have died by 1850); he married secondly Eliza J. Whitecotton on 1 Aug. 1850 in Putnam Co. (she was born about 1827, and died 11 Mar. 1903 in Hendricks Co.). Listed in the 1850 census for Greencastle Township, Putnam Co., IN, and in 1860 in Green Township, Hancock Co., IN; his widow is listed as head of the family in 1870 in Floyd Township, Putnam Co., IN, and in 1880 at Coatesville, Hendricks Co., IN. Shelton Burgess was a farmer in Putnam and Hancock Cos., IN. He probably died in one of these counties between 1860-70.

The Children of Shelton Burgess:

6a. **John L.** Born Jan. 1849 in Putnam Co., IN. Married Elizabeth S. Beckenhemer on 4 Aug. 1870 in Putnam Co. (died or divorced by 1876); married secondly Mary Elkins Riley on 6 Jan. 1876 in Hendricks Co. (she was born about 1847 in IN, and died 5 Nov. 1883); married thirdly Fannie Toney on 28 Feb. 1892 in Hendricks Co. Listed in the 1870 census for New Maysville, Putnam Co., IN with James H. Adair, and in 1880 in Hendricks Co., IN; he may be listed in the 1900 census for Putnam Co., IN boarding with Mickiel Freeley (with no family). John Burgess may have died on 15 May 1910 in Hendricks Co.

7a. **Charles (II).** Born about 1879 in Hendricks Co., IN. No further record.
7b. **Eliza F.** Born 19 Apr. 1882 in Hendricks Co., IN. Listed in the 1900 census for Floyd Township, Putnam Co., IN working as a servant for James L. Rogers. Eliza Burgess died unmarried on 3 Oct. 1904 at New Maysville, Putnam Co. Relationship not verified.
7c. **Daughter.** Born 26 Sept. 1883 in Hendricks Co., IN.

6b. **Sarah E. (II).** Born about 1852 in Indiana. Listed with her mother in the 1870 census. Married William Pierson on 30 Sept. 1880 in Hendricks Co. Has not been found in the 1900 census.
6c. **Atha.** Born Jan. 1854 in Indiana. Married William W. Craig on 23 Aug. 1871 in Putnam Co. (he died or they were divorced by 1880), and had children: *Eddie* (born 1872); *India* (born 1876, married Oliver M. Sparks). Listed with her mother in the 1880 census, and with her daughter (as Atha "Burgess") in the 1900 census for Hendricks Co., IN.
6d. **Emerine E. "Emma."** Born Jan. 1859 in Indiana. Listed with her mother in the 1870 census. Married William D. Mann on 15 Sept. 1877 in Hendricks Co., IN (he was born Feb. 1850 in IN), and had children: *Moses Willard* (born Nov. 1878); *Fanny E.* (born 30 Apr. 1887 in Hendricks Co.); *Lina P.* (born 30 Aug. 1891 in Hendricks Co.); *Mary* (born 25 June 1895 in Hendricks Co.). Listed in the 1900 census for Clay Township, Hendricks Co., IN.
6e. **Moses Willard.** Born 28 Dec. 1860 in Hancock Co., IN. See below for full entry.

[William (I)[1], Edward (I)[2], Garner (I)[3], John (I)[4], Shelton[5]]

MOSES W. BURGESS
(1860-1914)

OF HENDRICKS COUNTY, INDIANA

6e. **Moses Willard** *[son of Shelton]*. Born 28 Dec. 1860 at Coatsville, Hancock Co., IN. Married Ellen Pike on 2 Jan. 1884 in Hendricks Co., IN (she was born Sept. 1864 in IN); married secondly Celestia A. Rowan on 26 Mar. 1908 in Morgan Co., IN (she was born about 1883 in IN, and remarried Duneward Wright on 26 Feb. 1918 in Hendricks Co., IN). Listed in the 1880 census with his mother, and in 1900-10 in Clay Township, Hendricks Co., IN working as a farmer. Moses W. Burgess died on 29 (or 22) June 1914 at Amo, Hendricks Co., IN, but is buried in Coatsville.

The Children of Moses W. Burgess:

7a. **Rollie Ernest.** His name is also given as Rolla in the 1900 census. Born 19 Mar. 1885 at Amo, Hendricks Co., IN. Married Stella Pearl King on 29 Sept. 1907 in Hendricks Co., IN (she was born 1887, and died 7 Jan. 1969 at Marysville, CA). Listed in the 1920 census for Hendricks Co., IN. Rollie Burgess moved to Sacramento, CA in the early 1930s, where he worked as a night watchman for the Bercut Richards Packing Co. for 23 years. He died on 19 Dec. 1967 at Sacramento, Sacramento Co., CA, and is buried in the East Lawn Cemetery. His obituary mentions a "son," Norris Haig (probably a stepson).

8a. **(Miriam) Joyce.** Born 28 Aug. 1911 in Hendricks Co., IN. Married ___ Kennedy, and was living at Cupertino, CA in 1969. Joyce Kennedy died on 14 Apr. 1991 at Mariposa, Mariposa Co., CA.

8b. **Helen E.** Born about 1912 in Hendricks Co., IN. Married ___ Anderson, and was living at Wheatland, Yuba Co., CA in 1969.

8c. **Lois E.** Born 17 Mar. 1914 in Hendricks Co., IN. Married Shelton B. Farthing (he was born 5 Oct. 1906, and died on 12 Sept. 1985 at Placerville, CA). Lois Farthing was living at Placerville, El Dorado Co., CA in 1969. She died on 10 Mar. 1989 at Lodi, San Joaquin Co., CA.

7b. **Mamie Aria.** Born 15 Oct. 1887 at Amo, Hendricks Co., IN. Listed in the 1920 census for Hendricks Co., IN. Mamie Burgess died unmarried on 14 Apr. 1960, probably in Indiana.

7c. **Geneva L.** Born 5 Feb. 1903 in Hendricks Co., IN. Married Beverly Esmond Elliott (he was born 20 May 1907 at Ladoga, IN, son of Jesse Elliott and Flossie Pickle, and died 3 May 1970 at Indianapolis, IN). Listed in the 1920 census with her sister, Mamie. Geneva Elliott died in Aug. 1986 at Northfield, Cook Co., IL. Her granddaughter, Marjorie, married Myron Leroy Powell (div.), and lived at Richland, WA.

7d. **Max A.** Born 21 Feb. 1909 in Hendricks Co., IN. Married Marie Holbrook (she was born 26 Oct. 1904, and died 24 Nov. 1974, leaving six grandchildren). Max Burgess moved to the Sacramento, CA area in 1937, where he worked as a self-employed trucker. He died on 30 Aug. 1977 at Sacramento, Sacramento Co., CA, and is buried in the Memorial Lawn Cemetery. His obituary mentions two sisters (probably half-sisters), Vera Wright and Virgie Hubble (she was born 4 Feb. 1905, and died Nov. 1982 at Arlington, TX).

7e. **Ralph W.** Born about 1911 in Hendricks Co., IN. Married Lorene ___. Ralph Burgess was a cannery worker for Bercut Richards Packing Co. at Sacramento, CA. He is *not* the Ralph Burgess who was born 1 Sept. 1910 and died June 1982 at Oroville, CA.

BURGESS WAR SERVICE

The following chart provides a complete list of family members born with the surname Burgess who are believed to have served in every U.S. war prior to 1900, plus a list of known Burgess military dead in the twentieth century. Several served in more than one unit during the Civil War, and at least one (Charles Lafayette Burgess) served in both the Union and Confederate Armies.

Revolutionary War (1776-83)

Reuben (I)—service unconfirmed

War of 1812

Edward (VII)—Private, 4th Co., 7th NC Brigade—service unconfirmed
Mason Peyton—Private, 13th (Gray's) Regiment, KY Militia

Black Hawk War (1831)

Thomas (II)—Private, Nathan Boone's Co., U.S. Rangers

Mexican-American War (1845-48)

Thornton (II)—Private, Co. B, 2nd IN Volunteers

Civil War (1861-65)

Confederate Forces

Alexander Armistead—Private, Co. I, 1st VA Infantry—killed in action on 31 May 1862
Charles H.—Private, Co. D, 4th KY Cavalry—service unconfirmed
Charles Lafayette—Private, Co. E, 25th TN Infantry
Edward W.—Private, Co. F, 17th VA Infantry—killed in action on 1 June 1862
George Washington (VII)—Private, Co. C, 18th AR Infantry—service unconfirmed
Horace Peyton—Private, Co. H, 6th VA Cavalry
Isaac Washington—Corporal, Co. E, 25th TN Infantry
James Crawford—Sergeant, Co. H, 13th TN Cavalry
James Greenberry—Private, Co. D, 9th KY Mounted Infantry—died of disease on 22 Feb. 1863
James Marion (I)—Private, Co. I, 5th TN Cavalry
James Monroe—Private, Co. A, 12th VA Light Artillery
John H. (I)—Private, Co. G, 7th Battalion, NC Cavalry; Co. M, 7th Battalion, NC Cavalry; Co. C, Gibb's Prison Guard Battalion, NC Troops; Co. D, 42nd NC Troops
John M. (I)—Private, Co. K, 17th TN Infantry—service unconfirmed
John R.—Private, Co. F, 17th VA Infantry—killed in action on 1 July 1862
Joseph C.—Private, Co. K, 17th TN Infantry—service unconfirmed
Moses Franklin—Private, Co. A, 43rd VA Cavalry (Mosby's Raiders)
Paul Williamson—Private, Co. G, 9th KY Mounted Infantry
Thomas M.—Private, Co. E, 16th Regiment, NC Troops; Co. G, 7th Battalion, NC Cavalry; Co. M, 7th Battalion, NC Cavalry
William McCown—Private, Capt. William C. Quantrill's Co., Missouri Cavalry Scouts (Quantrill's Guerrillas)
William Shelton—Private, Co. A, 1st CSA Cavalry; Co. F, 7th KY Cavalry
William Simpson—Sergeant, Co. ?, 8th TN Cavalry; Co. H, 13th TN Cavalry

<u>*Union Forces*</u>

Archibald F.—Private, Co. D, 34th IA Infantry
Burlington Benjamin—Private, Co. K, 18th IN Infantry—died of disease on 24 Sept. 1862
Charles Lafayette—Private, Co. B, 1st TN Mounted Infantry
George Jefferson (I)—2nd Lieut., Co. B, 11th KY Cavalry
George Washington (VI)—1st Lieut., Co. A, 6th KS Militia
Harrison Monroe—Sergeant, Co. E, 5th (later 9th) MN Infantry; 3rd Ind. MN Light Artillery
Jacob Lawson (I)—Private, Co. K, 1st MN Heavy Artillery
James K. (I)—Private, Co. H, 43rd IN Infantry
James P.—Private, Co. B, 18th KY Infantry
John Harris—Private, Co. E, 2nd MN Cavalry
William (XII)—Private, Co. H, 25th IA Infantry—died of disease on 5 Sept. 1863
William F. (I)—Private, Co. G, 24th IN Infantry
William Henry (I)—Private, Co. FA, 22nd IN Infantry—service unconfirmed
William Thornton (I)—Private, Co. C, 111th IL Infantry

<u>Indian Wars (1840s-1890s)</u>

William W. (I)—said to have been in "regular service" in 1843

<u>Spanish-American War (1898)</u>

Avory V.—service unverified
Otis Asa—Private, Co. D, 21st KS Infantry
William Henry (VII)—Private, Co. A, 12th MN Volunteers

<u>World War I (1917-18; deaths only)</u>

Ira Ulysses—Private, Co. G, 119th TN Infantry—killed in action on 5 Sept. 1918

<u>World War II (1941-45; deaths only)</u>

William Conger—Private—killed in action in Jan. 1945

<u>Korean War (1950-54)</u>

No deaths known.

<u>Vietnam War (1963-75)</u>

No deaths known.

The highest ranking Burgess officer to date is Thomas Butler Burgess (1890-1968), who retired from the Army in 1951 as a full Colonel; Leslie Urban Burgess Jr. retired with the reserve rank of Colonel. The highest ranking Naval officer is Thomas's nephew, James Alan Burgess, a graduate of the Naval Academy at Annapolis, who retired with the rank of Commander. The highest ranking Air Force officers are Roy Walter Burgess (pictured above) and Scott Charles Burgess, both of whom retired with the rank of Major, and Major Charles Brent Burgess, who is currently serving. The military service of two early Burgesses, Major Edward Burgess and Captain James Burgess, is unknown; their titles may have been honorary.

THE BURGESSES BETWEEN THE WAR OF 1812 AND THE CIVIL WAR

The War of 1812 was a conflict with Great Britain which neither side really wanted, and which neither side pursued very aggressively. The United States had begun expanding west into the North American continent with the purchase of Louisiana Territory from the French in 1803. Britain still controlled Canada, and an American expeditionary force was sent north, but was ultimately repelled. The British sacked Washington, D.C., with little result, and the war's final battle, at which the British were decisively defeated at New Orleans in 1815, actually occurred after a peace treaty had been negotiated in Europe. For the first time we have evidence that Burgesses formally participated in a military conflict. Mason Burgess enlisted from Kentucky, and Edward Burgess of Rowan County, North Carolina probably served in that state's militia.

The net effect of the war was to confirm the U.S. in its western possessions, and to prompt a further wave of westward immigration by Americans seeking new opportunities and free land. During the five-year period from 1815-20, Mason Burgess moved his family from western Kentucky to southern Indiana, his brother William moved from the Shenandoah Valley of Virginia to south-central Ohio, and Thomas Burgess of Rowan County, NC resettled in central Tennessee in White (later Putnam) County. For the first time the Burgesses had left the old South, and many others soon followed in their footsteps, including my own great-great-great-grandfather, John Henry Burgess, who moved his family from Fleming County, Kentucky to Parke County, Indiana in 1824.

The Mexican-American War erupted in 1845 over the status of Texas, at that time an independent state on the verge of being annexed by the United States. The Mexicans rightly feared the growing power of their neighbor to the north, and attempted to protect their western colonies of California and New Mexico, and to re-annex Texas. The resulting conflict included an invasion of Mexico and the occupation of Mexico City by American forces, the defeat of the Mexican army, the brief independence of California, and the addition of huge new lands in the southwest to the American union. Thornton Burgess is the only member of the family known to have fought in this war.

The vast new lands that were now open to settlement meant that no man could be confined to the life that his father or grandfather had led. Waves of emigration became commonplace, with each new generation moving ever westward, buying into the promise that cheap land plus hard labor could mean a new life for anyone willing to expend the effort to develop the raw wilderness. The invention of steam engines, the building of the first railways and canals and government-sponsored road systems in the eastern states, speeded settlement into the undeveloped areas. Most travel, though, was still conducted by horse and carriage and wagon and foot, and most families moved in large protective groups, with near relatives and neighbors joining the trek into unknown territories. Some members of the Burgesses who stayed behind became wealthy as they accumulated goods and estates, and these new riches in turn allowed them the luxury of hiring servants or buying slaves to do the backbreaking labor necessary to maintain a large farm, and (by the 1850s) even to consider the possibility of sending their elder sons off to academies or to colleges.

The old established families in the South were the wealthiest Burgess relatives of their time, owning in several cases thousands of acres and hundreds of livestock. Among them was Armistead Burgess, the eldest son of Edward Burgess of Culpeper Co., Virginia, who was sent to the Virginia Military Institute in 1860, obviously in preparation for a life as a Southern gentleman. Unfortunately, it was not to be. The conflict between North and South, between slavery and freedom, between the industrialized northern states and the agrarian southern tier, between brother and cousin, was finally boiling to a head. Very few Americans, very few Burgesses, escaped the conflagration that followed.

T. F. & J. W. BURGESS' ORCHARD.
ON THE SNAKE RIVER.

The Peach Orchard of THOMAS FLEMING BURGESS *and* JESSE WALDEN BURGESS *on the Snake River, Near Wawawai, Washington, Circa 1886*

THE SECOND BRANCH

WILLIAM BURGESS
OF STAFFORD COUNTY, VIRGINIA

Chart III: William Burgess of Stafford Co., Virginia

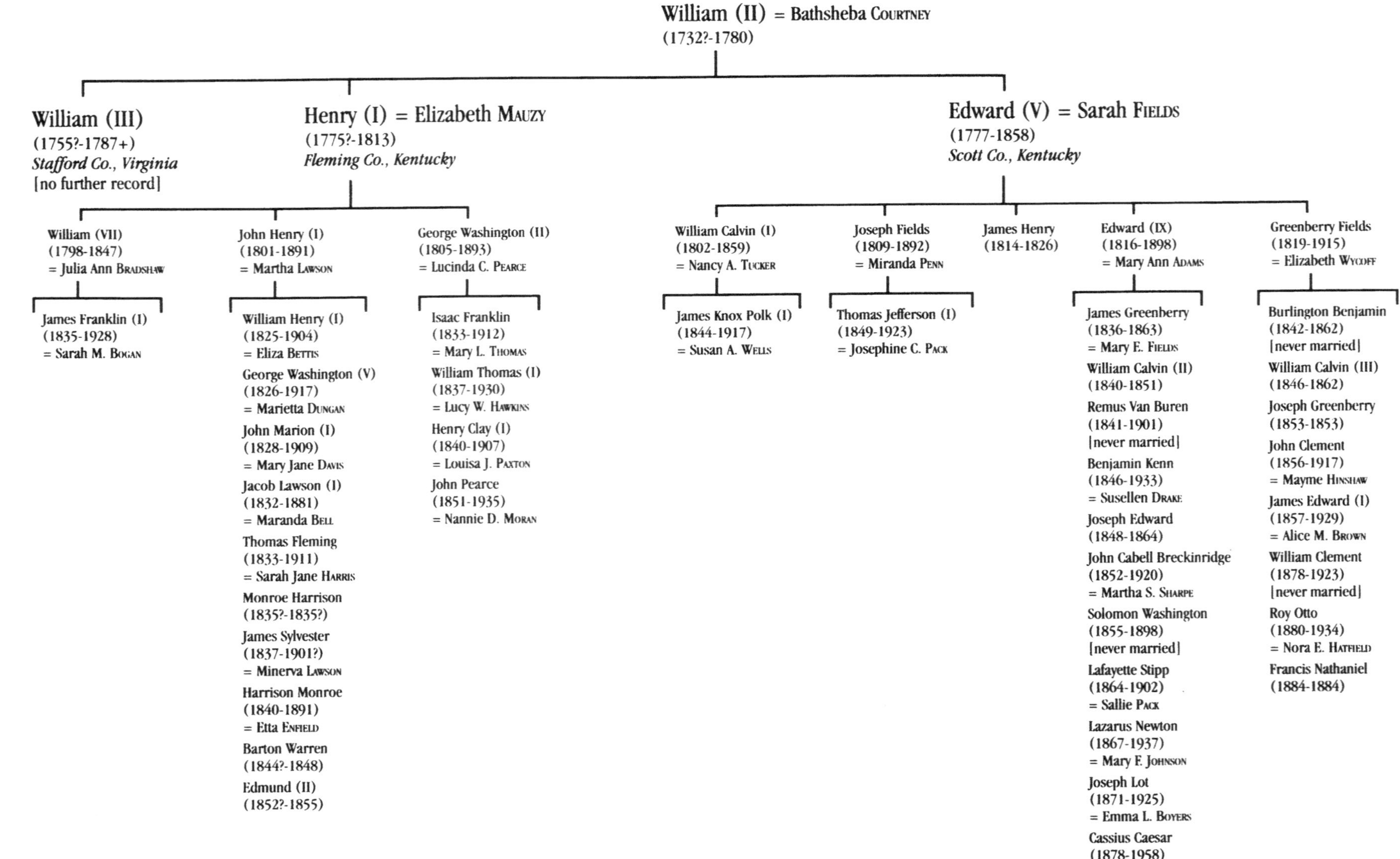

[William (I)[1], Edward (I)[2]]

WILLIAM BURGES
(1732?-1780)

OF STAFFORD COUNTY, VIRGINIA

3d. **William (II)** *[son of Edward (I)].* Born about 1732 in King George Co., VA. Married Bathsheba Courtney on 19 Jan. 1755 O.S. (*Overwharton Parish Register*) in Stafford (later King George) Co., VA. William Burges moved to the Accokeek Creek area of Stafford Co. with his brother, Garner Burges, in the early 1750s. He was named a co-executor of his father's estate (with Garner) in his father's will. His signature appeared on the 15 Oct. 1776 petition of the Stafford Co. freeholders to the Virginia House of Burgesses (the Legislature), asking that the boundary line between Stafford and King George Cos. be adjusted (the counties were subsequently realigned along their modern boundaries on 1 Jan. 1777); but he did not sign the Stafford Co. petition of May 1779. William Burges died about 1780; the inventory of his estate has been lost, but the index record survives (*Liber #N*, p. 410), citing a page number lying within a few pages of the Commissioners Poll (legislative election) of 1780 (p. 407). His relationship to the William Burges mentioned in his father's will is confirmed by the sale of the original Burgess lands in King George Co. in 1797, in which William's son Edward acted in his father's stead, William having been a co-executor of the original Edward's will.

Bathsheba Burges was born about 1734 in Stafford Co., possibly the daughter of William Courtney or John Courtney; after her first husband's death, she married a widower, Ralph Hughes, about 1781 (a Stafford Co. deed of 12 May 1781 [*Liber #S*, p. 63] mentions Ralph Hughes and ___ his wife), but in any case no later than 10 Oct. 1785, when, in the first of four deeds recorded in Oct. and Nov., Ralph Hughes and Bathsheba his wife sold their lands in Stafford Co. (see particularly *Liber #S*, p. 270). Ralph Hughes was born about 1726, son of John Hughes. He is missing from the Stafford Co. voters' list of Apr. 1786. The Hughes family moved to Bourbon Co., KY by 1787, when Ralph Hughes is listed on that county's first personal property tax roll; he bought 100 acres of land there on Flat Run on 20 Mar. 1787 from Isaac and Elizabeth Ruddle (*Deed Book #A*, p. 40). Ralph died by July 1803 (*Order Book #C*, p. 330); in his settlement deed (*Deed Book #6*, p. 128, dated 15 Nov. 1802, witnessed by Tho. Howard, John Jacobs, and "Henery" Burges, Bath-sheba's son), Bathsheba was given one-fourth of Ralph's land and two "Negroes" to maintain a home until her own death, after which the remaining property was to be divided among his own children, John, James, William, and George Hughes. Edward Burgess is noted as a debtor to Ralph's estate in his initial inventory (*Bourbon Co. Will Book #B*, p. 254, recorded at the Nov. 1804 court). Bathsheba Hughes died on 16 Sept. 1823 in Bourbon Co., KY (the date is recorded in her son Edward Burgess's family *Bible* record), aged about 86-88 years; her estate is probated in *Will Book #G*, p. 130-131. William and Bathsheba Burges undoubtedly had more children than those listed below, but their names and fates remain unrecorded.

The Children of William Burges:

4a. **William (III).** According to a family tradition among the descendants of Edward Burgess of Scott Co., KY, Edward had an older brother named William who served in the Revolutionary War. William, if he exists, had to have been born in 1755 or 1759 (probably the former). The 24 May 1779 petition of Stafford Co. freeholders to the House of the Burgesses (State Legislature), asking that courthouse be relocated to a more central position in the county, seems to confirm the story, since it includes the name of William Burgess, *Jr.*, the only such record known (his father would still have been alive at this time). This appears to be the same William Burgess who is listed on the Stafford Co. personal property tax rolls between 1784-87; the 1785 list, which includes the total number of white souls at each freehold, lists four whites under William's name, presumably himself, a wife, and two children. This cannot be Reuben Burgess's son, William, who is underaged and unmarried at this time, or any other known relative. William disappeared from the Stafford County records in 1788, either dying or moving away. Relationship not verified.

4b. **Margaret (III) "Peggy".** Born about 1757 in Stafford Co., VA. Married John Hughes by 1786 (he was born 24 Dec. 1756 [*Overwharton Parish Register*] in Stafford Co., VA, the son of Ralph Hughes, her stepfather, and Margaret Ferguson, and died Sept. 1829 in Bourbon Co., KY), and moved with them to Kentucky about 1786; they had at least the following children: *Ralph II* (died 1829); *Elizabeth* (born about 1800, living with John Todd in 1850-60); *Maria* (born 1802; married John S. Todd on 15 Dec. 1830 (he was a cousin of Mary Todd Lincoln), and had children: John [died June 1837]; James [died June 1837]; Noah H. [born 1838]); *Susan* (married ___ Bledsoe). John and Peggy Hughes sold their land in Stafford Co. on 7 Sept. 1786 (*Stafford Co. Liber #S*, p. 369). John is listed in the personal property records of Bourbon Co. from 1787-1829. Peggy is recorded as aged 95 years in the 1850 census for Bourbon Co., KY with John S. Todd (her son-in-law) and Betsy Hughes. She died on 22 Dec. 1852 at Ruddles Mill, Bourbon Co., KY, and is listed in the official Bourbon County death records as the daughter of William and Bathsheba Burgess of Stafford Co., VA, aged 95 years [sic].

4c. **Bathsheba (I) "Basha"** or **"Bashy."** She is also called **Barsheba**. Born about 1765 in Stafford Co., VA. Married James Hughes about 1789 (he was born about 1760 in Stafford Co., VA, son of Ralph Hughes, her stepfather, and Margaret Ferguson, and died 1812 in Bourbon Co.), and moved with them to Bourbon Co., KY about 1786. They had at least the following children: *Mason* (born about 1790, married Hannah Turley on 1 Nov. 1809, had children: James, and died 1847); *George* (married Christiana "Shanny" Parker on 30 May 1808 or Polly Case on 19 Dec. 1809, and died July 1840 near Paris, KY); *John M.* (born 1798 in Bourbon Co., KY, married Lucy Standeford on 27 Nov. 1824, and had children: Nancy M.; George S.; John J.); *Enoch* (born about 1800, married Polly Northcutt [or Nathart] on 28 Jan. 1822, living in Missouri in 1847); *Annis "Nancy"* (married ___ McGuffin, and had children: James M.). James Hughes is listed in the personal property tax records of Bourbon Co. from 1787-1812. His will (*Bourbon Co. Will Book #D*, p. 281, dated 15 Jan. 1812, probated Sept. 1812) mentions his wife, the five children listed above, and his brother, John; the probate record (p. 307-308) notes his brother-in-law, Henry Burgess (who by this time is a resident of Fleming Co., KY) as a debtor to his estate.

After Duncan's death, Bashy Hughes married Elias Duncan on 21 Aug. 1813 in Bourbon Co., KY (he also died before her). She moved to Missouri in Oct. 1837, back to Kentucky in Sept. 1838, to Calloway Co., MO in Aug. 1845, and back again in Fall 1847, living with her son, John Hughes, at Paris, KY. She is listed (aged 85 years) in the 1850 census for Franklin Co., KY with her son, John Hughes. Barsheba Duncan filed a lawsuit in the 1841 against some of her children and grandchildren (Bourbon Co. court records), alleging breach of contract and lack of material support. From these documents, it is clear that she was alive as late as mid-1852. A 12 Dec. 1851 letter from G. W. Hughes of Millersburg, KY to his brother (Daniel?) says: "...Old Aunt Peggy is still alive—don't know how her general health is at present—The balance of the family are well—Aunt Beersheba is living with one of her brothers in Scott County...." According to a deposition made in the above-mentioned lawsuit, "She is a woman of great imbecility. She knew nothing at all about business." Relationship not verified, but probable.

4d. **Henry (I).** Born about 1775 in Stafford Co., VA. See below for full entry.

4e. **Edward (V) "Ned."** Born 24 Nov. 1777 in Stafford Co., VA. See below for full entry.

A Letter from Bathsheba Hughes to Her Son, Mason Hughes, 1837

Dear son,

I am still firm in my mind to move out with you this fall provided you don't think it too much trouble to come for me. I wrote to Franklin Northcut this spring to come and move me out [to Missouri] this fall. I received his answer. He said he would come if I would do so and so. He had too many provisors [sic] which must be reduced to a certainty if he come to suit me. As I told him as plain as I could to come and sell my land and Negrows to the highest bidder and settle my business, and he should have what little was coming to me. I think he appeared somewhat doubtful of me. Now Mason, if you will come and sell my wright in my land and Negrows and settle all my business here, I will go out with you with out fail if life lasts, and live with you the ballance of my days. Mason, all I want is a support. I intend to relinquish all I have to you for a support in my last days, as they can't be many. Of course, Mason, I am bound to move somewhere this fall, as my wood is all gone, and John treated me like a stranger. So if you won't come for me, God nows what I shal do. Mason, have confidence in me, you may depend on my complying with every word. I say here if God will spare my life to see you, Mason, if you conclude to come, I would like for you to be here about the first of September so you may have time to settle my business. I don't intend to moove nothing but one bed and beding, therefore, I want you to conclude if you come whether or not wee had beter gow by water. Mason, I want you to write to me the same day you receive this leter, and let me now what I may depend on, and direct your leter to John S. Todd at Paris. My last request is, my dear son, don't fail to come. I am happy to say to you I am in good health at this time, and a fine crop a growing.

Your affectionate mother, Bashaba Huges

Mason, as respects Aunt Basha there is no doubt in my mind that she will comply with what she says. She will have to moove without doubt. I am satisfied she prefers to live with you. If you come you may depend on my returning with you. Yours with high esteem, John S. Todd.

[William (I)[1], Edward (I)[2], William (II)[3]]

HENRY BURGESS
(1775?-1813)

OF FLEMING COUNTY, KENTUCKY

4d. **Henry (I)** *[son of William (II)].* Born about 1775 in Stafford Co., VA. Married Elizabeth Mauzy on 12 May 1797 in Bourbon Co., KY (she was a daughter of Peter Mauzy, a Revolutionary War veteran who was born in 1751 in Stafford Co., VA, son of Henry Mauzy, and died in Fleming Co., KY on 15 Aug. 1841, aged 90 years), and Sarah Hughes (she was born 1760, possibly a daughter of Ralph Hughes, and died 1833). Listed in the Bourbon Co. personal property tax records of 1797 and 1803, in Fleming Co. from 1800-01 and 1804-13, and in the 1810 census for Fleming Co. Henry Burgess was a farmer in Bourbon and Fleming Cos., KY. He last appears in the official records on 5 July 1813, when he is appointed by the Fleming Co. court to work on the county roads. According to an account penned ninety years after his death by his grandson, Isaac Burgess, Henry was shot and killed at Vincennes, Indiana—this cannot be confirmed from Knox Co. (Vincennes) records. On 3 Mar. 1814 his eldest son, William, was apprenticed to a tanner (*Order Book #C*, p. 374), with Henry specifically being mentioned as deceased. Shortly thereafter, Elizabeth Burgess was granted administration of Henry's estate. Isaac Franklin Burgess calls his grandfather "Harrison Burgess" in a letter written in 1903 (see his entry).

The relationship between Henry, Elizabeth, and their six children is documented in a series of lawsuits filed between 1839-1856 in the Fleming Co. courts between the Burgess and Mauzy heirs (see particularly *Case #7119*), between John and Wash Burgess and the Rhodens, and between William Burgess's widow and a squatter on her land; Henry is specifically cited in these records as having come from Bourbon Co. Henry's relationship to his father and siblings can only be demonstrated circumstantially: Henry witnessed the settlement deed of his stepfather, Ralph Hughes, in Bourbon Co. on 15 Nov. 1802 (*Deed Book #6*, p. 128), and is listed as a debtor to the estate of his stepbrother and brother-in-law, James Hughes, who died in Bourbon Co. in 1812 (*Bourbon Co. Will Book #D*, p. 307). Henry's grandson, George Washington Burgess (V), married Marietta Dungan, granddaughter of Edward Burgess of Scott Co., KY, in 1850 in Harrison Co., KY. Marietta at this time was a ward of her uncle, Joseph Burgess, who gave his written permission for the marriage. George Burgess was raised in Indiana; Marietta Dungan was raised in Scott Co.—the two could not have met accidentally. This cousin relationship is confirmed by oral tradition among the descendants of George and Marietta Burgess. Henry named his oldest son William and his oldest daughter Bathsheba; Edward, his brother, named his oldest son William and his second daughter Bathsheba (the first daughter having been named for his wife's mother).

Elizabeth Mauzy Burgess was born about 1780 in Stafford Co., VA. She appeared on the tax lists as head of the family from 1814-1844, and deeded her property to her sons on 3 Apr. 1844; her estate was appraised on 28 May 1844 (*Fleming Co. Will Book #G*, p. 501). She left no will.

The Children of Henry Burgess:

5a. **William (VII).** Born 1798 in Bourbon Co., KY. See below for full entry.

5b. **John Henry (I).** Born 15 July 1801 in Bourbon Co., KY. See below for full entry.

5c. **Bathsheba (II)** (variously **Barsheba**) **"Sheba."** Born 6 Jan. 1803 in Bourbon Co., KY. Married Joseph Rhoden on 16 Dec. 1824 in Fleming Co., KY (he was born 15 Oct. [or Dec.] 1800 in Fleming Co., KY, probably the son of Thomas Rhoden and Susanna Beaty, and died on 26 June 1880 in Vigo Co., IN), and had children:

William Burgess RHODEN. Born 28 Dec. 1825 in Fleming Co., KY, married Nancy Harmon on 28 Oct. 1847 (she was born about 1831 in KY, and was living in 1880), and died 30 June 1885. Listed in the census records for the First District, Fleming Co., KY in 1850, in Fayette Township, Vigo Co., IN, in 1860, and in 1870-80 in Sandford, Elbridge Township, Edgar Co., IL, just on the county/state line. They had children:

Joseph Washington RHODEN. Born 4 Mar. 1849 in Fleming Co., married Mary E. Price in 1871, and died Sept. 1927. They had children: George W. (born 7 Oct. 1871 in Edgar Co., died 7 Dec.

1907); Sadie E. (born 1874 in Edgar Co., married Charles Reese, and had children: Joe); Franklin Edward (born May 1875 in Edgar Co., died 11 Apr. 1956); Bertha C. (born 22 Oct. 1879 in Edgar Co., died 14 Nov. 1930); Hubert A. (born 13 Dec. 1880 in Edgar Co., married Maud Tritt on 23 Aug. 1907 in Vigo Co., IN [she was born 1885, and died 1965], had children: Doyne [born 1918, died 1966], and died 1949); Tracy Otto (born 6 Jan. 1885 in Edgar Co., SEE BELOW); Monte (born 4 [or 11] Dec. 1886 in Edgar Co., IL, married Vernice Tritt on 28 Nov. 1911 in Vigo Co. [she was born 1887, and died 1978], and died 11 Dec. 1961); Mattie (born 31 Aug. 1888 in Edgar Co.); James (born Apr. 1896 in Edgar Co.); Omer D. (born 16 Apr. 1896 in Edgar Co., married Bonnie Mahan on 9 May 1920 in Vigo Co. [she was born 1895, and died 1942], and died 1954).

Tracy Otto *RHODEN* (born 6 Jan. 1885 in Edgar Co., married Ina Mae Stewart on 7 Feb. 1906 in Vigo Co. [she was born 18 Jan. 1887, and died 24 Dec. 1965], and died 29 May 1976, aged 91 years, at Sandford, Vigo Co., having had children: Ivan [born 1907 at Sandford, IN, and died about 1910]; Floyd [born 1909 at Sandford, IN, and died about 1911]; Clyde Ernest [born 11 June 1911 at Sandford, IN, and died 30 Mar. 1937]; James Kenneth [born 25 Aug. 1914 at Sandford, IN, married Doradine ___, had children: Maurice Leon {born 14 Mar. 1945, married Susanne Foertsch}; Marilyn Rose {born 12 Feb. 1949, married Timothy Barton, and secondly David Heaton}; Jeanette Lee {born 14 Jan. 1953, married Larry Stanfield, and secondly Austin Kendall}]; Katherine Virginia [born 10 May 1919 at Sandford, IN]).

Jane "Lida" RHODEN. Born Nov. 1850 in Fleming Co., married __ Wolfe, died 27 Nov. 1914.

(Barsheba) Elizabeth RHODEN. Born 14 Nov. 1854 in Fleming Co., married Alpheus Milton Hussong on 4 Sept. 1871 in Edgar Co., IL (he was born 31 July 1851 at Sandford, IN, son of Jacob H. Hussong and Margaret Smith, and died 2 Apr. 1890 at Hutsonville, IL, killed with his father in the explosion of a stave factory). They had children:

Lela Mary *HUSSONG* (born 10 Nov. 1874 in Illinois, married Waldo G. Watts on 19 June 1892 [div.] and married again to Watts after 1930 [he was born 1871 in Indiana, son of James W. Watts and Elizabeth E. Haymaker, married secondly Effie J. ___ {who died 1930}, and died May 1940], and raised two foster children: Arnold RAY; Evelyn Mae RHODEN [daughter of Perry Rhoden {SEE BELOW}], married secondly W. Lee Shickel on 1 July 1903 [div.; born Aug. 1879 in IN], married fourthly Everett Winters, and died 8 Feb. 1964 at Terre Haute, buried Hutsonville Cemetery).

Loma Pearl *HUSSONG* (born 25 Jan. 1876 in Indiana, married Elbert Staley Brown on 28 Mar. 1893 [he was born 9 May 1873, son of Theodore F. Brown and Susan Staley, and died 27 July 1953 at Terre Haute, IN, both buried Highland Lawn Cemetery], and died 13 Oct. 1969, aged 93 years, having had children: Raymond Theodore [born 3 Feb. 1896 at Sandford, IN, married Grace Coleman {she died 3 Feb. 1935}, and died childless on 1 Sept. 1960 at Indianapolis, IN, buried Highland Lawn Cemetery]; Elbert Vernon [born 26 Nov. 1904, married Mary Lou McMillin on 24 Mar. 1946 {she was born 3 July 1919, and died 3 Sept. 1993}, and had children: Donna {ad.; born 5 Nov. 1936, married Curtis Barcus}; Loma Jeanne {born 15 Dec. 1946}; Trenna {born 1 Apr. 1948}; Bonita {born 9 Jan. 1953}]).

Cleda *HUSSONG* (born Oct. 1877, married Fred C. Todd on 24 June 1896 in Vigo Co. [he was born 9 Jan. 1879, son of John P. and M. Jane Todd, married secondly Jessie Vermillion], had children: Oscar [born Sept. 1896], and died 1 July 1897, buried Rose Hill Cemetery, Sandford, IN).

Alpheus Brant *HUSSONG* (born 3 Nov. 1888 at Hutsonville, IL, married Mabel Isabel Claybaugh on 14 Sept. 1907 at Paris, Edgar Co., IL [she was born 21 Aug. 1890 at Hutsonville, IL, daughter of Oscar E. Claybaugh and Laura C. Helmick, and died 16 May 1968 at Danville, IN], and had children: Joe Oscar [born 3 Oct. 1908 at West Terre Haute, IN, married Dola Clatfelter about 1935 {div.}, and died 20 Mar. 1958, buried Roselawn Cemetery]; Mary Lela [born 14 Jan. 1916 at St. Mary of the Woods, Vigo Co., IN, married M. T. "Pete" Shalhout in Jan. 1935 at Danville, IL {div. 1937}, and had children: Barbara Lee {born 4 Nov. 1935 at Indianapolis, IN, married Raymond Allen Streib on 7 June 1957 at Danville, IL <div.; he was born 10 Nov. 1930, son of Carlton Streib>, and had children: Michael Alan <born 24 May 1958 at Indianapolis, IN>; Robert Louis <born 18 Apr. 1959 at Indianapolis, IN, married Linda Jeanne Hornbrook in Jan. 1986 at Indianapolis, and had children: Robert Kenneth |born 3 Oct. 1986 at Indianapolis|>; Barbara died on 24 Apr. 1987 at Indianapolis}; Mary Lela married secondly Louis Henry Rodney on 15 Dec. 1939 at Greenfield, IN {he was born 6 July 1915 at Danville, IL, son of Rollie W. Rodney and Rowena S. Pounds}, and had children: Judith Ann {born 25 Feb. 1944 at Indianapolis, IN, married Rodney Allen Schwartz on 14 Aug. 1966 at Danville, IL, and had children: Ryan Scott <ad.; born 15 May 1974 at Fort Wayne, IN>; Andrew Grant <ad.; born 19 Apr. 1977 at Fort Wayne, IN>; Daryn Matthew <born 5 Dec. 1978 at Fort Wayne, IN>}; Susan Elizabeth {born 24 Apr. 1945 at Indianapolis, IN, married David Louis Tyler on 24 Jan. 1965 at Avon, IN, and had children: Todd David <born 20 Nov. 1965 at Gary, IN, married Wanda Wilson in 1990 in CA, and had children: David James |born 30 July 1991 at Downey, CA|>; Tamara Sue "Tammy" <born 22 Sept. 1969 at Marion, IN, married Jeffrey Allan Chambers

on 17 June 1989 at Huntington, IN, and had children: Nathan Emmett |born 23 Nov. 1991 at Cleveland, OH|>}]; Alpheus Brant Jr. [born 6 Mar. 1922 at Sandford, IL, married Laura June Patterson on 28 June 1942 at South Bend, IN {she was born 30 June 1924, daughter of Virgil Lee Patterson and Stella May Hamilton}, and had children: Mary Lee {born 5 Mar. 1944 at Indianapolis, IN, married Tim Townsend on 2 Feb. 1976 in Florida <div.>}; Alpheus Brant III {born 22 June 1948 at Jacksonville, TN, married Mary Lynne Love on 24 Sept. 1978 at Lancaster, PA, and had children: Nicholas Brant <born 18 Aug. 1983 at Harrisburg, PA>}; Joseph Anthony {born 9 Sept. 1958 at Columbus, GA}; John Quentin {born 5 Feb. 1961 at Columbus, GA, married Denise Louise Davis on 9 July 1984 at Telford, PA, and had children: Zachary Orion <born 8 May 1989>}]).

(Barsheba) Elizabeth HUSSONG married secondly Perry Duck on 19 Mar. 1891 in Edgar Co., IL (he was born June 1858, son of John and Sarah Duck, and was killed in a train explosion on 13 Jan. 1907], and had children:

Paul Ira *DUCK* (born Jan. 1897 in Illinois, died Aug. 1918 while serving with the U.S. Army in France during World War I).

(Barsheba) Elizabeth DUCK died on 15 Dec. 1930 at Terre Haute, Vigo Co., IN, and is buried with her first husband in the New Hutsonville Cemetery, Hutsonville, IL.

Hollis K. "Rube" RHODEN. Born 16 Oct. 1855 in Edgar Co., IL, married Mary E. ___ in 1905 (she was born 1873, and was the widow of William H. Rhoden, his brother), and died July 1927.

Harrison R. RHODEN. Born 18 Mar. 1857 in Edgar Co., IL, married Lue Emma ___ in 1892, and had children: Clara (born Sept. 1898 in Edgar Co., IL). Harrison Rhoden died in Sept. 1935.

Emily "Emma" RHODEN. Born 31 Jan. 1859 in Edgar Co., married Samuel Bailey, lived in Vermilion Co., IL, and died in May 1935.

William H. RHODEN. Born 23 July 1861 in Edgar Co., married Mary E. ___ (she married secondly Hollis K. Rhoden, his brother), and had children: Perry O. (born 23 Jan. 1893 in Edgar Co., married Mary Barton on 8 Mar. 1913 in Vigo Co. [div. 1920], and had children: Oliver; Pauline; Evelyn Mae [born 17 Mar. 1916, raised by Lela Mary Hussong Watts, born 17 Mar. 1916, married Louis Todd]; Bernard [born about 1919]; Perry married secondly Ruby Lee, and died Aug. 1964, having had children: Ruth [married R. D. Albin]; Gladys Marie [married James Nichols]; Ronald); Irma E. (born 12 May 1895 in Edgar Co., IL, married Roy Hux on 1 Jan. 1916); Anna (born 1898 in IL); Minnie (married ___ Tagney and secondly Ross Tidd). *William H.* RHODEN died in Mar. 1899.

James Franklin RHODEN. Born 24 Oct. 1863 in Edgar Co., was crippled with rheumatism (so noted on the 1880 census record), and died unmarried on 28 Feb. 1911.

Minda Pearl RHODEN. Born 25 Jan. 1866 in Edgar Co., and died May 1930.

Rosa Bell RHODEN. Born 19 July 1872 in Edgar Co., married ___ Craig, lived at Mt. Carmel, IL, and died 28 Mar. 1956.

John W. RHODEN. Born 5 Feb. 1874 in Edgar Co., married Martha M. ___ in 1904 (she was born 1881), and had children: Lloyd O. (born 1909 in IN). *John W.* RHODEN died on 17 July 1953, possibly in Texas.

Bessie RHODEN. Born 24 Sept. 1877 in Edgar Co., married Pearl C. Riggs (born June 1877 in Indiana, son of C. A. and Celia Riggs), and had children: Leslie Fay (dau.; born Sept. 1897 at Hutsonville, IL). *Bessie* RIGGS died in 1971, aged 94 years, and is buried at Hutsonville, IL.

***Amanda D.* RHODEN.** Born 1828 in Fleming Co., KY, married David M. Fuqua in 1846 (he was the son of Washington R. Fuqua and Rebecca Wilson), and had children: *Martha J.* (married William H. McFarland); *Fleming S.*; *Bathsheba E(lizabeth?)* (married Jesse McFarland); *Joseph Burgess* (born 2 Oct. 1857 in Edgar Co., IL, married Ida V. Merring on 24 Nov. 1880 [she was born 11 Aug. 1861 at Buffalo, NY, daughter of Louis Merring and Anna Forrest], and had children: Herbert E. [born 19 Apr. 1883 at Terre Haute, IN]; Esther Cleone [born 17 Feb. 1887 at Terre Haute, IN, married Carroll H. Seldonridge on 4 Sept. 1907]). ***Amanda* FUQUA** died on 15 Nov. 1895 at Edgar Co., IL.

***Eunice* RHODEN.** Born about 1830 in Fleming Co., KY. She does not appear to be listed with Joseph Rhoden in the 1840 census, and she may have actually been a niece raised by Joseph.

***Emily E.* RHODEN.** Born about 1837 in Fleming Co., KY.

***Martha J. F.* RHODEN.** Born about 1842 in Fleming Co., KY.

Joseph and Barsheba RHODEN are listed in the 1830-50 censuses for the Third District, Fleming Co., KY. The Rhodens sold their land in Fleming Co. on 1 Dec. 1852, and moved to Elbridge Township, Edgar Co., IL, where they appear on the 1860 census. By 1870 they had moved just across the county/state line into nearby Fayette Township, at Sandford, Vigo Co., IN, and are also listed there in the 1880 census. Sheba Rhoden died there on 6 July 1880, a few days after her husband, and is buried with him in the Rose Hill Cemetery, near Sandford, Fayette Township, Vigo Co., IN. Mary Hussong Rodney has contributed greatly to this book; she currently lives at Englewood, FL.

5d. **(George) Washington (II).** Born 5 Mar. 1805 in Fleming Co., KY. See below for full entry.

5e. **Margaret (V)**. Born about 1809 (or 1811) in Fleming Co., KY. Married Simeon Harmon on 28 Feb. 1833 in Fleming Co. (he was born about 1811 in KY, brother of Elijah Harmon, who married Margaret's sister, Sarah A. Burgess; the marriage being conducted by her cousin, Rev. Thomas Mauzy, son of Peter Mauzy, her grandfather). Their children included: *John H(enry?)* (born about 1835); *James M.* (born about 1836); *Joab* (born about 1842); *Mary E.* (born about 1843); *Amanda J.* (born about 1845). Listed in the 1850 census for Fleming Co., KY; her husband appears there in 1860-70. Margaret Harmon evidently died in Fleming Co. between 1850-60.

5f. **Sarah A. (I)**. Born about 1811 (or 1809) in Fleming Co., KY. Married Elijah T. Harmon on 17 Feb. 1833 in Fleming Co. (he was born about 1812 in KY, brother of Simeon Harmon, who married Sarah's sister, Margaret Burgess; the marriage being conducted by her cousin, Rev. Thomas Mauzy). Their children included: *Wesley H.* (born about 1833, married Ellen Ann Scott, and had children: Sarah E. [born 23 July 1856 in Fleming Co.]; Elijah Washington [born 2 Sept. 1857, died 17 Sept. 1858]); *William* (born about 1835); *Morton E.* (born about 1838); *Minerva E.* (born about 1839, married John Preston on 2 Oct. 1858 in Fleming Co.); *John G.* (born about 1841); *Emily* (born about 1844); *James H.* (born about 1847). Listed in the 1850-70 censuses (listed as age 56 in 1870) for the Sherburne District, Fleming Co., KY. Sarah evidently died between 1870-80, since her husband, Elijah Harmon, is living alone with her brother and his brother-in-law, Wash Burgess, in the 1880 census.

INVENTORY OF ELIZABETH BURGESS

Inventory and appraisement of the personal estate of Elizabeth Burgess dec[d] made this 28th May 1844.

1 Cupboard and cupboard ware	$3.00
1 Sugar desk	.50
1 Breakfast table and candle stand	1.50
1 Bureau	2.00
1 Bed and furniture & 2 bedsteads	10.00
1 Frame chair & 1 keg	.25
1 Water bucket 25[cts] 1 Tea kettle 50[cts]	.75
1 Lott bacon & lott corn	1.90
1 Bay mare $10. 1 cow $7	17.00
1 Note on Joseph Rhoden due 25 Dec. 1842	153.62
1 do Washington R. Fuqua " 11 Apr. 1844	6.00
1 do do & Joseph Rhoden due 11 March 1845	11.00
1 do do & ditto " 11 March 1846	11.00
1 ditto ditto & ditto " 11 March 1847	11.00
1 ditto ditto & ditto " 11 March 1848	11.00
	$240.52

I certify the foregoing inventory contains all the personal estate of Elizabeth Burgess dec[d] which hath come to my hands.
May 28th 1844 .... G. W. Burgess, Adm.

Sales of the estate on 8 June 1844 were made to Daniel Harman, Thomas Todd, William Rhoden, Edward Moren, Thomas Rhoden, Geo. W. Burgess, James Moren, and Elijah Harman [sic].

Excerpts from Fleming County Case #7119, Burgess vs. Mausey

(November 1840)

To the Honorable the Judge of the Fleming Circuit Court in Chancery sitting, your orators William Burgess, John Burgess, George W. Burgess, Joseph Roden and Barsheba his wife, Elijah T. Harmon, and Sarah his wife formerly Sarah Burgess, and Simeon Harmon and Margaret his wife, heirs of Henry Burgess, deceased, and Elizabeth Burgess, widow of said Henry Burgess, deceased, humbly complaining respectfully represent to your honor, that on or about the [blank] day of 1810, the said Henry Burgess entered into an agreement with Peter Mausey for the purchase of a certain tract of land in the county of Fleming and State of Kentucky, for which a certain John Fowler then held the legal title. By said agreement it was stipulated that the said Mausey should purchase and take the title to himself a portion of said tract of land containing about one hundred and fifty acres, and that he should procure the legal title of the balance thereof, being about fifty acres for the said Henry Burgess and in his s[d] Burgess' name. And at the same time the said Henry Burgess paid into the hands of said Peter Mausey a certain horse of the full value of one hundred and fifty dollars, and also the sum of twenty pounds in money; which horse and money constituted the full price and consideration for said fifty acres of land: the said Mausey then agreeing to procure the title for said fifty acres of land from said Fowler, who then resided in Fayette county in said State, to which county said Mausey was about to go for the purpose of getting a deed of conveyance for said one hundred and fifty acres of land; having previously negotiated with the agent of said Fowler for the same, that is to say, for the whole of said tract, one hundred and fifty acres thereof being for himself, and fifty acres for said Henry Burgess. Said two parcels of land being divided by a certain division line passing through a fine spring, so as to give to each of them the benefits of said spring. After the payment of said consideration by said Henry Burgess, the said Peter Mausey paid the same and no other consideration over to said Fowler, but instead of getting a title for said parcel of fifty acres to and in the name of said Henry Burgess, said Peter Mausey fraudulently took a deed and procured the title from said Fowler in his own name for the whole tract, a copy of which deed is now herewith filed marked as voucher "A" and made a part of this bill. Upon the making of said agreement between said Henry Burgess and said Peter Mausey and the completion of the negotiation for the purchase of said land with William Prout, the agent of said Fowler, said Henry Burgess obtained the possession from said agent of said fifty acres of land, and held possession for several years—and then leased it to George Mausey, who had possession about [blank] years, and then gave possession to John Burgess who afterwards transferred the possession thereof to said William Burgess, who had possession about [blank] years, when the said Peter Mausey forcibly entered and took possession thereof, and has the possession ever since, a period of ten years. In the meantime, to wit, on the [blank] day of [blank] 1813, said Henry Burgess departed this life intestate, leaving said Elizabeth his widow and your other orators and oratrixes his heirs at law.

Your orators and oratrixes charge that by the law of the land, a trust in said fifty acres of land resulted to said Henry Burgess; he having paid the consideration and placed the same in the hands of said Mausey to procure the title, and said Mausey agreeing to obtain a deed for the conveyance of the same to said Henry Burgess. They also charge that said Peter Mausey received the rents on and profits of said fifty acres of land for ten years, and that he appropriated the same to his own use and benefit; they charge that the rents and profits so received by said Mausey were of the annual value of one hundred dollars. They further charge that said Peter Mausey had in the life time of said Henry Burgess often promised and agreed and [sic] with Henry Burgess to convey to him the legal title to said Henry. But which he failed to convey, and has ever since failed, and still fails, and refuses to do. They charge that in equity and good conscience said Peter Mausey is bound to convey to them the legal title of said parcel of fifty acres of land, according to the boundaries thereof and the division line aforesaid. Said division line running so as to cut off said fifty acres on the North West side of said two hundred acres, and to crop said spring in such manner as to give an equal part thereof to each of said parcels of land. The boundaries of said fifty acres will therefore be as follows, to wit, beginning at [large space], the same will be seen on reference to the inventory aforesaid, being on said evidence of said tract of land. In order that justice may be done in the premises your orators and oratrixes pray that said Peter Mausey be made a defendant to this bill, and that he be compelled to answer the same on oath; to set forth all the agreement made in relation to said purchase and the payment of the consideration for said fifty acres of land by said Henry Burgess; as well as all other matters and things herein contained, charged, and set forth. And upon final hearing that your honor order and decree that said Peter Mausey execute to your orators and oratrixes, widow and heirs as aforesaid, a good and sufficient deed of conveyance of said fifty acres of land; and they pray for all such further relief in the premises as to equity belong, and their case may require, and that said Peter Mausey be ordered to pay over to them such rents and profits of said land as shall appear to be due them from him and to surrender to them the possession of the said fifty acres of land.

—John S. Cavan, solicitor for compts.

The deposition of Jacob Lawson taken at the office of John S. Cavan, in the town of Flemingsburg, on the 17th day of February 1840:

This deponent being of lawful age and first duly sworn, deposeth as follows, to wit, he knows where the land lies on which Peter Mausey the defendent now lives—and which he occupies, but does not know how much there is in the tract. The land was originally the land of John Fowler, and was in possession of Henry Rice and Thomas Miller, and the said Peter Mausey and Henry Burgess the father of the complaintants, purchased the right of said Rice and Miller, and their right was only for the improvements so far as this respondent knows. They may have had a contract of purchase of the land. Said Rice and Miller were the first settlers on said land—and each of them had cabins on the land and some improvements, but deponent cannot tell what particular improvements—nor can he tell how lengthy they had been in possession—but thinks not many years. The defendant has been in possession of the land, deponent thinks, thirty years or upwards. Said Henry Burgess settled on part of the land occupied by Mr. Miller above named—and purchased the improvement of said Miller. The cabins of said Rice and Miller were not very far apart, not more, deponent thinks, than four or five hundred yards. The cabin of Rice stood near where said Mausey's house now stands, and the cabin of Miller stood in the direction of the house where William Browning now lives, being a north westwardly course from the cabin of Rice. This deponent was the first settler in the part of the country where said land lies.

Question by defendant's counsel: Did not Peter Mausey and Henry Burgess move from Bourbon County when they bought out the improvement rights of Rice and Miller?

Answer: They did, and Henry Burgess was the son in law of said Peter Mausey. Peter Mausey moved onto the land about two years after Henry Burgess. After Henry Burgess had been living on the land, some short time, he and Peter Mausey passed by my house on horseback and stopped a short time. I then understood from them that they bought out the claims of the beforementioned Rice and Miller, and as they were going in the direction of Bourbon, I supposed that they were returning to Bourbon County. This was before Peter Mausey moved onto the land. I did not hear them say anything at the time at having bought the legal title to the land from Fowler, the original proprietor.

Question by defendant: How long did Henry Burgess live on the land?

Answer: I cannot tell the length of time. I think that after he left he went back to Paris in Bourbon County. He afterwards returned to the neighborhood and lived some years, but I do not know whether he ever lived at the same place.

Question: Did Henry Burgess give up the possession of the land to Peter Mausey?

Answer: I do not know to whom. Jno. Mausey, a son of Peter Mausey, had possession of it after Henry Burgess left it for a considerable length of time.

Question: Was not Mr. Fowler a large proprietor of land in the neighborhood?

Answer: He was. I do not know at what time [he] sold it. The improvements of Miller and Rice above spoken of were on Fowler's land. Whether they had any liberty from Fowler to settle on the land I do not know. It was very customary then for a person to settle down on land without any right, and to sell out the improvements. Miller had been shifting about from one place to another, and had made and sold several improvements.

Question: Do you know of any agent that Fowler had attending to his land in Fleming?

Answer: At the time that P. Mausey & Henry Burgess moved on to the land, I do not know that Fowler had any agent in the neighborhood. Some time after that, Gen. Fletcher acted as the agent of Fowler. I do not know of Routt ever acting as the agent of Fowler in relation to his lands in this neighborhood.

Question: After Henry Burgess removed back from Bourbon, did he not live again near you, and did you hear of any claim that he set up to any part of the land in possession of Peter Mausey?

Answer: After he returned, he lived near me on my side of the branch from Peter Mausey's land. I did not hear of any dispute then. All the land was in Fowler's claims, and when he returned I think he lived on a part of the same land that was purchased of Rice and Miller, but not at the place he first settled on. And further deponent sayeth not.—Jacob Lawson.

The deposition of Henry Rice taken the 20th day of May 1840:

...At the time of purchasing the said improvements, said Peter Mausey stated that he was purchasing the improvement occupied by deponent for his son-in-law—and said Mausey at that time had no son-in-law but said Henry Burgess....Said Peter Mausey about a year or so after the purchase of the improvements purchased the said land and he paid horses for the land. One of the horses which went to pay for the land was gotten from John Mausey, a son of said Peter, and said John got another horse in his place from said Henry Burgess. Said horse of Henry Burgess was to go toward payment of the land. But it did not satisfy Fowler, and therefore John Mausey furnished one in its place. Burgess (said Henry) got possession of the land, which deponent understands to be the same now claimed by the complainants, being on the north western part of the tract, a few months, or a short time after said purchase of improvements was made, and retained the possession two or three years, and cleared and fenced and cultivated some of the land, but deponent cannot now say how much. Some time, deponent thinks about the time Burgess left said land, deponent heard Mausey say he would not make Burgess a title because he was in the habit of drinking, and also at same time that he had not paid him for the land, and stated that some difficulty had occurred between said Burgess and Mausey in relation to said land, said Burgess wanting Mausey to convey the legal title to him for the part he occupied....

Question by defendant: Do you know the reason why Henry Burgess left the land and moved away?

Answer: I understood it was because he & Peter Mausey had a difficulty about the land & Peter Mausey refused to make him a deed to any part of it. The exchange of horses above spoken of took place before the difficulty between Henry Burgess and Peter Mausey.

Question: At the time you heard Peter Mausey say he would not make a deed to H. Burgess for the land did he say he was very intemperate & that if he made him a deed he would run through & spend it?

Answer: I think P. Mausey remarked to me that H. Burgess was in the habit of drinking too much, & that he had not complied with his contract. I knew H. Burgess at the time, & I considered him very intemperate.

The response of Peter Mauzy, 10 Sept. 1839:

...This respondent denies most positively that he ever made a promise to the said Henry Burgess decd. to make him a deed to the said fifty acres of land in his life time or at any other time to any of his heirs or any other person. Your respondent does not know how it is that the said complainants can make allegations such as are contained in their Bill. He does not know how such things could have entered into their minds. This respondent never dreamed of any such thing & he had no idea that in his old age any such thing was to come to pass to disturb him in the peaceful possession of the little farm he has honestly labored & paid for with his own means & no other. He does not know with what other design the complainants could have filed their Bill against him but to harass and distress him & he does not know what evidence they may produce to sustain their claim. He charges, however, that the said complainants have no right whatever to maintain any such a suit against him: that none of the matters of their said Bill in relation [to] the pretended agreement between Henry Burgess & this respondent are true. He never made any such agreement; he never received any consideration from said Burgess to pay to Fowler for land, and the whole claim set up by the said complainants is false and fraudulent....—Peter Mauzy.

[William (I)[1], Edward (I)[2], William (II)[3], Henry (I)[4]]

WILLIAM BURGESS
(1798-1847)
OF FLEMING COUNTY, KENTUCKY

5a. **William (VII)** *[son of Henry (I)].* Born 1798 in Bourbon Co., KY. Married Julia Ann "Juliann" Bradshaw about 1831, probably in Bath Co., KY (she was born about 1815 in Bath Co., KY, the daughter of James and Mary Bradshaw, and sister of James Franklin Bradshaw, and apparently died in Indiana between 1860-70; see *Bath Co. Deed Book #N*, p. 284-287, dated 12 Aug. 1844, for the division of her father's estate, in which "Juliann Burgess, late Juliann Bradshaw, received Lot No. 3," and p. 322-323 of the same book for the deed in which William Burgess and Juliann his wife sell the land, and *Deed Book #S*, p. 157-158, in which "Julian Burgess wife of William Burgess deceased" of Parke Co., IN sold her portion of her mother's estate to her brother, James F. Bradshaw). First mentioned in the records of Fleming Co. on 23 Mar. 1814, when he was apprenticed to Robert Andrews to learn the art of tanning (*Order Book #C*, p. 417), and was then discharged in November of that year (*Ibid.*, p. 446). Listed in the Fleming Co. tax records in 1819 living with his mother, and separately from 1821-24, 1839-42, and 1845-47. Listed in the 1830 census for Bath Co., KY living unmarried with John Busbey, and in 1840 in Fleming Co. with one son under five, one between 5-10, two daughters under five, and one between 5-10. Moved to Bath Co. in 1842 on the death of his father-in-law, and was appointed constable there between 1842-44 (*Order Book #D*, p. 58). William Burgess was a farmer in Bath and Fleming Cos., KY. According to documents attached to a lawsuit filed in Fleming Co. by Juliann Burgess on 27 May 1854 (*Fleming Co. Case #12403*) to remove a squatter from the Burgess land, with depositions taken from William's two brothers, William died on 16 Sept. 1847 in Phillips Co., AR at the home of John McCloud, with a letter in his pocket from his brother, Wash Burgess. William had instructed Wash by mail in June of that year to move his family from their home in Fleming Co. to a plot next to his brother John's home in Parke Co., IN. Juliann is listed in the 1850 census of Green Township, Parke Co., IN next to John H. Burgess, and in 1860 in Russell Township, Putnam Co., IN, but has not been found in 1870 (however, a Julia A. Cast, wife of William Cast, born about 1823 in KY, appears in the 1870 census for Kirklin Township, Clinton Co., IN with her husband's son, Silas E. [born 1859 in OH]).

The Children of William Burgess:

6a. **Son.** Born about 1831 in Bath Co., KY; died between 1840-50.

6b. **Penelope (I).** Born about 1833 in Bath Co., KY. Sold her land in Fleming Co. in 1858. Married John R. Vancleave on 24 Nov. 1853 in Parke Co., IN. Not listed in the 1860 Indiana census index. She is *not* the "Lettia" Vancleve (born Apr. 1832 in KY) who married John S. Vancleve (born Dec. 1830 in IN), and is listed in the 1900 census for Vigo Co., IN.

6c. **James Franklin (I).** Born 12 Mar. 1835 in Bath Co., KY. See below for full entry.

6d. **Elizabeth P. (I).** Born about 1838 in Bath Co., KY. Living with her mother in 1850 (and also as a servant with Alexander Dougherty), but has not been found in 1860. She should not be confused with her cousin, Elizabeth F. Burgess, who married Jesse Hurst in Putnam Co., IN in 1860. Elizabeth Burgess died or married between 1850-60.

6e. **Minerva.** Born about 1840 in Fleming Co., KY; not listed in the 1850 census, but is mentioned in an 1857 lawsuit filed in Fleming Co., Co.

6f. **Norcissa "Nora."** Born about 1843 in Bath Co., KY. Listed in the 1850-60 censuses with her mother.

6g. **Lucinda (II) "Lucy."** Born about 1846 in Fleming Co., KY. Listed in the 1850-60 censuses living with her mother. Married Henry Cain on 28 Sept. 1865 in Clinton Co., IN (he was born about 1844 in OH), and had children: *James F(ranklin?)* (born Feb. 1870 in Clinton Co., married Cora Stewart on 18 Nov. 1891 in Clinton Co., and had children: Herbert [born 9 Nov. 1899 in Clinton Co., died May 1983 at Marion, IN]). Listed in the 1870-80 censuses for Kirklin Township, Clinton Co., IN, but has not been found in 1900-10; in 1870 Malinda Wells (born 1862 in IN) is working for them as a servant, and in 1880 Laura M. Johnson (born 1868 in IN, parents born KY) is also a servant.

JULIA ANN BURGESS VS. HICKERSON BELT

(Fleming Co., Kentucky Court Case #12403, 27 May 1854-March 1857)

To the Honorable Judge of the Fleming Circuit Court—your Petitioner would respectfully state that she was married to one William Burgess (now deceased) and that her and her said husband, William Burgess, formerly resided in the County of Fleming and State of Kentucky, and during coverture, and while residing in this state, said William Burgess, was seized and possessed of a certain tract of land in the county and state aforesaid, containing about 85 acres, one rood, and twenty five poles. She further states that said tract of land was deeded to her said husband, William Burgess, by Samuel Mers and wife on the 7th of Feby. 1842, for the consideration therein expressed—and said deed was duly acknowledged and recorded in the clerk's office of the Fleming County Court on the 22nd of Feby. 1842. She further states that her said husband has been dead about six years, that he died seized thereof, and that she has been credibly informed and believes that he died in the state of Arkansas. She states that said land above mentioned was paid for with her own separate money, and that dower has not been assigned to her, in the lands of her deceased husband, nor anything in lieu of dower. She further states that one Hickerson Belt, as she has been informed and believes, is in the possession of the tract of land above named, and has been using and enjoying the profits of the same. She also states that she has been deprived of the profits and rents of said dower interest, which is reasonably worth $100 per annum. Wherefore she prays that an account be taken of said rents and profits, and that she be decreed the same. She prays that the court will decree her dower in the said tract of land above named, and that a commissioner be appointed to assign and allot to her, said dower interest. She files herewith a certified copy of the deed above referred to, and makes it a part hereof. She prays for all appropriate and for general relief, as in duty bound, etc.—Trimble, for complainant.

Hickison Belt's response on 1 Sept. 1854:

Personally and of his own knowledge he knows nothing of their many allegations in the plaintiff's petition, but from the very best information he has been able to obtain by diligent examination and inquiry of the nearest relatives of William Burgess (of whom plaintiff claims to be the widow) is that the said William is still living herein and is not as alleged dead, he is from all the information he can get induced to believe that the plaintiff is not and never was the lawful wife of Wm. Burgess, and he therefore denies that William Burgess is dead and denies that the plaintiff is or ever was his lawful wife...

Deposition of John H. Burgess taken March 28, 1855, Parke Co., IN:

(First) To the best of my knowledge they was married in the year of 1832, the witness further states that he has visited the house of the said Burgess several times and that he recognized the said Julian as his lawful wife and also they lived the State of Kentucky about fourteen years & four months. The witness further states that to the best of his recollection, from letters only, I can say (viz.) from letter from the administrator that he died in Arkansas, Phillips County, Eight miles from Hellona, between the first of September & middle of October at the house of John McClouds, in 1847, also that I have received letter from the attorney of McClouds stating that he was attorney to settle up the estate of the said William Burgess deceased for said McCloud.—John H. Burgess.

Deposition of George W. Burgess taken March 28, 1855, Parke Co., IN:

(Second) The witness states to the best of his recollection that he has been at the said William Burgess' house frequently, and he recognized the said Julian as his lawful wife, the witness states that he has no particular recollection how long they lived in Kentucky or what time they was married, only he employed me by letter to move his wife Juliann Burgess and children from Kentucky to Indiana, which I done accordingly in the month of June 1847, the witness further states about the death of the said William Burgess, he only states what he knows from letter from the administrator that he died in Arkansas, Phillips County, eight miles from Hellona, between the first of September and the middle of October at the house of John McClouds in 1847....—George W. Burgess.

Deposition of Mark Haman taken March 28, 1855, Parke Co., IN:

(Third) To the best of my recollection I have all reason to believe that in regard to the marriage of William Burgess and Julian Burgess was married and lived together as husband and wife but no knowledge how long they lived in Kentucky. The witness further states that to his knowledge that George W. Burgess as I understood by request from said William Burgess moved his wife & children to Indiana. The witness further states that in regard to the death of the said William Burgess I read a letter directed to George W. Burgess from John McCloud stating that a man died at his house and I found a letter in his possession directed to William Burgess from George W. Burgess, Portland Mills, Indiana. The witness further states that I read a letter from L. Freeman Smith stating that John McCloud is administrator of William Burgess deceased who died (intestate) at the house of McCloud on the 16th day of September 1847.—Mark Haman.

[William (I)[1], Edward (I)[2], William (II)[3], Henry (I)[4], William (VII)[5]]

JAMES F. BURGESS, SR.
(1835-1928)

OF CLINTON COUNTY, INDIANA

6c. **James Franklin (I)** *[son of William (VII)].* Born 12 Mar. 1835 in Bath Co., KY. He may have married Elizabeth Y. Tippen on 8 Apr. 1863 in Putnam Co., IN (if so, she died before 1869). Married Sarah M. Bogan on 2 Mar. 1869 in Clinton Co., IN (she was born 25 June 1838 in OH, and died on 28 Dec. 1905 in Clinton Co., IN). Listed in the 1870-1910 censuses for Kirklin Township, Clinton Co., and in 1920 living with his son. James F. Burgess was a farmer in Putnam and Clinton Cos., IN. He died on 13 Jan. 1928 at Kirklin, IN, aged 92 years, and is buried with his wife in the Bogan Cemetery.

The Children of James F. Burgess:

7a. **Cenia Inez.** Listed variously as Inez F. or Ernestine. Born Mar. 1870 in Clinton Co., IN. Married Bert O. Corey (or Cory) on 21 Nov. 1894 in Clinton Co., and had at least the following children: *Carrie B.* (born 8 July 1896 in IN, married ___ Irby, and died Mar. 1986 at Whitestown, Boone Co., IN); *Frederick* (born 15 Jan. 1899 in IN, and died Jan. 1973 at Frankfort, Clinton Co., IN). Listed in the 1900 census for Clinton Township, Boone Co., IN, but has not been found in 1920.

7b. **(James) Franklin (II).** Born 27 Mar. 1875 in Clinton Co., IN. See below for full entry.

FRANK BURGESS OF CLINTON CO., INDIANA
[James Franklin (I)[6]]

7b. **(James) Franklin (II)** *[son of James Franklin (I)].* Born 27 Mar. 1875 in Clinton Co., IN. Married Cora Belle Hawkins on 23 Apr. 1898 in Clinton Co. (she was born 7 Feb. 1880, and died 5 May 1951). Listed in the 1900-20 censuses for Clinton Co., IN, and in the 1917 draft list for Clinton Co. Frank Burgess worked as a lumber yard manager in Kirklin, IN. He died there on 26 May 1965, aged 90 years, and is buried in the Crown View Cemetery.

8a. **(Milo) Claire.** Born 17 Jan. 1899 in Clinton Co., IN. See below for full entry.

8b. **John Floyd.** Born 25 Nov. 1901 in Clinton Co., IN; died there on 10 Dec. 1902, and is buried with his parents.

8c. **(Bernard) Ray.** Born 8 Dec. 1903 in Clinton Co., IN; died there on 11 Sept. 1904, and is buried with his parents.

8d. **Bert Bowers.** Born 15 Apr. 1907 in Clinton Co., IN. Married Betty Warriner on 16 Feb. 1938. Bert Burgess worked for 25 years for Delco Ramey before retiring. He currently lives at Anderson, IN.

8e. **Beulah Grace.** Born 25 July 1909 in Clinton Co., IN. Married Ross R. Baber on 29 Oct. 1933 (he died 31 Mar. 1950), and had children: *John William* (born 30 Nov. 1945); *Jane Marie* (born 25 Dec. 1947). A contributor to this book, she lives in the old family home at Kirklin, IN.

8f. **(Aletha) Lavene.** Born 4 Aug. 1912 in Clinton Co., IN. Married Steward Brown on 6 Oct. 1937, and had children: *Cora Sue* (born 6 June 1941). She lives in Hawaii.

CLAIRE BURGESS OF MARION CO., INDIANA
[James Franklin (I)[6], James Franklin (II)[7]]

8a. **(Milo) Claire** *[son of James Franklin (II)].* Born 17 Jan. 1899 (1898 in the Social Security and draft records) in Clinton Co., IN. Married Mary Elizabeth White on 25 Jan. 1930 (she died on 21 Dec. 1969). Listed in the 1917 draft register of Clinton Co., IN. Claire Burgess was a salesman in Indianapolis, Marion Co., IN. He died there on 3 Jan. 1970, and is buried in the Crown Hill Cemetery.

9a. **(James) Patrick.** Born 17 Mar. 1937 in Clinton Co., IN. Married Helen Gladys Early (div.); married secondly Alice Ann Stiles about 1967. Pat Burgess is a claims adjustor for Allstate Insurance Co. at Indianapolis, Marion Co., IN.

10a. **Sonja Lee.** Born 3 Feb. 1957 at Indianapolis, IN. Married Jeff Corlette.
10b. **Anthony Lenn.** Born 9 Mar. 1958 at Indianapolis, IN. He lives at San Francisco, CA.
10c. **Bryce Patrick.** Born 2 June 1968 at Indianapolis, IN.

9b. **William Edward (III).** Born 18 Sept. 1940 in Clinton Co., IN. Bill Burgess works in a manufacturing plant at Seattle, WA.
9c. **Barbara Louise (I).** Born 4 Dec. 1942 in Clinton Co., IN. Married Melvin Scott, and had children: *Pamela Lynn* (born 23 July 1960); *Breck Edward* (born 14 May 1969).

John Henry BURGESS *(1801-1891) and Martha "Patsy"* LAWSON BURGESS *(1807-1887)*

[William (I)[1], Edward (I)[2], William (II)[3], Henry (I)[4]]

JOHN HENRY BURGESS
(1801-1891)

OF BLUE EARTH COUNTY, MINNESOTA

5b. **John Henry (I)** *[son of Henry (I)].* Born 15 July 1801 in Bourbon Co., KY (so indicated in the patrons' list of *An Illustrated Historical Atlas State of Minnesota, 1874* [Chicago: A. T. Andreas, 1874, p. 387]). Married Martha "Patsy" Lawson on 18 Feb. 1824 in Fleming Co. (she was born 11 May 1807 in Fleming Co., KY, the daughter of Jacob Lawson [1763-1851] and Sarah "Sallie" Pollard or Rice [1770-1842], and died 30 Sept. 1887 in Blue Earth Co., MN). John Burgess is first listed in the Fleming Co. tax records in 1824, moving to Rush Co., IN shortly after his marriage. He returned to Fleming Co. in 1827, and is recorded there on the tax lists between 1828-31. In 1832 he moved his family to Green Township, Parke Co., IN near the small town of Portland Mills, on the border with Putnam Co., where he farmed and ran stock; he sold his land in Fleming Co. on 1 Oct. 1833 (*Deed Book #R*, p. 53), being listed as a resident of Parke Co. For several decades before the Civil War he operated a horse trading and shipping business with his brother George between Kentucky and Indiana. He helped found the first Christian Church at Portland Mills, IN in 1839, with Rev. John M. Harris as pastor. He is listed in the 1830 census for Fleming Co., in 1840-50 in Green Township, Parke Co., in 1860 just across the border in Putnam Co., and in the 1865-85 state and federal censuses for Blue Earth Co., Minnesota. He also appears on the 1851 tax list for Green Township, Parke Co.

In the fall of 1856 John H. Burgess moved his family to Blue Earth Co. by wagon train, a trip that took 42 days through untamed wilderness, settling five miles east of the present-day community of Mankato. Northeast of his farm his children helped found the small community of Burgess Mills (later renamed Eagle Lake for that nearby body of water). Attacks from the Sioux Indians became so fierce that a year later John and most of his family (except for sons William and Jacob) moved back to Putnam Co., IN, across the county line from their old farm. When the Indians had been subdued, he returned to Blue Earth Co. in the fall of 1860. He died on his farm, one mile southeast of Eagle Lake, on 20 July 1891, five days past his 90th birthday, and was buried next to his wife in the Burgess Cemetery, the land for which had been donated by him to the Christian Church at Eagle Lake (which still maintains it). John's obituary mentions seven surviving children out of eleven at the time of his death, but his wife's obituary (in 1887) mentions that she was the mother of fifteen children, of whom nine survived at that date.

In 1972 Cornelia DuBois wrote: "My mother [Harrison Monroe's daughter, Florence Burgess Andrews] told me of visiting the Lawson family in Flemingsburg, Kentucky, when she was 16 years old—in 1896. They had a big plantation and owned slaves. She said that her grandfather, John Henry, had run off with Patsy (Martha) Lawson when she was very young, probably 14 or 15, against her parents' wishes. They had fled on horseback to be married, and had taken a slave with them, who was Patsy's maid or mammy. I have the Lawson family Bible."

The Children of John H. Burgess:

6a. **William Henry (I).** Born 10 Jan. 1825 in Rush Co., IN. See below for full entry.
6b. **George Washington (V) "Wash."** Born 24 Aug. 1826 in Marion Co., IN. See below for full entry.
6c. **John Marion (I).** Born 25 Mar. 1828 in Fleming Co., KY. See below for full entry.
6d. **Lucinda Jane "Cindy."** Born 9 May 1830 (or 31 Jan. 1830, according to her family Bible record) in Fleming Co., KY. Married Thomas Reeder on 29 May 1851 in Parke Co., IN (he was born 29 July 1828, son of David Reeder and Nancy McNeal, and died 1880), and had children: *Mary J.* (born 1853 in IN); *Martha Marie "Mattie"* (born 24 Nov. 1854 at Portland Mills, IN, died 24 Jan. 1871 at Eagle Lake, MN, buried Burgess Cemetery); *Samuel W.* (born 1857 in IN); *David H.* (born 1859 in IN, became a physician, and was living in 1920); *Pheba A.* (born 1861 in IL); *Leona J.* (born 1863 in MN);

Thomas F. (born 1865 in MN); *(Dora) Belle* (born 1867 in MN); *Sarah D.* (born July 1869 in MN); *Laura* (born 1871 in MN); *John Wesley* (born 12 May 1872 in MN, married Grace Anna Hussey on 5 June 1907 in Polk Co., OR, and died 24 July 1964 at Eugene, OR, having had children: Lucinda May [married Bert Edwin Girton {he was born 19 Feb. 1896, and died 3 Dec. 1989 at Eugene, OR]); *Charles* (born 1876 in IA). Listed in the 1860 census for Rockville, Parke Co., IN, and from 1865-1900 in the federal and state censuses for Blue Earth Co., MN (in 1900 with her son-in-law, Elijah Pressnail). Lucinda Reeder died on 2 Oct. 1906 (or 4 Oct. 1906, according to her family record) in Blue Earth Co., and is buried in the Burgess Cemetery.

6e. **Jacob Lawson (I) "Jake."** Born 26 Jan. 1832 in Fleming Co., KY. See below for full entry.

6f. **Thomas Fleming.** Born 5 Feb. 1833 at Portland Mills, IN. See below for full entry.

6g. **Monroe Harrison.** Born about 1835 at Portland Mills, IN; died there as an infant, and is buried in the Mt. Pisgah Cemetery, Putnam Co., IN. Order and dates not confirmed.

6h. **James Sylvester "Vest."** Born Oct. 1837 at Portland Mills, IN. See below for full entry.

6i. **Harrison Monroe "Hack."** Born 20 Feb. 1840 at Portland Mills, IN. See below for full entry.

6j. **Martha A(nn?) (II).** Born 3 Dec. 1842 at Portland Mills, IN. Married Nelson W. Dickerson Jr. about 1861 (he died within the year), and had children: *Nelson W. III* (born 1862 at Eagle Lake, married Carrie ___, and died 1932); married secondly Freeman A. Cate on 30 Sept. 1866 in Blue Earth Co., MN (he was born 1836 in New Hampshire, served in the Union Army during the Civil War and was postmaster of Spier, MN, remarried Mary A. ___, and is listed with her in the 1885 census for Blue Earth Co.), and had children: *Moses P.* (born 22 Sept. 1867, died 22 May 1874, buried Burgess Cemetery); *John H(enry?)* (born 1870, married, and had children: Lola M. [born 6 July 1907, married ___ Starbuck, died 4 May 1989 at Forestville, MD]); *Gilbert R. "Bertie"* (born 1872, died 8 Sept. 1874, buried Burgess Cemetery); *Lois A.* (born 11 June 1876, died 15 Oct. 1880, buried Burgess Cemetery); *Lillian* (born Jan. 1878, married Tany Bahlky); *Freeman A. Jr.* (born July 1880). Listed in the 1865 census with her father, and in the 1870-80 state and federal censuses for Blue Earth Co., MN. Martha Cate died of consumption on 3 Jan. 1881 in Blue Earth Co., MN, and is buried in the Burgess Cemetery.

6k. **Barton Warren.** He was named for Barton Warren Stone (1772-1844), founder of the Christian Church. Born about 1844 at Portland Mills, IN; died there in 1848, and is buried in the Mt. Pisgah Cemetery.

Miranda Pickle wrote to her brother, George Washington Burgess, on 2 Sept. 1915, saying (among other things): "We have so much to be thankful for. We are both quite well, and the weather is fine. We have a nice comfortable home, and are surrounded by splendid neighbors; and, we have five of our children right here in town [Eagle Lake]. The rest of our children are scattered, but are all doing well....You wanted to know who lives on your old place. Well, there isn't any house on your old place, so there isn't anyone living there. There is not a stick of timber or building. Our son-in-law, John Cummins, owns it, and he could sell it for $150 per acre, but he won't take it. They have a fine, $3000 house in town, so they live here.

"And as for the children's graves [the infants of George Washington Burgess], they are kept nice and green, but ought to have gravestones, and they look bare and so forgotten. The rest of the family all have beautiful tombstones, and there are a great many beautiful monuments there [in the Burgess Cemetery]. Emma Wagoner has been here since school closed, she and her daughter Ruth, but they went back to Minneapolis Tuesday, as Ruth goes to school there, and Emma has a position there. You wanted to know about Harry Burgess; well, we don't know much about him, as he hasn't been here for a great many years. He is somewhere in Florida, don't know what he is doing. He did teach school for a while. He and his wife parted. She lives with their oldest son, Hugh Burgess, in Aberdeen, South Dakota. He is quite well off, he is an engineer on the railroad, he has a wife and two children. Their [Harry's] two girls are married, and live in Omaha, Nebraska. The oldest one [Jennie] married a master bricklayer, the other [Zazel] married a druggist. The girls were both trained nurses, and got big wages....

"Gabe was seventy-three the 18th of July, and I will be seventy next May the 7th, but we are real young. Well, Wash, we would like to do as you say, that is, to come and see you, and would like to come in our car, but it would be too tiresome for Dad to drive so far, so guess we won't come this Fall. We talk of going back to California again this Winter, but are not sure whether we will go or not. Brother John's son John was here and spent last Summer with us, and we had a fine time. He is begging us to come out there this Winter, if we don't go West. Maybe we will go down to Indiana for Christmas. I wonder if you are not getting tired of my rigamarole. I will have to stop and get dinner pretty soon. Gabe is playing the fiddle, and I wish you could hear him. So you will just have to come. I was so glad to hear from you and to hear that your children are so pleasantly located now. I hope you are both reasonably well and will write again soon. I forgot to tell you Mr. Braden died two years ago, Mrs. Braden lives with her son, and she is real thin and looks bad. I think you know their son married our daughter Ella; they live just across the street from us. Lots of love, and God bless you both: your sister and brother, G. A. & M. J. Pickle."

6l. **Miranda Jane "Nan" or "Mandy."** Born 7 May 1846 at Portland Mills, IN. Married Gabriel A. Pickle on 22 Mar. 1866 at Eagle Lake, MN (he was born 18 July 1842 at Fincastle, Putnam Co., IN, son of Carolyn [or Carl] Roshelle Pickle [originally Bickle] and Nancy Bundraunt, enlisted in Co. B., 54th Indiana Infantry, Union Army, during the Civil War, attaining the rank of Corporal, moved to Eagle Lake early in 1866, and died on 24 Oct. 1924 at Long Beach, CA, being survived by twelve children), and had children, some of whom spelled their name Pickel:

Alvah G. "Orvie" PICKLE. Born 1 (or 31) Jan. 1867 in Blue Earth Co., MN, and died 5 June 1867, buried Burgess Cemetery.

Carolyn B. "Carrie" PICKLE. Born 22 Mar. 1869 in Blue Earth Co., MN, married Fred Ingwerson of Mason City, IA; married two other times.

(Cora) Alice PICKLE. Born 17 Mar. 1870 in Blue Earth Co., MN, married John Cummins, and had children: *Donna*; *Marion*. She died at Mankato, MN.

John A. PICKLE. Born 24 Oct. 1871 in Blue Earth Co., MN, married Sadie ___, and had children: *Vern* (killed on a roller coaster at Long Beach, CA); *Jack* (had three children, and died at Long Beach); *Thelma*; *Herbert* (born 1905, accidentally shot on 2 Sept. 1910).

Henry V. PICKLE. Born 11 Mar. 1873 in Blue Earth Co., MN, married Bergine ___, had four daughters, and died at Mankato, MN.

Carl D. PICKEL. Born 14 Dec. 1874 in Blue Earth Co., MN, married Olive F. ___ (she died on 10 Apr. 1957), had one adopted child (Olive's niece): *Margaret*. Carl Pickle was a school teacher. He died on 5 Dec. 1954 at Long Beach, CA.

Bertha "Queen" PICKLE. Born 30 May 1876 in Blue Earth Co., MN, married ___ Cook, had two children who died young, and died at Mankato, MN.

Ella PICKLE (twin). Born 14 Feb. 1879 in Blue Earth Co., MN, married Clarence Braden, had children: *Merle*; *LaRene*. She died Feb. 1974 at Honolulu, HI (or Charles City, IA), aged 95 years.

Stella "Estelle" PICKLE (twin). Born 14 Feb. 1879 at Eagle Lake, married William Boegan, and secondly Charles Bryant, died 1942 in a train accident at Chicago, IL, buried Burgess Cemetery.

Charlotte Martha PICKLE. Born 21 Jan. 1881 at Eagle Lake, MN, married John Francis Bradish on 27 Dec. 1904 at Waseca, MN (he was born 23 Aug. 1882 at Janesville, MN, son of Col. William Peter Bradish and Mary McAweeney, and died on 16 Aug. 1963 at Van Nuys, CA); Charlotte died on 24 Dec. 1964 at Van Nuys, CA, having had children:

Glenis (married Arthur Amann [dec.], and had children: John Arthur [married Beryl Bevins, and had children: Arthur; Julie]; Nancy Ellen [married Dean Nordquist {div.}, and had children: Sandra Kay {married Arthur Libby}; Laura {died at age sixteen}; Martha]); *Verna Estelle* (born 21 Jan. 1909 at Cobden, MN, married Preston Daniel Dorsett on 29 Mar. 1928 at St. Cloud, MN [he was born 9 Aug. 1907 at Salt Lake City, UT, son of Daniel Hanks Dorsett and Marie Matilda Peterson, and died 16 Jan. 1968 at Minneapolis, MN], and died 27 Oct. 1979 at Minneapolis, having had children: Marjorie Elaine [married George Minarik {dec. <he was born 6 June 1972, and died Feb. 1982 at Minneapolis>}, and had children: Julie Ann {born 12 June 1958, married Chris Kotyk, and died July 1992, having had children: Brian; Megan}; Jean Elaine {married Scott Cates, and had children: Danielle Nicole}]; John Preston [married Mary Clemens, and had children: Sharon {stepchild; married and had three children, and died}; Susan {stepchild; married and divorced, with one child}; Anthony]; Charlotte Ann [born 16 Nov. 1940 at Minneapolis, MN, married George Dwight Church on 24 June 1961 {he was born 22 May 1937 at Norwich, CT}, and had children: Matthew Dorsett {married Kathy Lynn Schieb, and had children: Kimberly Anne}; Terri Lee {married R. Eric Lumpkin}; Joseph Mather]); *Queen Anne* (married Marion Haguewood [he was born 6 Feb. 1913, and died 27 Nov. 1988 at Van Nuys, CA]); *(Charlotte) Elaine* (married Neil Bullington, and had children: Brad; Diane [dec.]).

Frederick PICKLE. Born 11 Mar. 1883 in Blue Earth Co., MN, married Cora Swartz, and died childless at Chicago, IL.

Clarke M. PICKEL. Born 23 June 1885 in Blue Earth Co., MN, married Ellen "Nell" ___ (she died on 8 June 1946), had one adopted son: *Jack*. Clarke Pickel worked as a salesman, and died on 13 Oct. 1943 at Long Beach, CA.

Carmen PICKLE. Born 16 Apr. 1890 in Blue Earth Co., MN, married Arthur Schuyler, had children: *Corrine* (who married ___ O'Leary-Dallings), and died at Long Beach, CA.

Miranda and Gabriel PICKLE are listed in the 1870-1900 state and federal censuses for Blue Earth Co. They originally developed a mill with Jake Burgess southeast of Eagle Lake, and then farmed in LeRay Township. They moved to Long Beach, CA in 1921, after visiting the area for several winters previously. Both were members of the Christian Church. Miranda Pickle died on 17 Feb. 1932 at Long Beach, Los Angeles Co., CA, the last of her brothers and sisters to die. Both are buried in the Burgess Cemetery, Eagle Lake, MN.

Cornelia DuBois wrote on 3 Dec. 1972: "I remember making a visit to Eagle Lake to see Mother's aunt, Martha Pickle, who was the sister of my grandfather Burgess. She and Carl [sic] Pickle had 16 children, including two sets of twins and one set of triplets. She was an old lady and her children grown when we went to see her, in her white frame house—rather small, it seemed, for all those children—in Eagle Lake."

6m. **Child.** Born and died about 1848 at Portland Mills, IN.

6n. **Sarah Isabell.** Born 15 Nov. 1849 at Portland Mills, IN. Married Franklin W. Simonds on 13 June 1867 in Blue Earth Co. (he was born 21 May 1839 at Stowe, VT, son of John A. Simonds and Harriet Sanborn, worked as a traffic manager for Western Union Telegraph Co., married secondly Florence ___, and died 15 June 1929 at Topeka, KS, buried Topeka Cemetery), and had children: *John F.* (born 18 Dec. 1868 in Blue Earth Co., MN, died 15 Apr. 1940 at Glendale, CA); *Minnie M.* (born 26 May 1870 in Blue Earth Co., MN, died there 18 Feb. 1872, buried Burgess Cemetery); *Stella A.* (born 30 Sept. 1872 in NE, died unmarried on 27 June 1916 at Topeka, KS); *Eva G.* (born 24 Nov. 1874, died 29 July 1876); *Charles Loyl* (born 29 Oct. 1879 in IA, died 12 Apr. 1952 at Denver, CO); *Georgia Belle* (born 19 Apr. 1883 at Delta, IA, died 2 Sept. 1947); *Ray W.* (born 5 Aug. 1886 in IA); *Ted H. "Freddy"* (born 14 Nov. 1888 in IA, married, and had at least one son: Frank W. "Buster" [died as an infant on 24 June 1920 at Rock Island, IL]). Listed in the 1870 census for Blue Earth Co., MN. The Simondses later moved to Keokuk Co., IA, where they are listed in the 1880-1900 censuses for Delta City, Warren Township, and then to Topeka, KS. Sarah Simonds died on 15 Jan. 1909 at Topeka, KS; Frank Simonds is listed there in the 1910 census. A great-granddaughter, Mary A. Shields (granddaughter of Charles Loyl Simonds), lives at Anchorage, AK, and has contributed greatly to this book.

6o. **Edmund (II).** Born about 1852 at Portland Mills, IN; died there on 29 Jan. 1855, and is buried in the Mt. Pisgah Cemetery, Putnam Co., IN.

DEATH OF J. H. BURGESS, SR.

"Last Monday evening about nine o'clock, J. H. Burgess, Esq., one of the oldest and most respected citizens of Blue Earth County, quietly and peacefully passed away, at his home in Mankato Township. He was born in Kentucky, July 15th, 1801. He came to this county in the fall of 1855 [actually 1856], from Indiana, locating upon a farm near the present village of Eagle Lake, engaging in agricultural pursuits, and always made it his home. Mr. Burgess was a thoroughly honest and conscientious man, and during a residence of 36 years we do not believe that there is a man living or dead who could charge him with a dishonorable or even a mean act. His word was always esteemed as good as the best of bonds, and retired and unpretentious in manner, his presence always commanded the greatest respect. In his personal dealings with his fellow men he was the soul of honor. We recall an instance of many that from time to time came to our knowledge which illustrates the character of the man. One season being more successful in raising potatoes than farmers generally and having a surplus, he was applied to sell some to a neighbor. The prevailing price was 75 cents per bushel, and when asked his price he said 40 cents per bushel. He was told that they were worth 75 cents. He admitted that they sold for that price, but said that 40 cents per bushel allowed him a fair return for his labor, and would not sell at more than that price, adding that when potatoes were 25 cents or less, he could feed his surplus. This is characteristic of his dealings with his fellow men, and while he was a man of pronounced views, which he did not hesitate to express when called for, they were those of the highest sense of honor, integrity, and justice. Grandpa Burgess was the highest type of a good citizen and a true christian. He raised a family of eleven children—7 sons and 4 daughters—and seven remain to cherish his memory and enjoy the priceless legacy of a pure and well spent life. His wife died September 20th, 1887, and a few weeks ago he buried his youngest son. He was ill last spring, but it was his desire to pass his 90th birthday, and this reached he was ready and anxious to pass away. His desires were speadily gratified—without pain or suffering, he died peacefully and quietly, like the gradual going out of a feeble and flickering flame."—*Mankato Review*, 28 July 1891.

THE WILL OF JOHN H. BURGESS

(Blue Earth County Will Book #B, p. 278-279)

Know all men by these presents that I, John H. Burgess, of the Township of Mankato, in the County of Blue Earth, State of Minnesota, being in feeble health and of sound and disposing mind and memory, do make and publish this my last will and testament, hereby revoking all former wills by me at any time heretofore made. It is my will that all my just debts and funeral expenses be paid and discharged by my executors out of my estate as soon as conveniently may be after my decease. And I leave the charge of my funeral to the direction of the my said executors. I give devise and dispose of my entire real and personal [estate] save shall be necessary to pay all of my just debts and funeral expenses in the following manner, to wit:

It is my will that all my estate be equally divided share and share alike among my children now living and the children of those now dead, except—as is hereinafter directed. It is my will and I do direct that to the children of Martha A. Cate my daughter the sum of fifty dollars each to be paid to John Cate and Freeman Cate and Lillian Cate and Nelson W. Dickerson, to be held by the executors hereinafter named until the said minors shall have arrived at lawful age or shall be lawfully married in the meantime. The said account to be loaned at not less rate than the legal rate of interest, with good security, and said children to have the benefit of said interest.

To William H. Burgess my son fifty dollars. To Harrison M. Burgess my son, one dollar. To George W. Burgess my son, one eleventhh of all my estate. To John M. Burgess my son two hundred dollars. To Jacob L. Burgess my son, to his children one eleventh of my estate. To Lucinda J. Reeder my daughter two hundred and fifty dollars. To Thomas F. Burgess my son two hundred dollars. To James S. Burgess two hundred dollars. To Maranda J. Pickle my daughter one dollar. To Sarah Isabell Simonds my daughter one eleventh of my estate.

I further will and direct if there is any more of my estate than has been mentioned that it be equally divided among my living children and the heirs of my children that are dead. And lastly I do nominate and appoint my son Harrison M. Burgess and my son William H. Burgess and Charles F. Wagoner of the Town of Mankato Blue Earth County and State of Minnesota to be the executors of this my last will and testament. Signed sealed and published and declared this 2nd day of April in the year of our Lord one thousand and eight hundred and ninety one.

John H. Burgess his mark

Signed sealed published and delivered by the said John H. Burgess as and for his last will and testament in the presence of us who at his request and in his presence and in the presence of each other have subscribed our names as witnesses. Gabriel A. Pickle, Emma Wagoner.

The Obituary of Martha "Patsy" Burgess

"Mrs. J. H. Burgess died at her residence in Mankato Township last week and was buried at Eagle Lake on Sunday, her funeral being largely attended by her old and sympathising friends. She was born in Fleming County, Kentucky in 1807, and was in her 81st year. She was married to Mr. Burgess, who survives her, in 1824. They moved to Indiana, and came to this county in the fall of 1856, having resided in this county 31 years, excepting three years during the Indian Wars, commencing in 1882 [sic; actually 1857].

"Her death was the result of blood poison, originating from a very triveal [sic] cause. Some 5 or 6 weeks ago she was preparing dinner for a company of 15 persons and in digging potatoes in her garden pricked her hand with the sharp needles on a pumpkin vine. A painful sore followed, she suffering intense pain for 5 weeks, resulting in blood poison. She was the mother of 15 children, 9 of whom are living and all but 2 of whom were present at the funeral.

"The services were conducted by Rev. Stevenson of the Christian Church, assisted by the Rev. Hawley of the M.E. Church. Mrs. Burgess was a lady highly esteemed by a large circle of acquaintances and her death is a sad affliction for her venerable husband and family."—*Mankato Review*, 4 Oct. 1887.

REV. WILLIAM HENRY BURGESS
(1825-1904)

[William (I)[1], Edward (I)[2], William (II)[3], Henry (I)[4], John Henry (I)[5]]

REV. WILLIAM HENRY BURGESS
(1825-1904)
OF BLUE EARTH COUNTY, MINNESOTA

6a. **William Henry (I)** *[son of John Henry (I)].* Born 10 Jan. 1825 in Rush Co., IN (as indicated in the patrons' list of *An Illustrated Historical Atlas State of Minnesota, 1874* [Chicago: A. T. Andreas, 1874, p. 387]), or at Crawfordsville, IN, according to his obituary. Married Eliza A. Bettis on 10 Oct. 1845 in Parke Co., IN (she was born 5 Nov. 1827, and died 3 Apr. 1892 in Blue Earth Co., buried in the Burgess Cemetery); the marriage was conducted by the Rev. John M. Harris. Has not been found in the 1850-60 censuses; listed in the 1857 and the 1865-95 state and federal censuses of Eagle Lake, Blue Earth Co., MN; the 1865 census says he served in the Civil War (possibly in Co. FA, 22nd IN Infantry). The Rev. William Burgess preached his first sermon at age fifteen, qualifying as a minister for the Church of Christ; he served as founding pastor of the Eagle Lake Christian Church. After retiring from his pastorship, he moved to Brookfield, MO in 1902 to live with his son Henry, and died there on 6 Mar. 1904, being buried in the Rose Hill Cemetery, Brookfield, MO. A large portrait of William hangs in the Blue Earth Co. Historical Society, Mankato, MN.

DEATH OF W. H. BURGESS

"Last Lord's Day at three P.M. Wm. H. Burgess fell asleep in death at the home of his son, H. C. Burgess, in this city, lacking four days of completing 79 years and two months. The deceased had been in poor health and very feeble for several years. He was an active minister of the gospel for more than fifty years, having entered the ministry when quite a young man. His ministerial labors were mostly devoted to Eagle Lake and Mankato, Minn., and the surrounding country. His work in that state will remain a monument to his memory long after his body returns to dust. Wm. H. Burgess was born [in] Cranfordsville [sic; cited as Crawfordsville in an obituary published 12 Mar. 1904 in the *Brookfield Gazette*], Indiana, January 10, 1825. He married Miss Eliza Betts [cited as Bettes in the *Gazette* obituary] of Indiana in 1845. Eight children was [sic] born to them, four of whom are still living, as follows: John H., H. C., Thos. M., and Charles E.

"Father Burgess was a man of strong conviction. His whole being was devoted to the advancement of that which he thought right, and his soul abhorred that which he considered wrong. He was a positive ministry and his living harmonized with his preaching. He knew nothing of a compromise with evil or error, and opposed himself to both with unbating zeal.

"He was indeed a patriotic pioneer preacher. He believed that in the great essential truths of the Gospel the world should be united, and in matters of mere opinion and speculation he had the broadest charity for all.

"It has been our privilege to know the deceased about two years. He moved from Mankato, Minn. with his son H. C. Burgess and family to Brookfield about two years ago. He was elected by his brethren and sister in the church here as an elder and trustee last fall, and those who knew him best loved him most.

"He was indeed a man to be admired and loved. He belonged to a type of manhood peculiar to a day since passed, more is the pity. He did not look upon popular amusements and worldiness with the least degree of allowance. But when he could no longer thunder his protest against the improprieties, he believed the best, hoped for the best, and endured with a degree of patience that which he could no longer fight in the open.

"He was one of God's true noblemen, and looked upon his release from suffering as simply means by which he might pass to the reward which awaits the finally faithful. He talked of death as you and I talk of life, and clung to the promises as strongly as you and I cling to temporal favors in our earthly existence.

"The future to him was a reality, and not the figment of a disordered mind, and since his earth work had been accomplished, he longed for home, and surrounded by those who loved him, he fell asleep without a struggle or a murmur.

"The passing of such a man but newly emphasizes the need for another life. His full reward was not received here, and his highest ambition was not achieved here. Nature and relation proclaim it, and it must be so: 'Else whence this pleasing hope, this fond desire, this longing after immorality.' It is for this fair virtue of't must strive, against disappointment, penury, and pain. The everlasting day of God shall yet arrive, and man's immortal beauty bloom again.

"The funeral service was held from the family residence Thursday afternoon, after which the interment took place in the City Cemetery."—unknown Brookfield newspaper.

The Children of Rev. William H. Burgess:

7a. **John Harris.** Born 5 Nov. 1846 at Portland Mills, IN. See below for full entry.
7b. **(Henry) Clay (II).** Born 21 Oct. 1848 at Portland Mills, IN. See below for full entry.
7c. **(Thompson) Warren.** Born 26 Dec. 1850 at Portland Mills, IN; died there on 3 Mar. 1852, and is buried in Mt. Pisgah Cemetery, Putnam Co., IN.
7d. **Thomas Marshall (I).** Born 18 Dec. 1852 at Portland Mills, IN. See below for full entry.
7e. **Redella Alice "Ridda."** Born 24 Feb. 1855 at Portland Mills, IN. Married Lt. Charles Frederick Wagoner on 23 Aug. 1879 at Mankato, MN (he was born Feb. 1844 at Broome Co., NY, son of Smith Wagoner, served in the Union Army during the Civil War, remarried Ridda's first cousin, Emma Burgess, and died 1910 at Eagle Lake, MN), and had children:

Junia Mae WAGONER. Born 22 Aug. 1880 at Eagle Lake, MN, married Arthur Dexter Warner, and thirdly Addison H. Pease, and died childless on 31 July 1962 (or 1963) at Santa Monica, CA, buried Burgess Cemetery, Eagle Lake, MN.

James Guy WAGONER. Born 12 Sept. 1881 at Eagle Lake, MN, married Philadelphia Udora "Delphia" Higgins on 24 Oct. 1911 at Mankato, MN (she was born 24 Aug. 1883 in WI, daughter of Nathan Shaw Higgins and Betsy Adelaide Mallette, and died 13 Nov. 1969 at Alameda, CA), and died 30 Apr. 1945 at Eagle Lake, buried with his wife in the Burgess Cemetery, having had children:

James Guy WAGONER Jr. (born 13 June 1913 at Mankato, MN, married Lois Rachel Nebvedik [she was born 24 Feb. 1927 at LaCrosse, WI], and had children: James Charles [born 7 Dec. 1954 at LaCrosse, WI, married Glenda ___ in California, and had children: Angela Dawn {born 15 Apr. 1978}]; Michael Frederick [born 14 Mar. 1957 at LaCrosse, WI, married Kristine Marie Wojahn on 15 Sept. 1990 at LaCrosse {she was born 25 Mar. 1957 at LaCrosse, daughter of Robert Ernest Edward Wojahn and Anna Laura Beitlich}]).

Bessie Aurel WAGONER (born 14 Aug. 1915 at Eagle Lake, MN, married Carl John Joseph Zimmeth on 17 Aug. 1938 at St. Peter, MN [he was born 17 Oct. 1913 at Mankato, MN, son of Charles Zimmeth and Mary Hagen, and died 9 Jan. 1993 at Alameda, CA, buried Catholic Cemetery, Mankato], and had children: Geraldine June [born 15 Jan. 1940 at Mankato, MN, married Roger Allen Heath on 10 May 1958 at San Leandro, CA {he was born 8 Apr. 1937 at Sacramento, CA, son of James Smith Heath and Alice Raye Rowan}, and had children: Christian Scott {born 11 Apr. 1959 at Oakland, CA, married Roianne Pine on 3 Oct. 1987 at Hayward, CA <she was born 18 June 1955 at Oakland, CA, daughter of Roy Antone Pine and Marian Violet Showers, married firstly Dennis Warren Gately, and by him had children: LeAnn |born 18 May 1980 at Hayward, CA| >, and had children: Ryan James <born 25 Oct. 1990 at San Leandro, CA>}; Paul Allen {born 6 Feb. 1966 at San Leandro, CA}]; Sharon Lee [born 6 June 1945 at Alameda, CA, married Dennis Dean Parker on 5 Nov. 1966 at Alameda, CA {he was born 30 July 1942 at Davenport, IA, son of Cyril Parker and Mercedes Wallack}, and had children: Kimberly Ann {born 2 Nov. 1967 at San Leandro, CA, married Kevin Lee Gruidl on 20 Apr. 1991 at Livermore, CA <he was born 19 Sept. 1967 at Hayward, CA, son of Edward Lawrence Gruidl and Xenia Hazel "Ginger" Sparman>}; Michele Elizabeth {born 16 Nov. 1969 at San Leandro, CA}; Michael Joseph {born 14 Oct. 1972 at Walnut Creek, CA}; Kathleen Suzanne {born 14 Apr. 1977 at Walnut Creek, CA}]).

Robert Warren WAGONER (born 18 Sept. 1917 at Eagle Lake, MN, married Frances Georgene Holmes on 26 Oct. 1957 at Reno, NV [she was born 1 May 1929 at French Camp, CA, daughter of George Leslie Holmes and Etta Herron, married firstly Michael Francis Kelly on 28 Feb. 1948 at Stockton, CA, and by him had children: Michael Bruce {born 14 Nov. 1948 at Stockton, CA, married secondly Shirlee DeGregoris}], and had children: Kimberly Ann [born 23 May 1959 at Oakland, CA, and died 25 May 1959, buried Stockton Rural Cemetery]; Laureen Jeannie [born 2 Sept. 1961 at Sacramento, CA, married Richard Michael Conrey on 23 Mar. 1992 at Mount Hood, OR {he was born 27 Nov. 1950 at Portland, OR, son of Fred Leroy Conrey and Winifred Jeannie Marinkovic}; Laureen and Richard are both geologists]. *Robert WAGONER* died on 2 Dec. 1979 at Sacramento, CA, and is buried in the Lodi Memorial Cemetery. Frances Wagoner has contributed greatly to this book; she currently lives at Sacramento, CA).

Roy Elliott WAGONER (born 29 Jan. 1920 at Eagle Lake, MN, married Frances LaVerne Meyers on 5 July 1944 at Alameda, CA [she was born 21 Apr. 1920 at LaVerne, MN, daughter of

Francis Robert Meyers and Leila Elizabeth Kinney, and died 1 Nov. 1986 at Fremont, CA, buried Holy Sepulchre Cemetery, Hayward, CA], and had children: James Roy [born 25 Mar. 1946 at Oakland, CA, married Darlene Frances Ferri on 16 Apr. 1966 at Reno, NV {she was born 18 Feb. 1948 at Oakland, CA, daughter of Ferdinand Peter Ferri and Dorothy Ann Neyes}, and had children: Paul Anthony {born 9 Jan. 1966 at Castro Valley, CA, married Jacqueline ___ <div.>, and had children: Nicole Ann <born 7 Mar. 1985 at Hayward, CA>; Anthony Paul <born 16 Mar. 1987 at Hayward, CA>}; David Elliott {born 16 Apr. 1973 at Hayward, CA}]; Frank Carl [born 6 Nov. 1949 at Lynwood, CA, married Judy Marlene Hendriques on 24 Sept. 1972]; Patricia Jane [born 18 Nov. 1950 at Lynwood, CA, married Robert Lee Riley on 10 July 1971 at Fremont, CA {he was born 26 Dec. 1942 at Lebanon, MO, son of William Robert Riley and Phyllis Idema Barnes}, and had children: Lee Roibin {born 21 Nov. 1972 at Freemont, CA}; Robert Patrick {born 5 Mar. 1975 at Livermore, CA}; Tricia Rene {born 10 Sept. 1976 at Livermore, CA}]. Roy Wagoner died on 30 Jan. 1967 at Fremont, CA, and is buried in the Holy Sepulchre Cemetery, Hayward, CA).

***Child* WAGONER**. Born and died 1884 at Eagle Lake, MN, buried Burgess Cemetery.

Ridda WAGONER died (probably in childbirth) in 1884 at Eagle Lake, MN, and is buried in the Burgess Cemetery with her husband.

7f. **(Dora) Ann (I).** Born 2 Nov. 1857 at Eagle Lake, MN; died there on 22 Sept. 1871, and is buried in the Burgess Cemetery.

7g. **Charles Edward (I).** Born 4 Aug. 1861 at Eagle Lake, MN. See below for full entry.

7h. **Hetty Louisa.** Born 14 Feb. 1865 at Eagle Lake, MN; died there on 22 Sept. 1876, and is buried in the Burgess Cemetery.

7i. **May E.** Born July 1869 at Eagle Lake, MN; died there between 1870-75, and is probably buried in the Burgess Cemetery in an unmarked grave.

7j. **Son.** Born about 1872 at Eagle Lake, MN; died there in 1875, and is probably buried in the Burgess Cemetery.

JOHN HARRIS BURGESS OF BLUE EARTH CO., MINNESOTA

[William Henry (I)[6]]

7a. **John Harris** *[son of William Henry (I)].* Born 5 Nov. 1846 at Portland Mills, IN. Married Harriet V. "Hattie" Record(s) on 11 Oct. 1868 (she was born 28 Nov. 1844, and died 4 May 1869, buried Burgess Cemetery); married secondly Jane Saphronica "Jennie" Freeman on 1 Jan. 1878 at Eagle Lake (she was born 20 June 1855 in IN, the daughter of Valentine O. and Julia Freeman, and died 10 Apr. 1944). John H. Burgess enlisted in Co. E, 2nd Minnesota Cavalry, Union Army, during the Civil War, serving from 8 Nov. 1863 to 22 Nov. 1865; he participated in the roundup of Sioux Indians at New Ulm during the uprising of 1863. Listed in the 1880-1910 censuses for Blue Earth Co., MN; Jennie is listed as head of the family in 1920. John Burgess was a farmer on the family lands near Eagle Lake, MN. He died on 30 Sept. 1917 at St. Paul, MN, and is buried in the Burgess Cemetery.

THE OBITUARY OF JOHN HARRIS BURGESS

"John Harris Burgess of Eagle Lake at the St. Joseph's Hospital Sunday evening at seven o'clock from a complication of diseases. He had suffered for several years, becoming seriously ill two weeks before his death. Mr. Burgess will long be remembered by his many friends for his honesty, uprightness of character, and genial disposition. The deceased was married October 11, 1886 [sic] to Hattie V. Record, who died two years later. January 1 1878, he married Jennie S. Freeman, who with five children survive him. Mr. Burgess was born at Portland Mills, Parke County, Indiana, November 5, 1846, and at the age of ten moved with his parents to Eagle Lake, and with the exception of the years he served his country, and the three winters he spent at the Soldiers Home, the remaining years were spent at the old home near Eagle Lake. When Mr. Burgess was sixteen years of age, his father, Rev. Burgess, was eloquently pleading for parents to urge their sons to fight for their country, little thinking his own young son would be the first to respond to his call. He belonged to Company E, Second Minnesota Cavalry, and took active part in quelling the Indian uprising near New Ulm. His wife, his daughters, Mrs. G. W. Senecal of St. Paul, Miss Alberta Burgess of Eagle Lake, Miss Ida Burgess, Dassel, Minn., and one son, W. L. Burgess of St. Paul, were present at his bedside during his dying hours. The other son, Roy, of Mildred, Mont., was unable to come, but had visited his father during the summer. Old soldiers and comrades in the Civil War were the pallbearers. Rev. Groom of the Mankato Christian Church conducted the funeral services, which were held at the Christian Church at Eagle Lake."—Unknown newspaper.

8a. **Ellsworth C.** Born 4 May 1869 at Eagle Lake, MN; died on 28 Sept. 1870 at Portland Mills, IN, and is buried at the Mt. Pisgah Cemetery, Putnam Co., IN; a headstone was also erected in the Burgess Cemetery at Eagle Lake, MN.

8b. **Ella May "Alma."** Born 19 Oct. 1878 at Eagle Lake, MN. Married G. William Senecal on 25 Dec. 1899 at Eagle Lake, Blue Earth Co., MN, and had children: *Marie*; *(James) Lester* (born 21 July 1907, died Mar. 1983 at Three Rivers, MA); *Norman* (born 5 Apr. 1908, died May 1981 at West Springfield, MA); *Leroy "Roy"* (born 20 Nov. 1909, died June 1975 at Monson, MA). Alma Senecal died on 23 Mar. 1950 at St. Paul, MN.

8c. **(Daisy) Alberta.** Born 15 Mar. 1880 (4 Mar. in the county records) at Eagle Lake, MN. Listed in the 1920 census with her mother. Alberta Burgess was a nurse at St. Paul, MN, dying there unmarried on 13 Mar. 1966. She was the last person buried in the Burgess Cemetery, Eagle Lake, MN.

8d. **LeRoy Morton (I) "Roy."** Born 8 Feb. 1882 (12 Mar. in the county records) at Eagle Lake, MN. See below for full entry.

8e. **(William) Lloyd.** Born 7 June 1887 at Eagle Lake, MN. See below for full entry.

8f. **Ida Mildred.** Born 22 Aug. 1893 at Eagle Lake, MN. Married Sverre Kjarskow Wick on 21 Aug. 1924 in Blue Earth Co., MN (he was born 21 Aug. 1899 at Duluth, MN, and lives at Austin, TX), and had children: *Ronald Stanley* (he was born 26 May 1926 at Virginia, MN); *Allan Kaye* (twin; born 17 Jan. 1931 at Virginia, MN); *Barbara Mildred* (twin; born 17 Jan. 1931 at Virginia, MN). Ida Wick was the first person from Eagle Lake to graduate from Carleton College, Northfield, MN. She died on 20 Oct. 1971 at St. Paul, MN. Ronald S. Wick and his wife, Dee Wick, have contributed greatly to this book; they currently live at Austin, TX.

ROY BURGESS, Sr., OF GENESEE CO., MICHIGAN

[William Henry (I)[6], John Harris[7]]

8d. **LeRoy Morton (I) "Roy"** *[son of John Harris].* Born 8 Feb. 1882 (or 12 Mar., according to county birth records) at Eagle Lake, Blue Earth Co., MN. Married Jessie Lee Englerth on 1 Oct. 1905 at St. Paul, MN (she was born 29 Aug. 1882 [or 1883, according to her Social Security record], and died Jan. 1976 at Fenton, MI, aged 93 years). Roy Burgess was a carpenter and farmer in Minnesota and Michigan. He died on 3 July 1957 at Mt. Morris, MI, and is buried in the Chesaming Cemetery.

9a. **Lenore Alberta.** Born 1 Aug. 1906 at Eagle Lake, MN. Married Robert Pearce, and had children: *Robert Jr.* Lenore Pearce lives at Leesburg, FL.

9b. **LeRoy Morton (II) "Roy."** Born 4 Dec. 1913 in Custer (later Prairie) Co., MT. Married Margaret Elizabeth "Peg" Perry on 22 June 1940 at Chesaning, MI (she was born 23 Sept. 1921, daughter of Lester Perry and Agnes Azelton, and died 28 Sept. 1989 at Kansas City, MO, being cremated). Served as a 1st Lieut. in the Marine Corps during World War II. Roy Burgess Jr. worked in both engineering and sales for the Chevrolet Division of General Motors. He died on 4 Aug. 1985 at Morton, IL; he was cremated, with his ashes being scattered at the Little Big Horn National Monument, Custer Co., MT.

10a. **Diane Kay.** Born 26 Oct. 1946 at Flint, MI. Married Louis Johnson (he was born 10 Sept. 1939 at Peoria, IL), and had children: *Shelby Marie* (born 22 Nov. 1970 at Peoria, IL, was adopted by her stepfather, and uses the name McMorris; she enlisted in the U.S. Air Force, and is now a sergeant serving in Germany); married secondly Walter "Bud" McMorris on 7 May 1978 at Peoria, IL. Diane McMorris is a hair dresser at Kansas City, MO; Bud McMorris is a plumber.

10b. **Michael Roi "Mike."** Born 5 Jan. 1948 at Kansas City, MO. Married Shari McKelvey about 1968 (div.; she was born 15 Feb. 1948 at Paragould, AR). Mike Burgess served in the 82nd Airborne Division during the Vietnam War, attaining the rank of sergeant. He later worked as a police officer from 1978-82 for the community of Morton, IL, and as a manager of a night club at Bloomington, IL. At the time of his death he was working as an extraditor of county prisoners in Illinois. He died on 5 July 1990 at Sesser, Franklin Co., IN, and was cremated, his ashes being scattered at Morton, Tazewell Co., IL.

11a. **Stephanie Machelle.** She uses the surname Birkey. Born 4 Nov. 1968 at Ft. Bragg, NC. Stephanie Birkey is a graduate student in molecular biology at the University of Chicago.

11b. **Daughter.** Died young.

10c. **William David (II) "Bill."** Born 12 Nov. 1953 at Kansas City, MO. Served in the U.S. Marine Corps. Bill Burgess is a general construction manager at Cypress, CA.

LLOYD BURGESS OF RAMSEY CO., MINNESOTA
[William Henry (I)[6], John Harris[7]]

8e. **(William) Lloyd** *[son of John Harris].* Born 7 June 1887 at Eagle Lake, MN. Married Marie Meredith Goudy on 16 Nov. 1912 at St. Paul, MN (she died on 23 Oct. 1953). Lloyd Burgess was a bookkeeper for Swift and Co. at St. Paul, MN. He died there on 27 May 1950.

9a. **Willard Lloyd "Bill."** Born 8 Apr. 1915 at St. Paul, MN. Married Verne Lucille Johnson in 1940 (div.). Bill Burgess has worked as a certified public accountant, newspaper man, real estate salesman, and a construction worker. He died in Aug. 1986 at Houston, TX.

10a. **Craig Lloyd.** He was adopted by his stepfather, and uses the surname McKee. Born 13 Sept. 1942 at St. Paul, MN. Twice married (div.). Craig McKee manages a supermarket at Marne-on-the-St. Croix, MN.

HENRY CLAY BURGESS OF JACKSON CO., OREGON
[William Henry (I)[6]]

7b. **(Henry) Clay (II)** *[son of William Henry (I)].* Born 21 (or 22) Oct. 1848 at Portland Mills, IN. Married Ellen M. "Ella" French on 27 Dec. 1871 in Blue Earth Co., MN (she was born 22 June 1853 at Padeville, WI, and died 9 July 1927 at Medford, OR). Listed in the 1875-1900 censuses for Eagle Lake, MN (but not in the state censuses of 1885 and 1895). Moved to Brookfield, MO in 1901, and to Medford, OR in Dec. 1908 (listed there in 1920). Clay Burgess worked as a flour salesman, as General Manager of the Northwest (sales) Territory of Singer Sewing Machines for 25 years, and as a collector, and then as an advance man and travelling agent for the Andrews Opera Company, in which many of his children and grandchildren were involved as performers. He also served as Chairman of the Minnesota State Republican Committee, and was a lifetime member of the Masonic Fraternal Organization of Mankato, MN. He died on 18 Dec. 1928 at Medford, Jackson Co., OR, and is buried there in an unmarked grave in the Oddfellows Cemetery, next to his wife (whose grave has a stone).

8a. **Arthur Clay.** Born 30 Sept. 1872 at Eagle Lake, MN. See below for full entry.
8b. **Frank Oliver.** Born 30 Dec. 1874 at Oskaloosa, IA. See below for full entry.
8c. **William Henry (VII).** Born 17 Mar. 1878 at Eagle Lake, MN. See below for full entry.
8d. **Grace (I)** (nmn). Born 4 Jan. 1880 at Eagle Lake, MN. Married Jonas Wold on 9 Aug. 1904 at Brookfield, Linn Co., MO (he was born 18 Aug. 1872 in Norway, and died 7 Dec. 1946 at Medford, OR). The Wolds moved to North Dakota after their marriage, and then to Medford in 1908, where they owned and operated a drugstore; Jonas also worked at the Western Thrift Store in Medford. Jonas Wold's biography appeared in the May 1910 issue of *American Progress Magazine*. Although they had no children of their own, the Wolds adopted *Donald BURGESS*, son of Grace's brother, Bill, who became Donald Burgess Wold (see below). Listed in the 1920 census for Medford, Jackson Co., OR. Grace was living at San Francisco, CA in 1952, but died at Grants Pass, OR before 1961.
8e. **Stella (I)** (nmn). Born 19 Nov. 1884 at Eagle Lake, MN. Married Walker Francis Quisenberry in 1904 at Brookfield, Linn Co., MO (he died on 17 Jan. 1957 at Medford, OR), and had children: *Lois* (nmn) (born 9 Mar. 1905 at Brookfield, MO, married Fred Day, and had children: Janet [married ___ Hamilton]; *Lois* married secondly Slater Johnson, and thirdly Halbert Sylvanius Deuel, and lives at Portland, OR); *Janet* (born 1910, died young); *Philip Clay* (born 7 Feb. 1915 in OR, died 28 Nov. 1989 at Grants Pass, OR); *Jean* (nmn) (born 1916 in OR, lives at Keiser, OR). Living with her brother in 1920. Stella Quisenberry was a light opera performer with her husband. She died on 21 Sept. 1961 at Medford, Jackson Co., OR, and was cremated.
8f. **Robert Otis.** Born 5 Apr. 1887 at Eagle Lake, MN. Married Mable Florence Shaffer at St. Louis, MO (who survived him). Bob Burgess was a Sergeant in the 127th Field Artillery in France during World War I, and belonged to the Veterans of Foreign Wars. In early years he worked in light opera with his family, later settling at Yreka, CA. He died childless on 20 May 1952 at the Veterans Hospital, Oakland, CA, but was buried in Siskiyou Memorial Park, Yreka.

ARTHUR CLAY BURGESS OF JACKSON CO., OREGON
[William Henry (I)[6], Henry Clay (II)[7]]

8a. **Arthur Clay** *[son of Henry Clay (II)].* Born 30 Sept. 1872 at Eagle Lake, MN. Married Kitty P. Gebler in KY or TN (she was born Apr. 1877 in OH or IL, and died 10 June 1955 in Jackson Co.,

OR). Listed in the 1900 census with his father. Served as a 2nd Lieut. in the Minnesota National Guard. Art Burgess was a light opera comedian and singer for the Andrews Opera Co., Gordon Shay Opera Co., Boston Ideal Opera Co.; he was later associated with De Wolf Hopper, LaVelle Opera Co., Boston English Opera Co., *Rajah of Bong*, and Harvey Orr's Musical Comedies. When he left the road he bought a grocery store at Sidney, NE, then moved to Medford, OR in 1909, where he owned the Park Grocery Store. Listed in the 1920 census for Portland, OR, but moved in 1931 to Eugene, Lane Co., Oregon, where he had a store on the University of Oregon campus. He died there on 15 June 1933, and was cremated. His obituary calls him "the grand old opera singer."

"[Arthur Burgess's] life work was in the theatre, starting as a chorus boy with the Andrews Opera Company. He became a comedian and had leading roles, and later was a director with them. His brother Frank was in the theatre for a while, then moved to Sidney, NE, in 1917 and owned a music shop for many years. My husband [Ralph Burgess] was practically born in the theatre and was with different opera companies, mostly the Andrews Opera Company and the Joe Sheehan Company."—Ethel Hazelrigg Burgess, 1982.

9a. **Ralph Clyde (I).** Born 17 Nov. 1893 at Rockford, IL. Married Ruby V. Burker on 24 July 1913 at Medford, OR; married secondly Ethel Marie Hazelrigg on 17 Nov. 1916 at Chicago, IL (she was born 5 Jan. 1893 at Greensburg, IN, the daughter of Charles and Nora H. Hazelrigg, and stepdaughter of Nellie Andrews [of the Andrews Opera Company], and died 20 Nov. 1983 at Ashland, OR, aged 90 years). Ralph Burgess began touring with his parents at an early age, and he and his wife spent many years working as light opera actors and singers with the Andrews Opera Company and others; he and his father later operated grocery stores in Sidney, NE and Medford, OR, where he moved in 1925. He managed the Oregon State Liquor Store at Ashland, OR between 1935-60. He died on 9 Mar. 1973 at Ashland, and he and his wife are buried in the Hillcrest Memorial Park, Medford, OR.

Ralph C. Burgess Jr. wrote on 21 Mar. 1981: "My father and his father were both in show biz, working out of Chicago on the Redpath Circuit in the old Chataqua days, primarily in light opera, Gilbert and Sullivan musicals. My grandfather on my mother's side (Hazelrigg) was the musical director, and that's how my father met and married my mother. The Andrews Opera Co. was also in the picture, and many of these people came west and settled in the Rogue River Valley (Medford, Oregon). I tried following in their tradition, attended Pasadena Playhouse, met my wife, and we were in theatre for about eight years before our children were born."

10a. **Dorothy Jane.** Born 9 Nov. 1917 at Oak Park, IL. She graduated from the University of Oregon in 1939, majoring in music and education. Dorothy Burgess was an elementary school music teacher at Patrick Elementary School, Gold Hill, OR. She was a member of the Applegate Chapter of American Business Women, and was chosen its Woman of the Year for 1982-83. She belonged to the Episcopal Church. Dorothy died unmarried of cancer on 3 July 1982 at Medford, OR, and is buried in the Hillcrest Memorial Park, Ashland.

10b. **Ralph Clyde (II).** Born 7 July 1925 at Sidney, NE. Married Ellen Dolores Berry on 27 May 1951 at Medford, OR (she was born 11 June 1928 at Newark, OH, daughter of Frank T. Berry and Mildred Chapman). Ralph Burgess graduated from the Pasadena Playhouse College of Theatre Arts in 1950, worked as an actor with his wife in New York and Hollywood during the 1950s, and served on the Board of Directors of the Pasadena Playhouse Alumni and Associates. He subsequently worked as an insurance claims supervisor at Los Angeles, CA, living at Arcadia, CA. He retired in 1988, and now resides at Medford, OR.

11a. **Brenton Berry.** Born 1 Feb. 1957 at Pasadena, CA. Married Grace J. Buchhammer on 15 June 1991 (she was born 8 May 1964 at Glendale, CA, daughter of Edwin and Susana Buchhammer). Brent Burgess is a systems manager with the Bendix Corporation, working for the National Aeronautics and Space Administration at the Jet Propulsion Laboratory, Pasadena. He currently lives at La Verne, CA.

12a. **Brianna Jannette.** Born 8 Dec. 1993 at Pasadena, CA.

11b. **Tyler Chapman.** Born 19 June 1959 at Pasadena, CA. Married Shelley Lea Thomas on 13 Apr. 1990 in Clark Co., NV. Tyler Burgess works in electronics quality control for a helicopter parts manufacturer in Southern California.

11c. **Jason Paige "Jay."** Born 6 June 1962 at Pasadena, CA. Jay Burgess was a computer operator at the Jet Propulsion Laboratory, Pasadena, CA. He now works for Aaron Spelling Productions Inc., Los Angeles, CA. He currently lives at Pasadena, CA.

FRANK O. BURGESS OF CHEYENNE CO., NEBRASKA
[William Henry (I)[6], Henry Clay (II)[7]]

8b. **Frank Oliver** *[son of Henry Clay (II)].* Born 30 Dec. 1874 at Oskaloosa, IA. Married (Morna) Leata Forney (she was born 9 Nov. 1875, daughter of Maurice C. Forney, and died 1952). Frank Burgess was a singer and actor with his brothers for the Andrews Opera Company and other similar groups between 1895-1917. He settled at Sidney, NE in Aug. 1917, where he opened a music store. He died there on 3 Dec. 1935, and is buried with his wife in the Greenwood Cemetery.

9a. **Exie Etta**. Born 19 Dec. 1897 in Nebraska. Married Max Critchfield on 30 Aug. 1924 in Cheyenne Co., NE, and had children: *Maxine* (born 2 Jan. 1926, married Robert D. Kilby on 16 Apr. 1949, and had children: Jane Lynn [born 10 July 1954]; Marcia Ann [born 5 Nov. 1956]); *Marilynn "Lynn"* (born 8 July 1929, married Roger E. Sheets on 16 Dec. 1953, and had children: Cindy [born 23 Mar. 1960]; William Roger [born 10 May 1967]). Living with Maurice C. Forney, her grandfather, in the 1900 census for Kearney Co., NE. Exie Critchfield was an actress and performer for the Ferguson Light Opera Co. and other similar groups during the period between the wars. She died on 7 May 1966 at Indianapolis, IN.

9b. **Frances Lucille.** Born 19 June 1900 at Minden, NE. Married ___ Vacik about 1920, and secondly Goldwin Hubert "Bliss" Doran on 8 June 1927 at Sterling, CO (he died 1964), and had children: *Donna* (married Carl J. Schmidt, had three children, and lives at Sidney, NE). Frances Doran was an actress with her sister in various light comedy productions during and after World War I. She died on 28 Feb. 1971 at Sidney, NE, and is buried there in the Greenwood Cemetery.

WILLIAM H. BURGESS OF HALL CO., NEBRASKA
[William Henry (I)[6], Henry Clay (II)[7]]

8c. **William Henry (VII)** *[son of Henry Clay (II)].* Born 17 Mar. 1878 at Eagle Lake, MN. Married Florence Louise Bard about 1898 (she was born Aug. 1879 in MN, remarried ___ McOmie, and died 3 Feb. 1964 at Los Angeles, CA, buried in the Glen Haven Cemetery, San Fernando, CA); married secondly Josephine Marie Venuto on 7 June 1919 (she was born 17 June 1879 at St. Louis, MO, and died 11 Dec. 1967 at Grand Island, NE). Listed in the 1900 census for Bloomington, IL, and in 1920 at Medford, OR (his father and sister Stella are with him). William H. Burgess served as a musician in Co. A, 12th MN Infantry during the Spanish-American War, and as a Corporal in the 4th Development Co., 164th Depot Brigade in 1917, acting as a drill instructor until the end of World War I. Between wars he was a singer and performer for the Andrews Opera Company and others. He was living at Joplin, MO in 1927, and in South Dakota in 1936. He died on 6 Sept. 1943 at the Veterans Home, Grand Island, NE, and is buried in the Cemetery there with his second wife.

9a. **William Henry (IX).** Born 1 Mar. 1909 at Minneapolis, MN. Married Angela Christine Burbee on 3 Mar. 1934 in Los Angeles Co., CA (she was born 9 Oct. 1910 in PA, daughter of Charles E. Burbee Sr.). William H. Burgess Jr. was a clerk for Haas Baruch & Co. at Los Angeles in the 1930s-'40s, when he is listed in the directories there. He died on 2 Sept. 1990 at Temecula, Riverside Co., CA.

10a. **Carol Christine.** Born 27 Jan. 1936 at Los Angeles, CA. Married Richard Shrock, and lives at Palo Cedro, CA.

10b. **Donald Robert.** Born 27 Feb. 1939 at Los Angeles, CA. Married Chriselle E. "Kit" (Rivar) Brooks on 11 July 1969 in Los Angeles Co., CA (div.); married secondly Nancy L. Pitzer on 21 Oct. 1978 in Riverside Co. Don Burgess currently lives near Temecula, CA.

11a. **Chrisdon Rivar.** Born 30 Nov. 1969 at Tujunga, CA.

9b. **Donald Burgess.** Born 23 Dec. 1914 in MN. He was adopted by his aunt and uncle, Grace and Jonas Wold, his name being changed to Donald Burgess Wold. Married Marion or Marianne G. ___ (she is *not* the Marion Wold who died on 10 Apr. 1981 in Mendocino Co., CA, but she may be the Maryana L. Wold who was born 13 May 1909 and died 12 May 1984 at San Lorenzo, Alameda Co., CA). Donald B. Wold was an accountant and magazine salesman in the San Francisco area.

He died on 29 Oct. 1963 at Lone Pine, Inyo Co., CA, and is buried in the Golden Gate National Cemetery, San Francisco, CA; the service was conducted at Lafayette, Contra Costa Co., CA.

10a. **Son.**
10b. **Daughter.**
10c. **Daughter.**
10d. **Daughter.**
10e. **Daughter.**

THOMAS M. BURGESS OF BLUE EARTH CO., MINNESOTA

[William Henry (I)[6]]

7d. **Thomas Marshall (I)** *[son of William Henry (I)].* Born 18 Dec. 1852 at Portland Mills, IN. Married Laura A. Luthultz on 1 Jan. 1878 (she was born 19 May 1861 at Newcastle, IN, daughter of Joachim Luthultz, remarried Henry Mautner on 27 Mar. 1914, and died 1 Feb. 1943, buried in the Eagle Lake Cemetery, Eagle Lake, MN). Listed in the 1880-1900 censuses for Eagle Lake, Blue Earth Co., MN. Tom Burgess was a farmer on his family's lands, and also served as a wagonmaster for the Andrews Opera Company; during his later years he worked as a night watchman at Owatonna, MN. He died on 1 Apr. 1913 at Mankato, and is buried in the Burgess Cemetery.

THE OBITUARY OF THOMAS M. BURGESS

"Thomas M. Burgess of Eagle Lake died at a hospital in Mankato yesterday afternoon at three thirty o'clock, after a long illness of yellow jaundice. He had been ill most of the time since February, when he resigned his position as night foreman at the state school at Owatonna. Mr. Burgess has been a resident of Eagle Lake nearly all his life, and is a well-known and much-beloved man throughout Blue Earth County. Mr. Burgess was born in a small town in Indiana sixty-one years ago, and came to this county and settled near Eagle Lake with his parents when he was two years old. His father drove a team and prairie schooner from Indiana to Minnesota and homesteaded here. Up to four years ago he resided on a farm near Eagle Lake, but after his retirement from the farm, he accepted a position as night foreman at the state school at Owatonna. His brother, John H. Burgess, was an active soldier during the Indian uprisings near New Ulm. He has been an active member of the Christian Church at Eagle Lake for a great many years, and will be buried under the auspices of that church. Besides his wife, he is survived by four sons, a daughter, and three brothers. The children are: Mrs. E. M. Burgess of Gull Lake, Saskatchewan, Canada, C. E. Burgess of Frederics, Wisconsin, P. P. Burgess of Tracy, J. A. Burgess of Eagle Lake, and H. O. Burgess of Gull Lake, Saskatchewan. The brothers are J. H. Burgess of Eagle Lake, H. C. Burgess of Medford, Oregon, and C. E. Burgess of Eagle Lake. The funeral will be held from the Christian Church in Eagle Lake Sunday afternoon at two o'clock, and the services will be conducted by Elder Davidson. Interment will take place at the Burgess Cemetery at Eagle Lake."—unknown Mankato newspaper.

8a. **Edna Mildred.** Born 23 Oct. 1878 at Eagle Lake, MN. Married her first cousin, once removed, William Addison Burgess, about 1898 (he was born 15 Dec. 1875, and died 9 Nov. 1957). Edna M. Burgess lived with her family at Gull Lake, SK, Canada, in Blue Earth Co., MN, and at Minneapolis, MN. She died on 14 Nov. 1979 at the Angelus Nursing Home, Minneapolis, aged 101 years, 22 days, the oldest Burgess descendant on record to that date, and was buried in the Oak Hill Cemetery, Minneapolis. For her children, see her husband's entry.
8b. **Clinton Ernest.** Born 15 Dec. 1879 at Eagle Lake, MN. See below for full entry.
8c. **Phillip Paul Bliss.** Born 20 Nov. 1881 at Eagle Lake, MN. See below for full entry.
8d. **(Henry) Clay (III).** Born 10 Oct. 1890 at Eagle Lake, MN. See below for full entry.
8e. **Joachim** (nmn). Born 16 June 1896 at Eagle Lake, MN. See below for full entry.

CLINTON E. BURGESS OF POLK CO., WISCONSIN

[William Henry (I)[6], Thomas Marshall (I)[7]]

8b. **Clinton Ernest** *[son of Thomas Marshall (I)].* Born 15 Dec. 1879 at Eagle Lake, MN. Married Marie Ann Lundgren on 16 Aug. 1911 (she was born 5 Dec. 1891 at Lewis, WI, and died 30 May 1981 at Eau Claire, WI). Clint Burgess settled at Frederic, Polk Co., WI early in life, where he ran a livery barn before marrying; after his marriage, he and his wife bought a farm there, which they worked for the rest of their lives. He died on 19 July 1968 at Eau Claire, WI, but he and his wife are buried at the Reeve Cemetery, Reeve, Barron Co., WI.

9a. **Diavola Laura Ann.** Born 23 June 1912 at Lewis, WI. Married Fred Otto Aude on 15 June 1941 (he was born 15 Aug. 1905 at Chippewa Falls, WI, and died there on 10 Oct. 1977); married secondly Franklin Lemon in July 1990. Diavola Lemon continues to work the Aude family farm, at Chippewa Falls, WI.

9b. **Deloris Freda Maude.** Born 25 Mar. 1916 at Frederic, WI. Married Mark Cruzen in June 1939 (he died on 24 Jan. 1955), and had children: *Zoe Estelle* (born 5 Apr. 1941, married ___ Nelson, and had children: (Mark) Anthony "Tony" [married Bonita ___, and had children: Ryan; Daughter, and lives at Luck, WI]; Jeffrey Todd [married Tammy ___, and lives at Nashville, TN]); *Carol Ann* (born 25 Feb. 1942, married Ralph Schaber, had children: David [married, with one daughter]; Wayne [attends college at Lincoln, NE]; Susan [married, with one daughter], and lives at Dillingham, AK); *Gerald Mark* (born 24 Oct. 1945, married Norma ___, had one daughter, and lives at Hinsdale, IL); *Judy Margaret* (born 30 Aug. 1947, married Tom Tomerlin, and had children: Carol Ann [married ___ O'Daniel, and had children: Krista Nicole); *Lou Ellen* (born 27 Sept. 1948, married Michael Petty III, had children: Clinton Michael; Meridith Kaye, and lives at Trenton, NJ). Deloris Cruzen worked at the Madison Hospital for twenty-eight years before retiring; she now lives in a retirement community at Madison, TN.

9c. **Lucille Vivian.** Born 1 Dec. 1918 at Frederic, WI. Married Ralph Alton Cline on 28 July 1944 at Takoma Park, MD (he was born 11 Mar. 1912 at Williamsport, PA, was a registered nurse, and died 3 Oct. 1991 at Jersey Shore, PA), and had children: *Ralph Clinton* (born 8 Dec. 1945 at Takoma Park, MD, married Donna Sue Wharton on 25 Aug. 1968 at Riverside, CA, and had children: Jennifer Raelynn; both Donna and Ralph are educators at Loma Linda, CA); *Eldon Alfred* (born 15 Apr. 1950 at Madison, TN, and teaches music to children and works in counseling with the Health Department at Riverside, CA); *Edward DeWitt* (born 20 Aug. 1952 at Murfreesboro, TN, works as a lyric baritone, and is a professional singer of classical and religious music; he also works with the City Health Department, San Diego, CA); *Richard Lynn* (born 4 July 1958 at Murfreesboro, TN, married Cynthia Slater in Aug. 1982 [div. 1988]; he works as a pilot and captain for United Air Lines; he lives at Loma Linda, CA). Lucille Cline was a registered nurse for veterans' hospitals. She now lives retired at Loma Linda, CA.

9d. **Leta Marie.** Born 21 Jan. 1921 at Frederic, WI. Married William R. Brandemihl on 7 Sept. 1950 at Clear Lake, WI (he was born 30 Oct. 1918 at Baker, MT, and died on 6 Feb. 1992), and had children: *William Charles* (born 2 Aug. 1958 at Orafino, ID); *Lori Faye* (born 21 Nov. 1959 at Orafino, ID, married Jeffery England on 24 June 1984 at Hinsdale, IL). Leta and Bill Brandemihl were both registered nurses at Hinsdale, IL; they retired to Chippewa Falls, WI. Leta Brandemihl died there on 18 Aug. 1992.

9e. **Lyle Clinton.** Born 19 Feb. 1923 at Frederic, WI. See below for full entry.

9f. **Dale Elroy.** Born 20 Oct. 1932 at Clear Lake, WI. See below for full entry.

LYLE C. BURGESS OF LINN CO., OREGON

[William Henry (I)[6], Thomas Marshall (I)[7], Clinton Ernest[8]]

9e. **Lyle Clinton** *[son of Clinton Ernest].* Born 19 Feb. 1923 at Frederic, WI. Married Wanda Louise Adams on 19 Feb. 1946 at Hernando, DeSoto Co., MS (she was born 2 Feb. 1930 at Dyer, TN, daughter of Robert Howard Adams and Grace Goodwin). Lyle is a retired brick mason at Albany, OR.

10a. **Thomas Marshall (II).** Born 28 Dec. 1947 at Memphis, TN. Married Donna Fischer in 1967 (she was born 1 Jan. 1947 at Eau Claire, WI). Tom Burgess is a brick mason and photographer at Modesto, CA.

11a. **Morgan Marshall.** Born 8 Feb. 1969 at Eau Claire, WI.
11b. **Heather Louise.** Born 12 Feb. 1973 at Eau Claire, WI.

10b. **(Warren) Gregory.** Born 14 July 1952 at Memphis, TN. Married Lana Jean Bolman on 22 Oct. 1977 in Linn Co. (div. 1988). Greg Burgess is a process cameraman for the *Albany Democrat* newspaper; he lives at Lebanon, OR.

11a. **Sara Lynn (I).** Born 1 Feb. 1979 at Albany, OR.
11b. **Clinton Robert.** Born 25 Aug. 1981 at Albany, OR.

10c. **Larry Clinton.** Born 12 Oct. 1954 at Memphis, TN. Married Jacque Bittleston in Nov. 1980 (div.). Larry Burgess is a welder at Modesto, CA.

11a. **Janel Grace.** Born 12 Dec. 1981 at Eugene, OR.
11b. **Joseph Vaun.** Born 16 Mar. 1983 at Eugene, OR.

10d. **Barbara Louise (II).** Born 5 Apr. 1959 at Eau Claire, WI. Married Paige Andrew on 29 July 1978 in Linn Co., OR (div.); married secondly Henry Horn Jr. on 19 Sept. 1981 in Benton Co., OR (he works for Hewlett-Packard), and had children: *Marie Christine* (born 3 Sept. 1982 at Corvallis, OR); *Stefanie Louise* (born 23 Dec. 1984 at Corvallis, OR); *Kimberly Regina* (born 27 Sept. 1990 at Corvallis, OR). Barbara Horn lives at Corvallis, OR.
10e. **Randall Howard "Randy."** Born 8 Mar. 1961 at Eau Claire, WI. Married Jean Ann Travis on 19 Aug. 1992 at Corvallis, OR (born 28 Feb. 1961 at Milwaukee, WI). Randy and Jean Burgess both work for Hewlett-Packard at Corvallis, OR; they live at Philomath, OR.

DALE E. BURGESS OF DESCHUTES CO., OREGON
[William Henry (I)[6], Thomas Marshall (I)[7], Clinton Ernest[8]]

9f. **Dale Elroy** *[son of Clinton Ernest].* Born 20 Oct. 1932 at Clear Lake, WI. Married Jessie Mae Gray in 1952; married secondly Melody Ann Blatchley in 1978 (div. 14 Sept. 1988). Dale Burgess is a contractor and saw mill operator at Redmond, OR.

10a. **Crystal Kay.** Born 29 Sept. 1954 at Madison, TN. May have married Michael McJunkin on 27 Aug. 1972 in Linn Co., OR, and had children: *Aaron*; married secondly Mark Anderton, and had children: *Gama*; *George*. Crystal Anderton lives in New Zealand.
10b. **Terry Allen (I) "Bud."** Born 20 Sept. 1956 at Denver, CO. Married Karen JoAnn Bates O'Connor on 18 July 1986 in Deschutes Co., OR (div.). Bud Burgess is a rancher and building contractor at Redmond, Deschutes Co., OR.

11a. **Ashley Marie.** Born 3 Sept. 1987 at Redmond, OR.
11b. **Carrie Ann.** Born 6 Apr. 1989 at Redmond, OR.

PHILLIP BURGESS OF PIERCE CO., WASHINGTON
[William Henry (I)[6], Thomas Marshall (I)[7]]

8c. **Phillip Paul Bliss** *[son of Thomas Marshall (I)].* He was named for Phillip Paul Bliss, a well-known writer of religious hymns. Born 15 Nov. 1881 at Eagle Lake, MN. Married Ethel Lucille Clapp about 1908. He lived in New Orleans as a young man, where he learned to play the piano, particularly ragtime music. Phil Burgess was a railroad worker who helped install the first telegraph line across the Great Salt Lake in Utah. He also served as Postmaster of Brushy Knob, MO, and ran the trading post there. He died on 10 Dec. 1946 at Tacoma, WA, and is buried there in the Mountain View Cemetery.

9a. **Richard Phillip.** Born 27 Dec. 1908 at Huron, SD. See below for full entry.
9b. **Doris Ethel.** Born 5 Feb. 1910 at Tracy, SD. Married Irwin Vickers, and had children:
Donna Lee VICKERS. Born 12 Jan. 1927, married Jessie Bale (he died 1991), and had children: *Gary F.* (born 28 Jan. 1948, married, and had children: Shelly M. [born 27 July 1967]; Cory L. [born 16 July 1971]); *Cherrie L.* (born 15 Apr. 1949, married Dennis Kimsey, and had children: Jesse M. [born 9 Aug. 1967]; Jonah A. [born 26 Nov. 1971]); *Lore G.* (born 20 Sept. 1953, married ___ Hillis, and had children: Angela M. [born 29 Jan. 1970, married ___ Helu, and had children: Sydnye I. {born 7 Nov. 1987}; Jasmin N. {born 29 Apr. 1990}]; Lore married secondly Tito Podesta, and had children: Lucas T. [born 2 July 1982]; Matthew N. [born 21 Oct. 1990]); *Beverly N.* (born 15 July 1957, married Tracy Morgan, and had children: Gabriel K. [born 21 June 1976]; Beverly married secondly Sergio Arvizu, and had children: Sergio A. [born 19 Aug. 1983]; Krystle L. [born 22 Aug. 1984]; Marcos B. [born 31 Aug. 1987]).
Doris Burgess VICKERS married secondly Harold Hunter, and died on 31 Mar. 1988 at Heyburn, ID, being buried in the Rupert Cemetery, Rupert, ID.
9c. **Robert Thomas (I).** Born 10 Nov. 1913 at Watertown, SD. See below for full entry.
9d. **(Viola) Ruth.** Born 6 Sept. 1916 at Watertown, SD. Married Joseph M. Torres at Stockton, CA, and had children: *Thomas J. "Tommy"* (he died at age 47; he may be the Thomas Torres born 14 Mar. 1937 who died Aug. 1984 in CA); *Richard P. "Dickie"* (married, had three children, and died at age 24); Ruth married secondly Clarence A. Butcher (dec.), and thirdly David H. DeVol on 1 Aug. 1970 in Placer Co., CA (dec.), and fourthly Harold Robert "Hal" Pewitt on 10 Jan. 1979 at

Tombstone, AZ (he was born 25 Nov. 1917 at Laurel, MT). Ruth and Hal Pewitt live at Woodland, CA.

9e. **Nellie Mae.** Born 1 Aug. 1924 at Mountain View, MO. Married Ray Moore on 26 Apr. 1942 at Del Paso Heights, CA, and had children: *Sandra Lee* (born 30 Dec. 1942, married Kenneth Carlton, and had children: Raymond [born 31 Jan. 1961, and died 1991]; Robert David [born 3 Mar. 1968]; Brandie Lea [born 16 July 1971, married ___ Alledge]); *Kerry Sue* (born 11 July 1952, married ___ Beitman, and had children: Jennifer Nell [born 18 July 1982]; Brian Joseph [born 5 Oct. 1983]; Perry Robert [born 23 Aug. 1984]); *Kathleen Rae* (born 29 Oct. 1954, married ___ Sallander, and had children: Ramanda Mae [born 16 May 1973]; Trevor Vernon [born 26 Dec. 1982]). Nellie Mae married secondly Joseph Hickman on 16 Jan. 1970 at Davis, CA (he was born 2 Feb. 1919, and died 11 July 1992 at Richfield, UT). Nellie Hickman currently lives at Gold Beach, OR.

RICHARD P. BURGESS OF WASHOE CO., NEVADA

[William Henry (I)[6], Thomas Marshall (I)[7], Phillip Paul Bliss[8]]

9a. **Richard Phillip** *[son of Phillip Paul Bliss].* Born 27 Dec. 1908 at Huron, SD. Married Ruby Ellen Jones on 26 Oct. 1927 at West Plains, MO; married secondly Margaret Doris Boston about 1943, and thirdly Louise Parlanti about 1953. Dick Burgess was a TV, radio, and slot machine technician at Sparks, NV. He died there on 19 Apr. 1993.

10a. **Donald Leroy.** Born 2 Aug. 1927 at Brushy Knob, MO. Married Eva Amanda Eleonore Gross on 8 May 1953 at Herzogenaurach, West Germany (she was born 15 Aug. 1929 at Herzogenaurach). Don Burgess served 26 years in the U.S. Army, retiring as a Chief Warrant Officer in the Criminal Investigation Division in 1973; he later has worked as a Training Manager for the Military Banking Division of American Express Co., Nürnberg, West Germany. He now lives retired at Fürth, Germany.

11a. **Ronald Richard.** Born 4 June 1954 at San Antonio, TX. Married Pamela Sue Miller on 26 Aug. 1978 at Medford, Jackson Co., OR (she was born 30 Dec. 1955). Ron Burgess is an employee leasing manager for Barrett Business Services, Inc., Medford, OR. Pamela Burgess is co-owner of the Uniglobe Travel Agency at Medford.

11b. **Steven Bruce (I).** Born 13 Jan. 1958 at Heidelberg, West Germany. Married Vera Joan Simkins on 2 Nov. 1987 (she was born 14 Apr. 1961 at Baltimore, MD). Served three years in the U.S. Army, and later was a theater arts major at Southern Oregon State College, Ashland, OR, graduating with a B.S. in humanities. Steve Burgess has been a stock broker and (currently) a disk jockey for radio station KBOY in Oregon. He presently lives at Central Point, OR.

12a. **Jarrod Samuel.** Born 23 Apr. 1988 at San Francisco, CA.

11c. **Brian Ulrich.** Born 16 June 1965 at Nürnberg, West Germany. Married Sybille Grampp on 26 July 1991 at Fürth, Germany. Brian Burgess attended the University of Erlangen, Erlangen, Germany. Brian Burgess is a disk jockey for "Radio Gong" at Nürnberg, Germany; Sybille Burgess is a dental technician. They live at Fürth, Germany.

12a. **Kenneth Ronald.** Born 25 Aug. 1993 at Fürth, Germany.

10b. **Cleo Mae (I).** Born 26 Mar. 1932 at Medford, OR. Married Thomas David Hutchinson on 26 July 1952 at Reno, NV (he was born 2 Sept. 1925 at Oakland, CA, and died on 26 July 1987 at Medford, OR), and had children: *David Louis* (born 25 Mar. 1953); *Donna Kaye* (born 4 Sept. 1954, married Dennis Weber, and had children: Seth Adam [born 5 Aug. 1981]; Caitlin Anne [born 23 Nov. 1985]); *Scott Thomas* (born 5 Aug. 1963). With her husband, Cleo Hutchinson owned Hutchinson Produce for 22 years, and then operated the Hungry Bear Restaurant at Ashland, OR for seven years. She now works for a private post office at the Ideal Drug Store, Ashland, OR, and lives at Talent, OR. Her home was the site of a 1992 Burgess reunion for her branch of the family.

10c. **Lois Ione.** Born 19 May 1934 at Klamath Falls, OR. Married Martin Snyder at Beaverton, OR, and had children: *(Robert) Charles* (born 27 Aug. 1953, married, and had children: Travis [born 1975]; Sean [born 8 Oct. 1985]); *Michael Daniel* (born 28 Feb. 1955, married, and had children: Wyatt [born 13 Apr. 1976]; Emily Ann [born 5 Jan. 1984]); *Kathy Ellen* (born 14 Dec. 1956, married ___ McCord, and had children: Aaron [born 11 Jan. 1974]); *Kelly Jean* (born 29 Sept. 1962, married ___ Phillips, and had children: Jennifer [born 9 Sept. 1980]; Craig [born 12 Sept. 1982]; Gina [born 2 Aug. 1985]; Jessica [born 2 Nov. 1988]; Robert [born 21 Dec. 1989]). Lois married secondly Jean Bakke. Lois Bakke lives at Ketchikan, AK.

10d. **Darlene Joyce.** Born 8 May 1947 at Sacramento, CA. Married David Michael Bugica on 12 Aug. 1965 (div.), and had children: *Bradley David* (born 27 Mar. 1968 at Reno, NV); married secondly Stephen Alan Ingram on 31 Dec. 1983 in El Dorado Co., CA (div.). Darlene Burgess is a legal secretary for Duncan, Ball, Evans & Ubaldi at Sacramento, CA.

ROBERT T. BURGESS OF WASHINGTON CO., ARKANSAS

[William Henry (I)[6], Thomas Marshall (I)[7], Phillip Paul Bliss[8]]

9c. **Robert Thomas (I)** *[son of Phillip Paul Bliss].* Born 10 Nov. 1913 at Watertown, Codington Co., SD. Married (Lillie) Rosalina Chandler (she died in 1935, and is buried in the Oddfellows Cemetery, Medford, OR); married secondly Virginia Benjestorf about 1937 (div.); married thirdly Ruth Sessions on 13 May 1948; married fourthly Marsha Annette Smith on 10 Oct. 1970; married fifthly Janice Barlow on 3 Oct 1972 (div.). Bob Burgess has worked as a welder, millwright, railroad fire man, uranium prospector, mountain lion hunter, professional musician, and many others. At the age of fifteen he invented a new kind of brake shoe that was widely adopted. He drove the Alaskan Highway 29 times, and survived the disastrous Alaskan Earthquake of the 1960s. He later farmed near Elkins, Washington Co., AR. Bob Burgess died on 3 Apr. 1993 at Prairie Grove, AR, and is buried in a private cemetery at Viney Grove, Fayetteville, AR. Marsha Burgess lives near Fayetteville, AR; Janice Burgess lives at Kansas City, MO; Ruth Burgess lives at Milwaukie, OR.

10a. **Theodore Thomas "Ted."** Born 27 Apr. 1933 at Medford, OR. See below for full entry.
10b. **Delmer Robert.** Born 24 Sept. 1938 at Coos Bay, OR. See below for full entry.
10c. **Kenneth Hugh (I).** Born 19 June 1940 at Sacramento, CA. See below for full entry.
10d. **Jerry Phil (I).** Born 18 Feb. 1953 at Salmon, ID. See below for full entry.
10e. **Bobbi Ruth.** Born 16 June 1958 at Coeur d'Alene, ID. Married David Scogin, and had children: *Alicia Mae*; *Bonnie*; *Ben.*
10f. **Robert Donald (II) "Robbin."** Born 25 July 1971 at Truth or Consequences, NM. See below for full entry.
10g. **Joel Francis.** Born 18 Sept. 1972 at Truth or Consequences, NM; died there on 19 Sept. 1972.
10h. **Bethra Kay.** Born 16 Nov. 1973 at Deming, NM. Married Terry Hawkins (div.).
10i. **Burgess Lee "Burgie."** Born 28 Dec. 1973 at Truth or Consequences, NM.
10j. **Robert Thomas II "Bob."** Born 17 May 1976 at Belfair, WA.
10k. **Thomas Paul.** Born 13 June 1976 at Dallesport, WA.
10l. **Annette Lucille.** Born 30 Apr. 1978 at Tilly, AR.
10m. **Lois Vallee.** Born 14 Sept. 1978 at Hagerman, ID.
10n. **Ruth Marie.** Born 8 Sept. 1982 at Patrick, AR.
10o. **Ella Louise.** Born 8 June 1983 at Patrick, AR.
10p. **Martin Dudley.** Born 15 Feb. 1985 at Patrick, AR.
10q. **Chandler Clay.** Born 2 July 1986 at Fayetteville, AR.

THEODORE T. BURGESS OF KITSAP CO., WASHINGTON

[William Henry (I)[6], Thomas Marshall (I)[7], Phillip Paul Bliss[8], Robert Thomas (I)[9]]

10a. **Theodore Thomas "Ted"** *[son of Robert Thomas (I)].* Born 27 Apr. 1933 at Medford, OR. Married Mary Lou Threlkeld; married secondly Laurel Dodge on 11 Aug. 1979 at Puyallup, WA. Ted Burgess was a welder for the shipbuilding industry at Bremerton, WA. He currently lives at Belgrade, MT.

11a. **Karen Lynn (II).** Born 16 Oct. 1961 at Bremerton, WA. Married Kevin Lawing, and had children: *Aimee Victoria* (born 24 Oct. 1983); *Debra Lorene* (born 11 Mar. 1986); *Nickolaus Davis* (born 2 Feb. 1990).
11b. **Philip Thomas.** Born 20 Mar. 1970 at Tacoma, WA.
11c. **Megan Rose.** Born 29 Apr. 1983.
11d. **Cayce Paul.** Born 6 Mar. 1985.

DELMER R. BURGESS OF CURRY CO., OREGON

[William Henry (I)^6, Thomas Marshall (I)^7, Phillip Paul Bliss^8, Robert Thomas (I)^9]

10b. **Delmer Robert** *[son of Robert Thomas (I)].* Born 24 Sept. 1938 at Coos Bay, OR. Married Melodie Carolyn Waits on 6 Nov. 1959. Del Burgess works for the telephone company at Gold Beach, OR.

11a. **Sherry Lee.** Born 16 Dec. 1960 at Upland, CA. Married Howard Karp on 8 Aug. 1981 in Curry Co., OR, and had children: *Lyndsi Marie* (born 30 May 1982); *Mathew Ryan* (born 5 Oct. 1983); *Brittany Ann* (born 29 Nov. 1989).

11b. **Christine Rene.** Born 1 Apr. 1962 at La Mesa, CA. Married Johnnie Ward on 12 July 1980 in Curry Co., OR, and had children: *Tyler Del* (born 30 Dec. 1983); *Lacey Rea* (born 28 Nov. 1985).

KENNETH H. BURGESS, Sr. OF JACKSON CO., OREGON

[William Henry (I)^6, Thomas Marshall (I)^7, Phillip Paul Bliss^8, Robert Thomas (I)^9]

10c. **Kenneth Hugh (I)** *[son of Robert Thomas (I)].* Born 19 June 1940 at Sacramento, CA. Married Beverly Barnes; married secondly Linda Kaye Anderson on 12 June 1979; married thirdly Terry Lynn Ehred on 18 Dec. 1981 at Billings, Yellowstone Co., MT. Ken Burgess was a cable splicer for the telephone company at Billings, MT before retiring. He now lives at Phoenix, OR.

11a. **Kenneth Hugh (II).** Born 6 Feb. 1958 at Petaluma, CA. Married Paula J. Shore on 20 Jan. 1979 in Stanislaus Co., CA. Ken Burgess Jr. is a title manager for a company at Modesto, CA.

12a. **Vicki Lorraine.** Born 10 Feb. 1980 at Modesto, CA.
12b. **Kenneth Paul "Kenny."** Born 9 Oct. 1981 at Modesto, CA.

11b. **Ronald Del.** Born 16 Feb. 1959 at Petaluma, CA. Married Abby Lambert on 27 Feb. 1981 in Stanislaus Co., CA; married secondly Lois Ann Belt on 21 Nov. 1992 (she was born 3 Apr. 1954). Ron is a landscaper at Medford, OR.

12a. **Andrew Wayne.** Born 23 Oct. 1982 at Modesto, CA.
12b. **Toni Collene.** Born 8 Feb. 1984 at Modesto, CA.

11c. **Gary Wayne.** Born 12 July 1962 at El Cajon, CA. Gary Burgess is a large appliance salesman for Montgomery Ward at Salem, OR.

12a. **Rand Mason.** Born 30 Mar. 1988 at Modesto, CA.

11d. **Lisa Leanne** (ad.). Born 30 June 1976 at Bozeman, MT.

JERRY P. BURGESS, Sr. OF EL PASO CO., TEXAS

[William Henry (I)^6, Thomas Marshall (I)^7, Phillip Paul Bliss^8, Robert Thomas (I)^9]

10d. **Jerry Phil (I)** *[son of Robert Thomas (I)].* Born 18 Feb. 1953 at Salmon, ID. Married Diane Rae Long Sparks on 27 Aug. 1970 (div.; she was born about 1954 in Arizona, remarried ___ Tompkins, and was living at Clements, CA in 1972); married secondly Evangelina Bustillos on 9 Apr. 1972 (she was born 11 Oct. 1948); married thirdly Fara Ray on 13 Jan. 1977 (she was born 23 May ___). Jerry Burgess has been a dry wall installer, beekeeper, salesman, rancher, and insurance agent. He currently works at El Paso, TX.

11a. **Albert (IV)** (nmn) (ad.). Born 24 June 1967 at Las Vegas, NV. Married.

12a. **Amber.**
12b. **Daphny.**
12c. **Jasimine.**

11b. **Rafael Siegfried (I) "Lelo"** (ad.). Born 9 Jan. 1969 at Colonia Lebaron, Chihuahua, México. Married.

12a. **Cynthia (II).**
12b. **Rafael Siegfried (II).**

11c. **Jerry Moroni.** Born 23 May 1971 at Carlsbad, NM.
11d. **Mireya Jeanette** (ad.). Born 28 Dec. 1971 at Colonia Lebaron, Chihuahua, México. Married Foiny ___, and had children: *Ashley*; *Foiny Jr.*
11e. **John William (V).** Born 10 Sept. 1972 at Lodi, San Joaquin Co., CA.
11f. **Danila** (nmn) (ad.). Born 6 Oct. 1972 at Colonia Lebaron, Chihuahua, México. Married, and had children: *Mirrim*; *Linn.*
11g. **Daisy Ruth.** Born 2 June 1973 at Colonia Lebaron, Chihuahua, México.
11h. **Samuel Oliver** (ad.). Born 11 May 1974 at Colonia Lebaron, Chihuahua, México.
11i. **Jerry Phil (II).** Born 3 Aug. 1974 at Colonia Lebaron, Chihuahua, México.
11j. **(Flora) Lisa.** Born 20 Nov. 1975 at Colonia Lebaron, Chihuahua, México.
11k. **Jeremiah Thomas.** Born 18 Feb. 1977 at Colonia Lebaron, Chihuahua, México.
11l. **Aaron Jerry.** Born 25 June 1978 at Colonia Lebaron, Chihuahua, México.
11m. **Levi Jay.** Born 19 Mar. 1980 at Portland, OR.
11n. **Brian Timothy.** Born 17 May 1981 at Colonia Lebaron, Chihuahua, México.
11o. **Kristal Eva.** Born 20 Sept. 1982 at Las Cruces, NM.
11p. **Kami Ruth.** Born about 1984 at Colonia Lebaron, Chihuahua, México.
11q. **Amy.** Born about 1986 at Colonia Lebaron, Chihuahua, México.
11r. **Jereson.** Born about 1988 at Colonia Lebaron, Chihuahua, México.
11s. **Judy Melissa.** Born about 1990 at Colonia Lebaron, Chihuahua, México.

ROBBIN BURGESS OF WASHINGTON CO., ARKANSAS
[William Henry (I)[6], Thomas Marshall (I)[7], Phillip Paul Bliss[8], Robert Thomas (I)[9]]

10f. **Robert Donald (II) "Robbin."** Born 25 July 1971 at Truth or Consequences, NM. Married Malissa Ann Bryan on 1 June 1990 at Prairie Grove, Washington Co., AR (div.). Robbin Burgess was an E-4 technician for the U.S. Navy, working on sonar equipment installed in submarines. He now lives in Washington Co., AR.

11a. **Lindsay Nicole.** Born 18 June 1992 at San Diego, CA.

HENRY CLAY BURGESS OF SPOKANE CO., WASHINGTON
[William Henry (I)[6], Thomas Marshall (I)[7]]

8d. **(Henry) Clay (III)** *[son of Thomas Marshall (I)].* Born 10 Oct. 1890 at Eagle Lake, MN. Married Lenore Maxson on 27 July 1913 at Swift Current, SK, Canada (she was born 27 Sept. 1896 at Austin, MN, daughter of Roselle Maxson and Fanny Lyon, and died June 1976 at Spokane, WA). Clay Burgess was a salesman and manager for a lumber company. He died on 5 June 1972 at Spokane, WA, and is buried in the Greenwood Memorial Terrace.

9a. **Guy Willard.** Born 28 Jan. 1914 at Cabri, SK, Canada. Married Joyce Farrell on 27 July 1938 in Oregon. Dr. Guy Burgess was a chiropractor at McMinnville, OR. He died there on 18 Sept. 1968. Joyce Burgess lives at Salem, OR.

10a. **Clark Arthur.** Born 9 Mar. 1940 at Longview, WA. Married Valerie Klaiber on 26 Dec. 1968 at Indianapolis, IN. Clark Burgess is a technical manager for the Jet Propulsion Laboratory, Pasadena, CA. He lives at La Crescenta, CA.

11a. **Anthony Guy.** Born 17 Apr. 1970 at Glendale, CA. Anthony Burgess is a police officer for the City of Pasadena, CA. He currently lives at La Crescenta, CA.
11b. **Christian John.** Born 8 Sept. 1972 at Glendale, CA. Christian Burgess is a student at Pasadena City College. He currently lives at La Crescenta, CA.

10b. **Jerald Clay "Jerry."** His name was originally Jerald Dean Burgess. Born 26 Nov. 1945 at Portland, OR. Married Becky Anne McGinnis on 22 July 1972 at Las Vegas, NV (div.); married secondly Jan(ice) Eileen Dye on 23 Nov. 1986 at Loma Linda, CA (she was born 13 Oct.

1949 at Muncie, IN). Jerry Burgess spent twenty-four years in the United States Air Force, and served in Vietnam and in Operation Desert Storm (Kuwait, Iraq, Saudi Arabia); he now holds the rank of Lt. Col. in the USAF Reserves. Since retiring from the Air Force, he has worked as a commercial airline pilot, first with Western Airlines, and now with Delta Airlines. He lives at Redlands, CA.

11a. **Jordan Clay** (ad.). Born 27 Feb. 1988 at Loma Linda, CA.

10c. **Constance Florence "Connie."** Born 14 Jan. 1948 at Portland, OR. Married Jack Ziegler in 1968, and had children: *Richard Patrick* (born 2 Aug. 1970 at McMinnville, OR, married in 1993, and lives at Amity, OR); *Jackie Ann* (born 6 June 1975 at McMinnville, OR). Connie Ziegler currently lives at Salem, OR.

9b. **Margaret Samantha.** Born 13 Oct. 1915 at Portal, ND. Married Robert Waiting on 19 Apr. 1937, and had children:

Robert Blair WAITING. Born 12 Oct. 1938 at Spokane, WA. Married Carol Shriner (div.), and had children: *Gregory Clay* (born 28 Dec. 1958, married Cynthia Bennett on 25 Feb. 1984, and had children: Child [born Nov. 1993], and lives at Spokane, WA); *Chris Steven* (born 27 Nov. 1959 at Spokane, WA, and lives at Pullman, WA); *Kendall Allen* (born 19 June 1961 at Spokane, WA, married Ann Moore in 1988 at San Diego, CA, works as a diver in the U.S. Navy [currently stationed at San Diego], and had children: Kristin Nichole [born 15 June 1990 at Bremerton, WA]; Kelley Ann [born 6 Oct. 1991 at San Diego, CA]); *Denise Kathryn* (born 10 June 1968 at Spokane, WA, and works as a veterinary technologist at Medical Lake, WA). ***Robert B. WAITING*** currently works as a plumber at Spokane, WA.

Judith Dawn WAITING. Born 23 Apr. 1940 at Spokane, WA. Married Levi Perry on 20 Dec. 1958, and had children: *Byron Clay* (born 11 Dec. 1969 at Seattle, WA, married Tracy ___ in 1990, and lives at Lynnwood, WA). ***Judith PERRY*** lives at Lynnwood, WA.

Margaret WAITING currently lives east of Spokane, WA. She has contributed greatly to this book with her memories, pictures, and documents.

9c. **Zoe Loraine.** Born 24 Sept. 1920 at Humboldt, SD. Married Arthur Corbett on 30 Sept. 1941, and had children: *Bruce* (born 4 Mar. 1953, married, divorced, and had children: Brian; Brandi; he lives at Spokane, WA); *Carol Lynn* (born 31 July 1957, married Tim Simchuck on 4 June 1974 [div.], and had children: Ann Lorraine [born 14 Oct. 1975]; Michele [born 6 Jan. 1979]; Chris [born 10 Apr. 1980]). Zoe Corbett currently lives at Spokane, WA.

9d. **(James) Jeffrey.** Born 31 Jan. 1924 at Humboldt, SD. Married Martha Justine "Tina" Buford on 19 Aug. 1945 at Orlando, FL. Jeff Burgess was a senior project engineer for Kaiser Aluminum at Baton Rouge, LA before retiring in 1982. He currently lives at Stuart, FL.

10a. **James Michael.** Born 23 Jan. 1950 at Colorado Springs, CO. Married Christine Elizabeth Dolan on 17 Dec. 1972 at Spokane, WA (she was born 16 July 1952 at Van Nuys, CA). Jim Burgess owns a commercial real estate company, Mountain High Properties, at Salt Lake City, Utah.

11a. **Michael James (III).** Born 24 Nov. 1980 at Salt Lake City, UT.
11b. **Elizabeth (XXI)** (nmn). Born 11 Aug. 1985 at Salt Lake City, UT.

10b. **Joseph Jeffrey.** Born 2 June 1954 at Spokane, WA. Married Susan Sink. Joe Burgess is a biomedical engineer at Stuart, FL.

JOACHIM BURGESS OF LAKE CO., CALIFORNIA

[William Henry (I)[6], Thomas Marshall (I)[7]]

8e. **Joachim "Joe"** (nmn) *[son of Thomas Marshall (I)].* His name is also spelled Joachin; he was named for his grandfather, Joachim Luthultz. Born 16 June 1896 at Eagle Lake, MN. Married Elizabeth Martha Wager in Sept. 1915 (div. 1939; she was born 1895 in Brown Co., MN, and died 1969); married secondly Lillace Blanche Sheets on 19 June 1943 at Palo Alto, CA (she was born 25 Dec. 1894, and died Nov. 1984 at Lucerne, CA). Listed in the 1920 census for Pierce Co., WA, working at Ft. Steilacoom. Joe Burgess was a physical therapist for various governmental and private institutions. His lengthy unpublished memoir provides much background material on the Eagle Lake, MN Burgess families. He died on 7 Aug. 1980 at Lucerne, CA, and is buried with his second wife in the Upper Lake Cemetery.

9a. **(Clayton) James.** Originally christened Clay Joachim, he has also used the name James Clayton. Born 6 July 1915 at Portal, ND. Married Mary Jane Green on 27 Nov. 1941 (she was born 12 Apr. 1921 at Spokane, WA, daughter of Newton Green [1896-1978], the first cornet player for John Philip Sousa's Navy band, and later a musician on the Orpheum Circuit, and Marie Firby Baker [born 1896]; Mary was also a great-niece of George Bancroft [1800-1891], Secretary of the Navy and founder of the Naval Academy at Annapolis). Jim Burgess is an artist and draftsman; he has also worked as a security guard for the Alcoa Building in San Francisco (now retired). Mary J. Burgess is a certified nurse at Chico, CA.

10a. **Brio Marlisa.** Born 27 Apr. 1943 at San Francisco, CA. Brio Burgess won the Edward Arlington Robinson Fellowship in 1970, studying at the Edward MacDowell Colony in New Hampshire, for poetry, plays, paintings, and music she had composed during the period 1963-69. Her compositions include: *Briomindsound*, a sixty-minute audio cassette of piano harp music and poems by herself and others (1979); *Concentration Camp Blues* (piano harp and words, 1980); *Dame, Fame Remains* (piano harp and words, 1980); *Brio and Janis Oye* (experiment in sound, 1980); *The Painters' Song* (guitar and words, 1981); *Gypsy Melodies* (piano, 1982); *Prancing in Time* (piano piece, 1983); *Escape* (a ballet for piano harp, chains, and feet, 1983); *Sound Dreams* (piano and piano harp, 1983); *Moonshiner* (guitar background for a folk song selection sung by Gail Tolley, 1983); *Space Visions* (a four-act opera); and many others. She is a member of ASCAP, The Composer's Forum, The American Music Center, The International League of Women Composers, The Central Opera Service, and The Dramatists Guild, and a writer member of the Authors League at Albany, NY. Her biography has appeared in *The Dictionary of International Biography* (several volumes), *A Directory of American Poets and Fiction Writers*, and *The International Who's Who in Music*. Brio Burgess lives and works at Albany, NY, where she occasionally performs at the Half Moon Cafe and Mother Earth's.

10b. **James Joseph Michael.** Born 2 July 1946 at New Haven, CT. Jim Burgess is a rodeo worker and bull rope maker (under the name "Homer") at Half Moon Bay, California.

10c. **Christopher Paul Barrett.** Born 6 Aug. 1947 at San Francisco, CA. Married Kathryn J. Warner on 2 Apr. 1974 in Monterey Co., CA. Chris Burgess works for Rainbo Baking at Stockton, CA. He is also a champion homing pigeon breeder and racer.

10d. **Anthony Alexander "Tony."** Born 28 Aug. 1948 at San Mateo, CA. Tony Burgess is a part-time teacher at Marin College; he also works as a writer at San Rafael, California.

10e. **Mary Elizabeth (VIII) "Maribeth."** Born 26 Oct. 1950 at San Francisco, CA. Married Craig Olvin Starnes on 21 Feb. 1970 in Butte Co., CA (he was born 30 Sept. 1948, was a country and western guitar player, and died 26 Sept. 1992 at Chico, CA), and had children: *Starla* (born 9 June 1970 at Oroville, CA); *Jaydee Firby* (born 25 Jan. 1971 at Chico, CA); *Amber* (born 10 Aug. 1976 at Paradise, CA). Maribeth Starnes currently lives at Chico, CA.

10f. **Phillip Joseph.** Born 30 Apr. 1952 at San Francisco, CA. Married Mary Elizabeth Dolan on 26 June 1976 in Santa Clara Co., CA (she works as a registered nurse in obstetrics). Phil Burgess has been a boat builder of commercial fishing vessels and other ships at Moss Landing, CA, as well as a carpenter and artist. He currently lives at Chico, CA.

11a. **Suzannah Firby.** Born 14 Mar. 1978 at Salinas, CA.
11b. **Phillip Andrew.** Born 26 Mar. 1982 at Salinas, CA.

10g. **Veronica Mary.** Born 31 Mar. 1954 at San Francisco, CA. Married Richard Allen Hawkinson on 25 Aug. 1973, and had children: *Alan Lee* (born 23 Aug. 1974 at Sacramento, CA); married secondly Dennis Leslie Copenhaver on 18 June 1977, and had children: *Amy Rachel* (born 2 Feb. 1977 at Fairfield, CA); married thirdly Salvatore John Gigante on 28 June 1980 in El Dorado Co., CA. Veronica Gigante is a commercial artist at Placerville, CA.

10h. **Catherine Ann "Cathy."** Born 23 Nov. 1955 at San Francisco, CA. Married Joseph Brostek. Catherine Brostek was a housewife at Chico, CA. She died there on 5 Nov. 1974, and is buried in the Glen Oaks Memorial Park.

10i. **Andrew Edward "Andy."** Born 23 May 1957 at San Francisco, CA. Married Clare Kohlenburger. Andy Burgess was a supermarket manager for Mayfair Markets at Reno, NV. He died there on 19 Oct. 1992.

10j. **Peter Paul.** Born 29 June 1958 at San Francisco, CA. Pete Burgess is a Sergeant with the 1st U.S. Marine Brigade, stationed at Oahu, HI.

10k. **Sylvia Ann.** Born 9 Nov. 1961 at San Mateo, CA. Married. Sylvia Burgess is part owner of a carnival at San Antonio, TX.

CHARLES E. BURGESS OF BLUE EARTH CO., MINNESOTA

[William Henry (I)[6]]

7g. **Charles Edward (I)** *[son of William Henry (I)].* Born 4 Aug. 1861 at Eagle Lake, MN. Married Mary Agnes Buckley on 26 July 1890 in Blue Earth Co., MN (she was born 11 Apr. 1862, and died on 9 June 1954, aged 92 years). Listed in the 1900-10 censuses for Eagle Lake. Charley Burgess was a railroad telegraph operator, and also played in a Ringling Brothers dog-and-pony show, and traveled with an orchestra (he played the violin and piano); he later worked a small farm near Eagle Lake, MN. He died there on 13 Mar. 1918; a memorial marker appears in the Burgess Cemetery, but both he and his wife are actually buried in the Glenwood Cemetery, Mankato, MN.

8a. **Clara Alice.** Born 11 (or 18, according to Social Security records) May 1891 at Eagle Lake, MN. Married Harry Ross Jones on 3 Sept. 1913, and had children: *Joyce Harriet* (born 24 July 1914, married Kenneth Ogee, and lives at Warrington, PA); *Beatrice Grace "Betty"* (born 10 June 1916, married Harold Cramer, and died on 16 Mar. 1989 at Faribault, MN); *Constance Dawn "Connie"* (born 27 Apr. 1920, married Lloyd Bowen, and lives at Rochester, MN). Clara Jones was a piano teacher at Mankato, MN before losing her sight in her late 80s; she died on 6 Mar. 1989 at Mankato, aged 97 years.

8b. **Maude Frances.** Born 10 Nov. 1893 at Eagle Lake, MN. Married Lyle Austin, and had children: *Glenn* (born 11 May 1911, and died childless on 23 May 1961 at Mankato, MN); married secondly John Eckhardt; married thirdly Elmer Davis. Maude Davis was a school teacher and artist at Hot Springs, AR; she died there in 1983, aged 89 years. She may be the Maud Davis who was born 5 Nov. 1892, and died Feb. 1983 at Neelyville, MO.

8c. **(Charles) Benjamin.** Born 5 Mar. 1895 at Eagle Lake, MN. See below for full entry.

8d. **Glenn Edward.** Born Nov. 1896 at Mankato, MN. Married Evelyn Brown (she was born 16 Aug. 1897, worked as a school teacher, and died 11 Sept. 1993 at Kirkwood, IL, aged 96 years). Glenn Burgess was a telegraph operator at Kirkwood, IL. He later moved to Harlingen, TX, where he died childless on 8 Feb. 1977.

BENJAMIN BURGESS OF LA CROSSE CO., WISCONSIN

[William Henry (I)[6], Charles Edward (I)[7]]

8c. **(Charles) Benjamin** *[son of Charles Edward (I)].* Born 5 Mar. 1895 at Eagle Lake, MN. Married Dorothy Marie Scott on 27 June 1923 (she was born 7 July 1897, and died Jan. 1980 in WI or IL). Ben Burgess served in World War I in the Army Air Force as a balloon pilot; he later sold books, cars, and food products for the National Biscuit Co. He moved to La Crosse, WI in 1930, founding the La Crosse Dock Co. in 1939, and later Scott Burgess Inc., a fuel company specializing in coal, oil, furnaces, stokers, and water heaters. He was also a 32nd degree Mason, a Shriner, and a member of the Elks. Two years before his death, Ben Burgess began writing a history of the Burgess family, but died before completing more than the section on his own branch of the family. His work was transcribed by his daughter, Mary Redmann, who has allowed it to be used as background material for this genealogy. Ben Burgess died on 4 Mar. 1968 at La Crosse, WI, and is buried in the Oak Grove Cemetery.

9a. **Mary Katherine.** Born 3 Dec. 1925 at Ft. Dodge, IA. Married Delbert Floyd Redmann on 1 Mar. 1953 at LaCrosse, WI (he was born 10 Jan. 1922 in Mound Prairie Township, Houston Co., MN), and had children: *Katherine Elisabeth* (born 10 Dec. 1953 at LaCrosse, WI, married Richard Wood on 30 Nov. 1985 at Elk Grove Village, IL; she works as a trade show manager for Security Tag Co. at Clearwater, FL); *Mary Sue* (born 3 May 1956 at LaCrosse, WI; she works as a professional harpist at Chicago, IL). Mary Redmann contributed greatly to this book by transcribing her father's handwritten notes towards a history of the Burgess family. She has been a social worker, and currently lives at Park Ridge, IL. In 1994 she became the first person to join the Daughters of the American Revolution (DAR) through the line of Elizabeth Burgess Mauzy.

9b. **Scott Charles.** Born 29 Apr. 1927 at Chicago, IL. Married Margaret Hume on 24 Dec. 1951 at El Reno, OK. Scott Burgess was a graduate of Annapolis Naval Academy in 1950, and served as a pilot in the U.S. Air Force, attaining the rank of Major. After retiring from the service he owned and operated his father's fuel company, and worked as a sprinkler engineer at Chicago, IL. He also loved jazz, played the trumpet and trombone, and led the dance band at Annapolis. He died on 30 Aug. 1973 at Forest Park, IL, but is buried near El Reno, OK.

10a. **Charles Brent.** Born 24 Apr. 1956 at Brookline, MA. Married Somporn "Som" Boonsutat on 15 Sept. 1980. Charles Burgess received his B.A. from California Polytechnic State University, San Luis Obispo in 1978, and his M.S. in counseling in 1989 from the University of LaVerne, Riverside, CA. Major Charles Burgess is a mission crew commander (AWACS) in the U.S. Air Force, currently stationed at Tinker Air Force Base, OK.

11a. **Monica LeeLa.** Born 30 Sept. 1981 at Great Falls, MT.

10b. **Daniel Scott (I).** Born 3 Dec. 1959 at LaCrosse, WI. Married. Dan Burgess is a Captain in the U.S. Army Intelligence, currently stationed at Fort Hood, TX. He served in Operation Desert Storm (Kuwait and Iraq) in 1991, receiving the Bronze Star.

Excerpts from the Memoirs of Joachim Burgess (1970)

"Dad was a minister's son, and Mother came from a very religious family. Her people thought my father was a proper husband for her, so they became engaged. Father was a tall man, over six feet like myself, and a great lover of horses. I don't believe he ever had any formal training as a veterinarian, but he knew how to train and treat horses better than any man I ever knew. Originally Mother and Father planned to be married in the early spring. It was about the last of March 1877 when Dad saddled up and rode forth on what he thought would be his wedding day. In order to reach Grandfather Lethultz's [sic] house, he had to cross a stream; but by the time he reached there, the spring floods had washed out the flimsy bridge. Now he could have detoured and reached Grandfather's place by a longer way around, about fifteen miles longer, which would get him to Mother's late that night. He also could have removed all his clothes, rolled them up in a bundle, and tied them on his shoulders where they would keep dry. I guess he was thinking about only one thing, and that was getting to his prospective bride as soon as possible. Although the day wasn't too cold yet, the water in the stream would come up over his saddle, and chunks of ice were floating in it. His horse was reluctant about swimming that icy stream, but Dad raked him with spurs, and in they plunged and were soon on the other side. Now if Father had had dry clothes, he could, after wiping himself off, have put them on, perhaps building a fire, and all would have been well. As it was, he didn't have a dry thread on. To make matters worse, the weather suddenly turned freezing cold, and it began to sleet. He rode as fast as the horse could travel, but he had about five miles to go until he reached Grandfather's. When he did, he had to be literally chopped from the saddle and drug into the house. Hot toddies were administered, his icy clothes removed, and he was wrapped in warm blankets and put to bed. Poor Dad had pneumonia and wasn't physically able to get married until next New Year's Day, when Uncle John and Aunt Jennie were married at the same time in a double wedding."

The Children of Thomas Marshall Burgess: *Edna Mildred* (left, 1878-1979), *Phillip Paul Bliss* (back middle, 1881-1946), *Clinton Ernest* (back right, 1879-1968), *Joachim* (front middle, 1896-1980), *Henry Clay* (front right, 1890-1972)

[William (I)[1], Edward (I)[2], William (II)[3], Henry (I)[4], John Henry (I)[5]]

GEORGE WASHINGTON BURGESS
(1826-1917)
OF CARROLL COUNTY, MISSOURI

6b. **George Washington (V) "Wash"** *[son of John Henry (I)].* Born 24 Aug. 1826 in Marion Co., IN. Married his second cousin, Marietta Dungan, on 23 (or 22) Mar. 1850 in Harrison Co., KY (she was born 22 July 1833 in Scott Co., KY, daughter of Jesse Dungan and Margaret Burgess, and died on 2 Oct. 1920 in Carroll Co., MO; Marietta's uncle, Joseph F. Burgess, gave his written permission for his ward's marriage; on 7 Mar. 1855 George W. and Marietta Burgess of Parke Co., IN, and Joshua and Sarah Ann Fields [Marietta's sister] sold their interest in the estate of Thomas Dungan, Jesse Duncan's father, to their mother, Margaret Dungan of Harrison Co., KY [*Deed Book #25*, p. 281]; Marietta's relationship is also confirmed by her death certificate, which gives her parents' full names). Listed in the 1850 census living with his father, in the 1851 tax list for Parke Co., IN, in the 1860 census for Putnam Co., IN, in 1865-70 in Blue Earth Co., MN, in 1880 and 1910 in Morris Township, Carroll Co., MO, and in 1900 in Brookfield, Linn Co., MO. Wash Burgess lived near his parents in Parke Co., IN and Blue Earth Co., MN until 1873, when he moved his family to a farm about six miles southwest of Bogard, Carroll Co., MO, buying 120 acres of land there on 21 Mar. 1874 from John W. Smith (*Carroll Co. Deed Book #22*, p. 311). He died there on 22 Sept. 1917, aged 91 years, and is buried with his wife and some of his children in the Smith Cemetery near his farm. A lengthy biography of Wash (with photograph) appears in the 21 May 1914 issue of the *Carrollton Republican-Record*:

REPUBLICAN-RECORD READER 40 YEARS

"This week we present to our readers the well-known features of G. W. Burgess of Leslie Township, who has been reading the *Republican-Record* for more than forty years. Mr. Burgess was born August 24, 1826 in Marion County, Ind. While an infant, his parents moved to Kentucky, but returned to Indiana in 1832. In 1856 he went to Minnesota, making the trip overland. It took 42 days to make the trip. In the Spring of 1857, war broke out with the Indians, and the subject of this sketch passed through two Indian massacres. In the Fall of 1857 he returned to Indiana, and moved back to Minnesota in the Fall of 1860. At that time where he lived was nothing but a wilderness, inhabited by savage tribes with here and there a small settlement of civilized people. Mr. Burgess lived in Minnesota until 1873, and then came to Missouri, and settled on a farm six miles west of Bogard, where he continues to reside. On March 22, 1850 he was married to Miss Mary Dungan, in Harrison County, Kentucky. Of this union 11 children were born, only three of whom, John M. Burgess, Mrs. Nevada Payne, and Mrs. Martha Bush, are living. During the life time of Mr. Burgess, more changes have taken place than during any other two centuries in the world's history. Means of travel have been entirely revolutionized, means of communication by rail, telegraph, and telephone have placed the most remote parts of the earth in close proximity to the centers of population. The hand of civilization has changed the topography of the country and established many magnificent homes where wilderness abounded in the early life of Mr. Burgess. During the past few years Mr. Burgess has been in very poor health, and several times he was near death's door. We understand, however, that lately he has been feeling some better, and we sincerely trust that he may be spared many more years of usefulness, and enjoy the fruits of a well-spent life."

The Children of Wash Burgess:

7a. **John Marion (II).** Born 4 Mar. 1851 at Portland Mills, IN. See below for full entry.
7b. **Sarah M(arietta?).** Born about 1853 at Portland Mills, IN. Living with her parents in 1870, but died before 1880.

7c. **George T(homas?) (I).** Born 14 Dec. 1855 at Portland Mills, IN. Married Mrs. Lula L. Kennedy on 25 Nov. 1896 in Carroll Co., MO. Listed with his father in 1900. George T. Burgess was a salesman and grocer at Carrollton, MO. His brief biography appears in *History of Carroll County, Missouri* (St. Louis: Missouri Historical Co., 1881, p. 584, as noted below). He died childless on 23 Apr. 1899 on his parents' farm, and is buried with them in the Smith Cemetery. Lula is listed with his parents in the 1910 census, and is mentioned in a letter from George Washington Burgess as being alive in 1915.

"George T. Burgess was born in Putnam County, Ind., son of George W. and Mary A. Burgess, natives of Kentucky. George was educated in the mercantile business; after coming of age, he sold books and papers for a while, and afterwards sold sewing machines. In March 1881 he bought the grocery store of T. E. Willis in Carrollton, Mo., and is enjoying a large and extensive trade. Mr. Burgess is a member of the I.O.O.F."

7d. **Martha Ethleen "Mattie."** Born 22 Sept. 1858 at Portland Mills, IN. Married Cassius F. Bush on 27 July 1877 in Carroll Co., MO (he was born Aug. 1852 in OH), and had one child: *Flossie M.* (born 6 Dec. 1882 at Mandeville, MO, married Joseph Milligan in 1899 [he was born May 1880 in IA], and had children: Wilson [born May 1900]). Listed in the 1900-20 censuses for Pulaski, Prairie Township, Davis Co., IA. Mattie Bush was receiving county old age assistance with her daughter in Davis Co. between 1934-37.

7e. **Child.** Born about 1860 in Indiana; died young.

7f. **Child.** Born about 1862 in Minnesota; died young.

7g. **Mary Nevada "Vade."** Born 3 Dec. 1865 at Eagle Lake, MN. Married William E. Payne (he was born Oct. 1857 in MO, but died between 1913-23), and had children: *Roscoe* (born Oct. 1889); *Seymour* (born Apr. 1893); *Hazel Fern* (born Feb. 1898, married ___ Dunn, and secondly ___ Howard); *Gladys* (born after 1900). Listed in the 1900 census for Carroll Co., MO. Vade Payne died there on 14 July 1923, and is buried in the Smith Cemetery.

7h. **Child.** Born about 1867 at Eagle Lake; died young.

7i. **Henry A.** Born Mar. 1869 at Eagle Lake, MN; died there in Feb. 1870 (as listed in the Minnesota mortality census). Relationship not verified.

7j. **Ward.** Born 12 Dec. 1872 at LeRay Township, Eagle Lake, MN; died 31 Dec. 1874 in Carroll Co., MO, and is buried with his parents.

7k. **(Doctor) Allen.** Born 31 July 1875 at Bogard, MO; died there on 20 Dec. 1888, and is buried with his parents.

JOHN MARION BURGESS OF MARICOPA CO., ARIZONA

[George Washington (V)[6]]

7a. **John Marion (II)** *[son of George Washington (V)].* Born 4 Mar. 1851 at Portland Mills, IN. Married Alice Cornelia Tuttle on 28 July 1873 at Eagle Lake, MN, the marriage being conducted by his uncle, Rev. William H. Burgess (Alice was born 21 Aug. 1853 at Ogden, NY, and died 25 Dec. 1936 at Bristow, OK). Listed with his parents in the 1880 census, and in the 1900 census for Spearfish, Lawrence Co., SD, where he had moved in 1880. John M. Burgess was elected Justice of the Peace for Spearfish Precinct, DT (later SD) on 28 Nov. 1886, and City Assessor of Spearfish on 29 Apr. 1893. He moved to Phoenix, Maricopa Co., AZ in 1909, where he bought several fruit orchards, and is listed there in the 1920 census living with his daughter, Maud, and in the rural directories of Maricopa Co. from 1920-30. John Burgess died on 11 Jan. 1932 at Phoenix, and is buried in the Greenwood Cemetery with his wife and several of his children. A short, unpublished autobiography (later adapted into his obituary), now in the possession of his granddaughter, Fern Knight, provides important details on the Burgess family's move from Portland Mills, IN to Eagle Lake, MN in 1856 and 1860:

"John M. Burgess was born in Parke County, Indiana, 4 of March 1851. In September 1856 he, with his parents, relatives, and friends, thirteen wagons and seventy-five head of stock, started overland to Blue Earth County, Minnesota. The emigrant train moved slowly, resting Sunday. They passed through much unsettled country, timber, and prairie, seeing wild game of many kinds, building roads and many bridges. They settled near the Winnebago Agency, five miles from Mankato, Minnesota. The winter of '56/57 was very severe: snow fell to a depth of three feet. Most all of the stock died from cold and hunger. The last of April, news came that the Indians had broke out and killed some settlers at Spirit Lake. The Indians were soon subdued. His mother was in poor health; the shock from the Indian troubles did not help her, so his father with three other families returned to Putnam County, living there until September 1860, when they, with relatives and friends, returned overland with four wagons seven hundred miles to their wilderness home.

"Things went pretty well until the 18th of August 1862, when the Indians attacked New Ulm. Finally, the Indians were subdued. The Winnebago tribe was moved out of the country, and the country became prosperous. On the 28th of July 1873 John M. Burgess was married to Alice C. Burgess of Owatonna, Steele County, Minnesota. They moved that Fall to Carrollton, Missouri. [In] 1874 [they] moved to Oskaloosa, Iowa. In the Fall of 1875 moved back to Missouri, staying in Missouri until March of 1880, when with poor health and with three other men went overland to the Black Hills, Dakota Territory, landing there in May with health restored. On September 25th, 1880 he united with Spearfish Lodge No. 26, I.O.O.F., by invitation, was a member of that Lodge until his death, fifty-one years, three months, sixteen days. He was elected Grandmaster of South Dakota in 1905, went to Toronto, Canada as Grand Representative in 1906, into Saint Paul, Minnesota in 1907.

"[He] moved to Arizona in 1909, buying a fruit farm eight miles from Phoenix. Selling that in 1919 on account of his health, he then travelled four summers, living near Phoenix in winter. Then, his health being better, he planted a pecan grove which was beginning to bear nicely at his death. He also was a charter member of Ann Rebekah Lodge No. 4, I.O.O.F., Spearfish, South Dakota, and its first Noble Grand. He also was a member of the Camp Deadwood, Idaho. He loved the Order, he was a good Oddfellow at all times and places. He leaves a wife and five children, three girls, two boys: Mrs. W. H. Gardner of Los Angeles; Mrs. James M. Ellis, Bristow, Oklahoma; Mrs. M. Drane of Corsicana, Texas; Clyde Burgess of Phoenix, Arizona; George M. Burgess, Tempe, Arizona; twenty-three grandchildren, and eleven great-grandchildren."

8a. **Florence (I) "Flossie."** Her name is given as Flancy in the 1880 census. Born about 1877 in Carroll Co., MO. Married William H. Gardner (he was born about 1875 in IA), and had children: *Emerald* (born 1900 in WY); *Fahr* (born 1901 in SD); *Kenneth* (born 1903 in MT); *(Francis) Alan* (born 12 July 1905 in SD, and died 19 Mar. 1989 at Denver, CO); *William "Bill"* (born 21 July 1907, and died 13 June 1987); *Helen* (born 1912 in CO); *Zada*. Listed in the 1920 census for Boulder, Boulder Co., CO. Flossie Gardner lived at both Denver, CO and Los Angeles, CA, and had settled at Railroad Flats, CA by 1952. She is said to have died at Rifle, CO while visiting her brother, George, about 1955.

8b. **Clyde Durward**. Born 1 July 1885 at Spearfish, DT (later SD). See below for full entry.

8c. **Maud.** Born Feb. 1887 at Spearfish, DT (later SD). Married James M. Ellis Sr. by 1920 (he was born 3 Nov. 1884, and died July 1984, aged 99 years, at Bristow, OK), and had children: *James M. Jr.* (he may have been born 27 May 1909, and died 24 Apr. 1990 at Okmulgee, OK); *Velda*; *Aletha*; *Donald* (born 29 May 1918, and died Dec. 1986 at Okmulgee, OK). Listed in the 1920 city directory of Phoenix living alone, and in the 1920 census for Maricopa Co. with her father and husband. Maud Ellis was living at Beggs, Okmulgee Co., OK in 1952, and may have died there or at Bristow, Creek Co., OK about 1973. She may be the Maud Ellis who was born 6 Feb. 1890 and died Mar. 1982 at Pawhuska, Osage Co., OK.

8d. **George Marion (I)**. Born 5 June 1891 at Spearfish, DT (later SD). See below for full entry.

8e. **Evagiline Alica "Eva."** Born 8 Aug. 1892 at Spearfish, DT (later SD). Married as his second wife Meritt A. Drane about 1913, and had children: *Meritt A. Jr.* (born 31 July 1914, married Elizabeth Ann Mitchell, and lives at Dallas, TX); *Burgess Ellis* (born 30 Sept. 1919, and died Jan. 1978 at Brighton, IL); by his first wife Meritt A. Drane Sr. had children: *Ruth Thayer* (born 1908, married John L. King Jr. on 21 July 1928, and had children: John L. III [born 12 Aug. 1931, married, had five children, and died 7 Mar. 1973]); *Cora Frances* (dec.). Eva Drane lived at Dallas, TX from 1913-32, and at Phoenix, AZ from 1932-52. She died on 8 Oct. 1952 at Dallas, TX, but is buried with her parents in the Greenwood Cemetery, Phoenix, AZ. Ruth King currently lives at Denton, TX, and has contributed greatly to this book.

CLYDE BURGESS OF MARICOPA CO., ARIZONA

[George Washington (V)[6], John Marion (II)[7]]

8b. **Clyde Durward** *[son of John Marion (II)]*. Born 1 July 1885 at Spearfish, DT (later SD). Married Lillie Mildred Morrell on 14 Oct. 1914 at Phoenix, Maricopa Co., AZ (she was born 8 Sept. 1894 at Phoenix, AZ, daughter of Linsey Byron Morrell and Eva Brimmer, and died 18 Nov. 1971); married secondly Dorothy F. Trow Jedliska in 1973. Listed in the 1917 draft register and the 1920 census for Maricopa Co., AZ, and in the 1920-30 city directories of Phoenix. Clyde Burgess taught in a business education school in New Jersey from 1906-09, before moving to Phoenix in 1909. He was an office manager for Arizona Overland Co. until that firm failed during the depression, about 1930; he then served as office manager and accountant for Palmer Manufacturing Co. (an air cooling and conditioning company) for five years. He founded Triangle Auto Rebuilders in 1937, and operated it until his retirement in 1968. He died on 15 Feb. 1980 at Phoenix, AZ, aged 94 years, and is buried with his first wife in the Greenwood Cemetery.

9a. **(John) Byron.** Born 5 Feb. 1926 at Phoenix, AZ. Married Barbara Alice "Penny" Rice in 1947. Byron Burgess graduated from the University of Redlands and began teaching school at Bloomington, CA in 1947; he became a principal in 1950. After completing his M.A. at Redlands in 1956, he was a consultant to the California State Department of Education from 1958-59. He joined the Manhattan Beach, CA school district in 1959 as Assistant Superintendent of Schools. He was named Superintendent in 1972, and retired in 1986. He was Past President of the Manhattan Beach Chamber of Commerce, and a member of the Manhattan Beach Rotary Club, Manhattan Beach Coordinating Council, Los Angeles County School Administrators Association; and served as Assistant Moderator, Manhattan Beach Community Church, and on the Advisory Board of The Salvation Army. He died on 12 Jan. 1994 at Manhattan Beach, CA.

10a. **Steven Alan** (ad.). Born 26 Feb. 1956 at Los Angeles, CA. Married Traci Penex in 1986 (div.). Steve Burgess is a musician at San Diego, CA.

10b. **Susan Marie** (ad.). Born 22 Mar. 1958 at Newport Beach, CA. Married James Mark (div.), and had children: *Wayne Byron* (born 4 July 1977); *Justin* (born 4 May 1983).

GEORGE M. BURGESS OF MARICOPA CO., ARIZONA

[George Washington (V)[6], John Marion (II)[7]]

8d. **George Marion (I)** *[son of John Marion (II)].* Born 5 June 1891 at Spearfish, DT (later SD). Married Ruby Lucinda Young; married secondly Virginia Rice. Listed in the 1917 draft register of Maricopa Co. George Burgess was a farmer and produce market owner at Rifle, CO, Willis Springs, MO (where he was living in 1952), and Phoenix, AZ. He died on 6 Dec. 1981 at Phoenix, aged 90 years, and is buried in the Greenwood Cemetery.

9a. **John Marion (III).** Born 29 May 1916 at Phoenix, AZ. See below for full entry.

9b. **Velda Louise** (twin). Born 9 Oct. 1917 at Phoenix, AZ. Married Everett Vallas on 7 Oct. 1938 at Phoenix, AZ (he worked as a telephone technician), and had children: *(Evelyn) Lavone* (born 30 Dec. 1939 at Phoenix, AZ, married Ron R. Archer on 28 Aug. 1959 [div. 1981], and had children: Amy Lynn [married Frank Gallo, and had four children]; Ronda Ann [married Mike Trebitowski, and had three children]); *James Everett* (born 1 Sept. 1943 at Phoenix, AZ, married Melba Moore at Las Vegas, NV, and had children: Andrew James [born about 1975 at Phoenix, AZ]; David James [born about 1977 at Phoenix, AZ]; Andrea [born about 1981 at Phoenix, AZ]). Velda Vallas was a meat wrapper before retiring; she currently lives at Phoenix, AZ.

9c. **Verda Alice** (twin). Born 9 Oct. 1917 at Phoenix, AZ. Married Cecil Byrne, and had children: *Jane*; *Michael* (married Perri ___; Michael is an architect); *Gary* (married Norma ___; Gary is a bank president); *Roy* (dec.); Verda married secondly Robert Frehe. Verda Frehe is a retired superintendent of schools; she currently lives at Ontario, CA.

9d. **Fern Marrietta.** Born 1 June 1921 at Casa Grande, AZ. Married Russell Wayne Knight (dec.), and had children:

Elizabeth D. KNIGHT. Born 21 July 1943, married Thomas L. Wertner, and had children: *Tamra Kay* (born 26 June 1964, married Mark Edward Chapman, and had children: Christopher Mark [born 10 Feb. 1985]; Meghan Elizabeth [born 11 Nov. 1990]); *Timothy George* (born 20 May 1966, married Heather Lee Orme); *Tara Marietta* (born 13 Jan. 1968); *Trisha Maire* (born 2 Oct. 1972); *Tanya Sue* (born 30 Oct. 1974).

Russell Wayne KNIGHT Jr. Born 9 Apr. 1946.

Margret Ann KNIGHT. Born 10 June 1948, married Randy Seig.

Howard Ray KNIGHT. Born 24 Aug. 1949, married Nancy Patricia Keppler, and had children: *Traci-Anne* (born 30 Nov. 1969, married Allan Johnson [div.], and had children: Julia Anne [born 11 Sept. 1991]); *Kristina Rae* (born 11 July 1972).

Fern KNIGHT owned Fern Knight & Associates, a real estate office at Phoenix, before retiring. She generously supplied photocopies of her grandfather's biography and letters, and has contributed greatly to this book. She currently lives at Phoenix, AZ.

9e. **(Gwynetha) Ione.** Born 30 May 1923 at Phoenix, AZ. Married Joe F. "Lonnie" Basham on 18 Sept. 1954 in Orange Co., VA; married secondly Harry Barrett (a machinist), and had children: *Jane*; *Sherdia*; *Dan*; *Wayne*. Ione Barrett is a retired postal worker, currently living at Buckeye, AZ.

9f. **(Georgia) Marilyn.** Born 29 July 1925 at Phoenix, AZ. Married Everett Ellis (a gardener), and had children: *Cathy*; *Wayne*; *Suzie*. Marilyn Ellis is a retired nurse, currently living at Brea, CA.

9g. **Dorothy Maud.** Born 12 Nov. 1928 at Tempe, AZ. Married Robert Anderson (div.), and had children: *Rea*; *Robert*; *Alan*. Dorothy Anderson currently lives at Twenty-Nine Palms, CA.

JOHN M. BURGESS OF HIDALGO CO., TEXAS

[George Washington (V)[6], John Marion (II)[7], George Marion (I)[8]]

9a. **John Marion (III)** *[son of George Marion (I)].* Born 29 May 1916 at Phoenix, AZ. Married (Elsie) Louise Templin on 23 June 1939 at Phoeniz, AZ (she was born 19 Aug. 1917 at Converse, IN, the daughter of Arthur Eldridge Templin and Clara Bell Powell). John M. Burgess has been a farmer, truck driver, surveyor, carpenter, and an investor, and has also owned a number of businesses, including a hardware store, motel, gas station, clothing store, resort, mobile park, and a waterworks company. He currently raises citrus trees and lives at Edinburg, TX.

10a. **Itka Karroll.** Born 26 June 1941 at Huntsville, AR. Married Ronald LeRoy Troutman (a teacher and forester) on 22 Nov. 1961, and had children: *Cindy Lynn* (born 14 June 1962 at Springer, NM); *Roy Lee* (born 28 Apr. 1965 at Las Vegas, NM); *Robb Alan* (born 22 Aug. 1966 at Las Vegas, NM); *Kimberly Sue* (born 25 Dec. 1970 at Santa Fe, NM). Itka Troutman works as a secretary at Northland Pioneer College, She currently lives at Show Low, Navajo Co., AZ.

10b. **John Marion (IV).** Born 4 Apr. 1944 at Phoenix, AZ. Married Lolita Howland on 6 July 1968 (div. 1987; she was a sister of Edward Howland, who married John's sister, Cordy Burgess); married secondly Geraldine Irene "Geri" Swaggart on 17 June 1989. John M. Burgess Jr. owns and operates Burgess Pump Company, a water pumping business, at Eagle, Ada Co., ID.

11a. **David Harrington** (ad.). Born 1 Aug. 1967 at Fresno, CA.
11b. **Mark Allen (II).** Born 15 Jan. 1972 at Sacramento, CA.
11c. **John Marion (V).** Born 22 Oct. 1973 at Sacramento, CA.

10c. **Cordy Lane.** Born 26 Mar. 1950 at Peonia, CO. Married Edward L. Howland on 1 Nov. 1968 (div. 1991; he was a brother of Lolita Howland, who married Cordy's brother, John Burgess), and had children: *Cristy Ann* (born 1 May 1970); *Stacy Lynn* (born 3 Sept. 1971); Cordy married secondly Dave Abel (a college teacher) on 21 Mar. 1992. Cordy Abel is a secretary for the Navajo County Board of Realtors. She currently lives at Show Low, AZ.

JESSE WALDEN BURGESS (1857-1948; see page 124)
(CORA) ALICE PICKLE (1870- ; see page 83)

[William (I)[1], Edward (I)[2], William (II)[3], Henry (I)[4], John Henry (I)[5]]

JOHN MARION BURGESS
(1828-1909)

OF MONTGOMERY COUNTY, INDIANA

6c. **John Marion (I)** *[son of John Henry (I)].* Born 25 Mar. 1828 in Fleming Co., KY. Married Mary Jane Davis on 27 Oct. 1852 (she was born 13 Sept. 1827 at New Market, Montgomery Co., IN, daughter of Maj. Randolph Davis and Abigail Hoel (or Hole), and died there on 12 Sept. 1908). John M. Burgess moved to Montgomery Co. at the time of his marriage, and is listed there in Brown Township in the 1860-1900 censuses. A farmer all of his life, he died on 25 Aug. 1909 at New Market, IN, and is buried with his wife and many of their children in the Indian Creek Hill Cemetery.

The Children of John M. Burgess:

7a. **Daughter**. Born about 1853 in Montgomery Co., IN; died there an infant, and is buried with her parents.

7b. **William H(enry?) (IV).** Born 25 Jan. 1855 at Ladoga, IN. See below for full entry.

7c. **Mary E. (II).** Born 30 Aug. 1857 in Montgomery Co., IN; died there on 3 Nov. 1859, and is buried with her parents.

7d. **Nancy E. (II) "Nannie."** Her name is listed as Nancy A. in the 1860 census and in her first marriage record. Born Dec. 1859 in Montgomery Co., IN. Married Charles A. Caplinger on 27 Apr. 1878 in Montgomery Co. (div. 1899); married secondly Albert L. Hankins on 6 Jan. 1927 in Montgomery Co. Listed in the 1900 census with her father. Not in the county death records.

7e. **John Randolph.** Born 14 Apr. 1861 in Montgomery Co., IN. See below for full entry.

7f. **Abigail Mariah "Abbie."** Born 2 May 1863 in Montgomery Co., IN. Married Joseph F. Hite on 12 Feb. 1885 in Montgomery Co. (he was born June 1857 in IN, and died 4 Dec. 1920), and had at least the following children: *Elmer E.* (born 5 June 1886, married Vera M. Mullen on 26 Nov. 1913 in Montgomery Co., and died Mar. 1964 in WA); *Roy B.* (born 8 Nov. 1887, married Jennie Blanch Johnson on 15 Jan. 1908 in Montgomery Co., and died 1926); *(Otto) James* (born 20 Nov. 1889, married Anna A. Landes on 2 Aug. 1911 in Montgomery Co.); *(Dean) Charles* (born 1 Aug. 1892, and died July 1972 at Miami, FL); *Mary Ivyl* (her name is listed as Clara in the birth records; born 11 July 1894, married Ralph Harris Everhart on 15 Mar. 1918 at Louisville, KY [he was born 16 Sept. 1895, and died Mar. 1977 at Jamestown, IN], and died Aug. 1976 at Jamestown, IN); *George P.* (born Apr. 1897, died 20 Jan. 1913); *Forest* (born 11 Mar. 1902, and died Jan. 1985 at Trenton, NE). Listed in the 1900 census for Brown Township, Montgomery Co., IN. Abbie Hite died on 17 Dec. 1958, aged 95 years, at Crawfordsville, and is buried in the Indian Creek Hill Cemetery, New Market, IN.

7g. **Son.** Born about 1865 in Montgomery Co., IN; died an infant, and is buried with his parents (the actual dates of birth and death of this unnamed son and his unnamed sister are unknown, but they are mentioned on a group headstone with their parents).

7h. **(Martha) Emma.** Born 25 Dec. 1866 in Montgomery Co., IN; died there on 3 Aug. 1870, and is buried with her parents.

7i. **(Mary) Ida (I).** Born 9 Apr. 1868 in Montgomery Co., IN; died there unmarried on 24 Mar. 1888, and is buried with her parents.

7j. **Isaac N(ewton?).** Born 9 Sept. 1869 in Montgomery Co., IN; died there on 3 Aug. 1870, and is buried with his parents.

WILLIAM H. BURGESS OF MONTGOMERY CO., INDIANA
[John Marion (I)[6]]

7b. **William H(enry?) (IV)** *[son of John Marion (I)].* Born 25 Jan. 1855 at Ladoga, IN. Married Martha Josephine "Mattie" Benson on 5 Oct. 1876 in Montgomery Co. (she was born 19 May 1859 at Ladoga,

Montgomery Co., IN, the daughter of Seneca Benson and Susannah Himes, and died 3 Mar. 1940 at Chicago, IL). William H. Burgess was a farmer in Montgomery Co., IN. He is listed there in the 1880 census; Mattie appears as head of the family in 1900. He died on 18 Oct. 1885 at Ladoga, IN, and is buried with his wife and children in the Ladoga Cemetery.

8a. **Della Mae.** Born 1877 at Ladoga, IN; died there in 1879, and is buried with her parents.

8b. **Queen Ann.** Born 28 Nov. 1879 at Ladoga, IN. Listed in the 1900 census for Rush Co., IN working as a servant for Christian A. Lambert. Queen Burgess later worked as a clerk in Chicago before retiring to Crawfordsville, IN. She died there unmarried on 13 Dec. 1965, and is buried with her parents in the Ladoga Cemetery. She was a member of the Daughters of the American Revolution.

8c. **Forrest E.** Born 12 Mar. 1882 at Ladoga, IN. Married E. L. Harrigan on 14 Oct. 1939 at Delavan, WI. She was a member of the Daughters of the American Revolution. A tombstone with her name (but no date of death) appears next to her two sisters, but it is not known if she is actually buried there. Forrest Harrigan died in Dec. 1985 at Stoughton, WI, aged 103 years, 9 months, the oldest Burgess descendant of the main line on record.

8d. **(Harold) Omer.** Born 31 Mar. 1885 at Ladoga, IN. Married Helen Ruth Myers on 22 Feb. 1909 in Montgomery Co. (she was born 25 Feb. 1883, daughter of Noah Elias Myers and Elizabeth Porter McClelland, and died 1953). Listed in the 1920 census for Montgomery Co., IN living with his father-in-law. Omer Burgess was a high school history teacher at Crawfordsville, IN. He died childless on 25 July 1942 at Indianapolis, IN, but is buried with his wife in the Oak Hill Cemetery.

JOHN R. BURGESS OF MONTGOMERY CO., INDIANA

[John Marion (I)^6]

7e. **John Randolph** *[son of John Marion (I)].* Born 14 Apr. 1861 in Montgomery Co., IN. Married (Charity) Belle Coons on 24 Sept. 1884 in Montgomery Co. (she was born Aug. 1864 in IN). Listed in the 1900-20 censuses for Scott Township, Montgomery Co., IN. John R. Burgess was a farmer in Montgomery Co., IN. He died there on 3 July 1940, and is buried in the Masonic Cemetery.

8a. **William Franklin "Willie."** Born 21 Aug. 1887 at New Market, Montgomery Co., IN. Married Mary May Hodgkins on 16 Nov. 1913 in Montgomery Co., IN (she died before her husband). Listed with his father in 1900-20 censuses, and in the 1917 draft register of Montgomery Co. Willie Burgess was a farmer on his father's lands in Montgomery Co. He died childless on 20 May 1983 at the Golden Manor Nursing Home, Ladoga, IN, aged 95 years.

Four Sons of Jacob Lawson Burgess: Oliver B., Jacob Lawson Jr. "Lot," John Warren, William Addison

[William (I)[1], Edward (I)[2], William (II)[3], Henry (I)[4], John Henry (I)[5]]

JACOB LAWSON BURGESS, SR.
(1832-1881)
OF BLUE EARTH COUNTY, MINNESOTA

6e. **Jacob Lawson (I) "Jake"** *[son of John Henry (I)].* Born 26 Jan. 1832 in Fleming Co., KY. Married Maranda Bell on 9 Dec. 1852 at Fruit Hill, Vigo Co., IN (she was born 4 May 1834 in IN, and died 20 Jan. 1908 at Eagle Lake, MN). Said to have moved to Minnesota in 1854, and is listed in the 1857 State Census for Blue Earth Co., MN (he was one of two members of the Burgess family to remain in Minnesota during the Indian uprisings), and in the 1860-80 federal and state censuses for LeRay Township, Blue Earth Co., MN; his widow appears as head of the family between 1885-1900. Jake Burgess enlisted in the Mankato Home Guard on 14 Sept. 1862, and also served in Co. K, 1st MN Heavy Artillery, Union Army between 14 Feb. and 27 Sept. 1865. After returning home, he bought a farm one mile southeast of Eagle Lake, a mile east of his father's farm, where he built a mill with his brother-in-law, Gabriel Pickle, about 1870. In later life he became an attorney, and served as Justice of the Peace for both Mankato and LeRay Townships; he is said to have been one of the judges who presided over the trial of 38 Sioux Indians condemned to death for their part in the uprisings of 1863. In 1878 he bought land in Washington Territory near the farm of his brother, Tom, either as an investment or with the idea of eventually settling there. Jake Burgess died at his home of pneumonia on 12 Dec. 1881 (or 15 Dec., from his wife's pension deposition); he and his wife are both buried in the Burgess Cemetery. After his death, Maranda applied for a Civil War veteran's pension in his name.

The Children of Jake Burgess:

7a. **Harrison Alexander "Harry."** Born 20 Nov. 1853 at Portland Mills, IN. See below for full entry.
7b. **John Warren.** Born 23 July 1855 at Portland Mills, IN. See below for full entry.
7c. **George Franklin.** Born 12 Mar. 1857 at Eagle Lake, MN. See below for full entry.
7d. **Martha Eleonore "Matt(ie)."** Born 4 Aug. 1859 at Eagle Lake, MN. Married Egbert A. Cook about 1877 (he was born Dec. 1849 in WI), and had children:

Bert COOK. Born 26 Jan. 1878, married Ellen Hardie, and died childless on 1 Jan. 1970, aged 91 years.

George COOK. Born 2 July 1879, married Marie Dittert, had children: *Emma Belle* (born 28 May 1906, married Kenneth Chaffee, and secondly Clarence Currie (he was born 6 June 1892, and died Oct. 1972 at Elmore), and died 7 Nov. 1991 at Elmore, MN, having had children: Ardis Jacqueline [died 1929]; Lila Marie [married Enoch Newman, and had children: Marie {married Steve Anderson}; Donald {died at age eight}]; Marilyn Bell [dec.; married and had children: Kathy; Julie {dec.}; Jerry]); *Frances Martha* (born about 1909, married Rev. Russell P. Nelson on 5 Nov. 1965 [he was born 6 Sept. 1899, and died 17 Mar. 1986 at Winnebago], and lives at Winnebago, MN); *Georgia Marie* (born 23 Aug. 1911, married Elliott Sailor [he was born 6 Jan. 1896, and died 24 Mar. 1966 at Blue Earth], and died on 26 Nov. 1991 at Blue Earth, MN); *Crystal Vera* (born about 1916, married (Chester) Wallace Worden [he was born 9 Feb. 1916, and died 15 Apr. 1982], and had children: Wanda Jean [married David Patton]); *Anna Mae* (married Lawrence Feldick [dec.], and had children: Larry; George; *Anna* married secondly Harold E. Hutchins, and lives at Blue Earth, MN). ***George COOK*** died on 19 Sept. 1936.

(Jacob) Ernest COOK. Born Apr. 1883, married Effie ___, and had children: *Katherine* (dec.); *Austin* (born 12 Aug. 1915, married Louise ___, and died Mar. 1985 at Seattle, WA).

Ruthford Pearl COOK. Born 7 Feb. 1888, married and had children: *Olive* (married ___ Hansbery, and lives at Orting, WA); *Blanche* (married Kyle Wagg, and lives at Brewster, WA); *Martha* (married Vance Lake, and lives at Wenachee, WA); *Jessie* (married Willie Egbert, and lives at Spring Valley, CA). ***Ruthford COOK*** died on 11 Sept. 1974.

Emma Belle **COOK**. Born 7 Dec. 1890, married Floyd Blair, and had children: *Bethel* (married Lee Weimer); *Beryl* (dec.; married ___ Bracken); *Burton* (married Dorothy ___); *Bailey* (married Marge Pool, and lives at Winnebago, MN). ***Emma BLAIR*** died in Apr. 1984, aged 93 years.

Listed in the 1900 census for Elmore Township, Faribault Co., MN. **Mattie COOK** died on 7 Apr. 1936 at Blue Earth, MN.

7e. **(Sarah) Belle.** Born 24 Nov. 1861 at Eagle Lake, MN. Married Mortica Hastings about 1896 (he was born Mar. 1853 in NY), and children: *John M.* (ad.; born Oct. 1897, married Betty ___, and had children: John M. Jr. "Jack" [ad.; married and had children, and lives at Minnetonka, MN]). Listed in the 1900 census for Mason City, Cerro Gordo Co., IA. Belle moved to Brookfield, MO by 1902, where she had a one-third share in The Electric Medicine Co. with her brothers, John and George. She died on 20 Jan. 1910 at St. Joseph, MO, but was returned for burial to the Elmwood Cemetery, Mason City, IA.

7f. **Emma.** Born 8 Aug. 1863 at Eagle Lake, MN. Married Lt. Charles Frederick Wagoner about 1886 (he was born Feb. 1844 in Broome Co., NY, served in the Union Army during the Civil War, married firstly Emma's cousin, Redella Burgess, and died 1910 at Eagle Lake, buried Burgess Cemetery), and had children:

Meta WAGONER. Born Feb. 1887 in Washington. Died before 1956.

Logan True WAGONER. Born 1887 at Eagle Lake, MN, died unmarried of a brain tumor in 1909 at Eagle Lake, and is buried in the Burgess Cemetery. Not in the 1900 census.

Walter WAGONER. Born Aug. 1888. Died before 1956.

Alma WAGONER. Born Feb. 1890. Died before 1956.

Albert WAGONER. Born Jan. 1892. Died before 1956.

Ella WAGONER. Born Oct. 1894. Died before 1956.

Ernest WAGONER (twin). Born Nov. 1896. Died before 1956.

Otto WAGONER (twin). Born Nov. 1896. Died before 1956.

Ida WAGONER. Born Dec. 1898. Died before 1956.

Ruth Eleanore WAGONER. Born 29 Sept. 1899 at Eagle Lake, MN, married Howard Watkins Higgins on 20 Apr. 1929 at Pendleton, OR (he was born 4 July 1899, and died Mar. 1968), and had children: *Helen Ruth* (married V. Wayne Hazelbaker, and died childless in 1951); *Laura Lucille* (married Lloyd Henry Larson, and lived at Olympia, WA). Graduated from the University in Minnesota in 1920 with a degree in education, and received her master's degree in librarianship from the University of Idaho in 1953. Ruth Higgins was a teacher and librarian at Grangeville, ID, moving there in 1924, and later to Pendleton, OR and Avery, ID. She returned to Grangeville in 1947, retired in 1957, and died there on 31 Aug. 1989, the last of her brothers and sisters to die.

Emma WAGONER also raised the two children of her husband by his first marriage. Listed in the 1885 census for Blue Earth Co. as a caretaker for C. F. Wagoner's children, and in 1900 in Spokane Co., WA. Emma Wagoner lived most of her life at Grangeville, ID; she died on 11 June 1956 at Spokane, WA, aged 92 years, and is buried with her husband in the Burgess Cemetery, Eagle Lake, MN. Only two children survived her, Ruth Higgins, and her stepdaughter, Junia Pease.

7g. **(Jacob) Lawson (II) "Lot."** Born 22 May 1865 at Eagle Lake, MN. See below for full entry.

7h. **Oliver B(ell?) "Odd."** Born 12 Mar. 1868 at Eagle Lake, MN. Married Minnie Grace Waymer on 31 Dec. 1887 in Blue Earth Co. (div.; she was born Oct. 1865 in NY); married secondly Cora L. Cochran (she was born 1 Jan. 1870 at Farmington, KY, and died 12 Dec. 1944 at Los Angeles, CA). Listed in the 1900 census for Brookfield, MO. Odd Burgess was a school teacher at Kansas City, MO; he moved to Los Angeles by 1935, where he worked as a real estate broker. From 1938-48 he lived retired at the Pacific Home in Hollywood. He died there childless of Alzheimer's disease on 2 May 1949, and is buried with his second wife in the Hollywood Cemetery, Los Angeles, CA.

7i. **Jenny.** Born about 1871 at Eagle Lake, MN; died there on 25 Aug. 1875, and is probably buried in the Burgess Cemetery.

7j. **Newton.** Born 29 Mar. 1873 at Eagle Lake, LeRay Township, Blue Earth Co., MN; died there between 1875-80, and is probably buried in the Burgess Cemetery.

7k. **William Addison (II) "Willie."** Born 6 Dec. 1875 at Janesville, MN. See below for full entry.

7l. **Fred "Freddie."** Born Sept. 1879 at Eagle Lake, MN; died there between Dec. 1881 (alive at his father's death) and 1885, and is probably buried in the Burgess Cemetery.

HARRY BURGESS OF JACKSON CO., MISSOURI

[Jacob Lawson (I)[6]]

7a. **Harrison Alexander "Harry"** *[son of Jacob Lawson (I)].* Born 20 Nov. 1853 at Portland Mills, IN. Married Amelia "Emily" Conger (she was born 19 Apr. 1855 at Iola, WI, and died 15 Sept. 1945 at St. Paul, MN, buried in the Union Cemetery, St. Paul, MN); married secondly Lizzie ___. Listed in the

1880 and 1895 censuses for Blue Earth Co., MN, and in the Mankato directories for 1895 and 1897; his wife appears as head of the family in 1885 and 1900. Harry Burgess was a school teacher in Florida (he was living there in 1915, according to a letter written by his aunt, Miranda Pickle); during his later years, he worked as a salesman in Kansas City for his brothers' tire firm. He died there on 19 Aug. 1935, and is buried in the Green Lawn Cemetery, Kansas City, MO.

8a. **Jennie Bell.** Born 19 Apr. 1878 at Eagle Lake, MN. Married ___ Vaughn (a master bricklayer), and had children: *Hugh* (born about 1905, married Mane May ___). Jennie Vaughn was a registered nurse. She was living with her son, Hugh Vaughn, when she died in a Chicago suburb about 1955.

8b. **Hugh Howard.** Born 19 Sept. 1880 at Eagle Lake, MN. Married Myra May Woodworth on 4 Dec. 1906 at Rapid City, SD (she was born 5 Sept. 1879 at Sterling, IL, and died 17 Jan. 1960). Hugh Burgess herded cattle in the West River country during his youth, and later became a locomotive engineer in 1902 for the Pierre, Rapid City division of the Chicago and North Western Railroad, working out of Rapid City, SD. He was a Mason. He died on 4 Nov. 1960 at Rapid City, and is buried there in the Mountain View Cemetery. At his retirement in 1945, the following biography was published either in the *Rapid City Daily Journal* or in a newsletter of the Brotherhood of Locomotive Engineers:

"Bro. Hugh Burgess began firing an engine on the Chicago & North Western Railroad on August 22, 1902, and he said farewell to the throttle 43 years later, on September 22, 1945. He entered the service of the C. & N.W. at Huron, S.D., and was promoted to the position of locomotive engineer on August 25, 1906. Shortly thereafter, he was sent to Rapid City, S.D., to work work on the Pierre, Rapid City & Northwestern Railroad, which afterward became a part of the Chicago & North Western System. When the district between Rapid City and Pierre was made a division, Brother Burgess transferred to that division. Here he remained, working in both freight and passenger service, until his retirement. His last run was made on train No. 515. Becoming a member of the B. of L.E. in March, 1910, when he was initiated into Div. 213, Brother Burgess transferred to Div. 303 in 1921, but returned in January, 1932 to Div. 213, where he is still a member. He has been faithful to his B. of L.E. affiliation through the years. Brother Burgess's home is in Rapid City, S.D. However, during the summer months he may be found at his cabin on Rapid Creek, at Silver City, S.D., where he spends his time fishing. In November he is usually busy hunting deer. Members of Div. 213 extend best wishes to him for a long and happy retirement."

9a. **Edward Allen (I).** Born 8 Mar. 1908 at Rapid City, SD. Married Annie Laura Jane Murphy on 15 Mar. 1933 at Rapid City, SD (she was born 31 Dec. 1912, and died 28 Oct. 1987 at Ogden, UT). As a young man, Ed Burgess played for bands in the Rapid City area, and later worked for Rosenbaum Signs at Rapid City. He owned and operated Burgess Signs, a commercial art firm, for 23 years at Ogden, UT. He was an animal lover, railroad enthusiast, and avid photographer and animator. He and his wife were active members of the Utah Cine Arts Club, where he won many awards for his work. Shortly before his death he moved to Rapid City, SD to live with his niece, Kathleen Ann Murphy Perrigo. He died there childless on 14 Dec. 1989. Both he and his wife are buried in the Mountain View Cemetery, Rapid City, SD.

9b. **Kathryn Frances.** Born 5 May 1910 at Pierre, SD. Married Charles E. Heacock on 19 Dec. 1929 at Belle Fourche, SD (div.), and had children: *Marilyn Jean* (born 20 Dec. 1930 at Rapid City, SD, was adopted by Howard K. Fleming, married Joseph C. Carter Jr. at Mountain Home, ID, and had children: Craig M. [born 27 July 1954 at Pocatello, ID, married Margaret (Black) Burke on 20 Sept. 1986 {she had children: Robert Black BURKE <born 5 Mar. 1980>}]; James Hugh [born 10 Oct. 1958 at Idaho Falls, ID, and lives at Boise, ID]). Kathryn married secondly Howard K. Fleming on 25 Nov. 1943 at Rapid City, SD (he died on 1 Jan. 1994). Kathryn Fleming died on 16 Dec. 1993 at Boise, ID, and is buried with her second husband in the Mountain View Cemetery.

8c. **Zazel Ruth.** Born 11 July 1888 in South Dakota. Married Joseph E. Perry (he was a druggist, and died at Culver City about 1940), and had children: *William*; *Viola*; *Leslie* (or Lester); *Clyde* (born about 1922). Zazel Perry was a nurse at Omaha, NE and at Culver City, Los Angeles Co., CA. She died there on 3 Aug. 1944, and is buried in the Forest Lawn Cemetery.

8d. **Dale Omer.** Born 21 Apr. 1890 at Eagle Lake, MN. Married secondly Minnie E. ___. Dale Burgess was a conductor for the Union Pacific Railroad, working out of Council Bluffs, IA. He lived across the river at Omaha, NE for thirty years, and died there childless on 14 Apr. 1966. He is buried in the Cedar Lawn Cemetery, Council Bluffs, IA.

8e. **Mark Lorraine.** Born 1 Aug. 1895 at Eagle Lake, MN. Married Catherine Ellinor Stevens on 5 Feb. 1921 at Mapleton, MN (she was born about 1895 at Mapleton, MN, daughter of Charles Stevens and

Minnie Griggs, and lives at St. Paul). Served in the U.S. Army during World War I. Listed in the 1920 census for Blue Earth Co. Mark L. Burgess worked as a railway mail clerk out of St. Paul, MN. He died on 27 Mar. 1963 at North St. Paul, MN, and is buried in the Union Cemetery.

9a. **Jeremy Dale.** Born 12 July 1922 at Mapleton, MN. Jeremy Burgess died unmarried on 29 Nov. 1943 at St. Paul, MN, and is buried with his family in the Union Cemetery.

9b. **Helen May.** Born 23 Sept. 1923 at Mankato, MN. Married Ferdinand J. "Fred" Engelhart Jr. on 2 Oct. 1945 at St. Paul, MN, and had children: *William Mark* (born 29 Sept. 1947; he works as a taxi driver at St. Paul, MN); *Robert Francis* (born 28 Dec. 1950, married Cecelia Henny Tuggle in July 1980 [she died in 1984]; married secondly Linda Nesmith in 1988, and had children: Grant Robert [born 17 Feb. 1990]; Andrew James [born 15 June 1991]; he works as a banquet chef for the University of Colorado, Boulder, CO, and lives at Longmont, CO); *Judy Ann* (born 5 Jan. 1963, married Jean Karam on 29 Nov. 1989 [he was born 28 Oct. 1962 at Beirut, Lebanon], and had children: Xavier Jean [born 17 Apr. 1992]; *Judy KARAM* worked for the publisher Harcourt Brace Jovanovich at San Diego, CA before moving to Denver, CO; she now works as a commercial artist). Helen Engelhart lives at St. Paul, MN.

9c. **William Conger.** Born 2 Feb. 1926 at St. Paul, MN. He enlisted in the Army during World War II, and was killed in action in Europe in Jan. 1945, buried in the U.S. Cemetery at Eponal, France.

JOHN WARREN BURGESS OF JACKSON CO., MISSOURI

[Jacob Lawson (I)[6]]

7b. **John Warren** *[son of Jacob Lawson (I)].* Born 23 July 1855 at Portland Mills, IN. Married Sarah Anne "Sallie" Sugg on 18 Mar. 1877 in Carroll Co., MO (she was born 11 Oct. 1860 in MO, daughter of Thomas and Polly Sugg, and died on 9 July 1944 at Los Angeles, CA, buried Forest Lawn Cemetery). Listed in the 1880 census for Blue Earth Co., and at Brookfield, MO in 1900-10, having moved there about 1894. John W. Burgess operated a Singer Sewing Machine agency at Mason City, IA during the 1880s. With his younger brother, George, and his sister, Belle Hastings, he founded The Electric Medicine Co. at Brookfield during the 1890s, at one time employing a dozen salesmen selling patent medicines throughout the Midwest. In 1915, John and George moved to Kansas City, MO after liquidating their company, and established a new firm, the Burgess Patent Tire and Manufacturing Co., to produce automobile tires; John served as President of the company, with his brother George as Secretary/Treasurer. On George's death in 1925, the firm was dissolved, and John Burgess became a real estate broker. He died on 9 Nov. 1935 at Kansas City, and is buried there in the Greenlawn Cemetery.

A letter from John W. Burgess to his aunt, Marietta Dungan Burgess, widow of George Washington Burgess:

BURGESS TIRE COMPANY
THE TIRE THAT IS ALWAYS
READY, SAFE AND DURABLE

300 New Centre Bldg. — Bell Phone
15th and Troost — Grand 2030

Mrs. Marietta Burgess — Sept. 10, 1920
Bogard, Missouri

Dear Aunt Mary:

Sarah and myself just returned from a pleasant visit to the old home in Minnesota. We visited Uncle Gabe and Aunt Nan Pickle. They are growing old and feeble and gray. They were glad to see us and asked after you and family, and we gave them what little news we could.

We tried to locate the place where Uncle Wash's cabin stood, and the path that led down to the spring by the meadow; but every old landmark is gone. Truly the stranger's foot has crossed the sill in the dear old home country. The timber is most all gone, and the roads have been changed. There is a few of the large old elms still there, and the blackbirds would gather in them and were singing their last autumn songs before leaving for the south, the same as they did in days of yore. Very few wild ducks were on the lake at our old home lake, and a German lives on our old farm and has a large house and barn....

We visited Sister Mattie; they live on a farm, are doing well, and have grandchildren almost grown to womanhood. Mattie asked after you, and said: "May God bless that dear old aunt, and oh how I would like to see her." I told her we could not go there anymore, and she said it was truly a sad tragedy. It just breaks our hearts, but we can only say: God pity us all, and pray that "in the hereafter angels may roll the stone from the grave away."

My dear Aunty Mary, the gods know that I shall never forget how kind and good you and dear Uncle Wash have been to me, and the good counsel you always gave. If only I can live up to your teaching and the example that you and Uncle set by your daily lives, I will surely win the prize. Myself, brothers, sisters, and cousins owe much to our ancestors for their good advice and the good example they set. We can appreciate this all the more by living in the big city where so very few seem to care what they say or do. Will you be so kind as to forward this letter to your good boy John, my dear cousin, and tell him to write to me.

Oh yes, forgot to tell you that cousin Doctor David Reeder came to visit us a few weeks ago. We had a pleasant visit with him. I asked him to visit you and he said he would if I would go with him. He is a fine looking doctor, a loving cousin, and a manly man. He has a good practice, many wealthy patients, and a lovely home and family....

With kindest regards to you and yours, one and all,
I am as ever, your loving nephew
John W. Burgess

8a. **Warren William.** Born 20 July 1889 at Sioux City, IA. Married Ina Belle Walker on 27 May 1912 at Brookfield, Linn Co., MO (div.; she was born 1893 at New Cambria, MO, and died about 1968 at Kansas City, MO, buried in the Rose Hill Cemetery, Brookfield, MO); married secondly Anna Louise Lin(n)es in 1936 in Los Angeles Co. (she was born about 1912, and died on 16 Aug. 1956 in Los Angeles Co.); married thirdly Martha Dougherty (she died 3 Jan. 1965 in Los Angeles); married fourthly Mary J. ___ about 1966 (div.); married fifthly Dorothy L. Quiggle (Taulbee) on 2 Feb. 1967 in Los Angeles Co. (div.; she may have remarried Merle F. Morris on 11 July 1969 in Los Angeles Co.); married sixthly Stephanie Adams (Robinson) on 28 Nov. 1967 in Los Angeles Co. (she was born 1915, and died 5 Jan. 1968 in Los Angeles Co.); married seventhly Anne (Roberts) Higham on 27 Feb. 1968 in Los Angeles Co. (she was born about 1911, and lived at Marina del Rey, CA).

Warren Burgess moved to Kansas City with his father in 1915, and is listed there in the 1920 census. By 1920 he was President of F. A. Gray Advertising, and was also working as a salesman for his own company, Burgess & Johnson. He founded The Knox Company, an internationally-based pharmaceutical firm, about 1924, eventually serving as Chairman of the Board. He moved his company and his family (including his widowed mother) to Los Angeles in 1936. He died on 19 July 1969, the day before his 80th birthday, in Los Angeles Co., and is buried in the Forest Lawn Cemetery, Glendale, CA. After his death, the Knox Co., part of the Knox Group of affiliated corporations, was sold on 2 Feb. 1970 to Cooper Laboratories, Inc. of Mystic, CT for $7.5 million. Warren Burgess's personal estate was valued at his death at $5.5 million, making him probably the wealthiest Burgess on record, as well as the most married.

"Warren was the only one that daddy was close to, and Uncle John and Aunt Sarah, Warren's mother and father. They were the sweetest people that you could have known. He taught me how to pitch pennies and how to make interest. I would go to his office and he would always borrow a penny or nickel from me, and before I left he would decide that he had had my money long enough and give me back twice what he borrowed."—Betty Dean Burgess Carroll, 25 Jan. 1982.

9a. **Evelyn Roberta.** Her first name was originally Ethylend. Born 18 Jan. 1914 at Brookfield, MO. Married thirdly Louis J. Anderson on 2 Feb. 1948 (he was born 29 Nov. 1907, and died 9 May 1982). She may have appeared on the television program, *Sixty Minutes*, on 4 Jan. 1987. Evelyn Anderson died childless on 8 Feb. 1990 at Carmel del Mar, CA.

9b. **Virginia Lee (I) "Ginny."** Born 14 Jan. 1916 at Kansas City, MO. Married John Clark about 1935 at Kansas City, and had children: *Robert B.* (born 6 Mar. 1936, married Waldi ___, and had two children). Virginia Clark died about 1966 at Wichita, KS.

GEORGE F. BURGESS OF JACKSON CO., MISSOURI

[Jacob Lawson (I)[6]]

7c. **George Franklin** *[son of Jacob Lawson (I)].* Born 12 Mar. 1857 at Eagle Lake, MN, noted in the published histories of Blue Earth Co. as the first child born in that settlement. Married Mary Alice Davidson of Janesville, MN in 1880 (she was born July 1860 in WI, and died 27 Oct. 1941 at Los Angeles, CA, buried Forest Lawn Cemetery, Hollywood). Listed in the 1900-10 censuses for Brookfield, Linn Co., MO, and in the Kansas City directories from 1915-25; has not been found in the 1920 census.

George Burgess was a carpenter in early life in Minnesota and Cerro Gordo Co., IA, having moved to Mason City in 1882; he later became a partner in The Electric Medicine Co., and served as Secretary/Treasurer of The Burgess Tire and Manufacturing Co. He died on 20 May 1925 at Kansas City, MO, and is buried with his family in the Forest Hills Cemetery. He was a member of the Odd Fellows. His biography appears in the *History of Franklin and Cerro Gordo Counties, Iowa* (Springfield, IL: Union Publishing Co., 1883, p. 965):

> G. T. Burgess [sic] was born in Blue Earth Co., Minn., March 12, 1856 [sic]. His parents, J. L. and Miranda (Bell) Burgess, were natives of Indiana. They went to Minnesota in 1854, and were among the earliest settlers of Blue Earth County. Mr. Burgess went to school in the log school houses of the pioneers, and at fifteen learned the trade of carpenter and joiner, which he followed some years. He was married in 1880 to Mary A. Davidson, of Janesville, Minn. They have one child—Nellie. In 1882 Mr. Burgess came to Mason City. He is a member of the Oddfellows' Order at Mason City.

8a. **Nellie M. (I).** Born 8 June 1881 in LeRay Township, Blue Earth Co., MN. Married Treat P. Chapman about 1902 (he was born about 1878 in IL, served as Vice President of The Burgess Tire Co., and died about 1942 at Denver, CO), and had children: *Marjory* (born 1903 in MO); *June M.* (born Apr. 1917 in MO); *Gladys A.* Listed in the 1920 census for Kansas City, Jackson Co, MO, and in the 1941-50 city directories for Denver, CO. Nellie Chapman died on 15 May 1966 at Kansas City, KS.

8b. **Clifford Oliver.** Born 4 June 1889 at Sioux City, IA. According to his death certificate he was married (although no record has been found). Moved with his father to Kansas City in 1915, where he worked as a bookkeeper and stenographer until his father's death. In 1925 he and his mother moved to Los Angeles. He died childless on 30 Aug. 1927 in Los Angeles Co., but is buried with his family in the Forest Hills Cemetery, Kansas City, MO.

8c. **Geneva Rosina.** Born 13 June 1894 at Eagle Lake, MN. Married ___ Stone; married secondly (or vice versa) Roland A. Jenkins by 1925 (divorced or separated by 1941; he died on 15 May 1951 at San Francisco, CA, and is buried there in the Golden Gate National Cemetery). Geneva Jenkins moved to Los Angeles in 1925 at her father's death, and is listed there in the city directories through 1941 (but not in 1942, the last volume published). She is mentioned in her mother's obituary in Oct. 1941, and is said in a 29 Apr. 1967 letter from Leon Dean Burgess to his cousin Charles Benjamin to be living at Los Angeles, but has not been found in the California death index.

LOT BURGESS OF BLUE EARTH CO., MINNESOTA

[Jacob Lawson (I)[6]]

7g. **(Jacob) Lawson (II) "Lot"** *[son of Jacob Lawson (I)].* Born 22 May 1865 at Eagle Lake, MN. Married Helena H. "Lena" Morris on 28 Mar. 1894 (she was born 8 Oct. 1872 in Iowa, and died on 29 May 1907 at Eagle Lake, MN); married secondly Mayme Elizabeth Corbin about 1908 (she was born 1892, daughter of Wilbur A. Corbin, and died 1967). Listed in the 1895-1920 censuses of Blue Earth Co., MN. Lot Burgess was a farmer and stockbroker near Eagle Lake, MN. He died there on 18 Mar. 1944, and is buried with his two wives in the Eagle Lake Cemetery.

8a. **(Leon) Dean (I).** Born 12 July 1895 at Eagle Lake, MN. See below for full entry.

8b. **Evelyn Maranda.** Born 14 Oct. 1909 at Eagle Lake, MN. Married Reuben Plagemann, and had children: *Duane* (lives at Aurora, MN); *Dale* (lives at Britt, MN); *Virginia* (married ___ Masussi, and lives at Mt. Iron, MN); *Laurel* (married ___ McEnerny, and lives at Aurora, CO). Evelyn Plagemann died on 27 Aug. 1985 at Aurora, MN.

8c. **Genevieve.** Born 2 Feb. 1911 at Eagle Lake, MN; died there an infant.

8d. **Mildred Marie.** Born 27 May 1912 at Eagle Lake, MN. Married Arthur Johnson (dec.), and had children: *Deanna* (born 9 Mar. 1945, married ___ Ollila, and died Aug. 1986 at Minneapolis, MN, having had children: Denise [who lives at Brooklyn Center, MN]); *Linda M.* Mildred married secondly Ralph Stewart (dec.), and thirdly Gene Callahan. Mildred Callahan died on 5 Aug. 1988 at New Ulm, MN, and is buried in the Calvary Section of Riverside Cemetery, Blue Earth, MN.

8e. **Maurice George "Sparky."** Born 22 Feb. 1915 at Eagle Lake, MN. See below for full entry.

8f. **Milton Reuben.** Born 26 Dec. 1917 at Eagle Lake, MN. See below for full entry.

8g. **Vaughn Austin.** Born 13 Oct. 1929 at St. Clair, MN. See below for full entry.

8h. **Lowell Jacob.** Born 19 May 1934 at St. Clair, MN. He lives unmarried at Faribault, MN.

DEAN BURGESS OF JACKSON CO., MISSOURI

[Jacob Lawson (I)[6], Jacob Lawson (II)[7]]

8a. **(Léon) Dean (I)** *[son of Jacob Lawson (II)].* Born 12 July 1895 at Eagle Lake, MN. Married (Marion) Ruth Hornbuckle on 10 June 1915 at Warrensburg, MO (she was born 30 Sept. 1892 at Jefferson City, MO, and died 30 Aug. 1985 at Kansas City, MO, aged 92 years). Dean Burgess was a copywriter and director of the Canadian branch of The Knox Co. at Toronto, ON, Canada between 1934-54, having been hired by his first cousin, Warren W. Burgess, founder of the company. He died on 12 May 1979 at Kansas City, MO, and is buried with his wife in the Sunset Hill Cemetery, Warrensburg, MO.

9a. **Malcolm Winston.** His name is given as Malcom in Social Security records. Born 17 Mar. 1916 at Concordia, KS. Married Constance Yeager on 20 July 1941 (div.); married Frances Nelson (Taylor) on 13 May 1962; married sixthly (Edna) Florence Morrill Hallmark on 2 June 1974 in Los Angeles Co., CA. Malcolm Burgess was a security guard at Los Angeles. He died there on 23 Apr. 1984, and is buried in the Forest Lawn Cemetery, Hollywood, CA. Frances Burgess lives at Los Angeles, CA.

10a. **Ruth Collier.** Born 13 Dec. 1942 at Newburgh, NY. Married William Earl "Bill" Hyser about 1960, and had children: *Cindy Lou* (born 17 Sept. 1961 at Cornwall, NY, lives at Houston, TX); *Kevin Earl* (born 10 Feb. 1963 at Cornwall, NY, married Beth Ann Donton on 20 Mar. 1992, and had children: Amanda Nicole [twin; born 29 Mar. 1992]; Samantha Lynn [twin; born 29 Mar. 1992]; *Kevin* lives at Temple, PA). Ruth married secondly Gerald King Russell, and had children: *Marcia Ann* (born 25 Jan. 1965 at West Point, NY). Ruth married fifthly Kenneth Stasko on 15 Mar. 1975 at Dallas, TX. Ruth Stasko owns her own business, Admin Productivity Consultants, efficiency experts, at Houston, TX.

9b. **Betty Dean.** Born 25 July 1922 at Kansas City, MO. Married Alexander Lyle Ridley on 24 Aug. 1943 at Fort Erie, ON, Canada (he was born 4 Nov. 1923 at Indian Head, SK, Canada, worked for the Canadian National Railway and the Santa Fe Railroad, and died on 17 Jan. 1960), and had children: *Roger Dean "Taz"* (born 7 Feb. 1946 at Ft. Erie, ON, Canada, married Barbara Joy Wilson on 22 Apr. 1967 [div. 1977], and had children: David Alexander [born 16 July 1971 at Kansas City, KS, married 24 Aug. 1991]; *Taz* married secondly Deloris "Dee" White on 5 May 1978 [she is a supervisor at Southwestern Bell], and had children: Maria Christine [ad.; born 27 Oct. 1981 at Ft. Scott, KS]. *Taz RIDLEY* is a supervisor for AT&T at Lenexa, KS).

Betty Dean married secondly Don Eugene Carroll on 13 June 1965 at Kansas City, KS (he was born 17 June 1921 at Kansas City, KS, served as a master sergeant in the U.S. Air Force from 1942-62, and later worked as a maintenance man for various companies before retiring in 1983). Betty Dean Carroll currently lives at Kansas City, KS; she has contributed greatly to both editions of this book.

MAURICE BURGESS OF LARIMER CO., COLORADO

[Jacob Lawson (I)[6], Jacob Lawson (II)[7]]

8e. **Maurice George "Sparky"** *[son of Jacob Lawson (II)].* His first name was pronounced "Morris." Born 22 Feb. 1915 at Eagle Lake, MN. Married secondly Margaret Uppstrom; married thirdly Wilma Barr; married fourthly Florence Birdsill (she died on 3 Sept. 1993 at Berthoud, CO). Sparky Burgess was a truck driver, and operated a sanitation and iron service for many years in the Loveland, CO area. He died on 28 Sept. 1980 at Berthoud, CO, and is buried with his fourth wife in the Greenlawn Cemetery.

9a. **Joanne Carol.** Born 11 Feb. 1938 at Mankato, MN. Married Roger Fisher, and had children: *Dawn Marie* (born 11 Sept. 1957 at Mankato, married Anthony Nastansky on 15 Oct. 1977 at Shakopee, MN, works as a court clerk at the Thurston Co. Courthouse, Olympia, WA, and had children: Justin William [born 16 June 1982 at Fergus Falls, MN]; Carrie Marie [born 25 Nov. 1983 at Fergus Falls, MN]); *Laurie Lynn* [born 9 Dec. 1958 at Mankato, married Wilmer Louis Stier on 18 Aug. 1979 at Shakopee, and had children: Jeremy Allen [born 26 Jan. 1984 at Shakopee]; Lindsey Marie [born 8 Feb. 1986 at Shakopee]); *Rhonda Lee* (born 5 Aug. 1960 at Mankato, married Ricki Lynn Murray on 7 July 1988 at Las Vegas, NV, and had children: Samantha Amber "Sammie" [born 23 Feb. 1990 at San Diego, CA]); *David Allen* (born 26 Sept.

1962 at Mankato); *John Joseph* (born 7 July 1966 at Minneapolis). Joanne Fisher died of cancer on 29 Dec. 1991 at Edina, MN, and is buried in the Mt. Olive Cemetery, Mankato, MN. Rhonda Murray is an independent contractor with Young America Corporation, Shakopee, MN, and has also worked for H. & R. Block; she has contributed greatly to this book.

9b. **William Maurice.** Born 4 July 1939 at Mankato, MN. Married Mary Ann Shirley on 10 Feb. 1962. Bill Burgess served as an enlisted man in the U.S. Air Force; he also worked in the parts department of a Chrysler dealership. He currently lives retired at St. Peter, MN.

10a. **John William (IV).** Born 24 July 1964 at New Prague, MN. Married Gwen Lucas on 29 Sept. 1984. John Burgess works in a foundry at Le Sueur, MN, but lives at New Ulm.

11a. **Nicole Kay.** Born 4 Dec. 1985 at New Ulm, MN.
11b. **Joshua John.** Born 31 Mar. 1988 at New Ulm, MN.

9c. **Edward Lynn** (ad.). Born 1 June 1955 at Richmond, CA. Married Catherine Phillips; married secondly Michelle Hansen. Ed Burgess works for Kimato Brewing, manufacturers of non-alchoholic rice beverages. He lives at Loveland, CO.

10a. **Heath Aaron.** Born 22 Oct. 1975 at Denver, CO.
10b. **Wade Isaac.** Born 12 Sept. 1978 at Loveland, CO.
10c. **Katie Lynne.** Born 22 Feb. 1987 at Loveland, CO.

MILTON R. BURGESS OF BLUE EARTH CO., MINNESOTA

[Jacob Lawson (I)[6], Jacob Lawson (II)[7]]

8f. **Milton Reuben** *[son of Jacob Lawson (II)]*. Born 26 Dec. 1917 at Eagle Lake, MN. Married Mary Ellen Mason on 2 Aug. 1953 at Ft. Madison, IA (she was born 18 May 1917? at Mankato, MN, daughter of Samuel Clark Mason and Josephine Pierce). Mary Burgess is a retired nurse; by her first husband, ___ Mullen, she had children: *Josephine Jolene "Jody" MULLEN* (born 21 May 1951 at Mankato, MN, married Seldon Leighton, and had children: Kimberly Joy [born 1 June 1980 at Mankato, MN]; Jennifer A. [born 3 Mar. 1983]; Brian C. [born 8 Aug. 1986]). Milton Burgess was an engineer for Blue Earth Co., MN before retiring. He and his sons are the last cousins with the name Burgess still residing in Blue Earth Co., MN.

9a. **Milton Wayne "Jigger."** Born 8 Mar. 1955 at Mankato, MN. Married Terri Lee Lundberg (div.). Milton W. Burgess is an auto insurance claims adjuster at Denver, CO.

10a. **Bonnie Margaret.** Born 26 Sept. 1972 at Mankato, MN.
10b. **Timothy Wayne.** Born 4 Mar. 1978 at Mankato, MN.

9b. **Melvin Gene "Toby."** Born 1 July 1956 at Mankato, MN. Married Annie Saltwright (div.); married secondly Cindy Skarin (div.; by her first husband, ___ Skarin, she had children: *Chad* [born 28 Dec. 1977 at St. Peter, MN]). Toby married thirdly Mary Curtis on 2 July 1988. Toby Burgess works for a contractor at Mankato, MN.

10a. **Sara Lynn (II).** Born 12 Aug. 1979 at St. Peter, MN.
10b. **Shiane Gene.** Her name is pronounced Cheyenne. Born 25 Mar. 1982 at Sheridan, WY.
10c. **John Reuben.** Born 2 Dec. 1983 at Sheridan, WY.

9c. **Mark Jacob.** Born 22 Apr. 1958 at Braham, MN. Married Rachel Laechelt. Mark Burgess is a carpenter at Minneapolis, MN.

10a. **Matthew John.** Born 4 Nov. 1975 at Mankato, MN.

9d. **Michael Lee.** Born 25 Oct. 1963 at Mankato, MN. Mike Burgess works as a truck driver for Southern Minnesota Construction, Mankato, MN.

10a. **Mitchael Lee.** Born 25 Sept. 1983 at Mankato, MN.

VAUGHN BURGESS OF THURSTON CO., WASHINGTON

[Jacob Lawson (I)[6], Jacob Lawson (II)[7]]

8g. **Vaughn Austin** *[son of Jacob Lawson (II)].* Born 13 Oct. 1929 at St. Clair, MN. Married Haruko Oda in Japan about 1947 (div.); married secondly Bok Soon Lee in Korea about 1958 (div.); married thirdly Evelyn Mae Goldsby on 14 July 1967 at Olympia, WA (she was born 12 Feb. 1926). Vaughn Burgess served in the U.S. Army for 22 years, retiring with the rank of Master Sergeant; he later became a personnel officer for the State of Washington, Olympia, WA. He currently lives retired at Rochester, WA. Vaughn Burgess has contributed greatly to this book.

9a. **Robert Jacob.** He was adopted by Jaime De La Cerna, and changed his name legally to Francisco Michael "Frank" De La Cerna. Born 1 Oct. 1948 at Ft. Belvoir, VA. Married Judith Ann Boyce. Frank De La Cerna is the manager of a Volkswagen dealership in Santa Ana, CA.

9b. **Susan Lee (I).** Born 13 Oct. 1950 at Granite City, IL. Married and divorced, and had children: *Christina*; *Rodney Jr.*; *Sharlyn*; *Shawna*. Susan Burgess is a clerical worker at Honolulu, HI.

9c. **David Earl.** Born 13 Dec. 1955 at Landstuhl, West Germany. Married Keiko Miwa in Japan. David E. Burgess is a school teacher at Tokyo, Japan.

10a. **William Austin.** Born 20 Dec. 1981 at Olympia, WA.

9d. **Mary Ann (XII).** Born 30 Nov. 1959 at Seoul, Korea. Married ___ Kim (div.), and had children: *Alicia Marie* (born 14 Apr. 1985 at Flushing, NY). Mary Burgess is a homemaker at Olympia, WA.

9e. **James Lee (II).** Born 25 Mar. 1964 at Tacoma, WA. Jim Burgess is a construction worker at Tumon, GU.

WILL & EDNA BURGESS OF HENNEPIN CO., MINNESOTA

[Jacob Lawson (I)[6]]

7k. **William Addison (II) "Will(ie)"** *[son of Jacob Lawson (I)].* He was named for Addison W. Bell. Born 6 Dec. 1875 (or 15 Dec., according to his death certificate) at Janesville, MN. Married Edna Mildred Burgess, his first cousin once removed, about 1898 (she was born 23 Oct. 1878 at Eagle Lake, MN, daughter of Thomas Marshall Burgess and Laura A. Luthultz, and died on 14 Nov. 1979 at Minneapolis, MN, aged 101 years, then the oldest Burgess descendant on record). Listed in the 1900 census for Nicollet Co., MN. Shortly thereafter, Will moved his family to Gull Lake, SK, Canada, where he lived for many years. Will Burgess was a salesman. He died on 9 Nov. 1957 at Minneapolis, MN, and is buried in the Lakewood Cemetery.

8a. **Max Donald.** Born 26 Apr. 1899 in Nicollet Co., MN. Married Frances V. ___ about 1934 (she reportedly died shortly after their marriage). He was a hospital orderly in World War I for the U.S. Army, and continued in this profession when he returned to civilian life. Max Burgess died childless on 4 Dec. 1965 at Minneapolis, MN, and is buried in the National Cemetery, Ft. Snelling, MN.

8b. **(George) Avon.** Born 2 Aug. 1903 at Penora, AB, Canada. Avon Burgess was a hospital orderly at Hastings, MN, and later worked as a maintenance man at Minneapolis; he was also an accomplished pianist. He died unmarried on 6 Feb. 1954 at Minneapolis, MN, and is buried in the Lakewood Cemetery.

8c. **Eva Laura.** Born 9 Aug. 1908 at Gull Lake, SK, Canada. Married Fred J. Kline, and had children: *Sandra* (ad.; born about 1961). Eva Kline died about 1993 at Minneapolis, MN.

8d. **William Allen.** Born 9 Oct. 1910 at Gull Lake, SK, Canada. Married Ann M. ___ about 1952 (she died before him). Served in the armed forces during World War II. Bill Burgess was a television repairman. He died on 3 Apr. 1962 at Minneapolis, MN, and is buried in the National Cemetery, Ft. Snelling, MN.

9a. **Barbara (J.?) (II)** (ad.). Born about 1940 in MN. Married ___ Bennett, and was last known living (1973) on Irving Avenue at Minneapolis, MN. She may be the Barbara J. Bennett (wife of Dennis M. Bennett) who is listed in the 1970 Minneapolis directory living on Fillmore St.

[William (I)[1], Edward (I)[2], William (II)[3], Henry (I)[4], John Henry (I)[5]]

THOMAS FLEMING BURGESS
(1833-1911)

OF WHITMAN COUNTY, WASHINGTON

6f. **Thomas Fleming "Tom"** *[son of John Henry (I)].* Born 5 Feb. 1833 at Portland Mills, Parke Co., IN. Married Sarah Jane Harris on 1 Jan. 1857 at Quincy, Adams Co., IL (she was born 6 Dec. 1832 in Putnam Co., IN, the daughter of Rev. John Marion Harris and Jane Wilson, and reportedly died 23 Jan. [or Jun.] 1902 at Troy, Latah Co., ID [however, she is mentioned in a contemporaneous letter as being alive on 2 May 1902], buried in an unmarked grave in the Little Bear Ridge Cemetery, Troy, ID). Listed in the 1860 census for Mendon Township, Adams Co., IL, in 1865-70 in Blue Earth Co., MN, in 1880 in Whitman Co., Washington Territory (and in the 1883, 1885, 1887, and 1889 state censuses there), and in 1900 in Latah Co., ID; has not been found in the 1910 census.

Tom Burgess was a farmer, engineer, sawmill operator, miller, store owner, and shopkeeper at Eagle Lake, MN; he is said to have driven the first locomotive engine into Mankato, MN in 1862-63 (one family member said that Thomas remembered seeing Indians hanging from the trees along the train tracks; the Sioux insurrection of 1862 ended with the hanging of almost forty Sioux chiefs in Nov. 1862). In 1871 he built a general store in Eagle Lake. With his family he moved West about 1873 (or possibly 1878), travelling by wagon train or railroad (accounts vary) to San Francisco or Oregon, settling initially near the present-day community of Cottage Grove, OR (a Thomas Burgess and family are recorded as travelling the transcontinental railroad from Ogden, UT to San Francisco on 17 Feb. 1872, [*Railway Passenger Lists of Overland Trains to San Francisco and the West, Volume II*, by Louis J. Rasmussen {Colma, CA: San Francisco Historic Records, 1968, p. 25}]). In 1878 he moved to Whitman Co., WA Territory, where he homesteaded a 160-acre farm near Pullman (*Deed Book #H*, p. 457, dated 31 Aug. 1883, the northeast ¼ of Section 10, Township 14, Range 44 [now within the city limits]). On 25 June 1886 he and several of his sons bought a 30-acre fruit ranch on the east bank of the Snake River near the small community of Wawawai, on land now submerged by the Lower Granite Dam. A drawing of his farm appears as an unpaginated plate in a second or later printing of *Historical Sketches of Walla Walla, Whitman, Columbia, and Garfield Counties, Washington*, by Frank T. Gilbert (Portland, OR: A. G. Walling, 1882; the sketch is not included in the first printing); he is also mentioned in *Of Yesterday and the River*, by June Crithfield (Colton, WA: Crithfield, 1964, p. 25). On 3 Jan. 1892 he sold his land and moved to Kings Valley, OR. About 1898 he moved to the mountains near Troy, ID, later living with his son, Edwin Burgess, first in Troy, and then west of Winona, Whitman Co., WA. He died at Winona of septic poisoning and flu on 7 Feb. 1911 (the date is taken from his Bible record and a son's contemporary letter), and is buried in the Winona Cemetery; his tombstone, erected by his grandson, Fred E. Burgess, erroneously gives his middle name as Flemming and his birth year as 1834. Some of his letters and his family Bible record survive among his descendants.

"Tom Burgess's family had hardly reached Minnesota when the Civil War erupted and all the young men were subject to military draft. However, at this time a man could hire someone else to go in his place. So Thomas, who had a wife and two children, with a third on the way, hired a substitute. Some of his brothers, namely Jacob Lawson and Harrison Monroe, and his nephew, John Harris, served with the Union Army.

"My father [Jesse Burgess] told me many stories about his boyhood days at Eagle Lake. The boys learned to swim at an early age, and in the winter they skated and rode ice sleds, becoming quite accomplished young athletes. He also told me about Grandfather Tom driving the first locomotive into Mankato, but nothing about the Indian troubles they had about that time.

"Fred Burgess and his sister, Mable Morrison [sic], state that their father Edwin was only nine years old when they came West. Edwin was born in 1864, so that would fit with a date of 1873. Thomas had worked for the railroad long enough to earn passes for himself and his family, so they rode the Union Pacific to San Francisco, then by steamboat to Portland, Oregon. (However, see the statement of George Osmer Burgess under the entry of his father, George Walter Burgess, for a different account.)

"From Portland they journeyed to Cottage Grove, Oregon, near the family of Grandmother Sarah Jane Harris. There they lived for five years. My father told me how the boys loved to swim in the Willamette River, and what nice country it was.

"From Oregon they went by covered wagon with their livestock to Whitman County, Washington Territory. They had an Indian scare on the trip, but no actual trouble, and arrived safely at their destination. There Thomas and his son Jesse (my father) took out homesteads near the site of Pullman, Washington. In fact, the artesian well now supplying the water for Pullman is located on Jesse's original homestead.

"The family's next move was to a fruit ranch on the Snake River near Wawawai, Washington. All of the children by this time were married except Jesse, the oldest, and he and his father operated the orchard with hired help [including, occasionally, some of Jesse's brothers]. They hauled the fruit up the Lewiston Hill to the rail head at Colfax, where it was shipped to market. Must have been quite a trip with four horse teams, and it may have led them to finally sell the fruit ranch."—Paul D. Burgess Sr., 20 Jan. 1971 and 2 Feb. 1972.

"My brother Elmer was three months old when they went to Oregon. They left Pullman in June 1894. It took three months [for Edwin Burgess and his family] to reach Polk County, Oregon. Mabel was born at Kings Valley [in northern Benton Co.]—Independence was the post office. There was only a small store and a grist mill besides the post office. The family bought their flour there for 50¢ a sack, which lasted one week. They lived there three years. Times were very difficult; one winter they had only potatoes. My Dad [Edwin] worked all one day and received 50¢ which he used for a sack of flour. Myrtle remembers how happy they were to have bread."—Raymond O. Burgess, 1972.

"About our trip to Oregon, it didn't take three months and we landed at Buena Vista [eastern Polk Co.], where Grandpa and Grandma lived at the time. Grandpa and Uncle Hugh (Burgess) were operating the ferry across the Willamette River. Jesse Burgess came after Mama and family, and Uncle Ed's family and later Uncle David came but he didn't stay. From Buena Vista we moved to Kings Valley on railroad land and lived there about three years. Uncle Hugh and Aunt Mary were the first ones to go to Kings Valley. Grandpa went before we did so Grandma rode with us.

"After Grandmother's death [my mother's brothers] seemed to scatter. Mama [Ida Burgess] heard from them once in a while and Grandfather lived with us a lot. He would visit around with the families, but mostly he lived with Mama and Uncle Edwin. He died at Edwin's house, I believe; his son Fred took care of him and he has the Bible and all of Grandfather's things."—Theo Prather Finch, 1972.

"[About 1898] they purchased a hotel in Troy, Idaho. Things were not always rosy, and eventually Hotel Troy was sold and a small farm purchased. Grandmother Sarah passed away in Troy in 1902, and Thomas in Winona, Washington, in 1911."—Paul D. Burgess Sr., 20 Jan. 1971 and 2 Feb. 1972.

"Thomas Fleming Burgess and most of his brothers were born in Indiana, I have heard him say it was near Terre Haute. They grew up there and their boyhood play was often at their house under a large oak tree. The farming was done by spade (no plows then); later, after he moved to Minnesota, one of his neighbors walked forty miles to see a man plow with a team and steel plow. While a boy, Tom used a large work mare and a one-horse harrow to till ten acres in one day, and it was the talk of the neighborhood. I always enjoyed his stories about early-day activities. He later moved to Illinois, had a lawsuit with his neighbor, and won a dollar. His appointed lawyer was Abe Lincoln, and he often said that he knew Abe Lincoln personally and had been a lifelong Republican.

"He told about their house burning and everything in it. The older pioneer houses had no water except what was carried by hand. Grandfather Burgess became a steam engineer. When he had earned a pass he came to San Francisco by train, then by boat to Portland, and inland to Oregon City. When Whitman County, Washington, was made, he and family and the Rogers moved there. I think old man Rogers was a minister. Uncle Walter, Uncle Dave, and my father Edwin, all married three sisters of the Rogers family.

"Grandfather often told about fishing through the ice with a spear and an artificial minnow, playing it with a string to make it look natural. When a fish came near enough they speared it. He said he often had the largest fish. I have heard him say that when a storm was blowing the temperature could be sixty below zero. It was common to find a pile of snow on the floor blown through the keyhole. Edwin Burgess was nine years old when they left Minnesota. I can't tell you much of the life in Oregon, except they rented a farm, and like the rest of the early-day pioneers, lived off the country, mostly by hunting. Dad told tales of hunting with hound dogs. There were no hunting seasons. The pioneers lived off the land and their gardens, very little else. Most of the ammunition was home-molded bullets and hand-loaded shells. They had old muskets and a few shotguns.

"When they moved to Washington Territory, Uncle David was old enough to homestead for himself. I was born there. Grandfather Burgess and Uncle Jess had a peach orchard on the Snake River and father worked for them. Father took a pre-emption in the Texas Draw country near the place where Grandfather Park's father homesteaded. This place was to be ours for taking care of Grandfather in his old age. He died at the age of 78, sitting in his chair. He could not sleep in a bed, only in a chair because of asthma, and was so old [and deaf] we had to write on a slate so he knew what we were saying.

"Sometime before this Grandfather's brother [George Washington Burgess] came out from Missouri and visited us in Idaho. He was with Grandfather when we moved to Winona [about 1910]. He had quite a lot of money in a money belt. He went to Portland, Oregon, or somewhere else down there, and was never heard of again. Our thinking is that he might have been killed for his money [actually, he died in Missouri in 1917]. There was a wet fall in the wheat country and very little was harvested. Grandfather Burgess and Uncle Jess had moved to Kings Valley, near Independence, Oregon. Uncle Hugh Harris [actually Hugh Burgess], Grandmother Harris's brother, had a homestead there near Willow Creek. We kids played in the water. This was during the panic time of President Cleveland's administration [1893]. Evidently Grandfather Tom was with them all this time.

"Grandfather was a sort of local patrol state Indian fighter [in Minnesota] and was given the right to a state pension if he would come back to Minnesota State. He had a letter to that effect just before he died, and he talked about going back as soon as spring came. But he died in a very few minutes with septic poison and flu at our home in Winona, Wash. He lived with us in his last few years.

"Sarah Jane Burgess died at Troy, Idaho, and was buried in the Little Bear Ridge Cemetery in an unmarked grave. She died of an enlarged liver, perhaps cancer, about 1901 or '02. I remember it well. Ida May Burgess Ingram [her daughter] was present and Theo Prather Skinner [Ida's daughter]."—Fred E. Burgess, 1972.

The Children of Tom Burgess:

7a. **Jesse Walden.** Born 19 Oct. 1857 at Quincy, IL. See below for full entry.
7b. **David Monroe.** Born 19 Dec. 1859 at Quincy, IL. See below for full entry.
7c. **(George) Walter.** Born 10 Jan. 1862 at Eagle Lake, MN. See below for full entry.
7d. **Edwin (I)** (nmn). Born 25 Jan. 1864 at Eagle Lake, MN. See below for full entry.
7e. **(James) Hughes.** Born 11 Dec. 1865 at Eagle Lake, MN. See below for full entry.
7f. **Ida May (II).** Born 29 Mar. 1868 at Eagle Lake, MN. Married Silas Prather on 7 June 1882 at Pullman, WA (he was born 9 Dec. 1851 in Jackson Co., MO, and died 12 May 1892 at Pullman, Whitman Co., WA), and had children:

John Glenn PRATHER. Born 29 May 1883 at Pullman, WA, married Leola Mary Serles on 7 Nov. 1912 at Yakima, WA (she was born 14 June 1892 in Clay Co., KS, and died 8 Apr. 1958 at Yakima), worked as a shipbuilder and a truck driver for Consolidated Freightways, and died on 5 Dec. 1970 at Yakima, WA, having had children:

Delores Mary PRATHER (born and died 1913).

Glenn Marion PRATHER (born 31 Oct. 1914 at Port Townsend, WA, married Grace "Edith" Waite on 26 Oct. 1939 at Yakima, WA, and had children: (Glenna) Marlene; (Glenn) Marion Jr.; (Pamela) Kay; (John) Michael; Peggy Lee; Joseph Lindsey).

Vernon LeRoy PRATHER (born 29 Sept. 1916 at Seattle, WA, married Luella Harriett Sparks on 3 Mar. 1938 [div.], and had children: Barry Wilfred [born 4 Apr. 1939 at Ellensburg, WA, married Sharon Lee Mortimore {she was born 17 Oct. 1943, and died 2 Feb. 1985}, and had children: Eric {born 1969, killed with his father in 1987}; Liesl. Barry married secondly (Bonita) Kay (Bateman) McCormack, and had children: Brooks Barry; Kara Lynn; (Thane) Zackary. Barry Prather was a member of the first American team to successfully ascend Mount Everest in 1963, received the Hubbard Medal from President Kennedy, and died 5 Sept. 1987 in a car accident at Shaniko, OR]; Barbara Lynn [born 30 Aug. 1940 at Easton, WA, married James Alton Musselwhite on 14 June 1958 at Coeur d'Alene, ID {dec.}, and had children: Dennis Alton; Karen Lynn; Sharon Ann; Donald Allen; Barbara Lynn married secondly Robert David Keene, and had children: Sean Whitten; Barbara Lynn married thirdly Albert Llewellyn Beede on 22 Mar. 1980 {he was born 10 Nov. 1928 in Harney Co., OR}, and lives at Yakima, WA]; Judy Lou [born 19 Jan. 1942 at Seattle, WA, married Doyle "Doc" Burch {div.}, and had children: Kathryn Rae; Judy married secondly Charles "Chuck" Ferrari on 21 Oct. 1972 at Lancaster, CA, and had children: Kristen Charalene; Jason Charles; Judy lives at Lancaster]; *Vernon* married secondly Lee Cundy [she died in 1950], and thirdly Virginia Carol Lacy on 21 Jan. 1953 at Carmel, CA, and had children: Ceda [born 18 Feb. 1954, died 23 Mar. 1990 at Portland, OR]; Eva; Wes; Kit; Ami. *Vernon* lives at Portland, OR).

(Rayma) Audrey PRATHER (born 6 July 1918 at Seattle, WA, married Wilfred Peter Karp on 9 Sept. 1942 at Yakima, WA [he was born 8 Nov. 1916 at Williston, ND; dec.], and had children: Dennis Arlan [born 8 Dec. 1943 at Dillon, MT, married Marsha Bischoff on 20 May 1966 at Seattle, WA, and had children: Stephanie Diane {born 3 Dec. 1966 at Seattle, WA}; Dennis Arlen Jr. {born 25 Oct. 1967 at Seattle, WA}]; Raleigh Emerson [born 3 July 1945 at Everett, WA, married Jeanne Elizabeth Barclay on 21 May 1967 at Seattle, WA, and died Nov. 1978, having had children: Kiersten Elizabeth {born 10 Dec. 1969 at Lemoore, CA}]. *Audrey* married secondly Robert Page, and lives at Enumclaw, WA).

***Thomas Fleming* PRATHER.** Born 11 Oct. 1884 at Pullman, WA, died there 18 Oct. 1887.

***Theodosia Frances "Theo"* PRATHER.** Born 23 Nov. 1886 at Pullman, WA, married Ernest Eugene Finch on 10 Apr. 1907 at Bellingham, WA (he was born 25 Jan. 1880 at Beloit, KS, and died 6 Oct. 1958 at Seattle, WA), and had children: *Arthur E.* (born 21 Mar. 1908, died 14 May 1941); *Alta May* (born 29 Dec. 1911, married Lyle McInturff on 9 Feb. 1935 at Seattle, WA, and had children: Janice Lee [born about 1936, married W. J. Oas on 11 July 1957 at Seattle, WA, and had children: Russell Eugene {born 14 Aug. 1959}; Bryan Joseph {born 4 Oct. 1962}]). Theo Finch died on 3 Apr. 1989 at Seattle, WA, aged 102 years.

***Elsie June* PRATHER.** Born 21 June 1888 at Pullman, WA, married Walter Edward Gervais on 4 Jan. 1915 (he died in Dec. 1944), and died Feb. 1981 at Seattle.

Archie Marion* PRATHER.** Born 18 Aug. 1890 at Pullman, WA, married Cecelia Schaeffer (she was born 14 Feb. 1892 in IA), and had children: *Bryon Schaeffer* (ad.); ***Archie married secondly Amy Dahl on 15 Mar. 1927 (she was born 6 Mar. 1896 at Stanton, NE, and died May 1973 at Wausa, NE), and had children: *Ida* (born 6 Dec. 1927, married Dale Holmquist on 27 May 1949, and had children: David [born 1 Apr. 1951]; Beth [born 14 May 1954]); *Marian* (born 7 Apr. 1929, married Lowell Kohen in 1950, and had children: Scott [born 1952 at Louisville, KY]; Bradley [born 1 Dec. 1954 at Ammond, NE]); *Arnold* (born 27 Aug. 1930, married Betty Swanson on 1 Jan. 1950 at Wasau, NE, and had children: Pamela [born 14 Feb. 1954]; Kathy [born 2 Feb. 1955]; Connie [born 7 Apr. 1957]; Donna [born 21 Feb. 1959]); *John A.* (born 10 July 1932, married Polly Mauck in 1964, and had children: Elica [born 13 June 1966]; Paula [born 4 Feb. 1967]; Amy [born 13 Sept. 1969]); *Ralph* (born 22 Mar. 1936, married, and had children: Daniel [born 7 Dec. 1963]; Richard [born 27 Feb. 1965]; Elaine [born 5 May 1970]). ***Archie*** died Sept. 1972 at Wausa, NE.

***Arthur Silas* PRATHER.** Born 2 May 1892 at Pullman, WA, died 21 July 1902 at Troy, ID.

Ida May PRATHER married secondly Charles Lincolyn Ingraham on 1 June 1893 at Pullman, WA (div.; he was born 25 Jan. 1863 at Green Bay, WI, and died in May 1908 at Boca, CA), and had children:

Berniece Lora* INGRAHAM.** Born 22 June 1895 at Kings Valley, OR, married C. W. Bertch, had children: *Bonnie Jean* (married Robert F. Venema on 12 May 1946); ***Berniece married secondly Jack Martin.

***Alma Ethel* INGRAHAM.** Born 16 Dec. 1897 at Kings Valley, OR, married Harry William Shattuck on 5 Feb. 1919 at Seattle, WA, and died 23 May 1971 at Seattle, WA, having had children: *Norman*; *Julia*; *Robert*; *Marcia*; *William H.*

***Dwight Draper* INGRAHAM.** Born 19 Oct. 1900 at Troy, ID, married Josephine Luella Sullivan on 2 Dec. 1921 at Seattle, WA (she was born 28 May 1903 at Denver, CO, daughter of Maurice Sullivan and Clara Marie Bruce), and died Sept. 1982 at Seattle, having had children: *Judith Frances* (born 23 July 1941 at Seattle, WA, married Roland Sterrett on 24 Nov. 1961, and had children: Michael Dwight [born 10 Sept. 1970 at Bellevue, WA]).

Ida May INGRAHAM married thirdly Herman G. Conover on 1 July 1908 at Seattle, WA (div.), and fourthly Archie E. Agnew on 17 Oct. 1917 at Seattle, WA (he was born in Canada, and died 31 Oct. 1938 at Seattle). Ida Agnew died on 8 Mar. 1954 at Seattle, WA, and is buried in Acacia Memorial Park. Barbara Beede has contributed greatly to this book. The late Theo Finch also contributed greatly to this book, being one of the author's earliest Burgess correspondents.

7g. **John William (I).** Born 7 Oct. 1869 at Eagle Lake, MN; died there on 29 Sept. 1871, and is buried in the Burgess Cemetery.

7h. **Albert (II)** (nmn). Born 25 Aug. 1871 at Eagle Lake, MN; died there on 8 Apr. 1872, and is probably buried in the Burgess Cemetery.

7i. **Alma** (nmn). Born 11 Jan. 1873 at Eagle Lake, MN; died on 11 June 1881 at Pullman, WA in the typhoid epidemic which claimed her brother, Henry, and was buried on the family farm at Pullman, WA.

7j. **(Thomas) Henry (II).** Born 7 Sept. 1878 at Pullman, WA; died there on 5 June 1881 in the typhoid epidemic which claimed his sister, Alma, and was buried on the family farm at Pullman, WA.

"Just east of the land that had once been platted for the town of Wawawai [Washington], Thomas Fleming Burgess and his sons, Jesse and George, bought twenty-five acres located in the center of the bar [of the Snake River]. Here they planted an orchard of apples and prunes....In 1892 Mr. Holt bought the Burgess property....The fruit harvest in those days was all done by hand, which meant hiring literally hundreds of people. About twenty-three Chinese were employed to tend the gardens. The foreman of this crew was old Fong. These people were later housed in the old Jesse Burgess house, which became known as the China House. Half a hundred Indians or more set up their teepees along the creek, around the bend of the road from the Batty place. The Indians came every year and camped along the river or the creeks until about 1920; after that they stopped coming for the harvests."—*Of Yesterday and the River*, by June Crithfield (Colton, WA: Crithfield, 1964, p. 25 and 35).

JESSE WALDEN BURGESS OF BINGHAM CO., IDAHO

[Thomas Fleming[6]]

7a. **Jesse Walden** *[son of Thomas Fleming].* Born 19 Oct. 1857 at Quincy, IL. Married Carrie Saad on 20 Dec. 1903 at Troy, ID (she was born 17 Jan. 1878 at Ras al-Mattan, Syria, a descendant of a Christian Lebanese family which migrated to Spokane, WA about 1900, and died 6 Nov. 1958 at Santa Rosa, CA). Listed with his parents in the 1900 census, and in 1910 in the South Troy Precinct, Latah Co., ID. Jesse Burgess was a farmer and carpenter in Washington and Idaho, settling at Wawawai on the Snake River in 1887, and then at Troy, ID in 1903. He died on 22 Oct. 1948 at Blackfoot, ID, aged 91 years, and is buried with his brother, Hughes Burgess, in the Evergreen Cemetery, near Colville, Stevens Co., WA.

"My father decided to go to Portland during the 1870s and study music and bookkeeping. He was such a good penman that he was hired by the Behnke-Walker Business College as a penmanship instructor. Apparently this job enabled him to study the violin under Antonio Henrici. Dad's fingers were short and stubby, and Mr. Henrici made him a violin with an extra small neck. I have this violin in my possession; it is nearly a hundred years old, but I have never learned to play it, being too involved in playing baseball.

"Jesse Burgess paid $200 cash for a quarter section of land near Pullman, Washington [next to his father's land] on 2 May 1883; he had evidently earned enough money to buy the land instead of homesteading it. By 1887 Jesse and his father had developed a thirty-acre fruit orchard on a bar in the Snake River.

"Although he was the oldest, my father was the last of his brothers and sisters to marry. He and his father had returned to Troy, Idaho, from Oregon, and built the Hotel Troy, which they operated. One of the cook's helpers they hired was Carrie Saad, who with her brothers had just arrived from their native country of Lebanon. She and Jesse fell in love and were married in 1903. Dad brought the family back to town (Troy), and found whatever was available in the line of work. He was an excellent painter and sign maker, and in later years was school custodian. They stayed there until 1925, when they moved to Spokane to be with their oldest, son, Paul, who had gone there to work.

"There isn't much more to tell. My brother William and I followed the trade of our mother's family, that is shoe repairing."—Paul D. Burgess Sr., 2 Feb. 1972.

8a. **Paul David (I).** Born 31 Oct. 1904 at Troy, ID. Married Muriel Haney Jessup on 16 May 1926 and again on 28 Mar. 1939 at Boise, Ada Co., ID (she remarried Philip Sandham after her husband's death). Paul Burgess worked for Saad Shoe Stores at Spokane, WA, before owning and managing his own chain of shoe stores at Boise, ID. He also served as Mayor of Colville, WA from 1947-52, and managed the Colville Golf Course, worked as a sports promoter, was elected a Masonic officer, and was a well-known civic leader in Washington and Idaho. He moved to Spokane permanently in 1954, and lived there until his death. Paul Burgess was one of the original group of cousins who came together in 1970 to begin work on the Burgess genealogy. He died on 1 Dec. 1972 at Spokane, WA, and is buried in the Riverside Memorial Park. He is greatly missed. Muriel Sandham lives at Spokane, WA.

9a. **Paul David (III).** Born 4 Dec. 1928 at Spokane, WA. Dr. Paul D. Burgess Jr. is a speech pathologist and audiologist for the City of New York, working in a diagnostic unit. He lives and works at New York, NY.

9b. **Barbara Joyce.** Born 13 June 1937 at Boise, ID. Married Martin Price; married secondly Kenneth Berger. Barbara Berger lives at Spokane, WA.

8b. **(Jessie) Alice.** Born 5 Dec. 1905 at Troy, ID. Married (Edward) Curtis Trenholme (he was born 3 Oct. 1908, was a lumber industry magazine publisher, and died Feb. 1978 at Eugene, OR), and had children: *John*; *Peter*; *Alice*. Alice Trenholme died 3 June 1985 at Walnut Creek, CA.

8c. **Daisy Bell.** Born 16 Mar. 1907 at Troy, ID. Married John W. Shulsen on 3 Apr. 1955 (born 28 Sept. 1899, died Sept. 1981), and had children: *Michael* (ad.); married secondly Donald J. Otteson on 25 June 1977 at Sonoma (born 3 Sept. 1914, died 15 Oct. 1991). Daisy died Mar. 1993 at Sonoma.

8d. **Eva Catherine.** Born 24 Aug. 1908 at Troy, ID. Married fourthly Thomas Thompson (a certified public accountant). Eva Thompson died childless on 23 Dec. 1982 at Sonoma, CA.

8e. **William Henry (X).** Born 20 Feb. 1910 at Troy, ID. Married Erma L. Hilty (she was born 10 Mar. 1911, and died 10 Sept. 1977 at Sonoma). William H. Burgess owned a shoe shop at San Bruno, CA, and was also a professional singer. He died childless on 4 May 1991 at Sonoma, CA.

8f. **Myrtle May (II).** Born 12 Oct. 1912 at Troy, ID. Married Donald Clark (a taxi company owner), and had two adopted children: *Shirley*; *Cheri*. Myrtle Clark died on 19 Apr. 1981 at San Francisco, CA.

DAVID M. BURGESS OF WALLA WALLA CO., WASHINGTON

[Thomas Fleming[6]]

7b. **David Monroe** *[son of Thomas Fleming]*. Born 19 Dec. 1859 at Quincy, Adams Co., IL. Married Mrs. Matilda Jane "Tilda" (Rogers) Russell on 12 Aug. 1886 at Colfax, Whitman Co., WA (she was born 24 Feb. 1861 at Cottage Grove, OR, the daughter of Henry Milward Rogers and Paulina Whited, and sister of Rebecca Emiline Rogers [who married her brother-in-law, George Walter Burgess] and Sarah Loucinda Rogers [who married her brother-in-law, Edwin Burgess]; she married firstly ___ Russell, by whom she had children: *Minnie M.* [born 1884 in TX, married George Knowlton]; Matilda died on 11 Sept. 1935 at Yakima, WA). Listed in the 1900 census for Nez Perce Co., ID, in 1910 in the Melrose District, Nez Perce Co. (living separately from his wife), and in 1920 at Yakima, Yakima Co., WA. David Burgess was a farmer in Idaho and Washington, moving to Moscow, ID in 1886, and then homesteading in 1895 at Melrose (later Reubens), ID, where he lived for many years. He died on 19 Apr. 1935 at Walla Walla, WA, and is buried there in the Mountain View Cemetery.

8a. **(Sylvester) Waldon.** Born 9 Mar. 1888 at Moscow, ID. See below for full entry.

8b. **Ethel (II).** Born 11 Jan. 1890 at Moscow, ID; died there on 23 Sept. 1892.

8c. **Effie Elizabeth.** Born 14 Jan. 1893 at Moscow, ID. Married Leo W. Ball on 3 June 1914 (he died on 18 Aug. 1968), and had children: *Ione*; *Inez*; *Vivian*. Effie Ball was an early contributor to the Burgess genealogy. She died on 9 June 1984 at Sunnyside, WA, aged 91 years.

8d. **(Sarah) Edith.** Born 23 Sept. 1895 at Moscow, ID. Married John W. Butterfield on 1 Aug. 1918 (he was born 6 Feb. 1898, and died Jan. 1974 at Bellevue), and had children: *Johnnie*. Listed with her father in the 1920 census. Edith Butterfield died on 23 Dec. 1983 at Bellevue, WA.

8e. **Halsey William.** Born 20 Feb. 1898 at Reubens, ID. See below for full entry.

SYLVESTER W. BURGESS OF WHITMAN CO., WASHINGTON

[Thomas Fleming[6], David Monroe[7]]

8a. **(Sylvester) Waldon** *[son of David Monroe]*. Born 9 Mar. 1888 at Moscow, ID. Married Mary Elizabeth "Molly" Pace on 29 Nov. 1916 at Eldorado Springs, Cedar Co., MO (she died in Jan. 1952 at White Salmon, WA); married secondly Mamie McCoy about 1946. Waldon Burgess was a farmer most of his life; after retiring from the land, he worked as a maintenance man at Washington State University, Pullman, WA. He died on 22 Nov. 1953 at Moscow, ID.

9a. **Enola Hester.** Born 13 Mar. 1918 at Melrose, ID. Married Lester Clarence LaFollette on 27 Aug. 1937 at Galena, MO (he was born 24 Feb. 1916 at Jenkins, MO), and had children:

Ruby Lee LaFollette. Born 8 Nov. 1938 in Cedar Co., MO, married H. Wayne Busby on 27 Aug. 1956 at White Salmon, WA (div.), and had children: *Mary Josephine* (born 19 Dec. 1958, married Michael Gumm on 24 Oct. 1977 at Alpena, AR [div.], and had children: Michael Shane [born 9 June 1978]; Cody Lynn [born 19 May 1979]; Beau Vincent Brooks [born 4 Dec. 1981]). ***Ruby Lee*** married secondly Gerald Donald Sullivan on 28 May 1960 at Stevenson, WA (div.), and had children: *Colleen Yvette* (born 30 Dec. 1961, married Travis Lamar Wheatley on 23 Sept. 1977 at Alpena, AR [div.], and had children: Travis Lamar Jr. "T. J." [born 8 June 1978]; Felicia Alainna [born 8 Aug. 1981]; *Colleen Yvette* married secondly Dean Watson on 30 Dec. 1982 at Fayetteville, AR [div.], and had children: Zachary Dean [born 6 June 1985]; Jeremy Danial Beau [born 5 Feb. 1988]); *Geri-Lee* (born 4 Aug. 1963, married Billy Todd Smith on 18 Sept. 1982 at Huntsville, AR, and had children: Lacey Paige [born 2 June 1987]). ***Ruby Lee*** married thirdly Charles Edward McGill on 11 June 1967 at Carson City, NV (div.), and had children: *Charles Edward II* (born 17 Jan. 1968, married Debra Gail Riley on 11 June 1989 at Denver, AR, and had children: Levi Anthony [born 30 Dec. 1988]; Christopher Dayle [born 4 Mar. 1991]); *Jaimie Lorena* (born 23 Oct. 1970, and had children: Joshua Jaden DEAN [born 31 July 1989]; Jory Sean MCGILL [born 3 Oct. 1992]). ***Ruby Lee*** married fourthly Chester Allen Hardee on 19 Sept. 1978 at Cassville, MO (div.), and fifthly Kenneth Dale Herrington on 6 Oct. 1979 at Cassville, MO (div.). ***Ruby LAFOLLETTE*** lives at Green Forest, AR.

Lester Clarence LAFOLLETTE Jr. Born 27 Feb. 1941 at Wapato, WA, married Carol J. Clark on 21 Jan. 1961 at White Salmon, WA (div.), and had children: *Elaine Renee* (born 31 July 1961 at Hood River, OR, married Kenneth May on 28 June 1980 at Sedro Woolley, WA [div.], and had children: Rebekah Faith [born 16 Oct. 1981 at The Dalles, OR]; Jason Kenneth [born 19 Nov. 1983 at Portland, OR]; Vanessa Nicole [born 1 May 1985 at The Dalles, OR]); *Nancy Jo* (born 13 Jan. 1963 at San Pedro, CA, married Gary Michael Besse on 6 May 1978 at Galena, MO, and had children: Carol May [born 1 May 1979 at Harrison, AR]; Michael Joe [born 4 Nov. 1982 at Berryville, AR]); *Lester Clarence III "Skip"* (born 7 Aug. 1964 at White Salmon, WA, married Michelle Renee "Missy" Coss on 24 Apr. 1982 at Alpena, AR). *Lawrence Clarence Jr.* married secondly Patsy Ann Richards Von Goss on 4 Aug. 1979 at White Salmon, WA (by her first husband, she had children: Annamarie [born 30 June 1969 at St. Helens, OR, married Timothy Jay Jacob on 16 Apr. 1991 at Eureka Springs, AR, and had children: William Travis {born 7 May 1993}]; Danielle [born 8 Mar. 1971 at Astoria, OR, married Reggie Glen Smith on 11 Apr. 1988 at Berryville, AR, and had children: Keith Delbert {born 10 Jan. 1989 at Harrison, AR}; Russell Lee {born 8 Nov. 1990 at Harrison, AR}]).

Rosabelle LAFOLLETTE. Born 3 Sept. 1942 at Wapato, WA, married David Charles Hebeisen on 24 Dec. 1962 (he was born 14 May 1941 at Hamburg, MN), and had children: *David Todd* (born 7 Nov. 1963 at White Salmon, WA, married Joan Margaret Lervik in July 1988 [she was born 13 Sept. 1963 at Hibbing, MN], and had children: David Aaron [born 1 Nov. 1989 at Cambridge, MN]; Alexander Todd [born 17 Apr. 1992 at Cambridge, MN]); *Erik Weston* (born 21 Sept. 1965 at White Salmon, WA, married Amy Ekren in 1983 [div.], married secondly Debbi Petchner in 1988, and had children: Victoria Ann [born 22 Jan. 1993]); *Devin John* (born 9 June 1968 at Cambridge, MN, married Teresa Freeding [she was born 5 May 1970 at Minneapolis, MN]); *Jason Lee* (born 24 July 1969 at Cambridge, MN, married Ann Marie Kramshuster [she was born 6 Apr. 1970 at Mora, MN]); *Branda Rose* (born 17 Mar. 1971 at Alexandria, MN, married Cory Lee Helmbrecht on 27 Dec. 1991 [he was born 6 Dec. 1970 at Mora, MN], and had children: Cory Michael [born 10 June 1992 at Cambridge, MN]); *Buffy Lynnette* (born 5 Jan. 1975 at Alexandria, MN, married Gary Michael Udstean on 16 Oct. 1993 [he was born Sept. 1971]).

James Henry LAFOLLETTE. Born 16 Jan. 1944 at Yakima, WA, married June ___ on 2 Nov. 1962 at Bingen, WA (she was born 26 June 1947), and had children: *Tina Maria* (born 24 Aug. 1963, married Joseph William Manly on 27 Aug. 1980 at Spokane, WA [div.; he was born 25 Nov. 1959], and had children: Rebecca Maria [born 1 Jan. 1981]; William Joseph [born 25 Nov. 1981]; *Tina Maria* married secondly Mark Benjamin LaStafka on 14 Feb. 1987 at White Salmon, WA [he was born 19 Aug. 1956], and had children: Dustin Lee [ad.; born 10 May 1988]); *Timothy James* (born 22 Oct. 1965, married Denise Carlene McNabb on 21 June 1993 [she was born 7 June 1973], and had children: Jeremie Darek [ad.; born 28 July 1989]; Aaron Scott [ad.; born 10 Jan. 1991]); *Tonya LeAnn* (born 28 Jan. 1970, married Woody Owen Dowens on 22 July 1990 at Big Fork, MT [div.], and had children: James Michael [born 17 June 1991]; *Tonya* married secondly James Brian Trayer [he was born 21 Sept. 1974], and had children: Meagan Rebecca [born 10 May 1993]). ***James LAFOLLETTE*** currently lives at The Dalles, OR.

John Waldon LAFOLLETTE. Born 27 Sept. 1945 at Moscow, ID, married Ethel Jo Freeman in 1966 at Lewiston, ID (div.), and had children: *John William* (born 27 Apr. 1967 at Enterprise, OR, married Tomi Swatzell on 4 May 1990 at Homer, AK [she was born 9 Mar. 1970, and by her first marriage had children: Kimber Lee {born 27 Mar. 1986 at Homer, AK}], and had children: *John William Jr.* [born 20 June 1991 at Homer, AK]). ***John Waldon*** married secondly Joyce Jean Dunn on 24 Oct. 1970 at White Salmon, WA (she was born 15 Apr. 1951), and had children: *Jessica Jean* (born 31 July 1972 at Pullman, WA). ***John W. LAFOLLETTE*** served in Vietnam. He currently works as a real estate appraiser for the Clickatat Co., WA government.

Jeremy Lee LAFOLLETTE. Adopted May 1971.

Enola LAFOLLETTE has resided at Green Forest, AR since 1973.

9b. **Lois Edith.** Born 4 Aug. 1919 at El Dorado Springs, MO. Married Elton Light on 16 Sept. 1935 (div.); married secondly to Noble Bumgarten in 1937, and had children: *Jerry*; *Michael*; married thirdly James Hubbard. Lois Hubbard currently lives at White Swan, WA.

9c. **Henry Monroe.** Born 10 Oct. 1921 at Toppenish, WA. Married briefly and divorced, with no children. Henry M. Burgess is a retired hospital attendant in Seattle, WA.

9d. **Amy Matildia.** Born 3 Jan. 1923 at El Dorado Springs, MO. Married Gordon E. Sylling on 12 May 1941 (he died in Oct. 1985), and had children: *Daniel E.* (born 31 Mar. 1942, married Dorothy Brower on 13 May 1965, and had children: Scott Dean [born 30 June 1965, married Tracy A. White on 31 Jan. 1991, and had children: Amy Louise {born 23 Nov. 1991}]; Robin Lynn [born 23 July 1969]; Robert Lee [born 9 Sept. 1970]); *Richard Gordon* (born July 1943, died Oct. 1943); *JoyceAnn E.* (born 10 Jan. 1946, married Gary Traifal on 25 Feb. 1966 [div.], and had children: Shelly Lynn [born 24 Feb. 1967]; married secondly Jack F. Stokes on 13 May 1969, and had children: Gordon James). Amy Sylling currently lives at White Swan, WA.

9e. **Mary Belle (III).** She later spelled her name Marybelle. Born 4 Dec. 1930 at Chehalis, WA. Married Frank Graves in July 1950, and had three children. Marybelle Graves died on 15 Nov. 1978 at Yakima, WA.

9f. **Wilma Mae.** Born 2 Feb. 1932 at Chehalis, WA. Married Don Bryan in Nov. 1950, and had six children. Wilma Bryan currently lives at White Salmon, WA.

9g. **Betty Lou (II)** (twin). Born 23 June 1933 at El Dorado Springs, MO. Married Donald Titus (div.). Betty Burgess currently lives at Boise, ID.

9h. **Billie Lee (I)** (twin). Born 23 June 1933 at El Dorado Springs, MO. Married Patricia May Bowlin on 25 July 1956; married secondly Gayla Rae Butler Brady (a free-lance commercial artist and art instructor) on 10 June 1967. Bill Burgess was an Army enlisted man who served in Vietman, reaching the rank of SFC (E-7), Battalion Intelligence NCO. During his Army career he was a tank commander, Armor School Instructor, and military advisor to the Vietnamese Army. After retiring in 1973, he received his B.A. in Vocational Education from East Texas State University in 1980. He now works as an engineering supervisor for Sanger Harris Dept. Stores at Dallas, TX, and as a part-time instructor at Northland Junior College, Irving, TX.

10a. **Benjamin Lee.** Born 10 May 1957 at Stuttgart, West Germany. Married, with children. Currently serving in the U.S. Navy.

10b. **George Waldin.** Born 16 July 1958 at Neubrucke, West Germany. Lives in Washington State.

10c. **Billy (II)** (nmn). Born 31 May 1959 at Neubrucke, West Germany. Currently serving in the U.S. Navy.

10d. **Robert Wayne (II).** Born 22 Nov. 1961 at Ft. Lewis, WA.

10e. **Patricia Ann (IV).** Born 27 Mar. 1963 at Ft. Lewis, WA.

10f. **Clinton Scott Brady** (ad.). His original surname was Brady, his father, Joseph Clinton Brady, having died in Vietnam on 13 Dec. 1965. Born 23 Mar. 1966 at Dallas, TX.

10g. **Christine Allison.** Born 18 Mar. 1970 at Ft. Knox, KY.

HALSEY W. BURGESS OF WALLA WALLA CO., WASHINGTON

[Thomas Fleming[6], David Monroe[7]]

8e. **Halsey William** *[son of David Monroe].* Born 20 Feb. 1898 at Melrose (later Reubens), ID. Married Emma E. Layman on 27 Mar. 1921 at Yakima, WA (she was born 16 Aug. 1902, and died at Walla Walla in Aug. 1983). Listed in the 1920 census with his father. Halsey Burgess was a prominent dairy farmer, settling first at Yakima, WA by 1922, and then near Walla Walla, WA, where he served as General Manager of the Walla Walla Dairymen's Association, Director of the Walla Walla Production Credit Association, and Director of the Walla Walla Chamber of Commerce. His biography appears in *A History of the State of Washington*, by Lloyd Spencer (New York: American Historical Society, 1937, Volume IV, p. 676), and in *Who's Who for Washington, 1949-50* (Portland, OR: Capitol Publishing Co., p. 215). A member of the Baptist Church, Halsey Burgess died on 26 Apr. 1969 at Walla Walla, WA, and is buried in the Mountain View Cemetery.

9a. **Beverly Jean (I).** Born 9 Dec. 1922 at Yakima, WA. Married Dr. Harold Kenneth Latourette on 27 Oct. 1944 at New York, NY (he was born 10 Apr. 1922 at Seattle, WA), and had children: *Harold Kenneth Jr.* (born 1 Mar. 1947, died 31 July 1974); *Helen Denise* (born 28 May 1949, married Daniel Duffin on 6 Oct. 1969 [div. 1975], married secondly Frank Macioce Jr. in July 1988 at Summit, NJ, and had children: Theodore Kenneth [born 26 Apr. 1993]); *Lorene Michelle* (born 21 May 1954, married Michael Mark Chapman in Feb. 1973 [div. 1979], and had children: Michael Mark Jr. [born 15 Aug. 1973]; married secondly Ivo Romenesco in June 1986; Lorene Romenesco lives at Charlottesville, VA); *Marcia* (born 28 Apr. 1956, married Phillip Shady on 29 May 1981 at Lawrenceville, NJ, and had children: Paul [born 13 Jan. 1984]; Bethany [born 26 Apr. 1986]);

Stephen Scott (born 21 Apr. 1962, married Debra Salkind in Sept. 1987 at Washington Crossing, PA; they live at Arlington, VA). Beverly Latourette currently lives at Anacortes, WA.

9b. **(Margaret) Elaine (I).** Born 9 Nov. 1926 at Walla Walla, WA. Dr. M. Elaine Burgess is an Emeritus Professor of Sociology at the University of North Carolina, Greensboro, having previously taught at Duke University. She is the author of two books, *Negro Leadership in a Southern City* (Chapel Hill, NC: University of Carolina Press, 1962), and *An American Dependency Challenged* (Chicago: American Public Welfare Association, 1963); her biography has appeared in *Contemporary Authors*, *Who's Who of American Women*, *American Men and Women of Science*, and *Foremost Women in Communications*. She spends winters at her home in Greensboro, NC, and summers on Whidbey Island, at Couperville, WA.

9c. **Lorna Ann.** Born 11 Aug. 1930 at Walla Walla, WA. Married Dr. Ramon Ross on 7 June 1950 at Walla Walla, WA (div. 1975; he was born 1 Nov. 1929 at Walla Walla), and had children: *Jane Marie* (born 24 Aug. 1956 at Tacoma, WA); *Susan* (born 22 Aug. 1959 at Walla Walla, WA, married Jeffery Kawar in Aug. 1987 at San Diego, CA); *Michelle* (born 30 Nov. 1963 at San Diego, CA, married Michael Burns in Dec. 1990 at San Diego, CA, and had children: Rachael Marie [born 26 Aug. 1993]; they live at Oakland, CA). Lorna Ross currently lives at Tacoma, WA.

9d. **Georgia Jane.** Born 3 Mar. 1933 at Walla Walla, WA. Married William Kurtz on 9 Oct. 1959 at Walla Walla, WA (he was born 1 July 1933 in Iowa), and had children: *Melinda Jane* (born 16 July 1961 at Seattle, WA); *Anne Elaine* (born 22 Dec. 1964 at Seattle, WA). Georgia Kurtz currently lives at Seattle, WA.

9e. **(Charles) David.** Born 11 June 1939 at Walla Walla, WA. Married Janet English on 11 June 1960 at Walla Walla, WA (she was born 2 Feb. 1939 at Colville, WA). C. David Burgess has worked in finance most of his life; he was an executive with the Farm Credit Bank, Spokane, WA, retiring in Mar. 1990. He now works there for the Inland Empire Appraisal Co.

10a. **Brian David (I).** Born 9 Aug. 1961 Portland, OR. Married Holly Washkoska. Brian Burgess works for Johnson Wax at Racine, WI.

10b. **Beth Ann.** Born 11 Jan. 1963 at Colorado Springs, CO. Married Marty Price, and had children: *Bradley* (born 6 Sept. 1990). Beth Price is self-employed at Redmond, WA.

10c. **Brenda Elaine.** Born 6 June 1968 at Walla Walla, WA. She attended Spokane Falls Community College. Married Mark Servoss in Aug. 1991.

THE BIOGRAPHY OF HALSEY W. BURGESS

"The history of the rise and growth of the dairy industry in Washington has been noted in this work, but the reëmphasis of its importance to the development of the State cannot be overdone. Helsey [sic] W. Burgess is one of the many experienced men who have played prominent parts in this industry, both from the standpoint of manufactured products and of leadership in the Walla Walla Dairymen's Association. He is a native of Nez Percé County, Idaho, born February 18, 1898, son of David M. Burgess, who settled on a homestead in Idaho a year before his son was born.

"Helsey W. Burgess was reared on his father's farm, and as a boy learned the dairy business. As a young man, he came to the Yakima Valley, where he engaged in dairying, and where, for six years, he was engaged in the creamery business. During the past seven years, he has been actively interested in the manufacture of dairy products, as plant superintendent, and for four years has been the general manager of the Walla Walla Dairymen's Association. This association is a coöperative organization of about two hundred and fifty dairymen in the Walla Walla Valley region, and was organized in 1923. Among its purposes is the disposal of the members' milk and cream, eggs, and the purchasing of feed and supplies in large quantities. The Walla Walla plant of the association was built in 1927, and about thirty-three are employed. Butter, cheese, ice, cream, and allied products are made; eggs are shipped; and eight delivery trucks daily dispose of bottled milk and cream. The area this corporation draws from includes parts of Washington, Oregon, and Idaho, and a business exceeding a quarter of a million dollars annually is done. Branches are maintained in Touchet, Umapine, and Milton, Oregon. The officers of the company, which is incorporated, comprised, in 1935, Charles Baker, president and one of the original founders; C. H. McGilvrey, vice-president; C. M. Rader, secretary; Helsey W. Burgess, general manager; and Paul Hedger, H. G. Gordon, Ivar Williams, and Joseph Baker, board of directors. Mr. Burgess is a member and a director of the Walla Walla Chamber of Commerce, and a Rotarian.

"Helsey W. Burgess married Emma E. Layman, born and reared in the Yakima Valley. Her father is engaged in the grocery business at Toppenish, Washington. Mr. and Mrs. Burgess are the parents of four children: Beverley Jean, Margarite Elaine, Lorna Ann, and Georgia Jane."

GEORGE WALTER BURGESS OF BIGGAR, SASKATCHEWAN, CANADA

[Thomas Fleming[6]]

7c. **(George) Walter** *[son of Thomas Fleming].* Born 10 Jan. 1862 at Eagle Lake, MN. Married Rebecca Emiline (or Rebecka Emaline) Rogers on 10 Jan. 1887 at Colville, Whitman Co., WA (she was born 16 [or 14] May 1866 [or 1867] at Cottage Grove, OR, the daughter of Henry Milward Rogers and Paulina Whited, and sister of Matilda Jane Rogers [who married her brother-in-law, David Monroe Burgess], and Sarah Loucinda Rogers [who married her brother-in-law, Edwin Burgess], and died on 25 Oct. [or 11 Mar.] 1945 at Biggar, SK). Listed in the 1900 census for Latah Co., ID, and in 1910 in the Lenore District, Nez Perce Co., ID near the reservation of the Nez Percé Indians. Walter Burgess was a farmer in Washington, Idaho, Oregon, and near Biggar, SK, Canada, settling at Wawawai on the Snake River in 1887, at Lenore, ID about 1896, and then in Saskatchewan in the Spring or Summer of 1910, after the census was taken (1 Apr. 1910). He also worked as a timberman and railroad laborer in Idaho and Canada. Walter Burgess died on 30 Aug. 1942 at Biggar, SK; both he and his wife are buried in unmarked graves in the Biggar Cemetery.

"Regarding the statement by Ray Burgess, they could well have traveled [west] via train to start out, but most of the way was by wagon train. My father, George Walter Burgess, was twelve years old when they moved [from Minnesota to Oregon]; at that time a twelve-year-old was considered a man. He had his own wagon and team of oxen to take care of, his own rifle and other firearms as required at that time. He has told me on numerous occasions of the trip west, of fighting with the Indians, of taking his place in protecting the wagon train against the onslaught of the Indians. Although he was forced to kill Indians he was never proud of that fact. His sister Ida also told me how they would circle the wagons, the young children would take cover, while some of the women would help fight, loading the guns for the men and putting out fires. [Later,] the Chief of the Nez Percés, Chief Joseph, was a close and valued friend of my father. He was also known to your grandfather, Roy P. Burgess."—George Osmer Burgess, 31 Mar. 1981.

8a. **Horace M. "Liz"** (nmn). Born 28 Nov. 1887 at Wawawai, WA. See below for full entry.

8b. **Roy P.** (nmn). Born 19 May 1890 at Wawawai, WA. See below for full entry.

8c. **Dalpha** (nmn). Born 20 Sept. 1891 at Walla Walla, WA. Married Percy Watt (he died in 1918 in the great flu epidemic), and had children:

Daughter ***WATT***. Died 1918 in the great flu epidemic.

Clayton WATT. Died at age 14 during the 1920s.

Dalpha Burgess WATT married secondly James Skinner about 1925, and had children:

Florence Emiline SKINNER. Born 25 Oct. 1926 at Biggar, SK, Canada. Married Howard Presley (a farmer), and had children: *Edwin* (married Marleen Wieve, works as manager of a glass shop at Dawson Creek, BC, and had children: Anthony [married Amber ___]; Tanya); *Lois* (married Wayne Wooden [he teaches high school mechanics], and had children: Dart; Clifford; Dallas; Clinton; Lois and Wayne Wooden live at Dawson Creek, BC); *Minard* (married Alice ___, works as an electrical contractor at Langley, BC, and had children: Bufford; Twyla; Camelia; Breanna; Daughter). ***Florence PRESLEY*** was a school teacher before retiring. She and her husband currently live at Dawson Creek, BC.

James Walter SKINNER. Born 21 Aug. 1928 at Biggar, SK. Married Bertha Zacharias, and had children: *James* (married Darie ___, works as an accountant at Edmonton, AB, and had children: Cara; Andrew; Jody; Erica); *Mavis* (married Jim White [an accountant], and had children: Amanda; Tanya; Kendra; *Mavis* lives in Ontario, Canada); *Loreen* (married Randle Mantai, had children: Nathan; Daniel; Alysse; they work as school teachers at Edmonton, AB); *Pamela* (married Vern Landry, and had two children; they live at Grand Prairie, AB). In 1957 Jim Skinner moved his family to Hinton, AB and worked in the bush for one year. In 1958 he began working in the local pulp mill, and in 1968 he homesteading in the Blue Berry Mountain area of Northern Alberta. He later relocated to Grand Prairie, AB, where he worked in a pulp mill and farmed. The Skinners now live retired at Creston, BC.

Elsie Beatrice SKINNER. Born 8 Oct. 1930 at Biggar, SK. Married George Nicolson, and had children: *Alanna* (works as a secretary at Abbotsford, BC); *Janice* (married Mark Madsen [an electrician], and had children: Kyle; Child; *Janice* lives at Vancouver, BC); *Greg* (married Sherry ___, and works at a sawmill at Hinton, AB). The Nicolsons moved to Hinton, AB about 1960. Elsie Nicolson was a practical nurse, and George worked in the pulp mill at Hinton, AB. They currently live there retired.

Thomas William SKINNER. Born 2 Mar. 1932 at Biggar, SK. Married Karol ___ in 1959, and had children: *Gordon Thomas* (born 3 Mar. 1961, worked as an auto mechanic and in a food mission at Palmdale, CA); *Wanda Karol* (born 18 May 1963, married Harold Dawson, and had children: Jannell [born July 1986]; Jeremy [born Sept. 1992]; they live at Vanderhoof, BC). From 1953-54 Thomas Skinner farmed in the summers and fished during the winters on the Great Slave Lake in the Northwest Territories. In 1956 he moved to Hinton, AB to work in the bush, then began working at the pulp mill in 1958. He moved to Prince George, BC in 1966, where he works at the local pulp mill. Thomas Skinner has also had a cattle operation for many years. Karol Skinner works at the Prince George Regional Hospital.

Alice May SKINNER. Born July 1936 at Meadow Lake, SK. Married Hans Vidal (a farmer), and had children: *Roy* (married, works in the pulp mill at Meadow Lake); *Gary* (married Laurie ___, and had children: Kent, and works as an accountant at Meadow Lake, BC); *Lorenda* (married Darvin Friesen [he works for the School District of Meadow Lake as a repair and service man], and had children: Luke; Jessica; Joel; Solomon).

Dalpha SKINNER died on 16 Nov. 1974 at Dawson Creek, BC, Canada.

8d. **Harold M. "Dick"** (nmn). Born 3 Mar. 1895 at Walla Walla, WA. Married Myrtle Clark. Dick Burgess was a railroad fireman, logger, and farmer before being disabled in a train wreck. He returned to farming briefly, then was diagnosed with TB. He died on 28 Sept. 1958 at Meadow Lake, SK.

9a. **Alma Constance Glynn** (ad.). Born 4 Sept. 1930 at Regina, SK, Canada. Married Herbert Hill, and had five sons. Alma Hill lives at Kelowna, BC.

8e. **Evangeline** (nmn). Born 12 Oct. 1897 at Lenore, ID. Married Clifford Gordon Tricker at Biggar, SK, Canada, and had children: *Florence* (died at age 13 or 14 at South Salem, OR); *George Ellsworth* (born 26 Oct. 1917 at Biggar, SK, married Dorothy Nyberg [div.], and had children: Michael George); *Gordon* (born about 1922, married Maxine ___ [by her first husband she had a child: Janet]); *Rosetta* (born about 1927 at Salem, OR, married Donald Spear, and had four sons; may have married secondly Mike McFarland). Eva Tricker died on 26 Mar. 1980 at Salem, OR.

8f. **Leola Jessie May.** Born 9 Dec. 1901 (or 1902) at Lenore, ID. Married Hubert Hillman about 1922, and died on 24 Apr. 1992 at Airdrie, AB, Canada, aged 90 years, buried Cochrane Cemetery, Cochrane, AB, having had children:

(Ellen) May HILLMAN. Married Tony Riesling, and had children: *Jerome*; *Donald*; *David*; *Eva*; *Theresa*; *Michael*; married secondly ___ Zimmerman, and lives at Langley, BC, Canada.

(Charles) Arthur HILLMAN. Married Thelma B. McInnis, and had children: *Linda Anne* (married Conrad Bratushesky, and had children: Brian Conrad; Stacey Lynn); *Earl Arthur* (married Verna Hubbard, and had children: Trevor John; Georgina Eva); *Mavis Leola* (married Gordon Wayne Johnson, and had children: Richelle; April).

Walter George HILLMAN. Married Louise Fenton, and had children: *Joyce* (married Joe Hanna, and had children: John; Donald); *Robert* (married Alice Long); *Dianne* (married Kevin Yarkowski, and had children: Sheila; Troy Bruce). Walter Hillman lives at Breton, AB, Canada.

Lester Floyd HILLMAN. Married Shirley Keep, and had children: *Ronald* (married Terri Rose Bachmann, and had children: Tyson Marlin); *Katherine Ellen* (married Glen Allan Weir).

Ethel Margaret HILLMAN. Married Richard Buckler, and had children: *Laurinda* (married Kevin McPherson, and had children: Kyle Mitchell; Janelle); *Nancy* (married Wayne Annable, and had children: Christal; Tally Chantelle). Ethel Buckler lives at Airdrie, AB, Canada.

8g. **Henrietta (II) "Etta"** (nmn). Born 16 May 1905 at Lenore, ID. Married Donald Russel Speer, and had children: *Donald Russel Jr.* (married Doris ___, and had children: June; Faye; Carol; Kathy); *Arlo*. Etta Speer died on 27 Apr. 1976 at Red Deer, AB, Canada.

8h. **George Osmer**. Born 21 Apr. 1908 at Lenore, ID. See below for full entry.

HORACE M. BURGESS OF DOUGLAS CO., OREGON

[Thomas Fleming[6], George Walter[7]]

8a. **Horace M. "Liz"** (nmn) *[son of George Walter].* Born 28 Nov. 1887 at Wawawai, WA. Married Jessie Frost on 15 Dec. 1915 (she was born 21 Mar. 1892 at Lenore, ID, sister of Osmer Frost [from whom his brother and nephew were named], and died 14 Nov. 1918 at Biggar, SK, Canada); married secondly Beulah Belle Mabry on 14 Jan. 1922 (she was born 12 Nov. 1893, and died Jan. 1984 at Lewiston, ID). Horace Burgess was a farmer most of his life in Oregon. He died on 29 Dec. 1960 at Canyonville, OR, and is buried in the Winston Cemetery.

9a. **Ethel Louise (II).** Born 24 Dec. 1916 at Biggar, SK, Canada. Married Albert Mabry on 17 Mar. 1943 at Moscow, ID (he was born 17 June 1897 at Salt Lake City, UT, worked as a farmer, and died 28 July 1989 at Walla Walla, WA), and had children: *Karen* (born 30 Jan. 1944 at Cottonwood, ID; she works as a psychiatric technician); *Sharon* (born 7 Feb. 1947 at Cottonwood, ID); *Leray* (born 9 Aug. 1948 at Cottonwood, ID; he works as a restaurant chain owner). Ethel Mabry currently lives at Albany, OR.

9b. **Ronald Horace.** Born 30 May 1924 at Salem, OR. Married Vivian Charlotte Post on 15 Feb. 1945 at Moscow, ID (she was a teacher's aide). Ron Burgess worked for 30 years in the lumber industry in Oregon before becoming a maintenance man for the school district at Winston, OR.

10a. **Philip Ronald.** Born 9 Aug. 1946 at Moscow, ID. Married Sandra McBride on 21 Feb. 1970 at Denver, CO. Philip Burgess is a draftsman at Tempe, AZ.

11a. **Kevin Michael (II).** Born 11 Sept. 1975 at Corvallis, OR.
11b. **Jeffrey Todd.** Born 4 July 1977 at Tempe, AZ.
11c. **Melissa Lynn.** Born 23 May 1980 at Tempe, AZ.

10b. **Christine LuAnn.** Born 9 Feb. 1949 at Roseburg, OR. Married Bela "Bill" Von Tolmacsy in 1974 at Yakutat, AK, and had children: *Kristina* (born 1975); *Alex* (born 1980). Chris Von Tolmacsy was a teacher at Seward, AK. She died of cancer on 2 Aug. 1991 at Seattle, WA.

9c. **Callie Leola.** Born 3 Nov. 1926 at Siletz, OR. Married Harold M. Moore on 5 Nov. 1944 at Moscow, ID (he was born 24 Jan. 1910 at Pampa, WA, and worked as a farmer and a field man for a fertilizer company), and had children:

JoAnn Louise MOORE. Born 10 Nov. 1945 at Moscow, ID, married John W. Briney on 2 June 1962 at Moscow, ID, and had children: *Sandi L.* (born 8 Jan. 1963 at Moscow, ID, married Gregg G. Ybarra on 27 Mar. 1982 at Warden, WA, and had children: Rhett Victor [born 5 Oct. 1993 at Springfield, OR]); *Suzanna L.* (born 7 July 1965 at Moscow, ID, married Steven Crapson on 10 May 1986 at Warden, WA). JoAnn married secondly Robert Shockley on 4 May 1975 at Moscow, ID. JoAnn Shockley works for a daycare center.

Lloyd Raymond MOORE. Born 3 June 1947 at Moscow, ID, married Diana Gormsen on 1 June 1967 at Moscow, ID (div.), and had children: *Randy S.* (born 20 Nov. 1967 at Spokane, WA); *Clifton R.* (born 17 Mar. 1970 at Spokane, WA). Lloyd works as a body and fender man.

Harold Allen MOORE. Born 3 Dec. 1948 at Moscow, ID, married Cheri Diane Peck on 22 Feb. 1975 at Spokane, WA (by her first marriage, she had children: *Heather A.* [born 6 Oct. 1970 at Spokane, WA, married Greg Snelling on 24 Oct. 1987 at Warden, WA, and had children: Matthew T. {born 10 Mar. 1988 at Moses Lake, WA}]), and had children: *Aaron LeRay* (born 16 June 1976 at Moses Lake, WA). Harold Moore works as a field man for a fertilizer company.

Thomas Darrel MOORE. Born 16 Dec. 1949 at Moscow, ID, married Anne Wesner on 1 Dec. 1973 at Spokane, WA, and had children: *Leah Wesner* (ad.; born 25 Oct. 1981 in Korea). Thomas Moore works as a graphic designer.

Callie Burgess MOORE lives at Otis Orchards, WA.

9d. **Erdene Norella.** Born 5 Nov. 1928 at Willamina, OR. Married (Julius) Donald Coburn Jr. on 26 June 1948 at Spokane, WA (he was born 14 June 1926 at Spokane, WA, and worked as a custom picture framer), and had children: *Douglas Wayne* (born 7 July 1949 at Spokane, WA; he works as Director of Maintenance at Evergreen Helicopters of Alaska, Inc.); *Kathleen Louise "Kathi"* (born 7 Sept. 1951 at Spokane, WA, married ___ Ruby, and works as manager of Bookworld in Spokane); *Julie Dawn* (born 6 Apr. 1954 at Spokane; she works as a nurse). Erdene Coburn works as a secretary for a real estate firm in Spokane, WA.

9e. **Weldon Norvell.** Born 15 Jan. 1932 at Salem, OR. Married Ruth Melcum on 20 Jan. 1954 at Lewiston, ID. Weldon N. Burgess is a farmer at Craigmont, ID.

10a. **Dennis Duane.** Born 24 Feb. 1956 at Cottonwood, ID. Dennis is a mechanic at Craigmont, ID.
10b. **Denise Diane.** Born 29 July 1957 at Cottonwood, ID. Married Gary Hawk on 16 Mar. 1979. Denise Hawk works as a beautician at Lewiston, ID.

9f. **Roxanna Vernille.** Born 31 Oct. 1935 at Moscow, ID. Married Glenn Carlson on 27 June 1953 at Dillard, OR (he was born 17 Mar. 1932 at Sagola, MI, and works as an excavating contractor), and had children: *Eric* (born 30 June 1956 at Roseburg, OR; he works as a gill net fisherman and metal fabricator); *Flint* (born 28 June 1960 at Roseburg, OR; he works as an excavating contractor for a dump truck business). Roxanna Carlson lives at Hammond, OR.

ROY P. BURGESS OF CLACKAMAS CO., OREGON

[Thomas Fleming[6], George Walter[7]]

8b. **Roy P.** (nmn) *[son of George Walter].* Born 19 May 1890 at Wawawai, Whitman Co., WA. Married Edna Josephine Mathews on 15 Mar. 1914 at Biggar, SK (div.; she was born 21 May 1899 at Colville, Stevens Co., WA, daughter of William Thomas Mathews and Mary Magdalene Miller, married secondly Ray Mobley on 1 June 1932 [div.], thirdly a soldier about 1942 [div.], and fourthly Paul Feldman about 1974 [he was born 6 Apr. 1895 in IA, and died Sept. 1977 at Portland, OR], and died 24 June 1985 at Portland, OR). Roy Burgess married secondly Viola Hannon about 1930 (div.), thirdly Prudence E. Brunk about 1932 (she died 29 Nov. 1948 in Clackamas Co., OR), and fourthly Alvina Elizabeth (Keil) Pugh on 24 Sept. 1949 at Vancouver, WA (she was born 12 Nov. 1895, and died 31 May 1972 in Clackamas Co., OR; by her first marriage, she had children: *Eldon*; *Daughter* [married Donald DuRette]; *Daughter* [married Melvin DuRette]). Roy P. Burgess was a farmer in Canada until 1924, when he returned with his family to Oregon; he moved to Salem, OR in 1926, where he worked for 17 years as a guard for the Oregon State Penitentiary. In 1943 he moved to Canby, OR, where he took a position as a lathe operator and later as a night watchman for the Doernbecher Manufacturing Company's Coalca Sawmill at Canby, OR. He was a member of the Christian Church. He died on 28 Sept. 1954 at Oregon City, Clackamas Co., OR, and is buried with his third wife in Zion Memorial Park, Canby, OR.

9a. **Mary Paulina.** Born 3 Oct. 1916 at Biggar, SK, Canada. Married Ross Thompson (div.), secondly Ralph Wilson at Spokane, WA (div.), and thirdly Glenn Ernest Cleland on 16 October 1948 at Vancouver, WA (he was born 17 Mar. 1905 at Portland, OR, and died there on 22 Dec. 1991). Mary Cleland is an artist and sculptor at Portland, OR.

9b. **Osmer Ray "Ozzie."** Born 27 Jan. 1919 at Biggar, SK, Canada. Married Xenia Ione "Deanie" Greenlee on 23 June 1943. Ozzie Burgess is a retired lumber mill worker at Cottage Grove, OR.

10a. **Lynda Ione.** Born 7 Mar. 1948 at Cottage Grove, OR. Lynda Burgess died unmarried on 22 Aug. 1966 in Marion Co., OR.

10b. **Leon Dean (II).** Born 28 Oct. 1949 at Cottage Grove, OR. Leon Burgess works in a plant nursery at Cottage Grove, OR.

9c. **(Rebecca) Evangeline "Eva."** Born 27 Oct. 1920 at Biggar, SK, Canada. Married (Bernard) Brunel Richards on 22 Feb. 1939 at Salem, OR (div.), and had children: *Phyllis Jean* (born 6 Feb. 1940 at Salem, OR, married ___ Savage, and had children: Brent Alan [born 24 Feb. 1962, had children: Tyler James]); *Ruth Evelyn* (born 18 Sept. 1943 at Hillsboro, OR, married Dan Chase II, and had children: David Dean FERRARA [had children: Jason]; married secondly James Ferrara, and had children: Jennifer Jean; Gregory Gene; Joshua John; Bethany Christine; married thirdly Steven Allen, and had children: Zachary Cody); *John Roger* (born 15 June 1947 at Portland, OR, married Cecelia ___, and had children: Timothy). Eva Richards lives at Portland, OR.

9d. **(Roy) Walter.** Born 4 July 1922 at Biggar, SK, Canada. See below for full entry.

9e. **Margaret Evelyn "Peggy."** Born 1 Aug. 1924 at Swift Current, SK, Canada. Married Theodore Wilson Jones on 3 Nov. 1951 at Portland, OR, and had children: *Grant Lloyd* (born 27 Apr. 1954 at Portland, OR, married Elaine Evans on 17 Sept. 1977, and had children: Shannon Coleen [born 20 May 1983]; Trevor Wilson [born 15 Feb. 1986]); *Marsha Roberta* (born 28 Sept. 1955 at Portland, OR, married Drew Parsons on 13 June 1987, and had children: Tyler Patrick [born 7 Sept. 1988]; Nicholas Drew [born 11 Oct. 1990]); *Lee Arnold* (born 19 Jan. 1960 at Portland, OR, married Terry Ebbert on 6 June 1986, and had children: Austin Theodore [born 22 June 1990]; Nolan Lee [born 9 July 1992]). Peggy Jones currently lives at Portland, OR.

ROY WALTER BURGESS OF JACKSON CO., OREGON

[Thomas Fleming[6], George Walter[7], Roy P.[8]]

9d. **(Roy) Walter.** Born 4 July 1922 at Biggar, SK, Canada. Married Betty Jane Kapel on 15 Oct. 1945 at Spokane, Spokane Co., WA (she was born on 15 Sept. 1923 at Spokane, WA, the daughter of Andrew Kapel and Anna Kosnick [originally Kersnic]). Walt Burgess was a career officer in the U.S. Air Force, retiring in 1963 with the rank of Major. He owned a Chevron service station at Spokane, WA for six years, and the Royal Crest Motel at Medford, OR from 1969-72. He later became a school bus driver and Supervisor of the school busing system at Medford, OR, retiring from his position there in Aug. 1982. He and his wife currently live at Medford, OR.

10a. **Michael Roy.** Born 11 Feb. 1948 at Itazuke Air Force Base, near Fukuoka, Kyushu, Japan. Married Mary Alice (Wickizer) Rogers on 15 Oct. 1976 at Highland, San Bernardino Co., CA.

Mary Alice WICKIZER was born 21 June 1938 at San Bernardino, CA, the daughter of Judge Russell Alger Wickizer and (Wilma) Evelyn Gillispie Swisher; by her first husband, Floyd Edward Rogers, she had children: *Richard Albert* (born 10 Sept. 1957 at San Bernardino, CA, married Roseanne Sears in May 1980 at Moberly, Randolph Co., MO [div.]; married secondly Sheri LeAnn Clark on 7 July 1984 at Loma Linda, CA [she was born 9 Oct. 1961 at Fontana, CA, daughter of Gomer Gene "Bud" Clark and Linda Lou McAllister, and works as a veterinarian's assistant], currently works as Business Manager of the Borgo Press, and had children: Whitney Louise [born 6 July 1986 at Fontana, CA]; Dustin James [born 24 Apr. 1989 at Fontana, CA]); *(Mary) Louise* (born 21 Jan. 1960 at Concord, CA, married as his second wife Dr. Richard Douglas Reynnells II on 6 May 1987 at Redlands, CA [he was born 19 May 1947 in MI, son of Richard Douglas Reynnells and Helen Lucille Sirks, and currently works for the Dept. of Agriculture; by his first wife, Estella Chavez, he had children: Kathleen Janette {born 2 June 1970}; Michael Newton {born 6 Dec. 1971}; Steven Richard {born 2 Nov. 1973}; James Matthew {born 28 Oct. 1981}]; *Louise* works for the National Agricultural Library at Beltsville, MD; they had children: Russell Edward [born 25 May 1989 at Takoma Park, MD]; Samuel Douglas [born 15 Nov. 1993 at Takoma Park, MD]). ***Mary Burgess*** was Purchasing Agent at California State University, San Bernardino before resigning in 1981. Since then she has been Publisher of the Borgo Press, and has contributed immeasurably to this book with her suggestions, editing, and indexing. She has also authored or edited ten other books.

Michael BURGESS earned his A.B. in English literature and classical Greek at Gonzaga University in 1969, and his master's in library science at the University of Southern California in 1970. He joined the faculty of California State University, San Bernardino (California) on 1 Sept. 1970, working successively as Periodicals Librarian, Reference Librarian, Assistant Library Bibliographer, and Chief Cataloger; he was named Head of Collection Development in Sept. 1994. On 11 Oct. 1983 he entered the 10,000,000th bibliographical record into the international On-Line Computer Library Center (OCLC) cataloging database. He was promoted to full Professor on 1 Sept. 1984.

His first book was written in 1968-69 while still a student in college. In June 1975 he founded The Borgo Press, a library-oriented publishing company, and was Editor of Newcastle Publishing Co. of North Hollywood, CA from 1971-92. Under his own name and several pen names he has authored 70 books and 140 articles and reviews, and has edited more than 600 volumes, fifteen scholarly series, two journals, and six monographic reprint series. Biographies or interviews have appeared in: *Who's Who in America*, *Contemporary Authors* (3 volumes), *Who's Who in the World*, *Who's Who in the West*, *International Authors and Writers Who's Who*, *Who's Who in Genealogy and Heraldry*, *Who's Who in U.S. Writers, Editors & Poets*, *Contemporary Science Fiction Authors*, *The Writers Directory*, *Science Fiction and Fantasy Literature* (2 volumes), *Encyclopedia of Science Fiction*, *Fantasy Newsletter*, *The Bulletin of the Science Fiction Writers of America*, *Who's Who of Emerging Leaders in America*, and *Who's Who in California*, among others. A 176-page guide to his life and work was published in 1992 under the title *The Work of Robert Reginald: An Annotated Bibliography & Guide*. He received the Lifetime Collector's Award in Feb. 1993 and the 24th annual Pilgrim Award in June 1993 for his work as a bibliographer and scholar. He and his wife live at San Bernardino, CA.

10b. **Stephen Andrew.** Born 6 May 1951 at Hamilton Air Force Base, Marin Co., CA. Married Gina Rae Mann on 16 Mar. 1974 at Medford, Jackson Co., OR (she was born 19 Nov. 1955 at Lyons, NY, the daughter of Gabriel Francis Mann and Mary Jean Spoor). Steve Burgess is Senior Vice President of Sales and Operations for Krause's Sofa Factory, the largest made-to-order furniture company in the U.S., headquartered at Brea, CA. He previously held executive positions in a variety of industries, including computer technology. Gina Burgess is an insurance executive. Steve and Gina Burgess currently live at Yorba Linda, CA.

11a. **Allison Renae.** Born 28 Nov. 1979 at Portland, OR.
11b. **Andrew Ryan.** Born 31 Oct. 1988 at San Jose, CA.

10c. **Son.** Born and died Summer 1959 at Gunnison, CO.
10d. **Mark Eugene.** Born 8 July 1960 at Wichita, KS. Married Wang Shuju on 1 July 1984 at Bend, OR (div.); married secondly Laura Lynn Matin in Aug. 1994 (she was born 28 July 1959 at Portland, OR, and works as a dentist). Dr. Mark Burgess earned his D.V.M. degree in 1986 at Oregon State University. He has been a veterinary surgeon since Feb. 1987 at Raleigh Hills Veterinary Clinic, Portland, OR, specializing in exotic animals. He lives at Beaverton, OR.

10e. **Scott Alan (I).** Born 14 Apr. 1964 at Spokane, WA. Scott Burgess earned his bachelor's degree in computer science and mathematics in 1986 at Southern Oregon State College, and his master's degree in computer science in 1991 at Rutgers University. He is currently a Ph.D. degree candidate in computer science, specializing in artificial intelligence, at Oregon State University, Corvallis, OR. He has also written two books: *The Work of Reginald Bretnor: An Annotated Bibliography & Guide* (San Bernardino, CA: The Borgo Press, 1989); and *The Work of Dean Ing: An Annotated Bibliography & Guide* (San Bernardino, CA: The Borgo Press, 1990). He currently lives at Philomath, OR.

GEORGE O. BURGESS OF ABBOTSFORD, BRITISH COLUMBIA, CANADA

[Thomas Fleming[6], George Walter[7]]

8h. **George Osmer** *[son of George Walter].* Born 21 Apr. 1908 at Lenore, ID. Married Nettie Helen Schmor on 25 June 1933 at Meadow Lake, SK, Canada (she was born 10 July 1907 at Munich, ND, and died 12 Oct. 1988 at Abbotsford, BC); married secondly Ann (Niessen) Berg on 21 Apr. 1990 at Abbotsford, BC (she was born 30 June 1908 at Aberdeen, SK, daughter of Jacob and Elizabeth Niessen). George O. Burgess homesteaded in northern Saskatchewan during the 1930s. In 1940 he enlisted in the Royal Canadian Air Force, and served overseas for two years. He purchased a general store in Saskatchewan in 1945, but it burned in 1948. He then moved to British Columbia, and worked at as manager of a furniture store before being appointed Postmaster of Vedder Crossing, BC in 1955, where he served for fifteen years. He currently lives retired at Abbotsford, BC. George O. Burgess was the first Burgess relative the author consulted about putting together the family history, in 1970; he has contributed greatly to this book with his memories and good humor.

9a. **Lloyd Arthur.** Born 19 Nov. 1934 at Meadow Lake, SK, Canada. Married Sheila Dixon on 21 May 1955 at London, ON, Canada (div.); married secondly Kathy Sword on 30 June 1979. Lloyd Burgess served in the Royal Canadian Air Force for 12 years; he now owns his own TV and radio sales and service business at Vanderhoof, BC.

10a. **David Edward George.** Born 27 Oct. 1955 at Claresholm, AB, Canada. Married Valerie Fay Storfie on 28 Aug. 1979. David Burgess operated a home for teenagers for several years. He now owns a Radio Shack franchise at Port Hardy, BC, Canada, on Vancouver Island.

11a. **Colin David Craig.** Born 12 June 1981 at Williams Lake, BC, Canada.
11b. **Randall Matthew David** (ad.). Born 7 June 1983 in BC, Canada.
11c. **Wendy Miranda Yvonne** (ad.). Born 21 May 1985 in BC, Canada.

10b. **Kenneth Norman.** Born 15 June 1957 at Claresholm, AB, Canada. Married Vicki Lee Hieb (div.). Kenneth Burgess is a sawyer and heavy equipment operator for a sawmill in British Columbia.

11a. **Ian Landis.** Born 9 June 1977 at Enderby, BC, Canada.
11b. **Christina Jean.** Born 21 Oct. 1980 at Enderby, BC, Canada.

10c. **Dianna Helen Jean.** Born 24 Mar. 1959 at Portage La Prairie, MB, Canada. Dianna Burgess is an office worker at London, ON, Canada.
10d. **Paul Walter.** Born 23 Mar. 1968 at Vedder Crossing, BC, Canada.

9b. **Millar Roy.** Born 13 Oct. 1935 at Meadow Lake, SK, Canada; died there 18 Oct. 1935.
9c. **Lucille Blondina.** Born 13 Dec. 1936 at Hepburn, SK, Canada. Married William Fedoruk on 19 Oct. 1956 at Vancouver, BC, and had children: *(Robert) Dean*; *Alan Michael*; *Andrew*. Lucille Fedoruk currently lives at North Surrey, BC, Canada.
9d. **(Walter) Dean.** Born 13 Oct. 1939 at Meadow Lake, SK, Canada. Married Mila Milin (div.). Dr. W. Dean Burgess is a Professor of Mathematics at the University of Ottawa, ON, Canada.

EDWIN BURGESS OF WASHINGTON CO., IDAHO

[Thomas Fleming[6]]

7d. **Edwin (I)** (nmn) *[son of Thomas Fleming].* His name is listed in the 1865 census as Myron W. Burgess. Born 25 Jan. 1864 at Eagle Lake, MN. Married Sarah Loucinda Rogers on 28 Feb. 1886 at Moscow, ID (she was born on 19 Apr. 1868 at Cottage Grove, OR, daughter of Henry Milward Rogers and

Paulina Whited, and sister of Matilda Jane Rogers [who married her brother-in-law, David Monroe Burgess], and Rebecca Emiline Rogers [who married her brother-in-law, George Walter Burgess], and died on 2 Dec. 1886 of typhoid fever); married secondly Ella May Park on 6 May 1888 at Troy, Latah Co., ID (she was born on 20 Aug. 1872 at Oregon City, OR, the daughter of Robert Judson Park[e] and Lavina Jane Dearing, and died on 16 Oct. 1963 at Weiser, ID, aged 91 years). Has not been found in the 1900 census; listed in the 1910 census for the North Troy Precinct, Latah Co., ID. Edwin Burgess settled at Moscow, ID in 1886, moved to Troy in 1888, to Pullman later in 1888, to Kings Valley, OR in 1896, back to Troy in 1898, and to Winona, Whitman Co., WA in the fall of 1910. Edwin was a farmer and logger in Washington and Idaho for most of his life. He died on 24 Oct. 1933 at Weiser, Washington Co., ID, and is buried with his second wife in the Hillcrest Cemetery.

"I don't remember much about the Winona farm, as I was very young (3-9). I only remember power equipment for threshing was still pretty much of a novelty. There were in those days the old Rumley engines run on kerosine, the early-day tractors of the Case internal combustion type—compared to today's trim farming equipment, they were real monstrosities. Also the steam engines that we see parked around in various places today as novelties.

"We moved from Winona to Weiser, Idaho, in 1915. Dad bought a place five miles out of Weiser, by what was known as the Buttermilk Slough. The farm was sold to us as sub-irrigated, but was a big lie. My older brothers furnished father with enough money to buy a pumping plant, and Dad and I (12 years old) leveled this 20-acre piece of land with two horses and an old-time fresno. We kept milk cows (about 10 head, generally), and always raised our own pork, butchered on the farm. We sold milk and cream and eggs, and this constituted our living.

"We lived only a half mile from the Snake River. I owned a home-made boat when I was fourteen, and for several years I hunted on the Snake for ducks and geese. Later on they opened the pheasant season in that valley, and I became a good marksman with the shotgun, and kept the family well supplied with ducks and pheasants.

"Dad's health broke when he was about sixty years old. My brother Floyd was called home from the labor fields, and took over the farming of the property. Dad told him if he would support Dad and Mother and take care of the funeral arrangements that when that day came, he would deed Floyd the place there at Weiser. This took place in due time. I left the farm for the first time when sixteen, going to Powers, Oregon, near the coast, and worked in the logging camps. Dad came down after renting his property, and even though in ill health he took a nightwatchman's job (fire watch), and worked for several years. He returned to Weiser and died there in 1933. He, my mother, and Floyd are all buried in the Hilltop Cemetery in Weiser."

—Raymond O. Burgess

8a. **Anna (III).** Born and died 26 Nov. 1886 at Pullman, WA.

8b. **Pearl Ellen.** Born 2 Feb. 1889 at Pullman, WA. Listed in the 1910 census with her parents and son. Married Albert Earl Williams on 11 Jan. 1907 at Colfax, Whitman Co., WA (div.), and had children:

Lenus Earl WILLIAMS. Born 16 Oct. 1907 at Troy, ID, married Edith Mary Liedkie on 26 Mar. 1934 at Colfax, WA (she was born 28 Dec. 1912 at Woodland, ID), and had children: *Lou Mardell* (born and died 3 Mar. 1934 at Endicott, WA); *Bonita JoAnn* (born 3 July 1936 at Colfax, WA, married Everett Eligha Hill on 25 Oct. 1954); *Ella Jean* (born 26 June 1938 at Winona, WA); *Rodney Neal* (born 27 July 1947 at Colfax, WA); *Judith Gail* (born 18 Sept. 1951 at Colfax, WA). Lenus Williams died Jan. 1970.

Pearl Ellen WILLIAMS married secondly (Franklin) Monroe "Roe" Sayles on 15 June 1913 at Coeur d'Alene, Kootenai Co., ID or at Winona, WA (he was born 12 June 1891 at Cheney, WA, and died on 22 Mar. 1950), and had children:

Roda Muriel SAYLES. Born 11 May 1914 at Winona, WA, married William Jackson Inman on 5 June 1940, and had children: *Lee Ann* (born 18 Sept. 1944 at Oakland, CA); *Terrie Kay* (born 16 Feb. 1948 at Chewelah, WA); *William Roe* (born 30 Sept. 1950 at Colville, WA); *Dee Robert* (born 19 June 1955 at Mt. Vernon, WA). Roda Inman lived at Mt. Vernon, WA.

Norva Norma SAYLES. Born 28 Oct. 1915 at Winona, WA, married Albert Fox on 2 July 1933 (div. 1953; he was born 9 July 1913 at Coeur d'Alene, ID), and had children: *Ellen Lorraine* (born 25 Nov. 1936 at Winona, WA); *Daniel James* (born 21 Sept. 1938 at Winona, WA); *Dewayne Neal* (born 26 Nov. 1939 at Winona, WA); *Karen Pearl* (born 17 Mar. 1943 at Colfax, WA). Norva married secondly Ivan Ira Cook on 6 June 1955 (he was born 2 June 1916 at Revere, WA), and had children: *Duane* (born 9 Oct. 1939 at Spokane, WA); *Diane* (born 26 Sept. 1940 at Spokane, WA).

Ivan Roe SAYLES. Born 2 Aug. 1917 at Winona, WA, married Cordelia Mae Worley on 25 May 1941 at Rockford, WA (she died in 1946 at Pullman, WA), and secondly Velma Leona

Martin Sorrells on 6 June 1948 at Pullman, WA (she was born 25 May 1922 at Dillon, MT), and had children: *Gary Lee* (born 21 Apr. 1943 at Colfax, WA); *Sherry Lynn* (born 13 Feb. 1951 at Pullman, WA); *Carol Sue* (born 9 Nov. 1954 at Pullman, WA).

Dale Mac SAYLES. Born 20 Feb. 1920 at Winona, WA, married Vivian E. Vincent on 22 Jan. 1944 at Pullman, WA, and had children: *Susan Jane* (born 15 Jan. 1946 at Tillamook, OR); *Dennis Michael* (born 1 Sept. 1947 at Tillamook, OR); *Dixie Jean* (born 25 Apr. 1951 at Tillamook, OR); *Rodney Vincent* (born 4 Aug. 1952 at Tillamook, OR). ***Dale SAYLES*** lives at Rockaway, OR).

George Dee SAYLES. Born 20 Feb. 1924, married Ruth Elaine Nelson on 15 June 1947 at Coeur d'Alene, ID, and had children: *Greg Dee* (born 23 Nov. 1951 at Colfax, WA).

Pearl Mae SAYLES. Born 1 Oct. 1925, married Alvin Dotson on 5 June 1949 at Pullman, WA, and had children: *Pamela Jean* (born 29 May 1951 at Portland, OR); *Linda Pearl* (born 13 Feb. 1953 at Portland, OR). ***Pearl DOTSON*** lived in California.

Pearl and Roe SAYLES died on 22 Mar. 1950 near Price, Utah:

ROE SAYLES KILLED AS PLANE CRASHES IN UTAH

"Mr. and Mrs. Roe Sayles of Pullman were killed Wednesday afternoon where their light plane crashed and burned near Price, Utah. The couple, flying their own plane, were on the last leg of an air trip to Havana, Cuba and return, when the tragedy occurred. Information received here by their son, Ivan, indicated the plane had encountered a sudden storm two hours after leaving Grand Junction, Colorado, and crashed into a hill in a desperate effort to make a safe landing on a highway. First word of the tragedy reached Pullman Wednesday evening in a telephone call to local police from the police chief at Price, in the high country of east central Utah. Officer Kenneth Bell took the call, and notified Ivan, who then called back for additional details. The Price officer said the plane had crashed between 5:15 and 5:30 against a mountain about twenty-five miles northwest of Price during a storm. The wreckage burned, and the two victims, apparently killed instantly, also were badly burned. The Price police officer said that two Utah flyers had visited the scene of the crash, and reported that they believed Mr. Sayles was trying to make a landing when the plane struck."—*Pullman Herald*, 24 Mar. 1950.

8c. **Myrtle Belle.** Born 12 Jan. 1891 at Pullman, WA. Married William Edgar Holady on 12 June 1912 at Winona, WA (he was born 12 Nov. 1888 at Colfax, WA, and died 29 Jan. 1957 at Tucson, AZ), and had children:

Virgil Allen HOLADY. Born 3 May 1913 at Winona, WA, married Doris Laverne Burd on 2 Apr. 1938 at Caldwell, ID, and had children: *Virginia Ellen* (born 9 Dec. 1940 at Ontario, OR); *Patricia Kay* (born 19 Aug. 1943 at La Grande, OR); *Barbara Colleen* (born 16 Feb. 1947 at La Grande, OR).

William Edgar HOLADY Jr. Born 18 June 1915 at Winona, WA, married Carolyn Miltenberger on 27 Dec. 1938 at Weiser, ID, and had children: *William Edgar III* (born 17 Oct. 1939 at Payette, ID); *Wesley Franklin* (born 17 Aug. 1941 at Weiser, ID); *Michael Perry* (born 12 Nov. 1949 at Pendleton, OR); *Lawrence Dean* (born 13 Nov. 1951 at Pendleton, OR); *John Milton* (born 26 Oct. 1954 at Pendleton, OR).

Erma June HOLADY. Born 30 June 1917 at Spokane, WA, married Paul Lewis Brockus on 24 Jan. 1938 at Boise, ID, and had children: *Paul Lewis Jr.* (born 28 Aug. 1938 at Ontario, OR); *Erma Mae* (born 18 Oct. 1942 at Payette, ID).

Raymond Jesse HOLADY. Born 9 Nov. 1918 at Northport, WA, died there 3 Nov. 1919.

Myrtle HOLADY. Born 9 Sept. 1920 at Leavenworth, WA, died there 15 Sept. 1920.

Lewis HOLADY. Born 20 Jan. 1923 at Mabton, WA, died there on 27 Jan. 1923.

Floyd Lester HOLADY. Born 24 Oct. 1924 at Mabton, WA, married (Mary) Celia Arrita on 24 Aug. 1947, and had children: *Paula Kim* (born 6 June 1953); *Marsha Kaye* (born 17 Jan. 1954).

Iva May HOLADY. Born 3 Feb. 1928 at Klamath Falls, OR, died there on 5 Feb. 1928.

Myrtle HOLADY died on 7 Sept. 1973 at Ontario, OR.

8d. **Fred Earl.** Born 21 Mar. 1892 at Pullman, WA. Married Eliza Ann Horn on 19 Dec. 1922 at Coquille, OR (she was born 16 Oct. 1901 at Ellensburg, WA, daughter of William Arthur Horn and Phoebe M. Fortney, and died 8 Jan. 1968); married secondly Blanche Pickering about 1970. Fred E. Burgess served in World War I in France (117th Engineers); he later worked as a logger, farmer, and dairyman in Washington, Idaho, and Vale, OR, homesteading three different sites there and in Alaska (1958). He was elected District Superintendent of Irrigation for Malheur Co., OR, between 1936-46. In 1974 he published *Memoirs of Eighty Years of Farming* (Philadelphia: Dorrance & Co.), an autobiographical account of his life which includes much material on the Burgess family. He died on 11 Aug. 1986 at Boise, ID, aged 94 years, and is buried in Rosedale Memorial Gardens.

8e. **Elmer L.** (nmn). Born 6 Mar. 1894 at Pullman, WA. Elmer Burgess was a logger and farmer in Idaho most of his life; he inherited his brother's museum at Cambridge, ID, in 1967, and ran the facility until his death. He died unmarried on 30 June 1981 at Cambridge, and is buried in the Cambridge Cemetery.

8f. **Mabel D.** (nmn). Born 3 Mar. 1896 at Kings Valley, Benton Co., OR. Married Claude Charles Morrison on 21 July 1917 at Weiser, ID (he was born 20 June 1878 in MI), and had children:

Etta May MORRISON. Born 31 Mar. 1918 at Weiser, ID, died there 16 Apr. 1918.

Fred Charles MORRISON. Born 5 July 1919 at Weiser, ID, married Gladys Hattie Crapps on 13 June 1946, and secondly Betty Jean Wolford on 13 July 1950 at Tacoma, WA, and had children: *Fred Charles Jr.* (born 6 Oct. 1952 at Lawton, OK); *Danny Edwin* (born 19 Dec. 1953 at Lawton, OK); *Lillian Marie* (born 31 Jan. 1955 at Lawton, OK); *Gary Eugene* (born 25 Jan. 1956 at Bamberg, West Germany).

Neva D. MORRISON. Born 31 Mar. 1921 at Weiser, ID, married Paul Henry Pitzer on 22 July 1941 at Weiser, ID, and had children: *Sharon Elaine* (born 10 May 1944 at Portland, OR); *Linda Gayle* (born 7 June 1947 at Pendleton, OR); *Marian Lynn* (born 30 Jan. 1949 at Pendleton, OR); *Donna Lee* (born 2 Mar. 1953 at Pendleton, OR).

Claude Edwin MORRISON. Born 2 Feb. 1923 at Weiser, ID, married Barbara Jean De Brie on 22 Feb. 1947 at La Grande, OR, and had children: *Michael Edwin* (born 9 Dec. 1949 at La Grande, OR); *Patrick Charles* (born 13 Feb. 1951 at La Grande, OR).

Bonnie Jean MORRISON. Born 16 Apr. 1924 at Weiser, ID, married Melvin Otis Paul Neill on 6 May 1940 at Weiser, ID, and had children: *Ronald Dean* (born 27 Feb. 1941 at Weiser, ID); *Melvin Eugene* (born 12 Apr. 1942 at Weiser, ID); *Evalyn Kay* (born 9 May 1943 at Stanfield, OR); *Allan Ray* (born 9 Mar. 1951 at Pendleton, OR).

Edna MORRISON. Born 12 Oct. 1926 at Powers, OR, married W. D. Hurd on 10 Aug. 1948 at Boise, ID, and had children: *Dwight Dee* (born 15 May 1949 at Ontario, OR); *Diann Lee* (born 5 Feb. 1951 at Weiser, ID); *Darla Jean* (born 22 Apr. 1953 at Weiser, ID); *Teresa Nell* (born 16 Nov. 1954 at Weiser, ID).

Velda Irene MORRISON. Born 24 May 1930 in Malheur Co., OR.

Ralph Jay MORRISON. Born 13 Feb. 1935 at Weiser, ID.

Mabel MORRISON died on 24 Nov. 1976 at Weiser, ID.

8g. **Floyd Alva.** Born 26 Nov. 1898 at Troy, Latah Co., ID. Floyd Burgess was a farmer and grain mill operator at Weiser, ID; in 1966 he established the Cambridge Museum at Cambridge, ID. He died unmarried on 4 Oct. 1967 at Weiser, ID, and is buried in the Hillcrest Cemetery.

8h. **Iva Evelyn.** Born 27 Aug. 1904 at Troy, ID. Married Arthur Eugene Ford on 21 June 1931 at Baker, OR (he was born 23 Aug. 1909 at Midvale, ID), and had children: *Walter Edwin* (born 25 Apr. 1932 at Weiser, ID); *Jack Earl* (born 6 May 1934 at Cambridge, ID); *Dwane Lee* (born 6 June 1936 at Cambridge, ID); *Harold Eugene* (born 28 May 1938 at Cambridge, ID); *Ruby May* (born 10 Apr. 1940 at Cambridge, ID); *Wilma Jean* (born 18 June 1945 at Cambridge, ID). Iva Ford currently lives at Cambridge, ID.

8i. **Raymond Oscar.** Born 23 Oct. 1907 at Troy, ID. See below for full entry.

8j. **Virl** (nmn). Born 4 Jan. 1914 at Winona, WA. See below for full entry.

RAYMOND O. BURGESS OF CANYON CO., IDAHO

[Thomas Fleming^6, Edwin (I)^7]

8i. **Raymond Oscar** *[son of Edwin (I)]*. Born 23 Oct. 1907 at Troy, ID. Married Bessie Lorretta Frank on 5 Jan. 1938 at Salt Lake City, UT (she was born 31 Jan. 1913 at Frankburg, AB, Canada, daughter of David Frank and Amy Adelda Stanfield). Ray Burgess was a farmer, logger, dairyman, and carpenter in Oregon, Washington, Idaho, and New Mexico. He was one of the original group of Burgesses who came together in 1970 to begin working on the Burgess family history, and contributed greatly to this book. He died on 20 May 1992 at Fruitland, ID, and is buried in the Rosedale Memorial Gardens, Payette, ID. Bessie Burgess lives at Fruitland, ID.

9a. **Dd Rae.** Born 20 Oct. 1938 at Salt Lake City, UT. Married Robert LeRoy Thompson on 27 May 1960 at Salt Lake City, UT (he was born 6 May 1938 at Twin Falls, ID, son of Samuel Ward Thompson and Isabella Tomlinson), and had children: *Jana Maria* (born 26 Apr. 1961 at Provo, UT, married (Timothy) Daniel Dibble on 13 June 1985 at Salt Lake City, UT [born 21 Oct. 1963 at Los Angeles, CA, son of Stephen Eben Dibble and Linda Lee Fine], and had children: Kristin Kayleen [born 3 Feb. 1987 at Pasco, WA]; Joshua Adam [born 9 Aug. 1988 at Seattle, WA];

Jonathan Ryan [born 20 Sept. 1990 at Seattle, WA]; Jared Stephen [born 8 Oct. 1992 at Portland, OR]); *Kory Eli* (born 13 Aug. 1963 at Ogden, UT, married Jacqueline Mora Medina on 19 July 1986 at Dallas, TX [born 6 Apr. 1966 at Bogotá, Columbia, daughter of Alfredo Mora Valenzuela and María del Carmen Medina Moreno], and had children: Ashley Nicole [born 14 Dec. 1987 at Portland, OR]; Brittany Bodell [born 18 May 1989 at Portland, OR]; Courtney Love [born 17 Nov. 1991 at Vancouver, WA]); *Linda Joy* (born 5 Oct. 1971 at Vancouver, WA, married William Daniel Wilson [he was born 11 Dec. 1967, son of Lee Roy Wilson and Edna Elizabeth McCuller], and had children: Brooklyn Christine [born 19 July 1993 at Laguna Hills, CA]); *David Jeremy* (born 21 Aug. 1973 at Vancouver, WA); *Elaina Jill* (born 13 June 1980 at Nampa, ID).

9b. **J'Deane.** Born 3 July 1940 at Weiser, ID. Married as his second wife Lloyd Lester Bland on 7 Feb. 1961 at Lewiston, ID (div.; he was born 21 Aug. 1940 at Basin, WY, son of Lester Robert Bland and Estella Sims, and married firstly Dixie Lee Hyers), and had children: *Lana Dee* (born 8 Oct. 1961 at Walla Walla, WA, married Kevin Bubar [div.], and had children: Brandon Scott [born 24 Nov. 1980 at Walla Walla, WA]; *Lana* had children by John Sicocan: Tavis Mathew [born 11 Sept. 1992 at Walla Walla, WA]); *Jamie Scott* (born 15 Aug. 1964 at Walla Walla, WA, married Dena Dombrosky, and had children: Jarrett Scott [born 8 Nov. 1990 at Walla Walla, WA]); *Tony Allen* (born 1 Nov. 1967 at Walla Walla, WA, married Christine Larson on 15 June 1991, and had children: B.Devin Scott [born 8 Mar. 1993 at Walla Walla, WA]); *Holly Ann* (born 1 Dec. 1973 at Walla Walla, WA). **J'Deane** married secondly as his third wife Gene Kohler Edvalson on 26 Nov. 1977 at Boise, ID (he was born 14 July 1926 at La Grande, OR, son of Erick Theodore Edvalson and Lena Frieda Kohler, and the father of Gene David Edvalson [who married J'Deane's sister, Nola], married firstly Lila Ann DeGraw and secondly Katrina Yoha Dingamonsa, and died 13 Dec. 1983 at Boise, ID, buried Union, OR), and had children: *Eric Theodore II* (born 23 May 1979 at Caldwell, ID); *Brianne J'Deane* (born 14 Sept. 1981 at Caldwell, ID).

9c. **(Raymond) Kaye.** Born 12 Feb. 1943 at Ontario, OR. Married Sandra Fay Thornton on 4 Mar. 1967 at Los Angeles, CA (she was born 7 Jan. 1948 at Tulare, CA, daughter of John Merle Thornton and Juanita Joy Shahan). Kaye Burgess is a computer accountant at Los Alamos, NM.

10a. **(Raymond) Todd.** Born 21 Apr. 1971 at Newport News, Isle of Wight Co., VA.
10b. **(Patrick) Wade.** Born 8 Feb. 1973 at Riverside, CA.
10c. **(Justin) Clay.** Born 8 Aug. 1974 at Pasco, WA.
10d. **(John) Preston.** Born 27 July 1977 at Pasco, WA.
10e. **Glenna Kaye.** Born 28 July 1979 at Nampa, ID.
10f. **Aimee Joy.** Born 23 Nov. 1980 at Nampa, ID.
10g. **Lindsay Janae.** Born 20 Sept. 1985 at Pasco, WA.

9d. **David Edwin (I).** Born 14 Mar. 1946 at Portland, OR. Married Gearldine Ann Knight on 10 June 1967 at Mesa, AZ (she was born 27 Nov. 1949 at Mesa, AZ, daughter of Thomas F. Weaver and Margie James). David E. Burgess is a logger and auto body worker at Caldwell, ID.

10a. **Malya Loree.** Born 1 Oct. 1968 at Delta, Delta Co., CO. Married David Wayne Forsberg on 11 July 1986 at Caldwell, ID (he was born 12 Mar. 1966 at Caldwell, ID, son of Glen David Forsberg and Cheryl Hansen), and had children: *Leslie Nicole* (born 21 June 1988 at Nampa, ID); *Tyler Glen* (born 16 Sept. 1989 at Nampa, ID).
10b. **Latisha Ann.** Born 1 Apr. 1970 at Walla Walla, WA. Married Harland Drew Baker on 16 Dec. 1989 at Boise, ID (he was born 5 June 1966 at San Francisco, CA, son of Patrick D. Baker and Mary J. Mooney).
10c. **DeeAnn** (nmn). Born 12 May 1972 at Delta, CO.
10d. **Tambi Denise.** Born 27 Oct. 1973 at Grand Junction, Mesa Co., CO.
10e. **David Edwin (II).** Born 24 Oct. 1975 at Grand Junction, CO.
10f. **Joseph James.** Born 11 June 1977 at Grand Junction, CO.
10g. **Andrew Thomas.** Born 10 Apr. 1979 at Caldwell, ID.
10h. **Nathan Allan.** Born 27 Feb. 1981 at Nampa, ID.
10i. **Camillia Joleen.** Born 23 Nov. 1982 at Nampa, ID.
10j. **Adam Michael (II).** Born 11 Oct. 1986 at Boise, ID; died there on 12 Oct. 1986, and is buried in the Rosedale Memorial Gardens, Boise.

9e. **Sheila Loretta.** Born 30 May 1948 at Portland, OR. Married James David Russell on 8 Apr. 1968 at Las Vegas, NM (he was born 7 Aug. 1941 at Union City, TN, son of Edmond Darrell Russell and Lillie Belle Sullivan), and had children: *Marc Allen* (born 21 Dec. 1971 at Las Vegas, NM); *Brian James* (born 24 Jan. 1978 at Las Vegas, NM).

9f. **John Eldon (II).** Born 30 July 1951 at Pendleton, OR. Married Christine Lynn Andreatta on 9 Apr. 1977 at Grand Junction, CO (div.; she was born 31 Jan. 1959 at Glenwood Springs, CO, daughter of Rudolph Andrew Andreatta and Waunita Mae Bananto); married secondly as her second husband La Rinda Dee (Collins) Howe on 30 Nov. 1985 at New Plymouth, ID (she was born 7 Feb. 1967 at Riverside, CA, daughter of Lonnie Dal Collins and Carmen June Dodge, married firstly Terry Lee Howe). Served in the U.S. Army in the Vietnam War. John Burgess owns the B&B Lube Shop at Fruitland, ID.

10a. **William Lynn** (ad.). He uses the surname Andreatta. Born 25 June 1976 at Grand Junction, CO.
10b. **Carmen Diane** (ad.). She uses the surname Howe. Born 24 Jan. 1984 at Columbus, MT.
10c. **Paul John.** Born 6 Feb. 1986 at Billings, MT.
10d. **Keith James.** Born 1 Mar. 1987 at Caldwell, ID; died 4 June 1987 at New Plymouth, ID, and is buried in the Rosedale Memorial Gardens, Payette, ID.
10e. **Mariya Jolene.** Born 13 July 1988 at Nampa, ID.

9g. **Nola Marie.** Born 31 Jan. 1956 at Pendleton, OR. Married (Gene) David Edvalson on 21 July 1979 at Middleton, ID (div.; he was born 5 Mar. 1956 at La Grande, OR, son of Gene Kohler Edvalson [who married Nola's sister, J'Deane] and Lila Ann DeGraw), and had children: *Aaron David* (born 12 Feb. 1980 at Nampa, ID); *Daniel Scott* (born 24 July 1982 at Nampa, ID).

VIRL BURGESS OF BUTTE CO., CALIFORNIA

[Thomas Fleming[6], Edwin (I)[7]]

8j. **Virl** (nmn) *[son of Edwin (I)].* Born 4 Jan. 1914 at Winona, WA. Married Mabel Ruth Hulen on 4 Oct. 1936 at Payette, ID (she was born 13 Jan. 1913 at Ontario, OR, daughter of Thomas Jefferson Hulen and Anna May Stone, and remarried Euel Leslie Howard on 6 Sept. 1976 in NV [he was born 10 May 1913 at Drake Creek, AR]). Virl Burgess was a construction worker who invented a quick-release belt that was widely adopted. He died on 15 Aug. 1975 at Oroville, CA, but is buried in the New Cemetery, Payette, ID.

9a. **Thomas Edwin (I).** Born 17 Aug. 1938 at Payette, ID. Married Sandra Irene Baker on 7 Mar. 1963. Tom Burgess is a meat cutter at Nampa, ID.

10a. **Thomas Edwin II** (twin). Born 24 July 1963 at Fort Walters, TX.
10b. **Tobias Edward** (twin). Born 24 July 1963 at Fort Walters, TX.
10c. **Shelly Irene.** Born 5 Dec. 1965 at Marysville, CA.

9b. **Sherolyn Kay.** Born 5 Apr. 1943 at Portland, OR. Married Tex Nevada Spliethof on 20 July 1962 at Red Bluff, CA (he was born May 1936 at Red Bluff, CA), and had children: *David Rodney* (born 9 May 1965 at Oroville, CA); *Kelli Ann* (born 30 Mar. 1972 at Oroville, CA); Sherolyn married secondly James Carl Howard on 4 Oct. 1976 at Reno, NV (he was born 21 Aug. 1940 at Grants Pass, OR, son of Euel Leslie Howard and Flora Webb), and had children: *James Scott* (born 6 Aug. 1978 at Roseville, CA).
9c. **Lloyd Virl.** Born 3 July 1953 at Roseburg, OR. Married Karin Holcomb on 5 Oct. 1973; married secondly Tammy Taylor on 26 Dec. 1977 at Reno, NV (she was born 9 May 1959 at Oroville, daughter of Neil Taylor). Lloyd is a wallboard hanger at Oroville, CA.

10a. **Tyrel Neil.** Born 24 May 1979 at Oroville, CA.

JAMES HUGHES BURGESS OF STEVENS CO., WASHINGTON

[Thomas Fleming[6]]

7e. **(James) Hughes** *[son of Thomas Fleming].* He was named for James Hughes Harris, his uncle. Born 11 Dec. 1865 at Eagle Lake, MN. Married Mary Frances Culbertson on 8 Nov. 1890 at Moscow, ID (div.; she was born 11 Aug. 1872 at Crocker, MO, remarried John Mortenson, and died 7 Jan. 1928 at Spokane, WA). Has not been found in the 1900 census. Hughes Burgess lived at Troy, ID until about 1900. He then joined the bridge and tunnel crew of the Northern Pacific Railroad, settling at Spokane, WA. Later he and his oldest son homesteaded near Henry, ID, where he ranched and worked as a carpenter. He moved to Colville, WA in 1932, dying there on 5 Aug. 1945, and is buried with his brother, Jesse Burgess, in the Evergreen Cemetery.

8a. **Jesse Hugh (I).** Born 23 July 1893 at Troy, ID. See below for full entry.

8b. **(Matthew) Forrest.** Born 9 Aug. 1898 (or 1897) at Little Bear Ridge, Troy, ID. Married Lorraine Ziegler; married secondly Josephine Knapp; married thirdly Harriet Thorley (who survives him). Listed in the 1920 census for Spokane, Spokane Co., WA living with his stepfather, John M. Mortenson. Dr. Forrest Burgess was an optometrist at Colfax, WA, and later at Cedar City, UT. He died on 2 June 1965 at Cedar City, and is buried in the Cedar City Cemetery.

9a. **Nancy (VII)** (nmn) (ad.). Born 23 Oct. 1947 at Cedar City, UT. Married Ronald Wayne Worthen on 7 May 1965 at Cedar City, UT (div.). Nancy Burgess is a medical receptionist at Murray, UT, near Salt Lake City.

Dr. JESSE HUGH BURGESS OF WALLA WALLA CO., WASHINGTON

[Thomas Fleming[6], James Hughes[7]]

8a. **Jesse Hugh (I)** *[son of James Hughes].* Born 23 July 1893 at Troy, ID. Married Lucile Annette Stowell on 5 May 1915 at Coeur d'Alene, ID (she was born 2 Aug. 1897 at Poplar Lake, WI, remarried William H. Whelchel, died Dec. 1984, and had a daughter: Billie [married Johnny Turnbull]); married secondly Anna Sophia Carolina Hansen on 16 June 1930 in Stevens Co. (she was born 8 Dec. 1903 at Frederic, WI, and died Jan. 1960, buried Evergreen Cemetery, Stevens Co., WA). Listed in the 1920 census for Spokane, Spokane Co., WA. Dr. Jesse Burgess was an optometrist at Moscow, ID, Pullman, WA, and Walla Walla, WA. He died there on 25 Feb. 1980, and was cremated.

9a. **Jessie Lucile.** Born 9 Jan. 1916 at Spokane, WA. Married Woodrow Harold Nelsen on 30 Aug. 1936 at Spokane, WA (he was born 2 Aug. 1912 at Spokane, WA), and had children: *Kenneth Harold* (born 8 June 1938 at Spokane, WA, married Barbara Lynne Heaps on 8 Apr. 1960 at Spokane [she was born 16 Jan. 1940 at Salt Lake City, UT], and had children: Lisa Kristine [born 7 Apr. 1968 at San Jose, CA]; he works as a psychologist at Sacramento, CA); *James Woodrow* (born 8 June 1940 at Spokane, WA, married Sandra Lea Laughlin on 1 Aug. 1960 at Seattle, WA [div.; she was born 31 July 1942 in Canada], and had children: James Scott [born 2 May 1961 at Spokane, WA]; Tawnee Lea [born 15 Feb. 1964 at Spokane, WA, died Mar. 1993]; he works as an attorney at Monterey, CA); *Earl Robert* (born 12 May 1944 at Spokane, WA, married Conni Marie Fuller on 5 June 1965 at Spokane, WA [she was born 10 Aug. 1944 at Walla Walla, WA], and had children: Michael Robert [born 9 July 1968 at New York, NY]; he works as an attorney at Bellevue, WA). Jessie Nelsen currently lives at Spokane, WA.

9b. **Forrest Phillip.** Born 22 Dec. 1917 at Spokane, WA. Married Josephine "Jo" Block on 15 Apr. 1939 at Spokane, WA (she was born 19 Nov. 1918 at Spokane, WA, daughter of Nick Block and Olga Wuerch). Served in World War II with the U.S. Army as a Staff Sergeant in France. Forrest Burgess was Superintendent of Liquid Fuels at Fairchild Air Force Base, near Spokane, WA. He was one of the cousins who came together in 1970 to research the Burgess genealogy. He died of cancer on 26 Aug. 1989 at Post Falls, ID, buried Post Falls Cemetery.

10a. **Forrest William.** Born 11 Oct. 1942 at Spokane, WA. Married Yi (or Lee) Yon Sun on 25 Sept. 1963 at Seoul, South Korea (she was born 1 Mar. 1941). Forrest W. Burgess owns an advertising agency at Spokane, WA, where he also works as a cinematographer.

11a. **Forrest Maceroy.** Born 30 Nov. 1965 at Spokane, WA. Forrest Burgess graduated in 1989 from the University of Southern California School of Cinematography, majoring in film production. He currently lives at Los Angeles, CA.

10b. **Judith Annette "Judy."** Born 20 Nov. 1946 at Spokane, WA. Married Dennis William Phelan on 27 Apr. 1968 at San Francisco, CA (he was born 7 Aug. 1947 at Spokane, and works as a nurse), and had children: *Danielle Michelle* (born 17 Oct. 1968 at Spokane, WA, joined the U.S. Navy, married Stacey McClain on 29 Oct. 1988, and had children: Alexander Lee [born 12 Mar. 1993 at Aiea, HI]); *Dason Ahren* (born 9 Oct. 1976); *Jessica Dara* (born 20 Apr. 1981). Judy Phelan currently lives at Poulsbo, WA.

9c. **(Jesse) Hugh (II).** Born 1 June 1932 at Colville, WA. Married Sara Ann Landers on 23 Aug. 1956; married secondly Elsie Awai Abreu on 13 June 1968 at Honolulu, HI. Hugh Burgess earned his B.A. from the University of Idaho, his M.A. in architecture from Columbia University, and his D. Arch. at Rice University in 1980. He was formerly Dean of the School of Architecture, Arizona State University, Tempe, AZ from 1974-81, and since 1987 has been Dean of the School of Architecture at the University of Nevada, Las Vegas. His biography has appeared in *Who's Who in the West* and *Who's Who in the World*. He also co-edited the book, *Architectural Education and the University: Proceedings of the 70th Annual Meeting of the Association of Collegiate Schools of Architecture, 1982* (Washington, DC: Association of Collegiate Schools of Architecture, 1983).

10a. **Lawrence Peter (I)** (ad.). His surname was originally Abreu. Born 16 Sept. 1954 at Honolulu, HI. Married Beth Ann Rice on 1 July 1978. Lieut. Col. Lawrence P. Burgess, a 1976 graduate of West Point, earned his M.D. at the University of Hawaii, and has been a resident surgeon at Stanford University Medical Hospital and Walter Reed Hospital. He is an author of over thirty journal articles, three textbook chapters, and a textbook on otolaryngology. He is currently a medical doctor specialist in ear, nose, and throat surgery at Tripler Hospital, Honolulu, HI, and has co-authored the book, *Reanimation of the Paralyzed Face* (New York: Thieme, 1994).

11a. **Lawrence Peter (II).** Born 25 June 1980 at Honolulu, HI. Currently at student at Punahou Academy, Honolulu.

11b. **Brooke Maile.** Born 10 July 1984 at Honolulu, HI. Currently a student at St. Andrew's Priory, Honolulu.

10b. **Alexander Courtney "Alex."** Born 23 Feb. 1965 at Honolulu, HI. Alex Burgess earned his degree in chemical and petroleum engineering from King Fahd University of Petroleum and Minerals, Dhahran, Saudi Arabia. He currently works as a field engineer in Southeast Asia with Dowell Schlumberger (Eastern) Inc.

9d. **David Lee (I).** Born 25 Aug. 1934 at Spokane, WA. Married Esther Prins on 11 June 1955 at Moscow, ID (she was born 18 Mar. 1933 at Amsterdam, Netherlands, daughter of Dr. S. A. Prins and Rebecca Spiro-Frank, and was a survivor of the Holocaust, serving in the Dutch underground during World War II; she teaches at Walla Walla Community College). David Burgess is an artist at Walla Walla, WA.

10a. **Aaron Hansen.** Born 28 Feb. 1956 at Seattle, WA. Married Kathleen Pulfer in 1978 at Walla Walla, WA. Aaron Burgess is an artist and musician at Walla Walla, WA.

11a. **Jesse Lee.** Born 14 Mar. 1980 at Walla Walla, WA.

11b. **John David.** Born 20 Feb. 1983 at Walla Walla, WA.

10b. **Caitlin Ann.** Born 27 Feb. 1957 at Moscow, ID. Married and had one son. Caitlin Burgess is a Ph.D. candidate in statistics at Washington State University; she also works as a research assistant with a neurological institute at Walla Walla, WA.

10c. **Jesse Hugh III.** Born 11 Nov. 1958 at Moscow, Idaho. Married Nancy Dublinsky in Aug. 1988 (she works as a grade school teacher). Jesse Burgess graduated with a philosophy degree from Whitman College, Spokane, WA. He teaches English as a second language at Seattle, WA.

9e. **John Morgan Alexander.** His name was originally John Alexander Burgess. Born 7 May 1938 at Moscow, ID. Married Patricia Marie "Patti" Leslie on 31 Dec. 1970 at New York, NY (div.; she was born 3 Feb. 1938 at Hilo, HI, daughter of William Francis Leslie and Rose Yee); married secondly Kaipo Kincaid on 12 Apr. 1987. John Burgess earned his B.A. from the University of Idaho in 1961, and his J.D. there in 1964. He served as a law clerk from 1964-65, was admitted to the Hawaii Bar in 1966, was associate counsel, then supervising attorney for the Legal Aid Society in Hawaii, served as legislative assistant to Rep. Patsy Mink of Hawaii from 1968-69, as a deputy prosecuting attorney for the City of Honolulu during the early 1970s, and deputy public defender of Hawaii from 1972-73, public defender for the County of Hawaii, Hilo, 1973-76, taught at the School of Law, University of Hawaii during the late 1970s, and had a private practice for many years at Kamuela, HI in the 1980s. He was also an advisor to various political, social, and penal groups, particularly on the status of women; has lectured at the University of Hawaii and elsewhere; and is the author of several articles published in legal journals. In the early 1990s he began work on his Ph.D. in clinical psychology at the Saybrook Institute, San Francisco, with studies in Jungian psychology, dream interpretation, shamanism, and mythology. His biography has appeared in *Who's Who in the West* and *Who's Who in Government*.

10a. **William Francis Leslie.** Born 26 Mar. 1972 at Hilo, HI. William Burgess is a student and tattoo artist at Santa Rosa, CA.

[William (I)[1], Edward (I)[2], William (II)[3], Henry (I)[4], John Henry (I)[5]]

JAMES SYLVESTER BURGESS
(1837-1901?)

OF JEFFERSON COUNTY, ILLINOIS

6h. **James Sylvester "Vest"** *[son of John Henry (I)].* Born Oct. 1837 at Portland Mills, IN. Married his first cousin, Minerva Lawson, on 13 July 1856 in Parke Co., IN (she was born 30 Nov. 1840 in Fleming Co., KY, daughter of John Lawson and Constance Jones, and died 18 Dec. 1915 in Jefferson Co., IL). Listed in the 1860 census for Putnam Co., IN, in 1865 in Blue Earth Co., MN, in 1870 in Fleming Co., KY, in 1880 in Charleston, Coles Co., IL, and in 1900 in Farrington Township, Jefferson Co., IL; Minerva is listed as head of the family in 1910 (seven of eight children survive in 1900-10). Vest Burgess owned a sawmill at Eagle Lake, MN in 1864-65; he later worked as a locomotive engineer, moving to Illinois in 1878. After retiring, he bought a farm a few miles northeast of Mt. Vernon, IL, where he died between the summer of 1900 and the end of 1901. He and his wife are buried in unmarked graves at Well's Chapel Cemetery, near their home.

The Children of Vest Burgess:

7a. **(Mary) Oda.** Born Aug. (or Sept.) 1860 in Putnam Co., IN. Married Charles E. Carpenter on 29 Jan. 1879 in Fleming Co., KY (div.); married secondly Daniel Albert Crum on 15 Nov. 1886 in Coles Co., IL (he was born 26 Dec. 1831, and died 27 May 1899 in Coles Co., buried Pleasant Grove Cemetery), and had children: *Howard* (born Aug. 1887 in Coles Co., became a doctor in New York, and may have died in CT); married thirdly Walter DeLong on 19 June 1902 in Wayne Co., IL (he was born 1862 in Bureau Co., IL, son of John DeLong and ___ Moran). Listed in the 1880 census for Coles Co., IL living with her father and husband, and in the 1900 census for Coles Co. as a widower, with one of three children surviving; has not been found in 1910-20. **Oda Crum** bought a lot (#1064) in the Edgar Co., IL Cemetery on 12 Feb. 1901. She may have died at Independence, Warren Co., IN.

7b. **Alberta "Bertha."** Born Nov. 1862 at Eagle Lake, MN. Married George Robert Meredith on 27 Nov. 1884 in Coles Co. (he was born July 1841 in KY, and died 28 Mar. 1909 in Coles Co., IL, buried Dodge Grove Cemetery), and had children: *George Robert Jr.* (born Sept. 1885 in Coles Co., married Mary ___ [she was born 1893 in NE], listed in the 1920 census for Mattoon City, Coles Co., IL, and died 8 Oct. 1943 at Los Angeles, CA, buried Dodge Grove Cemetery, Coles Co.). Listed in the 1900-10 censuses for Coles Co., IL, but has not been found in 1920.

7c. **Laura Vanetta.** Born 27 Dec. 1864 at Eagle Lake, MN. Married ___ van Zeppeline, and had children: *Lillie* (born about 1884, married Ernest Garrison about 1903 [he died about 1927 in Jefferson Co., IL], and died in July 1956, having had children: Dorothy [born 27 May 1904, married Clyde Crask {he was born 2 Jan. 1901, and died Dec. 1986 at De Kalb, IL}, lived near De Kalb, IL, died Dec. 1980 at Creston, IL, and had children: Marita {married Warren Scott}; Marlene {married William Walters}]; Eva [married Edgar or Edward Bolin, died Feb. 1951, and had children: Joanne {married ___ Mayo}]; Audrey [married Pete Render]; Raleigh [or Rollie; married Swan Heyrew, secondly Edna Collvin, and thirdly Estella Rudolph]; Harold [born 23 June 1911, married Gladys Austin, died Apr. 1982 at Mt. Vernon, IL, and had children: Gary {twin}; Gloria {twin}; Glenda; Connie]; Howard [married Marlene Russell]; Wes [married Virginia Bodgett, and secondly Kay Trevell]; Juanita [married Edward Pressgrove]). **Laura** married thirdly Clarence O. Huff on 31 July 1902 in Jefferson Co., IL. Has not been found in the 1900 census; listed in the 1910 census for Jefferson Co., IL living next door to her mother. Laura Huff died of pneumonia and tuberculosis on 2 Feb. 1921 at Farrington, Jefferson Co., IL, and is buried in an unmarked grave in Well's Chapel Cemetery.

7d. **Jennie Isadore.** Born 6 July 1865 (or 1866) at Eagle Lake, MN. Married George Deihl Taylor on 12 Mar. 1883 in Coles Co., IL (he was born 16 Aug. 1855, and died 25 Sept. 1934 in Coles Co., IL), and had at least the following children: *(James) Mitchell "Mike"* (born 5 Mar. 1884 in KS, married Martha Jane Daily [she was born 10 Mar. 1881, and died 9 May 1965], and died Mar. 1979 at Kankakee, IL, aged 95 years, buried Janesville Cemetery); *Lucille* (or Luella; born 25 July 1886 in Cumberland Co., IL); *Ralph* (born 2 Dec. 1889 in IL, died May 1971 at Mt. Vernon, IL). Listed in the 1900 census for Dodds Township, Jefferson Co., IL. Jennie Taylor died on 22 Apr. 1959 in Coles Co., IL, aged 93 years, and is buried in the Janesville Cemetery, Pleasant Grove Township.

7e. **Elizabeth C(onstance?) "Lizzie."** Born 9 Jan. 1869 in Fleming Co., KY. Married George Chapman about 1889 (he was born May 1828 in NY, and may have died 1913), and had children: *Roy* (married Maud Gilmore); *Ernest* (died unmarried in a mine accident in Montana); *George Jr.*; *Norman* (born 16 Sept. 1898, died June 1972 at Seattle); *Homer* (died in an explosion; he may be the same as Emma's son); married secondly ___ Thayer. Listed in the 1900 census for Blue Earth Co., MN. Lizzie Chapman (so stated on her death certificate) died on 3 June 1949 at Seattle, WA.

7f. **Child.** Born about 1871 in Fleming Co., KY; died young.

7g. **Emma B.** Born Apr. 1873 in Fleming Co., KY. Married Henry Minnick Jr. on 27 Mar. 1892 in Coles Co., IL (div.; he was born about 1860 in Owen Co., IN, and appears to be listed in the 1920 census for Edgar Co., IL living with William H. Foy), and had children: *Mattie F.* (or *Maida*; born Oct. 1893); *Ruba M.* (born Oct. 1894); *Homer S.* (born Feb. 1896; he may have died in an explosion); *Clotill* (or Clothilde; listed as Irene H. in 1910; born Feb. 1899); *Vernon M.* (listed as *Cheuncey* in the 1910 census; born 1904); *Clarence E.* (born 1908); *Eva L.* (born 1911); *Florene*. Listed in the 1900-10 censuses for Chrisman City, Ross Township, Edgar Co., IL. Does not appear with her husband in the 1930 directory of Paris, Edgar Co., IL. She may have married secondly John T. Bishop (he was born about 1883 in IL), and be listed with him in the 1920 census for Grove Township, Jasper Co., IL. Said to have died between 1920-30 (however, a "Mrs." Minnick died in Edgar Co. on 12 Dec. 1912), and to have been buried at Mankato or Eagle Lake, MN. Not in the Illinois death index through 1938.

7h. **Alvin.** Born 15 Dec. 1876 (or 1874) in Fleming Co., KY. See below for full entry.

ALVIN BURGESS OF COLES CO., ILLINOIS

[James Sylvester[6]]

7h. **Alvin** *[son of James Sylvester].* Born 15 Dec. 1876 in Fleming Co., KY (however, Fleming Co. birth records give a date of 1874). Married Nancy L. Donoho on 16 Jan. 1914 in Jefferson Co., IL (she was born 6 Jan. 1881, daughter of John R. Donoho and Julia Williamson, and died 27 Jan. 1930 in Jefferson Co., IL). Listed in the 1917 draft register and 1920 census for Lee Co., IL. Alvin Burgess was a farmer in Jefferson, Lee, and Coles Cos., IL. He died 5 Mar. 1953 at Mattoon, IL, and is buried with his wife in Well's Chapel Cemetery, Jefferson Co.

8a. **Harry Lawson.** Born 23 June 1915 at Dixon, IL. Harry Burgess was a farmer on the family spread in northeast Jefferson Co., IL. He died there unmarried on 9 Dec. 1946, when a kerosene stove exploded and destroyed his home, and is buried with his parents in Well's Chapel Cemetery.

FIRE DESTROYS HOME; SON DIES, FATHER BURNED

"Harry Burgess, about thirty-three, was fatally burned and his father, Alvin Burgess, about seventy, suffered severe burns when their home in Farrington Township, about fifteen miles northeast of Mt. Vernon, was destroyed by fire early this morning. The father and son were brought to Good Samaritan Hospital at 5:30 o'clock this morning, and the son died at 11:20 A.M. Alvin Burgess was suffering from burns to his face and hands, and the seriousness of his condition was not definite early this afternoon. Details of the tragic fire were not immediately learned here. However, coroner Ben Roeder said friends told him that the fire occurred early today, and that the house was destroyed...."—*Mt. Vernon Register-News*, 9 Dec. 1946.

"Harry L. Burgess, 31, of Farrington Township, was fatally burned yesterday morning, when kerosene he poured into a stove to start a fire exploded, it was revealed this morning at an inquiry conducted here into the death by coroner Ben Roeder....Testifying at this morning's inquest, T. A. Mills, a neighbor of the Burgesses, said: 'About four o'clock yesterday morning I heard Mr. Burgess calling, but I didn't pay much attention to him, for I thought he was calling his stock. In a few minutes after I heard him calling, he came to my house in his night clothes, calling for help. Then I noticed the light from the burning house. I began calling and looking for Harry Burgess, because his father seemed to think he was still in the burning house. Later we found him in a field a short distance from his home. He was badly burned. He told me that he was building a fire, and that he poured some kerosene on the fire and it exploded. We brought him and his father to Good Samaritan Hospital.'"—*Mt. Vernon Register-News*, 10 Dec. 1946.

8b. **Helen Minerva.** Born 27 Mar. 1917 at Dixon, IL. Married Eddie Wiggins; married secondly Johnnie Pierce; married thirdly William Pierce, his brother. Helen Pierce died on 2 Dec. 1983 at Bluford, Jefferson Co., IL, and is buried in Well's Chapel Cemetery.

9a. **Ernie.** Born about 1937 in Jefferson Co., IL; died unmarried about 1957 at Lincoln, IL.

8c. **Alvin Forest.** Born Feb. 1919 at Dixon, Lee Co., IL; died there on 26 Mar. 1919, and is buried at Dixon, IL.

8d. **(John) Howard.** Born 20 Aug. 1920 at Dixon, IL; died 20 Jan. 1934 at Augusta, GA, and is buried with his parents in Well's Chapel Cemetery.

8e. **Henry (IV) "Hank"** (nmn). Born 5 Sept. 1922 at Dixon, IL. Married Margaret Jean Whipple on 20 Jan. 1945 at Princeton, Bureau Co., IL (she was born 31 Aug. 1926, daughter of Harry and Adah Whipple). Hank Burgess worked as a millwright for Northwestern Steel and Wire Co., Sterling, IL. He now lives retired at Walnut, IL.

9a. **Michael Dale.** Born and died 7 Oct. 1945 at Princeton, IL, and is buried in the Greenville Cemetery.

9b. **Peggy Sue.** Born 6 Nov. 1946 at Princeton, IL. Married Everett Sarver on 1 Oct. 1965 at Walnut, IL, and had children: *Diane Lee* (born 26 Mar. 1966 at Walnut, IL); *Michael Gene* (born 25 May 1967 at Walnut, IL); *Chad Allen* (born 18 Oct. 1977 at Walnut, IL). Peggy Sarver works for Shell Oil Co. at Walnut, IL.

9c. **Robert Maxwell** (ad.). Born 22 July 1957 at Sterling, IL. Married Cindy Landon on 10 Apr. 1976 at Walnut, IL. Robert Burgess is a carpenter for Princeton Farms at Princeton, IL.

10a. **Maxwell Michael.** Born 7 Oct. 1976 at Princeton, IL.

10b. **Melisa Ann.** Born 1 Dec. 1978 at Sterling, IL.

HARRISON MONROE BURGESS (1840-1891)*ORPHELIA DEYETTE ENFIELD (1860-1945)

[William (I)[1], Edward (I)[2], William (II)[3], Henry (I)[4], John Henry (I)[5]]

HARRISON MONROE BURGESS
(1840-1891)

OF BLUE EARTH COUNTY, MINNESOTA

6i. **Harrison Monroe "Hack"** *[son of John Henry (I)].* Born 20 Feb. 1840 at Portland Mills, IN. Married Orphelia Deyette "Etta" Enfield on 18 Apr. 1878 at Eagle Lake, Blue Earth Co., MN (she was born 15 Apr. 1860 in MN, daughter of James Enfield and Martha Pearson, remarried Julius Horvet [Minnesota State Chemist], and died 1945 at Mankato, MN, buried Glenwood Cemetery). Hack Burgess was a Sergeant in Co. E, 9th Regiment, 5th MN Infantry, Union Army, serving from 19 Aug. 1862 to 24 Aug. 1865, and was wounded at the battle of Brices Cross Roads, Lee Co., MS on 10 June 1864; he was also present as part of the guard for the hanging of 38 Sioux Indians at Mankato on 26 Dec. 1862. Early in life he was an advance agent for the Andrews Family Swiss Bell Ringers, precursors to the Andrews Opera Company. He worked as a carpenter, cabinet maker (some of his hand-made furniture, including desks and chairs, still survive among his descendants), and farmer near Eagle Lake, MN. He was also elected Justice of the Peace for Mankato Township and an elected member of the town board, and was considered a legal authority. Listed in the 1880-85 censuses for Blue Earth Co., MN. He died of consumption on 9 July 1891, eleven days before his father, and is buried in the Burgess Cemetery. After his death, Etta Burgess moved her family to Mankato, MN.

DEATH OF A GOOD MAN

"Mr. H. M. Burgess, one of the earliest settlers of Mankato Township, died at his home near Eagle Lake, on Thursday morning, the immediate cause of death being hemmorhage of lungs. He is the son of J. H. Burgess, esq., and his residence dates back to 1856. By calling he was a carpenter, but for many years has lived upon a farm engaging in agricultural pursuits. He enlisted in Company E, Ninth Regiment, in 1862, and though wounded at Brice Cross Roads, Ga. [sic], served his enlistment and was discharged with his regiment. Mr. Burgess was in poor health for many years, doubtless the result of his service in the army. He held the position of justice of the peace in Mankato Township for a number of years, and was a member of the town board. He was an upright, honorable gentleman, much esteemed by all who knew him, and in this township whenever his name was presented for office it always commanded a liberal support because of his integrity and general worth as a man. He was fifty-three years old, and his funeral last Friday afternoon was largely attended."—*Mankato Review*, 14 July 1891.

7a. **Florence (III) "Flossie"** (nmn). Listed in the birth records as Florinda; she was named for Florence Andrews, one of the stars of the Andrews Opera Company. Born 16 Nov. 1880 at Eagle Lake, MN. Married Dr. Roy Newbery Andrews in July 1906 at Minneapolis, MN (he was born 11 June 1884 at Mankato, MN, son of Dr. John Wesley Andrews, [a physician and a member of the Andrews family, who founded a troupe of travelling light opera singers and performers] and Jennie Cornelia French, and died 2 Dec. 1961 at Mankato, MN). Florence Andrews graduated from the University of Minnesota (one of the earliest college degrees in the family), and was a college professor and concert pianist. She died on 27 Nov. 1949 at Mankato, MN, and is buried with her husband in the Glenwood Cemetery.

Their only child, **Cornelia Deyette ANDREWS**, was born 9 May 1909 at Mankato, MN, married Cedric Rollin DuBois on 15 Oct. 1936 (he was born 15 Nov. 1908 at Mankato, MN, son of Edward Henry DuBois and Ethel Alvira Walrath, and died 7 June 1948 at Mankato), and had children:

Alice Deyette Florence DUBOIS. Born 22 Sept. 1938 at Mankato, MN, married Neil Vern Hamrin on 19 Dec. 1959, and had children: *John Edward* (born 28 Jan. 1967); ***Michelle Deyette*** (born 20 June 1969); ***Alice*** married secondly Del Holz on 21 Dec. 1970, and had children: *Aaron* (twin; born 7 Feb. 1972, just before midnight); *Matthew* (twin; born 8 Feb. 1972, just after midnight). ***Alice HOLZ*** lives at Bloomington, MN.

Carol Louise DuBois. Born 20 Sept. 1943 at Mankato, MN, married James Wackerbarth on 18 June 1972, and had children: *Amy* (born 10 Nov. 1974). ***Carol* WACKERBARTH** lives at Minnetonka, MN.

Cornelia ANDREWS DUBOIS died on 12 June 1981 at St. Louis Park, MN, and is buried at Mankato, MN. She inherited the Lawson family Bible from her mother, and wrote a young adult novel, *Singing Wheels* (Minneapolis, MN: Vanilla Press, 1979), loosely based around the history of the Andrews Light Opera Co., plus an unpublished manuscript, *A Medical History of Blue Earth County, 1852-1902* (1967), and an historical article, "Operatic Pioneers: The Story of the Andrews Family" (*Minnesota History* v. 33 [1953]: p. 317-325). She contributed greatly to this book.

7b. **Daughter**. Born 10 June 1881 in Blue Earth Co., MN, probably stillborn.

In 1972 Cornelia DuBois wrote: "Eagle Lake, about six miles 'in the country' [east of Mankato] had about 100 inhabitants then and about the same now. It is hardly more than a 'bend in the road.' However, the little house where my mother was born, on the original Burgess land, is still there, and there is a farmhouse on the original site of the log cabin built by John Henry Burgess and his wife, Patsy (Martha). The Burgess history is all in Eagle Lake. The Christian Church, the cemetery, were built and donated by the Burgesses. The church and cemetery are still there. The school house, which my mother said used to be across the street from the cemetery, and was later moved [north] onto the main road (I saw it there) is now gone....

"My other strong memories are of visits to the Burgess Cemetery, to my grandfather's grave, of walks through the lavender 'creeping Charlie' in the cemetery, and reading the old tombstones, including one which said, 'Remember me, as you pass by, As you are now so once was I, As I am now, so you will be, Prepare for Heaven and Eternity.' My mother also showed me the gravestones of a family which had been wiped out in a diphtheria epidemic. They are gone, too. In fact, there are few stones left in the old cemetery. Time, weather, and vandalism have taken their toll...."

George Washington ***Burgess*** *(1805-1893)*

[William (I)[1], Edward (I)[2], William (II)[3], Henry (I)[4]]

GEORGE WASHINGTON BURGESS
(1805-1893)

OF FLEMING COUNTY, KENTUCKY

5d. **(George) Washington (II)** *[son of Henry (I)].* Born 5 Mar. 1805 in Bourbon Co., KY (his published Bible record and tombstone state 1803, but census and tax records, and the Bible record of his daughter, Rebecca Peck, consistently support a date of 1805). Married Lucinda C. Pearce (or Pierce), reputedly a cousin of President Franklin Pierce, on 13 Sept. 1830 in Fleming Co. (she was born 1 Nov. 1813 in KY, and died on 1 Dec. 1851 in Fleming Co.). Listed in the census records for Fleming Co. between 1830-80 (in 1860 in the Elizaville District, and from 1870-80 in the Sherburne District), and in the tax records there from 1826. Wash Burgess was a farmer, horseman, and livestock trader near Sherburne, KY on the southern border of Fleming Co. with Bath Co. With his brother, John H. Burgess, he ran a horse trading company between Kentucky and Indiana in the decades prior to the Civil War. He is said to have supported the South during that conflict, breaking with his brother, and was sometimes called "Col." by his family. He died on his farm on 1 Feb. 1893, and is buried with his wife and many of their children in the Flemingsburg Cemetery, Flemingsburg, KY.

The Children of Wash Burgess:

6a. **(Isaac) Franklin.** Born 25 Feb. 1833 in Fleming Co., KY. See below for full entry.

6b. **Amanda Jane.** Born 21 Nov. 1835 in Fleming Co., KY. Listed with her father in the 1850-80 censuses for Fleming Co., KY, and in 1900-10 with her nephew, Harvey Magowan. Amanda Burgess helped raise her younger siblings after her mother's untimely death. She died unmarried on 13 Jan. 1916 in Fleming Co., and is buried with her parents in the Flemingsburg Cemetery.

6c. **(William) Thomas (I).** Born 12 Sept. 1837 in Fleming Co., KY. See below for full entry.

6d. **Mary (IX).** Born 9 July 1838 in Fleming Co., KY. Married John A. Hendricks on 13 Oct. 1856 in Fleming Co. (he was born 1811 in TN, and worked as a blacksmith), and had children: *William* (born 1859 in KY). She may be listed in the 1860 census for Somerset, Pulaski Co., KY, but has not been found in the 1900-20 censuses. Mary Hendricks died in Feb. 1923, apparently out-of-state (not listed in the Kentucky death index).

6e. **Henry Clay (I).** Born 25 Nov. 1840 in Fleming Co., KY. Married Louisa J. Paxton on 21 Dec. 1865 in Fleming Co. (she was born 1 Mar. 1846, and died 9 Apr. 1896); married secondly Dorcas Newcomb on 19 June 1900 in Fleming Co. (she was born about 1854 in KY, and survived her husband). Listed in the 1860 census with his father, in 1870 in the Flemingsburg District, and in 1880-1900 in the Sherburne District of Fleming Co.; Dorcas is living with Henry K. Crain in 1910. Henry Burgess was a farmer in Fleming Co. He died childless on 21 Sept. (or 17 Aug.) 1907 (the former date is confirmed by a contemporaneous letter) at his home near Tilton, KY, and is buried with his first wife in the Flemingsburg Cemetery.

6f. **Martha M.** Born 14 Nov. 1842 in Fleming Co., KY. Married George Washington Magowan (or Magowen) on 25 Jan. 1871 in Fleming Co. (he was born about 1842 in KY), and had children: *Lucinda "Cindy"* (born 1873, married ___ Doggett, lived at Sherburne, KY, and is buried in the Flemingsburg Cemetery); *George Washington Jr.* (born 1876); *(John) Harvey* (born 14 Mar. 1880 [or Sept. 1879] in Fleming Co., KY, married Jennie ___, and had children: Willie W. [born 1906]; Harland [born 1910]); *Lilla* (married ___ Price, and died at Cincinnati, OH). Martha Magowan died on 14 Mar. 1880 in Fleming Co., and is buried in the Flemingsburg Cemetery. George Magowan is listed with his brother-in-law, Wash Burgess, in the 1880 census.

6g. **Rebecca (III).** Born 10 Feb. 1845 in Fleming Co., KY. Married George Peck on 30 Oct. 1872 in Fleming Co. (he was born 18 Apr. 1837, and died 18 July 1914), and had children: *Sallie* (born 4 June [or Apr.] 1874, married ___ Allen, died before 1925, and is buried at Elizaville, KY); *Hattie* (born 30 May 1876, and died June 1943, buried with her parents); *George Washington* (born 1 Apr. 1878, and died

July 1925 when he fell under a wagon at Nepton, Fleming Co., KY, buried with his parents); *James Argo* (born 22 Oct. 1882, died 21 Dec. 1965, buried with his parents), all of whom died childless. Listed in the 1880 census for the Sherburne District, Fleming Co., KY. Rebecca Peck died on 18 May 1923 in Fleming Co., and is buried in the Flemingsburg Cemetery with her family. Her family Bible, giving the dates of birth and death of her parents and family, passed to Mary Burgess Saunders when the last of the Pecks died in 1965; she in turn gave it to the author of this book.

6h. **Elizabeth (XV) "Lizzie."** Born 23 Mar. 1847 in Fleming Co., KY; died there of tuberculosis on 10 Mar. 1857 (or 1858, according to the official death records), and is buried with her parents.

6i. **Lucinda B(athsheba?) "Lucy."** Born 1 Sept. 1849 in Fleming Co., KY. Married Daniel P. Hysong on 2 Sept. 1880 in Fleming Co. (he was born Sept. 1859, married secondly Almedia ___ [she was born July 1872, and died 1929], and died 1911, buried with his second wife in the Flemingsburg Cemetery), and had children: *Bathsheba "Bashie"* (born about 1881); *George Washington* (born Feb. 1885, married Ella Dorsey [div., living in 1982], had children: Ruby [born 13 Mar. 1909, married Jack Bernheim, worked as a school teacher, had children: Jackie Lee, and lived at Albuquerque, NM]; Charles W. [living at Winslow, AZ in 1982, and had children: Robert; Cranston; John]; and died 1950); *Harvey*. Listed in the 1880 census with her sister, Rebecca. Lucy Hysong died on 13 May 1888 in Fleming Co., and is buried in the Flemingsburg Cemetery; Daniel Hysong is listed in the 1900 census for Fleming Co., KY.

6j. **John Pearce.** Born 15 Nov. 1851 in Fleming Co., KY. See below for full entry.

Deplorable Accident

"Saturday morning last, George and James Peck, sons of the late Blind George Peck, living on the Elizaville Pike, went to Nepton for [a] load of coal. Having loaded their wagon at the Palmer coal yard, they started to drive out on the pike, James driving the team and George walking beside the wagon and holding down on the brake. Just as the wagon got on the pike, George attempted to climb on the wagon while in motion, but his foot slipped and he fell under the hind wheel of the wagon, which passed over his abdomen, crushing him so that death ensued in a few minutes. Deceased was a bachelor, about 47 years of age, and made his home with his brother and an unmarried sister. Funeral Monday and interment in the family lot in our cemetery. His brother and sister have our sympathy in this sad occurrence."—Unknown Flemingsburg newspaper.

A Letter from Minnie Zoeller Burgess

"R.R. #1, Hillsboro, Ky. Sept. 23[yd] 1907. Dear Brother, I don't know whether I can get my thoughts together to write what I want to or not. We had such a shock last Saturday night in the sudden death of Uncle Henry Burgess on whose farm we are living. The Christian Church were having a moonlight fate [sic] in his yard at Tilton & was about over when Uncle Henry fell dead or at least died in just a few moments. He had been ailing all summer but no one knew that it was heart trouble. Dr. said he overdone himself. He was helping freeze the cream and was returning from the tables with a freezer in one hand & lantern in the other when he fell. I was the second one to get to him. His wife was sitting on the porch near where he fell & she is an invalid & could not go to him. It was an exciting time. What I wanted to say to you is this: if the farm we are living on is sold, will you back us in buying it? Now I know you said you did not want to invest in land so far away, but I appeal to you with all my heart to help us out this time, for Uncle has made money off of this farm & I know we could and I feel like this is a golden opportunity. He leaves no heirs, an estate will have have [sic] to settled up soon. The general belief is that he has a will, but they have not found it yet, but if there is, it be known Monday, as it is court day. We are staying here with his wife until her daughters can come. Elijah attends to everything, for he was the only one knew how Uncle wanted things done. His Uncle was so fond of us & so pleased with E's work. E. has 30 acres of fine corn & 4 acres of tobaco [sic]. They had about $150 worth of hay cut. It is a well watered farm, good two story dwelling & barn & out buildings, a good place for sheep & stock. I feel like we could pay for it with a little time to do so. It is true land is right high now, but produce is high too. E. thinks the place will bring about $6000 and it is usually payable in 3 payments. I know you can help us out and certainly would appreciate it. You can take a morgage [sic] and should any thing happen it could be sold & get get [sic] your money back, so I don't see where you would be running any risk. Any body here would tell you there is not a steadier hard working man any where than Elijah. I hope & trust you will see fit to help us this once. Let me hear from you at once. I guess they will know something after Monday. About the money we owe you, I was not sure how much I got at Depot, but guess it was $20, so that makes it $60. I will attend to it as soon as possible. Love to all & tell Lizzie I will write to her Sunday. Your loving sister, Minnie."

[William (I)[1], Edward (I)[2], William (II)[3], Henry (I)[4], George Washington (II)[5]]

ISAAC FRANKLIN BURGESS
(1833-1912)

OF FLEMING COUNTY, KENTUCKY

6a. **(Isaac) Franklin** *[son of George Washington (II)].* His name is listed as I. F. L. Burgess in the 1860 census. Born 25 Feb. 1833 in Fleming Co., KY. Married Mary Louise Thomas on 13 Sept. 1860 in Fleming Co. (she was born 9 July 1841 in KY, daughter of Elijah Thomas and Permelia Hamlet Smith, and sister of William Thomas [who married Eliza Baltzelle], and died on 5 Feb. 1923 in Fayette Co., KY). Listed in the 1860 census for Fleming Co. working with Thomas Doherty as a merchant, and in 1870-1910 in the Sherburne District, Fleming Co.; Mary Burgess is listed with her son Elijah in 1920. Frank Burgess was a farmer and horse trader on his farmer's lands near Sherburne, KY. He wrote a letter in his declining years outlining what he believed to be the history of the Burgess family; in it he mentions visiting President Pierce at the White House in 1856 (see below). He died on 4 May 1912 in Fleming Co., and is buried with his wife in the Flemingsburg Cemetery.

The Children of Frank Burgess:

7a. **Permelia Thomas "Mamie."** Born 4 Dec. 1861 in Fleming Co., KY. Married James Fitch Hinton on 28 Nov. 1889 in Fleming Co. (he was born 11 May 1860, son of Thomas Jefferson Hinton and Sarah Ann Fitch, and brother of Jesse Hinton [who married Mamie's sister, Lida], and worked as an undertaker) and had children: *Mary Burgess* (born 9 Sept. 1890, died 17 Sept. 1890, buried Flemingsburg Cemetery with the dates "1898-1899"); *Kay Burgess* (born 17 Feb. 1892, married Jeannette Brewer of Paris, France, and died childless in Dec. 1969 at Louisville, KY); *Rena* (born 28 Mar. 1893, died 17 Jan. 1894); *Jesse Thomas II* (born 1 Sept. 1897, married Nell Paris, and died childless on 15 May 1922); *Anita M.* (born 29 May 1899, married Henry W. Gentry [his family owned the Gentry Tobacco Warehouse at Lexington and Paris, KY], and died childless on 9 Oct. 1964 at Lexington, KY); *Frances* (born 5 Mar. 1903, died unmarried in Mar. 1980 at Louisville, KY). Mamie Hinton died on 8 Feb. 1946 at Lexington, Fayette Co., KY.

7b. **Alvin Redmon.** Born 26 Mar. 1864 in Fleming Co., KY. See below for full entry.

7c. **Eliza Baltzelle "Lida."** Born 23 May 1869 in Fleming Co., KY. Married Jesse Thomas Hinton on 30 Dec. 1891 in Fleming Co. (he was born 24 Mar. 1865, son of Thomas Jefferson Hinton and Sarah Ann Fitch, and brother of James Hinton [who also worked as an undertaker, and who married Lida's sister, Permelia Burgess], founded J. T. Hinton & Son Funeral Home in Memphis, and died 15 May 1922), and had children: *(Frank) Frayser* (born 7 Dec. 1892, inherited his father's funeral home at Memphis, TN, and also worked as a professional photographer and composed music for the movie industry, was a published poet [but no books], and died childless on 23 Nov. 1950 at Memphis, TN); *Mary Louise* (born 5 Oct. 1897, died unmarried on 10 Mar. 1925). Lida Hinton died on 23 Nov. 1938 at Memphis, TN, and is buried with her husband and children in the Elmwood Cemetery, Memphis.

7d. **Elijah Thomas.** Born 11 Nov. 1872 in Fleming Co., KY. See below for full entry.

7e. **Harry Tolbert.** Born 21 Nov. 1877 in Fleming Co., KY. See below for full entry.

ALVIN R. BURGESS OF FLEMING CO., KENTUCKY
[Isaac Franklin[6]]

7b. **Alvin Redmon** *[son of Isaac Franklin].* Born 26 Mar. 1864 in Fleming Co., KY. Married Luttie D. Perkins on 18 Oct. 1888 in Fleming Co. (she was born 17 Nov. 1868, and died on 8 July 1955 in Fleming Co.). Alvin Burgess was a farmer on his father's lands in Fleming Co., KY. He died there on 12 Sept. 1906, and is buried with his family in the Flemingsburg Cemetery. Luttie Burgess is listed in the 1910 census for Fayette Co., KY working for Edward H. Dovak.

From the *Lexington Leader*, 12 Nov. 1902: "Mason County man shot on road to church. Maysville, Kentucky, Nov. 12th. Walter Peck, a young man, while on his way home from church last night from Flemingsburg, was waylaid and shot for an unknown cause. A man named Burgess was arrested. Information is that Peck died instantly."

Lexington Leader, 13 Nov. 1902: "Maysville, Kentucky, Nov. 13th. Alvin Burgess, who shot and killed Walter Peck, a fifteen-year-old boy, near Flemingsburg Tuesday night, was brought here last night for safe keeping. Word had been received that a mob would attempt to take Burgess from jail and Sheriff Robertson and deputies guarded the jail all night. The mob did not materialize, but is yet expected."

"Flemingsburg, Kentucky, Nov. 13th. A great deal of excitement prevails here over the killing of Walter Peck, age fifteen. Peck and several companions were returning from church at Tilton, and stopped on the road to build a temporary fence across the pike, and make the other members of the party, who were following behind, get out of their vehicles to clear the road. The action of the boys was purely in the way of a joke. While two of the young men were working with the fence, young Peck was sitting on his horse. Suddenly a man appeared in the dark with a pistol in each hand, and began firing. Young Peck was shot through the body and instantly killed. The others members of the party immediately fled and gave the alarm. Sheriff Collins arrested Alvin Burgess, age 30, who at first denied any knowledge of the crime, but later confessed and says that his intention was to frighten the boys, and that the killing was accidental. A great deal of indignation prevails in the neighborhood, and there is talk of dealing summarily with Burgess, who is a man of family."

8a. **Arthur Thomas (I).** His name is written "Auther" in his grandfather's Bible record. Born 3 Feb. 1890 in Fleming Co., KY. Married Glennie Lee about 1914 (she was born 3 Dec. 1890, and died 10 July 1963). Art Burgess worked for the Frisco Railroad and the Memphis Police Dept. Has not been found in the 1910 Kentucky Soundex. He died on 8 Mar. 1923 at Memphis, TN, and is buried in the Flemingsburg Cemetery.

9a. **(Luttie) Juanita.** Born 13 Apr. 1915 in Fleming Co., KY. Married George Robert Stokely (he was born 12 Feb. 1912, and died 28 Feb. 1973). Juanita Stokely died childless in Nov. 1986 at Memphis, TN.

ELIJAH T. BURGESS OF FLEMING CO., KENTUCKY

[Isaac Franklin[6]]

7d. **Elijah Thomas** *[son of Isaac Franklin].* Born 11 Nov. 1872 in Fleming Co., KY. Married Minnie Lee Zoeller on 5 Oct. 1897 at Tarboro, NC (she was born 29 Mar. 1874 in Bavaria, daughter of E. Zoeller, and died 4 Dec. 1948 [or 1945] at Cleveland, OH). Listed in the 1900-20 censuses for Fleming Co., and in the 1918 draft register of Fleming Co. E. T. Burgess was a farmer on his father's lands near Sherburne, and later on a farm near Tilton, both in Fleming Co., KY. He raced in the sulky races at Keeneland near Lexington, KY. He owned and had transcribed the family Bible once owned by his grandfather. Elijah Burgess died on 22 Mar. 1945 at Lexington, KY, and is buried with his wife in the Flemingsburg Cemetery. He and his wife helped raise Grace and Thomas Lytle, the children of their daughter, Kathryne.

8a. **Kathryne Zoeller** (twin). Born 23 Mar. 1899 at Hillsboro, Fleming Co., KY. Married Otho Taylor Lytle on 5 Jan. 1921 at Tilton, Fleming Co. (div.; he was born 8 May 1896 in Fleming Co., and died 13 June 1955 at Coral Gables, FL). Kathryne graduated from the Chicago School of Nursing by correspondence in the 1930s, and worked at Eastern State Hospital, Lexington, KY, and as a private nurse for terminally ill patients at Louisville. They had children:

Gracie Powers "Grace" LYTLE. Born 29 Dec. 1921 at Hillsboro, KY, married Frank Henry Polsgrove on 2 Jan. 1943 at Cleveland, OH (div. 1946; he was born 21 Nov. 1919 at Frankfort, KY, survived the attack at Pearl Harbor in 1941, and died 2 July 1956 at Frankfort), and had children: *Danny Taylor* (born 2 Mar. 1944 at Louisville, KY, was adopted by Edward Crocker, married Dorothy Hancock "Dottie" Armstrong on 12 Nov. 1977 at Frankfort, KY [she was born 2 Apr. 1947 at Frankfort; by her first marriage, she had children: Raymond S. ARMSTRONG {born 1 Aug. 1968?, married Stephanie Michelle Lance on 18 Oct. 1986, and had children: Stephanie Rae}; Chris {born 14 July 1972}], and had children: Sean Taylor [born 31 July 1981 at Winter Park, FL]; *Danny CROCKER* currently lives at Frankfort). *Grace* married secondly Edward Ray "Eddie" Crocker on 30 Nov. 1946 at Cleveland, OH (he was born 10 Aug. 1920, worked for the Cleveland Transit System, and died 5 Aug. 1958 at San Diego, CA). *Grace* married thirdly Robert Livingston Williams Jr. on

13 Aug. 1960 at San Diego, CA (div. 1968; he was born 10 June 1927 in Florida). ***Grace*** married fourthly Edward Charles Young on 18 Dec. 1968 at La Jolla, CA (he was born 11 June 1920 at Burdick, IN, retired from the Naval Reserve in 1980 with the rank of Lieut. Commander, and retired from California First Bank in 1981 after twenty years; by his first wife, he had children: *Gary Alan* [born 20 Apr. 1951 at San Diego, CA, married Cynthia Lynn Fleisher on 5 May 1984 at Austin, TX {she was born 2 May 1952 at Kankakee, IL}, and had children: Sarah Bennett {born 15 Aug. 1985 at Austin, TX}; Hannah Bloom {born 8 Oct. 1989 at Denver, CO}]). Grace Lytle graduated from Midway Junior College, Midway, KY in 1938, and later attended several modeling schools. She worked as a fashion and photographic model in Cleveland and San Diego during the 1940s. Grace and Ed Young currently live at Rancho Bernardo, near San Diego, CA.

Thomas Taylor LYTLE. Born 13 June 1923 at Hillsboro, KY, married (Rebecca) Winifred Lathram on 3 Oct. 1945 in Fleming Co., KY (div.; she was born 2 Aug. 1924 at Flemingsburg, KY), and had children: *Elsie Marie* (born 29 Dec. 1946 at Flemingsburg, KY, married Don Wayne Parker at Flemingsburg, KY, and had children: Cynthia Gail [born 28 Apr. 1964 at Flemingsburg, married Bryan Luther McMillen on 2 Jan. 1981 at San Diego, CA {div.}, and had children: Patrice Marie {born 25 Dec. 1981}; Kimberly Dawn {born 9 Dec. 1985}; Cynthia married secondly George Michael Deem on 2 Aug. 1987 {div.}, and had children: Bryanne Gail {born 26 July 1988}; Mari Rebecca {born 28 Feb. 1990}]; *Elsie* married secondly Hayward Nelson Averett on 12 Jan. 1980 at San Diego, CA [div.]; *Elsie* married thirdly Marty R. Mohney on 17 Nov. 1984 at Escondido, CA [he was born 29 Oct. 1955 at Valdosta, GA]); *James Thomas* (born 8 Nov. 1948 at Flemingsburg, KY, married Patsy Watson on 12 June 1970 at Las Vegas, NV [div.], married secondly Yolanda Sue Glover on 27 Mar. 1976 at Flemingsburg, KY [div.; she was born 19 Dec. 1951 at Mount Sterling, KY, daughter of William Preston Glover and Louise Blair Reynolds], and had children: Melissa Blair [born 3 Nov. 1978 at San Diego, CA]; *James LYTLE* lives at Flemingsburg, KY). ***Thomas Lytle*** married secondly Mary Lois Markic on 10 Aug. 1957 at Cleveland, OH (she was born 25 Aug. 1928 at Cleveland). Thomas Lytle was a combat infantryman in World War II, and participated in the Normandy Beach landing of 1944 and the Battle of the Bulge in the Winter of 1944. After operating a service station and farming equipment business in Kentucky, he moved to San Diego, where he owned a successful Shell Service Station. He currently lives at San Diego, CA.

Kathryne Zoeller LYTLE married secondly George W. French about 1938 (he was a male nurse at Eastern State Hospital). She was killed when the automobile being driven by her husband crashed into a wall on 8 Aug. 1945 near Lexington, KY. Grace Young has contributed greatly to this book.

8b. **Mary Ellis** (twin). Born 23 Mar. 1899 at Hillsboro, Fleming Co., KY, died there on 16 Aug. 1899.

HARRY T. BURGESS OF NICHOLAS CO., KENTUCKY

[Isaac Franklin[6]]

7e. **Harry Tolbert** *[son of Isaac Franklin]*. He was originally named Wood Burgess (so listed in the 1880 census), although his family Bible record states Harrison Tolbert, and his draft record gives Harry Talbott. Born 21 Nov. 1877 in Fleming Co., KY. Married Lou ___ about 1897 (she died Apr. 1899); married secondly Emma E. Kerns on 28 Nov. 1901 in Nicholas Co., KY (she was born 9 Apr. 1879, and died 13 Sept. 1966). Listed in the 1910-20 censuses for Nicholas Co., KY, and in the 1918 draft register there. Harry Burgess was a buyer for a wholesale grocery company at Carlisle, KY. He died on 17 Apr. 1955 in Fayette Co., KY, and is buried with his wife in the Carlisle Cemetery.

8a. **Nealya Thomas.** Born 30 Dec. 1904 at Carlisle, KY. Nealya Burgess was a school teacher at Memphis, TN before retiring. She enjoys travelling, and has circled the globe several times. She currently lives in a retirement home at Cynthiana, KY.

8b. **Lida Frances.** Born 13 Dec. 1907 at Carlisle, KY. Married Teddy Allan Poe (he was born 29 Jan. 1906, and died 6 Nov. 1967 in Fayette Co., KY), and had children: *Teddy Allan Jr.* (born 9 Jan. 1943, and currently lives at Carlisle, KY). Lida Poe was a school teacher before retiring. She was killed in an automobile accident on 28 Dec. 1991 at Carlisle, Nicholas Co., KY, and is buried in the Carlisle Cemetery.

8c. **Frank Kerns.** Born 19 Mar. 1914 at Carlisle, KY. Married (Alma) Pauline McClure on 22 Dec. 1941 in Knox Co., KY (she was born 24 Jan. 1910). Frank K. Burgess graduated from Union College in 1935, and received his master's degree in 1940 from the University of Kentucky. He was an administrative assistant for the Kentucky Department of Economic Security for 33 years, where he handled federal grants to state governments. He was a member of the Christian Church. He died on 23 Sept. 1993 at Lexington, KY (when the male line of Isaac Franklin Burgess became extinct), and was buried in the Frankfort Cemetery. Pauline Burgess lives at Frankfort, KY.

9a. **Nealya Susan** (ad.). Born 14 Mar. 1951 at Louisville, Kentucky. Married James Kinman Parish in 1973 (he died on 19 Nov. 1988), and had children: *Samuel Kinman* (born 22 Apr. 1980); *Sara Burgess* (born 29 Aug. 1983). Nealya Parish works in the Loans and Discounts Department at the Third National Bank, Nashville, TN.

A Letter from Isaac Franklin Burgess to His Daughter, Lida Hinton

Tilton, Ky., Feb. 11, 1903

Dear Lida,

This is the first opportunity I have had to answer your request and will try to give you the relations of our ancestors first. My grate granfather was general Christian Burgess born and raised in Ingland. My grate granmother was Mary Harrison also born and raised in Ingland. Here father was Thomas G. Harrison King of Ingland [sic]. Christian Burgess and wife and Benjamin Harrison Mrs. Mary Burgess brother emegrated to America in early life and settled in Maryland and afterward moved to Petersburgh Va. Christian Burgess & wife died having 9 children, seven sons and two daughters. He remarried and his first children all emegrated to Ky in 1787 and settled in Bourbon Co. Scott Co. Harrison Co. Mason Co. & Fleming. There names was Mordica Calvin Redmon Edwin Upton Joseph and Harrison Burgess. The latter was my granfather who was wounded in Ind in the year 1812 and died at Vincennes Ind. The Burgess family of Ky are all decens of General Christian Burgess or his two brothers which emegrated to Virginia in 1808 and some of their family to Ky later on. My granfather on my Mothers side was John Pearce a cousin of Franklin Pearce President of USA in 1856 at which time I visited him at the White House 28 of March 1856.

Benjamin Harrison was the father of Wm. Henry Harrison who was the father of Thomas Harrison who was the father of Benjamin Harrison who was the father of Lut. Rusill Harrison who married cousin Mary Saunders Cousin Alvins daughter. If you wish the histry of Quantrile I can give it to you in the future. His name was Henry Vollaney Burgess of Scott Co. Ky son of Calvin Burgess. Have not time to give you the full peticculars of all of them. We are all well. Write soon.

I. F. Burgess

Note: Although this account is a mishmash of fact, fantasy, and misinformation, I include it here for completeness, with the original spellings. The story about Quantrell/Quantrill is also wrong, having been investigated by the Union Army during the Civil War; and Henry Volney Burgess, although he existed, was not related to the Scott Co. Burgesses. Quantrell's band did include a relative, however, in the person of William McCown Burgess, who appears later in this book.

How a Hobby Has Been Made to Pay

"Yes, music has been my hobby all my life. I hummed tunes constantly as a boy, and my most cherished ambition has been to create, or rather to record, melodies that will reach to the very hearts of the millions....In all my compositions since that day, the melody and the bass—in fact the fundaments upon which my melodies have been fashioned, first have been fingered out on the guitar. I don't claim to be a musical technician...but I do feel and love melody. I have caught inspiration for the creation of melodies from humblest sources, and I have had the assistance of musical arrangers and experts to place in musical form all my compositions. I have made my hobby a commercial success, which to some extent has added to the great pleasure of helping make the world happy in song and music. I have never been disappointed in love. My compositions have come from the heart. They are part of me. I have never submitted a song for mechanical reproduction that has not been accepted."—Capt. (Frank) Frayser Hinton, *Tri-State Musical Journal*, Memphis, TN, 1 Apr. 1929.

Among his better-known songs were: "Clovita," "I'd Live All My Life Just for You," "Vida Española," "Napoli" (the theme song of a Paramount picture), "Have You the Time," and "Havana."

[William (I)[1], Edward (I)[2], William (II)[3], Henry (I)[4], George Washington (II)[5]]

WILLIAM THOMAS BURGESS
(1837-1930)

OF NICHOLAS COUNTY, KENTUCKY

6c. **(William) Thomas (I)** *[son of George Washington (II)].* Born 12 Sept. 1837 in Fleming Co., KY. Married Lucy W. Hawkins on 7 May 1863 in Nicholas Co. (she was born 1844 in Nicholas Co., daughter of Valentine and Dulcena Hawkins, and died of consumption on 27 Dec. 1877 in Nicholas Co., KY); married secondly Bertha Hawkins (her sister?). Listed in the 1860 census for Fleming Co., KY living with his father, and in the 1870-1920 censuses for Nicholas Co., KY. Tom Burgess was a farmer near Moorefield, KY. He died there on 5 Apr. 1930, aged 92 years, and is buried in the Mt. Zion Cemetery with his first wife and some of their children. His old house burned in 1985.

The Children of Tom Burgess:

7a. **Alice Lee.** Born 13 June 1864 in Nicholas Co., KY. Married Monroe Freeland Vice (he was born 24 Nov. 1861 in KY, son of Menaldo Botts Vice and Solrellda Williams, remarried Eva Blanche Capps after Alice's death, and died Sept. 15, 1922, buried with his wife Eva in the Mt. Zion Cemetery). Alice Vice died childless of tuberculosis on 20 July 1894 in Nicholas Co., KY, and is buried with her Burgess relatives in Mt. Zion Cemetery.

7b. **(William) Oscar.** Born 1866 in Nicholas Co., KY. See below for full entry.

7c. **(Oliver) Cosby.** Born 26 July 1868 in Nicholas Co., KY. See below for full entry.

7d. **Avory V(ice?).** Born 27 Aug. 1870 in Nicholas Co., KY. Said to have served in the Philippines during the Spanish-American War. Listed with his father in the 1900 census. He later moved to Macon, GA where he worked as a mail carrier. Avory Burgess was injured in a car accident on 26 Aug. 1931 at Macon, and died there unmarried of his injuries on 21 Sept. 1931. He was buried in the Mt. Zion Cemetery near Moorefield, KY.

7e. **Silas Frank.** Born Sept. 1873 in Nicholas Co., KY. See below for full entry.

7f. **Katherine Myrtle "Kitty."** Born Feb. 1875 in Nicholas Co., KY. Listed in the 1900 census for Nicholas Co. Married Thomas Jefferson Vice about 1894 (he was born 6 Jan. 1868, and died 16 Oct. 1956), and had children:

Chessie Owings VICE. Born 19 Dec. 1895 in Nicholas Co., KY, married Sarah Jane Kingsolver on 22 Mar. 1915 (she was born on 4 Feb. 1899 in Bath Co., KY, daughter of James Kingsolver and Fannie Sanders, and died 12 Aug. 1986 in Fleming Co., KY), and had children; *Carl Bascom* (born 7 Jan. 1917 in Nicholas Co., KY, married Edith Mae Pergrem on 29 Oct. 1937 in Mason Co., KY [she was born 9 May 1919 in Madison Co., KY, daughter of Henry Stone Pergrem and Mary Massie Davis], and died on 2 Feb. 1991 at Mayslick, KY, buried Mayslick Cemetery, having had children: Wanda Ruth [born 29 Aug. 1941, married Kenny Hickerson on 29 Mar. 1960, and secondly John Morgan on 16 May 1981]; Wayne Bascom [born 4 Sept. 1945, married Alberta Sharon O'Brien on 24 May 1969]; Sandra Gayle [born 9 Oct. 1948, married Charles Lacey Kackler on 4 July 1965]); *Frank Congleton* (born 2 Sept. 1918 in Nicholas Co., KY, married Sylvia Edith Grigson on 9 Feb. 1941 at Flemingsburg, KY [she was born 16 Apr. 1922 in Mason Co., KY, daughter of Richard Harold Grigson and Della Mae Kiskadon], and had children: Ronald Franklin [born 6 June 1942, died 21 Jan. 1960]; Janet Delleen [born 20 May 1947, married Thomas Lloyd MacDonald on 10 July 1965]; Steven Douglas [born 8 Nov. 1948, married Lois Ann Hord on 11 Nov. 1967]; Frankie Garland [twin; born 20 June 1953, married Karlyn Roberts Coatney on 31 Dec. 1972]; Frances Jacqueline [twin; born 20 June 1953, married Len Irwin on 4 Dec. 1976, and secondly Terrall Fererson on 1 Aug. 1986]); *Merrell Martin* (born 11 Apr. 1921 in Nicholas Co., KY, married Lorene Watson on 19 Jan. 1939 in Mason Co., KY [she was born 31 July 1920 at Sardis, KY, daughter of Orville Lee Watson and Betty Turner Frodge], and had children: Allen Owens [born 22 Aug. 1940, married Donna Douglas Leek on 12 Sept. 1959, and secondly Helen Faith Walker on 19 Mar. 1983]; Betty Jane [born 1 Oct. 1942, married Gerald Eugene Orme on 29 June 1962]; Patricia Lee [born 5 Sept. 1952, married David H. Fitzwater on 30 Aug. 1975, and secondly Gary W. DeVaughn on 25 Nov. 1983]; Anita Paige [born 21 Jan. 1957, married Darrell Wayne Ross on 21 May 1977]); *Emery Clay* (twin; born 18 July 1923 in Nicholas Co., KY, married Alice Dryden on 13 June 1946 in Mason Co., KY [she was born 15 Oct. 1927 in Mason Co., daughter of D. Lee Dryden and Emily LeBlond Lindsley], and had children: Richard Lee [born 8 Aug. 1947, married Dinah Sue Black on 20 Dec. __]; Sara Alice [born 31 Aug. 1949, married David C. Coates on 16 May 1971]; John Mark [born 30 July 1952, married Rebecca Ann Lee on 30 June 1979]); *Emma Catherine* (twin; born 18 July 1923 in Nicholas Co., KY, married Torrence Grover "June" Fritz Jr. on 9 Feb. 1944 at Lexington, KY [he was born 23 Apr. 1922 in Mason Co., KY, son of Torrence Grover Fritz and Katherine Mae Ryan, and died 1 Nov. 1961 at Washington, KY, buried Washington Catholic Cemetery, Mason Co., KY], and had children: Connie Ann [born 7 Dec. 1944, married William Thomas Carpenter on 29 Apr. 1967]; Timothy Ryan [born 23 July 1949, married Martha Lou Rawlings on 6 July 1973]; Judy Lynn [born 28 Oct. 1951, married William Scott Thompson II on 17 Apr. 1981]; Peggy Sue [born 28 July 1954, married David Allan Bowery on 17 Aug. 1985]; Randall Vice [born 31 Aug. 1959, married Jowana Lea Back on 14 Dec. 1981]; *Emma Catherine* died on 23 Oct. 1991 at Lexington, KY, buried Elizaville Cemetery, Fleming Co., KY). ***Chessie* VICE** died on 22 Apr. 1976 at Carlisle, KY, and is buried with his wife in the Elizaville Cemetery, Fleming Co., KY.

***(Thelma) Tivis* VICE.** Born 25 July 1900 in Nicholas Co., KY, married Eli W. Crockett (he was born 24 Feb. 1890, and died 28 Mar. 1982 at Lexington, KY), and had children: *Oliver Holmes* (born 2 June 1918 in Nicholas Co., KY, married Effie McFarland, and died on 24 Nov. 1973 in Fayette Co., buried in the Machpelah Cemetery, Mount Sterling, KY). ***Tivis* CROCKETT** died on 3 Dec. 1966 at Carlisle, KY, and is buried with her husband in the Carlisle Cemetery.

***Henry Clarence* VICE.** Born 17 Oct. 1905 in Nicholas Co., KY, married Gertrude Ellen Shrout on 16 Feb. 1926 at Mount Olivet, Robertson Co., KY (div.), married secondly Viola McDonald (she was born 11 Apr. 1905, and died 19 July 1990 at Cincinnati). ***Henry* VICE** died on 18 Feb. 1989 at Cincinnati, OH.

Kitty VICE died on 16 Apr. 1936 in Nicholas Co., and is buried with her husband in the Carlisle Cemetery. Much of the information on this family was supplied courtesy of John A. Vice, Ewing, KY, with additional material by Betty J. Orme.

7g. **Inez Mary "Ina."** Born May 1877 in Nicholas Co., KY. Ina Burgess was engaged to Oliver Clay, but fell out of a cherry tree early in Nov. 1900, breaking her back; she was hastily married to Clay on 6 Nov., and died there on 14 Nov. 1900. She is buried with her family in Mt. Zion Cemetery.

TWO ARE SHOT DURING FIGHT

"Two persons, one of them an innocent bystander, were shot early last night following an argument in front of 750 North Limestone Street. Les Burgess, 38, of Valley View, is in a serious condition in St. Joseph's Hospital, suffering from a gunshot wound in the left thigh. He lost considerable blood from the wound.

"Mrs. Eva Tipton, 21, had just emerged from a grocery store and was walking down the street when the shooting started, according to a report made to police. She was struck in the face and body by pellets from the shotgun. She was treated at St. Joseph's Hospital.

"Willie Rogers, 26, was arrested a short distance from the scene by patrolmen Marshall Jelley and Dillard Ross, on two charges of malicious shooting and wounding, and a charge of operating an automobile while intoxicated. Police said he fled the scene after the shooting, and was arrested on York Street. An additional charge of malicious shooting without wounding was placed against Rogers.

"Police said that they had had complaints all yesterday afternoon of someone shooting up the north end of town, and that they had been seeking Rogers in connection with the report."—*Lexington Herald*, 18 Oct. 1936.

OSCAR BURGESS OF FAYETTE CO., KENTUCKY

[William Thomas (I)[6]]

7b. **(William) Oscar** *[son of William Thomas (I)].* Born 1866 in Nicholas Co., KY. Married Hattie B. Brown on 20 Nov. 1895 in Bath Co., KY (she remarried Bennie Hagen on 5 May 1937). Listed in the 1920 census for Fayette Co., KY. Oscar Burgess was a real estate agent and carpenter at Lexington, KY from 1911 until his death on 7 Nov. 1926. Buried with his son in the Lexington Cemetery.

8a. **Lester T(homas?).** Born about 1902 in Nicholas Co., KY. Listed in the 1920 census living with his parents. Les Burgess was a laborer in Lexington, KY. He was accosted and shot at Lexington on 17 Oct. 1936, and died there unmarried of his wounds on 20 Oct. 1936. Buried in the Lexington Cemetery with his father.

WOUND IS FATAL TO LES BURGESS

"Les Burgess, 34, of Valley View, Ky., who was shot in the thigh Saturday night, as the aftermath of a quarrel, died in St. Joseph's Hospital yesterday afternoon at 5:50 o'clock. He was shot by a charge from a double-barrel shotgun.

"Willie Rogers, 26, was arrested on a charge of malicious shooting and wounding following the affray. The charge was changed to murder following Burgess' death. Rogers is being held in the Fayette County jail.

"Burgess was a son of Mrs. Hattie Burgess of Lexington, and the late W. O. Burgess, and was born in Nicholas County. Besides his mother, he is survived by six uncles: Omer and James Brown of Lexington, Jess and Kidwell Brown of Dayton, Ohio, Silas Burgess of Moorefield, and Vosby Burgess [sic] of Oklahoma, and his grandmother, Mrs. Fredonia Brown of Lexington. The body was removed to Kerr Brothers Funeral Home."—*Lexington Herald*, 21 Oct. 1936.

COSBY BURGESS OF LINCOLN CO., OKLAHOMA

[William Thomas (I)[6]]

7c. **(Oliver) Cosby** *[son of William Thomas (I)].* Born 26 July 1868 (or 1866) in Nicholas Co., KY. Married Etta Mae Vice on 7 Dec. 1892 in Bath Co., KY (she was born about 1868 in KY, daughter of George Allan and Mary Elizabeth Vice, and sister of Adda Vice [who married his brother, Silas Burgess]). Listed in the 1910 census for Davenport, Lincoln Co., OK, but had moved to Chandler, Lincoln Co., OK by 1914, and is listed there in the 1920 census. Cosby Burgess moved to Oklahoma about 1905, serving as Undersheriff of Lincoln Co. for twenty years. He was living at Chandler when his house burned down. He died of his injuries on 16 Sept. 1945 at Oklahoma City, OK.

8a. **Allen Thomas.** Born 14 Oct. 1893 in Nicholas Co., KY. Married Beatrix Jones (she was born 1897, and died 1952). Listed in the 1918 draft list of Lincoln Co., and served in World War I as a wagoner in the 29th Engineers. Listed in the 1920 census living with his father. Allen T. Burgess was an engineer for the Buffalo Northwest Railroad, and also served as County Clerk and Court Clerk of Murray Co., OK. He had a stepson who was sometimes called "Bobby Burgess." He died 23 Oct. 1934 at Sulphur, OK, but is buried with his wife at Oak Park Cemetery, Chandler, OK.

9a. **Jo Ann (I).** Born about 1923 at Chandler, OK. Married ___ Gage; married secondly Charles W. Scruggs (or Scroggs).

9b. **(Mary) Josephine.** Born 11 Aug. 1925 at Chandler, OK; died there on 14 Aug. 1925, and is buried with her parents.

8b. **(Raymond) Ward.** Born 28 Aug. 1896 in Nicholas Co., KY. Married Elizabeth Rork (who lives at Wetumpka, AL). Served in World War I as a Corporal in the 318th Butchery Co., QMC Corps. Ward Burgess owned a cafe at Chandler, OK. He died on 1 Feb. 1949 at Oklahoma City, OK, and is buried in the Oak Park Cemetery.

9a. **Bettye June.** Born 4 May 1931 at Hatfield, AR. Married Bob Slote, and had children: *Glenda Gail* (married ___ Stevens, and lived at Stamford, CT). Bettye Slote died of injuries suffered in an automobile accident on 30 Dec. 1978 at Redding, CA.

9b. **Allen Kent.** Born 9 Jan. 1936 at Chandler, OK. Married Lynn Fraser; married secondly Roslynn Russell on 20 May 1967. A Chief Master Sergeant in the U.S. Army, Allen K. Burgess currently lives at Wetumpka, AL.

10a. **Kevin Dwayne.** Born 21 May 1960 at Ft. Worth, TX.

10b. **Kelly Ann Elizabeth.** Born 27 Nov. 1961 at Ft. Worth, TX. Married Dean MacFarland, and lives in Alaska.

10c. **Kristy June Kathleen.** Born 27 May 1969 at Camp Springs, MD.

10d. **Marcy Ruth** (twin). Born 13 Dec. 1972 at Montgomery, AL.

10e. **Mitzie Gail** (twin). Born 13 Dec. 1972 at Montgomery, AL.

8c. **(Oren) Clair.** Born 22 Aug. 1908 at Davenport, OK. Married (Minnie) Othola ___ in 1934. Clair Burgess owned a coffee shop in a bus station at Tulsa, OK. He died there in Oct. 1984.

9a. **Glenda Margaret.** Born 12 Oct. 1945 at Oklahoma City, OK.

SILAS BURGESS OF NICHOLAS CO., KENTUCKY

[William Thomas (I)[6]]

7e. **Silas Frank** *[son of William Thomas (I)].* Born Sept. 1873 in Nicholas Co., KY. Married Ellen Nora Spencer on 22 Dec. 1892 in Fleming Co., KY (she died about 1893); married secondly Adda Raymond "Addie" Vice on 25 Nov. 1898 in Fayette Co., KY (she was born Mar. 1873, daughter of George Allan and Mary Elizabeth Vice, and sister of Etta Mae Vice [who married Silas's brother, Oliver Cosby Burgess], and died 19 Dec. 1953). Listed in the 1900 census for Bath Co., KY, with his father in 1910, and in 1920 census for Nicholas Co., KY. Silas Burgess ran the first postal route out of Moorefield, KY. He died on 17 June 1954 in Nicholas Co., KY, and is buried with his second wife in the Carlisle Cemetery.

8a. **William Fayne.** He was originally named Waverly Fayne Oscar, after a character in the novel *Waverly*, by Sir Walter Scott (1814). Born 9 July (or Sept.) 1899 in Nicholas Co., KY. Married Margaret Catherine "Maggie" Clark on 24 Nov. 1921 in Nicholas Co., KY (she was born 1 Apr. 1903). Listed in the 1917 draft register of Nicholas Co., KY. Fayne Burgess was a bus driver for Greyhound Bus Lines at Lexington, KY. He moved to Oklahoma in 1954, and died on 31 Mar. 1960 at Tulsa, OK, being buried on the land of his cousin, Clair Burgess.

9a. **(Mary) Loise.** Born 12 Nov. 1924 in Bath Co., KY. Married Murray Hardenbergh, and had four children; married secondly James Calvert Grugin. Loise Grugin currently lives at Lexington, KY.

FOUR BURGESS BROTHERS

(from left) *John Pearce BURGESS* (1851-1935) + *Henry Clay BURGESS* (1840-1907)
William Thomas BURGESS (1837-1930) + *Isaac Franklin BURGESS* (1833-1912)
(see pages 157, 147, 153, 149, respectively)

[William (I)^1, Edward (I)^2, William (II)^3, Henry (I)^4, George Washington (II)^5]

JOHN PEARCE BURGESS
(1851-1935)

OF FLEMING COUNTY, KENTUCKY

6j. **John Pearce** *[son of George Washington (II)].* Born 15 Nov. 1851 in Fleming Co., KY. Married Nannie D. Moran on 23 Dec. 1890 in Fleming Co. (div.; she was born 12 July 1871, daughter of James K. and Lucy Moran, remarried Joe K. Gilvin on 21 Oct. 1922 in Fleming Co., and died 7 Nov. 1933 in Nicholas Co., KY). Listed in the 1880 census with his father, and in the 1900 and 1920 censuses for Fleming Co., KY. John P. Burgess was a farmer in Fleming Co. He died on 25 July 1935 at Paris, Bourbon Co., KY, the last of his brothers and sisters to die, and is buried in the Mt. Zion Cemetery, Moorefield, KY.

The Children of John Burgess:

7a. **Serncy Clay.** Born 28 Sept. 1891 in Fleming Co., KY. See below for full entry.
7b. **David Wilson.** Born 8 Mar. 1893 in Fleming Co., KY. See below for full entry.
7c. **Lida Belle.** Born 18 May 1895 in Fleming Co., KY; died there on 12 Aug. 1896, and is buried in the Flemingsburg Cemetery.
7d. **Ethel Angeline.** Born 12 Jan. 1897 in Fleming Co., KY. Married Henry Leonard Faul in 1915 in Fleming Co. (he was born 31 Jan. 1871, and died 10 Dec. 1935), and had children: *Mildred* (born 31 July 1916, married Harold C. Graham [he was born 26 Oct. 1901, and died July 1987], and died Jan. 1983 at Franklin, OH, having had children: Alice Henrietta [born 7 May 1933, and married ___ Mills]); *Virgil Lee* (born 26 Apr. 1920, married Irene Farrel Congor [she died 2 Jan. 1966], and had children: Pauline Messmore [born 28 Sept. 19__]; Linda Carol [ad.; born 6 Jan. 1952]; Judith Lynn [ad.; born 17 Oct. 1954]; he lives at Springboro, OH); *Helen* (born 20 Sept. 1922, married Charles Apgar, , and died on 9 Mar. 1978 at Xenia, OH, having had children: Susan Charlene [born 10 Jan. 1946, died July 1965]; Jacqueline Kay; Dale Lynn); *Wilma* (born 7 July 1926, married William Kenneth Apgar, and lives at Xenia, OH); *Cecil C.* (born 22 Dec. 1932, married Helen Cain [div.], and lived at Lebanon, OH). Ethel Faul died on 6 Oct. 1963 at Lebanon, OH, and is buried in the Lebanon Cemetery.
7e. **Son.** Born 23 Sept. 1898 in Fleming Co., KY; died there young, buried Flemingsburg Cemetery.
7f. **Curtis Moran (I).** Born 18 May 1900 in Fleming Co., KY. See below for full entry.
7g. **Mary Florence.** Born 19 July 1902 in Fleming Co., KY. Married Irvin Estill Saunders on 25 Mar. 1920 in Fleming Co. (he was born 1897, and died 1943), and had children: *Demaree R.* (born 1920, married Gaynel Miller, and had children: Phyllis Jean [born 1948, married Harley Caum, and had children: Beverly Ann {born 1965}; Harley Jr. {born 1970}]; Michele [born 1952, married Karen Sue Leonard, and had children: Nicholas Leonard {born 1975}; Jason Curtis {born 1980}]); *(Earl) Glenn* (born 1922, married Anabel Lee Noble, and had children: Joyce Ann [born 1942, married Darrell Bradley Couch, and had children: Darrell Bradley Jr. {born 1963}; Brian Allen {born 1964}; Juliet Ann {born 1973}]; Robert Donald [born 1944, married Janice Davis, and had children: Delana Lynn {born 1968}]; James Ervin [born 1951]); *Donal Estill* (born 1924, married Helen Agnes Hughes, and had children: Terry Lynn [born 1951, married Owen Edward Meadows, and had children: Shawn Lynn {born and died 1975}; Dawn Rae {born and died 1975}; John Michael {born 1976}; Brandi Michell {born 1978}]). Mary Saunders worked as a nurse at Lebanon, OH. She was also a major contributor to this book, providing photos, documents, on-site visits to Fleming Co., and much precious information gathered from a lifetime of observations. She died on 10 Jan. 1983 at Lebanon, OH, and was buried in the Lebanon Cemetery. She is greatly missed.
7h. **Henry Franklin.** Born 9 Sept. 1904 in Fleming Co., KY. See below for full entry.
7i. **Minnie Armstrong.** Born 19 Oct. 1906 in Fleming Co., KY. Married Glenn Johnson on 28 Feb. 1929 at Cincinnati, OH (he was born 26 Aug. 1902, and died 17 Aug. 1984), and had children: *Alfred Gene*

(born 19 Jan. 1931); *Beulah* (born 10 Aug. 1932, married Martin Schredick, and had children: Deborah Lynn [married ___ McChesney]; *Beulah* lives at Jacksonville, FL); *Wayne* (born 7 Oct. 1933, and had children: Wayne Harding; Frank Floyd; *Wayne* lives at Cincinnati, OH); *Kenneth Lee* (born 30 Nov. 1934, lives at Lebanon, OH); *JoAnn Lucille* (born 13 Jan. 1937, married William Statler, and lives at Middleburg, FL). Minnie Johnson currently lives at Goshen, OH.

7j. **(John) Avery.** Born 5 Oct. 1909 in Fleming Co., KY. Avery Burgess died unmarried on 31 Dec. 1932 in Nicholas Co., KY (the official death record says 1 Jan. 1933), and is buried in the Mt. Zion Cemetery.

7k. **Leslie Hord.** Born 6 Dec. 1910 in Fleming Co., KY. See below for full entry.

SERNCY BURGESS OF BUREAU CO., ILLINOIS

[John Pearce^6]

7a. **Serncy Clay** *[son of John Pearce].* His first name is also spelled Surncey and Serency; he was named for the Serncy family, neighbors of the Burgesses. Born 28 Sept. 1891 in Fleming Co., KY. Married Bessie Lou Rigdon on 3 Apr. 1912 in Fleming Co. (she was born 10 Nov. 1887 in Fleming Co., daughter of George L. Rigdon and Susan Gourn, and died of flu on 16 Feb. 1920 at Princeville, IL); married secondly Grace Shinkle about 1924; married thirdly Lola Belle Mitchell Gilrin on 29 June 1929 in Nicholas Co., KY. Serncy Burgess was a farmer in Kentucky, Illinois, and Ohio. He died on 20 May 1971 at Lebanon, OH, and is buried with his first wife in the Princeville Cemetery.

8a. **William Clayton (I).** Born 7 June 1913 in Fleming Co., KY. Married Almeda Shields on 16 June 1934 in Nicholas Co., KY (she died in 1981 at San Diego, CA); married secondly Ruby Rebecca Ellswick on 1 Dec. 1945. William C. Burgess was a farmer, and an auto worker for fifteen years for the Ford Motor Co. at Sharonville, OH. He died on 13 Apr. 1984 at Lebanon, OH, and is buried in the Lebanon Cemetery.

9a. **William Clayton (II) "Billie."** Born 31 Aug. 1935 in Bourbon Co., KY. Married Juanita ___ about 1958 (div.); married secondly Edith Brown in 1959 (div.); married thirdly Beverly Gay Manning on 30 Aug. 1987 (div.); married fourthly Rhonda ___. Bill Burgess was a Master Sergeant in the Marine Corps, and worked as an investigator for the U.S. Dept. of Labor. He currently lives retired at Lebanon, OH.

10a. **Brenda Sue.** Born 9 Dec. 1959 at Dayton, OH. Married William Lewis, and had children: *Ryan*; *Jessica*. Brenda Lewis lives at Franklin, OH.

10b. **Kimberly Yvonne.** Born 26 May 1960 at Dayton, OH. Married Donald Howard, and had children: *Joe*; *Jimmy*. Kimberly Howard lives at Dayton, OH.

10c. **April Gay.** Born 3 Sept. 1963 at Dayton, OH. Married, and had children: *Timmy*; *Melvin*.

10d. **William Clayton III "W. C."** Born 9 Mar. 1965 at Pittsburgh, PA. W. C. Burgess served in the U.S. Marine Corps.

10e. **Brian Douglas.** Born 18 Feb. 1967 at Pittsburgh, PA. Married Angelia Eileen Hurley on 7 Mar. 1987 (div.; she was born 30 Jan. 1970).

11a. **Amber Nicole**. Born 10 Mar. 1988.

9b. **Roma Gene.** Born 29 Jan. 1938 at Waynesville, OH. Married Richard Goranson, and lives at San Diego, CA.

9c. **Eugene "Gene"** (nmn) (ad.). Born 18 Mar. 1943 at Ironton, OH. Married Shirley Lilly. Gene Burgess is a truck driver for Worthington Steel at Gratis, OH.

10a. **Kenneth Eugene.** Born 28 Oct. 1966 in Clinton Co., OH. Married Bonnie Sue Rigg on 16 Oct. 1986 in Butler Co., OH (she was the daughter of Gerald W. Rigg). Ken Burgess is a truck driver at Mason, OH.

11a. **Kyle Eugene**. Born 21 Feb. 1988 at Middletown, OH.

11b. **Christine Elizabeth**. Born 9 Dec. 1990 in Ohio.

10b. **Carla Jean.** Born 24 Apr. 1968 at Dayton, OH. Married Harold Lee Owsley, and had children: *Sarah Elizabeth* (born 12 Oct. 1992).

10c. **Rebecca Kathryn.** Born 19 Dec. 1974 at Middletown, OH.

10d. **Joseph Allen.** Born 28 July 1977 at Dayton, OH.

9d. **Betty Lou (III).** Born 20 Aug. 1946 at Dayton, OH. Married Steve Benner (div.); married secondly Hezzie Burchette in Nov. 1988. Betty Burchette lives at Blanchester, OH.

9e. **Thomas Allan (I).** Born 26 July 1949 at Dayton, OH. Married Freda Burgemeier (div.; she remarried Gary Powell [div.]). Tom Burgess worked at the Firestone Store, Carlisle, OH. He was killed on 18 July 1974 at Carlisle, OH, and is buried in the Lebanon Cemetery.

10a. **Dawn Annette.** Born 25 May 1966 at Middletown, OH. Married William A. Traylor, and had children: *Gregory Alan* (born about 1986). Dawn Traylor was killed on 14 July 1986 at Waynesville, OH, and is buried in the Miami Cemetery.

10b. **Thomas Allan (II)** (twin). Born Apr. 1968 at Middletown, OH; died there aged three days.

10c. **Rebecca Jean** (twin). Born Apr. 1968 at Middletown, OH; died there aged three days.

10d. **Lenn Michelle.** Born 26 Feb. 1971 at Middletown, OH.

9f. **Sandra Kay (I).** Born 19 Sept. 1950 at Lebanon, OH. Married Carlos Bachtel (div.), and had children: *Shannon Marie* (born 14 Oct. 1970 at Kettering, OH); married secondly Robert Lykins in May 1981 (he was born 13 Oct. 1949, and died in an accident in June 1981), and had children: *(John) Robert "Bobby"* (born 22 Dec. 1981 at Middletown, OH, and was adopted by Michael Faulkner); married thirdly Michael David Faulkner on 30 Nov. 1985 (he was born 15 Feb. 1954 at Dayton, OH, son of Craig and Helen Faulkner), and had children: *Carrye Helen* (born 2 Sept. 1988 at Kettering, OH). Sandra Faulkner is a real estate agent for Henkle and Scheuler Associates at Lebanon, OH. She has contributed greatly to this work.

8b. **Goldena Mae.** Born 22 Apr. 1915 at Princeville, IL. Married Thomas Logan Green in Bourbon Co., KY (he was born 29 Dec. 1912), and had children: *Wayne* (born 4 Sept. 1935, married Flora___, and had children: Monica [born 14 July 1957, married Curtis De Long {he was born 10 Oct. 1955}]); *Ronald* (born 11 Sept. 1939, married Carolyn ___, and had children: Donna Carol [born 17 Apr. 1963]; Jill [born 22 July 1966]; Douglas Allen [born 13 Oct. 1972]); *Thomas Logan Jr.* (born 14 Mar. 1951, lives at Lebanon, OH). Goldena Green has contributed greatly to this book; she lives at Lebanon, OH.

8c. **Inez Luna.** Born 8 Oct. 1918 at Princeville, IL. Married Dan Williams in Bourbon Co., KY, and had children: *Connie* (married ___ Spradlin); *Diane* (married ___ Williams). Inez Williams lives at Lebanon, OH.

8d. **(Morgan) Clay "Clayton."** Born 10 Feb. 1920 at Princeville, IL. Married Mary Louise Polk (div.). Served in the U.S. Army. Clayton Burgess was a car salesman and mechanic at Lebanon, OH before retiring. He died on 9 June 1989 at Winter Haven, FL, buried Miami Valley Memorial Gardens.

9a. **Ladena Faye.** Born 23 Nov. 1953 at Pell City, AL. Married Larry Robinson (div.); married secondly Wayne Rhoden. Ladena Rhoden lives at Port Charlotte, FL.

9b. **Roxena Kaye.** Born 10 Sept. 1954 in Warren Co., OH. Married Lonnie Sharp. Roxena Sharp lives at Springboro, OH.

9c. **Gregory Clayton.** Born 28 Nov. 1956 in Warren Co., OH. Greg Burgess lives and works at Winter Haven, FL.

9d. **Larry Allen.** Born 15 Feb. 1958 in Warren Co., OH. Married Tina Roberts. Larry A. Burgess owns his own catering and food handling service at Winter Haven, FL.

10a. **Angela Elaine.** Born 25 Mar. 1979 in Warren Co., OH.

10b. **Amanda Gail.** Born 2 Aug. 1981 at Dayton, OH.

8e. **Clifford Harlan.** Born 15 Sept. 1925 at Pleasant Plains, OH. Married (Margaret) Marie Dayberry. Clifford Burgess was a pipefitter at Cincinnati, OH. He now lives retired at Florence, KY.

9a. **Linda Marie.** Born 31 May 1947 at Covington, KY. Married Joel K. Brinkman (div.). Linda Brinkman lives at Florence, KY.

9b. **Gary Clifford.** Born 26 Dec. 1948 at Cincinnati, OH. Gary Burgess owns a restaurant at Covington, KY.

9c. **Rhonda Lee.** Born 12 Oct. 1950 at Mariemont, OH. Married Terry Brian Conley (div.). Rhonda Conley lives at Florence, KY.

9d. **Patricia Sue.** Born 19 Dec. 1953 at Mariemont, OH. Married Stephen T. Perry on 28 Apr. 1973 in Kenton Co. (pastor of the First Assembly of God). Patricia Perry lives at Madison, IN.

DAVID W. BURGESS OF BATH CO., KENTUCKY

[John Pearce[6]]

7b. **David Wilson** *[son of John Pearce].* Born 8 Mar. 1893 in Bath Co., KY. Married Mary Vaughn on 30 Jan. 1919 in Fleming Co.; married secondly Lucile Wightman on 26 Jan. 1932 in Fleming Co. (she was born 1 July 1915, and died 5 Aug. 1987 at Bethel, KY, buried Longview Cemetery). Listed in the 1917 draft register and 1920 census for Fleming Co., KY. Dave Burgess was a farmer near Bethel, Bath Co., KY. He died there on 2 Dec. 1972, and is buried in Bethel Cemetery.

8a. **Chessie Howard "Wolf."** Born 25 Oct. 1919 in Fleming Co., KY. Chessie Burgess was a Sergeant in the U.S. Army during World War II, and later farmed on his family's lands. He died unmarried on 21 Jan. 1979 at Dayton, OH, and is buried in the Bethel Cemetery.

8b. **Argie Elwood.** Born 6 Dec. 1923 in Nicholas Co., KY. Married Thelma Vice on 5 Feb. 1951 in Bath Co., KY (she was born 1929). Argie Burgess was a farmer on his family's lands near Bethel, KY. He was killed in a flood on 22 Apr. 1972 in Bath Co., KY, and is buried in the Bethel Cemetery. Thelma Burgess lives at Mount Sterling, KY.

9a. **Janice Fay.** Born 13 Apr. 1952 in Montgomery Co., KY.

9b. **Rita May.** Born 14 Aug. 1953 in Montgomery Co., KY. Married Bobby B. Kerns on 26 Apr. 1976 in Montgomery Co., KY.

9c. **Patricia Ann (III).** Born 10 Apr. 1955 in Montgomery Co., KY.

9d. **Karen Sue.** Born 22 Aug. 1957 in Montgomery Co., KY. Married Andrew C. "Bubby" Shields on 7 Apr. 1973 in Bath Co., KY.

9e. **David James.** Born 29 June 1961 at Hamilton, OH. Married Phyllis Lawson on 17 Apr. 1981 in Menifee Co., KY. Dave Burgess works as a stockman at Trojans, Mount Sterling, KY.

9f. **Sharon Kaye (II).** Born 19 June 1966 in Montgomery Co., KY. Married Insley G. Roland on 22 Sept. 1989 in Montgomery Co., KY.

8c. **George Roberts.** Born 22 Feb. 1934 in Bath Co., KY; died there 14 Nov. 1936, and is buried in Mt. Zion Cemetery.

8d. **Daughter.** Born and died 30 Dec. 1938 in Bath Co., and is buried in Mt. Zion Cemetery.

8e. **Emery Clay.** Born 22 Dec. 1940 (or 1939, according to his marriage record) in Fleming Co., KY. Married Rosa Dean Booth on 30 Oct. 1961 in Montgomery Co., KY (div.; she was born 29 May 1944). Emery Burgess was the last member of the family with the name Burgess to live in Fleming Co., owning a roadside store at Cowan Station; he now operates a pool room at Carlisle, KY.

9a. **Patsy Joe.** Born and died 2 Sept. 1962 in Montgomery Co., KY, and is buried in the Sharpsburg Cemetery.

9b. **Anna Lou.** Born 30 July 1964 at Mount Sterling, KY.

9c. **Doris Jean.** Born 9 Aug. 1965 at Mount Sterling, KY. Married Floyd Humphries on 10 Aug. 1981 in Fleming Co., KY.

9d. **Rosamary** (nmn). Born 2 Oct. 1971 at Carlisle, KY.

8f. **Nora Lee (II).** Born 13 Feb. 1945 in Montgomery Co., KY. Married Roger Helton on 15 Sept. 1960 at Mount Sterling, KY (div.), and had children: *Connie Lee* (born 26 Apr. 1962, married Dana Setters on 20 Oct. 1979, and had children: Wendy Michell [born 20 May 1980]; Andrew Allen [born 30 Jan. 1986], and lives at Mount Sterling, KY); *Lisa Gail* (born 3 Dec. 1963, married Mike Bellamy on 24 June 1983, and had children: Brandon [born 24 June 1986]; Lindsay LeeClay [born 16 Dec. 1991]); *Roger Daren* (born 8 May 1970, married Angie Norris on 19 Sept. 1991); *Shelly Denise* (born 19 Nov. 1973). Nora Helton currently lives at Mount Sterling, KY. She has contributed greatly to this book.

8g. **Clemmie Comly.** Born 13 Nov. 1947 (or 1949, according to his marriage record) at Sharpsburg, Montgomery Co., KY. Married Jennifer Ratliff on 29 Mar. 1974 in Montgomery Co. (she was born 7 Apr. 1956). Clemmie Burgess is a farmer at Bethel, KY.

8h. **Jimmy Edward.** Born 4 Apr. 1951 at Mount Sterling, KY. Married Mary Lou Bowles on 14 Apr. 1970 in Bath Co., KY (she was born 12 Mar. 1950). Jimmy Burgess is a farmer at Bethel, KY.

9a. **Jimmy Joe.** Born 23 Dec. 1972 at Mount Sterling, KY.

9b. **Samuel Edward (II).** Born 28 Dec. 1985 at Mount Sterling, KY.

9c. **Daniel Scott (II).** Born 13 Oct. 1989 at Mount Sterling, KY.

CURTIS M. BURGESS, Sr. OF CLARK CO., KENTUCKY

[John Pearce[6]]

7f. **Curtis Moran (I)** *[son of John Pearce].* Born 18 May 1900 in Fleming Co., KY. Married Bertha Lou Iker about 1923 in Montgomery Co. (she was born 17 Feb. 1898, and died on 3 July 1981). Listed in the 1918 draft register and 1920 census for Fleming Co., KY. Curtis Burgess was a farmer near Winchester, KY. He died on 9 Mar. 1955 in Fayette Co., and is buried in the Winchester Cemetery.

8a. **Roger Curtis.** Born 12 Sept. 1924 in Montgomery Co., KY. Married Dorothy Ellis Craig (she was born 5 Jan. 1927 in Montgomery Co., KY, daughter of Jesse Henry Craig and Sarah Alice Calvert). Roger Burgess served in the U.S. Army during World War II, and later worked for 28 years for the Dept. of the Army, Lexington-Bluegrass Army Depot, Lexington, KY. He currently lives retired near Paris, KY.

9a. **Jo Ann (III).** Born 12 Oct. 1944 at Winchester, KY. Married Sylvester Elton Stevens (he was born 6 July 1942, and died 17 Dec. 1978), and had children: *Angela Joy* (born 30 Mar. 1962 at Winchester, KY); *Joanna Lynne* (born 16 Nov. 1963 at Winchester, KY); Jo Ann married secondly Harold Wayne Hall (he was born 7 Dec. 1940), and had children: *Kevin Douglas* (born 25 June 1967 at Winchester, KY); *Russell Craig* (born 19 Nov. 1968 at Winchester, KY); *Robert Scott* (born 8 Mar. 1971 at Winchester, KY). Jo Ann Hall currently lives at Winchester, KY.

9b. **Diana Sue.** Born 7 May 1946 at Winchester, KY. Married Lester Wayne Combs (he was born 10 Sept. 1944), and had children: *Roger Clarke* (born 24 Oct. 1967 at Winchester, KY); *Leslie Michelle* (born 14 July 1973 at Lexington, KY). Diana Combs currently lives at Winchester, KY.

9c. **Roy Thomas.** Born 21 May 1947 at Winchester, Kentucky. Married Ella Louise Martin (she was born 7 Nov. 1954). Roy T. Burgess served in the U.S. Army during the Vietnam War. He works as a self-employed aluminum siding installer at Leesburg, FL.

10a. **Joseph Thomas (II).** Born 17 Jan. 1979 at Leesburg, FL.

8b. **Gladys Marie (II).** Born 30 Sept. 1926 in Montgomery Co., KY. Married Rev. Colby Ragland Jr., a Southern Baptist minister, on 26 May 1945 at Mount Sterling, KY (he was born 19 July 1926, and died 9 Oct. 1977), and had children: *Patsy Jane* (born 21 Jan. 1946 at Winchester, KY, married Melvin Cletus Conway on 20 Aug. 1976 [he was born 30 Oct. 1938], and lives at Frankfort, KY); *Peggy Jo* (born 25 Dec. 1948 at Lexington, KY, and lives at Lexington, KY); *Betty Sue* (born 17 Oct. 1952 at Winchester, KY, married John Lewis Robinson on 28 Apr. 1973 [he was born 14 Feb. 1945], and had children: Lori L. [born 8 May 1974 at Frankfort, KY]; Kelli Blair [born 30 Mar. 1982]; Betty Robinson lives at Frankfort, KY); *Beverly Kay* (born 14 Aug. 1964 at Versailles, KY). Gladys Ragland lives at Frankfort, KY.

8c. **Oscar Thomas "Bill."** Born 16 Mar. 1929 in Clark Co., KY. Married Ernestine Dixon (she was born 24 May 1927). Bill Burgess is a farmer near Winchester, KY; he and his wife hosted a family reunion of the Burgess family in the summer of 1982.

8d. **Edwin Lee (II).** Born 18 Aug. 1931 in Bath Co., KY. Married Sallie Hisle (she was born 27 May 1933, and died on 19 June 1988). Edwin L. Burgess was a trucker at Winchester, KY. He died on 19 Nov. 1990 at Mount Sterling, KY.

9a. **William Edward (IV).** Born 20 Aug. 1952 at Winchester, KY. Married (Printha) Sue Patrick on 8 June 1973 in Clark Co., KY. Bill Burgess is a laborer and drag racer at Winchester, KY.

10a. **William Russell.** Born 22 July 1975 at Winchester, KY.

9b. **Roger Allen.** Born 15 Jan. 1955 at Winchester, KY. Married Connie R. McGuire on 14 July 1973 in Clark Co. Roger Burgess is a tin metal worker at Lexington; he lives at Winchester, KY.

10a. **Rachel Ann.** Born 22 May 1976 at Winchester, KY.

9c. **Kathy Marie.** Born 3 Dec. 1957 at Winchester, KY. Married Thomas Horn (div.), and had one child.

9d. **Ermadine Sue.** Born 16 Oct. 1959 at Winchester, KY. Married (James) Donald Maupin on 11 Mar. 1978 in Clark Co., KY, and had two children.

9e. **Robert Lee (III).** Born 22 Mar. 1966 at Lexington, KY. Married Kimberly J. Parks on 25 Oct. 1985 in Clark Co., KY.

9f. **(Leslie) Anthony "Tony."** Born 15 Sept. 1967 at Lexington, KY. Married Mary M. Shearer on 30 June 1989 in Clark Co., KY.

8e. **Grover D.** (nmn). Born 28 Aug. 1933 in Nicholas Co., KY. Married Rebecca Sue Henry on 21 June 1960 in Clark Co., KY (div.; she was born 15 Jan. 1940). Grover Burgess is a farm worker at Winchester, KY.

9a. **Tina Carol.** Born 3 Dec. 1960 at Winchester, KY. Married Harold E. Murphy on 8 Dec. 1978 in Clark Co., KY; married secondly Johnny Dale Roseberry (he was born 5 Apr. 1954), and had children: *Jacinda Marie* (born 31 Mar. 1980).

9b. **Deborah Jo.** Born 15 Feb. 1962 at Winchester, KY. Married Michael William Miller on 2 May 1981 in Clark Co., KY (he was born 24 July 1960), and had children: *Michael William Jr.* (born 12 Jan. 1980).

9c. **Johnny Wayne.** Born 29 May 1963 at Winchester, KY.

9d. **Billy Clark.** Born 21 May 1965 at Winchester, KY.

8f. **Curtis Moran (II).** Born 18 Apr. 1938 in Nicholas Co., KY. Married Peggy Jo Lake on 17 Sept. 1960 in Clark Co., KY (div.; she was born 12 June 1944). Curtis Burgess Jr. is a truck driver at Winchester, KY.

9a. **Saundra Lynn.** Born 21 Feb. 1961 at Winchester, KY. Married Terry J. Salyers on 11 June 1976 in Clark Co., KY, and had children: *James Curtis* (born 20 Dec. 1976).

9b. **Rhonda Gayle.** Born 4 Oct. 1965 at Winchester, KY.

HENRY FRANKLIN BURGESS OF WARREN CO., OHIO

[John Pearce[6]]

7h. **Henry Franklin** *[son of John Pearce].* Born 9 Sept. 1904 in Fleming Co., KY. Married as her second husband Alice Clara Sheldt on 4 Aug. 1956 in Montgomery Co., KY (by her first husband she had four daughters). Served in the U.S. Army during World War II. Henry F. Burgess was a maintenance man at the Warren County Fairgrounds, Waynesville, OH. He died on 22 May 1986 at Dayton, OH, and is buried in Royal Oak Memory Garden, Waynesville, OH.

8a. **Henrietta Frances.** Born 10 Oct. 1956 at South Lebanon, OH. Married Scott Price, and had children: *Brian*; *Scott Jr.*; *Jason*; *Adam*. Living at Middletown, OH in 1986.

LESLIE H. BURGESS OF WARREN CO., OHIO

[John Pearce[6]]

7k. **Leslie Hord** *[son of John Pearce].* Born 6 Dec. 1910 in Fleming Co., KY. Married Georgia Gephart on 5 Jan. 1946 (she was born 23 Nov. 1911, and lives with her daughter, Rebecca). Leslie H. Burgess was a farmer and truck driver in Warren Co., OH. He died on 1 Feb. 1992 at Lebanon, OH, and is buried at Milford, OH.

8a. **John Edward (IV).** Born 18 June 1949 at Middletown, OH. Married Jane Nickel. John E. Burgess is a supervisor for SuperValue Stores. He lives at Mason, OH.

9a. **Aaron Leslie.** Born 31 July 1974 at Cincinnati, OH.

9b. **Amanda Jo.** Born 11 Mar. 1978 at Cincinnati, OH.

9c. **Adam Michael (I).** Born 2 Jan. 1981 at Cincinnati, OH.

8b. **Rebecca Jo "Becky."** Born 23 June 1953 at Middletown, OH. Married Stephen Yearout on 27 May 1977 at Morrow, OH (he works as an executive with Coopers and Lybrand), and had children: *Meghan Katherine* (born 11 May 1984 at Cincinnati, OH); *Joshua Burgess* (born 13 Aug. 1986 at Cincinnati, OH). Rebecca Yearout is a homemaker and part-time secretary at Hudson, OH.

[William (I)[1], Edward (I)[2], William (II)[3]]

EDWARD BURGESS, SR.
(1777-1858)

OF SCOTT COUNTY, KENTUCKY

4f. **Edward (V) "Ned"** *[son of William (II)].* Born 24 Nov. 1777 in Stafford Co., VA. Married Sarah Fields on 6 Feb. 1800 in Bourbon Co., KY. She was born Jan. 1781 in Maryland, the daughter of Joseph Fields, a Revolutionary War veteran from Frederick Co., MD, and Nancy Noland, both of whom had died by 1784; and was brought to Kentucky with her brother, Greenberry Fields, by their uncle, Abraham Fields, according to a long statement in Edward Burgess's surviving Bible record; Sarah Burgess died on 27 Nov. 1839 in Scott Co., and is buried with her husband.

Ned Burgess was brought to Kentucky about 1786 by his stepfather, Ralph Hughes, who settled near Paris, Bourbon Co., KY. In 10 Oct. 1797 he acted as legal heir of his father, William Burgess (who had been an executor for Ned's grandfather, Edward Burges), in selling the land that the original Edward had bought for his family in 1731 in King George Co., VA (*Deed Book #8*, p. 145-147); the other principals in the sale were the legal heirs of the senior Edward's other executor, Garner Burges. Hence, Ned Burgess is provably descended from Edward Burges of King George and Stafford Cos., VA. Ned appears on the tax lists of Bourbon Co. in 1799 and 1800, on the tax lists of Scott Co., KY from 1799-1857, and is listed in the census records there from 1810-50.

Ned Burgess settled on Eagle Creek in the eastern section of Scott Co. (the so-called "Turkey Foot District"), and systematically expanded his holdings until he had accumulated a large estate. On a hill overlooking his property he erected a house constructed to his exact specifications (which still survive in a letter owned by William Addison Thomson); this house burned some years after his death. He died on his farm on 26 Mar. 1858, probably the last of his brothers and sisters to die (the date is confirmed from the surviving handwritten instructions sent by his executors to the stone mason to purchase the original headstone for his grave). He was originally buried in a family plot set aside on his estate in the Old Elk-lick Cemetery; but when his lands were sold earlier in this century, the family disentombed all but one of the Burgess relatives buried there, and moved them in 1919 to a large plot in the southern section of the Georgetown Cemetery, Georgetown, KY, where they surround a small, Grecian-style temple emblazoned with the name "Burgess" across the top. Ned's Bible record still survives in his family. His probate record (*Scott Co. Will Book #N*, p. 363-365) mentions his nine children then living.

The Children of Ned Burgess:

5a. **Nancy (III).** Born 5 Jan. 1801 in Scott Co., KY. Married Cyrus Jaco on 9 Jan. 1821 in Scott Co., KY (he was born 26 May 1795, son of Theodore and Sarah Jaco, and died 7 Sept. 1877 in Shelby Co., IN), and had at least the following children:

Theadore JACO. Born 1822 in Scott Co., KY. Married Mary Price on 12 July 1849 in Scott Co. (she was born about 1819 in KY), and died 1907 in Shelby Co., IN, buried in the Mt. Pisgah Cemetery, having had children: *Nancy E.* (born 1856 in Shelby Co., IN); *Cordelia* (born 1858 in Shelby Co., IN). Listed in the 1860-70 censuses for Addison Township, Shelby Co., IN.

William Edward JACO. Born 17 Jan. 1826 in Scott Co., KY, married Mary Ann Newton on 2 June 1849 in Scott Co. (she was born 1832 in KY); married secondly his first cousin, Sarah Maria Drake, on 19 Aug. 1856 in Scott Co. (she was the daughter of Bathsheba Burgess and Henry Bruce Drake), and died on 5 Sept. 1898, buried Mt. Pisgah Cemetery, having had children: *James Edward* (born 4 May 1861 in Scott Co., KY, married his first cousin, Ellen Dora Drake, in Jan. 1890 in Scott Co., KY [she was the daughter of George E. W. Drake and Elvira Gurr], and died on 3 Jan. 1932 in Shelby Co., IN, having at least one child: Ethel Marie [born 21 Oct. 1897 in Shelby Co., IN, married Charles Albert Wood on 2 Feb. 1918 at Louisville, KY {he was born 26 Sept. 1891 at Toronto, ON, Canada, and died 10 Nov. 1925 at Indianapolis, IN}, and had children: (Rachel) Marie {SEE BELOW}]); *George S.* (born 1866, married Mary A. Marietta on 30 Apr. 1890 in Shelby Co., IN).

(Rachel) Marie WOOD (born 10 Aug. 1918 at Montgomery, AL, married secondly Andrew Lomen [he was born 17 Mar. 1914, and died Oct. 1975], and had children: Suzanne Marie "Suzi" [married Bill Ruona {son of Stuart and Rachel Ruona of Mooresville, IN}, and died about 1981, leaving one daughter: Michelle Suzanne {married ___ Ray, and had children: Suzanne Gale <born 23 July 1993>}]; Marie married thirdly Samuel W. DeFrees on 1 May 1976 at Mooresville, IN [he was born 9 June 1909, and died 28 Sept. 1981 at Mooresville, IN], and died 21 July 1984 at Indianapolis, IN, buried Washington Park North Cemetery. Marie DeFrees contributed greatly to this book).

Mariah E. JACO. Her name is also spelled Maria. Born 1833 in Scott Co., KY. Listed with her parents in the 1860 census.

Mary E. JACO. Born 1838 in Shelby Co., IN.

Calvin I. JACO. Born 1840 in Shelby Co., IN.

Nancy JACO is listed in the 1830 census for Scott Co., KY, and in 1840-60 in Addison Township, Shelby Co., IN. The Jacos settled in Shelby Co., IN about 1835. Nancy Jaco died there on 16 Mar. 1874, and is buried with her husband and two adult sons in the Mt. Pisgah Cemetery, just east of Shelbyville, IN.

5b. **(William) Calvin (I).** Born 5 Oct. 1802 in Scott Co., KY. See below for full entry.

5c. **Bathsheba (III).** Her name was also spelled Barsheba or Bashaba. Born 22 Aug. 1804 in Scott Co., KY. Married Henry Bruce Drake about 1829 (he was born 4 Jan. 1810, son of Thomas Drake and Rachel Peak [who was the daughter of John Peak, a Revolutionary War soldier, and Jamima Peak], and died 9 Mar. 1846 in Scott Co., KY), and had children:

James W. DRAKE. Born 1830 in Scott Co., KY, married Josephine Brockman on 10 June 1857 in Scott Co. (she was born 1827 in KY). Listed in the 1860 census for Scott Co., KY.

George Edward William DRAKE. Born 18 Jan. 1832 in Scott Co., KY. Served in the medical corps of the Confederate Army during the Civil War, and was stationed at Tunnel Hill, GA. He married Elvira M. Gurr on 18 Jan. 1866 in Houston Co., GA (she was born 13 Nov. 1840 in Houston Co., daughter of Samuel Gurr and Elizabeth Bishop, and died 17 Sept. 1901 at Sadieville, KY), and had children:

Remus Burgess "R.B." DRAKE (born 3 Feb. 1867, married Mary Lee Marshall on 22 Oct. 1891 [she died 5 Feb. 1901], and had children:

Harriett *DRAKE* (born 22 Aug. 1892, married Edmond C. "Gard" Polk on 17 Jan. 1909 [he was born 6 Sept. 1886, and died 3 Mar. 1962, buried Shirley, IN], and died 16 Aug. 1962, having had children: Marie Carrie [born 17 Aug. 1910 at Shirley, IN, married Bert Elsbury Sewell in 1929 {he was born 2 Apr. 1905, and died 4 June 1969}, and had children: Joseph Edmon {born Nov. 1929 at Shirley, IN, married Phyllis Joanne Stokes in 1950, and had children: Kathey Ann <born Nov. 1954, married Michael E. Riley in 1973, and had children: Joel Allen |born 2 Jan. 1982|; Luke Justin |born 10 Mar. 1983| >; Kris Joseph <born 27 Nov. 1957, married Evelyn Louise Carter in 1982>}]; Anna L. [born 2 Feb. 1912 at Shirley, IN, married Edward McKinley, and had children: Paul Edward {born 30 May 1934 at Shirley, IN, died 12 Aug. 1936}; Eleanor {born 1938 at Shirley, IN, married (Billie) Everett Savage, and had children: Keith; Vickie Lynn; Lessa; Timothy Allen}; Richard Leon {born 10 July 1943 at Shirley, married Roberta Ann Lacey, and had children: Richard Leon Jr. <born 19 Nov. 1965>; Ronald Lee <born 11 Aug. 1973>}]; Charles [born 10 Apr. 1917, married Velma "Peggy" Jones {she was born 11 Feb. 1916, and died 15 Mar. 1968}, and had children: Robert {born 1946}; Eugene {born 1948}]).

Bessie Lee *DRAKE* (born 21 May 1894 in Scott Co., married Dewey Southworth about 1917 [div.], and secondly William McKinley Callantine Berry on 6 May 1922 [he was born 19 May 1897 near Logansport, IN, was a tool and die maker and part owner of the Peerless Machine Co., and died 19 July 1936 in an automobile accident, buried I.O.O.F. Cemetery, Marion, IN], and died 17 Sept. 1982, having had children: Pauline E. [born 5 Aug. 1925, married Robert B. Marler on 1 Sept. 1946 {he was born 27 May 1925, served in the U.S. Navy during World War II in the Submarine Service, and has worked as a banker}, and had children: Stephanie Jo {born 15 Apr. 1948 at Marion, IN, married Robert Hamilton Foster on 22 June 1968 <he was born 23 July 1946 at Akron, OH>, and had children: Michille Ann <born 10 Nov. 1970 at Florissant, MO>; Robert <born 17 Oct. 1974 at Wyandotte, MI>}; John Randolph {born 16 Aug. 1950 at Indianapolis, IN, married Rebecca Lynn Williams on 24 June 1978 <she was born 9 Jan. 1952>, and had children: John R. <born 24 Sept. 1981 at Marion, IN>; Jason Todd <born 11 Mar. 1985 at Marion, IN>; Scott Joseph <born 17 Nov. 1986>}]).

Cerena Jane *DRAKE* (born 19 July 1896 in Scott Co., died 1918 at Marion, IN, buried I.O.O.F. Cemetery).

Julia Bell *DRAKE* (twin; born 9 Sept. 1898 in Scott Co., married Charles Sebray Neeley on 22 Oct. 1921 [he was born 1900, and died 23 Oct. 1961 at Marion, IN, buried Grant Memorial Park], and died 15 Feb. 1972 at Marion, IN, having had children: William [born 1923, married

Della Kendall, and secondly Goldie ___, and had children: Erma Jean {married Worley Gordon}; Norleen {married John Ressler}; William married thirdly Louise Riddle, and died 21 Jan. 1986]; Erma D. [born 1924, married Harold Gene Swank in 1945, and had children: Douglas; Gene Allen]; Francis [born 1925, married Margaret ___ in 1943, and had children: Penny L.; Tanya L.; Cindy S.; Dale W.; Judy A.]; Charles [married Phyllis ___, and had children: Jill; Steve; John]; Robert [married Sue Smithson, and had children: Rita; Bobby Sue]).

Laulie L. *DRAKE* (twin; born 9 Sept. 1898 in Scott Co., and died 6 Feb. 1901, buried with her mother).

Remus Burgess DRAKE married secondly Carrie Del Hensley on 8 Dec. 1904 [she was born 8 Apr. 1888, and died 16 May 1984?], and had children: John L. [born Oct. 1905, married ___ Humphrey, and had children: Katherine {born 11 June 1925, married Fred J. Noth, and secondly Jack D. Tardi <born 30 June 1931>}; Albert E. {born 12 June 1927, married Katherine Ashby <born 13 June 1927>, and had children: Alan Sanford <born 30 July 1953, married Hildegard Huettman>; Paul Steven <born 29 July 1956, married Robin Stringer>; Jane <born 16 Dec. 1957, married>; Philip David <born 25 Aug. 1959, married>}]; Clarine [born 16 Nov. 1906, died 23 Oct. 1939, buried Porter]. *Remus Burgess Drake* died on 1 Sept. 1948 at Porter, KY, buried in Porter Cemetery).

E. L. DRAKE (born 14 Oct. 1868, married, and had children: Frances; Sherman [never married]).

Martha S. "Mattie" DRAKE (born 23 Jan. 1869, married Oliver Taylor, and had children: Francis).

Elizabeth DRAKE (born 1 Dec. 1870, married Walter Green, had children: George Washington, and died 29 Oct. 1968, aged 97 years).

Thomas Jefferson DRAKE (born 23 Mar. 1872, married Dora Bell Gorham, and had children: Burgess Gorham "Buddy" [born 6 Oct. 1904, married Mary Ollie Ralston, and had children: Maureen; Louise; Betsy; Barbara; Larry; Donnie]; Ethel Janice [born 16 July 1905, married William Lewis Glass, and died 28 Sept. 1966]; Lutisha "Tisha" [born 18 Apr. 1906, married Murl Counterman on 24 Dec. 1924, and had six children]; Eunice H. [born 24 Feb. 1908, married Theron Meyers, and had children: Harold; Theron; J.; Eunice married secondly Jack Boles, and thirdly Carl Pulliam, and had children: Mariella; Eunice died 4 Apr. 1974]; Altandy "Tandy" [born 25 Dec. 1909, married Idella Turner Drake, and died childless 23 Dec. 1974]; Clarence L. [born 18 Mar. 1912, married Agnes Bowman, and died childless 14 Oct. 1949]; Forest "Chick" [born 10 Dec. 1913, married Diela Butcher, and secondly Marion Cote]; Walter B. [born 1 Jan. 1916, married Wallir Mae Butcher, and had children: Priscilla; Joan "Judy" {married ___ Crussare}, and both died on 5 July 1950]; Valeria Kathelean [born 18 Oct. 1917, married Clarence McGuinn {he died 1975/76}, and had children: David; Richard; Linda <married ___ Ruggle>; Valeria died 23 Jan. 1970]; Lela B. [born 17 June 1920, married Ivan F. Garner {he died 28 Sept. 1957}, and had children: Terry; Tony D.; Carol <married ___ Stines>; Lela married secondly Robert E. Gwinnup {he was born 8 Dec. 1917}]; Harold Thomas [born 24 Sept. 1924, married Charlotte Muller {born 1925, died 17 Mar. 1986}, and had children: Lucinda {married Larry Hosier}; Rebecca {married Jess Farrell}; Harold married secondly Louise ___, and had children: Patty {married ___ Stiety}; Harold died 17 Mar. 1967]).

Ellen Dora DRAKE (born 28 Dec. 1873, married her first cousin, James Edward Jaco, in Jan. 1890, and died 27 Dec. 1931 in Shelby Co., IN, having had at least one child: Ethel Marie [born 21 Oct. 1897 in Shelby Co., married Charles Albert Wood, and had at least one child: {Rachel} Marie DeFrees]).

George Washington DRAKE (twin; born 22 Jan. 1875, married Nan Barnett).

Charty DRAKE (born 22 Jan. 1875, died 15 Feb. 1876, buried Drake Cemetery).

Henry Bruce DRAKE II (born 6 Jan. 1877, married Maud Gorham, and had children: Henry Bruce III; Paul; Garnet [married Vern Lewis on 1 Aug. 1930 at Marion, IN]; Deloris [married Willis Spencer on 9 Sept. 1933]).

Penelope "Neppie" DRAKE (born 28 Aug. 1879 at Lytles Fork, KY, married Clarence Jones on 1 Oct. 1896 in Scott Co., KY [he was born 2 Oct. 1873 in Scott Co., son of John Jones and Ellen Humphrey, and died 27 Sept. 1940 at Marion, IN], had children: Son [born and died 1897]; John L. [born 17 May 1899 in Scott Co., married Helen Nieman, and died 1 Aug. 1979 at Marion, IN]; Orley Richard [born 16 Apr. 1901 in Scott Co., married Cecilia Hall, and died 9 Jan. 1979 at Marion, IN]; Roy Dallas [born 30 Nov. 1903 in Scott Co., married Emma Davis, and died 14 Mar. 1963 at Miami, FL]; Elzora Susan [born 27 Dec. 1905 in Scott Co., married Roy E. Pulley on 1 June 1924, and died 2 Nov. 1986 at Logansport, IN]; William Clarence [born 3 Apr. 1907 at Marion, IN, and died there 20 Mar. 1978]; Iva May [twin; born 27 Jan. 1909 at Marion, IN, married Emmett Chandler on 5 May 1927, and died 24 Oct. 1978 at Marion, IN]; Viva Frances [twin; born 27 Jan. 1909 at Marion, IN, married Arthur L. Walsh on 30 June 1929, and had at least the following children: Loretta L. {born 17 Apr. 1939 at Marion, IN, married Robert Phillips, and lives at Los Angeles,

CA}]; Odella Woodrow [born 22 Nov. 1913 at Marion, IN, died unmarried on 28 Feb. 1986 at Marion, IN]; Floyd Loomis [born 1 Jan. 1918 at Marion, IN, married Marietta Stewart on 10 Oct. 1930 at Marion, IN, and secondly Marjorie Clark on 12 Apr. 1941]. *Penelope JONES* died on 20 Jan. 1942 at Jonesboro, IN).

George E. W. Drake died on 20 Jan. 1880 at Lytles Fork (now Sadieville), Scott Co., KY, when he cut his own throat with a razor, and was buried with his wife in the Drake Cemetery.

Mary Ann DRAKE. Born 1835, married John Tucker on 13 July 1859 in Scott Co. (he was born 1826), and had children: Columbus; Burl; Frances; Eve.

Sarah Maria DRAKE. Born 22 Feb. 1836 in Scott Co., KY, married her first cousin, William Edward Jaco, on 19 Aug. 1856 in Scott Co., and died 2 Dec. 1924 in Shelby Co., IN, leaving children: *James Edward* (he was born 4 May 1861, married his first cousin, Ellen Dora Drake, and died 3 Jan. 1932; see her family for their children).

Susannah Ellen "Susellen" DRAKE. Born 1841, married her first cousin, Benjamin Kenn Burgess, on 7 Feb. 1867 in Scott Co., and died between 1880-1888, leaving one son, *James Edward*, listed under Benjamin Kenn's entry, below.

Bathsheba DRAKE is listed in the 1850 census for Scott Co., KY as head of her family, in 1860 with her son, James, and in the Scott Co. tax lists through 1865. Bathsheba Drake was a farmer in Scott Co., KY. She died there early in 1865 (her inventory, dated 21 Mar. 1865, appears in Scott Co. *Will Book #P*, pages 200-201, 215-216, and 280-281). Information on the Drake family was supplied by Mae Price, Pauline Marler, and Chris Glass.

5d. **Mariah (I).** Her name was also spelled Maria, and is listed on her tomb as Myriah. Born 22 Oct. 1806 in Scott Co., KY. Married George William Bates on 18 Oct. 1827 in Scott Co. (he was born 4 July 1806 at Berkshire, MA, son of William Randall Bates, and was killed by his nephew, Polk Burgess, on 7 Aug. 1866), and had children:

Sarah A. BATES. Born 24 June 1828, died 27 June 1828.

Mary A. BATES. Born 23 Apr. 1829, died 13 Nov. 1830.

William Edward BATES. Born 8 Aug. 1830, married Ann Eliza Reed on 26 June 1860 in Scott Co. (she was born 20 June 1837, and died 15 July 1912, buried Bates-Parker Cemetery). ***William Bates*** was a school teacher, magistrate, Deputy Scott Co. Clerk, and Judge; he died on 3 Jan. 1912, and is buried in the Lancaster Cemetery. His biography appeared in the *Biographical Cyclopedia of the Commonwealth of Kentucky* (Chicago: John M. Gresham Co., 1896, p. 233-234).

Richard Henry BATES. Born 12 May 1832, married Elizabeth F. Fleetwood on 22 Dec. 1857 in Scott Co. (she was born 14 Jan. 1835, and died 30 Mar. 1922 at Greensburg), and had nine children. Richard Bates worked as a stonemason and farmer, served in the Union Army during the Civil War, and died on 11 Sept. 1911 at Greensburg, IN.

George William BATES Jr. Born 26 Apr. 1834, married Estabine Burgess (unrelated) in 1864 in Brown Co., IL, lived at Versailles, IN, and died 7 Aug. 1912.

James Luther BATES. Born 15 Feb. 1836 at Shelbyville, IN, married Elizabeth Perry on 28 Aug. 1855, and died 4 Apr. 1865 in Scott Co.

Joseph M. BATES (twin). Born 2 May 1838 in Scott Co., married Martha Perry, lived at Decatur, IN, and died 13 Feb. 1864.

Horace G. BATES (twin). Born 2 May 1838 in Scott Co., married his first cousin, Sarah Fields Burgess, on 25 Jan. 1866, and died 24 Sept. 1909 in Shelby Co., IN, and is buried there in the Mt. Pisgah Cemetery; see her entry for his children.

Miranda Jane BATES. Born 22 Apr. 1840 in Scott Co., married Zephaniah Fields Jr. on 10 July 1860 (he was born 5 Feb. 1833, and died 12 Feb. 1923), and died 11 Mar. 1929, buried Sadieville Cemetery, having had thirteen children, among them: *John* (nmn) (born 25 Aug. 1870, married Beulah Benton Mulberry on 24 Dec. 1911 at Covington, KY [she was born 27 May 1896, and died 12 Mar. 1922], and died on 22 Sept. 1964 at Lexington, KY, buried Knights of Pythian Cemetery, Sadieville, KY, having had children: Mary Viola [born 2 Aug. 1913, married Roy Austin Marshall]; (Augusta) Mae [born 10 Mar. 1915 in Scott Co., see below]; Lucy Marie [born 11 May 1917, married Julius Janek]; James Woodrow [born 19 Feb. 1919, married Ada Anna Matuwuk, and secondly Caroline Birkenhauer, and died 18 Sept. 1967]; Cecil Ray [born 5 June 1921, was adopted by Jasper Crupper and Sadie Brooks, married Arva Jane McFarland, and died 1 May 1989]).

(Augusta) Mae FIELDS (born 10 Mar. 1915 in Scott Co., married Floyd Scott Price on 16 Mar. 1932 in Scott Co. [he was born 15 Sept. 1907, and died May 1983 at Georgetown, KY], and had children: Gayle Sanford [born 11 Sept. 1933 in Scott Co., died 18 Mar. 1940, buried Beards Cemetery]; (Earl) Wayne [born 15 Mar. 1939 in Scott Co., married Mary Puckett, and had children: Cynthia Dawn {born 17 Jan. 1966 at Cynthiana, KY}; Daryl Wayne {born 8 Aug. 1973 at Cynthiana, KY}]; (Warren) Demoree [born 26 Nov. 1942 in Scott Co., married Evelyn Carol Mullenex, and had chil-

dren: Bryan Matthew {born 8 Feb. 1977 at Lexington, KY}; Nathaniel Dane {born 3 Oct. 1979 at Lexington, KY}]).

John Thomas BATES (twin). Born 23 Feb. 1842, married Julia Ann Rogers on 20 Feb. 1868 in Scott Co. (she died 18 Nov. 1868); married secondly Susan Edith (Fitzgerald) Zeysing (she was born 8 Jan. 1837, and died 7 May 1920). ***John Bates*** died on 11 May 1914, and is buried in the Bates-Parker Cemetery.

Allen Genole BATES (twin). Born 23 Feb. 1842, married Martha "Mattie" ___, and died 3 Nov. 1908 in Decatur Co., IN.

Francis Marion BATES. Born 3 Feb. 1844, married Eliza Jane Patterson in Aug. 1872 (she was born 22 July 1849, and died 1 Oct. 1918), married secondly Emma Romans, and died 29 Nov. 1927, buried in the Bates Cemetery.

Walter Scott BATES. Born 18 Jan. 1846, died 25 Mar. 1848.

Charles Augustus BATES. Born 12 Feb. 1850, married Sarah E. Zeysing on 1 Sept. 1875 in Scott Co. (she died 1902), had eight children, moved to Indiana in 1906, and died 23 June 1930 at Greensburg, IN.

Mariah BATES is listed in the 1850 census for Scott Co., KY, and in 1860 living with Zephaniah Fields Jr. The Bateses farmed and owned a tavern near the Turkey Foot area of Scott Co. Mariah Bates died on 4 Apr. 1868 in Scott Co.; she and her husband are buried in the Old Elklick Cemetery. Her great-granddaughter, **Mae FIELDS PRICE**, is a major contributor to this book, providing photographs, documents, research, and her own memories; she currently lives at Georgetown, KY.

5e. **Joseph Fields.** Born 5 Feb. 1809 in Scott Co., KY. See below for full entry.

5f. **Margaret Ann (I).** Born 28 May 1811 in Scott Co., KY. Married Jesse Dungan about 1830 (he was the son of Thomas Dungan, and died between 1846-50), and had children: *Sarah Ann* (born 1831, married Joshua Fields); *Marietta* (born 22 July 1833, married her second cousin, George Washington Burgess [V], in 1850, and died 2 Oct. 1920 in Carroll Co., MO); *Nancy Elizabeth* (born 1835); *Maria(h) Frances* (born 1837, married her cousin, William Faulconer, son of Edmund Faulconer and Elizabeth Hedger, and grandson of Reuben Faulconer); *Leona F.* (born 1846). After her husband's death, Joseph Burgess provided for his sister's family, acting as his nieces' legal guardian until they came of age (he gave Marietta permission to marry in 1850). Listed with her father in the 1850 census, but moved to Harrison Co. in 1855, when Thomas Dungan's estate was divided, her two older daughters deeding their interest in that estate to Margaret on 7 Mar. 1855 in Harrison Co. (*Deed Book #25*, p. 281). Listed in the 1860-80 censuses for Cason's (6th) District, Harrison Co., KY, and in the tax records there as head of the family through 1881. She presumably died about 1881 in Harrison Co., KY, when she disappeared from the tax lists.

5g. **James Henry.** Born 8 Jan. 1814 in Scott Co., KY; died there on 8 June 1826, and is buried in the Georgetown Cemetery.

5h. **Edward (IX)** (nmn). Born 1 July 1816 in Scott Co., KY. See below for full entry.

5i. **Greenberry Fields.** Born 6 July 1819 in Scott Co., KY. See below for full entry.

5j. **Marietta "Martha."** Born 20 July 1824 in Scott Co., KY. Married as his second wife Thomas Creath White on 29 Apr. 1845 in Scott Co. (he was born 1817, son of Daniel W. White and Alice Threlkeld, and died 20 Jan. 1892; by his first wife he had children: *James K.* [born 1836, died childless]), and had children:

Mary Thomas WHITE. Born 1846.

Llewellyn Williams WHITE. Born 1848, married Margaret Mae "Maggie" Bane on 29 Mar. 1873 (she was born 25 Jan. 1856 in VA, and died 15 June 1914), and had children: *Alice Beatrice* (born 23 Jan. 1874, and died unmarried on 21 Jan. 1902); *Nanetta "Nettie"* (born 30 Aug. 1875, married John Leach Risk on 28 Apr. 1908 [he was born 14 Jan. 1875, and died 20 Feb. 1964], and had children: Louella [born 25 July 1909, married Henry Clelland Sanders on 17 Sept. 1936 in Fayette Co., KY {he was born 25 Sept. 1904 in Mercer Co., KY, and died 13 Jan. 1982 in Scott Co., buried Georgetown Cemetery}, and had children: John Clelland {born 28 Aug. 1941 in Mercer Co., married Nancy Ellen Farley on 29 Apr. 1961, and had children: Nancy Cumberland <born 7 Oct. 1962>; John Christopher <born 14 Dec. 1963>; Kelli Ann <born 24 Feb. 1966>}]; *Nanetta* died on 1 May 1967, aged 91 years, buried Georgetown Cemetery); *Birdie Mae* (born 23 Oct. 1877, married Daniel Dixon in 1897, and died childless on 6 Aug. 1974, aged 96 years, buried Turkey Foot Cemetery); *Thomas Cambridge* (born 11 Dec. 1879, and died unmarried on 2 Jan. 1969, buried White Family Cemetery); *Sarah Burgess "Sallie"* (born 21 Jan. 1882, married Walter Scott Fields on 15 June 1899 in Scott Co., and died 27 Jan. 1970, buried Turkey Foot Cemetery, having had children: Carl Wayne [born 8 June 1900, died 17 June 1901]). ***Llewellyn WHITE*** died on 17 Dec. 1921, and is buried with his parents.

Daniel Edward WHITE. Born 24 July 1850, married Angeline "Anna" Barnhill on 22 Dec. 1877, and died childless on 9 Dec. 1917, buried in the Vance Cemetery.

Joseph Calvin WHITE. Born 1853 (or 1855), married Carrie Sherritt Moreland, and died 1926, buried in the White Family Cemetery, having had children: *Edna Lyle* (born 20 Apr. 1900, married

William Walter Zwick, and had children: William Walter Jr.; Richard Calvin; Margaret Caroline "Peggy" [born Oct. 1926, married Frank Hays, and secondly Gentry Underwood]; *Edna* married secondly Walter Medley, thirdly ___ Whitesell, and fourthly George Herring, and died on 11 May 1979); *Oscar Calvin* (born 2 Feb. 1902, married Ethel Aubert, and had children: Paul [born 1946]; Oscar Calvin Jr. [born 1948, and died young]; Edna Earl [born 1950, died 1962]; Nancy Franklin [born 1952]).

Agatha Bathsheba "Gatha" WHITE. Born 20 Apr. 1858, married John S. Lay on 14 Sept. 1889, and secondly Calvin Parker, and died childless on 12 Mar. 1942, buried White Family Cemetery.

Nancy Maria "Nannie" WHITE. Born 11 Feb. 1866, and died unmarried on 17 Mar. 1889, buried White Family Cemetery.

Lula Green WHITE. Born 16 July 1869, and died 8 Jan. 1879, buried White Family Cemetery.

The WHITES are listed in the 1850-70 censuses for Scott Co., KY. Martha White died in 1890, and is buried in the White Family Cemetery. A descendant, Mrs. Henry Sanders, lives at Louisville, KY.

THE BIOGRAPHY OF WILLIAM EDWARD BATES

"William Edward Bates of Georgetown, Judge of the Scott County Court, son of George W. and Maria (Burgess) Bates, was born in Scott County, Kentucky, August 8, 1830. George W. Bates (father) was a native of Massachusetts, who came to Kentucky in 1826, locating in Scott County. In 1834 he removed to Indiana, and after spending two years in that state, he returned to his former home in Scott County, where he continued to reside until his death in 1886 [sic]. He was a fuller by trade, but after coming to Kentucky he devoted his attention to farming. He was a major of militia under the command of General John T. Pratt. He was a highly respected citizen and a worthy and upright member of the Christian Church....

"Maria Burgess Bates (mother) was born in Scott County, and was a resident of her native county until her death, April 8, 1888 [sic]. She was a most excellent woman whose chief characteristic was her devotion to her religion and to the Christian Church of which she was a member. Edward Burgess (grandfather) was born in Culpeper County, Virginia, in 1783 [sic], and was one of the first settlers of Scott County, where he was a farmer, and died in 1857. The Burgess family was descended from the Huguenots, who were driven out of France by Louis XIV in 1685, many of whom settled in Virginia and the Carolinas, and their descendants are everywhere highly honored and respected; being enterprising and intelligent, they are found in legitimate business pursuits and in the professions in almost every community. The ministers especially who belong to this sturdy race have wide influence in the South and West.

"William Edward Bates lived on his father's farm until he was twenty-four years of age. He was educated in the common schools of his day, and by close application he became well advanced in many of the English branches. He was married in 1860 to Annie E. Reed, daughter of James Reed of Scott County, after which event he returned to the farm, where he remained until 1890, during a part of which time—about nine years—he served as justice of the peace. In 1890 he was elected judge of the Scott County Court, and in 1894 was re-elected to that office, in both of which elections he was the candidate of the Democratic Party.... Judge Bates is the eldest of twelve children—eleven sons and one daughter—of George W. Bates, eight are now living. During the Civil strife the family was divided; two of the sons were in the Federal and two in the Confederate army, and latter two serving under General John Morgan. Two other brothers served for a short time only, one on each side of the conflict." *George and Mariah Bates are pictured below.*

[William (I)[1], Edward (I)[2], William (II)[3], Edward (V)[4]]

WILLIAM CALVIN BURGESS
(1802-1859)

OF SCOTT COUNTY, KENTUCKY

5b. **(William) Calvin (I)** *[son of Edward (V)].* Born 5 Oct. 1802 in Scott Co., KY. Listed in the tax records of Scott Co. from 1825-58, and in the 1830-50 censuses for Scott Co. Calvin Burgess owned a large farm near the convergence of the various branches of Eagle Creek ("The Turkey Foot") in the northeastern section of Scott Co.; on a hill overlooking his farm he built a log cabin, with various outbuildings and slave cabins and slave-built stone fences. He grew tobacco and raised horses, which he raced and showed at the Cynthiana Fairgrounds (in which he owned a share). He won nine silver cups at Cynthiana, some of which remain in the family to this day.

Calvin Burgess never married, but apparently had a son out of wedlock by his housekeeper, Nancy A. Tucker, and adopted him as his sole heir. Nancy was born 3 Sept. 1821, daughter of Mary Tucker, married Harrison A. Lynn on 6 Dec. 1849 in Scott Co., and died on 22 Nov. 1886 in Scott Co.; she is listed next door to Calvin in the 1850 census. Calvin died on his farm on 21 May 1859, and is buried, together with Nancy Lynn, his son, his son's wife, and several grandchildren, in a small family cemetery at the top of the highest hill on his estate, across the valley from his home. In his will (*Scott Co. Will Book #N*, p. 219-220, dated 18 Aug. 1858, probated May Court 1859), he gave his farm in Owen Co. to Antony G. T. Tucker (possibly Nancy's brother), with other bequests to John C. Hamilton and Mary Tucker (Nancy's mother), but left "unto James K. Polk Burgess my son all the remainder of my estate both real and personal."

The Children of William Calvin Burgess:

6a. **(James Knox) Polk (I).** Born 28 Mar. 1844 in Scott Co., KY. See below for full entry.

J. K. Polk Burgess (1844-1917)

[William (I)[1], Edward (I)[2], William (II)[3], Edward (V)[4], William Calvin (I)[5]]

POLK BURGESS
(1844-1917)
OF SCOTT COUNTY, KENTUCKY

6a. **(James Knox) Polk (I)** *[son of William Calvin (I)].* Born 28 Mar. 1844 in Scott Co., KY. Married Susan Ann Wells on 17 Apr. 1878 in Scott Co. (she was born 23 May 1859, daughter of Basil Wells, and died 17 Mar. 1934). Polk Burgess inherited his father's lands in the Turkey Foot district of Scott Co., where he farmed and raised horses; he appears in the census records there from 1860-1910 (in 1860 working for Samuel W. Green); Susan is listed with her son Willie in 1920. He dismantled his father's log cabin, and built a large frame house on the same site (it was destroyed by fire in 1978). On 7 Aug. 1866 he shot and killed his uncle, George Bates, in an argument over the the estate of his grandfather, Ned Burgess (through his father, he had received one full share). He was tried and convicted, but was eventually pardoned on 10 Jan. 1870 by Gov. Stevenson, and returned to his Scott Co. farm. He died there on 21 Mar. 1917, and is buried with his parents in his father's family cemetery. "Sadie Dunn told me that there was no doubt that Polk was Calvin's biological son. Nancy was still living there when Polk married, and Polk was the only child that Nancy ever had. Nancy's picture hung on the wall in the parlor until Joe Wheeler's wife redecorated."—Chris Glass, 1982.

The Children of Polk Burgess:

7a. **Flora** (nmn). Born 17 Jan. 1879 in Scott Co., KY; died there on 24 Nov. 1883, buried with her parents.

7b. **Motie** (nmn). Born 12 Sept. 1880 in Scott Co., KY. Listed with her father in the 1900-10 censuses, and with her brother, Willie, in 1920. Motie worked on the family estate; she was also an accomplished organist. She died there unmarried on 25 Aug. 1958, buried in an unmarked grave with her parents.

7c. **William Preston "Willie."** Born 13 Feb. 1882 in Scott Co., KY. Married Elizabeth "Lizzie" Dryden on 10 May 1920 in Harrison Co., KY (she was born 1889, and died 26 May 1971). Listed with his father in the 1900-10 censuses, and in the 1917 draft register and 1920 census for Scott Co., KY. Willie Burgess was a farmer and horse breeder on his father's estate; he died there childless on 22 Jan. 1972, and is buried with his wife in the Beard Cemetery.

7d. **Flavia Ann.** Born Jan. 1884 in Scott Co., KY. Married Grover Cleveland May on 14 Jan. 1926 in Scott Co. Listed with her father in the 1900-10 censuses, and with her brother, Willie, in 1920. Flavia May died childless on 11 Apr. 1935 in Scott Co. and is buried with her parents.

7e. **Scott "Jake"** (nmn). Born 19 Oct. 1885 in Scott Co., KY. See below for full entry.

7f. **Frank (I)** (nmn). Born 17 Nov. 1887 in Scott Co., KY. See below for full entry.

7g. **Lula Paxton.** Born 12 Nov. 1889 in Scott Co., KY. Married James Thomas Miley on 24 Dec. 1919 in Scott Co. (he was born 2 Feb. 1888, and died 6 June 1944), and had children: *Audra Mae* (born 5 Apr. 1921, married Garnett Florence on 23 Dec. 1947, and had children: Leon David [born 14 Apr. 1949]; James Dalon [born 19 Apr. 1951]; Betty Diana [born 8 Feb. 1954]; Carolyn Lou [born 15 Apr. 1956]); *Ruby Clay* (born 13 May 1923, married Barney Ritchie on 16 May 1942 [he was born 9 Aug. 1915], and died on 24 Feb. 1949, buried Beard Cemetery, having had children: James Miley [born 6 Oct. 1943, married Janice Faye Martin on 27 Nov. 1971, and had children: Jason {born 20 Feb. 1973}; Nathan {born 5 Sept. 1974}; Mathew {born 11 Nov. 1978}]; Jannette [born 8 Oct. 1945, married Larry Center on 27 Nov. 1968, and had children: Renee {born 9 Sept. 1969}]; Martha Rae [born 8 Mar. 1947, married Woodie Potter on 18 June 1970]); *James Carlton* (born 13 Nov. 1924, died unmarried in a gas explosion on 17 Feb. 1975, buried Beard Cemetery); *Anna Marie* (born 21 July 1929, married Virgil Antle on 23 Sept. 1949 [he was born 30 Sept. 1920, died 25 Nov. 1960], and had children: John Thomas [born 29 June 1950, killed in a car accident on 10 May 1968]); *Orville Ray* (born 5 Sept. 1933, married Pauline Collins on 20 June 1970, and had children: Timothy Ray [born 19 Apr. 1971]). Listed in the 1920 census with her brother, Willie. Lula Miley died on 4 Nov. 1979 at Georgetown, KY, and is buried with her husband in the Beard Cemetery.

7h. **(Ethel) Polk "Polkie."** Born 24 Jan. 1895 in Scott Co., KY. Married Jesse Lee Johnson on 3 Feb. 1921 in Scott Co. (he was born 8 Apr. 1896 in Scott Co., son of Joe Lee Johnson and Martha Ellen Mullen, and died on 25 July 1941 of Rocky Mountain spotted fever at Georgetown, KY), and had children:

James Knox "J. K." JOHNSON. Born 29 Nov. 1922 in Scott Co., married Hazel Sausman on 30 June 1944 at Lexington, KY (she was born 29 Dec. 1924 at Wilmore, KY), and had children: *Donna Kaye* (born 17 Sept. 1945 at Lexington, KY, married Jay Larue, and had children: James Scott [born 11 Oct. 1970]; Jennifer Lynn [born 10 Dec. 1971]; *Donna Kaye* married secondly David Smith, and lives at Honolulu, HI); *Patricia Anne "Patty"* (born 30 Nov. 1947 in Indiana, married Andrew Sean Pierce, and had children: Andrew Sean Jr. [born 30 June 1970]; Genevieve Shaw [born 24 Oct. 1972]; *Jamie Carol* (born 17 Feb. 1954 at Schenectady, NY, married Russell Hamada in Sept. 1991 in HI, and lives at Aiea, HI); *Melissa Jean "Lisa"* (born 23 Dec. 1960 at Lexington, KY, married William Andrew Forsythe at Lakeland, FL, and had children: William Andrew Jr. [born 16 Sept. 1985]; Christian Cross [born 12 Jan. 1990]). J. K. and Hazel Johnson live at Lexington, KY.

Eugenia JOHNSON. Born 25 Oct. 1924 in Scott Co., married (Walker) Finley Wallace on 1 June 1944 (he was born 24 May 1924 in Scott Co., and died 11 Mar. 1971 in Woodford Co., KY, buried Georgetown Cemetery), and had children: *Duane Thomas* (born 5 Oct. 1947 at Lexington, KY, married Betsy Carr on 15 July 1966 in Scott Co. [she was born 6 May 1951, and died 25 Mar. 1972 in a car accident, buried Crestlawn Memorial Garden], and had children: (Robert) Travis [born 27 July 1967, married Edye Johnson {unrelated; she was born 30 Nov. 1966} on 24 Feb. 1990]; Shannon Victoria [born 17 Dec. 1968]). ***Eugenia*** married secondly Jack R. Bell on 4 Dec. 1981 (he was born 31 Oct. 1928), worked as an accounting technician, and lives at Lexington, KY.

Owen Lee JOHNSON. Born 2 Oct. 1927 in Scott Co., married Mattie Florence Graves on 3 July 1947 at Georgetown, KY (she was born 26 Aug. 1928), and had children: *Pamela Lee* (born 11 May 1948 in Fayette Co., KY, married Donnie Doan on 11 May 1975 in Scott Co., and had children: Tara Lynn [born 3 Aug. 1979]); *Phillip Graves* (born 19 Aug. 1952 in Scott Co., married Nancy Scott on 19 Aug. 1975 [she was born 9 Dec. 1954], and had children: Jeremy Scott [born 7 Aug. 1976]); *Jesse Kevin* (born 28 Apr. 1954 in Scott Co., married Karen Southworth on 10 Mar. 1975, and had children: Jason Kevin [born 29 Sept. 1975]). Owen Johnson lives at Sadieville, KY.

Martha Anne JOHNSON. Born 15 Nov. 1929 in Scott Co., married Thomas Hurschel Marshall on 3 July 1947 at Georgetown, KY (he was born on the same day as his wife, and died 27 Dec. 1975 at Lexington, KY, buried Crest Lawn Memorial Gardens, Georgetown, KY), and had children: *Perry Thomas* (born 14 June 1948 at Georgetown, KY, married Sandy Lee Guynn on 27 July 1979 at Lexington, KY [she was born 29 Apr. 1955], and had children: Joshua Colby [born 22 May 1982]; Casey Thomas [born 14 June 1985]); *Danny Doan* (born 26 Nov. 1950, married Susan Gaines, and had children: Joseph Gaines [born 5 Apr. 1970]; *Danny* married secondly Judy Tackett, and had children: Sha Marie [born 8 Aug. 1971]; *Danny* married thirdly Melinda Sue Gibson, and had children: Danny Doan Jr. [born 29 July 1984]); *Peggy Anne* (born 15 June 1953 in Scott Co., married Jimmy Ray Offutt on 12 Feb. 1971 in Scott Co. [he was born 21 June 1953], and had children: Travis Ray [twin; born 1 Sept. 1972]; Trampus Ray [twin; born 1 Sept. 1972]; *Peggy* married secondly Gary Albert Riddle on 27 May 1977 [he was born 31 Oct. 1947], and had children: John Thomas [born 22 May 1980]; Melissa Anne [born 5 June 1983]); *Thomas Hurschel Jr.* (born 29 Sept. 1956 in Scott Co., married Sharon Kaye Stevens on 3 Aug. 1979 [she was born 26 May 1956], and had children: Ryan Thomas [born 25 Dec. 1982]); *Betty Eugenia* (born 11 Sept. 1957 in Scott Co., married Lonnie Wayne Pasley on 1 Jan. 1982 in Scott Co. [he was born 8 July 1953], and had children: Jacob Wayne [born 11 Dec. 1982]; Jesse Lee [born 7 Dec. 1985]). Martha Marshall lives at Georgetown, KY.

Polkie JOHNSON died of cancer on 20 Nov. 1958, and is buried with her husband in the Georgetown Cemetery. Martha Marshall and Eugenia Bell have contributed greatly to this book.

7i. **Joseph Wheeler (I).** Born 26 May 1899 in Scott Co., KY. See below for full entry.

SCOTT BURGESS OF SCOTT CO., KENTUCKY

[James Knox Polk (I)[6]]

7e. **Scott "Jake"** (nmn) *[son of James Knox Polk (I)].* Born 19 Oct. 1885 in Scott Co., KY. Married (Sarah) William "Willie" Tucker on 22 Aug. 1906 in Scott Co. (she was born 29 Aug. 1889, and died 14 Mar. 1931 in Scott Co., KY, the result of lingering injuries suffered when a tornado destroyed her home on 14 Mar. 1923, buried Davis Cemetery); married secondly Elizabeth Belle "Lizzie" Peak on 15 Jan. 1934 at Lexington, KY (she was born 10 Jan. 1913, and died 20 Sept. 1975). Listed in the 1910-20 censuses for Scott Co., and the 1917 draft register of Scott Co. Jake Burgess was a farmer and carpenter all his life in Scott Co., KY. He died there on 9 May 1971, and is buried with his second wife in an unmarked grave in the Hinton Cemetery.

8a. **Elmo** (nmn). Born 18 June 1907 in Scott Co., KY. Married Benjamin Franklin "Bennie" Jones on 4 June 1924 in Harrison Co., KY (he was born 23 Sept. 1897, and died 22 Apr. 1947); married secondly Arthur Huffman on 28 Jan. 1953 (he was born 8 Sept. 1897, and died 16 June 1969, buried Pythian Grove Cemetery). Elmo Huffman worked for several years at McKnight's Rooming House, Cynthiana, KY. She died childless on 28 Dec. 1985 at Corinth, KY, and is buried with her first husband in the Knights of Pythian (or Sadieville) Cemetery, Sadieville, KY.

8b. **(Lillie) Christine.** Born 18 Nov. 1912 in Scott Co., KY. Married Clarence Thomas "Tommie" Glass on 23 Nov. 1929 in Scott Co. (he was born 10 Oct. 1910, worked as a supervisor of rest areas for the Kentucky State Road Dept., and died on 10 Apr. 1984 at Georgetown, KY), and had children: *Wayne Tracy* (born 3 June 1930, married Faye Darlene Glass on 20 Oct. 1950 [she remarried George Young], and was killed by lightning on 1 June 1954, buried Caney Fork Church Cemetery, having had children: Paul Tracy [born 15 Mar. 1952, married Kathleen Marie Cleary on 17 Aug. 1974, and had children: Arizona Leigh {born 1 July 1978}]; Deborah Kaye [born 17 July 1953, married Donald Sieloff on 29 Aug. 1970]; Pamela Darlene [born 13 July 1954, married Michael C. Nettesheim on 11 June 1977]); *Gene Dale* (born 12 Sept. 1932, married Eula Mae Moss on 29 May 1958 at Georgetown, KY [she was born 3 Aug. 1931], and had children: David Wayne [born 8 Dec. 1959]; Gary Stephen [born 20 Mar. 1964]; *Gene* works as a calibration analyst for Avon, Lexington, KY); *Doyle Burgess "Pete"* (born 17 Mar. 1935 in Scott Co., KY, married Shirley Daniels on 3 July 1970 at Lexington, KY, and works as a staff assistance manager for IBM); *Ronald Thomas* (born 21 July 1944 in Scott Co., married Judy Arlene Williamson on 10 July 1965, and had children: Robin Ann [born 8 Apr. 1966]; Gregory Thomas [born 23 Sept. 1967]; Bradley Scott [born 19 Sept. 1971]; *Ronnie* married secondly Delores Gregg, and works as a truck driver). Chris Glass worked for an electrical parts factory, and later farmed in Stamping Ground in rural Scott Co., KY. A resident of Georgetown, KY, she has contributed many hours and many valuable documents to the research of this book, enriching it immeasurably.

8c. **Louise Catherine.** Born 1 Feb. 1936 in Scott Co., KY. Married J. W. Perkins on 17 May 1958 (he was born 14 Jan. 1937). Louise Perkins works in a pencil factory at Georgetown, KY, but lives at Deleplain, KY.

FRANK BURGESS OF SCOTT CO., KENTUCKY
[James Knox Polk (I)[6]]

7f. **Frank (I)** (nmn) *[son of James Knox Polk (I)].* Born 17 Nov. 1887 (or 1888, according to his draft record) in Scott Co., KY. Married Gertie Alice Barkley on 25 Aug. 1910 in Scott Co. (she was the daughter of Joseph F. Barkley and Almyra Munson, remarried Cleve Duncan on 24 Nov. 1934, and died on 2 June 1967 in Scott Co.). Listed in the 1917 draft register and 1920 census for Scott Co., KY. Frank Burgess was a farmer in Scott Co. He accidentally fell out of a loft in his barn in Sept. 1929, died from his injuries on 4 Nov. 1929, and is buried in the Georgetown Cemetery.

8a. **Odella** (nmn). Born 12 June 1911 in Scott Co., KY. Married Henry David Robertson on 18 June 1933 (he was born 12 Apr. 1911, brother of John Thomas Robertson, and died Jan. 1987), and had children: *(Henry) David II* (born 8 Sept. 1949). Odella Robertson lives at Lexington, KY.

8b. **Beatrice (II)** (nmn). Born 26 Aug. 1914 in Scott Co., KY. Married John Thomas Robertson on 31 Mar. 1934 in Fayette Co., KY (he died Oct. 1963), and had children: *Barbara Ann* (born 12 Jan. 1935, married D. C. "Bert" Myers on 8 Jan. 1953, and had children: Susan [born 1954]; Chris [born 1963]); *Shirley Thomas* (born 1 Oct. 1937, married Kenneth Houston on 20 July 1958, and had children: Sherry Len [born 12 June 1959]; Mark Thomas [born 3 Oct. 1963]; Tracy Ann [born 20 Jan. 1970]); *Betty Carolyn* (born 1 Mar. 1946, married (Harold) Scott Gardner on 12 June 1965, and had children: Jeffery Scott [born 14 Dec. 1966]; Lisa Carol [born 16 Dec. 1969]; Angelia Michelle [born 8 Aug. 1976]). Bea Robertson owned a grocery store at Muddy Ford, KY before retiring, and now lives at Georgetown, KY.

8c. **Aline** (nmn) (twin). Born 3 Dec. 1922 in Scott Co., KY. Married Melvin Faulconer on 4 Apr. 1942 in Scott Co. (div.; he was born 19 June 1911, died Apr. 1983 at Cynthiana, KY), and had children: *Sandra Sue* (born 2 July 1943); *Phyllis* (born 18 Sept. 1946); married secondly Gilmon "Bobbie" Curtsinger. Aline Curtsinger died on 22 Dec. 1978 at Lawrenceburg, KY.

8d. **Pauline** (nmn) (twin). Born 3 Dec. 1922 in Scott Co., KY. Married Biagio C. "Joe" Mangione on 11 Jan. 1946 in Fayette Co., KY (he was born 6 Nov. 1911, and died Sept. 1978 at Lexington, KY), and had children: *Charlene Burgess* (born 2 Dec. 1948); *(Paul) Michael* (born 14 June 1950).

Pauline married secondly Jack Barnes on 10 Jan. 1958 (he was born 30 Jan. 1923 in Harrison Co., KY, and died May 1982 at Cincinnati, OH), and had children: *Cathy* (born 15 Oct. 1959); ***Robbie*** (born 20 Aug. 1962). Pauline died of lung cancer on 20 Aug. 1988 at Cincinnati, OH, and is buried with her second husband in the Pythian Grove Cemetery, Berry, KY. "She was tall and blonde and very lovely, opposite of her twin sister Aline, who was short and a brunette."—Chris Glass.

JOE BURGESS OF SCOTT CO., KENTUCKY

[James Knox Polk (I)[6]]

7i. **Joseph Wheeler (I)** ***[son of James Knox Polk (I)].*** Born 26 May 1899 in Scott Co., KY. Married Amra Orpha Cox on 19 Sept. 1923 in Scott Co. (she was born 15 Oct. 1904, daughter of Hance and Nannie Sharon Cox, and died 15 July 1986 at Lexington, KY). Listed in the 1917 draft register of Scott Co., KY, and in the 1920 census living with his brother, Willie. Joe Burgess was a farmer on his father's lands in Scott Co., KY; he was living in his grandfather's house when it burned on 8 Feb. 1978. He and his wife were members of the Turkey Foot Christian Church. Joe Burgess later retired to Georgetown, KY, where he died on 6 July 1986; both he and Amra are buried in the Georgetown Cemetery.

8a. **Gilbert (II)** (nmn). Born 2 Apr. 1924 (or 26 Apr. 1923, according to Social Security records) in Scott Co., KY. Married (Theara) Faye Clem on 1 Apr. 1946 in Fayette Co. Gilbert Burgess worked at the Hoover Plant at Deleplain, KY. He died on 8 Nov. 1978 in Scott Co.

9a. **Alma Faye.** Born 19 June 1946 in Scott Co., KY. Married Charles "Chuck" Johnson, and lives at Lexington, KY.

8b. **Joseph Wheeler (II) "Junior."** Born 6 Sept. 1925 in Scott Co., KY. Married Lucille Dunn on 8 Nov. 1947 in Harrison Co., KY; married secondly (Eva) Marie Rankin on 23 Nov. 1966 in Scott Co. (div.; she was born 3 Aug. 1925). Served in World War II. Junior Burgess worked as an auto mechanic at Deleplain, KY. He was a member of the Turkey Foot Christian Church. He died childless of lung cancer on 7 Aug. 1988 at Lexington, KY, and is buried in the Georgetown Cemetery with his parents. "He was a charming, honest, and lovable person."—Chris Glass.

8c. **William Cecil.** Born 16 Sept. 1927 in Scott Co., KY. Married (Anna) Barbara Teegardner on 8 Aug. 1952 in Scott Co. Bill Burgess has worked in 14 different states as a signalman for the Southern Railroad. He currently lives in rural Scott Co., KY.

8d. **Ercell** (nmn). Born and died 15 Nov. 1931 in Scott Co., KY, and was buried in Calvin Burgess's family cemetery.

THE INDICTMENT OF POLK BURGESS

"We the Jury render a verdict that the said deceased [George Bates] came to his death by the evidence of said witnesses from a shot or shots fired from the pistol or pistols of Mr. Polk Burgess himself with the intent to kill."—*Coroner's Inquest, Turkey Foot, Ky., Aug. 9, 1866.*

"The Grand Jury this day made a report of the following indictments each endorces a true file. Issued Commonwealth of Ky. Case number 455 against James K. Polk Burgess. Murder. Nov. 23, 1866. That he did feloniously, wickedly, and of malice aforethought kill and murder George W. Bates by shooting him with a pistol loaded with gunpowder and leaden balls or other hard substance."—*Scott County Court, November Term 1866.*

"Polk Burgess, who is charged with shooting George W. Bates at Turkey Foot in Aug. of last year (from the effects of which Bates died the next day) and who has been at large ever since, came into town on Friday last and surrendered himself to Sheriff Tilford. He was bailed in the sum of $5000 to answer in the next term of the circuit court. James Fields, James Tucker, and Harrison Lynn were his surities."—*Georgetown News*, 11 Sept. 1867.

"Mariah Bates &C against J. K. P. Burgess. Petition ordered that the foregoing cause be continued." [Note: This was a civil suit brought against Polk Burgess by Mariah Bates and her brothers.]—*Scott County Suit #9203, Order Book #28, p. 251, 24 Nov. 1866.*

PETITION FOR A CHANGE OF VENUE IN CASE #9203

"The defendant in this action, James K. Burgess, states that he desires a change of venue in this case for the following reasons. He states that he verily believes that he can not have a fair trial of this case in Scott County, owing to the undue influence of the Burgess family.

"And he also states that there is an odium which attends himself and his defense which will as he believes prevent his having a fair and impartial trial in Scott County. He states that Marier Bates was the sister of defendant's father, William C. Burgess, and that she and her husband George Bates, who the defendant is charged with killing, and Joseph Burgess and Edward Burgess and all of William C. Burgess' brothers and sisters (Joseph Burgess and Edward both being brothers of W. Burgess) were greatly dissatisfied because said William C. Burgess dec'd adopted defendant as his own son and gave him by his will his whole estate—which they expected to own at his death, as he never was married.

"That Joseph Burgess and Edward Burgess are wealthy men and influential in Scott County, where they reside, and that they together with said George Bates and others have before and since the killing of said Bates, circulated and caused to be circulated false rumors of the cause and circumstances attending the killing of said Bates, greatly to the prejudice of defendant and causing great odium to exist against defendant, and a state of public opinion erroneous and prejudicial to defendant—which he believes would prevent a fair and impartial trail in said county—that in a suit now pending in this court instituted in the name of Marier Bates and as the next friend of her son Charles A. Bates, they executed bond for the sum of $40,000 with Joseph Burgess as surety claiming in said suit damages to the amount of $20,000—when no reasonable mind or person could have believed they could recover a judgment for as much as $5000.00 and sued out an attachment and caused it to be levied on a tract of land of about $12000.00, being nearly all the estate defendant then owned causing him great injury and thus shewing a disposition to oppress the defendant and to cast odium on his case and defense, which odium applied equally to his defense in this case of the Commonwealth against defendant. He therefore for these causes files this petition for and prays for a change of venue in this case."—James M. Shepard, attorney, 18 May 1868. The change of venue was granted to Fayette Co. on 19 May 1868 (*Scott Co. Order Book #29*, p. 113).

THE TRIAL

"March 1st, 1869. Case No. 455, Commonwealth of Ky. against James K. Burgess. The Commonwealth appeared by her Attorney, and the Defendant appeared in discharge of his recognisance, thereupon came a jury: John M. Garth, Wm. C. Graves, Josiah Pence, John J. Moore, Elly Blackburne, Joseph Y. Bond, Wm. H. Applegate, Joseph S. Simon, B. W. House, Reuben Powell, Joshua Talbot, George Fink, who being sworn according to law, the arraignment of the Defendant was dispensed with, by his consent and the consent of the Commonwealth and he pleaded not guilty to the charge in the indictment of the jury." (The trial then proceeded for the next two days.)

THE TESTIMONY

Squire Bates: Said his father told him "Polk had killed him."

Erastus Price: I was seventy-five or one hundred yards distant. Burgess came up and remarked that he had five loads for Bates and exhibited a pistol. About an hour afterward I saw Burgess firing on Bates and Bates attempted to fire and failing, ran. When Burgess pursued firing, I saw the wounds on ___ in the back.

Wm. Vance: I saw nothing.

E. T. Burgess: I was seventy-five yards off, and saw Polk come up to shop, and exhibiting a revolver said "here is five shots to kill old Bates with"—went to Vance's barroom, next saw him following up and firing upon Bates.

Mrs. Price: I saw Polk going toward Bates, then saw them Bates on the porch and Polk in the road. Polk said he had come to kill him and Bates said he had always been his friend. Polk saying he didn't care, he was going to kill him and had his pistol in his hand. Bates said he could shoot too, and went in and brought his horse pistol in his left hand and clenched half way up Polk began firing on Bates—Bates dropped his pistol and got over in the road. Polk still firing on him.

Zeph Fields: I saw Polk first at the barroom of Vance, then saw him going toward Bates and as he did so changed his pistols from right to left, then saw Bates on the porch and Polk in the road in front talking together, and Polk began to fire and shot several times before Bates got into the road. Polk's mother intervened. He persisted in the attack when Bates started first toward the creek then turned and ran up Oxford Road. Polk still pursuing and firing on him.

Charley Bates: I heard Polk make the threat at the shop, and I went home and told my father. Polk then came and called my father out, the old man declined and he [Polk] begged him to come saying gently "Come out—I want to talk to you," then pulled his pistol out with an oath, said he would shoot him. Bates then returned and got his pistol and came out front. Polk then began firing and shot four times. Bates advanced to the road and snapped his pistol. In the meantime I came out with the gun and snapped the gun at Polk.

THE VERDICT, 4 MARCH 1869

"We of the jury find James K. Burgess guilty of man slaughter and fix his punishment to two years confinement in the State Prison." He was remanded to prison on 11 Mar. 1869, arrived there on 26 Mar. 1869, and was pardoned by Gov. John White Stevenson on 10 Jan. 1870.

[William (I)[1], Edward (I)[2], William (II)[3], Edward (V)[4]]

JOSEPH FIELDS BURGESS
(1809-1892)

OF SCOTT COUNTY, KENTUCKY

5e. **Joseph Fields** *[son of Edward (V)]*. Born 5 Feb. 1809 in Scott Co., KY. Married Elizabeth Sharp in 1831 (she died six weeks later); married secondly Miranda Penn on 24 (or 21) Dec. 1839 in Scott Co. (she was born 1821, and died 1857). Listed in the 1840-80 censuses and tax records for Big Eagle Precinct, Scott Co., KY (listed with him in the 1870 census are two Black servants [formally slaves], Tony Burgess [age 15] and Susan Y. Burgess [age 16]). Joseph Burgess was a farmer, rancher, livestock breeder and trader, and realtor in Scott Co., KY; his large land holdings, amounting at one time to over 6000 acres, made him one of the wealthiest and most influential men in Scott Co.; he left a large personal fortune at the time of his death. His large mansion, fronted with ornamental Grecian columns, is considered to be the most splendid house of its type in northeastern Scott Co.; it is also the only old Burgess residence still surviving among the descendants of Ned Burgess. A popular novel, *Weeds*, by Edith Summers Kelley (New York: Harcourt, Brace & Co., 1923), used the Joseph Burgess estate as the basis for its background. Joseph Burgess was elected Justice of the Peace for Scott Co. from 1840-51. He died there on 20 Jan. 1892, and is buried with his wife and some of his children in the family cemetery behind his house.

The Children of Joseph Burgess:

6a. **Evaline P.** Her name is also spelled Evelyn. Born 1840 in Scott Co., KY. Married Sterling Paul "Jimmy" Smith on 13 Nov. 1868 in Scott Co. (he was born 2 Nov. 1842, and died 22 Jan. 1927), and had children: *Burgess S.* (born Jan. 1870, married Alice ___, and secondly Kate Fuller [she was born 1880, and died 1949], and died 1947, buried Georgetown Cemetery); *Sarah S. "Sally"* (born 5 Dec. 1872, married John A. Gano [born 1850], had children: Sterling [born 1899, married, and had children: Sally {who married ___ Hayes}], and died 7 Dec. 1958, buried Georgetown Cemetery). Living with her father in 1870. Evaline Smith died on 18 July 1931 in Scott Co., KY, aged 91 years, and is buried with her husband in the Georgetown Cemetery. Her son, Burgess Smith, owned a race horse farm and track in northern Scott Co.; the track which passed by their land is now called Burgess Smith Road. The Smiths inherited Joseph Burgess's mansion, passing it to Sally Gano and her descendants.

6b. **Sarah E. (I).** Born 9 Apr. 1842 in Scott Co., KY; died there on 6 Jan. 1857, and is buried with her parents.

6c. **Nancy E. (I) "Nannie."** Born May 1844 in Scott Co, KY. Married as his second wife Buford Hall on 23 Dec. 1868 in Scott Co. (he was born 8 Feb. 1827, son of William Hall, and died 13 June 1896; by his first wife he had children: *Lucy* [born 1862, married ___ Finley, and died 1898]), and had children: *Sallie* (born 17 Jan. 1870, married (James) Stucker Offutt on 15 Dec. 1891 in Scott Co. [he was born 14 Sept. 1868, and died June 1925], and died on 2 Mar. 1942 at Dayton, OH, having had children: Buford Hall [born 1894, died 1947]; James Stucker Jr. [born 12 Sept. 1903 at Georgetown, KY, lived at La-Grange, IL, and died May 1985 at Zephyrhills, FL]); *Linda* (born 1873, married Robert H. Anderson, and died 1962); *Mary* (born Sept. 1877, never married); *Buford Jr. "Blue"* (born Sept. 1879, married Lora Forwood [she was born 19 June 1893, and died July 1980 at Georgetown, KY], and died 10 Apr. 1946 in Scott Co., KY, having had children: Son [born and died July 1919]; Marion F.; Joe Burgess [who lives in Florida]; Buford III [a physician at Burr Ridge, IL]). Listed in the 1870 census for Georgetown, Scott Co., KY, and in 1900 in Scott Co. Nannie Hall died on 30 May 1914 in Scott Co., and is buried in the Georgetown Cemetery.

6d. **Son.** Born and died 1845 in Scott Co., KY, and is buried with his parents. Dates and order uncertain.

6e. **Penelope (III) "Neppie."** Born 12 Mar. 1847 in Scott Co., KY. Married James F. Musselman on 2 Dec. 1870 in Scott Co. (he was born 5 Dec. 1828 in Harrison Co., KY, married firstly Letha J. Hall on 23 May 1856 [she was born 19 Apr. 1832, and died 1 May 1860, having had children: *William S.* {died an infant}]), and had children: *Myra V.* (born 27 Nov. 1871); *Nannie H(all?)* (born 30 Oct. 1873); *Joseph*

Fields (born 4 Feb. 1878, married, and had one son; he graduated from the School of Engineering of the University of Kentucky, was a consultant in the building of the State Capitol at Harrisburg, PA, the housing properties at Muscle Shoals, AL, and plants for the Navy at Pelham Bay and for the Army at West Point; he was consulting engineer for the building of the Hotel Stadler, Buffalo, NY, for the Hotel Mayflower, Washington, DC, and for the Bank of the Manhattan Company, New York; he died on 6 Jan. 1926 at Bronxville, NY).

Neppie is listed with her father in the 1870 census. The Musselmans were living in Harrison Co., KY in 1882, when James's biography appears in the *History of Bourbon, Scott, Harrison, and Nicholas Counties, Kentucky*, by W. H. Perrin (Chicago: O. L. Baskin & Co., 1882, p. 601-602). In 1923 she was apparently living with her son, Joseph F. Musselman, in New York City, but was not mentioned in his 1926 obituary, and is not listed in the 1922-31 death indexes for the five boroughs of New York City, or in the Kentucky State death index.

6f. **Thomas Jefferson (I).** Born 22 Mar. 1849 in Scott Co., KY. See below for full entry.

6g. **Daughter**. Born and died about 1851 in Scott Co., KY, and is buried with her parents.

6h. **Elvessa B.** Born 10 Jan. 1854 in Scott Co., KY; died there on 29 June 1856, and is buried with her parents.

6i. **Son.** Born and died about 1856 in Scott Co., KY, and is buried with his parents.

Evaline P. BURGESS SMITH (1840-1931)
Sterling Paul "Jimmy" SMITH (1842-1927)
(see page 175)

[William (I)[1], Edward (I)[2], William (II)[3], Edward (V)[4], Joseph Fields[5]]

THOMAS JEFFERSON BURGESS I
(1849-1923)

OF SCOTT COUNTY, KENTUCKY

6f. **Thomas Jefferson (I)** *[son of Joseph Fields].* Born 22 Mar. 1849 in Scott Co., KY. Married Josephine C. Pack about 1874 (she was born 1 May 1855, the daughter of Dr. Richard F. Pack and Sarah Martha "Sadie" Emison [for whom the town of Sadieville, KY, was named], and first cousin of Sallie Pack, who married Lafayette S. Burgess, and died on 3 Feb. 1920). Listed in the 1870-1920 censuses for Scott Co. T. J. Burgess inherited some of his father's lands, and began adding to them, eventually becoming one of the largest land owners in Scott Co. He also traded in mules, horses, cattle, land, tobacco, and other goods, and was a principal founder of Sadieville, KY, located west of his estate, selling many of the original town plots. Josephine Burgess inherited her father's house, which is now known as the Tom Burgess Estate. Tom Burgess died intestate on 16 Feb. 1923 in Scott Co., and is buried with his wife in the Georgetown Cemetery. A short biography and photograph of T. J. Burgess appeared in ***The B. O.*** *Gaines History of Scott County*, by B. O. Gaines (Georgetown, KY: B. O. Gaines Printery, 1905, Volume 2, p. 170).

T. J. BURGESS DEAD

"Thomas J. Burgess, a prominent and wealthy farmer of Scott County, died at his home, Eagle's Nest, near Sadieville, Feb. 16. At the time of his wife's death in February 1921, Mr. Burgess suffered a general breakdown from which he never recovered. He was seventy-three years of age. Mr. Burgess was connected by birth and marriage with a number of the pioneer families of Scott County, and inherited from his father a large estate to which he added very materially during the years of his activity as a planter and stock breeder. His wife was a sister of Dr. John Pack of Georgetown, whose ancestors were prominent in the early development of Kentucky.

"The members of Mr. Burgess' immediate family left surviving him are: Mrs. Merle Whitney of Buffalo, N.Y.; Mrs. J. M. Fuqua of Danville, Ky.; Mrs. M. N. Burgess of Scott County; Mrs. Anthony A. McQuaid of this city. Funeral arrangements have not been completed on account of the absence of Mrs. Whitney, who was expected to reach Sadieville today."—*Lexington Leader*, 17 Feb. 1923.

LEADING STOCKMAN DIES

"Thomas Jefferson Burgess, 75 years old, died today at his country home, Eagles Nest, near Sadieville. He was the son of the late Joseph and Miranda Penn Burgess, and a descendant of William Penn. He was well known as an extensive stock and tobacco dealer, and was one of the largest land owners in the county. He was known locally as a scholar and philanthropist. He is survived by four daughters: Mrs. James M. Fuqua of Danville; Mrs. A. A. McQuaid of Lexington; Mrs. N. M. Burgess of Sadieville; and Mrs. M. B. Whitney of Buffalo, N.Y.; two sisters, Mrs. S. P. Smith of Scott County and Mrs. N. B. Musselman of New York City. Funeral services will be held at the family residence Monday morning at ten o'clock. Burial will follow in the Georgetown Cemetery. Pallbearers will be nephews of deceased: John A. Gano, Robert Anderson, Buford Hall, Burgess Smith, Joe Burgess, and Richard Burgess."—*Lexington Herald*, 18 Feb. 1923.

The Children of Tom Burgess:

7a. **Miranda.** Born 12 July 1875 in Scott Co., KY. Married Rev. James Melvin Fuqua (he was born 30 June 1873, was a Methodist minister, and died 23 May 1927). Living at Danville, Boyle Co., KY in 1923, but has not been found in the 1900 and 1920 Kentucky Soundexes. Miranda Fuqua died childless on 18 Apr. 1954 at Lexington, Fayette Co., KY, and is buried with her husband in the Georgetown Cemetery.

7b. **Elizabeth Pack.** Born 6 Sept. 1879 in Scott Co., KY. Married Anthony Ambrose McQuaid (eloped; he was born 13 Nov. 1869, and died 11 Jan. 1950). Has not been found in the 1900 Kentucky Soundex. Living at Lexington, KY in 1923, and is listed in the 1920 census for Lexington, Fayette Co., KY lodging with Jessie N. Wigginton. Elizabeth McQuaid died childless on 26 Jan. 1963 in Scott Co., and is buried with her husband in the Georgetown Cemetery.

7c. **Laura Stevenson.** Born 1 Jan. 1882 in Scott Co., KY. Married her first cousin, once removed, Noble Moses Burgess (he was born 7 Aug. 1880, son of John Cabell Breckinridge Burgess and Martha Susan Sharpe, and died on 25 Dec. 1953, buried Georgetown Cemetery). Listed in the 1920 census with her father. Laura Burgess died on 26 Feb. 1936 in Fayette Co., KY, and is buried in the Georgetown Cemetery. See her husband's entry for their children.

7d. **Joseph Richard.** Born 9 Feb. 1884 in Scott Co., KY; he died there on 18 June 1894 from the effects of a bad vaccination, and is buried with his parents.

7e. **Sadie.** She was named for her maternal grandmother, Sarah Martha "Sadie" Emison Pack. Born 18 Aug. 1886 in Scott Co., KY. Married Merle Bush Whitney Sr. (he may have been born 22 June 1885, and died Nov. 1965), and had children: *Josephine Ellen* (born 1 Sept. 1911, married Alva William Maischoss, and had children: Gail Elizabeth; Linda Laura); *Merle Bush Jr.* (born 12 Jan. 1918, never married). The Whitneys were living in Buffalo, NY in 1923, but retired to California. She reportedly died in 1966 in California, but is *not* the Sadie G. Whitney who died on 16 Apr. 1957 in Alameda Co., CA, and neither she nor her husband have been found in the California death index.

A BIOGRAPHY OF THOS. J. BURGESS (1905)

"Mr. Thomas J. Burgess [is] one of the wealthiest man, one of the largest landowners [of Scott County], and deals heavily in live stock and tobacco, and has made a great success. In 1904 it was reported that he made $30,000 on tobacco. He owns 3,916 acres of land. His wealth is known to no one but himself, but is approximately at several hundreds of thousands of dollars. He possesses every qualification of a business man, and being a liberal buyer, his value to the people in that portion of the county cannot be estimated. He resides on his farm near Sadieville, of which place he was one of the incorporators. He married Miss Josephine Pack, daughter of the late Richard Pack, and to this union four children were born—Miranda, Elizabeth, Laura, and Sadie." *His portrait appears below.*

[William (I)[1], Edward (I)[2], William (II)[3], Edward (V)[4]]

EDWARD BURGESS, JR.
(1816-1898)

OF SCOTT COUNTY, KENTUCKY

5h. **Edward (IX)** (nmn) *[son of Edward (V)].* Born 1 July 1816 in Scott Co., KY. Married Mary Ann Adams on 3 Jan. 1836 (she was born 7 Nov. 1814, daughter of Francis Adams and America Brennen [or Branham], and died of tuberculosis on 13 Dec. 1858); married secondly Sarah Elizabeth "Sallie" Davis on 21 Apr. 1861 in Scott Co. (she was born 19 July 1841, daughter of Elijah and Margaret Davis, and died on 21 May 1919 in Scott Co.). Listed in the 1840-80 censuses for Scott Co., KY; Sallie is listed as head of the family in 1900-10. Edward Burgess Jr. farmed large tracts of land in the Turkey Foot District of Scott Co., KY. He also inherited his father's family Bible, adding his own family's records; the Bible still survives among his descendants. Edward Burgess died on 28 Aug. 1898 in Scott Co.; he, his wife, and many of their children are buried around a large Burgess monument in the southern section of the Georgetown Cemetery.

The Children of Edward Burgess:

6a. **James Greenberry.** Born 12 Oct. 1836 in Scott Co., KY. See below for full entry.

6b. **Naomi.** Born 5 July 1838 in Scott Co., KY. Married (Benjamin) Thomas Hinton on 18 Sept. 1860 in Scott Co., and had children: *Mary Elizabeth*; *Sally* (one of whom married ___ Duncan, and had a granddaughter, Mrs. Leroy Jones Jr.). Naomi Hinton died on 5 May 1864 in Scott Co., and is buried with her husband in the Old Elklick Cemetery, on her father's lands.

6c. **William Calvin (II).** Born 12 Jan. 1840 in Scott Co., KY; died there on 10 May 1851, and is buried in the Georgetown Cemetery.

6d. **Remus Van Buren "Reem."** Born 5 Dec. 1841 in Scott Co., KY. Listed in the censuses through 1880 with his father, and in 1900 living with his brother, Ben. Reem Burgess was a farmer on his father's lands in Scott Co. He hanged himself in 1901 in the barn of his cousin, Polk Burgess, dying unmarried and childless, and is buried with his Burgess relatives in the Georgetown Cemetery.

6e. **Virginia (I).** Born 18 Aug. 1843 in Scott Co., KY; died there on 29 Mar. 1851, and is buried in the Georgetown Cemetery.

6f. **Benjamin Kenn.** Born 29 Aug. 1846 in Scott Co., KY. See below for full entry.

6g. **Joseph Edward.** Born 31 Aug. 1848 in Scott Co., KY; died there on 24 Aug. 1864, and is buried with his parents.

6h. **(Mary) Celestine "Tinie."** Born 22 Dec. 1850 in Scott Co., KY (or 18 Dec. 1851, according to her tombstone). Married Edmond Caesar Muddiman on 28 Sept. 1874 in Scott Co., KY (he was born 1852, and died 8 Sept. 1934 in Scott Co., KY). Tinie Muddiman died on 20 Jan. 1886 in Scott Co., and is buried in the Oxford Presbyterian Church Cemetery.

6i. **John Cabell Breckinridge.** Born 11 Mar. 1852 in Scott Co., KY. See below for full entry.

6j. **Solomon Washington "Sol."** Born 14 Aug. 1855 in Scott Co., KY. Sol Burgess was a farmer on his father's lands, dying there unmarried on 19 Feb. 1898. Buried with his family in the Georgetown Cemetery.

6k. **Nancy Jane (II) "Nannie."** Born 11 Feb. 1862 in Scott Co., KY. Married (John) Gano Shropshire on 15 Sept. 1885 in Scott Co. (he was born 21 Dec. 1860, and died 19 Jan. 1931), and had at least the following children:

Arden SHROPSHIRE. Born 9 July 1886, married Flora Tubbs (she was born 12 Sept. 1885, and died Apr. 1973 at Hendersonville, TN), and had children: *John Alonzo* (had children: Robert; Dorothy Jane); *Burgess Louise* (married Herbert Bates, and had children: Arden; John; Felix; Danny). Arden Shropshire died in Feb. 1964 in TN.

***Carrie Lorraine* SHROPSHIRE.** Born 27 Oct. 1887, married (James) Estill Cleveland (he was born 20 Dec. 1884, and died 1 Apr. 1933). She died on 26 Aug. 1979 in Scott Co., KY, aged 91 years, and is buried with her husband in the Georgetown Cemetery.

***Burgess S.* SHROPSHIRE.** Born 24 May 1889, married Felix H. Swope (he was born 1892, and died 20 Apr. 1958 in Scott Co.), and died on 23 Sept. 1972.

***Grover* SHROPSHIRE** (nmn). Born 17 Sept. 1890 in Scott Co., KY. Married Mattie Craig Burrier on 7 July 1919 (?) in Jessamine Co., KY (she was born 13 Sept. 1894, and died 15 Oct. 1966), and had children: *Grover Craig* (born 5 Dec. 1921 in Scott Co., married Mary Eloise Adams Brown on 1 Aug. 1952 at Lexington, KY [she was born Feb. 1921, and died]; married secondly Phyllis Ann Cox on 5 Dec. 1988 [she was born 2 Aug. 1924]; Grover C. Shropshire was a graduate of the U.S. Naval Academy, served as an admiral's aide, and later worked for Ashland Oil, Ashland, KY); *Nancy Clay* (born 6 Sept. 1923 in Scott Co., KY, married Paul Garrett Blazer Jr. on 24 Apr. 1948 in Scott Co. [he was born 31 Aug. 1919 at Chicago, IL, son of Paul Garrett Blazer Sr. and Georgia Frances Monroe], and had children: Nancy Monroe "Nan" [born 18 Aug. 1950 at Georgetown, KY, married James Dillon Tischer on 2 Oct. 1982 at Ashland, KY {he was born 7 Oct. 1949}]; Martha Frances [born 6 Feb. 1952 at Georgetown, KY, married Ben Curtis Smith on 15 July 1985 in Scott Co. {he was born 3 Aug. 1951}, and had children: Christopher Blazer {born 18 June 1987}]; Barrie Ann [born 2 Aug. 1956 at Ashland, KY, married Samuel Lyle Conner on 9 June 1978 in Scott Co., KY {born 28 May 1949}, and had children: Caroline Blazer {born 18 Aug. 1981}; Francis Clay {born 28 Oct. 1984}]; Nancy Shropshire Blazer earned her bachelor's degree in English from the University of Kentucky in 1945; her interests include the historical preservation and restoration of old Kentucky churches). Grover Shropshire was a farmer in Scott Co., and also sold real estate. He died there on 5 July 1962.

***Sarah Mai* SHROPSHIRE.** Born 11 Nov. 1900, died 11 Dec. 1900, buried with her parents.

Nannie SHROPSHIRE died on 12 Aug. 1920 in Scott Co., and is buried with her husband in the Georgetown Cemetery. Her granddaughter, Nancy Shropshire Blazer, lives at Ashland, KY.

6l. **Maria Antoinette.** Born 15 Oct. 1863 in Scott Co., KY; died there 23 Aug. 1864, and is buried in Georgetown Cemetery.

6m. **Lafayette Stipp.** Born 27 Nov. 1864 in Scott Co., KY. See below for full entry.

6n. **Lazarus Newton.** Born 30 Oct. 1867 in Scott Co., KY. See below for full entry.

6o. **(Joseph) Lot.** Born 6 July 1871 in Scott Co., KY. See below for full entry.

6p. **Hellena Ellen "Ella."** Born 4 Jan. 1873 in Scott Co., KY. Married Keller Current Thomson Sr. on 7 Apr. 1903 in Scott Co. (he was born 16 Oct. 1868, and died 15 June 1945), and had children:

***Addison Lafayette* THOMSON *II*.** Born 31 Jan. 1904 in IN. Married (Mary) Margaret Gray in 1946 (she was born 24 Feb. 1908 in Harrison Co., and died 20 July 1987 at Cynthiana), and had children: *William Addison "Billie"* (born 2 Apr. 1947 in Harrison Co., KY, married Eileen Jean Lancsak on 26 July 1970 at New Brunswick, NJ [she was born 22 Oct. 1947 at News Brunswick, NJ], and had children: Tracy Burgess [born 3 July 1972 at Lexington, KY]; Patricia Paige [born 5 July 1975 at Lexington, KY]; Addison Lafayette III [born 24 June 1984 at Cynthiana, KY]). Addison Thomson died on 15 Mar. 1972 in Harrison Co., KY, and is buried with his wife in the Battle Grove Cemetery. Bill Thomson lives on Grayland Farm, near Cynthiana, KY.

***Keller Current "K. C."* THOMSON *Jr*.** Born 7 Jan. 1906. Married Eddyth Elizabeth Jennings on 3 Sept. 1932 (she was born 10 Sept. 1905, and died 15 Feb. 1986), died on 6 Dec. 1971 at Louisville, KY, buried with his wife in the Battle Grove Cemetery, and had children:

Eleanor Clay THOMSON (born 23 Apr. 1936, married John Douglas Coner on 15 Aug. 1959 [he was born 23 Apr. 1939], and had children: John Douglas Jr. [born 7 June 1960, married Joyce Lee Bartnikowski on 25 Jan. 1984 {she was born 23 Jan. 1962}, and had children: Krista Elaine {born 19 Apr. 1987}; John Douglas III {born 22 July 1989}; Katelyn Mariah {born 6 May 1993}]; Kelley Elizabeth [born 23 Apr. 1962, died 28 July 1962]; Garret Clay [born 17 Feb. 1964, married Cristina Maria Gilliland on 22 Apr. 1987 {she was born 5 Nov. 1963}, and had children: Nancy Joy {born 18 Sept. 1988}; Eleanor Marie {born 8 Apr. 1991}]; Michelle Eleanor [born 22 Apr. 1970]).

Betty Burgess THOMSON (born 31 Dec. 1937, and had children: Kimberly Thu [ad.; born 7 June 1974]).

Alva Joyce THOMSON (born 30 Sept. 1939, and had children: Elizabeth Anh [ad.; born 20 Mar. 1974]; Betty and Alva Thomson live at Indianapolis, IN).

Keller Current "Bud" THOMSON *III* (born 2 Dec. 1941 at Louisville, KY, married Laura Frances Shipp on 30 Mar. 1962 [she was born 29 June 1940 at Lexington], and had children: Laura Kaye [born 2 Dec. 1962, married John Lawless in 1980 {div. 1987; he was born 8 June 1962}, and had children: Brian Douglas {born 23 Apr. 1981 at Covington, KY}; Laura Elizabeth {born 15 Jan. 1986 at Covington, KY}; Laura Kaye Thomson married secondly Clifford Anthony Bergman on 15 Oct. 1988 {he was born 24 Jan. 1962?; by his first wife he had children: Maranda Ann <born 3 Feb. 1980>; Benjamin Joseph <born 6 Feb. 1986>}, and had children: Nathan Christopher {born 26

Mar. 1991 at Edgewood, KY}; Daniel Conrad {born 13 Oct. 1992 at Edgewood, KY}; Laura Kaye is a registered nurse and Clifford Bergman is a plant manager for a steel fabrication plant; they live at Dry Ridge, KY]; Steven Keller [born 2 Nov. 1965 at Louisville, KY, married Teresa Lynn Webster on 26 Apr. 1988 {she was born 28 Aug. 1964}, and had children: Jacob Keller {born 15 Sept. 1990 at Edgewood, KY}; Steven Keller Thomson is a warehouse supervisor; Teresa is a hair stylist; they live at Walton, KY]; David Martin [born 7 Oct. 1968 at Covington, KY, works as a computer specialist for Johnson and Higgins Insurance, and is also a song writer and musician at Nashville, TN]. Bud Thomson is an inspector for the U.S. Dept. of Agriculture Food, Safety, and Inspection Service; Laura Thomson is an educator with the Northern Kentucky Cooperative for Education Services at Northern Kentucky University, Highland Heights, KY; they live at Independence, KY).

Garrett Douglas "Pat" THOMSON (twin). Born 17 Mar. 1908. Married Frances Phelps, and had children: *John*. Pat Thomson died on 12 Dec. 1991 at Big Pool, MD.

Joseph Lott "Jack" THOMSON (twin). Born 17 Mar. 1908. Married Elizabeth McKee on 22 Nov. 1938 at Cynthiana, KY (she was born 20 Jan. 1908, and died 23 Dec. 1984), and had children: *Jane Ann* (born 3 May 1940, married Emerson Harold "Em" Bell on 19 June 1965 [he was born 22 Nov. 1937, and died 2 Aug. 1987], and had children: Joseph Emerson [born 3 July 1967]; Garrett Hickman [born 17 June 1970]; Jane Ann Bell lives at Mystic, CT); *Joe McKee* (born 3 Mar. 1944, married Joann Marie Hutt on 19 Apr. 1975 [she was born 11 Aug. 1946], and had children: Bradley Scott [born 5 Jan. 1980]; Ashlee Ann [born 16 May 1981]; Kimberly Lynn [born 14 Apr. 1984]; Joe Thomson lives at Phoenixville, PA). Jack Thomson died on 13 Nov. 1968 in Harrison Co., KY, and is buried in Battle Grove Cemetery.

Ella Burgess THOMSON is listed with her mother in the 1900 census. She was a nurse in Scott and Harrison Cos. She died on 15 Sept. 1962 in Harrison Co., the last of her brothers and sisters to die, and is buried in the Battle Grove Cemetery, Cynthiana. She wrote a short unpublished history of her family based upon her memories of the accounts given her by her father and her older brothers. Margaret Gray Thomson inherited many of the Burgess papers from her mother-in-law, and contributed greatly to this book. Mrs. Thomson was born 24 Feb. 1908, lived much of her life on Grayland Farm, near Cynthiana, KY, and died there on 20 July 1987, being buried with her husband in the Battle Grove Cemetery, Cynthiana, KY. Her Burgess Bible record was transcribed by the author and published shortly after her death ("Edward Burgess of Scott County, Kentucky—His Family and the Family Bible Record," by Michael Burgess, in *Kentucky Ancestors, Quarterly of the Kentucky Historical Society* 24 [Summer, 1988]: 2-6).

6q. **Sarah Edward "Sallie."** Born 3 May 1876 (1875 on tombstone) in Scott Co., KY. Listed in the 1900-10 censuses living with her mother, and in 1920 living alone. Sallie Burgess died unmarried on 24 May 1924 in Scott Co., and is buried in the Georgetown Cemetery.

6r. **Cassius Caesar.** Born 25 Sept. 1878 in Scott Co., KY. See below for full entry.

"Abram Fields, administrator of Joseph Fields's estate, was a surveyor, and brought Sarah and Greenberry Fields to Kentucky. Abram married Johannah Peck in Montgomery Co., Maryland.... Nancy Noland Fields died in Montgomery Co. on 1 Jan. 1784. Her husband Joseph died the same year, same place. Johannah Fields died 15 Mar. 1807. Greenberry Fields, brother to Sarah and son of Nancy Noland, died in Kentucky 5 of Aug. 1819. Bathsheba Hews [died] 16 of Sept. 1823; [I] have heard the older boys say she was a sister of Edward 'Neddy' Burgess Sr. [actually, she was his mother, although he also had a sister of that name]. He ['Neddy'] was born 1777, was an Englishman, and had blue eyes and fair hair. He came to Kentucky in 1795; along with him came John Vance, Asher Hinton, Benjamin Carr, William Price, and Abram Fields who was married to Johannah Peck or Pack. Edward Burgess settled at Paris, Kentucky, and it is said the Indians fought them, so he came on to Elk Lick, Scott Co., Kentucky, and built a home on what Sarah calls the "Cash" Place, because after the Neddy Burgess house burned Cash bought the land from J. C. B. Burgess and put up a house on it and lived in it for a while. Neddy's house was two-story with an attic built of log. [On] Feb. the 6th, 1800 he was married to Sarah Fields, daughter of Nancy Noland and Joseph Fields. The house had two rooms to the front, plus the upstairs and a stairway to the attic. Behind the front of the house was a dog trot, and behind that the kitchens. There were carved walnut mantles and open fireplaces in every room."—Ella Burgess Thomson.

[William (I)[1], Edward (I)[2], William (II)[3], Edward (V)[4], Edward (IX)[5]]

JAMES GREENBERRY BURGESS
(1836-1863)
OF SCOTT COUNTY, KENTUCKY

6a. **James Greenberry** *[son of Edward (IX)].* Born 12 Oct. 1836 in Scott Co., KY. Married Mary Elizabeth Fields on 10 Aug. 1858 in Scott Co., KY (she was born 22 Aug. 1840, daughter of Zephaniah Fields Sr. and Mary Neale [Zephaniah remarried Gabraella Adams, sister of James's mother, Mary Ann Adams, on 6 June 1857 in Scott Co. {Gabraella was born 1822}], and died 15 Jan. 1874, buried in the Old Fields Cemetery, near Sadieville, KY). Listed in the 1860 census for Scott Co., KY. James Burgess was a farmer in Scott Co. He enlisted in Co. D., 9th Kentucky Mounted Infantry (the so-called "Orphan's Brigade"), Confederate Army, participating in the Battle of Shiloh in 1862. He died of illness on 22 Feb. 1863 at Chattanooga, TN (so noted on the company muster roll of Apr. 1863). His estate was inventoried in Scott. Co. on 9 May 1863 (*Will Book #O*, p. 138). Mary is living with Zephaniah and Gabraella (or Gabriella) Fields in the 1870 census.

The Children of James G. Burgess:

7a. **John Washington (I).** Born 8 Jan. 1860 (or 1859) in Scott Co., KY. Married Ida A. Estes on 3 Mar. 1881 in Scott Co. (she was born Feb. 1863 in KY, the daughter of W. and Notley C. Estes). Listed in the 1880 census with Gabraella Fields; Ida appears as head of the family in 1900, and is living with her daughter in 1910. John W. Burgess was a farmer on his father's land in Scott Co.; he died there on 11 Nov. 1886, and is buried in the Old Fields Cemetery, near Sadieville, KY.

8a. **Jessie G(abraella?).** Born Apr. 1885 in Scott Co., KY. Married Andrew T. Perkins (he was born 1875 in KY), and had at least the following children: *Earl B.* (born 1906); *Carl B.* (born 17 Mar. 1908, died Apr. 1974 at Lexington, KY). Listed in the 1910-20 censuses for Georgetown, Scott Co., KY. She may be the Jessie B. Perkins who was born 18 Nov. 1884 and died in 28 May 1971 at Barren, Hart Co., KY.

7b. **Mary Frances (I) "Mollie."** Born 21 Apr. 1862 in Scott Co., KY. Married William Vance "Bunk" Mulberry on 27 Mar. 1879 in Scott Co. (he was the son of Jacob and Lucinda Mulberry), and had children: *Durand Burgess* (born 17 Sept. 1880, died 5 Apr. 1926, buried with his parents); *(Jacob) Frederick* (born 19 Aug. 1882, died 15 Feb. 1929, buried with his parents); *Mary Elizabeth "Myrtle"* (born 12 Apr. 1885); *Maxie* (born 10 Aug. 1887, died 10 Aug. 1888); *Sarah Frances* (born 1889, married ___ Durwood, and secondly ___ Jones, and died 28 Sept. 1979); *Maxie Eller* (born 20 Nov. 1894, died 12 Jan. 1897). Mollie Mulberry died on 28 Jan. 1946 in Scott Co., and is buried with her husband in the Jacob Mulberry Cemetery.

[William (I)[1], Edward (I)[2], William (II)[3], Edward (V)[4], Edward (IX)[5]]

BENJAMIN KENN BURGESS
(1846-1933)

OF SCOTT COUNTY, KENTUCKY

6f. **Benjamin Kenn** *[son of Edward (IX)].* Born 29 Aug. 1846 in Scott Co., KY. Married his first cousin, Susan Ellen "Susellen" Drake, on 7 Feb. 1867 in Scott Co. (she was born 1841, daughter of Bathsheba Burgess and Henry Drake, and died between 1880-88); married secondly Frances "Fannie" True about 1889, possibly in Owen Co. (she died on 31 Jan. 1920). Listed in the 1870-80 censuses for the Caney Precinct, Owen Co., KY, and from 1900-20 in Scott Co. Ben Burgess was a farmer in Scott Co. He died there on 17 Mar. 1933, and is buried in an unmarked grave in the Beard Cemetery, Davis, KY.

The Children of Ben Burgess:

7a. **(James) Edward (III).** Born 14 Nov. 1873 in Owen Co., KY. See below for full entry.
7b. **Mary Vanetta.** She is called "Marie" in the 1920 census. Born 26 Aug. 1891 in Scott Co., KY. Married Raymond C. Miley on 20 Mar. 1920 in Harrison Co., KY (he was born 17 July 1896, and died 9 Feb. 1947). Listed in the 1920 census with her father. Mary Miley died childless on 15 Aug. 1964 in Harrison Co., KY, and is buried with her husband in the Beard Cemetery, Davis, KY.
7c. **Sarah Ella (II) "Sadie."** Born 13 Feb. 1893 in Scott Co., KY. Married Lucius Dunn on 16 Dec. 1915 in Harrison Co., KY (he was born 14 Jan. 1892, and died 3 Nov. 1982 at Cynthiana, aged 90 years), and had children:

Ruby DUNN. Born 28 Dec. 1916, married Stanley Hilton on 20 Dec. 1953, and had children: *Deborah Ann* (born 17 Nov. 1954 in Harrison Co., married James English); *Johnie Sue* (twin; born 13 Sept. 1956 in Harrison Co.); *Ruby Lou* (twin; born 13 Sept. 1956 in Harrison Co., married Jeff Stephens, and had children: Jessica Hall [born 20 Feb. 1981]). ***Ruby HILTON*** died on 14 Sept. 1956 in Harrison Co.

Emerson "Bud" DUNN. Born 15 May 1918, married thirdly Elaine M. Lewis, and had children: *Billie Ann* (married Timmy Yeomans); *David* (married Josie Sharp); *Stephen* (married Cathy ___). ***Bud DUNN*** lives at Florence, AL.

Sadie DUNN died on 30 Apr. 1984 at Cynthiana, KY, aged 91 years, and is buried with her husband in the Battle Grove Cemetery, Cynthiana, KY. Before her death, she was questioned extensively by her cousins, Christine Glass and Mae Price, and confirmed many of the stories about older members of the family.

JAMES EDWARD BURGESS OF SCOTT CO., KENTUCKY
[Benjamin Kenn[6]]

7a. **(James) Edward (III)** *[son of Benjamin Kenn].* Born 14 Nov. 1873 in Owen Co., KY. Married Lula Thomas "Lulie" Green on 12 Dec. 1889 in Scott Co. (she was born 7 Apr. 1871 in KY, and died on 24 Dec. 1934 in Scott Co.); married secondly Gladys Gillispie in 1935 (div.); married thirdly Christine Davies Jones on 7 Jan. 1937 (div.; she was born on 24 Apr. 1919, remarried his son by his first marriage, Clarence Marvin Burgess, on 7 June 1947, and died 2 Oct. 1981). Listed in the 1900-20 censuses for Scott Co., KY, and in the 1917 draft register of Scott Co. Ed Burgess was a farmer in Scott Co. He died on 3 Dec. 1956 at Cincinnati, OH, but is buried in the Porter Cemetery, Porter, KY with his first and third wives.

8a. **Owen Arthur.** Born 6 Oct. 1890 in Owen Co., KY. See below for full entry.
8b. **(Walter) Scott.** Born 24 Aug. 1892 in Owen Co., KY. See below for full entry.
8c. **Child.** Born and died about 1894 in Scott Co., KY.
8d. **Lafayette France.** Born 22 July 1895 in Scott Co., KY. See below for full entry.

8e. **(Ella) Florence.** Born 25 Jan. 1897 in Scott Co., KY. Married Roy Greene on 26 Dec. 1922, and had children: *Ruth* (born 8 Feb. 1924 in OH); *Mary Lou* (born 8 Nov. 1927 in OH, married Phillip Borgo, and had children: Denice; Michael; *Mary Lou* married secondly David Stowe). Florence Greene was a school teacher. She died on 22 Dec. 1976 in Ohio.

8f. **(Justis) Goebel.** Born 22 Dec. 1899 in Scott Co., KY. See below for full entry.

8g. **Ola Susan "Cat."** Born 8 Sept. 1901 in Scott Co., KY. Married Tensley Miranda Hamm on 11 Aug. 1934 in OH (he was born on 23 Sept. 1907, and died Feb. 1986 at Loveland, OH), and had children: *Janet Lorraine* (born 22 Oct. 1936, married Ronald Laverne Brooks on 22 Apr. 1961 [he was born 15 Aug. 1933], and had children: Ronald Lee [born 4 Aug. 1963]). Cat Hamm died on 22 Dec. 1981 in Ohio.

8h. **(Benjamin) Cam.** Born 23 Dec. 1903 in Scott Co., KY. See below for full entry.

8i. **Millie Frances.** Born 18 Oct. 1905 in Scott Co., KY. Married Hubert H. Witt on 28 June 1930, and had children: *Wanda* (born 11 Oct. 1932, married Humberto Bravo on 1 Mar. 1958 [he was born 13 Jan. 1930], and had children: Sally [born 3 July 1959]; Humberto Jr. [born 15 July 1960]; Wanda Jr. [born 18 Dec. 1961]); *Beverly Sue* (born 12 Aug. 1938, married Samuel A. Carter on 24 June 1961 [he was born 5 Aug. 1934], and had children: Marisa Faith [born 22 Sept. 1965]; Winnona Grace [born 21 Apr. 1967]; Nathan [born 21 Oct. 1972]). Millie Witt died on 22 Oct. 1991 at Cincinnati, OH.

8j. **(Lillie) Helen.** Born 14 Mar. 1908 in Scott Co., KY. Married Dave Covington on 12 May 1926 in Scott Co.; married secondly Wilbur Beard on 4 May 1935; married thirdly William Stevens on 12 Dec. 1941 (he was born 23 Feb. 1907, and died Nov. 1985 at Lancaster, KY). Helen Stevens died in Feb. 1985 at Lancaster, KY.

8k. **(Clarence) Marvin.** Born 22 Feb. 1910 in Scott Co., KY. See below for full entry.

8l. **Emery Helvy** (twin). Born 9 Nov. 1912 in Scott Co., KY. See below for full entry.

8m. **(Mary) Elva "Elvie"** (twin). Born 9 Nov. 1912 in Scott Co., KY. Married Bruce L. Houghton on 4 Jan. 1944 (he was born 19 Nov. 1907, and died Aug. 1986 at Cincinnati, OH), and had children: *Kathryn Susan* (born 30 Dec. 1949, married Timothy O'Brien on 25 Oct. 1975 [he was born 4 Nov. 1949]). Elvie Houghton lives at Norwood, OH.

8n. **Child.** Born and died about 1914 in Scott Co., KY.

8o. **Leon Lanham.** Born 15 Oct. 1915 in Scott Co., KY. Married Naomi Bryan on 17 June 1943. Leon Burgess currently lives at Akron, OH.

8p. **(Dorothy) Christine.** Born 14 Nov. 1917 in Scott Co., KY. Married William "Bill" Pool on 1 Dec. 1937 in Grant Co., KY; married secondly Luther Cook on 18 May 1940, and had children: *Frederick* (born 20 Dec. 1941, married Paula Lyons, and had children: Mark Alan [born 30 Dec. 1971]; Jamie [born 11 Apr. 1976]; *Patricia* (born 18 Oct. 1943, married William Sonnycalf on 2 Aug. 1963, and had children: Danielle Paige [born 19 Mar. 1967]; Christopher Scott [born 18 Dec. 1971]). Chris married thirdly Wally Clepper on 14 Dec. 1968.

8q. **Norma Gene.** Born 9 Sept. 1937 in Scott Co., KY. Married Harry Edmonds on 21 Nov. 1958 (he was born 6 Sept. 1932). Norma Edmonds lives at Norwood, OH.

8r. **Julia Yvonne.** Born 24 Aug. 1938 in Scott Co., KY. Married Teddy Lakes on 25 Jan. 1962 (or 1963).

8s. **James Wayne.** Born 13 Dec. 1939 in Scott Co., KY. See below for full entry.

8t. **Sue Carol.** Born 5 July 1941 in Scott Co., KY. Married Billy Joe James in Jan. 1959 (he was born 18 June 1932, and died 18 Oct. 1980), and had children: *Billy Wayne* (born 14 Aug. 1960 in Fayette Co., KY). Sue James lives at Lexington, KY; she has contributed greatly to this book.

8u. **Linda Fay (I).** Born 10 May 1943 in Scott Co., KY. Married Warren Kent Denniston on 14 Dec. 1963 (div. 1979).

OWEN ARTHUR BURGESS OF SCOTT CO., KENTUCKY

[Benjamin Kenn[6], James Edward (III)[7]]

8a. **Owen Arthur** *[son of James Edward (III)].* Born 6 Oct. 1890 (or 1891, according to his draft record) in Owen Co., KY. Married Margery Elizabeth Smith on 26 June 1916 in Scott Co. (she was the daughter of Elisha Smith); married secondly Hattie Frances Robey on 6 Jan. 1934 in Scott Co. Listed in the 1917 draft register and 1920 census for Scott Co., and served in World War I. Owen Burgess worked as an auto worker in the General Motors plant, Norwood, OH, and also farmed in Scott Co., KY. He died on 30 Oct. 1974 in Scott Co., and is buried in the Porter Cemetery.

9a. **Harold Webber.** Born 17 Jan. 1917 in Scott Co., KY. Married secondly Vera Reed Vance on 28 Dec. 1963 in Scott Co. Harold Burgess works for the U.S. Postal Service at Georgetown, KY.

9b. **Russell Eugene.** Born 28 Oct. 1934 at Norwood, OH. Married Mavis Lorean Baker on 4 Nov. 1972 in Scott Co. Russell Burgess drives a beer truck for the Sam Penn Co. at Porter, KY.

9c. **(Owen) Clayton.** Born 17 July 1936 at Norwood, OH. Married Mary Louise Gooden on 11 Jan. 1963 in Scott Co. (div.; she was born 30 Sept. 1946); married secondly ___. Clay Burgess is a farmer near Porter, KY.

10a. **Roy Scott.** Born 29 July 1963 in Scott Co., KY. He lives and works in Lexington, KY.
10b. **Mary Beth (II).** Born 6 Dec. 1967 in Scott Co., KY.
10c. **Douglas Clayton.** Born 29 Sept. 1972 in Scott Co., KY.

9d. **Lula Bell.** Born 12 May 1944 in Scott Co., KY. Married William Howard Sharp on 7 Feb. 1964 in Scott Co., and had children: *Aloma Lou*; *William Michael.* Lula Sharp lives in Georgetown, KY.

WALTER SCOTT BURGESS OF SCOTT CO., KENTUCKY

[Benjamin Kenn[6], James Edward (III)[7]]

8b. **(Walter) Scott** *[son of James Edward (III)].* Born 24 Aug. 1892 in Owen Co., KY. Married Frances Elizabeth Mulberry on 21 Dec. 1921 in Scott Co. (she was born 11 Apr. 1905, remarried Stamper White after her husband's death, died 23 Sept. 1959, and is buried with her first husband). Listed in the 1917 draft register and 1920 census for Scott Co., and served in World War I. Scott Burgess was a farmer in Scott Co., KY. He died there on 14 Jan. 1933, and is buried in the Knights of Pythian Cemetery, Sadieville, KY.

9a. **Arnetta Lee.** Born 23 Feb. 1924 in Scott Co., KY. Married James L. Davies, and had children: *La Merlin Faye* (born 8 Mar. 1945, married ___ Wolf); *Linda Day* (born 14 May 1946, married ___ Strascina); *Richard* (born 14 Dec. 1947). Arnetta Davies lives at Albuquerque, NM.

9b. **Eva May.** Born 23 Dec. 1925 in Scott Co., KY. Married Carl Dewey Lane (dec.), and had children: *Renoma Ray* (born 30 Sept. 1946; dec.); *Scott Walter* (born 5 June 1951, lives in Florida). Eva Lane lives at Seal Beach, FL.

9c. **Robert Lewis.** Born 2 Dec. 1927 in Scott Co., KY. Robert Burgess is an artist and musician at Albuquerque, NM.

LAFE BURGESS OF SCOTT CO., KENTUCKY

[Benjamin Kenn[6], James Edward (III)[7]]

8d. **Lafayette France "Lafe"** *[son of James Edward (III)].* Born 22 July 1895 in Scott Co., KY. Married (Ogla) Myrtle West on 24 Dec. 1920 in Scott Co. (she was born 2 Feb. 1902, daughter of George and Jennie West, and lives at Georgetown). Listed in the 1917 draft register of Scott Co., and served in World War I, and in the 1920 census with his brother, Walter Scott. Lafe Burgess farmed several large tracts of land in Scott Co. He died there on 14 Jan. 1975, and is buried in the Georgetown Cemetery. Myrtle Burgess lives at Georgetown, KY.

9a. **Paul Thomas.** Born 23 Oct. 1921 in Scott Co., KY. Married Adelle Downey on 24 Feb. 1946 at Dayton, OH (she was born 22 Mar. 1921 in Henry Co., KY, daughter of Oney and Mary Downey, and died on 20 Feb. 1994 at Lexington, KY). Paul Burgess managed his father's lands in Scott Co. before retiring. He died on 4 Feb. 1993, and is buried with his wife in the Georgetown Cemetery.

10a. **George Thomas (III).** Born 5 Feb. 1951 at Lexington, KY. Married Diania Sue Gillespie on 8 Aug. 1971 in Scott Co.; married secondly Elizabeth Ann Quinn on 23 Apr. 1977 in Scott Co. (she was born 31 Aug. 1957); married thirdly Sharon "Sherry" King in Feb. 1981; married fourthly Johanna Lynn Rogers on 28 Nov. 1987 in Campbell Co., KY (she was born 16 July 1956 at Covington, KY, daughter of Harry Coleman Rogers and Lois Jones; by her first husband, ___ Carr, she had children: *Leslie Marie* [born 26 Feb. 1978 at Lexington, KY]; *Justin Ryan* [born 21 Apr. 1983 at Lexington, KY]). George Burgess is a tool and die maker at Johnson Control, Georgetown, KY; Johanna Burgess is a nurse.

11a. **Mary Paula.** Born 4 Mar. 1974 in Scott Co., KY. Married Robert Douglas Fightmaster on 19 Oct. 1992 in Scott Co., KY.
11b. **Robert Lafe.** Born 15 July 1979 in Scott Co., KY.
11c. **Jennifer Marie.** Born 7 Dec. 1983 at Frankfort, KY.

GOEBEL BURGESS OF SUMMIT CO., OHIO

[Benjamin Kenn^6, James Edward (III)^7]

8f. **(Justis) Goebel** *[son of James Edward (III)].* His name is also spelled Justice and Justus; he was named for Kentucky Gov. William Goebel. Born 22 Dec. 1899 in Scott Co., KY. Married Leola Holm on 12 May 1934. Listed in the 1917 draft register of Scott Co., and in the 1920 census with his father. Goebel Burgess was a factory worker at Akron, OH. He died there in Oct. 1985.

9a. **Terry Lee (I)** (ad.). Born 14 May 1942 in OH. Terry Burgess was an auto mechanic at Akron, OH. He was killed in an auto accident on 24 May 1960 at Barberton, OH, and is buried in the Greenlawn Memorial Cemetery, Akron.

CAM BURGESS OF SUMMIT CO., OHIO

[Benjamin Kenn^6, James Edward (III)^7]

8h. **(Benjamin) Cam** *[son of James Edward (III)].* His name is given as Cam B. C. Burgess in the 1920 census. Born 23 Dec. 1903 in Scott Co., KY. Married Teresa Corey in Dec. 1941. Listed in the 1920 census with his father. Cam Burgess was a truck driver for Marathon Oil. He died on 19 June 1984 at Akron, OH.

9a. **Karen Ann.** Born 11 May 1942 at Akron, OH; died there on 6 Nov. 1952.
9b. **David Cam.** Born 23 Jan. 1947 at Akron, OH. Married Kathryn Lingenfilter. David C. Burgess works for B. F. Goodrich Company at Akron, OH.

10a. **(David) Scott.** Born 13 Aug. 1964 at Akron, OH.
10b. **Phillip Benjamin.** Born 22 Mar. 1979 at Akron, OH.
10c. **Erin Tommie.** Born 7 Nov. 1981 at Akron, OH.

9c. **Gary John.** Born 6 June 1948 at Akron, OH. Married Alice Marie Boring. Gary Burgess works for General Tire Co. at Akron, OH.

MARVIN BURGESS OF SCOTT CO., KENTUCKY

[Benjamin Kenn^6, James Edward (III)^7]

8k. **(Clarence) Marvin** *[son of James Edward (III)].* Born 22 Feb. 1910 in Scott Co., KY. Married Alma Dee Witt on 7 Mar. 1936 in Scott Co. (div.); married secondly Christine Davies Jones Burgess, his stepmother, on 7 June 1947 in Fayette Co., KY (she was born 24 Apr. 1919 in Scott Co., KY, the daughter of Norman and Lillie Belle Jones, and died on 2 Oct. 1981 at Georgetown, KY, buried Porter Cemetery). Marvin Burgess worked at Kentuckian Horse Farms, Georgetown before retiring; he now lives with his daughter, Lula.

9a. **Larry David.** Born 22 Jan. 1947 at Georgetown, KY. Married (Catherine) Teresa Smith. Larry Burgess works for the Burgess Tire Co., Corinth, KY.
9b. **Sherrel Landis.** Born 2 July 1949 at Georgetown, KY. Married Ted Sharpe on 7 Dec. 1968 in Scott Co., and had children: *Kim*; *Ted Jr.*; married secondly Tommy Davis in 1972, and had children: *Donald Wayne*; married thirdly Roger Thair. Sherrel Thair lives at Frankfort, KY.
9c. **Gloria Joan.** Born 20 Aug. 1950 at Georgetown, KY. Married Flem D. Warren on 6 Dec. 1966 in Scott Co. (he was born 14 Aug. 1944), and had six children; married secondly Orville Hubbard, and had children: *Orville Jr.*; *Amanda "Sunshine"*; married thirdly David Justice. Gloria Justice lives at Cynthiana, KY.
9d. **Rickie Clarence.** Born 15 Oct. 1951 at Georgetown, KY. Married (Marcellous) Hope Woolbert on 19 Aug. 1978 in Upper Deerfield Township, NJ (she was born 10 Dec. 1959 at Bluefield, WV, daughter of Larry Wayne Woolbert and Betty Lee Bevill). Rickie Burgess owns his own tire company at Perryville, KY.

10a. **Rickie Lee.** Born 8 July 1981 at Bridgeton, NJ.
10b. **Christine Kay.** Born 14 May 1991 at Danville, KY.

9e. **Lula May** (twin). Born 25 Sept. 1954 at Georgetown, KY. Married Jackie Pollard on 19 Mar. 1984 at Carlisle, KY, and had children: *Yoko Lillie Christine* (born 6 May 1984 at Georgetown, KY). Lula Pollard lives at Carlisle, KY.

9f. **Sandra Kay (III)** (twin). Born 25 Sept. 1954 at Georgetown, KY. Married Wiley Jordan on 27 Sept. 1975 in Knox Co., KY (div.), and had children: *Andrew Christian*; Sandra married secondly Mack McIntosh (div.), and had children: *Benjamin Eric.*

9g. **Randy (II)** (nmn) (twin). Born 1 Mar. 1958 at Georgetown, KY. His children are by his common-law wife, Della Jean Turner. Randy Burgess works for his brother, Rick Burgess.

10a. **Randy Bo.** He uses the surname Turner. Born 1 July 1980 at Georgetown, KY.

10b. **Ashley Jean.** She uses the surname Turner. Born 20 Mar. 1984 at Georgetown, KY.

10c. **Joshua.** He used the surname Turner. Born about 1986, died about 1988 at Lexington, KY, buried in the Lexington Cemetery.

9h. **Wendy** (nmn) (twin). Born 1 Mar. 1958 at Georgetown, KY. Married Trusten Romans on 24 May 1974 in Scott Co. (he was born 9 Jan. 1939, and died Apr. 1987 at Georgetown), and had children: *Trusten Jr.* (born 16 Mar. 1978); *Chrystle Ann* (born 26 Mar. 1979). Wendy married secondly Neveal T. Williams, and had children: *David* (born 1983); *Thomas* (twin); *Deana* (twin); *Ashley*; *Sarah* (twin); *Stephanie* (twin). Wendy Williams lives at Stamping Ground, KY.

9i. **Sheila Wray.** Born 15 June 1959 at Georgetown, KY. Married Wendell F. Centers on 12 Jan. 1981 in Scott Co., and had children: *Fallon Rae* (born 18 Jan. 1982). Sheila Centers lives at Frankfort, KY.

10a. **Justin Thomas.** Born 22 May 1979 at Georgetown, KY. He was adopted by his stepfather, and now uses the surname Centers.

EMERY BURGESS OF SCOTT CO., KENTUCKY

[Benjamin Kenn[6], James Edward (III)[7]]

8l. **Emery Helvy** (twin) *[son of James Edward (III)].* Born 9 Nov. 1912 in Scott Co., KY. Married Eleanora Braden on 10 Feb. 1937 in Grant Co., KY (she was born 17 Aug. 1918). Emery Burgess was a farmer in Scott Co. He died there on 8 Dec. 1978, and is buried in the Porter Cemetery. Eleanora Burgess lives at Georgetown, KY.

9a. **Mary Ann (X).** Born 30 Jan. 1943 in Scott Co., KY. Married Lloyd Thomas Adams on 29 Sept. 1961 in Scott Co., and had children: *Barbara Lynn* (born 9 June 1970). Mary Adams lives at Stamping Ground, KY.

JAMES WAYNE BURGESS OF HARRISON CO., KENTUCKY

[Benjamin Kenn[6], James Edward (III)[7]]

8s. **James Wayne "Buck"** *[son of James Edward (III)].* Born 13 Dec. 1939 in Scott Co., KY. Married (Beverly) Sue Moreland on 24 May 1960 in Scott Co. (she was born 18 Nov. 1942, daughter of Richard Moreland and Muriel Cook, and remarried Harold Owen Whitlock on 14 Oct. 1964); married secondly Diane Sara Lemmonds about 1968. Buck Burgess owns Burgess & Son Tire Distributor, Georgetown, KY, and lives on a small farm near Hinton, Harrison Co., KY.

9a. **Ronald Wayne "Ronnie."** Born 12 May 1961 in Scott Co., KY. Married Rebecca Rose Harrod on 20 July 1979 in Scott Co. (div.; she was born 23 July 1963); married secondly Barbara J. McCallister on 20 July 1982 in Scott Co. (div.); married thirdly Anita A. Griffith on 19 May 1989 in Scott Co. (she died on 2 Aug. 1991 at Georgetown, KY).

9b. **David Wayne.** Born 29 Sept. 1969 at Bridgeton, NJ. Married Alean D. Howard on 25 Nov. 1987 in Harrison Co., KY.

9c. **Brian Todd.** Born 7 Dec. 1971 at Bridgeton, NJ.

[William (I)[1], Edward (I)[2], William (II)[3], Edward (V)[4], Edward (IX)[5]]

JOHN C. B. BURGESS
(1852-1920)

OF SCOTT COUNTY, KENTUCKY

6i. **John Cabell Breckinridge** *[son of Edward (IX)].* Born 11 Mar. 1852 (1853 on tombstone) in Scott Co., KY. Married Martha Susan Sharpe on 23 Dec. 1875 in Scott Co. (she was born 14 Apr. 1859, daughter of A. J. Sharpe, and died 24 July 1933). Listed in the 1880-1920 censuses for Scott Co., KY. John C. B. Burgess was a farmer in Scott Co. He died there on 2 Nov. 1920, and is buried with his wife in the Georgetown Cemetery.

The Children of John Burgess:

7a. **Edmonia "Mona"** (nmn). Born 24 May 1878 in Scott Co., KY. Married James Wilson Collins (he was born 14 Feb. 1868, and died 11 Dec. 1938), and had children: *Jimmie Martha* (born 13 July 1899, married Ray Hopper [he was born 4 June 1901, and died Apr. 1984 at Lexington], and died May 1979 at Lexington, KY); *Pauline* (married Talton K. Stone [he was born 17 July 1906, and died Dec. 1987], worked as a teacher, and lives at Elizabethtown, KY); *Mary* (married ___ Mudd); *Lillian Burgess* (married ___ Smith, and had two daughters). Mona Collins died on 27 May 1948, and is buried with her husband in the Georgetown Cemetery.

7b. **(Noble) Moses.** Born 7 Aug. 1880 in Scott Co., KY. See below for full entry.

7c. **Mary Susan (I).** Born 5 Apr. 1882 in Scott Co., KY. Married Frank Gano (he was born 20 Feb. 1872, and died 20 Dec. 1953 in Scott Co.), and had children: *Burgess*. Mary Gano died on 25 July 1948 in Scott Co., and is buried with her husband in the Georgetown Cemetery.

7d. **Lillian M. (I).** Born 17 June 1886 in Scott Co., KY. Married Walter S. Powell (he was born 1884, and died 16 Feb. 1951 in Scott Co.), and had one step-daughter. Lillie Powell died on 5 Mar. 1959 in Fayette Co., KY, and is buried with her husband in the Georgetown Cemetery.

MOSES BURGESS OF SCOTT CO., KENTUCKY
[John Cabell Breckinridge[6]]

7b. **(Noble) Moses** *[son of John Cabell Breckinridge].* Born 7 Aug. 1880 in Scott Co., KY. Married his first cousin, once removed, Laura Stevenson Burgess (she was born 1 Jan. 1882, daughter of Thomas Jefferson Burgess and Josephine C. Pack, and died 26 Feb. 1936). Listed in the 1917 draft register and 1920 census for Scott Co., KY. "Mose" Burgess was a farm manager, land owner, and businessman in Scott Co., operating Burgess & Gano, a general merchandise store, at Sadieville, KY; part of his farm on Mallard Point is now a school and housing development. He died there on 25 Dec. 1953, and is buried in the Georgetown Cemetery.

8a. **Thomas Jefferson II "Jed."** Born 10 July 1906 in Scott Co., KY. Married Pauline Giles on 18 Jan. 1926 in Harrison Co., KY (she was born 1904 and died 1939, buried Beard Cemetery); married secondly Louise Mulberry Osborne on 31 July 1941 in Fayette Co., KY. Jed Burgess was a wool trader in Scott Co., and managed his father's estate, making him one of the largest landowners in Scott Co. He died there on 30 Apr. 1972, and is buried in the Georgetown Cemetery. Louise Burgess lives east of Sadieville, KY.

9a. **Thomas Jefferson III "Tommy."** Born 22 Mar. 1942 at Lexington, KY. Married Jane Leslie Lucas on 1 Dec. 1968 in Scott Co. (div.); married secondly Anga L. Wagers on 8 Nov. 1985 in Fayette Co. (div.). Tommy manages his father's lands in Scott Co., KY. He lives at Sadieville, KY.

10a. **Catherine Louise "Cathy."** Born 9 Feb. 1971 in Scott Co., KY.

[William (I)[1], Edward (I)[2], William (II)[3], Edward (V)[4], Edward (IX)[5]]

LAFAYETTE STIPP BURGESS
(1864-1902)
OF SCOTT COUNTY, KENTUCKY

6m. **Lafayette Stipp "Bud."** He is called Lewis Burgess in his obituary. Born 27 Nov. 1864 (or 1865, according to his tombstone) in Scott Co., KY. Married Sallie Pack (she was born 1867, a first cousin of Josephine Pack [who married Bud's cousin, T. J. Burgess], remarried Luke H. Paxton about 1906 [he was born 1853, and died 1943], and died 1942, by him having had one daughter: *Mary Alma* [born 13 Aug. 1907 at Sadieville, KY, married Glenn Haddon Thomas, was a registered nurse, and died 8 May 1989 at Lexington, KY {buried Georgetown Cemetery}, having had children: Mary Glenn {living at Lexington in 1989}]). Listed in the 1900 census for Scott Co. Bud Burgess owned a large farm in rural Scott Co. On 18 Nov. 1902 he was run over by an interurban train between Georgetown and Lexington, and died within a few hours; he is buried in the Georgetown Cemetery.

The Children of Bud Burgess:

7a. **Jessie Pack.** Born 6 Feb. 1890 in Scott Co., KY. Married Ernest M. Shirley (a postman), and had children: *Ernest M. Jr.* (married four times). Jessie Shirley died on 29 Dec. 1989 at Miami, FL, just short of her 100th birthday.

7b. **Theresa (II).** Born 24 Oct. 1891 in Scott Co., KY; died there on 29 Dec. 1891, and is buried in the John Pack Cemetery.

7c. **Helena Elizabeth.** Born 1 Jan. 1893 in Scott Co., KY. Helena Burgess was a nurse in Scott Co., KY. She died unmarried on 5 Feb. 1984 at Lexington, KY, aged 91 years, and is buried in the Georgetown Cemetery.

7d. **Anne Laythem.** Born 15 Feb. 1895 in Scott Co., KY. Died there unmarried on 28 Oct. 1918, and is buried in the Georgetown Cemetery.

7e. **Richard Lot "Dick."** Born 27 Feb. 1897 in Scott Co., KY. Married Vivian Chowning (she was born 1905, worked as a school teacher at Sadieville, and died 4 Feb. 1965). Dick Burgess was a farmer on his father's lands in Scott Co. He died there childless on 13 Nov. 1959, and is buried with his wife in the Georgetown Cemetery.

7f. **Joseph Stipp.** Born 27 July 1899 in Scott Co., KY. Married Nell Eugene Marshall on 31 Dec. 1935 (she was born 16 Aug. 1903 in Scott Co.). Served in the U.S. Navy during World War I. Joe Burgess was a farmer with his brother on the family lands, near Eagle Creek, Scott Co. He died on 4 Feb. 1984 at Lexington, KY, and is buried in the Georgetown Cemetery. Nell Burgess taught school for 43 years in Scott Co. She currently lives at Sadieville, KY.

8a. **Julia Ann (IV) "Julianna."** Born 4 Nov. 1944 at Lexington, KY. Married Jerry Minsky, and had children: *Arthur James* (born 5 Oct. 1970 at Everett, WA); married secondly Ronald La Fleche. Julia La Fleche owns a greenhouse at Lexington, KY.

WEALTHY FARMER KILLED ON ROAD TO GEORGETOWN

"Lewis S. Burgess, a prominent and wealthy farmer of Scott County, was mangled by a car on the Georgetown Interurban last night, and died an hour later from his injuries. The accident occurred about 6:30 o'clock five and a half miles from this city. To some extent it is clouded in mystery.

"The man was lying beside the track with his head and arms resting upon the outer rail. In the darkness he was not observed by the motorman until the car was almost upon him, and the headlight showed the prostrate form. The air brakes were instantly set, and the motor was reversed, but the car struck the man in the back, throwing his head against the right fore wheel, and then twisted his legs under the car, which slid over them, leaving a mass of quivering, mangled flesh and bones.

"The car was in charge of Motorman Barker and Conductor Bonfield, and left Lexington for Georgetown at six o'clock. The accident occurred near the gate of the Lascell residence, which is but a few hundred yards this side of the switch. Burgess was not killed by the immediate shock.

"He was carefully lifted onto the incoming car, which arrived here about 7:30 o'clock. The ambulance was notified and met the car. Upon arrival he was taken to the Saint Joseph's Hospital, where the traction company had Dr. F. O. Young in waiting to render all possible medical service. Death came within fifteen minutes after the hospital was reached. There was a long gash across the head and face, and both feet were cut off above the ankles, and the body was otherwise bruised. There was, however, no fracture of the skull. Upon the advice of the traction company, the remains were taken in charge by Milward, and prepared for burial.

"Up to that time, the man was entirely unidentified. In his pockets were found two tax receipts from the Sheriff of Scott County, dated November 8, showing that L. S. Burgess had paid the county and State taxes on about $20,000 worth of property in his own right, and as executor of C. C. Burgess; a receipted bill upon which the name of L. S. Burgess appeared; a blank check on a Sadieville bank; several pieces of white paper on which memoranda had been written in pencil; an unused vest pocket blank book; a pocket handkerchief; and eleven silver dollars.

"These articles were turned over by Dr. Young to President Younger Alexander of the company, and the theory was formed that the man was L. S. Burgess, and that his home at or near Sadieville. *The Herald* at once communicated with Sadieville, and learned that L. S. Burgess was a prominent farmer who lived with his wife and three children two miles from that place, and that he had not been seen at Sadieville that day. At the same time a messenger was sent by *The Herald* from Sadieville to the home of Mr. Burgess, asking that some member of the family be sent to the telephone.

"After the remains were taken to the undertakers, they were identified by Mr. William Beasley, clerk at the Phoenix Hotel, who had known Mr. Burgess quite well. Mr. Beasley, in fact, was confident that the dead man was Mr. Burgess from the description given of him by a *Herald* reporter, even before he reviewed the remains. As to how Mr. Burgess came to be on the track will perhaps never be known."—*Lexington Herald*, 19 Nov. 1902

LEWIS S. BURGESS WAS LYING ACROSS RAIL

"Lewis S. Burgess, a wealthy farmer who lived near Sadieville, Scott County, was run over and mangled by a motor car on the Georgetown and Lexington Road at 6:30 o'clock last night, and died two hours later at St. Joseph's Hospital, never having regained consciousness from the shock....

"A telephone communication was held with Mrs. Burgess shortly after the tragedy. The shock almost prostrated her. She said he left home Monday to go to Georgetown, but she did not know how he came to be alone halfway between Georgetown and Lexington on such an inclement night. Mr. Burgess is said to have been in the habit of drinking periodically, but at long intervals, and never to any serious extent, and it is believed in the absence of any other explanation that on this occasion he had been intoxicated and wandered out on the road, and becoming weary, had set down by the track, then fallen asleep, where he lay till the car struck him. There seems to have been no motive either for the suicide or foul play theory. He had no enemies that anyone seems to know of, and the presence of eleven dollars in his pocket shows that robbery had not been committed, and the circumstances surrounding his life were such as to indicate no reason to take his life. Mr. Burgess was a man of about thirty-six years of age, and was in prosperous circumstances. He was a son of the late C. C. Burgess of Scott County, and was engaged in the cattle business. He was a man of genial disposition, well educated, and very popular with those who knew him. He has a sister, Mrs. Gano Shropshire, living at Georgetown."—*Lexington Leader*, 19 Nov. 1902.

THE CORONER'S INQUEST

The inquest was held at the undertaking establishment of W. R. Milward, and the motorman and conductor were exonerated of any blame. The first witness was J. J. Bonfield, the conductor of the car at the time the accident occurred. He testified as follows:

"My name is J. J. Bonfield. First saw the deceased when he got on my car at Georgetown to come to Lexington. He got on just as it was leaving Georgetown. He was intoxicated at the time, and kept on grumbling about something in an undertone. I spoke to him and he said he wanted to get off at the next stop. I told him that the next stop was at the switch, but that he had better go on to Lexington. When we got to the switch, we stopped for a few minutes waiting for the other car to pass us. The car came in sight just as we stopped. There is no house at the switch, just a telephone box. He spoke about getting off, and I sought to persuade him not to do so. He was then standing up in the rear vestibule. I told him not to get off as we would soon start for Lexington. He replied that he knew his own business and could do as he pleased. He got off at the rear and walked to the front of the car. He then crossed the track in front of the car and went on to the pike. He appeared to start off to walk toward Lexington.

"When the other car got on the switch, I signalled the motorman to start, and he gave a warning with the whistle. He did not come back and we went on without him. We were late in reaching Lexington, and started back immediately. This was about ten minutes past six o'clock last night. We had reached a point about five miles from Lexington, this side of the switch, when I felt a shock and the emergency brakes were thrown on. I was sitting on the rear seat in the car at the time. The car came to a sudden stop. The motorman came running through the car and said to me, 'We have run over a man.' It was dark, and we took the headlight from the front of the car and placed it at the rear so as to see down the track. We could hear the man groaning. I could not see him, and I did not know who he was. The man was found lying by the side of the track, bleeding profusely from a wound in the head. Both feet were crushed. I then recognized him as the man who had got off my car at the switch as we were coming this way.

"The headlight was in front when we ran over him. The car was just going up McManus Hill; when a car is going uphill the light is deflected into the ground, and does not show as far as when the car is on a level grade.

"In answer to Coroner Malloy: the deceased got angry at me because I had requested him to take another seat, as he was sitting by the side of a colored woman. He told me he was coming to Lexington when he boarded the car. He was intoxicated because I saw him stagger as he walked and I could smell the liquor on him. The reason I asked him to change his seat is that I saw the colored passenger was annoyed, and I knew no sober white man would have sat down there. He displayed a hand full of silver. I asked him to move, just as I gave him the receipt for his fare. Our instructions in regard to intoxicated passengers are to take care of them just as far as we can. We never allow them or any passenger to get off while the car is in motion. The deceased got off the car in spite of my warning. Judging from the manner in which he spoke to me, I felt I would have trouble with him if I tried to keep him on. After he walked away from the car, I did not see him again until we picked him up after he had been struck.

"In answer to Juror Corbin: when we saw him after he had been struck by the car, his body was lying at right angles with the track, and he was bleeding.

"In answer to Coroner Malloy: the car was going at the rate of about twenty miles an hour. When a car is going at that rate of speed, it cannot be stopped with the reverse lever on inside three or four car lengths. It is impossible to stop the car in a shorter distance than an object on the track can be seen from the car at night. If a man is walking on the track, he can been seen in time to stop the car before striking him. But when a man is lying down on the track, it is difficult to see him."—*Lexington Leader*, 19 Nov. 1902.

Edward Burgess, Jr.
(1816-1898)
(see page 179)

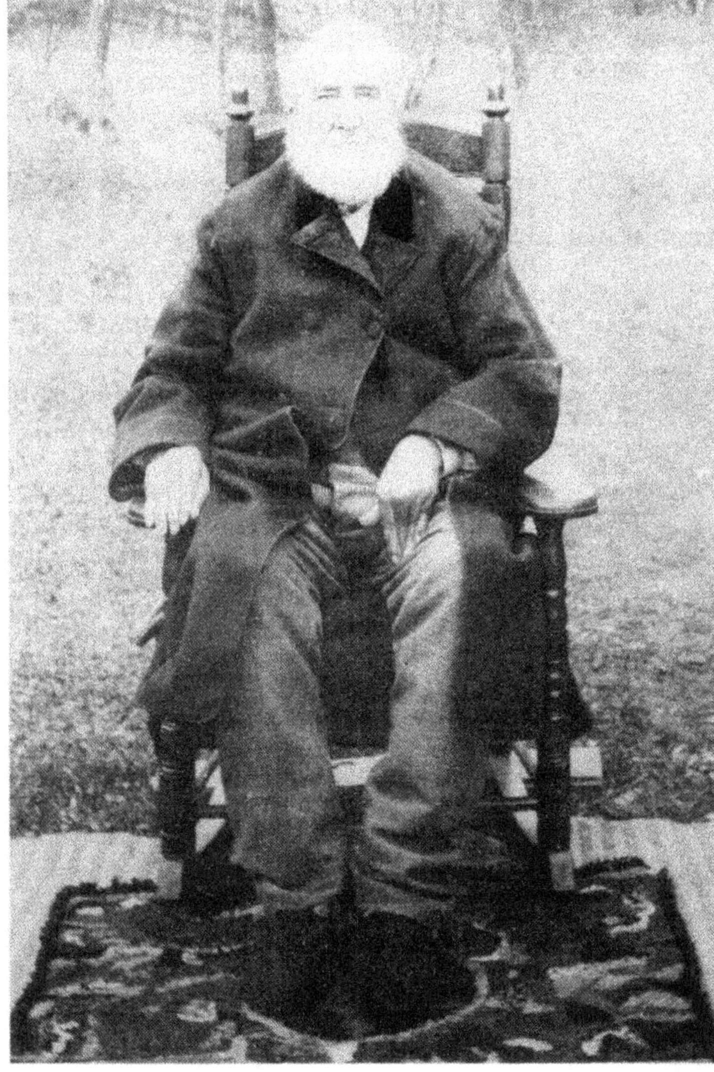

[William (I)[1], Edward (I)[2], William (II)[3], Edward (V)[4], Edward (IX)[5]]

LAZARUS N. BURGESS
(1867-1937)
OF ERIE COUNTY, NEW YORK

6n. **Lazarus Newton** *[son of Edward (IX)].* Born 30 Oct. 1867 in Scott Co., KY. Married Mary F. "Mollie" Johnson about 1889 (she was born 30 Nov. 1872 [or 1874], daughter of George F. Johnson, and died 1922). Listed in the 1900 census for Scott Co., KY living with George Johnson, and in 1910 in Fayette Co., KY (as "Lewis N."). Laz Burgess moved first to Corydon, IN, and then to Buffalo, NY by 1927, where he owned and operated a store at Delavan and West Streets; he also owned a farm at Williamsville, NY just outside Buffalo. He died on 31 May 1937, and is buried with his wife in the Georgetown Cemetery.

The Children of Laz Burgess:

7a. **Edward Caesar (I).** Born 3 Nov. 1890 in Scott Co., KY. See below for full entry.
7b. **Byron Lafayette.** Born 19 Aug. 1897 in Scott Co., KY. See below for full entry.
7c. **Margaret Helloise Lorrine.** Born 10 Oct. 1905 in Scott Co., KY. Married Elmer Hayes (he may have been born 30 Nov. 1911, and died Jan. 1987 at Buffalo), and had children. Margaret Hayes died on 1 Jan. 1980 at Buffalo, NY, and is buried in the Buffalo Medical School Cemetery. Her granddaughter, Marsha Anne Lorine Augustine "Mickey" Mayne, lives at Port Colborne, ON, Canada.
7d. **Daniel** (nmn) (ad.). Born 7 Apr. 1921 at Corydon, IN. See below for full entry.

EDWARD BURGESS OF HARRISON CO., MISSISSIPPI
[Lazarus Newton[6]]

7a. **Edward Caesar (I)** *[son of Lazarus Newton].* Born 3 Nov. 1890 in Scott Co., KY. Married Katherine ___ by 1910 (she was born 1891 in KY); married secondly Pauline Brown on 2 May 1931 at Edwards, MS (she was born 28 June 1910, remarried ___ Campbell, and died 14 July 1990 at Ocean Springs, MS). Listed with his father in the 1910 census. Ed Burgess worked at the Broadwater Beach Hotel at Biloxi, MS. He died there on 22 Dec. 1954, and is buried in the Southern Memorial Park Cemetery.

8a. **Edward Caesar (II).** Born 15 July 1932 at Biloxi, MS. Married Bonnie Grace Gillespie on 8 Nov. 1953 at Jackson, MS. Ed Burgess is a systems analyst with Trustmark National Bank, Jackson, MS.

9a. **Elise Gillespie.** Born 17 June 1956 at Hattiesburg, MS. Married Richard Steven Rogers on 24 Nov. 1974 at Jackson, MS, and had children: *Richard Aaron*; *Heather Anne.* Elise Rogers lives at Pearl, MS.
9b. **Emily Anne.** Born 20 Nov. 1960 at Jackson, MS. Married Glenn F. Boyce on 5 May 1983 at Jackson, MS, and had children: *Brittany*; *Danielle*; *Madeline.* Emily is a certified public accountant for MTEL Corp., Madison, MS.

8b. **Joy** (nmn). Born 26 Dec. 1934 at Vicksburg, MS. Married Lawrence Perkins, and had children: *Lawrence Jr.*; *Burgess Allen*; *Paula Steele.* Joy Perkins lives in Colorado.

BYRON BURGESS OF ERIE CO., NEW YORK
[Lazarus Newton[6]]

7b. **Byron Lafayette** *[son of Lazarus Newton].* Born 19 Aug. 1897 in Scott Co., KY. Married Violet Crampton about 1920 (she died 14 Nov. 1944). Living with his father in 1900. Byron Burgess moved to Buffalo, NY about 1921, where he worked as a railroad switchman and brakeman. He died there on 13 Feb. 1949, and is buried with his wife in the Elmlawn Cemetery.

8a. **Kenneth Newton.** Born about 1921 at Buffalo, NY. Married secondly H(ortense) Opal ___ (she was born 1 Oct. 1911, and died 30 Mar. 1989 at Sacramento, CA); married thirdly Joyce Elaine Chapman on 5 Sept. 1989 at Reno, Washoe Co., NV. Kenneth Burgess was last known living at Sacramento, CA.

9a. **Daughter**. These children are by his first wife.
9b. **Daughter**.

8b. **Donald B(yron?).** Born about 1923 at Buffalo, NY. Listed in the 1974 Buffalo city directory working for City Service Taxicab Co. He may have been born 19 Jan. 1926, and died Sept. 1974 in New York.

DANIEL BURGESS OF NIAGARA CO., NEW YORK
[Lazarus Newton^6]

7d. **Daniel** (nmn) (ad.) *[son of Lazarus Newton]*. His name was originally Daniel Edward Johnson, a son of Lazarus's wife's sister. Born 7 Apr. 1921 at Corydon, IN. Married Marjorie Jane Edwards on 10 Dec. 1942. Dan Burgess is a high school teacher of mathematics at Niagara Falls, NY.

8a. **Marcia Dale.** Born 19 May 1944 at Buffalo, NY.
8b. **Daniel Terrence.** Born 1 Nov. 1947 at Buffalo, NY. Married secondly Denise Catherine Sawtell on 8 Aug. 1981 at Las Vegas, Clark Co., NV. Daniel T. Burgess is a school teacher at Las Vegas, NV.

9a. **Kimberly Jane.** Born 26 Nov. 1968 at Mt. Vernon, OH.
9b. **Denise Elizabeth.** Born 28 Apr. 1970 at Mt. Vernon, OH.

8c. **Lynn Margaret.** Born 10 Oct. 1948 at Buffalo, NY. Married George Wayne Cellini on 5 Aug. 1972 at Las Vegas, Clark Co., NV.
8d. **Jo Anne.** Born 7 Feb. 1950 at Buffalo, NY.

Benjamin Kenn BURGESS (1846-1933) (page 183)

Ruth GREENE (1924-) (page 184)

Mary Lou GREENE (1927-) (page 184)

[William (I)[1], Edward (I)[2], William (II)[3], Edward (V)[4], Edward (IX)[5]]

LOT BURGESS
(1871-1925)
OF HARRISON COUNTY, KENTUCKY

6o. **(Joseph) Lot** *[son of Edward (IX)].* Born 6 July 1871 in Scott Co., KY. Married Emma Lovena Boyers on 18 Nov. 1897 at Covington, Kenton Co., KY (she was born 19 Feb. 1874 in KY, daughter of Jacob Marion Boyers and [Sarah] Elizabeth Allen, and died 22 Nov. 1950). Listed in the 1900 census for Scott Co., and in 1910-20 in Harrison Co., KY. Lot Burgess owned and managed 700 acres of land in Scott and Harrison Cos., KY. He died there on 14 Feb. 1925, and is buried with his wife in the Battle Grove Cemetery, Cynthiana, KY.

The Children of Lot Burgess:

7a. **Myra Allene.** Born Aug. 1899 in Scott Co., KY; died in July 1900 at Jacksonville, KY, and was originally buried in the Jacksonville Cemetery, but was later moved to the Battle Grove Cemetery with her parents.

7b. **Sarah Lewis.** Born 25 July 1901 in Scott Co., KY. Married (William) Ward Renaker on 7 Jan. 1933 in Harrison Co., KY (he was born 26 Sept. 1897, had an automobile business and raised angus cattle, and died 18 Apr. 1966, buried Battle Grove Cemetery, Cynthiana). Sarah Renaker inherited her father's lands in Scott and Harrison Cos., KY. She currently lives at Cynthiana, KY; her memories have added greatly to this book.

EMMA LOVENA BOYERS BURGESS (1874-1950)

[William (I)[1], Edward (I)[2], William (II)[3], Edward (V)[4], Edward (IX)[5]]

CASSIUS CAESAR BURGESS
(1878-1958)

OF DUBOIS COUNTY, INDIANA

6r. **Cassius Caesar "Cash"** *[son of Edward (IX)].* Born 25 Sept. 1878 in Scott Co., KY. Married Amelia Annie Hudgens on 22 Jan. 1906 in Fayette Co., KY (she was born 12 Nov. 1882, and died 25 Mar. 1938 in Carroll Co., KY). Listed in the 1900 census living with his brother, Lafe, and in the 1917 draft register and 1920 census for Scott Co., KY. Cash Burgess was a farmer and merchant in Scott Co., Carroll Co., and Grayson Co., KY, and near Corydon, Harrison Co., IN. He died on 15 Oct. 1958 at Huntingburg, IN, but is buried in the Owenton Cemetery, Owen, KY.

The Children of Cash Burgess:

7a. **(Joseph) Thomas (I).** Born 13 Mar. 1908 in Scott Co., KY. See below for full entry.
7b. **T. C.** (no given names). Born 13 Feb. 1910 in Scott Co., KY. See below for full entry.
7c. **Anna Mae (I).** Born 23 Mar. 1912 in Carroll Co., KY. Married Elwyn Deatherage on 8 Dec. 1933, and had children: *Gerald Holton* (born 19 June 1934, married ___ Cliene, had children: Chason; Gerald Holton Jr.; Donna); *Kerry Burgess* (born 20 Feb. 1937, had children: David; Kim); *Patricia Ann "Pat"* (born 10 Mar. 1940, married Bill Ransdell, and had children: Bill Jr.; Thomas). Ann Deatherage currently lives at Warsaw, KY.
7d. **Garrett Davis.** Born 8 Feb. 1914 in Scott Co., KY. See below for full entry.
7e. **Eva Gertrude Sue.** Born 3 Nov. 1921 in Scott Co., KY. Married Bernie Chitty on 18 Feb. 1942 in IN; married secondly Bill Hitchens. Eva Hitchens died on 30 Dec. 1966 in Iowa.

JOSEPH BURGESS OF DUBOIS CO., INDIANA
[Cassius Caesar[6]]

7a. **(Joseph) Thomas (I) "Tom"** *[son of Cassius Caesar].* His name was originally Pawtan Thompson Burgess, and he is listed in the 1920 census as Thompson Burgess. Born 13 Mar. 1908 in Scott Co., KY. Married Margaret Sebree on 23 Nov. 1934 in Carroll Co., KY (she was born on 6 Mar. 1916, the daughter of Charles D. and Maryn Lawrence). Tom Burgess was a phone maintenance man for the Southern Railroad at Corydon and Huntingburg, IN. He died on 6 July 1973 at Huntingburg, and is buried in the Fairview Cemetery. Margaret Burgess lives at New Albany, IN.

8a. **John Thomas (II).** Born 7 Apr. 1936 at Sanders, KY. Married Quanna Lynch (who remarried after her husband's death). John T. Burgess was a truck driver in Indiana. He was killed on 10 Aug. 1961 in a truck accident near Paulsboro, NJ, and is buried in the Fairview Cemetery, Huntingburg, IN.

9a. **Charles Clay.** Born and died 2 Oct. 1958 at Atlanta, GA, and is buried in the Ghent Cemetery, Carroll Co., KY.
9b. **John Thomas II (III).** Born 17 June 1960 at Atlanta, GA. Married Carol ___. John is a mechanic and truck driver at Winslow, IN.

8b. **Charlotte Virginia.** Born 12 May 1940 at Sanders, KY. Married James Philip Jones.
8c. **Garrett Harold.** Born and died 3 Nov. 1942 at Bedford, IN, and is buried in the Ghent Cemetery, Carroll Co., KY.
8d. **Thelma Jo.** Born 14 Nov. 1951 at Ghent, KY. Married Jimmy Ray Bye.
8e. **Sarah Elizabeth (VI).** Born 4 Aug. 1958 at Evansville, IN. Married John Dishmond Fields.

T. C. BURGESS OF ESTILL CO., KENTUCKY

[Cassius Caesar[6]]

7b. **T. C.** (no given names) *[son of Cassius Caesar]*. Born 13 Feb. 1910 in Scott Co., KY. Married Della Tyree on 29 Apr. 1939 in Estill Co., KY (she was born 20 Apr. 1920). T. C. Burgess was a farmer near Ghent, KY from 1928 until his retirement. He died on 30 Dec. 1992 at Carrollton, KY.

8a. **Billy Gene.** Born 6 May 1940 at Sanders, KY. Married Christine Beach on 20 May 1959 in Carroll Co., KY. Billy Burgess is a farmer near Ghent, KY.

9a. **William Gene.** Born 31 Mar. 1961 at Carrollton, KY. Married Sheila Williams on 26 June 1981 in Carroll Co., KY.

9b. **Anna Sue.** Born 26 Mar. 1968 at Carrollton, KY.

8b. **Joyce Elaine.** Born 26 Aug. 1945 at Ghent, KY. Married Larry Stephen Meadows in 1961, and had children: *Larry Stephen Jr.* (born 8 July 1962); *Becky Lee* (born 25 July 1966). Joyce married secondly William Harmon on 20 June 1970, and had children: *William Jr. "Billie"* (born 18 June 1971); *Shelly* (born 22 May 1975); *Shane* (born 29 July 1976).

GARRETT BURGESS OF CARROLL CO., KENTUCKY

[Cassius Caesar[6]]

7d. **Garrett Davis** *[son of Cassius Caesar]*. Born 8 Feb. 1914 in Scott Co., KY. Married Dorothy "Dottie" Walls on 7 Jan. 1942. Served in the U.S. Army in World War II. Garrett Burgess worked for Standard Oil Company at Carrollton, KY for 21 years. He died there on 10 Mar. 1967, and is buried in the Carrollton Cemetery.

8a. **Ronald Garrett.** Born 3 Jan. 1946 at Ghent, KY. Married Patricia Lyn Lowe. Ron Burgess is a Chief Petty Officer in the U.S. Navy.

9a. **Kristi Ann.** Born 17 Nov. 1970 at Richmond, KY.

9b. **Shannon Garrett.** Born 1 Dec. 1971 at Lexington, KY.

8b. **Patricia Carol "Pattie."** Born 26 Mar. 1951 at Covington, KY. Married Larry Lawrence; married secondly Michael Lewis. Pattie Lewis lives on a farm near Sanders, KY.

Elijah Thomas BURGESS (1872-1945)

Minnie Lee ZOELLER BURGESS (1874-1948?)

(see page 150)

[William (I)[1], Edward (I)[2], William (II)[3], Edward (V)[4]]

GREENBERRY FIELDS BURGESS
(1819-1915)

OF SHELBY COUNTY, INDIANA

5i. **Greenberry Fields** *[son of Edward (V)].* His name is also spelled Greenbury. Born 6 July 1819 in Scott Co., KY. Married Elizabeth Wycoff on 18 (or 15) Oct. 1841 in Scott Co. (she was born 18 May 1818 in KY, daughter of Nicholas and Susan Wycoff [or Wikoff], and died 16 Apr. 1853 in Shelby Co.); married secondly (Arthusa) Frances Wright on 17 Feb. 1855 in Shelby Co., IN (she was born 27 Jan. 1830 in KY, daughter of William and Sarah Wright, and died 15 Aug. 1871 in Shelby Co.); married thirdly Margaret A. Jacobs on 29 Apr. 1873 (she was born 8 June 1855 in Scott Co., KY, daughter of Nathaniel Jacobs and Margaret Sharp, and died 1938 in Shelby Co., IN). Listed in the tax records for Scott Co. from 1841-46. He moved to Addison Township, Shelby Co., IN in 1847 (his first farm was purchased from Thomas Zell on 29 Oct. 1849 [*Deed Book #2*, p. 14]), three miles east of Shelbyville, and is listed there in the censuses from 1850-1910 (four of five children of his third wife survive in 1910); Margaret Burgess is recorded as head of the family in 1920.

Green Burgess was a farmer in Shelby Co., IN. He died there on 2 Apr. 1915, aged 95 years, and is buried with his three wives, sister, and many of his children in the Mt. Pisgah Cemetery, east of Shelbyville, IN. His biography and a sketch of his farm (used as the cover of this book) appear in *Atlas of Shelby Co., Indiana* (Chicago: J. H. Beers & Co., 1880, p. 48), and a biography in *Chadwick's History of Shelby County, Indiana*, by Edward H. Chadwick (Indianapolis: B. F. Bowen & Co., 1909, p. 676-678). He was a Democrat and Baptist; his first two wives were Christians; his third wife was Catholic.

GREENBERRY F. BURGESS, ADDISON TOWNSHIP (1880)

"This old and respected farmer was born in Scott Co., Ky., July 6, 1819, and is the son of Edward and Sarah Burgess, nee Fields—he a native of Virginia and she of Maryland, who settled in Kentucky when children. There they grew to maturity, and Feb. 6, 1800 became man and wife, and spent the balance of their days in that State. Greenberry F. was the ninth in the family composed of Nancy, William C., Bathsheba, Maria, Joseph, Margaret A., James H., Edward, Greenberry F., and Marietta. His youth was passed in his native county, and in 1847 he moved to Shelby Co., Ind., settling in Addison Township. He was married in Scott Co., Ky., Oct. 16, 1841, to Elizabeth Wikoff, who was born in Kentucky May 18, 1818. She was the daughter of Nicholas and Susan Wikoff, natives of that State; they had the following children—Burlington B., who died in the Army Sept. 24, 1862; Susan D., deceased; William C., deceased; Sarah F.; Mary M., deceased; Maggie E.; and Joseph G., deceased. Mrs. Burgess was a member of the Christian Church, and died April 16, 1853. He was again married Feb. 17, 1855, to Arthusa F. Wright, daughter of William and Sarah Wright, natives of Kentucky, where she was born Jan. 27, 1830. The following children are the fruits of this union: John C., James E., Nannie G., Noah T., Belle [sic], Mary E., and one died infancy. This wife was also a member of the Disciples Church, and died Aug. 15, 1871. He was married a third time, April 29, 1873, to Margaret A. Jacobs, daughter of Nathaniel and Margaret Jacobs—he a native of Virginia, and she of Kentucky, who settled in this county in 1857, where Mrs. Jacobs is still living, her husband having died May 2, 1879. Mrs. Burgess was born in Scott Co., Ky., June 8, 1855, and has two children—Florence Helena and William Clement Burgess. Mrs. Burgess is an industrious, economical wife, and a faithful member of the Catholic Church. Mr. Burgess has always been a hardworking man, and it was by determined industry and frugal habits that he has been able to own today 256 acres of land. Politically, he has always been an unflinching Democrat. He is upright and honest in every transaction, and is truly one of "Old Shelby's" self-made men. A view of his home will be found in this book, denoting that he is considered one of the representative farmers of Addison Township." (The illustration appears on the cover of this genealogy.)

The Children of Greenberry Burgess:

6a. **Burlington Benjamin.** Born 3 Oct. 1842 in Scott Co., KY. Burlington Burgess was a private in Co. K, 18th Indiana Infantry, during the Civil War. He died of disease while serving on 24 Sept. 1862 at Helena, AR, and is buried in the Mt. Pisgah Cemetery.

6b. **Susan D.** Born 8 July 1844 in Scott Co., KY; died before 1850 (not listed in the census), and probably before 1847, since she is not buried with the rest of her family in the Mt. Pisgah Cemetery.

6c. **(William) Calvin (III).** Born 8 Mar. 1846 in Scott Co., KY; he collapsed and died on 24 Nov. 1862 in Shelby Co., IN (an obituary appeared in the *Shelby Volunteer*, 27 Nov.), and is buried with his parents in the Mt. Pisgah Cemetery.

6d. **Sarah Fields "Sallie."** Born Nov. (or May) 1847 in Shelby Co., IN. Married her first cousin, Horace G. Bates, on 25 Jan. 1866 in Shelby Co. (he was born 2 May 1838, son of Maria Burgess and George William Bates, served in Co. F., 51st Indiana Infantry, Union Army during the Civil War, and died 24 Sept. 1909), and had nine children (of whom seven survived in 1910), including: *Charles B.* (born May 1867); *Ellie* (born 1871); *William G.* (born Mar. 1874, married Josie E. ___ [she was born Oct. 1874, and died 1960], and died 1955, buried Mt. Pisgah Cemetery, having had children: Cleora E. [born July 1895, married Edwin Ward and had children: Helen; married secondly Don Hungerford]; Chandas [married Norma Towns {she was born 14 July 1909, and died Mar. 1973 at Shelbyville}, and had children: Carolyn {married ___ Hatfield, and lives at Orlando, FL}; Chandas Bates lives at Shelbyville, IN]); *Josie Lee* (born 30 Nov. 1877, died 28 July 1881, buried with her parents); *Herbert E.* (born Feb. 1880); *Artie M.* (born Oct. 1882); *Nannie B.* (born Feb. 1885); *Harry R.* (born May 1889). Listed in the 1870 and 1900-10 censuses for Addison Township, Shelby Co., IN. Sallie Bates died about 1927 in Shelby Co., IN, and is buried with her husband in the Mt. Pisgah Cemetery (he has a military monument for Civil War service, but she has no headstone).

6e. **Mary Miranda.** Born 7 Apr. 1849 in Shelby Co., IN; died there in 1853, and is buried the Mt. Pisgah Cemetery.

6f. **Margaret E. "Maggie."** Born 9 Nov. 1850 in Shelby Co., IN. Married Alfred F. Thompson on 26 Sept. 1889 in Shelby Co. Listed with her father in the 1880 census; has not been found in 1870. Maggie Thompson died in 1927 in Shelby Co., IN, and is buried in the Mt. Pisgah Cemetery.

6g. **Joseph Greenberry.** Born 27 Mar. 1853 in Shelby Co., IN; died there in 1853, and is buried in the Mt. Pisgah Cemetery.

6h. **John Clement.** Born 1 Mar. 1856 in Shelby Co., IN. Married Martha ___ (div. 1912); married secondly Mayme Frances Hinshaw on 4 May 1915 in Shelby Co. (she was born 12 Feb. 1887 in Shelby Co., daughter of John L. Mann and Cora O. Landingham, and remarried Roy Arbuckle). Listed with his father in the 1870-80 censuses, and in the 1900 census for Juneau, AK; Mayme appears as head of the family in 1920 in Shelby Co., IN. John C. Burgess was a hotel clerk in Shelby Co., IN and Alaska. He died childless in 1917 in Alaska, and is buried in the Mt. Pisgah Cemetery.

6i. **James Edward (I).** Born 14 Nov. 1857 in Shelby Co., IN. Married Alice M. Brown on 13 Nov. 1882 in Shelby Co. (she was born July 1865 in IN, and died 1941 in Shelby Co., IN). Listed with his father in the 1870-80 censuses, and in 1900-20 in Addison Township, Shelby Co., IN. James Burgess was a farmer in Shelby Co. He died there childless on 18 Apr. 1929, and is buried in the Mt. Pisgah Cemetery.

6j. **Nancy G. "Nannie."** Born 26 Aug. 1859 in Shelby Co., IN. Married John H. Fagel on 7 Nov. 1888 in Shelby Co. (he was born June 1859, and died 1933), and had children: *Child* (born 1889, died before 1900); *Bertha B.* (born Aug. 1891); *Goldie I.* (born 28 Oct. 1894, married Carl C. Cotton [he was born 1 June 1888, and died Sept. 1965, buried Mt. Pisgah Cemetery], and died Sept. 1985 at Shelbyville, aged 90 years, having had children: Florine); *Fred B.* (born 24 Sept. 1898, married B. Ellen ___ [she was born 1901, and died 1948], and had children: Fred B. Jr. [born and died 1924]; Fred married secondly Olive ___ [who survived him], and died Sept. 1985, aged 90 years, buried Mt. Pisgah Cemetery); *Mary F.* (born 1902; married Arnold Dow [he was born 6 Feb. 1897, and died Feb. 1978 at Shelbyville], and died childless). Listed with her father in the 1880 census, and in 1900-10 in Addison Township, Shelby Co., IN. Nannie Fagel died on 6 Aug. 1951 in Shelby Co., IN, aged 91 years, and is buried in the Mt. Pisgah Cemetery.

6k. **Child.** Born and died 1861 in Shelby Co., IN, and is buried with its parents.

6l. **(Noah T.) Belle.** Born 5 Aug. 1864 in Shelby Co., IN. Married Columbus Taylor Roberts on 8 Feb. 1888 in Shelby Co. (he was born 16 Nov. 1847 in Cabell Co., WV, and served as a minister), and had children: *(Ethel) Burgess "Burgie"* (born 26 Dec. 1891, married Fred McComas, had three children, and died May 1976 in West Virginia). Belle Roberts died on 2 Oct. 1892 at La Junta, CO (or she may be alive in 1909), and is buried in the Mt. Pisgah Cemetery. Burgie McComas did much unpublished research on the Burgess family.

6m. **Mary Etta.** Born about 1866 in Shelby Co., IN. Married David A. John(s) on 7 Aug. 1889 in Shelby Co., and is living in 1909. Has not been found in the 1900 Soundex for Indiana.

6n. **(Florence) Helena "Lena."** Her headstone gives her name as Helena Florence. Born Mar. 1877 in Shelby Co., IN. Married William R. Midkiff on 5 Dec. 1894 in Shelby Co., IN (he was born Aug. 1875, and died 1949). Listed in the 1900 census for Shelby Co., IN. Lena Midkiff died childless in 1959, and is buried in the Mt. Pisgah Cemetery.

6o. **William Clement "Bill."** Born 15 Sept. 1878 in Shelby Co., IN. Listed with his father in the 1900-10 censuses, and in the 1917 draft register for Shelby Co. Bill Burgess was a farmer and gambler in Shelby Co. He died unmarried on 27 Dec. 1923 at Shelbyville, and is buried in the Mt. Pisgah Cemetery.

6p. **Roy Otto.** Born 18 Nov. 1880 in Shelby Co., IN. See below for full entry.

6q. **(Grace) Leona.** Her name is given as Leona Grace in 1900. Born Nov. 1882 in Shelby Co., IN. Married Albert Byron Brown on 7 Aug. 1901 in Shelby Co. (he was born 8 June 1881, and died Nov. 1966 at Shelbyville, IN), and had children: *Burgess Byron* (married Mae Gable [now living at Fullerton, CA], and had children: Burgess Byron II; Jacqueline [married Milton Elithorpe]; Jay); *Ruth Pauline* (married Harry Payne, and secondly Bill Lowery, and thirdly Selmer Herheim, and lives at Bradenton, FL); *Margaret Helena* (born 7 Oct. 1906, listed in the 1920 census with her grandmother, married Richard Morris Osborne [he was born 7 Sept. 1901, and died Apr. 1974], and had children: Judith Anne [born 16 Dec. 1932, married James Arbuckle, and had children: Michelle {born 11 Apr. 1956, married Richard Le-Brous}; Byron Richard {born 4 Mar. 1959}; Judith married secondly James Marion Gilbert, and lives at Shelbyville]; Richard Morris Jr. [born 16 Dec. 1936, died 1940, buried Mt. Pisgah Cemetery]). Listed in the 1900 census with her father. Leona Brown died 1918 in Shelby Co., IN, and is buried in the Mt. Pisgah Cemetery.

6r. **Francis Nathaniel "Frankie."** Born 25 Feb. 1884 in Shelby Co., IN; died there on 2 May 1884, and is buried in the Mt. Pisgah Cemetery.

GREENBURY FIELDS BURGESS (1909)

"A worthy scion of a fine old pioneer family, and he himself a popular and venerable early settler who merits the praise due all hardy and honest men of this type, is Greenbury [sic] Fields Burgess of Addison township, Shelby County, Indiana, who was born in Scott County, Kentucky, July 6, 1819, the son of Edward Burgess, a native of Virginia, who married Sarah Fields on Feb. 6, 1800, a native of Maryland. After spending their long and useful lives on a farm, which they developed from the primeval forest, they both died in Scott County, Kentucky. Ten children were born to them, named as follows: Nancy, William C., Bathsheba, Joseph, Maria, Margaret, Edward, James Henry, Greenbury F., and Marietta.

"Greenbury F. Burgess received only a limited education in the old-time log school-houses. He remained at home until he was twenty-one years of age. In 1847 he came to Indiana, and began life for himself amid new conditions, locating in Addison township, Shelby County, where he secured land, which he at once began to clear and develop into a farm, erecting rude buildings, which, as he prospered by dint of hard toil and good management, gave way in time to more substantial buildings. He finally became the owner of two hundred and fourteen acres of valuable land. He cleared about one hundred acres of this himself. He has always been a very robust, rugged, and hard-working man, consequently he has succeeded. He has always carried on general farming in a manner that not only insured a good living from year to year, but enabled him to lay by quite a competency. He has devoted considerable attention to the raising of grain and various kinds of live stock. His farm is highly improved, and he has a good dwelling and substantial out-buildings, and an excellent orchard and garden.

"Mr. Burgess has been three times married, first on October 16, 1841, to Elizabeth Wikoff, of Kentucky, who was born May 18, 1818. She died April 16, 1853, and he married a second time on February 17, 1855, his second wife being Arthusa F. Wright, born January 27, 1830; she died August 15, 1871, and Mr. Burgess' third marriage was solemnized on April 29, 1873, to Margaret A. Jacobs, of Scott County, Kentucky, a daughter of Nathaniel and Margaret (Sharp) Jacobs, the former a native of Virginia, and the latter of Scott County, Kentucky. They came to Shelby County, Indiana, in 1851, and secured land in Liberty Township. Mr. Sharp [sic], who devoted his life to farming, died May 2, 1879, and his wife passed away October 22, 1894. They were the parents of thirteen children, namely: Malissa, Harvey, Maranda, Amanda, Mary, Susan, William, George W. and Thomas J. (twins); Narcissus; Margaret, wife of the subject of this review; Amanda [sic]; and Serelda.

"Greenbury F. Burgess' children by his first wife were: Burlington B., deceased; Susan D., deceased; William C., deceased; Sarah F.; Mary M., deceased; Maggie E.; Joseph G., deceased. The subject's children by his second wife were six, as follows: John C., James E., Nannie G., Noah T. Belle, Mary E., and an infant. The children by Mr. Burgess' third wife are: Florence Helena, wife of William Midkiff, of Liberty Township, Shelby County; William Clement, a farmer on the old home place; Roy Otto, a farmer in Addison Township, who married Nora Hatfield, on April 9, 1901, and they have two children, LaRue and

Gladys; Leona G., married Albert Brown, of Fort Benjamin Harrison, and to them three children have been born, namely: Burgess B., Ruth, and Margaret Helena; the fifth child of the subject and his third wife was Francis Nathaniel, who died May 2, 1884.

"Mr. Burgess has always been a Democrat. He is a member of the Baptist Church. He is truly self-made man, and has won the respect of a wide circle of friends and acquaintances in Shelby County. While feeble at the age of ninety years, owing to rheumatism, his health is otherwise unimpaired. His eyesight is particularly good, as he is enabled to read magazines and the finest print of the daily newspapers without glasses. It is a source of pleasure and satisfaction to him, and he devotes most of his time to reading."

Noble Moses BURGESS (1880-1953) and Housekeeper

(see page 188)

[William (I)[1], Edward (I)[2], William (II)[3], Edward (V)[4], Greenberry Fields[5]]

ROY OTTO BURGESS
(1880-1934)

OF SHELBY COUNTY, INDIANA

6p. **Roy Otto** *[son of Greenberry Fields].* Born 18 (or 19, according to his draft record) Nov. 1880 in Shelby Co., IN. Married Nora Ethel Hatfield on 9 Apr. 1900 in Shelby Co. (she was born 5 Oct. 1882, and died 5 Dec. 1964). Living with his father in 1900; listed in the 1910-20 censuses for Addison Township, Shelby, Co., IN, and in the 1917 draft register of Shelby Co. Roy Burgess was a farmer on his father's lands in Shelby Co., IN. He died there on 7 July 1934, and is buried with his wife in the Mt. Pisgah Cemetery.

The Children of Roy Burgess:

7a. **(Emerson) LaRue.** Born 30 July 1901 in Shelby Co., IN. See below for full entry.
7b. **(Gladys) Beryl.** Born 10 May 1903 in Shelby Co., IN. Married Harry Beryl Chambers on 16 Sept. 1923 in Shelby Co., and had children: *Harry Beryl Jr.* (born 19 Sept. 1924 in Shelby Co., and is Vice President and General Manager of NASA Tours, with TWA, at Cape Canaveral, FL). Beryl Chambers died in childbirth on 19 Sept. 1924, and is buried in the Mt. Pisgah Cemetery.
7c. **William Greenberry.** His name appears in the official birth records as John Burgess. Born 10 Sept. 1909 in Shelby Co., IN. Married Velda Mae Pollard on 10 Sept. 1927 in Shelby Co. (she was born 7 Mar. 1909, daughter of George W. Pollard and Laura Smith); married secondly Helen Louise (Sosbe) Peck on 29 Apr. 1939 in Shelby Co. Bill Burgess was an automobile salesman at Shelbyville, Shelby Co., IN. He died there childless on 3 Aug. 1993.
7d. **Kenneth Ferdinand.** Born 20 June 1912 in Shelby Co., IN. See below for full entry.
7e. **Reba Dean.** Born 5 Nov. 1915 in Shelby Co., IN; died there on 17 Sept. 1916.
7f. **Helen.** Born about 1917 in Shelby Co., IN; died there aged three months.

LARUE BURGESS OF MARION CO., INDIANA
[Roy Otto[6]]

7a. **(Emerson) LaRue** *[son of Roy Otto].* Born 30 July 1901 in Shelby Co., IN. Married Edith Kline. LaRue Burgess owned a tire and battery shop at Indianapolis, IN. He died there on 18 Nov. 1961, and is buried in the Crown Hill Cemetery.

8a. **Barbara (J.?) (I).** Born 11 Aug. 1927 in IN. Married Billy Scott. Barbara Scott died childless on 29 Dec. 1989 at Indianapolis, IN.
8b. **Kenneth Emerson "Sonny."** Born 27 Oct. 1935 at Indianapolis, IN. Married. Kenneth Burgess was an artist at New York City; he died there childless about 1992.

KENNETH BURGESS OF DELAWARE CO., INDIANA
[Roy Otto[6]]

7d. **Kenneth Ferdinand** *[son of Roy Otto].* His name appears in the official birth records as Harry Burgess. Born 20 June 1912 in Shelby Co., IN. Married (Margaret) Evelyn Judy on 9 May 1937 in Shelby Co. (she was born 16 Sept. 1913 at Bentonville, IN, daughter of Florian F. Judy and Bridella Belle). Ken Burgess has been a painter, shipping and receiving clerk, and maintenance man at Shelbyville High School (now retired). He currently lives at Muncie, IN.

8a. **Harry Allen (I).** Born 27 Jan. 1939 at Shelbyville, IN. Married Annette Henderson on 12 June 1960 in Shelby Co. (div.; she was born 25 July 1941 in Shelby Co., daughter of William C. Henderson and Lola Howe); married secondly Norma Jean Walton on 1 Mar. 1974 in Shelby Co. (div.; she was born 26 Oct. 1942 at Waldron, IN, daughter of Andrew F. Gaskill and Irene E. Krieger); married thirdly Regina Annette Goins on 10 May 1985. Harry Burgess teaches elementary choral and instrument music in the Decatur School District, Indianapolis, IN. He lives at West Newton, IN.

9a. **Michelle Denise.** Born 3 Oct. 1961 at Shelbyville, IN. Married Bruce Wayne Merrill in 1983 (div.); married secondly Eric Overhage. Michelle Overhage lives at Indianapolis, IN.

9b. **Andrew Allen.** Born 3 June 1975 at Beach Grove, IN.

9c. **Harry Allen II.** Born 29 Jan. 1987 at Franklin, IN.

8b. **Sandra Sue (II).** Born 8 May 1940 at Shelbyville, IN. Married Gary Lee Kautsky on 19 Mar. 1966 in Shelby Co., IN (he was born 25 Aug. 1939, son of LaVerne Kautsky and Lillian Neimeyer), and had children: *Lea Kay* (born 4 Mar. 1967); *Christi Elaine* (born 14 May 1968); *Stasy Lee* (born 25 Feb. 1970); *Chera Lynn* (born 3 June 1973). Sandra Kautsky is an elementary school teacher for a Christian school at Muncie, IN.

8c. **David Benton.** Born 21 Oct. 1942 at Shelbyville, IN. Married Ann Siegman (div.). David Burgess teaches English and speech at Parkview Junior High School, New Castle, IN.

The Family of *George Walter Burgess* (page 129): *G. W.* (back row), *Horace M.* (2nd row left), *Harold M.* (2nd row middle), *Rebecca Emiline* (2nd row right) *Roy P.* (front left), *Dalpha* (front right)

THE THIRD BRANCH

EDWARD BURGESS, JUNIOR OF FAUQUIER COUNTY, VIRGINIA

THE BURGESS COUNTRY SCHOOL, EAGLE LAKE, MINNESOTA, CIRCA 1896

D. Alberta Burgess (black hat, seated on left)*LeRoy M. Burgess (seated on right)
W. Lloyd Burgess (second row center, fourth from left)
Ella M. Burgess (top row, second from left)*Carl D. Pickel, teacher (standing on right)

SUSAN CATHERINE BURGESS UTTERBACK (1828-1912)
(see page 273)

THE BURGESSES BETWEEN THE CIVIL WAR AND THE SPANISH-AMERICAN WAR

The grievances which led to the outbreak of Civil War in 1861 were long-standing, and included regional rivalry between North and South, uneven economic development, industrialization, and governance, none of which in themselves would probably have caused conflict to erupt. The one irreducible issue, the fundamental difference that could never be papered over or wished away, was slavery. The southern half of the United States had developed an agrarian model based around large farms or plantations which were economically unviable without large pools of cheap labor. The northern tier of states also had its large farms, but featured many more independent growers with 50-to-200-acre plots that were largely self-sufficient, and that drew on a self-regenerating labor pool composed primarily of close family members and neighbors. The North had also begun to industrialize by 1860, and already had many more miles of railroads and other established transportion systems than the South, enabling the growers and manufacturers in the upper half of the country to get their goods and agricultural products to market that much quicker. Wealth in the South was concentrated in very few hands, and was much more static; in the North, the Great American Dream of rags to riches still ran rampant.

Still, slavery was the key issue over which war final broke out. The Burgesses had been slave owners from the time of the first Edward Burgess in the mid-1700s. Only the poorer members of the family (or those who had moved north of the Mason-Dixon line) had no slaves. When the first shots were fired by the South at Fort Sumter in the Spring of 1861, the Burgess family (as with so many others) split down the middle. Indeed, at least one family member served in both the Confederate and Union armies, and Burgess families in the border states of Tennessee and Kentucky sent their sons both ways. Only a handful of Burgesses were actually killed in action; more died of disease while on duty, and others came home after the war changed men, both physically and mentally, some with serious ailments that would eventually carry them off decades later.

Those families living in areas such as Johnson County, Missouri which had intermittent guerrilla warfare, were particularly devastated, with civilian Burgesses being slaughtered or displaced in various "military" actions. Many of these families suffered personal and financial losses that would affect them for generations, well into the early decades of the twentieth century.

Once again, however, a side effect of the conflict was a realization by the young men who participated in the war that there were other parts of America that might serve as future homes for their families; the latter decades of the nineteenth century featured further waves of emigration from the Midwest into the newly opened western territories. My great-great grandfather, Thomas Fleming Burgess, was one of these pioneers, settling with his family near Pullman, Washington Territory in 1878, and then on the Snake River, where he farmed and developed a fruit orchard.

Tom Burgess was also the first member of the family to list his occupation as "locomotive engineer," driving the first steam engine into Mankato, Minnesota about 1871. Although the majority of Burgesses were still farmers, the younger men were beginning to explore other, more interesting (and lucrative) occupations, including blacksmith, merchant, minister, and teacher.

Only a handful of family members had time to join or fight in the brief Spanish-American War of 1898, and none were killed, but the world they returned to was changing once again. The family farm began to appear increasingly less attractive to those who wanted to have a little money jingling in their pockets, and many of the younger Burgesses began considering the bright lights of the big city in the upper Midwest. In the late 1890s Garland S. Burgess moved his family from the hills of West Virginia to East Liverpool, Ohio, where they all (daughters included) worked in one of the many pottery factories being built there. Within a generation, some members of this group had moved a second time across the Ohio river into Beaver County, Pennsylvania to work in the steel plants rapidly being erected along America's major inland waterways.

By the onset of World War I (1914) factory employment was becoming commonplace and the waves of western migration to the fringes of the frontier had finally ended, the last such move taking place in 1910, when my great-grandfather, George Walter Burgess, removed his family from Troy, Idaho to Biggar, Saskatchewan, Canada. There was now no where else for the poor or disaffected to go but to America's rapidly-growing urban areas.

Chart IV: Edward Burgess of Fauquier Co., Virginia

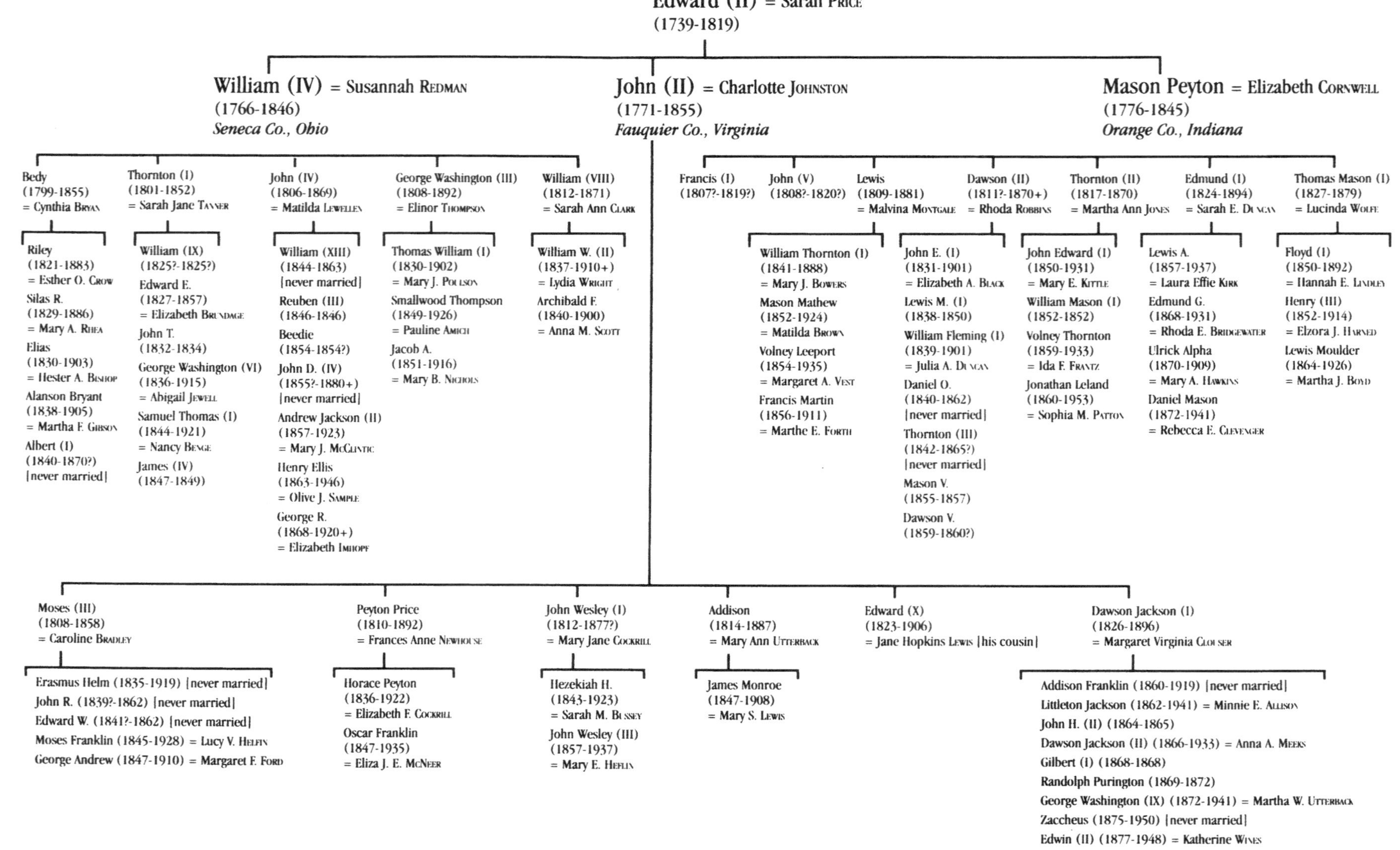
Edward (II) = Sarah Price
(1739-1819)
William (IV) = Susannah Redman
(1766-1846)
Seneca Co., Ohio
John (II) = Charlotte Johnston
(1771-1855)
Fauquier Co., Virginia
Mason Peyton = Elizabeth Cornwell
(1776-1845)
Orange Co., Indiana
Bedy (1799-1855) = Cynthia Bryan
Riley (1821-1883) = Esther O. Crow
Silas R. (1829-1886) = Mary A. Rhea
Elias (1830-1903) = Hester A. Bishop
Alanson Bryant (1838-1905) = Martha F. Gibson
Albert (I) (1840-1870?) [never married]
Thornton (I) (1801-1852) = Sarah Jane Tanner
William (IX) (1825?-1825?)
Edward E. (1827-1857) = Elizabeth Brundage
John T. (1832-1834)
George Washington (VI) (1836-1915) = Abigail Jewell
Samuel Thomas (I) (1844-1921) = Nancy Benge
James (IV) (1847-1849)
John (IV) (1806-1869) = Matilda Lewellen
William (XIII) (1844-1863) [never married]
Reuben (III) (1846-1846)
Beedie (1854-1854?)
John D. (IV) (1855?-1880+) [never married]
Andrew Jackson (II) (1857-1923) = Mary J. McClintic
Henry Ellis (1863-1946) = Olive J. Sample
George R. (1868-1920+) = Elizabeth Imhopf
George Washington (III) (1808-1892) = Elinor Thompson
Thomas William (I) (1830-1902) = Mary J. Poulson
Smallwood Thompson (1849-1926) = Pauline Amich
Jacob A. (1851-1916) = Mary B. Nichols
William (VIII) (1812-1871) = Sarah Ann Clark
William W. (II) (1837-1910+) = Lydia Wright
Archibald F. (1840-1900) = Anna M. Scott
Francis (I) (1807?-1819?)
John (V) (1808?-1820?)
Lewis (1809-1881) = Malvina Montgale
William Thornton (I) (1841-1888) = Mary J. Bowers
Mason Mathew (1852-1924) = Matilda Brown
Volney Leeport (1854-1935) = Margaret A. Vest
Francis Martin (1856-1911) = Marthe E. Forth
Dawson (II) (1811?-1870+) = Rhoda Robbins
John E. (I) (1831-1901) = Elizabeth A. Black
Lewis M. (I) (1838-1850)
William Fleming (I) (1839-1901) = Julia A. Duncan
Daniel O. (1840-1862) [never married]
Thornton (III) (1842-1865?) [never married]
Mason V. (1855-1857)
Dawson V. (1859-1860?)
Thornton (II) (1817-1870) = Martha Ann Jones
John Edward (I) (1850-1931) = Mary E. Kittle
William Mason (I) (1852-1852)
Volney Thornton (1859-1933) = Ida F. Frantz
Jonathan Leland (1860-1953) = Sophia M. Patton
Edmund (I) (1824-1894) = Sarah E. Duncan
Lewis A. (1857-1937) = Laura Effie Kirk
Edmund G. (1868-1931) = Rhoda E. Bridgewater
Ulrick Alpha (1870-1909) = Mary A. Hawkins
Daniel Mason (1872-1941) = Rebecca E. Clevenger
Thomas Mason (I) (1827-1879) = Lucinda Wolfe
Floyd (I) (1850-1892) = Hannah E. Lindley
Henry (III) (1852-1914) = Elzora J. Harned
Lewis Moulder (1864-1926) = Martha J. Boyd
Moses (III) (1808-1858) = Caroline Bradley
Erasmus Helm (1835-1919) [never married]
John R. (1839?-1862) [never married]
Edward W. (1841?-1862) [never married]
Moses Franklin (1845-1928) = Lucy V. Heflin
George Andrew (1847-1910) = Margaret F. Ford
Peyton Price (1810-1892) = Frances Anne Newhouse
Horace Peyton (1836-1922) = Elizabeth F. Cockrill
Oscar Franklin (1847-1935) = Eliza J. E. McNeer
John Wesley (I) (1812-1877?) = Mary Jane Cockrill
Hezekiah H. (1843-1923) = Sarah M. Bussey
John Wesley (III) (1857-1937) = Mary E. Heflin
Addison (1814-1887) = Mary Ann Utterback
James Monroe (1847-1908) = Mary S. Lewis
Edward (X) (1823-1906) = Jane Hopkins Lewis [his cousin]
Dawson Jackson (I) (1826-1896) = Margaret Virginia Clouser
Addison Franklin (1860-1919) [never married]
Littleton Jackson (1862-1941) = Minnie E. Allison
John H. (II) (1864-1865)
Dawson Jackson (II) (1866-1933) = Anna A. Meeks
Gilbert (I) (1868-1868)
Randolph Purington (1869-1872)
George Washington (IX) (1872-1941) = Martha W. Utterback
Zaccheus (1875-1950) [never married]
Edwin (II) (1877-1948) = Katherine Wines
Edward L. (1877-1942) [never married]

[William (I)[1], Edward (I)[2]]

EDWARD BURGESS, JR.
(1739-1819)

OF FAUQUIER COUNTY, VIRGINIA

3f. **Edward (II)** *[son of Edward (I)].* Born 27 Nov. 1739 O.S. in King George Co., VA (*St. Paul's Parish Register*). Married Sarah "Sally" Price on 20 Feb. 1765 in Stafford Co. (*St. Paul's Parish Register*; Sally was the daughter of Thomas Price [son of Thomas and Margaret Price] and Sarah Buckner [daughter of Anthony Buckner], and sister of Elizabeth Price, who married Edward's brother, Moses Burgess; she was born on 13 May 1743 in Stafford Co., VA [*St. Paul's Parish Register*], and died on 23 Nov. 1824 in Fauquier Co., VA). Edward witnessed the will of Henry Bussey on 16 Apr. 1764 in Stafford Co. (*Liber #O*, p. 476-77), but had moved to Prince William Co. by 1771, when his son John was born (as indicated on John's 1855 death record); he is listed on the personal property tax rolls of Prince William Co. from 1782-85 (the 1786 list is lost), and signed the 7 Apr. 1783 petition supporting Delegate Arthur Lee. In 1785 an Edward "Burge" paid rent to the estate of Joseph Tyler in Prince William Co. (*Prince William* County *Will Book #G*, p. 457-460). Edward moved across the county line into Fauquier Co. by 1787, and is listed there in the 1810 census and on the personal property tax records through 1819; he appraised John Redmon(d)'s estate on 25 July 1796 (*Will Book #3*, p. 23). Sally is noted as head of the family in 1820.

The identification of Edward Burgess of Fauquier Co. with Edward Burgess Jr., son of Edward Burgess of King George Co., can only be demonstrated circumstantially. Edward's marriage record in the *St. Paul's Parish Register* (then Stafford Co., now King George Co.) reads "Edward Burgess & ___ Price," the wife's first name being replaced with an underline (the minister apparently either misplaced or forgot the information when he wrote the names in his register some months after the event took place; other such instances occur regularly throughout this book, almost exclusively with the brides' first names). This same register earlier provided birth records for only one Price family, that of Thomas and Sarah Price. Female children of a proper age include: Anne (born 20 Dec. 1735), Margaret (born 10 Feb. 1738, married James Rollins), Elizabeth (married Moses Burgess, Edward's younger brother), Sarah (born 13 May 1743), Katherine (born 7 Feb. 1745), and Susanna (born 20 Mar. 1747), the latter three being the most probable candidates for a double brother/sister marriage, common in rural areas during this period. Significantly, the Price names were carried down in the family of Edward's middle son, John Burgess of Fauquier Co., VA, who named two of his children Peyton Price Burgess and Sarah Price "Sallie" Burgess (Sallie is one half of a twin pair, the other being named "Edward," obviously for the two grandparents on the father's side). While this is not conclusive, it does strongly suggest a connection between the two families, and such a connection can only be construed in a limited number of patterns, given the scarcity of Prices in the area. Also, the chronology and naming patterns of the Fauquier Co. Burgess family fit well with what we already know of Edward Burgess Jr.: the eldest son, William, is born just eighteen months after Edward and Sallie's marriage; another son, Mason, has an odd first name that probably derives from Mason French, father-in-law to Edward's sister Margaret. Finally, the 1785 rental record in Prince William Co. repeats a variation of the Burgess name (Burge) that has been documented in this family on a half dozen other occasions in the eighteenth century.

Edward Burgess died in Fauquier Co. on 4 Mar. 1819; his will (*Fauquier Co. Will Book #7*, p. 246-248, dated 4 Feb. 1819, probated 22 Mar. 1819), names as heirs his wife Sarah, and children William, John, Nancy White, Mason, Peggy Neale, Betsy Lewis, Sarah Cornwell, and Fanny Burgess, in that order, nominating as executors his son John (the only one still living in the area) and William R. Smith. A Fauquier Co. lawsuit, *John Burgess vs. William Burgess et al.* (30 Mar. 1825), mentions the surviving heirs of Edward and Sarah Burgess, and demonstrates that all of their daughters are alive at that date, and that William, Mason, and the Cornwells are "absent from this Commonwealth."

The Children of Edward Burgess Jr.:

4a. **William (IV).** Born 9 Oct. 1766 in Stafford or Prince William Co., VA. See below for full entry.

4b. **John (II).** Born 11 June 1771 in Prince William Co., VA. See below for full entry.

4c. **Ann (I) "Nancy."** Born about 1773 (or 1769) in Stafford or Prince William Co., VA. Married George White on 19 Jan. 1793 in Fauquier Co., VA (bond date, William Burgess providing the bond; George White died by 1810), and had at least the following children: *Sarah* (born about 1800, married her first cousin, Lewis French, on 27 Nov. 1822 in Fauquier Co. [bond date, John Burgess providing the bond for her and her sisters; Lewis French was born about 1800, son of Mason French and Ann Lewis]); *Elizabeth* (born about 1802, married John Drone on 24 Dec. 1822 in Fauquier Co. [bond date]); *Ann B(urgess?)* (born about 1805, married Alexander McDonald on 20 Dec. 1826 in Fauquier Co.); *Catharine* (born about 1807, mentioned as unmarried in her mother's will). Mentioned in her father's will. Listed in the 1810-20 censuses for Fauquier Co. as head of the family. Ann White died in Dec. 1826; her will (*Fauquier Co. Will Book #10*, p. 69, dated 5 Dec. and probated 25 Dec. 1826) mentions her "two single daughters, Catharine and Ann," and asks that her "Negro slave Philis & the money due from my father's estate be equally divided among my five children." Order and age uncertain.

4d. **Mason Peyton.** Born 14 Aug. 1776 in Prince William Co., VA. See below for full entry.

4e. **Margaret (IV) "Peggy."** Born about 1778 in Prince William Co., VA. Married John Neale on 20 Jan. 1801 in Fauquier Co. (bond date, with Edward Burgess providing the bond; the groom's name is listed as "Neile" on the bond). Mentioned in her father's will. The Rev. John Neale is believed to have been a son of Matthew Neale (who married Mary Burgess, daughter of Garner Burgess, Margaret's uncle), since the only John Neale (or Neile) mentioned on the 1800 personal property tax list for Fauquier Co. is a dependent male (over the age of twenty-one) listed with Matthew Neale; John is then recorded independently beginning in 1801. Listed in the 1810-20 censuses for Fauquier Co. with one son and three daughters, names unknown. Peggy Neale was living on 30 Mar. 1825, according to the probate records of her father, but may have died by 1826; John Neale may have remarried Lucy Martin, widow of John Martin, on 26 Oct. 1826 in Fauquier Co., and moved to Westmoreland Co. by Feb. 1827; however, he is listed in the 1830 census for Fauquier Co., aged 40-50 years. Order and age uncertain.

4f. **Sarah (IV) "Sallie."** Born about 1780 in Prince William Co., VA. Married Jeremiah Cornwell (or Cornwall) on 11 Apr. 1804 in Fauquier Co. (bond date; John Burgess provided the bond, and Edward Burgess gave permission for his daughter to marry; Jeremiah was born about 1770 in VA, and died 18 Aug. 1841 in Edgar Co., IL, aged 71 years), and had children: *Simon* (born 1811 in Jefferson Co., KY, and died 1840 in Edgar Co., IL, aged 29 years, buried with his parents); *Mary "Polly"* (born 1812 in Jefferson Co., KY, married William R. Johnson on 17 Sept. 1832 in Edgar Co., IL); *Burgess* (born 1818 in Jefferson Co., KY, married Sarah Doing on 1 Mar. 1838 in Edgar Co., and died 12 Apr. 1853, buried Pleasant Hill Cemetery); *Allen* (born 1820 in Jefferson Co., KY, died 1844 in Edgar Co., IL, aged 24 years, and is buried with his parents); *Sarah* (born 1822 in Jefferson Co., KY, married James D. Wilson on 30 Jan. 1842 in Edgar Co.); *Angeline* (born 29 Sept. 1823 in Jefferson Co., KY, married John R. Wilhoit on 18 Mar. 1847 in Edgar Co. [he was born 18 Apr. 1821, and died 7 Jan. 1913; his biography appears in *The History of Edgar County, Illinois* {Chicago: William LeBaron, 1879, p. 625}], died 31 May 1904 in Edgar Co., buried with her husband in the Grandview Cemetery, and had children: Sarah Elizabeth [born 1847 in Edgar Co., IL, died unmarried on 21 Dec. 1923, and is buried with her parents]; Cornelia F. [married F. Smith]; Owen E.; Mildred A.; Oscar; Louisa Emma "Lulu" [born 1860, died unmarried 28 Aug. 1939, and is buried with her parents]; Julius Y.); *Peyton* (or *Payton*; married Elizabeth ___, and is buried with his parents); *Hiram*. Mentioned in her father's will. Listed in the censuses for Jefferson Co., KY from 1810-1830. Moved to Kansas Township, Edgar Co., IL by 1840, when they are listed with their son in the censuses. Sarah Cornwell died on 26 Mar. 1846, aged 66 years, in Edgar Co., and is buried in the Cornwell Cemetery on the Ben Robinson farm. Her will (*Edgar Co. Will Book #2*, p. 34-35, dated 26 Mar. 1846, probated 6 Apr. 1846), mentions her six surviving children. Exact age and order uncertain.

4g. **Elizabeth (III) "Betsy"** or **"Eliza."** Born about 1785 in Prince William Co., VA (age 66 in 1850, age 74 in 1860). Married Charles Edward Lewis on 8 Dec. 1809 in Fauquier Co., VA (bond date, with John Burgess providing the bond; Charles was born between 1775-80, probably the son of Charles Lewis, and died before 1840), and had at least the following children: *Frances* (born about 1810, married William Kinsel on 5 Jan. 1830 in Fauquier Co. [he died by 1841], being specifically cited as a daughter of Charles, and may have had children: John W. [born 1831, listed with Elizabeth Lewis in the 1850 census and probably also in 1840]; *Frances* married secondly William Creel on 20 Dec. 1841 in Fauquier Co., specifically cited as widow of William Kinsel); *Son* (born 1813); *Daughter* (born about 1817, listed with her mother in the 1840 census, may have married ___ Shumate, and had children: Jane L(ewis?) [born about 1848, listed with Elizabeth Lewis in the 1850-60 censuses], and died about 1848); *Jane Hopkins* (born 22 July 1819 [according to the 1850 census] or 1822, married her first cousin, Edward Burgess, son of Elizabeth's brother, John Burgess, on 23 Sept. 1852 in Fauquier Co., and died 27 Oct. 1880); *Margaret* (born about 1821, listed with her mother in the 1850-60 censuses, two years younger than her presumed sister, Jane). Mentioned in her father's will. Living in Loudoun Co. on 29 July 1824, when Charles Lewis deeded to John Burgess his right in his wife's share of her father's estate (*Fauquier Co. Deed Book*

#28, p. 100). Listed in the 1810-20 censuses for Loudoun Co., VA, and in 1830-60 in Fauquier Co. (from 1840 with Elizabeth as head of the family); her nephew, Edward Burgess, is living with her and her unmarried daughters in 1850; also listed as head of the family on the Fauquier Co. tax lists through 1861. Elizabeth Lewis died in Fauquier Co. during the Civil War, between 24 May 1861 (when she last appears on the personal property tax lists) and 1865 (when such records were again maintained with some regularity). Exact order uncertain.

4h. **Frances (II) "Fanny."** Born about 1787 in Prince William Co., VA. Mentioned in her father's will as unmarried. Married French Utterback on 17 Mar. 1825 in Fauquier Co. (he was born 11 Apr. 1783 in the Germantown District of Fauquier Co., son of Harmon Utterback and Elizabeth Crump, and died 1857 [appraisal dated 17 Mar. 1857]). Listed in the 1830 census for Fauquier Co., VA with two sons and two daughters under the age of ten; French Utterback is listed there in 1840 (with two sons and two daughters and no wife) and 1850. Fanny Burgess signed a prenuptial agreement with her husband (*Fauquier Co. Deed Book #28*, p. 197-198, dated 15 Mar. 1825), which stated that "William Buckner, a child of the said Frances Burgess, is hereby recognised by the said French Utterback as his son." Her children included: *William Price* (originally *William BUCKNER*; born 9 Apr. 1824, married his first cousin, Susan Catherine Burgess, daughter of John Burgess, about 1850, and died 1 July 1901; see her entry for their children); *Robert Henry* (born about 1825, married Frances Bailey on 8 Dec. 1859 in Fauquier Co., and died on 6 Dec. 1899, having had children: Robert Henry Jr. [born 17 July 1860 at The Plains, and died unmarried on 22 Oct. 1935 at Culpeper, VA, buried Culpeper Cemetery]; James Arlington [born 1 Oct. 1861 at The Plains, VA, married Esther L. Kirby on 25 Nov. 1900, and had children: Robert M. {born 15 Nov. 1901, married Louise Brown, died Mar. 1972 at Alexandria}; Fannie E. {born 1905, married Walter L. Scales}; Emma J. {born 1907, married William Nichols}; Flossie M. {born 19 June 1909 at Culpeper, VA}]; Armistead [died unmarried]); *Sarah Elizabeth* (relation not verified; born about 1827, married Joseph Utterback, her cousin, on 23 Dec. 1845 in Fauquier Co., and had children: William F. [born 1847]; James H. [born Jan. 1850]); *Susan C.* (born about 1829, died between 1850-57); *Margaret E.* (born about 1831, married David W. McClanahan on 16 Dec. 1854 in Fauquier Co., and had at least the following children: Emma Fannie [born 1858 at The Plains, married her cousin, Millard Fillmore Utterback, on 9 Apr. 1882 in Fauquier Co.]). Fanny Utterback died about 1831 in Fauquier Co. Exact order and age uncertain.

THE WILL OF EDWARD BURGESS

In the name of God, Amen. I Edward Burgess of the County of Fauquire, being sick of body but of sound disposing mind and memory do hereby make my last Will and Testament in the manner and form following that is to say;

1st I desire that all my money which I may have on hand or due me shall be immediately applied to the payment of my just debts and funeral expences, and in case it should prove insufficient there shall be so much of the perrishable part of my Estate as shall be sufficient sold by my Executors herein after named to pay the same

2dly After the payment of my debts and funeral expences, I give to my wife Sarah Burgess all my Estate both real and personal for and during the term of her natural life, and after her decease I give the same to my children herein after mentioned, and to be enjoyed by them forever.

3dly I give to my son William Burgess the sum of forty pounds Virginia Currency to be paid out of that part of my Estate which I shall hereafter give to my son John Burgess to him or his heirs.

4thly I give to my son John Burgess Negro Judah Jean & Thomas and their increase to him and his heirs forever; by paying to William Burgess the sum of forty pounds as before mentioned to Mason Burgess the sum of forty pounds or his heirs & to Sarah Cornwell or her heirs the sum of forty pounds Virginia Currency.

5thly I do give to my dughter [sic] Nancy White, one Negro Girl Fillis and her increase to her and her heirs forever.

6thly I give to my son Mason Burgess or his heirs the sum of forty pounds Virginia Currency to be paid by my son John Burgess out of the Negroes which I have given him as before mentioned.

7thly I give to my daughter Peggy Neale one Negro girl Siller & her increase to her and her heirs forever.

8thly I give to my daughter Betsy Lewis one Negro girl Lydia and her increase to her and her heirs forever.

9thly I give to my daughter Sarah Cornwell the sum of forty pounds Virginia Currency or her heirs to be paid, by my son John Burgess out of the Negroes which I have given him as before mentioned.

10thly I give to my daughter Fanny Burgess two Negroes girls Delilah and Mariah and their increase to her and her heirs forever and one bed and furniture.

11thly I give to wife Sarah Burgess to dispose off [sic] as she thinks proper Lucy and Ailsy and their increase forever the balance of my Estate to be equally divided.

12thly And lastly I do hereby constitute and appoint my son John Burgess & William R. Smith my hole [sic] and sole Executors to this my last Will and Testament.

In testimony whereof I have hereunto set my hand and seal this 4th day of February in the year 1819.

Wm R Smith
French Utterback
James W. Wallace
Stephen Tomlin

his
Edward Burgess
mark

[William (I)[1], Edward (I)[2], Edward (II)[3]]

WILLIAM BURGESS, SR.
(1766-1846)

OF SENECA COUNTY, OHIO

4a. **William (IV)** *[son of Edward (II)].* Born 9 Oct. 1766 in Stafford or Prince William Cos., VA. Married Susannah "Suky" Redman on 26 Jan. 1793 in Fauquier Co. (bond date, bonded by James Turner, witnessed by O. Gwathmey; John Redman gave permission for his daughter to marry) in Fauquier Co., VA (she was born about 1774 in Prince William Co., daughter of John Redman and Elizabeth Calvert, and sister of Bedy Redman, and died 11 Mar. 1859 in Muskingum Co., OH). Listed in the tax records for Fauquier Co. in 1787, and again from 1790-91, 1793-96, 1800-1801, 1803-1804; listed in the land tax records from 1789-1802, when his name is written down but scratched out. He bought 100 acres of land, a farm called "Loon Hill," from Leonard and Elizabeth Hill in 1788 in Hamilton Parish (*Fauquier Co. Deed Book #10,* p. 64, dated 28 July 1788), on the east side of the main road to Falmouth, just above "Burnt Ordinary"; neighbors included James Markham and Lawrence Washington. He lost the farm through court proceedings in 1802. William Burgess was a farmer in Fauquier Co., VA; he moved to Shenandoah Co., VA about 1804, and appears on the tax lists there from 1805-16. He moved to Muskingum Co., OH by 1817, when his daughter married there. Listed in the 1810 census for Shenandoah Co., VA, and in the 1820-30 censuses for Muskingum Co., OH. William Burgess purchased land in Seneca Co., OH on 11 Feb. and 7 May 1833 (see *Deed Book #5*, p. 391 among others; his farm was located near the county line with Hancock Co.), and is listed there in Big Spring Township in the 1840 census. He died on 22 Feb. 1846 in Seneca Co., OH, but is buried in the Graham Cemetery, Hancock Co., OH, 1.5 miles from West Independence. His will (*Seneca Co. Will Book #2*, p. 8, dated 2 Sept. 1839, probated 9 Apr. 1850) mentions the children listed below. Susan Burgess is living with her daughter Elizabeth in 1850.

The Children of William Burgess:

5a. **Elizabeth (V).** Born about 1793 in Fauquier Co., VA. Married John Tanner on 21 Aug. 1817 in Muskingum Co., OH (he was born 11 Jan. 1793 in Muskingum Co., son of Edward Tanner and Sarah Brown, and brother of Samuel Tanner [who married Elizabeth's sister, Susan Burgess], and died 24 June 1859, buried in the Brushy Knob Cemetery, Muskingum Co., OH), having had children: *Samuel* (born 1819, married Catherine Flesher on 30 Mar. 1843); *Susan* (born 1823, married John Ramey on 15 Apr. 1847); *Caroline*; *John* (born 11 Dec. 1825 at Zanesville, OH, married Mary Ann Havens, and died 20 Feb. 1886 at Zanesville, buried Woodlawn Cemetery); *David* (born 1828, married Caroline Flesher on 12 May 1853, and secondly Louisa Redman on 5 Apr. 1866); *James* (born 1829); *Elizabeth* (born 1830, married Ezra T. Salisbury on 17 Apr. 1849); *Keziah* (born 1832, married ___ Pierson); *Sarah Ellen* (born 1833, married John Hammel on 2 Mar. 1851, and secondly Henry Baker on 13 Aug. 1853); *George W(ashington?)* (born 1836, married Abigail Stokey on 28 Aug. 1862). Listed in the 1830-50 censuses for Muskingum Co., OH; Elizabeth is listed as head of the family in 1860. Her date of death is unknown.

5b. **Lucinda (I).** Born about 1795 (or 1797) in Fauquier Co., VA. Mentioned in her father's will (1839), but does not appear to be listed with him in the 1820 census. She may have been the mother of Bede D. Burgess (see below). Exact age and order uncertain.

5c. **Son.** Born about 1797 (or 1795) in Fauquier Co., VA, and died young. Dates and order uncertain.

5d. **Bedy.** Born 31 Jan. 1799 in Fauquier Co., VA. See below for full entry.

5e. **Thornton (I).** Born 5 May 1801 in Fauquier Co., VA. See below for full entry.

5f. **Frances (III) "Fanny."** Born 19 Jan. 1803 in Fauquier Co., VA. Married Henry Flesher on 6 Sept. 1818 (?) in Muskingum Co., OH (he was born 16 Mar. 1800 in VA, son of Balser Flesher and Mary Brown, married secondly Elizabeth Lybarger on 13 Mar. 1845, and died 9 July 1873 in Muskingum Co., buried Finley Chapel), and had children: *Susan* (born 1819, married John Haines on 25 Mar. 1841 in Muskingum Co.); *John* (born 20 Feb. 1820, married Sarah "Lainey" Haines on 16 Aug. 1844 in Muskingum Co., and had children: George W.; Mary F. [married S. H. Snowden]; Landora S.; Emma J. [married

James W. Shultz]; Susannah; A. A.; Walter L.; Arthur S.; his biography appears in *The History of Union County, Ohio*, by Pliny A. Durant [Chicago: W. H. Beers, 1883, p. 618]); *Lucinda* (born 24 Dec. 1821, married James Trusel on 19 May 1842 in Muskingum Co., and died 15 Feb. 1890 at Spickard, MO); *Nancy* (born 1823, married David Crawford on 31 Oct. 1844 in Muskingum Co.); *Mary "Polly"* (born 1825, married Franklin Jones on 15 Oct. 1846 in Muskingum Co.); *George Washington* (born 8 Dec. 1829 at Falls, OH, married Catherine Figley on 10 Nov. 1853 in Muskingum Co., and secondly Phoebe Grives on 25 Apr. 1900, and died 24 Mar. 1917 at Zanesville, OH, buried Greenwood Cemetery); *Catherine A.* (born 1834, married William Martin on 26 Oct. 1854 in Muskingum Co., and secondly ___ Story); *William Henry* (born 1837, married Mary Ann Boylan on 3 July 1855 in Muskingum Co.); *Jacob B.* (born Oct. 1838, died 25 Oct. 1839, buried Finley Chapel Cemetery); *Elizabeth* (born 1839?); *Peter* (born 1841, married Sarah Jellyers Myres on 2 Mar. 1865 in Muskingum Co.). Listed in the 1820-40 censuses for Muskingum Co. Fanny Flesher died on 19 Mar. 1843 in Muskingum Co., OH, and is buried in Finley Chapel Cemetery, Falls Township. Henry Flesher is listed in the census records of Muskingum Co. from 1850-60.

5g. **Susanna (II) "Susan."** Born 6 Nov. (or 1 Jan.) 1804 in Fauquier or Shenandoah Cos., VA. Married Samuel Tanner on 28 Feb. 1822 in Muskingum Co., OH (he was born 1792, the son of Edward Tanner and Sarah Brown, and brother of John Tanner [who married Susan's sister, Elizabeth Burgess], and remarried Mary Ann Kinkaid), and had children: *Barbara* (born 1823, married John Alexander Cook on 25 Aug. 1842, and died at Odin, Marion Co., IL); *Sarah* (born 1825, married James Smith on 6 Mar. 1845); *Frances "Fannie"* (born 1827, married Balser Flesher on 28 May 1846, and died 21 Oct. 1889 in Muskingum Co., buried Finley Chapel Cemetery); *George Washington* (born 7 Oct. 1829 [or 1823], married Elizabeth Haines on 17 Oct. 1850, and died 2 Nov. 1896 in Muskingum Co.); *Caroline* (born 1831, married William Hayworth); *William E.* (born 1833, married Gertrude ___); *Elizabeth* (born 1835, married Josiah Flesher on 24 Jan. 1854); *Delila* (born 31 May 1837 [or 1839], died unmarried 1 Oct. 1856); *Ned* (born 1842); *Susanna* (born 24 Aug. 1844, married William Barnett on 23 Sept. 1863, and died June 1927 in Muskingum Co.). Listed in the 1830-50 censuses for Muskingum Co., OH. Susan Tanner died on 11 Oct. 1856 in Muskingum Co., OH, and is buried in the Brushy Knob Cemetery, Falls Township.

5h. **John (IV).** Born 29 Mar. 1806 in Shenandoah Co., VA. See below for full entry.

5i. **(George) Washington (III).** Born 3 Apr. 1808 in Shenandoah Co., VA. See below for full entry.

5j. **Isabelle.** Born 27 Feb. 1810 in Shenandoah Co., VA. Married John Barcus on 19 Nov. 1828 in Muskingum Co. (born 14 June 1807 in MD, son of George Barcus and Sarah Prichard, married secondly Fidelia Buck 1851, and thirdly Hannah Sparling in 1883, died 2 Oct. 1887 in Monona Co., IA), and had children:

William Burgess Barcus. Born 11 Sept. 1829, married Mary Jane McQueen (she was born 1840, daughter of Jeremiah McQueen and Rheuellen Fairall, and died 1923), and had children: *James Albert* (born 1857, married Martha Jane Wright [she was born 1864, daughter of Alexander Wright and Cyrena Tish], and died 1926, having had children: George Howard [born 1884, married Sylvia Inez Baughman, and died 1948, having had children: Ocie Irene {born 27 Apr. 1906, married Ernest Billman, died Nov. 1976}; Everett Starling {born 14 Jan. 1908, married Florence Chaney, died Mar. 1957}; Delpha Pearl {born 1912, married Hersel Boyd Locke, and died 1972}; Martha Gladys {born 1916, married Michael Anson Acord}; Bertha Flora {born 1918, married Thomas Gilbert Anderson}]: Louisa Estella [twin; born 30 Apr. 1886, married Edwin James Hunkins, died Sept. 1968]; Anna Oretta [twin; born 30 Apr. 1886, married Lewis W. Ramsey, died 1969]; Martha Florence [born 1889, married Joseph D. Dickerson]; Clara Belle [born 8 July 1893, married Delby Watson Ashcraft, died Mar. 1976]; Clarence Elmer [born 31 Mar. 1901, married Agnes Mary Hardesty, died Mar. 1978]); *Minerva Jane* (born 1860, married Clarence Washington Sterrett, and died 1905, having had children: Azor; Ira; Guy B. [born 12 Aug. 1892, died Mar. 1964]; Ura; Ocie [born 26 Aug. 1899, married ___ Grimes, died Jan. 1984]; Ola [married ___ Strouthers]); *Ella Oretta* (born 1862, married (Frank) Wallace Pound [he was born 1861, son of Samuel A. Pound and Lucinda Wilkins, and died 1923], had children: Rolla A. [born 19 Mar. 1886, married Bessie Florence Hamby, died Nov. 1979], and died 1914); *John Henry* (born 25 Oct. 1866, married Arminta Hancock [she was born 23 Oct. 1878, daughter of John Ramey Hancock and Elizabeth Bradfield, and died 17 Mar. 1965], had children: Ethel Clare "Sally" [born 1901, married John Canvas White, and died 1967 at Redlands, CA]; Herbert Spencer [born 23 Oct. 1904 at Martinsburg, OH, married Mary Pauline "Polly" Rogers on 26 Dec. 1945 {she was born 15 Feb. 1906 at Mount Vernon, OH}, and died June 1964, having had children: Mary Susan {born 23 Apr. 1947 at Newark, OH, married Kenneth Tulla Yost Jr. on 2 June 1968 <he was born 28 Feb. 1931 in Licking Co., OH>}]; *John Henry Barcus* died on 15 Jan. 1955); *Harvey C.* (born 1870, married Viola V. Mitchell [she was born 1876, daughter of William E. Mitchell and Elizabeth Wright, and died 1966], and died 1954, having had children: Thora Cleo [born 13 Dec. 1899, married Daniel Dotson, died Oct. 1982]; Walter [born 6 Oct. 1901, died Apr. 1970]; Lester [born 1909]); *George W.* (born 1873, married Florida Miller [she was born 1876, daughter of Willis Miller and Barbara Billman, and died 1954], and died 1947, having had children: Roy [born 1895?]; Lela [born 1896, married ___ Dunham]; Ira Earl [born 1899, died 1919]; Helen Patricia [born 1902, married

Carl C. Wells, and died 1975]; Vivian Ruth [born 1913, married Frank A. Weiss, and died 1954]); *(Printha) Florence* (born 1876, married Leeman T. Harris [he was born 1875, son of David Harris and Eunice Thrap, and died 1958], and died childless in 1956); *Charles Orlando* (born 13 Apr. 1879, married Florence McCraw, and died May 1967, having had children: Harry [died at three months]; Theodric [born 1905]; *Charles* married secondly Charlotte ___, and had children: Grace [married Frank Ruble]). ***William BARCUS*** died on 21 May 1907 at Newark, OH, and is buried in the Smith Chapel Cemetery.

George BARCUS. Born 1831, married Mahala Griffith, and died about 1866 at Red Rock, Marion Co., IA.

Samuel BARCUS. Born 13 Feb. 1835 near Newark, OH, married Elizabeth A. Webb on 27 Nov. 1860 in Muskingum Co. (she was born 8 Mar. 1840 near Newark, OH, daughter of Daniel Webb and Elizabeth Smith, and died 15 Oct. 1923 at Blencoe, IA), and had children: *Emma* (born 1861 in Licking Co., OH, married Robert Edward Lindley on 31 Dec. 1878 in Monona Co., IA, died 1894, and had children: Irvan, who was the grandfather of Shirley Montgomery of Buena Vista, CA). Samuel Barcus moved to Sherman Township, Monona Co., IA on 1 Oct. 1863. He died on 12 Sept. 1925 at Farm Home, Monona Co., IA, aged 90 years, and is buried in the Blencoe Cemetery.

Delilah BARCUS. Born 1837, married John Athey about 1854, and secondly David Loar on 11 May 1877.

John Henry BARCUS. Born 30 Apr. 1839, married Nancy Jane Ridenhour, and died on 16 Jan. 1906 at Newark, OH, buried Cedar Hill Cemetery.

James Tanner BARCUS. Born 5 Feb. 1843, married Abedience A. Redpath in 1865 at Red Rock, IA, and died on 12 Feb. 1923.

Juliann BARCUS. Born 1844, married Alba Burrell, and died 1929, buried Rocky Ford Cemetery, Licking Co., OH.

John and Isabelle BARCUS are listed in the 1830-40 censuses for Muskingum Co., and in 1850 in Licking Co., OH. Isabelle Barcus died on 22 Sept. 1850 in Licking Co., OH, and is buried there in the Pleasant Hill Cemetery.

5k. **William (VIII).** Born 14 Feb. 1812 in Shenandoah Co., VA. See below for full entry.

5l. **Julia Ann (I).** Born 20 June 1814 in Shenandoah Co., VA. Married Mark Thompson Fountain on 25 Feb. 1833 in Muskingum Co., OH (he was born 29 Dec. 1810 in NJ, worked as a potter, and died 8 Aug. 1851), and had children: *Martin* (born 1834, married Sarah Ann Atwell on 6 Mar. 1856 in Muskingum Co.); *James* (born 1836, married Mary E. Seanlin on 3 July 1862 in Muskingum Co.); *Sarah A.* (born 1837, married Wilson Bonnefield on 24 Apr. 1856 in Muskingum Co.); *Susan* (born 1840, married Jason Clapper on 7 Sept. 1859 in Muskingum Co.); *William* (born 1842); *Margaret S.* (born 1844, married Washington M. Bonnefield on 14 Feb. 1867 in Muskingum Co.); *Morgan* (born 1846, married Emaline Drumm on 1 Apr. 1874 in Muskingum Co.). Julia Ann married secondly Jacob Baird on 15 Apr. 1858 in Muskingum Co. Listed in the 1840-60 censuses for Muskingum Co. Julia Ann Baird died on 5 May 1899 in Mt. Sterling, OH, and is buried with her first husband in the Mt. Sterling Cemetery.

THE WILL OF WILLIAM BURGESS

September 2nd 1839

I Wm Burgess Senr of Seneca County and State of Ohio do make and publish this my last will and testament in manner and form following, that is to say

First it is my will that my funeral expenses and all my just debts be fully paid.

Second I give devise and bequeath to my beloved wife Susannah Burgess in lieu of her dower the one third part of all the [?] of every kind and one third of all the potatoes and flax hay corn & other productions of the soil [?} which shall be cultivated on the parsals owned by John Burgess and Wm Burgess Jn, being a part of the southeast quarter section No. Nineteen Township No. 1, north of range 13. And further I bequeath to sd wife all the live stock by me now owned and kept also my waggon and harness and house hold furniture and other items not particularly described or otherwise disposed of in this will during her natural life time as aforesaid, she however first disposing of a sufficiency thereof as aforesd to pay my just debts, and that at the death of my wife all the property hereby devised or bequeathed to her as aforesaid or so much thereof as may remain unexpended to be equally divided amonst our children eleven in number, viz. Elizabeth, Lucinda, Bedee, Thornton, Fanny, Susan, John, Washington, Isabelle, William, and Julian.

And lastly I hereby constitute and appoint my wife Susannah and John Burgess to be the executors of this my last will and testament revoking and anulling all former wills by me made and ratifying and confirming this and no other to be my last will and testament.

In witness whereof I have hereunto set my hand & seal the day & year above written.

William Burgess his mark

Witnesses included Isaac De Witt, William Mulholland. The estate sale occurred on 30 Apr. 1850. Buyers included the following relatives: William Burgess Jr., Thornton Burgess, Jacob Lantz, Philip Essex, John Baker, Edward Burgess.

[William (I)[1], Edward (I)[2], Edward (II)[3], William (IV)[4]]

BEDY BURGESS
(1799-1855)

OF MADISON COUNTY, IOWA

5d. **Bedy** *[son of William (IV)].* His odd given name derived from his uncle, Bedy (originally Bude or Obadiah) Redman, and appears in various spellings, including Bedy, Bede, Bedee, Bedey, Beedy, and Beede. Born 31 Jan. 1799 in Fauquier Co., VA. Married Cyntha Bryan on 30 Dec. 1820 [or 4 Jan. 1821, according to *Colonial Families*] (she was born 1 Nov. 1806 in VA, daughter of Morrison Bryan and Rhoda Johnson, and died 15 Nov. 1852 in Madison Co., IA); married secondly Sarah Jane (Tanner) Burgess, the widow of Thornton Burgess, his brother, on 5 Sept. 1854 in Wyandot Co., OH (she remarried James Bryan in Warren Co., IA in 1856). Mentioned in his father's will. Not found in the 1820 census (probably living with his father). Listed in the 1830-40 censuses for Greene Co., OH. Moved to Missouri (or possibly Iowa) in 1843, to Fairfield Township, Jefferson Co., IA by July 1848, and then to Madison Co., IA, where he is listed in the 1850 federal census and in the 1851 state census (with six individuals). Mentioned in an article on the "Bryan" family in *Colonial Families of the United States of America*, by George Norbury Mackenzie (Baltimore: 1917, Volume VI, p. 106). Bedy Burgess was a farmer in Ohio and Iowa. The unpublished diary of his daughter, Edna, indicates that Bedy had eleven children; not all of their names are known. He died on 19 Apr. 1855 at Winterset, IA, and is buried with his second wife in the Winterset City Cemetery. His settlement deed (*Keokuk Co. Deed Book #27*, p. 255-256, recorded 22 Feb. 1856) mentions his "heirs-at-law," but his younger sons, Alanson B. and Albert, both of whom are underaged at this time, are not listed, nor is Bede D. Burgess:

THE SETTLEMENT DEED OF BEDY BURGESS'S ESTATE

Know all men by these presents that we Riley Burgess and his wife Easter & Deliza Moorman & Joseph her husband & Silas R. Burgess and Mary his wife & Roda Ploughe and Robert her husband and Edna Richesson & George her husband & Elias Burgess & Hester Ann his wife heirs at law of the Estate of Bedy Burges deceased late of the County of Madison State of Iowa, for and in consideration of the sum of three thousand dollars, do hereby sell and convey unto John Landis of Madison & State of Iowa all our right, title, and intrest [sic] in & to the following real Estate, to wit the East half of the North-East quarter of Section No. Eleven "11" and the South East qr. of the South East qr. of Section No. Two "2" in Township No. Seventy Five "75" Range No. Twenty Seven "27" and the East half of the South West quarter of Section No. Thirty Six "36" in Township No. Seventy Six "76" N of R No. Twenty Seven "27" West containing two hundred acres more or less, and we warrant the title against all persons whomsoever witness our hands this 22 Day of February 1856.

The grantors were all living at this time in Keokuk Co., except for the Richessons, who signed from Madison Co.

The Children of Bedy Burgess:

6a. **Riley (I).** Born 14 Nov. 1821 in Greene Co., OH. See below for full entry.
6b. **Deliza D.** Born about 1823 (or 1825) in Greene Co., OH. Married Joseph Moorman on 10 Jan. 1842 in Highland Co., OH (he was born about 1818 in OH, and worked as a cabinetmaker), and had at least the following children: *Addison* (born 1843 at Independence, MO); *Sarah* (born 1844 in Iowa, married John Carmichael on 12 Apr. 1867 in Keokuk Co, IA). Listed in the 1850 census for Mahaska Co., IA, and in the 1860-70 censuses for Keokuk Co., IA. Has not been found in 1880, and is believed to have died by 1889.
6c. **Daughter.** Born about 1825 (or 1823) in Greene Co., OH; listed with her father in 1840, but died childless before 1856.
6d. **Son.** Born about 1827 in Greene Co., OH, but died by 1840.

6e. **Silas R.** Born 13 Feb. 1829 in Greene Co., OH. See below for full entry.

6f. **Elias.** Born Sept. 1830 in Greene Co., OH. See below for full entry.

6g. **Roda.** Born about 1832 in Greene Co., OH (noted as age 16 on her marriage license). Married Robert C. Plough(e) (or Plue or Plugh) on 19 June 1848 in Jefferson Co., IA at the home of Bedy Burgess (Robert was born about 1826 in IN, and worked as a carpenter), and had at least the following children: *Cynthia J.* (born about 1849 in Jefferson Co., IA, died by 1856); *Sarah Edna* (born 3 June 1852 in Iowa, died after 1906); *Louisa A. "Lou"* (born about 1853 in IA; married ___ Love); *William* (born about 1857 in KS); *Mary* (born about 1860 in IA, married ___ Boring); *Laura* (born about 1869 in IA, married ___ Hydorn). Listed in the 1850 census for Fairfield Township, Jefferson Co., IA, in the 1854-56 state censuses for Polk Township (next door to Silas Burgess), and in the 1870 census for Ozark Township, Anderson Co., KS. Has not been found in 1860 and 1880. By inference she died before 1903.

6h. **Edna Evelyn.** Born 7 Dec. 1833 in Greene Co., OH. Listed with her father in the 1850 census. Married George Richesson on 17 Oct. 1850 in Madison Co., IA (he died between 1856-66); married secondly William Martin in 1866 at Golden City, CO (he was born about 1823 [or 1828] in NY or KY). Has not been found in 1860; listed in the 1870-80 censuses for Golden City, Jefferson Co., CO, and in 1900 for Walden Town, Larimer (now Jackson) Co., CO. Edna Martin left a voluminous diary which provides much peripheral material on her immediate relatives. Among those mentioned are her brothers, Alanson and Elias Burgess, and her nephew, Balis Burgess; she also states that she was one of eleven children, two of whom died in infancy; . She adopted her niece, Harriet Octiva Burgess, after the latter's parents died young (see Harriet's entry for her family). Edna Martin died childless on 14 May 1915 at Golden, Jefferson Co., CO, the last of her brothers and sisters to die.

6i. **Alanson Bryant "Lancing."** Born July 1838 in Greene Co., OH. See below for full entry.

6j. **Albert (I).** Born 1840 in Greene Co., OH. He died unmarried about 1870 while "out West," according to the probate of his estate on 8 Apr. 1871 in Madison Co., IA.

An Excerpt from Edna Burgess Martin's Diary

"November 29, 1908. We are having a big snow, it began Saturday here, but had been snowing at Denver Friday. We have all of a foot here now & it's begun snowing again since breakfast. Well, I have lost my last sister-in-law the 19 of November, Ann Burgess, Elias' wife. She had always been so healthy I thought she would live to be old. I don't know just what her age was. She had a stroke of paralysis & only lived a couple of hours. Haven't heard yet if she spoke afterwards. So now I have lost both of my last sisters-in-law in one year, Martha last May & Ann in this month. Don't that beat anything that I am left alone of all of us! God knows why he has spared me so long."

Eliza Baltzelle BURGESS HINTON
(1869-1938) [see page 149]

[William (I)[1], Edward (I)[2], Edward (II)[3], William (IV)[4], Bedy[5]]

RILEY BURGESS
(1821-1883)

OF KEOKUK COUNTY, IOWA

6a. **Riley** *[son of Bedy].* Born 14 Nov. 1821 (or 14 Oct. 1822) in Greene Co., OH. Married Esther O'Dell Crow about 1843 (she was born Jan. 1824 in IN, and died 17 Oct. 1905 in Lincoln Co., IT [later OK], buried Stroud Cemetery). Listed in the 1850-80 federal and 1854-56 state censuses for Steady Run Township, Keokuk Co., IA (but is not in the 1844 state census for Keokuk Co.). Riley Burgess was a cooper and miller. He is said to have moved to Ray Co., MO in 1844, and to Keokuk Co., IA about 1846. He died there on 27 Mar. 1883, and is buried in the Rock Creek Cemetery. His widow is listed as head of the family in Keokuk Co. in 1900. In the 1860-70 censuses his ward, Sarah A. Burgess, orphaned daughter of Edward E. Burgess (his first cousin), is living with him.

The Children of Riley Burgess:

7a. **William (XII).** Born about 1844 at [Independence, Ray Co.?], MO. Listed in the 1860 census with his father. William Burgess is said to have been a brick mason, and to have moved back to Ray Co., MO, where he married and had two children. According to family tradition, William disappeared under mysterious circumstances (apparently murdered), and his wife moved the family back to Pennsylvania. No confirmation has been found, and William has not been found in the 1870 (or later) censuses.
7b. **Balis.** Born 1 Mar. 1846 at [Independence, Ray Co.?], MO. See below for full entry.
7c. **Mary Deliza.** Born about 1853 in Keokuk Co., IA; died there (or married) before 1870.
7d. **John D. (V).** Born Sept. 1860 in Keokuk Co., IA. Living with his father in the 1880 census. Listed in the 1889 state census for Pierce Co., WA with his brother, Balis Burgess, with his mother in the 1900 census, and with his nephew, John, in 1910. Said to have died childless at Stroud, Lincoln Co., OK.

BALIS BURGESS OF PIERCE CO., WASHINGTON
[Riley[6]]

7b. **Balis "Balie"** *[son of Riley].* Born 1 Mar. 1846 at [Independence, Ray Co.?], MO. Married Priscilla Amayza Mowrey on 26 July 1866 in Fairfield Co., OH (she was born 16 Jan. 1852 in Hardin Co., OH, and died 17 May 1908 in Bates Co., MO, buried Crescent Hill Cemetery); married secondly Lydia L. ___ about 1909 (she died in TN). Listed in the 1880 census in Des Moines Township, Boone Co., IA, in the 1889 state census for Pierce Co., WA (twice), and in 1900 in Lincoln Co., IT (later OK). He returned to Tacoma, WA by 1903, where he appears in the city directories through 1918, and in the 1910 federal census. Balis Burgess was a carpenter and contractor, and built a number of beautiful homes in the Tacoma area. He died at Tacoma on 18 (or 24) May 1918, and is buried in the Oakwood Cemetery, although he also has a stone in the Crescent Hill Cemetery, Bates Co., MO.

> "I have been told that Balis Burgess ran in the land race in Oklahoma, before it was a state, [in the part that was] called the Cherokee Nation (Dad was born there, in Lincoln Co., OK), also that one Burgess married a Crow Indian. Balis later was a carpenter who helped build many homes on the north end of Tacoma."—Balis M. Burgess Jr., 1985.

8a. **Anny May.** Born 14 Mar. 1868 in Boone Co., IA; died 9 July 1870 in Missouri.
8b. **George Riley.** Born 24 July 1872 in Boone Co., IA. See below for full entry.
8c. **John Franklin (I).** Born 6 July 1874 in Jefferson Co., IA. See below for full entry.
8d. **Beedy Shelton.** Born 29 Oct. 1876 in Boone Co., IA. See below for full entry.
8e. **Birty Willis.** Born 18 Oct. 1878 in IA; died there on 18 Dec. 1878.

GEORGE RILEY BURGESS OF KEOKUK CO., IOWA

[Riley6, Balis7]

8b. **George Riley** *[son of Balis].* Born 24 July 1872 in Boone Co., IA. Married (Sarah) Olive "Aide" Martin on 13 Nov. 1892 (she was born Jan. 1876 at Haysville, IA). Listed in the 1889 census with his father, in 1900 in Keokuk Co., IA, in the 1905-13 directories of Tacoma, WA, and in the 1910 census for Pierce Co., WA. In 1914 he settled near Harpville, Keokuk Co., IA, and is listed there in the 1915 state census (without his wife). George Burgess was a minister and carpenter. He died on 12 Jan. 1948 at Sigourney, IA, and is buried in the Bethel-Utterback Cemetery.

9a. **(Elbert) Earl.** Born 8 Dec. 1893 in Lincoln Co., IT. Listed in the 1914 directory of Tacoma, WA with his father. Enlisted in the U.S. Army Air Force in World War I, and served as a fighter pilot. Listed in the 1920 census for Los Angeles Co., CA. He died unmarried on 5 Feb. 1920 at Los Angeles, CA, but was buried in the Bethel-Utterback Cemetery, Sigourney, IA. His obituary stated:

> "Earl Burgess, a motion picture actor, was killed today when he fell 700 feet from an airplane on which was performing in the making of a comedy. Burgess was flying with Lieut. Walter Hawkins, an aviator. The actor was to cast off a dummy from the plane. In attempting this he fell. The camera man and director thought the falling body was the dummy, and continued photographing. They did not discover their mistake until they went to remove the supposed dummy from the telephone wires where it had alighted. Burgess was a professional 'stunt man' and had been employed in motion picture work for ten years. He was said to have been the first man to make a successful parachute jump from an airplane."—*New York Times*, 6 Feb. 1920.

9b. **James Franklin (III).** Born 3 Feb. 1896 in Lincoln Co., IT (later OK). Listed in the 1914 directory of Tacoma, WA with his father. Enlisted in the U.S. Army Air Force in World War I, and served as a fighter pilot. James F. Burgess died childless on 6 Jan. 1954 at Centralia, WA.

9c. **Roscoe.** Born 13 Feb. 1897 at Hayesville, Keokuk Co., IA; died there on 16 Feb. 1897, and is buried with his parents.

9d. **Isal Alice.** Born 24 Mar. 1900 at Haysville, Keokuk Co., IA. Married Guy Barber on 4 Jan. 1928 at St. Paul, MN (he was born 26 Mar. 1896, and died 22 Nov. 1988 at Sigourney, IA), and had children: *Son* (died in infancy); *Eleanor* (married Joe Kapfer). Isal Barber died on 1 Aug. 1970 at Sigourney, IA, and is buried in the Bethel Cemetery.

9e. **(Elma) Ruth.** Born 15 June 1906 at Tacoma, WA. Married ___ Parks, and had children: *James* (who lived at Lakewood, WA); married secondly ___ Clark. Ruth Clark died on 19 June 1985 at Norwalk, CA.

JOHN FRANKLIN BURGESS OF MEAGHER CO., MONTANA

[Riley6, Balis7]

8c. **John Franklin (I)** *[son of Balis].* Born 6 July 1874 on the Mowrey Homestead, Jefferson Co., IA. Married Isabella Bonnella Black on 21 Apr. 1895 in IT (she was born 8 Mar. 1875 in Scotland, and died 19 Apr. 1959 at Bremerton, WA). Listed in the 1889 census with his father, and in 1900-20 in Lincoln Co., OK (two of two children survive in 1910). Living at Tacoma in 1918. John Burgess died of cancer on 15 Aug. 1927 at White Sulphur Springs, Meagher Co., MT.

9a. **William Riley.** Born 4 Dec. 1899 in Lincoln Co., OK. See below for full entry.

9b. **Edna Dacygne.** Born 13 Feb. 1907 in Lincoln Co., OK. Married Ralph Bryant Madison on 28 June 1926 at Vancouver, WA (he was born 1 Aug. 1896, and died 4 Apr. 1977), and had children:

Barbara Maureen "Peggy" MADISON. Born 11 Sept. 1928, married Myron Stangler in 1946, and died of cancer on 14 Mar. 1984, having had children: *Maureen Barbara* (born 28 Sept. 1952, married Mike Ballard, and had children: Amanda Lynn [born 19 Jan. 1982]; Michelle Jean [born 9 Aug. 1983, died several days later]; Malissa Nicole [born 31 Jan. 1985]); *Robert Myron* (born 15 Mar. 1955, married Angie Magana on 17 May 1980, and had children: Shawn Robert [born 6 Dec. 1981]; Sheena [born 18 June 1985]); *Mark Alec* (born 6 Jan. 1959); *Pamela Dacygne* (born 15 Mar. 1961).

Frederick Llewellyn MADISON. Born 27 June 1933, and died childless of cancer on 29 Dec. 1986.

Edna Dacygne MADISON married secondly Bernard Blakly on 28 July 1982 at Bremerton, WA (dec.). Edna Blakly currently lives at Seabeck, WA.

9c. **Charles Ohman.** Born 30 July 1911 in Lincoln Co., OK. See below for full entry.

WILLIAM R. BURGESS OF LANE CO., OREGON
[Riley^6, Balis^7, John Franklin (I)^8]

9a. **William Riley** *[son of John Franklin (I)].* Born 4 Dec. 1899 in Lincoln Co., IT (later OK). Married Sylvia Lee Foglesong about 1919 (she was born 29 Nov. 1901, and died 21 Apr. 1973 in Clackamas Co., OR). Listed in the 1920 census for Tacoma, Pierce Co., WA. William Burgess worked as a dairyman for a trucking company. He died on 7 July 1983 at Eugene, Lane Co., OR.

10a. **John William (III).** Born 15 Feb. 1920 at Tacoma, WA. Married Marjorie Winifred Diehl Mitchell (she died 14 July 1964); married secondly Norma West on 25 June 1966. John Burgess is a retired cabinetmaker at Portland, OR.

11a. **John Marshall.** Born 14 Oct. 1944 at Bremerton, WA. Married Faith Taeko Nomura on 22 Apr. 1972 at San Francisco, CA (she was born 2 May 1943 at Honolulu, HI, daughter of Walter Tetsuo Namura and Torayo Minatodani). John Burgess lives at San Carlos, CA.

12a. **Christina Taeko.** Born 13 Apr. 1976 at Redwood City, CA.
12b. **Johanna Torayo.** Born 3 Jan. 1978 at Redwood City, CA.
12c. **David Marshall.** Born 1982 at Redwood City, CA.

11b. **Daniel James "Dan."** Born 29 Jan. 1946 at Portland, OR. Married Marla Kay Henriksen on 20 Apr. 1974 at Portland, Multnomah Co., OR. Dan Burgess works for the phone company at Salem, OR.

10b. **Edwin Lee (I).** Born 12 July 1925 at La Center, WA. Married Phyllis Ann Hayward on 30 Jan. 1949 in Clackamas Co., OR. Ed Burgess was a plumbing inspector for the state of Oregon before retiring. He currently lives at Aloha, OR. Phyllis Burgess has contributed greatly to this book.

11a. **Cheryl Ann.** Born 8 Nov. 1951 at Oregon City, OR. Married James Younger on 5 June 1976 in Lane Co., OR, and had children: *Sara Kathleen* (born 17 Aug. 1978 at Anchorage, AK); *Andrew Scott* (born 4 Nov. 1980 at Anchorage, AK). Cheryl Younger currently lives at Beaverton, OR.
11b. **Frederick William.** Born 4 Apr. 1954 at Oregon City, OR. Married Deanne White on 20 Sept. 1975 in Washington Co., OR (div.); married secondly Elaine Williams on 2 July 1983. Fred Burgess is a pilot in the U.S. Navy with the rank of Lt. Commander, currently stationed with the United Command at Stuttgart, Germany.

12a. **Angeline Sylvie.** Born 23 Feb. 1977 at Pensacola, FL.
12b. **Tayler Allen.** Born 17 May 1984 at Monterey, CA.

10c. **Walter Franklin "Walt."** Born 12 Apr. 1927 at Lacenter, WA. Married Peggy Arlene Allen on 27 Dec. 1953 at Eugene, OR (she was born 3 Mar. 1934 at Douglas, WY, daughter of Harvey Porter Allen and Pearl Marie La Fever). Walt Burgess is a retired elementary school principal; Peggy Burgess is a retired elementary school teacher. They currently live at Eugene, OR.

11a. **Nancy Joanne.** Born 10 Apr. 1957 at Eugene, OR. Married Fred Anderson on 28 Apr. 1979 in Lane Co., OR (div.). Nancy Anderson works in a restaurant at Eugene, OR.
11b. **Brent Allen.** Born 28 May 1961 at Eugene, OR. Married Suzanne Orem on 9 Sept. 1989 at Eugene, OR. Brent Burgess is a salesman for Frito-Lay at Eugene, OR.

12a. **Stephanie Orem.** Born 12 May 1986 at Springfield, OR.
12b. **Caleb Jordan.** Born 17 June 1990 at Eugene, OR.

11c. **Stuart Reid.** Born 21 Jan. 1966 at Eugene, OR. Married Liza Cruz on 15 June 1991 at Eugene, OR. Stuart Burgess is a high school teacher at Glendale, OR.

CHARLES O. BURGESS OF LANE CO., OREGON
[Riley^6, Balis^7, John Franklin (I)^8]

9c. **Charles Ohman** *[son of John Franklin (I)].* Born 30 July 1911 in Lincoln Co., OK. Married Bessie Pleninger on 1 June 1940 at Great Falls, MT (she was born on 15 May 1913 at Pittsburg, OK, daughter of Stanley Pleninger and Anna Zoubeck). Charles O. Burgess worked for the IRS before retiring. He now lives at Eugene, OR.

10a. **Bryant Ohman "Bob."** Born 10 June 1947 at Portland, OR. He may have married Kristine Smith on 23 Dec. 1978 in Jackson Co., OR (div. 1989). Bob Burgess is an engineering consultant for U.S. West Communications, Portland, OR.

10b. **Marilyn Kay.** Born 4 Dec. 1949 at Oregon City, OR. Married Ronald Peery on 1 July 1978 in Lane Co., OR (by his first marriage, he had children: *Scott*; *Suzanne*). Marilyn Peery currently lives at Eugene, OR.

10c. **Terry Lauren.** Born 19 Aug. 1955 at Roseburg, OR. Married Carolyn Jane Smith on 2 Aug. 1980 at Springfield, Lane Co., OR (div. 1992; she was born 31 Aug 1957 at Tillamook, OR, daughter of Claude Robert Smith and Barbara Lu Higbee). Terry Burgess is an aircraft mechanic at Springfield, OR.

11a. **Cory Robert.** Born 26 May 1981 at Springfield, OR.

11b. **Joel Scott.** Born 29 June 1984 at Springfield, OR.

BEEDY S. BURGESS OF PIERCE CO., WASHINGTON
[Riley^6, Balis^7]

8d. **Beedy Shelton** *[son of Balis].* His name is spelled Beidy in the 1900 census, and Beddy in 1910. Born 29 Oct. 1876 in Boone Co., IA. Married Nora B. B. Darr on 22 Sept. 1895 at Tacoma, WA (she was born 12 Nov. 1875 in IL, daughter of Madison Darr and Ann Cope, and died 12 Apr. 1920 at Tacoma, WA). Listed in the 1900-10 censuses for Lincoln Co., OK (five of seven children survive in 1910), and in 1920 in Pierce Co., WA. Listed in the 1904-1921 directories of Tacoma, WA, and again in 1945. Beedy S. Burgess farmed at Hendrix, OK before moving to Tacoma in 1911, and to Vashon Island in 1950. He died on 13 Nov. 1953 at Vashon Island, WA, and is buried in the Oakwood Cemetery.

9a. **Balis Madison (I).** Born 9 Oct. 1896 in Lincoln Co., Cherokee Nation, IT (later OK). See below for full entry.

9b. **Bert Bazzle.** His name is given as Birdie in the 1900 census, and as Bertie in 1910. Born 10 Mar. 1898 in Logan Co., Cherokee Nation, IT (later OK). See below for full entry.

9c. **Mazie Ann(a).** Her name is written Amazy in the 1900 census. Born 8 Mar. 1900 in Lincoln Co., Cherokee Nation, IT (later OK). Married Clifford M. Fuller on 15 June 1921, and had children: *Mrs. Donald Eklund.* Listed in the 1920 directory of Tacoma living with her father. Mazie Fuller was a physician's receptionist. She died on 17 Apr. 1968 at Seattle, WA.

9d. **(Esther) Mae.** Born 27 Oct. 1902 in Lincoln Co., Cherokee Nation, IT (later OK). Listed in the 1920-21 directories of Tacoma, WA living with her father. Married Norman L. Jones. Mae Jones died in Dec. 1990 at Tacoma, WA.

9e. **Lola Bell.** Born 7 July 1904 in Lincoln Co., Cherokee Nation, IT (later OK). Married Walter C. Nelson on 7 Sept. 1920; married secondly A. W. Sawyer. Living in 1968 at Seattle, WA. Lola Sawyer died on 19 Dec. 1975 at Fair Oaks, CA.

9f. **Sim Oscar.** Born 2 June 1907 in Bates Co., MO; died there on 19 Feb. 1909, and is buried in the Crescent Hill Cemetery.

BALIS MADISON BURGESS OF PIERCE CO., WASHINGTON
[Riley^6, Balis^7, Beedy Shelton^8]

9a. **Balis Madison (I)** *[son of Beedy Shelton].* Born 9 Oct. 1896 in Lincoln Co., Cherokee Nation, IT (later OK). Married Jeanette Elizabeth "Nettie" Carns on 18 June 1916 at Tacoma, WA (she was born 17 June 1898 at Clinton, TN, daughter of William Calvin Carns and Elizabeth Bell Brown, and died Aug. 1986?). Listed in the 1914-1921 directories for Tacoma, WA, and in the 1920 census for Pierce Co. Balis Burgess worked for Shell Oil Company for 32 years, and then as a gardener at Mountain View Memorial Park. He died on 11 June 1958 at Tacoma, WA, and is buried in the cemetery he tended. He was a member of the Christian Church.

10a. **Delores Mazie.** Her name is spelled Deloris in the 1920 census. Born 4 Dec. 1917 at Tacoma, WA. Married Lewis E. Whitney in 1937 at Port Orchard, WA, and had children: *Willard Calvin* (born 1938); *Leanne Jeanette* (born May 1941); *Brian Lewis* (born 1945).

10b. **Balis Madison (II).** Born 24 Jan. 1919 at Tacoma, WA. Married Jennetta Francis Morgan (she was born 10 Aug. 1918 at Tacoma, WA, daughter of Edward and Lois Morgan). Balis Burgess worked for the Shell Oil Company for 33 years, and then served 14 years as the manager of the Pierce County Garage at Eatonville, WA before retiring there. He has lived on the shores of Clear Lake for over fifty years.

11a. **Sharon Lee.** Born 7 June 1941 at Tacoma, WA. Married John A. Erickson (an architect with Erickson, McGovern, Tacoma, and Spanaway), and had children: *Kendra Michele* (born 1 June 1968 at Tacoma, WA); *Kerry Lea* (ad.; born 14 Aug. 1972). Sharon Erickson is a high school teacher of French at Eatonville, WA.

11b. **Susan Lois.** Born 9 Dec. 1942 at Tacoma, WA. Married Dale Curtiss (div.), and had children: *Tami Sue* (born 16 Nov. 1962 at Tacoma, WA, married Don Crisman, and had children: Tina); *Kyle Edward* (born 2 Mar. 1965 at Tacoma, WA, married Nicole Gruber in 1986); Susan married secondly Richard "Andy" Andrews. Susan Andrews lives at Eatonville, WA.

11c. **Candace Nora.** Born 22 June 1947 at Tacoma, WA. Married Dr. Michael J. Pine (a dentist), and had children: *David* (born 9 Feb. 1972 at San Francisco, CA); *Rebecca Michael "Becky"* (born 12 Dec. 1977 at Sacramento, CA). Candace Pine lives at Roseville, CA.

11d. **Balis Madison (III).** Born 17 Aug. 1953 at Tacoma, WA. Married Jacqueline K. Shaw about 1982 (she works for the Pierce Co. Prosecutor). Balis Burgess Jr. works as a maintenance man for the Pierce Co. Building Dept., Tacoma, WA.

12a. **Michael James (II)** (ad.). Born 1 Oct. 1972 at Tacoma, WA.

12b. **Bret Matthew.** Born 16 Apr. 1983 at Tacoma, WA.

BERT B. BURGESS OF PIERCE CO., WASHINGTON

[Riley[6], Balis[7], Beedy Shelton[8]]

9b. **Bert Bazzle** *[son of Beedy Shelton].* His name is listed as Bertis in the 1910 census. Born 10 Mar. 1898 in Logan Co., Cherokee Nation, IT (later OK). Married Ruth Gertrude Nelson in June 1918 (she may have been born 3 Apr. 1888, and died Mar. 1984). Listed in the 1913-1927 directories of Tacoma, WA, and in the 1920 census for Pierce Co. Bert Burgess was a truck driver at Tacoma, WA. He died there on 16 Feb. 1978, and is buried in the Washelle Cemetery.

10a. **Beverly Jean (II).** Born 14 June 1927 at Tacoma, WA.

10b. **Richard Bert.** Born 12 Dec. 1929 at Tacoma, WA. Married Thora Tauman. Richard Burgess died of a brain tumor on 26 May 1961 in Washington.

11a. **Jerry Richard Gellis.** Born 27 Nov. 1950 at Elgin, IL.

11b. **Mark Richard.** Born 13 July 1957 at Seattle, WA. Married Mary Schrader on 29 Dec. 1979 at Edmonds, WA (she was born 13 Sept. 1958 at San Mateo, CA, daughter of Dan Charles Schrader and Margaret Ackerman). Mark Burgess is an engineer for the Boeing Company, Seattle, WA.

12a. **Maria Alys.** Born 12 Dec. 1981 at Bellevue, WA.

12b. **Jill Elisabeth.** Born 11 May 1984 at Bellevue, WA.

11c. **Michelle Alys.** Born 10 July 1959 at Seattle, WA.

10c. **Jerol Ann "Jerry."** Born 17 Feb. 1938.

[William (I)[1], Edward (I)[2], Edward (II)[3], William (IV)[4], Bedy[5]]

SILAS R. BURGESS
(1829-1886)

OF RINGGOLD COUNTY, IOWA

6e. **Silas R.** *[son of Bedy].* Born 13 Feb. 1829 in Greene Co., OH. Married as Mary Ann Rhea on 28 July 1849 in Mahaska Co., IA (she was born 28 Sept. 1828 in VA, and died 11 Mar. 1904 at Kellerton, IA; she was a Methodist). Listed in the 1850 federal and the 1851 state censuses for Mahaska Co., IA, in the 1854-56 state censuses for Polk Township, Jefferson Co. IA, in 1860 in Osceola Township, Clarke Co., IA (he sold his land in Clarke Co. on 14 Feb. 1870 [*Deed Book #M*, p. 277]), and from 1870-80 in Lotts Creek Township, Ringgold Co., IA. Silas Burgess was a blacksmith in Ohio and Iowa, moving to the latter state in 1843. He died on 24 Sept. 1886 in Ringgold Co., IA, and is buried there in the Caledonia Cemetery. His widow appears as head of the family in the 1895 state and 1900 federal censuses for Kellerton town, Athens Township, Ringgold Co., IA.

The Children of Silas R. Burgess:

7a. **John N. (I).** Born 1851 in Mahaska Co., IA. See below for full entry.

7b. **Marcellus V.** (dau.). Born about 1853 in IA; died there between 1860-70.

7c. **(Anna) Eliza** (twin). Her name is also listed as Eliza Anna. Born Dec. 1855 in Jefferson Co., IA. Married John W. Taylor on 8 Jan. 1878 in Ringgold Co., IA (he was born Dec. 1855 in IA), and had at least the following children: *Morris G.* (born June 1879); *Maud S.* (born Sept. 1882). Listed with her father in the 1870 census, and with her husband in the 1900 census for Lotts Creek Township, Ringgold Co., IA.

7d. **James Rhea** (twin). Born Dec. 1855 in Jefferson Co., IA; died there before 1870.

7e. **Harriet J. "Hattie"** (twin). She was named for Harriet Carter. Born Oct. 1858 in Mahaska Co., IA. Married C. J. Morrison on 27 Dec. 1883 in Ringgold Co., IA (he was born about 1829, son of Robert Morrison and Mary A. Adair); married secondly (Samuel) Shelly Wood on 29 June 1898 at Saratoga, Carbon Co., WY. Listed in the 1900-10 censuses for Carbon Co., WY.

7f. **Carter Abraham** (twin). He was named for Abraham Carter. Born Oct. 1858 in Mahaska Co., IA (according to the 1895 census). Married and widowed by 1895. Living with his father in 1880, with his mother in 1895, and is listed in the county directory for Kellerton in 1899, and on the Ringgold Co. militia lists of 1878-1902; has not been found in the 1900 census; living with his brothers in the 1905 state census for Ringgold Co., IA, and in 1910 in Carbon Co., WY with his sister, Harriet; in 1920 he is an inmate in the Iowa Hospital for the Insane in Page Co., IA. Carter Burgess was a blacksmith. He apparently died childless.

7g. **Olive V.** Born 1860 in Clarke Co., IA. Married Jeremiah Swiga(r)t on 27 Nov. 1882 in Ringgold Co., IA (he was born 1859, son of Isaac Swiga(r)t and Frances Waller), and had children: *Ralph* (born 19 July 1884 in Ringgold Co., died 20 Dec. 1905); *Nina* (born 4 Aug. 1897 in Ringgold Co., married ___ Johnson, and died 20 Feb. 1943, buried Caledonia Cemetery). Olive Swiga(r)t died in Ringgold Co. in 1898, and is buried in the Maple Row Cemetery.

7h. **Willie A.** (dau.). Born about 1864 in Clarke Co., IA. Living with her mother in 1895, and is listed in the county directory for Kellerton, IA in 1899, but has not been found in 1900. She is listed with her brothers in the 1905 state census for Ringgold Co., IA, and is then unmarried.

7i. **Andrew Lincoln "Andy."** Born about 1865 in Clarke Co., IA. Married Julia L. ___ after 1910. Listed with his mother in the 1895 and 1900 censuses, in the county directory for Kellerton in 1899, on the Ringgold Co. militia lists of 1884-1908, in the 1905 state census for Ringgold Co., IA with his brothers, in the 1910 census for Carbon Co., WY with his brother, George, and in 1920 in Hickory Co., MO. Andrew Burgess was a blacksmith.

7j. **Nellie A.** Born Mar. 1867 in Clarke Co., IA. Married George W. Foster on 13 Oct. 1889 in Ringgold Co.

7k. **Cora E.** (twin). Born 4 Aug. 1870 in Clarke Co., IA (according to her marriage record); she was either a twin with Arlington Burgess, or was actually born in 1868 or 1869. Married Harry E. Scott on 3 Sept. 1894 in Ringgold Co. (he was born 1869 in IN, son of James and Margaret Scott), and had children: *Hattie D.* (born 1895 in IA); *Mona R.* (born 1898 in IA); *Margaret M.* (born 1900 in IA); *Burl M.* (born 1902 in IA); *Cleo C.* (twin; born 1907 in IA); *Leo H.* (twin; born 1907 in IA, died 1924 in Ringgold Co., buried Maple Row Cemetery); *Samuel S.* (born 1909 in IA). Has not been found in the 1900 census; listed in the 1910 census for Ringgold Co., IA. Cora Scott died in 1956, and is buried in the Maple Row Cemetery.

7l. **Arlington** (twin). Born 4 Aug. 1870 in Clarke Co., IA; died there on 15 Feb. 1871, and is buried with his father.

7m. **George E.** Born May 1873 in Ringgold Co., IA. See below for full entry.

JOHN N. BURGESS OF RINGGOLD CO., IOWA

[Silas R.[6]]

7a. **John N. (I)** *[son of Silas R.].* Born 1851 in Mahaska Co., IA (according to his second marriage record and the 1885 census). Married Fannie E. Pierson on 2 Dec. 1877 in Ringgold Co. (she was born about 1859); married secondly Etta Lutters on 23 Dec. 1896 in Ringgold Co. (she was born about 1869, daughter of John Lutters and Lois Raymond). Listed in the Ringgold Co. directory for 1899 in Riley Township, on the militia lists of Ringgold Co. from 1872-84, and in the 1885 state census for Kellerton, Athens Township, Ringgold Co., IA, but has not been found in the censuses of 1895-1910. John Burgess was a blacksmith, plasterer, and farmer in Ringgold Co., IA.

8a. **Daughter.** Born 15 Nov. 1880 at Caledonia, Ringgold Co., IA (according to the county birth records). She either died before 1885, or this is a misrecording of the birth of William F. Burgess.

8b. **William Fremon.** Born 14 Nov. 1881 in Ringgold Co., IA. Married (Mary) Jane ___ (she was born 1885 in IA). Living with his grandmother in 1895; listed in the 1917 draft register and in the 1915-20 censuses for Chariton, Lucas Co., IA. William F. Burgess was a miner for the Iowa Fuel Co.

8c. **Frederick Randalph.** Born 19 May 1883 in Lotts Creek Township, Ringgold Co., IA. He was engaged to Effie Cornett in Oct. 1911, but never married her. Married Umatilla "Tillie" Beals on 26 Feb. 1912 in Lucas Co., IA (she was born 26 Nov. 1891, and died 21 Dec. 1951). Living with his grandmother in 1895; listed in the 1915-20 censuses for Chariton, Lucas Co., IA, and in the 1917 draft register for Olmitz, Lucas Co. Fred Burgess was a blacksmith and miner in Lucas Co., IA. He died there on 19 Aug. 1962, and is buried with his wife in the Lincoln Cemetery.

9a. **Cleona L.** Born 1913 at Chariton, Lucas Co., IA. She is *not* the Cleona Wisler born 23 Apr. 1914 in IA who died June 1979 in CA.

8d. **Beryl F.** Her name is given as Mary Edna in her birth record. Born 5 June 1887 in Lotts Creek Township, Lucas Co., IA. Living with her grandmother in 1900, and with her uncles in 1905.

8e. **Maud(e) E.** Born 18 Aug. 1889 in Ringgold Co., IA. Married Ray C. Howard on 28 May 1910 in Ringgold Co., at Mt. Ayre, IA (he was born 1886 in IA, son of Austin Howard and Ellenor Briddnor [he may be the Ray Howard born 24 Aug. 1886 who died Dec. 1981 at Dallas Center, Dallas Co., IA]).

GEORGE E. BURGESS OF HICKORY CO., MISSOURI

[Silas R.[6]]

7m. **George E.** *[son of Silas R.].* Listed as George W. Burgess in the 1920 census. Born May 1873 in Ringgold Co., IA. Married Edna L. Higgens on 31 July 1904 in Ringgold Co., IA (she was born 1885 in IA, daughter of Frank Higgens and Mina McAminch). Listed with his mother in the 1895 and 1900 censuses, as a blacksmith in the county directory for Kellerton in 1899, on the Ringgold Co. militia lists of 1894-1904, in the 1905 census for Kellerton, Ringgold Co., IA living with his brothers, in the 1910 census for Carbon Co., WY, and in 1920 in Hickory Co., MO.

8a. **Doris L.** Listed as Doris E. Burgess in the 1920 census. Born about 1906 in Ringgold Co., IA.

[William (I)[1], Edward (I)[2], Edward (II)[3], William (IV)[4], Bedy[5]]

ELIAS BURGESS
(1830-1903)

OF MENDOCINO COUNTY, CALIFORNIA

6f. **Elias** *[son of Bedy].* Born Sept. 1830 in Greene Co., OH. Married Hester Ann Bishop in 1851 in Madison Co., IA (she was born Jan. 1833 [or 1835] in IN, and died 19 Nov. 1908 at Los Angeles, CA). Listed in the 1850 census with his father, in the 1854-56 state censuses (in 1854 there are two males and one female) and the 1860 federal census for Madison Co., IA, and in 1870-1900 in Mendocino Co., CA (eleven of fourteen children survive in 1900); he also appears in the 1876-98 Great Registers (voting lists) of Mendocino Co. (age 46 in Oct. 1876), but is not listed in the 1867-75 registers. Elias Burgess was a farmer near Willits, Little Lake Township, CA. He died there on 15 Sept. 1903, and is buried with other members of his family in the Little Lake Cemetery, Willits, CA (the common headstone simply states "Burgess"). Two settlement deeds filed in Mendocino Co. and dated 25 Feb. 1907 and 8 Mar. 1907 list all of Elias's heirs living at that time, including: (first deed) Hester Ann, John, Robert, Clayburn, Nora, all of Mendocino Co.; (second deed) Virginia F. and Ari Hopper of Yale District, BC, Mahala J. and Thomas Hopper of Spokane, WA, Samuel Burgess of Yale District, BC, Albert Burgess of Alameda Co., CA, Minnie Force of Nye Co., NV, Zelda Burgess of Los Angeles, CA, Alice Brown of Alameda Co., CA, Edmund McCracken of Kern Co., CA, Clarence McCracken of San Bernardino Co., CA. Hester Burgess is listed in the 1908 city Directory for Los Angeles living with her daughter Zelda. The estate of Hester Burgess was probated in 1910 (*Case #2175*) and that of Elias Burgess was probated on 8 July 1940 (*Case #6580*) by his daughter, Zelda Burgess, thirty-seven years after his death.

The Children of Elias Burgess:

7a. **Robert Ploughe.** Born Aug. 1852 in Madison Co., IA. See below for full entry.

7b. **Virginia F. "Jennie."** Born 11 June 1854 in Madison Co., IA. Married (Calvin) Ari Hopper on 24 Sept. 1871 in Mendocino Co., CA (he was born 18 Apr. 1845 in MO, son of William Hopper, and possibly the brother of Thomas B. Hopper [who married Jennie's sister, Mahala]), and had at least the following children: *Laura* (born 1873 in CA); *Hattie* (born 23 Feb. 1874 in CA, and married Thomas Humphrey on 27 Feb. 1896 in Stevens Co., WA, both listed as residents of Anaconda, BC, a mining camp one mile south of Greenwood, BC [where they are listed in the 1901 census], and had children: Irene M. [born 4 Apr. 1897 in BC]); *Lulu* (born 5 Sept. 1876 in CA, married William Powers, is listed in the 1901 census for Midway, BC, and had children: Violet [born 13 July 1895 in BC]); *Jenetta* (born 1878 in CA); *Alvin* (born 2 Apr. 1892 in Stevens Co., WA). Listed in the 1880 census for Calpella Township, Mendocino Co., CA; moved to Stevens Co., WA by 1892, and to Midway, BC, Canada in 1894, where she is listed in the 1901 census for the Rossland Riding District, BC (naturalized in 1900). Calvin Hopper's biography appears in the *History of Mendocino County, California* (San Francisco: Allen, Bowen & Co., 1880, p. 567). By inference Jennie Hopper died before 1930. A Calvin T. Hopper is living in Grand Forks, BC in 1938, working as a log operator.

7c. **Mahala Jane.** Born June 1856 in Madison Co., IA. Married Thomas B. Hopper on 29 Oct. 1871 in Mendocino Co. (he was born Jan. 1851 in MO, possibly the brother of Calvin Hopper, who married Mahala's sister, Jennie; he was a well-known hunter and guide, and may have died on 25 Sept. 1920 in Yolo Co., CA), and had at least the following children: *Rose*; *Ruby May* (born Apr. 1884 in WA). Has not been found in the 1880 California Soundex; the Hoppers moved to Spokane about 1890, and are listed in the 1900 census for Spokane, Spokane Co., WA, and in the Spokane, WA city directory in 1910. Mahala Hopper died of a heart attack on 4 July 1910 at Spokane, WA, and is buried in the Fairmount Cemetery. According to her obituary, she had lived in Spokane twenty years.

FAMOUS HUNTER'S WIFE DROPS DEAD

"Raising her hands to drive the flies from the door yesterday morning, only to reel suddenly and fall dying in the arms of Rose Hopper, her daughter, Mrs. Mahala Hopper, wife of Thomas Hopper, noted guide and friend of ex-President Roosevelt, was stricken down by heart trouble, to which she succumbed within 20 minutes. On getting up yesterday morning she apparently was in the best of health, having eaten a hearty breakfast and helped with the house work. The first intimation of anything wrong was when she reeled and fell. She had many friends in this city, having lived here 20 years, and in addition to her husband and daughter, is survived by six brothers and seven sisters, living in California and British Columbia. She was 54 years old. Arrangements for her burial will be made later. Mr. Hopper is one of the best known hunters in the west, and a number of times has led expeditions into the mountains for Roosevelt and his friends."—*Spokane Spokesman-Review*, 5 July 1910.

7d. **(William) Clayburn.** Born about 1858 in Madison Co., IA. See below for full entry.

7e. **Samuel H.** Born Dec. 1859 in Madison Co., IA. Married Mrs. Elizabeth B. (Frost) Ram(s)ey on 17 Oct. 1883 at Little Lake, Mendocino Co., CA (she was born May 1853 in MO). Listed in the 1882-98 Great Registers for Mendocino Co. (age 22 in Sept. 1882), and in the 1900 census for the Flat Creek District, Stevens Co., WA working as a quartz miner. Living at Midway, BC by 1907. In 1912 a Mrs. Elizabeth B. Burgess bought 160 acres of land at Danville, Ferry Co., WA, just across the Canadian border, and sold it again with her husband, Samuel H., in 1916. Sam Burgess is listed in the 1920 census for Spokane, Spokane Co., WA living alone, but died before 1930 (not in the Washington death indexes).

7f. **Sarah E. (III).** Born about 1862 in Mendocino Co., CA. Married John H. McCracken on 12 Mar. 1878 in Mendocino Co., CA, and had children: *Edmund* (born 1882?, living in Kern Co. in 1907); *Clarence* (born 1885?, living in San Bernardino Co. in 1907; he and his brother are living at Redding, CA in 1910; a possible grandson, Edmund McCracken, was born 11 Apr. 1910 in OR, and died at Portland on 3 Feb. 1990). Has not been found in the 1880 California or Oregon Soundexes. Sarah's sister, Zelda, stated in her 1940 probate of her father's estate that Sarah McCracken had died in 1888.

7g. **Albert B(ryan?).** Born 28 Apr. 1865 in OR. See below for full entry.

7h. **John Alvin.** Born Nov. 1866 (or 1867) in Mendocino Co., CA. Listed in the Sept. 1888, 1902, and 1906 Great Registers of Mendocino Co., CA (age 21 in 1888). Listed in the 1900 census for the Flat Creek District, Stevens Co., WA working as a quartz miner, was living in Mendocino Co. in 1907, and at Midway, BC by 1910. By inference he died before 1930.

7i. **Minnie (I).** Born 14 July 1869 in Mendocino Co., CA. Married (Carl) Emil Force (div.; he was born 1 Sept. 1876 in NE, worked as a furniture store manager, remarried Gerda ___ on 26 Nov. 1914 at Berkeley, CA, and died 26 Apr. 1937 at Fort Bragg, CA); married secondly George A. Otto about 1915 (he was born 23 Apr. 1868 in Germany, and died 7 Jan. 1927 in Sonoma Co., CA). Listed in the 1900 census for Riverside, Riverside Co., CA living alone; living in Nye Co., NV by 1907, and in Oakland, CA by 1910. Minnie Otto died childless on 17 Feb. 1933 at Santa Rosa, CA at the home of her sister, Nora, and was cremated at the California Crematory, Oakland, CA. Her obituary mentions Nora and Zelda as her only surviving siblings.

7j. **Leonard.** Born about 1872 in Mendocino Co., CA. Listed with his father in the 1880 census, and apparently died young in Mendocino Co. by 1900. Probably buried with his father in an unmarked grave.

7k. **Nora (II).** Born 22 Apr. 1874 in Mendocino Co., CA. Married Manuel Mathews Silva about 1896 (div. 1903), and had children: *William* (born July 1897); *Caroline* (born Oct. 1899); married secondly William P. Burns about 1910 (he was born 25 Nov. 1872, was a railroad engineer and banker, and died 23 Apr. 1941). Listed as head of her family in the 1900 census for Ten Mile River Township, Mendocino Co., CA. She and William Burns are living at Glen Ellen, CA in 1908. Listed in the 1910 census for Willits, Little Lake Township, Mendocino Co., CA, and in the 1935-1938 city directories for Santa Rosa, CA; her sister, Zelda, is living with her there in 1940; she is not in the 1947 directory. Nora Burns died on 22 June 1958 at Santa Cruz, CA, the last of her brothers and sisters to die, and is buried in the Odd Fellows Lawn Cemetery, Santa Rosa, Sonoma Co., CA. Neither the 1910 census nor her obituary mentions her children.

7l. **Zelda "Zell."** Born 31 Oct. 1877 (or 1879) at Willits, Mendocino Co., CA. Married Charles H. Bodle after 1910 (he was born 8 Jan. 1869 in IN, and died 7 May 1931 at Santa Rosa, CA, buried I.O.O.F. Cemetery, Santa Rosa, CA). Listed in the 1900 census for Riverside, Riverside Co., CA, and in 1910 at Willits, Mendocino Co., CA living with her sister, Nora. Listed in the 1902 and 1908 city directories for Los Angeles, CA. Living with her sister Nora at Santa Rosa, CA in 1940, when she probated her father's estate. Zell Bodle died childless on 12 Sept. 1947 at Alameda, CA. Her obituary mentions as sole surviving relatives her niece, Leah E. Wood, her nephew, M. L. Brown, and sister, Nora Burns.

7m. **Alice M. (I).** Born Jan. 1881 in Mendocino Co., CA. Living with her parents in 1900 working as a maid. Married William Henry Brown on 31 Mar. 1902 in Mendocino Co., and had children: *M. L. "Glenn"* (married Rose ___, living at Alameda in 1958). She was living at Alameda, CA in 1907. Listed in the 1910 census for Oakland, CA, and appears in the city directory there for 1930. Alice Brown died on 15 Mar. 1930 at Oakland, CA; her obituary mentions as survivors her son and her three sisters: Minnie, Nora, and Zelda.

ROBERT P. BURGESS OF MENDOCINO CO., CALIFORNIA
[Elias^6]

7a. **Robert Ploughe** *[son of Elias].* He was named for his uncle, Robert Ploughe, husband of Roda Burgess. Born Aug. 1852 in Madison Co., IA. Married Katharine E. Monroe on 11 Aug. 1885 in Mendocino Co., CA (div.?; she was born Apr. 1866 in Canada, and died 29 Apr. 1937 at Oakland, CA). Living at Garberville, CA in 1885. Listed in the 1900 census for Mendocino Co., CA, and in 1910-20 at Los Angeles, CA. Listed in the Great Registers of Mendocino Co. from 1875-1898 and in 1906 (age 23 in Aug. 1875), and in Sonoma Co. from 1902-04; he signed a deed in Mendocino Co. in 1907. Katharine is listed in the 1920 census for San Francisco, and in the 1930 city directory of Oakland. Robert Burgess may have died on 30 Jan. 1928 at Los Angeles, CA, but in any case before 1930.

8a. **Blanche Rainer.** Born 10 June 1889 in Oregon (according to early census records) or Washington (according to her death certificate and obituary). Married ___ Kane, and had children: *Thomas L.*; *Blanche* (married ___ Smith); *Muriel* (married ___ Bonini); married secondly James D. Daly. Listed in the Oakland, CA directories from 1935-43. Blanche Daly was a seamstress for the Oakland Towel Co. She died on 16 July 1958 at Oakland, CA.

CLABE BURGESS OF MENDOCINO CO., CALIFORNIA
[Elias^6]

7d. **(William) Clayburn "Clabe"** *[son of Elias].* Born about 1858 in Madison Co., IA. Married Mrs. Emma Adams on 15 June 1882 in Mendocino Co., CA (div.); married secondly Belle J. McCracken about 1888 (div. about 1900; she was born Mar. 1869 in CA, daughter of William J. and Mollie McCracken, remarried Edgar G. Aiken about 1904 [he was born 1862 in IL, worked as a city policeman, and died at Los Angeles on 26 July 1928], and died about 1940 at Riverside, CA). Listed in the 1880-86 and the 1902-16 Great Registers of Mendocino Co., CA (age 22 in July 1880) and in 1890 in Sonoma Co., in the 1897 special census of the City of Los Angeles with his second wife and children, in the 1910 census (age 52) for Little Lake Township, Mendocino Co., CA working as a ranchhand for S. E. Hamilton, in 1920 in Mendocino Co. with Luther Redemeyer; has not been found in 1900 (but his children are living with his parents). Clabe Burgess was a rancher and cowboy at Branscomb, CA. He died there on 20 Apr. 1921, and was apparently buried on the ranch where he worked. Belle Burgess appears in the 1900 census for Los Angeles working as a hotel chambermaid (living alone), in the 1902 city directory of Los Angeles as Mrs. Belle Burgess, and in the 1910 census with her new husband, her father, and her Burgess children (the daughters are now listed with the surname "Aiken").

8a. **Albert Elias.** Born Mar. 1889 in Mendocino Co., CA. Listed in the 1900 census living with his grandfather, in the 1910 census for Los Angeles with his stepfather, Edgar G. Aiken, in 1920 at Los Angeles, CA with his family, and in the city directories of Los Angeles from 1905-41 (with his stepfather through 1920). Mentioned in his stepfather's obituary in 1928. Married Emily H. Dewar about 1913 (she was born 20 Dec. 1894, the daughter of Edwin J. and Catherine Dewar, and died on 4 Aug. 1978 at Huntington Beach, CA). Emily is listed in the Los Angeles telephone directories through 1972. Albert E. Burgess was an electrician. He died on 15 Dec. 1946 at Portland, OR.

9a. **Catherine Belle.** Born 19 Jan. 1914 at Los Angeles, CA. Married James Burley McCallum (he was born 1 Dec. 1913, and died 21 July 1984 at Huntington Beach). Catherine McCallum worked as a machine inspector for Robert Shaw during World War II, and later as a sales clerk for Sears. She currently lives retired at Huntington Beach, CA.

9b. **Alberta Edith.** Born 19 July 1916 at Los Angeles, CA. Married Nicholas Iavenditti. Alberta Iavenditti worked as a machinist for Robert Shaw Co. She currently lives retired at Huntington Beach, CA.

8b. **Lola E.** Listed as Laura Burgess in the 1897 census; she used the surname Aiken before her marriage. Born Mar. 1890 in Sonoma Co., CA. Married Charles Couch. Listed in the 1910 census with her stepfather. Lola Couch died on 13 Dec. 1919 at Los Angeles, CA.

8c. **Edith A(lberta?).** She used the surname Aiken. Born Aug. 1892 in CA. Edith Aiken died about 1905 at Los Angeles, CA.

8d. **Leah E.** She used the surname Aiken before her marriage. Born 17 Apr. 1894 in CA. Married ___ Wood by 1919. Listed in the 1910 census with her stepfather. She is mentioned in Aiken's 1928 obituary, in the 1947 obituary of her aunt, Zelda Bodle, and in the 1958 obituary of her aunt, Nora Burns (she was then living at Pasadena, CA). Leah Wood was a real estate agent at Riverside, CA. She died there on 17 Mar. 1970, and is buried in the Forest Lawn Cemetery, Glendale, CA.

8e. **Lillian Rose "Lilly."** She used the surname Aiken. Born Dec. 1896 in CA. Listed in the 1910 census with her stepfather. Lilly Aiken died unmarried on 18 June 1917 at Los Angeles, CA, taking her own life by swallowing poison after being jilted by her boyfriend.

ALBERT B. BURGESS OF MENDOCINO CO., CALIFORNIA

[Elias^{6}]

7g. **Albert B(ryan?)** *[son of Elias].* Born 28 Apr. 1865 in Oregon, and is said to have been brought by his family to California at the age of three weeks. Married Ida Viola Cooper on 21 Apr. 1895 in Mendocino Co., CA (div.; she was born Mar. 1875 in CA). Listed in the 1886-98 Great Registers of Mendocino Co. (age 21 in Oct. 1886), but not thereafter; listed in the 1900 census for Mendocino Co., CA., in 1910 in Los Angeles Co., CA, and in 1920 in Humboldt Co., CA; he was living at Alameda, CA in 1907. Albert B. Burgess died on 3 Dec. 1923 at Willits, CA, and is buried there in an unmarked grave in the Little Lake Cemetery. Ida appears in the 1915 city directory for Santa Rosa, CA, and had moved to Oakland, CA by 1918.

8a. **Beatrice Lillian "Bea."** Born 28 Feb. 1897 at Laytonville, Mendocino Co., CA. Married Harry G. Garland on 26 May 1915 in Sonoma Co., CA (he was born 31 Mar. 1892, and died 6 May 1968 at Orland, CA), and had children: *Marion* (born 25 Apr. 1916, died May 1981 at Coos Bay, OR); *Norman* (lives at Aloha, CA); *Bernice* (married ___ Davis, and lives at Rogue River, OR); *Robert "Bob."* Living at Healdsburg, CA in 1915, but later settled to Coos Bay, OR. Bea Garland moved to Redding, CA in 1970, and then to Eureka, Humboldt Co., CA. She died there on 8 May 1982, and is buried in the Ocean View Cemetery.

8b. **Bernard Jennings.** Born 17 Feb. 1900 at Willits, CA. Married Emma Josephine Vanoni (she was born 7 Feb. 1903, and died 22 May 1934); married secondly Margaret Gosselin (who remarried William H. Brooks, and lives at Salem, OR). Listed in the 1917 draft register of Mendocino Co., CA, and in the 1920 census with his father. Bernard Burgess was a heavy equipment operator for the State of California. He died on 21 Feb. 1970 at Ukiah, CA, and is buried in the Little Lake Cemetery, Willits, CA.

9a. **Yvonne Emma.** Born 10 Oct. 1927 at Calistoga, CA. Married Raoul Flores; married secondly Stanley Sprague. Yvonne Sprague was a claims adjustor for the Unemployment Division, State of Oregon before retiring in 1991. She currently lives at Salem, OR with her stepmother and brother.

9b. **Albert Loren.** Born 2 Aug. 1929 at Lower Lake, CA. Married Elizabeth Perkins; married secondly Jeanine Powell (div.). Albert L. Burgess was a self-employed vending machine operator before retiring in 1992; he currently lives with his sister, Yvonne Sprague, at Salem, OR. He is believed to be the last descendant with the name Burgess in the line of Elias Burgess.

9c. **Richard Bernard.** Born 27 May 1932 at Woodland, Yolo Co., CA; died 15 Aug. 1932 at Crescent City, CA.

9d. **Phyllis Clara.** Born 21 May 1934 at Upper Lake, CA. Married Eldon L. Kellerhals (div.; he was born 18 June 1927, and died Jan. 1979 at Prineville, OR); married secondly Walter McLaughlin. Phyllis McLaughlin works for the Oregon State Department of Motor Vehicles, Salem, OR.

8c. **Lawrence Freadom "Larry."** Born 22 Apr. 1903 at Willits, CA. Married Selma Louise Gragg on 6 Sept. 1930 in Mendocino Co., CA (she was born 4 Mar. 1905 at Holmes, CA, and died 12 Aug. 1980 at Fortuna). Listed in the 1963 directory of Redding, CA. Larry Burgess was a truck driver in Northern California, moving to Sacramento in 1946, and to Redding in 1957. He retired in 1972 to Fortuna, Humboldt Co., CA, where he died childless on 12 June 1985.

[William (I)[1], Edward (I)[2], Edward (II)[3], William (IV)[4], Bedy[5]]

ALANSON BRYANT BURGESS
(1838-1905)
OF SONOMA COUNTY, CALIFORNIA

6i. **Alanson Bryan(t) "Lancing"** *[son of Bedy].* Born July 1838 (or 1837) in Greene Co., Ohio. Married Sarah J. Landers on 29 June 1856 in Madison Co., IA (she was born about 1838 in Putnam Co., IN, the daughter of John Landers and Sarah Burkett, and died between 1870-78); married secondly Martha Frances "Annie" Gibson on 4 July 1878 in Mendocino Co., CA (she was born Mar. 1864 at Willits, CA, daughter of Miles Gibson of Kings Co., CA, remarried a wagon master, C. H. Rudolph, moved with him to Cohasset, Butte Co., CA, and died on 21 May 1908 at Chico, CA). Listed in the 1870 census for Madison Co., IA, in the 1879 Great Register of Mendocino Co. (age 40 in Mar. 1879), in the 1890 and 1902 Great Registers of Sonoma Co., in the 1900 census for Sonoma Co., CA, and in the Santa Rosa city directory for 1904/05. He died on 27 July 1905 at Santa Rosa, Sonoma Co., CA, and is buried in an unmarked grave with his second wife in the McPeak Cemetery, Hacienda, CA.

EXCERPTS FROM EDNA BURGESS MARTIN'S DIARY

"October 25, 1903. Oh the loveliest morning we had, such beautiful weather for two weeks now, oh if it will only be this kind till my Brother [Alanson] gets here. Today Nannie & Sarah will be married, if Nannie's man gets there, my Brother's girls...."

"December 13, 1903. This last week has been cold & windy & threatening snow. It has snowed just a little & is cloudy this morning. I had a letter from my Brother's wife, and the disappointment didn't hurt him as I was afraid it would. They were going to write to me that they couldn't come on account of the failure of Nannie's marriage, as they would have no place to leave the little boy. I can't tell you how relieved I am that it didn't kill him."

"August 6, 1905. Still showery, almost every day it rains a little. Just enough to wet the grass so they have to stop haying for a while. It is very discouraging to the ranch men who are trying to make hay. Yet they were pleased to have it rain on the range. I got the sad news yesterday morning that my last Brother, who has been sick for the last six years, died the 27 of July. He suffered terribly at times. I wonder he lived as long as he did. He must have had an iron constitution in the first place & his will power was very strong. He was so determined to get well. So I am all that's left of eleven children. Two died young, but the others have all lived to middle age & over. Brother Elias was 71, he was the oldest, that is, he lived the longest except myself. I am near 72, and Alanson was 68. He had been married twice & left five children, three of them married, all able to make their own living."

The Children of Alanson Burgess:

7a. **John (IX).** Born about 1868 in Madison Co., IA; died there young after 1870.
7b. **Alanson Thomas.** Born 26 Oct. 1879 at Little Lake, CA. See below for full entry.
7c. **Mary Ann (VI).** Born Mar. 1881 in CA. Married August B. Lang on 26 Nov. 1898 in Sonoma Co., CA (div.; he was born Apr. 1876 in CA, remarried Mary's sister, Sarah, and may have died 18 Dec. 1955), and had children: *Archie R.* (born 13 Aug. 1902, died 1 Nov. 1981 at Dunsmuir, CA); *Mable* (born 1904). Mary Ann married secondly Harvey L. "Harry" Bennicuff in 1908 (a career Army man, he died on 11 Oct. 1949 in San Francisco, CA), and had children: *Harry L.* (born 16 Oct. 1908, and died 28 Feb. 1985 at Walnut Creek, CA); *Virgilia* (born about 1910); *Sadie "Babe"* (born about 1912, died young of tuberculosis). Listed in the 1900 census for Sonoma Co., CA. Mary Bennicuff died about 1930 of tuberculosis in Northern California; has not been found in the California death index.

7d. **Sarah Ethel.** Born 26 Oct. 1882 in Sonoma Co., CA. Said to have married on 25 Oct. 1903 (in Edna Martin's diary); married secondly Joseph Francis Halleran Sr. (a shoemaker) on 22 Nov. 1906 in Sonoma Co., CA (div.), and had children: *Joseph Francis Jr.* (born 1908, died 28 Feb. 1991 at Oakland, CA); *Bernal C.* (born 11 Jan. 1910, died 21 May 1976 in Alamada Co., CA). Sarah married thirdly her brother-in-law, August B. Lang, about 1938 (he was born Apr. 1876 in CA, married firstly Mary Ann Burgess, Sarah's sister, and may have died 18 Dec. 1955). Listed in the 1910 census for Oakland, Alameda Co., CA, and in the 1930 city directory for Oakland, but is not there in 1934. She died 19 Mar. 1968 at San Francisco, CA, and is buried in Cypress Lawn Memorial Park.

8a. **Wilbert.** Born Apr. 1901 in Sonoma Co., CA. Married about 1955 in Virginia. Listed in the 1920 census as an apprentice seaman at the Naval Air Station, San Diego, CA; has not been found in 1910. Wilbert Burgess enlisted in the U.S. Navy about 1918. He became a test pilot for the Navy, and was stationed in later years at Langley Air Field in Virginia. He died childless in 1989 at Asheville, NC.

7e. **Nancy Belle "Nannie."** Born 13 Apr. 1885 at Aptos, Santa Cruz Co., CA. Married firstly ___ on 25 Oct. 1903; her marriage is said in Edna Martin's diary to have failed in Dec. 1903. **Nannie** secondly George Milton Ball about 1909 (he was found wandering in the Mojave Desert in the early 1900s, with papers on him identifying him as George Ball; however, he suffered from partial amnesia for the rest of his life), and had children:

***Ollie Fernwood* BALL.** Born 31 Jan. 1910 at Stockton, CA, married Claire Belmont Knowles on 3 Mar. 1928 at Los Angeles, CA (he was born 9 Nov. 1908 at St. Joseph, MO, son of Henry Harry Weaver Knowles and Bessie Cecil Peterson, married secondly Kathryn Alice Shields, and died 20 May 1980 at Long Beach, CA), and had children: *Dorline Clair* (born 31 Jan. 1929 at Los Angeles, CA, married Everett Leonard Brown [later called Howard] on 22 Dec. 1949 at Los Angeles, CA [he was born 22 Sept. 1928 at Denver, CO, son of Albert Tillman "Alanzo" Howard and Maizie Isabell Brown, and died 17 July 1992 at Diamond Bar, CA, buried Oakdale Memorial Park, Glendora, CA], and had children: Sharon Yvonne [born 11 Dec. 1950 at Los Angeles, CA, married Glen Alan Goodrich on 6 May 1970 at Panama City, FL {div. 1975}; married secondly Sheridan Joseph Nault Jr. on 12 Nov. 1975 at Great Falls, MT {div.; he was born 23 Mar. 1943}, and had children: Shane Vernon {born 6 Apr. 1978}; Heather Marie {born 27 Aug. 1979}; Sharon married thirdly Bradley Curtis Johnson on 13 Jan. 1983 at Copenhagen, Denmark {he was born 28 Oct. 1949 at Tulare, CA, son of Robert Edward Johnson and Phyllis Earleen Spomer}; Sharon Johnson enlisted in the U.S. Air Force in 1969, was an administrative specialist, and retired in 1990; she now works at the University of Arizona, Tucson, AZ]; Michael Norman [born 1 Mar. 1952 at Los Angeles, CA, married Kimberly Sue Peterson on 9 Aug. 1983 at Denver, CO {she was born 16 July 1958}, and had children: David Lee {born 11 Oct. 1982 at Denver, CO}; Mike and Kim Brown both served in the U.S. Army; he currently works as a calibration specialist with United Tech, San Jose, CA]; Patricia Gale [born 1 Sept. 1954 at Los Angeles, CA; she has worked as a Mormon missionary, and is currently attending school at Diamond Bar, CA]; Gary Lee [born 12 Oct. 1955 at Artesia, CA, married Arsenia "Anita" Cabantoi on 23 July 1981 at Olongapo, The Philippines {she was born 29 Aug. 1951, daughter of Mariano Guiang and Julia Cabantoi}, and had children: Leilani Grace {born 12 Dec. 1982 at San Diego, CA}; Arleen Joy {born 3 Mar. 1984 at San Diego, CA}; Natasha Nicole {born 5 Apr. 1987 at San Diego, CA}; Gary works as an electrical engineer in the U.S. Navy]); *Christen* (died at birth).

Ollie Fernwood married secondly Paul Miller, and had children: *Gary Lewis* (born Aug. 1943 at Los Angeles, CA). ***Ollie*** married thirdly Charles Francis "Chuck" Blain, and died on 28 Feb. 1974 at Torrance, CA.

Melba Anna Held "Patsy"* BALL.** Born 22 Jan. 1912 at Mojave or Fresno, CA, married William Burton Grigsby on 31 Jan. 1932, and had children: *William "Bill"* (born 30 Nov. 1936 at Honolulu, HI, married Florence Geneva "Jean" Burk on 3 Mar. 1956 at Las Vegas, NV, and had children: Kimberly Ann [born 27 Oct. 1956 at Los Angeles, CA, married Robert Sidney Freeman on 17 Dec. 1977 at Stateline, NV]; Kip [born 1 Feb. 1958 at Lynwood, CA, died 22 Oct. 1966 at Robstown, TX, buried Sandia, TX]). ***Melba married secondly Leonard William Sherman in 1945, and died on 8 Jan. 1985 at Spokane, WA, buried Spring Canyon Cemetery, Grand Coulee, WA.

***Son* BALL.** Born about 1914, died young.

Nannie BALL married thirdly Albert A. Ables about 1916 (he was born about 1867, and died on 12 Aug. 1922 in Los Angeles Co.). **Nannie ABLES** married fourthly John G. Jadel about 1937 (he was born 28 Nov. 1892, and died 17 Aug. 1982 at Monterey Park, CA). Her two children went by the name Ables after her second marriage. She provided the information for her brother John's death certificate in 1908 (and was then living unmarried at Healdsburg, CA). Nannie Jadel died on 6 Apr. 1971 at Inglewood, CA, and is buried there in the Inglewood Park Cemetery.

7f. **William Bryant.** Born 8 Nov. 1887 at Aptos, Santa Cruz Co., CA. See below for full entry.

7g. **Olla "Ollie."** Born Mar. 1889 in CA. Listed in the 1907-08 Los Angeles city directories working as a laundress. Ollie Burgess died unmarried on 19 Sept. 1909 at Los Angeles, CA.

7h. **John E. (III).** Born 5 Oct. 1892 in Sonoma Co., CA. He died on 7 Sept. 1908 at Healdsburg, Sonoma Co., CA.

ALANSON T. BURGESS OF PLUMAS CO., CALIFORNIA

[Alanson Bryant[6]]

7b. **Alanson Thomas** *[son of Alanson Bryant].* Born 26 Oct. 1879 at Little Lake, Mendocino Co., CA. Married Susan Yeager about 1901 (she was born 13 Sept. 1881 at Traver, CA, and died 18 June 1970 at Redding, CA). Listed in the 1900 census for Napa Co., CA living alone, in the 1902 Great Register of Sonoma Co., and in the 1910 census for Stanislaus Co., CA working as a farmer; "Susie" is listed in the 1920 census for Napa Co., CA. Alanson was accidentally killed on 22 May 1914 when the belt on a donkey engine snapped at a logging camp near Quincy, Plumas Co., CA.

FATAL ACCIDENT AT THE QUINCY LUMBER COMPANY'S PLANT

"Last Friday, shortly after the noon hour, Hal Burgess, engineer in charge of one of the donkey engines used in yarding logs at the Quincy Lumber Company's plant east of Quincy, was crushed to death while trying to untangle a cable under the engine. It appears that the engine started in some unaccountable manner, while Burgess was thus engaged, and he was caught between the cable and the drum. At the time the accident happened Mr. Burgess' wife was nearby, she having come out to the mill with her three children to deliver her husband's lunch. She did not witness the actual tragedy. Mr. Burgess was still alive when he was released from the machinery, but he passed away before medical assistance could be secured. His left breast was badly crushed, and his body was badly cut and bruised. A coroner's inquest was held during the afternoon, and the jury returned a verdict in accordance with the facts above stated. Deceased came to Quincy several weeks ago from Sacramento, and his family later followed him here. Besides his widow, he leaves two sons and a daughter to mourn his loss....The tragic end of Mr. Burgess came as a heavy shock to the community. The sympathy of all our people is extended to the bereaved widow and children."—*Plumas National Bulletin*, 28 May 1914.

8a. **Charles Alanson.** Born 11 Oct. 1902 in Sonoma Co., CA. Married Lucille Bond (div.; she remarried ___ Jenson, and lived in India); married secondly Mildred Louise "Milly" Syfert about 1945 (dec.). Listed with his mother in 1920 attending Pacific Union College, Napa Co., CA. Listed in the Oakland, CA directories from 1921-43. Charles A. Burgess was a steel worker, consultant, and a steel inspector for the State of California, in Oakland, Mexico City, Sausalito, and Los Angeles. He currently lives retired at Woodland Hills, CA (or may have died 6 Nov. 1990 at Harbor City, CA).

9a. **Ethel May.** Born 18 Jan. 1923 at Oakland, CA. Married William Eggleston about 1947, and had children: *Charles Allen*; *Jo Ann*. Ethel Eggleston settled at Sacramento, CA in 1947, where she worked as a telephone operator for Pacific Telephone before her marriage. She died there on 16 May 1958, and is buried in Sierra Hills Memorial Park.

9b. **Alanson Gregory "Lance."** Born 1 June 1948 at Ciudad de México, DF, México. Married Sandra Jean "Sandy" McKenzie. Lance Burgess works for Nevada Bell, a Pacific Telesis Corporation, at Reno, NV.

10a. **Scott Alan (III).** Born 21 Jan. 1975 at Gardena, CA.

10b. **Kelly** (nmn). Born 2 Jan. 1979 at Torrance, CA.

9c. **Linda Louise (I).** Born 22 Sept. 1949 at Ciudad de México, DF, México. Linda L. Burgess works for an insurance company at Woodland Hills, CA.

8b. **Frances Alice "Franky."** Born 8 Feb. 1904 at Santa Rosa, CA. Married John Alfred Caswell on 10 Sept. 1925 at Yreka, CA (he was born 5 Aug. 1903 at Mt. Shasta, CA, and died 22 June 1969 at Alturas, CA), and had children:

(John) Gregory "Gary" CASWELL. Born 2 July 1929 at McCloud, CA, married Barbara Jean Manlapig on 12 June 1947 at Reno, NV (she was born 29 Mar. 1932 at Chandler, AZ), and had children: *Sandra Lynn* (born 8 June 1948, married Roger Crabtree in Reno, NV [he was born 3 Oct. 1950], and had children: Monica [born 18 Nov. 1977 at Colusa, CA]; John [born 19 Jan. 1980 at Colusa, CA]); *Stevan Michael* (born 29 Dec. 1949 at McCloud, CA, married Cindy Garnero on 21

Aug. 1971 at Reno, NV [div.], married secondly M. Kathleen Bennett on 31 Jan. 1988 [she was born 29 June 1960; by her first marriage she had children: Bryan BENNETT {born 19 Sept. 1985 at Redding, CA}], and had children: Sean [born 21 Mar. 1989 at Las Gatos, CA]; Mackenzie [born 30 Jan. 1992 at Woodland, CA]); *Barbara Suzanne* (born 13 Aug. 1951 at McCloud, CA, married Joseph Nadeker on 24 Jan. 1969 [he was born 29 June 1950, and died in an automobile accident on 23 Dec. 1979], and had children: Leslie [born 10 Sept. 1969]); *Patricia Anne* (born 23 Oct. 1954, married Wayne Mooney on 19 Dec. 1974 at Minot, ND [div.], and secondly Renney Doser on 22 June 1991 [by a previous marriage he had children: Stephan {born 2 Apr. 1986}], and had children: Shasta [born 14 Mar. 1993]). Gary Caswell is a college instructor at Redding, CA.

(Patricia) Suzanne "Sue" CASWELL. Born 12 Nov. 1933 at McCloud, CA, married Robert L. Sloss on 29 Jan. 1955 (he was born 31 Aug. 1928 at Lakeview, OR), and had children: *Laura Lee* (born 7 Mar. 1956 at Alturas, CA, married Michael Jordan [he was born 30 June 1957 at Weaverville, CA], and had children: Jesse Ryan [born 19 May 1988 at Alturas, CA]; Tyler James [born 29 May 1990 at Ontario, OR]); *Kerry Jane* (born 10 June 1957 at Alturas, CA); *Margaret Alice* (born 10 June 1958 at McCloud, CA, married Steve Malatesta on 9 June 1990 at San Anselmo, CA [he was born 6 Feb. 1956 at San Francisco, CA], and had children: Paul Joseph [born 1 Dec. 1991 at Kentfield, CA]; Annette Suzanne [born 20 May 1993 at Alturas, CA]); *John Robert* (born 8 Sept. 1961 at McCloud, CA, married Ann Marie Giusti on 8 Apr. 1988 at Fort Bragg, CA [she was born 16 June 1962 at Berkeley, CA], and had children: Anthony Robert [born 3 July 1990 at Alturas, CA]; Camille Suzanne [born 30 July 1992 at Concord, CA]). Robert and Sue Sloss are publishers of the *Modoc County Record* newspaper at Alturas, CA.

Frances CASWELL was a registered nurse who worked most of her professional life at a hospital at McCloud, CA. She died on 10 Apr. 1980 at Alturas, Modoc Co., CA.

8c. **Cecil Clare.** Born 1 Oct. 1911 at Irwin, CA. Cecil Burgess was a lumberman in Northern California, but after suffering an injury similar to that which killed his father, he worked as a commercial fisherman up and down the Oregon coast. He lived in later years at McCloud and Alturas, CA, but died unmarried on 22 July 1970 at Mt. Shasta, Siskiyou Co., CA.

WILLIAM B. BURGESS OF SAN FRANCISCO CO., CALIFORNIA

[Alanson Bryant^6]

7f. **William Bryant** *[son of Alanson Bryant].* Born 8 Nov. 1887 (or 1888) at Aptos, Santa Cruz Co., CA. Married Stella Frances Peterson on 3 July 1913 at Irwin City, CA (div.; she was born 4 Sept. 1895, daughter of Thomas and Minnie Adaline Peterson, married secondly ___ Fraser, and thirdly Lance Straham; after divorcing her third husband, she again used the surname Fraser; she died on 14 Jan. 1952 at San Francisco, CA). Listed in the 1905 directory of Santa Rosa living with his father, with his brother Alanson in the 1910 census, and in 1920 at Santa Cruz, Santa Cruz Co., CA. William B. Burgess was a carpenter for many years at Stockton, CA. He died on 12 Dec. 1958 at San Francisco, CA.

8a. **Lois Vida.** Born 15 Feb. 1915 at Santa Cruz, CA. Married Leo Francis Pacheco in 1932 (div.; he was born 3 Apr. 1906 at Mission San Jose, CA, son of Manuel Pacheco and Maybelle Margaret Rose, and died on 31 May 1984 at San Jose, CA), and had children:

Phillip Leon PACHECO. Born 20 Aug. 1933 at San Jose, CA, married (Darla) Kay Hall on 1 Oct. 1955 at Beeville, TX, and had children: *Mark Alison* (born 3 Oct. 1958 at San Antonio, TX, married Nancy Jean Pope on 14 Nov. 1987 at Houston, TX). Phil and Kay Pacheco have contributed greatly to this book; they live at Beeville, TX.

Lois Burgess PACHECO married secondly Charles Owen Chestnutt on 15 Dec. 1945 at San Antonio, TX (he was born 14 Feb. 1912 in Bee Co., TX, and died 18 June 1989 at Beeville, TX), and Charles Chestnutt had children:

Charles Burgess CHESTNUTT. Born 15 July 1947 at Beeville, TX.

Sarah Elizabeth CHESTNUTT. Born 1 Sept. 1948 at Beeville, TX.

Lois CHESTNUTT lives at Beeville, TX.

8b. **Jeanne Marjorie.** Born 29 Oct. 1921 at San Jose, CA. Married Orin Lewis "Jack" Sawtelle on 13 Oct. 1939 at Reno, NV (div.; he was born 8 Mar. 1918, and died 13 Aug. 1991 at Chula Vista, CA), secondly John DeNys (div.), and thirdly Ron Rowland (he died about 1990). Jeanne Rowland died on 19 Apr. 1989 at Salt Lake City, UT.

[William (I)[1], Edward (I)[2], Edward (II)[3], William (IV)[4]]

THORNTON BURGESS
(1801-1852)

OF HANCOCK COUNTY, OHIO

5e. **Thornton (I)** *[son of William (IV)].* Born 5 May 1801 in Fauquier Co., VA. Married Sarah Jane Tanner on 12 June 1823 in Muskingum Co., OH (she was born 16 Aug. 1806 in Muskingum Co., daughter of Edward Tanner and Sarah Brown, and sister of John and Samuel Tanner [who married Thornton's two sisters], and died 26 Sept. 1873, buried Indianola Cemetery). Listed in the 1830 census for Muskingum Co., OH, and in 1840-50 in Hancock Co., OH. Thornton Burgess was a farmer in Ohio. He died on 30 May 1852 in Hancock Co., OH, and is buried in the Graham Cemetery. Sarah Tanner Burgess remarried her brother-in-law, Bedy Burgess, on 5 Sept. 1854 in Wyandot Co., OH, and then moved her family to Warren Co., IA in 1856 after her second husband's death. She married thirdly James Bryan on 16 Sept. 1858 in Warren Co.

The Children of Thornton Burgess:

6a. **Harriett.** Born 20 Mar. 1824 in Muskingum Co., OH. Married John C. Baker on 9 Nov. 1844 (he was born about 1823 in PA), and had at least the following children: *William H.* (twin; born 25 Oct. 1845 in OH, died 1 Mar. 1848, buried Graham Cemetery); *Thornton E.* (twin; born 25 Oct. 1845 in OH, died 4 Mar. 1848, buried Graham Cemetery); *Fannie J.* (born 1846? in Hancock Co., OH, married Sanford Lincoln); *Sarah J.* (born 14 Jan. 1848 in OH, died 10 Mar. 1848, buried Graham Cemetery); *Albert T.* (born 31 Dec. 1849 in OH, died 1 May 1919, buried Indianola Cemetery); *Phebe Elizabeth* (born 14 Sept. 1852 in OH, married Henry Allen Stierwalt, and died in 1951, aged 99 years); *Leslie* (born 1854 in OH); *Daughter* (born 9 Jan. 1855 in OH, died 2 Feb. 1855, buried Graham Cemetery); *Edna Alice* (born 1856 in OH, married T. F. Brooks); *John W.* (born 1859 in Warren Co., IA, married Lora Randolph); *Abbie* (born 16 June 1861 in Warren Co., IA, died 16 July 1861, buried with her parents); *James H.* (born 1863); *Ava Ana*; *Adelpheus*. Listed in the 1850 census in Hancock Co., OH, and in 1860 in Warren Co., IA. Harriet Baker died on 3 July 1866 in Warren Co., IA, and is buried in the Indianola Cemetery.

6b. **William (IX).** Born about 1825 in Ohio; died there before 1830 (not listed with his father in the 1830 census), or at age sixteen.

6c. **Edward E.** Born 9 Feb. 1827 in Ohio. See below for full entry.

6d. **Mary Jane (I).** Born 14 May 1830 in Hancock Co., OH. Married Philip Essex Jr. on 27 Apr. 1848 in Hancock Co., OH, and had children: *John* (born about 1849, died young). Mary Essex died on 16 Feb. 1851 in Hancock Co., and is buried in the Graham Cemetery.

6e. **John T.** Born 10 Dec. 1832 in Hancock Co., OH; died there on 10 Aug. 1834, and is buried in the Graham Cemetery.

6f. **Elizabeth (XI).** She may actually be Kiziah Burgess. Born about 1834 in OH; died there about 1842, and is probably buried in the Graham Cemetery.

6g. **George Washington (VI).** Born 5 Oct. 1836 in Muskingum Co., OH. See below for full entry.

6h. **Kiziah.** Born 23 Aug. 1837 in Hancock Co., OH; died there on 30 Aug. 1846, and is buried in the Graham Cemetery.

6i. **Son.** Born and died 11 Aug. 1840 in Hancock Co., OH; buried in the Graham Cemetery.

6j. **Samuel Thomas (I).** Born 14 July 1844 in Hancock Co., OH. See below for full entry.

6k. **James (IV).** Born 3 May 1847 in Hancock Co., OH; died there on 4 Aug. 1849, and is buried in the Graham Cemetery.

[William (I)[1], Edward (I)[2], Edward (II)[3], William (IV)[4], Thornton (I)[5]]

EDWARD E. BURGESS
(1827-1857)
OF WARREN COUNTY, IOWA

6c. **Edward E.** *[son of Thornton (I)].* Born 9 Feb. 1827 (or 1828) in Ohio. Married Elizabeth Brundage on 13 June 1852 in Wyandot Co., OH (she was born 1830 in NY, and died 18 Sept. 1857 at Indianola, IA). Edward Burgess was a farmer in Ohio and Iowa. He died two months after his wife, on 18 Dec. 1857, at Indianola, Warren Co., IA, leaving their four young children orphans, and is buried in the Indianola Cemetery. After the almost simultaneous deaths of Edward and his wife, their young children were parcelled out among his cousins and uncles to raise as their own (as noted below).

The Children of Edward E. Burgess:

7a. **William Henry (III).** Born 8 Apr. 1853 in OH or IA. He was raised by his great-uncle, Wash Burgess. See below for full entry.

7b. **(George) Washington (VIII).** Born 5 Oct. 1854 in Warren Co., IA. He was raised by his great-uncle, William Burgess. See below for full entry.

7c. **Harriet Octiva "Hattie."** Born 7 Feb. 1856 at Winterset, Madison Co., IA. She was raised by her first cousin, Edna Evelyn (Burgess) Martin. Married as his second wife William C. Butler on 9 Aug. 1874 at Golden, CO (he was born on 14 Nov. 1843 at Pittsfield, MA, married firstly Frances A. McDowell on 1 Mar. 1864 at New Boston, IL, and by her had children: *Ida May* [born 19 Nov. 1864 at New Boston, IL]; *Harry Lee* [born 3 Mar. 1867 at Princeton, IL], and died of typhoid fever on 15 June 1883 at Pueblo, CO). Hattie had children: *Ernest F.* (born and died 5 May 1875 at Golden, CO); *Walter William E.* (born 20 Sept. 1876 at Pueblo, CO, died on 7 Apr. 1882 at Morrison, CO); *Maza Maud* (born 8 Oct. 1878 at Georgetown, CO, and died on 7 Apr. 1882 at Morrison, CO). **Harriet Octiva** married secondly Joseph Didimé Bourdon on 15 Apr. 1884 at Pueblo, CO (he was born 10 June 1854 at Montréal, PQ, Canada, son of Alexandre Bourdon and Tharsille Paiment, and died 31 Oct. 1915 at Pueblo, CO). Hattie and Joseph had children:

(Edna) Blanche BOURDON. Born 28 Nov. 1885 at Pueblo, CO, married William Herbert Urban on 28 Dec. 1903 at Pueblo, CO (he was born 13 Aug. 1879 at Mount Olive, IL, son of Georg Urban and Anna Marie Elisa Dierker, married secondly Anna Louise Roepe, and died on 13 Nov. 1963 at Springhill, KS). ***Blanche Urban*** died on 17 Nov. 1915 at Denver, CO, and is buried in the Roselawn Cemetery. They had children:

Leonard Henry D. URBAN. Born 26 Nov. 1904 at Pueblo, CO, married Diamond McEwen on 28 Dec. 1923 at Colorado, Springs, CO (she was born 25 Dec. 1904 at Murry, OH, daughter of Charles McEwen (Mahony) and Susie Ann Caroline Davis, married secondly Edwin Potter on 12 June 1950, and died on 26 July 1975 at Pueblo, CO, buried Valhalla Cemetery). Leonard married secondly Grace Brown Loud in 1935 (she was born 19 Feb. 1901, and died 10 May 1970 at Tampa, FL). Leonard Urban worked as the yardmaster for the Colorado and Western Railroad, attached to the C.F. & I. Steel Mill, Pueblo. He died on 4 June 1991 at Tampa, FL, but is buried in the Valhalla Cemetery, Pueblo, CO. Leonard and Diamond Urban had children:

Robert Lee *URBAN* (born 10 Nov. 1924 at Pueblo, CO, married Barbara Lucile Gilbert on 2 Jan. 1945 at Pueblo, CO [she was born 24 Mar. 1925 at Pueblo, daughter of Raymond Earl Gilbert and Mary Lucile Newell], and had children: Robert Lee Jr. [born and died 22 Oct. 1946 at Pueblo, CO]; Katherine Lucille [born 5 Oct. 1949 at Pueblo, CO, married Thomas Michael Healy on 12 June 1970 at Pueblo, CO {div.; he was born 1 June 1947 at Denver, CO, son of Thomas V. Healy and Jo Ann Daly}; married secondly Tommy Charles McKlem on 8 Jan. 1983 at Boulder, CO {he was born 7 Oct. 1951 at Pueblo, CO, son of Charles L. McKlem and Mary Ann Black}; Katherine McKlem is a school teacher at Lakewood, CO]; Gilbert Lee [born 16 Dec. 1952 at Pueblo, CO, married Lela Lee Ann Marshall on 19 Apr. 1974 at Pueblo {div.; she was born 11

Aug. 1955, daughter of Clinton and Maxine Marshall}, married secondly Cynthia Faye Rushton on 10 Mar. 1983 at Pueblo {born 29 Apr. 1960 at Greenwood, SC, daughter of James Ralph Rushton Jr. and Elmira Faye Wilson}, and had children: Trisha Jean {born 16 Sept. 1983 at Pueblo}; Twyla Dawn {born 10 Sept. 1987 at Pueblo}; Tessa Rose {born 27 Jan. 1991 at Pueblo}]; Curtis Leonard [born 11 Nov. 1953 at Pueblo, CO, married Lynette Marie Shern on 5 July 1975 at Pueblo {she was born 18 Mar. 1955 at Pueblo, daughter of Lennox L. Shern and Marie Louise Formico}, and had children: Kelsey Lynn {born 29 July 1983 at Pueblo}; Kyle Patrick {born 15 July 1986 at Pueblo}; Curtis Urban works for the Association of American Railroads at Pueblo]; Raymond Leslie [born 7 Nov. 1955 at Pueblo, CO, married Nina Kathryn Hall on 31 Dec. 1979 at Pueblo {she was born 5 Aug. 1956, daughter of William Homer Hall and Betty Marie Frobase}, and had children: Seth Rory {born 14 Feb. 1981 at Pueblo}; Shane Keeley {born 9 May 1982 at Pueblo}; Raymond Urban is the manager of Star Oil, Pueblo]).

Esther Louise *URBAN* (born 5 Apr. 1926 at Pueblo, CO, married William Stephan Beres on 6 Oct. 1946 at Pueblo [he was born 30 Sept. 1923, son of Stephan Beres and Julia August], and had children: William Stephan Jr. [born 16 Oct. 1949 at Pueblo, married Diane Sue Gaunt on 17 July 1976 at Salem, IN {she was born 24 Feb. 1952 at Decatur, IN, daughter of Bill Wayne Gaunt and Betty Cristina Young}, and lives at Geneva, IN]; Robert Leonard [born 4 Feb. 1953 at Pueblo, and lives at Pueblo, CO]).

Leona Blanche URBAN. Born 14 Dec. 1909 at Pueblo, CO, married Elbert Lee Willoughby on 3 July 1927 at Pueblo (he was born 7 Jan. 1906 at Sarcoxie, MO, son of Frank Willoughby and Mary Mann, and died on 7 Aug. 1954 at Kansas City, MO, buried in the Forest Hill Cemetery), and had children:

William Frank *WILLOUGHBY* (born and died 21 May 1928 at Pueblo, buried Roselawn Cemetery).

Donald Ray *WILLOUGHBY* (born 24 Sept. 1929 at Pueblo, CO, married Sharon Dee Wymore on 27 May 1950 [she was born 27 Jan. 1932 at Kansas City, MO, daughter of John Newton Wymore and Dorothy Juanita McCahon], and was killed 25 Apr. 1977 at Kansas City, having had children: Richard Dee [born 26 Feb. 1951 at Kansas City, MO, married Nancy Lee Haldiman on 25 June 1971]; Kerry Lynn [born 1 May 1952 at Kansas City, MO, married Joseph Samuel Still on 15 Jan. 1972 at Kansas City {div.; he was born 30 July 1950}]; Brenda Sue [born 20 Apr. 1954 at Kansas City, MO, married James William Fernandes on 9 Nov. 1974 at Kansas City {he was born 30 Jan. 1953 at Honolulu, HI, son of James Overton Fernandes and Ethel Lorraine Gouviea}, and had children: Heather Erin {born 15 Apr. 1978 at Stockton, CA}]; Julie Ann [born 3 June 1957 at Kansas City, MO]; Becky Ann [born 20 Dec. 1958 at Kansas City, MO]).

Elbert Lee *WILLOUGHBY* Jr. (born 23 Dec. 1930 at Pueblo, CO, married Verna M. Hilden on 1 Mar. 1952 at Honolulu, HI [she was born 7 Mar. 1926 at Laurium, MI, daughter of John A. Hilden and Edna A. Olson], works as the Chief of Police for Salt Lake City, UT, and had children: Matthew Lee [born 23 Dec. 1952 at Honolulu, HI, married Cordelia Pacheco on 14 Feb. 1976 at Pueblo, CO]; Mary Christine [born 25 Oct. 1954 at Kansas City, KS, married George Bernard Casey on 26 Dec. 1976 in Kentucky]; Timothy Urban [born 28 Feb. 1956 at Kansas City, KS]; John William [born 23 Sept. 1958 at Kansas City, KS]; Lizbeth Louise [born 9 Apr. 1960 at Kansas City, KS]; Jenny Lee [born 11 July 1963 at Kansas City, KS]).

James Louis *WILLOUGHBY* (born 1 Mar. 1934 at Kansas City, MO, married Nancy Harsh [she was born 20 May 1935 at Carpinteria, CA, daughter of Earl Dean Henry Harsh and Gladys Bernice Scott], and had children: Joanna Lee [born 18 June 1954 at Corona, CA]; Jimmy Dean [born 21 Dec. 1955 at Fort Leavenworth, KS, married Barbara Blossom on 29 Jan. 1976].

(Noma) Ethyl BOURDON. Born 23 Mar. 1890 at Pueblo, CO, married George Pryor Sinclair on 12 June 1912 at Pueblo (he was born 12 Sept. 1884 [or 1883] at Kincaid, KS, son of George P. Sinclair and Louisa Rebecca Stanton, and died on 1 Mar. 1971 at Pueblo, CO, buried Valhalla Memorial Gardens), and had children:

Walter Joseph SINCLAIR (born 21 May 1914 at Pueblo, Co, died there on 9 July 1914, buried Roselawn Cemetery).

Floreine Joy SINCLAIR (born 9 Aug. 1915 at Pueblo, CO, married Charles Elmer Bauer on 6 June 1936 at Pueblo [div.]; married secondly Graham Woodrow Wickizer on 29 May 1939 at Colorado Springs, CO [he was born 19 Jan. 1916 in Daviess Co., MO, son of Samuel Orville Wickizer and Nellie Jane Ratliff, and a cousin of the author's wife, Mary Wickizer Burgess, and died 23 May 1989 at Pueblo, CO]. Graham Wickizer moved to Colorado from Carrolton, MO in 1937, worked for CF&I at Pueblo, served as superintendent of the seamless tube mill, and retired in 1979. Floreine Wickizer is a life member of Beta Sigma Phi, and earned a certificate in child education from Colorado University. She lives at Boulder, CO. They had children):

Noma Nel *WICKIZER* (born 4 Sept. 1942 at Pueblo, CO, married Albert H. Hayden III on 5 May 1962 [div.; he was born 22 May 1942 at Pueblo, son of Albert H. Hayden Jr. and Ruth M. Burnett], and had children: Robert Dean [born 3 Aug. 1963 at Pueblo, married Tammera Smith on 11 July 1987 at Woodland Park, CO, and had children: Shannon SMITH {ad.; born 21 Dec. 1977}; Cassie Mae SMITH {ad.; born 31 Oct. 1985}; Samuel August Dean {born 29 Apr. 1988 at Colorado Springs, CO}; Justin Albert {born 29 Nov. 1989 at Colorado Springs, CO}]; Jeffrey David [born 30 Sept. 1965 at Pueblo, CO, married Donna Michelle Rosa on 25 Oct. 1987, and had children: Elizabeth Ruth {born 14 Feb. 1989 at Colorado Springs, CO}; Michael Thomas {born 1 Jan. 1992 at Colorado Springs, CO}]; Douglas Christopher [born 7 Feb. 1969 at Pueblo, CO]; Noma Nel married secondly Fred S. Mills on 29 Nov. 1991 [div.]. Noma Mills is a real estate broker for Century 21 at Woodland Park, CO).

Joyce Lynn *WICKIZER* (born 8 May 1945 at Pueblo, CO, married Martin Fredrick "Marty" Spritizer on 24 June 1967 [he was born 16 June 1944 at Gunnison, CO, son of John Michael Spritizer and Ann Cochevar], and had children: Melissa Dureen [born 5 Feb. 1969 at Pueblo, CO]; Tamara Lynn [born 9 Mar. 1971 at Pueblo, CO]; Karen Rochelle [born 8 Feb. 1975 at Pueblo, CO]. Marty Spritizer is a musician and draftsman; Joyce works at CF&I; they currently live at Widefield, CO).

Gary Walter *WICKIZER* (born 31 July 1952 at Pueblo, CO, married Jackie Arlene Caudill on 11 Feb. 1971 at Pueblo [she was born 15 Feb. 1956 at Fredrick, OK, daughter of Luther Caudill and Mary Effie Fielding], and had children: Krista Brea [born 12 Aug. 1972 at Pueblo, CO, married Charles Roland in 1990]. Gary Wickizer has worked as a psychiatric technician and painter at Colorado State Hospital).

George Terry *WICKIZER* (born 16 July 1955 at Pueblo, CO, married Kristina McGhee on 4 May 1982 at Pueblo, CO [she was born 29 Dec. 1951 at Pueblo, daughter of Edgar Randolf McGhee and Betty Ann Hollon], and had children: Shawn Winfield [ad.; born 16 Feb. 1977 at Pueblo]; Kristina Rhiannon [born 30 Nov. 1982 at Pueblo]. George Wickizer works for the City of Pueblo, CO).

Noma Ethyl SINCLAIR married secondly James P. Hennessey on 28 Dec. 1919 (he died 15 Nov. 1951 at Pueblo, buried Mountain View Cemetery), and thirdly Henry Schenk on 4 Mar. 1959 (he died 23 July 1982), and died on 1 Mar. 1982 at Pueblo, CO, aged 91 years, being buried in the Roselawn Cemetery.

Hattie BOURDON died on 18 Mar. 1922 at Pueblo, CO, and is buried with her second husband in the Roselawn Cemetery. Barbara Urban and Floreine Wickizer have both contributed greatly to this book.

7d. **Sarah Angeline.** Born 5 Sept. 1857 at Indianola, IA. She was raised by her first cousin, once removed, Riley Burgess, and is listed with him in the 1860-70 censuses. Married Franklin Pierce Pampel on 12 Mar. 1880 in Keokuk Co., IA, and had five children.

WILLIAM H. BURGESS OF BENTON CO., OREGON

[Edward E.[6]]

7a. **William Henry (III)** *[son of Edward E.].* Born 8 Apr. 1853 in Ohio or Iowa (death certificate). He was raised by his great-uncle, Wash Burgess. Married Mrs. Amanda Jane (Wycoff) White on 27 Dec. 1897 (she was born Jan. 1867 in MO, and died 8 Feb. 1939 in Benton Co., OR; by her first husband, ___ White, she had children: *Maxley A. "Jake"* [born Sept. 1882 in KS, killed near Arlington, OR in a car accident]; *Eva May* [born May 1892 in KS]; *Leslie H.* [born Jan. 1894 in KS]). Listed in the 1860 census for Warren Co., IA living with Mark W. Marshall, and in the 1900 and 1920 censuses for Smith Co., KS. William H. Burgess was a farmer in Kansas, at Pueblo, CO, and at Junction City, OR. He died on 11 Feb. 1941 at Monroe, Benton Co., OR, but is buried at Corvallis, OR.

8a. **(William) Edward (I).** Born 26 May 1900 at Smith Center, KS. Married Alpha Hall; married secondly Mrs. Marie C. (Decker) Kem on 17 Nov. 1943 (she was born 21 May 1903, and died on 20 July 1985 in Linn Co., OR). Listed in the 1917 draft register of Smith Co., KS, and with his father in the 1920 census. Ed Burgess was an auto mechanic; he moved to Corvallis, OR in 1929, and to Lebanon, OR in 1943. He died on 6 Aug. 1980 at Lebanon, Linn Co., OR, and is buried there in the I.O.O.F. Cemetery.

9a. **Parthene.** Her name is also written Artine. Born about 1921. Married ___ Seekins, and is said to have lived at Vancouver, WA before moving to Kansas.

8b. **(Etta) Octavia.** Born 4 Apr. 1903 at Pueblo, CO. Married (Andrew) Clark Bales on 8 May 1920, and had children: *John* (born 31 Aug. 1922); *Morris*. Octavia Bales died on 28 June 1987 at Junction City, Lane Co., OR.

8c. **Ethel Irene.** Born 14 Nov. 1907. Married Maurice Fagley, and had one daughter. Ethel Fagley died on 29 July 1934 at Hood River, OR.

8d. **(George) Asa "Ace."** Born 5 May 1911 at Reamsville, KS. Married Hazel Violet Johnson on 5 Feb. 1942 at Vancouver, WA (she was born 19 Feb. 1907, and died 14 Oct. 1980 in Lane Co., OR). Asa Burgess died childless on 4 May 1992 at Florence, OR.

WASHINGTON BURGESS OF SMITH CO., KANSAS

[Edward E.[6]]

7b. **(George) Washington (VIII)** *[son of Edward E.]*. Born 5 Oct. 1854 (or 1853, according to his tombstone) at Indianola, Warren Co., IA. He was raised by his great-uncle, William Burgess, and appears with him in the 1860 census for Warren Co., IA. Married (Mary) Frances "Fannie" Howell in Jan. 1875 in Clarke Co., IA (she was born 22 Oct. 1858 in VA, daughter of Mary L. Howell, and died 27 Apr. 1937 at Smith Center, KS). Listed in the 1900 and 1920 censuses for Smith Co., KS. Washington Burgess worked as mail carrier in Kansas, a miner in Pueblo, CO, and at various times owned the Burgess Laundry and a diner at Smith Center, KS. He died on 24 Jan. 1927 at Smith Center, KS, and is buried in the Fairview Cemetery.

8a. **Otis Asa.** Born 5 Nov. 1877 at Pomona, KS. See below for full entry.

8b. **(Chester) Vinton.** Born 13 Nov. 1879 in Phillips Co., KS. See below for full entry.

Rev. O. A. BURGESS OF MARION CO., OREGON

[Edward E.[6], George Washington (VIII)[7]]

8a. **Otis Asa** *[son of George Washington (VIII)]*. Born 5 Nov. 1877 at Pomona, Miami Co., KS. He was named for the well-known orator of the same name (but there is no known relation between the two families). Married Etta Emma McCarter on 31 Dec. 1900 (she was born 9 Jan. 1882 at Sarcoxi, Lawrence Co., MO, and died 13 Feb. 1963 at Fairfield, CA). Served as a Corporal in Co. D, 21st Kansas Infantry, during the Spanish-American War. O. A. Burgess owned a laundry at Phillipsburg, KS, then moved in 1906 to Spokane, WA, where he also worked in a laundry, and again to the Tacoma, WA area in 1918, where he is listed in the 1920 census for Pierce Co., WA. He later became a minister for the Christian Church (Church of God). Rev. O. A. Burgess died on 3 Feb. 1929 at Woodburn, Marion Co., OR. He and his wife are both buried there in the Belle Passi Cemetery.

9a. **(Frances) May.** Born 21 Sept. 1901 at Smith Center, KS. Married John Tom Myers Sr. on 23 Mar. 1919 (he was born 2 Feb. 1894 at Wawawai, WA, and died 19 July 1977 at Eugene, OR). She and her new husband are listed with her father in the 1920 census. May Myers died on 30 May 1983 at Gladstone, Clackamas Co., OR, and is buried with her husband in the Belle Passi Cemetery. Their children included:

***John Tom* M*YERS* *Jr*.** Born 2 Apr. 1920 at Tacoma, WA, married Virgil Elizabeth Olson (she was born 21 Oct. 1918 at Superior, WI), and had children: *John Tom III* (born 2 May 1941 at Oregon City, OR, married Linda Lee Wells [she was born 25 June 1943 at Paris, KY], and had children: Kyle Regan [born 1975]; Danika Paige [born 1977]); *Pamella Ann* (born 24 Feb. 1944 at Camp White, OR, married Allan Harold Doerksen [he was born 3 Apr. 1939 at Modesto, CA], and had children: Theresa Ann "Teri" [born 1966]; Jackie Lynn [born 1968]); *Cecelia Mae* (born 9 June 1949 at San Francisco, CA, married Thomas Frederic Newell [he was born 14 July 1949 at Portland, OR], and had children: Megan Jayne [born 1978]; Tucker Riley [born 1981]; Piper Joy [born 1985]; Tessa Rose [born 1987]).

***Lela May* M*YERS*.** Born 19 Oct. 1921 at Woodburn, OR, married Allen Salnave, and secondly Albert Wright about 1948, and had children: *Cathy Lea* (born 1949); *Albert Lon* (born 1949); *Thomas Wade* (born 1960). Lela Wright died on 17 Feb. 1967 at Fort Lewis, WA.

***(Otis Asa) Burgess* M*YERS*.** Born 19 May 1923 at Woodburn, OR, married Cara Lee Fisel, and secondly Dorothy Thompson, and thirdly Sylvia ___, and fourthly Desneiges ___, and had children: *Gail Frances* (born 1949, married ___ Jaynes); *Alice Ann* (born 1951, married ___ Feliciano). Burgess Myers died on 25 June 1967 at Oregon City, OR.

***Will J. "Bill"* M*YERS*.** Born 6 July 1927 at Oregon City, OR, married Betty Lettenmaier (she was born 21 June 1929 at Oregon City), and had children: *Jay Arnold* (born 25 Aug. 1949 at Oregon City, married Mary Pine, and had children: Jeffrey Warren [adopted out of the family, and had his name changed to Thornberg]; *Jay Arnold* married secondly Vickie Smith); *Roy Allen* (born 17 Aug. 1950 at Oregon City, married Linda Taylor Welter, and had children: Micky Mo [born 1974]; Louanne Erwin [born 1982]; Grant Michall [born 1982]); *Will J. Jr.* (born 5 July 1952 at Oregon City, married Penny Hulse, and had children: Justin Case [born 1972]); *Terry Lee* (born 16 Mar. 1954 at Oregon City, married Wendy Hallwyler, and had children: Danielle Lynn [born 1973]; Matthew Lee [born 1975]).

Marion Bird "Bob" MYERS. Born 28 Nov. 1928 at Oregon City, OR, married Shirley Welch (she was born 19 Mar. 1932 at Parkplace, OR), and had children: *Laura Lee* (born 29 July 1950, married Steven J. Weir, and had children: Stacey Elaine [born 1975]; *Laura* married secondly Alvie E. Wilcox [he was born 1 Jan. 1953 at Trumann, AR], and had children: David Allen [born 1981]); *Marion Bird "Bob" Jr.* (born 7 Nov. 1952); *Burgess* (born 7 Dec. 1971).

Bettie Olive MYERS. Born 19 Apr. 1931, married James Elwood Fegles (he was born 5 Mar. 1931 at Eugene, OR), and had children: *Michael James* (born 5 Apr. 1952 at Eugene, OR, married Garnet Leota "Chris" Forrest [she was born 19 Feb. 1954 at Port Angeles, WA], and had children: Caleb Michael [born 1977]; Joshua James [born 1979]); *Susan* (born 5 Oct. 1954, had children: Daniel James [born 1975 at Springfield, OR], married ___ Rodriguez, and had children: Nicholas William [born 1978 at Springfield]; Melissa Sue [born 1985 at Eugene, OR]; Andrew Michael [born 1990 at Salem, OR]); *Janice* (born 3 May 1956 at Springfield, OR, married James Marion Boechler, and had children: Kimberly Nichol [born 1980 at Springfield]; Andria Michelle [born 1982 at Springfield]; Nathan James [born 1985 at Springfield]); *Jennifer Jo* (born 20 June 1959, married Stafford Lee Owen II [he was born 15 Sept. 1957 at Danville, VA], and had children: Jacob Lee [born 1982]; Kyle James [born 1985]; Jessica May [born 1987]).

Dick Edward MYERS. Born 13 Dec. 1937 at Oregon City, OR, married Thresa ___, secondly Donna ___, thirdly Juanita Johnson, and had children: *Debra Ann* (born 1958); *Hugh* (born 1959); *Raymond Britten* (born 1960); *Edward Steward* (born 1963); *Sandra Kay* (born 1965, married ___ Edwards); married fourthly Lorna Sells, and had children: *Lisa Ann* (born 1971). Dick Myers died on 8 Jan. 1984.

John T. MYERS Jr. has contributed greatly to this book. He lives at Salem, OR.

9b. **Pearl Victoria.** Born 1 Sept. 1903 at Smith Center, KS. Married Audley P. Gregory about 1922 at Tacoma, WA (he was born 22 Sept. 1897 in ID, and died 14 Oct. 1976 at Modesto, CA), and had children:

Wilma Patricia GREGORY. Born 17 Feb. 1923 at Smith Center, married Melford Hubert Waterbury (he was born 24 May 1923 at Hayward, CA), and had children: *Sandra Rae* (twin; born 24 Oct. 1946, married Raymond L. Hunt [born 27 Apr. 1943], and had children: Ryan Chandler [born 19 Aug. 1969]; Christopher David [born 26 Oct. 1970]; Patrick Michael [born 23 Oct. 1976]); *Susan Kay* (twin; born 24 Oct. 1946, married Thomas James Carlin [he was born 11 Jan. 1943 in Stanislaus Co., CA], and had children: Jonathan Andrew [born 28 June 1973]; Niles Gregory [born 23 Apr. 1974]); *Kathi Lynn* (born 3 Apr. 1961, married James Russell Best [he was born 1 Apr. 1958 in IN], and had children: Jason Andrew [born 5 Oct. 1988]; Justin Michael [born 23 Jan. 1991]).

Margaret Ellen GREGORY. Born 15 Mar. 1928 at Oregon City, OR, married Robert Butterfield, and had children: *Victoria Louise* (born 10 May 1947, married Ronald Carter, and had children: Lisa [born 5 Dec. 1975]; Brent [born 9 Nov. 197_]); *Candace Kay* (twin; born 8 Oct. 1949, married David Thompson, and had children: Brittney [born 26 Sept. __]; Brian); *Constance Fae* (twin; born 8 Oct. 1949, married Fred Donnell, and had children: Shannon; Courtney); *(Garrett) Robert* (born 4 Aug. 1956, married Jill ___, and had children: Bart [born 25 Dec. __], and married secondly Beth ___).

Geraldine Lucille "Gerry" GREGORY. Born 6 Nov. 1931 at Montesano, WA, married Ray Bruce, and had children: *Steven* (born 3 Mar. 1951); *Terrance* (born 13 July 1954); *Gerry* married secondly Neil Gilton, and had children: *Gregory* (born 11 Aug. 1963); *Gerry* married thirdly Clifford D. Wise.

(Dennis) Douglas GREGORY. Born 22 June 1942 at Modesto, CA, married Karen Yornquist (she was born 19 Apr. 1942), and had children: *Michelle* (born 1 May __); *Niles D.* (born 13 June __).

Sandra Rae GREGORY. Born 1 Mar. 1944 at Modesto, CA, married Ray Bailey, and had children: *Mathew Ray* (born 1 July 1967); *Marcum* (born 24 July 1969, married); *Melanie* (born 12 Jan. 197_).

Pearl GREGORY died on 8 July 1980 at Modesto, CA.

9c. **Olive Amy.** Born 31 Oct. 1908 at Spokane, WA. Married Lynn Potter; married secondly Percy Chapelle on 2 Aug. 1945. Olive Chapelle currently lives at Mesa, AZ.

VINTON BURGESS OF SMITH CO., KANSAS

[Edward E.[6], George Washington (VIII)[7]]

8b. **(Chester) Vinton** *[son of George Washington (VIII)].* Born 13 Nov. 1879 in Phillips Co., KS. Married Nelsie Faye "Beckie" Pounds on 4 Aug. 1901 at Smith Center, KS (she was born 31 July 1882 at Thornburg, KS, daughter of Joel Dayton Pounds and Elizabeth Bruce, and died 30 Mar. 1965 at Smith Center, KS). Listed in the 1917 draft register and the 1920 census for Smith Co., KS. Vinton Burgess was a railroad worker in Kansas. He died on 21 June 1930 at Smith Center, Smith Co., KS, and is buried in the Fairview Cemetery.

9a. **George Dayton.** Born 22 Mar. 1903 at Pueblo, CO. Married and divorced. George Burgess was a civilian employee of the Camp Pendleton Marine Corps Base, near San Clemente, CA. He died childless on 9 Dec. 1960 at Albany, Benton Co., OR.

9b. **Doris Faye.** Born 27 Aug. 1905 at Smith Center, KS. Married Raymond Sutton on 23 Feb. 1929, and had children: *Berthada Rae* (born 1 Aug. 1937, and died 29 June 1982). Doris Sutton died on 26 June 1946 at Smith Center, KS.

9c. **Erma Twila.** Born 29 Sept. 1908 at Smith Center, KS. Married Garth Holmes on 3 Aug. 1932 at Norton, KS (he was born 10 Aug. 1903, son of Charles Edward Holmes and Beulah Macy), and had children: *(June) Joleen* (born 23 June 1933, married Everett McDowell on 25 Sept. 1955 [he was born 17 Sept. 1932, son of Glen McDowell and Helen Schalansky], and had children: Bradley [born 1 July 1956, married Rhonda Cosco on 31 May 1982]; Brenda [born 12 Sept. 1958, married Tim Heffel on 2 Aug. 1980]; Brian [born 23 Feb. 1961, married Debra Volker on 1 July 1984]; Brice [born 31 July 1962]; Blake [born 17 July 1963]; Beverly [born 11 Feb. 1966]; Beth [born 30 Jan. 1970]; Bridget [born 22 Sept. 1973]; Becky [born 8 Sept. 1978]; Joleen McDowell lives at Cairo, NE); *Joyce Jean* (born 19 Oct. 1934, married Earl Dean McGee on 28 Dec. 1952 [he was born 28 Aug. 1933, son of Earl McGee and Helen Carothers], and had children: Mitchell Dean [born 18 July 1954, married Deborah Smith on 31 May 1982]; Larry Michael [born 16 Aug. 1956, married Beverly Neibling on 1 Aug. 1976]; Marci Diane [born 15 June 1958, married Mark Overmiller on 21 Mar. 1981]; Murray Tod [born 27 Dec. 1964]; Joyce McGee lives at Agra, KS]); *Janet Juneil* (born 23 Nov. 1935, married Duane A. McDowell on 1 Aug. 1954 [he was born 24 May 1934, son of Glen McDowell and Helen Schalansky], and had children: Lana Jo [born 19 Oct. 1955, married Stephen Wells on 19 Jan. 1974]; Lori Jan [born 9 Nov. 1956, married Randall LaDow on 8 Aug. 1980]; Lance John [born 7 Sept. 1959, married Theresa Detwiler on 23 May 1982]; Lia Jayne [born 18 Feb. 1967]; Janet McDowell lives at Bellaire, KS); *Jeraldene Jo "Jerry"* (born 1 Aug. 1938, married Cecil Wayne Lambert on 21 Apr. 1960 [he was born 27 Nov. 1936, son of Cecil Lambert and Ruth Lorene Barrett], and had children: Clark Wayne [born 1 Sept. 1961, married Maribeth Grimes on 28 July 1981]; Crystle Dee [born 2 Feb. 1963]; Cally Jo [born 29 July 1967]; Cade Macy [born 15 Oct. 1977]; Jerry Lambert lives at Smith Center, KS). Erma Holmes currently lives at Smith Center, KS.

9d. **Chester Earl Howell.** Born 10 Jan. 1911 at Smith Center, KS. Chester Burgess was a general laborer in northern Kansas. He died unmarried on 14 Mar. 1984 at Osborne, Osborne Co., KS, and is buried in the Fairview Cemetery.

9e. **Charles Leonard (I)** (twin). Born 23 Sept. 1913 at Smith Center, KS. Married Vera Troxel on 22 Sept. 1943 at Stevenson, WA. Served in the U.S. Navy during World War II. He moved to Corvallis, OR in 1937, and then to Philomath in 1950. For twenty-two years he was the owner of the Philomath Cleaners, selling it in 1971, and then worked for Evans Products Division at Corvallis. Charles L. Burgess was a city councilman for the City of Philomath for ten years, and served eight years on the Philomath School Board; he was also a member of the Corvallis Elks Lodge #1413, and the International Order of Odd Fellows. He died on 20 June 1974 in Benton Co., OR, and is buried there in the Oaklawn Memorial Park Cemetery.

10a. **(Charles) Robert.** Born 19 May 1947 at Corvallis, OR. Robert Burgess attended school in Philomath, and was a member of the Odd Fellows Lodge there. He died unmarried of epilepsy on 16 June 1970 at Philomath, Benton Co., OR, and is buried there in the Oaklawn Memorial Park Cemetery.

9f. **Clarence Henry** (twin). Born and died 23 Sept. 1913 at Smith Center, KS (or 29 Sept., according to his tombstone); buried in the Fairview Cemetery.

9g. **Mildred Elizabeth.** Born 30 May 1916 at Smith Center, KS. Married Harold Hays; married secondly Woody Robinson. Mildred Robinson lives at Philomath, OR.

9h. **Arthur Woodrow.** Born 1 Sept. 1918 at Smith Center, KS. Married D. Elizabeth Lee. Listed in the 1963 directory for Corvallis, OR. Arthur Burgess was a lumber worker in Benton Co., OR. He died there on 24 May 1964. Elizabeth Burgess currently works for Pacific Northwest Bell, at Corvallis, OR.

10a. **Garey Lee.** Born about 1945 in Oregon. Married Sue ___; married secondly Eugenie Bonham on 29 Aug. 1981 in Benton Co., OR. Gary Burgess is a linestacker for Consumers Power Co., at Corvallis, OR.

11a. **Kimberly.**
11b. **(Garey) Arthur.**
11c. **Colin.**

9i. **(Mary) Marie.** Born 21 Mar. 1921 at Smith Center, KS. Married Fred Calkin, and had children: *Karen* (born 30 Oct. 1941, married ___ Lentz). Marie Calkin lives at Smith Center, KS.

9j. **Ivan Eugene (I).** Born 30 Nov. 1924 at Smith Center, KS. Married Laura Mae Rush on 3 Jan. 1944 at Smith Center, KS (she was born 24 Sept. 1924 at Howard, KS, daughter of John Henry Rush and Violet Guffey). Ivan Burgess worked for the U.S. Postal Service before retiring; he now works as an auction clerk at Smith Center, KS.

10a. **Theodore Lynn "Ted"** (ad.). He was Laura's son by her first marriage. Born 30 June 1943 at Kansas City, MO. Married Eileen Boch on 18 Aug. 1973. Ted Burgess works as a caretaker for a doctor at Faribault, MN.

11a. **Nathan Lynn.** Born 21 Dec. 1978 at Faribault, MN.
11b. **Nicole Marie.** Born 9 June 1982 at Faribault, MN.

10b. **Larry Neal.** Born 8 Oct. 1952 at Smith Center, KS. Married Judith Lambert on 26 May 1973. Larry Burgess is a school teacher at Smith Center, KS.

11a. **Luke Allen.** Born 9 Mar. 1978 at Smith Center, KS.
11b. **Blake Lambert.** Born 8 Aug. 1980 at Phillipsburg, KS.
11c. **Jada Yung Joo** (ad.). Born 8 Nov. 1985 in South Korea.

10c. **Kelly Vinton.** Born 7 May 1954 at Smith Center, KS. Married Becky Joy Hendrich on 18 Aug. 1978. Kelly Burgess is a school teacher at Randall, KS.

11a. **Vinton Hendrich.** Born 6 July 1980 at Wichita, KS.
11b. **Caleb John.** Born 12 Dec. 1983 at Beloit, KS.
11c. **Emily Joy.** Born 8 Apr. 1988 at Randall, KS.

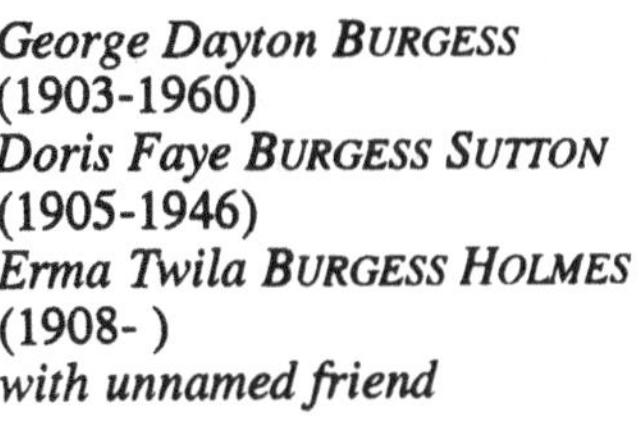

George Dayton BURGESS
(1903-1960)
Doris Faye BURGESS SUTTON
(1905-1946)
Erma Twila BURGESS HOLMES
(1908-)
with unnamed friend

On the back is a note:
"I am holding Erma"—Beckie

[William (I)[1], Edward (I)[2], Edward (II)[3], William (IV)[4], Thornton (I)[5]]

WASHINGTON BURGESS
(1836-1915)

OF WARREN COUNTY, IOWA

6g. **(George) Washington (VI)** *[son of Thornton (I)].* Born 5 Oct. 1836 in Muskingum Co., OH (according to his obituary). Married Abigail "Abbie" Jewell on 19 June 1862 in Bourbon Co., KS (she was born 14 June 1844 in IL, daughter of Eli Gilbert Jewell and Betsey Jane Brown, and died 22 Feb. 1886, buried Milo I.O.O.F. Cemetery); married secondly (Mary) Etta Dennis on 2 Mar. 1887 (she was born 22 Aug. 1864 in IA, daughter of William Robert Dennis and Lydia Ann Nelson, and died 6 June 1921 at Long Beach, CA). George W. Burgess served as a 1st Lieut. in Co. A, 6th Kansas Militia, Union Army, during the Civil War. He had previously been a Deputy Sheriff of Warren Co., IA from 1857-64, when he moved to Bourbon Co., KS. Listed in the 1860 census for Warren Co., IA living with John Baker, and in the 1865-70 censuses for Freedom Township, Bourbon Co., KS. He was Sheriff of Bourbon Co. from 1869-72. He returned to Warren Co., IA, and served as City Marshall of Indianola, Mayor of Milo, and Postmaster of Milo (1879-93, 1897, 1907). Listed in the 1880-1905 censuses for Warren Co., IA. Wash Burgess opened the first store in Milo, IA, later founding Burgess & Son, a real estate and insurance business. He moved to Long Beach, CA in 1905, where he died on 18 Dec. 1915, and is buried in the Sunnyside Cemetery. His biography appeared in *The History of Warren County, Iowa* (Des Moines, IA: Union Historical Co., 1879, p. 634), and in *The History of Warren County, Iowa, from Its Earliest Settlement to 1908*, by W. C. Martin (Chicago: S. J. Clarke Publishing Co., 1908, p. 744-748).

THE BIOGRAPHY OF GEO. W. BURGESS (1879)

"BURGESS, GEO. W., merchant, P.O. Milo; born October 5, 1836 in Hancock County, Ohio; came to Marion County in 1854, and to Indianola in 1856, and began the mercantile business in 1866, and moved to Hammondsburg in 1876, and moved his store and stock to Milo in July, 1879, where he keeps a full line of general merchandise; was First Lieutenant of Co. A, Sixth Kansas Militia; was ordered out by the government when Price made his raid through Missouri; was only out about two months when they were ordered back by the Governor; was deputy sheriff for six years in this county; has been town treasurer, constable, and is now justice of the peace; was under-sheriff in Kansas, and is now Postmaster with office in his store; was married June 19, 1862 to Abba, daughter of Eli Jewell, of Bourbon County, Kansas; have two children, Jennie, Eddie."

The Children of Washington Burgess:

7a. **(Sarah) Jennie.** Her middle name is given as Jane by John Myers, quoting William H. Burgess. Born 15 June 1865 at Ft. Scott, Bourbon Co., KS. Married Pearl Oscar "P. O." Busselle on 23 Oct. 1883 in Warren Co., IA, and had children: *Lelah E.* (born Apr. 1885, married ___ Greer); *Elsie M.* (born Jan. 1887); *Max W.* (born Aug. 1889); *Pearl M.* (dau.; born Oct. 1891); *Bernice B.* (born Oct. 1893). Living at Berkeley, CA in 1915. Jennie Busselle died on 18 Jan. 1942 at Alhambra, CA, and is buried in Sunnyside Cemetery.

7b. **Edward Jewell.** Born 3 Nov. 1868 at Ft. Scott, KS. See below for full entry.

7c. **Carrie (I).** Born about 1870 at Ft. Scott, KS; died young.

7d. **George (II).** Born about 1872 at Ft. Scott, KS; died young.

7e. **Lena.** Born about 1874; died young.

7f. **Harry (I)** (nmn). Born 6 Aug. 1882 at Milo, IA. Married Ora Belle ___ by 1917 (she was born 11 June 1891, and died 2 Jan. 1977 at San Bernardino, CA). Listed with his father in the 1900-05 censuses of Warren Co., IA, had moved to Long Beach, CA by 1915, is listed there in the 1917 draft register, and in the 1920 census for San Gabriel, Los Angeles Co., CA. Harry Burgess moved to Highland, CA by the 1920s, where he and his wife worked for the Citrus Association. He died there childless on 26 Dec. 1944, and is buried with his wife in the Mountain View Cemetery, San Bernardino, CA.

7g. **Abby.** Born and died 23 Dec. 1885 at Milo, IA.
7h. **Son.** Born and died 12 Aug. 1888 at Milo, IA.
7i. **Son.** Born and died 10 May 1891 at Milo, IA.
7j. **Leroy (I).** Born 14 Nov. 1892 at Milo, IA; died there 1894, buried in the Milo I.O.O.F. Cemetery.
7k. **Harley.** Born 7 Apr. 1898 at Milo, IA; died there on 10 Apr. 1898.

THE BIOGRAPHY OF GEO. W. BURGESS (1908)

"The history of Milo would be incomplete without mention of George Washington Burgess, who was born in Hancock County, Ohio, October 5, 1836, his parents being Thornton and Sarah (Tauner) Burgess. The paternal grandparents, William and Susan (Redman) Burgess, were natives of West Virginia, and made their home at the foot of the Blue Ridge Mountains, but at an early day in the development of Ohio, removed to Muskingum County, that state, and entered land from the government. The founder of the Burgess family in America came from Switzerland, and successive generations have manifested those sterling traits of character which have always marked the Swiss people.

"The maternal grandfather of our subject was Edward Tauner [sic] who, when about seventeen years of age, was captured by the Indians, and held as a prisoner by them for three and a half years, after which he was exchanged. It was the intention of the savages to kill the youth, and he was forced to "run the gauntlet." At the commencement of this, he was knocked down and while he was lying on the ground a squaw rushed in, picked him up, and carried him away. The squaw then claimed him as her own, and thus saved his life. It was his daughter Sarah who became the wife of Thornton Burgess, and unto this marriage were born ten children: Harriet, who married John Baker, of Indianola; William, who died at the age of sixteen years; Edward, who wedded Elizabeth Brundage; Mary Jane, the wife of Phillip Essex; John, who died in infancy; Elizabeth, who died at the age of eight years; James, and Samuel; and another who died in infancy. Samuel and George Washington are the only surviving members of this family. The father died in Ohio in 1852, and the mother, with her children, came to Warren County, Iowa, in 1854, arriving in Indianola in the Autumn of that year. Here she purchased a house, which is still standing, having for more than half a century been a witness of the changes which have occurred in the county.

"George Washington Burgess was now the main support of the family. He was only fourteen years of age when his father died, and it was at this time that he commenced his battle with the world. In 1857 he was appointed deputy sheriff of Warren County under Luke Bryan, and continued to fill the same position under the succeeding sheriff, John D. Ingalls. John J. Kozad was the third sheriff, and Mr. Burgess again served as deputy, but in 1864 resigned that position and made a trip to the Colorado gold fields. Not meeting with the success he had anticipated, he soon left and went to Bourbon County, Kansas, in the Fall of 1864. In 1869 he was elected sheriff of Bourbon County, and there remained until the Autumn of 1872, when he received word that his mother was growing quite feeble and needed his assistance and attention, so he resigned the office of sheriff and returned to Indianola, remaining there for about two years. During that time he was elected city marshal, which position he filled until 1875, when he traded for a stock of goods at Hammondsburg, his mother having passed away in 1874.

"In 1879, when the new town of Milo was just springing into existence, G. W. Burgess was the first man on the ground and removed his business house from Hammondsburg with the stock of goods and the buildings. He chose a location on the south side of the main street, and began business there June 27, 1879. He afterward turned his store around to face the north, and put a temporary foundation under it. The entire field which constituted the city of Milo had been sown to flax, which was then in full bloom, making the store building of Mr. Burgess appear rather lonely in its remoteness from other commercial undertakings. The railroad had just been completed and the first invoice of goods was unloaded in the flax field, as up to that time no depot had been erected. Mr. Burgess believed in the old saying regarding "the early bird," so he bent every energy to be the first one to locate on the new town site that he might gain the trade of the surrounding community. He enjoyed a good patronage as long as he remained in merchandizing, and was always an active citizen for the advancement of the interests of the town. As the years have passed, he has done much effective work for the upbuilding of Milo, and has performed many public duties here. He was the first postmaster of the town, receiving the appointment in October of 1879. He filled that office until March of 1892, when Grover Cleveland was elected, and although he was offered the position he refused to serve under a Democratic administration, and so resigned. When the Republicans came into power under President McKinley, he was once more appointed postmaster, and continued to serve until 1907, when he resigned.

"In 1885, having sold his stock of general merchandise, Mr. Burgess engaged in the real-estate loan and insurance business, under the firm name of Burgess & Son. In this connection he conducted an enterprise which brought him a goodly measure of prosperity. It is only during the past year or so that Mr. Burgess has been retired from active business, and is now enjoying a well-earned ease in a comfortable home surrounded by kind friends and neighbors who entertain for him the warmest regard. During the past three years he and his wife have spent the winter months at Long Beach, California, where Mr. Burgess has acquired quite a reputation as a skillful fisherman, holding the record of having landing the biggest Jew fish which has been caught there in years. He secured one fish weighing 240 pounds, and another of 185 pounds.

"Mr. Burgess was married June 19, 1862 to Miss Abbie J. Jewell, a daughter of Judge and Mrs. Eli Jewell, natives of Vermont and Illinois, respectively, and now residents of Kansas. The children of this marriage were Jennie, now the wife of P. O. Bussell of Kansas; Edward J., who married Lena Clevenger, and is a member of the firm of Burgess & Son, real estate loan and insurance agents at Milo; Carrie, George, Lena, and Abbie, all of whom died in infancy; and Harry, yet at home. The mother of these children died February, 1886, and on the 2nd of March 1887 Mr. Burgess was again married, his second union being with Mary Etta Dennis, a daughter of William Robert and Lydia Ann (Nelson) Dennis, who were natives of Kentucky and Ohio, respectively, and located in Ringgold County, Iowa, at an early day, before the county seat had been established there. The mother died in 1887, but the father still survives, and now lives in Missouri.

"Mr. Burgess is a charter member of Milo Lodge No. 409, A.F. & A.M., and also belongs to Milo Lodge No. 513, I.O.O.F. He has been a Mason for more than forty years. In politics he is a staunch Republican, supporting the party since Fremont became its presidential candidate. Beside being postmaster for many years, he was the second mayor of Milo, serving for five consecutive years, and has filled the office of justice of the peace and other local positions. Mr. Burgess is justly accounted one of the prominent and worthy representatives of Warren County, and though he has passed the allotted psalmist's span of threescore years and ten, in spirit and interests he seems yet in his prime, and is enjoying life and the opportunities which are afforded him for pleasure by reason of the fact that his former activity and success in business now enable him to live retired."

EDWARD J. BURGESS OF LOS ANGELES CO., CALIFORNIA

[George Washington (VI)[6]]

7b. **Edward Jewell** *[son of George Washington (VI)].* Born 3 Nov. 1868 at Ft. Scott, Bourbon Co., KS. Married Lena Leoti Clevenger on 23 July 1888 at Des Moines, IA (she was born 16 Jan. 1868 at Lacona, IA, daughter of John Clevenger and (Susan) Elizabeth Gray, and died 27 June 1940 at Los Alamitos, CA). Listed in the 1895-1905 censuses for Milo, Warren Co., IA, and at Long Beach, Los Angeles Co., CA in 1920; he was living at Milo when his father died in 1915. He moved to California by the 1920s; listed in the 1941 city directory of Long Beach, CA. Edward Burgess was a real estate broker and insurance agent (Burgess & Son). He died on 24 Nov. 1944 at Los Alamitos, CA, and is buried in the Sunnyside Cemetery.

8a. **(Edward) Byron.** Born 1 Jan. 1889 at Belmont, IA. See below for full entry.

8b. **Abbie Elizabeth.** Born 8 Mar. 1892 at Milo, IA. Married Clare Lennington "Carle" Williams on 6 Nov. 1908 at Albia, IA (he was born 11 Dec. 1887 at Linden, IA, the son of Ferdinand Aurelius Williams and Elizabeth M. "Lida" Moller, and died 3 Dec. 1953 at North Hollywood, CA), and had children: *Mary Ann* (born 2 Aug. 1911 at Milo, IA, married Virgil Jackson on 9 May 1932 [div.], and had children: Riley Edward [born 25 June 1936]; Terry Morris [born Dec. 1938]; *Mary Ann* married secondly Bart Peterson [div.], and thirdly William McGrath in Aug. 1956, and lives at Grants Pass, OR); *Betty Burgess* (born 20 Feb. 1915, see below); *(Edward) Kelly* (born 17 Mar. 1918 at Long Beach, CA, married Violet Mae Christensen in June 1940 [div.], and had children: Kelly Carle [born 3 Oct. 1942 at Long Beach, CA]; *(Edward) Kelly* married secondly Elizabeth Pierson in 1947 [div.], and had children: Kent [born 30 Nov. 1949 at Long Beach, CA]; *Kelly* died on 22 Oct. 1979 at Long Beach). Carle Williams's biography appears in *History of Long Beach and Vicinity* (Chicago: J. F. Clarke Publishing Co., 1927, Volume II, p. 323-325). Abbie Williams died on 17 June 1955 at Long Beach, CA.

Betty Burgess WILLIAMS was born on 20 Feb. 1915 at Long Beach, CA, married Vernon Arthur Williams on 2 Oct. 1937 at Beverly Hills, CA (he was born 30 Dec. 1911, son of Edward David Williams and Dorothy Katherine Lund, and died 18 Nov. 1969), and died 3 Mar. 1993 at Grants Pass, OR, having had children: *(Edward) David Jr.* (born 3 Sept. 1940 at Hollywood, CA, married Charlene Mary Berg on 2 May 1970, and had children: Edward David III [born 18 Apr. 1971 at Long Beach, CA]; Daniel Allen [born 2 Oct. 1973 at Long Beach, CA]); *Susan Elizabeth* (born 25 Oct. 1945 at Los Angeles, CA, married Ivan Jed "Ike" Mortensen on 16 Sept. 1966 at Long Beach, CA [he was born 29 Sept. 1940 at Rexburg, ID, and was a Naval officer and pilot before retiring, and now works as a commercial aviation pilot], and had children: Thomas Edward [born 29 Aug. 1973 at San Diego, CA]; Julie Elizabeth [born 30 Aug. 1976 at San Diego, CA]). Susan Mortensen is a member of the Church of Jesus Christ of Latter-Day Saints, and an accomplished professional genealogist. In 1988 she established a Burgess Clearing House to organize, preserve, and coordinate genealogical records of all Burgess families, and began publishing *The Burgess Bulletin*. She is also the author of *Burgess Families in the 1900 Soundex* (San Bernardino, CA: The Borgo Press, 1994), and a major contributor to this second edition of *The House of the Burgesses*.

8c. **(George) Dean** (twin). His name is given as Dean George Burgess in the official death records. Born 24 Jan. 1898 at Caloma, IA. Dean Burgess died unmarried on 6 May 1910 at Milo, IA, and is buried in the Milo I.O.O.F. Cemetery.

8d. **Dana Clevenger** (twin). Born 24 Jan. 1898 at Caloma, Marion Co., IA. Married Herbert Raymond Cole on 30 June 1917 in Warren Co., IA, and had children: *Erma "Jean"* (born 15 June 1918, married Ernest Atkinson [dec.], and secondly Richard "Vic" Vickery in Feb. 1987, and lives at Saraland, AL). Dana Cole died of tuberculosis on 12 Dec. 1924 at Los Angeles, CA.

BYRON BURGESS OF LOS ANGELES CO., CALIFORNIA

[George Washington (VI)[6], Edward Jewell[7]]

8a. **(Edward) Byron** *[son of Edward Jewell]*. Born 1 Jan. 1889 at Belmont, IA. Married Eva Elfa Starr on 17 Feb. 1909 (she was born 16 Oct. 1889, daughter of Frank H. Starr and Harriett Reeves, and died 8 Feb. 1973). Listed in the 1918 draft register for Milo, Warren Co., IA. Byron Burgess owned his own insurance business, Byron Burgess Co., at Long Beach, CA. He died there on 4 June 1954, and is buried in the Sunnyside Mausoleum.

9a. **Dean Franklin.** Born 10 Nov. 1910 at Milo, IA. Married Margaret M. Kiley. Dean Burgess owned and operated his father's insurance company after the latter's death. He died on 21 Aug. 1980 at Huntington Beach, CA.

10a. **Dean Byron.** Born 12 July 1941 at Long Beach, CA. Married Diane Williams on 19 Mar. 1967; married secondly Paula Stippec. Dr. Dean Burgess is an ophthalmologist at St. Louis, MO.

11a. **Bradley Byron.** Born 27 May 1977 at St. Louis, MO.

11b. **Jeffrey Daniel.** Born 22 July 1978 at St. Louis, MO.

9b. **Max Byron (I).** Born 15 June 1913 at Milo, IA. Married Helen "Bobbie" Drake. Max Burgess was a salesman for Marine Hardware Co. He died on 27 Dec. 1972 at San Pedro, CA, and is buried there.

10a. **Max Byron (II).** Born 29 June 1947 at Long Beach, CA. Married Robin Adler on 2 Mar. 1974 in Los Angeles Co., CA (div.); married secondly Lynda Carruthers about 1980 (div.). Dr. Max Burgess obtained his D.D.S. degree from Creighton University, Omaha, NE. He currently operates his own dental office at Huntington Beach, CA, and lives at Fountain Valley, CA.

11a. **Timothy Donald.** Born 3 Sept. 1981 at Long Beach, CA.

10b. **Starr Eva.** Born 2 Nov. 1953 at San Pedro, CA. Married Larry Malek (div.). Starr Burgess is an insurance adjuster in Southern California.

[William (I)[1], Edward (I)[2], Edward (II)[3], William (IV)[4], Thornton (I)[5]]

SAMUEL T. BURGESS, SR.
(1844-1921)

OF WARREN COUNTY, IOWA

6j. **Samuel Thomas (I)** *[son of Thornton (I)].* Born 14 July 1844 in Hancock Co., OH. Married Nancy Benge on 30 Nov. 1862 in Warren Co., IA (she was born 1 Apr. 1844 in IN, daughter of Thomas Benge and Dorcas Bales, and died 16 Apr. 1884 in Warren Co., IA, buried Indianola I.O.O.F. Cemetery); married secondly Della Conley on 3 Apr. 1892 in Warren Co., IA (she was born 13 Oct. 1862 in IA, daughter of Joseph M. Conley and Lydia A. Hinkle, and died 31 Mar. 1956 at Long Beach, CA). Listed in the 1860-1905 censuses for Otter Township, Warren Co., IA (in 1860 living with John Baker), and in the 1920 census for Pinal Co., AZ living with his son George. Sam Burgess was a farmer. He died on 4 May 1921 in Orange Co., CA, and is buried in the Sunnyside Memorial Park, Long Beach, CA.

The Children of Samuel T. Burgess:

7a. **Ellen Jane "Ella" or "Bell."** Born 6 Dec. 1863 in Warren Co., IA. Married Luke B. "Dug" Bloom on 8 Oct. 1885 in Warren Co., IA, and had children: *Gladys* (married ___ McCoy, and had children: Marlene J.); *Marvin E.* (born 29 Aug. 1905 in OK, and died 3 Jan. 1986 at Vista, CA). Listed in the 1900 census for Garfield Co., OK; she was living at Rio Oso, CA in 1921. Ella Bloom died on 20 Jan. 1950 at Compton, CA, and is buried in Sunnyside Memorial Park.

7b. **Clara M. (I).** Her name is also spelled Claira. Born 6 June 1865 in Warren Co., IA. Married Joseph A. Milligan (or Millican) on 12 Mar. 1885 in Warren Co., IA. Clara Milligan died on 24 Jan. 1886 in Warren Co., and is buried in the Indianola I.O.O.F. Cemetery.

7c. **Thomas Thornton.** Born 1 Dec. 1866 in Warren Co., IA. See below for full entry.

7d. **Sarah Alice "Sadie."** Born 13 Sept. 1869 in Warren Co., IA. Married George M. Bloom on 5 Aug. 1891 in Warren Co., IA (he was born 23 Sept. 1862, possibly the brother of Luke Bloom, and died 20 Oct. 1944). Living at Milo, IA in 1921. Sadie Bloom died on 24 Sept. 1949 in Warren Co., IA, and is buried in the Indianola I.O.O.F. Cemetery.

7e. **Samuel Thomas (II).** Born 3 Mar. 1872 at White Oak, Warren Co., IA. See below for full entry.

7f. **George Washington (X).** Born 5 Feb. 1875 in Warren Co., IA. Married Lois Edna B. ___ about 1904 (born about 1881). Living with his father in 1895; listed in the 1910 census for Coldwater Township, Grant Co., OK, and in the 1917 draft list and 1920 census for Casa Grande, Pinal Co., AZ. George Burgess was a farmer in Oklahoma and Arizona; he may be the George W. Burgess who appears in the 1948 city directory of Tucson, AZ. Living in 1950.

7g. **Henry Long "Doc."** Born 9 Dec. 1877 in Warren Co., IA. See below for full entry.

7h. **Louise E.** Born July 1880 in Warren Co., IA. Married Ira P. Pitman about 1900 (he was born Aug. 1875 in IA). Listed in the 1900 census for Belmont Township, Warren Co., IA, but was living at Stoughton, SK, Canada in 1921. Louise Pitman died between 1950-78, probably in Canada.

7i. **Hetty Fern.** Her name is also spelled Hettie. Born 19 May 1893 in Warren Co., IA. Married ___ Milligan. She was living at Nash, Grant Co., OK in 1921, and was the informant for her mother's death certificate. Hetty Milligan died on 2 May 1985 at Auburn, King Co., WA, aged 91 years.

7j. **Florence Loraine.** Born 7 Feb. 1897 in Warren Co., IA. Married Claud Andrew Graham on 26 Oct. 1915 in Los Angeles Co., CA (he was born 20 Sept. 1894, and died 28 Mar. 1969 at Garden Grove, Orange Co., CA), and had children: *Dorothy J.* (married ___ Duncan); *Claud Andrew Jr.* Living at Stockton, CA in 1921. Florence Graham died on 8 June 1978 at Long Beach, Los Angeles Co., CA.

THOMAS T. BURGESS OF ORANGE CO., CALIFORNIA

[Samuel Thomas (I)[6]]

7c. **Thomas Thornton** *[son of Samuel Thomas (I)].* Born 1 Dec. 1866 in Warren Co., IA. Married Cora E. Males on 24 Dec. 1894 in Warren Co., IA (she was born Feb. 1877 in IA, and died 9 Mar. 1912, age 36, buried in the Santa Ana Cemetery); married secondly Viola B. ___. Listed in the 1895 and 1905 state censuses for Warren Co., IA, and in 1900 in Garfield Co., OK living with his brother-in-law, Luke Bloom. He moved to Long Beach, CA in 1919, and is listed there in the 1941 city directory. Thomas T. Burgess was a freemason; he worked for the City of Long Beach Utilities Department. He died on 30 Jan. 1946 in Orange Co., CA, and is buried in the Santa Ana Cemetery.

8a. **Rex Leo.** Born 20 Aug. 1900 at Enid, OK. Married Opal Irene Mitchell on 26 Nov. 1925 in Orange Co., CA; married secondly Blanche Lorraine Matthews, daughter of Thomas Matthews and Ola E. Lacy (she was born 21 Feb. 1914, and died 4 Feb. 1949 in Orange Co., CA). Listed in the 1918 draft register of Grant Co., OK. Living in 1941 with his father. Rex Burgess was an accountant for the Shell Oil Company; his wife was Chief Clerk at the Naval Ammunition Department. He died childless on 4 Feb. 1949 in Orange Co., CA.

SAMUEL T. BURGESS, Jr., OF GRANT CO., OKLAHOMA

[Samuel Thomas (I)[6]]

7e. **Samuel Thomas (II)** *[son of Samuel Thomas (I)].* Born 3 Mar. 1872 at White Oak, Warren Co., IA. Married Elizabeth B. Mehaffey on 27 Feb. 1895 in Warren Co., IA (she was born Mar. 1876 in IA, and died 9 Nov. 1914, aged 38, buried in the Santa Ana Cemetery). Listed in the 1895-1900 censuses for Otter Township, Warren Co., IA, in 1910 in Coldwater Township, Grant Co., OK (five of six children then survive), and in 1920 at Nash, Grant Co., OK. Samuel Burgess was a farmer in Grant Co., OK. He died there on 26 Sept. 1947.

8a. **Son.** Born 11 Apr. 1896 in Otter Township, Warren Co., IA; died there on 14 Apr. 1896.

8b. **Merril Leroy.** Born 1 May 1897 at Milo, Warren Co., IA. Listed on the 1917 draft register of Grant Co., OK, and enlisted in the U.S. Army during World War I. Private Merril Burgess died unmarried during the great flu epidemic on 16 Nov. 1918 at Ft. Bliss, TX.

8c. **Ned Allen.** Born 3 Jan. 1900 at Milo, Warren Co., IA. Listed on the 1918 draft register of Grant Co., OK.

8d. **Lillian M. (II).** Born about 1905 in IT. Listed with her father in the 1910-20 censuses.

8e. **John S(amuel?).** Born about 1907 in OK. Listed with his father in the 1920 census. He may be the John Burgess born 14 Mar. 1907 who died Aug. 1983 at Tulsa, OK.

8f. **Nina Pearl.** Born 9 June 1909 at Renfro, Grant Co., OK. Married Floyd Daniel Greenlee on 9 June 1928 (div.; he was born 22 Apr. 1909 at Jones, OK, and died Apr. 1985 at Cottonwood, Yavapai Co., AZ), and had children: *Elizabeth Ann* (born 18 Mar. 1930 at Fallis, OK, married Artis Leelemy Bias on 22 July 1950, married secondly James Redway); *Nina Belle* (born 17 Feb. 1932 at Fallis, OK, married Albert Leonard Braham on 10 Jan. 1950, and secondly Jasper Worthen Houston on 3 June 1964; Nina is deceased); *Wanda Mae* (born 21 July 1934 at Fallis, OK, married Robert M. Farnsworth on 19 Dec. 1953; Wanda Farnsworth lives at Provo, UT); *(Phyllis) Colleen* (born 8 Mar. 1937 at Oklahoma City, OK, married Lars Mahlon Woolsey on 1 July 1954, and lives at Mesa, AZ); *Caroline Merle* (born 22 Nov. 1941 at Oklahoma City, OK, married Joseph Daniel Perez). Nina Greenlee died on 22 May 1951 at Mesa, Maricopa Co., AZ.

9a. **James Wesley (II).** He was adopted by his stepfather, and now uses the surname Greenlee. Born 5 Sept. 1927 at Oklahoma City, OK. Married Doris Elaine Hamsher on 15 Jan. 1950. James Greenlee currently lives at Wichita, KS.

DOC BURGESS OF GARFIELD CO., OKLAHOMA

[Samuel Thomas (I)[6]]

7g. **Henry Long "Doc"** *[son of Samuel Thomas (I)].* Born 9 Dec. 1877 (or 1876, according to his draft record) in Warren Co., IA. Married Sarah M. Bales about 1902 (she was born 24 May 1880, and died 12 July 1914 in MO, buried Indianola I.O.O.F. Cemetery); married secondly Minnie Myrtle ___ (she was born about 1886 in MO); married thirdly Evelyn M. (Johnston) Trower (she was born in 1880, and died Sept. 1939). Listed in the 1905 state census for Otter Township, Warren Co., IA, in 1910 in

Nashville Township, Grant Co., OK (one of one children survives), in the 1918 draft register of Grant Co., OK, and in 1920 in Rogers Co., OK. Living at Chelsea, OK in 1921. Doc Burgess was an auctioneer in Oklahoma; he died in 1950 at Covington, Garfield Co., OK, and is buried in the Covington Community Cemetery.

8a. **Loraine I.** Born 7 May 1903 at Milo, Otter Township, Warren Co., IA. Married Emmett Healy (he died before 1966); married secondly John T. Kennedy on 25 Oct. 1966 in Imperial Co., CA. Listed in the city directories of San Diego, CA from 1965-1982 (she was using the name Healy in 1982). Loraine Healy Kennedy died on 17 Jan. 1982 at San Diego, CA.

EDNA EVELYN BURGESS MARTIN (1833-1915)

[William (I)[1], Edward (I)[2], Edward (II)[3], William (IV)[4]]

JOHN BURGESS
(1806-1869)

OF HENRY COUNTY, IOWA

5h. **John (IV)** *[son of William (IV)].* Born 29 Mar. 1806 in Shenandoah Co., VA. Married Matilda Lewellen (or Lewallen or Luellen) on 6 Dec. 1838 (?) in Seneca Co., OH (she was born about 1821 in PA, and died about 1852 in IA, possibly in childbirth); married secondly Arzilla Oswalt on 18 Dec. 1853 in Henry Co., IA (she was born 25 Mar. 1833 in Carroll Co., OH, daughter of Samuel and Elizabeth Oswalt, and sister of Ellison Oswalt, remarried William Green Sample on 24 July 1879 in Henry Co. [he survived his wife], and died 11 Oct. 1900 at Mt. Pleasant, Henry Co., IA when her runaway carriage overturned). Mentioned in his father's will. Listed in the 1840 census for Seneca Co., OH, in the 1854 (two males, two females) and 1856 state censuses, and in the 1850-60 federal censuses for Jefferson Township, Henry Co., IA. His widow appears as head of the family in the 1870-1900 censuses for Henry Co. (seven of eight children survive in 1900). John Burgess was a farmer in Ohio and Iowa, moving to the latter state about 1843; he was deeded land from Henry Williams in Henry Co., IA on 25 Feb. 1848 (*Deed Book #G*, p. 287). He died on 17 Mar. (or 24 May) 1869 at Marshall, Henry Co., and is buried with his wife in the Greenmound Cemetery, Trenton Township (his tombstone gives his date of death as 24 May 1869, with John aged 62 years, 11 months, 25 days).

The Children of John Burgess:

6a. **Lovina.** Born 7 Jan. 1840 (or 1830) in Ohio; died on 10 Sept. 1846 in Henry Co., IA.

6b. **Lucy (II).** Born 12 Sept. 1842 in Seneca Co., OH. Married Ellison "Ellis" Oswalt on 31 Dec. 1860 in Henry Co., IA (he was born 25 [or 22] Oct. 1835 in Carroll Co., OH, son of Samuel and Elizabeth Oswalt, and brother of Arzilla Oswalt, Lucy's stepmother, and died 23 Mar. 1911 in Henry Co.), and had children: *(William) Isaac* (born 1861, married Martha McKenzie on 14 Oct. 1880, had three children, and died 19 Jan. 1934); *Matilda J.* (born 1864, married George York on 24 Sept. 1885, and had children: Della; Emma; Alpha [married ___ Batterson]; George Jr.); *James R.* (born 1865, married Elizabeth McClintic [she was born 1879, daughter of John and Elizabeth McClintic], and died 1941); *John* (born 1867, died unmarried); *Mary* (born 1872, married Alfred Johnson). Listed in the 1870-80 censuses for Henry Co., IA. Lucy Oswalt died on 27 June 1894 in Henry Co., and is buried in the Greenmound Cemetery.

6c. **William (XIII).** Born 1844 in Henry Co., IA (according to his military record). William Burgess was a farmhand for his father. He enlisted on 4 Aug. 1862 (age 18) at Marshall, IA in Co. H, 25th Iowa Volunteer Infantry, Union Army, and later participated in the Battle of Vicksburg. He was mustered out for disability on 20 Aug. 1863, and died unmarried of chronic diarrhea on 5 Sept. 1863 at Vicksburg, MS. After his death, his father applied on 22 Sept. 1866 for a pension in his son's name (Claim #138930), but never received one.

6d. **Reuben (III).** Born 11 Jan. 1846 in Henry Co., IA; died there on 30 Sept. 1846.

6e. **Sarah Jane (II).** Born 14 Feb. 1852 in Henry Co., IA. Married Charles Darneal on 2 Sept. 1875 in Henry Co. Listed in the 1860 census working as a domestic servant for Jack Luellen in Henry Co.

6f. **Beedie.** Born 1854 in Henry Co., IA; died there before 1856.

6g. **John D. (IV).** Born about 1855 in Henry Co., IA. Listed in the census records as an "idiot." He died unmarried in Henry Co. between 1880-1900.

6h. **(Andrew) Jackson (II).** Born 6 May 1857 in Henry Co., IA. See below for full entry.

6i. **Elizabeth Ann (I).** Born 16 Feb. 1859 in Henry Co., IA. Married Newton J. Sammons on 30 May 1872 in Henry Co. (he was born 1853, and died 1933), and had children:

Charles SAMMONS. Born 2 May 1873, married Ellen Campbell, and had children: *Willie*; *Harry* (he was raised by his grandparents; married Opal Bonney on 2 June 1923, and had children: Veryl [married Larue Lamb, and had children: Veryl Edward; Larry {married Jean ___}; Gary Lee; Dianna]; Geneva [married Warren Grooms, and had children: Larry Dean {married Margaret Brown, and had children: Rodney Dean <born 29 July 1967>}; Gary Lee {married Frances Conn}; Warren Leslie {married Nancy Keilkoff, and had children: Karen Sue <born and died 26 Oct. 1970>}; Gregory Allen; Nicky LeRoy]; Robert [married Shirley Miller, and had children: Robert Dean; Randy Lynn; Rickey]; Gerold [married Betty Houk, and had children: Jane Ann; Brenda Lee]; Harry Jr. [married Joyce Sylvester, and had children: Daughter {born and died 23 May 1963}; Harry III; Bruce Allan]; Denna [born 1940, killed in 1957 in a car accident]).

Mary SAMMONS. Born 27 Jan. 1875, married Joe Sample (he was born 21 Jan. 18__, and died 24 May 1899?), and had children: *Roy* (born 6 Jan. 1897, married Clara Orman on 31 July 1918 [she was born 19 Mar. 1900, and died 5 Apr. 1972], and died on 23 Dec. 1970 at Albia, IA, having had children: Iva [died in infancy]; Ralph [died in infancy]; Glenn [born 6 Oct. 1921, married Naomi ___, and had children: Terry Balwin {married Russell Pilcher, and had children}; Glendale Waynick; Sondra Nikie {married ___ Smith}; Eddie]; Wayne [married Grace Gray, and had children: Judy; Lee; Gary G. {married Twila Jean Anderson on 14 Feb. 1969, and had children: Gary Joseph <born 26 May 1970>; Son; David Glen <born 25 May 1973>}; Guy; Joyce; David]; Mary [married Marvin Prose, and had children: Dwayne {married Wanda Agen}; Marvin Jr.; Dennis]; Albert [born Betty ___]; Opal [married Kenneth Huber, and had children: Jimmy; Kimberly; Billy]); *Mary* (died in infancy).

Mary SAMMONS married secondly Frank Sample (he was born 3 Oct. 1868, brother of Joe Sample, and died 16 Dec. __), and had children:

Addie SAMPLE (born about 1901, married Roy Barnette on 5 June 1921 [he was born 8 Aug. 1893, died 12 July 1971], and had children: Ileta [born 10 May 1922, married James Smith on 29 Sept. 1940 {he was born 13 July 1914}, and had children: Carolyn {born 13 Jan. 1943, married Donald Reck on 31 July 1962 <he was born 9 July 1944>, and had children: Rodney Lee <born 11 Aug. 1963>; Lonnie Dean <born 18 Apr. 1966>; Tammy Lynn <born 29 May 1971>}; Robert {born 26 Dec. 1945}; Arlene {born 29 Oct. 1947, married Wayne Burrell on 14 July 1963 <he was born 17 Dec. 1944>, and had children: Bryan Wayne <born 3 May 1964>; Randy Edwin <born 15 Nov. 1967>; Robert Gene <born 15 May 1969>}; Roger {born 2 Jan. 1953}]; Betty [born about 1924, married Richard Glasser on 6 Mar. 1943 {he was born 13 Jan. 1919, died 23 Aug. 1982}, and had children: Ronda; Roxane; Ryan; Ross {born 10 Jan. 1970}]; Frank [born about 1926, married Helen Glasser, and had children: Wilma Jean {married Larry Eugene Klobnik on 1 Dec. 1967, and had children: Kris Eugene <born 25 Nov. 1968>; Kerry Brian <born 22 Sept. 1970>; Travis <born 31 May 1974>}; Debbie June {married James Sampson on 1 Sept. 1974}; Terry Gregory]; Melvin [born about 1928, married Dorothy Hinkle on 21 Feb. 1948, and had children: Daryl Dwayne {married Nancy Marie Amalang on 28 Aug. 1972}; Judith Ellen {married Jerry Lee Johnson on 29 Apr. 1973}; Russell; Jane Ann {married John L. Yocum Jr. on 6 Aug. 1977}; Leana; Steven Jay {married Diana Sue Fowler on 21 Dec. 1978}]; Irene [born 8 Aug. 1931, married Arthur Slack on 8 Aug. 1952 {he was born 15 Apr. 1920}, and had children: Donald Laverne {born 19 Sept. 1954}; Ronald {born 27 Oct. 1955, married Catherine Parks on 18 Sept. 1976}; Deloris Leanna {born 8 Dec. 1956}; Marc Alan {born 21 Oct. 1967}]; Barbara [born 4 Aug. 1936, married Virgil Rinehart on 17 July 1954, and had children: Shirley {born Nov. 1956}; Jane; Gary Lee]; Jack [born 4 Jan. 1942, married Rose Marie Gray on 6 Mar. 1965, and had children: Jeffrey Leroy {born 10 Sept. 1966}; Jerry Lee {born 14 Nov. 1967}; Johnie {born 7 Mar. 1969}; Julie {born 9 Feb. 1970}]).

Eva SAMPLE (born about 1903, married Dave Larson [he died 1984], and had children: Johnie [married Joyce Shilling, and had children: Leslie Joyce; Bobby Jean; Billie Joe]).

Frances SAMPLE (born about 1905, married Leonard Anderson on 16 Sept. 1941 [he was born 11 Nov. 1905, and died 17 July 1982]).

Eliza SAMMONS. Born 1877, married Charles Black (he was born 1873, and 195_), and had children: *Ocie* (born 26 Oct. 1896, married Jake Base, and died July 1979 at Fairfield, IA, having had children: Howard [married Nellie Glispy]; Arthur [married Frances Mae Bates, and secondly Edith Nordike]; Dale; Mildred; Frances; Edith; Dorothy); *Ray* (born 17 Aug. 1900, married Letha Swartz on 31 July 1924 [she was born 30 May 1904, and died 22 Nov. 196_], and died 4 Jan. 1979 at Ottumwa, IA, having had children: Marjorie [married ___ Hancock]); *Goldson* (born 18 June 1911, married Grace ___, and died 29 July 1986 at Bloomfield, IA); *Earl* (twin; born 28 June 1919, married Alma Hunt [she died 1942], and had children: Darrell; Donald [married Willa Mae Thompson]; Arbitina; Jerry; Dean); *Pearl* (twin; born 28 June 1919, married Walter Zulkie, had children: Patty [married Delbert Jim Simmons, and had children: Brian; Alisa], and died 2 Jan. 1947). ***Eliza SAMMONS*** died 195_.

Melissa SAMMONS. Born 1880, married Edward Ballard in 1896 at Mt. Pleasant, IA, and had children: ***Beulah*** (born 6 Feb. 1899, married Floyd Houseal, had children: Edward; Martha Bell [married Verlin Gorden, and had children: Donny; Bobby; Jackie; Marcia; Joey]; and died 25 Feb. 1980); *Floyd* (born and died 1900); *Hazel* (born about 1904, married Ralph Callison [he was born 15 Sept. 1894, died 3 Nov. 1967], and had children: Iola [married Eddie Bix, and had children: Shirley {married Richard Allie, and had children: Cash; Penny}; Gloria {married Philip Greer, and had children: Russell <twin; killed in an automobile accident on 1 Apr. 1972>; Sandra <twin>}; Linda {married Calvin Bently, and had children: Wayne}; Stanley; Connie; Pamala; Daughter {died at birth}]; Marjorie [married Lyle Smith, and had children: Steven; Sheila; Dennis; Rickie; Tena]); *Minnie* (born 16 Dec. 1907, married Harry Barnhill on 29 June 1957, childless); *Elizabeth "Libby"* (born 30 Jan. 1915, married Fred Benge [he was born 15 July 1908, and died 27 Sept. 1992 at Ottumwa], and died 12 Mar. 1992 at Ottumwa, IA, having had children: Freddie [married Donna LaRue, and had children: Terry {married Kathy Shepard in Feb. 1973, and had children: Shawn <born Feb. 1974>}; Penny]).

Ezra SAMMONS. Born 1884, and died unmarried about 1905.

Frank SAMMONS. Born 1892, and died unmarried in 1915.

Emily SAMMONS. Born 10 Mar. 1898, married Earl Campbell on 20 Mar. 1914 (he was born 19 Dec. 1889, and died 26 Nov. 1966 at Ottumwa, IA), and had children: *Ralph* (born 1915, died unmarried); *Thelma* (born 2 June 1917, married Edd Crain on 4 Dec. 1936, had children: Larry [born 13 Apr. 1938, married Mary Burkhardt on 5 Jan. 1969, and died 15 Sept. 1969 in an automobile accident]; Joyce [born about 1940, married Barron Boycel, and had children: Elaine; Debbie {born 1957, died of cancer on 22 Apr. 1969}; Cathy; Rusty]; *Thelma* died on 19 Feb. 1978); *Reggie* (born 4 Jan. 1924, married Penny ___, and had children: John Jay; Suberina). ***Emily CAMPBELL*** died on 7 June 1977.

Perry SAMMONS. Born 18 Oct. 1900, married Hester Workman on 19 Jan. 1921, and had children: *Harold* (died as an infant); *Henry* (born about 1923, married Mary ___, and had children: Peggy; David); *Wilbur*; *Kenneth* (married Ruth Mae Hewett [she was born 14 June 1932, and died 26 July 1974 at Ottumwa, IA], and had children: Keith; Danny; Mike; Angela Kay; Linda Marie; Tony); *Rose Marie* (died as an infant); *Edwin*; *Jerry B.* (twin); *Janet B.* (twin; died as an infant). ***Perry SAMMONS*** died on 17 June 1979.

Elizabeth SAMMONS died on 12 Nov. 1905.

6j. **Martha Alice** (twin). Born 3 July 1863 in Henry Co., IA. Married John W. Sammons on 2 Apr. 1887 in Henry Co., IA (he was born 12 June 1864, and died 23 Mar. 1932), and had children:

Arzilla SAMMONS. Born and died about 1888.

Arthur SAMMONS. Born 13 Feb. 1889, married Anna Brown on 12 Nov. 1912 (she was born 29 Aug. 1890, and died 20 Jan. 1987, aged 96 years), and had children: *Laurence* (born 12 Sept. 1915, married Mary Gilmore [she was born 3 Jan. 1909], childless); *Carl* (born 22 Apr. 1917); *Walter* (born 27 Oct. 1919, married his cousin, Margaret Maxcine Tracey, on 14 Nov. 1943 at Oletha, KS [she was born 23 June 1925]; see her entry for their children). ***Arthur SAMMONS*** died on 1 May 1950.

Ralph H. SAMMONS. Born 11 May 1891, married Etna Messer on 22 Oct. 1913 (she was born 10 July 1894, and died 11 May 1970), and had children: *Erma Frances* (born 8 May 1914, married Charles Cocherell on 17 Nov. 1932 [he was born 18 Nov. 1907, and died 30 Apr. 1981], and had children: Dorothy [born 22 June 1933, married Clarence H. Holcomb Jr., and had children: Holly Annette {died 21 Dec. 1979}; Sally Ann {born Feb. 1969}]; Marilyn [born 19 May 1934, married Donald Eugene Layden, and had children: Kimberly Dawn {born 13 May 1954, married Donald Lee Hines on 11 Nov. 1976 in Henry Co., IA <he was born 5 Feb. 1948>}; Kent Donald {born 20 Apr. 1959}; Barbara Elaine {born 8 Oct. 1962}]; Harold [born 18 Apr. 1938, married Shirley Joan Giberson, and had children: Kenneth Monroe {born 6 July 1963}; Karen Joan {born Jan. 1967, died Jan. 1976}; Martha {born 5 Nov. 1969}]); *William Patrick* (born 13 Dec. 1915, married Joan Johnson Wandling [she was born 7 Apr. 1926 at Chicago, IL], and had children: Robert [born and died 1952]; Gary William [born 5 Apr. 1953, married Judith Ann Scott on 25 Apr. 1978 {she was born 1 Aug. 1959}]; Susan Lynn [born 6 May 1957, married Thomas Engehill on 17 Aug. 1978 {he was born July 1953}, and had children: Nicholas Eugene {born 17 Apr. 1980}]; Bobby [born and died about 1958]); *Harold Lloyd* (born 1924, and died 1 Sept. 1925). ***Ralph H. SAMMONS*** died on 23 Aug. 1986.

Mamie M. SAMMONS. Born 13 May 1893, married Fred Messer on 3 Dec. 1913 (he died in 1918), and secondly Charles Farrell on 1 Oct. 1925 (he died in 1946), and died childless on 20 Oct. 1978.

Bonnie L. SAMMONS. Born 25 Sept. 1895, married George Swailes on 7 Apr. 1920 (he was born 19 Nov. 1896, and died Dec. 1958), and had children: *Esther* (born 11 May 1920, married J. D. Hotchkiss, and had children: Sally [born about 1945, married August Riccy, and had children: Mike]; Mike [born 12 Oct. 1947, and was killed fighting in the Vietnam War in Aug. 1967]); *Harold* (born 26 Apr. 1921, married Jean Newland, and had children: John; Don; Tom; Harold Swailes is an attorney and judge at Belle Plaine, IA); *Agness* (born 23 June 1922, married Darrell Hulen, and had children: Carolyn; Margaret); *Walter* (born 4 July 1923, married Winfred Wallace, and had children: Susan; Amy); *Martha* (born 16 Aug. 1924, married Raymond Herritage, and had children: Tresa; Bonnie); *Evelyn* (born 17 Mar. 1931, married Gordon Brannon, and had children: Joyce). ***Bonnie L. SWAILES*** died on 13 Jan. 1981 at Keosauqua, IA.

Alma F. SAMMONS. Born 4 Aug. 1898, married Josephus Messer on 17 Nov. 1919 (he was born 22 June 1896, and died 26 May 1979 at Mount Pleasant, IA), and had children: *Wilma* (married Bill Droz, and had children: Richard [married Ruby, and had an adopted child: Deanne]; *Wilma* married secondly Emet Bowers); *Blanche* (married Glen Anderson, and had children: Madilyn [married Jim Swailes, and had children: Mike; Susan]; Alma Lee [married Kent ___, and had children: Denice]; *Blanche* married secondly Herbert Byers, and had children: Joyce [married Harris Eugene Deck on 8 Jan. 1966 {he was born 15 Jan. 1945}, and had children: Susan Leanne [born 15 July 1966]; Joyce died 8 Apr. 1969); *Robert* (married Prisilla Westley [she died Dec. 1958], and secondly Marcelene White on 14 Feb. 1970); *Betty* (married Raymond Bogue, and had children: Patty; Robert). ***Alma MESSER*** died on 2 Dec. 1969.

Harry Clell SAMMONS. Born 4 May 1906, married Mercedes Ruby on 5 Feb. 1934 (she was born 8 July 1915), and had children: *Myra Alice* (born 22 June 1934, married James Burton Painter on 5 Feb. 1953 [he was born 19 Feb. 1934, and died Nov. 1985 at Ottumwa, IA], and had children: Charles Burton [born 5 Mar. 1954, married Laura Long on 18 Mar. 1978, and had children: Qwinten {born 22 May 1982}; Brenna]; Lawrence Clell [born 7 Nov. 1956, married Susan Carole Headley on 19 July 1982, and had children: Airen]; Marsha Sue [born 9 Dec. 1958, had children: Christopher Craig PAINTER, married Kerry Schack on 18 Nov. 1978, and had children: Erika Sue {born 28 Jan. 1979}]; Allen James [born 27 Nov. 1959]); *John Farrell* (born 11 Sept. 1938, married Roberta Burtlow Hollister, and had children: Johnnie Harry [born 8 May 1959]; *John* married secondly Carole Jane White Burden on 11 Feb. 1963, and had children: Douglas Burden [born Sept. 1959, married Cindy McCormick on 30 May 1981]; Byron Dale Burden; Ronda Sue [born 3 May 1969]); *Sharon Kay* (born 24 Sept. 1943, married Darrell Hemm on 7 Jan. 1964, and had children: Susanne Elaine [born 6 May 1964]; Edna Almyra [born 17 May 1967]). ***Harry SAMMONS*** died on 2 Jan. 1984.

Martha SAMMONS died on 19 Dec. 1944, and is buried in the Greenmound Cemetery.

6k. **Henry Ellis** (twin). Born 3 July 1863 in Henry Co., IA. Married Olive Josephine Sample on 16 Feb. 1892 in Henry Co. (she was a niece of William Green Sample, who married Henry's mother, Arzilla Oswalt Burgess). Listed in the 1900 census for Washington Township, Taylor Co., IA, and in 1920 at Ottumwa, Wapello Co., IA. Henry Burgess was a farmer in Wapello Co., IA. He died there without surviving children on 4 Jan. 1946.

7a. **Loyd.** Born 14 Jan. 1893 in Henry Co., IA; died there on 10 Oct. 1893, and is buried in the Wayland Cemetery.

6l. **(Mary) Emma.** Born 1 Oct. 1864 in Henry Co., IA. Married Andrew Jackson Lindbloom on 27 Sept. 1883 in Henry Co. (he was born 3 May 1857 in Sweden, and died 4 Mar. 1926 in CA), and had children:

Signe Charlotta LINDBLOOM. Born 5 July 1884, married Roy Finke, and had children: *Clara E.* (born 14 Aug. 1915, married Alfred H. Johnson [he was born 8 Apr. 1918], and had adopted children: Pauline [married Ernest E. Dicks on 3 Jan. 1974 in Iowa City, IA]; Virginia; Lloyd); *Everette R.* (born 28 Nov. 1916); *Lucille E.* (born 26 Feb. 1918, married George Miller Jr., and had children: Bonita; Glenda; Janet); *William A.* (born 23 May 1920, never married); *Ellis I.* (born 28 Nov. 1921, married Doris Fink, and had children: Jerry; Barbara); *Alice M.* (born 9 July 1923, married Magnus Ahmling). ***Signe Charlotta*** died on 15 Apr. 1964.

Francis David "France" LINDBLOOM. Born 16 Mar. 1888, and died 21 June 1897, buried with his parents.

Henry LINDBLOOM. Born about 1890, married Cora ___, and died childless.

Anna Arzilla LINDBLOOM. Born 18 Sept. 1897, married Raymond Tracey, and had children: *Margaret Maxcine* (born 23 June 1923, married her cousin, Walter Sammons, on 14 Nov. 1943 at Oletha, KS [he was born 22 Apr. 1919], and had children: Deana Kay [born 17 Aug. 1944, married Danny Murphy, and had children: Mark Jerome {born 13 May 1967}]; Larry LeRoy [born 22 Jan. 1946]; Virginia [born 25 Jan. 1947]); *Raymond Jr.* (born about 1925, married Norma C. Lee, and had children: Robert [married Kay Lewis, and had children: Vickey; Robin]; Judith Ann; Shirley Jean; Candy Lee; Theresa Ann; Walter Dale); *Ralph Dale* (born about 1930, married Shirley Leveke, and had children: David Joseph); *Thelma Jean* (born about 1933, married Frank Gardner, and had children: Linda Sue; Vicky Lynn; *Thelma* married secondly Robert LaMar). ***Anna Arzilla*** married secondly Harold Stewart (he was born 2 June __, and died 16 May 1961).

Mary Elizabeth LINDBLOOM. Born 4 Sept. 1901, married Everette Dalton, had children: Child (born and died 24 July 1920), and died in childbirth on 24 July 1920.

Emma LINDBLOOM died on 26 Feb. 1910, and is buried in the Greenmound Cemetery.

6m. **(Arennia) Bell.** Born 8 Apr. 1866 in Henry Co., IA. Married (Luther) Bruce Trowbridge on 11 Sept. 1886 at Rome, Henry Co., IA (he was born 26 Feb. 1866, son of John Darius Trowbridge and Amanda Jane Williford, and died 18 Feb. 1952), and had children:

Margaret Mae "Maggie" TROWBRIDGE. Born 3 Dec. 1886, married Edward Johnson Beckman on 9 Feb. 1907 (he was born 19 July 1875, and died 19 May 1941), and had children: *Dorothy Rae* (foster dau.; born 24 June 1913, married Clemmen Bellinger on 25 Apr. 1931 [he was born 20 Apr. 1910, and died 27 Mar. 1970], and had children: Patricia "Patty" [born 24 Oct. 1931, married William Spencer on 11 June 1950 {he was born 6 June 1929}, and had children: Deborah Lynn {born 5 Feb. 1951, married William Grey on 7 July 1973, and had children: Mathew Spencer <born 21 Feb. 1976>}; Susan Carol {born 13 Dec. 1954, died 16 Dec. 1954}]; Carol [born 30 June 1942, married Paul Edward Hinkson on 16 Nov. 1963, and had children: Chad J. {born 1 May 1969}; Amy Kathleen {born 15 Oct. 1970}]; *Dorothy Rae* married secondly William John Carlson). ***Maggie TROWBRIDGE*** died on 15 Sept. 1977, aged 90 years.

Sushanna TROWBRIDGE. Born 26 June 1889, married William Joel Grace on 23 Oct. 1910 at Eldon, IA (he was born 2 Feb. 1872, and died 15 Apr. 1936), and had children:

William Franklin GRACE (born 20 June 1914, married Edna Davis on 26 June 1935 [she was born 6 Mar. 1914, and died 25 Sept. 1971], and died Feb. 1974, having had children: Joyce Annette [born 4 July 1936, married Robert Fallitti on 1 Apr. 1955, and had children: Cheryl {born 5 Apr. 1956}; Robin {born 31 Aug. 1957}; Daniel {born 24 Mar. 1960}; Elizabeth {born 8 June 1963}]; Sandra [born 8 Sept. 1939, married James Bill Norman on 22 Mar. 1958 {div.}, and secondly Martin Jones about 1964, and had children: Michele Lynn {born 15 Jan. 1965}]; William Edward [born 21 Aug. 1940, married Nina McIntire, and had children: Linnette Elizabeth {born 10 Feb. 1970}]; Joel Franklin [born 30 July 1948]).

Mabel Louise GRACE (born 30 Dec. 1918, married Dale Smith, and had children: Helen Louise [born 10 Feb. 1938, married Leon Hogan on 12 May 1956, and had children: Judy Kay {born 25 Apr. 1957, married Craig Schwegen on 24 June 1977 in CA <div.>}; Helen Louise married secondly Arthur Eugene Hammon on 30 Aug. 1968]; William Roy [born 17 Nov. 1939, married Elizabeth Roberts on 23 Sept. 1968 {div.}, and secondly Noboka Miyazaki on 14 Dec. 1973 in Japan, and had children: Joseph Dean {born 17 Sept. 1974}]; Nancy Carol [born 9 Feb. 1943, married Lawrence Taylor on 14 Feb. 1960, and had children: Patricia Ann {born 2 Dec. 1960, married Richard Martin on 19 June 1979 <div.; he was born 18 Mar. 1961>, and had children: Tara Janine <born 13 Nov. 1979>; Christian Jane <born 11 May 1981>}; Lawrence Taylor Jr. {born 17 Feb. 1962, married Cheryl Ann Tertis on 2 May 1987 at Baton Rouge, LA}; Carol {born 28 May 1963, and had children: Michael Howard <born Mar. 1988>}; LeRoy {born 8 Aug. 1964}; Gregory Howard {born 24 July 1965, died in an automobile accident on 7 June 1985}; Tammy Sue {born 31 Oct. 1970, married Ashley Leonard in June 1987, and had children: Eric Gregory <born 9 Dec. 1987>}; Nancy Carol married secondly Clifford Roy Hendrickson {div.}]; Robert Dale [born 13 Oct. 1944, married Mary Brickenborne on 21 Feb. 1969 at Bremerton, WA, and had children: Tracey Lorene {born 12 Oct. 1970}]).

Sushanna GRACE married secondly Lyle Courter on 29 June 1955 (he was born 29 Nov. 1909, and died 8 Mar. 1988 at Galesburg, IL), and died on 29 June 1983, aged 94 years.

Ellen Easter TROWBRIDGE. Born 29 Mar. 1891, married Russell Smith on 21 Mar. 1912, and had children: *Louise Irene* (born 31 Oct. 1912, married Robert Lamphere, and had children: Twin Daughters [born and died about 1948]; James (born 31 Jan. 1949, married Dianne Kelly in May 1972, and had children: Angela [born 1977]). ***Ellen Easter SMITH*** married secondly Mathew Thomas Witham on 20 Oct. 1920 at St. Louis, MO (he was born 7 Nov. 1891, and died 10 Jan. 1969), and had children: *Ruth Gaines* (born 24 Sept. 1922, married Don Banter on 19 Nov. 1944, and had children: Carl [born 11 Dec. 1945, married Sandra Burley on 16 Jan. 1971, and had children: Ryan {twin; born 4 June 1976}; David {twin; born 4 June 1976}; Adam {born June 1980}]; Susan [born 27 Mar. 1949]; Donna [born 19 Dec. 1952, married Charles Anton Frisch on 20 Aug. 1978]); *Helen Isobel* (born 29 Jan. 1927, married Roy Trumbold on 8 Sept. 1944 [div.], and had children: Vickie [born 22 Feb. 1945, married Larry Reynolds on 14 Mar. 1964, and had children: Jeffery Michael {born 14 Aug. 1964}]; Mike [born 8 Feb. 1948, married Linda Seaford on 19 July 1970 {div.}, and had children: Steven Michael {born 4 Aug. 1971}; Gregory Mathew {born 25 Aug. 1973}; Lisa {born 1 Nov. 1976}]; Becky [born 16 Aug. 1950, married Clinton Heedy on 30 Aug. 1971, and had children: Chad Erick {born 29 Sept. 1973}; Ryan {born 31 Jan. 1977}; LeRoy {born 1 June 1980}]; *Helen Isobel* married secondly Don Reed [div.], and thirdly Bob Newman on 2 Sept. 1978]). ***Ellen Easter WITHAM*** died on 7 Apr. 1983, aged 92 years.

Amanda Marie TROWBRIDGE. Born 10 June 1893, married Clarence Henry Brauer on 23 Nov. 1911 (he was born 3 Mar. 1892, and died 4 Nov. 1961), and had children:

Marion Bruce BRAUER (born 5 Aug. 1915, married Gertrude Cully on 6 June 1936 [div.], and had children [later adopted out of the family]: Gail Aldene BLACK [born 28 Apr. 1937, married Maynard Polson on 3 May 1958 {he was born 30 Mar. 1935, and died May 1970}, and had children: Barton Lee {born 10 Oct. 1958}; Larry Dean {born 26 Jan. 1960}; Michael Eugene {born 8 Mar. 1961}; Jacqueline Ann {born 5 May 1964}]; Gloria Jeanne BLACK [born 16 Mar. 1939, married Miles Judd, and had children: Shelly Jeanne {born 16 May 1961}; Miles David {born 20 May 1962}; Katheryn Lynn {born 21 Jan. 1966}]; Marion Kent BLACK [born 5 Dec. 1940, married Ruth Yost on 4 July 1959 {she was born 4 Nov. 1942}, and had children: Marion Allison Lee {born 2 Feb. 1961}; Theresa Colleen {born 2 Jan. 1963}; by Mary Allen he had children: Marian Elizabeth {born 1962}; Marion Kent BLACK married secondly Virginia ___, and had children: Michael Kent {born 1967}; Michelle Kathleen {born 1970}; Marion Kent BLACK was killed in a motorcycle accident on 27 Aug. 1978 in IA]; *Marion Bruce* married secondly Louise Tipton on 2 Oct. 1944 [div.]; *Marion Bruce* married thirdly Ann Tomazeniski, and had children: Ronald Eugene [born 12 June 1949, married Cynthia Margaret Ferguson on 6 Sept. 1969, and had children: Ronald Eugene Jr. {born 9 Sept. 1975}]; Cheryl Kay [born 4 Sept. 1951, married David Allen Catron on 1 May 1970 at Pacoima, CA {div.}, and secondly Pete Ricardo on 25 July 1974]; Lavonne Lee [born 14 Dec. 1954]).

Myron Luther BRAUER (born 19 Aug. 1917, married Dorothy Starns on 16 Feb. 1942, and had children: Charles Edward [born 2 Mar. 1942, married Lucy Duval on 4 Sept. 1963 {div.}, and secondly Cheryl Bugman, and had children: Earl Edward {born 19 Feb. 1967}; Myra Mae {born Dec. 1972}; Charles Edward Jr. {born 24 Dec. 1974}]; Janice Marie [born 3 Dec. 1944, married Marion Richard Duval on 1 Dec. 1963, and had children: Ricky Glen {born 29 Nov. 1964}; Carolyn Marie {born 1 June 1966}; Richard Eugene {born 13 June 1967}]; Deana Lee [born 26 Feb. 1946, married Ronald Smith in Mar. 1966 {div.; he was born 1947}, and had children: Joe Michael {born 31 Nov. 1966}; Brian Edward {born 11 Apr. 1970}; Deana Lee married secondly Jack Long on 14 Sept. 1974]; Betty Jean [born 11 Jan. 1947, died 7 Oct. 1947]; James Howard [born 13 May 1950, married Vickie Ellen Barton on 4 Apr. 1970 {div.}, and had children: Chad Christopher {born 10 June 1976, died 14 June 1976}; James married Linda Kay ___ in 1978, and had children: Tiffany Lynn {born 2 Feb. 1979}]. *Myron Luther BRAUER* died on 15 July 1984).

Clarence Dean BRAUER (born 1 Nov. 1919, married Marjorie Johnson on 16 Aug. 1942, and had children: Constance Lou "Connie" [born 24 Aug. 1949, married Robert Little on 21 June 1969 {div.}, and secondly Howard Seymore on 22 Mar. 1974, and had children: Mathew Duane {born 17 June 1975}]; Dennis Dean [born 22 June 1955]. *Clarence Dean BRAUER* died on 27 Feb. 1983).

Henry Everette BRAUER (born 25 June 1921, married Arlene Lewis on 2 Dec. 1948 [div.], and had children: Gail Gene [born 19 Aug. 1953]. *Henry Everette* died on 25 Mar. 1981).

Gertrude Aldene BRAUER (born 28 Mar. 1924, and died on 29 June 1929).

Robert Max BRAUER (born 28 Aug. 1926, married Glenna Jane Martinsdale on 3 Dec. 1949 [she was born 14 Apr. 1924], and had children: Glenna Ann [ad.; born 22 May 1945, married Bruce Peterson on 22 Nov. 1963, and had children: Brett Marshall {twin; born 29 Apr. 1966}; Bret Michael {twin; born 29 Apr. 1966}; Kristian Michelle {born 10 July 1968}; Biron {born about 1970, killed in an automobile accident in 1985}]; Donna Carol [ad.; born 13 May 1947, married Harold Holgate on 26 Mar. 1966 {div.}, and had children: John Michael {born 8 Sept. 1967}; Joel Mathew {born 1 Oct. 1969}; Donna Carol married secondly James Dennis Schutz in 1973, and had children: Joshuah Wade {born 22 Apr. 1974}]; Nancy Lee [ad.; born 21 Sept. 1948, married ___ Smith {div.}, and secondly Gregory Quick, and had children: Jason Stewart {born 18 Sept. 1973}]; Robert Max Jr. [born 16 Apr. 1951, married Debra Sue Mejerus on 19 July 1972]; Cynthia Sue [born 26 Aug. 1952]; Tracy Lynn [born 27 Dec. 1957]; Jerri Sue [born 11 Sept. 1960]).

Howard Earl BRAUER (born 9 Apr. 1930).

Gerold Edward BRAUER (born 9 July 1933, married Mary Elizabeth Struth Thompson on 23 June 1956, and had children: Jerri Rosemarie [born 13 Jan. 1961, married Sam Parson on 12 Apr. 1980]; Jeffery Allen [born 5 Mar. 1962, married Jacque Cupples on 7 May 1987]; Jennifer Ellen [born and died 28 Oct. 1964]).

Amanda Marie TROWBRIDGE died on 3 May 1980.

Mabel Martha TROWBRIDGE. Born 24 Apr. 1896, married Eugene Alloysis Tolander on 23 June 1915 at Mt. Pleasant, IA (he was born 22 Oct. 1891, and died 31 Dec. 1984 at Swedesburg, IA, aged 93 years), and had children:

Lazzette TOLANDER (born and died 12 Aug. 1915).

Catherine Arrennia TOLANDER (born 31 Dec. 1916, married Lester T. Deck on 8 May 1940 [he was born 10 June 1916], and had children: Joy Louise [born 9 Nov. 1940, married David Schlater on 22 Oct. 1960 {he was born 9 May 1941}, and had children: Carol Ann {born 26 July 1961, married Duane Sauder on 31 Jan. 1981 <he was born 4 Nov. 1961>, and had children: Amanda Jo <born 17 Mar. 1983>; Roy Allen <born 12 July 1985>; Codi Lynn <born 24 Dec. 1987>}; Nancy Lynn {born 3 Dec. 1963 and died 25 Dec. 1963}; Tresa {born 2 Feb. 1970}]; Lester T. Jr. [born 14 Mar. 1942, married Patricia Roth on 7 June 1962 {she was born 6 Feb. 1942}, and had children: Barry Craig {born 1 Dec. 1962}; Bryan Trutman {born 24 Sept. 1964}; John Franklin {born 23 Oct. 1978}]; Ardith [born and died 5 Oct. 1943]; Harris Eugene [born 15 Jan. 1945, married Joyce Byers on 8 Jan. 1966 {she died 8 Apr. 1969}, and had children: Susan Leanne; Harris Eugene married secondly Debra McMillen on 3 Dec. 1973 {div.}, and had children: Brandon Eugene {born 14 Aug. 1974}; Jeffry Lee {born 22 Sept. 1975}; Harris Eugene married thirdly Billy Ingles Ford]; Linda [born 27 June 1947, married Jerry Messer on 25 Oct. 1968 {he was born 23 Sept. 1948}, and had children: Robert Patrick {born 28 June 1966}; Heather Lynn {born 16 Apr. 1973}]).

Martin Eugene TOLANDER (born 22 July 1919, married Doris Faubert on 30 Mar. 1952 [she was born 29 Feb. 1924, and died 16 Apr. 1982 at Cedar Rapids, IA], and had children: Jane Ann [born 28 Dec. 1954, married Donald Stark on 7 Aug. 1976 {div.}, and secondly John Michael Griffen, and had children: Michael Eugene {born 18 July 1978}]; Anita Lorene [born 18 June 1960, married J. J. Kauffman, and had children: Mindi Lynn {born 13 Jan. 1981}]).

Philip Everette TOLANDER (born 10 Aug. 1921, married Buretta Margaret Rutherford on 25 Sept. 1947 [she was born 22 Sept. 1929], and had children: Philip Loraine [born 29 July 1948, married Mary Patricia Brath on 30 Nov. 1974 at Las Vegas, NV {div.; she was born 30 July 1952}]; Rodney Eugene [born 2 Dec. 1949, married Jane Ann Gambarman {div.}, and secondly Jan ___ in 1984, and had children: Adam Rodney {born 21 Feb. 1986}]; Gregory Allen [born 28 Apr. 1951, married Martha Ann Garland on 14 Aug. 1970 {div.}, and secondly Barbara Lynn Duncan on 4 June 1977, and had children: Kari Macchelle {born 8 May 1979}; Rachel Tresa {born 4 Dec. 1985}]; Christopher Kent [born 30 Oct. 1960, married Kate ___ about 1986]; *Philip Everette TOLANDER* died on 16 Sept. 1985 at Fayetteville, AR).

Winona Evelyn TOLANDER (born 30 Sept. 1922, married Dean Hester on 10 Nov. 1944 [he was born 16 Mar. 1920], and had children: Deanne Sue [born 17 May 1946, married Raymond Lew on 27 Feb. 1965, and had children: Randall Eugene {born 3 Aug. 1966, married Angela Kay Stott}; Cynthia Sue {born May 1968, had children by Mike Blint: Amanda Sue <born 6 Mar. 1986>, married Kyle Lang on 7 Sept. 1986}]; Michael Dean [born 15 Aug. 1948, married Margaret Mary Sprankle on 23 Aug. 1970 {div.}, and secondly Robin Nical on 19 June 1976, and had children: Calvin {born 2 June 1979}]; Terry Gale [born 22 Sept. 1954, married Mary Styner on 29 Nov. 1980, and had children: Terri Ann {born 7 Nov. 1978}; Daniel John {born 3 Mar. 1981}; Kristi Jo {born 25 Feb. 1983}]).

Kenneth Irwin TOLANDER (born 11 Mar. 1924, married Norma Jean Faubert on 21 Sept. 1952 [she was born 25 Feb. 1931, and died 15 Oct. 1952], and secondly Beatrice Cox on 8 July 1960 [she was born 7 June 1929], and had children: Stephen Kenneth [born 4 Apr. 1961]; Russell Stewart [born 1 June 1962, married Lynn Rankin on 2 Aug. 1986]; John Allan [born 30 Aug. 1965]; Julie Ann [born 21 Apr. 1967, married Andrew Bittle on 25 July 1987]).

Harold Edward TOLANDER (born 1 Sept. 1925, married Beverly Jean Roberts on 16 Aug. 1946 [she was born 25 June 1929], and had children: Nicola Jean [born 20 July 1948, married Donald Sommes {div.}, and had children: Rodney; Shelly Lynn {born 14 June 1971}; Nicola Jean married secondly Gary Oldt, and had children: Justin Edward {born 14 Dec. 1976}]; Sandra Lee [born 19 Aug. 1950, had children: Anthony Todd {born 17 Dec. 1970}, married Richard Snyder, and had children: Chris]; Jimmy Edward [born 12 Apr. 1952]; Patricia Jean [born 1 Sept. 1953, and had children: Lonnie; Lesa]. *Harold Edward TOLANDER* died on 8 Oct. 1979 at Washington, IA).

Bruce Albert TOLANDER (born 28 Apr. 1928, married Evelyn Geraldine Gosenberg Randall on 16 July 1950 [she was born 8 Oct. 1922], and had children: Robert Darwin [ad.; born 11 Dec. 1946, married Nancy Jean Lamb on 23 Mar. 1965 {div.}, and had children: Robert Darwin Jr. {born 8 Mar. 1966}; Tamara Ann {born 12 July 1967, married ___ Klimp on 25 Oct. 1987}; Robert Darwin married secondly Sue Vandenburg, and had children: Dallas Dwayne {born 18 May 1970}; Robert Darwin also had children: Felisha Dawn {twin; born 17 Oct. 1986}; Mark Allan {twin; born 17 Oct. 1986}]; Geraldine Yvonne [ad.; born 19 Nov. 1947, married Joseph Robert Shaffer on 12 Dec. 1966 at Arvada, CO, and had children: Joseph Robert Jr. {born 21 June 1967}; Gerald Patrick {born 10 Apr. 1968}; Yvonne Marie {born 22 Oct. 1970}; Dawn Deanne {born 17 May 1972}; Geraldine Yvonne died on 28 Apr. 1974]; Patricia JoAnn [born 10 Aug. 1951, married Steven McNulty {div.}, and had children: Shawna Joan {born Mar. 1970}; Patricia JoAnn married secondly David Thomas {div.}, and had children: David Patrick {born 2 Sept. 1973}]; Ramona Jean [born 22 Apr. 1953, married Bruce Ferguson on 5 July 1971, and had children: Monique Rae Jean {born 18 Apr. 1972}; David Bruce {born 7 Sept. 1976}]; Dennis DeWayne [born 2 Sept. 1954, married Patti ___ {div.}, and had children: Jamie Christine {born 13 Apr. 1976}; Anthony]).

Richard Alloysis TOLANDER (born 12 July 1929, married Marilyn Joyce Woline on 29 May 1954 [she was born 6 Feb. 1934], and had children: David Wayne [born 10 Jan. 1955, married Debbie ___ in 1979, and had children: Abby J. {born 11 Sept. 1981}; Adam; Austin Michael {born 1

Aug. 1987}]; Duane Edward [born 22 Jan. 1956]; Ralph Eugene [born 26 Oct. 1958, married Debbie Ann Neal on 2 Jan. 1982 {div.}]).

Emma Louise TOLANDER (born 20 Jan. 1932, married Richard James Murphy, and had children: Becky Ann [born 12 Sept. 1952, married Kent Keeling on 29 Sept. 1973 {div.}, and had children: Brenna Larran {born 25 Aug. 1983}; Becky Ann married secondly Gary Perry, and had children: Amanda Laurie [born 25 Aug. 1986]).

Donald Earl TOLANDER (born 18 Apr. 1933, married Frieda Inga Mock on 8 May 1959 in West Germany, and had children: Klaus Peter [ad.; born 12 Feb. 1958 in West Germany, married Kimberly Jo Crew on 27 May 1981 in WY, and had children: Shannon Marilyn {born 22 May 1983}]; Billy Jo [born 5 Apr. 1960 in West Germany]; Walter Donald [born 2 Aug. 1961 in West Germany, married Deleith Parsons on 22 Nov. 1980, and had children: Weston Donald {born 24 June 1981}; Bret Wayne {born 14 July 1983}; De Ett {born 1985}]; Marilyn Inga [born 9 Nov. 1962 at Fort Knox, KY, married John Henry Sammons on 21 Feb. 1982 {div.}, and had children: Rosa Dawn {born 10 July 1985}]; Jimmy Russell [born 24 July 1966]).

Martha Mae TOLANDER (born 14 July 1934, married Richard James Murphy on 28 Oct. 1955 [he was the former wife of her sister, Emma], and had children: Joan Mae [born 10 July 1965]; Barbara Kay [born 6 Sept. 1968, married Gary Lammson in Dec. 1985, and had children: Amanda {born 9 Aug. 1986}]; Jeni Jay [born 24 Oct. 1969]).

Florence Ann TOLANDER (born 17 Mar. 1936, married Raymond Ernest Cambridge on 22 May 1954 [div.; he was born 1 Oct. 1931], and had children: Carl Ernest [born 9 July 1955, married Judith Ann Durva on 6 Nov. 1976, and had children: Nichola]; Florentine Raline "Tina" [born 13 June 1956, married Darwin Swartzenbruber, and had children: Aaron Jay {born 7 June 1983}; Hannah {born 1985}]; James Bernard [born 7 May 1960, married Melissa Jones on 6 June 1981, and had children: Molly; Joshua James {born 2 Feb. 1987}]; *Florence Ann* married secondly Stan Yeries on 3 Jan. 1975 [div.]).

John Bernard TOLANDER (born 23 Aug. 1937, and died unmarried in an automobile accident on 2 May 1956).

***Florence Arzilla* TROWBRIDGE.** Born 29 Apr. 1899, married Eness Emory "Dick" Hoffstatter on 2 May 1917 (he was born 21 Sept. 1885, and died 18 Feb. 1965 at Pecos, TX), and was childless.

***Frances Agness* TROWBRIDGE.** Born 13 Feb. 1902, married Dennis Huffstutter on 3 Jan. 1919 (he was born 18 Sept. 1896, and died 7 July 1977), and had children:

Elmer Bruce HUFFSTUTTER (born 14 July 1919, married Nadine Elsie Dodge on 9 May 1942 at Waynesville, MO [she was born 21 July 1923, and died 7 Dec. 1963], and had children: Lana Jean [born 7 Apr. 1944, married Roger Dale Booth on 29 Sept. 1969 at Rock Springs, AR {he was born 19 May 1944}, and had children: Luanne Daylene {born 18 Mar. 1962, married Larry Coatney on 15 Jan. 1981 at Lamar, MO <div.>, and had children: Karen Nadine <born 31 Aug. 1982>; Larry Dale <born 18 Dec. 1983>; Luanne Daylene married secondly Brian Williams}; Kelly Rene {born 22 Dec. 1963}]; Nancy Katheryn [born 13 June 1945, married Donald Gene Short on 31 Oct. 1964 at Lamar, MO {he was born 26 Aug. 1946}, and had children: Donald Bruce {born 1 Aug. 1965}; Steven Craig {born 1 May 1970}; Jacqueline Denice {born 20 Sept. 1972}]; Karen Francine [born 22 Aug. 1947, married Racine Denis Myers on 20 May 1965 at Liberal, MO {he was born 4 Oct. 1945}, and had children: Stephine {born 2 Sept. 1971}; Laura Jane {born 11 Mar. 1975}]; *Elmer Bruce* married secondly Rosa Lee Yost on 2 May 1965 at Diamond, MO [she was born 28 Apr. 1920]).

Robert George HUFFSTUTTER (born 17 Feb. 1921, married Helen Louise Tallman Smith on 18 Aug. 1946 at Ottumwa, IA [she was born 28 Mar. 1922], and had children: Linda Louise [ad.; born 23 Dec. 1943, married Richard Hanel on 10 Oct. 1964 at Mankato, MN {he was born 14 Dec. 1942}, and had children: April {born 26 Apr. 1966}; Curtis Richard {born 10 Dec. 1967}]; Barbara Lee [born 17 Apr. 1948, married Donald Foster on 2 Nov. 1968 at Mankato, MN {he was born 19 Dec. 1948}, and had children: Dean {born 4 Aug. 1970}; Craig George {born 27 July 1972}; Michele Leigh {born 28 Sept. 1974}]; Kathy Lynn [born 22 Oct. 1950, had children: Timothy John HUFFSTUTTER {born 13 Nov. 1984 at Baton Rouge, LA}, married Curtis Griesford on 6 Nov. 1976 {div.}, and secondly Gene Alan Swede on 24 Oct. 1981 {div.; he was born 5 Oct. 1956}, and thirdly Brian Riley on 9 Nov. 1983 at Baton Rouge, LA]).

***John Darius* TROWBRIDGE *II*.** Born 2 Oct. 1904, and died 14 Oct. 1904.

***Alice Jeannette* TROWBRIDGE.** Born 12 Sept. 1905, married Olen Harrison Gardner on 2 June 1925 at Ottumwa, IA (he was born 22 Nov. 1899, and died 5 May 1987), and had children:

Ethel Garnet GARDNER (born 8 Sept. 1926, married Robert Bruce Carl on 7 Aug. 1948 [he was born 3 Feb. 1920, and died 8 Nov. 1984], and had children: Barbara Ann [born 18 Nov. 1948, married Harlan Huffaker on 4 June 1965 at Omaha, NE {div.; he was born 8 Apr. 1928}, and had children: David Wayne {born 21 Oct. 1965}; Stewart Wade {born 20 June 1968, married Heike Rehse on 5 Jan. 1988, and had children: Christy <born 22 Mar. 1988>}]; Cassandra Jean [born 24

Apr. 1959, married Alan Lee Kelly on 25 June 1977 {div.; he was born 5 Jan. 1959}, and had children: Zebulan Ryan {born 24 Apr. 1978; adopted by his stepfather, and had his name changed to Zebulan Dale Minde}; Cassandra Jean married secondly Dale Minde on 4 Aug. 1979 {he was born 28 July 1955}, and had children: Daniel Carl {born 16 June 1982}; Aaron Jack {born 9 Jan. 1987}]; Bruce Olen [born 30 Dec. 1963, married Shelli Mabries on 1 Oct. 1983, and had children: Daniel Bruce {born 9 Feb. 1985}; Mathew Alan {born 4 June 1987}]).

Olen Harrison GARDNER Jr. (born 4 June 1928, married Donna Pearl (Renfrew) Henry on 30 June 1963 at Ottumwa, IA, and had children: William Olen [born 10 Feb. 1964, married Debra Sue McKee on 9 Nov. 1979 in MO, and had children: William Jason {born 20 Aug. 1979}]).

Cecelia Elsie GARDNER (born 29 July 1930, married Emery Edmund Polson on 28 Jan. 1950 [he was born 22 Feb. 1916, and died 14 July 1985], and had children: Lawrence Edmund [born 13 Jan. 1951, died 16 Jan. 1951]; Marvin Eugene [born 18 June 1952, died 20 June 1952]; Sarah Patsy [born 16 Oct. 1958, married Larry Webber on 23 Nov. 1979 at Hedrick, IA {div.; he was born 4 June 1959}, and secondly Wayne Brown on 12 Dec. 1987 {he was born 10 Jan. 1957}])

William Edward TROWBRIDGE. Born 2 Feb. 1909, married Dora Andrews (she was born 25 Feb. 1881, and died 25 Jan. 1979), and secondly Margaret Andrews on 4 July 1977, and died childless on 21 July 1987.

Bell TROWBRIDGE died 4 Jan. 1942 at Mt. Pleasant, Henry Co., IA. Alice Gardner lives at Hedrick, IA, and has contributed greatly to this book.

6n. **George R.** Born June 1868 in Henry Co., IA. See below for full entry.

THE OBITUARY OF ARZILLA OSWALT BURGESS SAMPLE

"Mrs. Sample was born March 25, 1833 in Carroll County, Ohio. She came to Iowa with her parents at age eleven. She married John Burgess December 18, 1853; there were nine children, five boys and four girls: Beedie, John, Andrew J., Elizabeth E., Henry E. and Martha, twins, Emma, Arennia, and George R. Beedie was an invalid and died at the age of fourteen. Two children and her first husband preceded her in death. She had eight children, the oldest fourteen, in 1879 when she married William Green Sample. He survives, as does seven children, twenty-four grandchildren, and five great-grandchildren. Mrs. William Sample was seriously injured in a runaway Wednesday [October 10, 1900]; she died Thursday at the home of her son-in-law, Bruce Trowbridge, west of K-Line tracks in Mt. Pleasant, at age 60, and is buried at Green Mound Cemetery, at Trenton, Iowa."—source unknown.

WILLIAM HENRY BURGESS
(1853-1941)
GEORGE WASHINGTON BURGESS
(1854-1927)
HARRIET OCTIVA BURGESS
(1856-1922)

Children of Edward E. Burgess
(see page 231)

[William (I)[1], Edward (I)[2], Edward (II)[3], William (IV)[4], John (IV)[5]]

ANDREW JACKSON BURGESS
(1857-1923)

OF BARTHOLOMEW COUNTY, INDIANA

6e. **(Andrew) Jackson (II)** *[son of John (IV)].* Born 6 May 1857 in Henry Co., IA. Married Mary Jane McClintic on 20 Apr. 1879 in Henry Co. (she was born 17 Aug. 1861, and died 23 Apr. 1951). Listed in the 1880 census for Tippecanoe Township, Henry Co., IA, in 1900 in Louisa Co., IA, and in 1920 at Hartsville, Bartholomew Co., IN. Jack Burgess died on 11 June 1923.

The Children of Jackson Burgess:

7a. **William Henry (VIII).** Born 14 Mar. 1880 in Henry Co., IA. See below for full entry.
7b. **Charles Elmer (I).** Born 10 Feb. 1882 at Merrimac, Henry Co., IA. See below for full entry.
7c. **Lee Riley (I).** Born 5 Apr. 1884 in Nebraska. See below for full entry.
7d. **Nellie Bell "Nelle."** Born 14 Sept. 1886 in Nebraska. Married Wilmot D. Boone on 16 July 1912 at Shanghai, China (he was born 27 Jan. __), and had children: *Wilmot Burgess* (born 25 Dec. 1913 in China, married Edith May Wallace on 11 Sept. 1938 [she was born 22 Nov. 1919], and had children: Muriel Ann [born 17 Apr. 1940, married Daniel O'Leary on 17 Aug. 1963, and had children: Brian Douglass {born 29 Sept. 1964?}; Cheryl Suzanne {born 13 Feb. 1968}]; David Arthur [born 23 Mar. 1946, married Dorinda Dee Ingles in Aug. 1970 {she was born 20 Sept. 1950}]); *Edward William* (born 3 May 1915 at Tsinan, China, married Jean Tiffany Youngs [she was born 12 Oct. 1918], and had children: Susanne Tiffany [born 27 Feb. 1945 in CA]; Andrea Rogers [born 19 Apr. 1948]; Diane Youngs [born 12 July 1950]; Caroline Frances [born 12 Nov. 1956]); *Mary Lucy* (born 1 Nov. 1918 at Tsinan, China, married John Walker Vincen on 18 July 1941 at Shanghai, China, and had children: John Wilmot [born 16 May 1946 at Shanghai, married Karen Lee Strickler on 12 Aug. 1972]; Edward Francis [born 28 Oct. 1947 at Kashing, China, married Sonya Thomas on 6 June 1970 {she was born 20 Aug. 1949}, and had children: Elsa {born 3 Nov. 1972}]; *Mary Lucy* died of polio on 22 Jan. 1952). Nellie and Wilmot Boone were missionaries in China through the mid-1940s. Living in 1966 at Tulsa, OK. Nelle Boone died on 29 Mar. 1973 in Hawaii.
7e. **Earl Harrison.** Born 21 Mar. 1889; died 6 Apr. 1890, and is buried in the Greenmound Cemetery, Henry Co., IA.
7f. **Ralph A(ndrew?).** Born 13 Jan. 1895; died 23 Feb. 1895.
7g. **Leota Genevia.** Born 3 Dec. 1900 in Louisa Co., IA; died there on 24 Mar. 1901.

WILLIAM H. BURGESS OF BROWARD CO., FLORIDA
[Andrew Jackson (II)[6]]

7a. **William Henry (VIII)** *[son of Andrew Jackson (II)].* Born 14 Mar. 1880 in Henry Co., IA. Married Mary Lucy "Mayme" Hall on 7 Dec. 1909 (she was born 4 Feb. 1883, daughter of Robert S. Hall, and died 1 Apr. 1965). Listed in the 1900 census for Center Township, Henry Co., IA living with Jephthah F. Yacum, and in the 1917 draft register and 1920 census of Indianapolis, Marion Co., IN. William Burgess was working as a branch manager for J. I. Case in 1918. He later settled at Ft. Lauderdale, FL. William Burgess died on 18 May 1971 in Broward Co., FL, aged 91 years.

8a. **Robert William (I).** Born 27 Aug. 1921. Married Jane Isabel Johnson (she was born 23 May 1919, and died 23 July 1969 at Ft. Lauderdale, FL). Living at Ft. Lauderdale, FL in 1975; last known living at Pompano Beach, FL.

9a. **Robert William (II).** Born about 1942. Married Virginia ___ on 1 Nov. 1969.
9b. **Gary.** Born 11 Aug. 1943. Married Judy ___ (she was born 24 Oct. 1943).

10a. **Child.**

9c. **Richard (III).** Born 7 Mar. 1946 (or 1947). Married Linda ___.

8b. **Joan (I)** (ad.). Born 18 Apr. 1924. Married Richard Huey on 16 June 1945 (he was born 7 Jan. 1924), and had children: *Barbara* (born 20 July 1946, married Steven Douglass Pechke [he was born 10 July 194_], and had children: Michael David {born 28 Sept. 1966}; Scott Dennis {born 24 Mar. 1969}]); *Donna Lee* (born 28 Jan. 1948, married Robert Lynn Paulson [he was born 14 Jan. 1946], and had children: Dana Lynn [born 3 Jan. 1966]; Kristin Leigh [born 13 Aug. 1969]).

Rev. CHARLES E. BURGESS OF SPOKANE CO., WASHINGTON

[Andrew Jackson (II)[6]]

7b. **Charles Elmer (I)** *[son of Andrew Jackson (II)].* Born 10 Feb. 1882 at Mer(r)imac, Henry Co., IA. Married Lois A. Mathews on 1 Jan. 1907 (she died 1957 at Boise, ID). Listed in the 1925-1936/37 city directories of Boise, ID. Rev. Charles E. Burgess was ordained a minister of the Disciples of Christ (Christian Church) in June 1908. He obtained his A.B. degree at the University of Missouri in 1910, his B.D. from Missouri Bible College, and an Honorary Doctor of Divinity degree at Gooding College, Idaho, in 1930. Charles Burgess served as pastor of Christian churches at Cohasset and Rochester, MN and at Boise, ID from 1924 to the late 1930s. He was also President of Child Welfare, under Minnesota State Board control, and of the Idaho Missions Council (1929), Chairman of the Southern Idaho Christian Missionary Society (from 1925), Vice-President of the Minnesota Anti-Saloon League, and Chaplain of the Idaho State Senate (from 1933). Other accomplishments include: founding a church at Las Vegas, NV; serving as Chaplain of the Idaho State Penitentiary; co-founding Northeast Christian College at Eugene, OR. He moved to Hawaii in 1937, to Riverside, CA in 1949, and retired to the Riverview Lutheran Home, Spokane, WA in 1964. Rev. Charles E. Burgess died on 13 July 1966 at Spokane, WA, but is buried in the Cloverdale Cemetery, Boise, ID. His biography appears in *Who's Who in the Clergy, Volume I, 1935-36* (New York: Who's Who in the Clergy, 1936, p. 172).

8a. **(Otis) Aylesworth.** Born 24 Aug. 1908 at Columbia, MN. Listed in the 1929-40 city directories of Boise, ID working as a chemist. O. A. Burgess died unmarried on 12 Feb. 1940 at Boise, ID from burns caused by an accidental explosion, and is buried there in the Cloverdale Cemetery.

8b. **Lucille Lois.** Born 16 Nov. 1910 at Cohasset, MN. Married Roy Bunn (who lives at Honolulu, HI), and had children: *Robert* (born 1933, married Frances Patsy Bull, and had children: Carol [born 1960]; Robin [born 1962]; Andrew Roy [born 14 May 1967]; Katheryn Burgess [born 28 July 1971]; *Robert* lives at Honolulu, HI); *Ronald* (born 1939). Lucille Bunn died in Dec. 1986 at Honolulu, HI.

8c. **Wilma Berniece.** Born 15 Feb. 1913 at Cohasset, MN. Married Frank Miller, and had children: *Sondra Marilyn "Sonnie"* (born 7 Oct. 1938 at Boise, ID, married Larry Alan Morrow on 7 Apr. 1957, and had children: Kevin [born 16 Nov. 1959 at Anchorage, AK, and died 19 July 1975]; Daniel Scott [born 19 Feb. 1959 at Anchorage, AK, and lives at Enumclaw, WA]; Terri Lynn [born 19 May 1961 at Anchorage, AK, married Douglas Clinton on 14 Dec. 1983 {div.; he was born 21 Sept. 1961}, and had children: Marissa Austin {born 24 Jan. 1991}; Terri married secondly Jeff James Dickson August on 28 Aug. 1993 {he was born 17 Feb. 1962}, and had children: Child {due Spring 1994}; Terri Dickson lives at Missoula, MT]; Steven Lee [born 2 July 1972 at Lincoln, NE, and lives at Pullman, WA]; *Sonnie MORROW* lives at Pullman, WA); *Lois Marie "Lori"* (born 11 May 1944 at Boise, ID, married Raymond A. Goolsbey on 1 Feb. 1965, and lives at Beaverton, OR); *Christine Ann "Chris"* (born 13 Mar. 1953 at Boise, ID, married Scott Lynn Robar on 1 Feb. 1975 at Spokane, WA, and had children: Brendon Scott [born 9 Oct. 1984 at Spokane]; Nathan Michael [born 30 Sept. 1988 at Spokane]; *Chris ROBAR* lives at Spokane, WA). **Wilma** married secondly James Siebert Stinnett, thirdly Lawrence "Larry" Stoner, and fourthly Jack B. Haymond (who lives at Spokane). Listed in the 1966-1986/87 city directories of Spokane, WA. Wilma Haymond died on 12 Mar. 1988 at Spokane, WA. Chris Robar has contributed greatly to this book.

8d. **Mildred Thelma "Millie."** Born 9 Dec. 1915 at Rochester, MN. Married Joseph Bailey (who lives at Buckholts, TX), and had children: *Michael Weldon "Micki"* (his name was originally David Gerald Bailey, but was legally changed; born about 1940, married Anita Starty on 6 June 1946 [she lives at South Windsor, CT], and had children: Karen; Alex; *Micki* died about 1980); *Marguerette LaLani "Marge"* (born about 1942, married ___ Gray, and secondly Wayne Shelton, and lives at Columbus, GA). Mildred Bailey lived in Guam. She died in June 1989 at Honolulu, HI.

LEE R. BURGESS OF MARION CO., INDIANA

[Andrew Jackson (II)[6]]

7c. **Lee Riley (I)** *[son of Andrew Jackson (II)].* Born 5 Apr. 1884 in Nebraska. Married Dixie Lorraine Forsythe on 3 May 1908 (she died on 21 Oct. 1918); married secondly Edith Harshman on 7 Feb. 1920. Listed in the 1920 census for Bartholomew Co., IN living alone. Lee Burgess died on 5 Sept. 1955.

8a. **Elva Lee.** Born 13 Apr. 1909 in IA; died on 12 Oct. 1909.

8b. **(Lula) Ellen.** Born 16 July 1910 in IA. Living with her grandparents in 1920. Married Claude Carter, and had children: *Dixie Bell* (married and had children); *Claude Jr.*; *Jane.* Ellen married secondly Clifford Steele, and had children: *Robert* (ad., the son of Jane Carter; married, and had children: Marjorie Annette [born 6 Sept. 1967]). Ellen Steele died in Nov. 1986 at Phoenix, AZ.

8c. **Charles A(ndrew?).** Born about 1920. Married.

9a. **Kathy.** Born about 1948. Married Bob Durham on 6 Feb. 1969.

8d. **Mary Margaret (I).** Born about 1922. Married, no children.

8e. **Lee Riley (II).** Born 14 Apr. 1924. Married Mildred J. ___ (she was born 6 June 1924). Lee Burgess worked for the Link Belt Railroad, and was later a building contractor. Listed in the 1949-71 city directories for Indianapolis, IN, and from 1972-78 in the Suburban directories living at Ravenswood, IN. He currently lives at Zionsville, IN.

9a. **Ronnie L(ee?) (III).** Born 15 Sept. 1948 in IN. Married Pamela Dee on 3 Dec. 1967. Listed in the Suburban Indianapolis directories at Ravenswood from 1972. He currently lives at Zionsville, IN.

10a. **Sharon Kelley.** Born 3 July 1969 in IN.

William Henry Burgess (1853-1941)
Amanda Jane Wycoff (1867-1939)

[William (I)[1], Edward (I)[2], Edward (II)[3], William (IV)[4], John (IV)[5]]

GEORGE R. BURGESS
(1868-1920+)

OF HENRY COUNTY, IOWA

6n. **George R.** *[son of John (IV)].* Born June 1868 in Henry Co., IA. Married Elizabeth Imhopf on 15 Apr. 1898 in Henry Co. (she was born 1875 in Switzerland). Listed in the 1900-15 censuses for Henry Co., IA (1910 in Jefferson Township, 1915 in Rome Township), and in 1920 in Davenport, Scott Co., IA. George R. Burgess was a farmer in Iowa and Minnesota.

The Children of George R. Burgess:

7a. **Mabel Arzilla.** Her name is spelled Mable in her birth record. Born 13 Jan. 1899 in Henry Co., IA. Married John D. Kincade on 3 July 1916 (he was born 24 Mar. 1886, and died 27 Oct. 1967 at Davenport, IA), and had children:

George Henry KINCADE. Born 22 Feb. 1918, married Dorothy Lavelle Alhern on 16 June 1945, and had children: *Corinne Lynne* (born 14 Feb. 1947, married Harry Lamb on 31 July 1965); *Marsha Ann* (born 12 July 1949); *Mark David* (born 21 Jan. 1954).

Delma Murine KINCADE. Born 5 Sept. 1920, married Max Wolf on 15 May 1937, and had children: *Patricia Ann* (born 23 Mar. 1939, married Jack Emmett Thomas on 9 Apr. 1955, and had children: Jack Emmett Jr. [born 7 June 1957]; Gloria Ann [born 25 Nov. 1960]; Kathleen Marie [born 22 Oct. 1961]; Brian Keith [born 30 Mar. 1963]; Mark Edward [born 6 Mar. 1964]); *Arlene Carol* (born 12 Feb. 1941, married Wayne Hildebrant on 15 Apr. 1957, and had children: Betty Ann [born 9 Mar. 1958]; Wayne Jr. [born 6 Feb. 1959]; James [born 9 Feb. 1960]; Raymond [born 14 July 1961]; Sherrel Lynn [born 2 Sept. 1962]); *Thomas Edward* (born 10 Mar. 1942, married Brenda A. Cassman on 11 Nov. 1965); *Karen Betty* (born 9 Oct. 1946, married Lyle Henders on 3 May 1964, and had children: Lyle Herbert [born 29 Nov. 1965]); *Kenneth Dean* (born 24 June 1950); *Valarie Jane* (born 28 Mar. 1954); *Dollinda Joanne* (born 5 July 1959); *Deama Louise* (born 9 Dec. 1960); *Debra Annette* (born 11 Sept. 1963).

Esther Ione KINCADE. Born 19 Feb. 1924, married Roy Long on 21 June 1944, and had children: *Jackie Jillene* (born 1 July 1947, married John Wochner on 17 July 1965); *Douglas William* (born 8 May 1954); *Donald Dayle* (born 6 Aug. 1959); *James Roger* (born 24 Oct. 1960); *John Wesley* (born 15 Feb. 1964).

Mabel KINCADE died in Nov. 1979 at Davenport, IA.

7b. **(Alonzo) Oscar.** His name is listed in various records as Elonzo, Lonzo, or Oscar E. Born 1 Jan. 1907 in Henry Co., IA. Married Mary Fick on 22 Mar. 1930. Oscar Burgess lived at Mizpah, Koochiching Co., MN. He died in Jan. 1982 at Wyoming, MN.

8a. **Jean Alice.** Her name is also given as Jane. Born 21 Nov. 1931. Married Warren Carlson on 21 Dec. 1948, and had children: *Wayne* (born 29 Mar. 1950); *Brian* (born 7 Nov. 1953).

7c. **Maxine Mae "Maxie."** Born 24 Sept. 1910 in Henry Co., IA. Married Fred Cernstische on 25 Dec. 1935, and had children: *Fred W.* (born 18 Feb. 1938, married Anna Mae Willis on 27 May 1964); married secondly Clarence Kane on 19 Nov. 1954 (he was born 12 July 1917, and died Aug. 1979 at Davenport). Listed in the Davenport, IA city directories through 1982.

[William (I)[1], Edward (I)[2], Edward (II)[3], William (IV)[4]]

GEORGE WASHINGTON BURGESS
(1808-1892)

OF SHELBY COUNTY, OHIO

5i. **(George) Washington (III)** *[son of William (IV)].* Born 3 Apr. 1808 in Shenandoah Co., VA, according to the county death records. Married Elinor "Ellen" Thompson about 1829 (she was born 17 Dec. 1810 in Muskingum Co., OH, and died 3 Feb. 1898 at Fosteria, OH). Listed in the 1830 census for Muskingum Co., OH, in 1840-50 in Shelby Co., OH (he was living in Seneca Co. in 1835), in 1860 in Putnam Co., OH (he moved there by 1854), and in 1870 in Washington Township, Hancock Co., OH; has not been found in 1880. Living in Randolph Co., IN by 1883. Wash Burgess died on 11 May 1892 at Port Jefferson, Shelby Co., OH, and is buried with his wife in the Glen Cemetery. The descendants of George Washington Burgess held an annual family reunion in Ohio for many years after his death, commencing about 1916, and continuing at least until at least 1936. Several printed reunion booklets listing his descendants in the male and female lines were also produced.

The Children of Washington Burgess:

6a. **Thomas William (I).** Born 24 July 1830 in Muskingum Co., OH. See below for full entry.

6b. **Julia Ann (III) "Julian."** Born Sept. 1832 in OH. Married Jacob Lantz on 15 Oct. 1848 in Seneca Co., OH (he was born 1824 in VA, and died between 1880-1900), and had children: *Mary E. "Mollie"* (born Feb. 1850, married Elisha Decker [not with his wife in 1880], listed with her parents in 1880, and had children: Dell D. [born 1877, married Bessie Hatcher, and had children: Francis M. {married Charles O. Dille, and had children: Robert Edward}; Delberta; Robert]; Burgess "Burt" [born Mar. 1880, married Emma Meister, and had children: Jacob; Burgess Jr.; (Ellen) Marie]; Julia [married Harry Jamison, and secondly Joe E. Aldrich, and had children: Rolland E.; Joseph D.]); *Arminda* (married Henry "Harry" Williard, and had children: Gertie [married Charles Hastings, and had children: Helen G.; Williard; Kenneth]; Abraham M. [married Minnie Burke, and had children: Henry Burke; Charles]; Lottie [married W. W. Donaldson]; William A.); *A. P.* (son; married Neal Holcomb, and had children: Clayton [married Pearl Fairbanks, and had children: Burdetta; Vera; Erma; Robert Alvin]; Hattie; Lee; Opel; Warren [married Mary Walker]; Lottie [married Jesse Graham, and had children: Mabel {married ___ Nisser}; Kenneth; Marveleen; Darjel; Ruth]; Fanny [married Otto Gaines, and had children: Keith; Dale]; Charley [married Gertrude Hathaway, and had children: Alvin; Donald]; Letha [married Rex Dyer, and had children: Janet; Lane; Virginia Rexean]); *Fanny* (married Daniel Krotz, and had children: Chauncey [married Lillias Hayes]; Orville C. [married Isabelle Zeigler, and had children: Frances {married Frank Orandel Baldwin, and had children: Frank Orandel Jr.}; Daniel; Richard J.]; Gertrude [married Wilson K. Hamlin, and had children: Virginia Lucille; Raymond Wilson]; Raymond H.); *Alice* (born 1856 in OH, married William Armstrong [he was born 1854 in OH], listed with her parents in the 1880 census, and had children: Ethlyn G. [born Apr. 1881 in OH, married Milton Tayer]); *Hattie* (born 1865 in IN, listed with her parents in 1880, married Charles Rhoades, and had children: Iona [married Eugene Lyman Scott, and had children: Dorothy Hattie; Carl Ernest Rhoades; Ioly Gertrude; Pershing James; David Ashley; Eugene Lyman Jr.; Gertrude Louise; Jeanetta Fae; Juanita May]; Julia [married Chauncey M. Vanderslice, and had children: Donelda May]). Julia Lantz is listed in the 1850 census for Seneca Co., OH, in 1880-1900 at Napoleon, Henry Co., IA, and in 1910 in Hancock Co., OH with her daughter, Hattie Rhoades.

6c. **Harriet (II) "Hattie."** Her name is also spelled Harriett. Born 20 Feb. 1835 at Tiffin, Seneca Co., OH, according to her death record. Married David Strallheim (or Strallum or Strahlem) on 28 Oct. 1852 in Shelby Co., OH (he died 1866), and had children: *Ellen E.* (married James E. Pierpont, and had children: Ida [married Ward Stephens, and had children: Ruth Pierpont]; Walter Strallum; Laura [married Granville Prentiss Taylor]; George W.); *George Washington*; *Minnie L.* (married Charles Maltby, and secondly Tell Berggren). Married secondly Enoch Rike in 1878 (he was born 1819, and died 7 Sept. 1881; his biography appears in the *History of Shelby County, Ohio* (Philadelphia: R. Sutton & Co., 1883, p. 312); married thirdly William A. Skillen on 6 May 1883 in Shelby Co. (he was Jan. 1822 in OH, and died 30 Nov. 1910). Listed in the 1900 census for Sidney, Clinton Township, Shelby Co., OH. Hattie Skillen died on 15 Apr. 1904 at Sidney, Salem Township, Shelby Co., OH, and is buried separately from her husband in the Glen Cemetery.

6d. **Susan (I).** Born 16 July 1837 in OH. Married Rev. Sampson Philip Albright in 1856 (he was born 22 Oct. 1827, son of Philip Albright and Catherine Strader, remarried Susan Riegle on 19 Aug. 1877 [1850-1918], and died 2 May 1914), and had children: *Edward T.* (born 6 Feb. 1857, died 29 Sept. 1875, buried Ithaca Cemetery); *Oliver B.* (born 1859, married Annie Rogers, lived at Kokomo, IN, and had children: Loren Sampson [married Nellie Post]; Elizabeth [married Rev. R. V. Johnson, and had children: Martha Jane]; Edward Chester [married Ruby

Hanson, and had children: Edward Hanson; Mary Ann]; Dale [married Alice Moore, and had children: Dale Moore; Marjorie Elizabeth; Edward Chester; Jack; Robert]); *Martha E.* (born 1861; died 29 Dec. 1862, buried Ithaca Cemetery); *Charles M.* (born 1862, married Elizabeth Coons, and had children: Mabel Grace [born 14 May 1896, married Minford Alspaugh {he was born 11 Sept. 1891, and died Dec. 1971}, and died Nov. 1985 at Lewisburg, OH, having had children: Phyllis Jean; James Burgess]; Howard Virgil; Harold Emerson; *Charles* married secondly Anna Mary Hecathorne); *Harriet "Hattie"* (born 1864, married Frank Lucas, and died childless); *Lilley T.* (born 1867, married William Lucas, and had children: Elizabeth [married Benjamin Field]); *George Wesley* (born May 1870, married Minnie Ellen Curl, and had children: May Elizabeth [married Harry Christian Dietrich, and secondly Albert Keich, and had children: Dorothy Albright]; Lillian Edna [married Harry W. Ackley, and had children: Jean Ruth; Harry Albright]; Helen Violet [married William Ross Miller, and had children: Jack Irving; William George]; Elmer Sampson; Josephine; George Thomas; Russell Bidwell [married Bessie Stump, and had children: Berman; Franklin; Billie]); *Daniel K.* (born 1872?, married May Detwiler, and had children; Constance [married Andrew Snow, and had children: Barbara Anne]; Celestian [married Rex Adams]; *Daniel* married secondly Margaret Weaver); *Grace Estelle* (born 1874?, married Frank Alexander Jones, and had children: Harold Albright; Helen Osee; *Grace* married secondly George Albert Wise, and had children: Ray Sampson; Ernest Albert; Grace Hattie; Leonard Lucas). Listed in the 1860-70 censuses for Twin Township, Darke Co., OH. Susan Albright died on 29 May 1876 in Darke Co., OH, and is buried in the Ithaca Cemetery; her husband and his second wife are also buried there (separately).

6e. **Nancy J. (II).** Born 31 July 1840 (or 1839) in Shelby Co., OH. Married Samuel McDougle (he died about 1875), and had children: *Julia* (born 1859?, had an illegitimate son: Clarence [married Clowe Williams, and had children: Lee; Ora]); *Eliza Ellen* (born 1860, married Emanuel C. Bowers, lived at Rawson, OH, and had children: Glenn [married Bernice Tisdale, and had children: William Clement; Glenn Jr.; Ruth Ellen; Betty Lou; Milton Wesley]; Alma [married Orville Smaltz, and had children: Marcella Luella; Fanny Laurene]); *Leonidas Irving* (born 1862, married Stella May Walter, and had children: Stella May Jr.; Edith Augusta; Leon Walter; Edward Gladstone; Warren Vincent [married Louise Henderson, and had children: Robert Bruce]; Leonidas Irving Jr.); *William Orton* (born 1864, and died childless); *Fannie "Ella"* (born 1866, married ___ Hipkins, and had children: Ralph Jr. [married Goldie Shutz, and had children: Edwin; Fanny Jane; Christina; Elizabeth; Julia Ann]; Floyd); *Amie* (born 1868?, died young); *Cora* (born 1870, married Daniel W. Reese, and had children: Hazel [married John Loucks Dillinger, and had children: John Loucks Jr.; Margaret Nancy; Daniel Franklin]; Presley [married Anna Moor, and had children: Vera]; Velzora [married Alfred Baumunk {he was born 22 July 1894, and died June 1967 at Findlay, OH}, and had children: Charlotte Ann; Burgess Ray]; Fanny [married P. Oran Downing]; Burgess [married Dorotha Mahugh]; *Cora* married secondly S. L. Bushong); *Lyman* (born 1874, married Estella Hunter, and had children: Velzora [married John P. Sayer, and had children: John Irvin; Delmer Wayne; Kathryn Alice]; Lamond [married Christina Henry, and had children: Barbara May; Freddy Lyman]). Nancy J. McDOUGLE is listed in the 1880 census for Putnam Co., OH, and in 1900 in Findlay Township, Hancock Co., OH with her son-in-law, Daniel W. Reese; she has not been found in 1910.

6f. **Fanny.** Her name is also written Fannie, and may originally have been Frances. Born 7 Mar. 1843 in Shelby Co., OH. Married Fred Wolfe on 20 Mar. 1862 in Putnam Co., OH, and had children: *Eura B.*; *Nellie* (married F. M. Melwee, and had children: Eula [married ___ Delhant, and had children: Francis Marion]); *Harry T.* (married Viola McNeal, and had children: Cammie [married Will H. Schinke, and had children: John McNeal; Mary Alene]); *Harry T.* married secondly Clara B. Dennis, and had children: Oneta B. [married Ernest N. Rayburn, and had children: Loleta Mae; Laurene Anne; Betty Jean; Ruth Elaine; Clara Ellen]; Carroll Wesley; Katherine Louise); *Jennie M.* (married H. Loran Huber, and had children: Earl B. [married Laura Kimball, and secondly Jennette Koogler]; Florence Alene [married William F. McNairy Jr. and had children: Jo Ann]); *Frank S.* (married Lura Patty); *Mae*. Fanny married secondly Albert Simpson (he was born 1840 in OH). Listed in the 1910 census for Findlay, Hancock Co., OH. Fanny Simpson died on 24 May 1923 in OH, and is buried in the Union Cemetery, West Independence, OH, on the border between Seneca and Hancock Cos.

6g. **Rachel (I).** Born 1845 at Salem, OH; died on 24 Nov. 1859 in Putnam Co., OH, and is buried in the Graham Cemetery, Hancock Co., OH.

6h. **Smallwood Thompson.** Born Aug. 1849 in Shelby Co., OH. See below for full entry.

6i. **Jacob A.** Born Dec. 1851 in Shelby Co., OH. See below for full entry.

6j. **Teressa A.** Her name is spelled Tressa on her tombstone, and Theresa in her biography. Born 26 Nov. 1854 in Putnam Co., OH. Married Jacob Nau on 28 Sept. 1871 in Hancock Co., OH (he was born 5 June 1847 in Württemberg, Germany, son of John Nau and Regina Wertz, and died 1910), and had children: *Ellen May* (born 24 Feb. 1873, married Rev. M. E. Gibson, and had children: Lowell; Helen [born 4 Nov. 1904, married G. Keen Van Curen, and died 13 Mar. 1988 at Tiffin, OH]; Emerson B. [married Beatrice Anderson, and had children: James Milton]); *John W.* (born 1 Mar. 1875, married Chloe Myers [she was born 1878], and died 1938, buried Union Cemetery, having had children: Lester [married Verna Dippelhofer, and had children: Olive Mae]; Walter [born 25 Aug. 1900, married Marie Wooster {she was born 29 Jan. 1903, and died 29 July 1990}, and died Aug. 1977 at Fostoria, OH, having had children: Maryell Lenore; John Charles]; Alice Belle); *Myrtle E.* (born 15 Oct. 1877, married T. V. Oxender, and had children: Opal [married John Cotton, and had children: James Robert]; Gladys [married Irvin H. Shick, and had children: Donna Mae; Evelyn]; Waldo Eckerd [born 23 May 1911, died May 1977 at Ashland, OH]; Marlowe J. [born 18 Jan. 1914, died Dec. 1985 at Ashland, OH]); *Blanche F.* (born 4 Sept. 1880, married P. M. Mowry, and had children: Vivian; Ruth Jeanette); *Bertha L.* (born 13 Aug. 1885, married Albert Heinz, and had children: Velma [married Robert Beamer]; Harold Adelbert; Margarite Maxine; Marie Elenore; Opal Kathryn); *Ray F.* (born 20 Oct. 1889, married Etho H. Bohn [she was born 1889], had children: Daughter [born and died 1913]; Thelma Lucille; and died 1953, buried Union Cemetery). Listed in the 1870 census with her parents, in 1880-1900 in Washington Township, Hancock Co., OH, and was living in 1932 at Dayton, OH. Teressa Nau died on 25 Aug. 1936 at Fostoria, OH, and is buried with her husband in the Union Cemetery, West Independence, OH. Jacob Nau's biography appears in *A Centennial Biographical History of Hancock County, Ohio* (New York & Chicago: Lewis Publishing Co., 1903, p. 354-55).

[William (I)[1], Edward (I)[2], Edward (II)[3], William (IV)[4], George Washington (III)[5]]

THOMAS WILLIAM BURGESS
(1830-1902)

OF JEFFERSON COUNTY, COLORADO

6a. **Thomas William (I)** *[son of George Washington (III)].* Born 24 July 1830 in Muskingum Co., OH. Married Mary Jane Poulson on 21 Aug. 1851 at Findlay, Hancock Co., OH (she was born 18 July 1832, daughter of Cornelious Poulson of Hancock Co., OH, and died 13 Nov. 1894 at Golden, CO). Listed in the 1860 census for Hancock Co., OH, and in the 1870-1900 censuses for Golden, Jefferson Co., CO (in 1900 with his son-in-law, Henry Robinson). Tom Burgess moved from Findlay, OH to Colorado by wagon train in Sept. 1865, arriving there on the last day of the month. He ran a boarding house at Guy Hill in Golden Gate Canyon, about halfway between Golden and Central City, and later owned the Burgess House in Golden, CO. He died on 24 July 1902 (his 72nd birthday) at Golden, CO, and is buried in the Golden Cemetery. His family Bible record survives with his granddaughter, Holly Fenton.

The Children of Tom Burgess:

7a. **Ellen Elizabeth (I).** Born 13 Feb. 1853 at Findlay, Hancock Co., OH; died there on 16 Apr. 1854, and is buried in the Graham Cemetery.

7b. **Flora Emma.** Born 12 May 1856 at Findlay, Hancock Co., OH; died there on 28 Feb. 1860, and is buried in the Graham Cemetery.

7c. **Charles Oscar.** Born 29 May 1858 in Hancock Co., OH; died on 30 Nov. 1866 at Golden, CO.

7d. **Lyman Emory (I).** Born 20 Sept. 1860 in Hancock Co., OH. Married Charlotte Sutcliffe on 28 Sept. 1898 at Warren, OH (she was born 31 May 1874 at Warren, OH, daughter of Ralph Sutcliffe and Aurelia S. Hart, and died 16 July 1960). Graduated from the Cincinnati College of Pharmacy, Cincinnati, OH. Lyman Burgess was a pharmacist at Golden, Denver, and Boulder, CO. Listed in the 1888-1905 city directories for Denver, CO. Lyman Burgess moved to Boulder, CO in 1905, where he opened his own drugstore, the Burgess Drug Co. He was an elected member of the Boulder City Council at the time of his death, and belonged to the Woodmen of the World, I.O.O.F., and the Methodist Church. He died of pneumonia on 10 June 1918 at Boulder, CO. His obituary stated: "When he was four years of age his parents came to Colorado, traveling by wagon train and driving a yoke of oxen." Charlotte Burgess is listed as head of the family in the 1920 census for Boulder, CO.

8a. **(Charlotte) Hollingsworth "Holly."** Born 11 Jan. 1900 at Denver, CO. Married Dr. Ward Caldwell Fenton on 29 Jan. 1923 at Waterloo, NE (he was born 6 Aug. 1898 at Rocky Ford, CO, worked as a physician, and died 19 June 1984 at Columbia Falls, MT), and had children:

Lawrence Lyman FENTON. Born June 1926 at Rocky Ford, CO, married Reta B. Hollister on 27 Mar. 1955 at Lamar, CO (she was born 12 Aug. 1932), and had children: *Hollis Sue* (born 16 Aug. 1956 at Rocky Ford, CO, married Kenneth Campbell in Nov. 1986, and lives at La Junta, CO); *Ward Christopher* (born and died 15 Aug. 1961 at Pueblo, CO). ***Lawrence FENTON*** currently lives at Ordway, CO.

Charlotte Louise "Sue" FENTON. Born 27 Nov. 1927 at La Junta, CO, married Daniel W. Conrad on 16 Aug. 1950 at Rocky Ford, CO (he was born 20 Nov. 1926 at Chicago, IL, and lives at Kalispell, MT), and had children: *Daniel Fenton* (born 22 Dec. 1952 at Aurora, IL, married Debbie Robbins on 14 May 1988 at Houston, TX [she was born 25 Nov. 1953 at Liberty, TX], and had children: Rebecca Anne [born 5 Sept. 1990 at Houston, TX]); *Sally Elizabeth* (born 12 Mar. 1955, married Christopher Delby on 16 Nov. 1979 at Barrington, IL [he was born 14 May 1955 at Berwyn, IL], and had children: Hannah Marie [born 9 Feb. 1987 at Whitefish, MT]; Elizabeth Ann [born 25 Dec. 1988 at Whitefish, MT]; Emma Christine [born 15 Aug. 1990 at Kalispell, MT]; Catherine Jean [born 13 July 1992 in MT]); *Peter Andrew* (born 28 Sept. 1957 at Hinsdale, IL, married Leslie Lenzi on 1 Apr. 1979 at Missoula, MT, and had children: Sarah [born 19 Sept. 1979 at Alberton, MT]; Adam [born 13 Apr. 1983 at Williston, ND]; Daniel Andrew [born 28 Jan. 1992]).

Holly FENTON currently lives at Kalispell, MT; she has contributed greatly to this book with her memories and documents.

8b. **Robert Lyman.** Born 13 Aug. 1914 at Boulder, CO. His birth is mentioned by his great-aunt, Edna Burgess Martin, in her unpublished diary. Married Cleo Elizabeth Mohr on 26 May 1937 (she was born 31 Dec. 1913 at Las Vegas, NV, daughter of Henry George Mohr and Lesta Cussins, and died 28 May 1986 at Denver). Robert Burgess was a pharmacist for several pharmaceutical companies in the Denver area. He died childless in June 1978 at Denver. Cleo Burgess was an accountant, and also served as National Secretary of the American Society of Women Accountants in 1966; her biography appeared in the 1972/73 edition of *Who's Who of American Women.*

7e. **Alice May.** Born 26 Apr. 1863 in Hancock Co., OH. Married Henry Rowland Robinson on 12 Apr. 1882 at Golden, CO, and had children: *Fred Burgess* (born 1 May 1883, married Mary Salzman); *Henry Wilson "Harry"* (born 9 Aug. 1888, married Louise Schmidt [she was born 10 May 1912, and died in Feb. 1984 at Littleton, CO], and had children: Alice Dolores; Henry Wilson Jr.; Rowland Edward); *Mary* (born 5 Oct. 1895, died 2 Apr. 1899); *Ruth Louise* (born 12 Mar. 1900, died unmarried in Jan. 1982 at Denver, CO). Listed in the 1900 census for Jefferson Co., CO. Alice Robinson died on 8 Mar. 1932 at Golden, CO, and is buried in the Golden Cemetery.

7f. **Frederick Arthur.** His name is given as Fred Arthur in his father's Bible record, but is usually listed as Frederick in the directories and census records. Born 25 Mar. 1866 near Golden, CO. Married Margaret Ann "Maud" Tucker about 1896 (she was born 15 Jan. 1878 in CO, and died Mar. 1967 at Denver, CO). Listed in the 1900 census for Gallup, Bernalillo Co., NM, in 1920 at Denver, CO, and in the 1889-1938 city directories of Denver; Margaret is listed as head of the family in the Denver directories from 1939-66. Fred Burgess was a pharmacist at Golden, a merchant in New Mexico, a plant operator for Apex Refining and Drilling Co., and helped manage the Savery Mushroom Co. at Denver. He lost an arm in a sawmill accident at the age of twenty-three. He died on 28 Apr. 1939 at Denver. Maud Burgess and Marion Geick later owned the Burgess and Geick Notions shop at Denver.

8a. **Marion Tucker.** Born 3 Nov. 1897 at Denver, CO. Married Elmer J. Geick, a bank clerk and bookkeeper, about 1922 (he was born 10 Apr. 1897, and died Dec. 1968), and had children: *Robert James* (he lives at Denver, CO); *Edward Frederick* (born 28 Aug. 1925, married Imogene English, and had children: Susan Yvonne; Ruth Melanie; and died Nov. 1984); *Margaret Ann* (born 1937, unmarried, currently lives at Denver). Listed in the Denver city directories from 1918-82, and in the 1920 census living with her father. Marion Geick was a shop owner with her mother at Denver, Co. She died there in July 1985.

8b. **Lyman Emory (II).** He was the son of Rose Tucker, Maud's sister. Born 26 Aug. 1899 at Gallup, NM. Married Myrtle Irene Mathews in 1922 (div.); married secondly Marie ___ about 1951. Listed in the Denver city directories from 1920-28, 1932-41, 1943-76, and with his father in the 1920 census. Lyman Burgess was a mechanic for Apex Refining and Drilling Co.; he also worked as a roadbuilder and as a mushroom farmer. He died in Oct. 1975 at Denver, CO.

9a. **(Marguerite) Yvonne.** Born 25 Mar. 1923 at Denver, CO. Listed in the Denver city directory in 1941 living with her grandmother. Married Roy John Stenholtz on 9 Nov. 1940 at Denver, CO (div.; he was born 6 July 1922 at Walden, CO, and lives at Los Alamos, NM), and had children: *Paulette* (nmn) (born 17 May 1941 at Denver, CO, and died unmarried 20 Nov. 1963 at Whittier, CA); *Johnnie Lee* (born 11 Dec. 1944 at Los Angeles, CA, and died 12 Aug. 1946 at Denver, CO); *Martin David* (born 10 Aug. 1946 at Denver, CO, married Susan Moreno, and had children: Kiley [born 25 Feb. 1974]; Courtney [twin; born 19 Jan. 1977]; Wiley [twin; born 19 Jan. 1977]). Yvonne married secondly Arthur Joseph Logsdon on 27 Oct. 1948 at Tijuana, Baja California del Norte, México (he was born 18 Aug. 1926, and died Jan. 1984 at Bradbury, CA), and had children: *Steven* (nmn) (born 10 Jan. 1950 at Inglewood, CA, married, and had children: Melissa Star; Melinda Jean "Mindy"; Timothy Steven; Michael William). Yvonne Logsdon worked as an astrologer and psychic before retiring; she lives at Fountain Valley, CA.

9b. **Margaret Ann (III).** Born 1952. Married Joseph Marcus on 24 Apr. 1976 at Denver, CO, and had two children.

9c. **Tony.** Born 1954.

10a. **Daughter.** Born 1993 at Denver, CO.

7g. **Mary Edna.** Born 1 Nov. 1871 near Golden, CO.; died there on 22 Feb. 1873.

[William (I)[1], Edward (I)[2], Edward (II)[3], William (IV)[4], George Washington (III)[5]]

SMALLWOOD THOMPSON BURGESS
(1849-1926)

OF COOK COUNTY, ILLINOIS

6h. **(Smallwood) Thompson "Com"** *[son of George Washington (III)].* Born Aug. 1849 in Shelby Co., OH. Married Pauline Amich about 1872 (div.; she was born Dec. 1849 in IN); married secondly Carrie V. Stinespring on 3 May 1900 in Warren Co., IN (she was born Apr. 1880 in IN, daughter of Liberty and Rachel E. Stinespring). Listed in the 1870 census for Perry Township, Marion Co., IN working for Garrett Sists, in 1880 in Morgan Co., IN in 1900 in Steuben Township, Warren Co., IN, in 1910 in Livingston Co., IL, and in 1920 in Lake Co., IN. Pauline Burgess appears as head of the family in the 1900 census for Marion Co., IN, and is living with her son Paul in 1920. Thompson Burgess was a farmer and laborer in Indiana and Illinois. He died of pneumonia on 6 June 1926 in Bremen Township, Cook Co., IL, and is buried in the Oak Forest Cemetery.

The Children of Smallwood Burgess:

7a. **(Amita) Belle.** Born Feb. 1873 in Indiana. Married Garret S. Toon on 2 Mar. 1889 in Marion Co., IN (he was born Oct. 1864 in IN), and had children: *Clifford* (born 31 Aug. 1890, died Jan. 1963); *Ethel* (born Mar. 1895); *Eva* (born Apr. 1897); *Daughter* (born 28 Mar. 1905 at Acton, IN). Listed in the 1900 census for Indianapolis, Franklin Township, Marion Co., IN, and was living at Acton, IN in 1910, when she attended a school reunion at the Bunker Hill School, Monroe Township, Morgan Co., IN. Not in the Indianapolis death index (through 1920).

7b. **Geneva E. "Neve."** Born Aug. 1874 in Indiana. Married James C. Woodruff on 29 Dec. 1898 in Marion Co., IN (he was born Mar. 1873 IN), and had children: *Harold* (born 14 Nov. 1899, died Sept. 1984 at Indianapolis); *Son* (born 19 Dec. 1906 at Indianapolis). Listed in the 1900 census for Indianapolis, IN, and was living at Indianapolis in 1910, when she attended the Bunker Hill School reunion noted above; listed in the 1940 city directory of Indianapolis. Said to have died in the 1940s.

7c. **George T(hompson?).** Born 12 Aug. 1876 in Indiana. Married May Hamlyn on 14 Dec. 1898 in Marion Co., IN (she was born 1875 in IN, and died 1931 in Marion Co., IN, buried Acton Cemetery). Listed in the 1900-20 censuses for Pike Township, Marion Co., IN; in 1910 he was living at Clermont, IN, when he attended the Bunker Hill School reunion noted above. George Burgess was a farmer at Acton, IN. He died there in Mar. 1963.

8a. **Ralph (II).** Born 1901 at Acton, IN.
8b. **Elsie.** Born 26 Sept. 1904 at Acton, IN.

7d. **Blanch.** Born about 1878 in Indiana. Not listed with her mother in the 1900 census, and is not mentioned in the Bunker Hill School reunion of 1910.

7e. **Frederic A.** (twin). Born 2 Mar. 1880 in Morgan Co., IN. Married Nellie G. ___ (she was born about 1880 in PA). Listed in the 1920 census for West Telford, Montgomery Co., PA on the Bucks Co. line.

8a. **Mildred D.** Born 1908 in PA.
8b. **Florence M.** Born 1910 in PA.
8c. **Grace N.** Born 1912 in PA.
8d. **Ruth C.** Born 1915 in PA.

7f. **Florence (II)** (twin). Born 2 Mar. 1880 in Morgan Co., IN. Married ___ Huffman. Living with her mother in 1900, and is noted as living at Acton, IN in 1910, when she attended the Bunker Hill School reunion mentioned above. Florence Huffman died in Nov. 1969 at Boggstown, IN.

7g. **Howard Clarence (I).** Born 17 Feb. 1882 in Morgan Co., IN. Married Ethel Smock about 1910; married secondly Maude ___ about 1923 (she was born 10 May 1889, and died Nov. 1972). Listed in the 1917 draft register of Marion Co., IN. Howard C. Burgess Sr. was a die setter for the Link Belt Co., Indianapolis, IN. He died there in Dec. 1967.

8a. **Bertha Mae.** Born 26 Nov. 1911 in Marion Co., IN. Married Jerrold Wence (he was born 5 July 1912, and died 1 Aug. 1988 at Cadiz, KY). Bertha Wence currently lives at Terre Haute, IN.

8b. **Howard Clarence (II).** Born 22 May 1924 at Edgewood, IN. Married Margaret Stephens (she remarried James Jansen, and lives at Indianapolis). Howard Burgess was a die setter for Link Belt Co. He died on 14 July (or Sept.) 1981 at Indianapolis, IN.

9a. **Kathryn Louise (II).** Born 5 Apr. 1948 at Indianapolis, IN. Married (Melvin) Richard Cohen, and lives at Mooresville, IN.

9b. **David Bruce.** Born 25 Dec. 1949 at Indianapolis, IN. Married Mary Kuklak (div.)

10a. **Kristine Renee.** Born 30 Oct. 1973 at Indianapolis, IN.

10b. **Lisa Ann (II).** Born 20 July 1976 at Indianapolis, IN.

9c. **Virginia Sue.** Born 25 Feb. 1954 at Indianapolis, IN. Died there unmarried in Sept. 1971.

9d. **William Howard (II).** Born 19 Aug. 1955 at Indianapolis, IN. Married Linda Williams.

10a. **Aaron William.** Born 7 Dec. 1978 at Indianapolis, IN.

7h. **Nettie M.** Born Apr. 1884 in Morgan Co., IN. Said to have died in the 1930s.

7i. **Julius Gordon "Jude."** Born 14 May 1886 in Morgan Co., IN. Married Viola L. ___ (she was born about 1890 in KY); married secondly Frances R. ___. Listed in the 1917 draft register and 1920 census for Marion Co., IN, and in the 1940 city directory of Indianapolis. Jude Burgess was a conductor for the C.C.C. & St.L. Railroad at Indianapolis, IN. He died in Indiana between 1964-68.

8a. **Millard G.** Born 1914 at Indianapolis, IN. Married Elmira M. ___. Listed in the 1940 city directory for Indianapolis, IN. Millard Burgess was a railroad conductor at Indianapolis before retiring. He was living at Indianapolis in 1970, but later settled at Noblesville, IN.

7j. **Paul Granville.** Born 16 July 1891 in Morgan Co., IN. Married Belle ___ about 1919 (she was born 1897 in IN). Listed in the 1917 draft register and 1920 census of Marion Co., IN, and in the 1945 city directory of Indianapolis. Paul Burgess was a welder and hammersmith for the C.C.C. & St.L. Railroad. He died in June 1969 at Greenwood, IN.

8a. **Mark.** He may be the Mark Burgess listed in the 1983 Indianapolis city directory as General Manager of Radio Shack, Greenwood, IN.

8b. **Mildred (I).**

8c. **Margaret (X).**

7k. **Corenne.** Born about 1901 in IL.

[William (I)[1], Edward (I)[2], Edward (II)[3], William (IV)[4], George Washington (III)[5]]

JACOB A. BURGESS
(1851-1916)

OF CHAFFEE COUNTY, COLORADO

6i. **Jacob A.** *[son of George Washington (III)].* Born Dec. 1851 in Ohio. Married Mary B. Nichols on 13 Dec. 1874 at Boulder, CO (she was born Nov. 1853 in IA, and died Sept., 1915 [obituary dated 15 Sept.]). Listed in the 1880 census for Gilpen Co., CO., and in 1900 in Salida, Chaffee Co., CO (four of four children then survive); has not been found in 1910. Jacob Burgess died in Jan. 1916 at Salida (obituary dated 1 Feb.), and is buried in the Fairview Cemetery.

The Children of Jacob Burgess:

7a. **Edna M.** Born June 1876 in CO. Married Frank C. Barlow (he was living at Marysville, CA in 1926, and died 26 Feb. 1935), and had children: *Samuel George* (lived at South Kortright, NY); *John Franklin* (lived at South Kortright, NY); *Harry Burgess* (died young); *Alva Carroll* (married Ruth Chestnut, and lived at La Salle, CO). Living with her parents in 1900; she is said later to have moved to Portland, OR. Edna Barlow died in childbirth in Aug. 1911; both she are her husband are buried in the Fairview Cemetery, Salida, CO.

7b. **Nellie B.** Born 12 Jan. 1878 in Gilpen Co., CO. Married George Fred Snell (he was born 1871, was Vice President of Jackson Lumber Co., and died Jan. 1937), and had children: *Florence Ione*; *Walter Burgess* (born 23 Oct. 1910, served in the 80th Infantry, U.S. Army during World War II, and died 25 Mar. 1951, buried Fairview Cemetery). Listed in the Salida, CO directories from 1916. Nellie Snell died on 31 Dec. 1966 (or 1965) at Salida, CO, and is buried in the Fairview Cemetery.

7c. **Florence Maud "Flora."** Born about 1881 in CO. Married Robert A. Hester, and had children: *Mary Bernice* (married Stewart Boulter, and had children: Robert Charles; she may have been born 2 Feb. 1900, and died Sept. 1982 at Greeley, CO); *William Jacob.* The Hesters are listed in the Denver city directories from 1917-26, but had moved to Atchee, Garfield Co., CO by 1932.

7d. **George Willis.** Born about 1883 in CO. Married Olive Belle Cartwright about 1916 (she was born about 1879 in IA, and died before 1926). Listed in the 1920 census for Denver, CO, and in the Denver city directories from 1918-33. George Burgess was a meat cutter.

8a. **Mary Elizabeth (VI).** Born Sept. 1917 at Denver, CO.
8b. **Florence Mabel.** Born Oct. 1919 at Denver, CO.
8c. **George William (I).** Born about 1921 at Denver, CO.

[William (I)[1], Edward (I)[2], Edward (II)[3], William (IV)[4]]

WILLIAM BURGESS, JR.
(1812-1871)

OF WARREN COUNTY, IOWA

5k. **William (VIII) "Jr."** *[son of William (IV)].* Born 14 Feb. 1812 in Shenandoah Co., VA. Married Sarah Ann Clark on 1 Jan. 1835 in Hancock Co., OH (she was born Jan. 1818 in MD, and was still living on 24 Sept. 1902, when she filed a pension application based on her son Archibald's service). Listed in the 1840 census for Jefferson Township, Muskingum Co., OH, in 1850 in Big Spring Township, Seneca Co., OH, in 1860 in Warren Co., IA; has not been found in 1870. William Burgess was a farmer in Ohio and Iowa. He died on 8 Nov. 1871 in Warren Co., IA, and is buried in the Indianola Cemetery. Sarah is listed in the 1880-85 censuses with her daughter, Margaret, at Pawnee, Smith Co., KS, and in the 1895-1900 state and federal censuses with her daughter, Isabell (three of six children survive in 1900). William Burgess Jr. also raised his orphaned nephew, (George) Washington Burgess.

The Children of William Burgess, Jr.:

6a. **William W. (II).** Born about 1837 in Hancock Co., OH. See below for full entry.

6b. **Mariah (II).** Born about 1839 in Hancock Co., OH; died 1850 in OH (as listed on the mortality census). Relationship not verified.

6c. **Archibald F.** Born 1840 in Muskingum Co., OH (the county so stated in his Army discharge papers). Married Anna M. Scott on 18 Nov. 1866 in Warren Co., IA (she died there in Oct. 1872). Archibald Burgess enlisted on 13 Aug. 1862 at Indianola, IA in Co. D, 34th Iowa Volunteer Infantry, Union Army, during the Civil War, served at the Battle of Arkansas Post, and was discharged on 19 Apr. 1863 for disability (chronic diarrhea, vertigo, and injury of right foot). Listed in the 1880 census with his sister, Margaret M. Brown. Archie Burgess was a farmhand and sheep herder in Iowa and Kansas. He moved to Cora, Smith Co., KS in the fall of 1879, then to Oxford, Furnas Co., NE by 1884, then back to Smith Co. again. He died of heart disease on 5 Mar. 1900 at Smith Center, KS, and is buried in the Fairview Cemetery. He received a pension for his service (Claim #429472, Certificate #592761); after his death, his mother applied to continue the pension, but was denied.

7a. **Child.** Born about 1867 in Warren Co., IA; died young.

7b. **Child.** Born about 1869 in Warren Co., IA; died young.

6d. **Margaret M.** Born 5 Apr. 1842 in Hancock Co., OH. Married Thomas Jefferson Brown on 6 Jan. 1859 in Warren Co., IA (he was born about 1837 in Indiana, possibly son of Thomas and Martha Brown, remarried Malinda ___ after his first wife's death [she was born 25 Sept. 1842, and died 1 Nov. 1914; by her first husband she had children: *Frank M. S.* {born 1869 in NE}; *Alice E. S.* {born 1871 in NE}; *George E. S.* {born 1874 in NE}; *Leo L.* {twin; born 1876 in NE}; *Lola* {twin; born 1876 in NE}]). Margaret and Thomas had children: *William T.* (born 1859 in IA); *Ellwood F.* (born 1867 in IA); *Chester C.* (born 1870 in IA); *Cornelius A.* (born 1872 in IA). Listed in the 1860 census for Warren Co., IA, and from 1880-85 at Cora, Pawnee Township, Smith Co., KS; T. J. Brown is further listed in the 1895-10 censuses for Smith Co., KS. Margaret Brown died on 2 Feb. 1891 in Smith Co., and is buried with her husband in the Cedar Hill Cemetery.

6e. **Susan (II).** Born 30 July 1843 in Hancock Co., OH. Married Eli Morris on 2 Sept. 1860 in Warren Co., IA (he was born 30 Aug. 1840 in IN, son of Jeremiah and Mary A. Morris, and died on 30 Oct. 1926), and had at least the following children: *Alfred* (born about 1863); *William J.* (born June 1876 in IA, married Agnes M. ___[she was born 1878, and died 1954], and died 1952, buried with his parents); *Amy H.* (or Abby) (born Dec. 1886 in KS, married ___ Seal, living at Riverton, NE in 1937); *Lou* (married ___ Hobart, living at Riverton, NE in 1937). Has not been found in the 1880 KS, IA, or NE Soundexes.

Listed in the 1900-10 censuses for Smith Center, Smith Co., KS. Susan Morris died on 1 Feb. 1915 in Smith Co., and is buried in the Fairview Cemetery.

6f. **Isabell J.** Born Feb. 1846 in Hancock Co., OH. Married William H. Flesher on 25 Dec. 1862 in Warren Co., IA (he was born Aug. 1840 in IL, the son of Benjamin and Caroline Flesher, and died 1922), and had five children. Listed in the 1880-1910 censuses for Smith Co., KS, first in White Rock Township, then in Lebanon Township (four of five children survive in 1900). Isabelle Flesher died in 1921 in Smith Co., and is buried in the Cedar Hill Cemetery.

THE PENSION DEPOSITION OF CAPT. JOHN M. LEE, 28 APR. 1884

"County of Furnas, State of Nebraska. In the matter of the claim of Archibald Burgess (No. 429742 for pension), late a private in Co. "D", 34" Iowa Infy. Personally appeared before me a notary public in and for the County and State above written, John M. Lee, late a Captain in the above named Co. and Regiment, who being by me first duly sworn on his oath, says that the above named Archibald Burgess who was a private in his Company, and while in the line of duty at Helena, Ark., on or about the 1st of January 1863, the said Burgess contracted Chronic Diarrhea and disease of Lungs, said diseases being brought on by exposure, and further aggravated while on the march from Miss. Riv. and White River to Arkansas Post during the month of January, 1863, said Burgess accompanying the Regiment to Chicago in Charge of Prisoners, where he became so weak that he had to be left in Hospital from where he was discharged in the month of April 1863 on account of said diseases contracted as above stated. And that said diseases was [sic] not brought on nor aggravate [sic] by the use of Intoxicating drinks, but while strictly performing his duty as a soldier. And the facts are known to me by the following facts, I was commanding said Company "D" during the time before mentioned, and know that said Archabald [sic] Burgess was in the line of duty when taken down with diarhea [sic] and was left at Hosptal [sic] at Chicago, and that I have no interest whatever in the prosecution of this claim for Pension, and that my Post Office address is Oxford, Furnas Co., Nebraska."—John M. Lee, late Capt., Co. D, 34 Iowa Vol.

DEPOSITION OF ELI MORRIS ON BEHALF OF SARAH ANN BURGESS

"Personally appeared before me the undersigned notary public, Eli Morris, aged 60 years, and Lee Starbuck, aged 46 years, both residents of Smith Centre, Kansas, who being duly sworn testify in relation to above mentioned claim as follows: We were well acquainted with Sarah A. Burgess and William Burgess during their married life. That William Burgess, husband of claimant, died in October 1872 [sic], and Sarah A. Burgess has never remarried. That we were also well acquainted with Archibald Burgess and his wife, Anna Burgess. That Anna Burgess died in October 1872, and that the only two children ever born to Archibald Burgess and Anna Burgess, died in infancy. That Archibald Burgess never remarried. That Sarah A. Burgess has no property of any kind or character, neither real nor personal, and that for more than twenty years she has been entirely dependent on her relatives for a living, and that there is not, and has not been during all that time, any one who was [under] any legal obligations to support her. For twenty years previous to the death of Archibald Burgess, he paid a large proportion of her living expenses. That after Archibald Burgess secured a pension for himself, every time he received his quarterly payment, he visited his mother, the claimant herein, took her clothing or shoes, and paid her a part of his pension money. That Sarah A. Burgess is too poor to look up and secure testimony as to the marriage of herself and William Burgess or a physician's affidavit as to date of his death. We knew Archibald Burgess before his marriage, and when he lived at home with his parents, William Burgess and Sarah A. Burgess. We believe it would be a difficult matter now, if not impossible, for claimant to secure record of his baptism, or of any public record of his birth, or of any witnesses who were present at his birth; but we know from a long acquaintance with his parents and himself that he was the son of William Burgess and Sarah A. Burgess, the claimant herein. That claimant has no property of any kind, no income from any source, and is totally unable to earn anything by her labor. That we are not interested in the event of this claim; that our Post Office address is Smith Centre, Kansas."—Eli Morris and Lee Starbuck, 8 Apr. 1901.

[William (I)[1], Edward (I)[2], Edward (II)[3], William (IV)[4], William (VIII)[5]]

WILLIAM W. BURGESS
(1837?-1910+)

OF SUMNER COUNTY, KANSAS

6a. **William W. (II)** *[son of William (VIII)].* Born about 1837 in Hancock Co., OH. Married Lydia Wright on 30 Nov. 1865 in Warren Co., IA (she was born about 1848 in TN, and died between 1880-85 in Sumner Co., KS). Listed in the 1850 census for Seneca Co., OH, in the 1860-70 censuses for Warren Co., IA, in 1880-85 in Gore Township, Sumner Co., KS, and in 1895 and 1910 in Mulvane Township; has not been found in the 1900 Soundex. William Burgess was a farmer in Iowa and Kansas. He or one of his two first cousins named William Burgess served in the Ohio Cavalry, and camped with the occupying federal troops in Fauquier Co., VA, during the Civil War (so mentioned in Ethel Burgess Harlan's notes). He apparently died in Kansas after 1910.

The Children of William W. Burgess:

7a. **(Sarah) Ella (I).** Born about 1867 in Warren Co., IA. Listed with her father in the 1885 state census of Sumner Co., KS, but died or married by 1895.

7b. **Ida (I).** Born about 1869 in Warren Co., IA. Listed with her father in the 1885-95 state censuses of Sumner Co., KS, but died or married by 1900.

7c. **Bruce.** Born about 1872 in Warren Co., IA. Listed with his father in the 1885 state census of Sumner Co., KS, but moved or died by 1895.

GEORGE WASHINGTON BURGESS (1836-1915)
(see page 238)

[William (I)[1], Edward (I)[2], Edward (II)[3], William (IV)[4], Lucinda (I)?[5]]

BEDE D. BURGESS
(1820?-1875?)

OF VIGO COUNTY, INDIANA

NOTE: The relationship of this branch to the line of William Burgess is uncertain, but it has been included due to the similarity between the odd given name Bede to Bedy, William's son. For the purposes of this genealogy, Bede D. Burgess will be considered the same generation level as William's grandson, or sixth generation.

6a. **Bede D. "B. D."** *[possible son of Lucinda].* Born about 1820 in Muskingum Co., OH (or possibly in Cincinnati, OH). Married Harriet Barnes on 9 Aug. 1842 in Muskingum Co. (she was born Aug. 1821 in OH, daughter of Daniel Barnes and Sarah Morgan, and died 15 [or 13] Jan. 1905 at Terre Haute, IN). He may be listed with his presumed grandfather, William Burgess, in the 1830 census for Muskingum Co., OH; Bede D. Burgess appears in Muskingum Co. as head of his family in 1850, in 1860 in Cloverdale Township, Putnam Co., IN (he bought a small house in Putnam Co. on 1 Jan. 1859 [*Deed Book #V*, p. 624, and sold it on 15 Sept. 1868 [*Deed Book #7*, p. 332]), and in 1870 in the 2nd Ward of Terre Haute, Vigo Co., IN. B. D. Burgess was a shoemaker at Terre Haute, IN, where he appears in the city directories from 1872/73-1874/75 (but is not listed in the next directory, 1876). Harriet Burgess appears as head of the family in the 1880 census, and is living with her grandson, Charles Burgess, in 1900, when just two of her children reportedly survive (the overall number of children is not given). B. D. Burgess apparently died at Terre Haute about 1875; both he and his wife are buried in the Woodlawn Cemetery, but only Harriet has a stone.

Bede D. Burgess may be a son of Bedy Burgess, of Lucinda Burgess (his sister), of some other member of the family, or he may be a foster child or unrelated; no relationship can be established or disproved from known records. On the one hand, the occurrence of a very unusual first name, plus B. D.'s initial appearance in Muskingum Co., OH, and the inclusion of an unidentified ten-year-old boy with William Burgess Sr. in the 1830 Muskingum Co. census, makes some connection plausible. However, there are several unrelated Burgess families in both Muskingum Co. and in neighboring Perry Co., although most of these have been eliminated as possible relatives through examination of probate records. Bedy Burgess's settlement deed in Iowa does not mention B. D. Burgess, although *all* of his other adult children are included (but two of the underaged siblings are not); on the other hand, B. D. would have had no rights to the estate had he been illegitimate or a foundling. Lucinda Burgess is mentioned in William's 1839 will as being an heir, but otherwise remains unaccounted for; her married name, if she had one, is unknown. The fact that B. D. was apparently apprenticed to a shoemaker, a profession uncommon in the Burgess family, and later married his employer's daughter, would suggest an individual who was orphaned or otherwise outside the usual family structure. His inclusion here should be regarded as speculative.

The Children of B. D. Burgess:

7a. **Sarah (VIII).** Born about 1843 in Muskingum Co., OH. Listed with her father in the 1850-60 censuses; no further record.

7b. **James Knox Polk (II).** Born about 1845 in Muskingum Co., OH. Listed in the Terre Haute city directories from 1872/73, in the 1870 census there with his father, and in 1880 with his mother. James K. P. Burgess was a teamster at Terre Haute, IN; he died there unmarried on 16 Feb. 1891 (or 23 Dec. 1890), and is buried in the Woodlawn Cemetery.

7c. **John W. (I).** Born 21 Jan. 1847 in Muskingum Co., OH. See below for full entry.

7d. **Rhoda.** Born Mar. 1850 in Muskingum Co., OH; died in Ohio or Indiana before 1860.

7e. **(Harriet) Ellen (I).** Born about 1857 in Putnam Co., IN. Listed as Harriet Burgess in the 1860 census, and as Ellen in 1870. As "Ella" Burgess she may have married James M. Miller on 21 Aug. 1877 in Vigo Co., IN. Has not been found in the 1880 Soundex. Relationship not verified.

7f. **Melissa B.** Born Dec. 1859 (or 1860) in Putnam Co., IN. Married Joseph Hamil(l) on 1 Oct. 1879 in Vigo Co., IN (he was born Oct. 1849 in OH), and had children: *Lewis J.* (born 23 July 1880, married Mary A. Minnick on 30 Apr. 1914 in Vigo Co., listed with his uncle, Lewis Burgess, in the 1900 census, and with his aunt, Minnie, in 1910); *Joseph Jr.* (born June 1883, died unmarried at age 19 on 28 Dec. 1901 at Terre Haute). Has not been found in the 1880 Soundex; listed in the 1900 census for the 9th Ward, Terre Haute, Vigo Co., IN.

7g. **Lewis H.** Born Jan. 1863 in Putnam Co., IN. Listed in the Terre Haute, IN city directories from 1878/79, and is recorded there in the 1900 census. Lewis Burgess was a railroad engineer at Terre Haute, Vigo Co., IN. He was killed in a train accident on 19 Oct. 1909 at Effingham, IL, dying unmarried and childless. He was living with his sister Minnie at the time of his death.

ENGINEER MEETS DEATH IN WRECK

"The Saint Louis-Pittsburgh train No. 44, conductor S. S. Smith; Engineer, Lewis H. Burgess, met with an accident at Effingham, Illinois, Tuesday evening at 7:45, in which engineer Burgess of Terre Haute lost his life. The train entered the house track switch at a point about 1500 feet east of the Illinois Central railroad crossing, and the engine was derailed and overturned. Engineer Burgess was caught beneath the engine, and was so badly injured that he died at 1:50 A.M. at the hospital where he was taken after being extricated. Fireman W. C. Harrison was climbing over the tank of the engine, preparatory to taking water at Effingham, and when the derailment occurred, he jumped from the tank, and was only slightly injured. Aside from a rather severe shaking up, none of the passengers were in any manner injured. A deadhead postal car, which was immediately behind the engine, was derailed and overturned. A mail car, a combination car, and a coach, which were the following cars, were all three derailed, but remained upright. The three remaining cars stayed on the track.

"The cause of the accident has not been ascertained, and as the track was considerably damaged, the exact cause may never be known. Division Superintendent Downing and his staff passed over the Division only the previous week, and inspected every main track and switch and found them to be in good condition. The last time that the switch was used was about 5:45 P.M., and the yard brakeman who handled it is positive that it was closed, and set for the main track. About 6:45 P.M., passenger train No. 7 passed this switch, and the engine man is positive that the track was clear at that time. After the derailment, the switch lock was found on the ground, and the top of the switch light was found thrown back and the cup overturned. The position of the train after the accident indicates that it started through the switch, and then the engine left the track at or near the frog. The buffet car and two sleepers of No. 44 which were not derailed, and an additional coach which was supplied at Effingham, was used to finish making up the train, and it was sent on with but slight damage.

"Mr. Burgess, who was fatally injured, was forty-six years old, and resided with his sister, Miss Minnie Burgess, in this city. The body was brought to this city Wednesday afternoon. Mr. Burgess is well known here, being a member of the Masonic, Elk, and various railroad orders. Arrangements for the funeral have not yet been made. The burial will be in Woodlawn Cemetery."—*Terre Haute Tribune*, 20 Oct. 1909.

7h. **(Sidney) Minnie.** Her unusual given name could be a nickname for Lucinda. Born 26 Oct. 1866 (or 1862) in Putnam Co., IN. Married Edward A. Slusser on 26 Jan. 1882 in Vigo Co. (div. 1885), and had children: *Son* (born 4 Feb. 1883); after her divorce she used the name Burgess. Minnie married secondly James I. Southard on 12 Dec. 1912 in Vigo Co. (he was born 12 Dec. 1856). Listed in the 1900 census for Terre Haute, Vigo Co., IN living with her nephew, Charles Burgess, with her brother Lewis in the 1906/07 directory of Terre Haute, as head of her family in the 1910 census (she claims to be a "widow" of 25 years in this census), and in the 1912/13 city directory. Minnie Southard died on 30 Mar. 1920, aged 54 years, at Terre Haute, Vigo Co., IN.

JOHN W. BURGESS OF VIGO CO., INDIANA

[Bede D.[6]]

7c. **John W. (II)** *[son of Bede D.]*. Born 21 Jan. 1847 in Muskingum Co., OH. Married Louisa Kelly on 7 Aug. 1870 in Vigo Co., IN (she was born Apr. 1854 in IN, and died 1922 at Terre Haute, IN). Listed in the city directories of Terre Haute beginning in 1872/73, and in the censuses from 1880-1920 (two of three children survive in 1910). John W. Burgess worked as a shoemaker with his father, and later as a railroad brakeman and switchman for forty-seven years (from 1873) for the Chicago & Eastern Illinois Railroad, at Terre Haute, Vigo Co., IN. He died there on 16 Jan. 1921, and both he and his wife are buried in the Woodlawn Cemetery. According to his obituary, he "was known as the oldest switchman in active service at Terre Haute."

8a. **Charles Henry (I).** Born June 1871 in Vigo Co., IN. See below for full entry.
8b. **James Thomas (II).** Born 11 May 1873 in Vigo Co., IN. See below for full entry.
8c. **Harriet (III) "Hattie."** Born 1877 in Vigo Co., IN. Married Andrew J. Evoy on 12 Apr. 1892 in Vigo Co., IN, and had children: *Mary G.* (born 13 Jan. 1895, listed with her grandparents in 1900). Hattie Evoy died on 23 Jan. 1898, aged 21 years, at Terre Haute, IN.

CHARLES HENRY BURGESS OF VIGO CO., INDIANA
[Bede D.[6], John W. (II)[7]]

8a. **Charles Henry (I)** *[son of John W. (II)].* Born June 1871 in Vigo Co., IN. Married Mabel Flowers on 23 Dec. 1895 in Vigo Co.; married secondly Mrs. Sadie E. (Cook) Wyatt on 1 June 1897 in Clay Co., IN (div.; she was born 18 Aug. 1868 in PA, and remarried Charles G. Burvill on 19 May 1906 in Clay Co.); married thirdly Grace E. Minnier about 1906 (she was born about 1879, and died 1954). Listed in the 1900-20 censuses for Vigo Co., IN, and in the 1899-1949 city directories of Terre Haute. Charles H. Burgess was a stone mason at Terre Haute, IN. He died there in 1950.

9a. **Henry Minnier.** Born 3 Apr. 1908 at Terre Haute, IN. See below for full entry.
9b. **Louisa Ann.** Born 19 Dec. 1911 at Terre Haute, IN. Married John Donnenhoffer (he was born 2 Nov. 1909, and died Sept. 1985). Louisa Donnenhoffer died in May 1986 at Terre Haute, IN.
9c. **Louis Bead (I).** Born 30 July 1914 at Terre Haute, IN. See below for full entry.
9d. **Ellen Elizabeth (II).** Born 23 Jan. 1920 at Terre Haute, IN. Married William Mann. Ellen Mann lives at Cataract Falls, IN.
9e. **Dorothy.** Born and died 1925 at Terre Haute, IN, aged two days.

HENRY MINNIER BURGESS OF VIGO CO., INDIANA
[Bede D.[6], John W. (II)[7], Charles Henry (I)[8]]

9a. **Henry Minnier** *[son of Charles Henry (I)].* Born 3 Mar. 1908 at Terre Haute, IN. Married Lucille "Anna" ___ by 1942; married secondly Ella L. ___ by 1947. Listed in the 1973 city directory of Terre Haute, IN. Henry M. Burgess was a coal strip miner near Terre Haute, IN. He died on 11 Nov. 1983 in Vigo Co.. Ella Burgess currently lives at Terre Haute, IN.

10a. **Charles Willard.** Born 26 Sept. 1942 at Terre Haute, IN. Married Jane A. Buckner; married secondly Kathy L. Buckner. Charles W. Burgess is a coal strip miner near Terre Haute, IN. He currently lives at Centerpoint, IN.

11a. **Michael Charles.** Born 2 Apr. 1963 at Terre Haute, IN.

12a. **Christy.**

11b. **Charles Henry (II) "Chuck."** Born 8 Dec. 1965 at Terre Haute, IN.
11c. **David Edward.** Born 12 Jan. 1967 at Terre Haute, IN.
11d. **Edward James (II).** Born 18 Oct. 1971 at Terre Haute, IN.
11e. **Joseph Lynn.** Born 1 Dec. 1976 at Terre Haute, IN.

10b. **John Henry (III).** Served in the U.S. Marines.

11a. **Son.**
11b. **Daughter.**

10c. **Mary Elizabeth (VII).**
10d. **Judith Ann (I).**
10e. **James William.** James Burgess currently lives at Terre Haute, IN.
10f. **Frank Edward.** Married Debra S.___. Frank Burgess currently lives at Terre Haute, IN.

11a. **Son.**
11b. **Son.**

10g. **Rocky Thompson.** Married and divorced.

11a. **Daughter.**

LOUIS "BUD" BURGESS OF VERMILION CO., ILLINOIS

[Bede D.[6], John W. (II)[7], Charles Henry (I)[8]]

9c. **Louis Bead (I) "Bud"** *[son of Charles Henry (I)].* Born 30 July 1914 at Terre Haute, IN. Married Edna Bridgewater by 1939; married secondly Clara Tabor by 1942; married thirdly Mary Allison; married fourthly Helen Curtis. Listed in the 1934-47 directories of Terre Haute, IN. Louis Burgess was a welder at Terre Haute, IN and at Danville and Muncie, IL. He died on 27 Aug. 1990 at Muncie, IL.

10a. **Carolyn Ann** (ad.). Her surname was originally Meeker. Born 18 Dec. 1945 at Danville, IL. Married Larry Alden.

10b. **Louis Bead (II)**. Born 6 May 1948 at Danville, IL. Married Diana Lomas. Louis Burgess is a truck driver at Covington, IN.

11a. **Louis Bead III "Buddy."** Born 31 Oct. 1977 at Danville, IL.

10c. **Gayle Ann.** Born 8 Oct. 1952 at Danville, IL. Married Thomas Mann.

JAMES T. BURGESS OF MARION CO., INDIANA

[Bede D.[6], John W. (II)[7]]

8b. **James Thomas (II)** *[son of John W. (II)].* Born 11 May 1873 in Vigo Co., IN. Married Elizabeth "Lizzie" Gauger on 31 Oct. 1898 in Vigo Co., IN (she was born June 1874, the daughter of Julius Ga(u)ger, is listed with her father in the 1900 census, and died 30 Jan. 1903 at Terre Haute, IN); married secondly Mary Gemmeke on 30 Nov. 1905 at Terre Haute, IN (she was born 11 May 1873). Listed in the Terre Haute city directories from 1899-1908, and with his father in the 1900 census. He moved to Indianapolis, IN, and is listed there in the 1917 draft register of Marion Co., in the census of 1920, and in the city directories from 1919-43. James Burgess Sr. was an iron molder for Byram Foundry Co. at Indianapolis, IN. He died there about 1943.

9a. **John Arthur.** Born Oct. 1899 at Terre Haute, IN. Living with his mother and grandfather in the 1900 census. John A. Burgess enlisted in Co. A., 113th Engineers, U.S. Army during World War I, and was shipped to France, where he was gassed in the Fall of 1918. Listed in the 1920 census living with his grandfather. After returning to Indiana, he lived with his uncle Charles for several years, before dying unmarried about 1924 at Terre Haute of his wounds.

9b. **Daughter.** Born 9 Dec. 1901 at Terre Haute, IN; she may have died young.

9c. **James Thomas (IV)**. Born 31 Aug. 1909 in Clay Co., IN. Married Audra M. ___. Served in the U.S. Navy during World War II. He and his sisters are listed in the 1920 census twice, once with their parents, and secondly with their aunt, Louise Connelly, in Vigo Co., IN; he is also listed in the city directories for Indianapolis from 1936-67; Audra appears as head of the house from 1968-75. James T. Burgess Jr. worked for U.S. Tire Company. He died in Jan. 1968 at Indianapolis, IN.

9d. **Helen L.** Born about 1911 at Indianapolis, IN. Listed with her sister Thelma in the 1936 city directory of Indianapolis. She is said to have moved to Denver.

9e. **Thelma M.** Born about 1913 at Indianapolis, IN. Listed with her sister Helen in the 1936 directory for Indianapolis, and alone from 1937-43 working as a saleswoman for G. C. Murray Co. She is said to have settled in Denver.

[William (I)[1], Edward (I)[2], Edward (II)[3]]

JOHN BURGESS
(1771-1855)

OF FAUQUIER COUNTY, VIRGINIA

4c. **John (II)** *[son of Edward (II)].* Born 11 June 1771 in Prince William Co., VA. Married Charlotte Johnston on 12 Nov. 1805 in Fauquier Co. (bond date; she was born 26 Nov. 1786 in VA, daughter of Moses and Duannah [or Diannah or Suannah] Johnston, and died on 1 May 1877 in Fauquier Co., aged 90 years). John Burgess remained in Virginia when his two brothers went west, working a mountain farm above Bethel, Fauquier Co., VA. His homestead was said to have been the site of a Civil War battle. Listed in the 1810-40 censuses for Fauquier Co., VA; he is living with his son, Addison Burgess, in Prince William Co. in 1850. Listed in the tax records in Fauquier Co. beginning in 1789. His will (*Fauquier Co. Will Book #26*, p. 209-210, dated 23 May 1855, probated 24 Dec. 1855) mentions his wife Charlotte, and children Edward (wife Jane H.), Dawson, Elizabeth, Margaret Leith, and Addison; probate records also mention John W. Burgess as a receiver of estate payments. Peyton Burgess is also provably a son from his own death record. John's family Bible record survived to modern times among the descendants of his son, Dawson, and was copied by Ethel Burgess Harlan about 1921. Charlotte Burgess appears in the 1860-70 censuses for Fauquier Co. with her son, Dawson Burgess. John Burgess died on 12 Dec. 1855 in Fauquier Co.; his official death record lists his parents, gives his age as 84, and mentions his county of birth.

Charlotte Burgess is named as a child of Moses Johns(t)on in the latter's will (*Fauquier Co. Will Book #3*, p. 439, dated 16 June 1803, probated 25 July 1803), which also mentions her siblings: Moses Jr.; David; Daniel; Nimrod; John; Mary; Hannah Boggess; Susanna Waddle; Margaret McMeekin. A subsequent guardianship proceeding (24 Oct. 1803) assigned Dianna Johnson (sic) control of Charlotte, Daniel, and Mary Johnson, orphans of Moses Johnson. Duannah's will (*Will Book #11*, p. 182, dated 16 May 1829, proven 25 Mar. 1830, witnessed by John Burgess), mentions Marshall K. Newhouse, son of her daughter Mary (or "Polly," who married Zebulon Newhouse on 23 Dec. 1811 in Fauquier Co., John Burgess providing the bond), and Mary Bray, "now wife of Timothy Bray."

The birth dates of John's children are taken from his family Bible record. There are a large number of cousin marriages recorded in this family, and many twin births.

The Children of John Burgess:

5a. **Margaret L. "Peggy."** Born 16 Aug. 1806 in Fauquier Co, VA. Married Benjamin R. (or C.) Leith by 1850 (he was born 11 Oct. 1813, and died before her). Listed in the 1850 census for Fauquier Co. with Benjamin Rector, and in 1860-70 with her husband in Fauquier Co. The Leiths lived outside Rectortown, VA near Peggy's brothers, Dawson and Addison Burgess. Peggy Leith died childless at the house of her brother-in-law and cousin, William Price Utterback, on 16 Sept. 1884.

5b. **Moses (III).** Born 2 May 1808 in Fauquier Co., VA. See below for full entry.

5c. **Peyton Price.** Born 9 May 1810 in Fauquier Co., VA. See below for full entry.

5d. **John Wesley (I).** Born 6 June 1812 in Fauquier Co., VA. See below for full entry.

5e. **Addison.** Born 20 Mar. 1814 in Fauquier Co., VA. See below for full entry.

5f. **Frances A.** Born 1 Apr. 1816 in Fauquier Co., VA. Married Presley G. Bradley (or Brady) about 1847 (he was born about 1819 in VA, brother of Caroline Bradley [who married Frances's brother, Moses Burgess], and worked as a carpenter), and had at least the following children: *(James) Taylor* (born 1848, married Alma ___, and had two sons who lived on the West Coast); *Emma* (born 1849, died before 1860); *William S.* (born 1853, married his cousin, Mary A. Burgess, daughter of Addison Burgess); *Winter P(ayne?)* (born 8 Jan. 1856, married ___ Hubbard in Texas [who died five days later], and secondly an Indian in Indian Territory). Listed in the 1850-70 censuses for Fauquier Co., VA. The Bradleys are said to have moved to Texas, but have not been found in the 1880 or 1900 Soundexes for TX or VA.

5g. **Mary (VIII).** Born 26 July 1818 in Fauquier Co., VA. Married Thomas McCormick about 1848 (he was born about 1823 in VA, and worked as a shoemaker and bookbinder), and had at least the following children: *Mary F.* (or *M.*) (born 1849); *Emma J.* (born 1851, married Lewis Mayhugh on 27 Oct. 1870 in Prince William Co., had children: Frank [born Feb. 1880], and died by 1882, when Lewis married Emma's sister, Anna); *Jeannette* (born Jan. 1852, listed unmarried with her mother in 1880-1900, and in 1910 with her sister, Annie, at Haymarket, Prince William Co.); *Charlotte B(urgess?)* (born 1854, listed with her parents in 1880); *John T.* (born 1856, married his cousin, Ida L. Rector, daughter of Bushrod Rector and Lucy Burgess, on 29 Nov. 1883); *Anna* (born Apr. 1858, living with her mother in 1880, married Lewis Mayhugh [the widower of her sister, Emma] on 7 Dec. 1882 in Prince William Co.; she may have married secondly B. B. Nails on 28 Dec. 1918). Listed in the 1860 census for Haymarket, Prince William Co., VA, and from 1870-1900 at Gainesville, Prince William Co., VA. Mary McCormick apparently died in Prince William Co. between 1900-1910. According to *Prince William: A Past to Preserve* (Manassas, VA: Prince William County Historical Commission, 1982, p. 70), the McCormicks' residence was a one-and-one-half-story small log house on a stone foundation with a large brick exterior chimney; "supposedly the oldest house in Haymarket, [it] was one of only four buildings which were not burned in November, 1862, when Union Soldiers set fire to Haymarket. It was spared, the story goes, when the occupant, a mother with children, delayed the troops until the order was rescinded."

5h. **Elizabeth (IX) "Betsy."** Born 3 Dec. 1820 in Fauquier Co., VA. Married her cousin, Marshall Knox "March" Newhouse, on 1 Feb. 1860 in Fauquier Co., VA (he was born about 1820 in VA, son of Zebulon Newhouse and Mary Johnston, and worked as a carpenter), and had children: *Jefferson Davis* (born 1863 in Fauquier Co., VA). Listed with her brother, Addison Burgess, in the 1850 census, in 1860 working as a seamstress for Charles H. Taverner (her husband is living with Dawson Burgess), and in 1870 with her brother, Edward Burgess. She is said to have died in West Virginia.

5i. **Edward (X) "Ned"** (twin). Born 30 Oct. 1823 in Fauquier Co., VA. Married his first cousin, Jane Hopkins Lewis, on 23 Sept. 1852 in Fauquier Co. (she was born 27 July 1822 in Fauquier Co., daughter of Charles Lewis and Elizabeth Burgess, and died 27 Oct. 1880). Listed in the 1850 census living with his mother-in-law, in 1860 with his brother-in-law, Thomas McCormick, in 1870-80 with his wife in Fauquier Co., VA, and in 1900 with John F. Armstrong. Edward Burgess was a farmer near Haymarket and New Baltimore, VA. He died childless on 3 Dec. 1906 in Fauquier Co.

5j. **Sarah Price "Sally"** or **"Sallie"** (twin). Born 30 Oct. 1823 in Fauquier Co., VA. Married Thomas A. Smith about 1847 (he was born about 1811 in VA, and was a retail merchant), and had at least the following children: *Sarah Margaret* (born 1848, married (George) Andrew Hulfish on 2 Oct. 1866 in Prince William Co., VA [he was born 1845 in VA], and had children: Sarah L. [born 1868]; Charles W. [born Mar. 1870]; Jane S. [born 1872]; George W. [born 1874]; Thomas A. [born 1876]; Raymond [born 1878]); *Bettie A.* (born 1852, died or married by 1870); *Ida* (born 1854, died or married by 1870); *John William* (born 1856, married Laura G. Belt on 3 Nov. 1875 in Prince William Co. [she was born 1855 in VA], and had children: Ida L. [born Oct. 1876]; Thomas A. II [born 1878]); *Tamzin* (born 1858, died by 1870); *George Washington* (born 13 Mar. 1860 at Haymarket, VA, married Mildred L. Foley on 22 Oct. 1879 in Prince William Co. [she was born 1862 in VA], and died May 1939 at Haymarket, Prince William Co., VA); *Jane* (born 1862). Listed in the 1860 census for Haymarket, Prince William Co., VA; her husband is recorded in the 1870-80 censuses for Gainesville, Prince William Co., VA. Thomas Smith's will (*Prince William Co. Will Book #U*, p. 210-211, dated 10 Dec. 1888, probated 4 Mar. 1889), mentions sons John and George, and son-in-law "G. A. Hirefish." Sally Smith apparently died between 1862-70 at Gainesville, VA.

5k. **Dawson Jackson (I) "Dorsey."** Born 6 May 1826 in Fauquier Co., VA. See below for full entry.

5l. **Susan Catherine.** Born 21 Nov. 1828 in Fauquier Co., VA. Married her first cousin, William Price Utterback (originally Buckner), about 1850 (he was born 9 Apr. 1824, a natural son of Frances Burgess, and adopted son of French Utterback, and died 1 July 1901), and had at least the following children: *Edmonia Jane "Ada"* (born 11 Aug. 1851 at The Plains, married John Thomas Cockrill on 31 Oct. 1877, and died there on 21 Nov. 1915, having had at least the following children: William Thomas; Edwin Clarence; Laura Lorena [born 15 May 1886, married her second cousin once removed, George Lewis Burgess, and died 1 June 1945 at Barboursville, WV; see George's entry for their children]); *Frances E. "Fanny"* (born 2 Aug. 1854, married Augustus R. "Gus" Mandley on 21 Dec. 1887 in Prince William Co., and died 3 May 1928, having had children: Mary Ida; Edward Durand); *Anna L.* (born 25 Oct. 1858, and died unmarried 20 May 1889); *Ernest M.* (born 28 Mar. 1862, married Edith Robertson, and died Sept. 1939); *Ida Jackson* (born 9 Aug. 1866, may have married Robert R. Cockrill on 6 Sept. 1883 in Prince William Co., and possibly secondly John Thomas Cockrill [widower of Edmonia Utterback], and died childless in 1954; her probate is recorded in *Will Book #67*, p. 305-306, dated 6 Jan. 1955; she may actually have been the daughter of James and Sarah E. Utterback); *Mary V. "Mamie"* (born 28 Aug. 1868, married Landon J. Cockrill on 15 Dec. 1888); *Martha W. "Mattie"* (born 23 Sept. 1870 [or 1873], married her first cousin, George Washington Burgess, and died childless on 24 Oct. 1940). Listed in the 1860-70 censuses for Fauquier Co., VA, in 1880 at Gainesville, Prince William Co., and from 1900-10 in Fauquier Co. with her son-in-law, John T. Cockrill. Susan Utterback died on 3 Mar. 1912 at The Plains, Fauquier Co., VA, and is buried in the Alton Cemetery, Bethel, VA.

THE WILL OF JOHN BURGESS

I John Burgess now residing in the County of Fauquier and State of Virginia, and of sound mind, though in declining health, make and declare the following my last will and testament, by it revoking and annuling any and all former wills made by me.

First—I give to my wife Charlotte Burgess during her natural life three of my slaves, namely, Scott and Tawney males, and my girl Judah, three feather beds with bedsteads and bed furniture, one bureau, two tables, six chairs, one p[?]ss, all the china and cracking ware and kitchen furniture and hogs I may die possessed of also two horses and two milck cows, her choice of all I may leave all which including the increase. At the death of my said wife, I give to be equally divided between them (except my son Edward, at whose request his wife Mrs. Jane H. Burgess is to have and receive the portion which otherwise would be his) to all my children as herein after the residue of my estate is given to them—

Secondly—I give to my sons Edward & Dawson to be paid to them by my executrix out of my estate before distribution fifteen dollars each unless it shall appear that subsequent to this date I pay to or for them the same, it being the amount I have advanced to each of my other children.

Thirdly—I give to my daughter Elizabeth who now resides with me in consideration of her previous services to myself and her mother and such as she may render hereafter, my boy Thornton now about six years old, to her and the heir or heirs of her body forever over and above an equal participation with her brothers and sisters in the residue of my estate or such part of it as I dont herein and herby particularly dispose of. I also give to Jane H. Burgess the wife of my son Edard [sic] besides the said Edwards distributable portion of my estate with his brothers and sisters (this as stated in the first section of this my will at his request) I give to her my infant slave boy now in her possession and care to her and her heir or heirs forever.

Fourthly—the entire residue of my estate after the payment of my just debts I give to all my children to be divided equally between them, share and share alike. And the shares of my daughter [no name mentioned] I give to them and the hair [sic] or heirs of their bodies and none other, and the hairs of my daughter Mrs. Margaret Leith and my son Dawson. I give to my son Addison Burgess in trust for the following uses and purposes and none other. He the said Addison Burgess is to permit his sister Margaret Leith and her husband to use and enjoy the share of the said Margaret Leith of my estate during the natural life of the said Margaret in kind if desirable to her to do so. Otherwise he is to so manage it as to make it productive yearly and pay over to her yearly the product thereof during her natural life and at her death said share to be distributed by the said Addison or such successor or trustee for the said Margaret and the said Dawson. Events may render necessary amongst all my children and the heir or heirs of such of them as may be dead equally and the said trustee is to act in the same manner with the share of the said Dawson Burgess except the said Dawson is not to use it in kind. It is to be made productive yearly and the yearly product to be paid over to the said Dawson or his assigns, unless it shall happen that the said Dawson shall have a legal hair or heirs. In such event happening this trust to the extent it opperates on the share of my estate given for the use of my son Dawson to cease and determine and said share place in the care and charge of a trustee for the use and benefit of such heir or heirs to whom I give the same absolutely at the death of the said Dawson.

Lastly—I constitute and appoint my wife Mrs. Charlotte Burgess executrix of this my last will and [?] testimony that is my will. I have set to it my hand and affixed my seal this 23rd day of May 1855.

John Burgess [his mark]

In the presence of us together John Burgess now residing in Fauquier County, Virginia, requested us to witness that he declared the foregoing to be his last will and testament. Test: Enoch H. Foley, John T. Howdershell, John D. Hirst.

[William (I)[1], Edward (I)[2], Edward (II)[3], John (II)[4]]

MOSES BURGESS
(1808-1858)

OF PRINCE WILLIAM AND FAUQUIER COUNTIES, VIRGINIA

5b. **Moses (III)** *[son of John (II)].* Born 2 May 1808 in Fauquier Co., VA. Married Caroline Bradley (or Brady) on 8 Sept. 1834 (bond date) in Fauquier Co. (she was born about 1813 in VA, possibly the daughter of Patrick [or Richard] Bradley [or Brady] and Osee Doughty, and sister of Presley G. Bradley [who married Moses's sister, Frances A. Burgess], and died after 1880). Listed in the 1840 census for Fauquier Co., and in the 1850 census for Prince William Co., VA. Caroline appears as head of the family in Prince William Co. in 1860, is recorded in 1870 in Fauquier Co. with William McCarthy, and in 1880 in Greenbrier Co., WV with her son, Erasmus. Moses Burgess was a farmer near the border of Fauquier and Prince William Cos. He is not mentioned in his father's estate papers, but is listed in the family Bible with his birth and death dates. He died of "spasms" on 5 Apr. 1858 in Frederick Co., accor-ding to the Prince William Co. death records.

The Children of Moses Burgess:

6a. **Erasmus Helm "Ras."** He was named for a well-known Fauquier Co. farmer. Born 22 June 1835 in Fauquier Co., VA. Listed as "blind and deaf" on the 1850 census, with his mother in the 1860-70 censuses, and in 1880 in Greenbrier Co., WV; in 1900 he is listed there with J. M. Knapp, and in 1910 he is recorded with Daniel Kirwen (his nephew-in-law) in Loudoun Co., VA. Ras Burgess was a farmhand in Virginia and West Virginia. He died unmarried on 22 Aug. 1919 at Sydenstricker Farm, Greenbrier Co., WV, and is buried there in the Calvary Cemetery.

6b. **Virginia A.** Born 21 Jan. 1837 in Fauquier Co., VA. Married her cousin, John Randolph Garrett, on 12 Aug. 1858 (the date is taken from the Garrett family Bible; he was born 22 Apr. 1837 in Fauquier Co., VA, son of Sydnor Garrett and Margaret Burgess French, and died 19 Nov. 1887), and had at least the following children: *Mason W.* (born 13 Aug. 1859, married Bert ___); *Anzonetta V.* (born 8 Mar. 1861, died 15 Nov. 1865); *Emma Randolph* (born 22 Feb. 1863, married James S. Settler on 20 Jan. 1881); *John Edward* (born 2 Nov. 1865, listed with his mother in the 1900 census); *Martha* (died young); *Moses Stanfield* (born 1871); *George Andrew* (born 1873); *Ashton J.* (born 1875); *Addie* (twin; born 6 Jan. 1877, died young); *Idabell* (twin; born 6 Jan. 1877, died young); *Eva May* (born Oct. 1879, listed in the 1900 census with her mother, married P. P. Williams). Listed in the 1860-80 censuses for Orleans, Marshall District, Fauquier Co., VA, and in 1900 in the Fairfield District, Henrico Co., VA. Virginia Garrett died on 26 Apr. 1904, and is buried with her husband in the Orlean Cemetery, Fauquier Co., VA.

6c. **John R.** Born about 1839 in Fauquier Co., VA. Listed with his mother in the 1860 census working as a farmer. John Burgess enlisted on 26 Apr. 1861 at Haymarket, VA (age 22) in the 17th Virginia Infantry, Confederate Army. He was shot in the head on 30 June 1862 on Frazier's Farm (near Richmond, VA) at the Battle of Malvern Hill, and was reportedly buried on his mother's farm.

6d. **Edward W.** Born about 1841 in VA. Listed with his mother in the 1860 census working as a carpenter. Edward Burgess enlisted on 26 Apr. 1861 at Haymarket, VA (age 21) in the 17th Virginia Infantry, Confederate Army. He was wounded on 1 June 1862 at the Battle of Seven Pines (east of Richmond, VA), and died on 14 June 1862 at Richmond Hospital #14 after his leg was amputated due to gangrene. He was reportedly buried on his mother's farm.

6e. **Mary Catherine (II) "Mollie."** Born about 1843 in VA. See below for full entry.

6f. **Moses Franklin.** Born 9 May 1845 in Prince William Co., VA. See below for full entry.

6g. **(Charlotte) Frances "Fanny."** Born Sept. 1846 in Prince William Co., VA. Married (William) Alpheus "Pump" Bray (possibly a cousin) on 24 May 1876 in Fauquier Co., VA (he was born Oct. 1838 [or 1836] in VA, and died about 1911), and had at least the following children: *William A(lpheus Jr.?) "Samuel"* (born 8 Nov. 1876); *Luther M.* (born 4 Dec. 1877); *Austin H.* (born 26 Apr. 1879, married

Emma Willis on 9 Jan. 1911); *John C.* (born Feb. 1880/81); *Earnest W.* (born Feb. 1883, listed with his father in the 1910 census); *Irene H.* (born Jan. 1886, listed with her father in the 1910 census). Living with Albert F. Garrett in 1860 and with her uncle, Presley G. Bradley, in 1870; listed in the 1880-1900 censuses for the Rappahannock District, Fauquier Co., VA; her husband is listed alone in the 1910 census for Fauquier Co. Fanny Bray died in Fauquier Co. between 1900-10 (she is not mentioned in her sister Mollie's obituary), and is buried in the Cedar Grove Cemetery (no dates), Fauquier Co., VA. William Bray's estate was probated on 31 Jan. 1911, mentioning Miss "I." Bray and William Bray as heirs.

6h. **George Andrew** (twin). Born Nov. 1847 in Prince William Co., VA. See below for full entry.

6i. **Georgianna** (twin). Her name is listed as George Annie in the 1850 census, and as Georgia A. in her obituary. Born Nov. 1847 in Prince William Co., VA. Married as his second wife John Burgess Lewis (her cousin?) on 18 Mar. 1884 in Fauquier Co., VA (he was born about 1836, son of William Buckner Lewis and Jane Lee, and brother of Mary Susan Lewis, who married Georgianna's cousin, James Monroe Burgess), and had children: *Ida Verona* (born 20 July 1887, worked as a housekeeper with her mother for her cousins, and died unmarried on 10 July 1981, aged 93 years, buried next to Zaccheus and Edwin Burgess in the Warrenton Cemetery). Listed with her mother in the 1870 census; she and her daughter are listed in 1910 with her cousin, Addison F. Burgess, working as his housekeeper, and in 1920 with her cousin, Edward L. Burgess, again working as a housekeeper. She died of pneumonia on 25 Feb. 1923 at New Baltimore, Fauquier Co., VA, and is buried in an unmarked grave in the New Baltimore Baptist Church Cemetery.

6j. **Alice (II).** Born Nov. 1849 in Prince William Co., VA. Married as his second wife Edwin Fletcher on 25 July 1876 in Fauquier Co., VA (he was born about 1836 in VA);, and had at least the following children: *John B(urgess?)* (born 1878); *Susanna* (born Dec. 1879, married Daniel Kirwen [he was born Aug. 1875 in VA], and had children: Lucille [born Oct. 1897]; Myrtle M. [born Nov. 1899]). Listed in the 1880-1900 censuses for the Scott District, Fauquier Co., VA (in 1900 with her son-in-law, Daniel Kirwen); listed with the Kirwens in the 1910 census for Loudoun Co., VA. Mentioned in Georgianna's obituary as living at Washington, DC in 1923.

6k. **(Sarah) Elisabeth "Sallie Bettie."** Born 9 June 1853 in Prince William Co., VA. Married ___ Luckett about 1877, and had one daughter: *Ravean C.* (or *C. E.*, according to the 1900 census; she was born Nov. 1878 in WV); she may also have earlier married James W. McDonald on 22 Nov. 1870 in Fauquier Co. Listed with her brother Ras in the 1880 census, and with her brother George in 1900-10 in Greenbrier Co., WV. Sallie Luckett died on 7 May 1924, probably in Greenbrier Co., WV. She is said by family members to have lost her mind.

(from left) Lila D. Burgess, Ashby Burgess Bodine, Herbert Hanback, Mary Alice Burgess, Ola O. Burgess

[William (I)[1], Edward (I)[2], Edward (II)[3], John (II)[4], Moses (III)[5]]

MOLLIE BURGESS
(1843?-1910)

OF GREENBRIER COUNTY, WEST VIRGINIA

6e. **Mary Catherine (II) "Mollie"** *[daughter of Moses (III)].* Born about 1843 in VA. According to an old family story, she was attacked and raped by a field hand named Smith in the summer of 1861, during the unrest caused by the Civil War, and had a son she raised herself. Listed in the 1870 census with her mother, and in 1880 with her sister and brother-in-law, William and Frances Bray; has not been found in 1900, but appears in the 1910 census living with her son; in all of the later censuses, her age and kinship are misrepresented. Mollie died unmarried on 8 May 1910 at Richlands, WV, and is buried with her family in the Calvary Cemetery. Her obituary mentions that she was survived by her sisters, "Mrs. Lewis and Mrs. Fletcher."

The Child of Mollie Burgess:

7a. **(Steven) Vincent** *[son of Mary Catherine (II)].* He is also called S. V. or Vince Burgess in some records. Born 28 Feb. 1862 in Fauquier Co., VA. Married Sarah Jane "Sallie" Crookshanks on 24 Feb. 1881 in Greenbrier Co., WV (she was born 2 July 1855 in Greenbrier Co., daughter of James Crookshanks and Elizabeth Jack, and died there on 29 Aug. 1945). Listed in the 1900-10 censuses for Greenbrier Co., WV, and in 1920 at Lewisburg, Greenbrier Co. living alone (his wife is then living with her daughter, Lelia). Vince Burgess was Sergeant Constable of Lewisburg, WV between 1919-30 (called "Chief" Burgess by all who knew him). He was also a high Mason of the Nobles of the Mystic Shrine. He died in July 1930 at Richlands, WV, and is buried with his wife in the Calvary Cemetery.

8a. **George Lewis.** Born 28 Feb. 1882 at Richlands, WV. See below for full entry.

8b. **Caroline "Carrie."** Born 5 June 1885 at Richlands, WV; died there on 2 Dec. 1895, and is buried in the Calvary Cemetery. According to Kathleen McClung, "she never walked nor talked."

8c. **Lelia Ada.** She was named for the heroine of the novel, *Lelia; or, The Siege of Granada*, by Edward Bulwer-Lytton (New York: Harper & Brothers, 1838). Born 17 Aug. 1888 at Richlands, WV. Married her first cousin, once removed, Taylor Scott Burgess, son of Moses Franklin Burgess, on 2 Jan. 1912 in Greenbrier Co., WV. Listed in the 1920 census for Greenbrier Co., WV. Lelia Burgess gave an account of her life to her granddaughter, Helen McClung. She died on 26 July 1977 at Washington, DC, and is buried in the Calvary Cemetery. See T. S. Burgess's entry for her children.

GEORGE L. BURGESS OF CABELL CO., WEST VIRGINIA
[Steven Vincent[7]]

8a. **George Lewis** *[son of Steven Vincent].* Born 28 Feb. 1882 at Richlands, WV. Married his second cousin once removed, Laura Lorena Cockrill, on 21 Dec. 1904 in Fauquier Co., VA (she was born 15 Feb. 1887 [or 1886] in Fauquier Co., daughter of John Thomas Cockrill and Edmonia Jane Utterback [who was the daughter of Susan Catherine Burgess], and died 1 June 1945 at Barboursville, WV). George Burgess owned a grocery story at Barboursville, Cabell Co., WV. He died there on 26 May 1950, and is buried with his wife in the Oak Lawn Cemetery, Huntington, WV.

9a. **Edmonia Viola.** Born 21 Sept. 1905 at Lewisburg, WV; died there on 15 Mar. 1907.

9b. **Vivian Irene (I).** Born 15 May 1907 at Harvey, Fayette Co., WV. Married Herbert Carl Lantz on 19 Apr. 1926 at Barboursville, WV (he was born 22 June 1902, was a famous football coach, and died 29 Jan. 1969 at Barboursville, buried Oaklawn Cemetery, Huntington, WV), and had children:

Laura Ann LANTZ. Born 7 Nov. 1927 at Farmington, WV, married John Flowers on 4 Oct. 1947 at Huntington, WV (he was born 31 Oct. 1926 at Huntington, son of George David

Flowers and Sarah Virginia Ferrell, and died 15 May 1969 at Point Pleasant, WV, buried Mason, WV), and had children: *John David* (born 3 Mar. 1948 at Huntington, WV, married Donna Lynnette Nash on 2 Nov. 1968 at Southside, WV [she was born 1 Jan. 1950 at Huntington], and had children: Coy Alden [born 21 Aug. 1972 at Huntington]; Cole Hunter [born 22 Oct. 1974 at Huntington]; Melody John [born 8 Nov. 1976 at Huntington]); *William Mac "Billy"* (born 10 Apr. 1950 at Huntington, WV, married Reida Lee Dolittle on 28 Dec. 1974 at Point Pleasant, WV, and had children: Joshua Reid [born Dec. 1986 in Korea]); *Sarah Virginia* (born July 1953 in Huntington, WV, married Monty Wayne Pearson on 11 Dec. 1971 at Henderson, WV, and had children: Wayne; William West; Monica Page).

***Helen Carol* LANTZ.** Born 7 Apr. 1937 at Barboursville, WV, married Paul Elworth Hess on 4 Aug. 1956 at Barboursville (he was born 13 Nov. 1936 at Morgantown, WV), and had children: *Paul Lantz* (born 29 July 1959 at Huntington, married Cynthia Lee Vicars on 20 Oct. 1979 at Oak Hill, WV [she was born 5 Dec. 1958], and had children: Laura Lynn [born 16 Apr. 1980 at Beckley, WV]; Stephen Lantz [born 15 Feb. 1983 at Beckley, WV]); *Teresa Ann* (born 28 July 1961 at Huntington, WV, married Michael Douglas Sauvageot on 29 June 1985 at Oak Hill, WV [he was born 26 Mar. 1962 in Kanawha Co., WV]); *David Barker* (born 14 Oct. 1962 at Huntington, WV, married Trudy Lea Monk on 10 Oct. 1981 at Oak Hill, WV, and had children: Thomas Paul [born 30 Sept. 1983 at Beckley, WV]; Amanda Carol [born 2 June 1987 at Beckley, WV]).

Vivian LANTZ died on 23 Oct. 1976 at Barboursville, WV.

9c. **Emerson Thomas.** Born 29 Mar. 1910 at Turkeyknob, Fayette Co., WV. Married Sadie Ellen Nelson on 20 Dec. 1940 (div.; she remarried Ferdinand Weinberger); married secondly Rebadene Nunnally on 7 Feb. 1958 (she was born 29 June 1915 in WV, and died 9 Apr. 1991 at Sebring, FL). Served in the U.S. Navy in World War II, and received a purple heart. Emerson Burgess worked for a truck parts company at Huntington, WV. He died there on 23 July 1972.

10a. **Dian.** Her name is also spelled Diane. Born 20 Oct. 1939 at Barboursville, Cabell Co., WV. Married ___ Willis (div.); married secondly ___.

9d. **Eloise Burton.** Born 18 Nov. 1921 at Lundale, Logan Co., WV. Married **James Dolliver Burgess** on 20 Dec. 1940 at Ironton, OH (he was born 9 Apr. 1920 at Barboursville, WV, worked as a security guard, and died 17 June 1974 at Huntington, WV, buried Blue Sulphur Cemetery, Ona, WV). Eloise Burgess currently lives at Mesa, AZ.

James Dolliver Burgess was the son of Hiram Grant Burgess [from an unrelated Burgess line] and Lena Mae Browning (married on 29 Aug. 1899 in Logan Co., WV). Hiram Grant Burgess was born 8 Dec. 1868, the son of Cornelius Burgess and Angeline Mullins (married 1867 in Logan Co., WV). Cornelius Burgess was born 1835, the son of Tandy Burgess and Elizabeth Browning (married 1826 in Logan Co., WV). Tandy Burgess was born 1800, the son of Thomas Burgess and Wynna Caudle Key (married 21 Dec. 1789 in Bedford Co., VA). Thomas Burgess was born 1755, the son of William Burgess (whose will was dated 1788 in Bedford Co., VA) and his wife Susanna. The information on James Dolliver's ancestry was supplied by James A. Burgess.

10a. **David Cockrell.** Born and died 20 July 1942 at Barboursville, WV.

10b. **James Anthony (II).** Born 20 Oct. 1943 at Huntington, WV. Married as her second husband Sandra Jeanette "Sandy" Richards on 27 Dec. 1969 at Joseph City, AZ (she was born 7 Oct. 1943 at Phoenix, AZ, daughter of Joseph Glenn Richards and Thelma Lauera Despain, and married firstly Richard Harvie Jordan on 31 Mar. 1963 [div.]). Jim Burgess owns a screen printing plant, Action Apparel and Advertising Specialties, at Mesa, AZ. He also published *Burgess, Mullins, Browning, Brown, and Allied Families*, a history of his own Burgess family (Parsons, WV: McClain Printing Co., 1978). He has contributed greatly to this book.

11a. **Glenn Alan** (ad.). Born 26 Nov. 1963 at Provo, UT. Married Marian Sawyer on 22 Aug. 1982 (div.); married secondly Larissa Aguilar on 5 July 1991 at Chihuahua, México (she was born 2 Sept. 1967 at Casas Grandes, Chihuahua, México). Glenn Burgess owns Visual Information Systems, proprietors of a touch television screen system, at Mesa, AZ.

12a. **Clint Anthony.** Born 22 Feb. 1983 at Mesa, AZ.

11b. **James David "Jim."** Born 27 May 1971 at Huntington, WV.

11c. **Celeste** (nmn). Born 13 July 1973 at Huntington, WV.

11d. **Steven Anthony**. Born 27 Apr. 1976 at Huntington, WV.

10c. **Linda Gail (II)**. Born 6 Mar. 1950 at Huntington, WV. Married Lawrence Eugene Sizemore on 14 June 1968 at Barboursville, WV, and had children: *Laura Gennae* (born 22 Jan. 1974 at Huntington, WV); *Lawrence Eugene Jr.* (born 7 Nov. 1976 at Huntington, WV); *Leslie Grace* (born 3 Nov. 1978 at Huntington, WV). Linda Sizemore lives at Fort Collins, CO.

THE BIOGRAPHY OF LELIA A. BURGESS

"My maternal Grandmother was born in a three-room log house on a farm outside of Lewisburg, West Virginia (Greenbrier County), on August 17, 1888, daughter of Vincent and Sally Jane Burgess. She was named after a heroine of a religious novel of the same name. Her father was a farmer on their 100 acres, on which he grew corn, wheat, and oats. There was a large fruit orchard, cane for molasses, wild berries that grew in abundance, and a creek kept stocked with trout by the government. Their cabin consisted of two bedrooms and a kitchen built over a fruit cellar. The home was heated by coal and wood stoves; clothes were ironed by big red irons which had to be kept constantly heated on the stove. Usually, two were used, one to iron with while the other was heating, then switched as the iron had cooled down. Her mama washed the clothes on a wooden wash board with water carried from the creek and heated on top of the stove. As there was no electricity in the cabin, their light came from kerosene lanterns, and they went to bed soon after dark ("going to bed with the chickens"), and arose with first light. Beds were feather mattresses, lain over straw on wooden planks. Her father cultivated the land with oxen at first, and then later on with horses. Her mother raised vegetable and flower gardens, and spent most of the summer canning vegetables, fruits, and some meats for the harsh winters ahead. Mama believed in three big meals a day for the man who worked in the fields, so the majority of her time was spent in food preparation. Her father owned his own farm, so he was able to come home for dinner in the middle of the day. "Granny," her maternal grandmother, lived with them and helped to raise the children as they came along. The first child was an older brother, George. Next came a sister, Carrie, who due to convulsions at one year resulting from teething, was retarded, and died before she was eight years of age."—Helen McClung, as told to her by Lelia Ada Burgess, 24 Nov. 1971.

Moses Franklin Burgess
(1845-1928)
Alice Virginia Hanback
(1863-1922)
Mrs. Kincaid of Catlett, VA
(relation unknown)

[William (I)^1, Edward (I)^2, Edward (II)^3, John (II)^4, Moses (III)^5]

MOSES FRANKLIN BURGESS
(1845-1928)

OF FAUQUIER COUNTY, VIRGINIA

6f. **Moses Franklin** *[son of Moses (III)]*. Born 9 May 1845 in Prince William Co., VA. Married Lucy Virginia Heflin on 23 Dec. 1875 in Fauquier Co., VA (she was born 15 Mar. 1855, daughter of George William Jackson Heflin and Hannah Hailey, and died 30 Mar. 1888); married secondly Alice Virginia Hanback on 20 May 1891 near Auburn, Fauquier Co., VA (she was born 14 Feb. 1863 in Fauquier Co., daughter of Silas B. Hanback and (Mary) Catherine Thayer, and died on 19 July 1922 in Fauquier Co.). Listed with his mother in the 1870 census, and in the 1880-1920 censuses for Fauquier Co., VA (seven of eight children of Alice survive in 1910). Moses Burgess enlisted in Co. A., Mosby's (43rd) Virginia Cavalry, Confederate Army, surviving numerous battles and raids behind enemy lines. He was a farmer in Fauquier Co., VA. He died on 23 May 1928 in Prince William Co., VA, and is buried in the Oakdale Church Cemetery. His family Bible record survives among the descendants.

The Children of Moses F. Burgess:

7a. **(George William) Wood.** Born 3 Nov. 1876 in Fauquier Co., VA. See below for full entry.

7b. **Carrie Franklin.** Born 18 Jan. 1878 in Fauquier Co., VA; died there on 31 July (or 1 Aug.) 1878.

7c. **James T.** His name is recorded in the official birth records as Moses Franklin Jr. Born 13 Apr. 1879 in Fauquier Co., VA. Married (Lillie) Brownie Neal on 7 Oct. 1903 in Greenbrier Co. (she was born 29 Sept. 1879, remarried William Middleton Walkup on 30 Apr. 1940, and died 3 Apr. 1967). Listed in the 1920 census for Lewisburg, Greenbrier Co., WV. Jim Burgess owned a general store on Route 60 in Greenbrier Co., WV. He died there childless on 21 Apr. 1928; both he and his wife are buried in the Calvary Cemetery.

7d. **Mossie Franklin.** Born 6 Sept. 1880 (or 1881) in Fauquier Co., VA. Married James H. Kincaid on 9 Nov. 1898 in Greenbrier Co., WV (he was born 16 Mar. 1879, and died on 22 Aug. 1963 at Hinton, WV), and had children:

***Mattie** KINCAID.* Born 20 Nov. 1899 in Greenbrier Co., WV, died there on 2 Mar. 1900.

Jessie Mae** KINCAID.* Born 6 July 1902 in Greenbrier Co., married Jesse Clarence Taylor on 1 Oct. 1919 at Sandstone, WV, and had children: *James Lee* (born 4 Mar. 1920 at Sandstone, died 14 Mar. 1920); *Virginia Pearl* (born 27 Feb. 1921 at Sandstone, married Denvil Eddie Tincher on 8 Oct. 1938); *Dainese Ella* (born 25 June 1923 at Sandstone, married Clarence Ames on 6 Mar. 1947, died 28 Aug. 1961); *Imogene Ruth* (born 27 July 1927 at Sandstone, married Fred Lyons); *Betty Josephine* (born 11 July 1928 at Sandstone, married Melvin Samuel O'Brien on 4 Feb. 1952); *Jay Coleman* (born 23 Mar. 1933 at Sandstone). ***Jessie Mae died on 13 Feb. 1947.

***Alice** KINCAID.* Born 19 Jan. 1904 in Greenbrier Co., married Thomas Crowe, and died on 7 Aug. 1978.

***Clara Hazeltine** KINCAID.* Born 29 Aug. 1905 in Greenbrier Co., married Stewart Lee Richmond on 1 Sept. 1922 at Oak Hill, WV, and had children: *James Lee* (born 21 Sept. 1923 at Hinton, WV, married Cecilia Jane Coogan on 1 May 1946); *John Edward* (born 22 Feb. 1926 at Hinton, married Lorna Jean Peterson on 27 Nov. 1946); *Margaret Alta* (born 14 July 1927 at Hinton, died there on 21 Jan. 1930); *Stewart Lee Jr.* (born 7 June 1929 at Hinton, married Eva Blanch Boland on 17 Sept. 1951); *Clara Louise* (born 19 Aug. 1930 at Hinton, married Leonard Nathan Neely on 20 Sept. 1947); *Carl Richard* (born 20 Sept. 1931 at Rutland, OH, married Betty Jean Basham on 16 Jan. 1951).

***Juneta** KINCAID.* Born 20 Sept. 1907 in Summers Co., WV, died there 19 Dec. 1907.

***Frank** KINCAID.* Born 12 Feb. 1909 in Summers Co., died there 1 July 1909.

Alta Louve KINCAID. Born 30 July 1910 in Summers Co., married Henry Gilmore Hutton on 17 Sept. 1929 at Cleveland, OH, had children: *Henry Gilmore Jr.* (born 29 Jan. 1931 at Rutland, OH, married Betty Jane Nunley on 11 Aug. 1951); *Kenneth Dewey* (born 28 Dec. 1933 at Dexter, OH, married Barbara Jean O'Keefe on 19 June 1955); *Doris Yvonne* (born 28 Oct. 1936 at Dexter, OH, married James Melvin McCombs on 19 Jan. 1953); *Marlene Kay* (born 2 Dec. 1938 at Rutland, OH, married George Leonard Rich at 21 Dec. 1956); *Barbara Jane* (born 8 Dec. 1940 at Rutland, OH, married Kenneth Harlan on 19 July 1957); *Herman Harvey* (born 30 June 1942 at Columbus, OH, married Sue Juanita Daniels on 21 Nov. 1961); *Alma Carolyn* (born 7 Aug. 1950 at Columbus, OH, married Roger Mays on 1 Aug. 1967). ***Alta HUTTON*** died on 31 Jan. 1982 at Columbus, OH.

Isabelle KINCAID. Born 20 June 1912 in Summers Co., died there 1 Sept. 1912.

Fred H. KINCAID. Born 25 Mar. 1914 in Summers Co., married Juanita McKinney.

Herman M. KINCAID. Born 5 Mar. 1919 in Summers Co., married Margaret Davis in 1946.

Mossie KINCAID died on 31 Aug. 1966 at Hinton, WV.

7e. **Lue Mat.** Her name may be short for Lucy Martha. Born 26 Mar. 1882 in Fauquier Co., VA; died there on 7 June 1884.

7f. **(Taylor) Scott (I).** Born 13 Sept. 1883 in Fauquier Co., VA. See below for full entry.

7g. **John Edward (I).** Born 10 Dec. 1885 in Fauquier Co., VA. See below for full entry.

7h. **Lucy Virginia (I) "Lue."** Born 14 Feb. 1888 in Fauquier Co., VA. Married Alex F. Williams on 24 July 1907 in Greenbrier Co., WV. Has not been found in the 1910 WV Soundex.

7i. **Ola O.** Born 10 Sept. 1893 in Fauquier Co., VA. Married Henry James Bodine on 28 Dec. 1912 at Washington, DC (he was born 27 Feb. 1889 at Nokesville, VA, son of Enoch Kennedy Bodine and Emma Florence Bryant, and died 24 Dec. 1945 at Washington, DC, buried Greenwich Presbyterian Church Cemetery, near Warrenton, VA), and had children:

Ashby Burgess BODINE. Born 29 Nov. 1913 in Fauquier Co., VA, married Frances Faye "Pat" Bohrer on 1 Aug. 1939 at Washington, DC (she was born 28 Sept. 1918 at Washington, DC, daughter of Alvin Shoemaker Bohrer and Euphemia Fortune "Faye" Cassidy, and died 1 Dec. 1991 at Prince Frederick, Calvert Co., MD), and had children: *Sharon Lynn* (born 6 Apr. 1943 at Washington, DC, married Paul Charles Stanley on 30 Oct. 1960); *Sandra Ann "Sandy"* (born 17 June 1944 at Washington, DC, married Stanley Maphis Haley Jr. on 1 June 1962); *Ashby Burgess II "Budd"* (born 24 June 1947 at Washington, DC, married Linda Jane Sanders on 15 July 1969); *Richard Bruce "Rick"* (born 26 Nov. 1952 at Washington, DC). Ashby Burgess Bodine Sr. died on 3 June 1993 at Port Republic, Calvert Co., MD, and is buried with his wife in the Rock Creek Cemetery, DC.

Robert Bruce "Bob" BODINE. Born 7 Aug. 1919 at Nokesville, TN, married Evelyn Gertrude Ashworth on 16 Nov. 1946 at Four Corners, MD (she was born 23 Mar. 1925 at Roanoke, VA, daughter of John Benjamin Ashworth and Pearl Belle Martin), and had children: *Robert Darryll "Bob"* (born 7 May 1947 at Washington, DC, married Georgette (Shanley) Owen on 12 May 1972, and secondly Karen Sue Hardy on 21 Oct. 1978); *John Scott* (born and died 22 Nov. 1952 at Cincinnati, OH); *(Linda) Renée* (born 10 Apr. 1954 at Cincinnati, OH, married Denton Hollis Rocky Jr. on 5 Feb. 1972, and secondly James Andrew Meador on 16 June 1982); *Randall Clay "Randy"* (born 17 Feb. 1956 at Bluefield, WV).

Ola BODINE died on 22 Apr. 1951 at Washington, DC, and is buried there in the Rock Creek Cemetery. Evelyn Ashworth Bodine currently lives at Roanoke, VA, and has contributed greatly to this book.

7j. **(Cleary) Franklin.** Born 29 Apr. 1895 at Catlett, Fauquier Co., VA. See below for full entry.

7k. **DeWitt Talmadge.** Born 21 Sept. 1896 at Alban, Fauquier Co., VA. See below for full entry.

7l. **Mary Alice (III).** Born 20 Jan. 1898 (or 1900, according to her tombstone) in Fauquier Co., VA. Married Herbert Hanback at Washington, DC; married secondly Clarence W. "Jack" Beggs (he was born 1903, and died 1957); married thirdly Sam Holiday. Mary Holiday died in 1962 at Warrenton, VA, and is buried with her second husband in the Rock Creek Park Cemetery, Washington, DC.

7m. **Lila Douglas.** Born 12 Oct. 1900 (or 1901) in Fauquier Co., VA. Married Alvin Suttle at Washington, DC; married secondly Fred Sonneman. Lila Sonneman died in Mar. 1978 at Silver Springs, MD.

7n. **Maud Virginia.** Her name is also spelled Maude. Born 12 Aug. 1902 in Fauquier Co., VA. Married Roy Hunt at Washington, DC; married secondly ___ King. Listed in the 1945/46 city directory of Washington, DC with her first husband. Maud King currently lives in a rest home in Maryland.

7o. **Ada Roosevelt.** Born 12 Oct. 1904 in Fauquier Co., VA. Married secondly Nat Karasik. Ada Karasik died in July 1989 at Adelphi, MD, and is buried in the George Washington Cemetery.

WOOD BURGESS OF WASHINGTON, DC
[Moses Franklin[6]]

7a. **(George William) Wood** *[son of Moses Franklin].* He was named for his grandfather, George William Jackson Heflin. Born 3 Nov. 1876 in Fauquier Co., VA. Married Clara Kraft on 27 Aug. 1920 at Washington, DC (she was born about 1892 at Baltimore, MD [age thirty in 1922], remarried John Hammond, and died on 11 July 1927 at Washington, DC, buried Mount Olivet Cemetery). Listed in the 1920 at Washington, DC. Wood Burgess worked as a chauffeur for the city of Washington, DC. He died on 1 Mar. 1923 at Washington, and is buried there in the Mount Olivet Cemetery.

8a. **Lucy Virginia (II).** Born 18 June 1921 at Washington, DC; died there on 20 June 1921, and is buried with her parents in the Mount Olivet Cemetery.

8b. **(George) William (II) "Bill."** Born 8 July 1922 at Washington, DC. After his parents' early death, he was sent to Lewisburg, WV, and raised by his Burgess aunts and uncles, living first with John E. Burgess and then with John's brother, Taylor Scott Burgess. Married Elizabeth Louise "Betty" Schneider on 27 Nov. 1948 at Washington, DC. Bill Burgess has worked as an FBI agent, as a Superintendent of Labor Relations for Union Carbide, and for the Atomic Energy Commission. He later worked as Deputy Director of the Security Division, U.S. Dept. of Energy, at the nuclear sites at Oak Ridge, TN, and since his retirement has served as a part-time security consultant.

9a. **Linda Louise (II).** Born 5 Dec. 1949 at Le Mars, IA. Married (Walter) Lee Payne on 4 June 1973 at Memphis, TN (he works as a dentist), and had children: *Brandon Christopher* (born 26 Oct. 1979 at Fairbanks, AK); *Lauren Ashleigh* (born 5 June 1983 at Fairbanks, AK). Linda Payne is a nurse at Fairbanks, AK.

9b. **Susan Ann (I).** Born 8 July 1951 at Le Mars, IA. Married Joseph Bicknell Marshall (div.), and had children: *Shannon Christine* (born 7 Nov. 1970 at Oak Ridge, TN; she works as an aeronautical engineer); *Rebecca Ann* (born 24 Mar. 1975 at Oak Ridge, TN; she currently attends the University of Tennessee at Chattanooga); married secondly L. William Varner Jr. (President of Zellweger Uster, Inc.). Susan Varner lives at Knoxville, TN.

9c. **Thomas William (II).** Born 27 July 1954 at Kingsport, TN. Tom Burgess works as a mechanical engineer for the Oak Ridge National Laboratory at Oak Ridge, TN.

9d. **Ann Louise.** Born 14 Oct. 1956 at Oak Ridge, TN. Married David Stewart (the manager of a Dodge Plymouth dealership). Ann Stewart is a dental hygienist at Oak Ridge, TN.

9e. **Mary Kathryn.** Born 11 Nov. 1957 at Oak Ridge, TN. Married Gary Hillis (div.), and had children: *(Samuel) Ryan* (born 27 Oct. 1979 at Oak Ridge, TN). Mary Burgess is a dental assistant at Oak Ridge, TN.

9f. **William Joseph.** Born 18 Mar. 1962 at Oak Ridge, TN. Married Tracy Jones in Apr. 1992. Bill Burgess is a mechanical engineer with Tennessee Eastman Corp., Kingsport, TN.

9g. **Janet Clare.** Born 6 Aug. 1965 at Oak Ridge, TN. Married Matthew Thornton on 21 Oct. 1989 at Oak Ridge, TN. Janet Thornton obtained her master's degree from the University of Tennessee College of Agriculture. She and her husband both work at the Agriculture Research Center, Greenville, MS.

SCOTT BURGESS OF GREENBRIER CO., WEST VIRGINIA
[Moses Franklin[6]]

7f. **(Taylor) Scott (I)** *[son of Moses Franklin].* Born 13 Sept. 1883 (or 1884, according to his tombstone) in Fauquier Co., VA. Married his first cousin, once removed, Lelia Ada Burgess on 2 Jan. 1911 in Greenbrier Co., WV (she was born 17 Aug. 1888 at Richlands, WV, the daughter of (Steven) Vincent Burgess and Sarah Jane Crookshanks, and died 26 July 1977 at Washington, DC). Listed in the 1910 census living with his future father-in-law, Vincent Burgess, and in 1920 at Lewisburg, Greenbrier Co., WV. Scott Burgess was a farmer in Greenbrier Co. He died there on 17 Feb. 1945, and is buried in the Calvary Cemetery.

8a. **Vincent Franklin.** Born 22 Nov. 1912 at Lewisburg, WV. See below for full entry.

8b. **Kenneth Lee.** Born 15 Dec. 1915 at Lewisburg, WV. See below for full entry.

8c. **Taylor Scott (II).** Born 4 Dec. 1917 at Lewisburg, WV. See below for full entry.

8d. **Sara Virginia.** Her name is listed as Sarah in the 1920 census. Born 19 Dec. 1919 at Lewisburg, WV. Married Raymond M. Lambert on 17 Oct. 1942 at Washington, DC (he died on 24 Nov. 1968), and had children: *Barbara Lee* (born 27 July 1943, married Jeffrey Lee Eagle on 24 Aug.

1963, and had children: Carrie Lee [born 29 Jan. 1964]; Lance Lee [born 20 Aug. 1969]); *Raymond Burgess* (born 25 Aug. 1944, and died in an automobile accident on 3 Sept. 1961); *Nancy V.* (born 11 Mar. 1952, married David R. Schwieson on 17 June 1972, and had children: Kirsten Ann [born 23 June 1979]; Paul David [born 17 Apr. 1982]). Sara married secondly James Nalley on 23 Jan. 1982 at Bowie, MD (he was born 14 July 1912, and died 20 Oct. 1988 at Bowie, MD). Sara Nalley is a former cashier at a food chain store. She now lives retired at Bowie, MD.

8e. **Beard Brown.** Born 31 Dec. 1921 at Lewisburg, WV. See below for full entry.

8f. **Kathleen Lorina.** Born 17 Feb. 1924 at Lewisburg, WV. Married Lillis Hill "Did" McClung, a cousin of the author's wife, Mary Wickizer Burgess, on 13 Feb. 1944 at Clifton Fords, VA (he was born 16 Feb. 1912, son of Newman B. McClung and Lucy H. Shumate, and died 5 Nov. 1986 at Frankford, WV), and had children: *Helen Joyce* (born 14 Sept. 1945 in Greenbrier Co., WV). Kathleen McClung was a secretary to the printers of Columbia First Federal Savings and Loan Association, Washington, DC, retiring in 1988. With her daughter, Helen McClung (a cousin to both the author *and* his wife), she settled in Laurel, MD, a few blocks from the author's stepdaughter, (Mary) Louise Reynnells. She then worked as a babysitter for the author's stepgrandson, Russell Edward Reynnells, from his birth in 1989 until her death. She and her daughter have contributed greatly to this book, drawing from their reminiscences, photographs, documents, and access to other family members. Kathleen McClung died on 12 Apr. 1992 at Laurel, MD; she was buried in the Burgess section of the Calvary Cemetery, Lewisburg, WV. She is greatly missed.

8g. **George William (III)** (twin). Born 17 Nov. 1926 at Lewisburg, WV. See below for full entry.

8h. **Isabell Mae "Bobbie"** (twin). Born 17 Nov. 1926 at Lewisburg, WV. Married Shelton W. Thigpen on 12 Dec. 1960 in North Carolina (he owns an accounting firm), and had children: *Dwayne Scott* (born 28 Aug. 1961). Bobbie Thigpen is an accounting assistant for her husband's firm at Silver Spring, MD.

8i. **Elizabeth Faye "Libby."** Born 1 Mar. 1929 at Lewisburg, WV. Married Alfred Sumner Hack on 28 Jan. 1950 at Washington, DC (he retired from the Metropolitan Police Department as a Lieutenant in 1984; he was later assigned as an investigator with the House of Representatives Select Committee on the assassinations of John F. Kennedy and Martin Luther King; he remarried Kay Ann Kramer on 18 Oct. 1980 at Roanoke, VA [she was born 25 June 1942; she worked as a special agent with the Federal Bureau of Investigation and the National Security Agency]), and had children:

Beverly Ann HACK. Born 22 Sept. 1955 at Washington, DC, married Robert Bess on 14 Oct. 1989 at Andrews Air Force Base, MD (he is a retired Chief Petty Officer in the U.S. Navy), received two degrees in public health and dental hygiene in 1976 and 1983 from East Tennessee State University, and works as a forensic psychophysiologist (polygraph examiner) with the Department of Defense; they live at Waldorf, MD.

John Robert HACK. Born 11 June 1958 at Washington, DC, married Susan Egan Dalsey on 15 Oct. 1988 at Laurel, MD, and had children: *Brandon Alfred* (born 13 June 1990); *Brian Austin* (born 15 Jan. 1993). John R. Hack graduated from Prince Georges Community College in 1978 and the University of Maryland in 1980, majoring in criminal justice; he joined the Montgomery County Police Department in 1982, and is currently a polygraph examiner assigned to the Forensic Science Division; Susan Hack works for Sprint as an event planner. They currently live at Brookeville, MD.

Libby HACK was a school bus driver in Maryland. She died on 19 Jan. 1980 at Oxon Hill, MD, and is buried in National Memorial Park Cemetery, Falls Church, VA.

8j. **Charlotte Ann.** Born 13 July 1931 at Lewisburg, WV. Married Paul D. Maynard on 16 May 1952 at Washington, DC (div.), and had children: *Gary D.* (born 14 Oct. 1954 at Columbia, MD). Charlotte married secondly George L. Ford on 7 Apr. 1961 at Washington, DC (div.), and had children: *Laura Jean* (born 24 May 1962, married Raymond Planas on 17 Nov. 1983); *Jeffery Porter* (born 16 May 1963). Charlotte Ford works as a clerk for the Student Loan Dept. of the University of Maryland. She lives at Laurel, MD.

VINCENT BURGESS OF WASHINGTON, DC

[Moses Franklin^6, Taylor Scott (I)^7]

8a. **Vincent Franklin** *[son of Taylor Scott (I)].* Born 22 Nov. 1912 at Lewisburg, WV. Married Mary Cecelia "Mae" Chambers on 18 Sept. 1939 at Washington, DC (she was born 17 Feb. 1917 at Washington, DC). Vincent Burgess was a bus driver for the DC Transit System at Washington, DC. He died there on 11 Dec. 1959, and is buried in the Mount Olivet Cemetery, Washington, DC.

9a. **Edward Vincent.** Born 21 Feb. 1942 at Washington, DC. Married Barbara Ann Klotz on 14 Dec. 1963 at Baltimore, MD (she was born 10 Sept. 1940 at Baltimore, MD, daughter of Eric Joseph Klotz and Esther Murray). Edward Burgess works for C&P Telephone Co. in Maryland.

10a. **David Vincent.** Born 17 Sept. 1964 at Washington, DC. Married Milne Dawn Reichard on 14 Nov. 1992 at Chapel Point, MD. David Burgess works as a salesman for Builders Supply and Lumber, La Plata, MD.

10b. **Joan Marie.** Born 14 Oct. 1966 at Washington, DC. Joan Burgess works as a collector for the NAFA Credit Union, Bowie, MD.

10c. **Stephen Paul** (ad.). Born 11 Jan. 1970 at Washington, DC. Married Hollie Reilly on 26 Sept. 1990 at Ironsides, MD.

11a. **Samantha Renée**. Born 26 Jan. 1990 at Clinton, MD.

10d. **Emily Elaine.** Born 18 Sept. 1973 at Washington, DC. Emily Burgess is a secretary for the Federal Bureau of Investigation.

9b. **James Steven (I).** Born 10 May 1947 at Washington, DC. Married Laura Lee Thomas on 27 July 1968 in Prince Georges Co., MD (she was born 7 May 1947 at Washington, DC). Jim Burgess is a certified public accountant at Leesburg, VA.

10a. **Gregory Vincent.** Born 19 May 1969 at Washington, DC.
10b. **Mark Steven (II).** Born 25 Feb. 1971 at Washington, DC.
10c. **Sarah Marie.** Born 29 May 1975 at Woodbridge, VA.
10d. **Matthew Lee (I).** Born 5 Mar. 1977 at Leesburg, VA.

9c. **Ann Cecelia.** Born 6 Jan. 1951 at Washington, DC. Married Joseph J. Bauer on 19 Sept. 1970 (div.), and had children: *Joseph Vincent* (born 25 Jan. 1973 at Washington, DC); *Jacqueline Marie* (born 16 July 1975 at Washington, DC); married secondly Juan Michael Kellar on 18 June 1983, and had children: *Jill Ann* (born 21 Nov. 1984 at Washington, DC).

9d. **Michael William.** Born 20 July 1954 at Washington, DC. Married Nancy D. Howe on 10 Jan. 1981. Michael W. Burgess is a business manager at Georgetown, Washington, DC.

10a. **Alison Marie.** Born 21 May 1983 at Fairfax, VA.
10b. **Katherine Louise (II) "Katie."** Born 4 June 1986 at Fairfax, VA.
10c. **Andrew Michael.** Born 30 Nov. 1992 at Fairfax, VA.

KENNETH BURGESS OF HERNANDO CO., FLORIDA

[Moses Franklin[6], Taylor Scott (I)[7]]

8b. **Kenneth Lee** *[son of Taylor Scott (I)].* Born 15 Dec. 1915 at Lewisburg, WV. Married Betty Woodward on 7 Aug. 1946 at Bradbury Heights, MD; married secondly Delores Irene Martin on 18 June 1949 at Washington, DC (she was born 3 Oct. 1921). Served in the Air Force during World War II. Kenneth Burgess worked for the Art Department of the *Washington Post* newspaper between 1936-41 and 1945-79. He currently lives retired at Spring Hill, FL.

9a. **Lawrence Martin "Larry"** (ad.). Born 21 Oct. 1947. Married Hedy Ann ___ on 21 Oct. 1979 (she was born 17 Dec. 1953). Larry Burgess works for Eastern Airlines in Florida.

10a. **Jeremy Charles.** Born 14 Dec. 1980.

9b. **Mark Wayne.** Born 26 Mar. 1953 at Poolesville, MD. Married Marsha Ann Reeves on 25 Jan. 1975 (she was born 27 Jan. 1951). Mark W. Burgess is a heavy equipment operator at Harpers Ferry, WV.

10a. **Keisha Marie.** Born 31 Dec. 1978 in WV.
10b. **Zachary Scott.** Born 15 Oct. 1981 in WV.

T. S. BURGESS OF PRINCE GEORGES CO., MARYLAND

[Moses Franklin^6, Taylor Scott (I)^7]

8c. **Taylor Scott (II) "T. S."** *[son of Taylor Scott (I)].* Born 4 Dec. 1917 at Lewisburg, WV. Married Irene Arnold on 3 Sept. 1946 in Kentucky (div.); married secondly Theda (Cooper) Burgess on 24 Dec. 1974 at Oxon Hill, MD (she was the widow of his brother, Beard Burgess). T. S. Burgess was a metropolitan bus driver. He currently lives retired at Temple Hill, MD.

9a. **Douglas Scott (I).** Born 15 Aug. 1954 at Forestville, MD. Married Kathleen O'Hara on 19 Mar. 1977 (div.; she was a sister of Margaret O'Hara [who married his brother, Steven]). Doug Burgess was an agent with the Drug Enforcement Administration, at Washington, DC. He was killed there on 13 (or 14) July 1986, and is buried in the Washington National Cemetery.

10a. **Taryn O'Hara.** Born 30 July 1978 in MD.

9b. **Steven Ray (I).** Born 13 May 1957 at Forestville, MD. Married Margaret O'Hara on 19 Jan. 1979 (she was a sister of Kathleen O'Hara [who married his brother, Douglas]). Steven R. Burgess is a Staff Sergeant with the U.S. Army, currently stationed at Ft. Belvoir, VA.

10a. **Steven Ray "Stevie" (II).** Born 8 Mar. 1980 at Stuttgart, West Germany.
10b. **Stephanie Lynn.** Born 22 Sept. 1983 at Washington, DC.

BEARD BURGESS OF WOOD CO., WEST VIRGINIA

[Moses Franklin^6, Taylor Scott (I)^7]

8e. **Beard Brown** *[son of Taylor Scott (I)].* Born 31 Dec. 1921 at Lewisburg, WV. Married Theda Cooper on 4 Aug. 1943 in Wyoming (she remarried his brother, T. S. Burgess, after Beard's death). Beard Burgess worked for Hope Gas Co. He died on 8 Feb. 1965 at Parkersburg, WV, and is buried there.

9a. **Lois Kay.** Born 10 Dec. 1945 at Parkersburg, WV. Married Charles G. Morris on 26 June 1967, and had children: *Mary Denise* (born 19 Aug. 1969); *Christopher G.* (born 25 Feb. 1971). Lois Morris is a school teacher at Keyser, WV.

GEORGE W. BURGESS OF LOUDOUN CO., VIRGINIA

[Moses Franklin^6, Taylor Scott (I)^7]

8g. **George William (III)** (twin) *[son of Taylor Scott (I)].* Born 17 Nov. 1926 at Lewisburg, WV. Married Betsy Richards on 17 Nov. 1950. Served in the U.S. Army in World War II. George Burgess was a mobile lounge leader for the Federal Aviation Administration at Dulles Airport, in Northern Virginia. He died on 25 Dec. 1983 at Leesburg, VA, and is buried in the Hillsboro Cemetery.

9a. **Colin Glenn.** Born 23 Sept. 1966 at Manassas, VA. Married Lisa Michele Carpenter on 20 June 1987. Colin Burgess works for the Leesburg Veterinary Hospital, Leesburg, VA.

JOHN E. BURGESS OF GREENBRIER CO., WEST VIRGINIA

[Moses Franklin^6]

7g. **John Edward (II)** *[son of Moses Franklin].* Born 10 Dec. 1885 (or 1886) in Prince William Co., VA. Married Rhoda Mae Morris on 19 Dec. 1911 in Greenbrier Co., WV (she was born 5 May 1889, and died 25 Nov. 1974). Listed in the 1910 census for Greenbrier Co, WV living with J. Washington Price, and in 1920 there with his family. John Burgess was a farmer in Greenbrier Co. near Lewisburg, WV. He died there on 17 May 1937, and is buried in the Calvary Cemetery.

8a. **(Mary) Ellen (IX) "Ella."** Born 17 Sept. 1912 in Greenbrier Co., WV. Ella Burgess drowned on 14 July 1914, when she fell into a cistern, and is buried in the Calvary Cemetery.
8b. **Louise Virginia (I).** Born 9 Feb. 1914 in Greenbrier Co., WV. Married Raymond Jesse Zicafoose on 23 Oct. 1932 in Greenbrier Co. (he was born 30 Oct. 1908, and died in May 1985 at Lewisburg, WV). Louise Zicafoose died childless on 6 June 1977 in Greenbrier Co., WV, and is buried in the Calvary Cemetery.

8c. **James Edward (IV).** Born 7 Apr. 1916 in Greenbrier Co., WV. Married Mary Alice Patton on 23 Oct. 1940 in Greenbrier Co. James Burgess died on 14 Nov. 1980 at Lewisburg, WV, and is buried there in the Memorial Gardens.

9a. **May Murneen.** Born 8 Jan. 1933 in Greenbrier Co., WV, daughter of Ethel May Flanagan.

9b. **Anita Mae.** Born 17 Oct. 1946 at Clifton Forge, VA. Married Dr. Joseph Emmett Shaver on 2 Aug. 1969 in Greenbrier Co., WV, and had children: *Britton* (born 18 June 1973); *Todd* (born Oct. 1974).

8d. **Robert Clarence.** Born 11 Sept. 1918 in Greenbrier Co., WV. Married Edith Muriel Vaughn in 1938. Robert C. Burgess was a security guard at the Greenbrier Hotel, White Sulpher Springs, WV. He died there on 25 Oct. 1972, and is buried in the Calvary Cemetery, Greenbrier Co.

9a. **Norma Gaye.** Born 18 Feb. 1941 in Greenbrier Co., WV. Married James R. Harrah on 9 May 1959, and had children: *Janet Lynne* (born 23 Feb. 1960, married Richard D. Waid on 17 June 1978, and had children: Jason Richard [born 4 Dec. 1984]; Erica LeAnn [born 12 May 1988]; Tyler Christian [born 30 Aug. 1991]); *Lori Gaye* (born 1 Dec. 1962, married Timothy J. Vallandingham on 22 May 1982, and had children: (Timothy) Chad [born 6 Mar. 1991]); *Sharon Leigh* (born 13 Oct. 1967, married Steven W. Whited on 13 Aug. 1988, and had children: Kayla LeAnn [born 29 Jan. 1993]).

9b. **Stephen Robert.** Born 15 Oct. 1949 at Covington, VA. Married Rebecca Middleton on 24 Aug. 1979 in Greenbrier Co., WV. Steve Burgess works as a production coordinator for Westvaco Corp. at Covington, VA. He currently lives in Allegheny Co., VA.

10a. **Sarah Beth.** Born 1984.

9c. **Nancy Jane (V).** Born 19 Feb. 1952 at Covington, VA. Married Donald S. Wiseman on 1 July 1972 in Greenbrier Co., WV (div.); married secondly Dr. Steven A. Smith on 26 May 1985 in Greenbrier Co., and had children: *Brandon Steven* (born 5 Jan. 1988); *Brittany Charlene* (born 9 Aug. 1990).

8e. **Hilda Mae.** Born 30 June 1920 in Greenbrier Co., WV. Married Hamilton C. Beall in 1937, and had children: *Carol Ann* (born 1946, married Ray Hanna, and had children: Kevin Ray [born 1971]). Hilda Beall lives at Lewisburg, WV. She has contributed greatly to this history.

FRANK BURGESS OF WASHINGTON, DC

[Moses Franklin[6]]

7j. **(Cleary) Frank(lin)** *[son of Moses Franklin].* Born 29 Apr. 1895 in Fauquier Co., VA. Married Lou French McLearen on 25 Nov. 1914 at Washington, DC (she was born 4 Dec. 1894 at Catlett, VA, daughter of Horace Marshall McLearen and Cynthia Ann Mark, and died 4 June 1973 at Fredericksburg, VA). Listed in the 1920 census for Washington, DC, and in the city directories there from 1923-32. Frank Burgess died on 26 June 1957 at Salisbury, MD.

8a. **Clinton Franklin (I).** Born 1 May 1916 at Catlett, Fauquier Co., VA. Married Vivian Elaine Woodworth on 2 Sept. 1939 in Fauquier Co., VA (she was born 14 Nov. 1916 at Washington, DC, daughter of John Ruben Woodworth and Ethel Arrison, and died on 23 Jan. 1941 at Washington, DC); married secondly Wilma Louverne Hernandez on 7 Mar. 1947 at Washington, DC (she was born 23 Aug. 1923 at Tarpon Springs, FL, daughter of Charles Emmanuel Hernandez and Sarah Susannah Brady). Clinton Burgess was Executive Director of the State Attorney's Office, Tampa, FL. He currently lives retired at Lafayette, LA.

9a. **Linda Lee.** Born 23 Jan. 1941 at Washington, DC. Married Charles McGoldrick, and secondly Robert L. Gibney, and thirdly ___ Hay.

9b. **Clinton Franklin (II).** Born 14 Dec. 1947 at Washington, DC; he died there on 15 Dec. 1947, and is buried in the Vereen Cemetery, Pasco Co., FL.

9c. **Robert Clinton "Buzz."** Born 12 Feb. 1955 at Tampa, FL. Married Marcia Ann Galvez on 31 May 1981 at Tampa, FL (div. 1983); married secondly Cathleen Mary Homb on 3 Mar. 1984 at Tampa, FL (she was born 12 Feb. 1957 at Monroe, WI, daughter of Raymond John Homb and Betty Belle Johnson). Buzz Burgess is currently Projects Manager for GTE at Dallas, TX.

10a. **Bradley Robert.** Born 1 May 1986 at Durham, NC.
10b. **Bryan Allen.** Born 31 Dec. 1987 at Durham, NC.

9d. **Rebecca Louverne.** Born 18 July 1957 at Tampa, FL. Married William Brent Young on 9 July 1978 and 30 Oct. 1979 (div.); married secondly Jerry Wayne Moore on 22 Dec. 1981 (div.; he was born 23 June 1949 at Scotts Hill, TN, son of James Fletcher Moore and Dorothy Jean Lancaster), and had children: *Sarah Fletcher* (born 3 Sept. 1982 at Nashville, TN); *Jerry Wayne Jr.* (born 28 Feb. 1984 at Lafayette, LA); married thirdly David Rhoton on 10 Sept. 1993 at Maui, HI.

8b. **Elizabeth May "Betty."** Born 2 Jan. 1918 at Catlett, VA. Married Winfred Lewis Brooks on 4 Mar. 1939 (div. 1974; he was born 10 May 1918 at Sweet Springs, WV, son of Artis Brooks and Mary Harrow), and had children: *Stephen Wayne* (born 29 Apr. 1942 at Washington, DC, married (Carol) Diane Tarbett on 7 Sept. 1963 [she was born 15 Mar. 1943 at Silver Spring, MD, daughter of William Tarbett and Mildred Haskin], and had children: Michael Stephen [born 9 Sept. 1965 at Silver Spring, MD, married Tammy ___, and had children: Laura Ashley {born 17 Mar. 1991}]; Douglas Wayne [born 5 Mar. 1970 at Silver Spring, MD]; Melissa Diane [born 12 Aug. 1977 at Silver Spring, MD]; Jason Travis [born 2 Sept. 1979 at Silver Spring, MD]); *James Allan* (born 1 Aug. 1944 at Washington, DC, married Judy Anderson on 28 Dec. 1968 [div.], and had children: Janet Elizabeth [born 8 Apr. 1971]; Jeffrey Stephen [born 9 Mar. 1974]; *James* married secondly Annabelle "Abby" (Goldkind) Lotenberg on 22 Feb. 1979 [she was born 26 Apr. 1947 at Washington, DC, daughter of Aaron and Rosalie Goldkind]); *Sharyn Elaine* (born 2 Sept. 1946 at Washington, DC, married Abraham "Abe" Gelber on 9 Oct. 1965 [div.], and had children: (Nathan) Eric [born 23 Mar. 1967 at Silver Spring, MD]; *Sharyn* married secondly Michael Krensky on 22 Dec. 1974 [div.], and thirdly Howard "Skip" Fry on 23 Feb. 1982). Betty Brooks currently lives at Silver Spring, MD.

DeWITT T. BURGESS OF WASHINGTON, DC
[Moses Franklin[6]]

7k. **DeWitt Talmadge** *[son of Moses Franklin]*. He was named for a well-known minister of the same name. Born 21 Sept. 1896 at Alban, VA. Married Geneva E. Fletcher on 29 Sept. 1920 in Fauquier Co. (she was born about 1894, and lived at Bealeton, VA). DeWitt T. Burgess was a railroad brakeman at Washington, DC. He died there in 1972.

8a. **DeWitt Fletcher "Dee."** Born 29 Mar. 1925 at Washington, DC. Married Mildred Yeatts on 7 Nov. 1952. Dee Burgess worked as a bus driver for Capital Transit before retiring. He now lives at Arlington, VA.

9a. **Karen Lynn (I).** Born 11 Mar. 1955 at Arlington, VA. Married secondly Michael A. Cosner. Karen Cosner currently lives at Keeling, VA.

8b. **Mildred Genevieve.** Born 6 Nov. 1928 at Washington, DC. Married William J. "Bruce" Hanback on 30 Nov. 1946 in Fauquier Co., VA (he was born about 1924 at Warrenton, VA). Mildred Hanback currently lives at Warrenton, VA.

[William (I)[1], Edward (I)[2], Edward (II)[3], John (II)[4], Moses (III)[5]]

GEORGE A. BURGESS
(1847-1910)

OF GREENBRIER COUNTY, WEST VIRGINIA

6h. **George Andrew** (twin) *[son of Moses (III)].* Born Nov. 1847 in Prince William Co., VA. Married Margaret F. "Maggie" Ford on 22 Feb. 1882 in Greenbrier Co., WV (she was born about 1860, daughter of James Ford, and died on 16 Feb. 1900 at Lewisburg; "she was lying in front of the fire asleep, and when she awoke her clothing was on fire; she ran out to her husband, but was badly burned"). Listed in the 1870 census with his mother, and in 1900-10 in Greenbrier Co., WV. George Burgess was a butcher at Lewisburg, WV. He died there on 16 Jan. 1910, from injuries suffered after being kicked by a horse, and is buried with his wife in the Calvary Cemetery.

The Children of George A. Burgess:

7a. **Wood Albert.** Born 1 Jan. 1883 at Richlands, Greenbrier Co., WV. See below for full entry.
7b. **Grover Cleveland.** Born 2 Dec. 1884 at Richlands, Greenbrier Co., WV. See below for full entry.
7c. **John Edward (III).** Born 4 Nov. 1887 at Richlands, Greenbrier Co., WV; died there on 1 Nov. 1893.
7d. **Son.** Born and died 10 Nov. 1889 at Richlands, Greenbrier Co., WV.
7e. **Vincent Lilburn "Dude."** Born 18 Mar. 1891 at Richlands, Greenbrier Co., WV. See below for full entry.
7f. **Grace Lewis.** Born 23 Dec. 1894 (or 1893) at Richlands, Greenbrier Co., WV. Married James Guy Levisay on 20 Mar. 1916 in Greenbrier Co. (he died 1958), and had at least one daughter: *Mildred* (who married Oscar King). Grace Levisay died on 19 July 1987 at Frankford, WV, aged 92 years, and is buried there. Her daughter, Mildred King, currently lives at Frankford, WV.
7g. **Gertrude Rebecca.** Born 5 Mar. 1897 at Richlands, Greenbrier Co., WV. Married Ross B. Hanna on 3 Feb. 1923 in Greenbrier Co.; married secondly Carl McClung. Listed in the 1920 census living with her uncle, Lilburn Crookshanks, at Frankford, Greenbrier Co., WV. Gertrude McClung died in 1975 at Weston, WV, and is buried in the Calvary Cemetery.

WOOD BURGESS OF GREENBRIER CO., WEST VIRGINIA
[George Andrew[6]]

7a. **Wood Albert** *[son of George Andrew].* Born 1 Jan. 1883 (or 31 Dec. 1881, according to Social Security records) in Greenbrier Co., WV. Married Cecil Virginia Brant on 19 Nov. 1908 at Greenbrier Co. (she was born 22 Apr. 1885, and died 21 Mar. 1941). Listed in the 1900-20 censuses for Lewisburg, Greenbrier Co., WV (in 1900 with James M. Rader). Wood Burgess was a farmer all of his life in Greenbrier Co.; his land was located across the road from Calvary Cemetery, where many Burgess relatives are buried. He died there on 25 Nov. 1962 of injuries received when he was hit by an automobile, and is buried with his wife in the Calvery Cemetery.

8a. **Ray Lewis "Tootie."** Born 10 Sept. 1909 in Greenbrier Co., WV. Tootie Burgess was a farmer on his father's lands in Greenbrier Co., WV. He died unmarried in 1990 at the Veterans Administration Hospital, Beckley, WV, and is buried in the Calvary Cemetery across from his farm.
8b. **(Margaret) Lucille (II).** Born 5 Sept. 1911 in Greenbrier Co., WV. Married Vernon Slayton (who died about 1966). Lucille Slayton was a nurse at Lewisburg, WV. She died there on 12 Aug. 1991.

GROVER BURGESS OF GREENBRIER CO., WEST VIRGINIA
[George Andrew[6]]

7b. **Grover Cleveland (I)** *[son of George Andrew].* His name is listed as James C. Burgess in the 1900 census. Born 2 Dec. 1884 in Greenbrier Co., WV. Married Lillie Withrow on 27 Sept. 1911 in Greenbrier Co. (she was born 27 June 1891, and died on 30 Oct. 1967). Listed in the 1910 census for Greenbrier Co., WV working for Dora S. Skaggs, and in 1920 at Lewisburg, Greenbrier Co. Grover Burgess was a farmer, and worked in later life for the West Virginia State Department of Roads. He died on 30 Aug. 1947 in Greenbrier Co., and is buried with his wife in the Calvary Cemetery.

8a. **(James) Ross(er).** Born 31 Aug. 1912 in Greenbrier Co., WV. He stepped on a nail, and died three weeks later of lockjaw on 16 June 1923, and is buried in the Calvary Cemetery.

8b. **Daughter.** Born 6 June 1914 in Greenbrier Co., WV; died there on 14 June 1914, and is buried in the Calvary Cemetery.

8c. **Reba M.** Born 16 June 1915 in Greenbrier Co., WV. Married Herman Hicks. Reba Hicks died about 1950 at Covington, VA.

8d. **Beulah Mae (II).** Born 8 Mar. 1917 at Lewisburg, WV. Married George Oliver Davis on 4 Aug. 1946 in Greenbrier Co.; married secondly Warren Hamilton. Beulah Hamilton died 1954 at Lewisburg, WV, and is buried in the Calvary Cemetery.

8e. **Grace Virginia.** Born 28 July 1919 at Lewisburg, VA. Married Forrest Hurt. Grace Hurt died on 11 June 1990 at Tustin, CA.

8f. **Cleveland Andrew.** His name was originally Grover Cleveland Burgess Jr. (II). Born 14 May 1922 in Greenbrier Co., WV. Married Frances Lockett Wilkerson on 24 Apr. 1943 in Greenbrier Co. Cleve Burgess was a high school teacher and coach. He died on 5 Mar. 1985 at Lewisburg, WV. Frances Burgess currently lives at Lewisburg, WV.

9a. **Donna Frances.** Born 11 June 1944 at Huntington, WV. Married Jerry Lambiotte (div.); married secondly Jack Hemm. Donna Hemm currently lives at East Moline, IL.

9b. **Andrea Lee.** Born 3 Aug. 1945 at Huntington, WV. Married William Louis Dankmyer on 3 Aug. 1968 in Greenbrier Co., WV. Andrea Dankmyer currrently lives at Colleyville, TX.

9c. **Rita Louise (II).** Born 5 Jan. 1948 at Logan, WV. Married Marvin W. Van Buren on 28 July 1969 in Greenbrier Co., WV. Rita Van Buren currently lives at Lewisburg, WV.

8g. **George Hill.** Born 1925 at Lewisburg, WV; died there in 1931 from injuries received when he was hit by a school bus, and is buried in the Calvary Cemetery.

8h. **(Mary) Essie.** She is called Essie May is her obituary. Born 31 July 1927 at Lewisburg, WV; died there of meningitis on 14 Oct. 1928, and is buried in the Calvary Cemetery.

VINCENT L. BURGESS OF SUMMIT CO., OHIO
[George Andrew[6]]

7e. **Vincent Lilburn (I) "Dude"** *[son of George Andrew].* His name is listed as S. V. Burgess in the 1900 census. Born 18 Mar. 1891 in Greenbrier Co., WV. Listed with his father in the 1910 census, and in 1920 at Akron, Summit Co., OH. Married Della ___ (she was born 25 Oct. 1895, and died Apr. 1983 at Cuyahoga Falls, OH). Served in World War I as a Corporal for the 335th Supply Co., QEC, U.S. Army. Dude Burgess is listed in the 1928-31 city directories of Akron, OH working for Goodyear. He died on 8 July 1946 at Akron, and is buried in the East Akron Cemetery.

8a. **George (IV).** Born about 1928 in Ohio. Last known living at Akron or Barberton, OH. Relationship not confirmed.

8b. **Vincent Lilburn (II).** Born about 1930 in Ohio. Married Helen V. Gray on 13 Oct. 1950 in Stark Co., OH. Listed in the 1957/58 city directory of Akron, OH working as an upholsterer, in the Barberton, OH city directory in 1962/63, and in the Uniontown city directory in 1974. Last known living at Cuyahoga Falls, OH.

[William (I)[1], Edward (I)[2], Edward (II)[3], John (II)[4]]

PEYTON PRICE BURGESS
(1810-1892)

OF FAUQUIER COUNTY, VIRGINIA

5c. **Peyton Price** *[son of John (II)].* Born 9 May 1810 in Fauquier Co., VA. Married Frances Anne Newhouse on 1 Jan. 1835 in Fauquier Co. (she was born 6 Aug. 1807 in VA, the daughter of Ziba Newhouse [who was the brother of Zebulon Newhouse] and Lydia Campbell, and died 2 Dec. 1880 in Fauquier Co.; another brother, Elias Newhouse, married Sallie, daughter of Bradford Dawson; and a sister, Sallie [born 1797], married Baylis Bruce of South Carolina). Listed in the 1840-80 censuses for Fauquier Co. (in 1870 as "Peyton B. Burgess"). Peyton Burgess was a farmer in Fauquier Co., VA. He died there on 8 Dec. 1892; his official death record gives the names of his parents, lists his age as 81 years, and provides the county of his birth. He was a Methodist.

The Children of Peyton Burgess:

6a. **Horace Peyton.** Born 17 Jan. 1836 in Fauquier Co., VA. See below for full entry.

6b. **Martha Frances.** Born 6 Mar. 1838 in Fauquier Co., VA. Listed in the 1860-70 censuses living with her father; listed in the 1900 census for Fauquier Co., VA. Martha F. Burgess died unmarried on 12 May 1908 in Fauquier Co., VA, and is buried with her brother, Horace.

6c. **Lydia Campbell "Lydie."** Born 29 July 1842 in Fauquier Co., VA. Married John Thomas McDonald on 25 Dec. 1866 in Fauquier Co. (he was born about 1843, son of Baylis McDonald and Eliza Collins, and died about 1928 when his will was probated [*Prince William Co. Will Book #2*, p. 106]), having had at least the following children: *Rosa Davenport* (born 1868); *Elizabeth Frances "Lizzie"* (born 1 Jan. 1871, married ___ Utterback, and died 8 Oct. 1947 at Haymarket, VA, buried there); *Clarence Merton* [or Morton] (born 4 July 1873, died 27 Apr. 1956 at Warrenton, VA, buried Union Cemetery, Leesburg); *Adelaide Jenesca "Addie"* (born about 1875, married Wesley White, and lived at Washington, DC); *John Cockran* (born 28 Jan. 1879); *Lena P.* (born 4 Jan. 1882 [or 1881], married Tom Peyton Smith, and died on 14 Aug. 1957 at Arlington, VA, buried Antioch Cemetery, Haymarket). Listed in the 1870-80 censuses for Fauquier Co., VA, and from 1900-1920 at Haymarket, Prince William Co., VA. Lydia McDonald died at Haymarket between 1920-28.

6d. **Oscar Franklin.** Born 15 Sept. 1847 at New Baltimore, VA. See below for full entry.

[William (I)[1], Edward (I)[2], Edward (II)[3], John (II)[4], Peyton Price[5]]

HORACE PEYTON BURGESS
(1836-1922)

OF FAUQUIER COUNTY, VIRGINIA

6a. **Horace Peyton** *[son of Peyton Price].* Born 17 Jan. 1836 in Fauquier Co., VA. Married Mrs. Elizabeth Frances (Moffett) Cockrill on 18 Dec. 1855 in Fauquier Co. (she was born 7 Aug. 1825, daughter of John T. Moffett, married firstly Robert Cockrill, and died 22 Feb. 1904); married secondly Emma O. Silcott on 7 Nov. 1907 in Fauquier Co. (she died before him). In addition to the children listed below, Horace P. Burgess had three stepchildren, listed in the 1860 census with the name Burgess: John C. Cockrill (born 1848), Robert Cockrill (born 1850), and Frances "Fanny" Cockrill (born 1852, died 1863 in the same diphtheria epidemic that killed her half-sister, Louise Burgess, and is buried in the Enon Baptist Church Cemetery); John and Robert are listed with their step-father in 1870.

Served in Co. H., 6th Virginia Cavalry, Confederate Army, during the Civil War; he was captured and imprisoned for ten months at Point Lookout Prison, MD, being released on parole in 1865. Listed in the 1860-1910 censuses for Fauquier Co., VA; in 1920 he is listed with his son-in-law, John A. Woolf. Horace Burgess was a farmer in Fauquier Co., VA, working the estate he called "Whitewood." He died there on 4 Dec. 1922, and is buried near Marshall, VA. He was a Methodist.

The Children of Horace P. Burgess:

7a. **Josephine Laws.** Born 14 Oct. 1856 in Fauquier Co., VA. Married John Andrew Woolf on 5 Jan. 1881 in Fauquier Co. (he was born 5 Oct. 1848, son of Henry M. Woolf and Elizabeth Dowell, and died 15 Apr. 1930), and had children:

(Samuel) Regester "Reg" WOOLF. Born 3 Nov. 1881, married Elsie Anna Hall, and had children: *James Marvin* (born 1914, married Dorothy Fisher, and had children: James; Susan); *Dorothy Anna* (born 1916, died May 1942); *Edna Mae* (born 1919, married Elmer Batzell, and had children: Peter; Stephen; Anne Louise). ***Reg WOOLF*** died on 3 Jan. 1924.

(Josephine) Elizabeth "Lizzie" WOOLF. Born 15 Apr. 1884, married Willis Mallory Foley (he was born 1874, and died 1954), and had children: *John Mallory* (born 1909, and died 1958); *Horace Burgess* (born 16 Sept. 1911, married Elizabeth Menefee, and died Nov. 1976 at Arlington, VA, having had children: James); *Elizabeth Josephine "Betty"* (born 1913, married Robert Victor Bailey Jr., had children: Robert Victor III, and died 15 Oct. 1973). ***Lizzie FOLEY*** died on 19 Mar. 1952 at Haymarket, VA, and is buried in the Marshall Cemetery.

Rosa Lee "Bee Bob" WOOLF. Born 23 Dec. 1885, and died unmarried on 27 Mar. 1982, aged 96 years.

Daughter WOOLF. Born 2 Jan. 1887; died young.

Catherine Andrea "Drew" WOOLF. Born 1 Jan. 1888, married W. T. Falls (he died July 1948), and secondly Christopher Lancaster, and died childless on 22 Aug. 1966.

Henrietta "Dett" WOOLF. Born 30 Sept. 1890, married William Henry Waters, and had children: *William Henry Jr.* (born 31 Mar. 1918, married Joyce Nichols, and died 11 Feb. 1992 at Washington, DC, having had children: William); *Mary Catherine* (born 1919, married Wilson Carmichael, had children: Catherine; James, and died 5 June 1970); *Robert Laws* (born 1922, married Mildred Summers, and had children: Charles). ***Dett WATERS*** died in Apr. 1979.

Eulalia "George" WOOLF. Born 12 Feb. 1893, and died 1990, aged 97 years.

(Mary) Cornelia "Nelie" WOOLF. Born 1 Apr. 1895, married Homer T. Heflin (div.), and had children: *Jeannette Woolf "Jean"* (married Hunter F. Payne, and had children: Paula Jeannette; Patsy Sue). ***Cornelia*** married secondly Theodore E. Rinker (he was born 3 Oct. 1900, and died 11 Dec. 1966), and died on 20 Nov. 1969.

Josephine Marion "Joe" WOOLF. Born 14 Dec. 1901, and died unmarried on 7 Feb. 1992 at Marshall, VA, aged 90 years.

John and Josephine WOOLF are listed in the 1920 census for Fauquier Co., VA. Josephine died on 9 Apr. 1945 in Fauquier Co., and is buried in the Marshall Cemetery.

Jean Payne wrote in 1993: "We live in Marshall, VA, very near (seven miles) Rectortown, where my Grandfather and Grandmother shopped, worshipped, and caught the train to travel the few places they went (besides buggy). Their farm house still stands and is used as a tenant house. Also still standing is the first field school, and the meat house. The log cabin has been torn down. The farm has changed hands a number of times, but I believe is now owned by Abe Polen. Of course, a large mansion has been built, and most of the farm land is landscaped."

7b. **Louise Alberta.** Born 22 Feb. 1859 in Fauquier Co., VA; died there in Mar. 1863 in a diphtheria epidemic, and is buried in the Enon Baptist Church Cemetery, near Marshall, VA, with her half-sister, Fanny Cockrill.

7c. **Winter Payne.** Born 3 Feb. 1861 in Fauquier Co., VA. See below for full entry.

7d. **Horace Turner.** Born 21 Feb. 1863 in Fauquier Co., VA. See below for full entry.

7e. **Melissa Alonza.** She was named for the heroine of an unidentified novel her father read during his ten-month stay in a Union Army prison camp. Born 25 Dec. 1865 (or 26 Dec. 1866) at Gordonsdale, Fauquier Co., VA. Married Frederick Hanson Duncan on 15 Sept. 1887 in Fauquier Co. (he was born about 1855, and died before 1923), and had at least the following children: *Luta B. "Sadie"* (born 28 June 1888, married ___ Kinnaird, and died Mar. 1973 at Christiansburg, VA); *Horace* (born 24 Oct. 1891, died Feb. 1969 at Marshall, VA); *Frederick Hanson Jr.*; *Emily* (born 1 Aug. 1896, married ___ Fishback, and died Apr. 1987 at Marshall, VA, aged 90 years); *Daughter* (married Arthur Allnutt, and was living at Washington, DC in 1958). Melissa Duncan died on 30 Mar. 1958 in Fauquier Co., aged 92 years, and was buried in the Marshall Cemetery.

7f. **Martha Pomeroy "Mattie."** Born 8 July 1868 in Fauquier Co., VA. Married William Eldridge Miller on 11 Feb. 1890 in Fauquier Co. (he was born about 1866 in Jefferson Co., WV), and had children: *Fannie E.* (born 11 Nov. 1890, married ___ Vaughn); *Hugh P.* (born 23 Nov. 1893); *Mattie Christian* (born 6 [or 9] Apr. 1896, listed with her grandfather in the 1900 census, married ___ Fewell, and died Nov. 1982 at Amissville, VA). Mattie Miller died on 19 Apr. 1896 at Rectortown, VA, and is buried in Ivy Hill Cemetery.

WINTER P. BURGESS OF FAUQUIER CO., VIRGINIA

[Horace Peyton[6]]

7c. **Winter Payne** *[son of Horace Peyton].* Born 3 Feb. 1861 in Fauquier Co., VA. Married Louisa Victoria Field on 25 Nov. 1886 in Fauquier Co. (she was born 25 Oct. 1861 in VA, daughter of Capt. Samuel Field and (Sarah) Virginia Summers, and died 27 Nov. 1925, buried in the Berg Cemetery). Listed in the 1900-20 censuses for Fauquier Co. (five of five children survive in 1910). Winter Burgess's farm "Greystone" was located three and one-half miles east of The Plains, on Route 15. He died there on 4 Mar. 1932, and is buried in the Mount Sharon Cemetery, Middleburg, VA.

8a. **(Horace) Field.** Born 11 Apr. 1888 in Fauquier Co., VA. Listed with his father in the 1900-20 censuses. Field Burgess was a farmer near The Plains, VA. He died there unmarried on 21 Nov. 1962, and is buried in the Mount Sharon Cemetery.

8b. **(George) Moffett.** Born 30 Dec. 1889 in Fauquier Co., VA. Listed with his father in the 1900-10 censuses, but not in 1920. Moffett Burgess was a farmer in the Mountsville-Philomont area, in Loudoun Co., VA. He died unmarried on 12 Apr. 1958 (or 1959) at Bristow, VA, and is buried in the Mount Sharon Cemetery, Middleburg, VA.

8c. **Virginia Summers.** Born 10 May 1892 in Fauquier Co., VA. Listed with her father in the 1900-20 censuses. Virginia Burgess was a farmer on her father's lands, near The Plains, VA. She died there unmarried on 16 May 1983, aged 91 years, and is buried in the Mount Sharon Cemetery.

8d. **Estelle Josephine.** Born 20 Sept. 1894 in Fauquier Co., VA. Married Louis Woodward Lightner on 3 Dec. 1919 (he was born 17 June 1896, son of Milton Hitt Lightner and Caledonia Green, and died 19 Nov. 1984 at Haymarket, VA), and had children:

***Louis Field** LIGHTNER.* Born 5 Feb. 1921 at Bonnie Brae Farm, Haymarket, VA, married Fannie Leach on 29 Nov. 1942 at Richmond, VA (div.), and secondly Thelma Lasbrook on 15 May 1957 (div.). ***Louis** LIGHTNER* died childless on 18 Sept. 1965 at Gainesville, VA, and is buried in the Stonewall Memorial Garden.

***George Moffett** LIGHTNER.* Born 23 July 1922 at Bonnie Brae Farm, Haymarket, VA, and died 1 Sept. 1926 at Warrenton, VA, buried St. Paul's Episcopal Church Cemetery, Haymarket.

Louise Green LIGHTNER. Born 16 Feb. 1924 at Bonnie Brae Farm, Haymarket, VA, married Russell Lewis Jamison on 11 Aug. 1963 at Haymarket, VA, and had children: *Russell Lewis Jr.* (born 8 May 1969 at Manassas, VA). ***Louise JAMISON*** currently lives at Haymarket, VA.

Ann Summers LIGHTNER. Born 9 Oct. 1925 at Bonnie Brae Farm, Haymarket, VA, married Sidney Armistead Park on 11 Sept. 1945 in Maryland (he was born 9 Apr. 1926), and had children: *David Louis* (born 20 Oct. 1949 at Washington, DC, married Phyllis Biondi on 16 Jan. 1973 [div.; she was born 1947], and had children: Beverly [born and died 7 Dec. 1973 at Washington, DC]; Jesse Lightner [born 26 May 1975 at Alexandria, VA]; Alexander Vincent [born 1 Feb. 1979 at Alexandria, VA]; Sophia A. [born 26 Aug. 1981, died 1 Sept. 1981]); *Vickie Jo* (born 29 July 1951 at Washington, DC, married Ronald Wayne Sullivan on 22 Jan. 1972 at Annandale, MD [he was born 23 Jan. 1951], and had children: Stacie Marie [born 13 Apr. 1976 in West Germany]; Todd Brent [born 13 June 1979 in NC]; Jodie Cathleen [born 26 July 1990 at Fairfax, VA]); *Patricia Ann* (born 29 Sept. 1956 at Washington, DC, married Frederick Kurtz Jr. on 6 June 1981 at Alexandria, VA [div.], and secondly Peter Montanino, and had children: Tyler Park [born 11 May 1993 at Fairfax, VA]); *Phillip Edward* (born 30 Nov. 1958 at Washington, DC, married Yvonne Trainum Morris on 20 June 1992 at Palmyra, VA [she had two children from her first marriage]).

(Estelle) Margaret LIGHTNER. Born 16 Feb. 1927 at Bonnie Brae Farm, Haymarket, VA, married Millard Chancellor Seay on 31 Aug. 1946 at Bonnie Brae Farm (he was born 8 May 1920), and had children: *Millard Lightner* (born 22 June 1948, married Kathleen "Cathy" Tomaskovic on 25 Oct. 1980 at Alexandria, VA, and had children: Jessica Michelle [born 23 June 1983 at Alexandria, VA]; John Robert [born 24 Sept. 1986 at Staten Island, NY]); *Pamela Louise* (born 4 Dec. 1950 at Alexandria, VA); *Richard Lee* (born 12 Aug. 1964 at Washington, DC); *Sandra Ann* (born 6 Sept. 1966 at Washington, DC). ***Margaret SEAY*** currently lives at Springfield, VA.

Helen Marie LIGHTNER. Born 10 Feb. 1929 at Bonnie Brae Farm, Haymarket, VA, married Elmer Everett Ray on 11 June 1950 at Haymarket, VA (he was born 16 Oct. 1921, and died 19 Nov. 1988), and had children: *Benjamin Everett* (born 15 Aug. 1953 at Alexandria, VA, and died 27 Dec. 1974 at Savage, MD, and is buried in the Pohick Church Cemetery, Fairfax Co., VA). ***Helen RAY*** currently lives at Savage, MD.

Charlotte Payne LIGHTNER. Born 30 Sept. 1930 at Warrenton, VA, married Thomas Lewis Hall on 20 June 1948 at Haymarket, VA (he was born 21 Jan. 1919), and had children: *Leslie Lee* (born 16 Aug. 1949 at Norfolk, VA, married Lynette Christine Scaggs on 26 Nov. 1976 [she was born 14 Sept. 1949], and had children: Mathew Scott [born 11 June 1978 at Norfolk, VA]; Andrew Layne [born 19 July 1980 at Norfolk, VA]; Mark Lindsey [born 10 Feb. 1982 at Norfolk, VA]); *Michael Lewis* (born 1 Apr. 1952 at Norfolk, VA); *Deborah Ann* (born 19 Feb. 1954 at Norfolk, VA, married Bruce Wayne Cross on 26 Apr. 1974 [div.], and had children: Bryan Wayne [born 19 July 1976 at Norfolk, VA]; Jaime Renee [born 7 Apr. 1978 at Norfolk, VA]; *Deborah Ann* married secondly Donald G. Kittle on 16 Aug. 1986 [div.], and had children: Jennifer Lea [born 11 May 1987 at Virginia Beach, VA]; *Deborah Ann* married thirdly Allen Greer on 31 July 1993); *Diane Estelle* (born 18 Sept. 1957 at Norfolk, VA, married Charles Milliken on 19 Aug. 1978 at Virginia Beach, VA [he was born 6 June 1955, and died 10 May 1986], and had children: Kendall Jo [born 3 Oct. 1984 at Virginia Beach, VA]). ***Charlotte Payne HALL*** died on 5 Oct. 1986 at Virginia Beach, VA, and is buried there in the Rosewood Memorial Park.

Estelle LIGHTNER lived at Haymarket, Prince William Co., VA. She died on 19 Jan. 1983 at Warrenton, VA, and is buried in the Stonewall Memorial Garden, Manassas, VA.

8e. **Oscar Wayland.** Born 28 Feb. 1899 in Fauquier Co., VA. Listed with his father in the 1900-20 censuses. Oscar Burgess was a farmer on his father's lands, near The Plains, VA. He died there unmarried on 13 Apr. 1965.

HORACE TURNER BURGESS OF FAUQUIER CO., VIRGINIA

[Horace Peyton[6]]

7d. **Horace Turner** *[son of Horace Peyton].* His middle name is also given as Thomas in some records. Born 22 Feb. 1863 in Fauquier Co., VA. Married Elizabeth Agnes "Bettie" Smith on 21 Nov. 1888 in Fauquier Co. (she was born 4 Mar. 1866, daughter of Henry Smith, and died 12 Jan. 1913); married secondly Mary Louise Glascock on 14 Jan. 1915 in Fauquier Co., VA (she was born 1 Nov. 1885, daughter of Ludwell and Sallie Glascock, and died 21 July 1967). Listed in the 1900-20 censuses for Fauquier Co., VA; four children out of seven children of Bettie survive in 1910. Horace T. Burgess was a cattle rancher and stock buyer, owning and operating Burgess, Brown & McClannahan (originally Brown & Burgess) in Fauquier Co., VA. He died on 12 Sept. 1943 at New Baltimore, VA, and is buried with his wives in the Warrenton Cemetery. His biography appears in *History of Virginia, Volume VI: Virginia Biography* (Chicago and New York: American Historical Society, 1924, p. 209).

8a. **Elizabeth Luke "Lizzie."** Born 10 Dec. 1889 in Fauquier Co., VA. Married William Pittman "Douglas" Kincheloe about 1914 (he was born 18 May 1895, and died 1 Aug. 1972), and had children: *Valerie* (born 24 Jan. 1915, married ___ Gilmore, was living at Washington, DC in 1968, and died Jan. 1989 at Waldorf, MD). Listed with her father in the 1910 census. Lizzie Kincheloe died on 2 Nov. 1918 in Fauquier Co., and is buried with her husband in the Warrenton Cemetery.

8b. **Mabel Frost.** Born 14 June 1891 in Fauquier Co., VA; died there on 21 (or 24) Apr. 1892, and is buried with her parents.

8c. **(Henry) Sidney**. Born 26 Nov. 1893 in Fauquier Co., VA. Married Kathleen Mary Mulvey on 4 Dec. 1917 (she was born 17 Nov. 1896, the daughter of James Mulvey [an Army captain who later served as head of security at the White House under seven U.S. presidents; he married secondly Martha Peterson, who served as head cook at the White House], and died 11 Nov. 1948). Listed in the 1920 census for Washington, DC. Sidney Burgess was a railroad worker. He was living at Mt. Rainier, MD by 1943, and died there on 27 Dec. 1962, being buried with his wife in the Ft. Lincoln Cemetery, Ft. Lincoln, MD.

9a. **James Horace**. Listed as Horace Mulvey Burgess in his grandfather's biography. Born 30 Sept. 1918 at Washington, DC. Married Margret Wilson on 11 June 1939; married secondly Dorothy Evelyn (Wilson) Gibson on 8 Jan. 1977 (by another father, she had children: *Linda Lea GIBSON*). James H. Burgess died on 28 June 1980 in Maryland.

10a. **James Mulvey**. Born 8 Dec. 1944. Married Linda Lea Gibson on 29 July 1967. James M. Burgess is a regional sales manager for the 3M Corporation. Linda Burgess works for the school system. They currently live at Greensboro, NC.

11a. **James Trevor**. Born 23 Sept. 1971. James T. Burgess works for Northwestern Life Insurance Company in Minnesota.

11b. **Kevin Michael (I)**. Born 3 May 1974. Kevin Burgess currently attends Guilford Technical Community College at Greensboro, NC.

11c. **Erin Lea**. Born 5 Sept. 1978.

10b. **William Sidney**. Born 5 Oct. 1951. Married Emily Marie Murray on 12 May 1980. William S. Burgess is Director of the Enforcement and Service Program for Maryland's Water Resources Administration. Emily Burgess is a dental technician. They currently live at Annapolis, MD.

11a. **Rebekah Lynn** (ad.). Born 1 May 1975. Rebekah Burgess attends Virginia Polytechnic Institute, majoring in forestry and wildlife.

9b. **Martha Betty**. Born 30 June 1922 at Washington, DC. Married Harold J. O'Brien (dec.). Martha O'Brien worked for the U.S. Department of Agriculture for 19 years before transferring to the Department of Health, Education, and Welfare as Head of the Information Section; she retired after more than 24 years of service. She currently lives at Adelphi, MD.

8d. **(Horace) Franklin Berkeley.** Born Oct. 1896 (or 1895) in Fauquier Co., VA. Married Elsie M. Fritz. Listed with his brother, Henry, in the 1920 census, and in the city directories of Scranton, PA from 1951-64. Frank Burgess was a mechanic for the Lackawanna Railroad, and also worked for Standard Oil Co. He died childless at Takoma Park, MD, and is buried with his wife in the Ft. Lincoln Cemetery, Ft. Lincoln, MD.

8e. **Agnes Lake.** Her middle name is also listed as Josephine. Born 12 Oct. 1897 in Fauquier Co., VA. Married Norvil Alva Wheeler, and had children: *(Norville) Alva Jr.* (married Irene S. ___, and lives at Woodville, TX); *Charlotte* (married Robert E. Hofma, and lives at Manassas, VA); *Katherine* (married Garland P. Timbrook, and lives at Leesburg, VA). Agnes Wheeler died on 15 Apr. 1976 at Fairfax, VA.

8f. **Son.** Born and died about 1917 in Fauquier Co., VA; buried with his parents.

8g. **Currell Tiffany.** Born Sept. 1919 in Fauquier Co., VA; died there in 1920, and is buried with his parents.

8h. **Mary Louise (II).** Born 30 Jan. 1921 in Fauquier Co., VA. Married Worth Anderson Martin on 4 May 1942 in Fauquier Co. (div.; he was born about 1917 in Webster Co., KY); married secondly Randolph Duffey. Living in Pensacola, FL in 1943. Mary Duffey currently lives at Lancaster, PA.

8i. **Frances Newton.** Born 7 July 1923 in Fauquier Co., VA. Married Albin Gray. Frances Gray currently lives at Warrenton, VA.

8j. **Alice Law.** Born 3 Oct. 1925 in Fauquier Co., VA. Married Charles T. Hanback Jr. on 2 Oct. 1944 in Fauquier Co. (he was born 24 Dec. 1926, was a well-known craftsman who constructed the cross over Robert Kennedy's grave and the eternal flame on John Kennedy's grave, and died on 23 July 1985 in Fauquier Co.). Alice Hanback died on 15 Mar. 1992 at Warrenton, VA, and is buried in the Warrenton Cemetery.

THE BIOGRAPHY OF HORACE T. BURGESS

"The successful record of Horace Turner Burgess as a farmer and stockman in Fauquier County was achieved from a beginning as a wage worker, and through the overcoming of many obstacles to prosperity. His reputation as a successful farm manager is thoroughly well established all over Fauquier County.

"He represents one of the older families of that county. It was established here in the early days by a Burgess ancestor who came from Scotland. Mr. Burgess' grandfather was Peyton Burgess, who was a native and life long resident of Fauquier County. He earned the respect of his fellow citizens by his industry as a farmer, and he followed that occupation all his life as a renter. He was a faithful worker in the Methodist Church. His wife, Frances Newhouse, was born in Fauquier County, and their children were: Horace P.; Miss Martha; Lydia, who became the wife of John McDonald of Haymarket, Virginia; and Rev. Oscar F., who lived at Catlett, Virginia.

"Horace Peyton Burgess, father of Horace T., was born in Fauquier County, and spent his active life in the vicinity of The Plains. His education was acquired in local schools when there was no work on the home farm, and it was in a similar manner that his son, Horace T., acquired most of his early schooling. When the war came between the states, he took his share of the danger and the duty of a soldier of the Confederacy, and was a member of the Sixth Virginia Cavalry, participating with his regiment in all its service until he was wounded. The last months of the war he spent as a prisoner at Point Lookout, Maryland. His wound came from a bullet through the fleshy part of the thigh, but he recovered, and it never troubled him in after life. When the war was over, he had to start his career from the very bottom, but his energy and good judgment enabled him to achieve financial independence when he was only fifty years of age. He was a good farmer, and also an excellent business manager. He took a serious interest in politics, although not as an aspirant to office, always voted as a democrat, and late in life became a member of the Methodist Church.

"Horace P. Burgess, who died November 17, 1922, married Mrs. Elizabeth Cockrill, the widow of Robert Cockrill. They were married before the war broke out. Her father was John T. Moffett, and she was born in Carters Run Valley, one of seven children. She died at the age of seventy-eight. Subsequently, Horace P. Burgess married Miss Emma Silcott, and he survived her. His children, all by his first wife, were: Josephine, wife of John A. Woolf; Winter P., of The Plains; Horace T.; Melissa, widow of Fred H. Duncan, of Marshall, Virginia; and Mattie, who died at Rectortown, wife of William Miller.

"Horace Turner Burgess was born near The Plains in Fauquier County, February 22, 1863. His birthplace was Gordonsdale Farm, but he spent his youth at Whitewood, which his father farmed for eighteen years. His privileges in school were chiefly at The Plains, and for three years he attended Captain Little's private school near Markham. When he was twenty-one years of age, Mr. Burgess went to work for his father as a farm hand, and for five years that was his method for getting experience and for getting ahead in the world. His wages were one hundred and fifty dollars a year and board, and he managed to save about a hundred dollars each year. His first effort at independent farmer was as a renter, located near the old Chief Justice Marshall farm. The three years he spent there brought him some profits each season, and he next rented the farm where he was born, and paid rent on that place for ten years. In all that time he was "getting ahead slowly," and he then continued renting St. Leonard, the country property now owned by Judge Barton Payne. He was at St. Leonard for a decade, and from there he moved to Huntley. His occupation at Huntley for a year was attended by considerable losses, and he had another experience of profitless farming the five years he rented Rhode Island farm. Since leaving Rhode Island, he has been proprietor of Chestnut Hill, known as the old Stone Farm. Chestnut Hill comprises a hundred acres, and he has handled it as a dairying and grazing proposition. He has a choice herd of Guernseys and Jerseys, the best in his experience for butter production, which is one of the chief sources of profit in his farm management.

"For a dozen years Mr. Burgess, in addition to his private business as a farmer, has been associated with the veteran stock buyer, E. W. Brown of Warrenton, in the firm of Brown and Burgess. They are the leading stock buyers and shippers of Fauquier County, and for years have been well known in the city markets of Baltimore and other cities. They have shipped many carloads of live stock from this section of Virginia to the firms of Blackshear and Company and Sundheimer at Baltimore, and the Rosling Packing Company at Washington.

"Mr. Burgess' first wife was Miss Bettie Smith, whom he married in Fauquier County November 21, 1889. She was a daughter of Dr. Henry Smith, a prominent citizen and member of a leading family in the Marshall District. Mrs. Burgess died in January 1913, and was the mother of the following children: Henry Sidney, a railroad man who lives at Washington City, and by his marriage to Catherine Mulvey has two children, Horace Mulvey and Martha Bettie; Elizabeth, who died as the wife of Douglas Kincheloe, leaving a daughter, Valarie; Frank, connected with the Standard Oil Company at Washington; and Agnes, who is the wife of Norvil Wheeler, of Wellington, Virginia, and the mother of a son, Alva.

"On January 14, 1915, Mr. Burgess married Miss Mary Glascock, daughter of Ludwell and Sallie (Glascock) Glascock. Her mother is a sister of Henry V. Glascock of a well known family of Fauquier County... Mr. and Mrs. Burgess have one daughter, Mary Louise. They have their church membership in the Carters Run Congregation of the Missionary Baptist denomination."

[William (I)[1], Edward (I)[2], Edward (II)[3], John (II)[4], Peyton Price[5]]

REV. OSCAR FRANKLIN BURGESS (1847-1935)

OF FAUQUIER COUNTY, VIRGINIA

6d. **Oscar Franklin** *[son of Peyton Price].* He was originally called Oscar Fitzalan Burgess, after a character in the novel, *The Children of the Abbey: A Tale*, by Regina Marie Roche (London: Minerva Press, 1796). Born 15 Sept. 1847 at New Baltimore, Fauquier Co., VA. Married (Eliza) Jane Ellen McNeer on 1 Mar. 1876 at Union, Monroe Co., WV (she was born 1 Sept. 1855, and died 9 Sept. 1919); Oscar married secondly (Mary) Margaret Milley Wilbur on 12 Oct. 1922 (she was born 18 Dec. 1854, and died 22 Jan. 1934). Listed in the 1870 census living with his father, in the 1880 census for Fairfield, Rockbridge Co., VA, and in 1910-20 in Fauquier Co. The Rev. Oscar F. Burgess attended Randolph Macon College, and was ordained a Methodist minister, serving as pastor of several churches at Fairfield and Catlett, VA. He died on 17 May 1935, and is buried with his two wives in Valley View Cemetery, Catlett, VA.

"My grandfather Oscar was a Methodist preacher, and lived in West Virginia, Virginia, and Maryland for most of his adult life. He began his ministry in 1874 in West Virginia, moving to Sterling, Virginia, by 1900, and then to Catlett, Virginia in 1907, where he retired in 1910. His church work kept him out of touch with most of his family except his own immediate kin: his brother and his sisters, children of Peyton Price Burgess. My mother, Ethel Burgess, got much of her information from 'sister Martha and sister Lydie,' and from Lydia's daughters, Lena and Addie. Addie was raised at Haymarket, and knew lots of the 'connections.' After Addie married Wesley White and moved to Washington she and mother used to get together and talk. I remember them laughing together. Cousin Addie enjoyed life and used to tell tales about the relatives. Mother got to know these folks after my grandparents moved to this area. I visited with Uncle Horace and his children: I remember Winter and his daughter Virginia. We used to visit 'Aunt Lydie' and Cousin Lena and Cousin Tom Smith at Haymarket. Cousin Addie said my grandfather Oscar, who had reddish hair and blue, blue eyes, and a cousin of his named Belle, were considered the handsomest couple in all Fauquier County! And I can still hear Cousin Lena telling my father: 'Now Ashlan, you bring Ethel and the children down again soon!'"—Frances Odor, 6 June 1986.

The Children of Oscar F. Burgess:

7a. **Ethel Coe.** Born 3 Nov. 1878 in Rockbridge Co., VA. Married Ashlan Fleetwood Harlan on 5 Jan. 1904 (he was born 28 July 1874, and died 22 Sept. 1949), and had children: *Ashlan Fleetwood Jr.* (born 19 Feb. 1906, married Helen Rachel Garrett on 12 July 1930, and died in Jan. 1982 at Williamsburg, VA, having had three children); *Frances McNeer* (see below). Ethel Harlan began researching the Fauquier Co. branch of the Burgess family about 1921, and left a treasure trove of family charts and papers which have contributed greatly to this work. She died 17 Jan. 1970 at Washington, DC, aged 91 years, and is buried in the Riverview Cemetery, Richmond, VA. Ethel Harlan was assisted in her labors by her daughter, Mrs. Frances Odor, who also contributed substantially to this volume.

Frances McNeer HARLAN was born 19 Sept. 1908 at Washington, DC. She married (Edbert) Franklin Odor Jr. on 28 July 1939 at Washington, DC (he was born 13 Nov. 1906 at Washington, DC, and died there on 30 Jan. 1985, buried National Memorial Cemetery, Suitland, MD). A resident for many years of northwest Washington, DC, Mrs. Odor currently lives at the Asbury Methodist Village, Gaithersburg, MD.

7b. **Aubrey Ashton.** Born 29 June 1880 in VA; died there on 19 Jan. 1881, and is buried in the Fairfield Cemetery, Fairfield, VA.

7c. **Oscar McNeer.** Born 18 Mar. 1882 in VA; died there on 24 Jan. 1883, and is buried in the Fairfield Cemetery, Fairfield, VA.

7d. **Norman Whitmore.** Born 30 Oct. 1885 at Aberdeen, MD. Married Jeanette Parkhill on 23 June 1920 (div.; she may have been born 27 Sept. 1897, and died Jan. 1977 at Fredericksburg, VA). Listed with his father in the 1910 census. He attended Randolph-Macon Academy, Front Royal, VA, and Washington and Lee University, Lexington, VA. Norman Burgess was the County Clerk for Rockbridge Co., Lexington, VA, and also worked as a legal clerk there. During World War II he was a purser on a liberty ship carrying American troops; his ship was scheduled for the 1944 invasion of Normandy, France, but was turned back by bad weather and then torpedoed; he was rescued with other crew members and spent some time recuperating in England. After the war he lived at Baltimore and at Washington, DC. He died on 12 Nov. 1950 at Washington, DC, and is buried with his parents at Catlett, VA.

8a. **Betty Jane.** Born 10 Apr. 1922 in Virginia. Married ___ Cutler.

7e. **Helen Peyton.** Born 14 Sept. 1893 in VA; died there on 3 Dec. 1893, and is buried in the Fairfield Cemetery, Fairfield, VA.

A Plucky Preacher

"During the Christmas holidays, we are told, a drunken bully for a time terrorized the town of New Castle, in Craig County, Va., and defied the officers who, if not afraid of him, were at least neglectful of their duty in not placing him under arrest. Disgusted with the situation and the bully's conduct, so the report goes, Rev. O. F. Burgess, the plucky Methodist preacher of that town, tackled the aforesaid drunken rowdy, and not being able to reason with him or control him otherwise, very properly thrashed him until he begged for a chance to get up and 'scoot.' He got the chance and 'scooted.' Shake, Brother Burgess, shake!"—*Salem Times-Register*, about 1904.

Ola O. Burgess Bodine (1893-1951) with son, Ashby Burgess Bodine (1913-1993) and mother, Alice Virginia Hanback Burgess (1863-1922), plus two unidentified children in three-wheeled automobile, 1914

[William (I)[1], Edward (I)[2], Edward (II)[3], John (II)[4]]

JOHN WESLEY BURGESS, SR.
(1812-1877?)
OF FAUQUIER COUNTY, VIRGINIA

5d. **John Wesley (I)** *[son of John (II)].* Born 6 June 1812 in Fauquier Co., VA. Married (Mary) Jane "Virginia" Cockrill (or Cockrell) on 20 Oct. 1840 in Fauquier Co. (she was born about 1822 in VA, the daughter of Hezekiah Cockrill, and died on 4 Mar. 1896). Listed in the 1850 census living with Hezekiah Cockrill, and in the 1860-70 censuses for Fauquier Co., VA with his family; listed in the personal property tax lists through 1876. John W. Burgess farmed in Fauquier Co. between Warrenton and Marshall, VA, and later between Liberty and Bealeton, VA. He died there between 1877-78, when he disappears from the tax records.

The Children of John W. Burgess, Sr.:

6a. **Sarah Anne.** Her middle name is also spelled Ann. Born Sept. 1841 in Fauquier Co., VA. Married Chandler Peyton Rector on 8 July 1869 in Fauquier Co. (he was born 8 Sept. 1839 in VA, the son of Thomas Rector, and died by 1928), and had at least the following children: *Alice J.* (born Aug. 1869, was unmarried in 1928); *James* (born July 1871, married Meta McCormick, his cousin [daughter of John T. McCormick and Ida L. Rector], on 2 Feb. 1899); *Mason J.* (born Dec. 1873, listed with his father in the 1910 census); *Tilden* (born 15 Apr. 1876); *Lewis* (born 1878). Listed in the 1870-1910 censuses for Fauquier Co., VA. Chandler Rector's will (*Fauquier Co. Will Book #50*, p. 389-90) was dated 21 May 1920, and probated 1 Mar. 1928. Sarah Rector died two days later, on 3 Mar. 1928, and is buried with her husband in the Bunker Hill Cemetery, Marshall, VA.

6b. **Hezekiah H.** Born 21 Dec. 1843 in Fauquier Co., VA. See below for full entry.

6c. **Charlotte T. (or A.).** Born Mar. 1845 in Fauquier Co., VA. Married William O. Caynor on 9 Nov. 1897 in Fauquier Co. (he was born Feb. 1847 in VA). Listed with her father in the 1870 census, and with her husband in 1900 in Fauquier Co., VA, but has not been found in 1910.

6d. **Lucy Francis.** Born Sept. 1847 in Fauquier Co., VA. Married Bushrod H. Rector on 8 Mar. 1866 in Fauquier Co. (he was born Oct. 1843 in VA, son of Thomas Rector, and brother of Chandler P. Rector [who married Lucy's sister, Sarah], and died about 1923), and had at least the following children: *Ida L.* (born 1867, married her cousin John T. McCormick on 29 Nov. 1883 in Prince William Co. [he was born Apr. 1856 in VA, son of Thomas McCormick and Mary Burgess]; *Ida* married secondly ___ Barron); *Lizzie J.* (born Feb. 1868 [or 1869]); *John* (born June 1875); *Laura B.* (married ___ Marshall); *Edward V.*; *Delia S.* (born Mar. 1880); *Welby S.* (born Apr. 1882); *Landon B.* (born Apr. 1886); *Emmett F.* (born 13 Aug. 1888, and died Dec. 1967 at Radford, VA). Listed in the 1870-1910 censuses for Fauquier Co., VA. Bushrod Rector's will (*Fauquier Co. Will Book #50*, p. 95, dated 7 Dec. 1916, probated 16 Jan. 1923) mentions surviving children Ide [sic] L. Barron, Laura B. Marshall, and sons Edward V. and Landon B. Lucy Rector died on 23 July 1925 at Belvoir, VA. Her obituary stated that she was survived by two sisters and a brother (no names are mentioned), plus three daughters and four sons.

6e. **Ellen.** Born Mar. 1850 in Fauquier Co., VA, and died there before 1860.

6f. **Hester Jane (II).** Born Apr. 1851 in Fauquier Co., VA. Married as his second wife John R. Heflin on 24 May 1887 in Fauquier Co. (he was born 10 Sept. 1838 in VA, son of John Heflin and Mary Ann Kearns, and died 27 [?] Nov. 1918 in an asylum in Fauquier Co.). Listed in the 1870 with her father, and in the 1880-1910 censuses for Fauquier Co., VA. Hester Heflin died on 20 July 1919 in Fauquier Co., and is buried with her husband in the Heflin Cemetery (no dates appear on their stones).

6g. **John Wesley (III).** Born 18 Feb. 1857 in Fauquier Co., VA. See below for full entry.

[William (I)[1], Edward (I)[2], Edward (II)[3], John (II)[4], John Wesley (I)[5]]

HEZEKIAH H. "BURR" BURGESS
(1843-1923)
OF FAUQUIER COUNTY, VIRGINIA

6b. **Hezekiah H. "Burr"** *[son of John Wesley (I)].* Born 21 Dec. 1843 in Fauquier Co., VA. Married Sarah M. "Sallie" Bussey on 23 Dec. 1869 in Fauquier Co. (she was born May 1847 in Fauquier Co., the daughter of William H. Bussey and Patsy Caynor, and died before her husband). Listed with his father in the 1870 census for Fauquier Co., in the 1900-10 censuses there with his family, and in 1920 with his son, Edward. Burr Burgess was a farmer near New Baltimore, VA. He died there on 6 June 1923, and is buried in the Warrenton Cemetery.

The Children of Burr Burgess:

7a. **Edward Lucien.** Born 16 May 1871 in Fauquier Co., VA. Married Myrtle Lovelace White on 31 Dec. 1916 in Fauquier Co. (she was born 3 Mar. 1881 [?], daughter of John J. White and Sarah Hanback, and died May 1933). Listed in the 1910 census with his father, and in 1920 with his family in Fauquier Co., VA. Edward Burgess was a farmer in Fauquier Co. He died on 15 Aug. 1961 at Hyattsville, MD, aged 90 years, and is buried with his wife in the Warrenton Cemetery.

8a. **Leslie Katherine.** Born 18 June 1919 in Fauquier Co., VA. Married secondly William Anthony Rehrey on 19 Aug. 1949 at Hyattsville, MD, and had children: *William Leslie* (born 22 June 1953 at Washington, DC, married Kathleen Carzon on 10 June 1988 in Maryland, and lives at Wilmington, NC). Leslie Rehrey currently lives at Hyattsville, MD.

7b. **Salena "Lena."** Born 10 Mar. 1873 in Fauquier Co., VA. Married (Hugh) Thomas Edwards on 6 Jan. 1897 in Fauquier Co., and had children: *Ashby Lee* (born 24 Apr. 1900, died May 1974 at Norfolk, VA); *Turner* (died before his mother); *Lena Katherine* (married Robert Bailey, and had five children). Lena Edwards died on 22 June 1958 at Warrenton, VA, and is buried in the Warrenton Cemetery. Her daughter, Lena Katherine Bailey, lived at Culpeper, VA.

7c. **Mason Curtis.** Born 29 Mar. 1875 in Fauquier Co., VA. Married Mary Ellen Huddleston on 17 June 1914 (div.; she was born 11 Dec. 1877, and died 25 Mar. 1959, buried Warrenton Cemetery). Living with his father in 1910; listed in the 1920 census for Fauquier Co., VA. Mason Burgess was a farmer in Fauquier Co. He died there on 2 June 1958, and is buried in the Remington Cemetery.

8a. **James Mason.** Born 24 Dec. 1916 in Fauquier Co., VA. Married Nancy Louise (Huddleston) Retchiff, but had no children. James M. Burgess was a farmer in Fauquier Co. He sold his land there in 1982 and retired to North Tazewell, VA. He was the last member of the family named Burgess living in Fauquier Co.

7d. **Hettie Gertrude.** Born 15 June 1877 in Fauquier Co., VA. Married John Shelton Cropp on 29 Dec. 1904 in Fauquier Co. (he was born 23 Apr. 1878, and died 2 Aug. 1948), and had children:

Herman Douglas CROPP. Born 5 May 1905 in Fauquier Co., VA. Married Blanche Mohler on 5 May 1923 (she died 1939), and had children: *Jeanne* (married Robert Cowan, and had children: Joan [married Thomas Wolfgang, and had children: Joan Marie]; Robert Jr. [married Rose Marie Simpkins, and had children: Laura {married David Allen Jones, and had four children}]); *Evelyn* (married Henry Westfall, and had children: Brian Douglas [married Judy Thompson, and had children: Ray Douglas; Jennifer Ann {twin}; Barbara Ann {twin}; Brian married secondly Carol Skates, and had one child]; Janet [married secondly David Barnes, and had two children]; Debra [married secondly Terry Lantz, and had one child]; *Evelyn* and Henry Westfall live at Ocean City, MD). ***Herman CROPP*** married secondly Katherine Francis (she was born 29 Jan. 1913, and died Jan. 1978 at Richmond, VA), and had children: *Anne Douglas* (married Joseph Bucker [an official with the U.S. State Department], had children: Shannon, and lives at Brussels, Belgium). ***Herman*** married thirdly Rebecca Rives about 1981 (she survives him). ***Herman CROPP*** died on 18 Apr. 1991 at Richmond, VA.

Margueritte C. CROPP. Born 1907 in Fauquier Co., VA. Married James Adams Millen, and had children: *James Adams Jr.*; *John Arthur Sterling* (married Elaine Yamada [div.]); *Richard Lyding* (married Candace Corby, and had children: Sage J.). ***Margueritte MILLEN*** lives at Sykesville, MD; she has contributed greatly to this book.

Edna CROPP. Born 12 Aug. 1909 in Fauquier Co., VA. Married Randolph Russell Payne (he was born 18 May 1911, and died Apr. 1980 at Ocala, FL), and had children: *Lawrence* (married Marjorie Ford [who died when her daughter Mary was three], and had children: Michael; Beth [married ___ Joiner {div.}, and had three sons]; Amy [married ___ Sakowski, and had one son]; Mary [married ___ McCoy]; *Lawrence* married secondly Barbara Beard [by her first marriage, Barbara had a daughter: Gail {married Joseph Luntz, and had one daughter}], and lives in Maryland); *Barbara* (married F. Sherman Shoemaker, had children: Eric; *Barbara* married secondly Charles Purvis in 1963, works as a producer of plays for the Ocala Community Theatre, and lives at Ocala, FL). ***Edna PAYNE*** died on 20 Aug. 1990 at Ocala, FL, but is buried in the Warrenton Cemetery, Fauquier Co., VA.

(James) Edward CROPP. Born about 1911. Married secondly Dorothy Wood, and had children: *Linda* (married secondly David Signori, and lives at Springfield, VA); *John* (lives at Falls Church, VA). ***Edward CROPP*** lives at Falls Church, VA.

Hettie CROPP died on 25 Mar. 1958, and is buried with her husband in the Warrenton Cemetery.

7e. **Lula Maud "Lulie."** Born 2 Jan. 1880 in Fauquier Co., VA. Married Albert Fletcher Edwards (he was born 13 Sept. 1877, and died 15 June 1944), and had children: *Clara* (born 15 Aug. 1904, married Daniel Luther Canard [he was born 23 Aug. 1903, and died Nov. 1975 at Warrenton, VA], and died Mar. 1974 at Warrenton, VA, having had children: Norma Lee [born 1930, and had three children]; Emily Folk [born 1932, married]; Daniel Luther Jr. [born 1934]; Charles; Carol Ann [married Bobby Rankin, and had four children]); *Alice* (born 1906, married Bernard C. DuBose [he was born 24 July 1902, and died Dec. 1971 at Raleigh, NC], and had children: Alice Bernice [born 1926, married Owen W. Reagan, and had four children]; Albert Louis [born 1947, and died 1985]; *Alice DUBOSE* lives at Raleigh, NC); *Betty* (born 1909, married William Johnson, and had children: Colleen Anne [born 1928, married Rev. T. H. Button, and had two children], and lives at Manassas, VA). Lula Edwards died on 7 Oct. 1964, and is buried with her husband in the Warrenton Cemetery.

7f. **(Mary) Ella.** Born 22 Oct. 1882 in Fauquier Co., VA. Married Ernest Carter Clatterbuck on 1 Feb. 1900 in Fauquier Co. (he was born 5 Sept. 1874, and died 5 Apr. 1912), and had children: *Elsie* (married ___ Norris); *Raymond*; *Roy*; *Ernest "Dick"*; *Nellie*; *Virgie Ann*; *Leslie Anderson*; married secondly Elisha Clatterbuck (his brother). Ella Clatterbuck died on 18 June 1960 in Fauquier Co., and is buried in the Warrenton Cemetery.

7g. **(James) Milton.** Born 10 Dec. 1884 in Fauquier Co., VA. Married Lillie Margaret Foster (she was the daughter of Z. M. P. Foster). Milton Burgess was a baker in Washington, DC. He died childless on 26 Aug. 1939 in a car accident in Fauquier Co., VA. Buried in the Remington Cemetery.

Milton Burgess, 55, Succumbs of Injuries in Highway Crash

"Milton Burgess, 55, of Washington, D.C., formerly of Warrenton, died in the Fauquier County Hospital Saturday night at seven P.M. following an automobile collision on the Lee Highway, just over the Prince William line, about six P.M. Burgess, it is understood, had been visiting relatives near Remington, and was on his way home when a car driven by Anthony Mozynski of Washington, D.C., struck his car. Burgess was said to have been thrown clear of his car. He died from a fractured skull, according to Hospital authorities. Mozynski, charged with manslaughter, was brought to the Fauquier County jail by State Officer L. E. Wetzel, and later carried to Prince William County, where he was turned over to authorities. The Mozynski party, in two cars, was returning to Washington, and was uninjured."—*Fauquier Democrat*, 30 Aug. 1939.

7h. **Clayton.** Born 12 Jan. 1887 in Fauquier Co., VA; died there in 1889.

7i. **Leslie York.** She was named for the heroine of an unidentified novel. Born 10 (or 11) Apr. 1889 in Fauquier Co., VA. Married "Shep" Kern; married secondly (Robert) Cleveland Scott. Leslie Scott died in 1955 at St. Louis, MO.

[William (I)[1], Edward (I)[2], Edward (II)[3], John (II)[4], John Wesley (I)[5]]

JOHN WESLEY BURGESS, JR.
(1857-1937)
OF FAUQUIER COUNTY, VIRGINIA

6g. **John Wesley (III)** *[son of John Wesley (I)].* His full name is given in the 1860 census. Born 18 Feb. 1857 (or 1855) in Fauquier Co., VA. Married Mary Elizabeth Heflin on 9 Aug. 1883 in Fauquier Co. (she was born 2 Feb. 1860 in Fauquier Co., the daughter of John R. and Susan A. Heflin, and died there on 14 June 1944). Listed in the 1900-20 censuses for Fauquier Co., VA; two of two children survive in 1910. John W. Burgess Jr. was a farmer in Fauquier Co. He died there on 24 Dec. 1937, and is buried in the Cedar Grove Cemetery, Bealeton, VA.

The Children of John W. Burgess, Jr.:

7a. **Benjamin Franklin (II).** Born 13 Oct. 1883 in Fauquier Co., VA. Married Maud(e) Loraine Kane about 1910 (she was born 6 Apr. 1891, daughter of Rosser F. and Annie B. Kane, and died 7 Feb. 1977 at Las Vegas, NV). Listed with his father in the 1910 census, and in 1920 at Alexandria, VA living with Robert L. Kane. He left Virginia in Oct. 1946, and eventually moved to Las Vegas, NV in 1971. Ben Burgess was a farmer and carpenter. He died on 8 Sept. 1974 at Las Vegas, NV, aged 90 years, but is buried at Gardena, CA.

8a. **Alvin F.** Living in Canada in 1977.
8b. **Elizabeth (XX).** Married ___ White. Living at Las Vegas, NV in 1977.
8c. **Child.**

7b. **Murray Clarence.** Born 16 Aug. 1885 in Fauquier Co., VA. Married Blanche L. Hale on 8 Dec. 1906 in Fauquier Co. (she was born 1888 in VA). Has not been found in the 1910 census, but his wife is living with her brother-in-law, Golden Ruffner, in Fauquier Co. (two of two children survive). Murray Burgess was a mail carrier for the U.S. Postal Service. He was living at Manilla, Crawford Co., IA in 1945, and at Harlan, Shelby Co., IA in 1946. He died in Iowa in Apr. 1970.

8a. **Evans M.** Born 19 Dec. 1907 in Fauquier Co., VA. Evans Burgess died in Sept. 1972 near Wilkes Barre, PA.
8b. **Roy M.** Born Apr. 1909 in Fauquier Co., VA. He may be listed in the 1954 Washington, DC directory; he may also be the Roy Burgess born 23 Mar. 1908/09 who died Dec. 1972 in Iowa.

[William (I)[1], Edward (I)[2], Edward (II)[3], John (II)[4]]

ADDISON BURGESS
(1814-1887)

OF FAUQUIER COUNTY, VIRGINIA

5e. **Addison "Add"** *[son of John (II)].* Born 20 Mar. 1814 in Fauquier Co., VA. Married Mary Ann Utterback on 18 Mar. 1845 in Fauquier Co. (she was born 29 Oct. 1817 at New Baltimore, VA, the daughter of Nathaniel Utterback, married firstly James A. Browning, and died 17 May 1852 in Prince William Co.); married secondly his first wife's cousin, (Mary) Olivia Utterback, on 8 Aug. 1853 at Washington, DC (she was born 7 Dec. 1825 at New Baltimore, VA, the daughter of Willis Utterback, is mentioned in a guardian's bond dated 28 Dec. 1829, and was living in Fauquier Co. in 1896; she may have died on 21 Feb. 1909 at Mannington, WV). Listed in the 1850-60 censuses for Prince William Co., VA, and in 1870-80 for the Centre District, Fauquier Co., VA. Addison Burgess was a farmer near Buckland, VA. He died there on 2 Nov. 1887, according to a funeral card surviving among his descendants.

The Children of Addison Burgess:

6a. **James Monroe.** Born 1847 in Prince William Co., VA. See below for full entry.

6b. **Julia Alice.** Born about 1849 in Prince William Co., VA. Listed with her father in the 1870 census. Married Isaac V. Knott(s) in May 1877 in Taylor Co., WV, and is said to have settled in SD. Has not been found in the 1880 soundex for VA and WV, or in 1900 in SD, ND, VA, and WV.

6c. **Mary A(nn?) (III).** Born (17?) May 1852 in Prince William Co., VA. Married her first cousin, William S. Bradley, on 13 Sept. 1876 in Fauquier Co., VA (he was born about 1853 in Fauquier Co., VA, son of Frances A. Burgess and Presley G. Bradley). Said to have moved to West Virginia, but has not been found in the 1880 Soundex for VA and WV.

EDWIN BURGESS (1864-1933) AND FAMILY about 1899 (see pages 134-35)
(from left) Fred Earl, Myrtle Belle, Mabel D., Ella May (Park), Pearl Ellen, Floyd Alva, Edwin, Elmer L.

[William (I)[1], Edward (I)[2], Edward (II)[3], John (II)[4], Addison[5]]

REV. JAMES MONROE BURGESS
(1847-1908)

OF BARBOUR COUNTY, WEST VIRGINIA

6a. **James Monroe** *[son of Addison]*. Born 1847 at Haymarket, Prince William Co., VA. Married Mary Susan Lewis on 17 Sept. 1868 at Richmond, VA (she was born 8 Dec. 1845 in Fauquier Co., VA, daughter of William Buckner Lewis and Jane Lee, and sister of John Burgess Lewis [who married James's cousin, Georgianna Burgess], and died on 20 July 1888 at Simpson, Taylor Co., WV, buried Simpson Cemetery); married secondly (Maude) Mona Utterback (she was born about 1878 in WV, daughter of George Utterback and Florence Fleming, and died on 25 Aug. 1940 at Morgantown, WV). Listed in the 1870 census for Upperville, Cedar Run Township, Fauquier Co., VA working as a merchant, and in 1880 in the Flemington District, Taylor Co., WV; has not been found in the 1900 census; his widow appears as head of the family in the 1910 census for the Philippi District, Barbour Co., WV. Served in Co. A, 12th Battalion, Virginia Light Artillery (later Capt. Utterback's Company), Confederate Army, participating in many battles, including Gettysburg, Fredericksburg, and Chancellorsville; he was taken prisoner late in the war.

James M. Burgess was educated at Bethel Academy, and was ordained a minister of the Baptist Church; he moved to West Virginia in 1874, where he worked as a school teacher, principal (of the Flemington School for seven years, at Flemington, WV), and a circuit preacher. He settled at Philippi, Barbour Co., WV, about 1891, where he had charge of six churches, and died there about 1908, being buried in the Philippi Cemetery (not in the county death indexes). His biography appeared in *The History of Barbour County, West Virginia, from Its Earliest Exploration and Settlement to the Present Time*, by Hu Maxwell (Morgantown, WV: Acme Publishing Co., 1899, p. 349-350).

THE BIOGRAPHY OF JAMES M. BURGESS

"JAMES M. BURGESS, born 1847 at Haymarket, Prince William County, Virginia, son of Addison and Mary A. (Utterback) Burgess, was married September 17, 1868 at Richmond, Virginia, to Mary S., daughter of William B. and Jane (Lee) Lewis. His second marriage was to Maude M., daughter of George and Florence (Fleming) Utterback. Children, Ora L., William A., James Edwin, Charles L., and Nela, the last named by his second marriage. He is a minister in the Baptist Church, and an Odd Fellow, and resides in West Philippi. He was educated at Bethel Academy, Virginia, and at New Baltimore, same State, and spent three years in the Confederate army, belonging to the artillery branch of the service, and took part in the battles at Fredericksburg, Chancellorsville, Gettysburg, Brisbane Station, The Wilderness, Spotsylvania Court-house, Hanover Court-house, Cold Harbor, Siege of Petersburg, New Market Heights, Dutch Gap, and many skirmishes. Although he had many narrow escapes, and was in the hardest fighting of the war, he escaped without a wound. Near the last days, he was taken prisoner. His great, great-grandfather Burgess was a Scotchman who settled in Virginia, and on the other side, his grandfather, Stephen Tompkins, was an Englishman, and also settled in Virginia. Mr. Burgess taught school fifteen terms, seven of them as principal of the Flemington school, and has been in the Baptist ministry seventeen years. In 1874 came to West Virginia, and spent twelve years at Flemington, where he had charge of four churches, and eight years at Philippi, where he had charge of six churches. He is an earnest advocate of education."

The Children of Rev. James M. Burgess:

7a. **Ora Lee.** Her name is given as Lora E. in the 1900 census. Born 21 Dec. 1868 in Fauquier Co., VA. Married Frank J. Jones about 1884, and had children: *Monroe C.* (born May 1885); *William Frank* (born 24 Apr. 1903, died 21 Apr. 1963). Listed in the 1900 census for the Barker District, Barbour

Co., WV. Ora L. Jones lived at Mannington, Marion Co., WV. She died there on 22 Aug. 1924, and is buried at Wheeling, WV.

7b. **William A(ddison?) (I).** Born 1870 in Fauquier Co., VA. William A. Burgess was a medical doctor, reportedly still attending medical school, when he died unmarried suddenly of typhoid fever (or a heart attack) on 25 July 1899 at Mannington, Marion Co., WV. He is buried with his father at the Philippi Cemetery.

7c. **(James) Edward (II) "Edwin."** His father's biography calls him James Edwin Burgess. Born 26 Sept. 1872 in Fauquier Co., VA. Ed Burgess was a soldier; he died of heart disease and typhoid fever on 20 July 1895 at Philippi, Barbour Co., WV, and is buried with his father at the Philippi Cemetery.

7d. **Charles Latelle.** Born 30 Aug. 1880 in Taylor Co., WV. See below for full entry.

7e. **Nela M.** Her name is given as Florence in her birth record, and is spelled Nellia in the 1910 census, and Neila elsewhere. Born 12 Oct. 1897 at Philippi, Barbour Co., WV. Married secondly James Null, and had children: *Kathleen* (dec.). Nela Null died on 29 Sept. 1953 at Morgantown, WV.

7f. **Elma Mae.** Born 10 Dec. 1900 at Philippi, WV. Married Dr. Walter Joseph Riley about 1925 at St. Louis, MO (he was born 24 May 1899, and died Jan. 1970 at Conover, NC), and had children: *Robert J.*; *William J.* Elma Riley died about 1972 at Conover, NC. Her son, Dr. William J. Riley, lives at Newton, NC.

CHARLES L. BURGESS OF OHIO CO., WEST VIRGINIA

[James Monroe[6]]

7d. **Charles Latelle** *[son of James Monroe].* Born 30 Aug. 1880 in Taylor Co., WV. Married Cora Blanch Snodgrass (she was born 9 July 1874, daughter of Ezekiel and Laverne Snodgrass, and died 11 Jan. 1933, buried in the Snodgrass Cemetery, Mannington, WV). Listed in the 1920 census for Wheeling, Ohio Co., WV. Charles L. Burgess owned The Burgess Co., specializing in carpets and furniture, at Wheeling, WV. He died there of a coronary thrombosis on 7 Oct. 1928, and is buried in the Greenwood Cemetery.

8a. **Charles Lee.** Born 30 Nov. 1909 at Mannington, WV. Married Virginia Anderson on 1 Dec. 1927. Charles L. Burgess was a 1st Lieut. in the Signal Corps of the U.S. Army; he later taught school at Wheeling, WV. He died there on 7 Feb. 1979, and is buried in the Halcyon Hills Cemetery. Virginia Burgess currently lives at Wheeling, WV.

9a. **Hope Elaine.** Born 18 Sept. 1928 at New Concord, OH. Married Morgan Clarke Bier on 2 July 1949, and had children: *Virginia Lee* (born 16 Apr. 1950 at Wheeling, WV, married Ronald Stuart Sapp of Wileyville, WV on 4 Aug. 1973, and had children: Kellie Sue [born 27 June 1975 at Glen Dale, WV, and had children: Catherine Scarlett {born 10 Aug. 1991 at Charleston, WV}]; *Morgan Clarke Jr.* (born 21 June 1957 at Wheeling, WV, died 22 June 1957, buried Greenwood Cemetery); *Rebecca Jo* (born 8 Apr. 1959 at Wheeling, WV). Hope Bier currently lives at Wheeling, WV.

9b. **Virginia Lee (III).** Born 17 Jan. 1930 at Wheeling, WV. Married Robert George Carle on 19 Sept. 1953, and had children: *Mark Robert* (born 11 Aug. 1958 at Wheeling, WV, died there in 1958, buried Stone Church Cemetery, Wheeling); *Melissa Ann* (born 2 Oct. 1965 at Wheeling, WV, married Scott Allan Richards on 23 June 1990, and lives at Wheeling). Virginia Carle currently lives at Wheeling, WV.

[William (I)[1], Edward (I)[2], Edward (II)[3], John (II)[4]]

DAWSON JACKSON BURGESS, SR.
(1826-1896)
OF FAUQUIER COUNTY, VIRGINIA

5k. **Dawson Jackson (I) "Dorsey"** *[son of John (II)].* His full name is given only on his son Dawson's death certificate. Born 6 May 1826 in Fauquier Co., VA. Married Margaret Virginia Clouser (or Clowser) on 11 Mar. 1859 at Washington, DC (she was born about 1841 in Frederick Co., VA, and died 16 July 1911 in Fauquier Co.). Living with his brother, Addison, in 1850; listed in the 1860-80 censuses for Fauquier Co.; Margaret is living with her oldest son in the 1900 census, and with Zaccheus in 1910; eight of ten children survive in 1910. In the 1880 census, an unidentified niece, Georgiana, age three, is also living with this family. Dawson Burgess was a farmer near New Baltimore, VA. He died there on 14 June 1896, and is buried with several of his descendants in the Little Georgetown Church Cemetery. His family Bible record survives in the possession of his great-grandson, Henry G. Weineke, Jr.

The children of Dawson Burgess:

6a. **Addison Franklin "Chat."** Listed as Sampson Burgess in the Fauquier Co. birth records. Born 12 Mar. 1860 in Fauquier Co., VA. Listed in the 1880-1910 censuses for Fauquier Co. Chat Burgess was a farmer all his life in Fauquier Co. He died there unmarried on 19 Feb. 1919, and is buried in an unmarked grave in the Broad Run Baptist Church Cemetery, New Baltimore, VA.
6b. **Littleton Jackson.** Born 1 Feb. 1862 in Fauquier Co., VA. See below for full entry.
6c. **John H. (II).** Born 12 Feb. 1864 in Fauquier Co., VA; died there on 18 Sept. 1865.
6d. **Dawson Jackson (II) "Dorsey."** Born 25 Feb. 1866 in Fauquier Co., VA. See below for full entry.
6e. **Gilbert (I).** Born 8 Jan. 1868 in Fauquier Co., VA; died there on 1 Sept. 1868.
6f. **(Randolph) Purington.** Born 29 Aug. 1869 in Fauquier Co., VA; died there on 7 Sept. 1872.
6g. **George Washington (IX).** Born 5 Mar. 1872 in Fauquier Co., VA. Married his cousin, Martha W. "Mattie" Utterback, daughter of Susan Catherine Burgess and William Price Utterback, both Burgess descendants (she was born 23 Sept. 1870 in Fauquier Co., and died there on 24 Oct. 1940). Listed in the 1920 census for rural Baltimore Co., MD. George Burgess was a farmer at Cockeysville, MD (where he was living in 1919) and near New Baltimore, VA. He died there childless on 1 Apr. 1941, and is buried with his wife in an unmarked grave in the Broad Run Baptist Church Cemetery, New Baltimore, VA.
6h. **Zaccheus.** His name is listed as J. Zaccheus in the 1880 census. Born 12 Apr. 1875 in Fauquier Co., VA. Listed in the 1900-20 censuses for Fauquier Co., VA. Zach Burgess was a farmer in Fauquier Co. He died there unmarried on 15 Feb. 1950, and is buried in the Warrenton Cemetery.
6i. **Edwin (II)** (twin). Born 23 Mar. 1877 in Fauquier Co., VA. See below for full entry.
6j. **Edward L.** (twin). His middle initial appears only in the 1941 estate settlement of his brother, George. Born 23 Mar. 1877 in Fauquier Co., VA. Listed in the 1900-20 censuses for Fauquier Co. with his mother and brothers. Edward Burgess was a farmer near New Baltimore and Gainesville, VA. He died there unmarried on 18 Apr. 1942, and is buried in an unmarked grave in the Broad Run Baptist Church Cemetery, New Baltimore, VA.
6k. **Mary Regina.** Born 3 Sept. 1880 in Fauquier Co., VA. Married her cousin, James Mars Johnson (sic; he was the son of Moses Johns(t)on Jr., and grandson of Moses and Duannah Johnston, whose daughter, Charlotte Johnston, married Mary's grandfather, John Burgess). Living with her mother and brother in 1910. Mary Burgess helped run her brothers' farm, living in an old house near New Baltimore, VA. She died child-less on 29 Mar. 1953, and is buried in the Warrenton Cemetery. Mary inherited the family papers of her father and grandfather, most of which were in turn saved by her niece, Evelyn Burgess Weineke.

[William (I)[1], Edward (I)[2], Edward (II)[3], John (II)[4], Dawson Jackson (I)[5]]

LITTLETON JACKSON BURGESS
(1862-1941)

OF FAUQUIER COUNTY, VIRGINIA

6b. **Littleton Jackson "B.B."** *[son of Dawson Jackson (I)].* Born 1 Feb. 1862 in Fauquier Co., VA. Married Minnie Elizabeth Allison on 26 Dec. 1883 in Fauquier Co. (she was born July 1865 in Fauquier Co., the daughter of John W. and Virginia M. Allison, and died 20 (?) Nov. 1905 in childbirth; after her untimely death her younger children were raised by Littleton's brothers and sisters). Listed in the 1900-20 censuses for Fauquier Co., VA (in 1920 living alone). Littleton Burgess was a farmer in Fauquier Co., VA; he died on 30 Mar. 1941, possibly at Washington, DC, and is buried in the Little Georgetown Church Cemetery.

The Children of Littleton Burgess:

7a. **Carrie (II).** Born 23 Aug. 1885 in Fauquier Co., VA; died there on 3 Apr. 1886.

7b. **John Dawson.** Born 28 Jan. 1887 in Fauquier Co., VA. See below for full entry.

7c. **Henry E. (II).** Born Dec. 1890 in Fauquier Co., VA. Listed with his father in the 1910 census, and with his uncle, George W. Burgess, in 1920. He died childless in 1940, possibly at Washington, DC, and is buried with his father. He may be the Henry Burgess (with wife Rosa) listed in the 1939 city directory for Washington, DC working as a taxi driver.

7d. **Evelyn "Eva."** Born 20 June 1892 in Fauquier Co., VA. Living with her father in 1910. Married Joe Janin about 1916 (he may have been born 19 July 1886, and died Oct. 1968 in MD), and had children: *Mary J.* (born about 1917, married ___ LeComte, and was living at Blairsville, GA in 1984). Living at Washington, DC in 1948, where she reportedly died.

7e. **Lillian.** Born 8 Feb. 1895 in Fauquier Co., VA. Living with her father in 1910; she may be listed with her cousin, Edgar Artis, in the 1920 census for Washington, DC. Lillian Burgess died childless before 1941, and is buried in the Cedar Hill Cemetery, Suitland, MD.

7f. **Nancy Jane (IV) "Nannie."** Born 24 Sept. 1898 in Fauquier Co., VA. Married Henry S. White about 1914, and had children: *Ashby H.* (born about 1915, and was living at Dunnellon, FL in 1984); *Margaret W.* (born 20 Nov. 1916, married ___ Turner, and died on 8 Jan. 1988 at Warrenton, VA); *Evelyn W.* (born about 1918, married ___ Hunnicutt, and was living at Culpeper, VA in 1984); *Harry W.* (born 11 June 1920, and died on 31 Dec. 1990 at Berkeley Springs, WV); *Mary E.* (born about 1922, married ___ Burrows, and was living at Arlington, VA in 1984); *Douglas E.* (born about 1930, and was living at Warrenton in 1984); *Maurice W.* (born about 1932, and was living at Great Falls, VA in 1984); *Helen* (born about 1934, married ___ Mayhugh, and lives at Warrenton, VA); *Wesley L.* (born about 1936, and was living at Aiea, HI in 1984). Nannie WHITE married secondly Wayne G. Garman (he was born 2 July 1896, and died Aug. 1964 in VA). Listed with her father in the 1910 census. She was living at Broad Run, VA from 1941-48, and later at Annandale, Fairfax Co., VA. Nannie Garman died on 8 Aug. 1961 at Arlington, Arlington Co., VA, and is buried in the Arlington National Cemetery.

7g. **Mary V(irginia?).** Born Mar. 1900 in Fauquier Co., VA. Mary Burgess died there unmarried in 1920, and is buried with her father.

7h. **Mamie E.** Born 1902 in Fauquier Co., VA. Listed with Zaccheus Burgess (and his brothers and sister) in the 1910 census. She died unmarried between 16 June 1932 (when she sued Lewis J. Allison, as recorded in the *Fauquier Co. Judgment Docket Book #3*, p. 48) and 1941.

7i. **Clara (II)** (nmn). Born 4 June 1904 in Fauquier Co., VA. Living with Zaccheus Burgess and his brothers and sister in the 1910 census. Married R. Carl Mitchell, and lived at Washington, DC for many years. Clara Mitchell died childless on 7 May 1984 at Fairfax, VA, and is buried in the Cedar Hill Cemetery, Suitland, MD.

7j. **Wesley D.** Born 20 Nov. 1905 in Fauquier Co., VA. Listed with John W. Allison (his grandfather) in the 1910 census. Married Elizabeth W. ___ (she was born 24 May 1907, and died Jan. 1976 at Milford, CT). Wesley Burgess was living at Bridgeport, CT in 1942, but later moved to Milford, CT, where he died in May 1970.

8a. **(Wesley) Rudolph.** Born about 1932. He was living at Devon, CT in 1984.

JOHN DAWSON BURGESS OF FAUQUIER CO., VIRGINIA
[Littleton Jackson[6]]

7b. **John Dawson** *[son of Littleton Jackson].* Born 28 Jan. 1887 (or 29 Jan. 1888) in Fauquier Co., VA. Married Annie H. Hurst (she died 1958). Listed in the 1920 census for Fauquier Co., VA. John Burgess was a farmer in Fauquier Co. He was hit and killed by a train on 20 (or 23) Sept. 1937 near Alexandria, VA, and is buried in the Little Georgetown Church Cemetery.

8a. **James Littleton.** Born 14 Oct. 1911 at Broad Run, VA. Jim Burgess served in the U.S. Army in World War II, and was wounded in Italy. He died unmarried on 25 Mar. 1968 at Salisbury, NC.

8b. **Frances Elizabeth.** Born 21 Feb. 1914 at Broad Run, VA. Married James George Vidi (he was born 12 Oct. 1912, and died Mar. 1975 in MD). Frances Vidi was living in Suitland, MD in 1959, but currently resides at Forestville, MD.

8c. **Lucille Virginia.** Born 4 Dec. 1915 at Broad Run, VA. Married James Jenkins. Living at Charlotte, NC in 1959.

8d. **Clarence Washington.** Born 1 Aug. 1918 near Broad Run, VA. Married Leona Poelcher. Clarence Burgess worked in a rayon production company before retiring. He currently lives near Maurerton, VA.

9a. **John Douglas.** Born 8 Aug. 1946 at Front Royal, VA. Lives at Woodstock, VA.

9b. **George Thomas (II).** Born 22 Apr. 1949 at Front Royal, VA. Lives at Maurerton, VA.

9c. **(Clarence) Wesley.** Born 3 Dec. 1955 at Winchester, VA. Lives at Woodstock, VA.

The Burgess Family at Meadow Lake, Saskatchewan, 1936 (p. 129-30)
(back left) Hubert & Leola Burgess Hillman, Myrtle Burgess, Etta & Don Speer, unknown, Art Hillman
(front left) Walter Hillman, unknown, Rebecca Burgess, unknown, G. Walter Burgess, Lester Speer Jr.

[William (I)[1], Edward (I)[2], Edward (II)[3], John (II)[4], Dawson Jackson (I)[5]]

DAWSON JACKSON BURGESS, JR.
(1866-1933)

OF FAUQUIER COUNTY, VIRGINIA

6d. **Dawson Jackson (II) "Dorsey"** *[son of Dawson Jackson (I)].* Born 25 Feb. 1866 in Fauquier Co., VA. Married Anna A. Meeks on 6 Jan. 1892 in Fauquier Co., VA (she was born June 1868 in Fauquier Co., the daughter of Charles H. and Susan F. Meeks). Listed in the 1900-20 censuses for Fauquier Co., VA (Susan Meeks is living with them in 1920). Dorsey Burgess was a farmer near New Baltimore, VA. He died there on 23 Aug. 1933, and is buried in an unmarked grave in the Broad Run Baptist Church Cemetery. He owned the family Bibles of his Burgess grandfather and father.

The Children of Dawson J. Burgess, Jr.:

7a. **LaClaire Marstellar.** He was named for LaClaire Arell Marstellar, a well-known Civil War soldier buried at Warrenton. Born 18 Jan. 1895 in Fauquier Co., VA. Listed with his father in the 1920 census. LaClaire Burgess was a farmer on his father's lands in Fauquier Co. He died there unmarried on 14 July 1925, and is buried in the Broad Run Baptist Church Cemetery, being the only one of the many Burgesses there to have a tombstone.

7b. **Evelyn Forrester.** Born 8 Sept. 1908 in Fauquier Co., VA. Married Henry George Wieneke Sr. (he was born 26 Sept. 1892, and died 6 Dec. 1961 at Warrenton, VA), and had children: *Henry George Jr.* (married, had children, and lives at Ocala, FL). She was living at Gainesville, VA in 1948. Evelyn Weineke owned several of the family Bibles and papers, some of which were lost after her death. Henry G. Weineke Jr. has the family Bible of Dawson Burgess Sr. Evelyn's granddaughter, Phyllis Cornwell, lives at Warrenton. Evelyn Weineke died in Dec. 1973 at Warrenton, VA, and is buried in the Manassas Cemetery, Manassas, VA.

A LETTER FROM D. J. BURGESS TO MRS. ASHLAN F. HARLAN

Gainesville, Va., R.F.D. #1, Box 70, June 7-1927.

My Dear Mrs. Harlan, Your letter of records of the Burgess family was handed me by Brother George W. Burgess. You have the records of John & Charlotte Burgess about correct—except—Dawson J. Burgess who married Miss Anna Meeks—Dawson Jr.—is a son of Dawson Burgess who is a brother of your grandfather, Peyton P. Burgess. You want the records of our ancesters to prove your wright to be come a member of the D.A.R. So I will give you all the information I have at hand. First, Edward Burgess, this is the family's records you need the most, and his ancesters. Now, John Burgess, a son of the above Edward Burgess, was born June 11-1771-and Sharlotte Johnson Burgess, his wife, was born November 12-1787-and was married November 12, 1805. John Burgess deceased December 12, 1855, aged 84 years, 6 m., and 1 day. I have no date of Charlotte death. I have no record of of [sic] the Johnson side of the House. This part of the record I have taken from the old family Bible. John Burgess had brothers William and Mayson Burgess. These brothers had large land grants from the Mexican Gov. The first grant was in 1835 of some 7 000 500 acres of land. This land was located in the State of Texas, then a part of the Gov. of Mexico. It appeared that they died without hires at law, and a wates [i.e., awaits] the hirs of one John Burgess to prove thire claims. I am sory I can not give you more information, but would advise you to [write to] my sister, Mrs. Mary R. Johnson Burgess of Warrenton, Va. She married James M. Johnson, and I think she has the old family Bible of the Johnson family. They are related all to the a childs family [sic]. You may get a lead to the Johnson side of the House. Whishing you every success in tracing our ancestry. Let me hear from you some time. And till me something a bout your self. If I get any information that will help you further, I will be glad to send it to you. Yours very truly, from your secon cousin, Dawson J. Burgess.

[William (I)[1], Edward (I)[2], Edward (II)[3], John (II)[4], Dawson Jackson (I)[5]]

EDWIN BURGESS
(1877-1948)

OF FAUQUIER COUNTY, VIRGINIA

6i. **Edwin (II)** (twin) *[son of Dawson Jackson (I)].* Born 23 Mar. 1877 in Fauquier Co., VA. Married Katherine "Kate" Wines on 10 May 1897 in Fauquier Co. (she was born about 1881 in Fauquier Co., the daughter of W. T. and Caroline Wines, and died Feb. 1917 in Fauquier Co.). Listed in the 1900-20 censuses for Fauquier Co.; six of six children survive in 1910. Edwin Burgess was a farmer in Fauquier Co., VA. He died there on 1 Oct. 1948, and is buried with his wife in the Warrenton Cemetery.

7a. **Irving Ashton.** Born 2 Sept. 1897 in Fauquier Co., VA. Has not been found in the 1920 census. Irving Burgess was a steeplechase jockey on Long Island, NY. He died at Hempstead, NY in Jan. 1985.

8a. **James Ashton.** He may live at Hempstead, NY.

7b. **Carlton Lee "Deacon."** Born 15 Dec. 1899 (or 1901, according to his death certificate) in Fauquier Co., VA. Married Ella May Grimsley on 6 Oct. 1923 in Fauquier Co. (she was born 27 Apr. 1894, and died 28 Sept. 1928); married secondly Lula Mayhugh on 25 Dec. 1929 (she died on 31 Mar. 1951). Listed in the 1920 census for Northumberland Co., VA living with Robert J. Martin. Deacon Burgess was a commercial painter in Warrenton (where he was living in 1948), and in Maryland. He died childless on 24 Jan. 1970 at Bethesda, MD, but is buried with his wives in the Warrenton Cemetery.

7c. **Douglas Morton (I).** Born 12 Feb. 1902 in Fauquier Co., VA. Married Ethel Ruby Haigler on 23 July 1925 at Washington, DC (div.; she remarried Earl Smith). Listed with his father in 1920; living at Rockville, MD in 1948. Douglas Burgess was a horse and hound trainer (for steeplechases and fox hunts), and Master of the Hunt for the Potomac Hunt Club. He died in Oct. 1975 at Rockville, MD.

8a. **Douglas Morton (II).** Lives at Poolsville, MD.
8b. **Kitty.**

7d. **Marie Evelyn "Elva."** Born 1904 in Fauquier Co., VA. Married Ross Payne (dec.), and lives at Arlington, VA.

7e. **Haldane Councel "Hallie."** He was also called Harold Burgess. Born 25 Nov. 1906 in Fauquier Co., VA. Married Celestinea Marian Conner on 2 Sept. 1933 (div.); married secondly Julia J. Edwards on 26 May 1949 in Fauquier Co. (she was born about 1923 at Upperville, VA). Hallie Burgess was a horse trainer for fox hunt clubs at Middleburg, VA (where he was living in 1948) and in Maryland. He died in Apr. 1974 at Rockville, MD.

8a. **Thelma Jean.**
8b. **Robert Langley.**
8c. **Walter.** He may be living at Silver Spring, MD.

7f. **Mabel (II).** Born about 1907 in Fauquier Co., VA. Married Edgar Grimsley, and had children: *James* (twin); *Julian* (twin; died at age 20); *Hal*; *Patsy* (dec.); *Child* (died at eight months).

7g. **Violet Virginia.** Born about 1909 in Fauquier Co., VA. Married Percival G. Crawford on 19 May 1928 in Fauquier Co. (he was born about 1907, and died Sept. 1949 or 1950), and had children: *David* (born about 1929); *Jacquelin* (born about 1933); *Gary* (born about 1947). Living at Arlington, VA in 1948. Violet Crawford died in July 1950 (or 1951) at Arlington, and is buried there in the National Memorial Park Cemetery.

7h. **Margaret Lucille (I).** Born 27 Apr. 1911 in Fauquier Co., VA. Married George L. Mayhugh on 2 Mar. 1929 in Fauquier Co. (div.; he was born 8 Aug. 1911 in Prince William Co., and died in May 1982 at The Plains, VA), and had children: *Eleanor* (married ___ Hyde, and lives in Fauquier Co.); *Carroll* (died 1934 at Virginia Beach, VA); *(George) MacArthur "Mack"* (born 1942, works as an attorney in Fauquier Co.). Margaret Mayhugh died Oct. 1989 at Warrenton, VA.

7i. **Edwin Maphis.** Born 25 Oct. 1915 in Fauquier Co., VA. Married Katharine Elizabeth Cubbage (she was born 8 Aug. 1918, and died 26 July 1968). Edwin Burgess was a horse trainer and farmer at The Plains, VA. He died there on 23 Dec. 1984, and is buried with his wife in the Warrenton Cemetery.

8a. **Peggy Carol.** Born 27 July 1939 at Warrenton, VA. Married Charles Clifton Gray on 12 Apr. 1959 in Fauquier Co., VA (he was born about 1936 at Broad Run, VA), and had children: *Stuart Edwin* (married and had two children). Peggy Gray was Secretary/Treasurer of V.D. & D. Inc., Warrenton, VA, a surveying company, before retiring. She is a breeder of Jack Russell dogs, and has a daycare center in rural Fauquier Co.

8b. **Joyce Ann.** Born 11 Dec. 1941 at Marshall, VA. Married Edward Nathan Sisk on 20 Oct. 1960 in Fauquier Co., VA (he was born about 1938 at Marshall, VA), and had children: *Scott* (married, and had two children); *Jeffrey* (married, and had one child); *Kevin*. Joyce Sisk is a secretary for the Fairfax Co., VA school board. She currently lives at Arlington, VA.

7j. **Katherine Sarah.** Born 5 July 1917 in Fauquier Co., VA. Married William Joseph Mayhugh on 22 Dec. 1934 in Fauquier Co. (he was born 25 June 1916, and died in Apr. 1984 at Gainesville, VA), and had children: *William Joseph Jr.* (born 7 Jan. 1942 at Warrenton, VA, married Julia House on 19 Aug. 1962 at Greenwich, VA, and had children: Michael Douglas [born 3 Sept. 1963 at Warrenton, VA]; Cheryl Lynn [born 10 Feb. 1965 at Warrenton, VA]; Dawn Marie [born 15 Jan. 1971 at Manassas, VA]); *Mary Elizabeth* (born 17 June 1947 at Warrenton, VA, married Gene Fairfax, and had children: Beth; Lisa); *Phyllis Lee* (born 12 Nov. 1952, married Gary Robbins, and had children: Katie; Kevin). Living at Nokesville, VA in 1948. Katherine Mayhugh currently lives at Manassas, VA.

Samuel Thomas Burgess Sr.
(1844-1921)
Della Conley Burgess
(1862-1956)
Florence Loraine Burgess Graham
(1897-1978)
(see page 242)

[William (I)[1], Edward (I)[2], Edward (II)[3]]

MASON BURGESS
(1776-1845)

OF ORANGE COUNTY, INDIANA

4d. **Mason Peyton** *[son of Edward (II)].* Born 14 Aug. 1776 in Prince William Co., VA. Married Elizabeth Cornwell on 15 May 1806 at Crab Orchard, Jefferson Co., KY (she was born 24 June 1787 in VA, daughter of Simon Cornwell, and died 17 Mar. 1872 at Stampers Creek, IN). Listed in the tax records for Fauquier Co. from 1793-1804, when his name is marked "De." (departed). Moved to Jefferson Co., KY, where he is listed in the 1810 census, and also in the 1806-1809 tax lists (the only ones extant from this period). His marriage bond and the 1806-1807 tax lists give his name as "Peyton Burges." Served in the 13th (Gray's) Regiment, Kentucky Militia, in the War of 1812. Moved to Orange Co., IN about 1819, and appears in the 1820-40 censuses there for Stampers Creek Township (in 1820 with three sons under the age of 10, and one aged 10-16); Elizabeth is listed with her son, Thornton Burgess, in 1850, and with another son, Thomas M. Burgess, in 1860 ("at rest"). Mason Burgess was a farmer in Orange Co., IN; his land was located in the NE ¼ of the NE ¼ of Section 2, Township 1 North, Range 2 (or 1) East, Stampers Creek Township. He died there on 29 Sept. 1845, and is buried with his wife and three descendants behind his former house, at Maeham Corner, on the south side of State Road 56, one and one-half miles west of Millersburg, IN. His surviving "heirs at law" are mentioned in a series of deeds dated 2 Mar. 1850 (*Orange Co. Deed Book #14*, p. 383-387 [two deeds]), in which his lands are partitioned as the settlement of a lawsuit brought by William Cornwell assignee of Dawson Burgess against his brothers and sisters: Thornton Burgess, Edmund Burgess, Lewis Burgess, James Baker and Sally his wife, Daniel Richardson and Phebe Ann his wife, Joseph Skinner and Polly his wife, Thomas M. Burgess, and Elizabeth Burgess widow of Mason Burgess.

The Children of Mason Burgess:

5a. **Francis (I).** Born 1807 in Jefferson, KY. According to a family story, she is said to have died at about the age of twelve (about 1819) from effects of a broken leg when she fell off a horse, while on the way from Virginia (or Kentucky) to Indiana, and was buried by the side of the road. Other than family tradition, no separate verification exists for Mason's two oldest children. Exact order and dates uncertain.

5b. **John (V).** Born 1808 in Jefferson Co., KY. The presence of an unidentified son born before 1810 on Mason's 1820 census record coincides with the family tradition of a son John who died young; he does not appear on the 1830 census. His inclusion here should be regarded as speculative. Exact order and dates uncertain.

5c. **Lewis.** Born 5 Apr. 1809 in Jefferson Co., KY. See below for full entry.

5d. **Dawson (II).** Born about 1811 in Jefferson Co., KY. See below for full entry.

5e. **Mary (VI) "Polly."** Born about 1813 in Jefferson Co., KY. Married Ezekiel Robbins on 29 Jan. 1835 in Orange Co., IN; married secondly Joseph Skinner; married thirdly ___ Taylor by 1881. Mary Robbins was living in 1851 in Orange Co., IN; she signed the receipt for her share of her father's estate in 1881 as "Mary Taylor."

5f. **Sarah (VI) "Sally."** Born 13 July 1815 in Jefferson Co., KY. Married Dr. James Baker on 3 July 1834 in Orange Co., IN (he was born 26 Mar. 1814 in Woodford Co., KY, and died 21 Apr. 1887), and had nine children, three of them living in 1884: *Elizabeth E. "Lizzie"* (married Jacob Marshall on 27 Dec. 1864 in Orange Co., and had children: James [had a son, Clotz]; John [a noted Christian minister, and had children: Bruce; Wilhelmina]; Golda M. "Goldie" [married Roy H. Oliphant]; Lydia A. [born 1871, married Joseph L. Cornwell on 4 Oct. 1891 in Orange Co. {he was born 1870, son of Harrison and Margaret Cornwell, and died 1940}, and had children: Altha {died young, buried Syria Cemetery}]; Laura E. [married Lemuel Joseph Pickens on 3 June 1888 in Orange Co., and had children: Oscar; Florence {married Bert Edwards}; Mary]; Cora [married ___ Mullins]; Orpheus [lived at Fort Worth, TX]); *(Almon) Vader* (born 14 Apr. 1853, married Jennie Lin Wells on 6 June 1877 in Orange Co. [she was born

23 Mar. 1854, and died 4 Mar. 1908], had children: Elva E. [born 1879, died 1924, buried with her parents]; Hattie [born 8 Sept. 1884, died 22 July 1901]; Bennie [born 25 Jan. 1892, died 20 Jan. 1901]; Child [born and died 29 Jan. 1895], and died 14 Jan. 1920, buried Stampers Creek Cemetery); *Sarah E.* (married Stephen M. Byrum on 6 Mar. 1878 in Orange Co.). Listed in the 1880 census for Orange Co., IN. She was a Methodist. Sally Baker died on 3 Feb. 1890 at Millersburg, IN, and is buried with her husband in the Stampers Creek Cemetery. James Baker's biography was published in *History of Lawrence, Orange, and Washington Counties, Indiana* (Chicago: Goodspeed Bros. & Co., 1884, p. 662):

THE BIOGRAPHY OF DR. JAMES BAKER

"Dr. James Baker, of Millersburg, was born in Woodford County, Ky., March 29, 1814. Immediately after this his parents moved to what is now Stampers Creek Township, Orange County, Ind., where the Doctor's home has ever since been. His education is not extensive, having been limited to the early country schools of his time. The first part of the Doctor's life was passed upon the farm, and he worked some at the shoemaker's trade. About the age of twenty-six years, he began the study of medicine at odd hours between his labors. Having sufficiently qualified himself, he began the practice of his profession about the year 1850, and has continued it ever since with good success. He is a member of the Christian, and his wife of the Methodist Episcopal Church. The Doctor is a Republican, and has been such ever since 1860, prior to which time he was a Whig. He was at one time Justice of the Peace of Stampers Creek Township, and is the present Postmaster at Millersburg. His nuptials with Miss Sarah Burgess were celebrated July 3, 1834, and the fruits of this union were nine children, only three of whom are now alive: Mrs. Lizzie Marshall, Almon V., and Mrs. Sarah E. Byrum. Dr. Baker is one of the highly esteemed citizens of Orange County, where he has lived to be one of its very old settlers."

5g. **Thornton (II).** Born 16 Aug. 1817 in Jefferson Co., KY. See below for full entry.

5h. **Phebe Ann.** Born 6 Nov. 1819 in Orange Co., IN. Married Daniel S. Richardson (or Richeson) on 20 Sept. 1846 in Orange Co. (he was born 2 Oct. 1823 in IN, and died 12 July 1902), and had children: *William* (born 11 June 1847 in Orange Co., IN, died 12 Aug. 1851, buried Trimble Cemetery); *Thomas Mason* (born 18 Jan. 1849 in Orange Co., IN, married Melvina L. ___ [she was born 13 Mar. 1850, and died 13 Dec. 1925], was a minister, and had children: Ellsworth [born 1870]; Minnie [born 1874]; Luella [born 1872]; *Thomas Mason* died on 10 Nov. 1911, and is buried in the Mount Pleasant Cemetery); *Addison* (born 1850 in Orange Co., IN, married Harriet M. ___ [she was born 1854, and died 1943], and had children: George [born 1874]; Fred [born 1877]; Any B. [born 1879]; *Addison* died in 1926, and is buried in the Mount Pleasant Cemetery; listed in the 1880 census for Wayne Co., IL); *Albert L.* (born 1852 in Orange Co., IN, married Nancy E. ___ [she was born 1852, and died 1934], and had children: Laura [born 1872]; William H. [born 1874]; Frank [born 1876]; Daniel [born 1878]; *Albert L.* died in 1925, and is buried in the Mount Pleasant Cemetery); *Volney* (born 1854 in Orange Co., IN, married Amanda ___, and is listed in the 1880 census for Wayne Co. next door to his parents); *John* (born 1856 in Orange Co., IN); *George F.* (born 1 Aug. 1858 in Orange Co., IN, died 29 Apr. 1864 in Wayne Co., IL, buried Mount Pleasant Cemetery). Moved to Illinois about 1860. Listed in the 1870-80 censuses for Brush Creek Township, Wayne Co., IL. Phoebe Richardson died on 21 Jan. 1899 in Wayne Co., IL, and is buried with her husband in the Mount Pleasant Cemetery.

5i. **Edmund (I).** Born 5 Feb. 1824 in Orange Co., IN. See below for full entry.

5j. **Thomas Mason (I).** Born 19 July 1827 in Orange Co., IN. See below for full entry.

[William (I)[1], Edward (I)[2], Edward (II)[3], Mason Peyton[4]]

LEWIS BURGESS
(1809-1881)

OF WAYNE COUNTY, ILLINOIS

5c. **Lewis** *[son of Mason Peyton].* Born 5 Apr. 1809 in Jefferson Co., KY. Married Malvina Montgale on 28 Oct. 1838 in Orange Co., IN (she was born 8 Nov. 1819, and died 11 July 1841); married secondly M(ary?) Alice "Alley" Warren about 1844 (she was born 20 July 1822 in IL, and died 10 July 1862); married thirdly Jane Hawkins by 1870 (surname unverified; she was born about 1815 in IN, and died between 1870-80). Listed in the 1850-80 censuses for Wayne Co., IL. Lewis Burgess was a farmer in Wayne Co. IL. He died there on 1 Jan. 1881, and is buried in the Mount Pleasant Cemetery with his first two wives.

The Children of Lewis Burgess:

6a. **William Thornton (I).** Born 11 July 1841 in Orange Co., IN. See below for full entry.

6b. **Elizabeth E. (I).** Born 30 Aug. 1845 in Wayne Co., IL. Married Joseph Slover about 1867 (he was born Aug. 1844 in IL), and had at least the following children: *Francis M(arion?)* (born 1868); *Sarah A.* (born Mar. 1870); *Georgiann* (born 1872, married Frank Brashear on 13 Feb. 1899 in Wayne Co.); *Louis* (born 1874); *John* (born Apr. 1877); *James* (born July 1880, married Clara C. Barnhouse on 24 Oct. 1900 in Wayne Co.); *William E.* (born Mar. 1883); *Omar* (or Elmer) (born July 1885, married secondly Mamie Bush on 20 Nov. 1911 in Wayne Co.). Listed in the 1870-1900 censuses for Wayne Co., IL. Elizabeth Slover died on 28 Feb. 1901 in Wayne Co., and is buried in the Mount Pleasant Cemetery.

6c. **Mary Ann (II) "Polly."** Born 3 Feb. 1847 in Wayne Co., IL. Married John Freelon Henson about 1867 (he was born 5 Aug. 1848 in IL, and died 5 May 1912), and had at least the following children: *Lewis M.* (born 1868); *Jeremiah E. "Jerry"* (born Mar. 1869); *Cordelia* (born 1871); *Reuben H.* (born 1873); *Parthelia* (born 1875); *Louvelia* (born 1876); *William* (born 1878); *Sophronia* (born 1880); *Jefferson M.* (born Aug. 1882, married Ona B. Ayers on 23 Dec. 1912 in Wayne Co.); *Frelon Henderx* (born 29 June 1884, married Nora Garrison on 9 Feb. 1903 in Wayne Co., married secondly Effie E. Daniels on 30 Sept. 1910 in Wayne Co.); *Versa P.* (born Apr. 1888, married Clarance A. Ellis on 15 June 1905 in Wayne Co.). Listed in the 1870-1900 censuses for Orchard Township, Wayne Co., IL. Polly Henson died on 28 Jan. 1906 in Wayne Co., and is buried in the Henson Cemetery.

6d. **Melvina Jane (I).** Her name is listed as Malvina on her tomb, but Melvina on her death certificate and in the census records. Born 28 Feb. 1849 in Wayne Co., IL. Listed with her father in the 1880 census. Married Joseph L. Brown on 22 July 1880 in Wayne Co., IL (he was born 1850, and died 1922). Listed in the 1900 census for Orchard Township, Wayne Co., IL. Melvina Brown died childless of the effects of an infected leg ulcer on 30 July 1926 in Wayne Co., IL, and is buried with her husband in the Mount Pleasant Cemetery.

6e. **Mason Mathew.** Born 9 Oct. 1852 in Wayne Co., IL. See below for full entry.

6f. **Volney Leeport.** Born 26 Sept. 1854 in Wayne Co., IL. See below for full entry.

6g. **Francis Martin.** Born 5 Mar. 1856 in Wayne Co., IL. See below for full entry.

6h. **Mahulda E. "Huldah."** Born 3 Apr. 1860 in Wayne Co., IL. Married A. J. Mosby on 4 Feb. 1881 in Wayne Co., IL; married secondly ___ Gilliland; married thirdly Philip Henson on 14 June 1891 in Wayne Co., IL (he was born 2 Dec. 1842, and died 4 Apr. 1919), and had at least the following children: *Evilena* (born July 1894); *Freddie* (born Nov. 1897). Listed in the 1880 census for Wayne Co., IL, and in 1900 with her family in Orchard Township. Huldah Henson died on 21 Apr. 1933 in Wayne Co., and is buried in the Henson Cemetery.

6i. **Cordelia A.** Born 30 Jan. 1862 in Wayne Co., IL; died there on 31 July 1862, and is buried in the Mount Pleasant Cemetery.

[William (I)[1], Edward (I)[2], Edward (II)[3], Mason Peyton[4], Lewis[5]]

WILLIAM THORNTON BURGESS
(1841-1888)

OF WAYNE COUNTY, ILLINOIS

6a. **William Thornton (I) "Will"** *[son of Lewis].* Born 11 (?) July 1841 in Orange Co., IN. Married Mary Jane Bowers about 1860 (she was born about 1840 in IN, and died Sept. 1878 in Wayne Co.); married secondly Elizabeth Holler in Oct. 1879 (she was born about 1834 in IN). Served in Co. C., 111th Illinois Infantry, Union Army, during the Civil War, and may be the William Burgess mentioned in Ethel Burgess Harlan's notes who was part of the occupying army in Fauquier Co., VA during 1864-65; after his death his daughter, Celia A. Jones, obtained a pension based on his service record. Listed in the 1870-80 censuses for Brush Creek Township, Wayne Co., IL. William T. Burgess was a farmer in Wayne and Clay Cos., IL. He died on 1 Jan. 1888 in Wayne Co., and is buried in the Onstott Cemetery, west of Xenia, Clay Co., IL.

The Children of William T. Burgess:

7a. **Melvina Jane (II) "Mollie."** Born 18 Sept. 1861 (or 1862, according to her death certificate) in Wayne Co., IL. Married Martin V. Miley about 1880 (he was born 1 Oct. 1855, and died 29 Aug. 1910), and had children: *Prentiss R.* (born Aug. 1881, married Rosabelle Milner on 23 Apr. 1905 in Wayne Co. [she was born 1885, and died 1919], had children: Opha Esther [born 26 Dec. 1909, died 12 July 1964], and died 1951, buried Mount Pleasant Cemetery); *John L.* (born Sept. 1884, married Myrtle Augusta Borton on 9 Dec. 1906 in Wayne Co., married secondly Nettie Byars on 25 May 1912 in Wayne Co., and died 1950, buried Mount Pleasant Cemetery); *Myrtle F. "Mertie"* (born May 1887, married Charlie Shannon on 29 Aug. 1907 in Wayne Co.). **Melvina MILEY** married secondly Gideon Bosley. Listed in the 1870 census for Wayne Co., IL with her parents, with John Webber in 1880 working as a servant, and with her family in the 1900 census for Orchard Township, Wayne Co., IL. Mollie Bosley died of breast cancer on 2 Dec. 1926 in Wayne Co., and is buried in the Mount Pleasant Cemetery.

7b. **Diantha Emma "Dicey"** or **"Dica"**. Born about 1863 in Wayne Co., IL (age 29 in 1892). Married William P. Barnard on 11 Jan. 1880 in Wayne Co., IL (he was born 1858 in IN, and died in the 1880s); Dicey married secondly James Scott (he was born about 1863, and died between 1887-90), and had children: *James Fred* (born 12 Mar. 1888, living with Melvina Miley in 1900, may have died June 1964 at Springfield, IL); Dicey married thirdly G. J. Mifflin on 8 Oct. 1890 in Wayne Co. (who died by 1892); Dicey married fourthly J(ames) Curtis Leathers on 11 Feb. 1892 in Wayne Co. (he was born Dec. 1867 in IL, son of Wesley Leathers, remarried Ida Clark in 1898), and had children: *Myrtle Jane* (born 15 Oct. 1892; living with her father in 1900). Listed in the 1880 census for Wayne Co., IL; her fourth husband appears there in 1900. Dicey Leathers apparently died about 1892 (possibly in childbirth) in Wayne Co., IL, and is buried in the Hale Cemetery with her first husband (no dates appear on her stone).

7c. **Lewis E.** Born Jan. 1866 (or 1867) in Wayne Co., IL. See below for full entry.

7d. **Amanda.** Born about 1868 in Wayne Co., IL; died there before 1880.

7e. **Jacob M(ason?).** Born May 1870 in Wayne Co., IL. See below for full entry.

7f. **Celia Ann (I).** Born 21 Sept. 1872 in Wayne Co., IL. Married Alfred B. Jones on 13 Aug. 1890 in Wayne Co. (he was born 1867, and died 1896), and had children: *Netta Mae "Nettie"* (born 29 Jan. 1895, married her second cousin, Chester L. Burgess, married secondly Tom Dilliner, and died July 1974 at Grove, OK). Celia married secondly Elisha Jones on 10 May 1897 in Wayne Co. (he was born 1867, son of Hiram Jones and Jane Judd, and died in 1949), and had children: *Audra Ines* (born 1 July 1898); *Lora Jane* (born 1 Aug. 1900, married ___ Hawkins, and was living at Johnsonville, IL in 1992); *Reba Katherine* (born 9 Aug. 1902, married ___ White, and was living at Mt. Vernon, IL in the 1980s). Celia Jones died in 1954 in Wayne Co., and is buried in the Wesley Chapel Cemetery.

7g. **Mahala.** Born about 1874 in IL. Listed with her parents in the 1880 census. She probably died young after 1880.

7h. **(William) Oliver.** Born 22 Nov. 1877 in IL. See below for full entry.

LEWIS E. BURGESS OF STEPHENSON CO., ILLINOIS

[William Thornton (I)[6]]

7c. **Lewis E.** *[son of William Thornton (I)].* Born Jan. 1866 (or 1867) in Wayne Co., IL. Married Stella Tumbleston on 14 Apr. 1889 (she was born Dec. 1872 in Ohio or Kentucky). Listed in the 1900-10 censuses for Wabash Co., IL, in the 1917 draft list for Freeport, Stephenson Co., IL, and in the 1920 census for Silver Creek Township, Stephenson Co., IL. He was living in 1953 at Frankfort, Will Co., IL.

8a. **Walter Edwin.** Born 9 Oct. 1893 at Mt. Carmel, IL. Listed in the 1917 draft list of Stephenson Co., IL (indicated as married), and in the 1920 census with his father (as "E. Walter Burgess"). Walter Burgess was a brakeman for the Illinois Central Railroad. He died in June 1971 at Rock Island, Rock Island Co., IL. A possible son is the Edwin Burgess who was born 21 May 1918 and died July 1986 at Rock Island, IL.

9a. **Son** (twin).

9b. **Son** (twin).

8b. **Omie Urwin.** Born 20 Dec. 1896 at Mt. Carmel, IL. Listed in the 1917 draft list of Stephenson Co., IL, and in the 1920 census with his father (as "E. Omie Burgess"). Omie Childless died childless in Jan. 1963 in Illinois.

8c. **Pans(e)y C.** Listed in the 1920 census (with her father) as C. Pansey Burgess; she later changed her name to Delores. Born about 1902 in IL. Married Clifford Soper (he was born 20 Jan. 1909, and died June 1983 at Rockford, Winnebago Co., IL).

JACOB M. BURGESS OF GIBSON CO., INDIANA

[William Thornton (I)[6]]

7e. **Jacob M(ason?)** *[son of William Thornton (I)].* Born May 1870 in Wayne Co., IL. Married Nevada "Vada" Henson about 1893 (div.; she was born Feb. 1875, and died 1939, buried Henson Cemetery); married secondly ___ after 1920. Listed in the 1900-10 censuses for Orchard Township, Wayne Co., IL, and in 1920 at Mt. Carmel, Wabash Co., IL (across the river from Gibson Co., IN), living with John McBride. He is said later to have moved to Princeton, Gibson Co., IN.

8a. **Olma E.** Born Dec. 1893 in Wayne Co., IL. Married. She may be the Olma Bach who was born 28 Dec. 1893, and died 27 May 1990 at Monticello, White Co., IN.

8b. **Bobby.** Born about 1923 in Gibson Co., IN.

8c. **Leroy (II).** Born about 1925 in Gibson Co., IN.

WILLIAM OLIVER BURGESS OF WAYNE CO., ILLINOIS

[William Thornton (I)[6]]

7h. **(William) Oliver** *[son of William Thornton (I)].* Born 22 Nov. 1877 in Wayne Co., IL. Married Amanda J. Henson on 19 Nov. 1903 in Wayne Co. (she was born 1881, daughter of William Henson and Mary Holler, and died 1962). Listed in the 1910 census for Wayne Co., IL living with Martin V. Miley, in the 1917 draft list of Wayne Co., and in the 1920 census for Wayne Co. Oliver Burgess was a farmer in Wayne Co., IL. He died there on 5 Nov. 1956, and is buried in the Mount Pleasant Cemetery.

8a. **(William) Oval.** Born 27 Oct. 1904 in Wayne Co., IL. Married (Marjorie) Faye Hoover in 1934 (she was the daughter of Elijah A. Hoover). Oval Burgess was a school teacher at Johnsonville, Wayne Co., IL. He died there on 18 July 1983, and is buried in the Mount Pleasant Cemetery.

9a. **(Farrell) Dean.** Born 14 Feb. 1935 in Wayne Co., IL. Married Charlene J. Swanson on 8 Oct. 1955 at St. Charles, IL (she was born 20 Feb. 1937 at St. Charles, IL). Dean Burgess worked for twenty years for Illinois Bell, and for ten years for J.T.'s general store, Yorkville, IL.

10a. **Edward Dean.** Born 24 Apr. 1956 at St. Charles, IL. Married Sherry White on 1 Mar. 1974 at Batavia, IL; married secondly Ellen Lockridge on 17 Feb. 1979 at Naperville, IL; married thirdly Lyla Upchurch on 12 Feb. 1993 at Elgin, IL. Ed Burgess works as a commercial construction superintendent, specializing in fresh water treatment and waste water treatment, at Geneva, IL.

11a. **Daniel Dean.** Born 2 July 1974 at St. Charles, IL.
11b. **Dorian Austin.** Born 6 June 1976 at St. Charles, IL.
11c. **Dayna Louise.** Born 4 Aug. 1980 at Aurora, IL.

10b. **Ronald Lee (II).** Born 2 May 1957 at St. Charles, IL. Married Teri J. Nepsted on 24 May 1980 at Batavia, IL. Ronald Burgess is a structural architect at Houston, TX.

11a. **Travis Dean.** Born 7 Nov. 1987 at Houston, TX.
11b. **Tyler Lee.** Born 30 Mar. 1990 at Houston, TX.

10c. **William Owen (II) "Bill."** Born 16 Apr. 1964 at Aurora, IL. Married Belinda Gruber on 26 July 1986 at Plattville, IL; married secondly Ann Birau on 28 Dec. 1991 at McHenry, IL. Bill Burgess works as a contract manager in new home construction, at Johnsburg, IL.

9b. **(William) Otis.** Born 31 Mar. 1937 in Wayne Co., IL. Married secondly Janet Cox (div.). Otis Burgess works for Fedders Corporation, an air conditioning manufacturer, at Effingham, IL.
9c. **Eloise Kaye.** Born 4 Sept. 1938 in Wayne Co., IL. Married John Phillips (died 20 Sept. 1992). Eloise Phillips owns an auto store and theater at Flora, IL.

8b. **Charles Parker.** Born 3 Aug. 1907 in Wayne Co., IL. Married Beulah Harrell, sister of Erma J. Harrell (who married his cousin, Freddie Burgess). Charles Burgess was a school teacher at Centralia, Marion Co., IL. He died there on 18 Nov. 1937, and is buried in the Mount Pleasant Cemetery, Wayne Co. Beulah Burgess lives at Streator, IL.

9a. **Wilma Romaine.** Born 11 Sept. 1927 at Xenia, IL. Married Glen Lee. Wilma Lee currently lives at Sugar Land, TX.
9b. **Rita Louise (I).** Born 28 Sept. 1935 at Orchardville, IL. Married Emil Ragusa; married secondly David Fowler. Rita Fowler currently lives at New Port Richey, FL.

NOTE: Unidentified (but almost certainly related) infant Burgesses buried in the Mount Pleasant Cemetery include: Cathy Lynn (1960-1960); Nancy Sue (I) (born and died 14 Oct. 1955).

[William (I)[1], Edward (I)[2], Edward (II)[3], Mason Peyton[4], Lewis[5]]

MASON MATHEW BURGESS
(1852-1924)

OF WAYNE COUNTY, ILLINOIS

6e. **Mason Mathew "Mase"** *[son of Lewis].* His middle name is given as Mathews on his death certificate. Born 9 Oct. 1852 in Wayne Co., IL. Married Matilda Brown about 1871 (she was born 30 Jan. 1853, daughter of John Brown and Narcissus Henson, and died 28 Aug. 1922 in Wayne Co.). Listed in the 1880 census for Brush Creek Township, Wayne Co., IL, and in 1900-20 in Orchard Township. Mason M. Burgess was a farmer in Wayne Co. He died there on 17 June 1924, and is buried with his wife in the Mount Pleasant Cemetery. The descendants of Mason M. Burgess have held an annual reunion in Illinois for the past forty years.

The Children of Mason M. Burgess:

7a. **Mahala Adline.** Born 7 May 1872 in Wayne Co., IL. Living with her father in the 1900-20 censuses. She was crippled from birth. Mahala Burgess died unmarried on 17 Nov. 1925 in Wayne Co., and is buried in the Mount Pleasant Cemetery.

7b. **Alice Elizabeth "Alley."** Her name is listed as "Anna" in the 1880 census. Born 15 Feb. 1874 in Wayne Co., IL; died there on 3 Oct. 1882, and is buried in the Mount Pleasant Cemetery.

7c. **John Lewis.** Born 15 Mar. 1875 in Wayne Co., IL. See below for full entry.

7d. **William Thornton (II).** Born 22 Feb. 1877 in Wayne Co., IL. See below for full entry.

7e. **Thomas Mason (II).** Born 16 Nov. 1878 at Orchardville, IL. See below for full entry.

7f. **(Levi) Edmund.** Born 22 Aug. 1880 in Wayne Co., IL. See below for full entry.

7g. **Narcissus Ellen.** Born 16 Apr. 1882 in Wayne Co., IL. Married William Lester Gaumer on 22 Dec. 1901 in Wayne Co. (he was born 1879, son of C. Harry Gaumer and Mary Coil, and brother of S. J. Gaumer, who married Narcissus's first cousin, Anna Burgess, and died on 15 June 1938), and had children. Narcissus Gaumer died on 7 July 1912, and is buried in the Pleasant Hill Cemetery. One of her descendants is Max Gaumer of Sterling, IL.

7h. **Joseph Marion.** Born 4 May 1884 in Wayne Co., IL. See below for full entry.

7i. **Floyd Monroe.** Born 1 Dec. 1885 in Wayne Co., IL. See below for full entry.

7j. **Mahulda Jane.** Born 11 Sept. 1887 in Wayne Co., IL. Married Robert M. Burroughs on 5 Feb. 1905 in Wayne Co. Mahulda Burroughs died on 7 Aug. 1913 in Wayne Co., IL, and is buried in the Mount Pleasant Cemetery.

7k. **Lora May.** Born 31 July 1889 at Orchardville, Wayne Co., IL. Living with her father in 1910. Married Ernest Noble Henson on 2 Mar. 1913 in Wayne Co. (he was the son of Jerry A. Henson and Rose May Burkett), and had at least the following children: *Kermit Woodrow* (born 16 July 1915, died Feb. 1967). Lora Henson died on 30 July 1961, and is buried in the Oak Knoll Cemetery, Mt. Sterling, Brown Co., IL.

7l. **Phillip Etzenhouser.** Born 27 June 1891 in Wayne Co., IL. See below for full entry.

7m. **Jesse Linla.** Born 11 July 1895 in Wayne Co., IL. See below for full entry.

JOHN LEWIS BURGESS OF WAYNE CO., ILLINOIS
[Mason Mathew[6]]

7c. **John Lewis** *[son of Mason Mathew].* Born 15 Mar. 1875 in Wayne Co., IL. Married Etta Ethel Ellis on 20 Jan. 1898 in Wayne Co. (she was born 21 Jan. 1874, and died Oct. 1966). Listed in the 1900-20 censuses and the 1917 draft list for Orchard Township, Wayne Co., IL. John L. Burgess was a farmer in Wayne Co. He died there on 28 Apr. 1937, and is buried in the Mount Pleasant Cemetery.

8a. **(Laura) Elberta.** Born 2 Mar. 1899 in Wayne Co., IL. Married Lyle Henson by 1920 (he was born 30 May 1896, and died June 1978 at Tampico, IL). Elberta Henson died on 6 Jan. 1976 at Tampico, Whiteside Co., IL.

8b. **William Mason (II) "Willie."** Born 1 Feb. 1901 in Wayne Co., IL. Married Verna Elizabeth Melton after 1920 (she was born 3 Jan. 1903, and died Oct. 1974 at Xenia, IL). Listed with his father in the 1920 census. Willie Burgess was a farmer in Wayne Co., IL. He died on 29 Jan. 1984 at Xenia, Clay Co., IL, and is buried in the Powers Cemetery.

9a. **Dean Edward.** Born 31 Mar. 1935 in Wayne Co., IL; died there on 10 Apr. 1935, and is buried in the Mount Pleasant Cemetery.

8c. **Edith Purl.** Born 7 Apr. 1906 in Wayne Co., IL. Married James Button Melton (he was born 16 Dec. 1905, and died Aug. 1977 at Lanark, IL). Edith Melton died on 5 Feb. 1986 at Lanark, Carroll Co., IL.

8d. **Roy Robert.** Born 4 May 1912 in Wayne Co., IL. Married secondly Betty M. Byers about 1943. Roy Burgess died on 11 Oct. 1984 at Xenia, Clay Co., IL.

9a. **Betty Joan.** Born 26 Feb. 1933 in Wayne Co., IL.

9b. **Bobby Leon.** Born 4 Aug. 1935 in Wayne Co., IL. He lives at Flora, IL.

9c. **Vicki Jo.** Born 1 Dec. 1944 in Wayne Co., IL.

9d. **Challice Lynn.** Born 6 Aug. 1947 in Wayne Co., IL.

9e. **Gregory L.** Born 21 Jan. 1954 in Wayne Co., IL. Married Bambi ___, and lives in rural Wayne Co., IL.

WILLIAM THORNTON BURGESS II OF WAYNE CO., ILLINOIS

[Mason Mathew^6]

7d. **William Thornton (II)** *[son of Mason Mathew].* Born 22 Feb. 1877 in Wayne Co., IL. Married Nora L. Ellis on 16 Feb. 1902 in Wayne Co., IL (she was born 1881, and died on 19 June 1965). Listed in the 1910 census for Wayne Co., IL. William T. Burgess was a farmer in Wayne Co. He died there of apoplexy on 20 Nov. 1917, and is buried in the Mount Pleasant Cemetery.

8a. **Bertha A. B.** Born 2 Oct. 1904 in Wayne Co., IL. Married Loren Wood on 12 Oct. 1920 in Wayne Co.; married secondly W. Lester Marpel in 1938 (he was born 11 May 1902, and died in Apr. 1979 at Hazelwood, MO). Bertha Marpel died on 3 Jan. 1979 at Hazelwood, St. Louis Co., MO, but is buried at Stewardson, Shelby Co., IL.

8b. **Son.** Born 31 Aug. 1910 in Wayne Co., IL; died there on 7 Sept. 1910, and is buried in Jacob's Chapel Cemetery.

THOMAS MASON BURGESS II OF WAYNE CO., ILLINOIS

[Mason Mathew^6]

7e. **Thomas Mason (II)** *[son of Mason Mathew].* Born 16 Nov. 1878 at Orchardville, Wayne Co., IL. Married (Mary) Elizabeth "Lizzie" Coil on 14 Aug. 1902 in Wayne Co. (she was born 1882, and died 1970). Listed in the 1910-20 censuses and the 1917 draft list for Wayne Co., IL. Tom Burgess was a farmer in Wayne Co., IL. He died on 12 Apr. 1953 at Mt. Vernon, IL, and is buried in the Mount Pleasant Cemetery.

8a. **Myrtle May (I).** Born 19 June 1903 in Wayne Co., IL. Married Ralph Cecil Henson (he was born 21 Feb. 1901, and died Mar. 1975 at Xenia, IL). Myrtle Henson currently lives at Xenia, Clay Co., IL.

8b. **Harlin Lester "Harley."** Born 1 July 1906 in Wayne Co., IL. See below for full entry.

8c. **Raymond Robert.** Born 18 Jan. 1909 in Wayne Co., IL; died there on 12 Jan. 1914.

8d. **Lora Rebecca.** Born 9 Mar. 1911 in Wayne Co., IL.

8e. **Oakley Burl.** Born 1 Mar. 1912 in Wayne Co., IL; died there on 22 May 1913.

8f. **Reba Opal.** Born 17 Jan. 1915 in Wayne Co., IL. Married Lawrence Thomas Austin. Reba Austin died on 11 Jan. 1969.

8g. **Arvel Owen.** Born 29 Jan. 1918 in Wayne Co., IL. See below for full entry.

8h. **Leta Fern.** Born 5 Dec. 1922 in Wayne Co., IL. Married Howard Lamar Towns.

HARLEY BURGESS OF WAYNE CO., ILLINOIS

[Mason Mathew[6], Thomas Mason (II)[7]]

8b. **Harlin Lester "Harley"** *[son of Thomas Mason (II)].* Listed as Lester Burgess in the 1920 census. Born 1 July 1906 in Wayne Co., IL. Married Elsie Ellis; married secondly Freida Ruth Thomason about 1936. Harley Burgess died on 14 Apr. 1972 at Salem, Marion Co., IL, and is buried in the East Lawn Cemetery.

9a. **Eber Eugene.** Born 1927 in Wayne Co., IL. Married Aline Thomas. Eber Burgess lives at Bluford, IL.

10a. **Eddie Eugene.** Born 14 Jan. 1956 in Jefferson Co., IL. Married Tina Marie Bean.

11a. **Tony Eugene.** Born 10 Apr. 1976 in Jefferson Co., IL.
11b. **Shawn Michael.** Born 26 Aug. 1978 in Jefferson Co., IL.

10b. **Robbin Ann.** Born 2 Aug. 1965 in Jefferson Co., IL.

9b. **Loren Ellis.** Born 15 Feb. 1928 in Wayne Co., IL. Married Barbara Jane Wood. Loren Burgess died on 21 Jan. 1979 at Webber, Jefferson Co., IL, and is buried in the Garrison Temple Cemetery.

10a. **Garry Ray.** Born 28 Aug. 1946 in Jefferson Co., IL. Married Judy Carol Gurganus.

11a. **Jason Ray.** Born 15 Sept. 1977 in Jefferson Co., IL.

10b. **Janice Sue.** Born 22 Sept. 1950 in Jefferson Co., IL.

9c. **Elbertia Ruth**. Her name is listed as Alberta in her birth record. Born 25 Sept. 1937 in Wayne Co., IL.
9d. **Carolyn Kay**. Born 12 June 1939 in Wayne Co., IL.
9e. **Larry Lester**. Born 27 Jan. 1942 in Wayne Co., IL.

ARVEL O. BURGESS OF JEFFERSON CO., ILLINOIS

[Mason Mathew[6], Thomas Mason (II)[7]]

8g. **Arvel Owen** *[son of Thomas Mason (II)].* Listed as Owen Burgess in the 1920 census. Born 29 Jan. 1918 in Wayne Co., IL. Married Reba Pearl Keene. Arvel Burgess lives at Mt. Vernon, IL.

9a. **Shirley Mae**. Born 4 Mar. 1939 in Wayne Co., IL.
9b. **Gary Owen**. Born 6 June 1941 in Wayne Co., IL. Died May 1981 in IL.
9c. **Beverly JoAnn**. Born 18 Oct. 1942 at Mt. Vernon, Jefferson Co., IL.

EDMUND BURGESS OF WHITESIDE CO., ILLINOIS

[Mason Mathew[6]]

7f. **(Levi) Edmund "Ed"** *[son of Mason Mathew].* Born 22 Aug. 1880 in Wayne Co., IL. Married Lillie Margaret Allein (or Allen; she died 6 Oct. 1960). Listed in the 1917 draft list for Wayne Co., IL, and in the 1920 census for Livingston Co., IL. Died 18 Dec. 1943 at Prophetstown, Whiteside Co., IL.

8a. **Franie Opal.** Born 16 Mar. 1905 in Wayne Co., IL. Married (William) Eldo Richardson on 16 Dec. 1927 (he remarried Lucie Vaughn on 16 Aug. 1990), and had children: *Darlene* (married Harold E. Siegman on 17 Apr. 1966). Franie Richardson died on 13 Jan. 1973 at Magnolia, Putnam Co., IL.
8b. **Ona Marie.** Born 29 Sept. 1907 in Wayne Co., IL. Married Eber Southard (he was born 11 Sept. 1906, and died July 1958). Ona Southard died on 15 July 1985 at Marshalltown, Marshall Co., IA.
8c. **(Wilbur) Marshall.** Born 27 Feb. 1910 in Wayne Co., IL. Married Nealia Shaheen. Marshall Burgess died childless on 8 May 1972.
8d. **Winnie Mae.** Born 11 June 1912 in Wayne Co., IL. Winnie Burgess currently lives at Moline, Rock Island Co., IL.
8e. **Teddy Forest.** Born 7 July 1914 in Wayne Co., IL. Teddy Burgess died childless on 20 Dec. 1991 at Milan, Rock Island Co., IL.

8f. **Ruby Loraine.** Born 23 Aug. 1916 in Wayne Co., IL; died there on 1 July 1918, and is buried in the Mount Pleasant Cemetery.
8g. **Ora LaDawn.** Her name is given as Mary Burgess in the 1920 census. Born 21 May 1919 in Wayne Co., IL. Married Lewis Olivier.
8h. **Ruth Genevieve.** Born 2 Dec. 1921 in Wayne Co., IL. Ruth Burgess lives with her sister Winnie.
8i. **Burnice Angeline.** Born 18 Nov. 1923 in Wayne Co., IL. Married Robert Ross. Burnice Ross died in Mar. 1987 at Prophetstown, Whiteside Co., IL.
8j. **(Jarvis) Lee.** Born 3 Oct. 1925 in Wayne Co., IL. Married Florence Jones. Lee Burgess currently lives at Twinsburg, OH.

9a. **Daniel Lee**. Born 13 Aug. 1956.
9b. **Donna Louise**. Born 5 May 1958.
9c. **Ronald Allen**. Born 8 Apr. 1966.

JOSEPH MARION BURGESS OF WHITESIDE CO., ILLINOIS
[Mason Mathew[6]]

7h. **Joseph Marion** *[son of Mason Mathew].* Born 4 May 1884 in Wayne Co., IL. Living with his father in 1910. Married Ethel Fraim on 6 July 1911 in Wayne Co., IL (she died in July 1943). Listed in the 1917 draft list for Clay Co., IL. Joseph M. Burgess was a professional musician. He died on 28 May 1957, and is buried in the Tampico Cemetery, Tampico, Whiteside Co., IL.

8a. **Celesta Augusta.** Born 25 Oct. 1911 at Johnsonville, IL. Married George Colvin. Celesta Colvin was last known living at Mt. Vernon, IL.

FLOYD MONROE BURGESS OF WHITESIDE CO., ILLINOIS
[Mason Mathew[6]]

7i. **Floyd Monroe** *[son of Mason Mathew].* Born 1 Dec. 1885 in Wayne Co., IL. Married Ida May Sinclair (or Sinkler) on 17 Jan. 1907 in Wayne Co. (she was born about 1889, daughter of James Sinclair [or Sinkler] and Margret Burkett, and died on 11 Feb. 1909); married secondly (Edith) Elsie Jones on 10 Dec. 1911 in Wayne Co. (she was the daughter of William E. Jones and Annie Lisenby, and died on 10 Nov. 1952). His two older children are living with their grandfather in 1910. Listed in the 1917 draft list for Wayne Co., IL, and in the 1920 census for Whiteside Co., IL. Floyd Burgess was a farmer in Whiteside Co., IL; he died there on 2 Oct. 1951, and is buried in the Riverside Cemetery, Sterling, IL.

8a. **James Virgil.** Born 22 Apr. 1907 in Wayne Co., IL; died there on 28 Apr. 1910. Listed in the 1910 census with his grandfather, Mason M. Burgess. Buried in the Powers Cemetery.
8b. **Idus.** Born 11 Feb. 1909 in Wayne Co., IL. Married Ruth Stromberg. Listed in the 1910 census living with his grandfather, James Sinclair, but has not been found in 1920. Idus Burgess was an auto mechanic at Flint, MI. He died there in June 1967.

9a. **William Allan** (ad.). Born 7 Dec. 1941.

8c. **Lula Fay.** Born 11 Sept. 1912 in Wayne Co., IL. Married Lawrence Greenwood. Lula Greenwood died on 14 June 1966.
8d. **Wilma May Hosea.** Born 14 Feb. 1917 in Wayne Co., IL. Married Arthur Foraker. Wilma Foraker died on 8 Sept. 1985 at Lubbock, TX.
8e. **Lester Monroe.** Born 18 Mar. 1925 in Wayne Co., IL. Married Irene Maxwell; married secondly Pauline Musselman. Lester Burgess currently lives at Stillman Valley, Ogle Co., IL.

9a. **Richard Lloyd**. Born 7 Mar. 1951.
9b. **Harold Leon**. Born 25 Sept. 1952. Harold Burgess died on 26 Oct. 1985 at Rockford, Winnebago Co., IL.
9c. **Daniel Lester**. Born 7 Mar. 1963.

PHILLIP E. BURGESS OF WHITESIDE CO., ILLINOIS
[Mason Mathew[6]]

7l. **Phillip Etzenhouser** *[son of Mason Mathew].* Born 27 June 1891 in Wayne Co., IL. Living with his father in 1910. Married Lulu Cecil Burroughs on 1 Aug. 1913 (she died 14 Jan. 1970). Listed in the

1920 census for Whiteside Co., IL living with his brother, Floyd. Phillip E. Burgess died on 6 Feb. 1967 at Tampico, Whiteside Co., IL, and is buried there in the Tampico Cemetery.

8a. **Freddie Roszelle.** Born 23 Mar. 1914 in Marion Co., IL. Married Arlene Musche on 6 Nov. 1938 (she was born 22 Feb. 1918, and died 5 Oct. 1979); married secondly Juanita Phillips. Fred Burgess was a farmer and highway maintenance man for the State of Illinois before retiring. He currently lives at Dixon, IL.

9a. **Darlene La Ferne.** Born 27 Feb. 1939. Married Ernest Farrell Durham. Darlene Durham lives at Sycamore, IL.

9b. **(Frances) Elaine.** Born 19 July 1940. Married Wayne Rubright in 1959. Elaine Rubright lives at Hayden Lake, ID.

9c. **(Kathryn) Joyce.** Born 27 June 1941. Married Robert O. Myers; married secondly William Volk. Joyce Volk currently lives at Dixon, Lee Co., IL.

8b. **George Woodford.** Born 6 May 1915 in Marion Co., IL; died there on 27 Aug. 1915, and is buried in the New Liberty Baptist Church Cemetery, Romaine Township, Marion, Co., IL.

8c. **Clyde Burl** (twin). Born 24 Aug. 1919 at Arrowsmith, IL; died there on 6 Dec. 1919, and is buried in the New Liberty Baptist Church Cemetery, Romaine Township, Marion, Co., IL.

8d. **Claude Murle** (twin). Born 24 Aug. 1919 at Arrowsmith, IL. Married Elizabeth Jane "Betty" Mayberry on 15 Apr. 1939 (she lives near Rock Falls, IL). Claude Burgess was a farmer. He died on 6 June 1987, and is buried in the Tampico Memorial Cemetery.

9a. **Patricia Ann (I).** Born 28 Mar. 1941 at Sterling, IL. Married Ronald Dickinson. Patricia Dickinson lives at Waterloo, IA.

9b. **Mary Susan (II).** Born 7 Mar. 1946 at Sterling, IL. Married Riley Smith. Mary Smith lives near Erie, IL.

8e. **Lyle Wayne.** Born 14 Apr. 1924 near Tampico, Whiteside Co., IL. Married Gracia Gene Lewis on 19 June 1949 (she was born 8 Feb. 1928, and died 4 Oct. 1964, buried Lusk Cemetery, Albany, IL); married secondly Jean Eleanor Hansen on 15 May 1965 (she was born 19 May 1923). Lyle Burgess was an accounting supervisor for the General Board of Pensions, United Methodist Church, Evanston, IL. He has also worked as an assistant head bookkeeper, State Bank and Trust Co. of Evanston, IL, and was a student minister for the Methodist Church. He is currently a tracer of missing persons for the General Board of Pensions. He has contributed greatly to this book.

9a. **Douglas Edward** (ad.). Born 6 Oct. 1959 at Moline, IL. Married Penny Mae Bremer. Doug Burgess is an electronics assistant for Northrop Corporation. He lives at Rolling Meadows, IL.

10a. **Shannon Lorraine.** Born 15 July 1980 at Arlington Heights, IL.

10b. **Adam Wayne.** Born 3 Apr. 1983 at Skokie, IL.

9b. **Mary Margaret (II).** Born 14 Mar. 1962 at Evanston, IL; died there on 15 Mar. 1962, and is buried in the Lusk Cemetery, Albany, IL.

9c. **Priscilla Louise.** Born 18 Feb. 1963 at Evanston, IL. Married Karl Madsen on 26 Sept. 1987, and had children: *Olivia Jean* (born 3 Apr. 1992 at Arlington Heights, IL). Priscilla Madsen currently lives at Elgin, IL.

JESSE LINLA BURGESS OF CLAY CO., ILLINOIS

[Mason Mathew[6]]

7m. **Jesse Linla** *[son of Mason Mathew].* His middle name is given as Linley in his draft record. Born 11 July 1895 at Orchardville, Wayne Co., IL. Married Ora Lou Goosetree (she was born on 5 Dec. 1902, and died 5 Aug. 1979 at Cisne, IL). Listed in the 1917 draft list for Clay Co., IL, and with his father in the 1920 census. Jesse Burgess was a farmer at Xenia, Clay Co., IL; he died there on 27 July 1969, and is buried in the Poplar Creek Cemetery.

8a. **Neil Kenneth.** Born 10 Oct. 1921 in Wayne Co., IL. Married Helen Louise Ward; married secondly ___. Neil Burgess lives at Salem, IL.

9a. **Cheryl Daun.** Born 12 Dec. 1947 in Wayne Co., IL.

9b. **Cindy Ruth**. Born 17 Dec. 1949 in Wayne Co., IL.
9c. **Carla Louise**. Born 28 Jan. 1957 in Wayne Co., IL.

8b. **Olaf Lavon.** Born 3 Aug. 1925 in Wayne Co., IL. Married Betty Jean McBride. Olaf Burgess currently lives at Brooksville, Noxubee Co., MS.

9a. **Judith Elaine**. Born 2 July 1948.
9b. **Tommy Ellis (I)**. Born 2 Mar. 1950; died 3 Mar. 1950.
9c. **Janice Lou**. Born 12 Mar. 1951.
9d. **Penny Sue**. Born 12 Dec. 1952.
9e. **Mary Jane (VI)**. Born 21 July 1962.

8c. **Earl Jerome.** Born 16 Dec. 1927 in Wayne Co., IL. Married Lela Mae Nichols. Earl Burgess currently lives at Xenia, IL.

9a. **Dennis Lee (III).** Born 9 Dec. 1955 in Wayne Co., IL.
9b. **Daughter.**

8d. **Ellis Eugene.** Born 20 July 1933 in Wayne Co., IL. Married Shirley Harrell. Ellis Burgess currently lives at Cisne, Wayne Co., IL.

9a. **Michael Eugene**. Born 16 Oct. 1953.
9b. **Marlys Ann**. Born 30 Jan. 1955.

Edna Blanche BOURDON (1885-1915)
Noma Ethyl BOURDON (1890-1982)
(see pages 231-232)

[William (I)[1], Edward (I)[2], Edward (II)[3], Mason Peyton[4], Lewis[5]]

VOLNEY LEEPORT BURGESS
(1854-1935)
OF WAYNE COUNTY, ILLINOIS

6f. **Volney Leeport** *[son of Lewis].* His middle name is also given as Leecord. Born 26 Sept. 1854 in Wayne Co., IL. Married Margaret Ann "Maggie" Vest about 1876 (she was born 27 July 1855 in Orange Co., daughter of Robert H. Vest and Sarah White, and died on 7 Oct. 1932 at Orchardville, IL). Listed in the 1880 census for Brush Creek Township, Wayne Co., IL, and in 1900-20 in Orchard Township. Volney Burgess was a farmer in Wayne Co., IL. He died there on 29 July 1935, and is buried with his wife in the Mount Pleasant Cemetery.

The Children of Volney L. Burgess:

7a. **(William) Halleck**. Born 1 Mar. 1877 in Wayne Co., IL. See below for full entry.
7b. **Lewis Mason**. Born 3 Sept. 1878 in Wayne Co., IL. See below for full entry.
7c. **(Sarah) Elizabeth (IV) "Lizzie."** Born about 1880 in Wayne Co., IL. Married (William) Riley Henson on 8 Dec. 1898 in Wayne Co. (he was born about 1877, son of Nicholas G. Henson and Amanda E. Holler, and brother of Laura Etta Henson, who married Sarah's brother, Lewis M. Burgess), and had at least the following children: *Homer L.* (born 7 Mar. 1901, died 7 Oct. 1990 at Rock Falls, IL); *Vernal Freddie* (born 8 Apr. 1907, died Feb. 1982 at Sycamore, IL); *Stanley Eber* (born 23 Apr. 1910, died Apr. 1976 at Iowa City, IA). Sarah Henson died in the 1950s at Dixon, Lee Co., IL.
7d. **(Emma) Josephine "Josie."** Born 12 Oct. 1883 in Wayne Co., IL. Married Sylvester Ward on 24 Aug. 1902 in Wayne Co. (he was born 1877, son of Thomas W. Ward and Martha Foster, and died 1953), and had children: *Dorothy* (who married ___ Talbert). She and her family are living with her father in the 1910 census. Josie Ward died in July 1962 at Wayne Co., IL, and is buried there in the Mount Pleasant Cemetery. Dorothy Talbert currently lives at Mt. Vernon, IL.
7e. **Robert Harvey**. Born 12 Apr. 1886 in Wayne Co., IL. See below for full entry.
7f. **Mary Ann (VII)**. Born 20 Aug. 1888 in Wayne Co., IL; died there on 17 Aug. 1889, and is buried with her parents.
7g. **Floyd (II)**. Born 5 Sept. 1890 in Wayne Co., IL. See below for full entry.
7h. **George Marion (II)**. Born 1 May 1893 in Wayne Co., IL. See below for full entry.

HALLECK BURGESS OF WAYNE CO., ILLINOIS
[Volney Leeport[6]]

7a. **(William) Halleck** *[son of Volney Leeport].* Born 1 Mar. 1877 in Wayne Co., IL. Married Katie C. Ellis on 12 Sept. 1900 in Wayne Co. (she was born 1881, and died 1967). Listed in the 1900 census living with his father, in 1910 in Wayne Co., IL, in 1920 in Lee Co., IL, and in the 1917 draft list for Wayne Co., IL. Halleck Burgess was a farmer at Dixon, Lee Co., IL. He died on 22 Jan. 1959 at Flora, Wayne Co., IL, and is buried in the Johnsonville Cemetery.

8a. **Chlorus Wiley Leeport.** Born 3 Oct. 1901 in Wayne Co., IL. Married Marie Kohler; married thirdly Mary ___. Chlorus Burgess died on 21 Oct. 1980 at Sterling, Whiteside Co., IL, and is buried in the Powers Cemetery.

9a. **Hubert N.**
9c. **Arthur.**
9d. **Richard (I).**

8b. **Archie Logan.** Born 5 July 1904 in Wayne Co., IL. Married Hazel Dunn. Archie Burgess died in Aug. 1969 at Colorado Springs or Denver, CO.

9a. **Gerald Francis.** He currently lives at Denver, CO.
9b. **William Carlton "Billie."** He currently lives at Colorado Springs, CO.
9c. **Karen (I).**

8c. **Wreatha Marie.** Born 13 Apr. 1907 in Wayne Co., IL. Married Ralph L. Lane (he was born 28 Feb. 1917, and died Jan. 1986 at Flora, IL). Wreatha Lane died in Dec. 1990 at Flora, Clay Co., IL.

LEWIS MASON BURGESS OF WAYNE CO., ILLINOIS
[Volney Leeport[6]]

7b. **Lewis Mason** *[son of Volney Leeport].* Born 3 Sept. 1878 in Wayne Co., IL. Married (Laura) Etta Henson on 5 Apr. 1900 in Wayne Co. (she was born 1883, daughter of Nicholas G. Henson and Amanda E. Holler, and sister of William Riley Henson, who married Lewis Mason's sister, Sarah Elizabeth Burgess, and died 1960). Listed in the 1900-20 censuses and 1917 draft list for Orchard Township, Wayne Co., IL. Lewis Burgess died on 20 Aug. 1953 in Wayne Co., and is buried there in the Mount Pleasant Cemetery.

8a. **Virgil Owen.** Born 24 Apr. 1902 in Wayne Co., IL. Married Katie Westmorland about 1927; married secondly Neva Weaver. He died on 16 July 1988 at Salem, Marion Co., IL, buried in the Mount Pleasant Cemetery.

9a. **Harold Lloyd.** Born 14 July 1928 in Wayne Co., IL. Harold Burgess died on 30 May 1992 at Olney, Richland Co., IL.
9b. **Virginia Lee (II).** She lives in Texas.

8b. **Freddie Everett.** Born 9 Oct. 1904 in Wayne Co., IL. Married Erma J. Harrell about 1923 (she was born on 17 Apr. 1905, sister of Beulah Harrell [who married his cousin, Charles Parker Burgess], and died Oct. 1983 at Xenia, IL). Freddie Burgess died on 28 Jan. 1969 at Xenia, Clay Co., IL, but is buried in the Mount Pleasant Cemetery, Wayne Co., IL.

9a. **Kenneth (III).** Born 2 July 1924 in Wayne Co., IL. Kenneth Burgess died in May 1981 at Xenia, Clay Co., IL.
9b. **Clacey Lionel.** Born 23 Jan. 1930 in Wayne Co., IL; died there on 13 Aug. 1931, and is buried with his mother in the Mount Pleasant Cemetery.
9c. **Kelley.** He lives at Orchardville, IL.
9d. **Camilla.**
9e. **Carroll.**

8c. **Gertie Elizabeth.** Born 14 Mar. 1907 in Wayne Co., IL. Married Joe Hoover (he was born 26 Oct. 1903, brother of Fay Hoover [who married William Oval Burgess, Gertie's cousin], and died in Sept. 1975 at Xenia, IL), and had children:

Thelma Marie HOOVER. Born 8 Feb. 1925 in Wayne Co., IL, married William A. Sloan on 5 Apr. 1947 at Flora, Clay Co., IL (he was born 18 Oct. 1923 at Flora, and died 16 Oct. 1986 at Olney, IL, buried in the Mount Pleasant Cemetery), and had children: *Gary Lee* (born 27 Mar. 1948 at East Saint Louis, IL, married Judy Kohn on 20 June 1970 at Flora [she was born 14 June 1949 at Chillicothe, OH], and had children: Vance Aron [born 13 Apr. 1974 at Flora]; Keith Allen [born 17 Aug. 1978 at Flora]); Gary L. Sloan currently lives at Flora, IL, and Thelma M. Sloan currently lives near Xenia, IL.

Mary Lou HOOVER. Married Robert Tadlock, had children, lives at Newport News.

Allen HOOVER. Born about 1930, and died about 1936.

Gertie E. HOOVER died on 27 Nov. 1979 at Xenia, Clay Co., IL, and is buried in the Mount Pleasant Cemetery.

8d. **Lloyd Wilber.** Born 21 Sept. 1909 in Wayne Co., IL. Married Vada Matchett; married secondly Elsie Waldbesser on 30 July 1936 (she was born 15 Oct. 1914). Lloyd Burgess died on 22 Aug. 1978 at Xenia, IL, and is buried in the Mount Pleasant Cemetery.

9a. **Betty (I).** Born about 1930.

9b. **Delorse Mae**. Born 10 Apr. 1936. Married Roy Eugene Flexter on 22 Mar. 1958 (he was born 10 Oct. 1935), and had children: *Pamela Sue* (born 26 Dec. 1958, married Robert Green on 16 Oct. 1982 [div.], and had two children); *Marty Eugene* (born 26 Apr. 1963, married Kimberly Lee Ann Simon on 26 Mar. 1986 [she was born 6 Aug. 1963], and had two children). Delorse Flexter lives at Waterford, MI.

9c. **(Lloyd) Eugene**. Born 7 June 1937. Married Lucy Robley Hubble on 26 Aug. 1956 (she was born 5 Dec. 1937). Gene Burgess lives at Flora, IL.

10a. **Brent Eugene**. Born 12 Nov. 1959. Married Becky Harrell on 25 May 1990 (she was born 30 Aug. 1964).

11a. **Dexter Clark**. Born 30 Oct. 1993.

10b. **Mark Kevin Robley**. Born 18 Jan. 1961. Married Kathryn Leigh King on 12 Oct. 1991.

11a. **Kara Kathryn**. Born 18 July 1992.

9d. **Billie Gene**. Born and died 1 May 1939, and is buried in the Mount Pleasant Cemetery.

9e. **Patsy Ann (I)**. Born 28 Jan. 1942. Married Gary Donoho (div.), and had children: *Trina Sue* (born 2 July 1965, married Darrell Kooy [div.], and had three children; *Trina* married secondly Roger Blanchett in Nov. 1990, and had one child).

9f. **Donald Ray**. Born 22 Aug. 1943. Twice married and divorced.

10a. **Sherry Lynn (I)**. Born 1 Apr. 1963. Married Scott David Organ on 31 Aug. 1985, and had one daughter.

10b. **Jeffery Don**. Born 2 Sept. 1970. Married Dawn Lee Frederick on 1 Aug. 1992.

10c. **Child**.

10d. **Child**.

9g. **Darrell Leon**. Born 5 Sept. 1949. Married Wanda May Brown on 4 June 1972 (she was born 10 Mar. 1953).

10a. **Tonya Lee**. Born 23 June 1978.

10b. **Vanessa Lynn**. Born 26 Feb. 1987.

9h. **Christine Diane**. Born 4 Dec. 1955. Married Robert Dagg on 23 June 1973 (he was born 2 May 1951), and had children: *William Wayde* (born 1 Oct. 1974); *Christopher Kyle* (born 26 Aug. 1979); *Robert Tyler* (born 5 Sept. 1983); *Lacey Jean* (born 10 Oct. 1987). Christine Dagg lives near Xenia, IL.

8e. **Cloyd Calloway**. Born 16 Aug. 1911 in Wayne Co., IL. Married Opal Greathouse on 14 Apr. 1934 in Wayne Co. (she was born 14 Nov. 1913, remarried Lawrence Shehorn on 12 Jan. 1963 in Clay Co., IL, and died Sept. 1987 at Elgin, Kane Co., IL). Cloyd Burgess died on 26 Jan. 1950 in Wayne Co., IL, and is buried in the Mount Pleasant Cemetery.

9a. **Milford Lavern**. Born 19 Mar. 1935 in Wayne Co., IL. Married (Vida) Joan Jarvis on 10 Sept. 1955 in Wayne Co. (she was born 8 Apr. 1934 in Marion Co., IL, daughter of Glenn Jarvis and Josephine Beattie). Milford L. Burgess currently lives at Elgin, IL; he has contributed greatly to this book.

10a. **Ricky Lavern**. Born 12 July 1956 in Marion Co., IL. Married Lauren Carr on 12 May 1979 at Independence, MO (she was born 15 Sept. 1959). Rick Burgess lives at Blue Springs, MO.

10b. **Diane Kaye**. Born 24 Mar. 1958 in Clay Co., IL. Married William Chapman on 25 Aug. 1979 in Cook Co., IL (he was born 5 Jan. 1957 in DuPage Co., IL), and had children: *William Timothy* (born 22 Dec. 1981 in Kane Co., IL); *Christopher Thomas* (born 27 Aug. 1985 in Kane Co.); *Sarah Nicole* (born 12 May 1987 in Kane Co., IL); married secondly William Melvin Hissam on 5 Aug. 1989 in Cook Co., IL (he adopted the three Chapman children in 1992). Diane Chapman lives at Elgin, IL.

10c. **Ronald Ray**. Born 27 Aug. 1965 in Kane Co., IL. Married Wendy Swain on 25 June 1988 in Cook Co., IL (she was born 21 June 1963 in Kane Co., IL). Ron Burgess lives at Elgin, IL.

11a. **Kevin Ronald.** Born 18 June 1990 in Kane Co., IL.
11b. **Kyle Marc.** Born 23 May 1993 in Kane Co., IL.

10d. **Cynthia Kaye.** Born 5 Jan. 1969 in Kane Co., IL. Married Gary L. Singery on 20 Nov. 1993 in DuPage Co., IL. Cynthia Singery lives at Bloomingdale, IL.

9b. **Shirley Darlene.** Born 4 June 1936 in Wayne Co., IL. Married Allen Thompson on 8 Oct. 1955 (div. 1980), and had children: *Teresa L.* (born 11 Aug. 1958 in Clay Co., IL, married Dale L. Ware on 2 Nov. 1980 in Cook Co., IL [he was born 29 Oct. 1961 in Kane Co.], and had children: Dustin [born 3 Oct. 1985 in Kane Co.]; Teresa Ware lives at Bartlett, IL); *Michael Allen* (born 30 June 1962 in Kane Co., married Hitomi Yamani on 14 Nov. 1987 in Japan [she was born 15 July __ in Japan]); Shirley married secondly Richard Werba in Kane Co., IL (he was born 3 Dec. 1929, and died on 14 Mar. 1991 at Elgin). Shirley Werba lives at Elgin, IL.

9c. **Charles Lewis.** Born 27 July 1938 in Wayne Co., IL. Married Jeanne Leathers on 19 July 1958 in Wayne Co. (div.; she was born 19 July 1940 in Wayne Co.). Charles Burgess lives at Woodstock, IL.

10a. **Jeffery Kent.** Born 24 Feb. 1961 in McHenry Co., IL. Married Varonica Craig on 24 July 1982.

11a. **Ryan Shane.** Born 16 Feb. 1988 in McHenry Co., IL.
11b. **Abigail Lee.** Born 5 June 1992 in McHenry Co., IL.

10b. **Jeanae Lee.** Born about 1963 in McHenry Co., IL. Married Brett Wood in 1986 in McHenry Co.

10c. **Gayla Jo.** Born 5 Oct. 1965 in McHenry Co., IL. Married Mark Weldon on 24 Dec. 1983. Gayla Weldon lives at Mobile, AL.

10d. **Charla Jeanne.** Born 28 July 1973 in McHenry Co., IL.

9d. **Judy Kaye.** Born 22 Apr. 1944 in Wayne Co., IL. Married Neil McGrew (div.), and had children: *Angie*; *Brian*; married secondly Lawrence Culbertson.

8f. **Oakley Bryan.** Born 2 Apr. 1914 in Wayne Co., IL. Married Mary Satterly. He currently lives at Salem, Marion Co., IL.

9a. **Lawrence O(akley?)** (ad.). Married Margie S. ___. Lawrence Burgess currently lives at Sandoval, Marion Co., IL.

10a. **Child.**
10b. **Child.**

8g. **Laura Etta.** Born 16 May 1917 in Wayne Co., IL. Married William Bennett on 17 Feb. 1934 in Wayne Co. (he was born 2 Mar. 1910, son of Doc P. Bennett and Lulu Boyle), and had children: *William Harold* (born 1 Jan. 1935 in Wayne Co., died 6 Jan. 1935); *Richard Boyle* (born 20 Nov. 1939 in Wayne Co., married Leta Diann Mayo on 6 Oct. 1961 [she was born 9 Mar. 1943 in Wayne Co], and had children: Tacey Boyd [born 8 Jan. 1964 in Wayne Co., married Cathy Lynn Allison on 10 June 1983 {she was born 18 Apr. 1965 in Marion Co.}, and had children: Derek Boyd {born 13 Nov. 1985 in Franklin Co., IL}; Dylan James {born 11 Feb. 1990 in Jefferson Co., IL}]; Bryan Wade [born 18 Sept. 1965 in Wayne Co., IL, married Judy Kaye Jones on 25 May 1984 {she was born 13 Nov. 1965 in Lake Co., IN}, and had children: Natasha Nicole {born 3 July 1987 in Jefferson Co., IL}; Mandy Kaye {born and died 26 Aug. 1990 in Jefferson Co.}; Drew Anthony {born 16 May 1992 in Jefferson Co.}]; Travis Lee [born 8 Mar. 1968 in Wayne Co.]; Shane Richard [born 17 Aug. 1971 in Wayne Co., married Jennifer Ann Jenkins on 11 Oct. 1991 {she was born 9 Oct. 1973 in Jefferson Co.}, and had children: Kole Allen Roy {born 8 Oct. 1993 in Jefferson Co.}]). Laura Bennett currently lives at Xenia, IL.

8h. **(Lewis) Ancil.** Born 16 July 1919 in Wayne Co., IL. Married Pauline Griffith; married secondly Lois Weaver; married thirdly Doris P. (Bennett) Jenkins on 1 May 1983 in Union Co., KY. He currently lives at Waverly, Union Co., KY.

9a. **Lilia.** Married ___ Hulbert. Daughter of the first wife.
9b. **Connie (I).** Married. Daughter of the second wife.

9c. **Lou Ann (II).** Married.
9d. **David Ancil.** Born 1955 in Wayne Co., IL; died there in 1956, and is buried in the Mount Pleasant Cemetery.

ROBERT HARVEY BURGESS OF WAYNE CO., ILLINOIS
[Volney Leeport[6]]

7e. **Robert Harvey** *[son of Volney Leeport].* Born 12 Apr. 1886 in Wayne Co., IL. Married Malissa J. Hufhines on 15 Sept. 1909 in Wayne Co. (she was born on 8 July 1885, daughter of T. W. Hufhines and Alice Upton, and sister of Harriet Hufhines [who married Robert's brother, Floyd Burgess], and died 12 Apr. 1910); married secondly Flossie L. Burkett in 1916 (she was born 10 Jan. 1899, and died 30 Jan. 1992 at Xenia, Clay Co., IL, aged 93 years). Living with his father in 1910; listed in the 1917 draft list and the 1920 census for Wayne Co., IL (no children in 1920). Robert H. Burgess was a farmer in Wayne Co., IL; he died there in 1951, and is buried in the Mount Pleasant Cemetery.

8a. **(Charles) Stanley.** Born 11 Apr. 1910 in Colorado; died there on 22 Apr. 1910, and is buried in the Mount Pleasant Cemetery. Listed with his grandfather in the 1910 census.
8b. **Howard.** Born 26 Aug. 1919 in Wayne Co., IL; died there on 3 Sept. 1919, and is buried in the Mount Pleasant Cemetery.
8c. **(Volney) Eugene.** Born 2 July 1921 in Wayne Co., IL. Married Marion ___. Gene Burgess died on 15 Nov. 1986 at Flora, Clay Co., IL.

9a. **Son.**
9b. **Son.**

8d. **Robert Lee (II).** Bob Burgess lives at St. Charles, MO.

9a. **Daughter.**
9b. **Daughter.**

8e. **George Burkett.** George Burgess lives at Xenia, IL.

9a. **Son.**
9b. **Daughter.**

FLOYD BURGESS OF WAYNE CO., ILLINOIS
[Volney Leeport[6]]

7g. **Floyd (II)** (nmn) *[son of Volney Leeport].* Born 5 Sept. 1890 in Wayne Co., IL. Married Harriet J. Hufhines on 22 June 1910 in Wayne Co. (she was born 7 Dec. 1890, daughter of T. W. Hufhines and Alice Upton, and sister of Malissa J. Hufhines [who married Floyd's brother, Robert Burgess], and died 22 Sept. 1987, aged 96 years). Listed in the 1910 census for Wayne Co. living with William Gaumer, in the the 1917 draft list for Wayne Co., and in the 1920 census there. Floyd Burgess was a farmer in Wayne Co., IL. He died there on 27 Mar. 1931, and is buried in the Mount Pleasant Cemetery.

8a. **(Rutha) Reah.** Born 22 Jan. 1911 in Wayne Co., IL. Married Virgil Sessions (he was born 15 July 1910, and died 28 Jan. 1991 at Flora, Clay Co., IL). Reah Sessions currently lives at Flora, IL. She has contributed greatly to this book.
8b. **Ruby Ester.** Born 29 Jan. 1913 in Wayne Co., IL. Married Henry Brown. Ruby Brown currently lives at Granite City, IL.
8c. **Eber** (nmn). Born 29 Nov. 1916 in Wayne Co., IL. Married Betty Barton. Eber Burgess currently lives at Flora, IL.

9a. **Debbie (I).**

8d. **Faye** (nmn). Born 12 Nov. 1920 in Wayne Co., IL. Married Buster Tadlock. Faye Tadlock currently lives at Flora, IL.
8e. **Versa Imogene.** Born 27 Jan. 1923 in Wayne Co., IL. Married Jack Markham (div.). Versa Markham currently lives at Flora, IL.

8f. **Volney Lincoln.** Born 12 Feb. 1925 in Wayne Co., IL. Married Joan Crawford; married secondly Lil ___. Volney L. Burgess currently lives at Gillespie, Macoupin Co., IL in the summer, and in Florida in the winter.

9a. **Randy (I).**
9b. **Sheila L.** Married Russell Shelton. She lives in Missouri.

8g. **Lawrence** (nmn). Born 6 July 1927 in Wayne Co., IL. Married Pauline Gill. Lawrence Burgess lives at Fairfield, Wayne Co., IL.

9a. **Gregg D.**
9b. **Brenda (I).**

GEORGE MARION BURGESS OF MARION CO., ILLINOIS

[Volney Leeport[6]]

7h. **George Marion (II)** *[son of Volney Leeport].* Born 1 May 1893 in Wayne Co., IL. Married Bessie Brown (she was born 1898 in IL). Living with his father in 1910; listed in the 1917 draft list for Wayne Co., and the 1920 census for Wayne Co. (with no children). George M. Burgess died in Texas, but is buried in Centralia, Marion Co., IL. He may be the George Burgess who died 19 July 1960 in Harris Co., TX.

8a. **Bobby Dean.** Twice married. Lives in West Germany.

9a. **George (V).**
9b. **Daughter.**
9c. **Son.** The first child of the second wife.

REDELLA ALICE BURGESS WAGONER
(1855-1884) [see page 87]

[William (I)[1], Edward (I)[2], Edward (II)[3], Mason Peyton[4], Lewis[5]]

FRANCIS MARTIN BURGESS
(1856-1911)

OF WAYNE COUNTY, ILLINOIS

6g. **Francis Martin** *[son of Lewis].* Born 5 Mar. 1856 in Wayne Co., IL. Married Martha E. Forth (or Fuller) about 1876 (she was born 7 Sept. 1861 in IL, and died 5 July 1922 when her car was hit by a freight train at Wayne City, IL, buried in the Orchardville Cemetery). Listed in the 1880 census for Brush Creek Township, Wayne Co., IL, and in 1900-10 in Orchard Township (in 1910 he with Kate Mills). Francis M. Burgess was a farmer in Wayne Co. He died there on 7 Dec. 1911, and is buried in the Mount Pleasant Cemetery.

The Children of Francis M. Burgess:

7a. **Edgar** (nmn). Born 20 Nov. 1877 in Wayne Co., IL. See below for full entry.
7b. **Child.** Born 1879, died 1880 in Wayne Co., IL, buried in the Mount Pleasant Cemetery.
7c. **Anna (II)** (nmn). Born 15 Feb. 1881 in Wayne Co., IL. Living with her father in 1900. Married Simon Jesse "Edgar" Gaumer on 3 Aug. 1902 in Wayne Co. (he was born 1881, son of C. Harry Gaumer and Mary Coil, and brother of William L. Gaumer, who married Anna's first cousin, Narcissus Burgess), and had at least the following children: *Lena Alberta* (born 2 July 1903 in Wayne Co.); *Fern* (married ___ Williams, and lives at Grand Junction, CO). Anna Gaumer died of pneumonia and childbirth on 13 Jan. 1919 at Wayne City, Wayne Co., IL, and is buried in the Mount Pleasant Cemetery.
7d. **Robert (I)** (nmn). Born 9 Nov. 1883 in Wayne Co., IL. See below for full entry.

EDGAR BURGESS OF KLAMATH CO., OREGON
[Francis Martin[6]]

7a. **Edgar** (nmn) *[son of Francis Martin].* Born 20 Nov. 1877 in Wayne Co., IL. Married (Ma)linda J. Brown on 8 Nov. 1900 in Wayne Co. (she was born 1885, daughter of Thomas Brown and Dora Woolf, and died 29 July 1947 in Jackson Co., OR). Listed in the 1910 census for Wayne Co., IL, and in the 1920 census for Skagit Co., WA. Edgar Burgess moved to Klamath Falls, Klamath Co., OR in 1925. He died there on 30 Nov. 1936, and is buried in the Linkville Cemetery.

8a. **Leona V.** Born about 1905 in Wayne Co., IL. Married Everett Gray (he was born 2 July 1908, and died on 26 Oct. 1988 at Grants Pass, OR). Living at Grants Pass at the time of her brother's death (1965). Leona Gray died at Grants Pass, Josephine Co., OR (or in Washington State) about 1970, and is buried in the Mausoleum at Grants Pass, OR; she has not been found in the Oregon State death index.
8b. **Eldo Francis "Slick."** Born 29 May 1909 at Xenia, Clay Co., IL. Married Marjorie Ellen Bailey on 4 June 1930 at Klamath Falls, Klamath Co., OR (she remarried Elmer Whitaker, and lives at Talent, OR). Listed in the Medford city directories from 1955-1959. Eldo lived variously in Klamath Falls and Tionesta, CA before moving to the Medford area about 1939, and to Ashland, OR in 1942. Slick Burgess was a partner in the White Spur Lumber Co. (a sawmill) in the Dead Indian area, and owned the White Fir Retail Lumber Yard at Ashland; he also made Crater Craft boats, and worked for the Parsons Box Factory. He died on 18 Jan. 1965 at Ashland, OR, and is buried in the Mountain View Cemetery.

9a. **Robert Leon.** Born 9 Nov. 1931 at Klamath Falls, OR. Married Darlene E. Watson on 5 Apr. 1957 in Jackson Co., OR (the same day as his brother's marriage). Served in the U.S. Army during the Korean War. Robert Burgess worked for Reter Fruit Co. He died childless on 9 Apr. 1989 at Eagle Point, OR, and is buried in the Veterans Administration National Cemetery, Medford, OR.

9b. **Garry Mitchell.** Born 18 Oct. 1935 at Klamath Falls, OR. Married June Genevieve Ritchison on 5 Apr. 1957 in Jackson Co., OR in a double wedding with his brother (she was born 1 June 1935 at Ashland, OR). Listed in the 1966-84 directories of Beaverton, OR. Garry Burgess was a designer and draftsman for Tektronics Co. for eighteen years, and has been a volunteer for the Washington Co. Youth Services. He currently owns and operates GMB Design Co. at Beaverton, OR, and teaches design classes at Rock Creek Community College. June Burgess is a mailroom coordinator for the Oregon Museum of Science and Industry.

10a. **David Rex.** Born 22 May 1964 at Portland, OR. Married Derinda Gean Heinz on 14 July 1984 (she was born 16 July 1965 at Hillsboro, OR). David Burgess is a cement worker at Beaverton, OR.

11a. **Meagan Rose.** Born 6 Nov. 1989 at Portland, OR.
11b. **MacKenzie Chase** (son). Born 2 Nov. 1993 at Portland, OR.

10b. **Linda Kay (III).** Born 25 Oct. 1966 at Portland, OR. Married Brad Hedricks on 29 Aug. 1987 (he was born 11 Aug. 1964 at Hillsboro, OR), and had children: *Melynda Kay* (born 14 Sept. 1991 at Fort Lewis, WA). Linda Hedricks has worked for the Columbia Co. Sheriff's Reserve Marine Patrol. Brad Hedricks works for the U.S. Coast Guard.

9c. **Eldeane Jane.** Born 6 June 1940 at Klamath Falls, OR. Married Frank Root, and had children: *Leonard Dean* (born 27 Mar. 1958, died 30 Mar. 1958); *Sue Ellen* (born 12 May 1961); *Mark Andrew* (ad.; born 22 Oct. 1967). Listed in the Medford, OR city directories from 1959-85. Eldeane Root is a proof runner for the *Medford Mail-Tribune*.

ROBERT BURGESS OF CLAY CO., ILLINOIS

[Francis Martin[6]]

7d. **Robert (I)** (nmn) *[son of Francis Martin]*. Born 9 Nov. 1883 in Wayne Co., IL. Married Juno Bandy on 25 Dec. 1904 in Wayne Co. (she was born 27 June 1885, daughter of J. C. Bandy and Ella McGregor, and died Dec. 1972 at Xenia, IL). Listed in the 1920 census for Xenia, Clay Co., IL. Robert Burgess owned a sawmill in Wayne City, Wayne Co., IL; he also worked as a banker at Xenia, IL, and farmed. He died on 29 Mar. 1963 at Xenia, IL, and is buried there in the I.O.O.F. Cemetery.

8a. **Zelma Faye.** Born 31 Jan. 1908 in Wayne Co., IL. Married Homer Wheeler (he was born 10 July 1903, and died Sept. 1983 at Flora, Clay Co., IL), and had children:

Robert Francis WHEELER. Born 5 Jan. 1942, married Mary Lou Reddish on 28 July 1962, and had children: *Lori Annette* (born 17 Aug. 1965, married Randy Poole on 1 Dec. 1984, and had children: Shaina Nicole [born 13 Apr. 1987]; Amy Lynette [born 26 Jan. 1991]; Kristen Anne [born 9 Mar. 1993]); *Gregory Wayne* (born 26 Oct. 1968). Zelma Wheeler died on 19 Oct. 1993 at Xenia, IL, and is buried with her husband in the Odd Fellows Cemetery, Xenia, OH.

8b. **Eileen Marie.** Born 10 Mar. 1917 at Xenia, IL. Married (Delsmer) Ora Tackitt, and had children:

Donnie Ray TACKITT. Born 8 Feb. 1939 in Clay Co., IL, married Nancy Irene Elliott, and had children: *Sherri June* (born 28 Feb. 1961 in Clay Co., IL; she was adopted out of the family). ***Donnie*** married secondly Kathryn Irene Mikesell (she was born 10 Oct. 1949 at Dent, OH), and had children: *Shane Ray* (born 16 Feb. 1969 at Dent, OH, married Patricia S. Stiles [she was born 20 Nov. 1968]); *Kathryn Eileen* (born 4 Aug. 1971 in Clay Co., IL). ***Donnie TACKITT*** currently lives at Flora, IL.

Linda Ann TACKITT. Born 12 Aug. 1940, married Frederick Drennan Duke on 17 Mar. 1960 at Culman, AL (div.), and had children: *Michelle Renee* (born 28 Dec. 1962 at Salem, IL, married ___ Daniels, works at Barnett Bank, and lives at Sarasota); ***Linda DUKE*** married secondly James L. Yarbrough on 25 June 1969 at Marked Tree, AR, and had children: *James Michael* (born 29 July 1971 at Akron, OH, works as a carpenter). ***Linda*** is a licensed massage therapist at Sarasota, FL.

William Robert "Billy" TACKITT. Born 23 Feb. 1942 at Hammond, IN, married Doris Ann Taylor on 1 July 1961 in Clay Co., IL (div. 1979), and had children: *William Scott* (born 13 Sept. 1964 at Huntington, IN, married Carole Burkett on 7 Feb. 1985 at Huntington, IN, and had children: Jordan Lee [born 13 Oct. 1988 at Huntington, IN]; Nicholas Robert [born 1 Nov. 1992 at Huntington, IN]); *Marshell Andrew* (born 5 Mar. 1974 at Huntington, IN, enlisted in the U.S. Navy). ***William Robert*** married secondly Judith Anne Hall on 2 July 1981 in Floyd Co., KY. He currently works for International Harvester in Ohio.

Patricia Sue *TACKITT*. Born 11 Mar. 1944 at Flora, IL, married Charles Lindal Reynolds on 23 May 1959 at Shawneetown, IL (he was born 17 Sept. 1940 at Metropolis, IL), and had children: *Angela Marie* (born 28 Jan. 1961 at Salem, IL, married Luther Dale Fender on 11 Feb. 1977 at Flora, IL, and had children: Joseph Dale [born 11 Aug. 1977 at Effingham, IL]; *Angela* married secondly Peter Lynn Robinson on 27 Dec. 1980 at Louisville, IL [he was born 15 Oct. 1960], and had children: Jessica Lynn [born 12 Sept. 1983 at Effingham, IL]; Angela is a factory worker for Spartons); *Charles Phillip* (born 11 Feb. 1964 at Chicago, IL, married Kittina Delyn Gouchenour on 9 July 1988 at Shawneetown, IL [she was born 22 Feb. 1969 at Effingham, IL], and had children: Chad Lindal [born 4 June 1990 at Effingham, IL]; Charles P. Reynolds is a cement truck driver for Monts); *Catherine Sue* (born 4 Jan. 1969 at Chicago, IL, and works for North American Lighting). Patricia Reynolds has been a factory worker; Charles L. Reynolds works for the Effingham Clay Fertilizer company.

Shirley Kay *TACKITT*. Born 4 Jan. 1946 at Olney, IL, married Larry Ray Coughlin on 7 July 1962 in Clay Co., IL (div.; he was born 9 Oct. 1940), and had children: *Barry Allen* (married Debbie Daggett on 6 June 1984 at St. Elmo, IL, and is a land surveyor at Carterville, IL); *Julie Lynn* (married Dennis Henry Duckwitz on 28 Sept. 1990, and had children: Rhiannan Denise [born 5 Aug. 1991]; Julie lives at St. Elmo, IL). Shirley married secondly Tom Henson on 24 Dec. 1982 at Xenia, IL.

Michael Joe *TACKITT*. Born 7 Dec. 1949 at Sinton, TX, married Bonnalyn Rose Sheffer on 9 Feb. 1974 in Champaign Co., IL (she was born 29 Aug. 1950), and had children: *Emily Rose Marie* (born 28 Apr. 1974, and by John Franklin Elmore had children: Danielle Michelle Rose ELMORE TACKITT [born 3 Aug. 1992]; Emily works at a bank); *Karen Elizabeth* (born 25 Aug. 1976 at Champaign, IL). Michael Tackitt served in the U.S. Air Force for four years; he currently works as a welder at Decatur, IL. Bonnalyn Tackitt works at Crafts at Champaign, IL.

Eileen Burgess TACKITT married secondly William Arlie McCormick (he was born 18 Sept. 1916, and died on 4 Dec. 1992, buried at Xenia, IL), and lives at Flora, IL.

[see pages 130, 132, 134]
Henrietta BURGESS SPEER (1905-1976)
Roy P. BURGESS (1890-1954)
George Osmer BURGESS (1908-)

[William (I)[1], Edward (I)[2], Edward (II)[3], Mason Peyton[4]]

DAWSON BURGESS
(1811?-1870+)

OF ORANGE COUNTY, INDIANA

5d. **Dawson (II)** *[son of Mason Peyton].* Born about 1811 in Jefferson Co., KY. Married Rhoda Robbins on 20 Nov. 1829 in Orange Co., IN (she was born 22 Nov. 1813, daughter of Daniel Robbins, and died 24 Aug. 1841, buried in Mason Burgess's family cemetery); married secondly Emily Cornwell on 3 May 1846 in Orange Co., IN (she was born about 1819 in KY, daughter of James Cornwell and Rebecca Bennett, and died on 1 Feb. 1885). Listed in the 1830-70 censuses for Stampers Creek Township, Orange Co., IN (in 1860 in North East Township). Dawson Burgess was a farmer in Orange Co., IN. He died there between 1870-80 (his share of his father's estate was paid in 1881 to his widow). He was probably buried in his father's small family plot, but his stone is missing.

The Children of Dawson Burgess:

6a. **Elizabeth A.** Born 1830 in Orange Co., IN. Married (Nelson) Dudley Vickrey on 22 Feb. 1855 in Orange Co. (he was born 1833 in IN, married secondly Mary A. Baker on 16 Oct. 1864 [she was the sister of James Baker, husband of Sarah "Sally" Burgess], and by her had children: *Allie E.* [born 1867]; *James D(udley?)* [born Jan. 1871, married Ida M. ___, and had children: Fred O. {born Aug. 1894}; Merle M. {born June 1896}; Emmett L. {born May 1900; he may have died July 1974 at Turlock, CA}]; *John* [married Julia A. Elliott on 29 Oct. 1874 in Orange Co.]; *Delbert O.* [born 10 Feb. 1879, married his cousin, Florence Lee Kirby, on 21 Feb. 1906 in Orange Co. {she was born 22 Nov. 1882, and died 18 Feb. 1920}, buried Stampers Creek Cemetery]; Dudley married thirdly Louisa Apple on 3 July 1879 in Orange Co., fourthly Mary J. Self on 28 Aug. 1892 in Orange Co., and died there on 8 Mar. 1900). Elizabeth Vickrey died in Orange Co. between 1855-64; Dudley is listed there in the 1870-80 censuses.

6b. **John E. (I).** Born 9 July 1831 in Orange Co., IN. See below for full entry.

6c. **Nancy J. (I).** Born 15 Oct. 1832 in Orange Co., IN; died there on 1 Nov. 1838, and is buried in Mason Burgess's family cemetery (the stone is now missing).

6d. **Mary J.** Born 23 Dec. 1833 in Orange Co., IN. Married James G. Stone on 2 Sept. 1852 in Orange Co. (he was born 11 Dec. 1831, and died 1 June 1915), and had children: *Nancy J.* (born 15 Sept. 1856, married Jacob Cornwell on 23 Oct. 1873 at Clay City, IL [he was born 1854, and died 1926], and died 21 Dec. 1920, buried Stampers Creek Cemetery, having had children: James Harley; Charles H.; Eva B.; Son [born and died 6 Dec. 1889]); *Julia A.* (born 24 May 1858, married Stephen American Trinkle on 22 Feb. 1903 in Orange Co. [he was born 1854], and had children: Ott Stone [married Sarah E. Limeberry on 19 Nov. 1902 in Orange Co.], and died 23 Oct. 1931, buried Stampers Creek Cemetery); *James W.* (born Aug. 1862, died 24 Dec. 1862, buried Old Methodist Cemetery); *Anna M. "Annie"* (born 4 Oct. 1863, married (Joel) William "Billy" McCoy on 25 Sept. 1880 in Orange Co. [he was born 20 Sept. 1860, and died 7 June 1944], and died 28 Jan. 1935, buried Stampers Creek Cemetery, having had children: Vallie [born 1881, died 1919]; Jennie [born 1883, died 1890]; Heber; Bertha [born 6 July 1896, married Ernest J. Magill on 30 Jan. 1916 in Orange Co.]); *Seth M.* (born 11 Dec. 1865, married Ella M. Boyer on 11 July 1885 in Orange Co., and died 17 Mar. 1913, buried Stampers Creek Cemetery); *Margaret E.* (born 4 Apr. 1869, married William J. Clevenger on 8 Jan. 1890 in Orange Co. [he was born 11 Apr. 1868, and died 22 July 1944], and had children: Homer H. [born 5 Sept. 1890, married Gladys Pollard on 16 Nov. 1919, and died May 1973 at Campbellsburg, IN]; Horace Emil [born 29 Mar. 1895, married Pearl Moon, had children: Philip {born 1926}; married secondly Winnie Hewitt on 22 Dec. 1950, and died Mar. 1968 at Linton, IN]; Margaret died on 27 Aug. 1938, buried Stampers Creek Cemetery); *Rhoda E.* (born 13 May 1871, died unmarried on 1 July 1890, buried with her parents); *Nellie F.* (born 8 Mar. 1873, married Edward J. Elliott on 20 May 1891 in Orange Co., and died 27 Feb. 194_, buried Stampers Creek Cemetery, having had children: Ora A. [born 2 Dec. 1891, married Nellie F. Hudelson on 21 Sept. 1913 in Orange Co.]; Jesse James [born 10 Feb. 1893, married Lena

E. Marshall on 9 Dec. 1911 in Orange Co., and died Oct. 1978 at Paoli, IN]; Mary [born 24 Sept. 1894, married Banks Kirby on 2 Dec. 1911 in Orange Co.]; Frankie [born 18 Mar. 1896, married Audley Mooday on 8 Oct. 1916 in Orange Co., and died 23 Feb. 1988 at Burlington, IA]; Edna [born 22 Sept. 1898, married Walter Mooday on 20 Oct. 1917 in Orange Co.]; Cecil [born 5 Jan. 1901, died Apr. 1970 at French Lick, IN]; Edith; Bruce [born 5 Jan. 1905, died Mar. 1982 at Paoli, IN]); *Dessie M.* (born 8 Sept. 1875, married Benjamin F. Barnard on 17 Nov. 1891 in Orange Co., and died on 13 Apr. 1916, buried Stampers Creek Cemetery); *(Mary) Belle* (married John H. McCoy on 26 June 1899 in Orange Co.). Listed in the 1880 census for Orange Co., IN. Mary Stone died on 7 Aug. 1913 in Orange Co., and is buried with her husband in the Stampers Creek Cemetery.

6e. **Sarah A. (II).** Born 15 Nov. 1835 in Orange Co., IN. Married Fleming L. Duncan Jr. on 25 Jan. 1854 (he was born 1 Aug. 1828, and died Aug. 1856); married secondly David Fisher on 4 Nov. 1859 in Orange Co. (he was born 31 Mar. 1823 in Orange Co., son of Thaddeus Fisher and Sarah Stine, and died on 7 Jan. 1893), and had children: *Mary E.* (born 23 Oct. 1860); *Eliza* (born 5 Nov. 1861); *James H.* (born 6 Dec. 1862, married Louisa Parish on 27 Sept. 1883 in Orange Co., and secondly his cousin, Della Daisy Burgess, on 30 Oct. 1895 in Orange Co.); *Margaret* (born 1864, died an infant); *Hattie B.* (born 15 Jan. 1866, married Milton J. Lindley on 29 Oct. 1884 in Orange Co.); *William G.* (born 16 Apr. 1867, died 11 Apr. 1895, buried with his parents); *Dawson V.* (born 5 Feb. 1869, died 7 Aug. 1870, buried Stampers Creek Cemetery); *Melvina B.* (born 22 May 1871, married Anderson J. Pickett on 11 Oct. 1893 in Orange Co.); *Thomas E.* (born 24 June 1873, married Rilla Martin on 21 Jan. 1894 in Orange Co.); *David O.* (born 2 Oct. 1875, married Lizzie Dillard on 16 Apr. 1900 in Orange Co.). Sarah Fisher died on 20 Apr. 1902, and is buried in the Stampers Creek Cemetery. David Fisher's biography is reprinted below:

> "David Fisher, son of Thaddeus and Sarah H. (Stine) Fisher,...was born in this county March 31, 1823. At that time the county was very new and very wild, numerous wild animals yet being found in the woods. He passed his youth without prominent event at hard work, and managed to obtain the rudiments of an education at the old subscription schools. Upon reaching manhood he began for himself on the farm. In 1859 he married Sarah Burgess, who was born in this county November 15, 1835. Eight of their ten children are living: Mary E., born October 23, 1860; Eliza, born November 5, 1861; James H., born December 6, 1862; Margaret, who died in infancy; Hattie, born January 15, 1866; William G., born April 16, 1867; Dawson, deceased; Melvina B., born May 22, 1871; Thomas E., born June 24, 1873; and David O., born October 2, 1875. Mr. Fisher has a fine farm of 480 acres. He is a member of the Baptist Church, a Republican, and cast his first vote for Henry Clay."—*History of Lawrence, Orange, and Washington Counties, Indiana* (Chicago: Goodspeed Bros. & Co., 1884, p. 608).

6f. **Lewis M. (I).** Born 21 Feb. 1838 in Orange Co., IN; died there on 25 Oct. 1850, and is buried in Mason Burgess's family cemetery (his stone is now missing).

6g. **William Fleming (I).** Born 5 Jan. 1839 in Orange Co., IN. See below for full entry.

6h. **Daniel O.** Born 24 (?) Aug. 1840 in Orange Co., IN. Daniel Burgess enlisted in Co. F, 50th Indiana Infantry, Union Army, on 1 Oct. 1861 for the term of three years, being described on his papers as age 21, with blue eyes, dark hair, height 5' 11½", with fair complexion. He died unmarried of typhoid fever on 7 Mar. 1862 on active service at Bowling Green, KY, and is buried in the Stampers Creek Cemetery.

6i. **Thornton (III).** Born about 1842 in Orange Co., IN. He does not appear with his family in the 1850-60 census records. According to family tradition, he died unmarried about 1865 while returning from Civil War duty, and is buried near Central Barren, Harrison Co., IN. Existence not verified.

6j. **Rebecca Ellen "Sis."** Born 9 May 1847 in Orange Co., IN. Married (John) Mack Lewis on 15 Sept. 1869 in Orange Co. (he was born 28 Aug. 1842), and had at least the following children: *Nora Lola* (born 1870, married Henry E. Simpson on 16 Nov. 1898 in Wayne Co., IL); *Daughter* (twin?; born and died 30 Apr. 1870, buried with her parents); *Malissa A.* (born 18 May 1874, died 18 Mar. 1875, buried with her parents); *Roszetta* (born 21 Feb. 1879, died 16 Mar. 1898, buried with her parents); *Burgess* (born 19 June 1882); *Thomas A.* (married Susie Barbara Reister, daughter of Stephen Reister, on 6 July 1903 in Orange Co.); *James* (he may be the James E. Lewis born 14 Feb. 1886 [sic] who married Josephine Hoffman on 17 Sept. 1908 in Orange Co.). Listed in the 1870 census with her father. Rebecca Lewis died on 1 Feb. 1885 in Orange Co., and is buried in the Stampers Creek Cemetery.

6k. **Melvina.** Born Dec. 1849 in Orange Co., IN. Listed with her father in the 1870 census.

6l. **Hester Ann.** Born about 1853 in Orange Co., IN. Married Fieldon F. Bridgewater on 11 Jan. 1877 in Orange Co. (he was born about 1853 in IN), and had at least the following children: *Arvey C.* (born 1878); *Ora* (born 1880). Listed in the 1880 census for North East Township, Orange Co., IN.

6m. **Mason V(olney?).** Born 22 July 1855 in Orange Co.; died there on 18 Dec. 1857, and is buried in the Stampers Creek Cemetery.

6n. **Dawson V(olney?).** Born Aug. 1859 in Orange Co., IN, and died there between 1860-70.

6o. **Caroline E. "Carrie."** Born about 1862 in Orange Co., IN. Married Albert N. Sevedge on 27 Jan. 1887 (or 1889) in Orange Co., IN. Listed with her sister, Rebecca, in the 1880 census.

[William (I)[1], Edward (I)[2], Edward (II)[3], Mason Peyton[4], Dawson (II)[5]]

JOHN E. BURGESS, SR.
(1831-1901)

OF ORANGE COUNTY, INDIANA

6b. **John E. (I)** *[son of Dawson (II)].* Born 9 July 1831 in Orange Co., IN. Married Elizabeth A. "Lizzie" Black on 28 July 1853 in Orange Co. (she was born 15 Aug. 1838 at Wheatland, IN, is living with her son, Jesse, in 1920, and died 8 Jan. 1927 at Paoli, IN). Listed in the 1850-80 censuses for Orange Co., IN, and with his son, Jesse, in 1900. John E. Burgess was a farmer in Orange Co., IN. He died there on 1 Feb. 1901, and is buried in Stampers Creek Cemetery.

The Children of John E. Burgess:

7a. **Lewis M. (II).** Born 4 July 1854 in Orange Co., IN, and died 18 July 1855, buried in the Old Methodist Cemetery. Relationship not verified.
7b. **(Lewis) Albert.** Born 15 Apr. 1858 at Wheatland, IN. See below for full entry.
7c. **Dawson (II).** Born 22 May 1860 in Orange Co., IN. See below for full entry.
7d. **Jesse (I).** Born 6 Apr. 1863 in Orange Co., IN. See below for full entry.
7e. **Alice (III).** Born 14 Nov. 1865 in Orange Co., IN; died there on 20 Sept. 1868, and is buried in the Stampers Creek Cemetery.
7f. **Ida Bell.** Born 23 Sept. 1867 in Orange Co., IN; died there on 16 Sept. 1868, and is buried in the Stampers Creek Cemetery.
7g. **Rhoda E.** Born 26 Apr. 1869 in Orange Co., IN. Married Leander Roberts on 9 Sept. 1886 in Orange Co. Rhoda Roberts died on 14 Apr. 1916 in Orange Co.
7h. **John E. (II).** Born 27 July 1877 in Orange Co., IN. Said by Carl C. Burgess to have been living in Kansas City, MO in 1911, but has not been found in the 1900-10 MO Soundexes.

LEWIS ALBERT BURGESS OF JASPER CO., IOWA
[John E. (I)[6]]

7b. **(Lewis) Albert** *[son of John E. (I)].* Born 15 Apr. 1858 at Wheatland, Knox Co., IN. Married Mrs. Sarah Agnes "Sallie" McLaughlin Prince on 9 Jan. 1884 in Orange Co. (she was born 11 Oct. 1853, daughter of Oliver McLaughlin, married firstly William Prince, and died 1 Mar. 1935). Listed in the 1880 census living with his father, in 1900 in Dallas Co., IA, and in the 1915 Iowa state census for Van Meter, Dallas Co., IA. Albert Burgess was a section gang worker for the Rock Island Railroad. He died of colon cancer on 24 Oct. 1933 at Newton, Jasper Co., IA, and is buried with his wife in the Van Meter Cemetery.

8a. **Lola Prince** (ad.). Born about 1877. Married Isaac N. Bickle (he was born about 1872, and died 4 July 1937 at Newton, IA), and had children: *Nada* (born 1 June 1898 at Van Meter, IA, married George Nelson [he died 1968], and had children: Jean, and died 8 Feb. 1980 at Newton, IA); *Helen* (born 11 Aug. 1901, married Don Albee, and had children: June; Loraine; *Helen* married secondly Ralph P. Woody, and died Apr. 1986 at Newton, IA); *Roy Wilson* (born about 1904, married Grace Ripple, had children: Bobbi; Mary [married ___ Jarnigan], and died 23 May 1931); *Bonnie* (married Wayne Selway, and had children: Harlan; Bobby); *Betty* (married Willard "Bud" Bewyer, and had children: Ronnie). Lola Bickle died on 10 Oct. 1937 at Newton, IA, and is buried with her husband in the Union Cemetery.
8b. **Albert Chesley "Allie."** Born Apr. 1885 in Monroe Co., IN. Married Grace E. Mason about 1915 (she was born about 1886 in IA). Listed in the 1915 state census and 1920 federal census for Newton, Jasper Co., IA working as a laborer. Allie Burgess died of influenza in Mar. 1923, and is buried in the Van Meter Cemetery.

9a. **Gail Cletus.** Listed as Cletis G. Burgess in the 1920 census. Born Aug. 1916 in Iowa. Married Rose Bernstein on 26 Nov. 1953 in Los Angeles, CA (she was born about 1913 in NY). Living at Hollywood, CA about 1970.

8c. **Oliver Edmond.** Born 18 May 1887 at Allen Creek, IN. See below for full entry.
8d. **Cletus.** Born about 1889 at Booneville, IA; died there of measles before 1900.
8e. **Carl Cecil.** Born 17 Aug. 1891 at Booneville, IA. See below for full entry.

OLIVER EDMOND BURGESS OF POLK CO., IOWA

[John E. (I)[6], Lewis Albert[7]]

8c. **Oliver Edmond "Ollie"** *[son of Lewis Albert].* Born 18 May 1887 at Allen Creek, Monroe Co., IN. Married Margaret Ann Wallace about 1913 (she was born 27 Jan. 1897 at Last Creek, ID, and died 25 Aug. 1945, buried Evergreen Cemetery, Brainerd, MN). Listed in the 1917 draft list for Jasper Co., IA. Ollie Burgess was an electrician for the Maytag Company. He died on 21 June 1968 at Des Moines, IA, and is buried in the Van Meter Cemetery.

9a. **(Genevieve) Maxine.** Born 22 Aug. 1914 at Colfax, IA. Married Harvey Clinton about 1930, and had children: *Harvey C. "Jack"* (born 31 Dec. 1931 at Van Meter, IA, died 5 June 1975 at Fremont, CA); *(Hugh) Eugene "Gene"* (born 8 Jan. 1935, married Patsy Door, had children: Tony; Michael; LeAnn; Dana, and died 13 Nov. 1973 at Fremont, CA); **Maxine** married Kelmer Moll on 12 Aug. 1967, and thirdly James Clair Staver (he was born 23 Apr. 1903, died Nov. 1973 at Fremont, CA). Maxine Staver died on 1 Sept. 1987 at Fremont, CA, and is buried in the Chapel of the Chimes Cemetery, Hayward, CA.
9b. **John Albert.** Born 18 May 1916 at Colfax, IA. Married (Geneva) Katherine Grim on 12 Sept. 1939 at Adel, IA (she was born 1 Apr. 1921 at Warrensburg, IL, daughter of Julius Vern Grim and Lucy Mae Fisher, and died 19 July 1992 at Des Moines, IA). John A. Burgess was an airplane pilot, truck driver, and diesel mechanic. He died on 2 Aug. 1972 at Des Moines, IA, and is buried with his wife in the Pine Hill Cemetery.

10a. **Shirley Ann (II).** Born 8 Apr. 1940 at Van Meter, IA. Married Richard Harry Messer on 30 Mar. 1956 at Des Moines, IA (he was born 6 Nov. 1933), and had children: *Ricky Harry* (born 28 Feb. 1958 at Des Moines, IA); *Mickey Albert* (born 26 Aug. 1959 at Des Moines, IA); *Vicky Ann* (born 9 Sept. 1960 at Des Moines, IA).
10b. **John Junior.** Born 20 June 1941 at Van Meter, IA. Married Terry Lynn Brown on 11 May 1963 (she was born 15 June 1945, daughter of James B. and Helen Brown). John Burgess is a farmer and diesel mechanic at Indianola, Warren Co., IA.
10c. **Katherine Jean.** Born 9 Sept. 1943 at Grimes, IA. Married Beldon Jack Wilson on 8 Mar. 1963 at Des Moines, IA, and had children: *David Allen* (born 22 Apr. 1969 at Des Moines, IA); *Thomas Allen* (born 2 Oct. 1971 at Des Moines, IA, died 3 Sept. 1991 at Des Moines, IA, buried Green Castle Cemetery, Mingo, IA); *Lisa Ann* (born 7 Mar. 1973 at Des Moines, IA). **Katherine WILSON** married secondly Thomas Allen Stewart on 18 Sept. 1976 at Des Moines, IA (he was born 23 Nov. 1942 at Des Moines, and died 11 Jan. 1992, buried Green Castle Cemetery).
10d. **Francis LeRoy "Butch."** Born 27 Jan. 1947 at Van Meter, IA. Married Shirley Elaine Evans on 7 May 1973 at Des Moines, IA (div.; she was born 24 Jan. 1952). Butch Burgess is a maintenance man for the West Des Moines school system; he also works as an auto body repairman in Des Moines.

11a. **Daughter.**

10e. **Janet Louise.** Born 24 Jan. 1949 at Van Meter, IA. Married Terry Edwin Burns on 23 Dec. 1968 at Grimes, IA (he was born 15 Jan. 1951), and had children: *Sonia Laray* (born 20 Nov. 1969 at Des Moines, IA, and is married, with children); *Terry Edwin Jr.* (born 3 Dec. 1971 at Des Moines, IA, and is married, with children); *Michael Shane* (born 1 Sept. 1974 at Des Moines, IA).
10f. **Diana Lee.** Born 2 Feb. 1952 at Des Moines, IA. Married Charles Robert Brown on 31 May 1969 at Des Moines, IA (he was born 1 Oct. 1948 at Newton, IA, the son of Charles Elias Brown and Catherine Jane Wade), and had children: *Christina Marie* (born 8 May 1970 at Des Moines, IA, married Jeffrey Gayle Crise on 28 Mar. 1992 at Des Moines, IA, and had children: Joshua Albert [born 8 Dec. 1992]); *Lori Lorraine* (born 7 Oct. 1972 at Des Moines, IA, married

Kelly Eugene Yokum [born 24 Apr. 1967]). Charles and Diana Brown own a farm at Baxter, IA; she previously worked for UPS at Colfax, IA. She has contributed greatly to this book.

10g. **Melvin Edmund.** Born 4 Oct. 1956 at Des Moines, IA. Married Cheri Campbell (she was born 4 June 1957). Melvin Burgess worked for the Great Plains Rag Co. He now lives retired at West Des Moines, IA.

11a. **Mindy Michell.** Born 26 Jan. 1976 at Des Moines, IA.
11b. **Misty Dawn.** Born 15 July 1979 at Des Moines, IA.

CARL BURGESS OF SAN BERNARDINO CO., CALIFORNIA

[John E. (I)[6], Lewis Albert[7]]

8e. **Carl Cecil** *[son of Lewis Albert].* Born 17 Aug. 1891 at Booneville, Dallas Co., IA. Married Fern Clearwater on 26 June 1912 at Booneville, IA (she was born 27 Nov. 1892, and died May 1984 in Iowa). Listed in the 1917 draft register for Newton, Jasper Co., IA. Carl Burgess worked as a telegraph operator for the Rock Island Railroad, bank clerk, salesman, and later as a traveling entertainer for school children. He lived at Newton, IA from 1913-35, in Marshalltown, IA from 1936-42, and at Yucaipa, CA from 1943-79, before moving back to Iowa. He died in June 1986, aged 94 years, at Baxter, IA, and is buried in the Union Cemetery, Newton, IA. In 1979 he published a book, *National Voice Throwing Champion* (Yucaipa, CA: U.S. Business Specialties), which tells about his life and his accomplishments as a ventriloquist.

9a. **Carl Junior.** Born 4 Apr. 1913 at Van Meter, IA. Married Judy Hummell. Carl Burgess died childless on 26 Sept. 1936 of appendicitis, and is buried in the Union Cemetery, Newton, IA.

9b. **Glen Russell.** Born 5 June 1914 at Van Meter, IA. Married Maxine Martin about 1936 (she was born 23 July 1917, and died in Mar. 1969 at Newton); married secondly Charlotte Dean in 1971. Glen Burgess worked for Maytag Company. He now lives retired at Newton, IA.

10a. **Michael Martin.** Born 21 Feb. 1937 at Newton, IA. Married Margery Bowers; married secondly Helen Raridon; married thirdly Frances Miles. Dr. Michael M. Burgess earned his Ph.D. in clinical psychology at Florida State University in 1964. He served as an assistant and associate professor of psychology at the University of Kansas Medical Center, Kansas City, KS from 1965-69, and as professor (and sometime Chair of the Department) at the University of Missouri, Kansas City, MO from 1969-76. Since 1976 he has had his own practice, Burgess Consultants, Inc. at Shawnee Mission, KS.

11a. **Mark David.** Born 29 Oct. 1954 at Des Moines, IA. He was adopted by his stepfather, E. A. McCardell Jr., and now uses that surname.
11b. **Michael Craig.** Born 23 Sept. 1956 at Belleville, IA.
11c. **Renee Annette.** Born 14 July 1959 at Panama City, FL. Married.
11d. **John Patrick.** Born 27 May 1965 at Kansas City, KS.

9c. **Paul Dwight.** Born 21 May 1922 at Newton, IA. Married Margery Summers at Carson City, NV. Paul Burgess was a sign painter and a designer of fuel and injection nozzles; he later worked as project engineer for Delavan Manufacturing Co., at Des Moines, IA. He and his wife were both killed in an automobile accident on 21 Dec. 1982 near Tama, IA, and are buried in the West Des Moines Cemetery.

10a. **Penelope Dee "Penny."** Born 24 Aug. 1950 at Des Moines, IA. Married John Kunkel, and had children: *Shannon* (born 1971); *Joel* (born 1974). Penny Kunkel lives at Lincoln, NE.

10b. **Timothy Lee.** Born 30 July 1955 at Des Moines, IA. Married Taressa Henderson. Tim Burgess is a computer programmer for Iowa State University, Ames, IA. He currently lives at Cambridge, IA.

11a. **Courtney Llewellyn.** Born 16 Feb. 1980 at Ames, IA.
11b. **Celeste Jean.** Born 20 Mar. 1982 at Ames, IA.

BERT DAWSON OF SPOKANE CO., WASHINGTON
[John E. (I)[6]]

7c. **Dawson (III) "Dorsey"** *[son of John E. (I)].* He adopted the name Bert G. DAWSON about 1903. Born 22 May 1860 in Orange Co., IN. Married Mary Jane Moore on 5 Dec. 1880 in Lawrence Co., IN (she was born 1862, daughter of David Moore and Elizabeth Hostitler, and died 4 Mar. 1898 at Tunnelton, IN); married secondly Bertha Jaynes in IL; married thirdly Dena M. Johnson (she was born 11 Mar. 1882 in SD, daughter of Gerdt W. Johnson and Susan A. Sutton, and died 14 July 1952 at Spokane). Listed in the 1880 census for Orange Co., IN working as a servant for Peter Hardman, in 1900 at Omaha, Douglas Co., NE living by himself, and in 1910 at Billings, Yellowstone Co., MT. Dawson Burgess (later Bert G. Dawson) was a minister and farmer. He later moved to Spokane, WA, where he is listed in the 1923 city directory working as a grocer. He died there on 8 Sept. 1925, and is buried in the Greenwood Cemetery. Two of his children used the surname Dawson.

"Uncle Dawson became a preacher. About 1899 Uncle Dawson and family visited his brother Albert. There were three children in his family: a girl 18, a boy 14, and a little girl about my age whose name was Mae. I don't remember anything about Uncle's preaching, but I do remember, very vividly, how crowded it was in our humble home, which had but four rooms. [There were] two families, ten people altogether, so sleeping quarters were quite crowded, but somehow mother managed to handle the problem quite satisfactorily. But how she managed to feed all of them is still a mystery, as it was quite a problem to get [enough] food for our own family. Perhaps Uncle Dawson had money to pay for their share, or perhaps my brothers brought home enough rabbits, fish, and ducks to help. The visitors stayed several months, after which they migrated out west to Montana, together with a farmer family from near Van Meter, the Crawfords."—Carl C. Burgess.

8a. **Claudia F.** Born 4 Oct. 1881 in Orange Co., IN; died on 19 Oct. 1889 in Lawrence Co., IN.

8b. **Henry E. (I) "Harry."** Born 28 Nov. 1884 in Orange Co., IN; died on 20 Oct. 1889 in Lawrence Co., IN.

8c. **Grace Lenore.** She used the surname Dawson before her marriage. Born 15 Dec. 1886 in Orange Co., IN. Married George W. Crawford, and had at least the following children: *Alice Cathryn* (who married ___ Ledum, and lives at Campbell, CA); *Harold Monroe*; *Leah Mae*; *Wayne*; *Mervian Frances*; *Donald Fred*. Grace Crawford died on 12 Sept. 1961 at San Jose, CA, and is buried in the Oak Hill Memorial Park.

8d. **Fred Oval.** He used the surname Dawson. Born 19 Sept. 1890 at Lexington, KY. Married Redina Dahl on 17 May 1913 at Billings, MT; married secondly Olga A. Bottiger. Listed with his uncle, Leander Roberts, in the 1900 census for Lawrence Co., IN (as Fred *Burgess*). Fred Dawson worked as a baggage handler and express messenger for the Union Pacific Railroad. He died childless on 11 June 1963 at Spokane, WA, and is buried in the Riverside Mausoleum.

8e. **(Ida) Mae (II).** She used the surname Burgess before her marriage. Born 19 Apr. 1894 at Orleans, IN. Listed with her uncle, Leander Roberts, in the 1900 census. Married Carey K. Crawford on 22 Apr. 1914 at Billings, MT (he was born 28 Dec. 1882, son of Robert M. Crawford and Kate Becker, and died 17 Nov. 1968 at McCleary, WA), and had children:

Cleo Katherine CRAWFORD. Born 14 May 1917 at Billings, MT, married Harold Lane, secondly Cleo Clemens, and thirdly Harry Limbocker, and died 20 Feb. 1985 at San Jose, CA.

Jean Lenore CRAWFORD. Born 20 June 1919 at Billings, MT, married Richard Bernard Breidenbach on 30 Jan. 1936 at Shelton, WA, and had children:

John Carey BREIDENBACH (born 24 Apr. 1937, married Linda Nevitt on 1 June 1960 [she was born 29 July 1942, and died on 23 May 1978], and had children: Lela Jean [born 8 Mar. 1962, married Ron Peterson in Aug. 1981, and had children: Lindsey Nicole {born Jan. 1985}; Philip Carey {born Sept. 1990}]; John Alan [born 23 Mar. 1964, married Diane ___, and had children: Carlee Elizabeth Diane {born 28 Dec. 1991}; married secondly Shelley ___ on 6 Sept. 1992]; John Carey Breidenbach married secondly Cindy Reade on 30 Jan. 1979).

Bobbette Mae BREIDENBACH (born 14 Jan. 1938, married Bobby Gene Fowler on 26 Apr. 1958 at San Antonio, TX, and had children: Barbara Jean [born 11 Nov. 1958, married Bennett Gum on 11 Sept. 1982, and had children: Charisa L. {born 12 June 1986}; Michael {born 16 Aug. 1988}]; Bobby Gene Jr. [born 9 Feb. 1960, serves as a Capt. in the U.S. Air Force]; Billy Richard [born 1 May 1962, married Beverly Smith on 19 May 1986, and had children: Ryan {born 31 July 1987}; Caitlyn {born 6 June 1989}; Kyle {born 19 Nov. 1991}]).

Richard Charles BREIDENBACH (born 2 Nov. 1939, married Holly Ann Horton on 12 June 1965 at Olympia, WA, and had children: Heidi Lynn [born 19 Feb. 1968, died 12 Jan. 1989];

Reid Alex [born 5 Dec. 1970, died 7 Dec. 1970]; Heather Anne [born 24 Dec. 1973, died 12 Feb. 1979]).

Mae ROBERTS died on 28 May 1955 at Olympia, WA. **Jean and Holly BREIDENBACH** have contributed greatly to this book. They both currently live at Olympia, WA.

8f. **Robert Dawson.** He used the surname Burgess. Born 26 July 1902 at Clay City, IL. Married Helen ___. Robert D. Burgess died on 12 July 1971 at Spokane, WA.

9a. **Mary Helen (I).** Born about 1925. She lives at Oakdale, CA.

JESSE BURGESS OF ORANGE CO., INDIANA

[John E. (I)[6]]

7d. **Jesse (I)** *[son of John E. (I)].* Born 6 Apr. 1863 in Orange Co., IN. Married Maggie Cooper on 17 Sept. 1890 in Lawrence Co., IN (she was born 1 Mar. 1858, and died between 1900-03); married secondly Carrie A. Wells on 27 Oct. 1903 in Orange Co., IN (she was born 1878 in IN). Listed in the 1900-20 censuses for Orleans Township, Orange Co., IN; three of five children survive in 1900. Jesse Burgess was a stonecutter in Orange Co. He died on 31 Dec. 1936 at Paoli, IN, and is buried in the Liberty Cemetery.

8a. **Noble.** Born 16 (or 14, according to his draft record) July 1891 in Orange Co., IN. Listed in the 1917 draft register of Orange Co., IN, and served in the 314th Cavalry and in the 63rd Field Artillery, U.S. Army, during World War I. Noble Burgess worked as a baker in Indiana and Ohio. He died on 30 Aug. 1950, and is buried in the Liberty Cemetery, Orleans, Orange Co., IN.

8b. **Earnest.** Born 6 July 1893 in Orange Co., IN; died there on 20 Mar. 1894, and is buried with his father.

8c. **Homer (II).** Born 7 Apr. 1895 in Orange Co., IN; died there on 1 June 1902, buried with his father.

8d. **Mabel (I).** Born Apr. 1898 in Orange Co., IN.

8e. **(Ray) Hazel.** Born 3 Apr. 1904 in Orange Co., IN. Living with her father in 1920. Married Varnie Jones on 24 Feb. 1921 in Orange Co., IN (div.; he was born 11 Mar. 1901, and died Feb. 1974 at Paoli, IN); married secondly George R. Buran on 16 Mar. 1925 in Orange Co.

8f. **Jesse (III).** Born 1906 in Orange Co., IN. Living with his father in 1920. Jesse Burgess Jr. died on 23 May 1954 in Orange Co., and is buried in the Fairview Cemetery.

9a. **Charles E. (II).** Born 1927 in Orange Co., IN; died there in 1928, and is buried with his grandfather. Relation not verified.

9b. **Phyllis C.** Born 1931 in Orange Co., IN; died there in 1933, and is buried with her grandfather. Relation not verified.

8g. **Alice M. (III) "Allie."** Born 15 May 1910 in Orange Co., IN. Married Evan E. Roll on 10 July 1928 in Orange Co., IN (he was born 22 Aug. 1906, and died Dec. 1982 at Paoli, IN), and had children: *Bettie J.* (born 20 Oct. 1928); *Georgia Louise* (born 7 Mar. 1931); *Alice* (born 28 Oct. 1935).

8h. **Russell (I).** Born 9 Sept. 1914 in Orange Co., IN. Russell Burgess died on 5 June 1990 at Orleans, IN.

Carl Burgess Remembers (1979)

"One event that stands out in my memory was the hot summer evenings [in Iowa], when my father would have us carry several chairs out to the yard, where we'd all sit awhile before retiring. My father would then light up a cigar, and when it was dark the light on the end of the cigar would glow brightly. I liked the aroma, and still do. The highlight of such evenings was catching lightning bugs. I wondered how they could make so much light. How quiet it was on such occasions. The only sound was the monotonous concert given by the invisible male crickets (my brothers called them tree toads), who never paused to wait for the applause. One of the less pleasant aspects of such evenings was the travel by horses and buggies on the extremely dusty road [in front of our place], particularly when a fast trotter came by. If the wind was from the north, all was well, but if it blew from the south, great clouds of dust would envelop us. Once I carried several buckets of water out to sprinkle on the street, but soon discovered that many barrels of liquid would be required to do the job. Not long after this we moved into a company house owned by a brickyard manufacturer, but the move proved disappointing, as dad was soon laid off. My father was without work for ten days, until he found work at Grundy Center, about thirty miles west of Van Meter. Our home was very lonely then, especially for me, because I couldn't understand why Papa had to be away for so long...."

[William (I)[1], Edward (I)[2], Edward (II)[3], Mason Peyton[4], Dawson (II)[5]]

WILLIAM F. BURGESS, SR.
(1839-1901)

OF ORANGE COUNTY, INDIANA

6g. **William Fleming (I)** *[son of Dawson (II)].* Born 5 Jan. 1839 in Orange Co., IN. Married Julia Ann Duncan on 27 Nov. 1862 in Orange Co. (she was born 7 May 1838, and died Sept. 1876); married secondly (Belinda) Jane Bridgewater on 26 Aug. 1877 in Orange Co. (she was born 4 Feb. 1851 in IN, and died after 1920). Served in Co. G, 24th Indiana Infantry, Union Army, during the Civil War. Listed in the 1870-1900 censuses for Stampers Creek Township, Orange Co., IN; his widow is listed as head of the family in the 1910-20 censuses (two of five children survive in 1910). William F. Burgess was a farmer in Orange Co., his land being located about ten miles east of Paoli, near Millersburg, IN. He died there on 13 Aug. 1901, and is buried in the Stampers Creek Cemetery.

The Children of William F. Burgess, Sr.:

7a. **Charles E. (I).** Born 26 Oct. 1863 in Orange Co., IN. See below for full entry.
7b. **Leroy Sherman.** Born 30 Aug. 1865 in Orange Co., IN. See below for full entry.
7c. **William Fleming (II) "Willie."** Born 9 Apr. 1867 in Orange Co., IN. See below for full entry.
7d. **(Julia) Etta.** Born 26 May 1869 in Orange Co., IN. Married Herman Cornwell on 5 Dec. 1894 in Orange Co. (he was born Dec. 1874 in IN), and had children: *Audrey M.* (born 7 Feb. 1897, married Ray R. Trinkle on 29 Aug. 1915 in Orange Co.); *Lois* (born 8 Aug. 1905, married Earl Holmes on 28 June 1924 in Orange Co.). Listed in the 1900 census for Stampers Creek Township, Orange Co., IN. Etta Cornwell died on 29 Mar. 1933, and is buried in the Stampers Creek Cemetery.
7e. **(Sarah) Rhoda.** Born 11 Apr. 1871 in Orange Co., IN. Married William Robert Martin on 15 Feb. 1896 in Orange Co., and had children: *Hazel Marie* (born 18 Nov. 1896, married Ray Chastain on 25 May 1915 in Orange Co., and died June 1975 at Salem, IN). Rhoda Martin died on 14 Apr. (or 22 July) 1899 in Orange Co., and is buried in the Stampers Creek Cemetery. William Martin is listed in the 1900 census for Stampers Creek Township, Orange Co., IN. Their granddaughter, Doris Martin, lives at Orleans, IN.
7f. **Polly Ann (II).** Born 3 May 1876 in Orange Co., IN. Married John Sailor on 22 Sept. 1892 in Orange Co. (he was born May 1869 in IN), and had at least the following children: *Heber B.* (born 1 July 1893); *Allie F.* (born 15 Nov. 1894, married Orville E. Reed on 1 Jan. 1915 in Orange Co., and died Nov. 1985 at Bedford, IN, aged 91 years); *Blanche M.* (born 12 Oct. 1897, married Merle S. Troth on 26 June 1926 in Orange Co., and died Mar. 1984 at Orleans, IN). Polly Sailor died on 25 July 1906 in Orange Co., and is buried there in the Stampers Creek Cemetery.
7g. **Emma E. (II).** Born 28 Oct. 1878 in Orange Co., IN. Married William W. Atkinson on 21 Oct. 1897 in Orange Co. (he remarried her cousin, Josie Estle Kirby), and had children: *Clarence R.* (born 3 Apr. 1899, listed with Emma's father in 1900, and with his Burgess grandmother in 1910-20, married Nellie Cornwell on 22 Dec. 1920 in Orange Co., and died 25 Jan. 1990 at Paoli, IN, aged 90 years). Emma Atkinson died on 22 Dec. 1899 in Orange Co., and is buried in the Stampers Creek Cemetery.
7h. **Melvina E. "Nellie."** Born 19 Aug. 1880 in Orange Co., IN. Married Floyd L. Wolfe on 7 May 1905 in Orange Co. (he was born 1881, and died 1921), and had children: *Cletus Earl* (born 14 June 1906); *Doris Pauline* (born 7 Apr. 1912). Nellie Wolfe died there on 10 Dec. 1917, and is buried in the Stampers Creek Cemetery.
7i. **(Clara) Ethel.** Her name is also spelled Chlorie. Born 4 July 1883 in Orange Co., IN. Married (James) Everett Coulter on 25 Jan. 1905 in Orange Co. (he was born 9 July 1878, and died 3 Aug. 1933). Ethel Coulter died on 27 Feb. 1907 in Orange Co., and is buried with her husband in the Stampers Creek Cemetery.
7j. **Amos Comart.** Born 26 Dec. 1887 in Orange Co., IN. See below for full entry.

CHARLES E. BURGESS OF ORANGE CO., INDIANA

[William Fleming (I)[6]]

7a. **Charles E. (I)** *[son of William Fleming (I)].* Born 26 Oct. 1863 in Orange Co., IN. Married Louella E. Cornwell on 4 Aug. 1885 in Orange Co. (she was born 1 Mar. 1862, daughter of Shelby and Jane Cornwell, and died 2 Jan. 1934). Listed in the 1900-20 censuses for Stampers Creek Township, Orange Co., IN; two of two children survive in 1900. Charles Burgess was a farmer in Orange Co. He died there on 12 Feb. 1934, and is buried in the Stampers Creek Cemetery.

8a. **(Clarence) Earl.** Born 4 July 1886 in Orange Co., IN. Married Blanche Rigney on 26 Aug. 1908 in Orange Co. (she was born 4 July 1886). Listed in the 1910-20 censuses for Orange Co., IN, and in the 1917 draft register there. Earl Burgess was a school teacher at Orleans, Orange Co., IN. He died there about 1960.

9a. **Merrill Charles.** Born 13 Jan. 1910 in Orange Co., IN. Married Lucille Velcein on 5 Apr. 1934. Merrill Burgess was a road engineer for the state of Indiana, working out of Mitchell, IN. He died there on 13 July 1969, and is buried in the Mitchell Cemetery. Lucille Burgess currently lives at Mitchell, IN.

10a. **Charles Edwin.** Born 7 Mar. 1935 at Orleans, IN. Married Annette Thielmeyer on 1 Dec. 1956. Charles Burgess lives at Cincinnati, OH.

11a. **Cindy Joy.** Born 19 Dec. 1959.
11b. **Sherri Diane.** Born 10 Apr. 1961.
11c. **Mark Allen (I).** Born 22 Oct. 1962. Mark Burgess is an enlisted man in the U.S. Army, now serving in West Germany.
11d. **Julie Ann.** Born 14 Sept. 1969.
11e. **Kevin Charles.** Born 30 Mar. 1973.

10b. **Barbara Ann (I).** Born 12 Jan. 1939 at Mitchell, IN. Married Dr. George Woodrow Sorrells Jr. on 4 June 1960, and had children: *Rhonda Gail* (born 17 Nov. 1962); *George Woodrow III* (born 29 May 1965); *Ann Rachelle* (born 3 Oct. 1966); *Trisha Lynn* (born 31 May 1971). Barbara Sorrells lives at Mitchell, IN.
10c. **Marilyn Jean.** Born 21 May 1944 at Crane, IN. Married Jerry Sadek on 6 Mar. 1971.
10d. **William Earl (II).** Born 24 Dec. 1946 at Mitchell, IN. Married Marie Ann Duncan on 1 Feb. 1966. William E. Burgess currently lives at Brownstown, IN.

11a. **David William (I).** Born 15 Sept. 1966. Married Melanie Brock on 8 Aug. 1987. David Burgess currently lives at Seymour, IN.
11b. **Debra Marie.** Born 18 Mar. 1970.
11c. **Todd Christopher** (ad.).
11d. **Wesley Ray** (ad.).

9b. **Maurine Ruth.** Born 27 Apr. 1913 in Orange Co., IN. Married Lon Beaty in Sept. 1933, and had children: *Carole Sue* (born 12 Nov. 1935 at Orleans, IN, and died there on 3 Apr. 1936); *Rhetta Ann* (born 24 Apr. 1937). Maurine Beaty currently lives at Cincinnati, OH.
9c. **Mary Edith.** Born 9 June 1919 in Orange Co., IN. Married Menlo Huston on 18 Dec. 1937, and had children: *Sidney Burgess* (born 28 July 1938); *Susan Earlene* (born 22 Feb. 1943). Mary Huston lives at San Antonio, TX.

8b. **Anna Jane.** Born 8 July 1894 in Orange Co., IN. Married Ramond Crockett on 10 Mar. 1915 in Orange Co., IN, and had at least the following children: *Buell*; *Charles Robert*. Listed with her father in the 1920 census. Anna Crockett died on 3 Feb. 1967 in Orange Co., and is buried in the Stampers Creek Cemetery. Buell and Charles Crockett currently live in Orange Co.

LEROY SHERMAN BURGESS OF ORANGE CO., INDIANA

[William Fleming (I)[6]]

7b. **Leroy Sherman** *[son of William Fleming (I)].* Born 30 Aug. 1865 in Orange Co., IN. Married Ella Mary "May" Stevens (or Stephenson) on 14 Oct. 1896 in Orange Co. (she was born 18 July 1871, daughter of Ben Stevens [or Stephenson] and Rachel Oldham, and died 12 June 1948). Listed in the 1900-20 censuses for Stampers Creek Township, Orange Co., IN; two of two children survive in 1900. Leroy Burgess was a farmer in Orange Co. He died there on 25 Oct. 1951, and is buried in the Stampers Creek Cemetery.

8a. **Lawrence Ray.** Born 3 May 1897 in Orange Co., IN. Listed in the 1917 draft register of Orange Co., IN, and in the 1920 census with his father. Lawrence R. Burgess was a farmer in Orange Co., IN. He died there unmarried in 1943, and is buried in the Stampers Creek Cemetery.

8b. **(Elta) Pearl.** Her name is spelled Alta on her birth record. Born 23 Sept. 1898 in Orange Co., IN. Married Raymond P. Strange on 24 Dec. 1919 in Orange Co., and had children: *Donald Roy* (born 6 Aug. 1921, and lives at Orleans, IN); *Julia Ellen* (born 23 Apr. 1923); *James Lee* (born 5 Sept. 1924); *Mary Lou* (born 6 June 1930); *Barbara R.* (born 28 Apr. 1932); *John Robert* (born 8 Feb. 1936). Pearl Strange died on 30 May 1983 in Orange Co.

8c. **Mabel Beatrice.** Born 2 July 1901 in Orange Co., IN. Listed with her father in the 1920 census. Married Archibald D. "Archie" Patton on 28 Apr. 1920 in Orange Co. (he died in 1951), and had children: *Carl Wayne* (born 29 Mar. 1921); *Charles Edward* (born 24 Dec. 1924); *Shirley* (married ___ Ruzich, and lives at Orleans, IN). Mabel Patton currently lives at West Frankfort, IL.

8d. **Rhoda Irene.** Born 22 Mar. 1904 in Orange Co., IN. Listed with her father in the 1920 census. Married (William) Arthur Hill on 12 Oct. 1929 in Orange Co., and had children: *Jacqueline J.* (born 15 Jan. 1935); *Linda Lou* (born 25 Oct. 1936). Rhoda Hill currently lives in Orange Co.

WILLIE BURGESS OF ORANGE CO., INDIANA

[William Fleming (I)[6]]

7c. **William Fleming (II) "Willie"** *[son of William Fleming (I)].* Born 9 Apr. 1867 in Orange Co., IN. Married Della E. Burton on 24 Oct. 1893 (she was born 1875, and died 22 Dec. 1899, buried Stampers Creek Cemetery); married secondly Laura E. Wells (she was born 1884 in IN). Listed with his father in the 1900 census, and in the 1910-20 censuses for Orange Co., IN. Willie Burgess was a carpenter. He died on 26 Oct. 1956.

8a. **Jewel J.** Born 5 Jan. 1905 in Orange Co., IN. Listed with her father in the 1920 census. Married Guy Burton on 25 Nov. 1925 in Orange Co. (he was born 31 Oct. 1904); married secondly Bennie Nail. Jewel Nail died on 19 May 1989 at Paris, Edgar Co., IL.

AMOS C. BURGESS OF OSCEOLA CO., FLORIDA

[William Fleming (I)[6]]

7j. **Amos Comart** *[son of William Fleming (I)].* Born 26 Dec. 1887 in Orange Co., IN. Married Martha Flo "Mattie" Crane about 1912 (she was born 20 Oct. 1893, daughter of (Thomas) Jefferson Crane and Amy Seithes, and died 27 Mar. 1919 at Paoli, IN, buried Stampers Creek Cemetery). Listed in the 1917 draft register of Orange Co., IN, and in the 1920 census living with his mother. Amos Burgess died Sept. 1968 at Saint Cloud, Osceola Co., FL.

8a. **Margueritte.** Born 25 Nov. 1913 in Orange Co, IN. Listed in the 1920 census with her father and grandmother. She is *not* the Marguerite Burgess (b. 1913) listed in *Who Was Who in American Art.*

8b. **Daughter** (twin). Born 1915, died before 1920.

8c. **Daughter** (twin). Born 1915, died before 1920.

8d. **Child.** Born and died 14 Aug. 1917 in Orange Co., IN, and is buried in the Stampers Creek Cemetery.

[William (I)[1], Edward (I)[2], Edward (II)[3], Mason Peyton[4]]

THORNTON BURGESS
(1817-1870)

OF CLARK COUNTY, ILLINOIS

5g. **Thornton (II)** *[son of Mason Peyton].* Born 16 Aug. 1817 in Jefferson Co., KY. Married Martha Ann Jones on 10 Feb. 1850 in Lawrence Co., IN (she was born 11 Feb. 1825, and died 4 July 1899 at Arcola, IL, buried in the Van Voorhis Cemetery, Douglas Co., IL). Served in Co. B, 2nd Indiana Volunteers, during the Mexican-American War (between 1846-47). Listed in the 1850 census for Stampers Creek Township, Orange Co., IN, and in 1860 in Jennings Township, Crawford Co., IN. Thornton Burgess was a farmer in Indiana; he moved in 1868 to Clark Co., IL. He died of tuberculosis on 24 Apr. 1870 at Westfield, Clark Co., IL, and is buried there in the Old Methodist Church Cemetery. His widow is listed as head of the family in the 1870 census for Westfield, Parker Township, Clark Co., IL, and in the 1880 census for Seven Hickory Township, Coles Co., IL; she had settled by 1887 in Douglas Co., IL. Martha Burgess obtained a pension based on her husband's war service, which she held until her death in 1899.

The Children of Thornton Burgess:

6a. **(John) Edward (I).** Born 15 Nov. 1850 in Washington Co., IN. See below for full entry.
6b. **William M(ason?) (I).** Born 8 Apr. 1852 in Orange Co., IN; died there on 16 Nov. 1852, and is buried in the Stampers Creek Cemetery.
6c. **Mary Ellen (III).** Born 30 Aug. 1854 in Orange Co., IN. Married Thomas J. Denny on 7 Dec. 1893 in Douglas Co., IL. Listed with her mother in the 1880 census. Mary Denny died on 27 Sept. 1918 in Douglas Co., and is buried in the Van Voorhis Cemetery.
6d. **Martha A(nn?) (III) "Mattie."** Born June 1856 in Orange Co., IN. Married John Henry Poulter on 20 Aug. 1877 (he was born on 5 Mar. 1859 at Paris, Edgar Co., IL, son of Harrison Poulter and Anna Waight; he invented the Leader Automatic Grain Weir, used to elevate, register, and convey grain; he then became a building contractor, and moved to Ardmore, OK in 1914, where he built homes and apartments, and was president of the Builders Exchange; he also was one of several men who helped carry Oklahoma state records from the old capital [Guthrie, OK] to the present-day capital of Oklahoma City). Their children included: *Fred H.* (born Mar. 1882 in IL, living at Wichita, KS in 1925); *George E.* (born 23 Feb. 1884 in IL, married Jennie Weaver, was living at Ardmore, OK in 1925, and died Sept. 1962 in TX); *William H.* (born Feb. 1890 in IL, served in World War I, married Ollie Moore, had children: Billie Ruth, and was living at Ardmore, OK in 1925); *Charles T.* (born Aug. 1896 in IL, married Lorena Wall, and had children: Charles John; George Allen, and was living at Ardmore in 1925); *Lorene Belle* (born 27 Aug. 1898 in KY, married Clay W. Patterson, an automobile dealer, had children: Anna Elaine, was living at Ardmore in 1925, and died Oct. 1988 at Arlington, TX, aged 90 years). Listed in the 1900 census for Kinman Township, Douglas Co., IL. The Poulters were living in Oklahoma as late as 1937. John Poulter's biography appears in *Oklahoma History South of the Canadian*, by John P. Gilday (Chicago: S. J. Clarke, 1925, Volume III, p. 1075-1076).
6e. **Volney Thornton "Vol."** Born Apr. 1859 in Orange Co., IN. See below for full entry.
6f. **Jonathan Leland.** Born 18 Nov. 1860 in Crawford Co., IN. See below for full entry.
6g. **Emma I.** Born about 1864 in IN. Married James A. Foster on 13 Jan. 1892 in Douglas Co. (he was born 1864 in IN, and died 1926). She died in Douglas Co. after her husband, and is buried in the Van Voorhis Cemetery (no dates appear on their stone). She may be the Emma I. Foster who died on 27 May 1929 at Chicago, IL.
6h. **(Sarah) Carrie.** Born 28 Apr. 1869 in Coles Co., IL (so stated on her marriage record). Married William F. Curry on 19 Feb. 1891 in Douglas Co. (he was born 1869 in Brown Co., IN, son of James Curry and Sarah Millsap). Carrie Curry died on 16 May 1892 in Douglas Co., and is buried next to her mother.

[William (I)[1], Edward (I)[2], Edward (II)[3], Mason Peyton[4], Thornton (II)[5]]

JOHN E. BURGESS
(1850-1831)

OF CASS COUNTY, MISSOURI

6a. **(John) Edward (I) "Ed"** *[son of Thornton (II)]*. Born 15 Nov. 1850 at Salem, Washington Co., IN. Married Mary Evelyn Kittle on 11 Jan. 1884 in Coles Co., IL (she was born at Rising Sun, IN, and died between 1892-1900); married secondly Nola Vaughn about 1912 (she was born about 1873, and died on 30 May 1924 at San Jose, CA). Listed in the 1880 census with his mother, and in 1900 in Douglas Co., IL working as a farmer; has not been found in the 1910-20 censuses. Ed Burgess later lived at San Jose, CA, at Denver, CO, and at Peculiar, Cass Co., MO, near Kansas City. He died in Missouri on 26 Dec. 1931.

The Children of John E. Burgess:

7a. **Pearl E.** (nmn). Born 30 Oct. 1884 at Hindsboro, Douglas Co., IL. Married Jim Burris, and had at least one child: *Opal L.* (she married ___ Tabor, and lives at Independence, MO). Pearl Burris died on 13 July 1961 at Peculiar, Cass Co., MO.

7b. **Emma Bell.** Born 9 Dec. 1886 at Hindsboro, Douglas Co., IL. Emma Burgess was a religious teacher and lay preacher; she founded Emmanuel Church at Boron, Kern Co., CA about 1946, which she operated until her death. She died unmarried on 11 Dec. 1985 at Lancaster, Los Angeles Co., CA, aged 99 years, and is buried in the Rose Hills Memorial Park, Pasadena, CA.

7c. **Harold H.** (nmn). Born 9 Mar. 1890 at Hindsboro, Douglas Co., IL. Married Louvisa A. "Louise" Schwartz (she was born 14 Sept. 1877, and died on 10 Oct. 1979 in San Joaquin Co., CA, aged 102 years). The Rev. Harold H. Burgess was a minister for the Assembly of God, at Boron, Kern Co., CA. He died childless on 29 Oct. 1975 at Lancaster, CA, and is buried in the Rose Hills Memorial Park, Pasadena, CA.

7d. **Owen Leon.** Born 22 Sept. 1892 at Hindsboro, Douglas Co., IL. Married Edith McCarty on 6 June 1935 at Carson City, NV (she was born 20 Feb. 1910 at Berkeley, CA). Owen L. Burgess came to California from Oklahoma in 1929, and worked variously for a hospital laundry, in the oil fields, and as a marine electrician for the shipyards in Stockton, CA. He died on 23 July 1982 at Stockton, just short of his 90th birthday, and is buried in Cherokee Memorial Park. Edith Burgess lives at Stockton, CA.

8a. **Marilyn Edith.** Born 13 Apr. 1938 at Livermore, CA. Married Claude Welch. Marilyn Welch currently lives at Carpinteria, CA.

8b. **Lyle Owen.** Born 8 May 1939 at Livermore, CA. Married Paula Giorgi. Lyle Burgess owns Rare Parts, Inc., selling and manufacturing steering and suspension parts for all vehicles back to 1930. He currently lives at Stockton, CA.

9a. **Dale Robert.** Born 15 Jan. 1964 at Stockton, CA. Dale Burgess earned a master's degree in computer science. He currently works as an independent computer consultant and as a consultant with the City of Stockton, CA.

9b. **Daniel Ryan.** Born 27 July 1972 at Stockton, CA. Dan Burgess works for Rare Parts, Inc., Stockton, CA.

[William (I)[1], Edward (I)[2], Edward (II)[3], Mason Peyton[4], Thornton (II)[5]]

VOLNEY THORNTON BURGESS
(1859-1933)

OF EDGAR COUNTY, ILLINOIS

6e. **Volney Thornton "Vol"** *[son of Thornton (II)].* Born Apr. 1859 in Orange Co., IN. Married Ida Florence Frantz on 1 Jan. 1890 in Douglas Co., IL (she was born 3 Feb. 1866 in Douglas Co., IL, daughter of Evans Frantz and Mary Ellen Barr, and died 22 Sept. 1900). Listed in the 1880 census with his mother, in the 1900 census for Sargent Township, Douglas Co., IL, in 1910 in Edgar Co., IL, and with his son, Clarence, in 1920. None of his family appears there in the county directory for 1930. Volney Burgess was a farmer at Cherry Point, Edgar Co., IL. He died there on 4 Mar. 1933, and is buried with his wife in the Barr-Johnson Cemetery, Paris, IL. Dorothy Burgess kindly supplied much of the information on the descendants of Vol Burgess.

The Children of Vol Burgess:

7a. **(John) Leslie.** Born 14 Feb. 1891 at Hindsboro, Douglas Co., IL. See below for full entry.

7b. **Clarence Chester.** Born 21 Nov. 1894 at Hindsboro, Douglas Co., IL. See below for full entry.

7c. **William Marian "Willie."** Born 11 July 1897 at Bowdre, Douglas Co., IL. Listed in the 1917 draft register of Edgar Co., IL, and in the 1920 census with his brother, Clarence. Twice married. Willie Burgess served in the U.S. Army during World War II. He died childless on 25 Oct. 1964 in Edgar Co., IL, and is buried in the Barr-Johnson Cemetery.

7d. **Bessie Ellen.** Born 26 Aug. 1899 at Bowdre, Douglas Co., IL. Married Eugene Lynch (he was born 9 Feb. 1899, and died 15 May 1976 at Paris, IL). Listed in the 1910 census living with Joseph S. Hopkins (she was raised by her aunt, Hannah Rossetta [Frantz] Hopkins), and in 1920 with her brother, Clarence. Bessie Lynch died childless on 14 Jan. 1967 at Riverdale, IL, and is buried with her husband in the Roselawn Memorial Cemetery, Terre Haute, IN.

JOHN LESLIE BURGESS OF COOK CO., ILLINOIS
[Volney Thornton[6]]

7a. **(John) Leslie** *[son of Volney Thornton].* Born 14 Feb. 1891 at Hindsboro, Douglas Co., IL. Married Callie Patterson on 23 June 1911 at Borton, IL (she was born 20 Mar. 1893 at Borton, daughter of John Patterson and Lucinda Plank, and died 27 Sept. 1959). Listed with his father in the 1910 census, in the 1917 draft register for Edgar Co., IL, and in the 1920 census for Brocton, Edgar Co., IL. Leslie Burgess was a railroad engineer for the Chicago and Eastern Illinois Railroad. He died on 6 Mar. 1971 at Chicago Heights, IL, and is buried with his wife in the Cedar Park Cemetery, Calumet Park, IL.

8a. **(Irma) Maureen.** Born 5 May 1912 at Borton, Edgar Co., IL. Married Arthur Preston Long on 22 Jan. 1944 (he was born 13 Feb. 1896 at Morgan Park, IL, died 19 Oct. 1986 at Harrisonburg, VA, and is buried at Eastlawn Memorial Gardens Mausoleum), and had children: *Sherril Ann* (born 14 Apr. 1945, married Omer Kenneth Brown on 17 Dec. 1966 [he was born 13 Apr. 1940], and had children: Omer Kenneth Jr. [born 14 June 1967]; Stacia Lynn [born 14 Nov. 1969]); *Philip Arthur* (born 20 Dec. 1947, married Tamra Jean Crandle on 1 May 1970 [she was born 13 Dec. 1947], and had children: Rebecca Jean [born 23 Jan. 1971]; Philip Arthur II [born 23 June 1973]). The Longs lived at Ivanhoe, IL until Arthur retired in 1960; they then settled on the Wiseman Farm, near Keezletown, VA, and finally (in 1983) at Harrisonburg, Rockbridge Co., VA.

8b. **Leslie Urban (I).** Born 30 Aug. 1914 at Paris, IL. See below for full entry.

8c. **Alvin Harold (I).** Born 11 Mar. 1919 at Borton, IL. See below for full entry.

8d. **Orville Eugene.** Born 3 Oct. 1921 at Paris, IL. Married Alberta Shelly on 24 Mar. 1957 (she was born 14 Apr. 1910 at Georgetown, KY). Orville Burgess was an engineer for the Indiana Harbor

Belt Railroad at Blue Island, IL. He died childless on 6 June 1976 at Park Forest, IL, but is buried in the Crestlawn Cemetery, Georgetown, KY.

8e. **(Malcome) Carlyle.** Born 27 Feb. 1928 at Chicago Heights, IL. See below for full entry.
8f. **John Thornton.** Born 17 Dec. 1929 at Chicago Heights, IL. See below for full entry.
8g. **Norman Keith (I).** Born 2 July 1931 at Chicago Heights, IL. See below for full entry.

LESLIE U. BURGESS OF COOK CO., ILLINOIS

[Volney Thornton[6], John Leslie[7]]

8b. **Leslie Urban (I)** *[son of John Leslie].* Born 30 Aug. 1914 at Paris, IL. Married Betty Marie Armstrong on 9 Nov. 1940 at Harvey, IL (she was born 12 Aug. 1917 at Chicago Heights, IL, daughter of Anthony Armstrong and Am Bell Burnett). Leslie Burgess was a welding engineer for South Suburban Welding and Heating Co., Chicago Heights, IL. He died on 15 Oct. 1986 at Harvey, IL, and is buried in the Cedar Park Cemetery, Calumet Park, IL.

9a. **Leslie Urban (II).** Born 20 Nov. 1944 at Harvey, IL. Married Karen Raven in 1965 at West Allis, WI (she was born 23 Sept. 1944); married secondly Claudia Ann Hiedelbrect on 22 Jan. 1973 (?) (she was born 23 Nov. 1952 at Newton, KS, daughter of Orville Hiedelbrect); married thirdly Ruth Keeng about 1981. Leslie Burgess Jr. enlisted in the U.S. Army on 30 Aug. 1963, served as a Green Beret, and later as part of the 863rd Reserve Engineers Batallion. He retired with the reserve rank of Colonel, returned to school, and obtained his B.A. degree from the University of Indiana in 1982. He now lives at Sierra Vista, AZ.

10a. **Linda Kristine.** Born 2 Dec. 1965 at Milwaukee, WI.
10b. **Joanne Marie.** Born 13 Apr. 1967 at Harvey, IL.
10c. **Angela Joy.** Born 2 Jan. 1974 at Joliet, IL.
10d. **Brian Kent.** Born 19 May 1975 in Kansas.
10e. **Amanda Lynn.** Born 9 Feb. 1977 in Kansas.
10f. **Michael Leslie.** Born 17 July 1984 in West Germany.
10g. **David William (II).** Born about 1986 in West Germany.
10h. **Elizabeth Sue.** Born about 1987.
10i. **Child.** Born Dec. 1988 at Sierra Vista, AZ.

9b. **Robert Wayne (I) "Bob."** Born 30 Sept. 1947 at Harvey, IL. Married Milogros "Millie" Bugtong Ablaza on 3 Sept. 1977 at Riverdale, IL (she was born 24 Nov. 1946 at Muñoz Nueva Ecija, The Philippines, daughter of Fortunato Ablaza and Gregoria Bugtong). Bob Burgess is an accountant. He currently lives at Hazel Crest, IL.

10a. **Christopher Ablaza.** Born 14 July 1979 at Chicago, IL.
10b. **Jennifer Ablaza.** Born 15 Nov. 1982 at Chicago Heights, IL.

9c. **Lawrence David "Larry."** Born 28 Sept. 1948 at Harvey, IL. Married Barbara Lea Gardner on 24 Dec. 1971 at Lansing, IL (she was born 1 Jan. 1954 at Ridgeway, PA, daughter of Keith Elvyn Gardner and Elaine Shirley Marie Straessley). Larry Burgess is a printer. He currently lives at Harvey, IL.

10a. **Cindy Marie.** Born 27 Jan. 1976 at Harvey, IL.
10b. **David Lewis.** Born 28 July 1978 at Harvey IL; died there of SIDS on 18 Sept. 1978, and is buried in the Oakridge Cemetery, Thornton, IL.
10c. **Julie Ellen.** Born 31 Mar. 1980 at Harvey, IL.
10d. **Lisa Elaine.** Born 14 May 1982 at Harvey, IL.

9d. **Richard Allen (I) "Ricky."** Born 27 Feb. 1952 at Harvey, IL. Married Donna Jean Baxter on 8 June 1973 at Wheaton, IL (she was born 9 Aug. 1955 at Virginia, MN, daughter of Howard Baxter and Emma Jean Carson). Ricky Burgess is a computer programmer. He currently lives at Dolton, IL.

10a. **Richard Allen II.** Born 17 Dec. 1975 at Harvey, IL.
10b. **Justin Michael (I).** Born 22 Apr. 1979 at Chicago Heights, IL.
10c. **Douglas Arthur.** Born 6 Jan. 1983 at Chicago Heights, IL.

ALVIN H. BURGESS OF COOK CO., ILLINOIS
[Volney Thornton^6, John Leslie^7]

8c. **Alvin Harold (I)** *[son of John Leslie].* Born 11 Mar. 1919 at Borton, IL. Married Genevieve Francis Kwaslk in 1946 at Chicago Heights, IL (div.; she was born 1 Nov. 1923 at Chicago Heights, and remarried Al Spillman); married secondly Marilyn Davis about 1950 (div.); married thirdly Helen Hood about 1955 (she was born 1930, and died 28 Dec. 1966 in IL). Alvin Harold Burgess was a fireman for the Indiana Harbor Belt Railroad, and a veteran of the U.S. Army, serving in the Aleutian Islands during World War II, and later in Korea. He died on 4 Aug. 1982 at Park Forest South (now University Park), IL, and is buried in the Evergreen Cemetery, Evergreen, IL.

9a. **Sharon Marie** (ad.). She was Genevieve's child by her first marriage, her original name being Deeshe. Born 19 May 1944 at Chicago Heights, IL. By a previous liaison, she had children: *Anthony Charles DEESHE* (now Spillman; married Jacqueline ___ on 16 July 1984, and had children: Anthony J. [born 12 May 1984]; Theodore [born 2 May 1985]; Sean [born 25 Nov. 1986]). Married John Gunderson on 14 Feb. __. Sharon Gunderson currently lives at Shobbona, IL.

9b. **Cindy Jean.** Born 25 Oct. 1946 at Chicago Heights, IL. Married Jerry Brown on 4 Mar. 1967 (div.), and had children: *Christine Louise* (born 4 Sept. 1967); *David Allen* (born 1 Nov. 1969). Cindy Brown currently lives at West Chicago, IL.

9c. **Patricia Ann (II) "Patty."** Born 2 Dec. 1947 at Chicago Heights, IL. Married Philip Smith (div.), and had children: *Annette* (born 13 June 1976). Patty Smith currently lives as Warrenville, IL.

9d. **Alvin Harold (II) "Buddy."** Born 22 Dec. 1948 at Chicago Heights, IL. Married Patricia Lee Kelly on 9 Mar. 1968 (div.; she was born 26 July 1949). Buddy Burgess is a tree trimmer and forester in Illinois. He currently lives at Wheaton, IL.

10a. **Timmothy Robert.** Born 3 June 1968 at Geneva, IL.

10b. **Scott Edward.** Born 20 May 1969 at Winfield, IL.

9e. **Marilyn Ann.** Born about 1951. Married ___ Canty. Marilyn Canty currently lives at Clinton, IN.

9f. **Gaynell Faith.** Born about 1953. Married ___ Riley. Gaynell Riley currently lives at Clinton, IN.

9g. **Robert (III).** Born about 1958 in Illinois. He was raised by his mother's parents in Oklahoma.

CARL BURGESS OF HILLSBOROUGH CO., FLORIDA
[Volney Thornton^6, John Leslie^7]

8e. **(Malcome) Carlyle** *[son of John Leslie].* Born 27 Feb. 1928 at Chicago Heights, IL. Married Juanita (Harland) Rossie on 31 May 1951 at Crown Point, IN (div.; she was born 5 Oct. 1925, and remarried Robert Cooper). Carl Burgess currently lives at Tampa, FL.

9a. **Robert Leslie.** Born 5 Mar. 1954 in Illinois.

JOHN T. BURGESS OF HILLSBOROUGH CO., FLORIDA
[Volney Thornton^6, John Leslie^7]

8f. **John Thornton** *[son of John Leslie].* Born 17 Dec. 1929 at Chicago Heights, IL. Married Carol Tanis on 19 Mar. 1950 (div.; she was born 25 Apr. 1931 at Chicago Heights); married secondly Lorraine Florence Bachar on 15 Apr. 1960 at Crown Point, IN (she was born 2 Aug. 1931, daughter of William Allen Bachar and Ella Ethel Kremal). John Burgess was a truck driver for a beer company, and later served as Deputy Marshall for the City of Harvey, IL. He retired in Dec. 1987, and died of cancer on 2 May 1990 at Tampa, FL.

9a. **Michelle Dawn.** Born 17 Oct. 1950 at Chicago Heights, IL.

NORMAN K. BURGESS OF COOK CO., ILLINOIS
[Volney Thornton^6, John Leslie^7]

8g. **Norman Keith (I)** *[son of John Leslie].* Born 2 July 1931 at Chicago Heights, IL. Married Dorothy Marie Sandifer on 25 Mar. 1950 at Joliet, IL (she was born 9 Feb. 1930 at Covington, KY, daughter of Thomas John Sandifer and Pearl Allie Hedger). Norman Burgess is a construction worker and cement truck driver at Chicago Heights, IL. Dorothy Burgess has contributed greatly to this book, providing much of the data on the family of Leslie Burgess.

9a. **Donna Rae.** Born 7 Mar. 1951 at Chicago Heights, IL. Married Marion Thomas Orendoff on 17 Jan. 1970 (div.), and had children: *Michael Keith* (born 19 Aug. 1970); *Sandra Lee* (born 23 Nov. 1971); *Thomas John* (born 15 Jan. 1974); *Norma Jean* (born 27 Feb. 1975). Married secondly Spencer Lee Clausen about 1977 (div.), and had children: *Jacqulyn Rae* (born 5 Sept. 1977). Married thirdly (Clifford) Fred Atkins on 19 Apr. 1985 at Miami, OK. Donna Atkins currently lives at Tampa, FL.

9b. **Debra Kay.** Born 8 Mar. 1952 at Chicago Heights, IL. Married James Paul Rote on 22 May 1971 at Chicago Heights, IL (he was born 18 Apr. 1952 at Grundy, VA, son of Robert Leonard Rote and Helen Louise Risley; he changed his name to Jerry Paul Risley in 1984), and had children: *Faith Ann* (born 18 Mar. 1972); *Hope Imogene* (born 7 Jan. 1975); *Paul James* (ad.; born 5 Sept. 1979 as Gary Allen Todd). Debra Risley currently lives at South Chicago Heights, IL.

9c. **Norman Keith (II).** Born 4 Oct. 1953 at Chicago Heights, IL. Married Linda Lou Cano on 19 Nov. 1977 (she was born 10 July 1960, daughter of Rudolfo Cano and Barbara Lee Middleton). Norman Burgess Jr. is a truck driver for Butternut Bread, Chicago, IL. He lives at Chicago Heights.

10a. **Christina Ann** (ad.). She uses the surname Cano. Born 5 Oct. 1975 in Indiana, and had children: *Adam Joshua CANO* (born 21 July 1991 at Gary, IN).

10b. **Norman Keith III.** Born 3 July 1978 at Chicago Heights, IL.

10c. **Aaron Edward.** Born 30 Jan. 1980 at Chicago Heights, IL.

10d. **Jennifer Lynn (II).** Born 14 Jan. 1982 at Chicago Heights, IL.

10e. **Candice Lee.** Born 18 June 1985 at Chicago Heights, IL.

9d. **Tammie Donnell** (ad.). Born 10 Jan. 1969 at Chicago Heights, IL.

CLARENCE CHESTER BURGESS OF EDGAR CO., ILLINOIS

[Volney Thornton[6]]

7b. **Clarence Chester** *[son of Volney Thornton].* Born 21 Nov. 1894 at Hindsboro, Douglas Co., IL. Married (Ida) Mae Rankins on 2 Oct. 1915 (she was born 28 Mar. 1892 at Isabell, IL, daughter of Green Rankins and Martha Davis, and died 12 Feb. 1977). Listed in the 1910 census with Alvin Forsythe, in the 1918 draft register for Edgar Co., IL, and in the 1920 census for Coles Co., IL. Clarence Burgess was a farmer and carpenter at Paris, Edgar Co., IL. He died there on 9 Jan. 1950, and is buried in the Barr-Johnson Cemetery.

8a. **(Clarence) Donald.** Born 25 Sept. 1916 at Oakland, IL. Married Nina Ruth Wheeler on 5 Oct. 1940 (she was born 23 Oct. 1918). Donald Burgess worked for Midwest Manufacturing at Paris, IL. He died there on 17 Feb. 1974, and is buried in the Pleasant Hill Cemetery, Kansas, IL. Nina Burgess currently lives at Ridge Farm, IL.

9a. **Darrell Donald.** Born 12 June 1943 at Paris, IL. Married Ruth Ann Megginson on 23 May 1965 (she was born 6 Aug. 1946). Darrell Burgess was a tool and die maker in Illinois. He died of cancer on 26 Feb. 1993 at Ridge Farm, IL, but is buried in the Pleasant Hill Cemetery, Kansas, IL. Ruth Burgess lives at Georgetown, IL.

10a. **Victoria Ann.** Born 2 July 1976 at Danville, IL.

9b. **Larry Dean (I).** Born 21 Jan. 1960 at Paris, IL. Married Barbara Ann Hall (div.); married secondly Debbie Griffon about 1988. Larry Burgess is an automobile mechanic at Chrisman, IL.

10a. **Paula Christine.** Born 5 Aug. 1980 in Illinois.

10b. **Isaac Caleb.** Born 12 Apr. 1989 in Illinois.

8b. **Russell (II).** Born and died 1918 at Oakland, IL, and is buried in the Oakland Cemetery.

8c. **(George) Owen.** Born 1 June 1920 at Oakland, IL. Married Betty Jane North on 16 Dec. 1945 (she was born 9 Nov. 1925 at Malta, MT, the daughter of William James North and Carrie May Fidler). Owen Burgess enlisted in the U.S. Army during World War II, was present at the invasion of Normandy in June 1944, and was wounded on 14 Sept. 1944 in Germany, receiving the Purple Heart.

After returning home, he worked as a machinist and supervisor for J. I. Case Tractor Co., and upon retiring in 1983 started his own shop, The Village Blacksmith. He was a member of the First Christian Church, and was a Mason. Owen Burgess died of cancer on 18 Feb. 1989 at Paris, IL, and is buried in the Barr-Johnson Cemetery. Betty Burgess owns a beauty shop, the Clip and Curl, at Paris, IL; her biography appeared in *Prairie Progress: A History of Edgar County, Illinois, 1880-1975* (Dallas, TX: Taylor Publishing Co., 1976, p. 354).

9a. **Georganna May**. Born 2 Nov. 1946 at Paris, IL. Married Donald Arthur North on 18 July 1965, and had children: *Bradley Burgess* (born 22 Aug. 1966); *Stephen Alexander* (born 13 June 1968); married secondly Harold McCormick on 6 July 1972, and had children: *Abbie Denise* (born 18 Apr. 1974); *Kelly Rae* (born 20 Apr. 1976). Georganna McCormick currently lives at Robinson, IL.

8d. **Lorraine Bessie**. Born 30 Aug. 1924 at Paris, IL. Married Ralph Eugene Closson on 9 June 1946 (he was City Commissioner of Charleston, IL from 1949-1953 and Mayor from 1953-57, and later worked as News Editor of the *Mattoon Journal-Gazette*), and had children: *Patricia Elaine* (born 5 Sept. 1947, married Joseph Edward Butler, and had children: Tammy Lynn; Joseph Mark); *James Eugene* (born 14 Mar. 1952, married Patricia Irene Hickerbottom, and had children: Michelle Elizabeth). Lorraine Closson was a registered nurse before retiring. She died on 26 July 1991 at Mattoon, IL, and is buried there at the Resthaven Memorial Gardens.

8e. **(William) Eugene**. Born 24 July 1927 at Paris, IL. Married (Wilma) Jean Coad in 1948 (div.); married secondly Eleanora Murphy (div.), and thirdly Betty Anderson (div.). Gene Burgess was a carpenter at Danville, IL. He died there on 31 Aug. 1993, and is buried in the Barr-Johnson Cemetery, Edgar Co., IL.

9a. **Wayne Eugene.** Born 20 July 1953 in Illinois. Married Twila Lee Smith on 15 Apr. 1978 (she was born 25 Oct. 1955, and works as a head start teacher at Neoga, IL). Wayne Burgess is a printer at Mattoon, IL.

10a. **Jessica Celeste.** Born 14 June 1979 at Charleston, IL.
10b. **Amanda Jean.** Born 1 Feb. 1982 at Charleston, IL.
10c. **Andrea Calleen.** Born 8 Jan. 1985 at Charleston, IL.

9b. **Gary Dennis.** Born 16 Apr. 1955 at Paris, IL. Married Minnie Duncan (div.). Gary Burgess is a land surveyor at Henderson, KY.

10a. **Corey Cagle**. Born 1980.
10b. **Tabitha.** Born Nov. 1981.
10c. **Stacie.** Born Apr. 1988.

8f. **Allen Lindley**. Born 4 Apr. 1931 at Chrisman, IL. Married Margaret Ann Lotze on 14 May 1955 at Terre Haute, IN (she was born 17 Oct. 1934 at Terre Haute, IN). Allen Burgess was a draftsman for USI Chemical Corporation, Tuscola, IL before retiring. He currently lives at Paris, IL.

9a. **Nancy Sue (II).** Born 25 Jan. 1957 in Illinois. Married Vernon Eugene Metcalf on 5 Mar. 1981, and had children: *Carter Allen* (born 17 Mar. 1983). Nancy Metcalf lives Oregon.
9b. **Michael Allen.** Born 10 Sept. 1959 in Illinois. Mike Burgess is a nuclear engineer at Atlanta, GA.

8g. **Connie Lee**. Born 6 June 1935 at Chrisman, IL. Married Wanda Maxine Hofmann on 18 Dec. 1958 at Paris, IL (she was born 4 Sept. 1937). Connie Burgess has been an engineer for the Illinois Dept. of Transportation since 1956. He and his family currently live at Paris, IL.

9a. **Stacy Lynn.** Born 22 Oct. 1966 at Paris, IL. Married Glenn Richard Strow on 6 June 1986 (he works for the Illinois Dept. of Corrections, Danville, IL), and had children: *Kirstin Courtney* (born 29 Apr. 1992 at Terre Haute, IN). Stacy Strow earned a degree in accounting at Wayne Community College in Goldsboro, NC, and currently works as an accountant at Terre Corp., Clinton, IN. They live at Paris, IL.
9b. **Stefanie Lee.** Born 6 June 1970 at Paris, IL. Stefanie Burgess graduated from Eastern Illinois University in May 1993, majoring in speech and communication, with minors in health communications and public relations. She currently works for K-Mart Corporation.

[William (I)[1], Edward (I)[2], Edward (II)[3], Mason Peyton[4], Thornton (II)[5]]

JONATHAN LELAND BURGESS
(1860-1953)

OF DOUGLAS COUNTY, ILLINOIS

6f. **(Jonathan) Leland "Lee"** *[son of Thornton (II)].* His name is spelled Johnathan on his tombstone. Born 18 Nov. 1860 in Crawford Co., IN. Married Sophia M. Patton on 19 Feb. 1889 in Douglas Co., IL (she was born 27 Apr. 1864 in Edgar Co., IL, the daughter of John M. Patton and Rebecca She, and died 31 July 1946). Listed in the 1880 census with his mother, and in the 1900-20 censuses for Bowdre Township, Douglas Co., IL. Lee Burgess was a farmer near Kemp, IL. He died there on 2 May 1953, aged 92 years, and is buried in the Van Voorhis Cemetery.

The Children of Lee Burgess:

7a. **Harley O.** Born 7 May 1890 in Douglas Co., IL; died there on 1 Mar. 1894, and is buried in the Fairland Cemetery.

7b. **Lula Pearl.** Born 19 Mar. 1894 (or 1890, according to her Social Security record) in Douglas Co., IL. Listed with her father in 1920. Married Ray Hallowell. Lula Hallowell died in Apr. 1984 at Oakland, Coles Co., IL, aged 90 years.

7c. **Everett Clayton.** His name appears as Evert Burgess on his death certificate. Born 24 Oct. 1895 in Douglas Co., IL (or 25 Oct., according to his birth record). Everett Burgess died unmarried of tuberculosis on 18 May 1916 in Douglas Co., and is buried in Van Voorhis Cemetery.

7d. **Stella May.** Born 31 July 1897 in Douglas Co., IL. Listed with her father in 1920. Stella Burgess died unmarried on 15 Aug. 1974 in Douglas Co., and is buried in the Van Voorhis Cemetery.

7e. **(Anna) Fern.** Born 15 July 1900 in Douglas Co., IL. Listed with her father in 1920. Married Trelly R. Redden in Sept. 1926 in Douglas Co. (he was born 19 Feb. 1898, and died Jan. 1966). Living at Tuscola, IL in 1953. Fern Redden died in Apr. 1986 at Camargo, Douglas Co., IL, and is buried in the Tuscola Cemetery.

7f. **Charles Leland.** Born 5 Sept. 1902 at Kemp, IL. Listed with his father in 1920. Married Nellie Hemingway on 11 Dec. 1925. Charles Burgess was a farmer at Arcola, IL, before retiring; he now lives in a rest home. Nellie Burgess continues to occupy the family farm at Arcola.

8a. **Rexford Lee "Rex."** Born 1 May 1932 at Kemp, IL. Married Barbara Ochampaugh on 12 Sept. 1959 at Chicago, IL. Rex Burgess is a painter at Rochester, MN.

9a. **Kathleen Kay**. Born 1 July 1961 at Sioux City, IA. Married Ian Richard Hick on 9 July 1988 at Rochester, MN.

9b. **Karen Kay**. Born 22 May 1964 at Sioux City, IA.

9c. **Kitty Kay**. Born 17 Sept. 1968 at Sioux City, IA. Married Tracy Allen Stromgren on 7 Oct. 1989 at Rochester, MN.

9d. **Kandia Kay**. Born 21 June 1972 at Rochester, MN. Married Bobby Glenn Hegland on 11 Dec. 1993 at Rochester, MN.

8b. **Ned Duane.** Born 16 July 1935 at Kemp, IL. Married Portia Ann Griffith on 14 Aug. 1960 in Douglas Co., IL; married secondly Evelyn ___. Ned Burgess died on 30 June 1987 at Johnson City, IL.

9a. **Molly Ann** (ad.).

9b. **Charles Duane** (ad.).

8c. **Gaythel Lu.** Born 30 Sept. 1941 at Kemp, IL. Married Jerry R. Mallady on 17 June 1961 in Douglas Co., IL. Gaythel Mallady currently lives at Filson, IL.

[William (I)[1], Edward (I)[2], Edward (II)[3], Mason Peyton[4]]

EDMUND BURGESS
(1824-1894)

OF ORANGE COUNTY, INDIANA

5i. **Edmund (I)** *[son of Mason Peyton].* His name is sometimes given as Edward Burgess in the records; "Edmund" may have been a nickname to distinguish him from his many cousins of the same name. Born 5 Feb. 1824 in Orange Co., IN. Married Sarah Elizabeth Duncan on 26 Jan. 1854 in Orange Co. (she was born 18 Sept. 1832 in IN, daughter of Fleming Duncan, and died 13 Nov. 1864); married secondly Rachel Ellis on 4 June 1865 in Orange Co. (she was born 21 Sept. 1843 in IN, and died 22 May 1882); married thirdly Permelia Stalcup on 5 Oct. 1892 in Orange Co. An Edward G. Burgess is listed as having served in Co. F, 29th Indiana Infantry during the Civil War; his identification with Edmund can be neither confirmed nor denied. Edmund Burgess joined the Gold Rush in California in the late 1840s; after returning to Orange Co. in 1853, he was robbed of $1,500 of gold, according to the *History of Lawrence, Orange, and Washington Counties, Indiana* (Chicago: Goodspeed Bros. & Co., 1884, p. 408). Listed in the 1860-80 censuses for Stampers Creek Township, Orange Co., IN (from 1860-70 as "Edward"). Edmund Burgess was a farmer in Orange Co., IN. He died on 3 Apr. 1894 at Millersburg, IN, and is buried in the Stampers Creek Cemetery.

The Children of Edmund Burgess:

6a. **Mittis Jane "Mettie."** Born 24 Oct. 1854 in Orange Co., IN. Married John Moore Dunlap on 28 Oct. 1880 in Wayne Co., IL, and had at least the following children: *William Edmond* (born 5 May 1882 in Wayne Co.). Mettie Dunlap died on 5 July 1889 in Wayne Co., and is buried in the Mount Pleasant Cemetery, Wayne Co., IL.

6b. **Lewis A.** Born 3 May 1857 in Orange Co., IN. Married (Laura) Effie Kirk on 23 Aug. 1885 in Orange Co. (she was born Nov. 1866 in IN, and died 1905). Listed in the 1900-20 censuses for Stampers Creek Township, Orange Co., IN (in 1920 living alone). Lewis Burgess lived on Locust Hill, west of Millersburg, IN. He died on 11 July 1937 at French Lick, Orange Co., IN of injuries received in an automobile accident, and is buried in the Stampers Creek Cemetery.

7a. **Maude E. "Maudie."** Born 19 July 1890 in Orange Co., IN. Married Herbert Hardin on 27 Feb. 1913 in Orange Co. (he was born 30 May 1886, and died Dec. 1966 at Rantoul, IL). Maude Hardin died on 13 Feb. 1990 at Rantoul, Campaign Co., IL, aged 99 years.

6c. **Sarah Elizabeth (III) "Sally."** Born Dec. 1859 in Orange Co., IN. Listed with her father in the 1870 census. Died unmarried.

6d. **Adina F. "Dina."** Born 28 May 1862 in Orange Co., IN. Married John W. Kirby on 8 Jan. 1882 in Orange Co., IN (he was born Aug. 1855, and died 1936), and had at least the following children: *Florence Lee* (born 22 Nov. 1882, married her cousin, Delbert O. Vickrey, on 21 Feb. 1906 in Orange Co. [he was born 10 Feb. 1879], and died 18 Feb. 1920); *Josie Estle* (born 8 Dec. 1884, married William W. Atkinson on 16 Apr. 1902 in Orange Co. [he married firstly her cousin, Emma E. Burgess]); *Child* (born and died 15 June 1886, buried with its parents); *Stella May* (born 2 Jan. 1893, married Ross Rutherford on 16 Feb. 1914 in Orange Co., and died on 18 Sept. 1988 at Paoli, IN, aged 95 years, having had children: Evelyn); *(George) Ermal* (born 17 June 1897, married Erma Newlin on 31 July 1918 in Orange Co. [she was born 1896], and died 17 Feb. 1922, buried Stampers Creek Cemetery); *Wesley Vaughn* (born 6 Mar. 1902, married Ruthe A. Roach on 2 Aug. 1922 in Orange Co., and died 23 July __). Listed in the 1900 census for Paoli Township, Orange Co., IN; four of four children then survive. Adina Kirby died on 9 Sept. 1935 in Orange Co., and is buried in the Stampers Creek Cemetery.

6e. **Polly Ann (I).** Born and died 1864 in Orange Co., IN.

6f. **(Mary) Ellen (V) "Ella."** Born Apr. 1866 in Orange Co., Indiana. Listed with Shelby Cornwell in the 1870 census. Married (William) Riley Moody on 5 Jan. 1888 in Orange Co. (he was born Nov. 1861 in IN), and had children: *Walter G.* (born Oct. 1888). Listed in the 1900 census for Orleans Township, Orange Co., IN.

6g. **Edmund G.** His name is given in the 1900-20 censuses as Edward G. Burgess. Born 27 July 1868 (or 1869) in Orange Co., IN (listed as age 12 in the 1880 census). Married Rhoda E. Bridgewater on 15 Nov. 1894 in Orange Co. (she was born 1861, daughter of William and Millie Bridgewater, and died on 22 June 1951, aged 90 years). Listed in the 1900-20 censuses for Stampers Creek Township, Orange Co., IN (in 1910 living with Isaac S. Bridgewater, his brother-in-law). Edmund G. Burgess died childless on 21 Aug. 1931 in Orange Co., and is buried in the Stampers Creek Cemetery.

6h. **(Ulrick) Alpha.** Born 28 Mar. 1870 in Orange Co., IN. See below for full entry.

6i. **(Daniel) Mason.** Born 11 June 1872 in Orange Co., IN. See below for full entry.

6j. **Lula.** Her name is listed as Elidie A. in the 1880 census. Born about 1875 in Orange Co., IN. Married Merle Wheat.

6k. **(Della) Daisy.** Her name is given as Evie D. in the 1880 census. Born July 1877 in Orange Co., IN. Married her cousin, James H. Fisher, on 30 Oct. 1895 in Orange Co. (he was born Dec. 1862, son of David Fisher and Sarah A. Burgess, married firstly Louisa Parish on 27 Sept. 1883 in Orange Co., by whom he had children: *Delbert* [born Aug. 1884]; *Lawrence* [born Oct. 1889]; *Earl* [born 6 June 1891, died Sept. 1974 at Greensburg, IN]). Listed in the 1900 census for Orleans Township, Orange Co., IN.

Matilda Jane ROGERS BURGESS (1861-1935)
Effie Elizabeth BURGESS (1893-1984)
Minnie M. RUSSELL (1884-?)
Sylvester Walden BURGESS (1888-1953)
David Monroe BURGESS (1859-1935)
[see page 125]

[William (I)[1], Edward (I)[2], Edward (II)[3], Mason Peyton[4], Edmund (I)[5]]

ALPHA BURGESS
(1870-1909)

OF WAYNE COUNTY, ILLINOIS

6h. **(Ulrick) Alpha "Alphie"** *[son of Edmund (I)].* Born 28 Mar. 1870 in Orange Co., IN. Married Mary Adeline Hawkins on 29 Jan. 1891 in Wayne Co. (she was born 19 Apr. 1870, daughter of John Hawkins and Amanda Bowers, remarried George Henson on 2 Apr. 1911 in Wayne Co. [he was born 1874, son of William A. Henson and Mary A. Holler], and died 29 Aug. 1938). Listed in the 1900 census for Orchard Township, Wayne Co., IL; his widow appears as head of the family there in 1910. Alphie Burgess was a farmer in Wayne Co., IL. He died there on 9 Sept. 1909, and is buried in the Mount Pleasant Cemetery.

The Children of Alphie Burgess:

7a. **Chester Lewis.** Born 20 Feb. 1894 in Wayne Co., IL. Married his second cousin, Netta "Nettie" Jones, about 1921 (she was born 29 Jan. 1895, daughter of Celia Ann Burgess and Alfred B. Jones, remarried Tom Dilliner after her husband's early death, and died July 1974 at Grove, OK). Listed in the 1920 census for Wayne Co., IL, living alone. Chester Burgess died childless of appendicitis and tuberculosis on 19 May 1927 at East St. Louis, IL, and is buried in the Mount Hope Cemetery.

7b. **Glenn Roger.** His name was originally Glenny Burgess, and his middle name is given as Rogers on his draft record. Born 24 Oct. 1895 (or 1896, according to his draft record) at Orchardville, Wayne Co., IL. Married Gussie Cleo Miley on 24 Nov. 1915 in Wayne Co. (she was born 5 Oct. 1898, daughter of Redic Miley and Violinder E. Border, and died 29 Aug. 1988 at Paxton, IL). Listed in the 1917 draft register for Clay Co., IL, and in the 1920 census for Wayne Co., IL. Glenn Burgess farmed and worked for the France Broom Co., near Paxton, Ford Co., IL. He died on 24 Oct. 1991, his 96th birthday, at Paxton, IL, and is buried there with his wife in the Glen Cemetery.

8a. **Willie Wesley.** Born 31 Oct. 1916 in Wayne Co., IL. Married Sylvia Henson on 11 Aug. 1939 at St. Louis, MO (she was born 23 Sept. 1920 in Wayne Co., IL, the daughter of John Thomas Henson and Nellie May Brown). Willie Burgess was a high school janitor at Paxton, IL. He now lives there retired.

9a. **Charles Lavern.** Born 17 Mar. 1940 in Marion Co., IL; died there on 23 Mar. 1940, and is buried in the Wesley Chapel Cemetery.

9b. **Cleo Mae (II) "Toots."** Born 31 Dec. 1940 in Marion Co., IL. Married Marvin Clarence Knell on 26 Dec. 1958 at Paxton, Ford Co., IL (he was born 26 Mar. 1937 at Dewey, IL, son of Samuel D. Knell and Leona Bressee, and works as an upholsterer), and had children: *Jerry Lee* (born 29 July 1971 at Gibson City, IL). Cleo Knell works at the Sorenson-Racion Factory, Paxton, IL.

9c. **Doris Irene.** Born 27 Oct. 1943 at Paxton, IL. Married Wilfred Ray Wagner on 27 Dec. 1963 at Paxton, IL (he was born 18 Nov. 1936 at Loda, IL, son of Raymond T. W. Wagner and Margaret Marie Davis). Doris Wagner manages the Pine Ridge Cemetery, Loda, IL. She has contributed greatly to this book.

9d. **William Wesley "Bill."** Born 21 July 1954 at Paxton, IL. Married Julie Ann King on 17 July 1976 at Paxton, IL (she was born 26 Nov. 1957 at Elmhurst, IL, daughter of Gerald Mack King and Judith Ann Hamowitz). Bill Burgess works for Krafts Foods at Champaign, IL, but lives at Paxton.

10a. **Gabriel Lee.** Born 7 Apr. 1979 at Urbana, Champaign Co., IL.

10b. **Joshua Allen** (twin). Born 23 June 1981 at Urbana, IL.

10c. **Joseph Anthony** (twin). Born 23 June 1981 at Urbana, IL.

9e. **Donna Marie.** Born 24 Aug. 1959 at Paxton, IL. Married Roger Alan Hustedt on 21 Feb. 1981 at Paxton, IL (he was born 17 Dec. 1956 at Champaign, IL, son of Kermit Henry Hustedt and Agnes Bernice Fossel). Roger Hustedt is a farmer, and Donna Hustedt currently works at the Sorenson-Racion Factory; they live at Elliott, IL.

8b. **Leonard Lesley.** Born 1918 in Wayne Co., IL. Listed with his parents in the 1920 census.

Steven Vincent Burgess (1862-1930) and wife, Sara Jane Crookshanks (1855-1945) [see page 277]

[William (I)[1], Edward (I)[2], Edward (II)[3], Mason Peyton[4], Edmund (I)[5]]

DANIEL MASON BURGESS
(1872-1941)

OF CLALLAM COUNTY, WASHINGTON

6i. **(Daniel) Mason "Mase"** *[son of Edmund (I)].* Born 11 June 1872 in Orange Co., IN. Married Rebecca Elizabeth Clevenger on 25 Dec. 1889 in Orange Co. (she was born 23 Apr. 1873 in IN, daughter of Azriah Clevenger and Patsy Lane, and died 5 Dec. 1902 at Port Crescent, WA, buried Crescent Beach Cemetery); married secondly as her second husband Mary Eugenia (Hall) Clevenger on 10 Aug. 1918 at Port Angeles, WA (she was born 26 Sept. 1876 in Bates Co., MO, daughter of Samuel M. Hall and Martha Jane Lamon, married firstly James Monroe Clevenger on 2 Dec. 1890 and by him had children: *Clara Hall* [born 19 Apr. 1897, married Burrell Vail, and secondly ___ Eacrett, and died May 1983 at Port Angeles]; *James Malcolm* [born 25 Jan. 1904, died about 1923 in a logging accident]; *Owen Kent* [born 23 July 1906 at Seattle, WA, died young]; *Howard Mason* [born 29 Sept. 1909, died Jan. 1964]; Mary Burgess died on 8 Mar. 1946 at Port Angeles, WA). Listed in the 1900 census for Stampers Creek Township, Orange Co., IN (four of four children then survive), and in 1910-20 in the Belleview Precinct, Clallam Co., WA. He also appears in the Port Angeles, WA rural directories from 1913/14-1939; Mary appears as head of the family beginning in 1941/42. Mason Burgess moved his family to Washington in late 1900, traveling by train to Seattle, and then by boat to Port Crescent, Clallam Co., WA, at that time a thriving community. He worked there as a logger, later purchasing the first logging truck used in harvesting operations in Clallam Co. He died on 4 Apr. 1941 at Port Angeles, Clallam Co., WA, and is buried in the Mount Angeles Cemetery.

The Children of Mason Burgess:

7a. **Alva Ovis.** Born 13 Oct. 1890 at Paoli, Orange Co., IN. See below for full entry.

7b. **(William) Noble.** Born 25 Oct. 1892 at Paoli, IN. Married Theresa E. Sullivan on 21 Sept. 1922 at Port Angeles, Clallam Co., WA (she remarried George Raoul Lamoureux). Served in World War I with the U.S. Army. Listed with his father in the 1920 census, and in the Port Angeles rural directories from 1923-32; his widow continues to be listed there through 1941. Noble Burgess was a logger in Clallam Co., WA, managing his own camp at Little River between 1932-34. He was injured in a logging accident, died childless on 29 July 1934, and is buried in the Mount Angeles Cemetery.

NOBLE BURGESS SERIOUSLY HURT AT LITTLE RIVER

"Noble Burgess, well known truck logging operator of Port Angeles, is in serious condition at the Davidson and Hay hospital following injuries sustained when a haul-back cable broke on the donkey engine and threw him forty feet through the air and crushed his left side against the donkey engine throttle. The accident occurred at Little River, where Burgess was logging....Five ribs on his left side were severely crushed, several of them puncturing the lung, and he was suffering frequent internal hemorrhages thoughout the night."

"William Noble Burgess, 41, one of the best known truck loggers and woodsmen on the Olympic peninsula, passed away at four o'clock Sunday morning, July 29th from injuries sustained while working in the woods at Little River last week....For several years he had been engaged in logging with his father, and also with E. E. Woolworth, but for the past two years he has been operating his own camp on Little River. He was an industrious logging operator, with a host of friends, and his death has shocked the community."—*Port Angeles Evening News*, July 26 and July 30, 1934.

7c. **Lillie Opal.** Born 21 July 1895 at Paoli, IN. Married William Wooding (he was born 6 Aug. 1894, and died Jan. 1942), and had children: *Kathlyn Eugenia* (born 14 Dec. 1914, married Carl Cary on 11

June 1931 at Port Angeles, WA, and died there on 6 Oct. 1990); *Ruth* (born about 1916, married Jess[i]e Epperson on 30 Mar. 1933 at Port Angeles, WA); *Opal* (born about 1918, married Marlin Schoeneman on 1 June 1937 at Port Angeles, WA). Lillie Wooding died in childbirth on 3 Jan. 1923 at Port Angeles, WA.

7d. **(Leona) Agnes (I).** Born 17 Feb. 1898 at Paoli, IN. She died of a lung abscess on 12 Sept. 1907 at Port Crescent, WA, and is buried in the Port Crescent Cemetery.

7e. **Mary Ellen (VIII).** Born 9 Nov. 1902 at Port Crescent, Clallam Co., WA. Married Thomas Vail on 28 Aug. 1920 at Port Angeles, WA (he was born 26 Nov. 1897, and died Jan. 1975 at Port Angeles), and had children: *Lewis H.* (he lives near San Diego, CA); *(Edwin) Eugene "Gene"* (born 7 Apr. 1925, and died Feb. 1975); *Betty* (married Glen Rudolph, living in 1994); *Alice* (married Vernon Elkhart Jr., married several other times, living in 1994); *Daniel* (died before his mother at Port Angeles, WA). Mary Vail died on 8 Aug. 1966 at Port Angeles, WA, and is buried in the Mount Angeles Cemetery.

7f. **Walter Daniel.** Born 30 Nov. 1918 at Port Angeles, Clallam Co., WA. See below for full entry.

ALVA O. BURGESS OF KITSAP CO., WASHINGTON
[Daniel Mason^6]

7a. **Alva Ovis** *[son of Daniel Mason].* His name appears as Alvin in the 1920 census. Born 13 Oct. 1890 at Paoli, Orange Co., IN. Married Grace Bicknell on 23 Dec. 1924 at Port Angeles, WA (she was born 8 Sept. 1904 at Kingston, Jamaica, daughter of Brooks Cameron Bicknell and May Scharschmidt, and remarried Arthur George Purdum on 5 Feb. 1976 [he was born 8 July 1902, and died Jan. 1982 at Bremerton, WA]). Served in World War I with the 346th Field Artillery Battalion in France. Listed in the 1920 census with his father, and in the Bremerton, WA city directories from 1948-68 (he moved to Bremerton in 1942); his wife appears as head of the family through 1976. Alva Burgess was a lumberman in Clallam Co., WA, and a machinist for the Puget Sound Naval Shipyard from 1942-57. He died on 15 Apr. 1968 at Bremerton, WA, and is buried in the Woodlawn Cemetery. Grace Burgess Purdum lives at Bremerton, WA.

8a. **Donald Raymond (I)** (twin). Born 16 Nov. 1926 at Port Angeles, Clallam Co., WA. Married Shirley Gaufin in Sept. 1955 (she remarried Linton James Rowan on 5 July 1992). Graduated from the University of Washington. Donald Burgess was an attorney at Portland, OR, eventually becoming Chief Title Officer for the Northwest Division of Trans America Title Insurance Company. He died there of cancer on 9 May 1987.

9a. **Donald Raymond (II).** Born 2 Dec. 1956 at Seattle, WA. Married Theresa Ann Fryberger (she was born 27 Sept. 1953, earned a Ph.D. degree, and works for the Department of Energy on low-level nuclear waste disposal). Donald Burgess graduated from Stanford University, and earned a Ph.D. degree in chemistry from Northwestern University. He works for the National Institute of Standards and Technology, U.S. Department of Commerce, at Washington, DC. He and his wife live in Maryland.

10a. **Anne Elizabeth.** Born 7 Nov. 1981 at Chicago, IL.
10b. **Stephen Christopher.** Born 16 Oct. 1983 at Gaithersburg, MD.

9b. **Timothy Alva.** Born 4 Jan. 1958 at Seattle, WA. Graduated from Seattle Pacific University. Tim Burgess died unmarried from injuries received when he was hit by a drunk driver on 26 (or 17) July 1980 at Portland, OR.

9c. **Andrew William.** Born 8 Sept. 1960 at Wenatchee, WA. Married Michelle Ann Parshal (she was born 31 Oct. 1961 at Seattle, WA, sister of Marilyn Parshal [who married Andrew's brother, Thomas Burgess]). Graduated from the University of Oregon with a degree in business administration. Andrew Burgess is a Food Services Director at Roseburg, OR.

10a. **Jamie Christopher.** Born 3 Jan. 1983 at Corvallis, OR.
10b. **Carey James.** Born 18 Oct. 1984 at Corvallis, OR.
10c. **Joshua Ryan.** Born 20 Sept. 1986 at Idaho Falls, ID.

9d. **Janna Marie.** Born 28 Nov. 1961 at Wenatchee, WA. Married Chester Orville Hoberg (he was born 17 May 1963), and had children: *Heather Chantal* (born 29 Oct. 1986 at Seattle, WA). Janna Hoberg graduated from Seattle Pacific University. She works as a school teacher at Seattle, WA.

9e. **Thomas Mason (III).** Born 17 Aug. 1965 at Bremerton, WA. Married Marilyn Kay Parshal (she was born 3 Nov. 1963 at Seattle, WA, sister of Michelle Parshal [who married Tom's brother, Andrew Burgess]). Graduated from Stanford University. Tom Burgess is a history teacher at a Catholic school at Redondo Beach, CA; Marilyn is a public school teacher.

8b. **Douglas Gordon** (twin). Born 16 Nov. 1926 at Port Angeles, Clallam Co., WA. Married secondly Beverly Lavens in Aug. 1958. Served as a 2nd Lieutenant in the U.S. Army Corps of Engineers, being commissioned in 1953, and served in Korea. He was also a crack rifle marksman, competing in various competitions for the Army during the 1950s. Doug Burgess graduated from the University of Washington. At the time of his death he was a forest manager for the U.S. Bureau of Land Management in Western Oregon. He died on 13 Feb. 1969 at Portland, OR.

9a. **Scott Alva.** Born 21 Mar. 1960 at Roseburg, OR. Married Debra Lynn Tyree in 1979 (she was born 2 July 1960, graduated from Auburn University, and works as a substitute teacher). Scott Burgess graduated with a degree in resources management Troy State University, Alabama. He now is a Master Sergeant in the U.S. Air Force, currently stationed at Mountain Home Air Force Base, ID, where he teaches military science classes.

10a. **Samuel Scott.** Born 9 Apr. 1980 at Sacramento, CA.
10b. **Susan Ann (II).** Born 21 Nov. 1981 at Sacramento, CA.
10c. **Serena Amber**. Born 24 July 1984 at Mountain Home, ID.
10d. **Savannah Crystal**. Born 30 Nov. 1986 at Mountain Home, ID.

9b. **Mark Randolph.** Born 23 June 1962 at Las Vegas, NV. Married Valerie Carlson (she was born 9 Nov. 1962 at Montebello, CA). Mark Burgess is a resaler specializing in jewelry and guns at Anchorage, AK.

10a. **Zachary Ryan.** Born 17 Apr. 1991 at Anchorage, AK.
10b. **Zane Daniel.** Born 3 Mar. 1993 at Anchorage, AK.

9c. **Kimberly Ann.** Born 26 Nov. 1965 at Salem, OR. Married Terry Edward Vrabec (he was born 10 Aug. 1962 at Park Ridge, IL), and had children: *Brandi-Jo* (born 16 Feb. 1990 at Soldotna, AK); *Thomas Douglas* (born 12 Feb. 1993 at Fairbanks, AK). Kim and Terry Vrabec both have degrees in police science. They currently live at Fairbanks, AK.

8c. **Robert Mason.** Born 6 Feb. 1941 at Port Angeles, Clallam Co., WA. Married Jerianne "Jeri" Gabrielson in Dec. 1962 (she works as Assistant Manager of the Social Security Office at Bremerton). Robert Burgess graduated from the University of Washington, worked briefly for the Puget Sound Naval Shipyard, and is listed in the directories of Bremerton, WA through 1966/67. Robert M. Burgess is a computer systems analyst for Puget Sound Naval Supply, Bremerton, WA.

WALTER D. BURGESS OF CLALLAM CO., WASHINGTON

[Daniel Mason^6]

7f. **Walter Daniel** *[son of Daniel Mason]*. Born 30 Nov. 1918 at Port Angeles, Clallam Co., WA. Married Reva M. Boggs. Listed in the directories of Port Angeles, WA from 1936-1980. Walter Burgess was a construction foreman for Clevenger Logging and Construction Co. at Port Angeles, WA, retiring in 1978, and was a member of International Woodworkers of America. He died there on 22 May 1989, and is buried in the Mt. Angeles Cemetery.

8a. **Sandra Jo "Sande."** Born 28 Aug. 1945 at Eureka, CA. Married David Mackey, and had children: *Tamra Jo* (born 22 Sept. 1962 at Port Angeles, WA; married William Kirkman [div.], and had children: Amber Nycole [born 27 Mar. 1981]; William Nicholas [born 3 Nov. 1986]); Sande married secondly Michael Clapshaw, and thirdly Warner E. Grose. Sande Grose is an antique dealer at Sequim, Clallam Co., WA. She has contributed greatly to this book.

[William (I)[1], Edward (I)[2], Edward (II)[3], Mason Peyton[4]]

THOMAS MASON BURGESS
(1827-1879)

OF ORANGE COUNTY, INDIANA

5j. **Thomas Mason (I)** *[son of Mason Peyton].* Born 19 July 1827 in Orange Co., IN. Married Lucinda Wolfe on 25 Oct. 1849 in Orange Co. (she was born 12 Dec. 1831, daughter of Henry Wolfe and Lucy Grigsby, and died 12 Nov. 1889). Listed in the 1850 census for Stampers Creek Township, Orange Co., IN living with Henry Wolfe (his father-in-law), and from 1860-70 there with his family; his widow appears as head of the household in 1880. Thomas Burgess was a farmer in Orange Co., IN. He died there on 27 Jan. 1879, and is buried with his wife in the Stampers Creek Cemetery.

The Children of Thomas M. Burgess:

6a. **Floyd (I)** (nmn). Born 22 Oct. 1850 in Orange Co., IN. See below for full entry.

6b. **Henry (III)** (nmn). Born 20 Dec. 1852 in Orange Co., IN. See below for full entry.

6c. **Louisa (I)** (nmn). Born 9 Jan. 1855 in Orange Co., IN. Married James Dudley Hackney on 5 Mar. 1872 in Orange Co. (he was born 17 Aug. 1840 in KY, son of Samuel and Mary Ann Hackney, and died 18 July 1918), and had at least the following children: *Lillie M.* (born 1874, married Ollie A. Boone on 28 May 1893 in Orange Co., and died 25 May 1915, having had children: Opal [died aged one month]; Durwood [born 27 Mar. 1909]; Harold [born 30 Mar. 1915, died 1 May 1952]); *Henry Herbert* (born 14 Oct. 1878, married Lydia J. Murray on 31 Oct. 1904 in Orange Co., and died Nov. 1969 [or 1936] at Newton, IA); *Leona B.* (born June 1886, married Cecil Allspaw on 19 May 1907, and had children: John Dudley [born 19 Mar. 1908, married Juanita G. Hendricks on 6 Oct. 1934]; Doris L. [born 28 Oct. 1910, married ___ Metzger on 6 May 1940]; Phyllis D. [born 21 July 1923, married Earl Carpenter on 3 Sept. 1948]). Louisa Hackney died on 15 Mar. 1898 in Orange Co., and is buried with her husband in the Stampers Creek Cemetery. James Hackney is listed in the 1900 census for Paoli Township, Orange Co., IN.

6d. **Mary Ann (IV).** Born 23 Apr. 1857 in Orange Co., IN. Married John V. McCoy on 31 Jan. 1877 in Orange Co. (he was born 5 Nov. 1850, son of Jackson McCoy and Sarah Van Cleave, and died 15 Jan. 1921), and had at least the following children: *Ora P.* (born Nov. 1878, married Charlie Strange on 2 July 1904 in Orange Co.); *Dessie May* (born 29 July 1881, died 30 Sept. 1882); *Ola Beatrice* (born 5 Sept. 1884, died unmarried in Apr. 1957 or 1961, buried Crown Hill Cemetery, Indianapolis, IN); *Everett O.* (born 17 Feb. 1887, died 9 July 1888). Listed in the 1900 census for Paoli Township, Orange Co., IN. Mary McCoy died on 3 Jan. 1936 in Orange Co., and is buried with her husband in the Stampers Creek Cemetery.

6e. **Elizabeth Ellen.** Born 21 July 1859 in Orange Co., IN. Married her first cousin, Charles Harrison Cornwell, on 3 Aug. 1885 in Orange Co. (he was born 26 May 1858, son of William H. Cornwell and Elton Wolfe [sister of Lucinda Wolfe], and died 15 Oct. 1893, buried Stampers Creek Cemetery), and had children: *(Elvet) Earl* (born 3 July 1880, married Ruby Hadley on 7 Feb. 1904, and died childless on 8 July 1959); *Chloe Olive* (listed as Clois in her birth record and Chlara in the 1900 census; born 10 Apr. 1883, married Frank Thomas on 18 Oct. 1903, and died 14 July __, having had children: Olive Bell [born 19 Nov. 1904, married Leonard C. Blevins on 21 June 1931, and died childless on 15 Feb. 1957]). **Elizabeth CORNWELL** married secondly James Jones on 16 Mar. 1899 in Orange Co. (he was born 19 Oct. 1837 in IN, served as a Quaker preacher and officer for the Union Army during the Civil War, and died 27 Sept. 1902, buried Beech Grove Cemetery, Paoli, IN next to his first wife). Listed in the 1900 census for Paoli Township, Orange Co., IN. Elizabeth Jones died on 3 Feb. 1943, and is buried in the Rosedale Cemetery, Mt. Clair, NJ.

6f. **Lucy Jane.** She is also called Lucinda in one record. Born 11 Nov. 1861 in Orange Co., IN. Married William Newton Pickens on 11 Feb. 1886 in Orange Co. (he was born 16 Feb. 1857, son of Louis Pickens and Sally Tegarden, and died on 29 Mar. 1941, buried Mount Pleasant Cemetery), and had children:

(Harold) Scott (born 16 May 1886, married Stella Cornwell, daughter of Patterson Cornwell and Kate Vest, on 4 July 1909 in Orange Co., and had children: Loren L. [born 3 Nov. 1914, married Ida Irene Quackenbush, and died 31 July 1942, buried New Cemetery, Paoli, IN]; Coleman [married Ida ___]; Doris; *Scott PICKENS* died on 28 May 19__); *Clois Opal* (born 14 June 1891, married Benjamin Harrison Jackson on 25 Dec. 1909 in Orange Co. [he was the son of John F. Jackson and Mary Edwards, and died 2 Apr. 1945, buried Stampers Creek Cemetery], and died 17 Aug. 1915, having had children: Paul Roger [born 1910, married Irene Baker, and had children: Gloria Irene {born 1931}; Roger Lee {born 1933}]; *Harold Lester* [born 1912, died unmarried 17 Feb. 1939 at Post Hospital, Fort Knox, KY]). Listed in the 1900 census for Paoli Township, Orange Co., IN. Lucy Pickens died on 12 Nov. 1908 at Lick Creek, IN.

6g. **Lewis Moulder.** Born 7 Feb. 1864 in Orange Co., IN. See below for full entry.

6h. **Lydia** (nmn). Born 24 May 1866 in Orange Co., IN. Married (Jacob) Kimball Van Cleave on 14 Aug. 1890 in Orange Co. (he was born 18 June 1865, son of James Van Cleave and Louisa [Hammersley] Wible, married firstly Clara Bell Hutchison, and died 19 Feb. 1950), and had children: *Omer Estes* (born 6 July 1891, married Wavie Myley, and died childless in Dec. 1972 at Mitchell, IN); *Harold Hobart* (born 22 Aug. 1896, married Artie Russell on 3 Sept. 1918, and had children); *Roy Cedric* (born 7 Sept. 1900, married Mildred P. Troth on 28 Feb. 1922 in Orange Co. [she was the daughter of Homer Troth], had children: Billie, and died 13 June 19__). Lydia Van Cleave died on 11 Dec. 1932 in Orange Co., and is buried with her husband in the Mitchell Cemetery.

6i. **Sarah (XII)** (nmn). Born 23 Dec. 1868 in Orange Co., IN. Married Volney Cornwell Galloway on 22 Oct. 1890 in Orange Co. (he was born 13 May 1869, son of William Lynd Galloway and Lucy Ann Cornwell, and died 2 Oct. 1938, buried Livonia Cemetery), and had children:

Elsie M. GALLOWAY. Born 23 Aug. 1891, married Earl H. Sweeney on 15 Apr. 1911 at Paoli, IN (he was the son of Allen B. Sweeney and Phoebe McNeely), and died childless on 14 Dec. __, buried Livonia Cemetery.

Alta F. GALLOWAY. Born 2 July 1893, married Benjamin F. Jones on 24 Dec. 1911 in Orange Co. (he was born 26 Mar. 1881, the son of William Jones and Phoebe Cornwell, and died 24 Apr. 1974 at Orleans, IN), and had children: *Samuel Ellis* (born 25 Jan. 1917, died 15 Oct. 1923 at Louisville, KY, buried Livonia Cemetery); *Louis F.* (born 26 Oct. 1920, married Sarah Rae "Sally" Stout on 20 Nov. 1946, and had children: Louann [born Oct. 1947, married Max Rutherford, and had children: Leah R.; Mark; Lindsey]; Sarah Lynn [born 18 Sept. 1956, married Terry Whiteman on 16 May 1982, and had children: Emmaline; Alex]); *M. Lucille* (born 26 Aug. 1923, married Arthur L. Crandall on 30 June 1943 [he was the son of Chester Crandall and Anna May Trinkle, and died 6 Sept. 1986], and had children: Janet Lee [born 26 May 1946 at Paoli, IN, married Daniel Fennessey on 27 June 1970, had children: Jody Ann {born 29 June 1971 at Bloomington, IN, and works as a nurse}; Casey Ginger {born 6 Oct. 1972 at Bloomington, IN}; Erin Kelly {born 31 Jan. 1975 at Washington, IN}; David {ad.; born 30 May 1984}; Richard {ad.; born 8 May 1985}; Janet Fennessey lives at Lacon, IL]; Bill F. [born 29 June 1947 at Paoli, IN, married Sandra Dean on 3 Mar. 1976 at Mitchell, IN, and had children: Courtney Lee {born 14 Nov. 1978 at Greenwood, MS}]; Carolyn Ann [born 22 Dec. 1948 at Paoli, IN, and works as an office manager at Mitchell, IN]; Dawn Rachelle [born and died 20 Nov. 1964, buried Mitchell Cemetery]); *Barbara Ann* (twin; born 5 June 1926, married James L. Dunn on 20 Nov. 1946 at Paoli, IN, and had children: Linda [born 20 Jan. 1948, married David Magner, and had children: Aaron {born 14 July 1973}; married secondly William K. Lane on 31 Aug. 1979]); *Bobby* (twin; born 5 June 1926, died 9 June 1926, buried Livonia Cemetery); *(James) Max* (born 5 Nov. 1928, married Betty Hamilton on 3 July 1948, and had children: Stephen Max [born 25 Dec. __, married Nancy Toliver, and had children: Amy; Kelly Jean {born 7 Mar. 1983, and died 8 Mar. 1983}]). *Alta F. JONES* died 15 Jan. 19__, and is buried in the Livonia Cemetery.

Sarah GALLOWAY is listed in the 1900 census for Stampers Creek Township, Orange Co., IN. She died on 31 Dec. 1942 in Washington Co., IN, and is buried in the Livonia Cemetery. Her grandson, Louis Jones, currently lives at Paoli, IN, and has contributed greatly to this book.

6j. **Cordelia (I)** (nmn). Born 31 July 1873 in Orange Co., IN. Listed with her sister, Sarah Galloway, in the 1900 census. Cordelia Burgess died unmarried of consumption on 7 (or 15) July 1906 in Orange Co., and is buried in the Stampers Creek Cemetery.

[William (I)[1], Edward (I)[2], Edward (II)[3], Mason Peyton[4], Thomas Mason (I)[5]]

FLOYD BURGESS
(1850-1892)

OF ORANGE COUNTY, INDIANA

6a. **Floyd (I)** (nmn) *[son of Thomas Mason (I)].* Born 22 Oct. 1850 in Orange Co., IN. Married Hannah E. Lindley on 27 Dec. 1878 in Orange Co. (she was born 10 Oct. 1854, daughter of Eli Lindley and Elizabeth Stout, and died 4 Feb. 1880); married secondly Barbara A. Kochenour on 7 May 1882 in Orange Co. (she was born 15 Mar. 1851, daughter of Isaac Kochenour and Anna Kagey, and died 13 Sept. 1884); married thirdly Mrs. Pauline "Lina" (Sparks) Foster on 25 Nov. 1886 in Orange Co. (she was born 5 Mar. 1865 in IN, and died 20 Apr. 1929). Floyd Burgess was a farmer in Orange Co., IN. He died there on 22 Jan. 1892, and is buried with his first wife in the Stampers Creek Cemetery. Pauline appears as head of the family in the 1900-10 censuses for Paoli Township, Orange Co., IN (one of two children survive in 1900).

The Children of Floyd Burgess:

7a. **Clyde Leslie.** Born 31 Mar. 1883 in Orange Co., IN. Married Anna Lee Geier on 9 Sept. 1911 at Helena, MT (she died 8 Jan. 1950); married secondly Deborah "Debbie" (Stout) Wells. Clyde Burgess lived at Helena, MT most of his life, but returned to Orange Co. shortly before he died childless on 26 May 1955. He was returned for burial to Montana.

7b. **Alice M. (II).** Born 21 Mar. 1885 in Orange Co., IN. Married Edward L. Hall on 18 Sept. 1904 in Orange Co., and had children: *Phillip A.* (born 4 Jan. 1908, died young). The Halls lived at Indianapolis, IN, and are buried there in the Crown Hill Cemetery.

7c. **Opal F.** Born 12 Sept. 1888 in Orange Co., IN; died there on 3 Nov. 1890, and is buried in the Stampers Creek Cemetery.

7d. **Minnie (II).** Born July 1890 in Orange Co., IN. Living with her mother in 1910. Married Frank McNutt in Jan. 1913 at Cincinnati, OH, and had children: *Frances*; *Mary Jane*; *Margaret*; *Barbara.* Minnie McNutt lived in Northern Indiana.

[William (I)[1], Edward (I)[2], Edward (II)[3], Mason Peyton[4], Thomas Mason (I)[5]]

HENRY BURGESS
(1852-1914)

OF WASHINGTON COUNTY, INDIANA

6b. **Henry (III)** (nmn) *[son of Thomas Mason (I)]*. Born 20 Dec. 1852 in Orange Co., IN. Married Elzora Jane Harned on 9 Oct. 1879 in Orange Co. (she was born born 27 Aug. 1860 in Orange Co., daughter of William Harned and Emmeline Maxeden, and died there on 12 Aug. 1884); married secondly Mattie Lindley on 29 Sept. 1886 in Orange Co. (she was born 28 May 1862, daughter of Eli Lindley and Mary Towell, and died on 14 Oct. 1888 at Livonia, IN, buried Stampers Creek Cemetery); married thirdly Julia Ann Hoar on 14 Aug. 1890 at Livonia, Washington Co., IN (she was born 24 Nov. 1852 in Indiana, daughter of Isaac Hoar and Dorcas (Paul) Guppy, and died 27 Dec. 1939 in Washington Co., buried Livonia Cemetery). Listed in the 1880 census for Stampers Creek Township, Orange Co., IN, and in 1900 in Washington Co., IN; Julia Burgess is listed there as head of the family in 1920. Henry Burgess was a storekeeper and undertaker in Vernon Township, Washington Co., IN. He died on 1 Apr. 1914 at Livonia, IN, and is buried in the Stampers Creek Cemetery, Orange Co., IN.

The Children of Henry Burgess:

7a. **Elma Dell.** Born 19 Jan. 1881 at Paoli, Orange Co., IN. Married Matthew Taggart on 9 Aug. 1905 in Orange Co. (he was the son of Hamilton Taggart and Margaret Marks, and died 30 Mar. 1942, buried Orleans Cemetery), and had children: *Margaret* (born 30 Aug. 1906, married Philip Raymond Myracek on 11 July 1937); *Mary* (born 13 May 1910, married Basil Franklin Rex on 21 June 1936, and had children: David Taggart [born 23 Feb. 1939]; John Burgess [born 16 Nov. 1945]); *Anah Lois* (born 4 Feb. 1917). Elma Taggart died in Apr. 1967 at Crown Point, Lake Co., IN.

7b. **Mary Emeline.** Her middle name is also written Emmeline. Born 23 Apr. 1882 in Orange Co., IN. Married Harley Franklin Hardin, an attorney, on 15 Sept. 1901 in Washington Co., IN (he was born 29 June 1876, son of Isaac Hardin and Susan Thomerson, and died 6 June 1958), and had children: *Belva Lorraine* (born 27 Sept. 1902 in Grant Co., IN, married Oscar Horace Barbre on 24 Dec. 1931, and died in Jan. 1977 at Marion, IN, having had children: Nancy Sue [born 10 Sept. 1933 at Marion, IN, died 13 Sept. 1933]; John Hardin [born 3 Sept. 1934, married Myra J. Hatter on 2 Dec. 1961]; Mary Ann [born 22 Oct. 1938, married Theodore Johnson in Sept. 1961]); *Esther Malinda* (born 27 Apr. 1905 in Grant Co., married Maynard W. Mylin on 16 Aug. 1944); *Forrest Franklin* (born 28 Sept. 1906 in Grant Co., married Marjorie E. [Burkette] Barnes on 30 Dec. 1934 [she died 5 Apr. 1957], and had children: Robert [ad.]; *Forrest* died 5 Dec. 1955); *Frances Elzora* (born 23 May 1909 in Grant Co., married Clair Lester Stafford on 27 June 1934, and had children: David Clair [born 5 Feb. 1940]); *Carl Henry* (born 1 Aug. 1915 in Grant Co., married Blanche Hall on 23 Dec. 1943, and had children: Hettie Jill [born 12 Dec. 1947]). Mary Hardin died in Dec. 1973 at Marion, Grant Co., IN. Harley Hardin's biography appears in *Indiana and Indianans: A History of Aboriginal and Territorial Indiana and the Century of Statehood*, by Jacob Piatt Dunn (Chicago & New York: The American Historical Society, 1919, Volume III, p. 1355-56).

7c. **Mattie Leana.** Her name is listed as Leana M. in the 1900 census. Born 26 Sept. 1888 at Livonia, IN. Married William Claude Wright on 25 Nov. 1908 (he was the son of George Lincoln Wright and Maggie Margaret McPheeters). Mattie Wright died on 31 May 1934 in Washington Co., IN, and is buried in the Livonia Cemetery.

7d. **Lawrence Henry.** Born 1 June 1893 in Orange Co., IN. See below for full entry.

LAWRENCE H. BURGESS OF WASHINGTON CO., INDIANA

[Henry (III)[6]]

7d. **Lawrence Henry** *[son of Henry (III)].* Born 1 June 1893 at Livonia, Washington Co., IN. Married Elsie Faye Radcliff on 22 Mar. 1916 in Washington Co. (she was born 31 July 1893, daughter of Benjamin Radcliff and Martha Ellen Newly, and died 29 Nov. 1988, aged 95 years). Listed in the 1920 census for Washington Co., IN. Lawrence Burgess was a farmer near Campbellsburg, Washington Co., IN. He died there in Mar. 1975, and is buried in the Livonia Cemetery.

8a. **Maurice Henry.** His name is spelled Morris in the 1920 census. Born 29 Mar. 1918 at Livonia, Washington Co., IN; died on 3 Apr. 1928 at St. Edwards Hospital, New Albany, IN, and is buried in the Livonia Cemetery.

8b. **(Benjamin) Eugene.** Born 6 Oct. 1920 in Washington Co., IN. See below for full entry.

8c. **Dorothy Faye.** Born 26 June 1923 in Washington Co., IN. Married Jefferson Boyd Nickell Jr. on 16 Apr. 1949 at Memphis, TN (he was the son of Jefferson Boyd Nickell Sr. and (Carrie) Elizabeth Frizelle), and had children: *Henry Boyd* (born 22 Aug. 1950 at Memphis); *Donald Paul* (born 28 Dec. 1954 at Memphis, married Janeen Lynch, had children: Jeffrey, and lives at San Diego, CA). Dorothy Nickell lives at Memphis, TN.

8d. **Mary Frances (III).** Born 26 June 1928 in Washington Co., IN. Married Clifford Vance Moon on 14 Dec. 1946 (he was the son of Roy Moon and Olive Busick), and had children: *Karen Sue* (born 12 Aug. 1958 at Bedford, IN, married Kenneth Howard Simmons on 30 June 1979, and had children: Christopher Brandon [born 26 Feb. 1981]; Matthew Aaron [born 25 Feb. 1987]); *Dale Allen* (born 13 Jan. 1963 at Bedford, IN); *Patricia Denise* (born 16 Jan. 1972 at Salem, IN). Mary Moon currently lives lives at Orleans, IN. She has contributed greatly to this book.

8e. **Annabel Lee.** Born 23 Sept. 1933 in Washington Co., IN. Married Haskel Cleek on 13 Apr. 1957 at Salem, IN, and had children: *Donna Faye* (born 24 June 1959, married Terry Ray Hurst on 7 June 1980, and had children: Andrea Dawn [born and died 18 Dec. 1980]; Kristen Faye [born 5 Jan. 1982]; Jennifer Renee [born 20 July 1983]); married secondly Darrell Medlock in 1964. Annabel Medlock died on 1 May 1988 at Campbellsburg, IN.

EUGENE BURGESS OF WASHINGTON CO., INDIANA

[Henry (III)[6], Lawrence Henry[7]]

8b. **(Benjamin) Eugene** *[son of Lawrence Henry].* Born 6 Oct. 1920 in Washington Co., IN. Married Helen Frances Rutherford on 11 Oct. 1940 (she was the daughter of Charles M. Rutherford and Carrie Florence Jackson, and died in Apr. 1973). Gene Burgess is a farmer near Campbellsburg, Washington Co., IN.

9a. **Ernest Lee "Ernie"** (ad.). His surname was originally Turner. Born 22 Mar. 1949 in Washington Co., IN. Married Susan Eunice Evans about 1972. Ernie Burgess is a farmer on his father's lands near Campbellsburg, IN.

10a. **Donavon Eugene.** Born Nov. 1972 at Livonia, IN.
10b. **Lawrence Lee.** Born about 1974.
10c. **Robert Daniel (I).** Born about 1976.
10d. **Helen Sue.** Born about 1978.

[William (I)[1], Edward (I)[2], Edward (II)[3], Mason Peyton[4], Thomas Mason (I)[5]]

LEWIS MOULDER BURGESS
(1864-1926)

OF ORANGE COUNTY, INDIANA

6g. **Lewis Moulder** *[son of Thomas Mason (I)].* Born 7 Feb. 1864 in Orange Co., IN. Married Martha Jane "Mattie" Boyd on 26 Mar. 1885 in Orange Co. (she was born 10 Nov. 1861, daughter of Jesse Boyd and Elizabeth Ellen Howell, and died 28 Dec. 1939). Listed in the 1900-10 censuses for Paoli Township, Orange Co., IN; four of four kids survive in 1900, three of seven in 1910. Lewis Burgess was a farmer in Orange Co. He died there on 15 Mar. 1926, and is buried with his wife in the Lick Creek Cemetery.

The Children of Lewis M. Burgess:

7a. **Dessie** (twin). Born and died 23 June 1887 in Orange Co., IN, buried Lick Creek Cemetery.
7b. **Jessie** (twin). Born and died 23 June 1887 in Orange Co., IN, buried Lick Creek Cemetery.
7c. **Everett Owen.** Born 3 Dec. 1888 in Orange Co., IN. Married Amanda Mae Noblitt on 29 Apr. 1908 in Orange Co. (she was born 7 Oct. 1889, daughter of Leander Noblitt, and died 22 Feb. 1977). Listed in the 1917 draft register of Orange Co., IN. Everett Burgess was a farmer in Orange Co., IN. He died on 15 Mar. 1945 at Louisville, KY, but is buried in the Community Cemetery, Paoli, IN.

8a. **Charles Austin.** Born and died 18 Jan. 1912 in Orange Co., IN.
8b. **Mable Olive.** Born 4 Nov. 1914 in Orange Co., IN. Married Edwin Fleming Trimble on 10 Sept. 1933 in Orange Co. (born 1 Mar. 1913 in Orange Co.), and had children: *(Mary) Jeanette* (born 12 Dec. 1935, married Phillip Haworth on 20 Feb. 1955, and had children: John Edwin [born 16 Apr. 1962, married Michelle Gibson on 13 Aug. 1988, and had children: Ashlie Nicole {born 9 Aug. 1990}; Jordan Wayne {born 22 Aug. 1993}]; Phyllis Jeanne [born 21 Aug. 1964, married Robert Heinrich on 28 May 1983, and had children: Robert Grant {born 23 Dec. 1985}; Christopher Phillip {born 26 Apr. 1989}]). Mable Trimble lives near Paoli, IN, and has contributed greatly to this book.
8c. **Grant Noblitt.** Born 12 Apr. 1918 in Orange Co., IN, died there in 1922.

7d. **Daughter**. Born 6 Apr. 1892 in Orange Co., IN, died there on 11 Apr. 1892.
7e. **Floyd B.** Born 29 Sept. 1893 in Orange Co., IN, died there on 15 Apr. 1902, buried Lick Creek.
7f. **Raymond Elwood.** Born 23 Aug. 1896 in Orange Co., IN. Married Hildred Lapping (daughter of William Lapping and Susie Cravens). Listed in the 1917 draft register of Orange Co., IN. Raymond Burgess was a baker, and also worked for the City of Clarksville, IN government. He died in Apr. 1985 at New Albany, Floyd Co., IN.

8a. **Billy Lewis.** Born 20 Jan. 1931 in Orange Co., IN. Married Bette Vance. Bill Burgess died on 30 Mar. 1993 at Milton, FL.

9a. **Kenneth (IV).**

10a. **Daughter.**

9b. **Jeffrey.** Married.

10a. **Danielle.** Born 21 July 1985.
10b. **Daughter.**

7g. **Lillie Eva.** Born 23 Jan. 1900 in Orange Co., IN. Married Charles M. Hill on 27 Aug. 1919 in Orange Co. (he was born 27 Feb. 1895, and died Mar. 1981). Lillie Hill lives at English, IN.

THE FOURTH BRANCH

MOSES BURGESS OF ORANGE COUNTY VIRGINIA

Exie Etta BURGESS CRITCHFIELD (1897-1966)

Frances Lucille BURGESS DORAN (1900-1971)

Starring in "Martha," Ferguson Light Opera Co. Circa 1920

Three

Acting

Brothers

About 1910

ROBERT OTIS BURGESS
(top)

FRANK OLIVER BURGESS
(right)

ARTHUR CLAY BURGESS
(left)

THE BURGESSES BETWEEN THE SPANISH-AMERICAN WAR AND WORLD WAR II

At the beginning of the twentieth century, the majority of Burgesses were still tilling the soil, despite the fact that some of the younger members of the family were rapidly moving into smithing, the railroad industry, and a few of the professions, including law and medicine. Within a generation these tentative moves away from the soil would become an avalanche.

The outbreak of World War I in 1914 found the United States officially neutral, ill-prepared for the trench warfare which soon engulfed the European continent. But America's sympathy for Great Britain and the depredations of the German U-boats inexorably pushed the U.S. into an official declaration of war in 1917. For the first time since the Civil War, a universal draft was enacted, and young men by the thousands registered at the newly-erected local draft boards. The draft was conducted in three stages, at first only affecting those in a narrow age group, but later being expanded in 1918 to cover all men aged 18-45.

The delay in getting men trained meant that significant numbers of American soldiers did not actually arrive in Europe until mid-1918, where they were immediately used to bolster and replace the tired Allied units. The addition of U.S. troops significantly altered the course of the war, shortening what was probably an inevitable outcome. Only one Burgess soldier was killed in the war, but many others participated, and at least one other member of the family died a few years later of lingering ailments caused by gas warfare. The Germans surrendered on 11 November 1918, the American troops came home, and the world was changed irrevocably, as the U.S. for the first time assumed an ongoing role as one of the world's superpowers.

The world to which the soldiers returned was also changing. The United States heartland was industrializing, and the young men and women who might previously have been satisfied with life on the family farm could not resist the lure of the bright lights and relatively good money in the steel, auto, and manufacturing industries burgeoning in Ohio, Pennsylvania, Illinois, and Michigan. Burgesses by the dozens left the hills of Tennessee and Kentucky and the farms of Indiana, Ohio, Illinois, Iowa, and Minnesota to work in the mills and plants of the upper Midwest, often forming little colonies of friends, neighbors, and family transplanted from one particular area. Many of these factory workers would spend ten, twenty, thirty years laboring in the plants, and then return with their retirement checks to the sunnier, less hectic rural areas from which they had originally come.

America became a nation on the move: the widespread rail system, the establishment of a national road network, plus the cheap availability of automobiles made transportation readily available for families who previously might have spent all or most of their lives within ten or twenty miles of their original birthplace—or who at the best could have expected to move only once or twice in their lifetimes, with all of the dislocation that entailed. Like many of his cousins, my grandfather, Roy P. Burgess, left the uncertainties and disasters of farm life in rural Saskatchewan in 1924, and moved his family back to Oregon, where he secured regular employment as a prison guard at the Oregon State Penitentiary. The promise of a weekly paycheck during the 1920s and '30s more than outweighed the joys of trying to coax a crop from the sometimes reluctant prairie soil.

But the prosperity of the postwar years vanished quickly with the stock market crash of 1929 and the great depression that followed. Many of the Burgess families just barely managed to scrape by, working at whatever jobs they could find, or raising some of their own food in backyard gardens. Those living in the dustbowl states of Kansas and Oklahoma had particularly hard times, some of them moving on to California, where jobs were more plentiful and the climate less extreme. By 1941, as America geared up for war once more, the economy was showing slow signs of recovery, and the world was again rushing headlong toward international conflict.

Chart V: Moses Burgess of Orange Co., Virginia

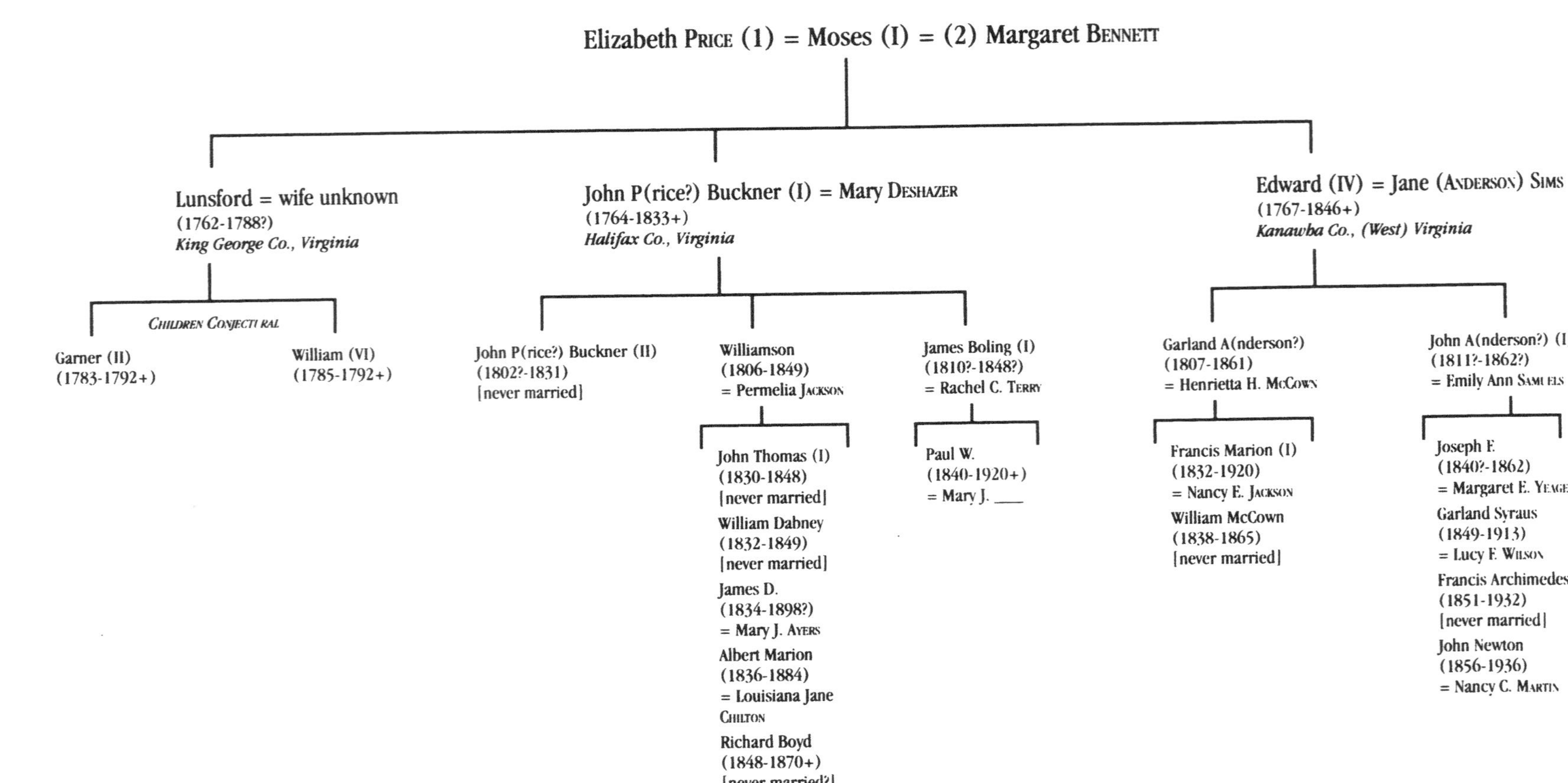

Elizabeth Price (1) = Moses (I) = (2) Margaret Bennett
Lunsford = wife unknown
(1762-1788?)
King George Co., Virginia
Children Conjectural
Garner (II)
(1783-1792+)
William (VI)
(1785-1792+)
John P(rice?) Buckner (I) = Mary Deshazer
(1764-1833+)
Halifax Co., Virginia
John P(rice?) Buckner (II)
(1802?-1831)
[never married]
Williamson
(1806-1849)
= Permelia Jackson
John Thomas (I)
(1830-1848)
[never married]
William Dabney
(1832-1849)
[never married]
James D.
(1834-1898?)
= Mary J. Ayers
Albert Marion
(1836-1884)
= Louisiana Jane Chilton
Richard Boyd
(1848-1870+)
[never married?]
James Boling (I)
(1810?-1848?)
= Rachel C. Terry
Paul W.
(1840-1920+)
= Mary J. ___
Edward (IV) = Jane (Anderson) Sims
(1767-1846+)
Kanawba Co., (West) Virginia
Garland A(nderson?)
(1807-1861)
= Henrietta H. McCown
Francis Marion (I)
(1832-1920)
= Nancy E. Jackson
William McCown
(1838-1865)
[never married]
John A(nderson?) (I)
(1811?-1862?)
= Emily Ann Samuels
Joseph F.
(1840?-1862)
= Margaret E. Yeager
Garland Syraus
(1849-1913)
= Lucy F. Wilson
Francis Archimedes
(1851-1932)
[never married]
John Newton
(1856-1936)
= Nancy C. Martin

[William (I)[1], Edward (I)[2]]

MOSES BURGESS
(1742-1796)

OF ORANGE COUNTY, VIRGINIA

3g. **Moses (I)** *[son of Edward (I)].* Born 2 Dec. 1742 O.S. in King George Co., VA (*St. Paul's Parish Register*). He may have been named for Moses Lunsford, a neighbor of the Burgesses who was born 1718 in Northumberland Co., son of John Lunsford and Elizabeth Swanson. Married Elizabeth Price on 30 May 1762 in Stafford Co., VA (*St. Paul's Parish Register*) (she was born 3 June 1741 [*St. Paul's Parish Register*], the daughter of Thomas Price and Sarah Buckner [who was the daughter of Anthony Buckner and Sarah Ellis, a sister of John Buckner, and a niece of Catherine Ellis], and sister of Sarah Price, who married Edward Burgess Jr., Moses's older brother; and died between 1771-84 [probably in the late 1770s]). Moses BURGESS is believed to have married secondly before 1784 (perhaps as early as 29 Apr. 1778, when he and John Bennett witnessed the will of Price Roach [*King George Co. Will Book #A-1*, p. 392, which names William Bennett as executor of Roach's estate) Margaret "Peggy" Bennett, daughter of Cossom(b) Bennett and Katherine Bunbury, and sister of William, John, Charles Ellis, Mason, and Mildred Bennett King, and granddaughter of Catherine Ellis (see *King George Co. Will Book #2*, p. 257-259, dated 2 Feb. and probated 3 July 1800, for the will of her brother, William ["...the rest and residue of my estate I wish to be sold & the proceeds divided between my sister, Peggy Burges—Behethlem Kirk, and Hannah King a blind girl daughter to Thomas King dec^{d}..."). Peggy died in Orange Co., VA between Mar. of 1815 and 15 Mar. 1816 (when the first inventory of her husband's estate took place), probably by 10 Sept. 1815, when the orphaned children of her stepdaughter, Sarah Faulconer, were adopted by Samuel Faulconer Jr.; by 1816 the Moses Burgess estate was dropped from the Orange Co. tax lists, and the first settlement of the estate was made by Samuel Faulconer Jr. At least one researcher has suggested that Peggy Bennett was the wife of Reuben Burgess, Moses's younger brother, but the *St. Paul's Parish Register* gives Reuben's wife's surname as Stribling (the Striblings were next-door neighbors of the Burgesses in King George Co.), and several of the Stribling families followed Reuben Burgess to Albemarle Co., buying land very close to the Burgess farm. Although there is no direct statement that Peggy Burgess is Moses's wife, the association between the two families is clearly established in the Roach deed and suggested in the guardianship record of Garner Burge (see below), Lunsford Burges's presumed son; also, since Moses Burgess was dead in 1800, he need not have been mentioned in Bennett's will as Peggy's husband.

Moses Burgess was a farmer in King George Co., VA, apparently remaining on his father's lands, two miles northwest of the town of King George, near Comorn, Virginia. He is mentioned in his father's will in 1759 as an underaged son, and is listed in the personal property tax records there from 1782-1783 (1784 is missing). In the Spring of 1779 he is recorded having exchanged $147 of worthless Continental Congress banknotes for newly-issued currency, his residence being given as Westmoreland Co. (*Claim #464*, indexed in *National Genealogical Society Quarterly* 46(4) [December, 1958]: 172). On 5 Nov. 1784 he purchased 239 acres of land in Orange Co., VA from Stephen Smith, the farm lying on the head branches of the Matapony River (*Orange Co. Deed Book #18*, p. 398-399), with Moses specifically being mentioned as having come from King George Co.; neighbors noted on the deed include: William Gaines, George Riden, Thomas Faulconer, William Sullivan, and ___ Chapman. Moses's will (*Orange Co. Will Book #3*, p. 415, dated 11 May 1796, probated 23 Jan. 1797) mentions as legatees his three daughters by his second marriage, and makes his son, Edward, and his widow, Margaret, joint executors. The administration of his estate encompassed thirty-six years, not being finally settled until 1832. The estate divisions of 1816 and 1832 mention all of his surviving children except Edward, who had already deeded away his rights to his father's estate (see *Orange Co. Will Book #5*, p. 145, dated 15 and 27 Mar. 1816, for the inventory of his wife's estate, and *Will Book #7*, p. 544-546 and 548-551, dated 27 Apr. 1816, recorded 27 Nov. and 24 Dec. 1832, for final accounting and division). Moses is listed on the Orange Co. tax lists from 1785-1796 (19 May); his estate remains on the rolls through 1815. The arrangement of children in this family is based upon their order in Moses's will and in his estate settlements.

The Children of Moses Burgess:

4a. **Lunsford.** Born 20 Sept. 1762 in King George Co., VA (*St. Paul's Parish Register*). Lunsford Burgess was a farmer in King George Co., Virginia, apparently remaining on his father's lands when Moses Burgess moved to Orange Co., VA in 1784. Listed in the tax records for King George Co. in 1785 and 1787-88 (in 1787 as "Burge," with no males over 21), but is not mentioned in his father's will (1796) or in the later estate divisions and accountings (beginning in 1816), nor are his two supposed children, despite the fact that all other known children or grandchildren except Edward Burgess are meticulously recorded there. He presumably died before the settlement of his father's estate, probably between 1788-1789, when he is dropped from the tax rolls.

However, two guardianship records in Spotsylvania Co. (*Liber #N*, p. 188-189, dated 3 Jan. 1792, witnessed by William Bronaugh [who was the son of David Bronaugh and grandson of Jeremiah Bronaugh Sr. of King George Co.], Edward Herndon, and Lewis Holladay), just across the Rappahannock River from King George Co., mention two orphaned children of "Leonard Burge." The repetition of the unusual given name "Garner" for the oldest of these children suggests that they may have been offspring of Lunsford Burgess. No further record has been found for these orphans or for Leonard Burge or even for a Burge family in the area, although a Gardner "Burge" *is* recorded on the tax and census lists of Halifax Co., VA between 1810-30 (on the border between Virginia and North Carolina, in the same county where John P. B. Burgess eventually settled), changing his name to Burgess by the 1830 census (his descendants *all* use the name Burgess). No evidence has been found to establish any provable connection between this family and the boy, Garner Burge. The first of the guardian deeds (p. 188) appears below; the second (p. 189) is identical, except that William Burge is apprenticed to John Steward "to learn the art and business of a planter and farmer."

> This indenture made this third day of January in the year of our Lord one thousand seven hundred & ninety-two Between Edward Herndon, Lewis Holladay & William Bronaugh overseers of the poor in the District (N°. 2) in the County of Spotsylvania of the one part and Charles Bennet (black smith) of the same County of the other part **Witnesseth** that the said overseers in pursuance of an order of the County Court of Spotsylvania, doth put and bind to him the said Charles Bennet one orphan boy by the name of Garner Burge (son of Leonard Burge decd) aged eight years the 20th day of last March to serve him the said Charles Bennet as an apprentice until he shall arrive to the age of twenty one years, during all which time the said apprentice his said Master shall faithfully serve & his lawful commands obey—And the said Charles Bennet on his part doth hereby convenant and agree with the said overseers that he will use his endeavours to teach his said apprentice the trade and art of a Blacksmith and find and provide for him good and sufficient dish clothing washing and lodging fiting for such apprentice during the time of his service and shall also teach or cause him to be taught to read write & arithmatic (including the Rule of Three) and at the expiration of his apprenticeship shall pay him three pounds ten shillings current money of Virginia freedom dues. **In Witness** whereof the parties to these presents have hereunto set their hands and seals the day and year first above written. [Signed by the overseers and by Charles Bennett [sic], and recorded 6 June 1792].

5a. **Garner (II).** Born 20 Mar. 1783 in VA. He was apprenticed to Charles Bennet(t) on 3 Jan. 1792 in Spotsylvania Co., VA (Bennett may be the same Charles Ellis Bennett who was born 23 Aug. 1752 in King George Co. [*St. Paul's Parish Register*], son of Cossum Bennett and Catharine Bunbury, a brother of Margaret Bennett, Moses Burgess's second wife, and a major beneficiary in his brother William Bennett's 1800 will: "My tract of land in this county [i.e., King George Co.] near the court house, containing by estimation about two hundred and twenty acres, I wish and do hereby will to be divided between my brother, Charles Bennett, and my sister, Mildred King...but should he die without heir or heirs [implying that Charles had none in 1800], he is to hold the lands only during life, and after his death without lawful issue, my will is that it shall again be annexed to the part it is taken from, & go with the other part to my sister Mildred King, wife to Matthew King..." [*King George Co. Will Book #2*, p. 258]). Relationship not verified, although probable.

5b. **William (VI).** Born 20 Nov. 1785 in VA. He was apprenticed to John Steward on 3 Jan. 1792 in Spotsylvania Co., VA (Steward [or Stewart] may be related to Humphrey Steward, who bought the original Burgess land in King George Co. in 1797; the former's will [*Spotsylvania Co. Will Book #K*, p. 148, dated 22 July 1821, probated 5 Nov. 1821], mentions a son, William). If Garner and William are grandsons of Moses Burgess, why are they not listed in his detailed estate accountings? There are several possibilities: 1) that they both died before Moses did at the end of 1796; 2) that they were adopted into another family and took the surname of their new father; 3) that they were illegitimate and thus not eligible to share in the estate; 4) that neither Moses nor his executors were aware of the children. Relationship not verified, although probable.

4b. **John P(rice?) Buckner (I).** Born 5 Apr. 1764 in King George Co, VA. See below for full entry.

4c. **Edward (IV).** Born 2 Apr. 1767 in King George Co., VA. See below for full entry.

4d. **Nancy (I).** Born about 1775 in King George Co., VA. See below for full entry.

4e. **Sarah (III).** Born about 1777 in King George Co., VA. Married Samuel Faulconer Jr. on 14 May 1798 in Orange Co., VA (bond date, "Edmund" Burgess [presumably her brother Edward] providing the bond; Samuel was the son of Samuel Faulconer Sr. and Elizabeth Moseley Newman, and the brother of Reuben Faulconer, whose daughter married Sarah Burgess's cousin, John Garner Burgess of Harrison Co., KY), and had children:

Burgess ***FAULCONER.*** Born about 1800 in Orange Co., VA (according to the 1850 census). On 12 Mar. 1828 he was deeded 55 acres by his guardian, Samuel Faulconer of Spotsylvania Co., as part of his inheritance [*Spotsylvania Co. Deed Book #BB*, p. 372-373], and then a month later deeded his original inheritance, another 55-acre plot, to his cousin, James Faulconer [p. 374-375]). He married Mary Proctor on 10 Dec. 1830 in Spotsylvania Co. (she was born about 1795). Listed in the 1830-50 censuses for Berkley Parish, Spotsylvania Co. Burgess Faulconer was a farmer in Spotsylvania Co. He died there childless in 1853. His will (*Spotsylvania Co. Will Book #U*, p. 54, dated 25 Jan. and probated 7 Mar. 1853) left all of his estate to his wife during her lifetime (but "none of the Proctor family is not to have any thing to do with any part of my estate in no manner whatever"), thereafter to be divided between his friends Thomas H. Lumsden and Oscar F. Almond.

Sarah ***FAULCONER.*** Born about 1802 in Orange Co., VA. She may be the Sarah Mason mentioned in her aunt Nancy's 1844 will.

Samuel FAULCONER is listed in the 1810 census for Spotsylvania Co., but this may be his cousin of the same name. Samuel the husband of Sarah died by 19 Feb. 1811, when Samuel Faulconer "Junior" of Spotsylvania Co., James Faulconer, Thomas Moore, James Underwood, Elizabeth Faulconer, Jemima Faulconer, and Delphy (Philadelphia) Faulconer deeded a portion of his estate (55 acres of land plus household goods) to Burgess Faulconer (*Spotsylvania Co. Deed Book #S*, p. 350-353); Sarah may have died before 1810, but in any case by 1815. On 11 Sept. 1815 Samuel's cousin, Samuel Faulconer Jr. of Spotsylvania Co. (he was born 16 July 1757 in Orange Co., VA, served in the Revolutionary War, and died in Spotsylvania Co. on 9 Apr. 1833), executed a bond to secure to "Burgess Faulconer & Sally Faulconer orphans of Samuel Faulconer deceased all such estate or estates as now or are or hereafter shall appear to be due to the said orphans when and as soon as they shall attain to lawful age" (*Orange Co. Will Book #I/J*, p. 37). Presumably Samuel then raised both children to adulthood.

4f. **Catharine Ellis.** Born about 1783 in King George Co., VA. See below for full entry.

4g. **Mildred Lunsford "Milly."** Born about 1785 (or 1787) in Orange Co., VA (age 65 in the 1850 census, age 73 in 1860). Married William Almond on 22 June 1807 in Louisa Co., VA (bond date, John D. Watkins providing the bond; William Almond was born in the 1780s, and died in Orange Co. in 1849 [the appraisal of his estate is mentioned in *Orange Co. Will Book #11*, p. 90, dated 23 Apr. 1849, although no probate has been found]). The Almonds may be listed in the 1810 census for Campbell Co., VA, and in 1830-40 in Orange Co., VA (in 1830 with two boys aged 10-15 [one of them believed to be Barnett Almond, Catharine Ellis Burgess's son], and two daughters, one 10-15 and one under 5); Mildred is listed in the 1850-60 censuses for Berkley Parish, Spotsylvania Co., VA (in 1860 with her daughter, Martha McCracken). In 1818 William Almond deeded his children the Negroes which Mildred Almond had received from her father's estate (*Spotsylvania Co. Deed Book #V*, p. 348; see Catharine Ellis Burgess's entry for further details). Milly and William Almond had children:

Amanda E(llis?) ALMOND. Born about 1808 in VA. Mentioned in her father's deed of gift in 1818.

Margaret Lunsford ALMOND. Her middle initial is listed as L^d. in her father's 1818 deed of gift, the same notation used for her mother's name in that document. Born about 1810 in VA, married Reuben Crawford on 12 Jan. 1833 in Orange Co. (Mason B. and Barnet Almond providing the bond, with Margaret specifically being mentioned as a daughter of William Almond), and had children: *Oliver G.* (born 1837, living with his grandmother in 1850); *(Reuben) Beverly* [born 1843, living with his grandmother in 1850-60); *Margaret L. CRAWFORD* apparently died between 1843-50, and probably by 1844, when her aunt, Nancy Burgess Long, left a legacy to Margaret's children.

Mason B(ennett?) ALMOND. Mentioned in his father's deed of gift in 1818. Born 1812 in VA, became a physician and school teacher, and provided the marriage bond for his sister, Margaret. Listed in the 1850 census living with his mother (without wife or family), and from 1860-80 at Troymans, Berkley Parish (later Livingston Township), Spotsylvania Co., VA. He married Julia G. ___ about 1840 (she was born about 1820 in VA), and had children: *Clarina* (or Corina) (born 1840); *Liston* (born 1842); *Isabella* (born 1845); *Columbus* (born 1848); *Marion* (born 1851); *Welford B.* (born 1854); *Beauregard Columbia* (born 1858).

Martha Jane M. ALMOND. Born 1828 in VA. Married Michael McCracken on 18 Dec. 1856 in Orange Co., VA (he was born 1832 in Ireland, probably the son of Thomas and Ellen McCracken, who are living next door to him in 1860). Mentioned as a legatee in the will of Catharine Ellis Burgess (Mildred's sister) in 1849. Listed with her mother in the 1850 census, and with her husband and his relatives in 1860 at Danielsville, Berkley Parish, Spotsylvania Co., VA.

William and Mildred ALMOND probably also raised Barnett Burgess Almond, son of Catharine Ellis Burgess, who is frequently associated with this family. Milly Almond is mentioned as a legatee to her father's estate in the 1816 and 1832 accountings, and as a legatee of her sister Catharine's estate in 1854. She died in Spotsylvania Co. between 1860-70.

4h. **Lucy (I).** Born about 1790 in Orange Co., VA. She is mentioned in her father's will, but died childless before the settlement of her father's estate (1816).

THE WILL OF MOSES BURGESS

In the name of God Amen. I Moses Burgess of Orange County in the State of Virginia, being very sick and weak in body but of perfect mind and memory, thanks be to God for the same & Calling to mind the mortality of my body & knowing that it is appointed for all men once to die do make and ordain this my last will and testament

That is to say principally & first of all I give and recommend my soul into the hands of God that gave it me and as for my body I recommend it to the Earth to be decently buried in a christian like manner at the discretion of my Executors hereafter named nothing doubting but at the general resurrection I shall receive the same again by the mighty power of God. And as touching such worldly Estate wherewith it hath plesed [sic] God to bless me with in this life I give devise and dispose of it in the same in the following manner and form Viz[t].

Imprimis. First my will & desire is that all my just debts be paid by my Executors they raising the money out of my Estate—

Item. I give & bequeath to my beloved wife Margaret Burgess all my whole Estate real & personal consisting of lands, negros, stock & house hold furniture during her natural life or widowhood and at Margaret Burgess's or my wife's death the whole of the negros that came by Elizabeth Burgess to return to her children that then is living & to be equally divided amongst them—

Item. I also give to my daughter Catharine Ellis Burgess, Mildred Lunsford Burgess and Lucy Burgess the negros that came by Margaret Burgess named Syllar, Mary and Edmond & their increase to my above mentioned Catharine, Mildred & Lucy Burgess to them and their heirs forever. Observing an equal division to be made between them by my Executors at the death of Margaret Burgess also my houshold furniture stock & land to be sold & equally divided among my children then living of both families & And [sic] do appoint my beloved wife, John Procter & my son Edward Burgess Executors of this my last will & Testament revoking disannulling and making void all former wills & bequests by me made ratifying and confirming this and no other to be my last will & Testament

In witness whereof I have hereunto set my hand and seal this eleventh day of May one thousand seven hundred and ninety-six being the twentieth year of the commonwealth—

Signed Sealed pronounced
& delivered in presence of

Moses Burgess [Seal]

Andrew Mountague
David Falkner [his mark]
Michael McDonald

At a court held for Orange county on Monday the 2nd of Jan[y] 1797 this last will & Testament of Moses Burgess dec[d]. was moved by the oaths of David Falkner & Andrew Mountague and ordered to be recorded—Teste, James Taylor C.O.C.

INVENTORY OF THE ESTATE OF MOSES BURGES DECEASED MARCH 15TH, 1816

George a man	$500
Franky a woman	$300
Hariot a girl	$150
Bombary a boy	$120
Negroes belong second wife [total]	$1170
Winney a young woman	$400
Mary a woman	$300
Winston a boy	$270
The Estate [total]	$970
Sorrel mare	$20
Dark bay mare	$20
[total of horses]	$40

Appraisers include John Lancester, William Wright, Edmund Lancaster

Division of the Negroes Belonging to the Estate of Moses Burges dec[d]

27 Apr. 1816, by James Nelson, Administrator, Will Book 7, p. 544-546

First wife's Negroes:

George a man	$500
Frankey a woman	$300
Harriet a girl	$150
Bumbary a boy	$120
[total]	$1070

Samuel Faulconer in right of Edward Burges a legatee as per his recipt, Negro man George $500 (to pay $232.50)=$267.50

Samuel Faulconer guardian for Burges Faulconer and Sarah Faulconer orphans of Sarah Faulconer dec[d] formerly Sarah Burges as per his recipt, Negro girl Harriet $150 (Cash from George $117.50)=$267.50

Nancy Burges as per her recipt Negro Frankey $300 (Frankey to pay $32.50)=$267.50

John P. Burges as per his recipt Negro boy Bumbary $120 (Cash from George $115, cash from Frankey $32.50)=$267.50

Second wife's Negroes:

Winney a woman	$400
Mary a woman	$300
Watson a boy	$270
[total]	$970

William Almond in right of his wife and Catherine E. Burgess as per their recipt in full have received the above Negroes Winney, Mary, and Watson

11 September 1832 the above division examined by the undersigned & proven satisfactory vouchers produced from each legatee that they have received the said Negroes. Given under our hands the day and date above written. Tho[s] Ross, Rich[d] Richards, Edm[d] Ross. At a quarterly court continued and held at the Courthouse on Tuesday the twenty seventh of November 1832, this division of the slaves of Moses Burgess deceased was entered into court in order to be recorded.

*NOTE: "Receipt" is consistently spelled "recipt" in the above records. Edward Burgess is not mentioned in the division because he sold all rights to his father's estate while his mother was still alive, on 22 Apr. 1815, to Samuel Faulconer (*Orange Co. Deed Book *#26, p. 302-303).*

[William (I)[1], Edward (I)[2], Moses (I)[3]]

JOHN P. B. BURGESS, SR.
(1764-1833+)

OF HALIFAX COUNTY, VIRGINIA

4b. **John P(rice?) Buckner (I)** *[son of Moses (I)]*. Born 5 Apr. 1764 in King George Co., VA; the *St. Paul's Parish Register* gives his name as John Buckner Burgess. Listed in his father's 1832 final accounting as John P. Burgess. John is listed in the tax records of Orange Co., VA from 1788-92 and again in 1796 and 1799. He then moved to Prince Edward Co., VA, where he is listed in the tax list of 13 Mar. 1800 as "John P. B. Burgess." He married Mary "Polly" Deshazer about 1800 (she was born between 1775-84, the daughter of a wealthy land owner, John Deshazer Sr., and sister of Martha Deshazer, who married Thompson Jackson; she died between 1820-30 in Halifax Co., VA). After the marriage, John and his family disappeared from the tax records for a nine-year period. In 1807, Mary's father, John Deshazer, died, leaving part of his land to his daughter, and naming John Burgess as one of his executors (with John Deshazer Jr. and Zachariah Rice). At this point the Burgesses again returned to Prince Edward Co., with John being listed in the tax records through 1818 as "John P," and under the same name in the 1810 census. John Burgess forced the division of his father-in-law's estate when he filed suit against the other heirs (*Order Book #18*, p. 281, dated 17 Oct. 1814); he then sued John Deshazer Jr. for defamation of character (same book, p. 311), but lost the case in Aug. 1815. These actions evidently caused much bitterness between the two families, a rancor which surfaced again in 1831 after his wife's death.

John Burgess sold his land in Prince Edward Co. on 4 Nov. 1818 (*Deed Book #16*, p. 448 and *#17*, p. 31), and moved his family to neighboring Halifax Co., VA by 13 July 1819, when he bought a 364-acre farm from William Terrell on Piney Creek (*Deed Book #28*, p. 344). He is listed there on the real estate tax rolls from 1819-33, and in the 1820-30 censuses. Upon his oldest son's death in 1831, John was sued by his late wife's brother, John W. Deshazer (administrator of the estate of John P. Burgess Jr.), for nonpayment of a loan the son gave the father. John Sr. was ultimately forced to pay $234.77 plus court costs and interest, first by mortgaging and then selling all of his personal property, including lands, goods, and slaves (the most significant of these deeds is recorded in *Halifax Co. Deed Book #37*, p. 580, dated 9 May 1830). One of these slaves, Bombary or Bumberry, appears to be the same Negro "boy" allotted him as part of his father's estate, being specifically mentioned by name in Moses Burgess's final accounting of 1832 (the settlement having actually been made sometime after Apr. 1816). Following liquidation of his estate, John continues to be listed on the personal property tax rolls of Halifax Co., VA until 1833; on 28 Jan. 1833 he granted power of attorney to his lawyer to settle any further debts, evidently in preparation for his departure from the county (*Deed Book #40*, p. 478).

A year later, on 14 Jan. 1834, a Mrs. Rebecca McAlpin is mentioned in the *National Banner and Nashville Daily Advertiser* as having died at the residence of Mr. John Burgess, who presumably was living either in Nashville itself, or in rural Davidson Co., TN. This John does not appear in the 1830 census for Davidson Co., but is listed there in 1840 with his (new) wife. His presumed daughter, Elizabeth R. Burgess, who marries William Stack or Stark in neighboring Robertson Co. in 1840, appears in the 1850 census for Davidson Co., living with her husband and with Priscilla Burgess (born about 1783 in Virginia), an innkeeper, believed to be this John's wife. Priscilla died in 1858 in Robertson Co.; her inventory (*Will Book #17*, p. 580, dated 7 June 1858) mentions a slave, Nathan; her granddaughter, Ann Dabbs, is the principal legatee. The connection between John Burgess of Halifax Co., VA and Davidson Co., TN has not been proven, but seems at least possible given the close proximity of John's sons, Williamson and Boling Burgess.

The Children of John P. B. Burgess:

5a. **John P(rice?) Buckner (II).** Born about 1802 in Virginia. Listed in the personal property tax records of Prince Edward Co., VA, between 1818-19 (age 16+, not specifically named), and in Halifax Co., VA between 1826-31. He died there unmarried in 1831, when the $234 owed to him by his father resulted in a lawsuit between the Burgesses and Deshazers; his inventory (*Will Book #15*, p. 421, dated 23 Apr. 1831, and *#16*, p. 243-44, 275) mentions a horse, watch, and miscellaneous personal property; the sales of his estate (28 Feb. 1831) mention purchases by his father.

5b. **Son**. Born about 1804 in Virginia, died between 1810-20.

5c. **Williamson.** Born 12 Nov. 1806 in Virginia. See below for full entry.

5d. **Daughter**. Born about 1808 in Virginia.

5e. **(James) Boling (I)**. Born about 1810 in Prince Edward Co., VA. See below for full entry.

5f. **Daughter**. Born about 1812 in Prince Edward Co., VA.

5g. **Elizabeth R.** Born about 1818 in Prince Edward Co., VA. Married William W. Stark (or Stack) on 18 Feb. 1840 in Robertson Co., TN (he was born about 1819 in TN), and had children: *John* (born 1844 in TN); *Clari* (born 1846 in TN); *Alberton* (born 1848 in TN). Listed in the 1850 census for rural Davidson Co., TN with Priscilla Burgess (born in VA about 1783), her presumed mother or stepmother, working as innkeepers. Has not been found in the 1860-70 TN census indexes. Her inclusion here should be considered speculative.

THE PROMISSORY NOTE OF JOHN P. BURGESS SR.

On demand I John P. Burgess Sr. do promise to pay or cause to be paid unto John P. Burgess Jr. the just and full sum of too [sic] hundred and thirty four dollars and 77 cents, for value recd. of him as witness my hand and seal this 23rd day of April one thousand eight hundred thirty.

Boling J. Burgess John P. [his mark] Burgess Sr.

Thomas Fleming BURGESS *(1833-1911)* [see page 120]

[William (I)[1], Edward (I)[2], Moses (I)[3], John Price Buckner (I)[4]]

WILLIAMSON BURGESS
(1806-1849)

OF ROBERTSON COUNTY, TENNESSEE

5c. **Williamson** *[son of John Price Buckner (I)].* Born 12 Nov. 1806 in Virginia. He may have been named for Williamson Foster, mentioned as a legatee in John Deshazer Sr.'s will. Married his first cousin, Permelia Jackson, on 1 Apr. 1830 in Robertson Co. (she was born 5 Oct. 1812 in Prince Edward Co., VA, the daughter of Thompson Jackson and Martha Deshazer [who was the daughter of John Deshazer Sr.], and died of tuberculosis in Sept. 1869 in Robertson Co., TN). Williamson Burgess is listed in the 1829 tax list of Halifax Co., VA with John P. Burgess Sr. and Jr. He moved to Robertson Co., TN by 2 Feb. 1830, when he bought 198 acres of land on Sulfer Fork from Elias Lawrence (*Deed Book #V*, p. 11); he is also said to have lived in Lewis Co., TN during the 1830s. Listed in the 1840 census of Robertson Co. with four sons and one daughter.

Williamson Burgess was a farmer and school teacher, his land being located east of Adams, TN; he was also elected Justice of the Peace for Robertson Co. in 1840. He died there on 15 Dec. 1849 in the typhoid epidemic which also claimed his eldest surviving son (confirmed from the 1850 mortality census). His wife appears as head of the family in the censuses of 1850-60; her estate was probated in Robertson Co. on 20 Oct. 1869 (*Will Book #18*, p. 402). Both are buried in unmarked graves in the Williams Cemetery. His family Bible record survives in the possession of the heirs of Myrtle Garrison. Much of the information on this branch derives from the memories of Myrtle Garrison and the research of Phillip A. Gowan (see *Byrns/Jackson: A Record of Their Probationary State* (Brentwood, TN: Gowan, 1982).

The Children of Williamson Burgess:

6a. **John Thomas (I).** Born 6 Dec. 1830 in Robertson Co., TN; died there on 26 Jan. 1848, and is buried with his parents.

6b. **William Dabney.** His middle name is also given as Dunn. Born 11 May 1832 in Robertson Co., TN. He died on 3 Dec. 1849 in the same typhoid epidemic that claimed his father, as mentioned in the 1850 mortality census.

6c. **James D(eshazer?).** Born 9 May 1834 in Robertson Co., TN. See below for full entry.

6d. **Albert Marion.** Born 25 Mar. 1836 in Robertson Co., TN. See below for full entry.

6e. **Martha Louise.** Born 5 Jan. 1839 in Robertson Co., TN. Married John W. Chilton on 11 Jan. 1857 in Robertson Co. (he was the brother of Louisiana Chilton [who married Martha's brother, Albert Burgess, in a joint wedding ceremony], and died before 1900), and had at least the following children: *Permelia* (born 1858, married John Perdue, had children: Wiley Everett [born 17 Oct. 1892, married (Maude) Marie Zimmerman on 18 Nov. 1932 {she was born 10 May 1905, and died Oct. 1982}, and died childless on 1 July 1979]; *Permelia* died about 1940); *Anna Martha* (born 1862, married secondly Fred Crant, and thirdly ___ Nichols, and died childless about 1947); *Jane* (born 1864); *Sally* (born Feb. 1867 in TN); *George* (born 1871, married, and had two children who died young). Not in the 1860 TN census. Listed in the 1900 census for East Fork Township, Clinton Co., Illinois. Said to have died about 1913 at Patoka, Marion Co., IL, but has not been found in the 1910 census.

6f. **(Mary) Catherine (I).** Born 10 Nov. 1840 in Robertson Co., TN. Married Henry Washington Williams on 14 Apr. 1861 in Robertson Co. (he was the son of David Williams, and died about 1915), and had children:

Thomas F. WILLIAMS. Born Apr. 1863, married Paralee W. Woodard on 4 Dec. 1895 (she died between 1903-10), and had children: *(Elmer) Clarence* (born 6 Oct. 1896, and died childless in Dec. 1977 at Memphis, TN); *Jesse Frank* (born Feb. 1899, died unmarried about 1977); *Carrie G.* (born about 1903). Thomas F. Williams is listed with his parents in the 1910 census. He died about 1925.

Eudora C. "Bessie" WILLIAMS. Born May 1865, listed with her parents in the 1910 census, and died unmarried after 1910.

Permelia Elizabeth WILLIAMS. Born Dec. 1866, listed with her parents in the 1910 census, and died unmarried about 1920.

William Ramey WILLIAMS. Born 25 July 1872, married Beulah Briggs on 29 Dec. 1898 (she was born 11 Oct. 1878, and died 27 Oct. 1913), and had children:

William David WILLIAMS (born 7 Dec. 1899, married Musa Belle A. Stoddard on 14 Nov. 1929 [she was born 27 Oct. 1907], and had children: William Robert [born 2 June 1932, married Brigitte Jehn on 4 Sept. 1959 {she was born 13 Sept. 1935}, and had children: Annelise Brigitte {born 18 Jan. 1961}; William Eric {born 4 Mar. 1964}]; Earl David [born 29 Apr. 1937, married Gwendolyn Lee Gibson on 15 Aug. 1959 {she was born 9 Mar. 1936}, and had children: Constance Yvonne {born 15 Apr. 1962}; Glen Robert {born 13 May 1964, died 9 June 1964}; Glen David {born 2 June 1965}]. *William David WILLIAMS* died on 27 Apr. 1950).

Virgil Smith WILLIAMS (born 5 Dec. 1901, married Ethel Earline Barnes on 30 June 1923 [she remarried Howard Frank Warner, widower of Virgil's sister, Esther Pearl], and had children: Elizabeth [born 9 July 1924, married James Edwards Rodgers on 29 Aug. 1942, and had children: James Edward Jr. {born 25 Sept. 1953}]; Virgil Leon [born 5 July 1926, married Grace Pewitt on 8 Apr. 1949, and had children: David Leon {born 10 Nov. 1954}]; Richard Eugene [born 11 Jan. 1932, married Betty Murray on 28 Dec. 1951, and had children: Richard Eugene Jr. {born 13 May 1953, married Paula Jean Wright on 15 Mar. 1974, and had children: Cherie Dawn <born 1 Mar. 1976>; Richard Eugene III <born 6 Jan. 1979>; Jonathan Paul <born 25 July 1981>}; Stephen Bruce {born 8 Mar. 1955, married Kelly Dale Cooper on 23 Sept. 1978, and had children: Kristopher Andrew <born 8 May 1981>}; Laura Lynn {born 11 Feb. 1958, married Darrell Eugene Boman on 2 Apr. 1977, and had children: Cameron Eugene <born 20 Mar. 1979>; Christie Lynn <born 21 Apr. 1981>}; Jonathan Brent {born 23 Aug. 1962}; Patrick Andrew {born 8 Jan. 1969}]; Joyce Ann [born 21 Dec. 1940, married Wayne Michael Cavender on 29 May 1959, and had children: Wayne Michael Jr. {born 18 Nov. 1960}; Mark Lee {born 9 May 1967}; Elizabeth Michelle {born 22 July 1971}]. *Virgil Smith WILLIAMS* died on 4 July 1973).

Esther Pearl WILLIAMS (born 29 Nov. 1903, married Howard Frank Warner [born 15 July 1908, married Ethel Williams, his sister-in-law, and died Feb. 1985], and died 30 July 1981).

Roy Lee WILLIAMS (born 25 July 1906, married Marie Emma Powell on 4 Sept. 1948, and died childless on 8 June 1976).

Bradley Briggs WILLIAMS (born 19 Apr. 1909, married Annie Christine Griffin on 15 Mar. 1940, and had children: Margaret Carol [born 18 Dec. 1944, married James Charles Miller Jr. on 15 Sept. 1967 {he died 11 Apr. 1982}, and had children: James Charles III {born 26 May 1975}]).

Henry Buford WILLIAMS (born 1 Apr. 1910, married Alice Ruth Brooks on 30 June 1939, and had children: Buford Wayne [born 3 June 1941, married Pamela Swafford Mabry, and had children: Buford Wayne Jr. "Beau" {born 12 May 1971}; Katherine Elizabeth {born 5 Oct. 1973}]. *Henry Buford* died on 29 Mar. 1980).

William Ramey WILLIAMS died on 29 May 1929.

Charles C. WILLIAMS. Born Aug. 1876, married Verdie ___, and died childless about 1950, buried in the Spring Hill Cemetery, Madison, TN.

Mary Lucy WILLIAMS. Born 5 Apr. 1878, married John Isham Moon on 30 Apr. 1899 (he was born 1866, and died 1941), and had children:

Henry Eunice MOON (born 16 July 1900, married Angeline Wilson on 31 May 1918, and had children: Robert Eunice [born 28 July 1921, married Lucy Gower on 12 Feb. 1948, and had children: Carolyn {born 22 Aug. 1950, married Ricky Bryant, and had children: Kevin <born 8 June 1975>; Keith <born 7 July 1978>}; Robert Henry {born 5 Oct. 1953, married Beverly Lambert, and had children: Robert Phillip <born 1 Sept. 1978>}; Janice {born 5 Apr. 1959}]; Aubrey Hassen [born 20 Aug. 1923, married Dollie Wilma Hunter, and had children: Audrey Diane {born 4 June 1949, married John Howard Goff on 3 May 1969, and had children: Angela June <born 8 Mar. 1971>; Brian Howard <born 24 Mar. 1973>}; Aubrey Dennis {born 5 July 1950, married Deborah Lynn Knight on 11 Aug. 1970, and had children: Kathy Rae <born 20 May 1973>}; Danny Mike {born 3 Mar. 1954, married Amy Jean Thomas on 25 Sept. 1974, and had children: Joseph Aubrey <born 5 May 1979>; Patricia Michelle <born 11 Nov. 1981>}; Aubrey Hassen died on 21 Mar. 1968]. *Henry Eunice* died on 28 Aug. 1979).

Clara Bell MOON (born 5 Apr. 1902, married Johnnie Richard Clinard on 21 Aug. 1927, and had children: (Ellen) Marie [born 11 Aug. 1931, married secondly Wilbern Edgar Krisle, and had children: Bonnie Justine {born 8 July 1955, married Bob Davies, and had children: John Kevin <born 23 July 1975>}; Wilbern David {born 30 June 1957, died 10 Jan. 1958}; Cynthia Darlene {born 4 Apr. 1958}; Johnnie Mark {born 14 Jan. 1961, married Denise Louise Hall}; Rachel Anne {born 10 Sept. 1963}]; Katherine Frances [born 11 July 1935, married Ralph Willis]; Johnnie Richard Jr. [born 10 Apr. 1937, married Genevieve ___, and died childless about 1965]; Isham Lonzie [born 24 Aug. 1942, married Carolyn Thaxton, and had children: Stacy Lynn {born 27 Dec. 1962}; Kimberly {born and died about 1964}; Isham married secondly Lucille Worrell, and thirdly June ___]). *Clara Bell* died on 13 Mar. 1974.

William Felix MOON (born 9 Aug. 1905, married Eura Ellis, and had children: Barbara Barker [born 18 Mar. 1927, married James Clyde Byrd, and had children: Dotsy Marie {born 1 Aug. 1944, married Homer Haley Jr. on 15 Feb. 1963, and had children: Marie Lucille <born 25 June 1964>; Jeffrey Dwayne <born 10 July 1965>}; Barbara Barker married secondly Jewell Warren, and had children: Barbara Gayle {born 13 June 1947, married Gary Haddad, and had children: Tina <born 15 July 1967, married ___ Wallace>; David <born 12 Dec. 1970>; Barbara Gayle married secondly Jim Jager, and had children: Jennifer Marie <born 16 Sept. 1980>} Shirley Faye {born 2 Nov. 1953, married Michael Stuard, and had children: Alana Michelle <born 11 Dec. 1978>; Kelly Ann <born 16 Sept. 1980>}; Barbara Barker married thirdly Roy Anderson, and had children: Mary {twin; born 23 Mar. 1960}; Martha {twin; born 23 Mar. 1960}].

William Felix MOON married secondly Maudie May Baker, and had children: Lucy Mae [born 21 July 1937, married Charles Wayne Watts on 18 May 1957, and had children: Sheila Jane {born 24 Mar. 1958, married Robert Draper Quarles on 10 July 1981}; Terry Wayne {born 1 July 1961}]; William Sory [born 16 Aug. 1940, married Norma June (Holman) Bagby]. *William Felix MOON* died in Sept. 1984 at Springfield, TN).

Mary Jane MOON (born 4 Dec. 1906, married Harvey Hanner Hunter on 8 Oct. 1939, and had children: Robert Owen [born 17 Dec. 1939]; Thomas Warren [born 29 Oct. 1943, married Laura (Hite) Stacy on 11 Aug. 1965, and had children: Jana Stacy {born 28 Dec. 1962}; April {born 23 Apr. 1973}; Thomas Warren Jr. {born 1 July 1975}]; Jimmy Wayne [born 21 Feb. 1946, married Martha Jane Blick in Dec. 1968, and had children: Julia Lynn {born 24 June 1969, married}; Jimmy married secondly Marie Tabb on 2 Mar. 1972, and died on 23 Oct. 1972]).

James Rogers MOON (born 26 Sept. 1912, married Ruth Elizabeth Clinard on 1 Oct. 1932, and had children: John William [born 8 Mar. 1935, married Frances Felts, and had children: Wendell Earl {born 8 Aug. 1962, died 26 Apr. 1979}; Michelle Dawn {born 12 Aug. 1966}; John William married secondly Connie Jones, and thirdly Charlene Morris]; Wilburn Rogers "Bubba" [born 20 Mar. 1937, married Virginia Louise King on 4 Sept. 1960, and had children: Nathan Lee {born 20 Sept. 1965}; Evelyn Michelle {born 6 June 1979}; Bubba married secondly Cecelia Juaneece Travis on 3 Oct. 1981]. *James Rogers MOON* died in the 1980s).

Daisy Blonde MOON (born 28 Apr. 1919, married Ranel Elvis Farmer on 24 Dec. 1939, and had children: Rebecca Ann [born 28 Dec. 1941, married Carl Ray Goostree on 16 June 1965, and had children: Ginger Ann {born 6 Jan. 1966}; Jeffrey Ray {born 21 Jan. 1972}; Rebecca married secondly Fred Brooks]; Jerry Lynn [born 24 Apr. 1945, married Diana Lynn Matthews on 1 May 1971]; Sarah Elaine [born 9 Mar. 1950, married Anthony Bruce Knight on 1 May 1971, and had children: Stephanie Elaine {born 25 Jan. 1976}; Kristen Leanne {born 28 Dec. 1979}]; Michael Henry [born 29 May 1955]).

Mary Lucy MOON died on 12 Dec. 1942.

Joseph Marion WILLIAMS. Born 18 Aug. 1882, married Lena Rivers Lemons on 5 Sept. 1909, and had children:

Mary Odell WILLIAMS (born 22 Nov. 1910, married Stanley Edward McGlothan on 23 July 1927, and had children: Thelma Fay [born 21 Mar. 1930, married Glenn Arthur Deuser on 21 May 1949, and had children: Mark Steven {born 16 Nov. 1952, married Ruth Ann Smith on 14 June 1975, and had children: Brett Christopher <born 19 Dec. 1978>; Lara Michelle <born 3 Apr. 1981>}; Jeffrey Alan {born 23 Feb. 1954, married Asha Swarup on 26 Dec. 1977}; Greg Edward {born 5 Oct. 1958}; David Scott {born 8 July 1961}]; Loyce Jean [born 3 May 1931, married William Lee Wheeler on 10 June 1950, and had children: Michael {born 4 Apr. 1955}; Terri Ann {born 3 Aug. 1962}]; Vera Louise [born 22 Dec. 1933, married John Stafford Mattingly on 4 Dec. 1959, and had children: Karen Beth {stepchild; born 18 Sept. 1956, married Alfred Baker Ganote on 27 Aug. 1978, and had children: Brian A. <born 9 Feb. 1982>}; Dianne Marie {born 12 Jan. 1961, married Michael Bough on 27 July 1980}; Vera Louise died in Apr. 1985 at New Albany, IN]).

Herbert Marion WILLIAMS (born 11 Sept. 1913, married Winona Alice Kirkpatrick on 17 Apr. 1938, and had children: Carolyne Faye [born 5 July 1939, married Thomas Lehnertz on 3 Sept. 1966, and died childless on 18 Nov. 1977]; Marolyne Louise [born 11 Jan. 1941, married Paul Wesley Diggs on 15 July 1967, and had children: Richard Paul {born 13 July 1968}; Denise Louise {born 14 Mar. 1971}]; Paul Marion [born 23 Jan. 1942, married Shelly Seratt in July 1966, and died childless on 24 June 1975]; Stephen Joseph [born 2 Oct. 1949, married Rebecca Corosco on 30 Jan. 1981, and had children: Ardena Rebecca {born 16 Mar. 1982}]. *Herbert Marion WILLIAMS* died on 13 May 1974).

Cora Ruby WILLIAMS (born 10 Sept. 1919, married Rex Spears, and died childless on 3 Apr. 1977).

Bernice Louise WILLIAMS (born 22 Apr. 1924, married DeWitt Moffett McCloy on 19 Oct. 1946).

Joseph Marion WILLIAMS died 3 Nov. 1970.

Catherine and Henry WILLIAMS owned a farm near Adams, TN, and are listed in the 1900-1910 censuses for Robertson Co., TN. Catherine is said to have died there about 1913, and is buried in an unmarked grave in the Williams Cemetery, on her farm, located near the original Burgess land.

6g. **(Permelia) Susan.** Born 2 Aug. 1842 in Robertson Co., TN. Married Ambrose Hatcher on 25 Nov. 1869 in Robertson Co., TN, and had one child who died young. The Hatchers owned a farm near Adams, TN. Susan died there on 30 Nov. 1911, and is believed to be buried in an unmarked grave in the Williams Cemetery.

6h. **Sarah Elizabeth (II) "Maundie."** Born 31 July 1844 in Robertson Co., TN. Listed in the 1900 census for Robertson Co., TN. Sarah Burgess died unmarried on 23 Nov. 1911 at Adams, Robertson Co., TN.

6i. **Richard Boyd "Dick."** Born 2 Apr. 1848 in Robertson Co., TN. Listed in the 1870 tax list of Robertson Co., TN, and in the 1870 census for Logan Co., KY, just across the county line. According to the *Goodspeed Histories of Tennessee*, Robertson Co. Section (Nashville, TN: Goodspeed Publishing Co., 1886, p. 850-851), "At a special term of the [Robertson County] court held in March of 1870, Thomas Clinard and Richard Burgess were tried for the murder of a man named Smith. Clinard became possessed of the idea that Smith had bewitched him [through the influence of the 'Bell Witch,' a local superstition], and according to his statement of the case, he, with the assistance of Burgess, attempted to arrest Smith. The latter drew a revolver and fired, when Clinard emptied both barrels of his shotgun into him. During the trial the subject of witchcraft was thoroughly discussed, and the jury were probably somewhat influenced by their own superstitions. A verdict of 'not guilty' was returned." Dick Burgess left the county shortly thereafter, and never returned. His further fate is unknown.

6j. **(Louisiana) Jane.** Born 26 Sept. 1849 in Robertson Co., TN. She is listed with her brother Albert in the 1870 census. No further record.

Myrtle Garrison wrote in 1983: "Yankees came and occupied the Burgess home [during the Civil War], where Mrs. Burgess was raising her large family. The Yankees took the family's only horse and most of the food. Sausage had been stored in corn shucks and the Yankees found it and ate everything there. Later, Mrs. Burgess found that the corn shucks had been infested with flies, and was glad that the Yankees had eaten all of the sausage."

[William (I)[1], Edward (I)[2], Moses (I)[3], John Price Buckner (I)[4], Williamson[5]]

JAMES D. BURGESS
(1834-1898?)

OF ROBERTSON COUNTY, TENNESSEE

6c. **James D(eshazer?)** *[son of Williamson].* Born 9 May 1834 in Robertson Co, TN. Married Mary Jane Ayers on 3 Nov. 1861 in Robertson Co. (she was born 24 July 1843 in TN, daughter of Washington Ayers and Nancy Johnson, and died on 28 Sept. 1923 in Robertson Co.). Listed in the 1860-80 censuses for Robertson Co.; his wife appears as head of the family from 1900-20. Listed in the tax records for Robertson Co. from 1869-84 (there is a gap in the records hereafter). James Burgess was a farmer near Cedar Hill, TN. He died there between 1887-1900, and is buried in the Cedar Hill Cemetery, Cedar Hill, TN.

The Children of James D. Burgess:

7a. **(James) Ella.** Born Mar. 1862 (or 1863) in Robertson Co., TN. Married Elias Drake on 30 Dec. 1885 in Robertson Co. (he was born Oct. 1865 in TN, and died about 1911), and had at least the following children: *Boyd E.* (born Apr. 1888); *Maggie J.* (born Dec. 1889); *Frank L.* (born June 1891); *Bessie M.* (born Dec. 1892); *Jessie L.* (born July 1894); *Robbie E.* (born Mar. 1897); *Charles H.* (born Oct. 1898); *Mattie P.* (born 1901); *Anna M.* (born 1904). Listed in the 1900-10 censuses for the Sixth District, Hohenwald, Lewis Co., TN. After Elias Drake's death, some of the children were farmed out, since Ella could no longer care for them. She died after 1925 in Lewis Co. or at Hayti, Pemiscot Co., MO, where some of her descendants settled.

7b. **Sidney Johnson.** Born 17 Dec. 1866 in Robertson Co., TN. See below for full entry.

7c. **Margaret Allen "Maggie."** 11 Born Apr. 1868 in Robertson Co., TN. Married Ephraim Noel "Eafe" Knight on 21 May 1890 in Robertson Co. (he was born 7 July 1869, and died 25 May 1941), and had children:

Ephraim Noel KNIGHT Jr. Born 1891, died young.

Ruth Cleveland KNIGHT. Born 1892, married Herman Chandler, and had children: *Ethel Mae* (born 29 Sept. 1913, married Neal Holcomb, and secondly Eugene Burton, and died childless on 15 Sept. 1975); *Sophia Lillian* (born 5 Feb. 1915, married William Arsteller Melis on 4 Feb. 1950, and secondly James William Billings on 11 Oct. 1974); *Katherine Hickson* (born 17 Jan. 1917, and died unmarried in Apr. 1984); *Anna Margaret* (born 18 Jan. 1920, married Willie Thomas Price, and died childless on 17 Feb. 1959); *Child* (born and died about 1921). ***Ruth*** died in Apr. 1921.

Ralph KNIGHT. Born Apr. 1894, died about 1901.

Ruby KNIGHT. Born 1897, died before 1900.

Robert Washington KNIGHT. Born 13 June 1899, married Cecelia Dorothy Wotier on 17 Mar. 1944, and died childless on 30 July 1990 at Springfield, TN, aged 91 years.

Mary Queenelle KNIGHT. Born 15 Sept. 1902, married Robert Lee Johnson on 22 Dec. 1928, and had children: *Clara Olieta* (born 5 Apr. 1929, married Richard Ardle Rawls on 27 July 1951, and had children: Ardle Lee [born 31 Aug. 1953, married Suzanne Schlosser on 19 June 1971]; Cynthia Lynne [born 7 Dec. 1958]); *Ernest Donald* (born 29 Mar. 1930, married Ophie Kathryn Witt on 27 Sept. 1952, and had children: Vicky Lynn [born 27 Aug. 1953, married Thomas Bernard Wilson on 29 Aug. 1971, and had children: Thomas Mark {born 17 July 1973}; Valery Lynn {born 2 Feb. 1976}; John Robert {born 7 Aug. 1980}]; Donna Sue [born 15 July 1957, married Sammy Lee Crabtree in Sept. 1974, and had children: Kathy Denise {born 12 Apr. 1975}]; John Bruce [born 1 Nov. 1959, married Susan Renee Manis on 4 Oct. 1980]); *Robert Ray* (born 12 Apr. 1932, married Juanita Belt, and had children: Thomas Wayne [born 3 Jan. 1957]; Kenneth Ray [born 11 Mar. 1958]; Gary Knight [born 25 June 1959]; Karyn Elizabeth [born 17 Oct. 1962]; Mary Juanita [born 26 Oct. 1968]); *Arthur Wendell* (born Oct. 1934?, died at eighteen months). *Mary KNIGHT* died on 1 June 1980.

Cecil Sory KNIGHT. Born 29 Oct. 1904, married Eunice Myrtle Lear on 17 Nov. 1934, and had children: *Hazeline Lear* (born 18 July 1938, married Robert Joseph Mills on 23 Aug. 1959, and had children: Michael Joseph [born 27 Jan. 1968]; Lisa Michelle [born 20 Nov. 1972]).

Clara Ovena KNIGHT. Born 5 May 1908, married Robert Hancock, and died childless on 15 Aug. 1955.

Margaret and Eafe KNIGHT lived at Springfield, TN. Maggie died there on 3 Mar. 1942, and is buried in the Cross Plains Cemetery.

7d. **Eugene M. "Gene."** Born 6 Apr. 1870 (or 4 Apr. 1869) in Robertson Co., TN. Listed in the 1910-20 censuses with his mother. Gene Burgess died unmarried on 31 Mar. 1954 at Tullahoma, TN, and is buried in the Maplewood Cemetery.

7e. **(Charles) Bishop.** Born 20 May 1872 in Robertson Co., TN. See below for full entry.

7f. **Mary Elizabeth (III).** Born about 1875 in Robertson Co., TN. Listed with her father in the 1880 census, but is said to have died young shortly thereafter.

7g. **Fanny Lee.** Born 8 Sept. 1877 (or 1879, according to her death certificate) in Robertson Co., TN. Married James A(llen?) "Jim" Smith on 24 Jan. 1900 (he was born 12 Nov. 1870, and died 27 Oct. 1937), and had children: *James Allen "Speedy"* (born 18 Dec. 1900, married Bonna Leorta Felts about 1946, and died childless on 7 July 1976); *Louise* (born about 1902, married Frank D. Baker, and had children: Betsy Lee [married ___ Bushee]). Fanny Smith died on 3 Feb. 1949 at Cedar Hill, TN, and is buried in the Ward Cemetery.

7h. **Boyd L.** Born 1879 (or 1877) in Robertson Co., TN; died there in Jan. 1880 (as listed in the 1880 mortality census), age 1 year. Relationship not verified.

7i. **Clara Ovena.** Born Aug. 1881 in Robertson Co., TN. Listed with her father in the 1900 census, but is said to have died unmarried about 1901 in Robertson Co.

7j. **Walter L.** Born May 1884 in Robertson Co., TN. See below for full entry.

7k. **(Edward) Brown (I).** Born 10 Apr. 1887 in Robertson Co., TN. See below for full entry.

SIDNEY J. BURGESS OF ROBERTSON CO., TENNESSEE
[James Deshazer[6]]

7b. **Sidney Johnson** *[son of James Deshazer].* Born 17 Dec. 1866 (or 1867) in Robertson Co., TN. Married Mont(i)e Maud Cobb about 1899 (she was born 21 Sept. 1878, and died 29 Apr. 1950). Listed in the 1900-20 censuses for Robertson Co., TN. Sidney Burgess was a farmer, liveryman, and carpenter near Springfield, TN. He died there on 4 Sept. 1939, and is buried with his wife in the Elmwood Cemetery, Springfield, TN.

8a. **Beulah Mae (I).** Born 28 Sept. 1899 in Robertson Co., TN. Married Guy Payne. Beulah Payne died childless in Oct. 1984 at Springfield, TN.

8b. **John Ferris "Tobe."** Born 20 Oct. 1902 in Robertson Co., TN. Married (Nancy) Lucille Moon on 3 Oct. 1944 in Robertson Co. (she was born 28 Mar. 1903, and died Dec. 1984). Listed with his father in the 1920 census. John Burgess was a railroad worker. He lives retired at Cedar Hill, TN.

8c. **Felix Albert.** Born 5 Aug. 1904 (or 1905, according to Social Security records) in Robertson Co., TN. Married Ossie Mae Scruggs on 6 Mar. 1934 in Robertson Co. (she was born 12 Apr. 1903, and died Nov. 1980). Felix Burgess worked for the telephone company in Robertson Co. He died childless in July 1980 at Cedar Hill, TN.

8d. **Geneva A. "Genevie."** Born 21 Sept. 1907 (or 24 Sept. 1906) in Robertson Co., TN, and died there on 21 Nov. 1909 (or 1908).

8e. **Edd Wilbert.** His middle name was supposed to have been Woolard. Born 1 Feb. 1910 at Cedar Hill, TN. Married Linda Harris on 7 Aug. 1938 (she died on 4 Sept. 1959); married secondly (Cynthia) Ann Hewell on 30 Dec. 1967. Edd Burgess worked in various department stores before buying his own Western Auto outlet at Guthrie, KY. He lives retired at Cedar Hill, TN.

9a. **(Dorothy) Sue.** Born 28 July 1939 at Cedar Hill, TN. Married George W. Batey in 1986 [div.]. Sue Burgess is a physical therapist at Springfield, TN.

8f. **George Ivan.** Born 17 July 1915 in Robertson Co., TN. Married Christine Lavada Hardin on 15 Dec. 1943 (she remarried Clarence Buttrey [dec.], and lives at Nashville, TN). George Burgess was an electrician for the TVA at Springfield, TN. He died there on 22 Feb. 1975, and is buried in the Robertson County Memorial Gardens.

9a. **John Ray.** Born 8 May 1946 at Springfield, TN. Married Elaine Picard on 8 June 1968. John R. Burgess is a computer systems analyst for State Industries at Pleasant View, TN.

10a. **Barbara Ann (III).** Born 12 Sept. 1969 at Nashville, TN.
10b. **Deborah Lynn (III).** Born 31 Mar. 1971 at Nashville, TN.

9b. **Lucinda Ann.** Born 12 Oct. 1953 at Springfield, TN. Married Ernest Sidney Mitchell on 11 Nov. 1972, and had children: *Steven Trinity* (born 14 Apr. 1974); *Michelle Marie* (born 28 Nov. 1975); *Dustin Allen* (born 16 Oct. 1977). Lucinda Mitchell lives at Springfield, TN.

CHARLES BISHOP BURGESS OF DAVIDSON CO., TENNESSEE

[James Deshazer[6]]

7e. **(Charles) Bishop "Bish"** *[son of James Deshazer].* Born 20 May 1872 in Robertson Co., TN. Married Georgia Ellen James on 18 Sept. 1898 in Robertson Co., TN (she was born Feb. 1880, and died 24 June 1924). Listed in the 1920 census for Eastland, Davidson Co., TN. Bish Burgess moved to Nashville, TN, where he is listed as a carpenter and railroad worker in the city directories from 1918-60. He died there on 22 Apr. 1960, and is buried in the Mount Olivet Cemetery.

8a. **Mamie Lee.** Born 12 Nov. 1900 in Robertson Co., TN. Married Robert Franklin Caughey, and had children: *Robert Burgess* (born 14 Oct. 1920, married Anna ___, had two children, and lived at Nashville); *Sarah Ellen* (born 1 Apr. 1922, married M. R. Tracey, and secondly Vernon John Sundquist on 13 Oct. 1951, and had children: Kristina [born 26 May 1966]; Sarah Sundquist lived at Sedona, AZ); *Charles C.* (born 21 Jan. 1923, died 9 Apr. 1931). Listed with her father and husband in the 1920 census. Mamie Caughey died on 10 Jan. 1948 at Chicago, IL, but was buried in Tennessee.
8b. **James Vernon (I).** Born 6 Sept. 1904 at Greenbrier, Robertson Co., TN. Married Mary Roach; married secondly Mary Christine Waldon in 1945. Jim Burgess worked as a mechanic for the Armored Transport Co., and later as a dispatcher for the Belle Meade Police Dept. Listed in the 1934-42 city directories for Nashville. He died there on 20 Feb. 1955, and is buried in the Mount Olivet Cemetery.

9a. **James Vernon (II).** Born about 1946 in Nashville, TN.
9b. **Arthur Thomas (II).** Born about 1948 in Nashville, TN.

8c. **Jesse Clinton.** Born 1906 in Robertson Co., TN. Married Alice Hawkins; married secondly Geneva ___ (who died in 1975). Listed in the 1934 directory for Nashville. Jesse Burgess was a clerk at Chicago, IL, where he died in 1957. His children are by his first wife.

9a. **Grace (IV).**
9b. **Allen (I).**

8d. **Hallie Mae.** Born 23 Aug. 1908 in Robertson Co., TN. Married George R. Speaker Jr. Living at St. Louis, MO in 1955. Hallie Speaker died childless on 4 Sept. 1964.
8e. **(Charles) Edward (II).** Born 12 June 1913 at Nashville, TN. Married Jimmie Madeleine Baltimore on 25 Feb. 1938. Listed in the city directories for Nashville from 1937. Ed Burgess was a mechanic. He died on 4 Apr. 1991 at Nashville, TN.

9a. **Charles Leonard (II).** Born 1 Aug. 1941 at Nashville, TN. Married Patricia Slaughter (div.); married secondly Nancy Breseman. Listed in the city directories of Nashville from 1961-65. Charles Burgess is a supervisor for Capt. D's restaurant chain at Dallas, TX.

10a. **John Leonard.** Born 15 Apr. 1968 at Nashville, TN.
10b. **Lisa.** Born 2 Sept. 1971 at Dallas, TX (?).

9b. **(Douglas) Eugene.** Born 5 July 1953 at Nashville, TN. Married Sallie Holmes (or Wood) on 3 July 1982. Gene Burgess is an architectural millworker, building custom doors and windows, at Madison, TN.

WALTER L. BURGESS OF ROBERTSON CO., TENNESSEE
[James Deshazer[6]]

7j. **Walter L.** *[son of James Deshazer].* Born May 1884 in Robertson Co., TN. Married Minnie Parker on 23 Nov. 1929 in Robertson Co., TN (who survived him). Listed with his mother in the 1910-20 censuses. Walter Burgess died on 12 Feb. 1950 at Springfield, TN, and is buried in the Doyle Cemetery.

8a. **Charles E. (III)** (ad.). He was the son of Elvin McClain and Mattie Bell Stark. Born 14 Mar. 1935 at Springfield, TN; died there on 30 May 1935, and is buried in the Elmwood Cemetery.

BROWN BURGESS OF ROBERTSON CO., TENNESSEE
[James Deshazer[6]]

7k. **(Edward) Brown (I)** *[son of James Deshazer].* Born 10 Apr. 1887 in Robertson Co., TN. Married Violet Marshall on 4 Oct. 1919; married secondly Nannie Aileen Richardson on 14 Nov. 1920 (she was born 30 June 1896, and died Nov. 1973). Listed with his mother in the 1920 census. Brown Burgess died on 7 May 1955 in Robertson Co., and is buried the Elmwood Cemetery, Springfield, TN.

8a. **Edward Brown (II).** Born 6 Nov. 1921 in Robertson Co., TN. Married (Lillian) Marguerite Merriman in June 1942 (she was born 24 Jan. 1923). Ed Burgess is a retired steel mill worker, currently living at Utica, KY.

9a. **Beverly Jean (III).** Born 13 Jan. 1944 at Takoma Park, MD. Married Robert Sutton, and had children: *Samuel*; *Seth*. Beverly Sutton lives at Point of Rocks, MD.

9b. **Michael Edward (I).** Born 1 Apr. 1947 at Indianapolis, IN. Married (Dorothy) Jean "Jeannie" Hoover. Mike Burgess works as an air conditioning and refrigeration specialist at Owensboro, KY.

10a. **Michael Edward (II).** Born 28 Nov. 1971 at Owensboro, KY.

EDWIN BURGESS
(1864-1933)
[see page 134]

[William (I)[1], Edward (I)[2], Moses (I)[3], John Price Buckner (I)[4], Williamson[5]]

ALBERT MARION BURGESS
(1836-1884)

OF ROBERTSON COUNTY, TENNESSEE

6d. **Albert Marion** *[son of Williamson].* Born 25 Mar. 1836 in Robertson Co., TN. Married Louisiana Jane "Eliza" Chilton on 11 Jan. 1857 in Robertson Co. (she was born 4 Apr. 1830, sister of John W. Chilton [who married Albert's sister, Martha Louise Burgess, in a joint ceremony], and died on 12 May 1897). Listed in the 1860-80 censuses for Robertson Co., and in the tax records there from 1869-1884, when his name is marked "deceased." Albert Burgess was a farmer in Robertson Co., TN. He died there on 12 Mar. 1884, and is buried with his wife in the Sory Cemetery. A settlement deed (*Robertson Co. Deed Book #44*, p. 502-503, dated 1 Oct. 1898) lists the heirs surviving at that time: James M. and Mary E. Burgess, Permelia "Amelia" J. Burgess, Lee Anna Burgess, Walter D. Sugg, James B. Sugg, Charles A. and Lucinda Strange, William T. and Drewcilla Burgess. The Sugg brothers held a note against the estate; Leona Unger is not mentioned.

The Children of Albert M. Burgess:

7a. **(Martha) Elizabeth.** Born 14 May 1858 in Robertson Co., TN; died there on 28 Aug. 1861.

7b. **William Thomas (II) "Billie."** Born 10 Sept. 1859 in Robertson Co., TN. Married Mrs. Drusilla Elizabeth "Drue" (Holloway) Kinney on 25 Dec. 1894 (she was born 12 Jan. 1854, daughter of Jack Holloway and Susan Sory, and died on 2 Aug. 1952, aged 98 years). Listed in the 1900 census for Robertson Co., but later moved to Henderson, KY. Billie Burgess was a railroad worker in Kentucky. He died childless on 1 Feb. 1927 at Henderson, but is buried in the Red River Baptist Church (Adams Cemetery), Robertson Co., TN.

7c. **James Marion (II).** Born 25 Jan. 1861 in Robertson Co., TN. See below for full entry.

7d. **Mary S.** Born 28 June 1862 in Robertson Co., TN; died there on 24 June 1863.

7e. **Permelia Jane "Mellie."** Born 9 June 1863 (or 1860, according to her death certificate) in Robertson Co., TN. Married William M. Strange on 27 Feb. 1899 in Robertson Co. (he was born 14 Mar. 1875, and died 15 July 1899); married secondly George Washington Ogg on 28 Sept. 1904 in Robertson Co. Listed with her father in the 1900 census for Robertson Co., TN. Mellie Ogg died childless on 17 June 1930 in Robertson Co., and is buried in the Adams Cemetery.

7f. **Leana "Anna"** (twin) (nmn). Her name is spelled Leanna in her family record. Born 22 Mar. 1865 in Robertson Co., TN. Leana Burgess died unmarried on 10 (or 19) Mar. 1901, and is buried in the Sory Cemetery with her parents.

7g. **Leona (I) "Ona"** (twin) (nmn). Her name is spelled Leonna in her family record. Born 22 Mar. 1865 in Robertson Co., TN. Married James Henry Unger on 19 Mar. 1889 (he was born 4 Feb. 1865, brother of Mary Ellen Unger [who married Leona's brother, James Burgess], and died on 6 Apr. 1930), and had children:

Emmett Morrow UNGER. Born 12 Oct. 1892, married Nina Marable on 16 June 1917, and had children:

Elizabeth Bell UNGER (born 25 Apr. 1918, married Dan Jim Bullard, and had children: Sarah Jean [born 8 May 1944, died June 1944]; Gordon Melvin [born 5 Dec. 1946, married Carolyn Ann Barker on 7 Jan. 1967, and had children: Danny Lee {born 5 Sept. 1967}; Melissa Ann {born 5 Dec. 1978}]; Linda Faye [born 14 June 1948, married Tommy Parchman in July 1966, and had children: Nina Gail {born 10 Dec. 1966}; Linda Beth {born 1 Feb. 1976}; Sarah Margaret {born 15 July 1978}]; Nancy Dianne [born 1 Mar. 1952, married Harvel Dale Martin on 11 June 1966, and had children: Judy Dianne {born 7 Oct. 1967}; Barbara Ann {born 24 Aug. 1969}]; Debra Sue [born 1 July 1959, married Jerry Elliott on 11 Oct. 1980]; *Elizabeth* married secondly Buddy Gray on 28 Aug. 1966).

Virgil Morrow UNGER (born 27 Jan. 1920, married Nellie Frances Hittenhause, and had children: Lawrence Eugene; Nancy [married ___ Green]).

Mable Louise UNGER (born 20 Nov. 1922, married E. W. Warfield in Oct. 1944, and had children: Patricia Louise [born 26 Mar. 1945, married Jerry Wayne Pentecost, and had children: Shari Lynn {born 29 Sept. 1964}]; James Vernon [born 11 Oct. 1946]; Phillip Ray [born 2 Nov. 1949, married Diane Ross, and died 6 May 1970]; Martha Jean [born 4 June 1953, married Robert Lee Stanley on 7 Oct. 1972, and had children: Phillip Scott {born 18 Feb. 1972}]; Charles Michael [born 10 Nov. 1957, married Cindy Rivers on 13 Oct. 1979, and had children: Michael Shane {born 13 May 1982}]; Norma Elaine [born 18 Mar. 1960, married Jerry Wayne Baggett on 29 Nov. 1980]; Paul Christopher [born 30 Oct. 1966]).

James William UNGER (born 13 Jan. 1925, married Maxine Dortch on 10 Dec. 1945, and had children: Donald Wayne [born 15 Nov. 1946, married Linda Jean Marler on 13 Sept. 1968, and had children: Jennifer Lynn {born 6 Aug. 1970}]; James LeRoy [born 2 Nov. 1948, married Myra Elaine Penrod on 3 June 1967, and had children: James Andrew {born 13 Aug. 1969}]; JoAnne [born 7 Nov. 1951, married Burt Lee Fields on 20 July 1967, and had children: Burt Lee II {born 19 Feb. 1969}; Eric William {born 7 June 1970}; Jason Aaron {born 10 Dec. 1974}]).

John Emmitt UNGER (born 22 Apr. 1927).

Charles Raymond UNGER (born 24 Dec. 1929, married Sarah Elizabeth Jones on 4 May 1950 [she remarried Charles E. Claxton], had children: Cathey Elaine [born 3 Aug. 1954, married Brad Guerin on 27 Mar. 1976, and had children: Selina Nicole {born 22 Dec. 1977}]; *Charles* died on 6 Feb. 1954).

Mary Frances UNGER (born 22 Oct. 1931, married James Tilton Smith on 12 Oct. 1948, and had children: James Blonden [born 28 Aug. 1949, married Teresa Eileen Dreden, and had children: Jamie Lynn {born 4 July 1979}]; Donald Ray [born 16 Nov. 1953, married Judy Swill, and had children: Mandy Ray; Ramey Ann]; Ricky Lynn [born 25 July 1955, married Vicky Lynn Beacham]; Jeffrey Lee [born 3 Sept. 1957, married Helen Hooper, and had children: Brenda Lee {born 23 Dec. 1975}]; Charles Tracy [born 7 July 1962, married Jana Musser, and had children: Charles Tracy Jr. {born 12 May 1980}]; Anita Kay [born 26 Aug. 1968]).

Robert Clifton UNGER (born 16 Nov. 1934, married Frances Magglen Atkins on 5 Nov. 1956, and had children: Sandra Jean "Sandy" [born 17 Feb. 1958, married Dannie Gene Wyatt on 21 June 1975, and had children: Daniel Lynn {born 21 Feb. 1976}]; Larry Dale [born 30 Apr. 1959, married Robin Brooks, and had children: Larry Dale Jr. {born 7 Apr. 1977}; Michael {born 14 Jan. 1979}; Jesse Aaron {born Aug. 1982}]; Beverly Sue [born 18 Dec. 1962, married Joseph Fred Hubbs in May 1977, and had children: Robert Gregory {born 5 May 1978}]; Timothy Wayne [born 24 Oct. 1966]; Jeffrey Lynn [born 5 Aug. 1970]). ***Emmett*** married secondly Maggie Hutton. ***Emmett UNGER*** died on 2 Nov. 1972.

Beulah May UNGER. Born 24 Apr. 1894, married Deward Belmont Lemmons on 23 June 1912, and had children:

Dorris Boyd LEMMONS (born 9 Aug. 1913, married Carmie Lucille Lane on 19 June 1939, and had children: Sharon Athene [born 14 Mar. 1941, married Malcolm Felix Pace on 14 Dec. 1958, and had children: Tammie Jo {born 29 Sept. 1959}; Thomas Lloyd {born 2 Oct. 1962}]; Betty Karene [born 19 June 1945, married James Edwin Pace on 1 July 1961, and had children: James Gregory {born 15 May 1962}; Cathy Lynn {born 26 Oct. 1964}; Julie Dawn {born 11 Sept. 1970}; Jamie Gail {born 3 Feb. 1974}]; Barbara Lynn [born 19 Feb. 1954, married Gary Donley in May 1969, and had children: Jeremy Scott {born 17 Sept. 1970}; Brian Keith {born 9 Mar. 1974}; Melissa Lynn {born 23 May 1975}; Tammie Shea {born 6 Nov. 1976}]).

Buford Calvin "Red" LEMMONS (born 18 June 1915, married Frances Dunn, and had children: Frank [born about 1930]; *Red LEMMONS* married secondly Myrtle Carlea "Pete" Turner on 29 Apr. 1941, and had children: Shirley Annette [born 30 Sept. 1941, married James Bobby Worley on 24 Dec. 1960, and had children: Theresa Ann {born 27 Dec. 1963}; Jamie Lynn {born 26 May 1968}; Shirley married secondly Robert Elwood Turner on 24 May 1978]; Buford Calvin Jr. [born 29 June 1943, married Marylynn Gillespie on 28 Sept. 1979]; James David [born 5 May 1946, married Nancy Jean Raye on 31 Dec. 1967, and had children: Michael David {born 18 Sept. 1968}; Christopher Dwayne {born 5 Oct. 1970}; James David married secondly Ewa Maria Szewz on 18 Dec. 1980]).

Belford Lester LEMMONS (born 21 Apr. 1917, married Albie Bryant, and had children: Jeaniece Ann [born 23 June 1937, married Harry Joseph Dumas on 31 Mar. 1955, and had children: Jeaniece Patricia {born 3 July 1956, married Michael Anthony Peppers on 26 Mar. 1977, and had children: Shawn Michael <born 21 Oct. 1977>; Roxanne Lynn <born 28 Feb. 1981>}; Michelle Maria {born 9 July 1958, married Stephen Owen on 11 Sept. 1982}; Collette Renee {born 12 Jan. 1967}]; Donald Wayne [born 4 Oct. 1940, married Nancy Jane Marquis on 6 July 1963, and had children: Heather Ann {born 20 Aug. 1969, uses the surname Vaughn}; Samantha Elizabeth {born 31 Jan. 1976, uses the surname Vaughn}]; *Belford Lester* married secondly Marie Faulkner, and had children: Donald Wayne (II) [born 28 May 1947, married Debbie Lynn Rose in 1966, and died May 1967, having had children: Melissa Ann {born 30 Mar. 1967}]; Joanne [born 9 Jan. 1950, died 15 Dec. 1965]; *Belford Lester* married thirdly Marin Faye Walker, and had children: Frank Luther [born 1958?, married Genevieve Griffin on 26 Aug. 1970, and had children: Genny Donessa {born 11 May 1971}; Anna Marion {born 27 Oct. 1976}]; Brenda Lou [born 16 Sept. 1960, married Donald Lee Francett on 13 Oct. 1979, and had children: Donald Wayne {born 28 Sept. 1980}]; Douglas Belford [born 9 Sept. 1962]).

Joe Frank LEMMONS (born 24 Apr. 1919, married Pauline Priest, and had children: James Lee [born 7 May 1940, married Nancy Elizabeth Haley on 15 July 1971, and had children: James Lee Jr. {born 16 Jan. 1972}; Joe Franklin {born 21 Dec. 1973}]; Betty Jo [born 7 June 1941, married David Elwood Sutter on 16 Aug. 1961, and had children: David Elwood Jr. {born 17 Apr. 1962, married ___ Dickens, daughter of country western star "Little Jimmy" Dickens}; Donna Elaine {born 29 Mar. 1963, married Scott McEwing}; Dianna Elisa {born 3 Feb. 1965, married ___ Ball on 15 Oct. 1988}]; *Joe Frank* married secondly Nelda June Huffman, and had children: Lois June [born 26 Oct. 1948, married Ronnie David Hays on 30 June 1968, and had children: Alex David {born 12 Apr. 1969}; Lawrence Randall {born 7 Nov. 1970}; Bobby Joe {born 26 Nov. 1974}]; Jo Elaine [born 11 Apr. 1950, married Roger Dale Downen on 24 Mar. 1978, and had children: Christopher Brian {born 23 Dec. 1976}; Teresa Marie {born 2 Jan. 1980}; Amanda Fern {born 30 Mar. 1982}]; *Joe Frank* married thirdly Helen Cross).

Beulah LEMMONS died on 9 Mar. 1969.

(Myrtle) Vastie UNGER. Born 29 June 1898, married ___ McMillan, and had children: *Mildred* (married ___ Wheaton). ***Vastie MCMILLAN*** died in 1918 at Guthrie, KY.

(Jimmie) Marie UNGER. Born 18 June 1900, married John Douglas Miles about 1917, and had children:

Elizabeth Lee MILES (born 21 July 1918, married Charles Burnett Sheets, and had children: Gertrude Joyce [born 28 Nov. 1942, married Larry Lynn Starr on 14 Aug. 1957, and had children: Larry Lynn Jr. {born 2 Aug. 1959, married Carol Ann Kondik on 5 Sept. 1981}; John Douglas {born 5 June 1960}; Joyce Leann {born 5 July 1962}]; Linda Lee [born 31 Oct. 1945, married Raymond Clark Yoho, and had children: Karen Elizabeth {born 10 Apr. 1963}; Robin Lynn {born 11 June 1964, married Donald Mark Wharry on 11 June 1982, and had children: Joshua John <born 24 Nov. 1982>}; Linda Lee married secondly Samuel Allen Ward in 1968, and had children: Charles Burnett {born 9 July 1968}; Samuel Allen Jr. {born 2 June 1969}]; Charlene Jo [born 12 Mar. 1949, married Michael Owen Long on 2 Sept. 1966, and had children: Michael Owen Jr. {born 16 Apr. 1967}; Beryl Joseph {born 29 Aug. 1969}; Charlene married secondly Dale Alan Polley on 13 Dec. 1981]; Charles Burnett Jr. [born 28 Mar. 1951, married Pamela Jean Gunn on 4 Nov. 1970, and had children: Charles Willard {born 9 Feb. 1978}; Elizabeth Holly Marie {born 2 Sept. 1979}]).

Johnnie Loraine MILES (born 25 Sept. 1923, married Leroy Everhart in 1939, and had children: Joseph [born 3 Jan. 1940, married, and had two children]; James [born 10 Jan. 1941, and died Sept. 1941]. *Johnnie Loraine* married secondly Joseph Mihalko in 1945, and thirdly Willard Bennett Hooper on 24 Oct. 1955, and had children: Troy Willard [born 6 Oct. 1964]).

Gladys Monita MILES (born 20 June 1926, married Raymond Frederick DeFranco on 21 May 1947, and had children: Ellen Darlene [born 22 Feb. 1949, married Joseph Aperfine, and had children: Charles Raymond {born 1 Sept. 1969}; Monita Marie {born 18 Apr. 1973}; Ellen married secondly Glen Brady]; Raymond Frederick Jr. [born 26 Sept. 1950, married Kathy Debar, and had children: Raymond Frederick III {born 2 Nov. 1969}; Tammy Lynn {born 27 Sept. 1973}; Raymond Jr. married secondly Elida Petrella]; James Douglas [born 10 Nov. 1952]).

Margaret Louise MILES (born 16 Mar. 1928, married Harvey Thomas Cline, and had children: Trudy Ann [born 24 Nov. 1943, married Larry Ray Boyett on 5 July 1962, and had children: Steven Burl {born 8 Jan. 1965}; Penny Lee {born 19 Oct. 1966}; Kristi Lynn {born 4 May 1968}]; Thomas Harvey [born 26 Jan. 1946, married Sharolyn Gayle Kimbrough on 23 May 1969, and had children: Jay Maxwell {born 2 Dec. 1969}; Scott William {born 14 May 1972}]. *Margaret Louise* married secondly Nile Branham on 7 Sept. 1973).

Marie MILES died in May 1971.

Virgie Lou UNGER. Born 6 June 1902, died young in a fire.

Anna Inez UNGER. Born 20 Mar. 1904, married John Konopko about 1923, and had children: *Joseph Frank* (born 4 Jan. 1925, married Evelyn Joan Gilbert on 8 July 1952, and had children: Pamela Ann [born 18 Jan. 1955, married Gary Francis Lawson on 4 Feb. 1978, and had children: Hunter Allan {twin; born 11 June 1981}; Morgan Taylor {twin; born 11 June 1981}]; Michael

Joseph [born 17 Nov. 1957, married Lynn Ann Scribner on 6 Feb. 1982]; Joanna Lynn [born 23 July 1959]). ***Anna KONOPKO*** died on 13 Feb. 1978.

Leona UNGER died on 21 June 1921 in Stewart Co., TN, and is buried in the Lowery (or Jess Nolan) Cemetery, Cumberland City, TN.

7h. **Lucinda (III) "Cindy"** (nmn). Born 14 Oct. (or 4 Sept.) 1866 in Robertson Co., TN. Married Charles A. Strange on 28 Nov. 1895 in Robertson Co. (he was born Feb. 1874, and died 1948), and had children: *(Verda) Blanche* (born 18 Jan. 1899, married Benjamin Ogg [he was born 27 Aug. 1893, and died 15 Oct. 1964], and died childless on 30 July 1960); *Annie C.* (born 1904, married ___ Wilson, and died childless in 1936). Lucinda Strange died on 1 Nov. (or 31 Oct.) 1943 in Franklin Co., TN, and is buried in the Elmwood Cemetery.

JAMES MARION BURGESS OF ROBERTSON CO., TENNESSEE

[Albert Marion[6]]

7c. **James Marion (II) "Jim"** *[son of Albert Marion].* Born 25 Jan. 1861 at Adams, Robertson Co., TN. Married Mary Ellen Unger on 25 Dec. 1884 in Robertson Co. (she was born 24 May 1867, daughter of John Unger Sr., and sister of James Henry Unger [who married James's sister, Leona], and died 30 Oct. 1959 at Detroit, MI, aged 92 years). Listed as a farmer in the tax records for Robertson Co. for 1883-1906, and in the censuses of Robertson Co. for 1900-20. Jim Burgess died on 2 Nov. 1933 (or 3 Nov., according to his death certificate) in Robertson Co., and is buried with his wife in the Red River Baptist Church Cemetery.

8a. **George Lee.** Born 12 Mar. 1886 in Robertson Co., TN; died there on 7 Apr. 1886, and is buried in an unmarked grave in the Sory Cemetery.

8b. **Lou Eddie.** Born 5 Mar. 1888 in Robertson Co., TN; died there on 10 Aug. 1888, and is buried in an unmarked grave in the Sory Cemetery.

8c. **Ernest Ewing "Buddy."** Born 22 June 1889 at Adams, TN. Married Helen Sheets on 21 June 1919 in Robertson Co. (she was born 16 May 1888, and died 7 Apr. 1972). Living with his father in 1920. Listed in the 1918 draft register of Robertson Co., TN. Buddy Burgess was a farmer and banker at Adams, TN. His short genealogy of the Burgess family appears in *Historical Sketches of Adams, Robertson County, Tennessee and Port Royal, Montgomery County, Tennessee, from 1779 to 1968,* by Ralph L. Winters (Clarksville, TN: S. J. Winters, 1968). He died childless on 23 May 1973 in Robertson Co., and is buried in the Red River Baptist Church (or Adams) Cemetery.

8d. **(Willie) Ethel.** Born 2 Aug. 1891 at Adams, TN. Married John Thomas Unger on 10 Dec. 1911 in Robertson Co. (he died 19 Apr. 1974), and had the following children:

(Horace) Lyndal UNGER. Born 7 Aug. 1916, married Frances Eloise Winters on 5 Nov. 1940, and had children: *Carl Randolph* (born 1 Jan. 1942, married Carol Sue Rowe, and had children: Lyndal Allen [born 6 Mar. 1962]; Christopher Eugene [born 9 Nov. 1965]); *John Winters* (born 9 Sept. 1954). Lyndal Unger currently lives at Ocala, FL.

Ruby Lucile UNGER. Born 19 Feb. 1921, died 10 Sept. 1921.

(Mary) Wilma UNGER. Born 23 Sept. 1922, married D. Edward Decker on 4 May 1947, and had children: *David Edward* (born 5 Apr. 1949, married Wendy Knodel on 6 June 1971, and had children: Melissa [born 11 June 1976]; Elizabeth [born 8 July 1978]); *Daniel Scott* (born 6 June 1951, married Irene Ann Siebenga on 30 Aug. 1974, and had children: Katherine Jessica [born 8 Nov. 1979]; Christina Laura [born 31 Aug. 1981]); *Norma Jean* (born 16 Feb. 1954, married Fred Nerio on 22 Aug. 1976, and had children: Rachel Renee [born 4 Aug. 1978]); *James Michael* (born 15 Mar. 1957, married Jerie Lee Chaffin on 5 Aug. 1978, and had children: Jenessa Lynn [born 12 July 1979]; Joshua Moses [born 16 Feb. 1981]).

Ethel UNGER died on 19 May 1972 in Robertson Co., and is buried in the Red River Baptist Church (or Adams) Cemetery.

8e. **(Mattie) Myrtle.** Born 12 Dec. 1896 at Adams, TN. Married Thomas Edward Garrison on 16 Mar. 1919 (he was born 5 June 1893, and died 22 Oct. 1984 at Springfield, TN, buried in the Old Springfield Cemetery), and had children:

Thomas Edward GARRISON Jr. Born 26 Jan. 1920, died 25 Sept. 1920.

James Junior GARRISON. Born 1 May 1921, married Lilla Lee Crabb on 16 Nov. 1940, and had children: *Terry Lee* (born 30 Apr. 1941, married Barbara ___, and had children: Michael [born 25 Nov. 1963]; Lori [born 20 Oct. 1964]; Bernie [born 5 Dec. 1965]; Cheryl [born 2 Dec. 1968]). ***James GARRISON*** secondly Rosemary Laramie, and died on 31 May 1991 at Belleville, MI.

Myrtle Allene GARRISON. Born 11 May 1924, married Landis Randall Hallman on 17 Apr. 1941, and had children: *Linda Ruth* (born 20 May 1943, married T. J. Lloyd, and secondly

William Percy "Pete" Cook on 5 July 1974, and had children: James Matthew [born 30 Nov. 1981]); *Landis Randall Jr.* (born 11 Aug. 1946, married Peggy Nickson, and had children: Janice Louise [born 28 July 1965]; Darren Dewayne [born 30 July 1966]; Tammy Lynn [born 15 July 1967, married]; Randy Gene [born 8 Oct. 1969]; *Landis* married secondly Jeannie (Webb) Nelson, and had children: Randall Bryant [born 25 Aug. 1978]; *Landis* married thirdly Sandra Brady); *Larry Edward* (born 8 June 1949, married Cindy ___, secondly Brenda (King) Spain, and thirdly Paula ___); *Betty Joyce* (born 2 Oct. 1953, married Jerry Atler, and had children: Cora Nicole [born 14 Sept. 1977]); *James David* (born 21 Feb. 1956, married Joyce Ann Hobgood, and had children: James Randall [born 13 Feb. 1974]; Thomas Edward [born 9 Dec. 1975]; Steven Curtis [born 27 Oct. 1978]); *Mary Myrtle* (born Apr. 1958, married Charles Smith on 17 Jan. 1977, and had children: Lisa Marie [born 15 Feb. 1981]); *Patricia Darlene* (born 26 Mar. 1959, married James McQuiston, and had children: Jason Claude [born 9 Sept. 1978]). Myrtle Hallman lives at Springfield, TN.

Elmer Ryce "E. R." GARRISON. Born 29 Oct. 1927, married Nancy Lee Hooks on 28 June 1952, and had children: *Pamela Lee* (born 23 July 1953, married Benjy White in 1972, and had children: Ginger Lee [born 26 May 1972]); *Tommy Calvin* (born 28 Mar. 1956, married Eva ___); *Nancy Lou* (born 21 May 1958, married Terry Toms in June 1979). *E. R.* married secondly Betty Lou Snoddy on 18 Apr. 1963, and had children: *Betty Renee* (born 18 Apr. 1963); *Mary Catherine* (born 21 June 1968). ***E. R. GARRISON*** currently lives at Charlotte, NC.

Jewell Mervin GARRISON. Born 22 July 1930, married Lois Elizabeth Timmons on 28 Oct. 1950, and had children: *Andrew Jewell* (born 19 July 1956, married Debbie ___, and had children: Michael Andrew [born 23 Feb. 1975]); *Kenneth Douglas* (born 20 Aug. 1959); *Mitchell Louis* (born 15 May 1963); *Julie Beth* (born 28 Oct. 1966). ***Jewell GARRISON*** currently lives at Charlotte, NC.

(Dorothy) Geraldine GARRISON. Born 12 Dec. 1936, married Bruce Thomas Smith in 1955, and had children: *Cindy Lynn* (born and died 13 Apr. 1958); *Dorothy Bruce* (born and died 17 Oct. 1961). ***Geraldine*** married secondly Gathron Austin Weakley on 8 June 1962 (by his first marriage, he had children: *Jerry Michael* [born 26 Feb. 1952]; *Teresa Fay* [born 24 Nov. 1954]). ***Geraldine WEAKLEY*** lives at Ashland City, TN.

Myrtle GARRISON contributed immeasurably to this book through her personal memories and preserved records. She lived in later years at Ashland City, TN, but died on 4 Nov. 1992 at Springfield, TN, aged 95 years. She is buried in the Elmwood Cemetery.

8f. **(Bettie) Lorena.** Born 26 Aug. 1899 at Adams, TN. Married (Jack) Comer Gardner on 29 May 1923. Lorena Gardner died on 22 June 1984 at Detroit, MI.

8g. **Roy Hawkins.** Born 6 Sept. 1901 at Adams, TN. Married Jean "Jennie" Williams in Aug. 1935. Living with his father in 1920. Roy Burgess was a truck driver at Detroit, MI. He moved back to Springfield in 1981. He died there childless a few months later, on 8 Oct. 1981, but was returned for burial to Detroit.

[William (I)[1], Edward (I)[2], Moses (I)[3], John Price Buckner (I)[4]]

JAMES BOLING BURGESS
(1810?-1848?)

OF LOGAN COUNTY, KENTUCKY

5e. **(James) Boling (I)** *[son of John Price Buckner (I)].* Born about 1810 in Prince Edward Co., VA. Married (as "Boling J. Burgess") Rachel C. Terry on 30 Jan. 1840 in Robertson Co., TN (she was born 1811/14 in KY, the daughter of William and Elizabeth Terry). He witnessed the debt between John P. Burgess Sr. and Jr. on 23 Apr. 1830, signing himself "Boling J. Burgess." Listed with his father in the 1830 census, in the 1833 personal property tax list of Halifax Co., VA, in the 1839 tax list for Logan Co., KY, and in the 1840 census for Robertson Co. Boling Burgess apparently died in Logan Co., KY about 1848; his widow is listed there with her parents in the 1850 census, as head of her family in 1860, and in the 1870 census for Nashville, Davidson Co., TN. Rachel Burgess is also listed intermittently in the 1871-96 city directories of Nashville, but has not been found in Nashville's death index. She apparently died there between 1896-1900 (she has not been found in the 1900 Soundex).

The Children of Boling Burgess:

6a. **Paul W(illiamson?).** Born Dec. 1840 in Logan Co., KY. See below for full entry.
6b. **Lucy (III) "Lula."** Born about 1843 in Logan Co., KY. Listed with her mother in 1860-70, working as a school teacher, but has not been found in 1900.
6c. **(Anna) Emily.** Born about 1845 in Logan Co., KY. Listed with her mother in the 1860 census. Married Robert A. Carbon on 8 Oct. 1863 in Logan Co., KY. She does *not* appear to be the Black woman, Emily Carbin (aged 37 years), who is listed in the 1870 census for Muhlenberg Co., KY.
6d. **Sarah (X).** Born about 1848 in Logan Co., KY. Listed with her mother in the 1860-70 censuses, working as a dressmaker. However, she does *not* appear to be the Black woman, Sarah Burgess (aged 50 years), who is living at Nashville, TN in 1900.

[William (I)[1], Edward (I)[2], Moses (I)[3], John Price Buckner (I)[4], James Boling (I)[5]]

PAUL W. BURGESS
(1840-1920+)

OF SUMTER COUNTY, SOUTH CAROLINA

6a. **Paul W(illiamson?)** *[son of James Boling].* Born Dec. 1840 in Logan Co., KY. Married Mary J. W___ about 1866 (she was born Nov. 1840 in SC, and died between 1910-20). Served in Co. G, 9th Kentucky Mounted Infantry, Confederate Army, during the Civil War; he was captured at Whippoorwill Bridge in Nov. 1861, imprisoned for two years, exchanged, re-entered active service, and was wounded at the Battle of Chickamauga in Sept. 1863. After the War, Paul Burgess farmed in Sumter Co., SC, where he is listed in the 1870-1910 censuses for Rafting Creek Township (four of four children survive in 1900 and 1910), and in the 1920 census for Kershaw Co., SC living with his son-in-law, Wesley Hendrix. Paul Burgess was a miller and farmer in South Carolina. He died there after 1920.

The Children of Paul Burgess:

7a. **James B(oling?) (II)**. Born Sept. 1866 in South Carolina. See below for full entry.
7b. **Sarah A. G.** Born about 1869 in Sumter Co., SC. Married by 1900. By inference she is married and living in 1910.
7c. **Ida D.** Her name is given as Irine in the 1880 census. Born July 1872 (or 1875) in Sumter Co., SC (although the census taker gave her birthdate as July 1885 in 1900, he listed her before her sister Celia, and gave her age as 24). Married Wesley Hendrix about 1905 (he was born 1863 in SC, and worked as a manager), and had children: *Birdie* (born 1906 in SC). Listed with her father in the 1900 census, and in 1910-20 in DeKalb Township, Kershaw Co., SC.
7d. **Celia D.** Her name is spelled Sealia in the 1880 census. Born June 1874 (or 1879) in Sumter Co., SC. Listed with her father in the 1900 census, but is married and living elsewhere by 1910.

JAMES BURGESS OF KERSHAW CO., SOUTH CAROLINA
[Paul Williamson[6]]

7a. **James B(oling?) (II)** *[son of Paul Williamson].* Born Sept. 1866 in South Carolina. Married Clara ___ about 1890 (she was born Dec. 1869 in SC). Listed in the 1870-80 censuses with his father; he may be living in 1900 in Providence Township, Sumter Co., SC, and in 1910 in Kershaw Co., SC. One of one children are living in 1900, two of five in 1910. The relationship of the James Burgess listed in the 1900-10 censuses to his earlier counterpart has not been confirmed; the later James does not use a middle initial, and states in both censuses (1900-10) that his father was born in SC. Has not been found in 1920. James Burgess was a farm laborer in South Carolina.

8a. **Theresa (I).** Born Sept. 1889 in Sumter Co., SC.
8b. **Clara M. (II)**. Born Aug. 1909 in Kershaw Co., SC.

[William (I)[1], Edward (I)[2], Moses (I)[3]]

MAJ. EDWARD BURGESS
(1767-1847?)
OF KANAWHA COUNTY, (WEST) VIRGINIA

4c. **Edward (IV)** *[son of Moses (I)].* He is called Edmund in his sister Sarah's bond record; this may have been a nickname used to distinguish him from his many cousins named Edward. Born 2 Apr. 1767 in King George Co., VA (*St. Paul's Parish Register*). Married Jane (Anderson) Sims about 1804, probably in Hanover Co., VA (she was born before 1765, daughter of Henry and Elizabeth (?) Anderson, and died on 4 Mar. 1843 in Kanawha Co., WV; she married firstly John A. Sims about 1791 [he drowned about 1792], and had a daughter: *Patsy* [she was born posthumously in Apr. 1793; her guardian, Hudson Martin Jr. of Nelson County, sued Edward Burgess in 1809 {see *Augusta Co., VA Judgments*, O.S. 192/N.S. 68, 1809, and the later lawsuit mentioned below}; Patsy died by 1844]). Listed in the Orange Co., VA tax lists from 1790-99. Edward was living at Luray, Page Co., VA in 1805 when his daughter was born. He may be the Edward Burgess mentioned in the *Statutes at Large of Virginia* (1835, Volume III, p. 196) as a convict in the Virginia State Penitentiary from 1800-1804 (he has not been found during this period). He is called "Major" in his wife's obituary, but his war service (if any) is unknown.

Edward Burgess moved his family to Kanawha Co. by 2 Sept. 1806, when he is mentioned in an Orange Co. deed as being of Kanawha Co. He bought 286 acres on the north side of the Elk River in Kanawha Co., VA (later WV) on 10 Feb. 1807 (*Kanawha Co. Deed Book #C*, p. 113-114), where he operated a salt furnace for several years between 1810-13 (see *Edward Burgess and William Nickle vs. John Welch and Joseph Cobb* [*Kanawha Co. Court Case #1812-5*, plus related suits filed in 1814, 1822, and 1825], and *The Antebellum Kanawha Salt Business and Western Markets*, by John E. Stealey III [Lexington: University Press of Kentucky, 1993, p. 17-18 and 204]). Edward built his home near Moore's Dam, three and a half miles above Charleston, and is listed on the tax lists of Kanawha Co. from 1807-45. Two deeds recorded in Orange Co., VA confirm that Edward Burgess son of Moses Burgess moved to Kanawha Co. (see particularly *Orange Co. Deed Book #24*, p. 185-186, dated 2 Sept. 1806, in which Edward Burgess of Kanawha Co. sold "the Negro man James he purchased of his father's estate"; and *Deed Book #26*, p. 302-303, dated 22 Apr. 1815, witnessed by William Almond, Burgis Faulconer, Nancy Burgess, Thomas Colemand, and John Chevis, in which Edward Burgess of Kanawha Co. sold "a tract of land belonging to the estate of the late Moses Burgess" and relinquished "all claims he may have in said estate" to his cousin, Samuel Faulconer of Spotsylvania Co., VA). Has not been found in the 1810 census for Kanawha Co., but is listed in the 1820-40 censuses there, with two young sons and a daughter (in 1820 with two other grown men aged 26-45). He was an executor for his father's estate, but resigned when he left Orange Co.; Samuel Faulconer, a cousin of Samuel Faulconer, his brother-in-law, was appointed in his place. He is mentioned in his father's final estate accounting of 1832. He mortgaged his land on 16 Aug. 1844 (*Deed Book #N*, p. 598) to pay the debts he owed his two sons, and sold the farm on 24 Mar. 1845 to Sara Walker (*Deed Book #O*, p. 106).

The alignment of the Kanawha Co., WV Burgess families is a difficult problem, exacerbated by the lack of any probate records for Edward Burgess. The John M(eredith) Burgess who appeared there in 1811, married Judith Cobb(s), and had sons Fleming Cobb, Thomas C., and George Washington Burgess, was born, according to an oral tradition among his descendants, in Beaverdam, Hanover Co., VA (but there is also a Beaverdam Creek in Orange Co.). A Thomas Burgess is listed in the tax records of Hanover Co. in 1790-91, at about the time of John M.'s presumed birth, and may be his father. A close examination of existing evidence has not found any evidence that the John M. and Edward lines share a common heritage.

Garland A. Burgess is known to be a son of Edward Burgess; deeds and legal records tie these two men to John A. Burgess. All three men left the county simultaneously in 1845, moving to the same county in Missouri. Similarly, deeds and legal records tie together Thomas C., Fleming C., and Washington Burgess. No other correlations can be established between individuals in the two respective groupings. In an extensive lawsuit filed in Kanawha Co. in 1844 (*Hudson Martin, Guardian of Patsey Sims De-*

ceased vs. Edward Burgess et al., Kanawha Co. Court Case #1844-20, concerning a disputed purchase of several Negroes, Milly and Watsy), Garland A. Burgess responded in Edward's name, being specifically mentioned as his son, and stated that Edward had moved to Missouri "in the month of October 1845," and that his mother had died "on the 4th of March 1842" (actually 1843; see the obituary below); it is clear that Edward was still living in Nov. 1846 when the suit was finally dropped. Edward apparently died in Johnson Co., MO between 1847-50, since he has not been found in the 1850 census for MO or WV.

The Children of Edward Burgess:

5a. **Elizabeth Anderson.** She was evidently named for her mother's aunt, Elizabeth "Betsey" Anderson. Born 13 Nov. 1805 at Luray, Page Co., VA. Married Joseph Chancelor Kendall on 10 Dec. 1823 at Kandalia, Kanawha Co., VA (later WV) (he was born 9 Feb. 1798 in King George Co., VA, son of James Kendel and Rebecca Wroe [or Rowe], and died on 27 June 1865 at Kandalia, WV). Listed in the 1850 census for Kanawha Co., VA (later WV), and in 1860 living with her daughter, Biddy Clay. Elizabeth and Joseph had children:

Rebecca Jane KENDALL. Born 7 Nov. 1824 at Sanderson, Kanawha Co., VA (later WV). Married George Washington Hill on 27 Nov. 1848 in Kanawha Co. (he was the son of Moses Manning Hill and Felicity Boone Vanbibber, and brother of Margaret R. Hill [who married Rebecca's brother, James Edward]). Rebecca Hill died on 1 Mar. 1909 at Kandalia, WV.

James Edward KENDALL. Born 28 Feb. 1828 at Elk Creek, Kanawha Co., VA (later WV). Listed with his parents, wife, and son in the 1850 census working as a millwright. Married Margaret R. Hill (she was born 26 Jan. 1825 in Nicholas Co., VA [later WV], daughter of Moses Manning Hill and Felicity Boone Vanbibber, and sister of George Washington Hill [who married James's sister, Rebecca], and died about 1855 at Kandalia), and had children: *Ernest Augustus* (born Mar. 1850); *Elizabeth Josephine* (born 15 June 1852 in Kanawha Co., married Joel Preston Connor on 18 July 1867 in Kanawha Co. [he was born 20 Oct. 1847 in Kanawha Co., son of Preston Connor and Rachel Kendall, and died on 28 Aug. 1903 in Kanawha Co.], and died on 31 Mar. 1893 in Kanawha Co., having had children: Minnie Ellen [born 18 Apr. 1869 in Kanawha Co., married Henry Oscar Wyatt on 24 Dec. 1893 in Kanawha Co., and died 4 Dec. 1907 in Kanawha Co.]; Stella Ann [born 1 Mar. 1872 in Kanawha Co., married Henry Lafayette Graves in 1896, and died on 15 Oct. 1956 at Charleston, WV]; Hallie Kendall [born 6 Dec. 1874 in Kanawha Co., died 17 Aug. 1892]; Mahala [born 20 Mar. 1875 in Kanawha Co., died young]; Ernest Virginius [born 5 Feb. 1877 at Mink Shoal, WV, married Carrie Lovelia James on 21 June 1903 at Big Otter, Clay Co., WV, and died 25 July 1961 in Kanawha Co.]; Howard George [born 10 Jan. 1880 in Kanawha Co., married Minnie Willard on 4 July 1904 in Kanawha Co., and died 28 June 1961 in Kanawha Co.]; Joseph E. [born Feb. 1881, died young]; Hubert Edward [born 5 Dec. 1882 in Kanawha Co., married Ida Page on 20 Oct. 1907 in Kanawha Co., and died 7 Aug. 1967 at Charleston, WV]; Noble Floyd [born 12 Aug. 1885 in Kanawha Co., married Lena Louise Edwards on 6 Oct. 1908 at Charleston, WV {she was born 30 Apr. 1886 in Putnam Co., WV, daughter of Squire Riggs Edwards and Elizabeth Shoal, and died 14 Dec. 1959 at Charleston, WV, buried Connor Cemetery}, and died 4 Aug. 1961 at Charleston]; Bessie Rachel [born 6 Sept. 1888 in Kanawha Co., married Harper Glenn, and died 11 June 1911 in Kanawha Co.]; Frank Eugene [born 2 Nov. 1891 in Kanawha Co., married Blodwin M. Pugh, and died 3 June 1956 at Morgantown, WV]).

Noble and Lena CONNOR had children: Bernard Granvel (born 14 July 1909 at Charleston, WV, married Leona Estell Arbogast on 28 Feb. 1937 at Charleston, and died 13 Feb. 1992 at Columbus, OH); Harold Fredrick (born 25 Dec. 1911 at Charleston, and died 15 Nov. 1912); Joel Edwards (born 16 Dec. 1913 at Charleston, WV, married Frances Margarite Bacon on 21 Feb. 1935 at Charleston, and died there on 26 Apr. 1989); Eugene Westfall (born 10 Mar. 1916 at Charleston, WV, married Ann Lee Teets on 7 Mar. 1941 at Beckley, WV); Mary Louise (born 8 July 1918 at Charleston, WV); Mildred Elizabeth (born 13 Apr. 1920 at Charleston, WV, married Maxwell Earlington Anderson on 7 June 1946 at Charleston); Noble Floyd Jr. (born 23 Oct. 1924 at Charleston, WV, married Margaret Barry on 28 Aug. 1948 at Charleston [she was born 13 Apr. 1927 at Charleston, daughter of David Barry Jr. and Margaret Rachel Wilson], and had children: Donna Celeste [born 21 June 1951 at Charleston, married Paul Edward Webb on 15 May 1973 at Marmet, WV]; Mary Emily [born 6 Apr. 1954 at Charleston, married Charles William Gerwig on 8 Sept. 1984 at Charleston]; Barry Noble [born 18 Aug. 1959 at South Charleston, married Delia Louise Finks on 20 June 1981 at Charleston]).

James Edward KENDALL married secondly Elmira C. Guthrie on 1 July 1858 in Kanawha Co. (she was born 31 Dec. 1835), and had children: *Frederick Amos* (born 12 May 1859 at Blue Creek, Kanawha Co., married Minnie Price, and died 5 May 1950 in Kanawha Co., aged 90 years); *James Floyd* (born 1862 at Blue Creek); *Albert E.* (born 1865 at Blue Creek); *Madora J.* (born 1868 at Blue Creek); *Junius E.* (born 29 June 1870 at Blue Creek); *Francis J. "Frank"* (born 1872 at Blue Creek); *Almira E.*

(born 1876 at Blue Creek). Listed in the 1880 census for Kanawha Co. James E. Kendall died on 23 July 1914 in King George Co., VA, and is buried there on Poplar Farm.

***Biddy Ann Chancelor* KENDALL**. Born about 1832 in Kanawha Co., VA (later WV). Married Burwell W. Clay on 19 Aug. 1852 in Kanawha Co., and had children: *Rhoda E.* (born 1853); *Burwell W. Jr.* (born 1857). Listed as head of the family in the 1860 census for Kanawha Co., VA (later WV).

Elizabeth *Anderson* KENDALL died on 23 Jan. 1879 (Kanawha death records) or 21 Jan. 1880 (according to her tombstone) at Kandalia, Kanawha Co., WV. The Kanawha Co. death certificate gives both of her parents' full names, and her place of birth. Noble Connor Jr. has contributed greatly to this book.

5b. **Garland A(nderson?).** Born 22 Aug. 1807 in Kanawha Co., VA (later WV). See below for full entry.
5c. **John A(nderson?) (I).** Born about 1811 in Kanawha Co., VA (later WV). See below for full entry.

THE OBITUARY OF JANE ANDERSON BURGESS

(*Kanawha Republican*, Mar. 11, 1843)

"Died at her residence in Kanawha County, 3 miles from Charleston, on Saturday the 4th, inst., Mrs. Jane Burgess, wife of Maj. Edward Burgess, in the 78th year of her age. This worthy matron had experienced a large share of infirmity for several years, but the disease which brought her thus maturely to her grave was a paralytic stroke, accompanied by apoplexy, which speedily terminated her life. Mrs. B. was born in Hanover County, Virginia, and in early life became a respectable member of the Methodist Episcopal Church. She emigrated to Kanawha in the year 1806, where she has resided ever since. Shortly after her location in Kanawha, she rejoined the Methodist Church, when Methodism was first introduced in this valley, and ever after lived as she died, a worthy member of the same. She was a loving wife, a tender and affectionate mother, a kind mistress, and a charitable neighbor."

Rebecca Emiline Rogers Burgess (1866-1945)
[see page 129]

[William (I)[1], Edward (I)[2], Moses (I)[3], Edward (IV)[4]]

REV. GARLAND A. BURGESS
(1807-1861)
OF JOHNSON COUNTY, MISSOURI

5b. **Garland A(nderson?)** *[son of Edward (IV)].* He may have been named for Garland Anderson of Davie Co., NC, or for his mother's family. Born 22 Aug. 1807 in Kanawha Co., VA (later WV). Married Henrietta H. McCown on 30 Aug. 1831 in Kanawha Co. (she was born 4 Jan. 1814 in Kanawha Co., VA [later WV], daughter of Mathew McCown and Mary Magdalean Bowyer, and sister of Col. James Madison McCown [who married Caroline Francis Burgess], and died on 16 Feb. 1879 in Johnson Co., MO). Listed in the Kanawha Co. tax records from 1830-31 and again from 1839-45, with his father in the 1830-40 censuses, and in the 1850-60 censuses for Post Oak Township, Johnson Co., MO (William McCown, age 13, is living with them in 1860); his widow appears there in 1870 in Madison Township. Mentioned as a son of Edward Burgess in a lawsuit filed against his father in Kanawha Co. in 1844 (*Kanawha Co. Court Case #1844-20*), and moved within a year to Post Oaks Township, Johnson Co., MO. There he bought several tracts of land with his brother, John, one in the southeast quarter of Section 15 (*Johnson Co. Deed Book #G*, p. 198, dated 1 Apr. 1846), with the exception of two acres of land conveyed to the trustees of the Post Oaks Church for church grounds and cemetery.

Rev. Garland A. Burgess was ordained in Oct. 1837 as a minister for the Methodist Episcopal Church South. He died on 22 Sept. 1861 in Johnson Co., aged fifty-four years, one month (his will was probated on 12 Apr. 1866 [*Will Book #J*, p. 337]); he and his wife are buried in the Old Smyrna (or Post Oak) Cemetery, Centerview Township, near where his church stood (it burned on the night of 22/23 Mar. 1862, at the same time his brother's house was torched by Union troops), and which now is completely overgrown. Henrietta Burgess was cofounder (with Simon Taylor and others) of the Fairview, MO Methodist Episcopal Church in 1867. Her will was probated on 22 Feb. 1879 (*Will Book #V*, p. 93).

The Children of Rev. Garland A. Burgess:

6a. **Francis Marion (I).** Born 9 Sept. 1832 in Kanawha Co., VA (later WV). See below for full entry.

6b. **Mary Jane (II).** She was named for her two grandmothers. Born Jan. 1835 in Kanawha Co., VA (later WV). Married David W. Ripley on 5 Feb. 1856 in Johnson Co., MO (he was born 1834 in TN, son of William and Martha Ripley, and died about 1880 in MO), and had at least the following children: *Frances J.* (born about 1857 in MO); *Angeletta L.* (born about 1859 in MO, married ___ Teator); *William David* (born about 1863); *Virginia L.* (born about 1867, married Sylvestor Rayburn); *Hattie M.* (born about 1869); *Minnie Etta* (born about 1871 in MO, married Edward Dodd [he was born about 1876 in Canada]); *Charles D.* (born about 1877). Listed in the 1860 census for Post Oak Township, Johnson Co., in the 1885 Territorial census for Columbia Co., WA, in 1900 in Seattle, King Co., WA living with her daughter, Angeletta, and in 1920 at Denver, Arapahoe Co., CO with her son-in-law, Edward Dodd. Listed in the 1904-20 city directories of Denver, CO. Mary Ripley apparently died at Denver about 1920.

6c. **(William) McCown "Mack."** He was named for William McCown, a cousin of his mother's family. Born 6 Jan. 1838 in Kanawha Co., VA (later WV). Listed with his father in the 1860 census. Witnessed the will of his grandmother, Mary McCown, on 24 Mar. 1860 in Johnson Co, MO. Mack Burgess enlisted as a Private in Capt. William C. Quantrill's Co., Missouri Cavalry Scouts (Quantrill's Guerrillas), operating behind Union lines. After he returned to Johnson Co., he was ambushed and killed, evidently in retaliation for his war service, dying unmarried on 2 Oct. 1865, and was buried with his parents in the Old Smyrna (or Post Oak) Cemetery.

6d. **Harriet Elizabeth.** She was named for her mother's sister Harriet and father's sister Elizabeth. Born 21 Apr. 1839 in Kanawha Co., VA (later WV). Married as his second wife Simon Taylor on 31 Aug. 1854 in Johnson Co., MO (he was born 20 Dec. 1825 at Grape Island, Tyler Co., VA [later WV], and married firstly Martha Austen on 13 July 1848, by whom he had children: *Laura J.* [born 1849]; listed in the

1850 census for Wilson Hollow, Johnson Co., and died 18 July 1899 at Waitsburg, WA), and had at least the following children:

Henrietta Burgess TAYLOR. Born about 1855 in Johnson Co., MO, married Francis "Frank" Wooldridge (or Woldridge), and died before 1911.

Eliza E. TAYLOR. Born 18 Nov. 1858 in Johnson Co., MO, died there on 19 Oct. 1859, buried Old Smyrna Cemetery.

Charles McCown TAYLOR. Born 10 Jan. 1859 in Johnson Co., MO, married Nannie E. White on 4 Feb. 1880 in Johnson Co. (she was born 1858), and had children: *Lula* (born Feb. 1880); *Estella* (born 1883). *Charles M. TAYLOR* died in 1923, and is buried in the Waitsburg Cemetery.

William McCown "Mack" TAYLOR. Born 31 Jan. 1861 in Johnson Co., MO, married Flora R. Kinyoun on 18 Sept. 1889 at Columbia, WA (she was born 1868), and had children: *Harriet Elizabeth* (born 1891); *Laura E.* (born 1894). *Mack TAYLOR* married secondly Lillian A. Devall (she was born 1867), and had children: *Florence G.* (born 1900). *Mack TAYLOR* died in 1944, and is buried in the Waitsburg Cemetery.

John F. TAYLOR. Born 7 Sept. 1863 in Johnson Co., MO. *John TAYLOR* died on 8 Dec. 1904 at Waitsburg, WA, apparently unmarried, and is buried in the Waitsburg Cemetery.

Garland Burgess TAYLOR. Born 30 June 1866 in Johnson Co., MO, married Anna M. Fuller in 1895 (she was born 1869), and had children: *Joseph G.*; *Ben F.*; *Garland E.*; *Henrietta*. *Garland B. TAYLOR* died in 1903 [or 1923], and is buried in the Waitsburg Cemetery.

(James) Walter TAYLOR. Born 20 Jan. 1873 in Johnson Co., MO, married Bonnie A. Brockman on 7 Oct. 1896 in WA (she was born 1875), and had children: *Herman W.* (born 1898); *Helen U.* (born 1899); *Charles Floyd* (born 1906). *Walter TAYLOR* died in 1932, and is buried in the Waitsburg Cemetery.

The TAYLORS are listed in the 1860 census for Post Oak Township, Johnson Co., MO. They settled in 1880 at Waitsburg, Walla Walla Co., WA, coming west to San Francisco by rail, then by boat to the Walla Walla area (according to Henrietta's obituary). Listed in the 1880 census for Walla Walla Co., WA, possibly in the 1887 state census for Walla Walla Co., WA (the record is very faint), and in the 1910 census for Waitsburg, Walla Walla Co., WA. **Henrietta TAYLOR** died on 9 Aug. 1911 at Waitsburg, WA, and is buried with her husband and her sons in the Waitsburg Cemetery.

6e. **Julia A.** Born 20 Feb. 1842 in Kanawha Co., VA (later WV); died on 20 Nov. 1845 in Johnson Co., MO, and is buried with her parents.

[William (I)[1], Edward (I)[2], Moses (I)[3], Edward (IV)[4], Garland A.[5]]

FRANK M. BURGESS
(1832-1920)

OF WALLA WALLA COUNTY, WASHINGTON

6a. **Francis Marion (I) "Frank"** *[son of Garland Anderson].* Born 9 Sept. 1832 in Kanawha Co., VA (later WV). Married Nancy E. Jackson on 12 Oct. 1854 in Johnson Co., MO (she was born 9 Jan. 1833 in MO, and died on 11 July 1882 in Bates Co., MO, buried in the Rogers Cemetery); married secondly Nancy Catherine "Nannie" Lotspeich on 20 Nov. 1883 in Henry Co., MO (she was born 24 Dec. 1848 in Henry Co., MO, and died on 19 June 1914 at Waitsburg, WA). Listed in the 1860 census for Post Oak Township, Johnson Co., MO, in 1870 in Madison Township, and in 1880 in Centre View Township. He moved his family in 1890 to Waitsburg, Walla Walla Co., WA, and is listed there in the 1900-20 censuses. Frank Burgess was a farmer at Waitsburg, WA. He died there on 8 Apr. 1920, and is buried with his second wife in the Waitsburg Cemetery. His obituary mentions his three surviving children.

FRANCIS M. BURGESS LAID TO REST

"Francis Marion Burgess, who died at his home in this city last Thursday morning, April 8th, was buried Friday afternoon at 2:30 o'clock. The funeral was held at the Methodist church, Rev. J. E. Garver officiating. Francis Burgess was born in Kenowka county [sic], West Virginia, Sept. 6, 1832, and was therefore 87 years old at the time of his death. He moved to Missouri with his parents in 1845 and in 1854 was married to Nancy E. Jackson. Of this union three children were born, Henry, Roland [sic] and Emma. This wife died and in 1883 he married Nancy Lotspeach. They moved to Waitsburg in 1890, Mrs. Burgess dying here in 1914, which left Mr. Burgess alone. His daughter, Mrs. Emma Kelly, was with him at the time of his death."—*Waitsburg Times*, 16 Apr. 1920.

The Children of Frank Burgess:

7a. **(Henry) Bascomb.** Born July 1855 in Johnson Co., MO. See below for full entry.

7b. **Garland N.** Born about 1858 in Johnson Co., MO. See below for full entry.

7c. **Emma E. (I).** Born 30 Nov. 1868 in Johnson Co., MO. Married John DeWitt Kelley on 8 Nov. 1887 in Bates Co., MO (he was born 17 Nov. 1820, and died 17 May 1909), and had children: *Ida* (married ___ Kirby, and lived at Ozark, MO); *Sallie* (married ___ Hathaway, and lived at Chicago). The Kelleys moved in 1890 to Waitsburg, Walla Walla Co., WA with the Taylors and Burgesses; Emma is listed in the 1920 census living with her father, but has not been found in 1900. Emma Kelley died on 1 Oct. 1960 at Walla Walla, WA, aged 91 years, and is buried with her husband in the Waitsburg Cemetery.

7d. **A.** [full name and sex unknown]. Born about 1890 in Waitsburg, WA, and died there before 1900. A small field stone ("A.B.") set next to its mother's grave is the only surviving memorial to this infant.

During the Civil War, "A detail of Foster's men surrounded a house where John Brinker and Frank Burgess were, a short distance south of Warrensburg. Brinker and Burgess made a sudden dash, killed and wounded two of [Major Emory] Foster's men, and escaped. Foster's men burned the house, and killed the owner for harboring Brinker and Burgess."—*The History of Johnson County, Missouri*, by Ewing Cockrell (Topeka, KS: Historical Publishing Co., 1918).

BASCOMB BURGESS OF BATES CO., MISSOURI
[Francis Marion (I)[6]]

7a. **(Henry) Bascomb** *[son of Francis Marion (I)].* Born July 1855 (or 1856) in Johnson Co., MO. Married Melvina Curtney on 6 July 1879 in Johnson Co. (div.?; she was born 1857 in NC); married secondly Martha C. Fitzgerald on 17 Oct. 1886 in Bates Co., MO (she was born June 1860 in MO). Listed in the 1880 census for Centre View Township, Johnson Co., MO, and in the 1900-10 censuses for Bates Co., MO (five of seven children survive in 1900). Bascomb Burgess was a farmer near Rich Hill, MO. He died there on 31 (or 15) Dec. 1936, and is buried in the Greenlawn Cemetery.

8a. **Samuel (II).** Born Apr. 1880 in Johnson Co., MO. Has not been found in the 1900 census.

8b. **Francis Marion (III) "Frank."** Born 5 Apr. 1883 in MO. Married (Mary) Melvina "Vina" ___ about 1914 (she was born about 1898 in MO). Listed in the 1900 census for Cass Co., MO working as a farmhand for Theodore Gundrum, possibly in 1910 at Charleston, Mississippi Co., MO, in 1920 in Bates Co., MO (age 36), and in the 1917 draft list for Bates Co., MO, with his next of kin being given as Mary Melvina Burgess. He died on 23 Sept. 1922 in Bates Co., and is buried in the Greenlawn Cemetery. Relationship not verified.

9a. **Alice M. (IV).** Born about 1915 in Bates Co., MO. She is the only child listed with her parents in 1920.

9b. **Maude Irene.** Born 9 Dec. 1917 in Bates Co., MO; died there on 14 Jan. 1918, and is buried in the Greenlawn Cemetery.

9c. **Frances Marion.** Born 10 Jan. 1919 in Bates Co., MO; died there on 13 Feb. 1919, and is buried in the Greenlawn Cemetery.

8c. **Laura B.** Born Aug. 1887 in MO.

8d. **Wesley Gray.** Born May 1891 in MO. See below for full entry.

8e. **Lavina A.** (variously Levina). Born Mar. 1893 in MO. Living with George Fitzgerald (her uncle) in 1900-10. Married Elmer H. Randall on 10 Apr. 1912 in Bates Co., MO (he was born 1884, and died 1955, buried Pleasant Grove Cemetery).

8f. **Cordelia (II) "Cordia."** Born Apr. 1896 in MO. She was hired by Mathew G. McCown to work as a housekeeper and nurse for him and his mother, Caroline Francis Burgess McCown, Cordelia's nonagenarian cousin by marriage, and stayed with McCown as his common-law wife for seven years (he was born 1858 in Johnson Co., MO, son of James Madison McCown and Caroline Francis Burgess, and worked as a telegraph operator and farmer). After McCown was arrested for murder in 1921 (see below), he married Cordelia on 25 Aug. 1921 in Johnson Co. to keep her from testifying against him, and although convicted, received a light sentence. Two years later, he was accused of killing another man, and when the sheriff came to their home on 6 Oct. 1923 to arrest him, he disappeared out the back door, never to be seen again. He is said either to have thrown himself down a well, or to have gone west to his brothers in Idaho and Montana. Their children included: *Eugene Albert* (born 1917); *Dorene Elizabeth* (born 1919); *James E.* (born and died Feb. 1921). After McCown vanished, Cordelia divorced him on grounds of abandonment, and married Paul L. Hicks about 1925 (he was born 7 Apr. 1904, and died 23 Apr. 1962), and had children: *Edith Pauline* (born 31 July 1926, married John Andrews, and died on 4 Feb. 1973, buried in the Greenlawn Cemetery). Listed in the 1910 census for Bates Co., MO working as a servant for J. E. Clemens. Cordelia Hicks died on 18 Feb. 1950 in Bates Co., and is buried with her second husband in the Greenlawn Cemetery.

8g. **Nellie M. (II).** Born Nov. 1898 in MO. Married W. M. Kennedy on 8 Feb. 1915 in Bates Co., MO, and had children: *Lester* (born 14 Dec. 1918, and died 28 Dec. 1972 at Nevada, MO, buried Greenlawn Cemetery); married secondly ___ Wolfenbarger. Nellie Wolfenbarger died on 14 Feb. 1966 in Bates Co., MO, and is buried in the Rich Hill Cemetery.

8h. **Edna A.** Born about 1904 in Bates Co., MO.

ANOTHER MURDER

"Johnson County has another murder case on hands, caused by the murder committed Saturday forenoon of last week [20 Aug. 1921], about 10 o'clock, at the Matthew McCowan farm, ten or twelve miles southwest of Warrensburg. Sheriff Duncan, Prosecuting Attorney Chaney, and Coroner Bolton were summoned to the McCowan farm by the murder soon after it happened. The news of the tragedy was not known about town until after noon. The officers were summoned by McCowan.

"A coroner's jury of six men, composed of A. C. Prather, R. F. Graham, C. W. Hamith, J. L. Johns, R. R. Graham and J. H. McMurphy, was impaneled. After hearing the evidence in the case the jury returned a verdict to the effect that the dead man, Ernest Morford, has come to his death by a gunshot wound caused by a gun held in the hands of Matthew McCowan.

"According to the evidence produced before the coroner, Cornelia Burgess [sic], McCowan's common law wife, was the only near witness to the murder. There were other witnesses at a distance, but not close enough to hear the conversation.

"*Standard-Herald* is not in the habit of trying to give the evidence before the case is tried in court, but from the evidence given at the inquest the following story is practically correct: McCowan and the Burgess woman had been living together for the past seven years. Three children have been born to them. Last spring McCowan hired the murdered man, Ernest Morford, to work for him on the farm. McCowan and the Burgess woman had difficulty some time ago and separated, she going an eighty [acre farm] belonging to McCowan some distance away from the home farm. McCowan outfitted her with team, farming implements, cow, chickens, etc. Morford quit the employ of McCowan and went to work with the Burgess woman. Saturday, Morford and the woman went to the McCowan farm to get some corn, etc. Morford took the corn home, and the woman remained. When Morford returned and started to drive the team in at the gate, he was stopped by McCowan and ordered to drop the lines and get out of the wagon. He did so, and McCowan shot him with a load of buckshot, the shot taking effect in the neck and side of the head, killing the victim instantly. McCowan then turned the gun on the Burgess woman, who was carrying their six-months-old child in her arms. The woman ran into the barn and hid behind a truck. She was followed by McCowan, but she evidently talked him out of the idea of shooting her. McCowan was arrested and brot [sic] by Sheriff Duncan, and is in jail awaiting action of the officials. Attorneys M. D. Aber and W. E. Suddath have been retained to defend McCowan."—*Warrensburg Standard-Herald*, 26 Aug. 1921. McCown's name is consistently misspelled McCowan throughout this article, and Cordelia Burgess is erroneously called Cornelia.

McCOWN GIVEN JAIL SENTENCE

"The jury in the McCown murder trial returned a verdict Thursday night of last week after deliberating seven hours, found the defendant guilty and assessed the defendant's punishment at six months in the county jail and a fine of $500. The verdict is not a popular verdict, as it is contended that if the defendant is guilty the punishment was not adequate, and if not guilty he should have been given his liberty. It is reported that from the start the jury stood four for conviction and eight for acquittal. There is so much talk that one hardly knows what to believe. The way the thing stands the defendant had as well to be paroled. A man stealing chickens would be sent to the penitentiary for from three to five years, but McCown was declared guilty of murder in some degree, and escaped with a jail sentence and a fine. The opinion expressed on every hand to the effect that he was guilty or not guilty, and he should have had a penitentiary sentence or acquittal is right. An injustice has been done Mr. McCown or society. Such meting out of justice is the cause of mob violence. We trust there will never be another case of the kind in Johnson County."—*Warrensburg Standard-Herald*, 5 Mar. 1922.

WESLEY BURGESS OF BATES CO., MISSOURI

[Francis Marion (I)[6], Henry Bascomb[7]]

8d. **Wesley Gray** *[son of Henry Bascomb].* Born May 1891 in Missouri. Married Pearl Bel(l)man about 1918 (she was born 11 Feb. 1898, and died on 20 Aug. 1969). Listed in the 1920 census for Weir, Cherokee Co., KS. Wesley Burgess was a farmer and handyman near Rich Hill, Bates Co., MO. He died there in the summer of 1946, and is buried in the Greenlawn Cemetery. In addition to the children listed below, he may also have had the following sons (according to Ivan Burgess): Jack Bee, Samuel Dale, Jacob, and Robert Sam. A stepson, Udell Canader (age 3), is listed with the family in 1920.

9a. **James Richard (I) "Buck."** Born 23 Nov. 1919 at Weir, Cherokee Co., KS. Not with his family in the 1920 census. Married Bonnie Shofield, a nursing aide, in 1947. Buck Burgess served in the U.S. Army during World War II; after the war he returned to Bates Co., where he worked as a heavy equipment operator for the Missouri State Highway Dept. He now lives retired at Butler, Bates Co., MO.

10a. **Frances Irene.** Born Aug. 1948 at Rich Hill, MO. Married Jesse Caine; married secondly Edward Jones. She lives at Rich Hill, MO.

10b. **James Richard (IV).** Born Dec. 1949 at Rich Hill, MO. Married ____. Jim Burgess was a Sergeant in the U.S. Army for twenty-two years, before retiring from the service in 1987; he now works as a security guard in Colorado Springs, CO.

11a. **Nyles Wesley.** Born 1972.
11b. **Vernon Lee.** Born 1974.

9b. **Vernon Dale (I) "Skeeter."** Born 13 June 1922 in Bates Co., MO. Skeeter Burgess served in the U.S. Army during World War II, and was wounded at Normandy in June of 1944. He later returned to Bates Co., where he worked as a handyman. He died unmarried at Rich Hill on 14 Nov. 1974, and is buried in the Greenlawn Cemetery.
9c. **Ivan Eugene (II)** (twin). Born 22 Aug. 1927 in Bates Co., MO. Married Hisako Omiya on 1 Nov. 1949 at Sapporo, Japan (she was born 1 Nov. 1928 in Japan, was a school teacher at the Clover Park School and later ran her own day care service, the Burgess Mini Center, and died on 14 June 1989 at Tacoma, WA). Listed in the directories for Tacoma and Tacoma Suburban from 1968. Ivan Burgess served for 22 years in the U.S. Army, retiring in Nov. 1966, and then worked for the Washington State Department of Social and Health Services for 21 years before retiring. His hobbies included fishing and hunting. He died on 22 Sept. 1990 at Tacoma, WA, and is buried with his wife in the Mountain View Memorial Park.

10a. **Kathleen Eugene.** Born 1 Jan. 1955 at Colorado Springs, CO. Married Cecil Brown, and had children: *Janette Marie* (born 9 Apr. 1980 at Klamath Falls); *Thomas Eugene* (born 20 Mar. 1985 at Klamath Falls); *Emily Sue* (born 4 Apr. 1988 at Klamath Falls). Kathleen Brown is a teacher at Klamath Falls, OR.
10b. **(Ivan) Eugene (III).** Born 6 Sept. 1955 at Tripler Army Hospital, HI. Married Christine Bailham. Gene Burgess works at Western State College. He lives at Spanaway, WA.
10c. **Rose Eugene.** Born 2 June 1959 at Tripler Army Hospital, HI. Married Bryan McCoy, and had children: *Joshua*. Listed with her father in the 1981 directory of Tacoma.

9d. **(Ida) Geraldine** (twin). Born 22 Aug. 1927 at Rich Hill, MO; died there on 15 June 1931, and is buried in the Greenlawn Cemetery.
9e. **Harland Gray.** Born about 1935 at Rich Hill, MO. Married Marion F. Shelton on 6 Oct. 1970 at Winner, Humboldt Co., NV. Harland Burgess was an enlisted man in the U.S. Army for twenty-five years before retiring to Nevada. Said to have died about 1980 at Reno, NV.

10a. **Son.** Born about 1971 at Reno, NV.

BUD BURGESS OF BATES CO., MISSOURI
[Francis Marion (I)[6]]

7b. **Garland N. "Bud"** *[son of Francis Marion (I)].* His middle initial is listed as "G" in the 1870 census. Born about 1858 in Johnson Co., MO. Married Malissa J. Frisbie about 1878 (she was born 1 June 1858 in MO, and died on 3 Mar. 1939 in Bates Co., buried Greenlawn Cemetery). Listed in the 1880 census for Centre View Township, Johnson Co., MO, and in the 1900-10 censuses for Bates Co., MO (three of six children survive in 1900, two of six in 1910). Apparently died after his wife (1939), and is probably buried with her in an unmarked grave.

8a. **Francis Marion (II) "Frank."** Born Mar. 1880 (or 1879, according to cemetery records) in Johnson Co., MO. Living with his father in 1900. Married Susie Mann on 28 July 1902 in Bates Co. (her name is given as Augusta on his death certificate and cemetery record; she remarried Charles McCoy). Frank Burgess died on 30 May 1909 in Bates Co., and is buried in the Greenlawn Cemetery, Rich Hill, MO.
8b. **Vern Vallie.** Born 6 Dec. 1889 (or 1888, according to his draft record) in MO. Married Margie Rogers on 24 Dec. 1916 in Bates Co. Listed in the 1917 draft register of Bates Co., MO; he may be listed in the 1920 census for Kansas City, Jackson Co., MO. Vern Burgess was a semi-professional prize fighter in the U.S. Navy, serving four years about 1910; after retiring from the service, he worked as a barber in Bates Co., MO. He died there childless on 10 May 1977, and is buried in the Greenlawn Cemetery.
8c. **Nettia.** Her name is also spelled Nita and Neta (on her marriage record). Born Sept. 1897 in Bates Co., MO. Married S. Irvin (or Erven) Campbell on 12 Sept. 1913 in Bates Co., MO.

[William (I)[1], Edward (I)[2], Moses (I)[3], Edward (IV)[4]]

JOHN A. BURGESS
(1811?-1862)

OF JOHNSON COUNTY, MISSOURI

5d. **John A(nderson?) (I)** *[son of Edward (IV)].* Born about 1811 in Kanawha Co., VA (later WV). Married Emily Ann Samuels on 27 Dec. 1838 in Kanawha Co. (she was born June 1819 in [Kanawha Co.?], VA [later WV], daughter of Greenbury Samuels and Esther Slack, is said to have been of Indian descent, and died in 1903 in Kanawha Co., being the first person to be buried in the Burgess Cemetery, Poca District, Kanawha Co., WV). Listed in the tax records for Kanawha Co. from 1833-34 and 1837-45. Living with his father in 1840. He bought land in Johnson Co., MO on 1 Apr. 1846 (*Deed Book #G*, p. 198), and is listed in the 1850 census there for Post Oak Township; by 1860 he had moved just across the county line, into Tebo Township, Henry Co., MO. John Burgess was a farmer in West Virginia and Missouri. He supported the Confederacy during the Civil War, and was either killed in the raid by Federal soldiers on the Burgess house on the night of 22 Mar. 1862, in which three family members were shot down as they tried to escape, and the Burgess home and store burned, or died shortly thereafter of natural causes (the traditional family accounts differ; see the stories below). His widow returned with her family to Poca Township, Kanawha Co., WV, where she is recorded as head of the family in the censuses of 1870-1900 (four of five children survive in 1900).

The Children of John A. Burgess:

6a. **Joseph F.** Born about 1840 in Kanawha Co., VA (later WV). Married Margaret E. Yeager on 30 Aug. 1860 in Pettis Co., MO (next to Johnson Co.). Listed with his father in the 1860 census. He may be the "Dow" Burgess remembered by his family as having been killed by Indians, but was more likely killed in the 22 Mar. 1862 night raid by Union troops on the Burgess home, which killed two or three family members.

7a. **Georgiana.** Born about 1861 in Missouri. She was either the daughter of Joseph F. and Margaret Burgess (more likely), or of Hester Jane and Richard Burgess (see below). Married James L. Simpson on 24 Mar. 1889 in Fayette Co., WV, and had children: *Ernest W.* (born Sept. 1892); *Sarah* (born Oct. 1894). Georgiana Burgess is listed with her grandmother in the 1870-80 censuses (the 1880 census specifically identifies her as a grandchild). She died in Kanawha Co. about 1894. Her two children are listed in the 1900 census with her grandmother, Emily Burgess, and E(a)rnest Simpson with his father in 1910.

6b. **(Hester) Jane (I) "Jennie."** She was named for her two grandmothers. Born about 1844 in Kanawha Co., VA (later WV). Married **Richard B. BURGESS** on 30 Aug. 1860 in Johnson Co., MO (he was born 4 Aug. 1839 in Carroll Co., MD, son of Richard H. Burgess [a tavern owner in Frederick Co., MD who was born 7 Apr. 1808, died 23 Apr. 1847, and is buried in the Haughs Lutheran Church Cemetery, Ladiesburgh, MD], and Henrietta Stimmel, and died on 22 Mar. 1862 during the raid on the John Burgess home by Federal troops, being buried with the family in the Old Smyrna Cemetery; he is listed with the John A. Burgess family in the 1860 census, which was taken on 16 Aug.); married secondly John Wesley Ellis on 3 Apr. 1863 in Johnson Co.; married thirdly John H. Perry on 12 Sept. 1871 in Kanawha Co., WV. Living with her father in 1860, and with her mother in the 1870 census. Has not been found in the 1880-1900 West Virginia soundexes; however, by inference she is living in 1900, according to her mother's census record.

6c. **Garland Syraus.** Born 30 Mar. 1849 in Johnson Co., MO. See below for full entry.

6d. **(Francis) Archimedes "Ark."** Born 15 Dec. 1851 (1853 on his tombstone, but the 1860 census suggests 1851) in Johnson Co., MO. Listed with his mother in the 1900 census for Kanawha Co., WV. Ark

Burgess died unmarried and childless on 15 June 1932 in Kanawha Co., aged 77 years, 6 months (Frank Robertson providing the information), and is buried in the Burgess Cemetery, Kanawha Co., WV.

6e. **John Newton.** Born 10 Aug. 1856 in Johnson Co., MO. See below for full entry.

The Union Army burned the homes and churches of several Confederate supporters in March of 1862, as they systematically rounded up or killed sympathizers of the CSA guerrilla forces. The accounts below dramatically describe the incident involving the Burgess family:

A report filed by Brigadier General James Totten, U.S. Army, on Mar. 26, 1862, contained the following: "On the evening of the 19th instant, Capt. Thomas W. Houts, Missouri State Militia, Commander of the State Militia at Warrensburg, having received information of the whereabouts of concealed powder, sent fifteen men under Lieut. A. W. Christian to bring in the same to Warrensburg. The detachment was entirely successful, finding 125 kegs of powder (a portion of it damaged), buried in different places on the plantation of Mrs. Sarah B. Brinker, near Warrensburg. On the evening of the 22nd instant, Capt. Houts also sent twenty men under Lieut. J. M. Jewell to arrest several armed men who were supposed to be concealed in the house of Mrs. Burgess, about ten miles southwest of Warrensburg (this was in Post Oaks Township). Lieut. Jewell proceeded to the house, and silently surrounded it. A woman, assuring him that there were no men in the house, opened the door. Instantly the rebels, four in number, sprang out, firing upon our men, who promptly returned fire. It is thought that one of the party escaped unhurt; the other three were killed on the spot. Our loss was one killed and one badly wounded. The house was burned to the ground."

This report and a series of similar incidents led to an official investigation of the abuses of the State Militia, ordered by the U.S. Army Headquarters of the Central District, Missouri on 5 Apr. 1863, as noted below:

HEADQUARTERS DETACHMENT, 1ST IOWA CAVALRY

Warrensburg, Mo., 17 Apr. 1862

Testimony as to cause and manner of death of Jas. A. Turley;
burning of house, furniture, etc., of Col. McCowan and Mrs. Brinker;
Shooting of Mr. Burgess & his brother and burning of their dwelling;
and killing of Piper & burning of houses of Oliphant, Doak, Thompson, and Janes

Major, Pursuant to your order of April 16th, 1862, I having called to my assistance Capt. A. G. McQueen of Co. A, Lieut. D. A. Kerr, both of 1st Iowa Cavalry, proceeded to carry out the instructions of special orders #27 date April 5th 1862 issued from Headquarters Department of Central Missouri at Jefferson City, Mo., and being constituted a board of investigation were duly sworn and elicited the following testimony, to wit:

3.—In regard to the shooting of Mr. Burgess and his brother and the burning of their dwelling.

Thomas Black being duly sworn, testified:

I am a member of Capt. Hout Company of Mo. S.M. as a private, now stationed at this fort. Was 26 years of age last February. I do not know the two Burgesses, have heard of them. I know the place where they lived but do not know the name of it. I can't say that I do know how they came by their death. Can't say exactly how long since they were killed. I was out one night when two men were killed, don't know their names, about 4 wks ago. It occurred 6-8 miles from town. I was in command of the squad, Lieutenant Jewell was with us but I had Command. I was then orderly Sergeant in Hout's Co., since reduced in rank by order of Genl. Totten. We left here about 6 o'cl PM, proceeded to Wards House, searched for Mr. Ward—failed to find him—thence went to another House—the House was opened and found some firearms, also one bushwhacker—whom we brought along as prisoner. Crossing the yard between his House and the fence he started to run in the dark when I fired and shot him. Left the body there, then went to another House, searched without finding either arms or bushwhackers. After searching several other Houses we came to one where I dismounted 8 of the men, stationing them around the House, mostly behind, with instructions to let no one escape out of the House. I then demanded admittance at the front door. A lady inside told me there was no men inside, to give her time to dress. I told her she might take as long time as she desired if there were no men in the House, that I wished to search inside before leaving. Only 2 of my men went to the rear of the House although I had ordered the 8 nearly all there. As I went in I requested an inner door on my left opened, she refused. I then ordered one of my men to break it open. He struck with his rifle against the door, when two shots were fired through the back door, killing one and wounding one severely of my men—two men had rushed out the back door at the same time—one was fired at by one of my men but although he fell, both escaped into the brush. I then went into the House again and searched. Found a man in bed, asked why he didn't get up and open the door when I called for it. He told me he was afraid we would kill him. Told him if he wasn't a bushwhacker he need not be afraid as we wouldn't kill anyone except bushwhackers. I made him get up and dress, after that asked him the two men were who had escaped, he answered Dave Greenlee & John Brinker (I knew both noted bushwhackers, both while in a Company of about 40 had only a short time before shot at me among the Militia hitting me 4 times). I asked why he harbored such persons in the House. He said, he couldn't help it and begged not to kill him. I told him I didn't want to kill him. While there talking with him outside the House took fire. Can't say who set it on fire. Knowing that one man was dead and another badly wounded, I told my men to take them away from the burning House. Looking around again I saw the prisoner running to the rear of the House where some 6 to 8 women were also running for the brush. I "halted" him, but he continued running when I fired, killing him dead. Took the dead and wounded men to a House near by, dressed the wounded man myself. The owner of the House told us not to leave him there as about 200 bushwhackers were near to whom the 2 who had escaped would run and we certainly be attacked if we remained there and if the wounded man was left alone they would kill him. We borrowed an ox team from a farmer half a mile distant and in it carried the dead and wounded men into town, arriving in town about daylight. I do not know who burnt the House.

R. F. Logan, being duly sworn, testified:

I live west of here about 18 miles—at present belong to Capt. Hout's Company of State Militia, am 25 years of age, a carpenter by business. I was on the same Scout during which the 2 Burgesses were killed, but saw neither of them killed myself. I do not know them personally. Lt. Jewell commanded the Scout. I saw the House burnt, do not know who set it on fire. I don't think any of them had a drop of liquor with them even. I dismounted among the 8 at the second house, heard Sergeant Black order the men 3 times to go to the backdoor, only two did go. I was ordered by Sergt. Black to break open an inner door. Did so then heard the report of two pistols at the rear door. Knew they were none of our arms. Went out and saw one of our men lying there nearly dead, went into the House again and heard the 3rd shot which I understood is the one killing Burgess. When we first went to the front door Sergeant Black ordered the door opened. They fussed around a long time it seems to me fully 10 minutes before they opened it. I don't know what was said. Lieutenant Jewell was in Command when the House was burnt. I don't know why it was that I received orders from Sergt. Black. Lieut. Jewell I understood was in Command, he remained mounted until the firing then dismounted. He was with us during the whole scout.

[see page 92]
Frank Oliver BURGESS (1874-1935)
(Morna) Leata FORNEY BURGESS (1875-1952)

[William (I)[1], Edward (I)[2], Moses (I)[3], Edward (IV)[4], John Anderson (I)[5]]

GARLAND SYRAUS BURGESS
(1849-1913)

OF COLUMBIANA COUNTY, OHIO

6c. **Garland Syraus "Garl"** *[son of John Anderson (I)].* His middle name is also written Syracuse. Born 30 Mar. 1849 in Johnson Co., MO. Married Lucy (or Louisa) Frances Wilson on 20 (or 28) Jan. 1877 at Ripley, Jackson Co., WV (she was born 1 Jan. 1854 in Fauquier Co., VA, daughter of Sidnor B. Wilson and Henrietta Childes, and died on 18 Dec. 1928 at East Liverpool, Columbiana Co., OH). Listed in the 1880-1900 censuses for Ripley, Jackson Co., WV (the 1900 record scrambles the names and dates of his children). In 1906 he sold his farm in Jackson Co. to his son, Herbert (*Deed Book #71*, p. 35), and moved to East Liverpool, Columbiana Co., OH, where he appears in the 1910 census for Liverpool Township (six of six children then survive). Listed in the 1906/07-10 city directories of East Liverpool, OH; his widow appears as head of the family there from 1912/13-1929, and also in the 1920 census. Garl Burgess was a farmer in Jackson Co., WV, and a pottery worker in Columbiana Co., OH. He died of the effects of a stroke on 1 June 1913 at East Liverpool, OH, and is buried with his wife in the Spring Grove Cemetery, Liverpool Township.

The Children of Garl Burgess:

7a. **Herbert Lee.** Born 18 Nov. 1877 at Ripley, Jackson Co., WV. See below for full entry.
7b. **Rudolph Pearl (I).** Born 7 Mar. 1879 at Ripley, Jackson Co., WV. See below for full entry.
7c. **Iva Dell "Ivy."** Born 4 May 1882 at Ripley, Jackson Co., WV. Married James McIntosh about 1908 (he was born about 1885), and had children: *Kathleen G.* (born about 1909, married ___ Tritten); *Gloria M.* (born July 1917, married ___ Palmer; she may be the Gloria Palmer born 12 Feb. 1915 who died in Jan. 1991 at East Liverpool, OH). Listed in the 1906/07-08 and 1928 city directories of East Liverpool, OH, and also in the 1920 census there. Ivy McIntosh died after 1950 in Ohio.
7d. **Leslie M. "Lessie."** Born 27 Feb. 1888 at Ripley, Jackson Co., WV. Married ___ Hanley after 1910, and secondly James H. Grafton (he was born 7 July 1892, and died Oct. 1970 at East Liverpool), and had at least the following children: *Ruth Ann* (married ___ Corfello); *Daniel.* Not listed in the 1900 census record, but appears with her father in 1910 working as a pottery decorator, and in the 1906/07-1915/16 city directories of East Liverpool, OH, in the 1920 census for East Liverpool (with no children), and in the city directories through 1957/58. She apparently died at East Liverpool about 1958.
7e. **Eugene Jessie.** Born 3 Apr. 1893 at Ripley, Jackson Co., WV. See below for full entry.
7f. **Garnet Franklin.** Born 7 Oct. 1895 at Ripley, Jackson Co., WV. See below for full entry.

HERBERT L. BURGESS OF BEAVER CO., PENNSYLVANIA
[Garland Syraus[6]]

7a. **Herbert Lee** *[son of Garland Syraus].* Born 18 Nov. 1877 at Ripley, Jackson Co., WV. Married Martha Louise Lyons on 16 Apr. 1899 in Jackson Co., WV (she was born 15 Mar. 1882, daughter of John Franklin Lyons and Mary Margaret Davis, and died on 19 Feb. 1951 in Beaver Co., PA). Listed in the 1900-10 censuses for Jackson Co. Herbert Burgess bought his father's land in 1906, and then sold it on 13 Sept. 1917, moving to Aliquippa, Beaver Co., PA, where he is listed there in the 1918 draft register and in the 1920 census. He was an entrepreneur, a guard at a water station, and a carpenter. Herbert also sang bass with various evangelical singing groups in West Virginia at the turn of the century. He died on 8 Sept. 1950 at Aliquippa, and is buried with his wife in the Woodlawn Cemetery.

8a. **Hallie Odell.** Born 11 Aug. 1899 at Ripley, Jackson Co., WV. Married Archie Wilson Murphy on 30 Apr. 1921 at Woodlawn (later Aliquippa), Beaver Co, PA (he was born 21 May 1892, and died Feb. 1954), and had children:

Natheleen Evelyn MURPHY. Born 14 Nov. 1921 at Woodlawn, PA, married (Harold) James Vaughan on 10 Apr. 1940 in Sewickley, PA, and had children: *Douglas Murphy* (born 20 Dec. 1944 at Aliquippa, PA, married Geraldine Vincent, and had children: Morgan Douglas [born 20 Mar. 1978]; Travis Taylor [born 21 Apr. 1980]); *Craig William* (born 13 Sept. 1951, married Lina Tateso, and had children: Melissa Ann [born 15 Aug. 1977]; Ryan Michael [born 9 Mar. 1981]); *Lisa Laverne* (born 5 Oct. 1960; Lisa Murphy is an electrical engineer on the research faculty of Carnegie-Mellon University, Pittsburgh, PA; she also is an occasional flautist and pianist with the Butler Symphony Orchestra). ***Natheleen VAUGHAN*** teaches piano, music theory, and voice at Aliquippa, PA; she has contributed greatly to this book.

Gilbert Brooks MURPHY. Born 8 Oct. 1924, married Swaleta Hinman, and secondly Irene Young, and had children: *Jane Ellen* (born May 1963, married Mark Pryzbolac), served as a policeman at Aliquippa, PA for fourteen years, and then as an assistant supervisor of the Erie office of the Pennsylvania Liquor Control Board. ***Gilbert BROOKS*** died on 13 July 1977 at Erie, PA, and is buried there in the Laurel Hill Cemetery.

John Franklin MURPHY. Born 23 Apr. 1928, married Dorothy ___, and had children: *Lorraine Joyce* (born Jan. 1967); *John Franklin Jr.* (born posthumously in Mar. 1968), and died Nov. 1967.

Travis Lee MURPHY. Born 28 Oct. 1930, married Nancy Grula, and had children: *Kevin Lee* (born June 1960, married Judy Shook, and had children: James Travis [born 1990]; Renis Brooks [born Nov. 1992]).

(Martha) Ardele MURPHY. Born 11 Sept. 1934, currently lives at New York City.

Hallie MURPHY was a midwife in Beaver Co., and she also worked for American Bridge Co. She died in May 1968, and is buried with her husband in the Woodlawn Cemetery, Aliquippa, Beaver Co., PA.

8b. **Raymond Pearl.** Born 11 Jan. 1901 at Ripley, Jackson Co., WV. See below for full entry.

8c. **Dale Keith (I).** Born 16 July 1902 at Ripley, Jackson Co., WV. See below for full entry.

8d. **(Evelyn) Dolly.** Listed as Ocal Burgess in the birth records. Born 6 Oct. 1904 at Ripley, Jackson Co., WV. Dolly Burgess died of heart failure on 13 Mar. 1921 at Aliquippa, PA, and is buried in the Woodlawn Cemetery. She is said to have been a beautiful and popular student; when she died, her high school closed for a day in her honor.

8e. **Garland Lee.** Born 13 Jan. 1907 at Ripley, Jackson Co., WV. See below for full entry.

8f. **Virginia Valentine.** Born 14 Feb. 1911 at New Sheffield, Beaver Co., PA. Married Russell Perkey on 25 Sept. 1933 (?), and had children: *Russell Jr.* (born 29 May 1931, married Anita Thomas, and had children: Cheryl [born 28 Apr. 1958, married Neil Cantor]; Beverly [born 3 May 1959]; Deborah [born 26 July 1960]); *(Martha) Elaine* (born 13 Aug. 1933, married Dr. James Durenzo, and had children: Victor James PERKEY [ad.; born Aug. 1954]; Marlaine [born 1959, married Paul Olshanski]; James Jr. [26 Nov. 1962, married Jennifer Shiberly]); *Dale Benton* (born 7 Nov. 1938, married Linda Tyler). Virginia Perkey worked in the Jones and Laughlin Steel Mill, Beaver Co. She currently lives at Aliquippa, PA.

8g. **Eugenia Frances "Jean."** Born 29 Oct. 1916 at New Sheffield, Beaver Co., PA. Married Samuel Marcus on 2 Apr. 1934; married secondly William Allen about 1942. Jean Allen worked in the Jones and Laughlin Steel Mill, Beaver Co. She currently lives at Aliquippa, PA.

RAYMOND P. BURGESS OF BEAVER CO., PENNSYLVANIA

[Garland Syraus[6], Herbert Lee[7]]

8b. **Raymond Pearl** *[son of Herbert Lee].* His middle name is given as Carl on his marriage license. Born 11 Jan. 1901 at Ripley, Jackson Co., WV. Married Mary Allein Davis on 14 Feb. 1922 at New Cumberland, Hancock Co., WV (she was born 14 Dec. 1903 at Pittsburgh, PA, died of kidney failure on 27 Oct. 1946 in Beaver Co., PA, and is buried in the Woodlawn Cemetery); married secondly Helen E. Riddle in 1950 (she was born 18 Mar. 1915, and died on 12 Feb. 1989). Raymond Burgess was a railroad and construction worker. He died on 10 June 1952 in Chippewa Township, Beaver Co., PA, killed by a truck while working on Pennsylvania State Route 51, and is buried in the Woodlawn Cemetery, Aliquippa, PA.

"Although Dad only went to third grade, which wasn't unusual in his day, he had an almost perfect command of proper English. I think he felt ashamed of his lack of education, so he made sure he spoke correctly. He also played guitar by ear, and we used to have great singing times. He had a great voice, and loved to sing."—Mary Louise Vaughn, 1992.

9a. **Ray Lee.** Born 23 Oct. 1922 at Aliquippa, PA. Married Katherine Powell; married secondly Mrs. Ruth Townsend, mother of his first two children (by her first husband, she had children: Wendy; Toby); married thirdly Rita ___ about 1964. Served as a Sergeant in the U.S. Army Air Force during World War II. Ray Burgess was a foreman for A.M.P., an electronics company, at Mount Joy, PA. He died in June 1967 at Lancaster, PA in an automobile accident, and is buried there.

10a. **Michael (I).** Mike Burgess is a contractor at Lincoln, VT.
10b. **Lee.** Lee Burgess is an attorney at Nashville, IL.
10c. **Lee Ray.** Born about 1965 at Lancaster, PA. He may be living in Vermont.

9b. **William Ralph "Bill."** Born 21 July 1924 at Aliquippa, PA. Bill Burgess was a steel worker at Kentucky Steel before being drafted at the beginning of World War II. He served as a Technical Sergeant in Co. B., 771st Field Artillery Battalion, U.S. Army. He died unmarried while serving, killed in a truck accident on 2 June 1945 in West Germany; his body was returned for reburial on 29 Jan. 1949 in the Woodlawn Cemetery, Aliquippa, Beaver Co., PA.

9c. **Robert David (I) "Butch."** Born 19 Apr. 1926 at Rochester, PA. Married Carolyn Elizabeth "Carrie" Mills on 10 Nov. 1951 at Hagerstown, Washington Co., MD (she was born 3 Nov. 1931 at Huntingdon, PA, and worked as a school teacher). Served in the U.S. Navy from 1943-46. Butch Burgess was a school teacher in the Mechanicsburg School District, Mechanicsburg, PA before retiring. He now lives at Mount Holly Springs, PA.

10a. **Fredric Ray "Fred."** Born 17 June 1955 at Carlisle, PA. Fred Burgess is a newspaper editor for the *Carlisle Sentinel*, Carlisle, PA.

10b. **James Joseph "Jimmy Joe."** Born 12 Apr. 1958 at Carlisle, PA. Married Susan Elizabeth Peffer on 19 Dec. 1981 at Shippensburg, Cumberland Co., PA (she was born 10 Nov. 1960). Jim Burgess is an elementary school principal at Carlisle, PA.

11a. **Benjamin John (II).** Born 3 Sept. 1986 at Harrisburg, PA.

9d. **Edith Allein "Sis."** Born 11 July 1928 at Aliquippa, PA. Married Chalmer Dean Strosnider on 22 Oct. 1949 at McDonald, Washington Co., PA (div.; he was born 23 Oct. 1927 at Washington, Washington Co., PA), and had children: *Neil Edwin* (born 25 June 1950 at Beaver Falls, PA, married, and had children: Sarah Louise [born 22 June 1975]; Brooke M. [born 17 Mar. 1978]); *Dean Lee* (born 4 Mar. 1952 at Beaver Falls, PA, married, and had children: Carter [born 30 Sept. 1986]; Colin [born 30 Dec. 1988]; Sean [born 29 June 1992]); *Jay Kurt* (born 13 Jan. 1954 at Beaver Falls, PA, married, and had children: William [born 16 July 1980]; Annie [born 4 June 1982]; Jay [born 19 Sept. 1990]); *Mark Boyd* (born 26 July 1957 at New Brighton, PA, married, and had children: Blake [born 23 June 1985]; Marlie [born 23 Sept. 1987]). Sis Strosnider graduated from Geneva College in 1966. She worked as a fourth grade school teacher in North Sewickley Township, Beaver Co., PA before retiring.

9e. **John Richard (I).** Born 17 Feb. 1930 at Aliquippa, PA. Married Dolores "Ducky" Anderson in 1947 (div.); married secondly Mary Marie Muntean Evans on 18 Dec. 1967 at Ellwood City, Lawrence Co., PA. John Burgess worked as a millwright for forty years at the Monaca Vasco Teledine Mill, Beaver Co., PA before retiring.

10a. **Lynda.** Born 1947 in PA. Married Gary Lee Starr about 1966 (he was born about 1941), and had children: *Wanda* (born about 1967, had children: Son [born 1985, adopted out of the family], and died on 19 Feb. 1988 at Coraopolis, PA); *Gary Lee Jr.* (married and had children: Leon); *James "Jimmy."* Lynda Starr died in 1971 at Rochester, Beaver Co., PA.

10b. **John Richard (II).** Born about 1949. John Burgess lives at West Montgomery, IL.

11a. **Rachel (II).**
11b. **Julie.**
11c. **Marsha.**
11d. **Steven.**

10c. **Susan (III).** Born about 1952. Had four children.
10d. **Brenda (II).** Born about 1955. Married ___ Dillan about 1979, and had children: *Benjamin* (born about 1980); *Nathan* (born 1982).
10e. **Robert (II).** Born about 1960.

9f. **James Roy "Murphy."** Born 18 May 1931 at Aliquippa, PA. Married Edith Hilka "Edie" Forsman on 31 Oct. 1950 at Beaver, PA (she was born 16 Feb. 1937 at Avon, Allegheny Co., PA). Murph Burgess is a carpenter in Brighton Township, Beaver Co., PA.

10a. **William James "Bill."** Born 9 July 1951 at Rochester, Beaver Co., PA. Married Christine Ann Turbish on 23 May 1970 at Monaca, Beaver Co., PA (she was born 14 June 1952).

11a. **Megan Lynne.** Born 6 Feb. 1973 at Washington, DC.
11b. **Sarah Elizabeth (VII).** Born 12 Oct. 1977 at Rochester, Beaver Co., PA.
11c. **Nathan Ian.** Born 11 Aug. 1981 in Brighton Township, Beaver Co., PA.

10b. **Edith Hilka "Edie."** Born 10 Dec. 1952 at Rochester, PA. Married James Walter "Jim" Nicols on 20 Mar. 1971 at Beaver, PA (he was born 14 Dec. 1950), and had children: *Wendy Jo* (born 24 Feb. 1972 at Rochester, Beaver Co., PA); *James Luke* (born 21 Oct. 1975 at Rochester, PA); *Marja Eileen* (born 26 Jan. 1982 at Rochester, PA, died Nov. 1983 of meningitis); *Jeremiah Ray* (born 5 Mar. 1985 at Rochester, PA).
10c. **Joseph David "Joe."** Born 31 May 1954 at Rochester, PA.
10d. **David Allan (II) "Dave."** Born 22 Dec. 1955 at Rochester, PA. Married Shannon Luking.

11a. **Sheena Marie.**
11b. **Joseph (II).**

10e. **Ray Pearl.** Born 7 June 1957 at Rochester, PA. His common-law wife is Lorrain Yolande St. Esprit (she was born 2 June 1955).

11a. **Marla Ray.** Born 12 Aug. 1988 at Elizabeth City, Pasquotank Co., NC.

9g. **Mary Louise (III).** Born 15 Nov. 1932 at Aliquippa, PA. Married John Lee "Jack" Vaughn on 20 Mar. 1954 at Beaver, PA (he was born 28 May 1934), and had children: *Karen Louise* (born 25 Nov. 1954 at Rochester, Beaver Co., PA, married William Fields in 1973 at Winchester, VA [div.], and had children: (William) Andrew "Andy" [born 18 Apr. 1974 at Denver, CO]; *Karen Louise* married secondly Anthony "Tony" Wawrzonek on 21 Oct. 1977 [he was born 19 Jan. 1952 at Ridway, MN], and had children: Kate Vaughn [born 27 July 1978 at Rochester, PA]; Jill Elizabeth [born 10 June 1980]); *Beth Ann* (born 15 Sept. 1956 at Rochester, PA, married Peter John Tabacchi on 15 Dec. 1979 at Beaver, PA [he was born 17 Mar. 1957], and had children: Eugene Marx "Gino" [born 14 Mar. 1982 in Germany]; Kristie Elizabeth [born 19 Dec. 1984 in Germany]; Daniel John [born 24 Jan. 1985 at Fort Belvoir, VA]); *Tracy Lynn* (born 27 Dec. 1960 at Rochester, PA, married Robert Duffy on 20 Sept. 1992); *Lee Marx* (born 18 Apr. 1973 at Rochester, PA).
9h. **Karen Elizabeth.** Born 13 Dec. 1940 at Rochester, PA. She married Joseph Edward "Joe" Hardy on 9 Aug. 1958 at Wexford, Allegheny Co., PA (he was born 24 May 1936 at Kokomo, IN), and had children:

(Joseph) Kirk HARDY. Born 7 Mar. 1959 at New Brighton, Beaver Co., PA. Married Kathleen Mary Dunn on 16 Oct. 1982 at Golden, CO (div.); married secondly Robin Lynn Clodgu on 29 Oct. 1988 (she was born 21 Oct. 1959), and had children: *Kevin Robert* (born 30 Nov. 1992 at Irvine, CA). Kirk Hardy is a geologist at Laramie, WY.

Brian Thomas HARDY. Born 18 Jan. 1960 at New Brighton, PA. Married Lisa Kay McClure on 7 May 1982 at Beaver, PA (she was born 19 July 1962), and had children: *Andrew Thomas* (born 21 Nov. 1982 at Beaver, PA); *Amber René* (born 2 Aug. 1984 at Chambersburg, PA); *Katelyn Noél* (born 19 Dec. 1988 at Altamonte Springs, FL); *Caleb John* (born 14 Apr. 1993 at Orlando, FL). Brian Hardy currently lives at Orlando, FL.

Susan Eileen "Sue" HARDY. Born 14 Oct. 1961 at Beaver Falls, Beaver Co., PA, married Noé Carl Scherer on 30 July 1983 at New Brighton (he was born 9 Apr. 1959), and had children: *Jessica Eileen* (born 9 Jan. 1987 at Beaver); *Noé Jacob* (born 8 Sept. 1988); *Molly Karen* (born 4 May 1990).

Janet Lynne HARDY. Born 3 Oct. 1962 at Beaver Falls, PA.

Kirk HARDY has contributed greatly to this book; he currently lives at Laramie, WY.

9i. **(George) Edward.** Born 20 Oct. 1942 at Rochester, PA. Edward Burgess attended Franklin Marshall College, Lancaster, PA, earning his master's degree in hospital administration, and served two years in the Peace Corps in Senegal, and also served in the U.S. Navy as a Corpsman. He later worked as an intensive care nurse, and currently is an administrative supervisor for Kaiser Hospital at San Francisco, CA.

9j. **Donald Ralph "Pete."** Born 24 Aug. 1945 at Rochester, PA. Pete Burgess earned his master's degree in education in 1967 at Indiana University of Pennsylvania, and served in the Peace Corps in Malaysia. He later worked as a school teacher at Newport, RI, as a bookkeeper for Yankee Book Peddler, and currently for Metropolitan Insurance Co. at Providence, RI.

DALE K. BURGESS OF BEAVER CO., PENNSYLVANIA

[Garland Syraus[6], Herbert Lee[7]]

8c. **Dale Keith (I)** *[son of Herbert Lee].* Born 16 July 1902 at Ripley, Jackson Co., WV. Married Susan Irene Young on 15 Dec. 1924 (she was born 13 Feb. 1904 at Pittsburgh, PA, and died on 19 Oct. 1976 at Aliquippa, PA). Dale K. Burgess was a steel worker for over forty-five years for Jones & Laughlin Steel, Aliquippa Works, in Beaver Co., PA, retiring as a foreman in the boilerhouse in 1967. He was also a charter member of the Hopewell Township Volunteer Fire Department, Aliquippa, PA, and remained active until his death. He died on 26 Mar. 1983 at Aliquippa, PA, and is buried there with his wife in the Woodlawn Cemetery.

9a. **Dale Herbert.** Born 31 Aug. 1925 at Aliquippa, Beaver Co., PA. Married Helen Louise Dull on 15 Aug. 1947 (she was born 21 June 1929). Dale Burgess worked for Jones & Laughlin Steel, Aliquippa Works for over thirty years as an assistant foreman and millwright in the 30-inch round mill maintenance department. Dale H. Burgess died on 22 July 1976 in Beaver Co., PA., and is buried in the Woodlawn Cemetery. Helen Burgess currently lives in Hopewell Township, near Aliquippa, PA.

10a. **Dale Keith II.** Born 13 Apr. 1948 at Rochester, PA. Married Suzanne Clifford (div.). Served in the U.S. Air Force and U.S. Air Force Reserve. Dale K. Burgess is a bank officer at Portland, ME, and currently resides at Saco, ME.

11a. **Heather Sue.** Born 1 Nov. 1974 at Brewer, ME. Married Sean Andrews.

10b. **David Allan (I).** Born 11 Nov. 1954 at Rochester, PA. Married Diane Kay Ahlum in 1977 (div.); married secondly Kim Louise Frankett on 23 Feb. 1990 at Mendon, VT (she was born 17 Aug. 1960 at Phillipsburg, NJ). David Burgess earned his B.S.M.E. degree at Carnegie-Mellon in 1976. He works as a mechanical engineer for Air Products, Allentown, PA. He currently lives at Alburtis, PA.

11a. **Nathan Dale.** Born 14 June 1981 at Bethlehem, PA.
11b. **Taylor Rianne.** Born 3 Jan. 1994 in Beaver Co., PA.

10c. **Debra Lee.** She now uses the legalized name, Debra Burgess Yawor. Born 14 Jan. 1957 at Rochester, Beaver Co., PA. Married Alex Brian Yawor on 11 Aug. 1979 (he was born 7 July 1956 at Sweickley, PA), and had children: *Megan Alexandra* (born 27 May 1990). Debra Yawor is a management analyst and technical records manager for the Federal Aviation Administration; Brian Yawor is a model maker and prototype fabricator. They live near Boston, MA.

9b. **James Edward (VI).** Born 28 Jan. 1927 in Beaver Co., PA. Married Ruby Lois Shaddock on 11 Sept. 1947. Living at Hopewell, PA in 1976. Jim Burgess was a steel worker in Beaver Co. for twenty-eight years. He died on 19 Sept. 1990 at Aliquippa, PA. Ruby Burgess currently lives at Aliquippa, PA.

10a. **Janet Lynn.** Born 26 June 1949 in Beaver Co., PA. Married William David Heinbaugh on 20 June 1969, and had children: *Scott David* (born 30 Oct. 1972). Janet Heinbaugh is a legal secretary at Aliquippa, PA.

10b. **Judith Ann (II).** Born 15 July 1952 in Beaver Co., PA. Married Vincent Louis Gill on 23 Sept. 1972, and had children: *Michael Vincent* (born 15 Aug. 1975); *Jason Daniel* (born 30 July 1978). Judith Gill lives at Aliquippa, PA.

10c. **Donald Bruce.** Born 1 Oct. 1956 in Beaver Co., PA. Married Karen Egen on 7 Feb. 1978 (div. 1982); married secondly Jennifer Lundon. Donald B. Burgess lives at Riverside, CA.

11a. **Danielle Marie.** Born 18 June 1979 in Beaver Co., PA.
11b. **Rachel (III).** Born 16 June 1986 in Beaver Co., PA.
11c. **Jessica.** Born 27 May 1990.

9c. **William David (I).** Born 10 Aug. 1928 in Beaver Co., PA. Married secondly AnnaLou Carroll on 22 May 1954. Bill Burgess was a steel worker in Beaver Co. for thirty-five years. He now lives retired at Imperial, PA.

10a. **Bruce Carroll.** Born 21 Nov. 1956 in Beaver Co., PA. Married Katrina "Tina" Mitrakos on 7 May 1983. Bruce Burgess is a dining room supervisor at Camp Hill Prison, PA. He lives at Halifax, PA.

11a. **Amanda Carroll.** Born 14 Dec. 1983 in PA.
11b. **Heather Nicole.** Born 15 Nov. 1985 in PA.

10b. **Daniel Beason.** Born 15 Jan. 1960 in Beaver Co., PA. Daniel B. Burgess is a computer associate for Environmental Controls at Silver Spring, MD.
10c. **Cheryl Anne.** Born 27 Nov. 1964 in Beaver Co., PA. Married Eric Shurilla on 5 Sept. 1992. Cheryl Shurilla is a nurse at the Allegheny Trauma Unit, Pittsburgh, PA, and lives at Northside, PA.

GARLAND L. BURGESS OF TEXAS
[Garland Syraus[6], Herbert Lee[7]]

8e. **Garland Lee.** Born 13 Jan. 1907 at Ripley, Jackson Co., WV. Married Noémi Brocard on 25 July 1932. Garland Burgess currently lives near Fort Worth, TX.

9a. **(Martha) Francine.** Born 1932 at Aliquippa, PA. Twice married. Lives at Fort Worth, TX.
9b. **Henri Pierre.** His name is also listed as Henry Burgess. Born 1935 at Aliquippa, PA. Married secondly Paula Stangl. Henri Burgess owns a bakery at Ambridge, PA.

10a. **Son.**
10b. **Son.**
10c. **Laurie Ann.**

RUDOLPH P. BURGESS, Sr. OF BEAVER CO., PENNSYLVANIA
[Garland Syraus[6]]

7b. **Rudolph Pearl (I)** *[son of Garland Syraus].* Born 7 Mar. 1879 at Ripley, Jackson Co., WV. Married Josephine Pelley about 1903 (she was born 8 Nov. 1881 at Cameron, WV, and died 13 Feb. 1951 at New Brighton, PA). Listed in the 1900 census for Bridgewater Borough, Beaver Co., PA (as Rude Burgess), in the 1906/07 city directory of East Liverpool, OH, and in the 1918 draft register and the 1910-20 censuses for New Brighton Borough, Beaver Co., PA, working as an iron molder; he continues to be listed there in the directories through 1939, working as a landscaper. Rudolph P. Burgess died on 23 Feb. 1941 at New Brighton, PA, and is buried there with his wife in the Grove Cemetery.

8a. **Robert Lee (I).** Born 5 Sept. 1904 in Beaver Co., PA. See below for full entry.
8b. **Leslie Franklin (I).** Born 18 Mar. 1906 in Beaver Co., PA. See below for full entry.
8c. **Rudolph Pearl (II).** Born 23 Sept. 1909 in Beaver Co., PA. See below for full entry.
8d. **Kenneth (I).** Born 7 Sept. 1910 at New Brighton, PA. Married Helen Groves (by her first husband, she had children: *George W. ROBERTS*). Kenneth Burgess was a garage foreman for the Pennsylvania Department of Highways. He lived at New Brighton, PA, but died childless on 1 June 1967 at Greenville, Mercer Co., PA.
8e. **Fred (II) "Lefty."** Born 18 July 1913 at New Brighton, PA. See below for full entry.
8f. **Norman P.** Born Jan. 1923 at New Brighton, PA; died there on 2 June 1923, and is buried with his parents.

ROBERT L. BURGESS OF BEAVER CO., PENNSYLVANIA

[Garland Syraus[6], Rudolph Pearl (I)[7]]

8a. **Robert Lee (I)** *[son of Rudolph Pearl (I)].* Born 5 Sept. 1904 in Beaver Co., PA. Married (Cecilia) Pauline Kenney on 26 Aug. 1925 in Beaver Co. (she was born 8 July 1906, daughter of R. Jefferson Kenney), and died on 15 Nov. 1982). Robert L. Burgess was the night superintendent for the Townsend Company Rivet Mill (later Textron). He died on 2 Oct. 1975 at New Brighton, PA, and is buried in the Sylvania Hills Memorial Park.

9a. **Robert C.** Born 12 Mar. 1926 at New Brighton, PA; died there on 17 Mar. 1926, and is buried in the Irvin Cemetery.

9b. **Betty Lou (I).** Born 17 Nov. 1927 at New Brighton, PA. Married James Mohney, and had children: *James Lee* (born 25 July 1950, married, and had children: Robin; Kathryn Susan); *Jocinda Lee* (born 18 Nov. 1951, married, and had children: Cari); *Gary Vance* (born 12 Mar. 1955, married, and had children: Timothy; Amy; Andrew; John Michael); *Paula Joann* (born 13 Feb. 1963, married, and had children: Jessie; Kaleigh). Betty Mohney currently lives at Clearfield, PA.

9c. **Robert Rudolph.** Born 16 Jan. 1933 at New Brighton, PA. Married Alice Marie Teaford. Bob Burgess is the manager of a condominium complex at Conway, SC. (803-347-3601)

10a. **Lori Colleen.** Married and had two children.

10b. **John Robert (I).** Married.

11a. **Daughter.**

11b. **Son.**

9d. **(Lois) Joan.** Born 19 July 1935 at New Brighton, PA. Married Richard Duerr Bailey, and had children: *Trudie Lynn* (married Pat Adams [div.]; married secondly Glen Ristich, and had children: Monique LeeAnn); *Leslie Ann* (married Chawn Wallace, and had children: Stephnie Susan; Chawn Jr.). **Joan** BAILEY married secondly Dr. Byron M. Walls. Joan Walls currently lives at Yorba Linda, CA.

LESLIE F. BURGESS, Sr. OF BEAVER CO., PENNSYLVANIA

[Garland Syraus[6], Rudolph Pearl (I)[7]]

8b. **Leslie Franklin (I)** *[son of Rudolph Pearl (I)].* Born 18 Mar. 1906 in Beaver Co., PA. Married Margaret McGowan on 3 July 1926 at Patterson Heights, PA (she was born 10 Oct. 1906). Leslie Burgess owned and operated the Burgess Auto Body Shop at New Brighton, PA, retiring in 1966 after forty years. He died on 15 July 1979 at New Brighton, PA, and is buried in the Sylvania Hills Cemetery.

9a. **Leslie Franklin (II).** Born 31 Mar. 1927 in Beaver Co., PA. Married Jean McCowin. Les Burgess lives at Homewood, PA.

10a. **Judy Rae.**

10b. **Keith Allen.**

10c. **Merrily** (nmn).

9b. **Donald Lee (III).** Born 5 Oct. 1931 in Beaver Co., PA. Married Gloria Krause. Don Burgess lives at Pompano Beach, FL.

10a. **Doreen Sue.** Married ___ Roadman.

10b. **Donald Lee (IV).**

10c. **Lisa Ann (I).** Married ___ Quitoni.

10d. **William Leslie "Billy."**

9c. **Nancy Eileen.** Born 21 Aug. 1936 in Beaver Co., PA. Married John Hutchinson, and had children: *Ann Margaret* (born 29 Nov. 1966, married Anthony Berry on 19 Mar. 1994 in Beaver Co.); *Brian John* (born 6 Nov. 1970). Nancy Hutchinson is a school teacher at New Brighton, PA.

9d. **Ruth Ann.** Born 2 Oct. 1944 in Beaver Co., PA. Married William Maybray (div.), and had children: *Danielle Renée* (married ___ Bobbin); *Leslie Ann* (married ___ Mercier); *William Richard*; *Chad Alan*. Ruth married secondly Michael Shane. Ruth Shane lives at New Brighton, PA.

RUDOLPH P. BURGESS, Jr. OF CUYAHOGA CO., OHIO

[Garland Syraus[6], Rudolph Pearl (I)[7]]

8c. **Rudolph Pearl (II) "Rudy"** *[son of Rudolph Pearl (I)].* Born 28 Nov. 1907 in Beaver Co., PA. Married Emma Kappen. Rudolph Burgess died in Mar. 1960, probably at Cleveland, OH.

9a. **Gloria.** Married Ronald Cantwell, and had one son. Gloria Cantwell was last known living in Arizona.

FRED "LEFTY" BURGESS OF BEAVER CO., PENNSYLVANIA

[Garland Syraus[6], Rudolph Pearl (I)[7]]

8e. **Fred (II) "Lefty"** *[son of Rudolph Pearl (I)].* Born 18 July 1913 at New Brighton, PA. Married Edwina Winnail (she was born 16 May 1917 in PA, and died Aug. 1984 at Whittier, CA). "Lefty" Burgess played for a year (1938) as the main pitcher for the minor league baseball team, the Beaver Falls Browns (sponsored by Cleveland). He later worked as a supervisor for Ajax Hardware Corporation. He died on 18 July 1978, his 65th birthday, at Whitter, CA.

9a. **Fred (III).** Fred Burgess was working as a restaurateur at Whittier, CA in 1978.
9b. **(Rudolph) Geoffrey.** Living in California in 1978.
9c. **Patricia "Patsy."** Never married. Living in California in 1978.
9d. **Edwina Kay "Eddie."** Married ___ Edwards. Living in California in 1978.

EUGENE J. BURGESS OF COLUMBIANA CO., OHIO

[Garland Syraus[6]]

7e. **Eugene Jessie** *[son of Garland Syraus].* Listed in the 1900 census as Jesse J. Born 3 Apr. 1893 at Ripley, Jackson Co., WV. Married Emma Elizabeth Schenk about 1919 (she was born 14 June 1901 at Beloit, OH, daughter of Christ and Mary Gemtler, worked as a china decorator at Homer Laughlin China Co., and died 5 Nov. 1982). Listed with his father in the 1910 census working as a pottery decorator and artist, in 1920 at Carrollton, Carroll Co., OH, in the city directories of East Liverpool, OH from 1910-1914/15, and at Wellsville, PA through 1968. Eugene Burgess was a pottery liner decorator at Homer Laughlin China Co, retiring in 1963. He died of a heart attack on 1 Nov. 1969 at Wellsville, Columbiana Co., OH, and is buried there with his wife in the Springhill Cemetery.

8a. **Aileen Emma.** Listed as Genevieva A. in the 1920 census. Born 1920 in Columbiana Co., OH. Married Fred Boso (he was born 1 June 1919, and died 5 Apr. 1990 at East Liverpool, OH), and had children: *Karen K.*; *Alan*. Aileen Boso currently lives at Wellsville, OH.
8b. **Robert Eugene (I).** Born 1921 in Columbiana Co., OH. Married Rose M. Grafton. Robert Burgess lives at Scottsdale, AZ.

9a. **Robert Allen.**
9b. **Rebecca Jhaneane.**
9c. **Nanette Louise.**

8c. **Keith Alan.** Born 20 May 1934 in Columbiana Co., OH. Living at Pittsburgh in 1969 and at New York City in 1982. Keith Burgess died unmarried and childless on 19 Sept. 1991, and is buried in the Springhill Cemetery beside his parents.
8d. **Sandra Karen "Sandy."** Born 18 Nov. 1941 in Columbiana Co., OH. Married Arlie E. Palmer (div.), and had children: *Edward Keith* (born 7 July 1968); *Steven Arlie* (born 11 Mar. 1972). Sandy Palmer is a school teacher at Crafton, PA, a suburb of Pittsburgh.

GARNET F. BURGESS OF COLUMBIANA CO., OHIO

[Garland Syraus[6]]

7f. **Garnet Franklin** *[son of Garland Syraus].* Listed in the 1900 census as Rudolph P. Born 7 Oct. 1895 at Ripley, Jackson Co., WV. Married Margaret I. Switzer on 18 Dec. 1924 at East Liverpool, OH (she was born 31 July 1902 at East Liverpool, OH, daughter of Earnest Switzer and Minnie Hutchison, and died there on 28 Dec. 1983). Listed in the 1920 census with his mother, and in the 1912/13-1967 city directories of East Liverpool, OH; his widow appears there from 1968-83. Garnet Burgess worked as a blacksmith at Ripley, WV, as a traveling pottery salesman for twenty-five years for Taylor, Smith & Taylor, Chester, WV (just across the Ohio River from East Liverpool), and as a pottery decorator there. He later worked as a decorator for Hall China, East Liverpool, OH, and then for Sterling China at Wellsville, OH for over fifteen years. Garnet died on 27 Nov. 1966 at East Liverpool, Columbiana Co., OH, and is buried with his wife in the Riverview Cemetery. He was a Methodist.

8a. **John Allen (I) "Jack."** Born 24 Nov. 1931 at East Liverpool, OH. Married Alma J. Hyder about 1952 (she was the daughter of John C. Hyder and Minnie I. Kinsey). Listed in the 1951 city directory for East Liverpool. Served as a 2nd Lieut. in the U.S. Army from 1954-56. Jack Burgess earned his B.S. in mechanical engineering from the University of Cincinnati in 1954, and his M.B.A. at Xavier University in 1960. He worked as an engineer for Westinghouse, Pittsburgh, PA, from 1962-79, and as a quality assurance manager at Muncie, IN from 1979-89 and at Aiken, SC since 1989. He has also written forty technical papers and one book: *Design Assurance for Engineers and Managers* (New York: Marcel Decker, 1984). He currently lives at Aiken, SC.

9a. **Christel Lynne.** Born 14 Jan. 1953 at Cincinnati, OH. Married Russell Nichols on 28 May 1977 (he served as an Army officer before retiring), and had children: *Jenna Nichole* (born 10 June 1980 in West Germany). Christel Nichols earned her bachelor's degree in secondary education from Clarion State College, Clarion, PA in 1975, and her master's degree in social counseling from Hood College, Fredericksburg, MA in 1986. She currently works as executive director of a social agency at Washington, DC. Christel and Russell Nichols live at Hanover, MD.

9b. **Michael James (I).** Born 6 May 1955 at El Paso, TX. Married Nanci M. Fullet on 22 Oct. 1977 (she was the daughter of William and Patricia Fullet). Mike Burgess earned his B.S. in mechanical engineering from Virginia Polytechnic Institute and State University, Blacksburg, VA in 1977, and his master's degree in mechanical engineering from Ohio University in 1990. He has worked as an engineer for DuPont since 1977. Mike and Nanci Burgess currently live at Little Hocking, OH.

9c. **Jack Warren.** Born 22 Apr. 1959 at Cincinnati, OH. Married Amy Kemp on 20 June 1981 (she was the daughter of Richard and Norma Kemp). Jack Burgess graduated from the U.S. Naval Academy at Annapolis, MD in 1981. After completing his five-year tour of duty as a Naval officer, he was employed by RCA in New Jersey. In 1989 he received his M.B.A. from Carnegie-Mellon University, Pittsburgh, PA, and took a job in marketing with Harris Electronics. Jack and Amy Burgess currently live at Melbourne, FL.

10a. **Jessica Raye.** Born 22 Aug. 1986 at Marlton, NJ.

10b. **Kaitlyn Michelle.** Born 11 July 1989 at Pittsburgh, PA.

9d. **Ronald Joseph.** Born 24 Apr. 1963 at Pittsburgh, PA. Married Julie A. Campbell on 16 Aug. 1986 (she was the daughter of Dale and Gloria Campbell). Ron Burgess received his B.S. in aeronautical engineering from Purdue University in 1986, and his M.S. in mechanical engineering from Washington University, St. Louis, MO in 1989. He is currently employed as a structures engineer with McDonnell-Douglas. Ron and Julie Burgess live at St. Louis, MO.

10a. **John Allen (III).** Born 22 Aug. 1991 at St. Louis, MO.

[William (I)[1], Edward (I)[2], Moses (I)[3], Edward (IV)[4], John Anderson (I)[5]]

REV. JOHN NEWTON BURGESS (1856-1936)

OF KANAWHA COUNTY, WEST VIRGINIA

6e. **John Newton** *[son of John Anderson (I)].* Born 10 Aug. 1856 in Johnson Co., MO. Married Nancy Catherine "Nannie" Martin on 14 Dec. 1881 in Kanawha Co., WV (she was born May 1857 at Poca, Kanawha Co., WV, daughter of William B. Martin and Nancy D. Johnson, and died on 29 June 1936 at Sissonville, WV). Listed in the 1900-1920 censuses for Kanawha Co., WV. The Rev. John N. Burgess was a Methodist circuit minister at Sissonville, WV, near Grapevine Creek; on 1 Feb. 1886 he purchased sixty acres of the Bruen Grant at Pigeon Roost, WV. He died on 25 Apr. 1936 at Sissonville, WV, and is buried with his wife and descendants in the Burgess Cemetery, in the Grapevine area of northern Kanawha Co., WV. The Cemetery was donated from his land, but is currently owned by the estate of Robert Benjamin Baldwin, following a trade of land between him and the Rev. Burgess.

Rev. Burgess was a supply (lay) minister for the United Methodist Church South from 1913-33. From 1913-18 he served in the Charleston District, from 1919-22 in the Parkersburg District, and from 1923-33 again in the Charleston District. Among the many churches that he served were: Trinity, Sissonville, Bias Chapel, New Hope, and Baber Agee. A supply minister was usually appointed by the district presiding elder in the absence of an ordained minister. The churches on his circuit were several miles apart, and Rev. Burgess traveled on horseback to serve them. During the years he served as minister of Baber Agee Methodist he resided in the church parsonage on Rocky Fork.

Lura Baldwin wrote in 1993: "One of Grandpa's circuit horses was named 'Dick.' Grandpa did not wear a necktie: he thought they were frivolous, and he always wore a black suit and white shirt with detached collars. Grandma would iron them until they were stiff. He did not allow banjos to be played in the house, and he did not believe that airplanes would carry passengers as predicted. He was very kind and gentle, and I don't remember him ever raising his voice. He was tall and very thin, even looked frail in his later days, probably due to his heart condition; he had dark brown hair, a fair complexion, and blue eyes. Grandpa always had prayer at every meal, and also family prayer every evening. Once I remember him laying his hand on my hand as he prayed especially for me.

"One time Uncle Marvin came for Mom and I in a car to go see Grandpa. Uncle Bub and Uncle Ernest were there, holding him up so he could breath easier. I remember it had snowed the morning he died. The funeral was at the house the next day. Grandma's funeral was at the house also; she died two months later. She had asthma, and had not been well for several years, with shortness of breath and coughing. She reportedly died from an asthma attack, but it was probably from congestive heart failure. Everyone else in the family called them Pap and Ma, but my family called them Grandpa and Grandma.

"Grandma had red hair, a fair complexion, and blue eyes, and was of medium build. She always wore an ankle-length black dress and a black bonnet when she went outdoors. She also wore a beautiful brooch on the front of her dress, in the center of the Peter Pan collars of that time.

"Grandpa tended a large peach orchard back on the hill, and would give us two to three bushels of peaches for canning each year. He also grew apples and tobacco for his own use. Water was carried from a natural spring across the hill from the house. This spring never went dry, and serviced several families during times of drought. He also kept hogs, chickens, and a milk cow. There wasn't a road to their place, you had to travel in the creek bed. They were always glad to see us come, which was only about twice each year; although we only lived about three miles apart, farm duties and travel time made it difficult.

"After his death, my mother was deeded the home place. The house was an L-shaped Jenny Lynn, with a large fieldstone hearth and fireplace, which serviced both the bedroom and sitting room. I recall a coffee grinder which hung on the kitchen wall, a large woodbox, and a cast iron wood-burning stove. All the windows in the house were hung with white or ecru lace curtains. These had to be washed and starched by stretching on a wooden frame. All their furniture was marble-topped. There was also what Grandma called a 'cinnamon vine' which grew outside the sitting room window; it was very fragrant (like cinnamon) when in bloom. The seed pods looked like tiny potatoes, and were about as large as a person's thumb.

"I was sixteen years old when we moved to Pigeon Roost. My Dad added on to the back of the home place, then tore down the original house to finish ours. He also rebuilt the barn, and a lot of people came to the barn raising: Uncle Ernest, Uncle Marvin, Hansford and George Boggess, and Greenbury 'Green' Sisson were ones I recall. Uncle Ernest's land was beside ours. Aunt Bertha was given money for her share. My Dad bought Uncle Bud and Aunt Ina's share of the land, a total of 53 acres."

The Children of Rev. John N. Burgess:

7a. **Bertha Blanch (I) "Sister."** Born 23 Dec. 1883 (or 1882) at Sissonville, WV. Married (William) Marshall "Mart" Sigmon on 31 Mar. 1903 in Kanawha Co. (he was born 31 Mar. 1882 at Sissonville, son of Shields Sigmon and Elizabeth J. Reece, and died on 23 May 1933), and had children:

Son SIGMON. Born and died 1904, buried Burgess Cemetery.

Ocie Oakley SIGMON. Born 28 Aug. 1905 at Sissonville, WV. Married Lando Gibson, and had children: *Billy Ray* (born 8 Feb. 1927 at Charleston, WV, married Isabelle H. Duty on 18 July 1947 at Charleston [she was born 31 Mar. 1931 at Chapmanville, WV], and had children: Belinda Joyce [born 3 July 1948 at Charleston, married Charles Bernard Nestor on 6 Aug. 1966 at Lanham, MD {he was born 6 Aug. 1947 at Washington, DC}, and had children: Christine Lee {born 23 June 1968}; Charles Bernard II {born 13 Mar. 1969}; Amy Catherine {born 19 Feb. 1978}]; Billie Jean [born 20 Oct. 1952 at Washington, DC, married Freeman Brand in Maryland, and had children: Maxwell {born 26 Dec. 1972}; Billie married secondly Robert Ellington in Maryland {he was born 23 Mar. 1951}, and had children: Amanda Jean {born 23 Nov. 1980}]; Douglas Wayne [born 23 July 1958 at Washington, DC, married Marie ___ on 28 Nov. 1989 at Manassas, VA]).

Ocie Oakley SIGMON married secondly Sherman Bostic (he was born 1910, brother of William Bostic [who married Ocie's sister, Eupha], and died 1945, buried Burgess Cemetery), and had children: *Pansy Lou* (born and died 1944, buried Burgess Cemetery). ***Ocie Oakley SIGMON*** also had children by Jessie Withrow: *Madeleine Delores "Sissy"* (married Jessie Facemire, and had children: Demona Lorena; Jessie Diane; *Sissy* married secondly Phillip Smith, and had children: Delilah Rose; Phillip Dale; Lois Ann; Robin Lynette; Cammy Lynn; Shannon Heath; Herbert Rocky Lee [died at age two]; by other fathers she had: Franklin Delano BOSTIC [born 28 June 1952, adopted by his aunt, Eupha Bostic {see below}]; Cherita Eileen BOSTIC [born 21 Sept. 1953 at Charleston, raised {but not adopted} by Elmer Hansford and Heather Eileen (Bostic) Burdette, married Larry Bradley Scott, and had children: Larry Jason Bradley; Heather Elizabeth; John Christopher; Cherita married secondly Ronald Lee Myers]; Robert Wesley BROWNING); *Mary Kathryn* (married Robert Munsey, and had children: Kathy; Bobby; Joe; Jessie; Tammy Jean [adopted by Eugene and Maxine Young, and renamed Rebecca Allison YOUNG]; Billy). By an unknown father ***Ocie*** also had: *Phyllis Jean* BOSTIC (by an unknown father she had children: Sharon Elizabeth BOSTIC [adopted by her aunt, Eupha Bostic {see below}]; Steven BOSTIC [adopted by Delbert and Lorene Blankenship]). ***Ocie BOSTIC*** died on 25 Aug. 1952, and is buried in the Reese Cemetery, Sissonville.

Eupha Hazel SIGMON. Born 28 Apr. 1908 at Sissonville, WV. Married William Franklin Bostic on 9 Sept. 1928 at Sissonville (he was born 22 June 1903 at Sissonville, brother of Sherman Bostic [who married Eupha's sister, Ocie], and died Mar. 1985, buried Bostic Cemetery), and had children:

Freda Mae BOSTIC (born 24 Jan. 1930 at Charleston, married Denver Ray Holmes on 19 June 1954 at Sissonville [he was born 29 Jan. 1930 at Tuppers Creek, and died 3 Jan. 1987, buried John Beane Cemetery], and had children: Rebecca Ann [born 5 Jan. 1960 at Charleston, married Anthony L. Thaxton, and had children: Crystal Ann {born 3 Feb. 1978 at Charleston}; Steven Ray {born 15 Mar. 1979 at Charleston}]).

(Heather) Eileen BOSTIC (born 29 Mar. 1931 at Charleston, married Elmer Hansford "Hank" Burdette on 28 June 1951 at Tuppers Creek, WV [he was born 2 Feb. 1932 at Sissonville], and had children: Jeffrey Hansford [born 24 Mar. 1959 at Charleston, married Sandra Kay Wolfe on 1 July 1978 at Sissonville {she was born 10 June 1960 at Charleston}, and had children: Cynthia Leigh {born 1 Jan. 1980 at Charleston}; Melinda Dawn {born 2 Nov. 1981 at Charleston}]; Anthony Allen [born 18 Sept. 1960 at Charleston, married Gloria Sue Burdette on 3 Nov. 1979 at Sissonville, and had children: Kista Renee {born 17 Apr. 1980 at Charleston}]; Christian Andre [born 18 Oct. 1962 at Charleston, married Linda Danay Page in July 1984 at Sissonville, and had children: Christian Andre II {born May 1985 at Charleston}]; Nicholas Patrick [born 23 Aug. 1966 at Charleston, married Serena Mae McMillion on 29 June 1991 at Sissonville]).

Mina Blanch BOSTIC (born 25 June 1938 at Charleston, married Hurley Eugene Bailey on 24 Aug. 1960 at Charleston [he was born 24 Aug. 1939 at Charleston], and had children: Jennifer

Suzette [born 12 Aug. 1961 at Charleston, married Michael Anthony Wyatt {he was born 21 Nov. 1958}, and had children: Jessica Leann {born 15 Apr. 1981}; Jamacia Roseann {born 27 May 1983}]; Joseph Eugene [born 29 Jan. 1963 at Charleston, married Sharon Summers, and had children: Bobbi June Yvonne {born 5 Apr. 1986 at Charleston}; William Joseph {born 22 June 1990 at Charleston}]; Eupha Jane [born 23 Sept. 1964 at Charleston, married Richard Lester {born 20 Jan. 1964}, and had children: Jeremy Richard {born 17 Feb. 1983 at Charleston, died there 13 May 1983}; Joshua Allen {born 10 Oct. 1989 at Charleston}]; James David [born 15 Aug. 1968 at Charleston]; Geril Matthew [born 15 June 1970 at Charleston]).

William Rex BOSTIC (born 1 June 1940 at Charleston, married Kay Frances Withrow on 29 June 1963 at Charleston [she was born 9 June 1944 at Charleston], and had children: Lisa Gail [born 27 Apr. 1964 at Charleston, married Ralph O'Neil Casto {he was born 26 Feb. 1952}, and had children: Kristen Elizabeth {born 8 June 1987 at Charleston}]; William Rex Jr. [born 19 Mar. 1968 at Charleston]). *William Rex* married secondly Julie Ann Staunton in Aug. 1991.

Jannice Lorraine BOSTIC (born and died Dec. 1950 in Kanawha Co., buried Burgess Cemetery).

Franklin Delano BOSTIC (ad.; born 28 June 1952 at Charleston, married Karen Sue Smith on 4 Aug. 1972 at Sissonville [she was born 13 Apr. 1955 at Charleston], and had children: Travis Franklin [born 5 Feb. 1973 at Charleston]; Maggie Mae [born 23 Nov. 1977 at Charleston]; *Franklin* married secondly Kelly Gwen Miller on 28 May 1988 in Ohio [she was born 22 Jan. 1966 at Charleston]).

Sharon Elizabeth BOSTIC (ad.; married Kenneth Estep, and had children: Kenneth; Lorrie; Lisa; *Sharon* married secondly Richard Moss, and had children: Lawson).

Eupha Hazel SIGMON died on 18 May 1964 at Sissonville, WV, and is buried in the Bostic Cemetery.

Nannie Pearl SIGMON. Born 14 Nov. 1910 at Sissonville, married Estil James "Chet" Moss on 4 Feb. 1933 at Sissonville (he was born 25 Mar. 1911 at Sissonville, and died on 29 Nov. 1979, buried in the John Beane Cemetery), and had children: *Robert Lee* (born 12 Oct. 1940 at Sissonville, married Jewel Margaret Moss on 2 July 1963 at Sissonville [she was born 16 Feb. 1944 at Sissonville], and had children: Mark Steven [born 18 Sept. 1969 at Charleston]); *Son* (born and died Feb. 1946 at Sissonville, buried Burgess Cemetery); *Connie Marie* (born and died 30 Dec. 1950 at Charleston, buried John Beane Cemetery).

Son SIGMON. Born and died about 1912, buried Burgess Cemetery.

Olaf Merle SIGMON. Born 14 Mar. 1915 at Sissonville, WV, married James Emerson Fisher on 23 May 1936 at Charleston (he was born 12 Oct. 1914 at Sissonville, and died on 29 June 1989 at Milton, WV, buried Forrest Memorial Park), and had children: *Shirley Faye* (born 27 Jan. 1938, married Lyman Darrell Niceley on 16 Feb. 1957 [he was born 3 July 1937], and had children: Darla Sue [born 19 June 1960 at Columbus, OH, married Gregory Allen Baker on 4 Nov. 1981 at Columbus, and had children: Sean Gregory {born 3 Apr. 1985 at Columbus}; Kaylee Jean {twin; born 29 July 1990 at Columbus}; Corey James {twin; born 29 July 1990 at Columbus}]; Dena Marie [born 11 July 1965 at Columbus, OH, married Benjamin Lafuze on 20 July 1985 at Columbus, and had children: Nicole Marie {born 2 Mar. 1988 at Columbus}]); *June Evelyn* (born 4 June 1941, married Ronald Shannon "Butch" Thompson on 10 Oct. 1969).

Vernon Estes SIGMON. Born 8 May 1917 at Sissonville, WV, married Delcie Smith at Sissonville (she was born 9 Dec. 1923 in Kanawha Co.), and had children: *Emmett Darrell* (born 30 Jan. 1942 at Charleston, WV, married Janet Wolfe on 3 July 1965 at Sissonville [she was born 27 Apr. 1948 at Charleston], and had children: Rhonda Lynn [born 1 Feb. 1966 at Charleston, married James Payne {he died 1991}, and had children: Cassie Lynn; Kayla Dawn; Rochelle Nicole; Rhonda married secondly Edgar Boggess]; Sherry Ann [born 14 Mar. 1967 at Charleston, and had children: Brandon Allen {born 20 Sept. 1987 at Charleston}]; Darrell Ross "D. R." [born 20 June 1972 at Cleveland, OH, and by Lorrie Estep had children: Megan Leann Nichole {born May 1992}; Darra Dawn {born Apr. 1993}]; Kelly Dawn [born 24 Mar. 1974 at Charleston]).

Vernon Estes SIGMON married secondly Thelma Pearl Newhouse on 12 July 1952 at Sissonville, WV (she was born 24 June 1923 in Kanawha Co.), and had children: *John Larry* (born 13 Aug. 1952 at Charleston, WV, married Rita Shaffer, and had children: Tracey Dawn; Alisha Nicole; *John* married secondly Joyce ___, and had children: Angela Mae); *Mazie Mae* (born 24 Nov. 1954 at Charleston, WV, married Kem Palmer, and disappeared about 1975); *Marilyn Sue* (born 2 May 1957 at Charleston, WV, married William Daniels about 1976 [div.; he was born 18 Mar. 1957], and had children: Wesley Adam [born 12 June 1981 at Charleston]); *Glennis Dale* (born 27 Dec. 1958 at Charleston, WV, married Diana Kay Boggess [she was born 30 June 1964 at Charleston], and had children: Glennis Matthew [born 26 Mar. 1982 at Charleston]); *Rena Aline* (born 30 June 1960 at Charleston, WV, married Daniel Perkins, and had children: Daniel Jr.); *William Gerald* (born 16

Mar. 1963 at Charleston, WV, married Tammy Smith, and had children: Travis); *Rocky Allen* (born 13 Mar. 1965 at Charleston, married Sabrina Stewart, and had children: Rocky Allen II; Brittany Kay); *Vernon Estes Jr.* (born 30 June 1967 at Charleston, WV, married Pamela Lawrence, and had children: Mindy Sue; Amanda Lynn).

Glennis Elwood SIGMON. Born 1919 at Sissonville, WV, married Freda Humphreys (she was born 27 Nov. 1922 at Sissonville), and had children:

Clement Edward SIGMON (born 22 Nov. 1939 at Charleston, married Patricia Ann Curry [she was born 16 Sept. 1938], and had children: Roger Dale [born 18 Sept. 1961, married Kim McMillion, and had children: Roger Dale II {born 3 Oct. 1978 at Charleston}; Roger married secondly Tracy Leigh O'Connor {born 12 Oct. 1966 at Charleston}, and had children: Brandy Nichole {born 24 Apr. 1983}; Summer Sierra {born 19 Jan. 1992 at Charleston}]; *Clement* married second (Laura) Victoria "Vicky" Blake on 18 Apr. 1971 at Charleston [she was born 22 Sept. 1949 at Charleston], and had children: Russell Edward [born 27 Aug. 1970 at Charleston, and had children: Kelsey Jean {born 23 Mar. 1992}]; Rhonda Ileen [born 16 July 1974 at Charleston, married William Harrison Pauley, and had children: William Brandon {born 20 June 1992 at Charleston}]).

Joyce Ann SIGMON (born 11 Aug. 1941 at Charleston, WV, married (Gerald) William "Bill" Richter on 12 June 1960 at Decatur, IL (he was born 29 Mar. 1940 at Rockbridge, IL), and had children: Lisa Michelle [born 3 Apr. 1961 at Alleny, IL, married Larry Diebold {he was born 15 Sept. 1961 at Lancaster, CA}, and had children: Michelle Lynn {born 22 Feb. 1978}; Kelly Ann {born 7 Feb. 1980}; Holly Rayan {born 17 Aug. 1983}]; Jeffery Allen [born 10 May 1962 at Pomona, CA, married and divorced]; Sandra Kaye [born 23 May 1964 at Hawthorne, CA, married Joseph Thomas Alyea on 2 Aug. 1989 at Lancaster, CA {he was born 22 Jan. 1967 at Newhall, CA}, and had children: Nichole Marie {born 3 Sept. 1989}]).

Glenda Ileen SIGMON (born Oct. 1943 [posthumously], died 12 Dec. 1946 [or 1945] at Sissonville, buried Burgess Cemetery).

Glennis Elwood SIGMON died on 15 Apr. 1943, and is buried in the Burgess Cemetery.

Mazie Mae SIGMON. Born 6 May 1921 at Sissonville, WV, married Asa Eldon Wolfingbarger on 27 Apr. 1940 at Greenup, KY (he was born 16 July 1917 at Sissonville, son of Emmons H. Wolfingbarger and Mary Alice Campbell, and died 19 July 1983, buried John Beane Cemetery), and had children: *Charlotte Larue* (born 25 Jan. 1943, married Ira Wesley "Speedy" Miller [he was born 8 Oct. 1942], and had children: Tammy Jean [born 20 Apr. 1963 at Charleston, married Robert Thomas Tobias on 14 Aug. 1981 at Girard, OH {he was born 19 Mar. 1961 at Warren, OH}, and had children: Cynthia Larue {born 8 Jan. 1985 at Warren, OH}; Tammy married secondly Calvin Thomas Sullivan on 4 Mar. 1993 at Jelico, TN {he was born 14 Apr. 1955 at Versailles, KY}]; Kelly Gwen [born 22 Jan. 1966 at Charleston, married her cousin, Franklin Delano Bostic, on 28 May 1988 at Niles, OH {div.}]); *Karen Lou* (born 19 Oct. 1947 at Charleston, WV, married Dana Gwinn Kees on 29 Mar. 1970 at Sissonville [he was born 8 Sept. 1947 at Charleston], and had children: Dana Sean [born 2 May 1974 at Charleston]; Justin Thomas [born 26 May 1979 at Charleston]). ***Mazie Mae WOLFINGBARGER*** died on 11 Nov. 1990, and is buried in the John Beane Cemetery.

Verlie Virginia SIGMON. Born 30 Oct. 1923 at Sissonville, WV, married Edgar Miller Patton on 7 Apr. 1944 at Guthrie, WV (he was born 30 June 1917 in Roane Co., WV, and died on 1 Apr. 1991, buried Cunningham Memorial Park, St. Albans, WV), and had children: *Susan Kay* (born 6 Sept. 1945 at Charleston, married (Floyd) William "Billy" Regalia on 17 Feb. 1965 at District Heights, MD [he was born 16 Sept. 1945 in CA], and had children: Robin Beth [stepchild; born 13 Apr. 1961, married Mike ___, and had children: Samantha Michelle]; Matthew Scott [born 27 Aug. 1965, married Gail ___, and had children: Matthew Scott II; Joshua; Christopher]); *Paul Edgar* (born 21 Aug. 1947 at Charleston, married Brenda Craddock in Nov. 1967 at District Heights, MD, and had children: Paula Gail [born Feb. 1971 at Washington, DC, married Harold Wentz in 1992, and had children: Danielle Renee PATTON]; *Paul* married secondly Susan Paulette Goodwin [she was born 4 Mar. 1967], and had children: Jennifer Lynn [born Oct. 1978 in Jefferson City, MO]; Tara Elizabeth [born Feb. 1983 at South Charleston, WV]); *Fern Janilea* (born 23 July 1950 at Charleston, married Keith Willis, and had children: Sherry Lynne [born Feb. 1969 at Washington, DC, married Ronald Ashley]; Rebecca Sue [born 23 Oct. 1970 at Washington, DC, married Christopher Douglas Thompson, and had children: Christopher Douglas Jr. {born July 1992}]; *Fern* married secondly Kenneth Glenn Bays, and had children: Kenneth Glenn Jr. [born Jan. 1980 at Washington, DC]; Kelly Virginia [born Dec. 1981 at Washington, DC]); *Anna Lynne* (born 16 July 1951 at Charleston, married Richard Edward Holcombe on 6 Sept. 1969 at District Heights, MD [he was born 28 Apr. 1946 at Porterdale, GA], and had children: Phillip Edward [born 5 Aug. 1970 at Washington, DC, married Catherine Sovine in 1992 {she was born May 1971 in Thailand}, and had children: Carley Elaine {born 6 Sept. 1993 in WV}]; Karen Anne [born 3 July 1971 at Washington, DC]; Joan Marie [born 7 Apr. 1974 at Cheverly, MD]).

Bertha Blanch SIGMON died on 4 Nov. 1967 at Charleston, WV, and is buried with her husband in the Burgess Cemetery, Sissonville. Her granddaughter, Karen Kees of Sissonville, WV, has contributed greatly to this book.

7b. **Orien Cleveland.** Born 6 Oct. 1884 at Sissonville, WV. See below for full entry.

7c. **Ernest Kennell.** Born 29 May 1887 at Sissonville, WV. See below for full entry.

7d. **Essa E. "Essie."** Born June 1889 at Sissonville, WV; died there after 1900, and is buried in the Burgess Cemetery.

7e. **Ina Pearl.** Born 11 Feb. 1892 at Sissonville, WV. Married Benjamin Franklin Griffith on 13 Nov. 1910 in Kanawha Co. (he was born 4 Mar. 1887 at Sissonville, WV, son of Daniel Alexander Griffith and Melinda Jane Jordan, and died 30 Aug. 1945 at Beckley, WV), and had children:

***Oran Jackson** GRIFFITH.* Born 22 Jan. 1912 at Sissonville, WV, married Edith Moles on 10 Oct. 1936 at Raleigh, WV (she was born 15 May 1909 at Raleigh, WV), and died 31 Jan. 1993 at Goshen, Elkhart Co., IN, having had children: *Bertha May* (born 5 Jan. 1938 at Raleigh, WV); *Glenda* (born 19 Feb. 1941 at Raleigh, WV, married Freasure Treadway); *Gladys* (born 28 May 1942 at Raleigh, WV, married Warren Stover); *Yvonne* (born 6 Oct. 1943 at Raleigh, WV, married William Jackson); *Oran Jackson Jr.* (born 21 Mar. 1946 at Raleigh, WV, married Marilyn Jean Dooley at Goshen, IN); *Carol* (born 19 Oct. 1948 at Raleigh, WV, married Thomas Fellers); *Wanda "Snookie"* (born 16 Nov. 1950 at Raleigh, WV).

***Vernon Eugene** GRIFFITH.* Born 22 Nov. 1913 at Sissonville, WV, died there about 1914.

***Macy Blanche** GRIFFITH.* Born 19 Feb. 1915 at Sissonville, WV, married Charlie Wriston at Raleigh, WV, and died 23 Nov. 1986 at Beckley, WV, having had children: *Trilba*; *Violet*; *Jack*; *Lou*.

Luverna Gladys GRIFFITH. Born 21 May 1917 at Sissonville, WV, married Calvin Allen Duncan on 23 Aug. 1935 at Milburn, WV (he was born 6 Feb. 1909 at Brushy Creek, KY, son of Landon Timothy Duncan and Louisiana Daniels, and died there on 1 July 1959 at Brushy Creek, KY, buried Foster Cemetery), and died 30 Jan. 1977 at Troy, OH (buried Casstown Cemetery, Casstown, OH), having had children:

Allen Timothy DUNCAN (born 16 Jan. 1936 at Milburn, WV, married Edith Bowling on 24 July 1958 at South Portsmouth, KY [div.; she was born 29 Dec. 1937 at Greenup, KY, and married secondly ___ Woodlief], and had children: Timothy Lynn WOODLIEF [born 31 July 1959 at Mansfield, OH, was adopted by his mother's second husband, married Susan René Kipp on 30 Dec. 1979 at Miami, FL {she was born 20 Jan. 1959 at Miami}, and had children: Veronica Adelle {born 3 Feb. 1985 at Miami}; Sabrina Michelle {born 5 July 1990 at Miami}]).

Bethel Lou DUNCAN (born 3 Jan. 1938 at Raleigh, WV, married James Marshall Stephens on 7 July 1953 at Greenup, KY [he was born 6 Apr. 1926 at Greenup, KY, son of Thomas Stephens and Annie Marshall, and died 2 June 1980 at Greenup, buried with his wife in the Quillen Cemetery], and died 14 Apr. 1978 at Ashland, KY, having had children: Debra Jo [born 18 Apr. 1954 at Ashland, KY, married Henry Brown on 8 Oct. 1972 at Greenup, KY {he was born 8 Dec. 1951 at Ironton, OH, son of Earl Brown}, and had children: Earl James "Jamie" {born 11 Apr. 1979 at Greenup, KY}; Brandon Eugene {born 10 June 1983 at Greenup, KY}]; Glen Dale [born 9 Sept. 1955 at Little White Oak, KY, married Bonita Sue Stephens on 25 Aug. 1980 at Greenup, KY, and had children: Jason Dale {born 5 Jan. 1981 at Greenup}; James Paul {born 7 Mar. 1982 at Greenup}; Salissa Ann {born 30 Dec. 1983}; Brittany Rachelle {born 11 May 1985}]; Robin Kay [born 7 Apr. 1957 at Greenup, married Glen Paul Logan on 14 Feb. 1976 at Warnock, KY {he was born 18 Oct. 1957 at Greenup}, and had children: Christopher {born 16 Nov. 1979 at Greenup}]; Brent Irwin [born 29 Oct. 1958 at Greenup, married Nancy Louise Gauze on 12 Aug. 1989 at Highpoint, NC, and had children: Calvin Brent {born 6 June 1991 at Highpoint, NC}; Erica Louise {born 5 July 1993 at Highpoint, NC}]; James Randall [born 10 Dec. 1961 at Greenup, KY, married Pamela Kinncer at Frankfort, KY, and had children: Kasey Michelle {born 28 Apr. 1987}; Jared Clay {born 26 Dec. 1992 at Frankfort, KY}]).

Carolene DUNCAN (born 16 Mar. 1940 at Brushy Creek, KY, married Ellis Earl Keeton on 17 Dec. 1954 at Russell, KY [div.; born about 1932 at York, KY, son of Lonnie Keeton and Nora Holbrook]; *Carolene* married secondly Raymond Greathouse at Mansfield, OH [div.], and had children: Brenda Louise [born 29 Aug. 1956 at Mansfield, OH, married Tracy Edmon Roszek on 25 Apr. 1987 at Jacksonville, FL {he was born 23 Feb. 1960 at Garden Grove, CA, son of George Edmund Roszek and Peggy Ann Haney}, and had children: Benjamin Duncan {born 21 Oct. 1988 at Jacksonville, FL}; Lacy Noel {born 12 Dec. 1991 at Jacksonville, FL}]; Raymond Keith [born 16 Oct. 1957 at Mansfield, OH, married, had children: Joey, and died 3 Sept. 1988 at Mansfield, OH]; *Carolene* married thirdly Henry Paul Carmel [div.; he was born 31 Jan. 1917 at Mansfield, OH], and had children: Kandi Lea [born 6 May 1960 at Mansfield, OH, married Frank Powell, and had children: Denielle Lea {born 17 Sept. 1977 at Jacksonville, FL}]; Derek Jan [born 30 Sept. 1964 at Mansfield, OH, married Gwendolyn Lee Pullen on 16 June 1984 at Jacksonville, FL {she was born 30 Apr. 1963 at Arlington, VA, daughter of Elwood L. Pullen and Juanita Amos Yancy}, and had children: Christina Lee {born 9 Dec. 1988 at Jacksonville, FL}]; *Carolene* married fourthly William Snow on 21 Oct. 1977 at Green Cove Springs, FL [he died about 1979 at Green Cove Springs, FL, and is buried in Dry Ridge, KY]; *Carolene* married fifthly William Loyd on 16 Aug. 1980 [div.]).

Wayne DUNCAN (born and died 1944 at Brushy Creek, KY, buried Foster Cemetery).

Lowell Franklin DUNCAN (born 6 June 1946 at Portsmouth, OH, married Susie Howard on 16 July 1966 at Big White Oak, KY [div.; she was born 5 Aug. 1949 at Big White Oak, daughter of John Lewis Howard and Eva Burton], and had children: Jeffery Lowell [born 25 Mar. 1967 at Portsmouth, OH, married Lori Lebounty in 1984 in WV {she was the daughter of Robert Lebounty and Shirley Long}, and had children: Brandon Jeffery {born 1 Jan. 1984 at Columbus, OH}]; Tammy Sue [born 7 Aug. 1969 at Marion, OH]; *Lowell Franklin* married secondly Alice Marie Large on 16 Oct. 1977 at Marion, OH [she was born 15 Oct. 1952 at Marion, OH, daughter of Edgar Large and Alice Green], and had children: Eric Douglas [ad.; born 13 June 1972 at Marion, OH, married Sherry Cavenaugh on 5 Dec. 1992 at Lawrenceville, GA {she was born 7 Feb. 1974 in PA, daughter of Michael Cavenaugh and Debbie Lutz}, and had children: Joshua Edgar {born 27 Jan. 1993 at Lawrenceville, GA}]).

Daryl Lee DUNCAN (born 31 Jan. 1948 at Portsmouth, OH, married Penny Arlene McMullen on 11 Apr. 1970 at Troy, OH [she was born 8 Apr. 1954 at Troy, OH, daughter of Ronald Everett McMullen and Helen Lucille Bissett], and had children: Tabatha Lee [born 5 Dec. 1970 at Troy, OH, and by Michael Todd Lewis Jackson had children: Ty Landen {born 16 Aug. 1990 at Dayton, OH}; married Darrell Paul Skeens on 11 Jan. 1992 at Troy, OH {he was born 9 Nov. 1955 at Xenia, OH, son of Arthur Skeens and Maggie Cantrell; by his first marriage, he had children: Jaden Paul <born 22 Mar. 1976 at Dayton, OH>; Colista Deanna <born 15 Dec. 1978 at Dayton, OH>}, and had children: Mackenzie Lyn {dau.; born 1 Sept. 1992 at Troy, OH}]; Tina Lyn [born 2 Aug. 1973 at Troy, OH]). *Daryl L. DUNCAN* lives at Troy, OH, and has contributed greatly to this book.

Donna Jewel GRIFFITH. Born 31 Aug. 1919 at Sissonville, WV, married Howard Maynor on 5 Feb. 1940 at Tazewell, VA (he was born at Raleigh, WV), and had children: *Glennis Howard* (born 1 June 1940 at Raleigh, WV, and died 20 Dec. 1987); *Roger Dale* (born 21 Oct. 1941 at Raleigh, WV); *Zelma Yvonne* (born 5 Dec. 1942 at Raleigh, WV, and died there 8 May 1950); *Neamon* (born 16 July 1944 at Raleigh, WV); *Freddie Gene* (twin; born 9 Aug. 1946 at Raleigh, WV); *Teddy Dean* (twin; born 9 Aug. 1946 at Raleigh, WV); *Sharon Kay* (born 31 Oct. 1947 at Artie, WV, married Harry Page Williams on 19 June 1964 at Artie, WV [he was born 19 May 1944 at Clear Creek, WV, son of Page Williams and Ethel McBride], and had children: Pamela Jane [born 29 Jan. 1967 at Detroit, MI, married Paul Williams {div.}]); Kimberly Michelle [born 28 May 1971 at Oakland, MI, married Chris Taylor on 12 July 1987 at Raleigh, WV]); *Michael Clint* (born 23 May 1949 at Artie, WV, married Lessie Mae Webb on 13 Nov. 1967 at Wayne, MI [she was born 24 Feb. 1949 at Charleston, WV, daughter of Warner Webb and Edith Marie Linville], and had children: Tina Marie [born 1 Apr. 1969 at Wayne, MI]; Donna Michelle [born 8 Aug. 1970 at Wayne, MI, married Lacy Lloyd Lusk on 8 Sept. 1990 at Dorothy, WV]); *Sandra Faye* (born 24 Mar. 1951 at Clear Creek, WV, married Chester Gale Pack on 21 Nov. 1969 at Hazel Park, MI [he was born 13 June 1949 at Flat Top, WV, son of Howard Pack and Mary McBride], and had children: Crystal Gail [born 1 Dec. 1971 at Madison Heights, MI, married Brian Davis on 20 Oct. 1990 at Raleigh, WV]; Meagon LaDonna [born 25 May 1975 at Beckley, WV]; Matthew Shane [born 19 Oct. 1978 at Beckley, WV]).

Lovell Ray GRIFFITH. Born 23 Nov. 1921 at Sissonville, WV, married Opal Maynor at Raleigh, WV (she was born Sept. 1918 in WV, and died 27 Oct. 1991 at Raleigh, WV), and died 20 Feb. 1974 at Clear Creek, WV, having had children: *Patricia*; *Floyd* (born about 1945 at Raleigh, WV); *Sambo* (born about 1951 at Raleigh, WV).

Lester Alvin GRIFFITH. Born 4 Mar. 1923 at Sissonville, WV, married Betty Dillion, and died on 24 Nov. 1977 at Detroit, MI, having had children: *Melody Ann*; *Ina May*.

Norma Arbutus GRIFFITH. Born 21 Jun. 1928 at Raleigh, WV, married Clina Griffith on 1 Mar. 1953 at Madison, WV (he was born 3 Apr. 1925 at Boone, WV, son of Dowten Griffith and Margariete Conkle, and died 2 Mar. 1991 at Sandusky, MI), and had children: *Kenneth James* (born 12 Nov. 1954 at Detroit, MI, married Mary Spencer [div.]); *Connie Lynn* (born 5 Feb. 1956 at Pontiac, MI, married Tim Kruger); *Karen Frances* (born 3 Dec. 1959 at Pontiac, MI, married Ronald Wright); *Kathy* (born 15 Oct. 1961 at Sandusky, MI, married Bruce Scruggs [div.]); *Teresa Jean* (born 27 Apr. 1967 at Sandusky, MI, married Donald Webster).

***Esther Dremalee* GRIFFITH.** Born 3 Feb. 1932 at Raleigh, WV, married Richard "Dickie" Dunbar, and died 20 Aug. 1982 at Toledo, OH, having had children: *Justin* (born at Toledo, OH).

Benjamin Franklin* GRIFFITH *Jr. Born 17 Feb. 1935 at Raleigh, WV, married Phyllis French (daughter of Wade and Sadie French).

Ina GRIFFITH died on 3 Mar. 1981 at Beckley, Raleigh Co., WV, but is buried with her husband in the Burgess Cemetery, Sissonville, Kanawha Co., WV.

7f. **Icy Elura.** Her middle name is also written Lura; she was named for her aunt, Icy Johnson. Born 9 June 1895 at Sissonville, WV. Listed with her father in the 1920 census. Married (John) Franklin Robinson on 20 Dec. 1922 in Kanawha Co., WV (he was born 25 Apr. 1892 in Kanawha Co., and died 25 July 1965), and had children:

***Lura Colleen* ROBINSON.** Born 19 Oct. 1923 at Sissonville, WV, married Arthur Herman Baldwin on 7 Apr. 1946 (he was born 13 June 1920 in Kanawha Co., and died 7 Jan. 1993), and had children: *Nancy Margaret* (born 23 Apr. 1947 at Charleston, WV, married John Franklin Shinn, and had children: Melissa Lura [born 21 Mar. 1972, married Charles Brian Stowers on 17 Sept. 1993]; *(Ronald) Travis Franklin* (born 28 Apr. 1951 at Charleston, WV, married Ann Leslie Whittington on 26 Sept. 1981, and had children: Daniel Whittington [born 27 Jan. 1984]; Andrew Keatley [born 7 May 1991]; Travis Baldwin is employed as a learning specialist for the Kanawha County Schools, and Ann works as a psychiatric nurse supervisor at Shawnee Hills Community Mental Health Center; they live at Charleston, WV). ***Lura* BALDWIN** lives at Sissonville, WV.

***Leota Maxine* ROBINSON.** Born 12 Mar. 1925 at Sissonville, WV. Married ___ Robinson, and lives at Charleston, WV.

***Edythe Irene* ROBINSON.** Born 8 Sept. 1926 at Sissonville, WV. Married Clair E. Kreider (he worked for AMP Inc., an electronics firm, before retiring), and had children: *Kenton Eugene* (born 1 May 1949, married Charlene Kolak, and had children: Kendra Elizabeth [born 18 May 1969, married Jeff Wilbur, and had children: Caleb Johnathon {born 29 Aug. 1993}]; Christen Ruth [born 17 May 1972, married Dale Largent on 31 July 1993]; Katie Irene [born 28 Mar. 1975]; Kevin Arthur [born 6 Oct. 1976]; Clairissa Anne [born 16 Dec. 1981]); *Carol Anne* (born about 1952, married Edward Saner, and had children: Michael Joseph [born 16 Jan. 1978]; Shannon Ilene [born 13 Sept. 1982]). ***Edythe* KREIDER** lives at Elizabethtown, PA.

***Gertrude Verdean* ROBINSON.** Born 10 Apr. 1928 at Sissonville, WV. Married Harold Richard Taylor on 6 Nov. 1954, and had children: *Harold Richard Jr.* (born 4 Oct. 1955); *Paul Douglas* (born 24 Jan. 1962, married Carol Lynn Matheny on 1 Sept. 1984, and had children: Joshua David [born 11 Mar. 1987]). ***Gertrude* TAYLOR** lives in Kanawha Co., WV.

***Kermit Lee* ROBINSON.** Born 20 Feb. 1931 at Sissonville, and died there 24 Feb. 1931, buried Oscar Gibson Cemetery.

***Betty Justine* ROBINSON.** Born 11 Mar. 1932 at Sissonville, WV. Married Gaynel Abbott on 25 Apr. 1952 at Clendenin, WV, and had children: *Pamela Lynn* (born 22 Dec. 1954, married Ronald Harper, and had children: Gaynel [born 29 Dec. 1975]; Martha [born 7 Oct. 1978]; *Pamela* married secondly Lue Rios in 1991); *Patricia Diane* (born 23 July 1956, married Justin Smith at Elkview, WV, and had children: *Justin Jr.* [born 13 July 1976, and had children: Andrew {born 12 Jan. 1993}]). ***Betty* ABBOTT** lives at Roane Co., WV.

***Lexie Orilla* ROBINSON.** Born 8 Apr. 1935 at Sissonville, WV. Married ___ Dooley, and had children: *Edward*; *Betty Janice*; married secondly Cecil Jones, and had children: *Charlotte*. ***Lexie* JONES** lives in Kanawha Co., WV.

***(Bethel) Yvonne* ROBINSON.** Born 6 June 1938 at Sissonville, WV. Married Glen W. Beverage on 26 Dec. 1958 (he was born 8 May 1928), and had children: *Glenna Evon* (born 1 May 1964, married Paul Mihalak, and had children: Tiffany Marie [born 31 July 1992]).

Icy Burgess ROBINSON died on 4 July 1943 at Sissonville, WV, and is buried with her husband in the Robinson Cemetery, on Grapevine Creek, in northern Kanawha Co., WV. Travis Baldwin has contributed greatly to this book.

7g. **Merle M. "Merlie."** Born Jan. 1899 (or 1898) at Sissonville, WV; died young after 1900, and is buried in the Burgess Cemetery. She may be the "M." Burgess listed in the Kanawha Co. birth records as having been born 1898.

ORIEN C. BURGESS OF KANAWHA CO., WEST VIRGINIA

[John Newton[6]]

7b. **Orien Cleveland "Bubby"** *[son of John Newton].* His name was pronounced "Orin," and is variously spelled Orian or Oran. Born 6 Oct. (or 22 Oct.) 1884 at Sissonville, WV. Married Almeda Spencer on 29 Nov. 1906 in Kanawha Co., WV (she was born about 1884 in VA). Listed in the 1910-20 censuses for Kanawha Co., WV. Bubby Burgess was a timberman near Charleston, WV. He died there on 27 June 1970, and is buried in the Spencer Cemetery, Grapevine.

8a. **Iva Pearl "Ivy."** Born 12 Sept. 1907 at Sissonville, WV. Married Farlet Hencil "Forest" Counts on 24 Oct. 1926 in Kanawha Co. (he was born 30 Mar. 1905, and died 24 May 1968), and had children: *Pearlie Mae* (born and died 12 Nov. 1927); *Vivian Pauline* (born 1 Feb. 1930 at Chelyan, WV, married Cecil Edward Lucas on 14 June 1947 at Chelyan [he was born 26 Nov. 1919, and died on 27 June 1978], and had children: June Marie [born 6 Apr. 1952, married Forrest Dale DeVees on 26 June 1970, and had children: Christopher Dale {born 26 Oct. 1973}; Melanie Lynn {born 28 June 1977}]; Joyce Lynn [born 7 Aug. 1954, married Howard David Lavender on 30 Mar. 1972, and had children: Jason David {born 4 Nov. 1977}; Chad Edward {born 15 Mar. 1980}; Angela Dawn {born 28 Apr. 1983}]; Tony Edward [born 19 July 1964, married Lynette Suzanne Suttle on 11 Aug. 1984, and had children: Zachary Craig {born 11 Sept. 1988}; Parker Jamenson {born 21 July 1991}]); *June Marie* (born 17 June 1932, died 17 Sept. 1934). Ivy Counts lives with her daughter, Vivian Lucas, near Charleston, WV.

8b. **Arnie** (dau.). Born 23 Feb. 1909 at Sissonville, WV; died there on 3 (?) Mar. 1909.

8c. **Denver Earl (I) "Den."** Born 25 July 1910 at Sissonville, WV. See below for full entry.

8d. **Cloa M.** Her name is spelled Chloa in the 1920 census. Born 1912 at Sissonville, WV. Married Blake Litton, and had children: *Raymond*; *Ronnie*; *Larry*; *Barbara*. Cloa Litton lives at Houston, TX.

8e. **Una.** Born 16 June 1914 at Sissonville, WV; died there before 1920 (not in the census).

8f. **Okey Orian.** Born 24 Sept. 1916 at Sissonville, WV. Married Mabel Belcher. Okey Burgess died childless on 26 Sept. 1970 in WV, and is buried in the Belcher Cemetery.

8g. **Louise Alice "Losie."** Born 24 May 1918 at Sissonville, WV. Married ___ Patton; married secondly ___ Kirby. Losie Kirby died on 5 Jan. 1945 in Kanawha Co., WV, and is buried in the Spencer Cemetery.

8h. **Radie.** Born about 1922 at Sissonville, WV. Married Jimmy Mullins, and lives at Blount, WV.

8i. **Cleo Addison** (son). Born 17 June 1924 (or 1925, according to his birth record) at Sissonville, WV. Married Elizabeth ___. Cleo Burgess was a miner at Elkview, WV. He died there childless in a house fire on 18 Nov. 1961.

DENVER BURGESS OF KANAWHA CO., WEST VIRGINIA

[John Newton[6], Orien Cleveland[7]]

8c. **Denver Earl (I) "Den"** *[son of Orien Cleveland].* Born 25 July 1910 at Sissonville, WV. Married Ruth Glassburne in 1933 in Kanawha Co. Den Burgess was a miner and lumberman in Kanawha Co. He died there on 3 July 1964, and is buried in the Spruce Cemetery, Cinco, WV.

9a. **Alton Clifford.** Born 26 May 1938 in Kanawha Co., WV; died there on 15 Aug. 1938, and is buried in the Hicks Cemetery.

9b. **Denver Earl (II).** Born and died 13 Dec. 1939 in Kanawha Co., WV, and is buried in the Hicks Cemetery.

9c. **Kenneth Maynard "Kenny."** Born 11 May 1941 at Cinco, WV. Married Beulah Mae Keller. Kenny Burgess lives at St. Albans, WV.

10a. **Kenneth Wayne.** Born 6 Apr. 1964 at Blount, WV.

10b. **Karen Lynn (III).** Born 7 June 1965 at Blount, WV.

9d. **Carol Jean (I).** Born 29 Sept. 1943 at Sissonville, WV.

9e. **Son.** Born 1 May 1950 at Tad, WV.

9f. **James Allen.** Born 30 Mar. 1959 at Tad, WV.

ERNEST K. BURGESS OF KANAWHA CO., WEST VIRGINIA

[John Newton[6]]

7c. **Ernest Kennell** *[son of John Newton].* Born 29 May 1887 at Sissonville, WV. Married Martha Alice Griffith on 24 Feb. 1910 in Kanawha Co. (she was born 27 Feb. 1891, the daughter of Daniel Alexander Griffith and Melinda Jane Jordan, and died 28 Mar. 1964 at Charleston, WV). Listed with his father in the 1910 census, and in the 1920 census for Kanawha Co., WV. Ernest Burgess died on 26 Jan. 1972 at Clendenin, Kanawha Co., and is buried with his wife in the Burgess Cemetery, Sissonville, WV.

8a. **Eva Everal.** Born 4 Aug. 1910 at Sissonville, WV. Eva Burgess currently lives at Charleston, WV.

9a. **Jackie** (nmn). Born and died 1937 in Kanawha Co., WV; buried in the Burgess Cemetery.

8b. **Marvin Ezra.** Born 15 Sept. 1912 at Sissonville, WV. See below for full entry.

8c. **Alpha Thelma.** Born 24 Nov. 1914 at Sissonville, WV. Married (Carl) McClelland "Mack" Martin on 10 Dec. 1936 in Kanawha Co., WV (he died 20 Oct. 1941, buried Conley Cemetery, Minnard, WV), and had children:

Helen Mae MARTIN. She was raised by her grandparents, Ernest and Martha Burgess. Born 31 Mar. 1940, married Ralph Naylor on 26 Sept. 1958 at Charleston, WV, and had children: *Debra Ann* (born 9 Aug. 1959 at Charleston, died 14 Feb. 1968 at Charleston, buried John Deane Cemetery); *Mary Louise* (born 2 Apr. 1965 at South Charleston, WV, married David McClanahan Jr. in July 1981 at Sissonville, WV [div.], and had children: Michael David [born 18 Jan. 1982]; Holly Nicole [born 18 Aug. 1983]; Mary Louise married secondly Gary Marc Lennant in 1992 at Catlettsburg, KY).

Ernest Carl MARTIN. Born 31 May 1942 (posthumously) at Sissonville, WV, married Ferabelle (or Fairy Belle, the name which appears on her tombstone in the Burgess Cemetery [no dates]) Parsons on 26 July 1964, and had children: *Carla Jane* (born 2 Apr. 1965 at South Charleston, WV, married William Ray Bryant on 12 Sept. 1980 at Gadsten, AL, and had children: Joshua Travis [born 15 Mar. 1984 at Charleston]; Beth Aron [born 26 Nov. 1988 at Charleston]; Carla Bryant lives at Walton, WV); *Ferabelle* (born and died Mar. 1960 at Charleston, WV, buried Burgess Cemetery); *Cara June* (born 29 Apr. 1967 at Charleston, WV, married Mike Stevens on 18 Nov. 1984 in Roane Co., WV; she lives at Walton, WV); *Camelia Jeane* (born about 1969, married Roger Lee Bryant on 4 Oct. 1986 at Roane Co., WV, and had children: Roger Lee Jr. [born 29 Sept. 1987]; Rusty Logan [born 29 Dec. 1989]; Camelia Bryant lives at Walton, WV); *Christopher Jason* (born 24 Apr. 1972 in Roane Co., WV). ***Ernest Carl MARTIN*** died on 1 July 1990 at Charleston, WV, and is buried in the Burgess Cemetery, Sissonville.

Alpha Thelma MARTIN married secondly Elmer Vicey Chapman on 5 Oct. 1943 in Kanawha Co. (he was born 10 Aug. 1910, and died on 2 Jan. 1976 at Goshen, IN), and had children:

Ruth Ann CHAPMAN. Born 25 Oct. 1944 at Charleston, WV, married Hubert Shaffer in 1959 in Jackson Co., WV, and had children: *Lyndall Lee* (born 26 June 1969); *Leticia Ann* (born 7 Apr. 1976). ***Ruth*** Shaffer lives at Leray, WV.

Nellie Jean CHAPMAN. Born 17 Mar. 1946 at Charleston, WV, married Raymond Reese on 12 July 1969 at Youngstown, OH, and had children: *Nathan Todd* (born 4 Apr. 1971 at Youngstown, OH); *Aron Ray* (born 25 July 1973 at Youngstown, OH). She lives at Lutonia, OH.

Marilyn Lou CHAPMAN (twin). Born 2 June 1947 at Sissonville, WV, married Kenneth Parsons in Mar. 1965 in Roane Co., WV, and had children: *Deanna* (born 26 Sept. 1965 at Charleston, WV, married, and had four children); *Kenneth Jr.* (born 13 Feb. 1969 at Goshen, IN). ***Marilyn*** married secondly Pete Schiock on 3 May 1975 in Indiana. She currently lives at Goshen.

Carolyn Sue CHAPMAN (twin). Born 2 June 1947 at Sissonville, WV, married Bobby Vaughn on 19 July 1969 at Goshen, IN, and had children: *Scott Allen* (born 12 Apr. 1972 in IN); *Sandra Renee* (born 7 Dec. 1977 at Greenwood, MS). Carolyn Vaughn currently lives at Goshen, IN.

Judy Hilda CHAPMAN. Born 19 Feb. 1949 in Jackson Co., WV, married Ralph Fields Jr. on 15 June 1968 in Roane Co., WV, and had children: *Timothy Johnny* (born 9 Jan. 1971 at Spencer, WV); *Shelly Nicole* (born 10 Aug. 1977 at Spencer, WV). Judy Fields lives at Walton, WV.

Joseph Kennell CHAPMAN. Born 25 Jan. 1951 in Tyler Co., WV, married Regina Justice in 1971 (div.), and had children: *Herbert Shane* (born 10 Oct. 1975); ***Joseph*** married secondly Reva Randolph in Oct. 1981 in Roane Co., WV (div.), and thirdly Charlotte ___. ***Joe CHAPMAN*** lives in North Carolina.

(Charles) William "Billy" CHAPMAN. Born Feb. 1952 in Tyler Co., WV, married Rebecca Horn in 1971 in Indiana (div.), and had children: *Sean Charles* (born 1 Nov. 1973 in IN); *Joshua Dewey* (born 11 Feb. 1975 in IN); *Adam Craig* (born 12 Oct. 1978 in IN); *Travis Clayton* (born 17 Feb. 1981 in IN); *Samuel Jordan* (born 8 Mar. 1983 in IN). Billy Chapman lives at Goshen, IN.

Georgia Alice CHAPMAN. Born 5 Sept. 1954 in Hancock Co., WV, married Dell Spurlock in May 1971 in Roane Co., WV (div.), and had children: *Anthony Dale "Tony"* (born 10 Oct. 1971 at Goshen, IN); *Eric Shawn* (born 2 Oct. 1973 in IN). ***Georgia*** married secondly Alan Hinley on 5 May 1978 (div.), and thirdly Larry Moore on 17 Oct. 1981 in Roane Co. (div.). By another father ***Georgia*** had children: *Chelsey Dawn* (born 8 Oct. 1992); she lives at Ripley, WV.

Sheila Lynn CHAPMAN. Born 29 Mar. 1954? in Roane Co., WV. She lives at Charleston, WV.

Alpha Thelma CHAPMAN died on 9 Nov. 1967 at Charleston, WV, and is buried with her second husband in the Hunt Cemetery, Vicars Ridge, Roane Co., WV.

8d. **Delphia Merle "Delphie."** Born 3 Jan. 1917 at Sissonville, WV. Married Clarence Delbert Olive on 12 Jan. 1935 in Kanawha Co., and had children: *Child* (born and died 1936, buried Burgess Cemetery); *Billy* (born and died 1937, buried Burgess Cemetery); *(Dale) Eugene* (born 22 Feb. 1941 at Sissonville, WV, married Sally Carder [div.], and secondly Lola Wilkinson Vicars, and lives in NC); *Judy Kay* (born 23 Sept. 1953 at Charleston, WV, married Richard Hobbstett [div.], had children: Richard Jr., and lives at Vienna, WV). **Delphie** OLIVE died of lung cancer on 19 Oct. 1963 at Sissonville, WV, and is buried there in the John Beane Cemetery.

8e. **Ivan Beverley.** Born 20 Dec. 1918 at Sissonville, WV. Married Henrietta Chandlar in Aug. 1967 in Kanawha Co. (she was born 31 Dec. 1932, and died July 1978 at Charleston, WV). Served in World War II. Ivan Burgess was an auto mechanic at Charleston, WV. He died there childless on 2 Feb. 1991, and is buried with wife in Cunningham Memorial Park, St. Albans, WV.

8f. **Glow Wayne.** Born 3 May 1921 at Sissonville, WV. Married Sylba Burdette about 1952 in Kanawha Co. (she was born 26 Mar. 1907, and died on 9 Apr. 1974 at Charleston, WV, buried Boyd Burdette Cemetery, Tuppers Creek, WV). Served in World War II as a private in the U.S. Army. Glow Burgess was a truck driver for the City of Charleston, WV. He died there childless on 19 Dec. 1984, and is buried in the Burgess Cemetery.

8g. **Orva Oval.** Born 31 Oct. 1922 at Sissonville, WV. Married Okey Earl "Buster" Chapman on 28 June 1946 in Roane Co., WV (he was born 1 July 1917, and died 3 June 1973, buried Burgess Cemetery), and had children: *Alma Faye* (born 13 Nov. 1951 at Charleston, WV, and currently lives at Charleston); *Connie Sue* (born 26 Sept. 1953 in Kanawha Co., married Tommy Handshare in 1972 [he was accidentally electrocuted two weeks after their marriage, and is buried in Legacy Memorial Gardens, Tyler, MT]; married secondly Randy Erwin Shillings in 1973 [he died 30 July 1991], and had children: Randy Erwin Jr.; Tammy; Kimberly Jo; *Connie SHILLINGS* currently lives at Kelly's Creek, WV). **Orva** married secondly Edward Pauley.

9a. **LeRoy (III)** (nmn). Born 2 July 1944 at Sissonville, WV; died there in Oct. 1944, and is buried in the Burgess Cemetery.

8h. **Bertha Blanch (II).** Her name appears in the birth records as Allyn. Born 7 Oct. 1924 at Sissonville, WV. Married Ernest William Ellis on 18 Apr. 1942 (he was born 17 Oct. 1924, son of William Hansford Ellis and Gracie May Elkins, and died on 7 Apr. 1990, buried Burgess Cemetery), and had children:

Kathryn Aileen ELLIS. Born 5 Apr. 1943 at Charleston, WV, married Everette Ellis Horton on 31 Jan. 1960 (he was born 11 Nov. 1941, son of Clarance Horton and Ruth Holt), and had children: *Natalie Ann* (born 15 June 1963 at Altus, OK, married Gregg Upton); *Sherry Tereace* (born 11 June 1965 at Ankara, Turkey, married Mark Lisjak); *Everette Ellis Jr.* (born 21 Sept. 1966 at Chicapee Falls, MA).

Wilda Ernestine ELLIS. Born 12 May 1945 at Charleston, WV, died there 23 Dec. 1945.

Ernest William ELLIS Jr. Born 31 Oct. 1946 at Charleston, WV, married Sharon Smith on 24 Nov. 1964 at Charleston (div.; she was the daughter of Robert and Catherine Smith), and had children: *Yolaunda Faye* (born 1965 at Charleston, WV); *William Riley* (born 1967? at Highpoint, NC); *Ernest* married secondly Zeola Hill (div.), and had children: *Joseph* (born 1973 at Charleston, WV); *Ernest* married thirdly Doris Knuckles (div.), and had children: *Ernest William III* (born 1 Apr. 1975 at Cleveland, OH); *Ernest* married fourthly Robin Barnette (div.), and had children: *William Casey* (born 24 July 1979 at Charleston, WV); *Ernest* married fifthly Mary Towsend, and sixthly Jackelin Curtis.

Donzel Dean ELLIS. His name is also spelled Donsal. Born 12 Nov. 1947 at Charleston, WV, married Lea Ann Winnell on 12 July 1968, and had children: *Lisa Renee* (born 15 Nov. 1975 at Charleston); *Donzel* married secondly Rose Taylor on 4 July 1976, and had children: *Deana Beth* (twin; born 21 Feb. 1978 at Charleston); *Donna Rose* (twin; born 21 Feb. 1978 at Charleston); *Donzel* died on 10 Aug. 1977, and is buried in the Burgess Cemetery.

Wanda Marie ELLIS. Born 22 June 1950 at Charleston, WV, married John Goodwin on 18 July 1968 (div.; he was the son of Oscar Goodwin and Lois Pickins), and had children: *Martha Grace* (born 16 July 1970 at Charleston, married Brian Ketron on 16 Oct. 1993).

Lonzel Albert ELLIS. Born 7 Mar. 1953, married Mollie Kate Martin on 22 Nov. 1974 (she was born 13 July 1950, daughter of Hugh Martin and Beatrice Price), and had children: *Lonzel*

Albert Jr. (born 15 Aug. 1975 at Charleston); *Christopher Michael* (born 6 July 1978 at Charleston); *Shawn Richard* (born 1 Feb. 1982 at Charleston); *Heather Renee* (born 14 Dec. 1983).

***Paul Randall* ELLIS.** Born 16 May 1956, married Jan Deniece Weekly on 18 July 1987 (she was the daughter of Richard Lee Weekly and Delores Claudine Rowan), and had children: *Nicole Deniece* (born 5 Oct. 1979 in Greenbrier Co., WV); *Joshua Paul* (born 8 June 1989 at Charleston, WV).

MARVIN BURGESS OF KANAWHA CO., WEST VIRGINIA

[John Newton[6], Ernest Kennell[7]]

8b. **Marvin Ezra** *[son of Ernest Kennell].* Born 15 Sept. 1912 at Sissonville, WV. Married Thelma Florence Fisher in 1937 (she was born 13 Jan. 1920, and died 10 Sept. 1946); married secondly Cora Cunningham Mandy in 1949. Marvin Burgess died on 26 Jan. 1988 at Charleston, WV, and is buried with his first wife in the Fisher Cemetery, Sissonville, WV.

9a. **Bobby Ray.** Born 14 Mar. 1938 on Grapevine Creek, near Sissonville, WV. Married Mary Elizabeth Grinstead on 7 Nov. 1963 at Catlettsburg, KY (she was born 2 Feb. 1941, and works as a nursing supervisor). Bob Burgess is a retired police officer for the city of South Charleston, WV, where he currently resides.

10a. **Mark Edward (II).** Born 18 July 1967 at South Charleston, WV.
10b. **Susan Ray.** Born 11 Aug. 1971 at Charleston, WV.

[see page 150]
Kathryne Zoeller Burgess Lytle (1899-1945)

[William (I)[1], Edward (I)[2], Moses (I)[3]]

NANCY BURGESS LONG
(1771?-1844)

OF SPOTSYLVANIA COUNTY, VIRGINIA

4d. **Nancy (I)** *[daughter of Moses (I)].* She is also called Ann in one record; this may have been her original name. Born about 1775 in King George Co., VA. Married Joshua Long in Spotsylvania Co. about 1838, signing a prenuptial marriage agreement (*Spotsylvania Co. Deed Book #HH*, p. 83-85) (he was born about 1776, may have married firstly Frances Dawson on 16 Jan. 1821 in Orange Co., had at least one daughter: *Susan E.* [married Philip F. Kinzer on 3 June 1845 in Orange Co.], and is listed in the 1850 census for the Eastern District [Berkley Parish], Spotsylvania Co., VA living with Molly Perry). Mentioned in the final 1832 estate accounting of Moses Burgess as having received her portion of her father's estate on 26 Jan. 1828. She may be listed in 1830 in Spotsylvania Co. with Samuel Faulconer, and in the 1840 census for Orange Co., VA with Joshua Long; Long continues to be listed in 1850 in Spotsylvania Co.

Nancy Burgess Long owned a tavern near The Wilderness in western Spotsylvania Co., VA (not far from the Orange Co. border). She died there in 1844. Her will (*Spotsylvania Co. Will Book #R*, p. 216-217), several earlier deed records, and her marriage contract, all mention her (apparently) natural son, James Burgess Faulconer, later called James T. Faulconer by his father; James is also acknowledged in the will of Samuel Faulconer as the latter's son (*Spotsylvania Co. Will Book #N*, p. 498-499, dated 24 Oct. 1820, probated 3 June 1833). This is the same Samuel Faulconer who adopted the two orphaned children (Burgess and Sarah Faulconer) of Nancy's sister, Sarah, in 1815, and who served, briefly, as executor of Moses Burgess's estate.

The Children of Nancy Burgess:

5a. **James Burgess FAULCONER.** He is called James T. Faulconer by his father. Born about 1809 in Orange Co., VA. He was deeded 55 acres of land by his cousin, Burgess Faulconer, on 11 Apr. 1828 (*Spotsylvania Co. Deed Book #BB*, p. 372-375; this is not the same parcel deeded to Burgess Faulconer a month earlier, but appears to be the farm adjoining Samuel Faulconer's land that was deeded to Burgess Faulconer by his Faulconer aunts and uncles in 1811 as his share of his father's estate [*Spotsylvania Co. Deed Book #S*, p. 350-353]). Married Eliza L. Brightwell on 26 Nov. 1835 in Spotsylvania Co., VA (she was born 1812 in VA, and died after 1853). Probably listed in the 1830 census for Spotsylvania Co. with his mother and Samuel Faulconer, and in the 1840-70 censuses for Danielsville, Berkley Parish (later Livingston Township), Spotsylvania Co., VA. James Faulconer inherited his mother's inn and part of his father's farm in rural Spotsylvania Co., VA. He died there childless in 1895; his will (*Spotsylvania Co. Will Book #AA*, p. 458, dated 18 May 1874, probated 6 May 1895), mentions one surviving heir, Mrs. Eliza A. Orr (relation unknown).

THE MARRIAGE CONTRACT OF NANCY BURGESS AND JOSHUA LONG

This indenture made the fifteenth day of August in the year of our Lord eighteen hundred and thirty eight between Joshua Long of the County of Spotsylvania of the first part, and Nancy Burgess of said County of the second part, and Lewis Rawlings of said County of the third part. Whereas a marriage is shortly intended to be had and solemnized by the permission of God by and between the said Joshua Long and the said Nancy Burgess, and whereas the said Nancy Burgess is possessed of certain personal estate, consisting of the following negroes, to wit; one woman named Frankey, one other woman Milley, and her child named William, and one other woman named Malinda, and whereas it hath been agreed that the said Joshua Long should, after the intended marriage, had [sic], receive and enjoy during the joint lives of them the said Joshua Long and Nancy Burgess. But should the said Joshua Long die before the intended wife Nancy Burgess, then she is to have the sole and only disposal of the above described property notwithstanding her coverture (?), and whereas it hath also been agreed, that in case the said Nancy Burgess should survive her said intended husbon [sic] Joshua Long, that she should not have or claim any part of the real or personal estate whereof the said Joshua Long should die seized or possessed, only one hundred acres of land lying in Glady Run and being the same land on which the mill formerly stood, this she is to have and enjoy for her life; Now this indenture Witnesseth, that in pursuance of the before recited agreement, and in consideration of one dollar of lawful money, to the said Nancy Burgess in hand paid by the said Lewis Rawlings, at and before the ensealing and delivery of these presents, the receipt whereof is hereby acknowledged, she the said Nancy Burgess by and with the privity, consent and agreement of the said Joshua Long testified by his being made a party to and his sealing and delivery of these presents hath granted bargained assign, transfer'd and set over, and by these presents doth grant, bargain, sell assign transfer, and set over, unto the said Lewis Rawlings his executors, administrators, and assigns all the said negroes, to wit: Franky, Milley, and her child named William, and Malinda, with all the futer increace [sic] of the female slaves. To have and to hold the said property hereby conveyed unto the said Lewis Rawlings his executors, administrators and assigns. Upon Trust nevertheless, and to and for such intents and purposes and under such provisoes and agreements as are herein after mentioned, that is to say, in Trust for the said Nancy Burgess and her assigns until the solemnization of the said intended marriage Then when Trust, that the said Lewis Rawlings, his executors administrators and assigns, shall and do permit, the said Joshua Long, during the joint lives of the said Joshua Long and Nancy Burgess his intended wife, to have receive take and enjoy all the interest and profits of the said property hereby assigned, to and for the support of the said Long, and his intended wife, Nancy Burgess, and from and after the decease of them the said Joshua Long and Nancy Burgess, then upon Trust that he the said Lewis Rawlings, his executors administrators and assigns, shall and do assign transfer and pay over all the said property to the said Nancy Burgess, in the event of her surviving her intended husbon [sic] Joshua Long, but if she the said Nancy Burgess die before her intended husband Joshua Long, then he the said Lewis Rawlings is to pay it over to such person or persons as she shall direct by her last will and testament; to the intend that the same may not be at the disposal of, or subject to the control, debts, forfeiting or engagements, of the said Joshua Long her intended husband. In witness whereof the parteys have hereunto set their hands and affixed their seals, the day and year first above written. Joshua Long, Nancy [her mark] Burgess, Lewis Rawlings.

The contract was witnessed by Thos. M. Horn and Linah M. Hodges, filed 17 Dec. 1838, and noted as "exe[d] and del[d] L. Rawlings."

The Will of Nancy Burgess Long

In the name of God amen, I Nancey Long of the County of Spotsylvania and the State of Virginia being weak in body, but of sound mind and disposing memory, for which I thank God, and calling to mind the uncertainty of human life and being desirous to dispose of all such worldly estate as it hath pleased God to bless me with—I give and bequeath the same in manner following, that is to say, first I desire that all of my just debts and funeral expenses be paid out of my Estate—Secondly, I give to my son James Burgess Fauconer my farm and tavern that I purchased of John Layton during his life time, and to the lawfull heirs of his body forever, provided he shall leave any such heirs at his death, but in the event he should have no such heirs of his body, I desire that my Executor hereinafter named shall sell the said farm and tavern above named for the best price that can be obtained and to divide the money ariseing [sic] from such sale equally between the children of my neces [sic] Sarah Mason and the children of Margrit Crawford, to be enjoyed by them forever—and Thirdly I desire that my Executor hereinafter named shall sell all my negroes that I may leave at my death giving the negroes the liberty of chuseing [sic] there [sic] Master, and out of the money ariseing from the sale of my negroes I desire that my nephew Burgess Faulconer shall have one hundred dollars provided he is living at the time of my [__] death and the balance of the money ariseing from the sale of my negroes I give to my son James Burgess Fauconer to be enjoyed by him for ever, and lastly I do hereby constitute and apoint [sic] my friends Thomas M. Horn, Mason B. Almond, and Barnett Almond Executors to this my last will and testament, hereby revoking all other former wills or testaments by me heretofore made. In witness whereof, I have hereunto set my hand and affixed my seal this six day of May 1844.

Nancey [her mark] Long.

The will was witnessed by Joseph H. Robinson, Robert Richards, and Catharine Richards, and was probated on 3 Sept. 1844. The executors declined to serve, and James Faulconer was appointed administrator of the estate.

THE WILL OF SAMUEL FAULCONER

In the name of God amen I Samuel Faulconer of the County of Spotsylvania in the state of Virginia being very sick and weak in body but of perfect mind and memory thanks be to God for the same and calling to mind the mortality of my body and knowing that it is appointed for all men once to die do make and declare this my last will and testament that is to say principally and first of all I give and recommend my soul unto the hands of God, that give it and as for my body I recommend it to the earth to be decently buried in a christian manner at the discretion of my exetors [sic] here after named nothing doubting but at the general resurrection I shall receive the same again by the mighty power of God, and as touching such worldly estate where with it hath pleased God to bless me with in this life I give devise and dispose of the same in the following manner and form vizt.—Imprimis. First I give all my estate to my son James T. desiring all my just debts to be be paid out of the estate my desire is for Burgess Faulconer to be first executor Nancy Burgess second on condition after deeding all her estate to her son James Faulconer if not to be avoid. I desire the said Nancy Burgess to have a house and home during her living a single life also one feather bed and furniture and half dozen plates two basons one desk acknowledging this to be my last will and testament revoking disannulling and making void all form [sic] wills and bequeaths by me mad [sic] ratifying and confirming this and no other to be my last will and testament—In witness whereof I have hereunto set my hand and seal this twenty forth day of October eighteen hundred and twenty. Samuel [his mark] Faulconer.

The will was witnessed by John Almond, Nenton Sullivan, William Almond, Bolles Faulconer, with a codicil added: "N.B. I desire my sister Jemima Faulconer to have a house and home her life living single." The will was probated on 3 June 1833. Burgess Faulconer and "Ann" Burgess refused to act as exectors, and James Faulconer was appointed in their stead.

[William (I)[1], Edward (I)[2], Moses (I)[3]]

CATHARINE ELLIS BURGESS
(1783?-1849)

OF ORANGE COUNTY, VIRGINIA

4f. **Catharine Ellis** *[daughter of Moses (I)].* She was named for her great-grandmother, Catherine Ellis. Born about 1783 (or 1790) in King George Co., VA. Listed in the 1830-40 censuses for Orange Co., VA living alone. Catharine Burgess was a farmer in Orange Co., VA. On 2 Nov. 1818 (1819 in the deed book) she made a deed of gift to her natural son, Barnett Burgess (*Spotsylvania Co. Deed Book #V*, p. 347, filed 5 Apr. 1819), in which she gave him the slaves she had received as part of her father's estate; the deed was directly followed by a similar grant from William Almond to his children then surviving, dated and filed the same day. She died there unmarried in 1849. Her will (*Orange Co. Will Book #11*, p. 58-59, dated 30 Nov. 1848, probated 26 Feb. 1849; with appraisals on 28 Oct. 1850 [*Will Book #11*, p. 244] and 27 Apr. 1854 [*Will Book #12*, p. 81]), mentions as legatees her sister, Mildred L. Almond, niece Martha J. M. Almond, and her natural son, Barnett Burgess, later called Barnett Burgess Almond. No father is mentioned.

The Children of Nancy Burgess:

5a. **Barnett Burgess** ALMOND *[son of Catharine Ellis].* He is called Barnet Burgess in his mother's 1819 deed of gift, but always used the surname Almond in later life, and was probably raised by the Almond family. Born Nov. 1815 (or 1813) in Orange Co., VA. Married Ann S. Webb (?) about 1840 (she was born Mar. 1822 [or 1825] in VA, and died between 1900-10). He sold all of his interest in the estate of Jessie B. Webb to Catharine Burgess (his mother) on 12 Sept. 1845 (*Orange Co. Deed Book #40*, p. 55). Listed in the 1840-1900 censuses for Berkley Parish (later Livingston Township), Spotsylvania Co., VA (in 1840 with a wife and no children); three of eight children survive in 1900. Barnett Burgess Almond was a shoemaker and farmer in Spotsylvania Co. His brief obituary, in the 29 Dec. 1904 issue of the *Fredericksburg Free Lance*, headlined "Death of an Old 'Fiddler'," mentions that he "had furnished music for the dancing public for fifty or sixty years." He died there on 9 Dec. 1904.

6a. **Alverda A.** ALMOND. Born Aug. 1843 in Spotsylvania Co., VA. Married Edward H. Gordon on 15 June 1896 in Spotsylvania Co., VA (he was born May 1843 in VA, and died about 1910 [his name is scratched off the census]). Listed in the 1850-1900 censuses with her parents, and in 1910-20 with her brother, Winston. Alverda Gordon died childless after 1920.

6b. **(Ethelwin) Alexander** ALMOND. Born Apr. 1845 in Spotsylvania Co., VA. Listed in the 1850-1900 censuses with his parents, and in 1910-20 with his brother, Winston. Alexander Almond was a carpenter. He apparently died unmarried after 1920.

6c. **Leonidas S.** ALMOND. Born about 1847 in Spotsylvania Co., VA. Listed in the 1850-1880 censuses with his parents. Leonidas Almond was a farmhand in Spotsylvania Co. He died there, apparently unmarried, before 1900.

6d. **Elonzo** ALMOND. Born about 1849 in Spotsylvania Co., VA. Listed in the 1850 census with his parents, but died there before 1860 (probably by 1857).

6e. **Winston S.** ALMOND. Listed in the 1860-70 censuses as Monilva or Monilda Almond. Born 22 Feb. 1852 in Spotsylvania Co., VA. Married Nellie O. Peacher about 1905 (she was born 4 Dec. 1881 in VA, and died 15 Aug. 1970 at Adelphi-Chillum [near Hyattsville], MD). Listed in the 1860-1900 censuses with his parents, and in 1910-20 in Spotsylvania Co., VA. Winston Almond was a watchmaker in Spotsylvania Co. He died there on 31 Jan. 1937, and is buried in the Confederate Cemetery, Spotsylvania, VA.

7a. **Daisy V. ALMOND.** Born 9 May 1905 in Spotsylvania Co., VA. Married ___ Haina (he may be the William Haina who was born 15 July 1904, and died May 1971 at New Carrollton, MD). Daisy Haina was living at Riverdale, MD in 1970. She died in Apr. 1978 at Burlington, IA.

7b. **Flora M. ALMOND.** Her name is also spelled Floura or Flouna. Born about 1911 in Spotsylvania Co., VA. Married ___ Jett. Flora Jett was living at Spotsylvania, Spotsylvania Co., VA in 1970. She is *not* the Flora Jett whose obituary appears in 24 Dec. 1980 issue of the *Fredericksburg Free Lance-Star*, but may be the Flora Jett who was born 3 Dec. 1912, and died 2 Oct. 1992 at Mesa, AZ.

6f. **Laura A. ALMOND.** Born 14 Aug. 1854 in Spotsylvania Co., VA; died there before 1860.

6g. **Leonzo C. ALMOND.** His name is given as Leonzia in 1870. Born about 1857 in Spotsylvania Co., VA. Listed with his parents in the 1860-80 censuses for Spotsylvania Co. Leonzo Almond was a farmhand in Spotsylvania Co. He died there, apparently unmarried, before 1900.

6h. **Florida D. "Flora" ALMOND.** Born 18 Sept. 1859 in Spotsylvania Co., VA. Listed with her parents in the 1860-80 censuses for Spotsylvania Co. Flora Almond was a musician in Spotsylvania Co. She died there, apparently unmarried, before 1900.

THE DEED OF GIFT FROM CATHARINE BURGESS TO HER SON

Know all men by these presents that I Catherine Burges of the county of Orange and State of Virginia for and in consideration of the natural love and effection [sic] which I bear to my son Barnet Burges of the county and state aforesaid as well as for the further consideration of one dollar to me in hand paid by the said Barnet Burges at or before the ensealing and delivery of these presents the receipt whereof is hereby acknowledge [sic] have given and granted and by these presents do give and grant unto the said Barnet Burges his executors administrators and assigns a negroe woman slave named Mary and her child named Emilly and all there [sic] future increase one sorrel mare three head of cattle and there future increase one bed and furniture and one chist to have and to hold the above named property and all its future increase unto the said Barnet Burges his executors administrators and assigns forever and the said Catherine Burges for herself her executors and administrators the above named property unto the said Barnet Burges his executors administrators and assigns against the claim of her the said Catherine Burges her executors administrators and against the claim of all and every other person or persons whatsoever shall and will warrant and forever defend by these presents. In witness whereof I have hereunto set my hand and seal this 2. day of November 1819 [sic].

Cathrine [his mark] Burgess [sic]

Witnessed by Richard Richards, John Sulivant, Francis Sulivant, and filed 5 Apr. 1819 [sic]. A margin note to the left of the deed states: "1850 Feby 4th—The original deed is del^{d} to B. B. Almond."

THE DEED OF GIFT FROM WILLIAM ALMOND TO HIS CHILDREN

Know all men by these presents that I William Almon of the county of Spotsylvania and State of Virginia for and in consideration of the natural love and affection which I bear to my children Barnet Amanda E. Almon Mason B. Almon and Marget [sic] L^{d}. Almon and all the futer [sic] increase of my present wife during of [sic] my life of the county and state aforesaid as well as for the further consideration of one dollar to me in hand paid by the said children Amanda E. Almon Mason B. Almon Margaret L^{d}. Almon at or before the ensealing and delivery of these presents the receipt whereof is hereby acknowledged have given and granted and by these presents do give and grant unto the said Amanda E. Almon Mason B. Almon Margaret Ld Almon their executors administrators and assigns a negroe woman by the name of Winney and her child by the name of Mary and a negroe boy by the name of Watson and all their future increase to have and to hold the above named negroes Winney Mary and Watson and all their future free from the claim or claims of any other person or persons whatsoever shall and will warrant and forever defend them by these presents but is understood and intended that the above named property shall remain in the possession of my present wife Mildred L^{d}. Almon for her use during her life. In witness whereof I have hereunto set my hand and seal this 2. day of Novembember [sic] 1819 [sic].

William Almon [sic]

No witnesses are noted. The deed was filed 5 Apr. 1819 [sic]. Teste (for both deeds): Richard S. Stevenson, C.S.C.

[uncle-in-law of Garland Anderson Burgess]

JOHN MEREDITH BURGESS
(1790?-1842?)

OF KANAWHA COUNTY, (WEST) VIRGINIA

NOTE: No direct genealogical connection between the John Meredith Burgess line and the Moses Burgess line has yet been established, except that John Meredith's daughter married the brother of Garland A. Burgess's wife, and the two families either traveled together or at least settled in the same area of Johnson Co., Missouri in the 1840s. This may or may not be a coincidence, but it is enough, in this writer's opinion, to warrant inclusion of this family. For the purposes of this genealogical history, John Meredith Burgess will be considered the same generation level as Garland Burgess's father—that is, fourth generation. Much of the information on the McCowns and their Burgess connections has been supplied courtesy of Diane and Del Poole and Peggy Carlston.

4a. **John Meredith (I)** *[uncle-in-law of Garland Anderson].* Born about 1790 at Beaverdam, Hanover Co., VA, or in Albemarle Co., VA (according to different family traditions; it should be noted, however, that there are Beaverdam Creeks in Orange Co. and elsewhere in Virginia). Married Judith "Judy" Cobb (or Cobbs) in 1812 in Kanawha Co., VA (later WV) (she was born 1796 in Kanawha Co., VA [later WV], the daughter of Fleming Cobb, a scout and Indian fighter [he was born 23 Sept. 1768 in Ablemarle Co., VA, and died 10 Jan. 1846, buried Cobb Cemetery {now located on the Kanawha Country Club property}], and Sarah "Sally" Morris [she was born 1775 at Donnally's Fort, Greenbrier Co., VA {later WV}, and died 23 Oct. 1856, buried Cobb Cemetery]; her brothers included Thomas Upton Cobb, Roswell Cobb [stabbed to death in Mar. 1851], and possibly Hiram Cobb; Judy Burgess's date of death is unknown, but she was buried in the Cobb Cemetery). John was arrested in 1812 along with Hiram Cobb for beating John Dawson (*Kanawha Co. Court Case #1812-2*), and is noted in the record as being a cooper; he was fined $100. Listed in the personal property tax lists of Kanawha Co. from 1811-1830, and again from 1837-1838, and in the 1820 census for Kanawha Co. (but no other census there; in 1820 he has three sons under the age of 10). He appears to have moved either to another county in West Virginia, or to southern Ohio, and died there at an unknown date. The children listed below cannot absolutely be verified, but are so closely associated with each other in the legal records of Kanawha Co. as to constitute a distinct family group. Said to have been buried in the Cobb Cemetery, South Charleston, Kanawha Co., WV.

The Children of John Meredith Burgess:

5a. **George Washington (IV)**. Born 1813 at Spring Hill, Kanawha Co., VA (later WV). See below for full entry.

5b. **Fleming Cobb (I)**. Born 25 Jan. 1815 at Spring Hill, Kanawha Co., VA (later WV). See below for full entry.

5c. **Thomas C(obb?)**. Born about 1817 at Spring Hill, Kanawha Co., VA (later WV). See below for full entry.

5d. **John D. (I)**. Born about 1820 at Spring Hill, Kanawha Co., VA (later WV). A John D. Burgess is mentioned as an heir (through the right of Judith Cobb Burgess) in the estate records of Fleming Cobb, in which Moses Ward received "the share and rents, issues and property, issuing out of the estate of Fleming Cobb, by purchase from Fleming Burgess and by descent and distribution from John D. Burgess, both who were the owners of shares or interest in the said estate, and where Thomas, has only drawn from Roswell Cobb, administrator, $54.76" (when Roswell Cobb was murdered in 1851, Moses Ward was appointed his successor as administrator). This seems to indicate that he died childless shortly after his mother's death (1856). He does *not* appear to be the John Burgess born about 1819 who is listed in the 1850 census for Mason Co. and the 1860 census of Fayette Co. as "deaf and dumb."

5d. **Caroline Francis**. Born 21 Nov. 1821 at Spring Hill, Kanawha Co., VA (later WV). Married Col. James Madison McCown on 29 Aug. 1836 in Lawrence Co., OH (he was born about 1817 [or 1815] in Kanawha Co., VA [later WV], son of Mathew McCown and Mary Magdalean Bowyer; as a young man he worked on steam boats on the Ohio River, and before leaving Kanawha Co. was elected Colonel of a militia company; he later served as a Lieut. Colonel in the 2nd Missouri Cavalry, Confederate Army during the Civil War; after the war he went into business and died on 8 July 1867 at Warrensburg, MO of yellow fever contracted while on a trip to New Orleans, being buried in the Smyrna Church Cemetery, Centerview, MO). Caroline Burgess McCown is mentioned in the estate accounts of her grandfather, Fleming Cobb. The McCowns had children:

William H. "Billy" McCOWN. Born 4 Oct. 1839 (or 1842) in Kanawha Co., VA (later WV), married Gilly A. Bridges on 4 Oct. 1870 at West Plains, MO (she was born Dec. 1853), and had children: *James* (born 1872, married Margaret Smith); *Fanny* (born 1876); *William* (born 1878, married May Gosney, and had seven children); *Henry* (born 1880); *Mamie* (born 1882); *Nellie* (born 1884, married Harry J. Carr). ***William H. McCOWN*** attended Cumberland University, Lebanon, TN, served as a Captain in the Confederate Army during the Civil War, worked as an attorney, and died at Piedmont, MO. He was captured in Johnson Co. during the war, ostensibly coming to get his mother and "take her to Texas to be with her brother," who can only be George Washington Burgess. "On August 7, 1885 Wm. H. McCowan [sic] was shot to death in a barber shop operated by Harry S. Lamb and Simon Conrad by a telegraph operator named Flynn."

Mary Francis McCOWN. Born 19 Dec. 1840 in Henry Co., MO, and died unmarried of typhoid fever on 8 Nov. 1860 in MO, her death being reported in the *St. Louis Christian Advocate*.

Martha Ellen "Mattie" McCOWN. Born 28 Apr. 1843 in MO; married George Roderick Foster on 4 May 1860 in Johnson Co., MO (he was born 20 July 1834 in Logan Co., KY, son of James Foster and Elizabeth Hornbuckle Simpson, remarried Bertha Price in 1881, and died on 9 Apr. 1896 at Valley City, MO), and had children:

Mary Lee "Molly" FOSTER (born 24 Aug. 1861, married Ledbetter Thomas Ward in Dec. 1881 at Pleasant Hill, MO [he was born 1846 in TN], and had children: James Gordon [born 1883, married Leota Bannister, and died Oct. 1932 at Kansas City, KS]; Carola Cleveland [born 1885, married Frank Webb, and died on 20 Apr. 1944 at Stockton, MO]; Nannie Mace [born 1888, married August Newman, had children: Mary Lu, and died 29 Nov. 1941]; Fred Foster [born 1894, married Lola McMillan]; *Mary* died on 23 Dec. 1937, and is buried with her husband in the Stockton Cemetery, Stockton, MO).

James McCown FOSTER (born 2 Apr. 1866 at Allenton, MO, married Mattie Lynn, and died childless in Oct. 1932 at Kansas City, KS).

George Roderick FOSTER Jr. (born 23 Jan. 1869 at Allenton, MO, married Ada Frances Archer on 20 Sept. 1893 at Kansas City, MO [she was born 23 May 1876 at Kansas City, MO, and died 12 Dec. 1952 at Long Beach, CA], and died 30 Mar. 1934 at Stockton, MO [buried Stockton Cemetery], having had children: Jessie Bartlett Elizabeth [born 18 Oct. 1895 at Kansas City, MO, married Carl Paul Ockel on 3 Dec. 1910 at Denver, CO {he was born 13 Dec. 1892 at Milwaukee, WI, and died 29 Feb. 1948 at Denver, CO}, and had children: Mellissa Margaret {see below}; Jessie Bartlett Elizabeth married Harold Evans Yetter on 5 June 1919 at Golden, CO {he was born 25 Nov. 1894 at York, NE, and died 20 Apr. 1983 at Sun City, AZ}, and died Dec. 1977 at Sun City, having had children: Harold Hannan, married Jennie ___, and had children: Jennifer Louise <married Frank Watson>; Susan}]).

<u>Mellissa Margaret</u> FOSTER. Born 15 Mar. 1914 at Denver, CO, married Haskell Jolley Clark on 2 Jan. 1939 at Tijuana, Baja California Norte, México (he was born 27 Oct. 1912 at Lovell, WY), and had children: Margaret Ann "Peggy" (born 8 Apr. 1945 at Hollister, CA, married Kenneth Lee Johnson on 21 Dec. 1966 at Los Angeles, CA [he was born 12 June 1942 at Yuba City, CA], and had children: (Clark) Douglas [born 17 Jan. 1968 at Redondo Beach, CA, married Ada Mirna Gómez-Pérez on 10 Aug. 1991 at Toronto, ON, Canada {she was born 11 Apr. 1971 at San Salvador, El Salvador}, and had children: Madison Lael {born 7 Oct. 1993 at Albany, NY}]; Jody Lynne [born 23 Jan. 1970 at Torrance, CA, married Michael Robert Land on 21 Nov. 1992 at Los Angeles, CA {he was born 13 Sept. 1966 at Lynwood, CA}, and had children: Child {due Sept. 1994}]; Jennine Dawn [born 22 July 1971 at Torrance, CA, married Brian Keith Boling on 23 May 1992 at Ontario, CA {he was born 18 Feb. 1966 at Knoxville, TN}, and had children: Brandilyn Rene {born 29 Sept. 1991 at Anaheim, CA}; Kaylissa Ann {born 13 Mar. 1994 at Fontana, CA}]; "Peggy" married secondly Roger Wayne Hendricks on 27 July 1974 at Bellflower, CA [he was born 1 Oct. 1940 at Compton, CA, and died 5 Jan. 1983 at Upland, CA], and had children: Mellissa Margaret [born 17 Jan. 1976 at Harbor City, CA]; "PEGGY" married thirdly Dennis Price Carlston on 25 Apr. 1987 at Ontario, CA [he was born 13 Mar. 1943 at Salt Lake City, UT]). Peggy Carlston has contributed greatly to this book.

William Yancey FOSTER (born 2 May 1877 at Allenton, MO, married Ivah Catherine Barnes [she was born 2 Nov. 1891, and died 24 Jan. 1971], and had children: Martha Ann [born 4 May 1923 at Springfield, MO]; William Roderick [born 16 June 1924 at Springfield, MO, married Ruth Bernice Schumacher on 28 Dec. 1946, and had children: David Barnes {born 18 Sept. 1949 at St. Louis, MO, married Susan Atterbury in 1975, and had children: Scott H. <born 1976>; Linda R. <born 1980>}; James Walter {born 19 Jan. 1951 at Dallas, TX, married Gale Gainer in 1978, and had children: Daniel

J. <born 1971>; Lindsey M. <born 1980>}; Robert McCown {born 25 Dec. 1952 at Dallas, TX}; Barbara Jean {born 19 July 1955 at Dallas, TX, married John A. Jarvin}; Catherine Ann {born 13 June 1961 at Dallas, TX}; William R. Foster is a petroleum engineer at Dallas]. William Y. Foster was a teacher and principal in Cedar and Vernon Cos., MO. He was elected Superintendent of Schools for Vernon Co. in 1907, serving until 1915. He died 2 Sept. 1948 at Springfield, MO, and is buried there with his wife in the Greenlawn Cemetery).

Mattie FOSTER died on 6 Mar. 1878 at Allenton, MO, and was buried with her husband in the Sunset Hill Cemetery, Warrensburg.

(James) Sanford "Samp" MCCOWN. Born 16 Nov. 1845 at Warrensburg, MO, served as a private in Co. F, Capt. Waddell's Co., 16th Missouri Infantry, Confederate Army, and was living unmarried in 1915 at Walla Walla, WA. He died there childless on 24 May 1931.

Charles Calhoun MCCOWN. Born 23 Jan. 1848 at Warrensburg, MO, married Eugenia A. Ferguson on 25 Dec. 1873 at Allenton, MO (she was born May 1853, and died 20 Dec. 1920), and had children: *Stella Price* (born 1874, married William Cyrus Coleman [born 1867, died 1954], and died 1940, having had children: Floyd Hugh [born 1901, married Alice Johnson {born 1899}, and had children: Sally {born 1934}]; Elgin Hilbert [born 1903, married Emma ___, and had children: Patsy {born 1934}]; Bernadine [born 27 Nov. 1905, married Harry Averill, and secondly ___ Kincaid, and died Sept. 1966 at Spokane, WA]; Helen [born 1909, married Ransom Vard Summers {he was born 18 Apr. 1902, and died 6 Oct. 1988 at Tacoma, WA}, and had children: Diane Louise {born 1929, married Delbert Monty Poole <born 1927>}; Adelle Bertine {born 1934, married John Christian Hauf <born 1931>}]); *Cora* (born 1875, married Aaron D. Sampsel [born 1865], secondly ___ Williams, and thirdly Henry M. Haag [born 1865]; *Cora* died in 1944); *Mary* (born 1877, died 1881); *Florence* (born 22 Oct. 1880, married Gilbert Peter Chriss [born 1871]; *Florence* married secondly Ezra Edmund Dill [born 1891, died 1965], and died Dec. 1975 at Boise, ID, aged 95 years); *Lillian* (twin; born 20 Jan. 1884, married Guy H. McConaughey [born 1883, died 1918], and had children: Lois [born 1910, married Jack Edwards]; *Lillian* married secondly Samuel Bollinger [born 1866, died 1948], and died July 1974 at Portland, OR, aged 90 years); *Hugh Brinker* (twin; born 20 Jan. 1884, married Anna Fern Pickard [born 1885, died 1965], and had children: Madolyn Fern [born 1912]; Guy Hugh [born 1913, married Edna Enis McGrath]; Ruth [born 1914, married Doyle Scott]; Grace Lillian [born 1918, married Norman Fowler]; *Hugh* died 1960). ***Charles Calhoun MCCOWN*** was living at Middleton, ID in 1911; he died on 6 Dec. 1924 at Emmett, ID, and is buried in the Morris Cemetery, Boise, ID. His biography appeared in *Portrait and Biographical Record of Johnson and Pettis Counties, Missouri* (Chicago: Chapman Publishing, 1895, p. 345-346). Del and Diane Poole have contributed greatly to this book.

John W. MCCOWN. Born Dec. 1853 at Warrensburg, MO. Married Christina Braun about 1890 (she was born 1860). He was a commercial traveler in 1896 at Kansas City, MO. Listed as a druggist in the 1900 census for Kansas City, MO. He died there in 1914.

George Walter MCCOWN. Born 22 May 1857 at Warrensburg, MO. Married Cora Mertine Johnson on 25 Feb. 1914 in Custer Co., MT (she was born 1872, and died 1951), and had children: *Olive* (born 1894, married Emil A. Tomkewitz [he was born 1882], and died 1931); *Kenneth Walter* (born 1918, married Adeline Matilda June Redmer). ***George MCCOWN*** died on 7 Jan. 1924 at Beebe, MT, and is buried in Miles City Cemetery.

Mathew G. MCCOWN. He is called Robert G. McCown mentioned in his father's will. Born about 1858 at Warrensburg, MO. Married Cordelia Burgess, his cousin, on 25 Aug. 1921 in Johnson Co., MO (see her entry for their children). He disappeared in 1923, and was never heard from again.

Virginia Davis MCCOWN. Born May 1861 at Warrensburg, MO, married James W. Smith on 8 Dec. 1880 in Johnson Co., MO (div. 1890), and had children: *Hilda* (born 1881); *Caroline Francis* (born and died 1883, buried Pisquah Cemetery); *Jesse McCown* (born 1884, died 1887, buried Pisquah Cemetery); *Birdie* (born 1887, married Lovely Vurn). Listed in the 1900 census for Warrensburg, Johnson Co., MO. Virginia died on 19 Mar. 1918 at Kansas City, MO, and is buried there in the Elmwood Cemetery.

The MCCOWNS moved about 1837 from Kanawha Co. to Post Oak Township, Johnson Co., MO, becoming a prominent family there; James McCown was elected County Clerk of Johnson Co. in 1848, and Circuit Clerk in 1856. By 1850 he was reported to be the tenth most prosperous land owner in Johnson Co. But the onset of the Civil War in 1861 divided the county between supporters of the Union and the Confederacy, the McCowns and Burgesses siding with the latter cause. The McCowns' house was burned on 23 Mar. 1862, the morning after several of the Burgesses were killed and their own house destroyed, and Caroline fled the county with her family until the war ended. ***Caroline F. MCCOWN*** died on 28 Aug. 1915 in Johnson Co., MO, aged 94 years, and is buried in the Sunset Hill Cemetery, Warrensburg. The account below reveals much about the passions stirred by the onrush of Civil War fever:

Early in 1861 the State of Missouri conducted a special election to select delegates to a state-wide convention to discuss possible secession from the Union. There were avid supporters of both sides residing in Johnson

County. Supporting the new Confederacy were Col. James Madison McCown, 44, the Virginia-born Circuit Clerk, and his attorney son, Billy, 22, who worked actively for the pro-secession candidates. On the other side were such leading citizens as Marsh Foster, the 24-year-old County Clerk of Johnson Co., who had backed Stephen A. Douglas for president in the 1860 election.

James Eads, editor of a local newspaper formerly edited by Foster, became concerned over the McCowns' campaigning, and warned his readers that "there are runners out, be on your guard. Don't be influenced to vote for Secessionists in the guise of Union." This agitated the McCowns, and on Election Day, February 18th, they went to Eads and demanded to know if the editorial referred to them. Eads admitted that it did. The elder McCown called Eads a liar, and the two drew pistols. Bystanders intervened to prevent violence.

Soon afterwards, Marsh Foster met Eads and the two talked. Billy McCown saw the encounter, and remarked: "I saw Marsh Foster give Eads a pistol, and damn him, I will kill him for it!" Apparently hoping to affirm his suspicion, Billy McCown approached Foster and asked to borrow his pistol. He complied with the young attorney's request.

Late in the day, Benjamin Grover, a respected citizen, anticipated trouble. He approached McCown and asked him to take his son and go home. He warned that McCown "would get into difficulty and kill somebody or somebody will kill him." McCown thanked him for his "kindness," but said he and his son could take care of themselves. When the polls closed, Foster was called into the courthouse to certify the returns. As he entered, he remarked to Justice of the Peace John Campbell that the law officer "would have fun tomorrow in taking these fellows for drawing their pistols in the street."

This was just the provocation that Billy McCown was waiting for. He snapped: "Marsh Foster, you are a God damned rascal!" Foster replied that McCown should give up his guns before making any further insulting remarks to him. McCown responded by giving Foster a pistol belong to a Dr. Noble. He then drew the gun he had borrowed from Foster and fired, missing his mark. McCown ran toward the south door of the courthouse, as Foster fired back and missed. Reaching the door, McCown turned and shot; Foster returned fire, both missing again. McCown was intercepted by his father, who asked if he was hurt; learning that Billy was not, the elder McCown drew his pistol and entered the door. He fired at Foster and the County Clerk shot back; again, both missed. Foster's pistol jammed; he turned to the window to examine the weapon. Despite Campbell's urgings that he stop, McCown took deliberate aim and shot Foster through the heart. Foster died almost immediately.

Six witnesses swore that the Colonel shot him as described. The McCowns were arrested and put into the county jail, but a mob soon formed demanding summary punishment. Grover, Emory S. Foster (the victim's older brother), and former Sheriff George W. Houts intervened. Speaking from the steps of the jailhouse door, they urged the crowd to disperse, and to allow the law to take its course. Had the crowd known the course the law would take, the jail would undoubtedly been stormed. Although the record is foggy, apparently neither of the McCowns were ever convicted. Both joined the Confederate Army and survived the Civil War. The elder McCown died on July 8, 1867.

The above account is excerpted and rewritten from an article by Bruce Reynolds in the *Warrensburg Daily Star-Journal*, 5 Apr. 1978, who in turn extensively quoted a contemporaneous letter penned by James M. Foster.

DEATH OF MRS. MCCOWN

"Mrs. Caroline Frances McCown passed away last Saturday [28 Aug. 1915] at the home of her son, Matthew McCown, in Chilhowee Township. This remarkable woman had reached the age of 94 years, having been born in 1821, the year of Missouri's admission as a state. She lived for 3 quarters of a century in Johnson County. Since 1866 she has been a widow, her husband, Col. James McCown, dying in that year of yellow fever in New Orleans. Mrs. McCown was remarkable in her splendid courage under conditions that tried the souls of the strongest men. She had seen more of the deep tragedy of life than falls to the lot of most people. Up to the beginning of the war the McCown family was one of the leading families of Warrensburg. When the trouble came on, Col. McCown espoused the Southern side and tragedy began. The husband and grown son had to leave and her fine home was burned over her head. She was turned out penniless but undismayed. From a leading society woman she became the head of her family and nobly met the duty, displaying a wonderful strength of character and resource. For years she has lived at peace, tenderly cared for by her son Matthew, and she has at last gone to join the husband whom she loved. She leaves five children, Mrs. Virginia Davis, of Kansas City; Samuel McCown, Washington; Chas. McCown, of Idaho; George, in Wyoming; and Matthew, of this county. The funeral was held in the Cemetery Chapel last Monday at 2 o'clock by Rev. C. L. Stouffer, and her body laid to rest in the Warrensburg Cemetery, in plain sight of the location of her old home as a happy bride and mother."—*Warrensburg Standard-Herald*, 3 Sept. 1915.

THE BIOGRAPHY OF CHARLES C. MCCOWN

"CHARLES C. MCCOWN has been engaged in agricultural pursuits for about twenty-five years on the farm which he still owns and cultivates, and which is located on section 26, township 45, Johnson County. He has served as Justice of the Peace for two terms, and has also held other official positions. He comes from a well known and respected family in these parts, the name being associated with the upbuilding of this region from its pioneer days.

"The father of Mr. McCown, James McCown, was born in Kanawha County, W. Va., in 1815, and on reaching manhood married Caroline F. Burgess, a native of the same county, born in 1821. A few years later the young couple moved from West Virginia to Missouri, settling in Henry County, near Calhoun. About 1845 they moved to a farm in Chilhowee Township, this county, where Mr. McCown entered land. In the course of time his possessions numbered about 1500 acres of finely improved farm land, besides lots in Warrensburg. Most of this was lost during the war, and by going security for friends. He was very generous, and never knew how to say no to those who applied to him for assistance. In Henry County he held the offices of Constable and Sheriff, and after coming here was made County and Circuit Clerk and Recorder, serving as such for three terms. When a young man, he was for some time engaged in steam-boating on the Ohio River, and before leaving his native state was elected Colonel of a militia company.

"Early in 1861 James McCown raised a company for a Missouri regiment, of which he was elected Colonel. Afterward, the Third and Fifth Confederate Infantries were consolidated, and he continued to serve in the same capacity. In 1862 he went east of the Mississippi River and took part in many important battles, among them being Baker Creek, Corinth, Chickamauga, those of the Georgia campaign, and many others. He was at Ft. Blakely at the time of its surrender, and soon afterward joined his family at Waco, Tex., where they were then living. They returned to Johnson County, where they were obliged to begin at the bottom round of the ladder once more, for though they had formerly been in affluent circumstances, they now had nothing left. Mr. McCown formed a partnership with E. A. Nicholson, an attorney, and on one of his business trips through Texas, Louisiana, and Kentucky, contracted an illness which resulted in his death, July 8, 1868. For years he was a member of the lodge and chapter of Masons at Warrensburg, and held offices at different times. Politically, he was always a strong Democrat. In religious faith he was a member of the Southern Methodist Church, to which his widow still belongs. She is now making her home in Warrensburg.

"The following children were born to James McCown and his wife: J. S., who is connected with one of the Washington State institutions at Walla Walla; Charles C., our subject; John W., a commercial traveler of Kansas City; George, a stockraiser; Mathew, who is connected with the Missouri, Kansas & Texas Railroad; Virginia D., wife of James Smith of Warrensburg; William H., a promising young attorney who died at Piedmont, Mo.; Mary, who died in 1860; and Mattie, formerly the wife of George R. Foster, of Saint Louis County, Mo., but now deceased. Two of the sons, J. S. and W. H., were in the Confederate Army. The latter was a Captain and held a Colonel's commission. He was actively engaged in many noted battles, among which were Lexington, Wilson Creek, and Springfield, Mo. In the last-named encounter, he received severe wounds. The other brother was in the battles of Pea Ridge and Vicksburg, being under his father's command and in Parsons' Brigade.

"Charles C. McCown was born in January, 1848, in this county, and attending school in Warrensburg. During the war he was with his father for a time, though he was really much too young to be in the service. Nevertheless, he carried a musket at the Battle of Dry Wood. In 1863 he went with the other members of the family to Texas, and as he was the eldest of the children, he was for the time being the protector and the head of the family, the father being at the front. They first located in Dallas, then moved to Georgetown, and finally to Waco, where the Colonel met them at the close of the war.

"On Christmas Day, 1873, Charles McCown married Eugenia, daughter of James T. Ferguson, who is now living in Kansas City. Mrs. McCown was born in St. Louis, and by her marriage became the mother of six children, five of whom are living, namely: Stella, Cora, Florence, and Hugh and Lillie, twins; Mary died in childhood.

"For about a quarter of a century Mr. McCown has been engaged in agricultural pursuits on his present farm, and is a thoroughly practical and well posted business man. His homestead comprises eighty acres of very fertile land on which stand good buildings. In his political belief he is a Democrat. With his good wife, he holds membership with the Methodist Episcopal Church South, and has officiated in the congregation as Steward."

[John Meredith (I)[4]]

CAPT. GEORGE WASHINGTON BURGESS
(1813?-1875)

OF BENTON COUNTY, MISSOURI

5a. **George Washington (IV)** *[son of John Meredith (I)]*. Born 1813 (or 1811, according to his obituary) at Spring Hill, Kanawha Co., VA (later WV). Married Mary J. Venable on 19 Apr. 1838 in Kanawha Co. (she was born Apr. 1817 in VA, is listed in the 1900 census for St. Louis with her daughter and son-in-law, John B. English [four of eight children survive in 1900], and died on 3 Mar. 1901 at St. Louis, buried Old St. Marcus Cemetery). George is not mentioned in the estate records of Fleming Cobb, but had numerous dealings with Fleming C. and Thomas C. Burgess, his presumed brothers, until he left the county; he may have received his inheritance before his departure. He appears to be the unnamed brother of Caroline F. Burgess McCown mentioned as living in San Antonio (a Confederate-controlled area) during the Civil War. Listed in the 1840 census in Cabell Co., VA (later WV), in 1850-60 in Lindsey Township, Benton Co., MO, and in 1870 in Roscoe Township, St. Clair Co., MO. Capt. George W. Burgess was a steamship pilot in West Virginia, serving as master of the steamboat *Kanawha*, and in Ohio and Missouri; he moved to the latter state about 1844 (contrary to the statement in his obituary); he also farmed in Benton Co. In later life he was a trustee of the town of Roscoe, MO. He died on 8 Nov. 1875 in Benton Co.

The Children of George Washington Burgess:

6a. **Sarah C. (I) "Sally."** Her middle initial is listed as "E." in the 1900 census. Born Feb. 1839 in VA (later WV). Married John B. English on 20 June 1860 in Benton Co., MO (he was born Dec. 1836 in MO), and had at least the following children: *Louise* (born Dec. 1868 in MO, married Louis Nichols [he was born Oct. 1861 in MO], and had children: Hugo G. [born June 1897 in MO]); *Daughter* (married Hardy Mears [he was born Jan. 1864 in MO], and had children: Frank [born May 1888]; Harry [born Mar. 1891]; Jonie [born Apr. 1893]; Marian [born Jan. 1899]). Listed in the 1900 census for St. Louis, St. Louis Co., MO.

6b. **Child.** Born about 1841 in VA (later WV); died before 1850.

6c. **L. Francis.** Born about 1843 in VA (later WV). Listed with her father in the 1870 census. Married C. C. Armstrong on 29 Feb. 1872 in St. Clair Co., MO. Has not been found in the 1880 Soundex for Missouri.

6d. **Emily B.** Born about 1845 in Benton Co., MO.

6e. **Mary V.** Born about 1847 in Benton Co., MO. Listed with her father in the 1870 census. Married Henry C. Smith on 1 Mar. 1871 in St. Clair Co., MO (he was born about 1846).

6f. **Charles W.** Born Apr. 1850 in Benton Co., MO. Listed with his father in the 1870 census. Charlie Burgess died unmarried in June 1875 in Benton Co., five weeks before his brother, Johnnie.

6g. **George (I).** Listed with his father in the 1870 census. Born about 1853 in Benton Co., MO.

6h. **John D. (III) "Johnnie."** Listed with his father in the 1870 census. Born about 1855 in Benton Co., MO. Johnnie Burgess died unmarried in July 1875 in Benton Co., five weeks after his brother, Charles.

THE OBITUARY OF GEORGE W. BURGESS
(*Obituaries of Missouri*)

"Capt. George W. Burgess was born near Charleston, VA, in 1811; removed to Missouri in 1839, enduring many hardships; settled in Warsaw, Benton Co., where he died 8th Nov. 1875....There was never a stain on his life of sixty-four years. He leaves a wife and five children to mourn his loss....Also in June 1875, our brother Charles W. Burgess in his twenty-third year, five weeks later our baby brother, Johnnie D., in his sixteenth year. Truly the hand of the Lord is heavy upon us."—abstracted from *St. Louis Christian Advocate*, 6 Jan. 1876.

[John Meredith (I)[4]]

FLEMING COBB BURGESS
(1815-1883)

OF KANAWHA COUNTY, (WEST) VIRGINIA

5b. **Fleming Cobb (I)** *[son of John Meredith (I)].* Born 25 Jan. 1815 near Spring Hill, Kanawha Co., VA (later WV). Married Adelia (or Adelaide) Margaret Wood on 24 Dec. 1835 in Kanawha Co. (she was born 11 Oct. 1818 at St. Albans, VA [later WV], daughter of Bazzle A. Wood and Elizabeth Dudding, and died 10 Feb. 1865 at St. Albans, Kanawha Co., WV); married secondly (Margaret) Ann (or "Margarita") Harshbarger about 1867 (she was born about 1830 in VA). After their marriage, they settled near Browns Creek, Kanawha Co. to be near her parents. Mentioned in the estate accounts of his grandfather, Fleming Cobb. Listed in the 1850-80 censuses for Kanawha Co., and appears there in the tax lists from 1833. Fleming C. Burgess was a farmer in Kanawha Co. all of his life. He sold his personal property to his brother, George Washington Burgess, on 15 Oct. 1838 (*Kanawha Co. Deed Book #K*, p. 359), and then leased it back again; he again mortgaged his property to Thomas C. Burgess (his brother) and others on 14 Aug. 1845 (*Deed Book #O*, p. 231). His biography, with those of his son and grandson, appears in *West Virginia and Its People*, by Thomas Condit Miller and Hu Maxwell (New York: Lewis Publishing Co., 1913, Volume II, p. 474-475). He died on 5 Feb. 1883 at St. Albans, Kanawha Co., and is reputedly buried in the Woods Cemetery.

"Cousin Fannie told me one day while I was visiting her in her home in Huntington, when she was most ninety years (she was most ninety-four when she died), she told me that he [Fleming Cobb Burgess] had such good manners and morals (both of these are cut off the same bolt of cloth). She said her mother would dress her twins, Annie and Fannie, in their white Sunday dresses and once a year (summertime) they would go up to visit her grandfather and grandmother Ann Harshbarger in Milton, West Virginia. Grandmother Adelia W. Burgess died in 1865, the year cousin Fannie was born. He would come in from the field, wash his face and hands, and don a little black coat. When they came to the table, he would ask the blessing and help each child's plate, and when he began to eat, they could also.

"He had married Ann Harshbarger of Milton, West Virginia. Adelia had died during childbirth. There were several children from the family which needed a mother's care, so he just had to have a wife to help him raise his small children. There was a child Bettie born of this union, making his twelfth child. I certainly want to meet Grandmother Ann when I get to Heaven. She must have been a fine person to assume a ready-made family. Cousin Fannie said, 'Lillian, there was something back of that man.'"—Lillian Burgess Royal, 17 Aug. 1983.

The Children of Fleming C. Burgess:

6a. **James Washington.** Born 22 May 1837 near St. Albans, Kanawha Co., VA (later WV). See below for full entry.

6b. **Hester Anne Rogers.** She was named for a well-known religious writer. Born 1839 (or 1840) in Kanawha Co., VA (later WV). Married George L. Thomas on 1 Feb. 1860 in Kanawha Co. (he was born about 1839), and had at least the following children: *Hellenia D.* (born 1861); *Henry R.* (born 1863); *Emma B.* (born 1865); *William L.* (born 1868); *Mary Alice* (born 1870); *Etta C.* (born 1872); *Benjamin W.* (born 1874); *Lucy A.* (born 1877); *Frank E.* (born Mar. 1880). Listed in the 1880 census for Kanawha Co., WV; has not been found in the 1900 WV Soundex.

6c. **John Meredith (II).** Born 14 May 1842 in Kanawha Co., VA (later WV). See below for full entry.

6d. **(Mary) Elizabeth (I).** Born about 1846 in Kanawha Co., VA (later WV). Married Nicholas Ready on 27 Sept. 1865 in Kanawha Co., and had children: *Missouri* (born 1866 in VA). **Mary Elizabeth** married secondly Peter Provost about 1871, and had children: *Annie L.* (born 1872); *Cora* (born 1874); *Julia C.* (born 1876); *Edward L.* (born 1878). Listed in the 1880 census for Kanawha Co. She deeded her share of her father's estate on 15 Feb. 1884 (*Deed Book #25*, p. 486+). Has not been found in the 1900 WV Soundex.

6e. **William Henry (II).** Born about 1848 in Kanawha Co., VA (later WV); died there on 22 Jan. 1854.

6f. **Judith Cobb "Judea."** Born 4 Dec. 1850 in Kanawha Co., VA (later WV). Married William A. Bowles on 12 Nov. 1868 in Kanawha Co. (he was born 29 Aug. 1846 in VA, and died 12 Dec. 1911), and had at least the following children: *Thomas E.* (born Jan. 1879 in WV); *Ambrose S.* (born July 1883 in WV); *Alvilla* (born Oct. 1885 in WV). Judea Bowles deeded her share of her father's estate in 1886 (*Deed Book #25*, p. 486+). Listed in the 1900 Soundex for Putnam Co., WV. She died on 20 Sept. 1912 in Putnam Co., and is buried with her husband in the Bowles Cemetery.

6g. **Henry A. W(ood?).** Born 6 June 1855 in Kanawha Co., VA (later WV). See below for full entry.

6h. **George E(dgar?) (II).** Born 20 Feb. 1858 in Kanawha Co., VA (later WV). See below for full entry.

6i. **Margaret A(delia?) "Maggie."** Born 20 July 1860 in Kanawha Co., VA (later WV). Married John N. (or H.) Draper on 4 Oct. 1877 in Kanawha Co. (he was born Apr. 1851 in VA), and had children: *Emma* (born Feb. 1884 in WV); *Olie* (born Dec. 1887 in WV); *Virgie* (born Oct. 1888 in WV); *George H.* (born Oct. 1890 in WV); *Fleming* (?) (born Feb. 1893 in WV); *William W.* (born Jan. 1895 in WV); *Charles A.* (born Mar. 1897 in WV); *Homar F.* (born Jan. 1899 in WV). She was living in Lincoln Co., WV on 29 July 1885, when she deeded off her share of her father's estate (*Deed Book #25*, p. 486+). Listed in the 1900 Soundex for Lincoln Co., WV.

6j. **Fleming Cobb (II).** Born 9 Apr. 1865 in Kanawha Co., WV. See below for full entry.

6k. **Elizabeth E. (II) "Bettie."** Born about 1867 in Kanawha Co., WV. Married Eugene Norris (or Morris) by 1889. Listed with her father in the 1880 census. She deeded off her share of her father's estate on 24 Jan. 1889 (*Deed Book #51*, p. 392+). Has not been found in the 1900 WV Soundex. Said to have died young in West Virginia.

THE BIOGRAPHY OF FLEMING C. BURGESS, JAMES W. BURGESS, WILLIAM H. BURGESS (1913)

"Fleming C. Burgess was born in Virginia, and was of the old pioneer farmers in Kanawha County, West Virginia, where he passed the closing years of his life, and where his death occurred in the year 1883. He was of English ancestry, the founder of the Burgess family in America having settled in Virginia in an early day. He married Adelia Woods, who died in 1865.

"James W., son of Fleming C. Burgess, was born in Kanawha County, West Virginia. He was reared to maturity on his father's farm and in due time became a farmer himself. He died in 1905, and his cherished and devoted wife, whose maiden name was Elizabeth Harmon, survives him, and now maintains her home at Huntington, West Virginia. Mr. and Mrs. Burgess had two children: Dr. William Henry, mentioned below; Dr. Thomas D., who is engaged in the work of his profession at Louisa, Kentucky.

"Dr. William Henry Burgess, son of James W. and Elizabeth (Harmon) Burgess, was born in Kanawha County, West Virginia, September 16, 1867. He passed his early life on the old homestead farm, and received his rudimentary educational training in the neighboring district schools. Subsequently, he attended the graded school at St. Albans, and as a young man he began to do railroad work in order to obtain money for a medical course. He began firing on the Chesapeake and Ohio Railroad in September, 1888, and in due time became an engineer. He filled the position of engineer on the above road until 1904, when he was matriculated as a student in the Louisville Medical College at Louisville, Kentucky, in which well-ordered institution he was graduated as a member of the Class of 1907, duly receiving the degree of Doctor of Medicine. His first practice was at Matewan, Mingo County, West Virginia, where he was associated in medical work with his brother, Dr. Thomas D. Burgess. For two years Dr. Burgess was a resident of Matewan, and in 1909 he came to Williamson, where he conducts an individual practice. Dr. Burgess makes a specialty of the diseases of the throat, nose, and eyes, and is considered an expert in this particular line of work. He is a man of most generous impulses, and is always ready to relieve the worthy distressed and needy who come to him for medical aid. His quiet and unselfish manner fully characterizes his pure Christian spirit and innate kindliness of heart, traits which make him decidedly popular with all classes of people. Dr. Burgess is a valued and appreciative member of the West Virginia State Medical Society and the American Medical Association. He still retains his membership in the Brotherhood of Railroad Engineers and Firemen, and in the Scottish Rite Branch of Masonry, has reached the 32nd degree. He is a Republican in politics, and his religious faith is in harmony with the tenets of the Methodist Episcopal Church South.

"On March 2, 1899 Dr. Burgess married Mary Ella Byars, a native of Shelby County, Kentucky, where her birth occurred January 17, 1873. Mrs. Burgess is a daughter of Francis Byars, who was a prominent stock-farmer in Shelby County, Kentucky during his lifetime, and who died about the year 1892. Dr. and Mrs. Burgess have no children."

[John Meredith (I)[4], Fleming Cobb (I)[5]]

JAMES WASHINGTON BURGESS
(1837-1904)

OF CABELL COUNTY, WEST VIRGINIA

6a. **James Washington** *[son of Fleming Cobb (I)].* Born 22 May 1837 near St. Albans, Kanawha Co., VA (later WV). Married Elizabeth Ann Harmon on 11 May 1860 in Cabell Co., VA (later WV) (she was born 15 Mar. 1840 at Huntington, Cabell Co., VA [later WV], daughter of Eli Ferdinand Harmon and Peggie Brumfield, and died on 13 Feb. 1921 at Huntington, WV). Listed in the 1860 census with his parents and new wife, in 1870-80 in Kanawha Co., WV, and in 1900 in Huntington, Cabell Co., WV; his widow appears as head of the family there in 1910-20. James W. Burgess was a farmer in Kanawha and Cabell Cos. He died on 9 Sept. 1904 at Huntington, Cabell Co., WV, and is buried with his wife in the Springhill Cemetery.

The Children of James W. Burgess:

7a. **Victoria Evelyn.** Born 10 Feb. 1861 near St. Albans, Kanawha Co., VA (later WV). Married Dr. Gaston Anderson Shumate on 11 Sept. 1883 in Kanawha Co. (he was born 5 Dec. 1850 in Giles Co., VA [later WV], and died 4 Mar. 1914), and had children:

Edgar Burgess SHUMATE. Born 7 July 1884. Married Fannie Lee Moses.

Gaston Anderson SHUMATE Jr. Born 27 Sept. 1886. Married Margaret Ruth Carpenter on 1 Sept. 1914 at Dallas, TX (she died 8 June 1989), and had children: *Nancy Jane* (born 18 May 1922, married Albert Carl Michaelis Jr. on 11 July 1942 [he died 5 Feb. 1953], and had children: Nancy Jane Jr. [born 27 June 1945, married Paul Harris Davis on 18 July 1967 {div.}, and had children: Kristen Elizabeth {born 22 May 1971}; Carrie Suzanne {born 28 Oct. 1974}; Nancy Jr. married secondly Joe Bourne in Sept. 1978, and died 17 Nov. 1983]; Victoria Lynne [born 4 Jan. 1950, married Peter Blancke Bartholow on 21 July 1973, and had children: Peter Blancke Jr. {born 19 Jan. 1978}; David Shumate {born 23 Nov. 1979}; Sarah Elizabeth {born 3 Sept. 1981}]. *Nancy Jane MICHAELIS* married secondly Frederick Jonathan Knieff on 18 Mar. 1955 [div.], and had children: Frederick Jonathan Jr. [born 7 Oct. 1956]. *Nancy Jane KNIEFF* married thirdly Jefferson Edwin Miller Jr. on 9 June 1984 [div.]). *Gaston Anderson III* (born 29 May 1924, never married). Gaston A. Shumate Jr. died on 19 Mar. 1925, and is buried with his wife in the Forest Lawn Cemetery, Dallas, TX. *Nancy MILLER* has contributed greatly to this book.

Adelia Margaret SHUMATE. Born 12 Nov. 1888. Married Dr. Uriah Vermillion.

Dorsey Cullen SHUMATE. Born 3 Feb. 1891, and died 19 Sept. 1911.

Hunter McGuire SHUMATE. Born 27 Mar. 1893. Married Carrie Peck. Hunter Shumate died in May 1971 at Irvine, KY.

Frances Naomi SHUMATE. Born 16 Apr. 1895.

Evelyn Elizabeth SHUMATE. Born 25 Apr. 1897, died 9 July 1923.

Gertrude Gregory SHUMATE. Born 24 May 1899. Married Taylor F. Johnston.

Willie Marie SHUMATE. Born 17 Mar. 1901, and died unmarried in Feb. 1982 at Princeton, WV.

Ruth Virginia SHUMATE. Born 25 June 1903. Married Philip Crosbie.

Thomas Dickinson SHUMATE. Born 7 Aug. 1906. Married Lillian Weir. Thomas Shumate died in May 1978 at Richmond, KY.

Victoria SHUMATE was a school teacher. She died on 24 July 1943 at Glen Lyn, WV.

7b. **Adelia Margaret "Ada."** Her name was also written Adda Marguerite, and as Adelaia on her tombstone. Born 27 Mar. 1863 near St. Albans, Kanawha Co., VA (later WV). Listed with her father in the 1870-1900 censuses, and with her mother in 1910-20. Adelia Burgess died unmarried on 9 Sept. 1937 at Huntington, WV, and is buried there in the Springhill Cemetery.

7c. **Frances Corrie "Fannie"** (twin). Born 19 June 1865 (or 29 June, according to her birth record) near St. Albans, Kanawha Co., WV. Listed with her father in the 1870-1900 censuses, and with her mother in 1910-20. Fannie Burgess was a professor at Marshall College (now Marshall University), Huntington, Cabell Co., WV. She died there unmarried on 22 Feb. 1960, aged 94 years.

7d. **Anna Laurie "Annie"** (twin). Born 19 June 1865 (or 29 June, according to her birth record) near St. Albans, Kanawha Co., WV. Anna Burgess died unmarried in 1888 at Huntington, Cabell Co., WV, and is buried in the Springhill Cemetery.

7e. **William Henry (VI)**. Born 16 Sept. 1867 near St. Albans, Kanawha Co., WV. Married Mary Ella Byers on 2 Mar. 1899 (she was born 17 Jan. 1873 in Shelby Co., KY, daughter of Francis Byers [or Byars]). Listed in the 1910-20 censuses for Williamson, Mingo Co., WV. According to the biography of his grandfather, William worked for the Chesapeake and Ohio Railroad from 1888-1904, becoming an engineer. He saved his money to attend medical school, and graduated from Louisville Medical College in 1907. His first practice was established at Matewan, Mingo Co., WV, where he was associated with his brother, Tom. In 1909 he established a practice at Williamson, WV, specializing in diseases of the nose, throat, and eyes. He was a member of the West Virginia State Medical Society, the Brotherhood of Railroad Engineers and Firemen, and the Scottish Rite Branch of Masonry. Dr. William Burgess is said to have died in 1948 in WV (however, a William H. Burgess who died on 4 Apr. 1924 is buried in the Springhill Cemetery with the other Burgesses). He reputedly had an illegitimate daughter (name unknown).

7f. **Thomas Dickinson (I)**. Born 15 Dec. 1869 near St. Albans, Kanawha Co., WV. See below for full entry.

THOMAS D. BURGESS OF LAWRENCE CO., KENTUCKY

[John Meredith (I)[4], Fleming Cobb (I)[5], James Washington[6]]

7f. **Thomas Dickinson (I)** *[son of James Washington]*. Born 15 Dec. 1869 near St. Albans, Kanawha Co., WV. Married **Willie Jane Burgess** on 12 Apr. 1899 in Lawrence Co., KY (div.; she was born 2 Mar. 1869 at Gallup, Lawrence Co., KY, daughter of **Thomas Jefferson Burgess** [a descendant of the unrelated Edward Burgess line of Lawrence Co., KY] and Onolda Zaida Garred, and died on 16 Mar. 1952 at Louisa, KY, buried Pine Hill Cemetery); married secondly Bess Harris after 1910. Listed in the 1900 census for Mingo Co., WV, and in 1910 at Louisa, Lawrence Co., KY. Dr. Tom Burgess was a physician in West Virginia and Kentucky, eventually establishing a practice at Louisa, Lawrence Co., KY. He died on 24 June 1943 at Shelbyville, Shelby Co., KY, but is buried at Huntington, Cabell Co., WV.

Thomas Jefferson Burgess was born 27 Sept. 1834, son of George Revel Burgess and Emily Layne Johns, and died 20 Feb. 1900 at Gallup, Lawrence Co., KY. George Revel Burgess was born 26 Nov. 1806, son of John Burgess and Jane Shannon, and died 21 Sept. 1872 at Gallup, KY. John Burgess was born 15 Feb. 1777 in Bedford Co., VA, son of Edward Burgess and Nancy Ann Francis, and died 1 Mar. 1858 at Dearborn, Platte Co., MO. Edward Burgess was born Oct. 1744, and died 23 Dec. 1835 in Lawrence Co., KY.

8a. **Elizabeth Ann (II)**. Born 14 July 1902 at Matewan, Mingo Co., WV. Married Kit Carson Elswick on 2 Sept. 1924. Elizabeth Elswick died on 21 Apr. 1978 at El Cajon, San Diego Co., CA.

8b. **Thomas Dickinson (II)**. Born 4 Dec. 1904 at Matewan, Mingo Co., WV; died there on 8 July 1905.

8c. **Cornelius Jefferson**. Born 22 Feb. 1907 at Matewan, Mingo Co., WV. See below for full entry.

8d. **Julia Jane**. Born 12 Sept. 1909 at Louisa, Lawrence Co., KY; died unmarried on 30 Sept. 1928.

CORNELIUS J. BURGESS OF GILES CO., VIRGINIA

[John Meredith (I)[4], Fleming Cobb (I)[5], James Washington[6], Thomas Dickinson (I)[7]]

8c. **Cornelius Jefferson "Neil"** *[son of Thomas Dickinson (I)]*. Born 22 Feb. 1907 at Matewan, Mingo Co., WV. Married Lou Elaine Waybright on 2 June 1933 at Greenup, Greenup Co., KY (she was born 2 Aug. 1908 at Ripley, Jackson Co., WV, daughter of James Otmer Waybright and Lucile Parsons). Neil Burgess lived at Narrows, VA, but died on 29 July 1987 at Roanoke, VA.

9a. **Thomas Dickinson III**. Born 15 Feb. 1937 at Williamson, Mingo Co., WV. Married Diana Faye Moore on 1 Oct. 1960 at Harrisonburg, Rockingham Co., VA (div.; she was born 1 Sept. 1942 at Harrisonburg, daughter of Edward Carl Moore and Beulah Elizabeth Sisk); married secondly Sandra Sue Mann on 15 June 1990 (div.). Thomas D. Burgess currently lives at Narrows, VA.

10a. **Tanya Danielle.** Born 27 Oct. 1961 at Danville, Pittsylvania Co., VA. Married Joseph Donald Reardon on 27 Apr. 1985, and had children: *Kelsey Elaine* (born 12 June 1987 at Harrisonburg, VA); Tanya married secondly Garey Dane Hulvey on 10 Mar. 1990, and had children: *Alexander Dane* (born 27 Oct. 1990 at Harrisonburg, VA); *Blair McKenzie* (born 29 Feb. 1992 at Harrisonburg, VA).

10b. **Thomas Dickinson IV.** Born 15 Jan. 1963 at Danville, Pittsylvania Co., VA. Married Manuela Lucero González on 10 Feb. 1985 at Rota, Spain (she was born 10 Nov. __).

11a. **Thomas Dickinson V.** Born 29 July 1985 at Rota, Spain.
11b. **David Anthony.** Born 1 July 1987 at Harrisonburg, VA.
11c. **Heather Lynn.** Born 26 May 1990 at Laurel Park, MD.

10c. **Jefferson Moore.** Born 28 Feb. 1964 at Danville, Pittsylvania Co., VA. Married Jill Renae Place on 30 June 1990 at Manti, Utah.

11a. **Jackson Tanner.** Born 1 Aug. 1993 at Salt Lake City, UT.

10d. **Diana Layne.** Born 22 Feb. 1966 at Danville, Pittsylvania Co., VA. Married Jay Arthur Ballard on 26 Apr. 1986 (he was born 14 Oct. 1959, son of Arthur Jay Ballard and Doyne Ilene Nelson), and had children: *Elizabeth Ilene* (born 4 Apr. 1987 at Provo, UT); *Virginia Rose* (born 28 Sept. 1988 at Harrisonburg, VA); *Thomas Jefferson* (born 21 Mar. 1990 at Harrisonburg, VA); *Robin Jayne* (born 10 Jan. 1992 at Staunton, VA).

(see page 90) *ARTHUR CLAY BURGESS* (1872-1933)

[John Meredith (I)[4], Fleming Cobb (I)[5]]

JOHN MEREDITH BURGESS II
(1842-1931)

OF KANAWHA COUNTY, WEST VIRGINIA

6c. **John Meredith (II)** *[son of Fleming Cobb (I)].* Born 14 May 1842 in Kanawha Co., VA (later WV). Married Nancy Ellen Reynolds on 4 Mar. 1862 in Kanawha Co. (she was born 11 Mar. 1840 at Milton, Cabell Co., VA [later WV], and died 7 Dec. 1935, aged 95 years, buried Cobb Cemetery). Listed in the 1860-1920 censuses for St. Albans, Washington Township, Kanawha Co., VA/WV. John M. Burgess died at St. Albans on 26 Aug. 1931.

7a. **William Henry (V).** Born and died 1863 (aged six weeks) in Kanawha Co., VA (later WV).
7b. **James Fleming.** Born May 1864 in Kanawha Co., WV. Married Ellen E. Scott on 28 Oct. 1885 in Kanawha Co. (she was born July 1869 [or 1868] in WV, and died 1933). Listed in the 1900 census for Montgomery, Fayette Co., WV, but has not been found in 1910. Jim Burgess died childless on 3 Dec. 1945, and is buried in the Springhill Cemetery, Huntington, WV.
7c. **Lillian Ann "Lillie."** Born 1866 in Kanawha Co., WV. Lillie Burgess died unmarried in Kanawha Co. on 16 June 1895.
7d. **Frazier Dean.** Born 24 Mar. 1868 in Kanawha Co., WV. See below for full entry.
7e. **Carrie Adelia.** Her middle initial is given as "D" in the 1900-10 censuses. Born May 1872 in Kanawha Co., WV. Listed with her father in the 1900-10 censuses. Carrie Burgess died unmarried on 17 July 1916 in Kanawha Co.

FRAZIER D. BURGESS OF KANAWHA CO., WEST VIRGINIA
[John Meredith (II)[6]]

7d. **Frazier Dean** *[son of John Meredith (II)].* Born 24 Mar. 1868 in Kanawha Co., WV. Married Ida Mae Chapman (she was born 18 Feb. 1870 at Clinton, OH, and died 3 Oct. 1954 at St. Albans, WV). Listed in the 1900-20 censuses for St. Albans, Kanawha Co. Frazier Burgess was four times elected Mayor of St. Albans, WV. He died 29 July 1954 in Kanawha Co., WV.

8a. **Wayland Dean (I).** Born 15 Apr. 1894 in Kanawha Co., WV. See below for full entry.
8b. **Garland Pritchard.** Born 24 Aug. 1895 in Kanawha Co., WV. See below for full entry.
8c. **Lillian Marie.** Born 5 July 1897 in Kanawha Co., WV. Married Omer E. Royal about 1920 (he was born 13 Aug. 1894, and died Nov. 1967 at Charleston), and had children: *Robert Frazier* (born 4 Sept. 1921 in Mercer Co., WV); *Richard Curtis* (born 24 June 1928 in Mercer Co., WV). Lillian Royal currently lives in a nursing home at South Charleston, WV.
8d. **Randall Wesley.** Born 24 Feb. 1902 in Kanawha Co., WV. See below for full entry.
8e. **Dorothy Delphine.** Born 24 Apr. 1904 in Kanawha Co., WV. Married John Campbell Hall on 14 June 1922 (he was born 27 June 1896, and died 3 Sept. 1958), and had children: *John Campbell Jr.* (born 5 Aug. 1924); *Norma Jean* (born 3 Jan. 1928, married Robert Burwell Williamson Jr.). Dorothy Hall died in Sept. 1986 at Wilmington, NC.
8f. **James Frazier (I).** Born 6 Aug. 1910 in Kanawha Co., WV. See below for full entry.

WAYLAND D. BURGESS OF KANAWHA CO., WEST VIRGINIA
[John Meredith (II)[6], Frazier Dean[7]]

8a. **Wayland Dean (I)** *[son of Frazier Dean].* Listed as John W. Burgess in the 1910 census. Born 15 Apr. 1894 in Kanawha Co., WV. Married (Jewel) Ethel Lovejoy on 12 Feb. 1916 (div.; she was born 12 Jan. 1899 in WV, and died 5 Sept. 1962); married secondly Virginia Morton Green on 3 July

1936 (she was born 12 July 1904). Listed in the 1920 census for Charleston, Kanawha Co., WV. Wayland Burgess died on 23 Nov. 1966 at St. Albans, Kanawha Co., WV.

9a. **Virginia Vera.** Born 22 Apr. 1916 in Kanawha Co., WV. Married Leonard Boggess on 25 Nov. 1946 (he was born 28 Aug. 1922). Virginia Boggess died in Aug. 1987 at Ripley, WV.

9b. **Wayland Dean (II).** Born 3 Apr. 1937 in Kanawha Co., WV. Married Melva Jean Toler on 6 Dec. 1958 (she was born 9 July 1938). Wayland Burgess is a teacher and principal at Bridgeport, WV.

10a. **Pamela Jean (II).** Born 12 Jan. 1962 at South Charleston, WV. Attended Ohio State University.

10b. **Stephen Dean.** Born 6 May 1964 at South Charleston, WV.

GARLAND P. BURGESS OF KANAWHA CO., WEST VIRGINIA

[John Meredith (II)[6], Frazier Dean[7]]

8b. **Garland Pritchard** *[son of Frazier Dean].* Born 24 Aug. 1895 in Kanawha Co., WV. Married (Velma) Pearl Holmes (she was born 15 July 1896 at Syracuse, OH, and died 6 May 1986 at Charleston, WV). Listed in the 1920 census for Kayford, Kanawha Co., WV. Garland Burgess was an accountant. He died on 17 Apr. 1973 at St. Albans, WV.

9a. **Harold Dean (I).** Born 1 Aug. 1917 at Kayford, WV. Married Freda Doris Smith (she was born 15 Sept. 1916 at Gary, WV). Harold Burgess is a retired chemical engineer for Union Carbide, currently living at Mount Pleasant, SC.

10a. **Harold Dean (II).** Born 17 Dec. 1942 at Gallipolis, Gallia Co., OH; died 13 Dec. 1945 in Kanawha Co, WV.

10b. **(William) Patrick.** Born 1 Mar. 1945 at South Charleston, WV. Married Susan Mecum (she was born 3 Mar. 1946). Dr. Patrick Burgess is a physician at Charlotte, NC.

11a. **Geoffrey Pritchard.** Born 6 Nov. 1968 at Princeton, NJ. Geoff Burgess is an attorney.

11b. **Jason Shade.** Born 3 Aug. 1971 at Princeton, NJ. Jason Burgess is currently attending medical school.

11c. **Gillian Mecum.** Born 5 June 1979 at Birmingham, AL.

11d. **Collin Patrick.** Born 11 Nov. 1982 at Charlotte, NC.

10c. **Natala Sue.** Born 9 Feb. 1948 at South Charleston, WV. Married Winfred Junior Auvil (he works as a logger), and had children: *Lyndon Dean* (born 8 Feb. 1971); *Emily Doris* (born 4 Jan. 1975). Natala Auvil is a teacher and nurse at Buckhannon, WV.

10d. **Sally Ann (I).** Born 15 Aug. 1950 at South Charleston, WV. Married Michael Alvaro Blessing (he was born 6 Sept. 1949 at Gallipolis, OH, and works as a chemical engineer for Union Carbide), and had children: *Aaron Matthew* (born 27 Dec. 1975 at South Charleston, WV); *Stephanie Ann* (born 31 Aug. 1979 at South Charleston, WV). Sally Blessing has contributed greatly to this book; she lives at Scott Depot, WV.

10e. **Gregory Preston.** Born 29 Mar. 1956 at South Charleston, WV. Married Nancy Dickerson (she was born 15 Mar. 1958 at Greenville, SC). Greg Burgess is a financial counselor living near Greenville, SC.

11a. **Christopher John.** Born 3 Sept. 1978 at Greenville, SC.

11b. **(Gregory) Adam.** Born 10 Oct. 1984 at Greenville, SC.

9b. **Mary Frances (II).** Born 15 June 1921 in Kanawha Co., WV. Married William Robert Wills (he was born 10 Oct. 1917, and is a retired newspaper editor), and had children: *William Robert Jr.* (born 31 Jan. 1941, married Verna Lee Smith [she was born 12 Aug. 1943], and had children: Deborah Marie [born 14 Aug. 1964]; William Robert III [born 6 June 1968]); *Lois Ann* (born 10 Dec. 1945, married Charles F. Mills, married secondly Anthony Sokola about 1974, and had children: Andrea [born 12 Mar. 1975]). Mary Wills lives at Beckley, WV.

9c. **Dorothy Marie.** Born 9 Dec. 1923 in Kanawha Co., WV. Married Donald Walter Finn on 17 Feb. 1945 at Charleston, WV (he was born 25 Dec. 1918, worked as a chemical engineer for Union Carbide, and currently lives at Columbia, SC), and had children: *Nancy Carolyn* (born 25 May 1946, married Earl Robertson [he was born 14 Sept. 1945], and had children: Karen Lynn [born 17 June 1969]); *Patricia Lee* (born 2 Apr. 1949, married Kerry Allen MacPherson [he was born 14 Oct. 1950], and had children: Douglas Carl [born 17 Jan. 1982]; Patricia MacPherson lives at Cary,

NC); *Donald Paul* (born 20 Dec. 1950, married Karen Craige; they both work as chemical engineers, and live at Louisville, KY). Dorothy Finn has contributed greatly to this book; she currently lives at St. Albans, WV.

RANDALL W. BURGESS OF KANAWHA CO., WEST VIRGINIA

[John Meredith (II)[6], Frazier Dean[7]]

8d. **Randall Wesley** *[son of Frazier Dean].* His name is listed as Randolph in the 1920 census. Born 24 Feb. 1902 in Kanawha Co., WV. Married Martha Dunlap about 1922. Randall Burgess died on 27 Oct. 1979 at Charleston, WV.

9a. **Betty Josephine.** Born 23 Sept. 1923 in Kanawha Co., WV. Married Edward Lewis Suptic about 1951, and had children: *Joanne Burgess* (born 25 Apr. 1952); *Cathy Jo* (born 25 Sept. 1954); married secondly Charles Edmond Temple (he was born 23 July 1914). Betty Temple lives at Satellite Beach, FL.

9b. **Kathryn Louise (I).** Born 4 Feb. 1925 in Kanawha Co., WV. Married Francis John "Frank" Nardi, and had children: *Barbara Ann* (born 18 Feb. 1945); *Nancy Carol* (born 18 May 1947); *Deborah Kay* (born 21 July 1952). Kathryn Nardi currently lives at Roanoke, VA.

JAMES F. BURGESS OF KANAWHA CO., WEST VIRGINIA

[John Meredith (II)[6], Frazier Dean[7]]

8f. **James Frazier (I)** *[son of Frazier Dean].* Born 6 Aug. 1910 in Kanawha Co., WV. Married Bess Edna Milhollin about 1929 (div.); married secondly Marjorie Elizabeth (Morris) Bailey about 1935 (she was born 20 May 1914, and died Dec. 1979 at St. Albans, WV). Jim Burgess worked for the St. Albans Fire Dept. and for Union Carbide. He now lives retired at St. Albans, WV.

9a. **James Frazier (II).** Born 6 July 1930 at Hinton, WV. Married Patricia Lee Ewing (she was born 18 Sept. 1931). Jim Burgess works for the Stainless and Alloy Department of the McDunklin Corporation, making pipe valves. He lives at Dunbar, WV.

10a. **Steven Patrick (I).** Born 20 Sept. 1952 at San Antonio, TX. Steve Burgess is a musician and carpenter.

10b. **James Ewing.** Born 11 Nov. 1953 at Wilmington, OH. Married Sarah Miragliotta. Jim Burgess is a musician.

11a. **Noah James.** Born 24 May 1972 at Charleston, WV.

10c. **Peggy Lee.** Born 4 Aug. 1955 at Charleston, WV. Married Stephen Turkovich III.

10d. **Mary Beth (I).** Born 27 Mar. 1959 at Charleston, WV. Married Marc Winters.

10e. **Joseph Brian.** Born 4 Aug. 1961 at Cincinnati, OH. Joe Burgess is a bartender.

9b. **Frances Kay.** Born 4 June 1943 at Charleston, WV. Married Jack Edwin Holmes, and had children: *Barry Lee* (born 9 Dec. 1969); *Nicholas James* (born 2 Oct. 1979).

9c. **John Meredith III.** Born 29 Jan. 1949 in Kanawha Co., WV. Married Beverly Joyce Ashley on 11 Oct. 1975. John Burgess currently lives at Charleston, WV.

10a. **Scott Christopher.** Born 1 July 1979 at Charleston, WV.

10b. **Justin Michael (II).** Born 6 July 1982 at Charleston, WV.

[John Meredith (I)^4, Fleming Cobb (I)^5]

HENRY A. W. BURGESS
(1855-1884+)

OF PUTNAM COUNTY, WEST VIRGINIA

6g. **Henry A. W(ood?)** *[son of Fleming Cobb (I)].* Born 6 June 1855 in Kanawha Co., VA (later WV). Married Mrs. Julia Ann E. McClanahan on 8 Feb. 1877 in Kanawha Co., WV (she was born about 1852, married firstly ___ McClanahan, and had children: *John A.* [born 1871]; *Rebecca F.* [born 1872]). Listed in the 1880 census for the Union District, Kanawha Co., WV, but had moved by 12 Feb. 1884 to Putnam Co., WV, when he deeded off his share of his father's estate (*Kanawha Co. Deed Book #25*, p. 486+). Neither he nor his wife have been found in the 1900 Soundex. Said to have moved to Ohio.

7a. **Berta Ann "Birdie."** Born 25 Dec. 1877 in Putnam Co., WV.
7b. **Lucy (IV).** Born June 1879 in Kanawha Co., WV.
7c. **Ralph (I).** Born about 1881. Said to have moved to Columbus, OH.
7d. **Albert (III).** Born about 1883. Said to have moved to Columbus, OH.
7e. **Ersa F.** Born 28 Oct. 1886 in Kanawha Co., WV. Listed with her uncle, John M. Burgess, in the 1900 census.

[John Meredith (I)[4], Fleming Cobb (I)[5]]

GEORGE E. BURGESS
(1858-1920+)

OF KANAWHA COUNTY, WEST VIRGINIA

6h. **George E(dgar?) (II)** *[son of Fleming Cobb (I)].* Born 20 Feb. 1858 in Kanawha Co., VA (later WV). Married Laura E. Riffle on 21 Apr. 1881 in Kanawha Co. (she was born 28 Feb. 1857, and died 25 Apr. 1900); married secondly Leah Jividen on 23 Mar. 1901 in Putnam Co., WV (she was born 1862 in WV). Listed with his father in the 1880 census, in the 1900 census for the Union District, Putnam Co., WV, and in 1920 in Dunbar, Kanawha Co., WV. Living on 18 Dec. 1883 in Kanawha Co., WV, when he deeded off his share of his father's estate (*Deed Book #50*, p. 439). George E. Burgess was a painter.

7a. **Robert E.** Born 28 Feb. 1882 in Kanawha Co., WV. Robert Burgess died unmarried on 13 Mar. 1900 in Putnam Co., WV, and is buried in the Bowles Cemetery.
7b. **Della (II).** Born Nov. 1883 in WV. Married Charles Craig on 19 Dec. 1904 in Putnam Co., WV.
7c. **Walter S.** Born 22 Jan. 1885 in Kanawha Co., WV. Married Clarinda Turner on 2 Aug. 1909 in Mason Co., WV. Listed in the 1920 census for Middleport, Meigs Co., OH, across the Ohio River from Mason Co. Walter Burgess died in June 1954 in WV.

8a. **Grace (III).** Born Apr. 1909 in WV.
8b. **Carrie L.** Born Feb. 1912 in WV.

7d. **Ethel (I).** Born and died about 1887, buried Bowles Cemetery. Dates and order uncertain.
7e. **Leota P.** Born Apr. 1888 in WV.
7f. **Carra I/J. "Carrie."** Born Jan. 1890 in WV. Married John Walker on 17 Mar. 1906 in Putnam Co.
7g. **Kattie.** Born about May 1892, died Aug. 1892, buried Bowles Cemetery. Dates and order uncertain.
7h. **Fleming Cobb (IV) "Flem."** Born Sept. 1894 in WV. Married Mary Belle Green (she was born 1897 in Ohio, and may have died 1927, buried Maple Grove Cemetery). Listed in the 1920 census for Boonville, Warrick Co., IN.

8a. **Gladys.** Born 1906 in Ohio.
8b. **Frank (II).** Born 1908 in Ohio.
8c. **Ethel Louise (I).** Born 8 Oct. 1916 at Boonville, IN.
8d. **Walter Calvin.** Born 1 Jan. 1919 at Boonville, IN. He may have died Nov. 1979 at Stuttgart, AR.
8e. **William (XV).** Born 1921 at Boonville, IN; died there on 9 June 1921, and is buried in the Maple Grove Cemetery, Boon Township, Warrick Co., IN.

7i. **Rabra Bell.** Born 1895 in Putnam Co., WV; died there on 16 Apr. 1899, buried Bowles Cemetery.
7j. **William S. (II) "Willie."** Born 5 Apr. 1897 in Putnam Co., WV. Married Roxie Leona Higginbotham on 26 Nov. 1917 in Mason Co., WV (she was born 12 Nov. 1898, daughter of M. A. Higginbotham and Dora Marshall, and died 25 Sept. 1939 in Mason Co.). Listed with his father in the 1920 census. Willie Burgess died in Oct. 1982 at Charleston, WV, but is buried with his wife in the Bowles Cemetery, Putnam Co., WV.

8a. **Rayma.** Born Aug. 1918 in WV.
8b. **Child.**
8c. **Child.**
8d. **Hellen Ester.** Born 4 Mar. 1925 in Mason Co., WV.
8e. **William George Mattison.** Born 11 June 1927 in Mason Co., WV.
8f. **Frances Elinor.** Born 25 Sept. 1939 in Mason Co., WV; died there on 27 Sept. 1939, buried with her parents.

[John Meredith (I)[4], Fleming Cobb (I)[5]]

FLEMING COBB BURGESS, JR.
(1865-1920+)

OF MONTGOMERY COUNTY, OHIO

6j. **Fleming Cobb (II)** *[son of Fleming Cobb (I)]*. Born 8 Apr. 1865 in Kanawha Co., WV. Married Minnie E. ___ (she was born Sept. 1873 in OH, and died 1903, buried Springhill Cemetery, Huntington, Cabell Co., WV). He was living in Kanawha Co. on 27 Sept. 1886, when he deeded off all interest in his father's estate (*Deed Book #51*, p. 391+). Listed in the 1880 census with his father, and in 1900 and 1920 at Dayton, Montgomery Co., OH (in 1920 living alone).

7a. **Kate M.** Born Sept. 1890 in WV. Said to have married ___ Williams, and moved in Florida. She may be the Kate Williams who was born 12 Sept. 1890, and died June 1976 at Tampa, FL.

7b. **Grace (II).** Born May 1898 in OH.

Charles Dudley Burgess (1870-1940) with family and employees working in the Wessel orchard *(see page 523)*

[John Meredith (I)[4]]

THOMAS C. BURGESS
(1817?-1880+)

OF MASON COUNTY, (WEST) VIRGINIA

5c. **Thomas C(obb?)** *[son of John Meredith (I)].* Born about 1817 at Spring Hill, Kanawha Co., VA (later WV). Married Judith B. "Judea" Smoot on 26 Oct. 1843 in Kanawha Co. (she was born July 1823 in Fauquier Co., VA, and died after 1900). Mentioned in the estate accounts of his grandfather, Fleming Cobb. Listed in the tax and census records of Kanawha Co., (West) Virginia through 1857, when he sold his farm. He moved to Hartford, Mason Co., WV, where he is listed in the census records from 1860-80. Thomas C. Burgess was a cooper for the Hartford Salt Factory, Hartford City, WV; he apparently died in Mason Co. between 1880-1900; Judea Burgess is listed as head of the family in the 1900 census for Hartford City, Mason Co., WV (ten of twelve children then survive).

The Children of Thomas C. Burgess:

6a. **George Edgar (I).** His name is given as Edgar G. in his marriage record. Born about 1847 in Kanawha Co., VA (later WV). Married Imogene Harper on 23 Mar. 1868 in Mason Co., WV (she was born 1848, daughter of William W. Harper, and died Sept. 1869, possibly in childbirth). Listed in the 1850-60 censuses with his father. By inference he is living in 1900.

7a. **Nora (I).** Born 1869 in Mason Co., WV. Listed in 1880 with her grandfather, William Harper.

6b. **John D. (II).** Born about 1848 in Kanawha Co., VA (later WV). Listed in the 1850-60 censuses with his father. By inference he is living in 1900.

6c. **(Francis) Angeline.** Born 1 Jan. 1850 in Kanawha Co., VA (later WV). She may have married Samuel D. Hanna on 15 Dec. 1867 in Mason Co., WV. Married Thomas Bumgarner about 1869 (he was born 1833 in WV), and had at least the following children: *Myrta* (born 1870); *Cora* (born 1872); *Curtis* (born 1874). Listed in the 1870 census with her parents and new husband, and in 1880 in Mason Co., WV. She died there on 21 Feb. 1923, and is buried in the Brown Cemetery.

6d. **Charles A.** Born about 1852 in Kanawha Co., VA (later WV). Listed in the 1860-70 census with his father. Charles Burgess was a cooper. By inference he is living in 1900.

6e. **Anna O.** Born about 1853 in Kanawha Co., VA (later WV). Married Lawrence Kinney (or Kenny) on 29 Nov. 1869 in Mason Co., WV. By inference she is living in 1900.

6f. **(Thomas) Flournoy.** His name is listed as Henry Flournoy in the Kanawha Co. birth records. Born 4 Feb. 1855 in Kanawha Co., VA (later WV). Listed in the 1860-80 censuses with his father. Flournoy Burgess was a cooper. By inference he is living in 1900.

6g. **William (XIV).** Born 25 Feb. 1857 (or 1858) in OH (so indicated in the 1860 census). He died on 30 June 1879 in Mason Co., WV (county death records).

6h. **James (VI).** Born Dec. 1859 in Mason Co., VA (later WV; noted as an infant male in the 1860 census). Listed with his father in the 1860-80 censuses, and with his mother in 1900. James Burgess was a cooper.

6i. **Joseph (I).** Born about 1862 in Mason Co., VA (later WV). Listed with his father in the 1870-80 censuses. By inference he is living in 1900.

6j. **Estella C.** Her name is also spelled Stella. Born about 1864 in Mason Co., WV. Married John Albert Young on 20 Apr. 1886 in Mason Co., WV. By inference she is living in 1900.

6k. **Nancy (IV) "Nettie."** Born 22 Aug. 1866 in Mason Co., WV. Living with her mother in 1900. Married Columbus Long on 31 Jan. 1903 in Mason Co., WV (he was born 1870, and died 9 Mar. 1908 in Mason Co.), and had at least the following children: *Gladys M.* (born 20 July 1904 in Mason Co.).

6l. **Fleming Cobb (III).** Born Jan. 1870 in Mason Co., WV; died there in Apr. 1870 (as indicated on the 1870 mortality census).

THE FIFTH BRANCH

Reuben Burgess, Senior
of Rowan County, North Carolina

The Old Burgess Home Near Troy, Idaho:
George Walter Burgess and Family, Circa 1909
(from left) Horace M., Mrs. Rebecca, Harold M., G. W., Roy P.
(front row) George O., Henrietta, Leola May, Evangeline

Chart VII: John Meredith Burgess of Kanawha Co., (West) Virginia

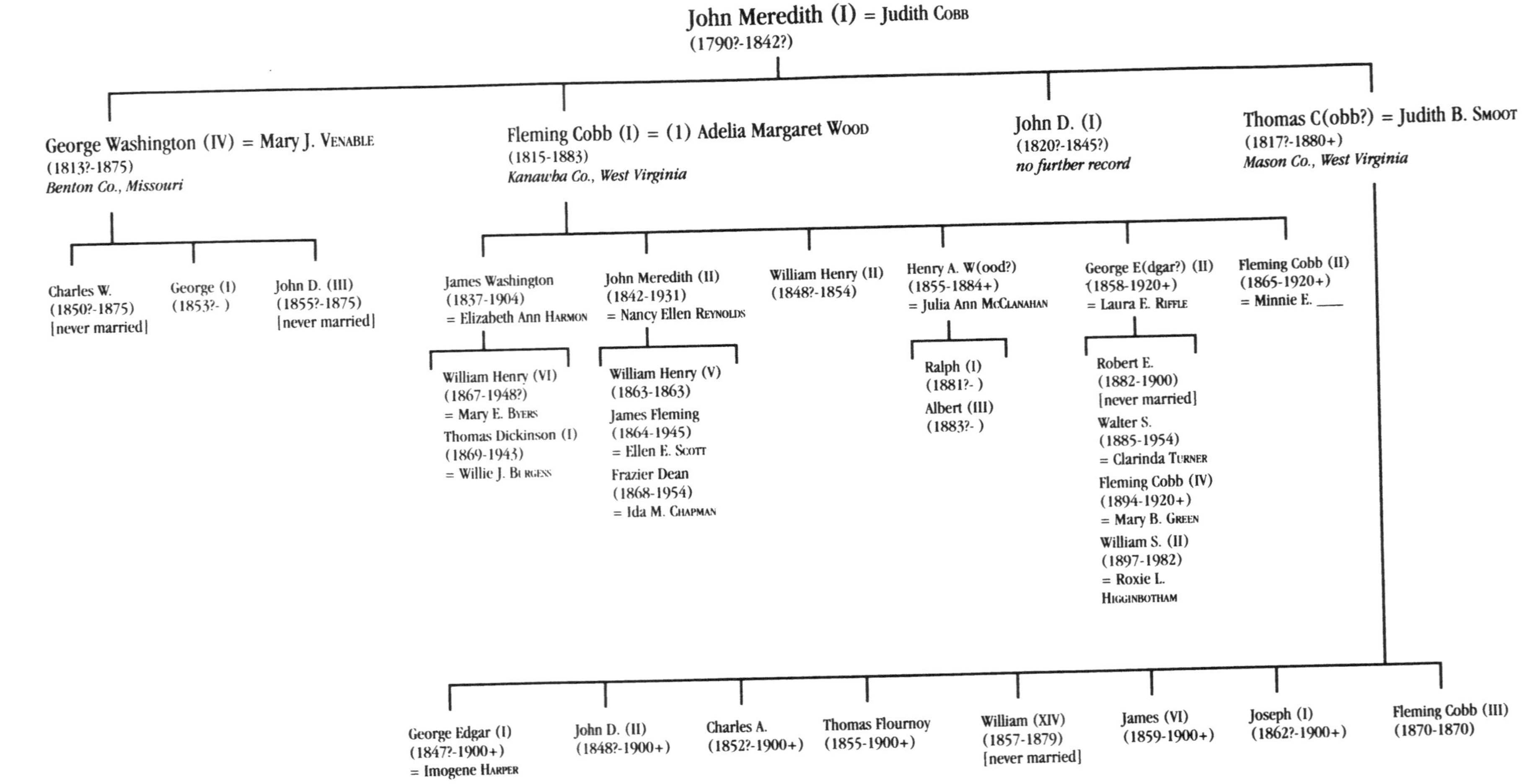

John Meredith (I) = Judith Cobb
(1790?-1842?)
George Washington (IV) = Mary J. Venable
(1813?-1875)
Benton Co., Missouri
Fleming Cobb (I) = (1) Adelia Margaret Wood
(1815-1883)
Kanawha Co., West Virginia
John D. (I)
(1820?-1845?)
no further record
Thomas C(obb?) = Judith B. Smoot
(1817?-1880+)
Mason Co., West Virginia
Charles W.
(1850?-1875)
[never married]
George (I)
(1853?-)
John D. (III)
(1855?-1875)
[never married]
James Washington
(1837-1904)
= Elizabeth Ann Harmon
John Meredith (II)
(1842-1931)
= Nancy Ellen Reynolds
William Henry (II)
(1848?-1854)
Henry A. W(ood?)
(1855-1884+)
= Julia Ann McClanahan
George E(dgar?) (II)
(1858-1920+)
= Laura E. Riffle
Fleming Cobb (II)
(1865-1920+)
= Minnie E. ____
William Henry (VI)
(1867-1948?)
= Mary E. Byers
Thomas Dickinson (I)
(1869-1943)
= Willie J. Burgess
William Henry (V)
(1863-1863)
James Fleming
(1864-1945)
= Ellen E. Scott
Frazier Dean
(1868-1954)
= Ida M. Chapman
Ralph (I)
(1881?-)
Albert (III)
(1883?-)
Robert E.
(1882-1900)
[never married]
Walter S.
(1885-1954)
= Clarinda Turner
Fleming Cobb (IV)
(1894-1920+)
= Mary B. Green
William S. (II)
(1897-1982)
= Roxie L.
Higginbotham
George Edgar (I)
(1847?-1900+)
= Imogene Harper
John D. (II)
(1848?-1900+)
Charles A.
(1852?-1900+)
Thomas Flournoy
(1855-1900+)
William (XIV)
(1857-1879)
[never married]
James (VI)
(1859-1900+)
Joseph (I)
(1862?-1900+)
Fleming Cobb (III)
(1870-1870)

THE BURGESSES BETWEEN WORLD WAR II AND THE PRESENT DAY

When Pearl Harbor was attacked in December 1941, the United States immediately entered World War II, which had already been in progress for two years on the European continent. Once again, the Burgess family responded generously with its young men and women, who enlisted in great numbers as war fever swept the nation. Burgesses served in every part of the military, but particularly in the Army and the Air Force. Although only one Burgess was killed in the fighting, many others were wounded or suffered debilitating injuries. By the time the war ended in 1945, dozens of family members had participated.

The world to which these men and women returned was permanently altered. Prior to this time, the American military had been downsized immediately following each major conflict and the draft ended. However, during the late 1940s the United States assumed the role of world policeman, and its rivalry with the Soviet Union mandated that the armed services be kept permanently enlarged to deal with the new global threat. Now many Burgesses encountered foreign cultures directly for the first time by actually living and serving among them. The maintenance of the draft and the two-years service it required also allowed many young men to see parts of America they had never before experienced. The institution of the G.I. Bill in the 1940s provided many of these Burgesses with a practical way of attending college, and for the first time every young person with the drive and ambition and intelligence could actually further his or her own education; others like my father, Roy W. Burgess, made a career of military life, both as officers and enlisted men, and more than a few brought back foreign wives from their overseas assignments.

Life was good in the Fifties and Sixties, with high-paying jobs readibly available in both the blue and white collar sectors. American industry was at its peak, providing the world with cheap, reliable goods of all kinds. American agriculture became the breadbasket of the world. The proliferation and expansion of the freeway system and inexpensive automobiles made frequent cross-country moves a fact of life for many families, spreading Burgess families into every state and every major metropolitan area, but simultaneously severing or straining the ties that bind all families together.

The Korean and Vietnamese Wars had their share of Burgess participants, men and women who served honorably and suffered their own measure of injuries, physical and mental. But the latter half of the twentieth century also saw an increasing number of Burgess men and women who made notable contributions to the advancement of science, engineering, medicine, psychology, religion, literature, and many other fields of endeavor, leaving small but positive signposts that they had made a positive difference with their lives. By the 1970s attendance at universities became commonplace, even expected, and more family members were finally able to achieve something close to their potential, a potential that had often been lost in earlier generations. The world was moving towards the information age, and the Burgess family moved with it, into occupations that reflected society's preoccupation with computers, data retrieval, and automation. So it is that I, a tenth-generation descendant of William Burges of King George Co., Virginia, spend most of my day in front of a computer, buying and cataloging materials for an academic library, and writing and editing books in my leisure time. As I write these words, as they flash on the screen before me, I wonder what Will Burges would think of me amidst this technology if he could see his great-great-great-great-great-great-great-grandson reflected back some three hundred years to his era.

As we near the end of the second millennium of the Christian era, we simultanously approach the 300th anniversary of the arrival of our Burgess family in North America. Soon William Burges's descendants will reach unto the thirteenth generation. Were he alive today, he could not imagine or understand the enormous changes that have altered the world almost beyond recognition. From an agrarian, highly stratified colony that owed allegiance to Queen Anne of England, we have become a tumultuous, even riotous collection of disparate nationalities and cultures striving to make itself a nation. He would not understand. But perhaps he would still recognize something of himself in the tens of thousands of his offspring who live today. You and I, all of us who share the Burgess name, we are the living threads which tie our family inexorably to the past. And to the future.

Chart VI: Reuben Burgess of Rowan (later Davie) Co., North Carolina

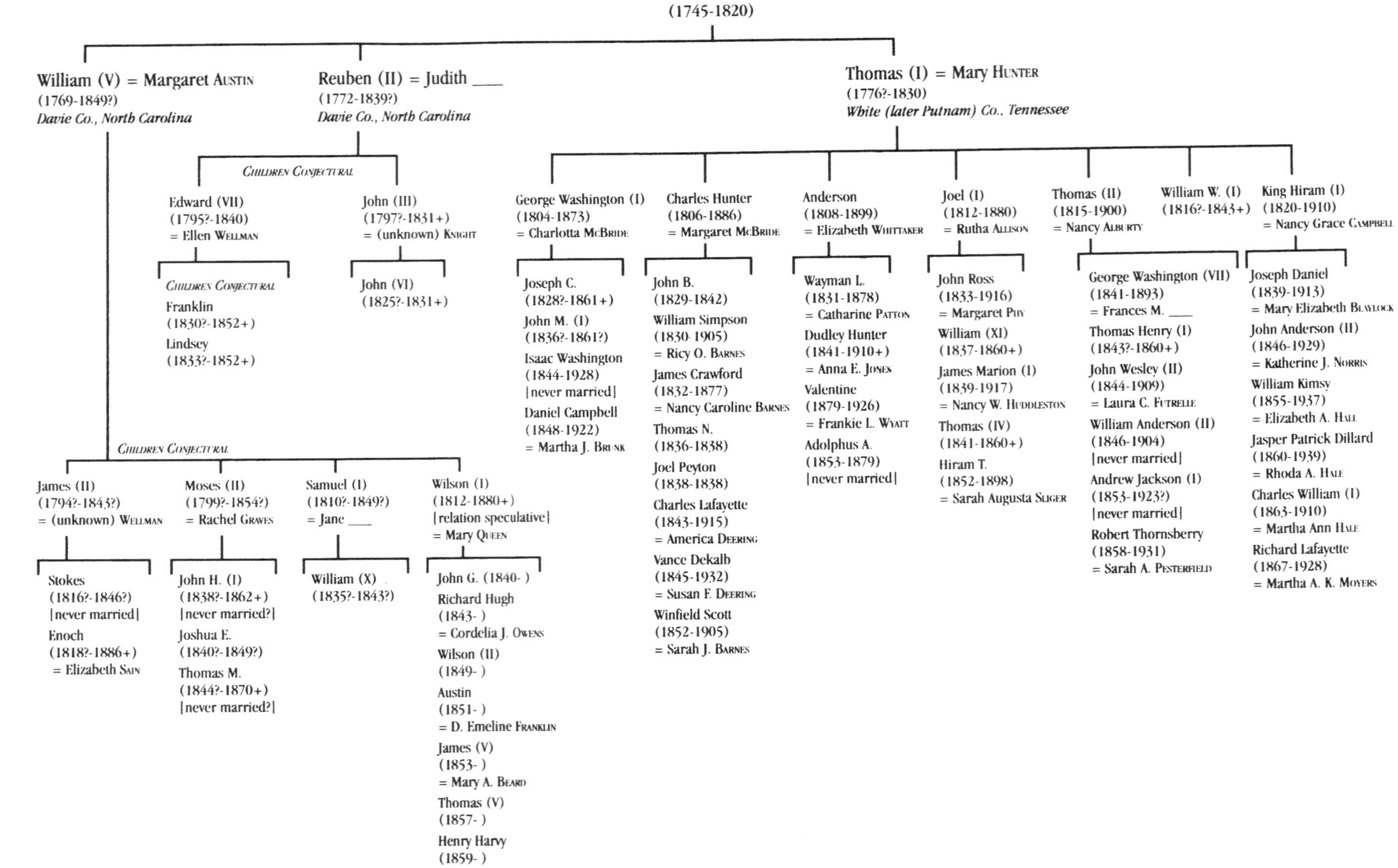

Reuben (I) = Margaret Stribling
(1745-1820)
William (V) = Margaret Austin
(1769-1849?)
Davie Co., North Carolina
Reuben (II) = Judith ___
(1772-1839?)
Davie Co., North Carolina
Thomas (I) = Mary Hunter
(1776?-1830)
White (later Putnam) Co., Tennessee
Children Conjectural
Edward (VII)
(1795?-1840)
= Ellen Wellman
John (III)
(1797?-1831+)
= (unknown) Knight
Children Conjectural
Franklin
(1830?-1852+)
Lindsey
(1833?-1852+)
John (VI)
(1825?-1831+)
George Washington (I)
(1804-1873)
= Charlotta McBride
Joseph C.
(1828?-1861+)
John M. (I)
(1836?-1861?)
Isaac Washington
(1844-1928)
[never married]
Daniel Campbell
(1848-1922)
= Martha J. Brunk
Charles Hunter
(1806-1886)
= Margaret McBride
John B.
(1829-1842)
William Simpson
(1830-1905)
= Ricy O. Barnes
James Crawford
(1832-1877)
= Nancy Caroline Barnes
Thomas N.
(1836-1838)
Joel Peyton
(1838-1838)
Charles Lafayette
(1843-1915)
= America Deering
Vance Dekalb
(1845-1932)
= Susan F. Deering
Winfield Scott
(1852-1905)
= Sarah J. Barnes
Anderson
(1808-1899)
= Elizabeth Whittaker
Wayman L.
(1831-1878)
= Catharine Patton
Dudley Hunter
(1841-1910+)
= Anna E. Jones
Valentine
(1879-1926)
= Frankie L. Wyatt
Adolphus A.
(1853-1879)
[never married]
Joel (I)
(1812-1880)
= Rutha Allison
John Ross
(1833-1916)
= Margaret Pitt
William (XI)
(1837-1860+)
James Marion (I)
(1839-1917)
= Nancy W. Huddleston
Thomas (IV)
(1841-1860+)
Hiram T.
(1852-1898)
= Sarah Augusta Sliger
Thomas (II)
(1815-1900)
= Nancy Alburty
George Washington (VII)
(1841-1893)
= Frances M. ___
Thomas Henry (I)
(1843?-1860+)
John Wesley (II)
(1844-1909)
= Laura C. Futrelle
William Anderson (II)
(1846-1904)
[never married]
Andrew Jackson (I)
(1853-1923?)
[never married]
Robert Thornsberry
(1858-1931)
= Sarah A. Pesterfield
William W. (I)
(1816?-1843+)
King Hiram (I)
(1820-1910)
= Nancy Grace Campbell
Joseph Daniel
(1839-1913)
= Mary Elizabeth Blaylock
John Anderson (II)
(1846-1929)
= Katherine J. Norris
William Kimsy
(1855-1937)
= Elizabeth A. Hall
Jasper Patrick Dillard
(1860-1939)
= Rhoda A. Hale
Charles William (I)
(1863-1910)
= Martha Ann Hale
Richard Lafayette
(1867-1928)
= Martha A. K. Moyers
Children Conjectural
James (II)
(1794?-1843?)
= (unknown) Wellman
Stokes
(1816?-1846?)
[never married]
Enoch
(1818?-1886+)
= Elizabeth Sain
Moses (II)
(1799?-1854?)
= Rachel Graves
John H. (I)
(1838?-1862+)
[never married?]
Joshua E.
(1840?-1849?)
Thomas M.
(1844?-1870+)
[never married?]
Samuel (I)
(1810?-1849?)
= Jane ___
William (X)
(1835?-1843?)
Wilson (I)
(1812-1880+)
[relation speculative]
= Mary Queen
John G. (1840-)
Richard Hugh
(1843-)
= Cordelia J. Owens
Wilson (II)
(1849-)
Austin
(1851-)
= D. Emeline Franklin
James (V)
(1853-)
= Mary A. Beard
Thomas (V)
(1857-)
Henry Harvy
(1859-)

[William (I)[1], Edward (I)[2]]

REUBEN BURGESS, SR.
(1745-1820)

OF ROWAN (LATER DAVIE) COUNTY, NORTH CAROLINA

3h. **Reuben (I)** *[son of Edward (I)].* Born 12 Feb. 1744/45 O.S. in Stafford (later King George) Co., VA [*St. Paul's Parish Register*]. Married Margaret Stribling on 1 Sept. 1765 in King George Co. (*St. Paul's Parish Register*; the register states ___ Stribling, but is followed in quick order by the births of their first children, with her given name listed as Margaret; she was born 10 Mar. 1743/44 O.S. in King George Co., VA [*St. Paul's Parish Register*], daughter of Thomas Stribling and Jane Thomas, and died about 1826 in Rowan Co., NC, when Reuben's estate was divided; Margaret's maiden name is confirmed by oral tradition among the descendants of this family [see the Hinkle family file in the Davie County Public Library, Mocksville, NC]). He is said in the Hinkle family record to have served in the Revolutionary War (but no proof of service has been found). Listed on the Stafford Co. personal property tax rolls from 1783-1788 (with nine whites in 1785), and on the Albemarle Co., VA tax rolls from 1789-1799. The Striblings moved with the Burgesses to Albemarle Co., with Thomas Stribling purchasing a farm next door to the Burgess land on 12 Apr. 1792 (*Deed Book #10*, p. 379-86, witnessed by Reuben, Reuben's son William, and Benjamin Ro(d)gers, believed to be Reuben's son-in-law). Reuben sold his land in Albemarle Co. on 5 Jan. 1799 (*Deed Book #13*, p. 19, 26), and moved to Rowan Co., NC (the section that became Davie Co. on 29 Dec. 1836) later that year; in his first deed there (*Rowan Co. Deed Book #17*, p. 714-15, dated 1 Dec. 1799) Reuben bought 520 acres of land from Jacob Trout, and is specifically cited as being "of the county Albemarle of State of Virginia"; the estate adjoined the land of Caspar (or Gaspar) Sain, on Dutchman Creek, and was located near or in the present town of Mocksville. Fifty acres of this land was sold to Hugh Wilson on 20 Nov. 1806 (*Deed Book #19*, p. 947); Wilson had previously bought (in July 1806) 142 acres from Joshua Hawkins adjoining the Burgess farm (*Deed Book #19*, p. 950). Reuben is listed in the 1800-20 censuses for Rowan Co., NC, and in the early tax records and surviving merchants' books of Rowan Co. and the Mocksville area.

Reuben Burgess Sr. was a farmer in Virginia and North Carolina. He died in Rowan Co. in the Summer of 1820; his will (*Rowan Co. Will Book #H*, p. 60-63, dated 18 Sept. 1817, the codicil dated 22 May 1820) was probated on 21 Aug. 1820, the last previous court session having ended on 20 May. The document also mentions Elizabeth McDowel(l), "the orphan child I raised," and is witnessed by son-in-law Ebenezer Nelson, Sam'l. Austin (the executor), and B. Bryan. Six years later, on 20 Aug. 1826, after the death of Margaret Burgess, Reuben's surviving heirs all cosigned a deed selling his remaining estate (*Deed Book #29*, p. 55-59). Reuben was probably the last of his brothers and sisters to die.

The Children of Reuben Burgess:

4a. **Mary (IV).** Born 7 July 1767 in Stafford (later King George) Co., VA [*St. Paul's Parish Register*]. Married Benjamin Rogers (the name confirmed from the Hinkle family records of Frances Hinkle Foster; Benjamin lived near the Burgesses in Albemarle Co.), and had children: *Lewis* (born about 1795 in VA, married his grandfather's ward, Elizabeth McDowell, on 10 Dec. 1817 [bond date] in Rowan Co., NC, and died after 13 Sept. 1819 [when he is recorded buying goods at Nesbitt's Store], but in any case by 22 May 1820, when he is noted as deceased in the codicil to his grandfather's will); *Mary N. "Polly"* (born 1803 in VA [so stated in 1850], married Daniel Sport on 19 Dec. 1830 in Rowan Co., NC [bond date; he died between 1839-41], and had children: Susannah [born 1832, apparently never married]; William B(urgess?) [born 1835, married Nancy C. ___ about 1859]; Daniel [born 1839]; *Mary SPORT* married secondly Andrew Hinkle about 1841 [her cousin?; he died 1845], by whom she had one son: George Washington (see below). *Mary HINKLE* is listed in the 1850-80 censuses for Davie Co., NC working as a spinner and housekeeper. She died there in the first half of 1900 [before the census was taken], aged 97 years). **Mary Burgess ROGERS** died between 1803-17 in Rowan (later Davie) Co., NC.

George Washington HINKLE was born 3 Aug. 1842 in Davie Co., NC, served in the Civil War in the Union Army, married Mrs. Susannah (Dwiggins) Conrad on 28 Jan. 1864 in Davie Co. (she was the widow of Philip Conrad [who was killed in the Civil War], and died before 1868), and had children: *Frances Louetta* (born 1864, married ___ Foster, listed with her grandmother in the 1870 census, and died childless at Cooleemee, NC about 1940; her memories and family Bible record, written down in the 1930s by Mrs. J. T. Baity of Mocksville, provided much background information on these families). ***George Washington HINKLE*** married secondly Mrs. Mary A. (Foster) Seaford in 1868 (she was born about 1834 in NC), and had children: *(Susannah) Maggie* (born 1868, married ___ Potts, and had many children); *Jessie A.* (born 1874, married, had six children, and was living at Cooleemee, NC in the 1930s); *Pinkney L.* (born 1877, died without living children); *Lillie* (born 1880, married ___ Boger, and had one son). Listed in the 1880 census for Davie Co., NC. ***George Washington HINKLE*** died on 17 July 1919 in Davie Co., NC, and is buried near Church Center.

4b. **William (V).** Born 15 June 1769 in Stafford (later King George) Co., VA. See below for full entry.

4c. **Reuben (II).** Born 14 June 1772 in Stafford (later King George) Co., VA. See below for full entry.

4d. **Molinde "Millie."** Her name is also written Malinda. Born about 1774 in Stafford (later King George) Co., VA. Married George Nelson by 1800 (he may have been a brother of Ebenezer Nelson, who married her sister, Franky Burgess; his will [*Rowan Co. Will Book #G*, p. 125, dated 1809, no probate date] mentions wife Melinda, brother Moses Nelson, but no children), and had one son and three daughters (names unknown). Molinde Nelson is mentioned in the 1826 settlement deed of the heirs of Reuben Burgess Sr.; she appears in the 1800-30 censuses for Rowan Co., NC, living next to Reuben and Edward Burgess, and in the 1840 census for Davie Co. Her half acre of land was sold for debts on 1 May 1840 (*Deed Book #3*, p. 361). She died by 1 Mar. 1845, when Henry R. Austin was appointed administrator of her estate (*Davie Co. Court Minutes #1*, p. 511).

4e. **Thomas (I).** Born about 1776 in Stafford (later King George) Co., VA. See below for full entry.

4f. **Frances (I) "Franky."** Born about 1782 in Stafford (later King George) Co., VA. Married Ebenezer Nelson on 11 July 1800 in Rowan Co., NC (bond date, William Burgess providing the bond; he was born 24 July 1777 in Rowan Co., NC, possibly a brother of George Nelson [who married Millie Burgess, Franky's sister], and died 1846 at Palmyra, MO; his intestate estate was probated on 5 July 1847 in Marion Co., MO [*Record of Wills, Letters, Etc. #B*, p. 439]), and had at least four sons and two daughters, among them: *Diadema* (born 1814 in NC, married Tillman Roberts on 4 Sept. 1833 (?) in Marion Co., MO, and had children: Isaac [born 1834]; Paulina [born 1836]; Ebenezer Nelson [born 1838]; John J. [born 1840]; Josephine [born 1842]; Tillman L. [born 1844]; listed in the 1840-60 censuses for Marion Co., MO); *(Ebenezer) Nesbit* (born 1816; see below); and possibly *Hiram* and *Benjamin Franklin*. Mentioned in her family's settlement deed of 1826. Listed in the 1800-20 censuses for Rowan Co., NC, and in 1830-40 in Fabius Township, Marion Co., MO. After receiving her portion of her father's estate, she and her husband sold their land in Rowan Co., and moved about 1828 to Palmyra, Marion Co., MO (they sold one acre of land in Mocksville on 28 Feb. 1828 to the Mocksville Academy [*Deed Book #2*, p. 599]). Ebenezer Nelson was a carpenter, cabinet-maker, and farmer. Franky Nelson died in 1833 at Palmyra, MO.

(Ebenezer) Nesbit NELSON was born 23 Sept. 1816 at Mocksville, Rowan (later Davie) Co., NC, and moved with his parents to Missouri. He married Lucetta Morehead on 24 Dec. 1840 in Marion Co., MO (she was born 1822 in Fauquier Co., VA, and died 25 Dec. 1864 in Marion Co., MO), and had children:

Morehead (born 1842 in MO, married Lucy Gordon [she was born 1839 in KY, possibly the daughter of Obedience Gordon, and died 1904], listed in the 1870 census for Marion Co., MO, and died 1889, having had children: Burgess [born 1867, died 1884]; Ira [born 1868, died 1869]; Ora [born Dec. 1869, married Benjamin Phears in 1890, and died 1941, having had children: Mallie Ray {born 22 June 1891, died unmarried in Oct. 1972 at Perry, MO}; Nellie Fay {born 1893, died 1981}]; Floy [born 10 Jan. 1872, and died Feb. 1968 at Troutdale, OR]; Morehead Jr. [born 1875, died 1956]; G. C. [born 1877, married Bessie May Kimball in 1906, and died 1944]; Gordon [born 1879, died 1957]; Guy [born 1883, married Susie Lennington in 1920 in Pike Co., MO {she was born 1902, and died 1965}, and died 1965, having had children: Son {born and died 1921}; Ivan Wade {born 29 Mar. 1922, married Mary Rufkohr in 1940, and died 19 Mar. 1988 at Bowling Green, MO, having had children: John H. <born 1941>}; Retha Mae {born 1925, drowned in 1931}; Vera {born 1926, married James A. Orf in 1947, and had children: Sandy <born 1948>; Paula <born 1949>; Duane <born 1950>; Pamela <born 1953>; Ronnie <born 1954, died 1988>; Aaron <born 1956>; Jeffery <born 1957>; Barbara <born 1958>; Dwight <born 1960>; Shari <born 1963>; Patricia <born 1965, died 1994>; Valorie <born 1967>; Scott <born 1970>}; Gale Dean {born 1929, married Joyce Stambaugh in 1957, and had children: Kenneth <born 1957>; Bryan <born 1959>; Clifford <born 1961>; Lisa <born 1965>}; Lucy {born 1932, married Thomas Skillman in 1954, and had children: Harold <born 1953>; Blake <born 1956>; Melissa <born 1958>; Denton <born 1961>}; Glen Harold {born 1935, married

Dorothy Barton in 1955 <she was born 1936, and died 1975>, and had children: Audrey Lynn <born 1957, married Virgil Jones Jr. in 1975 |he was born 1950|, and had children: Jarred Lee |born 1976|; Ryan Glynn |born 1979|; Nicole LaDawn Mayol |born 1981|>}; Nina Mae {born 1937, married James Mudd in 1953, and had children: Michael Henry <born 1954>; Nina married secondly John Drainer in 1957, and had children: Diane <born 1958>; Dawn Marie <born 1961>; John Robert <born 1963>}; Fred Wayne {born 1939, married Mary Maiden in 1960, and had children: Allen <born 1962>; Russell <born 1964>; Lavona <born 1971>}]; Vera [born 1885, married Glen Bowen, and died 1958]). Audrey Nelson Jones has contributed greatly to this book.

(Mary) Francis "Fannie" (born 1846, married Dr. James P. Frame [he was born 1839 in MO], and had children: Clarence [born Mar. 1870]); *Elizabeth* (born 1848, married J. T. Hall); *John H.* (born 1851, died unmarried); *James T.* (born 1854); *William Frost* (born 1857, married Josephine Wilson in 1883, and died 1920, having had children: Georetta Mae [born 1885, married John Bogener Jr. in 1908, and died 1922]; Edna [born 28 Aug. 1887, married John Bogener Jr. in 1922, and died June 1982 at Quincy, IL); *Joseph* (born 1859, died between 1860-70); *George L.* (born 1864).

Nesbit NELSON married secondly Virginia Ann Lillard on 12 Nov. 1871 in Clark Co., MO (she was born 20 Jan. 1835 in Culpeper Co., VA), and had children: *Lillard* (born and died 1872); *Ezra* (born and died 1875). Served in Capt. John H. Curd's Company, First Missouri Regiment, during the Seminole War against Chief Osceola in Florida in 1837-38. Listed in the 1850-60 censuses for Marion Co., MO, and in 1870 in Lewis Co., MO. Dr. Nesbit Nelson was a school teacher, doctor, and minister. He moved to Lewis Co., MO in Feb. 1866, and to Clark Co., MO in Nov. 1871, and died there in 1899, buried on his farm near Kahoka, MO. His biography appears in *History of Lewis, Clark, Knox, and Scotland Counties, Missouri* (St. Louis & Chicago: Goodspeed Publishing Co., 1887, p. 941-942).

4g. **Winny.** Her name is also written Vinny on her marriage record, and may actually have been Winifred. Born about 1784 in Stafford (later King George) Co., VA. Married John Hinkle on 7 Jan. 1813 in Rowan Co., NC (bond date; he died between 1820-30), and had one son and one daughter (names unknown). Mentioned in her father's settlement deed of 1826. Listed with her father in 1800-10, and in the 1820-30 censuses for Rowan Co., NC. She may have moved to Illinois with Henry Hinkle.

THE BIOGRAPHY OF NESBIT NELSON

"N. Nelson, M.D., a prominent physician and Baptist minister, was born at Mocksville, in Rowan (now Davie) County, N.C., September 23, 1816. His parents, Ebenezer and Frances (Burgess) Nelson, were natives of Rowan County, N.C., and Albemarle, Va., and born July 24, 1777 and 1782, respectively. After their marriage in North Carolina they came to Marion County in 1828, and entered land near Palmyra. The mother died in 1833, and the father survived her until 1846. The father was a cabinet-maker and carpenter, but engaged in farming chiefly. Our subject was educated in Marion County principally, and at the age of twenty-three began teaching school. During his pedagogue days he began reading medicine, and afterward practiced, together with farming and other business. He received his medical education in the St. Louis Medical College, located at Philadelphia, Marion County, and began practice, and also devoted several years to his favorite study, theology. He was ordained as a minister in March, 1865, and since then has been preaching. In February, 1866, he moved to Gilead, in Lewis County. He there took a medical partner, Dr. Frame, that he might continue preaching also. He moved to his present farm [in Clark County] in November, 1871, and is still engaged in his professions, and in farming. His wife, Lucetta Morehead, was born in 1822 in Fauquier County, Va., and came to Missouri in 1835. She was married December 24, 1840, and her death occurred December 25, 1864. She was the mother of seven children. In November, 1871, Virginia Lillard, a native of Culpeper County, Va., became his wife. She was born January 20, 1835, and the following year her parents came to Missouri. Her children are deceased. Our subject's children are Morehead, Mary F. (the wife of Dr. J. P. Frame), Elizabeth (the wife of J. T. Hall), John H., James T., William F., and George L. Our subject is very prominent, both as a physician and a minister, and in his evangelical work has built up two churches in Clark County, and one in Lewis. Politically he is a Democrat, and first voted in 1840 for that party. Our subject's family, excepting the oldest son, are members of the Baptist Church. He served in the Florida war of 1837-38."

THE WILL OF REUBEN BURGESS

In the name of God, Amen

I Reuben Burgess Senr. of the County of Rowan, and State of North Carolina, being in perfect health & of sound mind & memory, thanks be rendered unto God for his mercies, considering the mortality of this frail body, the immortality of the Soul, that it is appointed for all men once to die, and after death to stand befor [sic] the awful Judge of Heaven and Earth to give an account of the deeds done in the body, whether they be good or evil, do hereby, & in consequence of the aforesaid important considerations, make this my last will and testament.

First, I recommend my soul ento [sic] the hands of Almighty God who gave it hoping to receive the same again at the great day of the Resurrection, and to enjoy the same felicity of the Angels in Heaven.

Secondly, I recommend my body to the Earth to be buried in decent Christian burial at the discretion of my Executors hereafter specify'd. And as it hath pleas'd God in his mercy to bless me with some worldy substance, I give & bequeath the same in manner and form following Viz.

First, I give and bequeath unto my beloved wife, Margaret Burgess after my just debts are paid, every thing of which I am ^{now} posses'd, or should be posses'd at the time of my decease during her natural life or Widowhood.

Secondly, I give & bequeath unto my son Thomas Burgess one Shilling & no more.

Thirdly, I give & bequeath unto ~~my~~ Elizabeth Dowel an orphan child whom I rais'd, one feather bed and furniture together with a small pine chest.

Fourthly, I give and bequeath unto my granddaughter Polley Rogers one feather bed & furniture.

Fifthly, after the deceace or marriage ^{of} my beloved wife, Viz., the said Margaret Burgess, it [sic] my absolute will and desire that my grandsonson [sic] Lewis Rogers should become an equal heir with my surviving children provided he continues with his grandmother Viz the ^{said} Margaret Burgess during her natural life or widowhood.

Sixthly, it is my will and desire that after the decease or marriage of my beloved wife aforesaid all the remaining part of my property not previously specified should be equally divided amongst my said surviving children, & as aforesaid Lewis Rodgers included.

Lastly, I hereby nominate and declare Captain Samuel Austin the whole & soul ^{sole} [sic] Executor of this my last will and testament.

In witness whereof I the said Reuben Burgess Senr. hath this eighteenth of September in the year of our Lord one thousand eight hundred & seventeen affix'd both his hand and seal in the presence of us.

Sign'd, Seald, and deliver'd to the said Capt. Samuel Austin for the purpose within specify'd.

Attest Reuben Burgess [Seal]

Witnessed by B. Bryan, Saml Austin Jr. [?], Lewis Rodgers

[CODICIL]

I Reuben Burgess sound in mind but weak in body do make & publish the following alteration in my foregoing will

Namely, Whereas Lewis Rogers having deceased since the time of making said will, I do therefore give and bequeath to my other heirs as mentioned in the will aforesaid, all that portion of my Estate bequeathed to him the said Lewis Rogers to be equally divided and do hereby exclude said Rogers or his heirs from any party, claim or inheritance whatsoever in my Estate except such property as I have heretofore bequeathed to Elizabeth Dowell, wife of said Lewis Rogers Dec^{d}

Signed and sealed and acknowledged in our presence this 22nd of May 1820.

Test Reuben Burgess [Seal]

Witnessed by Saml Austin Jr. [?] and Ebenezar Nelson

THE SETTLEMENT DEED OF REUBEN BURGESS'S ESTATE

This indendure made the __ day of March in the year of our Lord one thousand Eight hundred and twenty six Between Reubin Burgess, William Burgess, Milly Nelson, Ebenezer Nelson and his wife Franky Nelson, and John Hinkle and his wife Winny Hinkle of the County of Rowan and the State of North Carolina of the one part, and John Clement of the county of Rowan and the state of North Carolina of the other part—Witnesseth, that the said Reubin Burgess, Wm Burgess, Malinde Nelson, Ebenezer Nelson and his wife Franky Nelson, and John Hinkle and his wife Winny Hinkle, for and in consideration of the sum of Forty four Dollars, to them in hand paid by the said John Clement, the receipt whereof the said Reubin Burgess, William Burgess, Malinda Nelson, Ebenezer Nelson and his wife Franky Nelson, and John Hinkle & his wife Winny Hinkle, doth hereby acknowledge, hath given granted bargained and sold aliened and confirmed and by these presents, doth give grant bargain and sell alien and confirm unto the said John Clement his heirs and assigns forever, all that tract peice or parcel of Land situate lying and being in the county of Rowan and state aforesaid, on the waters of Dutchmans Creek, being part of a tract Caspar Sain formerly owned and purchased by Reubin Burgess dec^{d}, being part of his Lands, Begining at a black oak grub or tree corner of said John Clements land running thence West One hundred and twelve poles to a Stake or stone on Ebenezer Nelsons line, thence North sixty three poles to a stake or stone on A. G. Carters line, thence East one hundred and twelve poles to a black oak on said John Clements line, thence South to the beginning, Containing forty four acres be the same more or less, the said Land fell to the beforenamed persons by heirship as per will of their father, Reubin Burgess Senr dec^{d}—And also the woods, ways, waters, and water courses and all and every the appurtenances thereunto belonging or in any wise appertaining and the reversion and reversions remainder and remainders rents issues and profits of the aforesaid lands and premises and every part thereof and all the Estate right title interest claims property and demand whatsoever of the said Reubin Burgess, William Burgess, Milly Nelson, Ebenezer Nelson and his wife Franky Nelson and John Hinkle and his wife Winny Hinkle, of, in, and to the Land and premises hereby granted To have and to hold the aforesaid lands and premises with the appurtenances unto the said John Clement his heirs and assigns to the proper use and behest of the said John Clement his heirs and assigns forever, and the said Reubin Burgess, William Burgess, Milly Nelson, Ebenezer Nelson and his wife Franky Nelson and John Hinkle and his wife Winny Hinkle for themselves and their heirs the aforesaid land and premises and every part thereof against themselves and their heirs and against the claim or claims of all and every other person or persons whatsoever to the said John Clement his heirs and assigns shall and will forever warrant and defend by these presents In Testimony whereof Reubin Burgess, William Burgess, Milly Nelson, Ebenezer Nelson and his wife Franky Nelson and John Hinkle and his wife Winny Hinkle hereunto set their hands and affixd their seals the day and year first above written.

Witnesses included: Littleberry R. Rose, Thomas McNeely Esq. The date on the first line of the deed is blank; the document was filed on 16 May 1826, and accepted at the August 1826 court session.

[William (I)[1], Edward (I)[2], Reuben (I)[3]]

WILLIAM BURGESS
(1769-1849?)
OF DAVIE COUNTY, NORTH CAROLINA

4b. **William (V)** *[son of Reuben (I)].* Born 15 June 1769 in Stafford (later King George) Co., VA [*St. Paul's Parish Register*]. Married Margaret "Peggy" Austin on 3 Sept. 1793 in Albemarle Co., VA (bond date, with Reuben Burgess providing the bond, John Carr witness; Margaret was born about 1774 in Maryland, the daughter of James Austin of Calvert Co., MD [who died young] and ward of Henry Austin, and apparently died between 1840-50; her parentage is established in a brief unpublished "Record of the Austin Family" written by Rev. William Austin in Feb. 1857 [located in the McCubbins papers in the Rowan Public Library, Salisbury, NC], which also mentions that James's brothers Samuel Austin and Henry Austin and brother-in-law William Marshall settled in Albemarle Co. [and later came to Rowan Co. with the Burgesses]). William Burgess was a farmer in Virginia and North Carolina. He and "Peagey" sold their land in Albemarle Co. on 5 Jan. 1799 (*Deed Book #13*, p. 26), and moved with his father to Rowan (later Davie) Co., NC, where he appears in the census records for 1800 and from 1820-30; he has not been found in 1810, although he may be living with his father; listed in 1840 in Davie Co., NC (which was split off from Rowan Co. in 1836). Listed on the voting register of 11 Aug. 1825 (and thereafter). William Burgess received 67 acres of land on Elisha Creek from Samuel Austin, his uncle-in-law, in 1803 (*Deed Book #21*, p. 431), lying next to the farms of Ebenezer Nelson and Walter Gaither, and sold it to Littleberry R. Rose on 24 June 1809 (*Deed Book #21*, p. 623). William and Samuel Austin then sold 35 acres of land on Dutchman Creek to Littleberry R. Rose on 27 Feb. 1819 (*Rowan Co. Deed Book #25*, p. 894). William received 50 acres of land from Samuel Austin in July 1819 (*Deed Book #30*, p. 881), and with his wife regranted it on 26 Dec. 1829 to their son, Samuel Burgess (*Deed Book #30*, p. 927); the farm adjoined the parcels of Jeremiah Wellman, Jacob Booe, John Nail(e), and Jeremiah Williams. William apparently died between 3 Aug. 1848 and 2 Aug. 1849 (when he disappeared from the voting lists).

According to the census records for Rowan and Davie Cos., NC, William and Reuben Jr. had between them five or six sons, of which only one, Samuel, can be absolutely attributed to his father (William); another, Wilson, cannot be firmly established as belonging to this family. The other four boys can be divided into two age groups: James and Edward born in the early 1790s, and John and Moses born in the mid to late 1790s; two pairings are possible: James and John with Edward and Moses, or Edward and John with James and Moses. The situation is complicated by the fact that both families apparently lived together, and intermingled freely among themselves. The key to this family appears to be the breakdown of the daughters. William can be shown from census records to have had two daughters born after 1800, and Reuben to have had three daughters, one born just before 1800, and two just after. If Juda Burgess is the wife of Reuben Burgess Jr., as seems very probable (William's wife Peggy is still alive in Dec. 1829), then Mary and Sarah Burgess are daughters of Reuben Jr., since they are mentioned in two records as daughters of Juda. Of the three remaining women, Drucilla and Elizabeth are paired with their presumed brother, Moses Burgess, who provided bonds for their marriages, leaving only Nancy, who is identified as a sister of Edward Burgess in the 1816 Nesbitt's Store account books. Therefore, Edward Burgess is probably a son of Reuben Burgess Jr., and Moses Burgess is likely a son of William Burgess; it follows that James Burgess is a son of William Burgess, and John Burgess (who bonded Edward's marriage) is a son of Reuben Burgess Jr. None of this can be proven, despite an exhaustive search of published and unpublished records in Davie and Rowan Cos., NC, and in the Archives Branch of the North Carolina State Library in Raleigh, NC; however, this is the likeliest interpretation of the known facts. William's land was located on Dutchman Creek in 1837 (see Davie Co. *Deed Book #1*, p. 45).

The Children of William Burgess:

5a. **James (II).** Born about 1794 in Albemarle Co., VA. See below for full entry.
5b. **Moses (II).** Born about 1799 in Rowan (later Davie) Co., NC. See below for full entry.

5c. **Drucilla "Drusy."** Born about 1802 (or 1803) in Rowan (later Davie) Co., NC. Married Bennett Rogers (her cousin?) on 20 Jan. 1827 in Rowan Co. (bond date, Moses Burgess providing the bond; Bennett was born about 1798 in VA), and had at least the following children: *Margaret* (born 1829); *Rebecca* (born 1831); *Lydia* (born 1833, may have married ___ Nail [a Lydia Nail was deeded 5.75 acres of land by Bennett Rogers on 27 Feb. 1860, in *Deed Book #4*, p. 396]); *Mary S. "May"* (born 1837); *Elizabeth* (born 1839). Listed in the 1830 census for Rowan Co., NC, and from 1840-60 in Davie Co., NC; has not been found in 1870; listed in the land tax lists from 1843-51 with 50 acres of land in the Mocksville District, and from 1855 with 117 acres. Drucilla and her sister Elizabeth are believed to be sisters of Moses Burgess, who provided their marriage bonds. Drusy Rogers apparently died in Davie Co. between 1860-70.

5d. **Elizabeth (VII).** Born about 1807 in Rowan (later Davie) Co., NC. Married Eli W. Coble on 31 Jan. 1828 in Rowan Co. (bond date, Moses Burgess providing the bond). Has not been found in the 1830 census or thereafter. Elizabeth and Drucilla are believed to be sisters of Moses Burgess, who bonded both their marriages. An Elizabeth Coble married Peter Turner on 23 Jan. 1830 in Rowan Co.

5e. **Samuel (I).** Born about 1810 in Rowan (later Davie) Co., NC. See below for full entry.

5f. **Wilson (I).** Born about 1812 (or 1815 or 1818) in Rowan (later Davie) Co., NC. Married Mary Queen on 10 Apr. 1837 in Davie Co. (she was born about 1817 in NC). Wilson Burgess is recorded as trading at the Kelly & Gaither store in Mocksville, Davie Co., NC beginning on 24 Mar. 1836, and is listed on the insolvents' tax list of 31 Aug. 1839 for Davie Co. He moved west to Haywood Co., NC by 1850, when he is listed in the census there. His relationship to this line has not been proven, and his inclusion here should be regarded as speculative.

6a. **Sarah Ann (I).** Born 1838. Married M. M. Messer on 31 Jan. 1858 in Haywood Co.
6b. **John G.** Born 1840.
6c. **Richard Hugh**. Born 1843. Married Cordelia Jane Owens on 18 Mar. 1869 in Haywood Co.
6d. **Elizabeth P. (II).** Born 1845.
6e. **Mary L.** Born 1847.
6f. **Wilson (II).** Born 1849 in Haywood Co., NC.
6g. **Austin.** Born 1851 in Haywood Co., NC. Married D. Emeline Franklin about 1871.

7a. **Margaret (IX).** Born 1872 in Haywood Co., NC.
7b. **Elizabeth Jane (III).** Born 28 Feb. 1875 in Haywood Co., NC. Married George Washington Davis. Elizabeth Davis died on 26 Mar. 1937 at Tekonsha, MI.
7c. **J. W. Gain.** Born 1878 in Haywood Co., NC.

6h. **James (V).** Born 1853 in Haywood Co., NC. Married Mary A. Beard on 6 Feb. 1880 in Haywood Co.
6i. **Thomas (V).** Born 1857 in Haywood Co., NC.
6j. **Henry Harvy**. Born 1859 in Haywood Co., NC.

[William (I)[1], Edward (I)[2], Reuben (I)[3], William (V)[4]]

JAMES BURGESS
(1794?-1843?)

OF DAVIE COUNTY, NORTH CAROLINA

5a. **James (II)** *[presumed son of William (V)].* Born about 1794 in Albemarle Co., VA. Married ___ Wellman, daughter of John Wellman (verified from subsequent land deeds of Enoch Burgess), about 1815 (she died before 1820); by Sarah "Sally" Potts he may have had an illegitimate daughter, Sarah (the older Sarah was born about 1801 in NC, possibly the daughter of Peter Potts, and may be living with him in the 1830-40 censuses). Listed in the A. Nesbitt's Store Day Book in 1816 with entries: "James Burgess per wife" and "James Burgess per J. Foster." Listed in the 1820-30 censuses for Rowan Co., in 1840 in Davie Co., and in the tax records of both counties through 1843. Listed on the voting register of 11 Aug. 1825 (and thereafter). James Burgess was a farmer in Rowan (later Davie) Co., NC. He purchased 48 acres of land from his presumed cousin, John Burgess, on 26 Sept. 1818 (*Rowan Co. Deed Book #25*, p. 199), and another 24 acres from Kannon Brown on 10 Jan. 1819 (*Deed Book #25*, p. 229), all three plots situated on Bear Creek, having been sold as part of the estate division of Daniel Hendricks to John Burgess and Gaspar (or Caspar) Sain. On 18 Apr. 1840 he was forced to mortgage his remaining 63.5 acres of land on Dutchmans Creek and all his personal property to Ephraim Gaither, trustee of Berry Foster and Radford Foster, for a bond "for the cost of jail fine and prison fees lately determined in the superior court for Davie Co. at Spring term 1840 drawn payable to Thomas Foster and wife for the sum of $138.42" (*Davie Co. Deed Book #1*, p. 288). He apparently died or left Davie Co. about 1843. Exact relationship not verified.

The Children of James Burgess:

6a. **Stokes.** Born about 1816 in Rowan (later Davie) Co., NC. Stokes Burgess was a farmer in Davie Co., NC. He died there unmarried about 1846; on 9 Jan. 1847 his brother Enoch (his sole heir) sold Stokes's half share of John Wellman's estate (*Davie Co. Deed Book #2*, p. 540).

6b. **Enoch.** Born about 1818 in Rowan (later Davie) Co., NC. See below for full entry.

6c. **Sarah (VII).** Born about 1837 in Davie Co., NC, the daughter of Sally Potts. She may be the Sarah Ann Burgess who is mentioned on an undated Davie Co. school list of the 1840s. Listed in the 1850 census for Davie Co. living with her mother (as "Sarah Potts"), and in 1860 with G. A. Bloom. Married Jonathan Smith on 5 Feb. 1868 in Davie Co., and is noted on the marriage bond as being the daughter of James Burgess. Has not been found in the 1870 census for Davie Co. Relationship not verified.

[William (I)[1], Edward (I)[2], Reuben (I)[3], William (V)[4], James (II)[5]]

ENOCH BURGESS
(1818-1886+)
OF DAVIE COUNTY, NORTH CAROLINA

6b. **Enoch** *[son of James (II)].* Born about 1818 in Rowan (later Davie) Co., NC, although one of his daughter's death certificates states he was born in Union Co., NC. Married Martha "Patsy" ___ about 1836 (she is mentioned in the Gaither & Johnston merchant ledger book on 21 Feb. 1837 through 29 Mar. 1839, was enrolled with her husband in the Mocksville Methodist Episcopal Church on 27 July 1838, and died about 1840); married secondly Elizabeth "Bettie" Sain on 17 Sept. 1845 in Davie Co. (bond date; she was born about 1819 in Rowan [later Davie] Co., NC, and died in Davie Co. about 1900). Listed in Davie Co. tax lists from 1843-72+, in the 1840 census living next door to his father, and in the 1850-80 censuses for the Mocksville District, Davie Co., NC (his wife is listed as head of the family in 1870, and Enoch has not been found in this census); he appears on the land tax records there with 36 acres through 1858, and with 67 (or 69) acres through at least 1872.

Enoch Burgess inherited through his deceased mother ___ Wellman (whose first name does not survive) the second half of Lot #2 of John Wellman's estate, which was divided between the two Burgess brothers; since Stokes Burgess died unmarried between 1846-47, Enoch was able to sell both halves by 1850 (*Davie Co. Deed Book #1*, p. 86, 3 Feb. 1838, and *Deed Book #2, p. 540*, 9 Jan. 1847; Wellman's Lot #1 went to Elizabeth Wellman, John's daughter, who married Littleberry R. Rose, and Lot #6 to Dolly Wellman and her husband, James Chaplin; the disposition of the remaining pieces is unknown). Enoch Burgess later bought a farm about four miles outside of Mocksville, Davie Co., NC. He died in Davie Co. between 1886-1900; his wife's estate was probated on 20 Aug. 1900 (but she is not listed in the 1900 census); both are believed buried in unmarked graves in the Sain Cemetery.

The Children of Enoch Burgess:

7a. **Elizabeth (XIII).** Born about 1836 in Davie Co., NC. Mentioned on the school list of 1 July 1842 as the older child. Died young.

7b. **John (VII).** Born about 1838 in Davie Co., NC. Mentioned on the school lists of 1 July 1842 and 1843, but is dropped (presumably dead) in 1844.

7c. **Milton.** Born about 1846 in Davie Co., NC; died there young between 1850-1860.

7d. **(Louisa) Jane.** Born 27 Aug. 1849 in Davie Co., NC. She apparently never married, but had an illegitimate son by an unknown father. Jane Burgess continued to operate the family farm after her parents' death. She died of measles on 4 Mar. 1917 at her farm in Davie Co., and is buried in an unmarked grave in the Oak Grove Cemetery.

8a. **James Madison "Jim."** He spelled his name Burges; his middle name is given as Martin on his tombstone and obituary, but Madison on his death certificate. Born 13 May 1866 in Davie Co., NC. Listed in the 1880-1900 censuses for Davie Co., NC with his family; has not been found either in the 1870 or 1910 censuses; listed in the 1920 census for Davie Co., NC. James Burges was a farmer with his mother and aunt on his family's lands, inheriting the property from his aunt Sallie in 1938. He died there unmarried on 17 June 1942, the last male representative of his family in Davie Co. and the last known descendant of his great-grandfather, James Burgess, and is buried in the Oak Grove Cemetery (the only Burgess there with a tombstone).

7e. **Sarah C. (II) "Sallie."** Born 30 Dec. 1852 in Davie Co., NC. Listed with her parents in the censuses through 1880, and with her nephew, James Burges, in 1900 and 1920. Sallie Burgess was a farmer in Davie Co. on the family lands near Mocksville, NC. She died there unmarried on 19 Jan. 1938, and is buried in an unmarked grave in the Oak Grove Cemetery.

7f. **Mary E. (I).** Born about 1855 in Davie Co., NC. Living with her father in the censuses through 1880, but apparently died there unmarried before 1900. Not mentioned in her mother's probate record.

Wedding Picture of John Washington Burgess and Etta Leach
28 January 1900
(see page 473)

[William (I)[1], Edward (I)[2], Reuben (I)[3], William (V)[4]]

MOSES BURGESS
(1799?-1854?)

OF DAVIE COUNTY, NORTH CAROLINA

5b. **Moses (II)** *[presumed son of William (V)].* Born about 1799 in Rowan (later Davie) Co., NC. Married Rachel Graves on 17 Aug. 1833 in Rowan Co. (bond date, Wilson Rose providing the bond; Rachel was the daughter of George Graves, and died between 1843-50). He served as bondsman for the marriages of his two presumed sisters, Drucilla and Elizabeth Burgess, and sold his interest in George Graves's estate on 12 Oct. 1840 to Lemuel Bingham (*Davie Co. Deed Book #1*, p. 326). Listed on the insolvents' tax list of 25 Nov. 1841 (and was taken into custody by the sheriff on 2 Mar. 1842 for debts), and in the 1840-50 censuses for Davie Co. (listed with him in 1850 is Sally Hightower [age 47]; also listed in the 1850 census for Davie Co. is William M. Graves [probably his brother-in-law] and William's son, Burgess Graves). Listed on the voting register of 11 Aug. 1825 (and thereafter). Moses Burgess was a farmer in Rowan (later Davie) Co. He was appointed overseer of the road from Graves Bridge to Ely Carter's gate on 28 Jan. 1837 in Davie Co. He died there between 4 Aug. 1853 (when he voted) and 1 Mar. 1854, when his orphaned children were apprenticed. Exact relation not verified, but probable.

The Children of Moses Burgess:

6a. **(Sarah) Elizabeth (I).** Born about 1835 in Rowan (later Davie) Co., NC. Mentioned in various school lists of the 1840s in Davie Co. as Sarah E., Sary E., or Elizabeth Burgess. Elizabeth Burgess was a seamstress in Davie Co. She died there unmarried between 8 Mar. 1856, when she is mentioned in a surviving merchant's record book, and 21 June 1856, when her small estate was sold.

6b. **John H. (I).** Also called John M. Burgess in some records. Born about 1838 in Davie Co., NC. Mentioned in various school lists of the 1840s. He was apprenticed on 1 Mar. 1854 to Bennett Rogers, his presumed uncle, and again on 28 Aug. 1855 to James W. Shuck. Listed in the 1860 census for Davie Co. with his brother and M. Bean, a farmer for whom they both worked, but is not mentioned on the 1865 election list. John Burgess enlisted in the Confederate Army on 1 Feb. 1862 in Davie Co. in Co. C., Major Gibbs's Prison Guard Battalion, North Carolina Troops (also called Co. D, 42nd Regiment, North Carolina Troops), and also served with his brother, Thomas Burgess, in Co. G. and Co. M, 75th Regiment, 7th Battalion, Confederate Army, during the Civil War. He either died during the war, or never returned to Davie Co.

6c. **Joshua E(dward?).** Born about 1840 in Davie Co., NC. Mentioned on the school list of Dec. 1847 (unnamed), and is named on the 1848/49 list as a son of Moses Burgess, but apparently died there before 1850.

6d. **Thomas M.** Born about 1844 in Davie Co., NC. Mentioned in various school lists of the 1840s. Apprenticed on 1 Mar. 1854 to Bennett Rogers, his presumed uncle, and again on 28 Aug. 1855 to Robert Orrill. Listed in the 1860 census for Davie Co. with his brother and M. Bean, a farmer for whom they both worked. Tom Burgess served in Co. G. and Co. M, 75th Regiment, 7th Battalion, Confederate Army, during the Civil War, and later in Co. E., 16th Battalion, North Carolina Troops (being transferred on 11 July 1864); he was captured on 1 Apr. 1865 at Hatcher's Run, VA, but was released on parole on 17 June 1865. He then returned to Davie Co., where he is listed in both the 1865 voters' list and in the 1870 census for the Mocksville District, working as a teamster for Lucinda Taylor. He has not been found thereafter.

[William (I)[1], Edward (I)[2], Reuben (I)[3], William (V)[4]]

SAMUEL BURGESS
(1810?-1849?)

OF DAVIE COUNTY, NORTH CAROLINA

5e. **Samuel (I)** *[son of William (V)].* Born about 1810 in Rowan (later Davie) Co., NC. Married Jane ___ about 1830 (she was born about 1807 in Rowan [later Davie] Co., NC, and remarried John Massey on 29 Nov. 1849 in Davie Co. [witnessed by James and I. P. Ellis; John Massey was born about 1784 in Franklin Co., NC]). Sam Burgess's relation to his wife is confirmed from unpublished lists of school children enrolled in the Davie County schools in the 1840s. Listed in the 1840 census for Davie Co., on the insolvents' tax list of 31 Aug. 1839 (and again on 25 Nov. 1841), and in the tax records through 1848; Jane Massey appears there in 1850 with her surviving Burgess children. Sam Burgess was deeded land by his parents in Rowan (later Davie) Co. in 1829 (*Deed Book #30*, p. 927), being specifically mentioned as the son of William Burgess. He last appeared on the official list of voters on 3 Aug. 1848, but is not on the list of 2 Aug. 1849, apparently dying in the interim.

The Children of Samuel Burgess:

6a. **Daughter**. Born about 1831 in Rowan (later Davie) Co., NC; died or married before 1850.

6b. **Margaret (VI)**. Born about 1833 in Rowan (later Davie) Co., NC. Mentioned on the school lists of 1 July 1842 through Sept. 1850 for the Tenth District. Listed with her mother and stepfather in the 1850 census.

6c. **William (X)**. Born about 1835 in Rowan (later Davie) Co., NC. Mentioned on the school lists of 1 July 1842 and 1843, but is dropped (presumably dead) in 1844.

6d. **Penelope (II)**. Born about 1837 in Davie Co., NC. Listed on the 1843-44 list school list of Davie Co., but is dropped (presumably dead) in 1845.

6e. **Elinor.** Her name is listed as Elender on the Sept. 1850 school list of Davie Co. for the Tenth District. Born about 1838 in Davie Co., NC. Listed with her mother and stepfather in the 1850 census.

6f. **Rebecca (II)**. Her name is listed as Rebecky on the Sept. 1850 school list of Davie Co. for the Tenth District. Born about 1840 in Davie Co., NC. Listed with her mother and stepfather in the 1850 census.

[William (I)[1], Edward (I)[2], Reuben (I)[3]]

REUBEN BURGESS, JR.
(1772-1839?)

OF DAVIE COUNTY, NORTH CAROLINA

4c. **Reuben (II)** *[son of Reuben (I)].* Born 14 June 1772 in Stafford (later King George) Co., VA [*St. Paul's Parish Register*]. Believed to have married Judith "Juda" ___ about 1794 in Albemarle Co., VA. Moved to Rowan Co., NC with his father in 1799. Listed in the census records for Rowan Co. from 1800-30, but not in 1840; he is also recorded on the tax list of 1830 with 34.75 acres of land (which he bought from Cannon [or Kannon] Brown on 28 June 1820 on Bear Creek in Rowan Co. [*Deed Book #26*, p. 174], adjoining Littleberry R. Rose's and William Knight's lands, witnessed by Samuel Austin and Jesse Brown, but which is never accounted for in either the probate records or deed books). Listed on the voting registers of 11 Aug. 1825 and Aug. 1833. Reuben Burgess Jr. was a farmer in Rowan (later Davie) Co., NC. He is last mentioned in the official records on 1 Mar. 1839, when he was assigned road work by the Davie Co. Court (*Minute Docket 1837-47*, p. 115), but he did not vote in the election of Aug. 1838, and apparently died there before 1840 (not listed in the census). Judith Burgess deeded away her property to her grandchildren in 1848 (*Davie Co. Deed Book #3*, p. 92, dated 12 Apr. 1848, recorded Nov. 1848). She died there before 1850 (has not been found in the 1850 census). See the comments under Reuben's brother, William Burgess, concerning their children.

The Children of Reuben Burgess, Jr.:

5a. **Edward (VII).** Born about 1795 in Albemarle Co., VA. See below for full entry.

5b. **John (III).** Born about 1797 in Albemarle Co., VA. See below for full entry.

5c. **Nancy (II) "Nannie."** Born about 1800 in Rowan (later Davie) Co., NC. Mentioned in A. Nesbitt's Store Day Book in 1816 as buying goods ("Edward Burgess by daughter Nancy" [sic], which probably should have read "by sister Nancy"; several other records in this book state: "Edward Burgess per little sister" and "Miss Nancy Burgess"). Married Jonathan Nelson (her cousin?) on 18 June 1824 in Rowan Co. (bond date, David Jacobs providing the bond; he may have served in the North Carolina House of Commons in 1825, and died about 1840, not being listed in that census). Nannie was allotted a year's relief provisions by the Davie Co. Court on 28 Aug. 1841 (*Minute Docket 1837-47*, p. 281), and had at least four children (two sons and two daughters), among them: *Decatur* (born 1823 in NC, listed with his mother in the 1850 census as an "idiot"). Listed in the 1830 census for Rowan Co., NC; Nancy is listed as head of the family in the 1840-50 censuses for Davie Co., NC. Nannie Nelson apparently died between 1850-60 in Davie Co., NC.

5d. **Sarah (V) "Sally."** Born about 1803 in Rowan (later Davie) Co., NC. She is mentioned as a daughter of Juda Burgess in a surviving record book of a Mocksville merchant, A. Nesbitt, as buying goods from his store in 1816 ("Juda Burgess by daughter Sally"). Married as his second wife Samuel Austin on 12 Nov. 1832 in Rowan Co. (bond date; he married firstly Tammy Suckey, and may have died by July 1836, when a Sally Austin, widow of Samuel, is mentioned as purchasing goods in the Kelly & Gaither merchant ledger book [p. 27]); she may have remarried ___ Hightower and be listed with Moses Burgess in the 1850 census. Sally Austin sold a slave in 1841 in Davie Co., and is mentioned as a tax delinquent in 1843. It should be noted that there were several Samuel Austins in Davie Co., all cousins to each other.

5e. **Mary (V) "Polly."** Born about 1805 in Rowan (later Davie) Co., NC. Listed as buying merchandise at the Kelly & Gaither store about 1835. Married Joseph Daniel about 1836 (he was born about 1811 in NC), and had at least the following children: *Son* (born 1837, died before 1850); *Amanda Anne "Mandy"* (born about 1840, married Joseph A. Hendricks [or Hendrix] on 16 Nov. 1870 in Davie Co. [he was born 1828 in NC, and died 1904], worked in a factory, and died 5 Feb. 1908, buried Cherry Hill Cemetery, having had children: Mary M. [married Buford Vernon, and had children: Beulah M.]; Julia A. [married ___ Thompson]; Lula A. [married Randolph Wood, and had children: Dinah; Paul]; George Mc.; Thomas J.; John A.); *Emily J.* (born 1844, married Henry J. Beeker on 15 Aug. 1865 in Davie Co.); *Samuel* (born

1845); *Nancy M.* (born 1857). Mentioned in her mother's settlement deed of 1848, and is listed in 1835 buying goods at the Kelly & Gaither store in Mocksville ("Miss Polly per mother"), at which point she is still unmarried. Listed in the 1840-80 censuses for Mocksville town, Davie Co., NC, and in 1863 as a member of Sain's School House; Amanda and Nancy are listed with their parents in 1870-80 in Mocksville Township, and Amanda is also listed separately with her husband in 1880 in Jerusalem Township (Mary is again listed with her daughter). Mary Daniel died in Davie Co. between 5 Aug. 1881 and Dec. 1885 (probably the latter year), when two settlement deeds are recorded (*Deed Book #10*, p. 550, dated 13 May 1843, recorded 31 Dec. 1885; *Deed Book #11*, p. 306, dated 5 Aug. 1881, recorded 26 Feb. 1886).

THE GIFT OF JUDITH BURGESS TO HER GRANDCHILDREN

Know all men by these presents that Judith Burgess, for and in consideration of one dollar to me in hand paid, the receipt whereof is hereby acknowledged, and the love & affection I have for my two Grand-children, namely; Mandy & Emily Daniel, and for the further purpose of making them some compensation for the tender care that my daughter Mary Daniel has been pleased to bestow on me, I do hereby give to my fore-named grandchildren as above named the following articles 1 bed & furniture, 2 bedsteads, one Table, one chest, 1 Black Cow named Black, also one calf which now sucks, one looms & tacklings, one spinning wheel, one cubbard & contents, 2 pots, 1 spider, 4 chairs. In witness whereof, I have hereunto set my hand & seal, this 12th day of April 1848.

Witnessed by L. R. Rose; recorded November term 1848.

The McCaleb Family

(from left, back row) *John William McCALEB, David Crockett McCALEB, Samuel Crawford McCALEB*
(front row) *Elizabeth LANE McCALEB, David Robinson McCALEB, Synthia BURGESS McCALEB*, two grandchildren

[William (I)[1], Edward (I)[2], Reuben (I)[3], Reuben (II)[4]]

EDWARD BURGESS
(1795?-1840)

OF DAVIE COUNTY, NORTH CAROLINA

5a. **Edward (VII) "Ned"** *[presumed son of Reuben (II)].* Born about 1795 in Albemarle Co., VA. Married Ellen "Nellie" Wellman on 31 May 1817 in Rowan Co., NC (bond date, John Burgess providing the bond; she may be a sister or cousin of the unknown Wellman girl who married James Burgess, although she does not appear to have received one of the six divisions of John Wellman's land). Listed in the 1820-30 censuses for Rowan Co.; his widow, Ellen Burgess, is listed as head of the family in 1840, but has not been found in 1850, by which time she had apparently either died, remarried or moved away; also listed on the voters' registers of 10 Aug. 1816 and of 11 Aug. 1825 (and thereafter). He is believed to have served in the Fourth Co., Seventh North Carolina Brigade, in the War of 1812 (other members on the muster roll for this company include Jacob Booe, Daniel Booe, George Graves, and William Glasscock, all familiar names from Rowan [later Davie] Co.). Ned Burgess was a farmer and blacksmith on his family's lands in Rowan (later Davie) Co., dying there in early 1840 (Ellen petitioned the Davie Co. Court on 25 May 1840 for a widow's year's relief). Edward is mentioned as a "father" (evidently a misrecording of "brother") of Nancy Burgess in the A. Nesbitt's Store Day Book in 1816, and is also noted in that register as having several shots of whiskey with John Burgess and Reuben Sr., and in other listings as "Edward Burgess per mother," "Edward Burgess per little sister," and "Ned Burgess." He is listed next to Reuben Burgess Jr. in the 1820 census. Three little girls enrolled in the Mocksville Methodist Church in Apr. 1842 are believed to be his daughters, but this cannot be confirmed. Exact relationship not verified.

The Children of Ned Burgess:

6a. **Daughter**. Born about 1818 in Rowan (later Davie) Co., NC; listed with her mother in the 1840 census.

6b. **Daughter**. Born about 1820 in Rowan (later Davie) Co., NC; listed with her mother in the 1840 census.

6c. **Chloe E.** Born about 1822 in Rowan (later Davie) Co., NC. Mentioned (as Cloey Burgess) in the Gaither & Johnston ledger book as buying goods on 20 Jan. 1838; her account was settled on 25 June 1838 by Joseph Daniel, Reuben Burgess Jr.'s son-in-law, which would seem to confirm a relationship with that branch of the family. Listed with her mother in the 1840 census. Enrolled in the Mocksville Methodist Church in Apr. 1842. Relationship not verified, but probable.

6d. **Deby E.** Born about 1824 in Rowan (later Davie) Co., NC. Listed with her mother in the 1840 census. Enrolled in the Mocksville Methodist Church in Apr. 1842. Relationship not verified.

6e. **Louise (I).** Born about 1827 in Rowan (later Davie) Co., NC. Listed with her mother in the 1840 census. Enrolled in the Mocksville Methodist Church in Apr. 1842. Relationship not verified.

6f. **Franklin.** Born about 1830 in Rowan (later Davie) Co., NC. Listed with his mother in the 1840 census, as an enrolled member of Eaton's Baptist Meeting House, Cana, Davie Co. in Sept. 1845, and on the Davie Co. school list of 27 Sept. 1847 (in the Ninth District). He and his presumed brother were both dropped from the church rolls on 26 Oct. 1852: "On motion according to a late established rule of the church, Bro. Franklin and Lindsey Burgess were excluded from the fellowship thereof on account of their being absent from the state without being heard from by the church." Neither he nor Lindsey Burgess have been found in the 1850-60 censuses. Relationship not verified.

6g. **Lindsey.** Born about 1833 in Rowan (later Davie) Co., NC. Listed with his mother in the 1840 census, as an enrolled member of Eaton's Baptist Meeting House, Cana, Davie Co., in Sept. 1845 (as "Leindsey Burgess"), and on the Davie Co. school list of Oct. 1848 (in the First District). He and his presumed brother were both dropped from the church rolls on 26 Oct. 1852. Relationship not verified.

[William (I)[1], Edward (I)[2], Reuben (I)[3], Reuben (II)[4]]

JOHN BURGESS
(1797?-1831+)

OF ROWAN (LATER DAVIE) COUNTY, NORTH CAROLINA

5b. **John (III)** *[presumed son of Reuben (II)].* Born about 1797 in Albemarle Co., VA. Married ___ Knight about 1817 in Rowan Co., NC (William Knight's farm adjoined the land of Reuben Burgess Jr.; John's unnamed wife was the daughter of William Knight and Martha [Hendricks?], and died between 1825-30). Mentioned in A. Nesbitt's 1816 Store Day Book with several entries, including: "John Burgess for J[n] Henkle," and "Edward Burgess Dr. pr J[no] Burgess." Listed in the 1820-30 censuses of Rowan Co., NC next to James Burgess. He received two lots of 24 acres each on Bear Creek about 1818, either as an heir of Daniel Hendricks (through his wife or mother), or by purchase (but no deed is recorded), and sold them to his presumed cousin, James Burgess, on 26 Sept. 1818 (*Rowan Co. Deed Book #25*, p. 199). Listed on the voting register of 11 Aug. 1825. John Burgess was a farmer in Rowan (later Davie) Co., NC. His children are mentioned as heirs in the will of his uncle-in-law, John Knight (*Rowan Co. Will Book #H*, p. 541, dated 24 Sept. 1831: "I give and bequeath to my sister-in-law, Martha Knight, relict of my late brother William, during her natural life the interest on two notes due me by John Beard Jr. each for three hundred dollars, and also the interest on a note due by Moses A. Locke for two hundred and seventy-five dollars; after the death of my said sister-in-law, I give and bequeath to her grandchildren, Matilda, Martha, and John, the children of John Burgiss, the whole of the aforesaid notes..."). After receiving this legacy, John apparently moved away almost immediately, since he does not appear again in any records of either Rowan or Davie Co., and is dropped from the voters' list of 8 Aug. 1833. The Davie Co. census taker made a margin note on the original copy of the 1840 census: "Left between 1830 & 1840 John Burgess." Exact relationship not verified.

The Children of John Burgess:

6a. **Matilda.** Born about 1818 in Rowan (later Davie) Co., NC.
6b. **Martha (I).** Born about 1820 in Rowan (later Davie) Co., NC.
6c. **John (VI).** Born about 1825 in Rowan (later Davie) Co., NC. He may be the John Burgess who married Barbara E. Keller on 29 Jan. 1846 in Davie Co., NC (she is later mentioned in the will of her father, John Keller, as "Barbry E. Burgess" [*Will Book #1*, p. 136, dated 4 Apr. 1849, probated Sept. 1857]).

[William (I)[1], Edward (I)[2], Reuben (I)[3]]

THOMAS BURGESS
(1776?-1830)

OF WHITE (LATER PUTNAM) COUNTY, TENNESSEE

4e. **Thomas (I)** *[son of Reuben (I)].* Born about 1776 in Stafford (later King George) Co., VA. Married Mary "Polly" Hunter about 1800. Moved to Rowan (later Davie) Co. in 1799 with his father; listed in the 1800-10 censuses for Rowan Co., NC (and is married by 1800, with no children, both individuals being 16-26 in age). Thomas sold his 73 acres on Mill Creek in Rowan Co., NC on 3 Sept. 1814 to Bottom Nailor (*Deed Book #23*, p. 245), and moved to White Co., TN (the section which later became Putnam Co.), where he bought land from William Stinson on 8 Feb. 1815 (*Deed Book #F*, p. 121). Listed in the tax records there from 1816-29, and in the 1820-30 censuses for White Co., TN (in 1820 with the following family: 4 males under 10, 2 males 10-16, 1 male 16-18, 1 male 16-26, 1 male 45+, 1 female under 10, 1 female 10-16, 1 female 26-45; 1830 gives: 2 males 10-15, 1 male 15-20, 1 male 50-60, 1 female 5-10, 1 female 10-15, 1 female 50-60). Thomas Burgess was specifically disinherited by his father, and does not appear on the 1826 settlement deed, probably because he had already received his stake when he moved to Tennessee. According to a brief family history published by his son, Anderson, in *A History of the Pioneer Families of Missouri*, by William S. Bryan and Robert Rose (St. Louis: Bryan, Brand & Co., 1876, p. 206), Thomas Burgess son of Reuben Burgess drowned in 1830 at the Trousdale Ferry Crossing of the Cumberland or Falling Water River, near Gordonsville, TN, leaving the eleven children listed below in the order given (a twelfth child recorded in the census records apparently died young); he is said to have been buried near Carthage, TN.

Mary Hunter Burgess was born 1778 in NC, daughter of Charles and Eva Rosannah Hunter (the relationship is verified through Charles Hunter's will [*Rowan Co. Will Book #G*, p. 6, dated 9 Feb. 1808], which mentions wife Eve Rosannah Hunter, and children Valentine, John, Mary Burgess, Hannah, Betsy, Susannah, Nelly, Rachel, Rosannah, and Lidia). She appears in the 1840 census for White Co. as head of the family (with one daughter aged 20-30), and in 1850 living with her son, Charles. Mary Hunter Burgess died on 20 Aug. 1859 in Putnam Co., TN, and is buried in the Howard Cemetery. Some of the data on the Allison descendants of this branch is partially based on research conducted by Della P. "Pat" Franklin, and published in her book, *Allison Connections* (Cookeville, TN: Della P. Franklin, 1988).

The Children of Thomas Burgess:

5a. **Elizabeth (VI) "Betsy."** Born 7 Oct. 1800 in Rowan (later Davie) Co., NC. Married David Bradford about 1819 (he was born 14 June 1797, son of William Bradford and brother of Jacob Bradford [who married Elizabeth's sister, Margaret Burgess], and died 22 June 1887, aged 90 years; the Bradford heirs [as enumerated in *White Co. Book #Q*, p. 184, dated 3 Nov. 1837, recorded 3 Oct. 1849] included: David, Richard, Nancy [wife of ___ Hooten], Mary "Polly" [wife of John Phy], Margaret [wife of William Brown], William K., Thomas J., Bennett, Jacob, Daniel, John A.), and had at least the following children: *Daughter* (born 1820); *William Simpson (I)* (born 1825-29); *Thomas* (born 1834); *John* (born 1837). Listed in the 1820-30 censuses for Jackson (later Putnam) Co., TN (in 1830 next door to Joel Burgess), in 1840-50 in White (later Putnam) Co., TN, and in 1860-80 in Putnam Co., TN (in 1860 and 1880 in the 1st Civil District, and in 1870 in the 16th District, next door to her niece, Mary Crowley). Betsy Bradford died on 26 Nov. 1882 in Putnam Co., and is buried with her husband in the West Cemetery.

5b. **Son.** Born about 1802 in Rowan (later Davie) Co., NC; listed with his father in the 1810 census, but apparently died between 1810-20. He may be the same as the William W. Burgess listed below.

5c. **(George) Washington (I).** Born 8 Jan. 1804 in Rowan (later Davie) Co., NC. See below for full entry.

5d. **Charles Hunter.** Born 16 May 1806 in Rowan (later Davie) Co., NC. See below for full entry.

5e. **Anderson.** Born 24 Apr. 1808 in Rowan (later Davie) Co., NC. See below for full entry.

5f. **Margaret Elizabeth "Peggy."** Born 15 Feb. 1809 in Rowan (later Davie) Co., NC. Married Jacob Bradford about 1833 (he was born 1813 in Sumner Co. or White Co., TN, son of William Bradford and brother of David Bradford [who married Peggy's sister, Elizabeth Burgess], and died 1891 at Maysville, DeKalb Co., MO), and had children:

William Simpson BRADFORD *II*. Born 1834 in White Co., TN. Married Mary M. Collin on 18 Apr. 1858 in DeKalb Co., MO.

Richard C. BRADFORD. Born 1837 in White Co., TN. Married Ellen Berk on 25 Jan. 1855 in DeKalb Co., MO (she was born 1834, and died 1917), and had children: *Richard N.* (born 1865, died 1892, buried Wamsley Cemetery); *Daniel B.* (born and died 1872, buried Wamsley Cemetery). Richard C. Bradford homesteaded in 1857, served in the 43rd Missouri Volunteers during the Civil War, and died 1901, buried Wamsley Cemetery.

Polly BRADFORD. Her name may actually have been Mary. Born 1839 in White Co., TN. She may have died young in Missouri.

Elizabeth BRADFORD. Born 1840 in White Co., TN; died 1847 in DeKalb Co., MO, and is buried with her parents.

Winfield H. "Winney" BRADFORD. Born 1841 in DeKalb Co., MO. Married Caroline M. Gregg on 13 Nov. 1862, and had children: *Winney J.* (born 1863, died 1867, buried with her parents); *Son* (born and died 1866, buried with his parents); *Daniel* (born 1868, died 1870, buried with his parents). W. H. Bradford died 1881, and is buried in the Wamsley Cemetery.

John A. BRADFORD. Born 1842 in White Co., TN, married Sarah L. Archer on 1 Sept. 1867 in DeKalb Co., MO (she was born 1850, and died 1929), and had children: *William R.* (born 1868, and died 1923, buried Wamsley Cemetery); *Charley B.* (born 1892, died 1895, buried with his parents). John Bradford served on the Wamsley School Board in 1881. He died in 1926 in DeKalb Co., and is buried in the Wamsley Cemetery.

Thomas W. BRADFORD. Born 1844 in DeKalb Co., MO, died there in 1860 (after the census), and is buried with his parents.

Nancy J. BRADFORD. Born 1846 in DeKalb Co., MO. Married Andrew J. Parker on 1 Sept. 1867 in DeKalb Co., MO (in a double wedding with her brother, John).

Daniel Boon BRADFORD. Born 20 Apr. 1848 in Adams Township, DeKalb Co., MO. Married Emily Jenna Stagner on 23 Dec. 1870 at Cameron, DeKalb Co., MO (she was born 22 Oct. 1854 at Dubuque, IA), and had ten children, including: *Lester* (born 1882, died 1892, buried Wamsley Cemetery); *Ida M.* (born 1890, died 1891, buried Wamsley); *Roy* (born and died 1896, buried Wamsley). Daniel B. Bradford settled at Guymon, Texas Co., OK, and is buried in the Elmhurst Cemetery.

Winney L. BRADFORD (dau.). Born Nov. 1849 in DeKalb Co., MO; died young.

Margaret BRADFORD. Born 1852 in DeKalb Co., MO. Married Sampson Lewis on 26 Sept. 1871 in DeKalb Co., MO, and died 1931, buried Wamsley Cemetery.

Margaret BRADFORD is listed with her husband in the 1840 census for the 12th District, Jackson Co., TN (the section that later became Putnam Co.). The Bradfords moved to Missouri in 1843, settling in Clinton Co. for six months, before relocating to Stewardsville, DeKalb Co., MO. They are listed in the 1850-60 censuses for DeKalb Co., MO; both are mentioned in a contemporaneous letter written on 20 Feb. 1882 to their relatives back in Tennessee as being then resident in Clinton Co., MO. Peggy Bradford died on 22 Dec. 1889 at Maysville, DeKalb Co., MO, and is buried with her husband in the Wamsley Cemetery, Cameron, MO. Daniel's descendant, Lorraine Bradford, lives at Placerville, CA.

5g. **Joel (I).** Born 17 Apr. 1812 in Rowan (later Davie) Co., NC. See below for full entry.

5h. **Thomas (II).** Born 15 May 1815 (or 1814) in Rowan (later Davie) Co., NC, or on the way west, or in White (later Putnam) Co., TN. See below for full entry.

5i. **William W. (I).** Born about 1816 in White (later Putnam) Co., TN. Mentioned in Anderson Burgess's autobiography as one of Thomas Sr.'s children, being listed in order between Thomas Jr. and Mary, and in Anderson's 22 Feb. 1843 letter to Charles Burgess as then being in the "reglar servic" (presumably serving in the U.S. Army, although he has not been found in the 1833-46 regular Army enlistment rolls; see Anderson Burgess's entry for both documents). He may be the William W. Burgess who is mentioned in one transcription as being buried in the Lovelady Cemetery (the stone no longer survives).

5j. **Mary (VII) "Polly."** Born 9 Feb. 1818 in White (later Putnam) Co., TN. Living unmarried with her mother in the 1840-50 censuses. Married as his second wife J. A. "Joab" Barnes on 10 Jan. 1870 (he was born 27 Feb. 1812, and died on 30 Oct. 1897, buried Howard Cemetery); married secondly Corder Lollar on 23 Sept. 1903 (he was born 3 June 1820, and died on 1 June 1906). Listed in the 1860-1900 censuses for the 1st District, Putnam Co., TN. Polly Burgess was a farmer in Putnam Co. She deeded her land in 1907 to her nephew, Isaac Burgess (*Putnam Co. Deed Book #Z*, p. 184; he was living with her in 1900). She died childless on 11 Feb. 1910 in Putnam Co., aged 92 years, three days after the death of her brother Hiram, the last of her brothers and sisters to die; her obituary calls her "Mary Burgess."

5k. **(King) Hiram (I).** Born 6 June 1820 in White (later Putnam) Co., TN. See below for full entry.

5l. **Eleanor R. "Ellen" or "Nellie."** Her name is listed by James Z. Burgess as Mary Eleanor. Born 26 Jan. 1822 in White (later Putnam) Co., TN. Married Bethel Bowman on 6 Apr. 1840 in White Co., TN, Rev.

Levi Parker performing the ceremony (Bethel was born about 1820 in TN, and died after 1856), and had at least the following children: *Lucinda* (born 1841 in TN); *Hiram* (born 1843 in TN, living in Putnam Co. in 1870); *Cantrell* (born 1845 in TN); *John* (born 1848 in TN, living in Putnam Co. in 1870); *Charles* (born 1850 in Madison Co., IA); *Norman*; *Hickman*; *Elizabeth J. "Lizzie"* (born Aug. 1856 in TN, married George W. Spears [he was born June 1852 in TN], and had children: Araminta A. [born Oct. 1890]).

Nellie BOWMAN married secondly Bill Farris (he died before 1900). Listed in the 1850 census for Madison Co., IA (but is not there in 1860), and in 1900 in White Co., TN (six of six children then survive), living with her daughter, Lizzie Spears, but has not been found in the 1860-80 censuses. Nellie Farris died on 27 Oct. 1906 in White or Jackson Co., TN.

A Letter from Jacob and Margaret Bradford to Charles Burgess, 1879

"January the 26th 1879. Clinton Co., Mo. Dear Brother and Sister, after a long time delay I take my pen in hand to rite you a few lines. I will in form you that we are all well hoping thes lines may find you all well. I have nothing strange. Times is hard, every thing [__]. Our crops the past year was only tolerable good. We had a storm in August that ingered our corn. I maid about 100"30 [sic] bushel of wheat. We had a big snow fell about the 10th of December and it tis on yet. We had fine slaying and very cold about newyear. I got a letter from Valentine Burgess a few days ago the[y] was not very well. Waymon L. Burgess dide the 14th of Oct. last, that is Anderson Burgess son. Well, Brother, I sole my hogs 2 weeks ago for 2 cents a pound groce, the[y] braught me 55 dollars c[ents] 50. I went and paid my tax whitch was 30 dollars and 6 cents. Well, Brother, I baught me a fine calf. I paid $25 dollars for him when sucking. He is a little over 2 year old, his half brother has sole for 75 dollars. I have 25 cattle. I want to know where Charles L. Burgess is and Isaac is and how the[y] are dooing. Well, Brother, I have good houses that will see me and your sister while we live. We have plenty to doo us but I mite a had 1000 on in trust, but I went security in the bank and had to pay $400 like a man, I dont greave over spilt milk. I dont ow[e] a dollar to no man. I have a good waggon and team [*line illegible*] pride and cut my grain and grass. I put up 5 rick (?) of timothy hay last fall. I have a little money on in trust. I was offerd 1000 dollars for 40 akers of my land and I did not take it. It was a part of my farm. Our children is all married, we have one gran son with us that we raised. Tell Charles L. that his aunt wants to see him. We wold like to see you all. I want you to right soon, gives us all of the knews. I will give the price of sum things: wheat 70c bushel, oats 15c, horses $50 to 75 dollars, coffee 4 lbs, shugar 9 lbs, calico 5 to 8c yard, salt $1.50 a barrel. We make our oan molasses. Well, Brother, your Sister wants to see you, she ante [i.e., ain't] very stout tho. I wold tell you that she can get a meal of vituals as quick as enny girl tho. You mite thin[k] that I wanted to brag, I dont want to we[a]ry your patience, and I will close. Right soon. This from your Brother and Sister, Jacob and Margarett Bradford, to Charles and Margarett Burgess. Tell Charles L. that Sindy is married and lives in Cameron, the[y] wold like to see him back and dance around the wash tub. Tell Brother David I want him to right. If you can't read this take it to Brother and he can tell me how Lotty Burgess is getting along."

The First Deed of Thomas Burgess in Tennessee

"This indenture, made this eight day of Febuary [sic] in the year of our Lord one thousand eight hundred and fifteen between William Stinson of the County of White and State of Tennessee of the one part and Thomas Burgess of the county and state aforesaid of the other part, Witnesseth that the said William Stinson for and in consideration of the sum of three hundred dollars to him in hand paid, the receipt whereof is hereby acknowledged, hath and by these presents doth grant, bargain, sell, alien, enfeoff, and confirm unto the said Thomas Burgess his heirs and assigns forever, a certain tract or parcel of land, containing three hundred and thirty four acres, lying and being in the county of White and state aforesaid, Being in section No. seven, as will appear by conveyance from Isaac Taylor to James and William Stinson, atturney in fact for John W. Keever and William P. Anderson, lying and as follows, Begining [sic] on a black oak runing [sic] north two hundred and fourteen poles, Lollers Corner, thence due east with John Lollar's line one hundred and sixty poles to Joseph McBrids [sic; actually Joseph C. McBride] line corner to a stake thence with said McBrides line south ninty four poles to a hikory bush thence with his line due east one hundred and sixty poles to a post oak on the auld line of said section No. Seven thence south one hundred and twenty poles to a black oak then west three hundred and twenty poles to the begining. With all and singular the woods, water courses, profits, commodities, hereditaments, and appurtenances whatsoever to the said tract of land belonging or appertaining: And the reversion and reversions, remainder and remainders, rents and issues thereof and all the estate, right, title, interest, property, claim, and demand, of him the said William Stinson and heirs and assigns forever, of, in, and the same, and every part or parcel thereof, either in law or equity, To Have and To Hold the said three hundred and thirty four acres of land with the appurtenances, unto the said Thomas Burgess, his heirs and assigns forever, in Witness whereof I have hereunto set my hand and affixed my seal the day and date above ritten [sic]."

William Stinson

The deed was witnessed by Thomas Bounds and Joseph Hunter, and recorded on 24 Oct. 1816.

[William (I)[1], Edward (I)[2], Reuben (I)[3], Thomas (I)[4]]

GEORGE WASHINGTON BURGESS
(1804-1873)

OF PUTNAM COUNTY, TENNESSEE

5c. **(George) Washington (I)** *[son of Thomas (I)].* Born 8 Jan. 1804 in Rowan (later Davie) Co., NC. Married Charlotta McBride about 1823 (she was born 18 July 1803 in VA, daughter of Joseph C[rawford?] McBride and Elizabeth Brimmer, and sister of Margaret McBride [who married Wash's brother, Charles Burgess], and died 24 Apr. 1880 in Putnam Co., TN). Listed in the 1830-50 censuses for Jackson Co., TN (the part that later became Putnam Co.; in 1840 they are living in the 12th District, with Elizabeth McBride next door, and have three sons [one aged 10-15] and four daughters [one aged 15-20]), and from 1860-70 in the 1st District, Putnam Co., TN. Wash Burgess was a farmer in Putnam Co., TN. He died there on 26 Mar. 1873, and is buried with his wife in the West Cemetery.

The Children of Washington Burgess:

6a. **Synthia.** Born 12 Mar. 1824 in Jackson (later Putnam) Co., TN. Married (David) Robinson McCaleb [later McCalib], her cousin, in 1844 (he was born 5 July 1820 in NC, son of John McCaleb and Catherine Allison, served in the Confederate Army during the Civil War, married secondly Margaret Bunch [or Munch] on 14 Sept. 1884 in Carroll Co., AR [she was born 10 Nov. 1849, and died 7 Sept. 1941, aged 91 years, leaving one child: *(Margaret) Louise* {born 26 Nov. 1887, married Walter Newton Hall on 23 Aug. 1903, and had children: Troy Oliver <born 4 Feb. 1905, married Esther Lucy Forshes on 3 July 1947, and died Aug. 1978, leaving children: Troy Oliver Jr. |born 16 Jan. 1949 at Memphis, TN| >}]; John McCaleb died on 1 Jan. 1894 in Washington Co., AR). Synthia and John McCalib had children:

Charlotte Catherine "Lottie" McCaleb. Born 26 June 1845 in Jackson Co., TN. Married George Andrew Alberty on 19 Aug. 1868, and had children: *Cynthia Valenda "Lenna"* (born 25 June 1869 in Washington Co., AR, married Horace McFarland in Dec. 1888 at Fort Smith, AR, had nine children, and died May 1942 at Mullins, TX); *Calvin Petty* (born 9 July 1871 in Washington Co., AR, married Ida Whitlock in 1903, and died 21 July 1945 at Mullins, TX); *Annie Welm* [born 9 June 1873 in Washington Co., AR, married ___ Petty, and died 1896 at Muskogee, OK); *David Wa'ter* (born 20 Feb. 1877 in Washington Co., AR, married Willie May Blain in 1898, had one son, and died 19 July 1956 at Oroville, CA); *John Gophus* (born 8 July 1879 in Washington Co., AR, died 1896 in Muskogee Co., OK); *Edna Beatrice* (born 10 May 1887, married Willard Robert Luther, and had children: Alleene [who lived at Carmel, CA]; *Edna* married secondly John Caughey, and died 29 Sept. 1964 at Salinas, CA). Lottie Alberty died on 26 Jan. 1908 in Howard Co., TX.

Matilda Frances McCaleb. Her name is given as Frances Matilda on her tombstone. Born 27 Aug. 1846 in Jackson Co., TN, married John Carter about 1867, and had children: *William D. "Willie"* (born about 1870, married Fanny ___); married secondly Rufus Alexander Allen in 1874 (he was born 3 Mar. 1849 at Jackson Co., TN, and died 8 Aug. 1908 at Houston, TX), and had children: *Rufus Loma* (born 11 Nov. 1879 at Comanche, TX, died unmarried of measles on 17 Aug. 1898 at San Francisco, CA while serving in the U.S. Army during the Spanish-American War); *Lona Vashti* (born 18 Feb. 1882 at Cleburne, TX, married William Peyton Easley on 14 Sept. 1900 at Houston, TX [he was born 28 Sept. 1868 at Princeton, KY, and died 5 Oct. 1939 at Houston], and had children: Alma [married Ray Kuhn, and had children: Barbara {married ___ Spencer}; Joyce {married ___ Stewart}; Dewey; Patricia {married ___ Krasse}]; Frances [married ___ Hunziker, and had children: Doris Mae {married ___ Anderson}]; Robert Allen [had children: Robert Allen Jr., Ronald, Douglas, Marie; (Johnny) Peyton {dec.}]; *Lona Vashti* died in July 1984 at Houston, TX, aged 102 years); *John Samuel* (born 11 Mar. 1885 in Comanche Co., TX, married Doris Walters in 1915, and had children: Jess; Rufus Patton; John; Travis; *John Samuel* married secondly Dorothy "Jimmie" Clifton, and had children: Mike; *John Samuel* died 2 Mar. 1961 at Paluxy, TX); *Nannie Mae* (born 28 June 1887 at Towash, TX, married Robert Rhett Sanders Jr. on 14 Oct. 1906 at Houston, TX [he was born 4 Dec. 1883 in Chester Co., SC, and died 8

Sept. 1964 at Coney Creek, TX], and had children: Robert Rhett II [who had children: Camille]; Ruby [married ___ Dike]; *Nannie Mae* died on 13 Jan. 1965 at Houston, TX); *Ida Beatrice* (born 30 Sept. 1890 at Paris, TX, married Louis Ernest Roberts on 16 Sept. 1907 [he was born 30 Jan. 1888 at Morgans Point, TX, son of John Edward Roberts and Nancy Rose, and died 7 Dec. 1970 at Houston], and died on 9 Sept. 1975 at Houston, TX, having had children: (Donnie) May [born 8 June 1909 at Morgans Point, TX, married Louis F. Hunger on 6 Jan. 1937 {he was born 13 Aug. 1908 at Palestine, TX, son of Edward and Annie Elizabeth Hunger, and died childless on 13 May 1954 at Houston, TX}]; Ernest Samuel [born 2 Oct. 1912 at Morgans Point, TX, and had children: Donnie Sue {born 27 Mar. 1945 at Houston, married Sheldon Moore}]; Frances Lynn [born 9 Jan. 1922 at Houston, TX, married Howard Davis Wilborn on 9 Jan. 1945 at Houston {he was born 10 Sept. 1922 at Kennedy, TX, son of James Aaron and Nina Mearl Wilborn}, and had children: Lynn Kay {born 31 July 1955 at Houston}]). ***Matilda Frances Allen*** died on 15 Jan. 1915 at LaPorte, TX, and is buried with her husband in the Hollywood Cemetery, Houston.

John William [or Washington] McCaleb. Born 1848 in Jackson Co., TN, married Elizabeth "Dicie" Lane, died in California, and had twelve children, including: *Thomas* (born 5 May 1878, married Lilly Ann McMahen, and died 1954 at Sedro Wooley, WA); *David Crockett* (born about 1886, served as a physician, married Addie Lee Watson, had children: William [married Marguerite Monk, and served as the manager of the Chamber of Commerce, Edinburg, TX]; Cynthia [born about 1910, and worked as a librarian at the McAlister, OK high school]); *William*; *Bert* (lived at Sedro Wooley, WA); *Everett* (lived at McAlister, OK); *Fannie*; *Betty* (married ___ Whiteside, and died in 1904); *Cora* (married ___ Bullard, and lived at Wright City, OK).

Anderson Loranzia McCaleb. Born 1853 in Jackson Co., TN; died between 1860-70.

(Thomas) Ira Allison McCaleb. Born 19 Mar. 1856 in Jackson Co., TN, married Mary Garrett on 16 Jan. 1879, and had eleven children, including: *James*; *Elizabeth "Lizzie"*; *Dovie A.* (born 3 Aug. 1883, died 18 July 1896, buried Antioch Cemetery); *John*; *Allison Larenzo* (born 11 Feb. 1888 at Fayetteville, AR, married Hazel M. Dozier on 6 Jan. 1914 in Haskell Co., TX, and died 19 July 1971 at Anderson, CA). Ira McCaleb died on 20 Jan. 1916 in Washington Co., AR.

Samuel Crawford McCaleb. Born 4 Apr. 1858 in Washington Co., AR. He died unmarried on 20 Jan. 1916 at Antioch, AR, and is buried in the Antioch Cemetery.

William Robinson McCaleb (twin). Born 16 Mar. 1861 in Washington Co., AR. Married Laura Evaline Reed on 9 Nov. 1879 in Arkansas (she was born 5 Oct. 1860, daughter of Samuel King Reed and Martha Ann King, and died 6 Nov. 1959 at Stilwell, OK, aged 99 years), and had children:

Lonny Cosmo McCaleb (born 21 Sept. 1880 at Rule, Carroll Co., AR, married Donna Leach on 18 Oct. 1905 [div.], and had three children; married secondly Ada Dick on 5 Oct. 1916, had two children, and died on 26 June 1966 at Vinita, OK).

Samuel David McCaleb (born 27 Aug. 1883 at Cane Hill, Washington Co., AR, married Luella Welchel on 12 Dec. 1908, had three children, and died 11 Aug. 1949 at Vinita, OK).

Vernie Ett McCaleb (born 31 Aug. 1886 at Dutch Mills, Washington Co., AR, married Charles Matthew Roller, had nine children, and died 1 Jan. 1970 at Lincoln, AR).

Dollie Beatrice McCaleb (born 18 Nov. 1888 at Dutch Mills, AR, married Ollie Dave Hembree on 12 Dec. 1908, had one son, and died 9 Oct. 1972, buried Stilwell Cemetery, Stilwell, OK).

Labon White McCaleb (born 19 July 1892 at Dutch Mills, AR, married Mary Elizabeth Ervin on 22 Mar. 1918 at Stilwell, Washington Co., OK [div.; she was born 22 Mar. 1896 at Mexico, MO, daughter of Samuel Brown Ervin and Mary Elizabeth Patton], and died 6 Apr. 1973, buried Austin, TX, having had children: (Harold) Kenneth [born 19 Feb. 1920 at Stilwell, OK, married Margaret Elinor Baughman on 28 June 1945 at Joplin, MO {she was born 9 Nov. 1920 at Neosho, MO, daughter of Clarence Hubert Baughman and Freada Phoebe Bushner}, and had children: Robert Donald {born 14 Aug. 1958 at Knoxville, TN, married Patti Lane Powell on 17 Apr. 1982 at Prattville, AL <she was born 17 Feb. 1959, daughter of Horace Powell and Nadine Weldon>, and had children: Laura Catherine <born 2 Mar. 1986 at Cleveland, TN>; Leah Lane <born 27 Aug. 1988 at Cleveland, TN>; Landon Robert <born 23 Feb. 1993 at Cleveland, TN>}; Kenneth McCaleb was a Captain in the U.S. Air Force, and graduated with a B.S. degree in mechanical engineering from the University of Oklahoma; he worked at Oak Ridge for ten years, and at NASA for twenty-five years; he and his wife live at Huntsville, AL]; Bettie Illaree [born 16 Nov. 1921 at Stilwell, OK]).

Son McCaleb (born and died 16 May 1897 at Dutch Mills, AR).

Laura Buena McCaleb (born 7 Dec. 1898 at Dutch Mills, AR, married Augustus Weatherford West on 17 Dec. 1916, had five children, and died 20 May 1988 at Stilwell, OK, buried Stilwell Cemetery). ***William R. McCaleb*** was a merchant and farmer in Arkansas and Oklahoma. He died on 15 Oct. 1943 at Stilwell, OK, and is buried with his wife there in the New Hope Cemetery.

Mary Jane MCCALEB (twin). Born 16 Mar. 1861 in Washington Co., AR, married James J. Ince on 20 Mar. 1879 in Washington Co. (he was born 1858, changed his name to James Madison Ince because he had a cousin of exactly the same name, and died at Mullin, TX, buried Mullin Cemetery), and died 28 May 1927 at Mullin, TX, having had children: *Ora S.* (born 4 July 1880 in Hill Co., TX, married Dr. A. J. Wells on 26 Feb. 1899); *Nora* (born and died 4 June 1882 in Hill Co., TX); *Oma S.* (born 22 Nov. 1883 in Hill Co., TX, married Charles Corse on 18 Oct. 1903, and died 12 Oct. 1969); *James Ernest* (born 7 May 1884 in Hill Co., TX, married Tribie Slack); *Bertha Beatrice* (born 19 Jan. 1886 in Hill Co., TX, married Emil Mayer on 20 Jan. 1904, and died 16 June 1946 in an automobile accident, having had children: Norris Robert [born 13 Apr. 1906, and had children: Norris Robert Jr. {lives at LaPorte, TX}; Hulbert {lives at Pasadena, TX}; Norris Sr. died on 10 Sept. 1981]; Florena Mary [born 29 Mar. 1910 in Washington Co., TX, married Lee U. Stephens {he was the son of Walter Morgan Stephens and Claudie A. Ellis}, and died 18 Nov. 1992, having had children: Bette Lee {married Elmo Mays, and had children: Sharon Kay <married Lynn Pattillo>; Shirlee Jean; Sandra Lee; Suzanne Roi; Bette lives at Panacea, FL}; Mona Faye {married Don Looper <he died 4 May 1987 in Wharton Co., TX>, and had children: Lance <born 1 Nov. 1967 in Wharton Co., TX, married Karen Roberson on 17 Dec. 1988, and had children: Lorne>; Lainee <born 11 Aug. 1969, and had children: Denane>; Mona married secondly Max Cloud on 8 Oct. 1989 in Wharton Co., TX <he died 20 Aug. 1993>}; Steve K. {born 10 Oct. 1945 in Wharton Co., TX, married Joy Spears, and had children: Steva Kay <born 14 May 1960>; married secondly Lynette Daniels on 27 July 1968 at Iago, TX, and had children: Melisa Lynette <born 18 Feb. 1974, died 21 July 1984 in MS, buried Wharton, TX>}]; Woodrow Lester [born 15 Aug. 1914, and had children: Ronald Earl; Peggy; Connie]); *David Wilson* (born 10 May 1888 in Hill Co., TX); *Mary* (born 7 June 1891 in Hill Co., TX, married Til McPherson on 17 Sept. 1925, and died in California); *Lizzie Lilian* (born 22 July 1896 in Hill Co., TX, married Fred Perkins); *Margaret Charlotte* (born 9 June 1898 in Hill Co., TX, married Wesley Stark on 3 May 1920, and died in 1976); *Willa* (born 18 July 1901 in Brown Co., TX, married Frank Haber on 18 Nov. 1922); *Earl C.* (born 4 Apr. 1905 at Mill, TX, married Louise Milbourne on 25 Jan. 1941, and died 3 July 1964). Mona Looper Cloud lives at Boling, TX, and has contributed greatly to this book.

(William) David Crockett MCCALEB. Born 26 Apr. 1863 in Washington Co., AR, married Margaret Elizabeth Wells (she was born 10 Jan. 1863, daughter of Thomas Wells), worked as a medical doctor, died 9 July 1925, and had children:

Maud MCCALEB (born 22 Dec. 1886, married William P. Blevins, and had children: Margaret Elizabeth [born 6 Mar. 1921, married Bernard Parth, and had children: Emelie Beth {born 19 Apr. 1951}]).

David Preston MCCALEB (born 4 Mar. 1888, married Evelyn Embree, was a Captain in the U.S. Army during World War I, ran for U.S. Congress from Texas, died at Los Angeles, CA, and had children: Paul Tyler [married Dorothy Rellike on 6 Apr. 1952]; David Embree [born 9 Apr. 1918 at Belton, TX, and is a skilled painter and sculptor]; Daniel Hodge [twin; born 8 May 1924, married Carolyn Harris, and had children: Darrel Douglas]; Joseph Wells [twin; born 8 May 1924]).

Togwell L. MCCALEB (born 5 Feb. 1892, died childless at Laredo, TX).

Donathan Cecil MCCALEB (born 28 Sept. 1893, lived at Dallas, TX, and had children: Elizabeth; Joan; Jamie).

William Douglas MCCALEB (born 20 Dec. 1895, married [his wife died six weeks after him], was murdered on 7 Jan. 1930 at the Mexican border while serving with the U.S. Border Patrol, and had children: James David).

Synthia Patience MCCALEB (born 21 July 1897, died 7 July 1899).

Cephus Arigustis "Gus" MCCALEB (born 25 Aug. 1899, killed in action in 1918 while serving with the U.S. Army in France, leaving one son).

Kettie Davey MCCALEB (born 11 Jan. 1901, married ___ Cooper).

Bemeth B. MCCALEB (born 29 Dec. 1903, lived at Laredo, TX, and had children: Elsie Louisa).

David MCCALEB is listed in the 1840 census for Jackson Co., TN eight doors from his future father-in-law, in the 1850 census for Jackson Co. next door to Washington Burgess, and in the 1860-80 censuses for Washington Co., AR. Synthia McCaleb died in Washington Co. on 21 Jan. 1884, and is buried with her husband in the Antioch Cemetery, Morrow, AR.

6b. **Ibba "Ibby."** Her name may have been short for Isabella. Born 21 Sept. 1825 in Jackson (later Putnam) Co., TN. Living with her father in 1850. Married William Stephen Crawley (or Crowley) about 1852 (he was born 1 July 1827 in TN, son of James Y. and Anania Crawley, is listed in the 1850 census in Washington Co., AR with Shadrack Murray and his future brother-in-law, Joseph C. Burgess, and died in 1921), and had children: *Stephen H.* (born 16 Nov. 1853, and died 1933, buried Strickler Cemetery); *Martha Rebeka* (born 21 July 1855, SEE BELOW); *Joseph C.* (born 8 July 1857); *Mary Alisabeth* (born 25 June 1859); *Charlooty Livina* (born 27 May 1861); *Washington Burgess* (born 12 Apr. 1863).

***Martha Rebeka* CRAWLEY** was born 21 July 1855, married Alfred Douglas Strickler on 18 July 1880, and had children: *Sarah Nevada* (born 19 Nov. 1882 at Strickler, AR, and died 6 Mar. 1966 at Buffalo, OK); *Mary Tilford* (born 11 July 1887 at Strickler, AR, married Oscar Miles Sharp on 25 Dec. 1910 at Strickler, and had children: Orval Douglas [born 16 July 1912, married Jewel Reiff in 1935, and had children: Shirley Ann {married ___ Lowry}; Orval Douglas married secondly Marie ___ in 1947, and had children: Norman; Orval Douglas died 30 Sept. 1982 at Liberal, KS, and was buried in the Sharp Cemetery, Prairie Grove]; Hiram Wayne [born 16 Jan. 1917, married Glendora Virginia Powell on 31 Dec. 1941 at Jefferson City, MO, and had children: Betty Jo {born 27 Dec. 1942, married James Arthur Ezell on 31 July 1964, and had children: Elizabeth René <born 22 May 1969>; Marianne <born 20 Apr. 1972>}; James Donald "Jim" {born 26 Jan. 1945, married Dolores Kaye Ostie on 21 June 1969, and had children: Serenity Kaye <born 10 Nov. 1972>; Kimberly Vale <born 8 Feb. 1974>; Summer Leigh <born 12 July 1978>; Stevenson James <born 28 Nov. 1980>; Jim Sharp is a medical doctor at Fayetteville, AR}]; Oscar Miles Jr. "Ottie" [born 14 May 1919, married Jo Lee West on 10 Oct. 1946, and had children: Jimmy Wayne {born 26 Dec. 1948}; Oscar Miles Jr. married secondly Marian Bell Bushong on 12 Sept. 1981]; Marion James "Jay" [born 10 Feb. 1925, married Patricia Ann Trout in 1957, and had children: William Andrew {born 14 Jan. 1958}; Jay was killed in an automobile accident on 30 Jan. 1970 at Fort Nelson, BC, Canada, and is buried in the Sharp Cemetery, Prairie Grove, AR]).

Ibba CRAWLEY is listed in the 1860 census for Washington Co. She died in childbirth on 12 Apr. 1863, and is buried with her husband in the Strickler Cemetery.

> "At the time of Ibba's death, the Civil War was in progress, so William [Crawley] moved his family deep into the wooded area toward Cane Hill. They constructed a cabin, cleared land for a garden and to grow corn. Their mother had already died, so the minor children were in the woods alone. They moved household furnishings, food, a team of oxen, and the other necessities to the cabin. He did this for the safety of his children. Martha told the incident when her father returned from the war, and was ill. He told her he had been followed, and if anyone came to the cabin, she was to detain the person at the door, which she did. This enabled William to climb out of the window at the back of the cabin, go around the house, and shoot the man who was being detained at the front door. They returned to their home on Old Wire Road after the war, and found that it had been used as a hospital. Soldiers had been buried in the meadow in front of the house [but were later removed and reburied]."—Hiram Wayne Sharp.

6c. **Joseph C(rawford?).** Born about 1828 in Jackson (later Putnam) Co., TN. Listed with his father in the 1840 census, and in the 1850 census for Washington Co., AR with Shadrack Murray and his future brother-in-law, William Crawley, but has not been found in 1860. Joseph Burgess witnessed the deed of his brother, John M. Burgess, who purchased land on 12 Oct. 1861 in Washington Co. He may have served in Co. K., 17th Tennessee Infantry, Confederate Army, during the Civil War. He has not been found after the war.

6d. **Thomas (III).** Born about 1834 in Jackson (later Putnam) Co., TN. Listed with his father in the 1850 census, but has not been found in 1860 or later.

6e. **John M. (I).** Born about 1836 in Jackson (later Putnam) Co., TN. Listed with his father in the 1850 census, but has not been found in 1860. He moved to Washington Co., AR, where he bought land on 26 Aug. 1861 from John and Polly Oliver (*Deed Book #O*, p. 336), recorded "at the request of John M. Burgess" on 12 Oct. 1861 (perhaps preparatory to joining the army), with his brother Joseph witnessing the deed, and his brother-in-law, D. R. McCalib, acting as Justice of the Peace. He may have served in Co. K., 17th Tennessee Infantry, Confederate Army during the Civil War, or in Co. I, 34th Arkansas Infantry. He died by 1870, since his land was sold on 23 Aug. 1870 by his parents (*Deed Book #Y*, p. 71), with John specifically mentioned as being deceased.

6f. **Martha (II)** (twin). Born 21 Aug. 1838 in Jackson (later Putnam) Co., TN. Married John Robert Harris about 1868, and had at least the following children: *Rebecca L. "Becky"* (born 1869); *Sarah Charlotte* (born Jan. 1872, died 1875, buried with her mother). Listed in the 1860 census with her father, and in 1870 in the 16th Civil District, Putnam Co., TN. Martha Harris died there in Jan. 1872, and is buried in the West Cemetery. Becky Harris, her daughter, is living with Martha's brother, Isaac Burgess, in 1880.

6g. **Rebecca (I)** (twin). Born 21 Aug. 1838 in Jackson (later Putnam) Co., TN. Married John Ra(w)leigh Allison about 1863 (he was born 24 Mar. 1840, son of Joseph Allison and Cynthia Stone, and died 6 June 1912 [or 1913]), and had children:

(John) Isaac "Ike" ALLISON. Born 19 Mar. 1864, married Mattie Robinson, and had children: *(William) Hershal* (born 14 Feb. 1890, died 6 Oct. 1958, and had children: Raymond; Ralph [married Mary Alice ___, and had children: Susan; Katherine; Robert]); *Fannie Mae* (born 7 Oct. 1892, married Dr. ___ Caldwell, and died 17 Sept. 1946); *Milbra Rebecca* (born 24 Dec. 1894, married Charlie Norton on 3 Oct. 1915 in Putnam Co., and died 14 Jan. 1956, buried Allison Cemetery, having had children: Kenneth; Glen Gilbert [born 1 Nov. 1931]; Beulah Louise [born 9 Feb. 1936, married ___ Delany, and lives at Sparta, TN]; and possibly Lewis and Earl); *Martha Ethel "Mattie"* (born 7 Apr. 1897, married Thomas Leslie Passons on 8 June 1922 in Putnam Co. [he was born 9 June 1889, and died on 20 Mar. 1969], and died on 27 Nov. 1985, having had children: Thomas Leslie Jr. [born 7 Apr. 1923, married Helen Degnan, and lives at Barberton, OH]; Julia Ethel [born 2 Feb. 1925, married David H. Lennox {he was born 14 June 1925}, and had children: Peter Geoffrey {born 26 Mar. 1947, married Linda Arthur and secondly Terry Brown}; Linda Ann {born 22 Nov. 1948}]); *(Zina) Hubert* (born 22 June 1898, married Florence ___ at Minneapolis, MN, and had children: Zina Hubert Jr.; Richard; Joan [married ___ Kruger]; Child); *Maude Lee* (born 31 July 1900, married Joe Wheeler Webb on 15 Aug. 1921 in Putnam Co. [he died Feb. 1967], and had children: Joe Wheeler Jr. [married Billie Bradford, and had children: Barbara; Deborah]). ***Ike*** married secondly Julia Ann Caruthers on 30 Mar. 1901 in Putnam Co., and had children: *Joe Milton* (born 11 June 1902, married Mattie Lee Ferrell on 31 Dec. 1924 [she was born 25 June 1901], and had children: Nancy Jean [born 3 Aug. 1926, married James H. Harrison, and had children: Bronwyn {born 28 Dec. 1960}; Bryn {born 25 Aug. 1962?}]; Joe Ferrell [born 14 Dec. 1933]; Hugh Milton); *Helen Vio* (born 1 Sept. 1904, married W. Prentice Roark on 24 Sept. 1926 in Putnam Co. [he was born 3 Sept. 1904], had children: Janet, and lived at Franklin, KY); *Harry Horace* (born 11 Apr. 1907, married Josie Blair at Birmingham, AL, and had children: John Blair); *Beulah Beatrice* (born 11 Apr. 1909, married Robert Delaney). ***Dr. Ike ALLISON*** was a physician; he died on 21 June 1936, and is buried in the Cookeville City Cemetery.

Martha A. ALLISON. Born 1866, married Milton Bartlett (he was born 1844, and died 1921), died 1937, and had children: *Effie* (born 1885, married Henry Sadler, and died childless); *Eulola* (married James Deathridge); *Milton Jr.* (married Sarah ___).

Charlotta "Lottie" ALLISON. Born 1868, died young.

Rebecca Jane ALLISON. Born about 1870, married Cee Exum, and had children: (Jim) Howard.

Bird P. ALLISON. Born 27 Apr. 1872, married Moniza Caroline Bussell on 22 Aug. 1891 in Putnam Co. (she was born 5 Aug. 1872, the daughter of Greene Lawrence Bussell, and a cousin of William Wade Bussell, and died 1955), died 15 Feb. 1945, and had children: *Virgil Van C.* (born 22 Apr. 1892, married Mary Ann Tipton Copeland on 2 June 1917 in Putnam Co. [she was born 19 Oct. 1894, and died Oct. 1969], served as an attorney, and died 16 Jan. 1946, having had children: Virgil Van C. Jr. [born 26 Aug. 1918, married Edna Pugh, and died 9 Mar. 1963]; Joe Putnam [born 21 July 1920, married Hazel ___, and had children: Ray; Michael; Jackie; Carson]; John Robert [born 2 June 1921, married Dorothy "Dot" Fitzpatrick on 20 Jan. 1942 {she was born 17 Feb. 1923}, and had children: John Robert II {born 18 Oct. 1946, married Pat Goodwin Jones}]; William Burgess [born 5 Sept. 1925, married Rebecca Moore on 7 Apr. 1946, and had children: Grier {born 17 May 1947, married Wallace Collins, and had children: Cassell <born 26 June 1972>}]; William married secondly Helen Garner Jones on 24 Aug. 1963 {she was born 23 Dec. 1923}]); *John Amo* (born 2 Aug. 1898, died 12 Aug. 1901, buried Cookeville City Cemetery).

Bettie ALLISON. Born 1876.

Rebecca Burgess ALLISON is listed in the 1860 census with her father, and in the 1870-1910 censuses for the 16th Civil District, Putnam Co., TN. She died there on 16 Apr. 1925, and is buried with her husband in the West Cemetery.

6h. **Mary (X)**. Born 1840 in Jackson (later Putnam) Co., TN. Married (Solomon) Robert Crowley (or Crawley) about 1862 (he was born about 1840 in TN), and had at least the following children: *Washington Burgess* (born 1863); *John R.* (born 1865 KY); *Samuel J.* (born 1866); *Mary Jane* (born 1868); *Dicy E.* (born 1873); *William T.* (born 1874); *Isaac M.* (born 1876); *Russell L.* (born 1879). Listed in the 1860 census with her father, and in 1870-80 in Putnam Co., TN (1870 in the 16th District, 1880 in the 8th); neither she nor her children have been found in 1900, by which time they had apparently moved out-of-state.

6i. **Elizabeth (XIV)**. Her name is listed as Mary Elizabeth Burgess by James Z. Burgess in his book, but no corroboration has been found elsewhere. Born 29 Aug. 1842 in Jackson (later Putnam) Co., TN. Married Leonidas Lisander Lindsey about 1862 (he was born about 1840, son of Joseph A. Lindsey and Mary Gentry, and may have died in 1863 [but in any case by 1870], possibly in the Civil War), and had children:

John Isaac LINDSEY. Born 24 Mar. 1863, married Mary Marinda Lee on 13 Dec. 1891 in Putnam Co. (she was born 3 Nov. 1868, daughter of Harmon Young Lee and Malinda Whitehead, and died 25 May 1951). J. I. Lindsey inherited the farm of his uncle, Isaac W. Burgess, in 1928. He died in Putnam Co. on 17 June 1941, buried West Cemetery, having had children:

Ulah Solona LINDSEY (born 3 Sept. 1892, married Mansfield Roberts on 12 Apr. 1915 in Putnam Co., died 17 June 1960, and had children: Zola May [born 22 May 1915, married her cousin, Joda Grant Burgess {see his entry for her children}]; Nola Frances [born 7 Aug. 1916?, married Winfield Thomas]; Lola Sabrina [born 27 Apr. 1918, married Dow Maxwell on 25 Feb. 1940]; (Mary) Flossie [born 1 May 1920, married Everett Henley]; Cordie Magdalene [born 2 May 1922, married J. P. Stanley on 14 Jan. 1939]; Floyd [twin]; Lloyd [twin]; M. J. [born 1 June 1926, married Billie Pritchard on 25 Dec. 1948, and had children: Benny Ray {born 19 July 1951, married Glenda Foster}; Terry Lynn {born 15 Mar. 1954, married Beverly Evans}; Marty Jay {born 19 Dec. 1958}; Randall Leon {born 15 Apr. 1965}; Paul Edward {born 19 Oct. 1970}]; Betty Jane [born 7 Mar. 1930, married Charles "Jigs" Robinson]; Kenneth Ray [born 1 June 1933, married Mildred Ladell Saylors on 16 June 1951 {she was born 26 Sept. 1930, daughter of Joseph Bethel Saylors and Allie Enid Maxwell}, and had children: Danny Wayne {born about 1952, married Diana Whiteaker <she was born 7 Feb. 1954, daughter of J. B. Whiteaker and Ruth Bumbalough>, and had children: Dustin Wayne <born 12 Jan. 1983>}]).

Martha Elizabeth LINDSEY (born 1 Oct. 1893, died 30 Aug. 1894).

John Isaac LINDSEY Jr. (born 31 Dec. 1894, married Bertha Mae Clemons on 17 Apr. 1915, and had children: Valous Rhe "Vallie" [born 7 Apr. 1916, married Mary Judd, and had children: Johnny Rhe; Mary Elizabeth; Valerie Ann]; (John) William "Willie" [born 14 Dec. 1917, married Chloe B. Medley, and had children: Sharon Kay; Karen Sue; Sandra; Deborah Lynn; Dennis Jerome]; Vinnie Vaylene [born 9 Feb. 1920, married Walter Roberts on 12 Aug. 1940]; Willard Leon "Purt" [born 30 Aug. 1925, married Rose Marie Carraway, and had children: Barbara {married Edd Sharpe}; Wayne; James {married Sadie Rhea}]; Veda Carrie [born 16 Oct. 1928, married Lamar Dew, and had children: William Sullivan "Billy"; Lindsey Phillip; Rebecca Lee; Mary Elizabeth; Rachel Vaylene]; (Mary) Elizabeth [born 11 May 1932, married Luther Burton]; (James) Delmos [born 30 Dec. 1933, married Connie Sue Chaffin on 30 Aug. 1958 {she was born 2 May 1941, daughter of James Keith Chaffin and Joyce Marie Love}, and had children: Katherine Elaine {born 24 June 1959, married Wayne Anthony Han <he was born 4 Oct. 1957>, and had children: Wayne Anthony Jr. <born 28 Jan. 1977>}; Calvin Dain {born and died 17 June 1960}; Carolyn Sue {born 29 Aug. 1961}; Gary Dale {born 10 Oct. 1962}; Karen Jo {born 18 Sept. 1965}]; Rebecca Ann [born 4 Apr. 1940, married Waymon J. Wallace on 27 Aug. 1958 {he was born 13 June 1935, son of William Carroll Wallace and Minnie Betty Ann Montgomery, and died in a construction accident on 22 Apr. 1987, buried Cookeville City Cemetery}, and had children: Vinnie Ann {born 17 Aug. 1961, married ___ Hassler}]).

Alma Young "Scrooch" LINDSEY (born 11 July 1896, married Jessie L. Roberts on 6 June 1920 [she was born 28 Feb. 1904, daughter of Andrew Johnson Roberts and Amelia Hale, and died on 17 Apr. 1936]; *Alma* married secondly Orpha Cronk on 11 Mar. 1939 in Putnam Co. [she was born 25 Oct. 1901, and died on 16 Feb. 1951], and died in Mar. 1978 at Cookeville, TN, having had children: Truman; Thurman Cronk).

(Mary) Frances LINDSEY (born 15 June 1898, married Sam Monroe LaFever on 4 Sept. 1936 [he was born 5 Jan. 1901, son of George Washington LaFever and Winnie Ora Belle Wilhite, and died on 9 Apr. 1979], and died on 27 Dec. 1980, the same day as her sister, Cynthia, having had children: Mary Belle [born 21 June 1939, married Lem Samuel Hickey on 23 Oct. 1961 {he was born 5 Jan. 1939, son of James Samuel Hickey and Alma Lillian Coleman}, and had children: Edward Alan {born 11 May 1962}; Danita Rose {born 21 Sept. 1963}; Lisa Ann {born 22 Jan. 1965}; Rita Diane {born 5 Sept. 1966}]).

Cynthia Charlotte LINDSEY (born 18 Dec. 1899, married George Levester "Slim" Bray on 21 Aug. 1921 in Putnam Co. [he was born 16 Sept. 1899, son of John M. Bray and Frances Eleanor "Fannie" Gentry], and died on 27 Dec. 1980, two hours before her sister, Mary, having had children: Mildred Modean [born 3 June 1925 in Putnam Co., married Laurence Grady Grimes on 18 Apr. 1947 {he was born 1 Apr. 1924, son of William Eldridge Grimes and Maggie Jane West}, and had children: James Laurence "Jimmy" {born 15 Oct. 1948, married Sandra Gail Bray on 9 Apr. 1971 <div.; she was born 24 July 1951, daughter of John Douglas Bray and Frances Irene Bean>, and had children: Christi Nicole <born 22 Nov. 1971>; Jimmy married secondly Amy Virginia Smith}; Rona Gail {born 21 Sept. 1952 in Overton Co., TN, and had children: Joseph Brent <born 7 June 1973>}]; Alma Eulene [born 27 Sept. 1930, married Jerry Wallace Montgomery on 28 Mar. 1949 {he was born 31 July 1928, son of Jesse N. Montgomery and Mae Carmichael}, and had children: Jerry Michael {born 20 Oct. 1949, married Linda Houghton on 1 Sept. 1979 at Dallas, TX, and had children: Catherine <born 6 May 1978>}; Robert Lee {born 8 June 1956, married Sherry Liles on 10 Dec. 1976}; Gary Lynn {born 28 May 1961}]; Charles Levester [born 24 Sept. 1932, and lives at Valley Park, MO]).

William Leon LINDSEY (born 11 Aug. 1902, married Mamie Hawkins on 21 Oct. 1923, and died Apr. 1980 at Randlett, OK, having had children: Cletis Leon; Joe Larrel).

Jewel Hixie LINDSEY (born 16 Dec. 1904, died 11 Oct. 1909).

Dulah Malinda LINDSEY (born 28 Sept. 1908, married William Haskell Judd on 12 May 1936 [he was born 8 Sept. 1912, son of Jim Judd and Eliza Howell, and died 23 Feb. 1974, buried with his wife in the West Cemetery], and died 29 Dec. 1976, having had children: Willie Duraine [born 15 June 1938 in Putnam Co., married Mary Kathleen LaFever on 21 Sept. 1956 {div.; she was born 3 Aug. 1941, daughter of Robert LaFever and Georgia Cleo Tallant}, and had children: Teresa Ann {born 30 July 1957}]; Martha Vayalene [born 26 May 1941 in Putnam Co., married Josephas Gregory at Miami, FL, and had children: Joie Dewayne {born 1 Feb. 1961, married Nancy Hutchison, and had children: Jennifer Rochelle <born 11 Oct. 1983>}; Regina Vayelene {born 16 May 1963, married Clinton Steward, and had children: Christina Vayelene <born 6 Feb. 1980>; Jason Clinton <born 2 Mar. 1981>; Dustin Joe <born 7 June 1983>}; Joseph Lynn {born 29 Oct. 1968}]).

Elizabeth Burgess LINDSEY married secondly Craven M. Shanks between 1870-80, and had children:

Van Everett SHANKS. Born 187_, married Ellen Maynard, and had children: *Virgil* (born 11 Dec. 1901, married Dorothy Whitehead, and died Dec. 1970 at Baxter, TN, having had children: Solon [born 24 Dec. 1927, died 6 Mar. 1993 at Silver Point, TN]; Bill; J. V.; Mac; Fred); *Mary* (married John Boyd); *Audie* (married ___ Brewington); *Haskel*; *Fred*; *Novie D.* (died at age 13); *Erma* (married ___ Dyer); *Juanita*; *Ellen Katherine* (married ___ Anderson).

Elizabeth is listed with her father in the 1870 census (as Elizabeth Linsey), and is listed with Shanks, three step-children, and her son in the 1880 census for the 17th District, Putnam Co., TN. Elizabeth Shanks died on 25 July 1925 in Putnam Co., and is buried in the Smellage Cemetery.

6j. **Isaac Washington "Ike."** Born 6 July 1844 (or 1842, according to his death certificate) in Jackson (later Putnam) Co., TN. Served in Co. E, 25th Tennessee Infantry, Confederate Army, during the Civil War, enlisting on 19 Dec. 1862 at College Grove, TN, and fought at the Battle of Murfreesboro shortly thereafter. Has not been found in the 1870 census; listed in the 1880 census for the 1st District, Putnam, Co., TN, living with his mother and niece, and in 1900 with his aunt, Mary Barnes; he appears there as head of the family in 1910. Isaac Burgess lived in Oregon as a youth, working as a professional gambler; he later returned to Putnam Co., TN, where he farmed on the lands of his aunt, Mary, who deeded him her farm in 1907 (*Deed Book #Z*, p. 184). He donated a plot from his land to help establish the Burgess School. He died unmarried of nephritis on 19 Jan. 1928 in Putnam Co., and is buried in the West Cemetery. He was the last of his brothers and sisters to die.

ISAAC BURGESS DIES THURSDAY IN HIS 83RD YEAR

"Isaac Burgess, aged 83, died at his home near Burgess School Thursday afternoon. He was the last of a family of 12 to pass away. 'Uncle Ike,' as he was familiarly called, made several trips to the West in his younger days, living for some time in the state of Oregon. He died within half mile of his birthplace. He is survived by a host of relatives. Funeral services were conducted by Rev. J. D. Harris and Grover Stewart, Friday, after which the remains were interred in the West Cemetery."—*Putnam County Herald*, 23 Jan. 1928.

6k. **Charlotte.** She is called Charlotte Burgess Jr. in an 1878 deed. Born 18 May 1847 in Jackson (later Putnam) Co., TN. Married John A. Roberts after 1880 (he was born 11 Feb. 1829, and died 13 Aug. 1904), and had children: *Andrew Johnson* (married Amelia Hale and/or Tilly Bray, and had children: Arville [born 3 Aug. 1899, married Dimple Ivene Veteto, and died Mar. 1976 at Mountain City, TN]; John; Jessie L. [born 28 Feb. 1904, married her cousin, Alma Young Lindsey, on 6 June 1920]; Willie [married Oakley Thomas]; Clode; Lawrence; Myrna Gail [married Ronnie Jones]; Nell [married Erb Ray]; Cecil [married Gladys Cass]; Ed; Dean). Listed with her father in the 1870 census, and with her brother, Isaac Burgess, in 1880. Charlotte Roberts died on 12 Jan. 1912 in Putnam Co., and is buried with her husband in the West Cemetery. A descendant, Cloyd Roberts, currently lives at Cookeville, TN.

6l. **Daniel Campbell**. Born 19 May 1848 near Cookeville, Jackson (later Putnam) Co., TN. See below for full entry.

NOTE: An unidentified female, M. A. Burgess (sic), aged one year, is listed with D. R. McCalib and his wife Synthia (Burgess) in the 1870 census after their own children. This girl is almost certainly related, probably the daughter of John M. Burgess or one of his brothers. No further record has been found, and she presumably died or moved away before 1880.

[William (I)[1], Edward (I)[2], Reuben (I)[3], Thomas (I)[4], George Washington (I)[5]]

DANIEL CAMPBELL BURGESS
(1848?-1922)
OF WASHINGTON COUNTY, ARKANSAS

6l. **Daniel Campbell** *[son of George Washington (I)].* His middle name is given as Camel in his family Bible record. Born 19 May 1848 near Cookeville, Jackson (later Putnam) Co., TN. Married Martha Jane Brunk on 30 Mar. 1871 at Fly Creek, Washington Co., AR (she was born 18 June 1851 in Virginia, grew up in Austin, TX, moved to Clyde, AR in 1868, and died 23 May 1936). Listed in the 1880-1900 censuses for Washington Co., AR, but has not been found in 1910; five of nine children survive in 1900; listed in the 1920 census with his son, Thomas Burgess. Daniel Burgess moved to Washington Co., AR in 1868, and on 23 Aug. 1870 purchased the farm of his late brother, John (*Deed Book #Y*, p. 71), near Cane Hill, AR, on the border between Arkansas and Indian Territory (later Oklahoma). He died there on 24 Oct. 1922, and is buried with his wife in the Reece Cemetery, near Fly Creek, at Morrow, AR.

The Children of Daniel Burgess:

7a. **Mary Jane (III).** Born 22 July 1872 at Clyde, Washington Co., AR. Married James Newton "Jim" Mattox on 22 Jan. 1889 in Washington Co., and had children: *Emmett* (born 2 Apr. 1890, died 11 Feb. 1942); *Ernest* (born 1894, died 1982). Mary Mattox died on 18 Apr. 1897 at Evansville, AR.

7b. **John Washington (II).** Born 24 Jan. 1874 at Clyde, Washington Co., AR. See below for full entry.

7c. **Ada Ellen.** Born 18 Mar. 1876 at Clyde, Washington Co., AR. Married Phelix Grundy Pennel on 30 Dec. 1894 in Washington Co. (he was born 20 July 1873, and died 7 Apr. 1936), and had children:

***(Thomas) Edgar* PENNEL.** Born 18 Dec. 1895 at Clyde, AR, married Gladys Eve Davis on 23 Dec. 1917 (she was born 17 Sept. 1897, and died 5 Apr. 1989], worked as a farmer and carpenter, and died 11 Nov. 1965, buried Lakeview Gardens Cemetery, Wichita, KS, having had children: *Lorraine*; *Dora Grace "Happy"*; *Eugene*.

***(Daniel) Walter* PENNEL.** Born 7 Dec. 1897 at Morrow, AR, married Viola May Reed on 16 Sept. 1917 (she died 16 Mar. 1969), and had three children who all died at birth; married secondly Goldie Whinery on 1 Feb. 1972 (she was born 2 Dec. 1898, and died 15 July 1972); married thirdly Fay Vaughn on 3 Nov. 1972; Walter Pennel was an ordained Methodist minister who lived near Morrow and Lincoln, AR. He died on 22 Nov. 1986 at Westville, OK.

***Laura Etta* PENNEL.** Born 5 Feb. 1900 at Morrow, AR, married Walter K. Winsted on 11 Sept. 1918 at Morrow (he was a farmer and served as elected Mayor of Satanta, KS), moved to Evansville, AR, and died of tuberculosis on 11 July 1939 at Norton, KS (buried Satanta Cemetery, Satanta, KS), having had children: *Irene*; *Talmadge "Tally"*; *Felix*; *Ernest*; *John*; *Oletta*.

***James Clarence "Johnnie"* PENNEL.** Born 6 Sept. 1902 at Morrow, AR, married Laverna Maude Cates on 28 Feb. 1932 (she died 12 Aug. 1990 at Wentzville, MO), worked as a barber at Lincoln, AR, and died on 28 Sept. 1986 at Fayetteville, AR, buried with his wife at Summers, AR, having had children: *Jackie Warren* (married, had children: Teresa; Tamera "Tammy"; Danny; Jackie Pennel works as a chiropractor, and lives at Grove, OK).

***(Oren) Marvin* PENNEL.** Born 28 June 1907 at Morrow, AR, married Gladys Marie McCamish on 5 Aug. 1928 (div. 1948); married secondly Cora Cunningham on 17 Nov. 1950, worked as a mechanic for Knights Manufacturing Co. at Broken Arrow, OK, and died there on 5 Dec. 1969, buried at Rogers, AR.

***(Samuel) Emmett* PENNEL.** Born 3 June 1913 at Morrow, AR, died 19 May 1915.

***Margie Rowena* PENNEL.** Born 16 May 1916 at Morrow, AR, married Clifford Hampton Bradley on 23 July 1932 at Fayetteville, AR (div.), and had children: *Betty Jean* (died at birth); *Carol* (married ___ Phillips, and had children: Connie Lucie; Cynthia "Cindy"; married secondly Bill Chapin, and lives at Catoosa, OK); *Joann*. In 1941 the Bradleys settled at Sallisaw, OK, where Clifford Bradley went into business with Margie's cousin, Emmett Mattox. She later lived in Kansas and

Springdale, AR, where she worked successively for Moore's Manufacturing, Kroeger's, and K-Mart. Margie Bradley has contributed greatly to this book.

Ada PENNEL died on 14 July 1955 at her daughter Margie's home at Sallisaw, OK, and is buried with her husband in the Cox Cemetery, Morrow, Washington Co., AR.

7d. **(Sallie) Luvenia "Venia."** Born 21 Apr. 1878 at Clyde, Washington Co., AR. Married Walter J. Parker on 30 Dec. 1896 in Washington Co. Venia Parker died in Jan. 1900 at Holbert, OK.

7e. **Samantha Alice.** Born 12 Nov. 1880 at Clyde, Washington Co., AR; died there on 22 Nov. 1894.

7f. **Thomas Walter.** Born 27 Aug. 1883 at Evansville, Washington Co., AR. See below for full entry.

7g. **Cora Tennessee.** Born 7 Nov. 1887 at Clyde, Washington Co., AR. Married William C. "Will" Mintz on 30 Dec. 1906 in Washington Co. (he died 31 Oct. 1957), and had children: *Leona Alice* (born 20 Sept. 1908 at Weir, KS, married ___ Presley [he died 2 July 1975], and had four children); *Ila Juanita* (born 1910, died 30 May 1910); *Veta Trewhitt* (born 28 Apr. 1911 at Clyde, AR, married ___ Barnum, had three children, and died 11 Apr. 1988 at Chanute, KS); *Garl Burgess* (born 7 Nov. 1912 at Clyde, AR, and had one son, and died 22 Jan. 1977 at Russell, KS); *Hubert* (born 28 Apr. 1916 at Stilwell, OK, had one son and one daughter, and lives at Chanute, KS); *Wayne* (born 11 July 1918, had one daughter, and lives at Martinez, CA); *Luretta Josephine* (born 26 Jan. 1920, married ___ Kirkpatrick, had four children, and died 26 July 1982 at Topeka, KS). Cora Mintz died on 7 Nov. 1984, her 97th birthday, at Chanute, KS. Leona Presley worked at the Stilwell Mercantile from 1943-87, when she retired; she currently lives on her farm at Stilwell, OK, and has contributed greatly to this book.

7h. **Daughter.** Born 15 Sept. 1889 at Clyde, Washington Co., AR; died there on 16 Sept. 1889.

7i. **Leona Elizabeth.** Born 11 Aug. 1893 at Clyde, Washington Co., AR. Married John Cohea on 10 Oct. 1915 in Washington Co. (he was born 16 July 1889, and died Nov. 1967 at Hobbs, NM; by his first marriage he had children: *Dorothy* [who married her first cousin by marriage, Lee Burgess]; *Daughter*). Leona Cohea died childless on 8 Mar. 1964 at Hobbs, Lea Co., NM.

Margie Bradley wrote in 1993: "All of Ada and Phelix Pennel's children were raised on a farm near Morrow, Arkansas. We raised all of our fruits and vegetables, raised hogs and cattle, milked cows, churned milk and made our own butter. Dad butchered hogs and beef for our meat, Mom raised turkeys, guineas, and chickens. They furnished us meat and eggs. We raised acres of strawberries for market. Also grew sorghum cane, used in a horse-drawn sorghum mill, we hand-fed stocks to extract the juice to boil and skim and cook down into sorghum molasses. Dad was also a carpenter, and helped build houses. All of our farm machinery was pulled by mules or horses. We raised lots of apples. Dad would take the old wood-covered wagon, loaded with apples, and would be gone for a week to Fort Smith, Van Buren, and various other towns to peddle them out so we could have money to buy shoes and material to make our clothes. Mom made most of what we wore. She had a foot treadle sewing machine we were lucky to have (there was no electricity). We used kerosene lamps and burned wood in the fireplace, and had an old wood-burning cookstove. We bathed in an old washtub, had an old outhouse privy, washed our clothes on a rub-board with lye soap Mom made. We had a hand-dug well in the yard, we used a rope on a pulley and a bucket to draw the water from the well. Dad took our shelled corn to a gristmill and had it ground into meal for cornbread. He had wheat ground into flour for our other cooking needs. Before any cars [reached our area], we went everywhere in wagon or horse-drawn buggy. Then Dad's first car came along, a Model-T. In later years he traded it for a Chevrolet. He didn't get to drive for very many years; he died at age sixty-two in 1936."

JOHN W. BURGESS OF LOS ANGELES CO., CALIFORNIA

[Daniel Campbell[6]]

7b. **John Washington (II)** *[son of Daniel Campbell].* Born 24 Jan. 1874 (or 1873, according to his draft record) at Clyde, Washington Co., AR. Married Etta Nora "Pet" Leach on 28 Jan. 1900 in Washington Co., AR (she was born May 1876 [or 1877] in AR, and died 16 Apr. 1943 in Reagan Co., TX); married secondly Ava Rogers about 1944 (she died about 1950). Listed in the 1900-20 censuses and 1918 draft register for Washington Co., AR. John W. Burgess was a farmer at Clyde, AR; he moved in 1925 to Best, Reagan Co., TX, and lived there until his first wife's death in 1943. He then moved back to Washington Co., where he remarried, and finally to Los Angeles Co., CA, where he lived with his daughter, Mae Sumrall. He died on 23 June 1954 at Florence, Los Angeles Co., CA, but he and his first wife are buried together in the Cox Cemetery, Washington Co., AR.

8a. **Mae Evelyn.** Born 1 Feb. 1901 in Washington Co., AR. Married (James) Alvin Sumrall Sr. on 22 Nov. 1919 in Washington Co. (he was born on 24 Apr. 1898, and died on 16 Feb. 1973 at Salinas, CA), and had children: *James Alvin Jr. "Gordon"* (born 8 Dec. 1920, died 11 Aug. 1985 in Santa Cruz Co., CA); *Eldon B.* (born 27 Jan. 1924, died 1 Aug. 1981 at La Mirada, CA); *Alvina* (married

___ Kemp, and was living at Reno, NV in 1983). Living at Florence, Los Angeles Co., CA in 1954, but moved to Salinas in 1965. Mae Sumrall died on 1 Aug. 1983 at Salinas, Monterey Co., CA, and is buried with her husband in the Garden of Memories Cemetery.

8b. **(Jessie) Jewel.** Born 8 Aug. 1903 in Washington Co., AR. Married (Hugh) Morris Simpson on 26 Sept. 1920 in Washington Co., AR (born 13 Sept. 1902, and died Aug. 1970 at Merriam, KS), and had children: *Erma Etta* (born 21 Mar. 1921, married Clay Wold, and died on 12 Mar. 1992 in WA); *(Morris) Clifton* (born 31 Mar. 1929 at Montecito, WA, married Lula Bell Harris in Nov. 1953 at Tacoma, WA [she was born 1929, and died 1986], had children: Diane; Rosemary; Sandra; Douglas; Perry; Joel, and lives at Sumner, WA). **Jewel SIMPSON** married secondly Owen Avery (div.), and thirdly Alan Opine about 1950 (he was born 5 Nov. 1910 in CA, and died Sept. 1985 at Albuquerque, NM). Jewel Opine died in an automobile accident in Dec. 1973 near Spanaway, WA.

8c. **(Sarah) Louvena "Winnie."** Her name is listed as Sarah in the 1910 census and Luvena in 1920, and Lovena in her marriage record. Born 5 July 1906 in Washington Co., AR. Married Jewel J. (nmn) Schaible Sr. on 10 July 1924 at Van Buren, Crawford Co., AR (he was born 18 Nov. 1902 at Van Buren, AR, and died 26 May 1979 at Big Lake, TX), and had children:

Robbie Lee SCHAIBLE. Born 13 Mar. 1925 at Van Buren, AR, married John Allen "Buddy" Winn in 1944 at Del Rio, TX (he operated a service station at Big Lake, TX for 25 years before retiring), and had children: *Linda Joyce*; *Carol Dea*; *Nancy Kay*; *Allen Wayne*; *Janet Lou.*

Marcia Dea SCHAIBLE. Born about 1927, married Leonard "Lefty" Hough in 1948, and died 1968, buried Glen Rest Cemetery, Big Lake, TX.

Jewel J. "Buck" SCHAIBLE Jr. Born 1928 at Best, TX, married Barbara Langston in 1950, and had children: *(Larry) Kent* (married Margaret Orms at Midland, TX, and had children: Andrew Kent; Daniel Brian; Kent Schaible lives at Houston, TX); *Leslie Karen* (she works as a chemical engineer for Boehringer Mannheim at Houston, TX). Buck Schaible owns and operates Schaible's Grocery at Big Lake, TX. He has contributed greatly to this book.

Louvena and Jewel SCHAIBLE worked on a dairy at Texon, Reagan Co., TX, and later moved to Best, TX, where she ran a small variety store. In 1936 they bought a dairy at Texon, which they operated until 1943. They then bought a grocery store (Schaible's Grocery) at Big Lake, TX, and built a new store there in 1953. They retired in 1967. Louvena died on 1 Aug. 1989 at Big Lake, Reagan Co., TX, and is buried with her husband in the Glen Rest Cemetery, Big Lake, TX.

8d. **(Malcomb) Lee.** His name is listed as Malcolm in the 1910 census, as Lee in 1920, and as Lee Malcomb on his death certificate. Born 21 Nov. 1909 in Washington Co., AR. Married Dorothy Cohea, his first cousin by marriage, about 1934 (div. 1943, and remarried); married secondly Annie McGee (she was born 18 July 1912, and died 28 Apr. 1988 at Glendale, CA). Lee Burgess was a truck owner who hauled supplies for the oil fields in Texas and New Mexico; he moved to Glendale, Los Angeles Co., CA, during the 1940s, and worked as a carpenter and later as a civilian construction worker in Vietnam during the Vietnam War. He died on 11 Mar. 1986 at Glendale, CA.

9a. **Johnny Lee.** Born about 1935. He was raised by John and Leona Cohea (his great-aunt). Served in the U.S. Army during the Korean War. Johnny Burgess worked for the U.S. Postal Service, and was last known living at Hobbs, NM about 1980.

9b. **Linda Kay (I).** Born about 1938.

8e. **Tersie L.** Born Nov. 1914 in Washington Co., AR; died there on 6 Jan. 1915, and is buried in the Cox Cemetery.

8f. **James D(aniel?).** Born 14 July 1921 in Washington Co., AR; died there on 30 Sept. 1924, and is buried in the Cox Cemetery.

THOMAS W. BURGESS OF CRAWFORD CO., ARKANSAS

[Daniel Campbell[6]]

7f. **Thomas Walter** *[son of Daniel Campbell].* Born 27 Aug. 1883 at Evansville, Washington Co., AR. Married Mary Melvina "Mollie" Baugh on 14 Dec. 1913 at Morrow, Washington Co., AR (she was born 2 Feb. 1896 in Indian Territory [later Oklahoma], just across the border from Evansville, AR, and died 27 Jan. 1972). Listed in the 1918 draft register and 1920 census for Washington Co., AR. Tom Burgess was a farmer at Cane Hill, Washington Co., AR, and also worked in the produce business for thirty years at Van Buren, Crawford Co., AR. He died on 27 Aug. 1965 at Van Buren, AR, and is buried there with his wife in the Gill Cemetery.

8a. **Naomi Alice.** Her name is spelled Neoma in the 1920 census. Born 13 Oct. 1914 at Cane Hill, Washington Co., AR. Married Loyce Glidewell on 29 Nov. 1930 (div.), and had children: *Norma*

Nadine; *(Lois) Jeannene*. Married secondly Paul Rapier on 17 July 1937 (he was born 15 Feb. 1912, and died Apr. 1975 at Van Buren, AR), and had children: *Paula Juanita*; *Danny Gayle*. Naomi Rapier died on 22 Mar. 1973 at Van Buren, Crawford Co., AR.

8b. **Ernest Daniel.** His name is spelled Earnest in the 1920 census. Born 25 Feb. 1917 at Cane Hill, AR. Married (Laura) Elizabeth "Bess" Adams on 3 July 1939 (she was born 25 Mar. 1923, and died 9 Mar. 1992 at Fort Smith, AR, buried Gracelawn Cemetery, Van Buren, AR). Ernest Burgess currently lives at Van Buren, Crawford Co., AR.

9a. **Thomas Wayne "Tommy."** Born 29 Apr. 1940 at Van Buren, AR. Married Sharon Shockley on 27 July 1963. Tom-my Burgess currently lives at Van Buren, AR.

10a. **Angela Dawn**. Born 25 Aug. 1964 at Fort Smith, AR. Married Michael Green (div.).

10b. **Jeffrey Ernest.** Born 7 July 1966 at Van Buren, AR.

9b. **John Allen (II) "Johnny."** Born 18 Nov. 1943 at Van Buren, AR. Married Betty Biggerstaff on 10 Oct. 1965, and secondly Edna Cox on 27 Feb. 1970. Johnny Burgess curreny lives at Van Buren.

10a. **(Rodney) Michael.** Born 17 Nov. 1967 at Van Buren, AR.

10b. **Judy Elizabeth.** Born 10 Sept. 1975 at Fort Smith, AR.

8c. **Martha Geneva "Bill."** Her name is spelled Geneiva in the 1920 census. Born 13 Sept. 1919 at Cane Hill, AR. Married Robert Daugherty on 13 July 1940 (div.), and had children: *(Janet) Sue*; *Bobbie Jo*; *Thomas Edward "Tommie."* Geneva Daugherty lives at Tulare, CA.

8d. **Ila Mae.** Born 7 Feb. 1922 at Cane Hill, AR. Married (Virgil) Frank Lincks in 1938 (div.), and had children: *Jimmy Frank*; *Ronnie Don*. Married secondly Manning R. Cameron on 6 Nov. 1950 at Van Buren, AR, and had children: *Pamela*. Ila Cameron lives at Rialto, CA.

8e. **Roxanna Rowena "Roxie."** Born 9 Nov. 1924 at Cane Hill, AR. Married Warren D. Moore on 14 Aug. 1943 at Douglas, AZ, and had children: *Kenneth Wayne*; Dr. *Timothy Dean*; *Sheryl Ann*. Roxie Moore currently lives at Poteau, OK.

8f. **Joe Homer.** Born 3 Sept. 1927 in Washington Co., AR. Married Lois Williams on 19 Dec. 1948. Joe H. Burgess was a sales representative for twenty years for John Morrell & Co., and then worked as a sales manager for John Garner Meats, Van Buren, AR before retiring at the end of 1992. He currently lives at Fort Smith, AR.

9a. **Jo Dawna.** Born 15 Dec. 1952 at Fort Smith, AR.

9b. **Stephen Joe.** Born 13 June 1957 at Fort Smith, AR. Married Patricia Preston on 7 May 1983 (div.). Steve Burgess is a sales representative for Bayer Electronics, Fort Smith, AR.

10a. **Preston Bradley**. Born 16 June 1987 at Fort Smith, AR.

9d. **Mark Edward (I)** (twin). Born 8 May 1959 at Fort Smith, AR. Married Jan Willis on 21 June 1986. Mark Burgess works as a computer programmer for Baldor Electric, Fort Smith, AR.

10a. **(Phillip) Taylor**. Born 1 Jan. 1988 at Fort Smith, AR.

10b. **Weston Edward**. Born 14 Sept. 1990 at Fort Smith, AR.

9c. **Mike Anthony** (twin). Born 8 May 1959 at Fort Smith, AR. Married Cynthia Megeebee on 27 Nov. 1981. Mike Burgess works as a division sales manager for Bar S Foods, Oklahoma City, OK.

10a. **Alexandra Nichole**. Born 9 June 1986 at Oklahoma City, OK.

10b. **Elizabeth Michelle**. Born 30 Mar. 1990 at Oklahoma City, OK.

8g. **Peggy Louise.** Born 1 May 1933 at Cane Hill, AR. Married James Edward Baber on 28 June 1952 at Waldron, AR (he was born 25 July 1933 at Van Buren, AR, son of Veachel Elonzo Baber and Cora Manasco), and had children: *Ricky Burgess* (born 31 Dec. 1954 at Richland, WA, married Rebecca G. Price on 1 Nov. 1974); *Robin Diane* (born 17 May 1956 at Fort Smith, AR, married William C. Collins on 26 Apr. 1991); *(James) Randall "Randy"* (born 21 Mar. 1960 at Eureka Springs, AR, married Christina Johnson on 25 Oct. 1985 [div.]); *Rhonda Leigh* (born 1 May 1972 at Newport, AR).

8h. **Robbie Lee.** Born 15 June 1935 at Cane Hill, AR. Married Jack E. Toothaker on 17 Feb. 1956, and had children: *(Jack) Keith*; *Katherine Lynn "Kathy"*; *Leslie Alan*.

[William (I)[1], Edward (I)[2], Reuben (I)[3], Thomas (I)[4]]

CHARLES HUNTER BURGESS
(1806-1886)
OF PUTNAM COUNTY, TENNESSEE

5d. **Charles Hunter** *[son of Thomas (I)].* Born 16 May 1806 in Rowan (later Davie) Co., NC. Married Margaret "Peggy" McBride about 1828 (she was born 15 Feb. 1808 in TN, daughter of Joseph C. McBride and Elizabeth Brimmer, and sister of Charlotta McBride [who married Charles's brother, George Washington Burgess], and died 22 Dec. 1891). Moved to Tennessee with his father. Listed in the 1830-50 censuses for White (later Putnam) Co., TN, and from 1860-80 in the 1st District, Putnam Co., TN; in 1830 they have one son under five, in 1840 one son 10-15, two sons 5-10, one daughter 5-10, one daughter 0-5 years of age. He signed the 11 Feb. 1854 petition to the Tennessee State Legislature requesting that Putnam Co. be established. Charles H. Burgess was a farmer in Putnam Co., TN, and a member of the Christian Church. He died there on 7 Dec. 1886, and is buried with his wife in the Howard Cemetery. Much of the information on this family is based on the work of James Z. Burgess Sr. and his book, *Burgess History: A Tennessee Pioneer* (Atlanta, GA: James Z. Burgess, 1976).

On 7 Mar. 1859 Charles Burgess purchased a ten-year-old slave named Isaac from James J. Bohannon. At the end of the Civil War, after all the slaves were freed, Isaac signed an agreement on 5 Mar. 1866 to continue working for Charles Burgess, and himself assumed the surname Burgess. A large, unrelated Burgess family descends from this line.

The Children of Charles Burgess:

6a. **John B.** Born 15 Apr. 1829 in White (later Putnam) Co., TN; died there in Nov. 1842, and is buried in the Lovelady Cemetery.

6b. **William Simpson.** Born 24 Aug. 1830 in White (later Putnam) Co., TN. See below for full entry.

6c. **James Crawford.** Born 28 July 1832 in White (later Putnam) Co., TN. See below for full entry.

6d. **Elizabeth (XII) "Betsy."** Born 9 Jan. 1834 in White (later Putnam) Co., TN. Married Andrew R. Massa on 30 Mar. 1862 (he was born 4 Apr. 1842, was a prominent local politician and a member of the Tennessee Legislature [see below], and died on 31 Jan. 1915), and had children:

(Sarah) Naomi MASSA. Born 1 Feb. 1863, married Paris Carr (he was born 29 Jan. 1847, son of "Big" John Carr and Perlina West, and died 11 Dec. 1921), and died 19 Aug. 1900, having had children: *Lee*; *Benton M.* (married Martha Lewis, and died 12 Dec. 1952).

(Margaret) Susanne "Ann" MASSA. Born 9 June 1864, married James J. Carr (he was born 1858, son of "Little" John Carr and Sarah Roenas West, and died in 1930), and died 26 June 1900, buried with her husband in the West Cemetery, having had children: *Mertie M.* (born 26 Aug. 1884, married her cousin, (Pretteman) Payne Burgess, and died 19 Sept. 1960—see his entry for their children); *Citha Uretta* (born 19 July 1886, married David Franklin Goodwin on 26 Mar. 1904 [he was born 1881, son of John W. Goodwin and Harriett Deering, and died 1919], and had children: Leon [born 6 Aug. 1906, died 29 July 1919, buried Goodwin Cemetery]; Odell [born 1 Nov. 1908, and died Feb. 1984 at Rockwood, TN, buried Goodwin Cemetery]; Edna Lee [born Apr. 1912]; John David [born 25 Mar. 1917, and died Aug. 1981 at Cookeville, TN, buried Goodwin Cemetery]; *Citha* married secondly William Wade Bussell in 1921 [he was born 4 Feb. 1891, son of George Presley Bussell and Sarah Elizabeth Worley, and died 6 Oct. 1962, buried Cookeville City Cemetery], and had children: Hugh Mansfield [born 14 June 1922, married Jeanne Duclos on 20 July 1942 {she was born 23 July 1923, daughter of Émile Louis Duclos and Mabel Eaton}, and had children: Hugh Daguerre {born 6 Jan. 1945}; Adrienne {born 19 June 1949}; Wade Armand {born 26 May 1951}; Suzanne Denise {born 14 June 1953}, and lives at Cookeville, TN]). Jeanne Bussell has contributed greatly to this book.

(Mary) Jane MASSA. Born 1866, married Erastus H. Davis (he was born 1870, and died 1946), and died childless in 1943, buried Judd Cemetery.

(Jarusha) Alabama "Bama" MASSA. Born 5 Feb. 1868, married William H. Barr on 21 Dec. 1884 (he was born 23 May 1867, son of Jacob Barr and Hixey Adeline Martin, and died 2 Dec. 1941), and died 29 Sept. 1937, buried Judd Cemetery. They had children: *Etta Lillian* (born 20 May 1887, married Isaac Medley on 10 Apr. 1904, and had children: Erwin [born 6 Dec. 1905]; Virgil E. [born 16 Jan. 1908]; Clara [born 13 Sept. 1910, died 28 Nov. 1913]; *Etta MEDLEY* died in 1978 at Little Rock, AR, aged 91 years); *Elmer Etheridge* (born 14 Dec. 1889, married Arlie Davis on 13 Apr. 1913 [she was born 6 July 1893, daughter of Henry Franklin Davis and Laura Parlee Carr, and died 26 Jan. 1916, buried West Cemetery], and had children: Edith Marie [born 20 Dec. 1915]; Elmer E. [dau.; born 4 Dec. 1910]; *Elmer* married secondly Beulah Frances Farley in 1917, and died on 25 Oct. 1918, buried West Cemetery); *Clay Evans* (born 17 Jan. 1893, married his cousin, Dimple Ray, on 1 May 1930 [she was born 15 May 1901, daughter of Joseph Robinson Ray and Sarah Ann Burgess, and died 25 Feb. 1976], and died 3 Feb. 1970); *Mary E.* (born 23 Oct. 1897, may have married ___ Nash); *Rebecca C.* (born 11 Sept. 1905).

Nancy C. MASSA. Born July 1869. No further record.

Leanora B. "Lee" MASSA. Born 22 July 1875, married Jess H. Pendergrass (he was born 1869, and died 1938), and died 17 June 1937, buried with her husband in the West Cemetery, having had children: *Horace* (born 24 Aug. 1906, and died 26 June 1908, buried with his parents).

The MASSAS are listed in the 1870-80 censuses for the 8th Civil District, Putnam Co., TN. Betsy Massa died there on 18 Apr. 1909, and is buried with her husband in the West Cemetery.

Andrew R. MASSA was elected to the Tennessee House of Representatives for the 56th-57th General Assemblies between 1909-13, representing Putnam County as a "Free Democrat." His biography appears in *Biographical Directory of the Tennessee General Assembly, Volume III, 1901-1931*, by Ilene J. Cornwell (Nashville: Tennessee Historical Commission, 1975), p. 457.

6e. **Thomas N.** Born 12 Feb. 1836 in White (later Putnam) Co., TN; died there on 6 Dec. 1838, and is buried in the Lovelady Cemetery.

6f. **(Joel) Peyton.** Born 22 Jan. 1838 in White (later Putnam) Co., TN; died there in (December?) 1838, and is buried in the Lovelady Cemetery.

6g. **Nancy Jane (I).** Born 17 Dec. 1839 in White (later Putnam) Co., TN. Married Robert Peek Jr. about 1857 (he was born 28 Mar. 1836, and died 11 Aug. 1919), and had children:

Elizabeth Frances PEEK. Born 24 Nov. 1857, married J. S. Moore in 1898, and secondly Silas Matthew Harvey Taylor (he was born 12 July 1853, and died 15 Oct. 1939), and had children: *Jessie Ann* (born 25 Mar. 1902, married Johnnie J. Wright on 23 Mar. 1919 [he was born 6 Mar. 1901], and had children: Edna Frances [born 4 Jan. 1920, died 9 Jan. 1923]; Lillie Florence [born 26 Jan. 1922, married Earl Otis Burgess on 10 Nov. 1945, and had children: Patricia Lynn {born 17 Dec. 1943?, married Steven Wayne Webb on 3 June 1966}; Vickie Diane {born 30 Oct. 1949}]; James Taylor [born 18 Nov. 1924, married Sylvia Gentry on 25 Apr. 1943, and had children: Ronald Taylor {born 15 May 1947, married Althea Mai Wells on 22 Dec. 1967, and had children: Rhonda Michelle <born 26 July 1972>}; Daryl Randall {born 29 Mar. 1951, married Carolyn Kay Williams on 12 Sept. 1971 <she was born 31 Jan. 1952>}; Tilda Angelita {born 7 Apr. 1954}]; Johnnie J. Jr. [born 14 Nov. 1928, married Wilma D. Ledora Williamson on 25 Sept. 1947 {she was born 8 July 1929}, and had children: Johnnie J. III {born 8 Mar. 1949, married Elizabeth Ann Taylor on 28 May 1971, and had children: John Charles <born 25 July 1972>}; Margaret Deadria {born 7 Apr. 1951, married David Barlow on 28 May 1971 <he was born 29 Feb. 1948>}; David Williamson {born 10 Oct. 1954}; Allen Brice {born 23 Sept. 1957}]. *Jessie* married secondly Tom Jeff Farris on 2 Nov. 1933, and had children: Donald; Tommy Jean; Geraldine [born 23 Oct. 1938, married William C. Sessions on 5 Sept. 1959 {he was born 24 Jan. 1924}, and had children: William C. Jr. {born 26 Aug. 1961}; Helen Elizabeth {born 27 Oct. 1964}; Rebecca Ann {born 3 Apr. 1969}]. *Jessie FARRIS* died on 4 Nov. 1938). ***Elizabeth TAYLOR*** died on 9 Feb. 1942.

David Peyton PEEK. Born 23 Sept. 1859, married Mary Alabama Davis (she was born 8 Mar. 1866, and died 20 Sept. 1962, aged 96 years), and had children:

Henry Vestal PEEK (born 15 Feb. 1884, married Arlie Bell Davis on 6 Sept. 1906 [she was born 7 Oct. 1875, and died 14 Feb. 1927], and had children: Eugene Peyton [born 25 Nov. 1907, married Winnie Corene Briggs on 12 May 1934 {she was born 24 Nov. 1914}, and had children: Norman Eugene {born 15 Nov. 1935, married Ava G. Sunderland on 4 Sept. 1960 <she was born 1 Jan. 1935>, and had children: Mary Charlene <born 19 Aug. 1964>; Daniel Norman <born 9 July 1966>}; Mary Eleanor {born 11 Aug. 1937, married Robert Carl Kurzynske on 12 June 1960 <he was born 7 Jan. 1939>, and had children: Terryn Diane <born 14 June 1961>; Mary Michelle <born 8 June 1962>}; Marvin Leon {born 21 Aug. 1946}]; Eula Mary [born 12 Nov. 1909, married Virgil Raymond Black on 31 Dec. 1932 {div.}, and had children: Lawrence Raymond {born 11 June 1937, married Doris Jean Dierce on 28 Aug. 1960 <she was born 8 June 1941>, and had children: Shirley Jean <born 19 June 1961>; Kevin Raymond <born 23 June 1962>; James Patrick <born 23

Apr. 196_>; Mary Elizabeth <born 10 Jan. 1972>}; Eula Mary married secondly Earl F. Liegler]; Archie Dillard [born 15 July 1911, married Ruth C. Casey on 8 Mar. 1944 {she was born 9 Nov. __}]; Henry Lawrence [born 1 May 1913, married Mary Virginia Wagners on 30 May 1939 {she was born 25 Jan. 1917}, and had children: Robert Lawrence {born 26 Jan. 1942}; Ronald William {twin; born 6 Mar. 1944, married Sylvia Jane Schottgen on 19 Dec. 1970 <she was born 4 Aug. 1950>}; Bonnie Ann {twin; born 6 Mar. 1944, married Ralph Worthington Keith on 6 Sept. 1964 <he was born 15 Oct. 1942>, and had children: Christopher Scott <born 31 Jan. 1969>; Caryn Christy <born 10 Nov. 1970>}; Gerald Redman {twin; born 19 Dec. 1945, married Linda Durgee Card <she was born 30 Mar. 1949>, and had children: Sean Michael <born 19 Dec. 1972>}; Jane Alma {twin; born 19 Dec. 1945, died 21 Aug. 1958}]; Argo [born 14 Mar. 1916, married Bessie Lee Ford on 1 Sept. 1940, and had children: Robert Ford {born 22 Mar. 1942, married Barbara Houlette on 14 Aug. 1964 <she was born 24 Feb. 1945>}]). *Henry V. PEEK* died in May 1918.

Claude Herman PEEK (born 5 July 1885, married Lou Banks on 4 July 1909, and had children: Edna Mae [born 30 May 1910, married B. A. "Jack" McCreary on 11 May 1930 {he was born 18 July 1908}, and had children: Sharon Kay {born 17 Mar. 1945}]; Mary Elizabeth [born 30 July 1918, married Cecil Thomas Overby on 18 Dec. 1939 {he was born 12 June 1918}]; Claudine [born 18 Oct. 1922, married Robert Aaron Lofland on 3 Sept. 1946 {he was born 10 Dec. 1921}, and had children: Robert Aaron Jr. <born 2 Oct. 1961>}).

Zona PEEK (born 6 June 1887, died young?).

Lillian Ann PEEK (born 22 Mar. 1889, died young?).

Lula Mae PEEK (born 28 July 1891, married Robert William Williams in 1930 [he was born 23 Dec. 1890]).

Sterling Martin PEEK (born 28 Dec. 1893).

Pascal PEEK (born 18 Dec. 1895, married Vivian Hatchett on 18 Dec. 1917 [she was born 20 Sept. 1899], and had children: Virginia K. [born 27 Mar. 1936, married Kenneth Lyle Chestnut on 12 Sept. 1959 {he was born 26 Dec. 1926}, and had children: Andrew Timothy {born 19 Dec. 1966}]).

Marvin Jennings PEEK (born 26 Sept. 1897, married Alma V. Bradley on 14 July 1925, and had children: Marvin Jennings Jr. [born 3 June 1927, died 25 June 1952]. *Marvin J. PEEK* died on 14 July 1935).

Ruby Almira PEEK (born 19 Jan. 1903).

Arlia Edith PEEK (born 17 Feb. 1906, married David Edward Sellers on 25 Nov. 1931 [he was born 17 Jan. 1904], and had children: John Thomas [born 2 Aug. 1945, married Betty Darlene Lawson on 3 May 1968 {she was born 23 Aug. 1946}]).

David PEEK died on 6 Feb. 1934.

Charles Thomas PEEK. Born 16 Feb. 1862, married Ollie Elizabeth Buck (she was born 13 Feb. 1866, and died 4 Oct. 1939), and died 29 Aug. 1891, having had children:

Cora Frances PEEK (born 27 Jan. 1889, married John Washington Pointer on 25 Oct. 1908 [he was born 21 Nov. 1886], and had children: Robert Lee [born 28 Mar. 1911, married Lola Mae Byrd in Apr. 1938, and had children: Sammie Lyn {born 20 May 1939, married Edward Lewis Martin in 1960 <he was born 22 Feb. 1935>, and had children: Mark Edward <born 3 May 1963>; Allen Stewart <born 10 Mar. 1966>}; Mary Frances {born 8 May 1943, married William Burnhardt Hains Jr. on 15 Mar. 1963 <he was born 29 Sept. 1943>, and had children: Elizabeth Marie <born 13 Aug. 1966>; Joseph William <born 6 Nov. 1967>}; Robert Lee Jr. {born 14 Oct. 1944, married Martha Ellen Manning on 29 Aug. 1970 <she was born 1 June 1949>, and had children: Robert Lee III <born 3 Aug. 1973>}]; John Allan [born 20 Oct. 1915, married Avannah Jones on 18 May 1935 {she was born 17 Dec. 1916, and died 26 Nov. 1946}, and had children: Barbara Ann {born 14 June 1936, married Melvin Hayward Brown on 16 Aug. 1958 <he was born 27 Aug. 1937, and died 28 Dec. 1972>, and had children: Michael Hayward <born 16 Aug. 1959>; Gregory Stephen <born 26 Nov. 1964>}; John Allan Pointer married secondly Rohbell Bates {she was born 21 June 1928}, and had children: Syble Amanda {ad.; born 28 June 1946, married Robert Tidwell <div.>, and had children: Monty Christopher <born 31 Aug. 1971>}; James Edward {born 21 Jan. 1951}.

Robert Hickman PEEK (born 14 Nov. 1890, married Addie Jane Bragg on 17 May 1912 [she was born 7 Mar. 1894], and died 1 Apr. 1930, having had children: Thomas Woodrow [born 11 Feb. 1913, died 11 Nov. 1954]; Robert Hickman Jr. [born 1 Sept. 1914, married Alice Larkin on 28 July 1938, and had children: Judith Kay; Robert married secondly Nancy ___, and had three children]; William Newton [born 28 Oct. 1921, married Essie Mae Jackson on 18 May 1939, and had children: William Newton Jr.; Thomas]; Joel Richard [born 4 Nov. 1926, married Helen Marcella Dargis on 12 Aug. 1947 {she was born 11 Nov. 1924}, and died 5 Oct. 1962, having had children: Richard Joel {born 27 May 1948}; Robert Charles {born 15 Mar. 1951}]; James Bragg [born 1 July 1930, married Dorothy H. Fitzgibbon on 15 Dec. 1962 {she was born 12 Apr. 1925}]).

***James Burr* PEEK.** Born 12 Apr. 1864, married Mary Cordelia West (she was born 14 Dec. 1868, and died 14 Apr. 1952), and died 17 Jan. 1957, aged 92 years, having had children:

Pearl Darthula PEEK (born 22 July 1887 in Putnam Co., married Robert Lee Cawthon on 23 Dec. 1913 at Atlanta, GA [he was born 16 Aug. 1891, and died 18 Apr. 1982], and died 24 Dec. 1988, aged 101 years, buried Roselawn Cemetery, Atlanta, GA, having had children: Nina Vivian [born 25 May 1915 in Butts Co., GA, married Jack Daniel Selman on 15 June 1935 at Atlanta, GA {he was born 31 July 1914, and died 20 June 1961}, and had children: Amy Jacqueline {born 13 Aug. 1936 at Atlanta, GA, married Jerry Lane Kintigh on 27 Sept. 1958 at Atlanta <he was born 15 Oct. 1932>, and had children: Lane Dwight <born 8 Dec. 1965 at Pittsburgh, PA>; Laura Cawthon <born 17 Nov. 1968 at Pittsburgh, PA>}; Beverly Jo {born 2 May 1938 at Atlanta, married David Thomas James on 5 Mar. 1960 <div.; he was born 13 Oct. 1939>, and secondly Lester L. Heath in 1977 <born 3 Feb. 1939>}; Rita Caroline {born 7 Feb. 1944 at Atlanta, GA, married Edward Alan Riffle on 15 Feb. 1964 <div.; he was born 12 Mar. 1941>, and had children: Marion Yvonne <born 21 Feb. 1966, married Ty Martin Bittner on 10 Aug. 1991 |he was born 25 Dec. 1965|, and had children: Wesley Martin |born 29 Aug. 1992|>; Rita married secondly John Albert Goeble on 9 Sept. 77 <he was born 21 Apr. 1948>}; James Daniel {born 3 Apr. 1945 at Atlanta, married Brenda Fay Moody on 5 Oct. 1963 <she was born 10 Nov. 1945>, and had children: Lorrie Ann <born 18 Feb. 1967, married James Lester Murphy on 22 Dec. 1984, and had children: Danielle Kaylan |born 18 Apr. 1987|; James Andrew |born 17 Jan. 1990|; Taylor Hays |born 25 July 1992|>; James Daniel Jr. <born 14 Nov. 1969, married Joyce ___ on 28 Dec. 1991 |div.|>; James Daniel Sr. married secondly Sandra ___ on 2 Apr. 1992}]; Ruby Leola [born 30 Dec. 1917 in Butts Co., married Henry Keith on 10 Mar. 1939 {he was born 5 Dec. 1914}, and had children: Robert Marshall {born 28 Sept. 1942 at Atlanta, GA, married Leanne McGinnis on 19 June 1965 <she was born 19 Jan. 1944, and died 24 Oct. 1987>, and had children: Robert Perry <born 24 Sept. 1972>; Robert Marshall KEITH married secondly Phyllis Ann Simmons on 10 June 1989 <she was born 22 Apr. 1948>}; Regina Ann {born 5 Jan. 1947, married Gary Lee May on 6 June 1969 <he was born 30 July 1946>, and had children: Jennifer Leanne <born 23 Sept. 1971>; Keith Hill <born 13 Dec. 1974>}; Ruby Keith died on 17 Jan. 1957]; (Robert) Stanley [born 11 Feb. 1922 in Butts Co., GA, married Doris Roberts Gilford on 12 May 1946 at Atlanta, GA {she was born 7 July 1917, and died on 20 Dec. 1967}, and secondly Geraldine McDonald Freeman on 15 Aug. 1969 at Cookeville, TN {she was born 12 May 1928}; Stan Cawthon was Chief Deputy Marshal for the City of Atlanta, GA before retiring]).

Rettie Beulah PEEK (born 9 Mar. 1889, died unmarried on 20 Dec. 1907).

Samantha Della PEEK (born 29 Mar. 1891, married Ura Arno Brogden on 8 July 1917 [he was born 23 Jan. 1895], and had children: Mary Elizabeth [born 24 Sept. 1918]; Helen Louise [born 12 Mar. 1921, married James V. Hensley Jr. on 25 July 1954 {he was born 13 Dec. 1924}, and had children: James V. III {born 24 May 1956}; Barbara Louise {born 3 Oct. 1961}]; Douglas Edwin [born 12 Feb. 1923, married Daisy Wallin on 15 Mar. 1942 {she was born 20 Oct. 1921}, and died on 17 Oct. 1950, having had children: Douglas Edwin Jr. {born 16 Oct. 1945, married Judy Evelyn Wallace on 1 June 1969}; Martha Sue {born 23 Mar. 1948, married Carl Michael Sasser on 31 May 1970 <he was born 23 Aug. 1946>, and had children: Dewey Michael <born 6 Aug. 1971>}]).

Nancy Pauline PEEK (born 16 Mar. 1893, married William Tolbert Thompson [he was born 19 May 1892, and died 17 Oct. 1960]).

Dillard Stephen PEEK (born 26 July 1895, married Maggie Ada Ford on 25 Dec. 1921 [she was born 25 May 1898], and had children: Dorothy Inez [born 29 Oct. 1922, married Leonard Wood Davis on 2 Apr. 1945 {he was born 4 June 1919}, and had children: Wayne Durell {born 2 Jan. 1947, married Tana Marie Judd on 18 Dec. 1966 <she was born 7 Feb. 1948>}; Connie Sue {born 17 Sept. 1948, married William David Fisher Jr. <he was born 19 Mar. 1946>, and had children: Shannon Kyle <born 15 Aug. 1970>}; Joyce Elaine {born 10 Dec. 1951, married Jimmy Allen on 10 Oct. 1970 <he was born 8 Jan. 1951>, and had children: Stephen Lance Ephriam <born 30 Jan. 1973>}; Donna Ann {born 24 Sept. 1953}; Karen Gay {born 26 Sept. 1956}; Kenneth Lance {born 21 Nov. 1959}]; Norma Elise [born 23 Dec. 1934]; Anita Faye [born 27 Apr. 1939]).

Virgie Dowel PEEK (born 30 Oct. 1897, married Tilbert Harrison Bice on 17 Mar. 1917 [he was born 27 Sept. 1889, and died 22 Mar. 1958], and had children: Margaret Iola [born 5 May 1918, married Chester Matt Brown on 11 Sept. 1936 {he was born 4 Nov. 1918}, and had children: James Harrison {born 17 June 1937, married Joyce Carol Gentry on 13 May 1961}; Martha Virginia {born 9 Feb. 1939, married Robert Elroy Martin on 1 Jan. 1958 <he was born 23 Apr. 1932>, and had children: Susie Lyn <born 20 Oct. 1962>; Michael Keith <born 25 Apr. 1964>; Connie Jean <born 28 Jan. 1966>}; Chester Matt II {born 30 Jan. 1942, married Gail Ann Buell on 24 Nov. 1963 <she was born 14 July 1944>, and had children: Chester Matt III <born 27 July 1965>; Karen

Marie <born 30 Sept. 1966>; Stephen John <born 3 Aug. 1968>; Juli Ann Denise <born 12 Oct. 1972>}]; Tilbert Harrison Jr. [born 4 Aug. 1924, married Pearlie Mae Boatman on 4 June 1948 {she was born 2 June 1932}, and had children: Kenneth Harrison {born 24 Aug. 1954}]).

Amy Frances PEEK (born 6 June 1900, married William Dow Ensor on 12 Feb. 1922 [he was born 17 Mar. 1896, and died 23 Nov. 1949], had children: Child [born and died Aug. 1922], and died 16 Aug. 1922).

Mary Althea PEEK (born 21 Sept. 1904, married Virgil Clarence Jones on 24 Dec. 1923 [he was born 19 May 1905], and had children: Martha Alene [born 6 Nov. 1924, married Joseph Clarence Britt on 22 Dec. 1967 {he was born 9 Feb. 1936}]).

Vallie Kate PEEK (born 24 June 1907, married George Thomas Choate on 3 Mar. 1945 [he was born 4 Feb. 1910], and had children: Linda Kay [born 24 Jan. 1946, married James Harvey Wynne on 2 Sept. 1965 {he was born 27 Apr. 1944}, and had children: Virginia Katherine {born 7 Jan. 1969}; Amy Elizabeth {born 13 Aug. 1974}]).

Margaret A. PEEK. Born 26 Sept. 1865, married Lee Cantwell, and died 10 Dec. 1887, having had children: *Ridley Lee* (born 6 Dec. 1887).

Robert Lee PEEK. Born 30 Apr. 1867, married Lou Verna Phifer on 10 Oct. 1889 (she was born 18 Jan. 1870, daughter of Joseph P. Phifer and Mary Jane Bradford, remarried Dow Bell in 1894, and died 12 June 1919), and died 3 Feb. 1894, having had children: *Jayanna* (born 9 July 1890, died 6 Dec. 1915); *Arvel* (born 8 Sept. 1895, died 3 Dec. 1913); *Viola* (born 11 July 1897, and died 27 Dec. 1916). Lou and her children all died of tuberculosis, and are buried together in the Brown's Mill Cemetery.

Vance Dillard PEEK. Born 10 Apr. 1869, married Nora Della ___ (div.; she was born 18 Jan. 1874, and died 5 Apr. 1941), and had children:

Martin S. PEEK (born 19 Apr. 1894, married Lelia Belle Lewis on 18 Mar. 1917 [she was born 12 Dec. 1898, and died 18 Feb. 1928], and died 19 Jan. 1960, having had children: Lelia Grace [born 11 June 1918, married Donald L. Winn {he was born 28 Aug. 1921}, and had children: Jean Marie {born 4 Oct. 1943, married Mendell Dicks Morgan Jr. on 7 Dec. 1963 <he was born 29 Nov. 1940>, and had children: Mendell David <born 16 Jan. 1965>}; Donald L. Jr. {born 19 Dec. 1944, married Montine Cannon in Oct. 1965 <she was born Oct. 1944>}]; Nora Jean [born 9 Sept. 1923, married William Harrell Lewis on 15 Apr. 1944 {he was born 15 Dec. 1916}, and had children: William Harrell Jr. {born 15 Apr. 1945, married Marchia K. Anderson on 18 May 1968 <she was born 21 Nov. 1947>, and had children: William Craig <born 8 Dec. 1968>; Bradley Paul <born 2 Mar. 1972>}]).

Mary Maude PEEK (born 26 Nov. 1896, married James Other Hall in 1914 [he died 21 July 1915], and had children: James Lewis [born 21 July 1915, was adopted by his stepfather and used the surname Furman, married Eula Faye Whitson on 11 Aug. 1942 {she was born 1 Nov. 1919}, and had children: Robert Edmond {born 14 June 1943, married Carolyn Carlson on 11 Jan. 1972}; James David {born 1 Apr. 1949}; Patricia Faye {born 23 Nov. 1950, married Thomas Nelson Minyard on 18 Dec. 1971?}]. *Mary Maude HALL* married secondly Robert Wood Furman about 1923, and had children: Kenner Maude [born 25 May 1924, married Ernest Custus Beard on 10 Aug. 1945 {he was born 8 Aug. 1921}, and had children: Michael Furman {born 15 Mar. 1951, married Valerie Kay Shubert on 8 Sept. 1973 <she was born 8 June 1953>}; Laura Ruth {born 8 Dec. 1955}]; Roberta Harriet [born 23 Aug. 1927, married Albert Henry McInnis on 17 Apr. 1948, and had children: Jana Marie {born 18 Apr. 1951}; Jo Ann Bruce {born 2 May 1954}]).

Vance Dillard PEEK married secondly Emma Elizabeth Ferguson about 1907 (she was born 18 July 1872, and died 17 Nov. 1918), and died 13 Mar. 1956, having had children: *Ellen Doris* (born 1 May 1908, married Reino Mikael Rossi on 28 Dec. 1938 [he was born 14 May 1909]); *Dillard Ferguson* (born 17 June 1910, married Marjorie Laraine Thompson, and died 7 Oct. 1939, having had children: Dawson [born 21 Dec. 1936?]); *Evelyn Frances* (born 19 Jan. 1915, married Robert Byrd Chapman on 28 Oct. 1933 [born 2 Sept. 1909], and had children: Janice Eileen [born 28 Dec. 1939, married James E. Lanterman on 29 Aug. 1962 {born 6 June 1939}, and had children: Robert Earl {born 3 May 1964}]; Beverly Diane [born 27 Dec. 1942, married Louis Charles Strohmeyer on 29 Oct. 1961 {he was born 1 May 1936}, and had children: Scott Lee {born 29 Jan. 1967}; Karen Beth {born 27 Sept. 1970}]).

Nancy Jane PEEK Jr. Born 8 Dec. 1871, married James Calvin Matthews (he was born 15 July 1859, and died 2 Mar. 1902), and died 27 Oct. 1895, having had children: *Ridley Beal* (born 9 Dec. 1894, married Sally Gertrude Turney [she was born 9 July 1898], and died 2 Jan. 1969, having had children: Jessie Arnold [born 19 Nov. 1919, married John Bright Miller on 30 Dec. 1941 {he was born 20 Nov. 1920}, and had children: Rebecca Jean {born 6 Nov. 1946}; John Stephen {born 18 Oct. 1948}; Sandra Jo Anne {born 28 May 1959}]; James Harold [born 23 Oct. 1921, married Ethel Mae Mendenhall on 31 Aug. 1948 {she was born 30 Jan. 1929}, and had children: Raymond Lawrence {born 5 July 1949}; Regina Lee {born 6 Oct. 1950, married Habib Mouflen Salloum on 1 Sept. 1972}; Duane Clark {born 19 Dec. 1951}; Douglas Carl {born 16 Jan. 1953}; Deborah Lynn {born 21 Mar. 1954}; Renee Corrine {born 19 Jan. 1957}]; Larry Doyle [born 7 Jan. 1923, married Therese Marie Sanders on 3 Apr. 1946 {she was born 29 June 1927}, and had children: Anita Marie {born 1 Apr. 1947, married Michael David Pologi on 20 Apr. 1968 <he was born 30 May 1945>, and had children: Kenneth Alan <born 30 Jan. 1970, died 31 Jan. 1970>; Tara Marie <born 21 Jan. 1972>}; Jerry Wayne {born 21 Jan. 1951, married Kathleen Frances Disalvo <she was born 3 Jan. 1952>}]; Carlos Leroy [born 22 Sept. 1925, married Frances Jane Wohnhas on 27 Aug. 1948 {she was born 20 June 1927}, and had children: Peggy Ann {born 21 Dec. 1949, married Marc William Messaros on 26 June 1971 <he was born 3 Sept. 1948>}; Alan Frank {born 12 Mar. 1953}]; Norma Jean [born 15 Dec. 1927, married Glenn Robert Burkholder on 11 Sept. 1948 {he was born 6 Aug. 1919}, and had children: Bruce Allen {born 9 Jan. 1951}; Mark Alvin {born 11 Nov. 1953}]).

Dorinda C. PEEK. Born 26 Mar. 1874, married Robert Lee Davis (he was born 27 Feb. 1870, and died 22 Feb. 1917), and died 3 Jan. 1913, having had children:

Oscar Wesley DAVIS (born 6 May 1893, married Myrtle Chandler on 5 June 1923 [she was born 3 Oct. 1897], and had children: Dorena).

Lillie Lee DAVIS (born 30 Oct. 1897, married Marshall Lee Wright on 15 June 1919 [he was born 16 Aug. 1895], and died 26 May 1963).

Ben Wheeler DAVIS (born 13 Feb. 1902, married Carris Mai Kirby on 9 June 1926 [she was born 9 June 1905], and had children: Frances Madeline [born 22 Dec. 1927, married Max William Coulton on 6 Jan. 1945, and had children: Karen Mai {born 11 July 1948, married Klein Shaw Gilhousen <he was born 13 Apr. 1942>, and had children: April Louise <born 6 Feb. 1969>; Phillip Jason <born 25 Oct. 1972>}; Terry Allen {born 18 July 1950, married Marie Quattrocchi on 25 Aug. 1972}; Cathy Lynn {born 21 Jan. 1952, married Victor Van Decarr on 20 Feb. 1971, and had children: Rachel Ann}; Frances Madeline married secondly Rex Lance Frame {he was born 21 Apr. 1925}, and had children: Kevin Patrick Madwell]; Thelma Joyce [born 5 Jan. 1931, married Robert Charles Drewyor {div.}, and had children: Barbara Caroline {born 17 Apr. 1950, married Stanley David Getter on 30 Sept. 1967, and had children: Carrie Dianne <born 18 Sept. 1968>}; Roxanne Marie {born 5 Aug. 1952}; Kenneth Archer {born 29 Aug. 1956}; Robert Charles {born 1 June 1958}; Brian Michael {born 7 Apr. 1965}]; Shirley Pauline [born 1 Apr. 1933, married Earl Leroy House on 2 Sept. 1950 {he was born 19 May 1928}, and had children: Stephen; Joel; Jeff]; David Gerald [born 5 Apr. 1944, married Judy McKee on 3 Feb. 1963 {she was born 8 Dec. 1942}, and had children: Michael Allen {born 27 Feb. 1964}; Christine Lynne {born 10 Apr. 1971}]).

Teddy Talmadge DAVIS (born 20 Sept. 1904, died 22 Dec. 1918).

Sadie Francis DAVIS (born 19 Nov. 1906, and died unmarried on 15 Sept. 1966).

Nola DAVIS (born 25 Feb. 1909, married Henry Young Thompson on 15 Feb. 1930 [he was born 10 Feb. 1905], and had children: Walter Leon [born 26 June 1935, died 6 Aug. 1941]; Norma Jean [born 17 June 1938, married Dudley J. Delffs <he was born 21 Sept. 1929>]; Janice Marie [born 24 Oct. 1948, married Carle Weaks Jr. on 23 Sept. 1967 {he was born 9 Aug. 1944}]).

Robert Lee DAVIS Jr. (born 27 May 1911, married Maggie Goodwin, and had children: Talmadge; Bobbie Charles).

John Porter PEEK. Born 11 Mar. 1875, died 26 Aug. 1886.

Mary Dee PEEK. Born 26 Jan. 1878, married Albert Lon "Abbie" Boatman (he was born 18 Dec. 1871, and died 10 June 1951), and died on 19 Mar. 1954, having had children:

Cora Alma BOATMAN (born 14 Nov. 1894, married Louis Homer Carr on 24 Dec. 1919 [he was born 23 Jan. 1893], and had children: Homer Horace [born 7 Sept. 1920, married Lillian Marie Whitson on 8 Sept. 1943 {she was born 30 Nov. 1917}, and had children: Gary Gene {born 15 Dec. 1946}; Carolyn Marie {born 1 Feb. 1951}; Jimmy David {born 26 Jan. 1953}; Robert Horace {born 1 Apr. 1954}]; Eva Mildred [born 16 Nov. 1921, married George W. Miller on 29 June 1942, and had children: Barbara Aline {born 18 Mar. 1944}; Ronald Myrl {born 16 Aug. 1945}; Donald Gerald {born 13 Mar. 1947}; George Gaylan {born 11 May 1949}; Shirley Ann {born 8 Sept. 1956}; Debbie Sue {born 20 Mar. 1958}]; Bolivar Howard [born 29 Nov. 1922, married Nettie Jim Johnson on 19 Feb. 1947 {she was born 15 Feb. 1928}, and had children: Linda Carol {born 19 Dec. 1953}; Billy Gene {born 20 Mar. 1957}]; Donald Hubert [born 3 Nov. 1923]; Myrl Louis [born 9 Mar. 1926, died 3 Feb. 1945]; Mabel Emmogene [born 22 Apr. 1927, married Howard McCulley in Mar. 1946 {he was born 19 Mar. 1922}, and had children: Jerry Wayne {born 28 June 1946}; Sandra Faye {born 20 Aug. 1949}; Diane Yvonne {born 14 Nov. 1951}; Phillip Alan {born 4 Feb. 1957}]; Olcie Lee [born 23 Sept. 1928, married Amy Jewel Whitson Gates on 2 July 1967 {she was born 4 May 1926}]; Norma Faye [born 28 Oct. 1935, married Norman Oliver Pheasant on 25 Aug. 1954 {he was born 3 Nov. 1932}, and had children: Richard Mark {born 11 Sept. 1957}; Kevil Neal {born 17 Nov. 1962}]).

Charlie Clarence BOATMAN (born 3 Oct. 1896, married Dora Thompson [div.], and had children: Elsie May [born 6 Oct. 1918, married Gilbert Crabtree on 10 Dec. 1940 {he was born 30 Oct. 1914}, and had children: David Harvey {born 9 Nov. 1941}; Frieda Dianne {born 19 Jan. 1944, married Cecil Eugene Holder on 1 Aug. 1964 <he was born 16 Aug. 1940>}; Jeffrey Lynn {born 30 Aug. 1945, married Geneva Fay Clark on 26 Dec. 1969}]. *Charlie BOATMAN* married secondly Lillian Aline Davidson on 14 Dec. 1924 [she was born 18 Oct. 1905], and had children: Mary Emmeline [born 17 Oct. 1925, married Noble Howard on 24 July 1948 {he was born 8 Oct. 1923}, and had children: Brenda Jean {born 2 May 1949}; William Noble {born 17 Sept. 1954}]; Hallie Christine [born 13 July 1927, married Robert Lynn Draper on 31 Aug. 1952 {he was born 21 June 1918}, and had children: Adelia Lynn {born 29 Aug. 1955}; Mary Ann {born 27 May 1958}]).

Robert Edgar BOATMAN (born 21 Dec. 1898, died 23 Sept. 1902).

Nancy Alice BOATMAN (born 13 Sept. 1901, married Joe Spiros Corones on 25 June 1919 [he was born 25 Oct. 1896, and died 24 Dec. 1970], and had children: Jimmie S. [born 20 Apr. 1921]; Johnny [born 18 Dec. 1922, died 16 May 1924]; Marian [born 15 May 1924]; Lee T. [born 7 July 1925, married Emmy Lou Miller on 14 May 1944 {born 25 June 1927}, and had children: Joseph Lee {born 10 Aug. 1945}; Cathy {born 13 Jan. 1948}; Johnny {born 13 Sept. 1953}]. *Nancy CORONES* married secondly Walter Baine Barr on 2 Aug. 1937 [he was born 2 Mar. 1884, and died 1956]).

Harvey Lee BOATMAN (born 27 Apr. 1903, married Clara Genevia McElroy on 8 Mar. 1937 [she was born 16 May 1904], and had children: Jimmie Lee [twin; born 14 Aug. 1938, married Sherly Anna Turner on 30 Dec. __ {she was born 5 Apr. 1942}, and had children: Donna Coleen {born 26 Aug. 1960}; Robert W. {born 26 Jan. 1962}; James Otis {born 31 Jan. 1964}; Jesse Lee {born 7 July 1965}]; Jesse Gordon [twin; born 14 Aug. 1938, married Kathryn Louise Herlevic on 6 Feb. 1970 {she was born 11 Dec. 1941}, and had children: Mary Kathryn {born 8 Apr. 1961}; Pamela Gail {born 6 June 1963}; Thomas Lee {born 5 Oct. 1964}]).

Zebedee BOATMAN (born 10 May 1905, married Ann Thomas on 18 June 1929 [she was born 14 May 1907], and died 7 Oct. 1966, having had children: Fred Carl [born 11 Jan. 1935, married Coleen Terese Airhart on 8 Sept. 1962 {she was born 17 Mar. 1939}, and had children: Kenneth Joseph {born 27 Sept. 1963}; Kathleen Marie {born 23 Oct. 1965}; Kevin Joseph {born 12 July 1968}]; Carolyn Ann [born 16 Dec. 1939, married Thomas James Waldron on 20 Nov. 1960 {he was born 17 Feb. 1938}, and had children: Thomas James Jr. {born 11 Aug. 1961}; Evelyn Ann {born 4 Oct. 1962}; James Andrew {born 4 Jan. 1965}; Gregg Callen {born 28 Nov. 1967}]).

Vaughda Frances BOATMAN (born 31 July 1907, died 4 Aug. 1908).

Vallie Dimple BOATMAN (born 16 May 1909, married Wilber Osmer Brown on 27 Apr. 1941 [he was born 5 Oct. 1904], and had children: Robert Louis [born 1 Feb. 1943, married Paula Jim Robertson on 14 May 1969 {she was born 21 July 1946}, and had children: Michael Robert {born 28 Mar. 1974}]; David Eugene [born 19 May 1947]; Mary Frances [born 4 May 1950, married John C. Wood on 29 June 1973 {he was born 8 Mar. 1946}]).

Venoy Ernestine BOATMAN (born 8 Sept. 1913, married William Kelly Ament on 29 Oct. 1938 [he was born 6 July 1913], and had children: Joan Pearl [born 21 Mar. 1941, married James Roy Constant on 16 Apr. 1960 {he was born 9 Dec. 1934}, and had children: Jay Deane {born 3 Mar. 1963}; Rhonda Jo {born 4 Aug. 1964}]; William Keith [born 6 Dec. 1942, married Sally Cowen on 11 Mar. 1967 {she was born 25 Sept. 1946}, and had children: Byron Keith {born 19 Apr. 1965}; Robert Kelly {born 22 Oct. 1970}]).

Fred Ray BOATMAN (born 8 Feb. 1916, married Willette Brotherton [she was born 27 Sept. 1916], and died on 4 July 1970, having had children: Ronnie Ray [born 31 Jan. 1942, married Betty Jo Smallwood on 28 Oct. 1963 {she was born 23 Feb. 1946}, and had children: Ronnie Ray Jr. {born 8 Oct. 1964}; Michael Shawn {born 31 Jan. 1973}]; Kathy Marie [born 21 Dec. 1954]; Jeffery Lynn [born 25 Dec. 1955]).

Bethley Blanton BOATMAN (born 16 Apr. 1919, married Christine Pippin on 13 June 1944, and had children: Arkley Douglas [born 20 June 1942]; *Bethley* married secondly Cleatus Ovella Luna on 8 Mar. 1947 [she was born 19 Oct. 1928], and had children: Brenda Sue [born 20 June 1948, married Gary Dalton Mayberry on 9 Aug. 1968 {he was born 4 Oct. 1946}, and had children: Angela Rechelle {born 19 July 1969}; Wanda Gay {born 22 Oct. 1953}]).

Margaret May BOATMAN (born 31 May 1921, married Ralph Bullington on 22 Sept. 1942 [he was born 31 Mar. 1917, and died 13 June 1944], and had children: Stanley Ralph [born 28 July 1943, married Judy Boyd on 9 Oct. 1964, and had children: Timothy Boyd {born 18 Sept. 1966}; married secondly Joyce Marie Owens]. *Margaret BULLINGTON* married secondly Grady DeWitt Smith on 12 Nov. 1947 [he was born 19 Apr. 1914]).

The PEEKS are listed in the 1860-80 censuses for Putnam Co., TN (1870 in the 15th District, 1880 in the 1st District). **Nancy PEEK** died on 16 Oct. 1891 in Putnam Co., and is buried with her husband in the Salem Cemetery.

6h. **Dorinda "Deanna."** Born 1 Jan. 1842 in White (later Putnam) Co., TN. Married Isaac E. Lollar about 1862 (he was born 23 Feb. 1842, and died 20 May 1870, buried Howard Cemetery), and had children:

Lizzie LOLLAR. Born 15 Apr. 1863, married John Adam Rice (he was born 27 Apr. 1860, and died 19 Sept. 1940), and died 4 Oct. 1942, having had children: *Ada* (married Foster Daniels, and had children: Elizabeth [married ___ Hale]; Louise); *Norma Elizabeth*; *Sara Reta* (born 15 June 1891, married Sam Jones [he was born 1 Mar. 1884, and died 13 Dec. 1957], and died 6 Nov. 1967, having had children: Gladys [married Hasten Dotson]; Dot [married Johnny Bradford]; Lellinwin [married Clifford Lollar]; Willine [married ___ Clark]); *Amy Ethel* (born 24 Feb. 1893, died 21 Feb. 1971); *Carl* (born 30 Dec. 1896, died 12 May 1908); *Velma* (born 21 Sept. 1900, married Whitten Wright, and had children: Oliver James [born 27 Aug. 1921, married Peggy Lee, and had children: James Lee; married secondly Adele Kay Peabyhouse on 1 Oct. 1970 {she was born 29 Oct. 1927}]); *Odis Dillard* (born 1 Oct. 1902, married Ethel Cunningham, and had children: Bethel [born 1922, married Bricy Stamps]; Betty Jean [born 1932, married Lemon Bray, and had children: Sharon; Lequida; Tim; Betty married secondly W. C. Burgess, and had children: Lesa]); *Oakley V.* (born 21 Mar. 1904); *Oliver* (born 22 Sept. 1906, married Elizabeth Hunter on 31 May 1937).

James Waymon LOLLAR. Born 12 Apr. 1865, married Sarah V. ___ about 1889 (she was born 24 May 1871, and died 28 July 1890), and secondly Matilda G. ___ about 1892, and died 15 Jan. 1950, having had children: *Norma* (born 20 Jan. 1893, died 5 Jan. 1969); *Hobert* (born 1896, married Tilla Presley, and had children: Robert; Delbert; Erma; *Hobert* married secondly Lillian Trobaugh); *Claude*; *Reed* (born 1901, married Erma Jones, and died 1956, having had children: Billie Reed [born 23 Feb. 1932, married Kathleen Rogers {she was born 10 Jan. 1934}, and had children: Billy Rogers {born 18 Jan. 1952}; Robert Reed {born 9 Sept. 1961}]; James D. [married Harriet Hays, and had children: James Michael; Victor; Paul Anthony]; Leslie Tony [married Joe Brumbalough, and had children: Vicky]; Myrl Dean [married Kendrick Mullins, and had children: Mary Beth]); *Willie* (married ___ Trobaugh, and had children: Waymon; Helen); *Bertha* (married Haskel Martin, and had children: Printiss; Kenneth); *Pearl* (married Harold Ruppert); *Hugh*; *Clay*.

Leoma LOLLAR. Born 20 Aug. 1867, married George Monroe Howell (he was born 17 Aug. 1860, and died 10 Jan. 1949, and is buried with his wife in the Boiling Springs Cemetery), and died 1944, having had children: *Tillman Cantrel* (born 28 Aug. 1884, married Ella Meyers, and had children: Haskell [married Margaret ___]; Willard [married Eileen ___]; *Tillman HOWELL* died on 3 Feb. 1917, buried Boiling Springs Cemetery); *Dorina* (born 15 July 1886, married Haskel Farley and secondly Will Sadler, and died 18 Nov. 1975); *Claude* (born 20 July 1888, married Amanda Williams, and died 1 Jan. 1969); *George Leslie* (born 20 Feb. 1890, married Brimy Judd, and died on 18 May 1974); *Isaac Rustus* (born 21 Mar. 1892, died Mar. 1977, buried Boiling Springs Cemetery); *Mansfield* (born 5 Mar. 1894, married Bessie Cash [she was born 28 Mar. 1909], died June 1983); *James Dexter* (born 6 Nov. 1897, married Edith Ford, had children: Richard, and died 28 Apr. 1967); *Richard Elmer* (born 16 May 1899, and died 11 Nov. 1918, buried Boiling Springs Cemetery); *Shelia* (born 20 Aug. 1901, married Ella Howell, and died Sept. 1987, having had children: Betty Sue [married James Langford]; Donald [married Betty A. Flatt]; Bobby [married Barbara ___]; Harold [married Patsey ___]); *Una* (born 11 Dec. 1903, married Clay Hicks, and died 9 Nov. 1991, having had children: Marie [married James Key, and had children: Patricia; Betty]; Helen [married Keith Jones, and had children: Alan]; Earl); *Dillard* (born 29 Apr. 1906, married Ina Stultz, and had children: Daughter [born and died 30 Jan. 1925, buried Boiling Springs Cemetery]; Winell [born 2 Dec. 1926, married Bessie Lee Martin {she was born 29 June 1933}]; Dimple [born 26 Dec. 1929, married Delbert Elrod]; Wilene [born 20 Apr. 1932, married Lillard Maxwell {he was born 4 Sept. 1929}]; Joyce [born 11 Nov. 1932, married James Robert Bean {he was born 31 Dec. 1934}, and had children: Mario Robert {born 21 Apr. 1972}]; Lorraine [born 5 Mar. 1940]); *Erby* (born 29 Aug. 1909, married Esther Knowland, and had children: James); *Ina* (born 10 Sept. 190_, married Wallace Browder).

Dorinda LOLLAR married secondly William Massa about 1877 (he was born 1831, and died 31 Jan. 1891), and had children:

Addaville MASSA. Born 21 May 1878, married Columbus Robert Howell (he was born 28 Jan. 1872, and died 4 May 1960, and is buried with his wife in the Boiling Springs Cemetery), and died 26 [or 21] Jan. 1943, having had children: *Gina* (born 24 Aug. 1895, married Oliver Bussell [born 24 Jan. 1892, and died 10 May 1963, buried with wife in Boiling Springs Cemetery], and died 19 Nov. 1965, having had children: Aradell [married Wanda Waites]; Artis [married Charlene Thompson]; Berie [married Betty Whitehead]); *Erma Gladys* (born 4 Feb. 1900, married Benton Worley, and died 29 Dec. 1922, buried Boiling Springs Cemetery, having had children: Lorraine); *Estes Clemie* (born 10 May 1902, married Flossie Lafevor, and died on 11 Sept. 1950, buried Boiling Springs Cemetery); *Orville Ertle* (born 1 Mar. 1904, married Bertha Cunningham, and had children: Orville Ertle Jr. [married Opal Morgan]; Carlos D. [married Elsie Thomas]); *Orley Dexter* (born 6 Sept. 1907, married Stella Cunningham, and died Apr. 1985, having had children: Shirley [married Ray Cannon]; Marlene [married John

Newland]); *Hobert Clifton* (born 2 Sept. 1910, married Manelle Maxwell, and had children: Faye [married Eldon Carwald]).

***Dillard* MASSA.** Born 2 Feb. 1880, married Nancy Farley and had children: *Lola F.* (born 12 Oct. 1906, married Emmett E. Smartt, and died 3 Apr. 1948); *Mildred B.* (married Arthur Piepmier); *James D.* (married Betty ___, and had children: Mike; Mark). ***Dillard* MASSA** married secondly Callie Brown, and died 5 Aug. 1956.

***Norman* MASSA.** Born 12 Apr. 1881, married Elizabeth Brown (she was born 18 July 1881, and died 13 June 1953), and died 6 Apr. 1947, having had children: *Clifford Thurman* (born 3 Apr. 1907, married Henrietta Jared, and died 25 Apr. 1958, having had children: Clifford Thurman Jr. [married ___ Bowman, and had children: Barbara]).

***Oakley Dexter* MASSA.** Born 19 Oct. 1882, married Mattie Stanton (she was born 28 Dec. 1890), and died 30 Mar. 1952, having had children: *William Stanton* (born 11 Jan. 1912, married Hazel Wallace [she was born 25 Apr. 1912], and had children: Margaret [born 2 Apr. 1938, married George Dixon Jr., and had children: Elizabeth Ann {born 24 Dec. 1959}; Katherine Ruth {born 18 Jan. 1961}; George III {born 30 Jan. 1962}]; William Stanton Jr. [born 1 Oct. 1942, married Pat Tracy, and had children: William Stanton III {born 17 Nov. 1961}; Philip {born 13 Dec. 1965}]; *William S. MASSA* married secondly Margaret Hembre [she was born 27 Nov. 1912]); *Ruth* (born 18 Sept. 1922).

***Adar* MASSA.** Born 4 June 1885, and died unmarried on 17 Oct. 1904.

Dorinda MASSA was living with her father in 1860-70, and with George Massa in 1880 in the 16th Civil District, Putnam Co., TN. She died on 10 Dec. 1916 in Putnam Co., TN, and is buried in the Boiling Springs Cemetery.

6i. **Charles Lafayette.** Born 27 Sept. 1843 in White (later Putnam) Co., TN. See below for full entry.

6j. **Vance Dekalb.** Born 17 Oct. 1845 in White (later Putnam) Co., TN. See below for full entry.

6k. **Margaret (VII) "Peggy."** Born 3 Sept. 1847 in White (later Putnam) Co., TN. Married Isaac Ephram Elrod about 1870 (he was born 22 Feb. 1836, and died 2 Apr. 1919), and had nine children, including: *Charles* (born 1871); *William* (born 1873); *John* (born 1875); *Mary S.* (born 6 June 1880, died 3 Jan. 1933, buried with her parents); *Leana* (born Feb. 1888); *James* (born Oct. 1890). The Elrods had moved to Johnson Co., IL by Aug. 1873, to Pottersville, Howell Co., MO by 1877, to Ava, Douglas Co., MO by 1879, and to Norwood, Wright Co., MO by 1881, where they are listed in the 1900 census for Clark Township. By Mar. 1906 the Elrods were living in Indian Territory (later Oklahoma). Peggy Elrod died on 30 Oct. 1922 in Wright Co., MO, and is buried with her husband in the Retherford Cemetery, near Norwood, MO. A granddaughter, Imojeanne Lawson, lives at Montrose, MO.

"Norwood, Wright County, Mo., January the 12th 1887. Dear Mother, I will write you a letter to let you know I received your kind [letter] and was proud to hear from you but I am awful sorrow to hear of the death of my dear father. I will never see him no more in this world but I hope wee [sic] will meet in heaven where there will be no sickness. Mother, your letter did ask me who was advising me. There is no body advising me. But I heared my father was dead & I could not get any more news. I wrot & could not get no answer. I did write to Mr. Capshaw in Cookville to let me know how things lay. I would a come in there last summer to seen you all but my helth was bad. I had plenty of money to come on. So no more a bout that. Mother, I wish I could see you one time more. I only come in to see you but if I come I will not come until the weather gets warm, and I will have time to hear from you before I start. My helth is better now than it has bin in a long time. Give me best respects to all my brothers & sisters & friends. As to the estate I only want a equal part with the rest. Write to me as soon as you get this letter & give me the news. So no more but remains your loving daughter until I dye. Margart Elrod to Margrit Burgess."

6l. **(Mary) Leoma.** Born 29 May 1850 in White (later Putnam) Co., TN. Married John Jefferson Lollar about 1868 (he was born 5 Dec. 1848 [or 1846], and died on 22 May 1918), and had children: *Robert Alonzo* (born 15 Dec. 1869, married Rebecca Martin, and died 7 May 1942); *Isaac* (born 4 Aug. 1871, died 1892); *(Margaret) Vernia* (born 19 July 1873, married Lum Elrod, and died 1954); *Winfield* (born 2 Oct. 1875, died 31 Oct. 1875); *Joseph Samuel* (born 2 May 1878, married Sarah Almedia Worley on 29 Aug. 1899 [she died on 18 July 1907], and secondly Ella Avo Goolsby [she was born 24 Sept. 1884, and died 12 Apr. 1967], and died 14 Apr. 1944); *Dillard Monroe* (born 16 Oct. 1880, married Georgia Lambert [she was born 23 Jan. 1889, and died 7 Dec. 1910], and secondly Fannie Goolsby, and died 13 Aug. 1942); *Mentia* (born 28 Mar. 1883, married Riley Johnson, and had children: Holly; Cleo); *Wayne Franklin* (born 22 Mar. 1885, married Annie Gossage [she was born 28 Sept. 1884, and died 7 July 1972]); *Jane* (born 19 May 1888, married Jim Judd, died May 1973); *Dorinda* (born 19 Dec. 1890, married Norman Slagle). Listed in the 1880 census for the 16th Civil District, Putnam Co., TN. Leoma Lollar died on 3 Nov. 1926, and is buried with her husband in the Howard Cemetery.

6m. **Winfield Scott.** Born 25 Feb. 1852 in White (later Putnam) Co., TN. See below for full entry.

[William (I)[1], Edward (I)[2], Reuben (I)[3], Thomas (I)[4], Charles Hunter[5]]

WILLIAM SIMPSON BURGESS
(1830-1905)
OF WHITE COUNTY, TENNESSEE

6b. **William Simpson** *[son of Charles Hunter].* Born 24 Aug. 1830 in White (later Putnam) Co., TN. Married Ricy Ozenia Barnes on 13 Mar. 1855 (she was born 3 June 1834, and died 13 Feb. [or Mar. or Dec.] 1912). Listed in the 1860-1900 censuses for White Co. In 1851 William Burgess started for California, but stopped to spend three years in Kansas and Missouri. He returned to Tennessee in 1854, where he purchased 1200 acres of land in what is now White Co. (*Deed Book #U*, p. 92, 1861). He enlisted on 15 Sept. 1862 in White Co. in the 8th Tennessee Cavalry, Confederate Army, during the Civil War, serving as a Sergeant in that unit and also in Co. H, 13th Tennessee Cavalry. He was captured in 15 Dec. 1864 at Athens, TN, but was released on parole the following spring. William S. Burgess was a farmer in Putnam and White Cos., TN. With his brother, Winfield Burgess, he owned a large water mill on the first three falls of the Falling Water River, on the border between White and Putnam Cos.; the land was later donated to the State of Tennessee to become Burgess Falls State Park. He died on 30 July 1905 in White Co., and is buried with his wife in the Cherry Creek Presbyterian Church Cemetery, White Co., TN. His biography appears in *The Goodspeed Histories of Cannon, Coffee, DeKalb, Warren, and White Counties* (Nashville, TN: Goodspeed Publishing Co., 1887, p. 862-63):

"William S. Burgess, a prominent citizen and a well-known enterprising planter of White County, and resident of the Twelfth Civil District, was born in Putnam County August 24, 1830. He is the son of Charles and Margaret (McBride) Burgess. His father was of Irish descent, a native of North Carolina, born in that State in 1806, and died in Putnam County December 6, 1886. He was engaged in agricultural pursuits, and made life a fair success. He was a member of the Christian Church, and died in that faith. Mr. Burgess' mother's ancestors came from Scotland. She was a native of White County, born in 1808. She is still living, a resident of Putnam County. Mr. Burgess is the second of thirteen children. He secured a common-school education, which has been supplemented by extensive reading. At the age of twenty-one, he went West with the intention of going to California, but when he reached Missouri, unfavorable news of the Pacific Coast caused him to stop in that State. He was one of the first settlers of Kansas. For three years he gave his attention to farming in Kansas and Missouri. In 1854 he returned to his father's home, and purchased a farm in White County, where he lived five or six years. In the Fall of 1862 he entered the Confederate States Army, and joined the Eighth Regiment of Cavalry, commanded by General Dibrell. He served with credit the remainder of the war with this general, and took part in many of the battles and skirmishes fought. December 1864 he was captured while on a scouting expedition, and kept prisoner of war until the Battle of Nashville. In the Spring of 1865, after an absence of three years, he returned home and resumed farming. Mr. Burgess has been an active business man. He began with nothing but an honest heart and a strong will, and now owns 1,200 acres of land in White County, also a half-interest in a large water mill on Falling Water Creek, near the Putnam County line. The falls on the streams are remarkable beyond description. There are four falls, Mr. Burgess and his younger brother, Winfield, owning the first three. On March 13, 1855 he was united in marriage to Miss Ricy O. Barnes, a most excellent lady, who was born June 14, 1834, and reared in White County. To this union have been born three children—one son and two daughters. Although not a member of the church, Mr. Burgess and wife are in sympathy with the Baptist Church."

The Children of William S. Burgess:

7a. **(Thomas) Alonzo.** Born 5 July 1860 in White Co., TN. See below for full entry.

7b. **Mary Louise (I).** Born 24 Nov. 1863 in White Co., TN; died there unmarried on 29 Oct. 1881, and is buried in the Cherry Creek Presbyterian Church Cemetery.

7c. **Alice (IV).** Born 17 Aug. 1867 in White Co., TN. Married A. Sid Alcorn on 24 Dec. 1885 (he was born 28 Mar. 1863, and died 19 Jan. 1921), and had children:

Robert Simpson ALCORN. Born 2 Apr. 1887, married Mary E. Matlock on 24 Dec. 1913 (she was born 30 Oct. 1890, and died Sept. 1974 at Pleasant Hill, TN), and died 1957, buried with his wife in the O'Conner Cemetery.

Sam ALCORN. Born 20 Apr. 1889, married Rennie Sullivan on 3 Aug. 1922 and secondly Golden ___ on 25 Apr. 1924, and died on 24 Sept. 1961.

Minnie ALCORN. Born 24 Sept. 1892, married Lonnie Stewart, and died on 2 Feb. 1961, having had children: *William Sidney* (born 23 Dec. 1920, married Rose M. Sherrell [she was born 20 Apr. 1919], and had children: Lutricia [born 26 Mar. 1941, married Wallace Neal, and had children: Stanley {born 7 Dec. 1969}]).

Will A. ALCORN. Born 12 Dec. 1894, married Florence Whitson (she was born 10 Mar. 1896, and died on 1 Aug. 1971), having had children: *Alec* (married Rennie Hart); *Eugene* (born 11 Oct. 1920, married Mary Ruth Peck [she was born 25 Aug. 1924]); *Fred* (born 10 Aug. 1924, married Mildred Swindle [she was born 23 Nov. 1932], and had children: Deborah [born 15 Feb. 1955]; Sherry [born 26 Dec. 1957]); *Albert* (married ___ Jones). ***Will ALCORN*** died on 3 Oct. 1952, and is buried with his wife in the O'Conner Cemetery.

Althea ALCORN. Born 19 Jan. 1897, married Dallas Carmichael England (he was born 23 June 1893, and died on 13 Feb. 1960, buried O'Conner Cemetery), and died Jan. 1982 at Sparta, TN, having had children: *Mary Alice* (born 22 June 1916, married Joe Little [he was born 6 Dec. 1915], and had children: Joe P. [born 4 Feb. 1940, married Becky Ford {she was born 19 Sept. 1940}, and had children: James Ford {born 24 Mar. 1964}; John P. {born 19 Sept. 1966}; Mary Elizabeth {born 7 July 1970}]; Betty L. [married ___ Evans]); *Son* (born and died 17 Dec. 1917, buried with his parents); *Eloise* (born 13 May 1921, married James L. Massey); *Jean* (born 5 Nov. 1924, married Carlyle Ruttledge, and had children: Dwight R. [born 3 June 1946, married Karen ___, and had children: Amy {born 2 Feb. 1971}; Child {born 15 Jan. 1975}]); *Don* (born 7 Nov. 1933, married Kay Hasten [she was born July 1932], and had children: Deborah E. [born 23 Apr. 1956, married Ronald Foster]; David E. [born 29 Dec. 1958]; Lori E. [born 13 May 1970]).

Encina ALCORN. Born 30 Oct. 1899, died unmarried on 1 Feb. 1931.

Carabell ALCORN. Born 21 Feb. 1902, married Frank Fisher on 31 Aug. 1921 (he was born 21 Aug. 1896), and had children: *Frank Jr.* (born 20 July 1922, married Anna Boguslasuski on 10 Feb. 1944 [she was born 26 Feb. 1917], and had children: Mary Carolyn [married Angelo D. Angelus, and had children: Brad {born 12 Aug. 1974}; Adam {born 16 Jan. 1976}]); *Shirley A.*

Josephine ALCORN. Born 20 July 1908 (or 1906), married Frank Sullivan on 6 Jan. 1924, and had children: *Richard Denton* (born 22 Jan. 1925, married Wilene Eller [she was born 21 Apr. 1923], and died on 22 June 1966, buried O'Conner Cemetery, having had children: Richard Lynn [born 28 Dec. 1947, died 17 Sept. 1961, buried with his father]; Judy Sharon [born 6 Feb. 1951]). ***Josephine SULLIVAN*** married secondly Van England (he was born 9 Jan. 1908, and died on 10 Aug. 1964), and died on 9 Sept. 1992 at Sparta, TN.

Alice ALCORN died on 18 May 1941, and is buried with her husband in the O'Conner Cemetery.

ALONZO BURGESS OF WHITE CO., TENNESSEE

[William Simpson[6]]

7a. **(Thomas) Alonzo** *[son of William Simpson].* Born 5 July 1860 in White Co., TN. Married (Sarah) Emiline "Emma" Terry on 16 Mar. 1882 (she was born 31 Aug. 1862, daughter of Elijah Washington Terry and Angeline Abigail Campbell Denton, sister of Jesse Vincent Terry, and granddaughter of Samuel Denton [who furnished the cotton bales for the breastworks of Andrew Jackson at the Battle of New Orleans in 1815], and died on 24 Feb. 1931). Listed in the 1900-20 censuses for White Co., TN. Alonzo Burgess was a farmer, miller, and lumberman in White Co., TN. He died there of pneumonia on 10 Mar. 1937, and is buried with his wife in the Cherry Creek Presbyterian Church Cemetery.

8a. **Mertie Lou (I).** Born 2 Apr. 1883 in White Co., TN. Married William Aaron Miller on 27 Dec. 1898 in White Co. (he was born 4 Jan. 1877, and died 1955), and had children: *Jule* (born 14 Sept. 1900, married Collon Miller Johnson on 18 Sept. 1920 [he was born 25 Sept. 1891, and died 2 Mar. 1966], and died May 1989, having had children: Louise [born 16 July 1921, married Norman Kemper, and had children: Norma Elaine {married Jimmie Harris, and had children: Amy Louise}; Lavenia Jo {married William Colleen}; William Collon]; Joe [born 18 Aug. 1927, married Lavena Brooker]); *James S.* (born 9 May 1902, died 1 June 1902); *Joe Everett* (born 29 Sept. 1908, married Mae ___, and died Dec. 1973 at Detroit, MI, having had children: Agnes Louise; Ray); *Herbert*

Gaines (born 29 Feb. 1916, married Thelma Harvey, and died on 20 May 1993 at Cookeville, TN, buried at Haleyville, AL, having had children: Herbert Gaines Jr. [born 13 Feb. 1939, married secondly Vernelle Hicks, and had children: (William) David {born 12 Nov. 1955 at Haleyville, AL, married Deborah Faye Thrasher, and had children: Isaac Chase <born 15 Nov. 1985 at Jasper, AL>; Kathrine Blaine <born 11 Aug. 1988 at Jasper, AL>; David Miller is a carpet salesman in Alabama}]). Mertie Miller died on 12 Apr. 1954 in White Co., and is buried in the Cherry Creek Presbyterian Church Cemetery. Herbert Miller Sr. lives at Dixon, Pulaski Co., MO.

8b. **(Lucy) Lela (I).** Born 26 Oct. 1884 in White Co., TN; died there unmarried on 13 Aug. 1898, and is buried in the Cherry Creek Presbyterian Church Cemetery.

8c. **Robert Taylor.** Born 8 Oct. 1886 in White Co., TN. See below for full entry.

8d. **Daisy Angeline.** Her middle name is also given as Angelina. Born 9 Nov. 1888 in White Co., TN. Married T. J. R. "Bud" Scott in 1903 (he was born 14 June 1880, and died 12 Nov. 1906); married secondly David L. Scott about 1908 (he was born 26 Apr. 1886, and died 29 Oct. 1957), having had children: *General W.* (born 20 Jan. 1909, died 28 Mar. 1970, buried Scott Cemetery); *Thomas* (married Jane Borden, and had children: Mildred [married ___ Knowles]; Tommy). Daisy Scott died on 11 Nov. 1965 in White Co., and is buried with her two husbands in the Scott Cemetery.

8e. **Lola C.** (nmn). Born 13 Dec. 1890 in White Co., TN. Married Clark Scott on 28 Feb. 1909 in White Co. (he was born 2 Apr. 1882, and died 21 Jan. 1969), and had children: *Emma Frances* (born 7 Feb. 1914, died 13 Dec. 1928, buried with her parents); *Lafayette M.* (married Dimple Howard, and had children: Peggy; Ronnie; Beverly; Sandy; Becky); *Bobby*; *Juanita* (married Flora Mackie, and had children: Bobby [married Regina Woods]; Brenda M. [married Jack Ware]; Angie; Glenn); *Charles* (married ___ Bray). Lola Scott died on 20 Dec. (or Feb.) 1957 in White Co., and is buried with her husband in the Scott Cemetery.

8f. **Jessie Ann** (twin). Born 10 Aug. 1894 in White Co., TN; died there on 8 Apr. 1896, and is buried in the Cherry Creek Presbyterian Church Cemetery.

8g. **Willie Alice** (twin). Born 10 Aug. 1894 in White Co., TN. Living with her father in 1920. Married Robert L. Demps on 30 June 1929 in White Co. (he was born 20 Sept. 1894, and died 17 May 1959), and had children: *Emma J.* (born 5 July 1930, married Clay Officer, and had children: Teresa; Alice R. [married Tharon Howard]; Robert Martin; Nancy Elizabeth [married W. R. Hyder]). Willie Demps died on 15 Jan. 1987 at Sparta, White Co., TN, aged 92 years, and is buried with her husband in the Cherry Creek Presbyterian Church Cemetery.

8h. **Elijah Bryan** (twin). Born 27 Apr. 1897 in White Co., TN. See below for full entry.

8i. **Simpson Cline** (twin). Born 27 Apr. 1897 in White Co., TN. Married Sallie Lela Geer on 7 Jan. 1922 in White Co., TN and again on 17 Oct. 1979 (div.; Sallie was born 8 Aug. 1894, and died 1993 in White Co., aged 99 years); married secondly Rachael Christine Hendersen (she was born 1919, and died 1967). Listed in the 1917 draft register and the 1920 census for White Co., TN living with H. R. Terry. Simp Burgess was a lumberman and farmer in White Co.; in later years he served as Chief of Police of the town of Sparta, Tenn. Although he was childless, he raised several of his sister Lizzie's children. He died there in Feb. 1980. He and his first wife are buried in the Cherry Creek Church of Christ Cemetery.

8j. **(Young) Jerry Baxter.** Born 17 Oct. 1899 in White Co., TN. Married secondly Mable Medlin (she was born July 1916, and died 1993 at Cassville, TN). Listed in the 1917 draft register of White Co., TN, and with his father in the 1920 census. Jerry Burgess was a hog and cattle trader in White Co., TN. He died there childless on 26 June 1973, and is buried with his wife in the Peeled Chestnut Cemetery, White Co.

8k. **(Sarah) Elizabeth (V) "Lizzie."** Born 18 Nov. 1901 in White Co., TN. Married James Alexander Geer on 14 Jan. 1918 in White Co., TN (he was born 6 Feb. 1896, and died Nov. 1983 at Sparta, TN), and had children: *Son* (born and died 1919, buried with his parents); *Gus Alexander* (born 22 Mar. 1920, married (Rebecca) Lucile Copeland, and had children: Ronald Gus [born 27 Feb. 1944]; Twila Rebecca [born 5 May 1947]); *Avis Ruth* (born 13 Nov. 1922, married Reed Demps); *James Lloyd* (born 12 Mar. 1927); *Sarah Elizabeth* (born 8 Sept. 1928, married Lester Baker, and had children: Debra); *Martha Flo* (twin; born 2 Aug. 1935, married J. W. Lee, had children: Sharon [married Terry Whitson]; Jeffrey [married ___ Stublin]; and lives at Sparta, TN); *Mary Jo* (twin; born and died 2 Aug. 1935, buried with her parents); *Pattie Lee* (born 12 Oct. 1943, married Carl England). Lizzie Geer died on 28 July 1960 in White Co., and is buried with her husband in the Cherry Creek Presbyterian Church Cemetery.

8l. **Blanche Oka "Mistie."** Born 21 Aug. 1903 (or 1902) in White Co., TN. Living with her father in 1920. Married (Joshua) Owen Kinnard on 7 Sept. 1930 in White Co. (he was born 10 June 1908, and died June 1985 at Sparta, TN), and had children: *James Haggerd* (born 10 Feb. 1933, married Frankie Hendrickson on 14 Feb. 1960 [she was born 5 Sept. 1940], and had children: Emily Terry [born 11 Sept. 1964]; Mary Rebecca [born 12 May 1967]); *Lenora M.* (born 27 Apr. 1935, married

Glenn Guy, and had children: Retisue; Ross; Bobby Rex [born 1955, died 1957]). Mistie Kinnard died on 20 Sept. 1983 at Sparta, White Co., TN.

8m. **Samuel Denton (I).** Born 7 June 1905 in White Co., TN. See below for full entry.

ROBERT T. BURGESS OF WHITE CO., TENNESSEE

[William Simpson[6], Thomas Alonzo[7]]

8c. **Robert Taylor** *[son of Thomas Alonzo].* Born 8 Oct. 1886 in White Co., TN. Married Beatrice Randolph on 23 Dec. 1905 in White Co. (she was born 25 Oct. 1889, and died on 23 July 1946); married secondly Maggie England on 29 Nov. 1955 in White Co. (she was born 6 Aug. 1896, daughter of Carl and Bob Bilbrey, had children by her first marriage: Bransford ENGLAND [living at Sparta, TN in 1986]; Dimple ENGLAND [living at Cookeville, TN in 1986]; Dora Lou ENGLAND [who married Merle Bandy, and was living at Sparta, TN in 1986], and died 1 Apr. 1986 at Sparta, TN). Listed in the 1918 draft register and the 1910-20 censuses for White Co., TN. Robert Burgess was a farmer in White Co., TN, and also served as the Tax Assessor for White County through 1964, when he retired. He died on 31 [or 25] May 1975 at Sparta, TN, and is buried there with his first wife in the Highland Cemetery.

9a. **Terry Laramore.** Born 27 Aug. 1906 in White Co., TN. Married Inez Riley. Terry Burgess died childless in an air crash in June 1940 at Akron, OH, but is buried in the Highland Cemetery, White Co., TN.

9b. **Malcolm Patterson.** Born 17 Aug. 1908 in White Co., TN. See below for full entry.

9c. **(Lucy) Lela (II).** Born 7 Oct. 1910 in White Co., TN. Married Klodus Weaver on 6 Nov. 1932 in Putnam Co., TN (he was born 18 Mar. 1909, and died 31 Jan. 1989 at Sparta, TN), and had children: *Robert Lynn* (married ___ Hickey); *Roy*; *Mary Jo.* Lela Weaver lives in rural White Co., TN.

9d. **Mertie Lou (II).** Her name is listed as Myrtle on her marriage certificate. Born 1 Jan. 1913 in White Co., TN. Married Billy L. Kinnard, cousin of J. Owen Kinnard, on 13 Jan. 1933 in Putnam Co.; married secondly Jimmy Castner. Mertie Castner lived in Michigan. She died on 27 Oct. 1984, and is buried in the Highland Cemetery.

9e. **William Richard "Bill."** Born 5 June 1916 in White Co., TN. Married Nina Heston (or Hestand) on 21 Mar. 1936 in White Co. (div.; she moved to Indianapolis after their separation); married secondly Jessie Ray Phifer about 1940 (she was born 10 Oct. 1917, remarried James C. Bratcher, and lives at Cookeville, TN). Bill Burgess served in World War II. After returning home from the service in Nov. 1945, he was seriously injured in a car accident on 17 Feb. 1946 at Sparta, White Co., TN, and died the following day while being transported to Nashville, being buried at Sparta in the Highland Cemetery.

10a. **Edward Richard "Eddie."** Born about 1937 in White Co., TN. Eddie Burgess was last known living at Indianapolis, IN.

10b. **Carolyn Terry.** Born 27 Sept. 1942 in White Co., TN. Married Avery Roberts, and had children: *Travis Lee* (born 7 Aug. 1969 in Iran). Carolyn Roberts lives at Baxter, TN.

9f. **Geneva Frances.** Born 6 Jan. 1919 in White Co., TN. Married Ray T. Brady, an automobile dealer. Geneva Brady currently lives in Putnam Co., TN.

9g. **Betty Jean (I).** Born 6 Apr. 1930 in White Co., TN. Married Clifford Mills on 6 Sept. 1959 in White Co., TN (he was born 13 July 1928), and had children: *Roger* (born 10 Nov. 1966). Betty Mills currently lives in Michigan.

MALCOLM P. BURGESS OF FRESNO CO., CALIFORNIA

[William Simpson[6], Thomas Alonzo[7], Robert Taylor[8]]

9b. **Malcolm Patterson** *[son of Robert Taylor].* Born 17 Aug. 1908 in White Co., TN. Married (Vivian) Ruth Golden on 31 July 1928 in White Co. Malcolm Burgess was a water well driller near Fresno, CA, moving there about 1931. He now lives retired at Oakhurst, CA.

10a. **(Robert) Ronald (I).** Born 17 Mar. 1932 near Fresno, CA. Married Marjorie Woodfin; married secondly Dorella Shute Harris on 20 Apr. 1962 in Fresno Co.; married thirdly Jone M. Talmage Eades on 16 Mar. 1966 in Fresno Co., CA; married fourthly Delores Smith. Ron Burgess was a building contractor at Fresno, CA. He died there on 14 Aug. 1990, and is buried in the Belmont Memorial Cemetery.

11a. **Robert Ronald (III).** Born 14 Feb. 1963 at Fresno, CA. Married Suzan D. Smith Losorwith on 12 Aug. 1984 in Shasta Co., CA.

12a. **Dorian R.** (dau.). Born 2 Aug. 1985 at Fresno, CA.

11b. **Michael Wayne.** Born 4 Aug. 1968 at Delta, CO.
11c. **Matthew George.** Born 5 Sept. 1970 at Delta, CO.

10b. **Donald Lynn (I).** Born 12 Sept. 1936 at Fresno, CA. Married Sharon Henry; married secondly Roberta Joan White on 6 Mar. 1964 in Fresno Co.; married thirdly Cathy Jones on 20 Apr. 1979 in Mariposa Co. Don Burgess owns and operates Don Burgess Construction Co. at Fresno, CA.

11a. **Donald Lynn (II).** Born 25 Feb. 1959 at Fresno, CA. Married Colleen C. Coelho on 9 Feb. 1985 in Monterey Co., CA. Don Burgess Jr. works for his father's construction company at Fresno, CA.
11b. **Kellene Rene "Kelly."** Born 9 Sept. 1960 at Fresno, CA. Married Darrell Graef.
11c. **Stewart Lynn.** Born 16 Oct. 1964 at Fresno, CA. Stewart Burgess is a student at California State University, Fresno.

10c. **Nancy Laurine.** Born 19 Feb. 1944 at Fresno, CA. Married James V. Phillips on 23 June 1962 in Fresno Co. (he was born 12 Jan. 1941, and died 19 Dec. 1989), and had children: *Wendy Rebecca* (born 20 Oct. 1966 at Fresno, CA); *Scott Eric* (born 23 Jan. 1971 at Hanford, CA). Nancy Phillips works for the U.S. Postal Service at Fresno, CA.

ELIJAH B. BURGESS OF WHITE CO., TENNESSEE
[William Simpson[6], Thomas Alonzo[7]]

8h. **Elijah Bryan "Lige"** (twin) *[son of Thomas Alonzo].* Born 27 Apr. 1897 (according to his Social Security record) or 1896 in White Co., TN. Married Pauline Pennington on 5 Mar. 1932 (she was born 18 Feb. 1909 at New Middleton, TN, and lives at Sparta, TN). Listed in the 1917 draft register of White Co., and with his father in the 1920 census. Lige Burgess was a carpenter at Sparta, TN. He died there in Jan. 1986, and is buried in the Highland Cemetery.

9a. **Thomas Lonzo.** Born 17 Feb. 1933 at Sparta, TN. Married Jean Johnson; married secondly Betty Burns. Tom Burgess is a retired partner in the accounting firm of Deloitte & Touche, Nashville, TN.
9b. **Bryan Elijah.** Born 27 Oct. 1937 at Sparta, TN. Married (Freddie) Kathryn Kirby on 10 June 1961 in White Co., TN (she was born 20 Aug. 1942); married secondly Jerry Livesay; married thirdly Leslie Hindman (a technical writer for the University of Alabama Medical Center). Dr. Bryan Burgess is an engineer for Bell South, Birmingham, AL. His biography has appeared in *Who's Who in the South and Southwest*. He and his wife live at Ashville, AL.

10a. **Belinda Carol.** Born 23 July 1962 at Huntsville, AL. Married Leonard A. Gentry on 10 Sept. 1982 in Putnam Co., TN; married secondly Thomas West at Birmingham, AL.
10b. **Susan Selene.** Born 10 Aug. 1964 at Huntsville, AL. Married Dr. Kenneth Urquhart at Birmingham, AL.
10c. **Paula Rae.** Born 1 Aug. 1966 at Lewisburg, TN. Married Bryan Cook at Birmingham, AL.
10d. **Wendy Judith.** Born 24 May 1972 at Huntsville, AL.

SAMUEL D. BURGESS, Sr. OF WHITE CO., TENNESSEE
[William Simpson[6], Thomas Alonzo[7]]

8m. **Samuel Denton (I)** *[son of Thomas Alonzo].* Born 7 June 1905 in White Co., TN. Married Ora Lee Bumbalough on 31 Oct. 1926 in White Co. (she was born 7 Sept. 1905, and died Oct. 1983 at Chattanooga, TN). Sam Burgess was a trucker in Tennessee most of his life. He died on 26 May 1982 in White Co., and is buried with his wife in the Oaklawn Cemetery.

9a. **Samuel Denton (II).** Born 4 Jan. 1929 at Sparta, TN. Married Barbara Saxton on 31 Aug. 1957 (she was born 11 Jan. 1936). Sam Burgess has worked for Dupont Corp. since 1948. He lives at Chattanooga, TN.

10a. **Lea Ann.** Born 26 Oct. 1959 at Chattanooga, TN.
10b. **Samuel Denton III.** Born 16 Oct. 1961 at Chattanooga, TN.

A Civil War Letter from William Simpson Burgess to His Wife

"Camp Florance, Alabama, March 2th, 1863, Zina. The opportunity will admit my writing a few lines. I have no news of importance to write. We had a fight at Port Hutson which went in our favor. We burnt one of these ironclad steamers and damaged several others, drove them all back except one it passed through but was damaged. All this was done without the loss of a man. It is in the papers that Missouri has rebelled against Lincoln's administration had taken the assault and all the arms and called on the south to help them. General Marmaduke (?) was on his march to aid them with another general. This is good news for us. If it be true, the war is nearly at a close. There is no expectation of a fight at this place, we have nothing to do but watch the river. I think we will stay here till the river gets down. Colonel Dibrel has laid in a requisition to move to Sparta to recruit. If it is granted him we will be there by the first of June, which will suit me very well. I would like to be at home then to pay notary for [__]. If I am not there pay the notary and the clerk will make the retitle. If somebody hasn't got the money you can get it without collecting your debt. I have not heard from Louis (?) but once since I left, then he was mending slow. I would like to hear from him, I want you to write when you get this and give me all the news and tell [__] to write. Our boys has been out aconscripting and met with some yankees that was posted (?). They told us that they [had] come to our men to be pardoned (?). They said there was twenty good as they and they also stated that there was 2 regiments at Corinth [Miss.] and they have nearly all left and gone home. It is also reported that the yankee men at Vicksburg was deserting and coming to us army every day and I saw it in a paper last night that there have been 134 officers resigned and gone home. If we hold our position till the waters gets down the yankees is bound to fall back. There is no doubt but we will hold our position. I have hopes this war will close this summer. It is the general oppinion of the citizens. I thought when we come here the Alabamans would scorn us but I find them more sociable than the Tennesseeans and give us the name of being the best behaved soldiers that they ever saw. A lady in Florance made us a song and James is going to send it home; I thought Tenn. was backwar[d] and not doing her part in this war but she is going to be one of the brightest stars in the Confederacy. Tell your mother and Frances (?) I have not read any lines from them. Yours truly, William S. Burgess."

CORA TENNESSEE BURGESS
(1887-1984)
[see page 473]

[William (I)[1], Edward (I)[2], Reuben (I)[3], Thomas (I)[4], Charles Hunter[5]]

JAMES CRAWFORD BURGESS
(1832-1877)

OF WHITE COUNTY, TENNESSEE

6c. **James Crawford** *[son of Charles Hunter]*. Born 28 July 1832 in White (later Putnam) Co., TN. Married (Nancy) Caroline Barnes about 1853 (she was born about 1830 in TN, and died on 1 Oct. 1893). Listed in the 1860-70 censuses for White Co., TN; Nancy Burgess appears as head of the family in 1880. Enlisted on 15 Sept. 1862 in White Co., TN in Co. H, 13th Tennessee Cavalry (Gore's Cavalry), Confederate Army, during the Civil War, eventually reaching the rank of Sergeant; he was captured on 15 Dec. 1864 at Athens, TN, and was paroled on 8 Jan. 1965 at Louisville, KY. James C. Burgess was a farmer in White Co., TN, buying land there about 1854. He died there on 2 June 1877, and is buried with his wife in the Cherry Creek Presbyterian Church Cemetery.

The Children of James C. Burgess:

7a. **(Jemima) Frances.** Born 7 Oct. 1854 in White Co., TN. Married Robert Nelson Terry on 17 Jan. 1879 in White Co. (he was born 14 Aug. 1852, remarried Virginia Austin in 1906, and died 27 Dec. 1935), and had children:

James Washington TERRY. Born 19 Mar. 1880, married Elizabeth "Bessie" Holsapple, and died 10 Sept. 1941, having had children: *Mary Frances* (born 16 Oct. 1914, married John B. Lee, and had children: James William [born 8 Oct. 1941 at Cookeville, TN, married Homa Soltani, and had children: Frances B.; Justin Montega]; Mary Carolyn [born 5 June 1945 at Cookeville, TN, and works as Picture Editor for the *New York Times*]; Frances Kay [born 22 Nov. 1947, married James Carroll Raines, and had children: James William; John Keith]).

William Smith TERRY. Born 30 Oct. 1882, married Sophia Haston, and died 26 Sept. 1941, having had children: *Robert Vann* (married Elizabeth Cantrell); *Frances Juanita* (married Benton Poor, and had children: Bennie; Neva Jane); *Warren Reed* (married Treva Sullivan).

Cora Florence TERRY. Born 7 Jan. 1885, married William Andrew Jernigan, and died Feb. 1973 at Chattanooga, TN, having had children: *Cicero Terry*; *Jewell Ruth* (married Charles Zieman, and had children: Charles Jr.); *James Robert* (married Mary Webster, and had children: Terry Lewis; Peggy Beth); *William Andrew Jr.* (married Jean ___, and had children: Margaret; Betty; Cora Sue; Brice); *Buford*; *John Paul*.

Joseph Lee TERRY. Born 28 Nov. 1886, and died unmarried on 5 July 1907.

Effie Ann TERRY. Born 31 July 1888, married Riley Dalton Davis on 1 June 1911, and died Feb. 1986 at Savannah, GA, aged 97 years, having had children: *Bessie Elnora* (born 17 Sept. 1912, married William Johnson Lewis [he was born 28 May 1901, and died on 3 July 1966], and had children: William Davis [born 25 July 1944, married Barbara ___, and had children: Christy; Billy]); *Robert Dalton* (born 19 Nov. 1917, married Geraldean Daniel); *Gene Franklin* (born 14 Sept. 1925); *Nancy Ann* (born 26 Nov. 1928, married John Potter Davis [he was born 13 July 1933], and had children: John Potter Jr. [born 6 Jan. 1957]).

Harvey Roll TERRY. Born 31 July 1890, married May McBride, and had children: *Joseph Lee* (born 23 Sept. 1913, married Sallie Brogden, and had children: Phil [born 18 July 1936, married Laurence Bumbalough, and had children: Debbie {married Jim Pollard}; Elaine; Michelle; Lissa]); *Edith Louise*; *Robert Franklin* (married Mary Alice Bort, and had children: Bobby; Louise); *Paul Howard* (married Geneva Kell, and had children: Billy; Randall; Russell). ***Harvey TERRY*** secondly Grace Weaver, and died Jan. 1985 at Sparta, TN, aged 94 years.

Nancy Pearl TERRY. Born 28 June 1892, married Charles Meek (he was born 1 June 1911), and had children: *Lyla Marie* (married Ray Cowden, and had children: Charles Marshall [married Nancy Overton, and had children: Marsha Gail {born 14 May 1953}; Charles Marshall Jr. {born 21 Sept. 1955}; Paul Douglas {born 21 May 1957}; Jeffrey Frederic {born 26 Feb. 1960}]).

Frances Harriet TERRY. Born 13 Aug. 1894, died Sept. 1894.

Frances TERRY died in childbirth on 13 Aug. 1894 in White Co., TN, and is buried in the Cherry Creek Presbyterian Church Cemetery.

7b. **Letta Margaret.** Her name appears on her tombstone as "Lettia." Born 25 Nov. 1856 in White Co., TN; died there on 16 Feb. 1862, and is buried in the Lovelady Cemetery.

7c. **William Hopkins.** Born 13 May 1859 in White Co., TN; died there on 8 Jan. 1862, and is buried in the Lovelady Cemetery.

7d. **Jefferson Beauregard.** Born 11 Aug. 1861 in White Co., TN; died there on 30 Jan. 1862, and is buried in the Lovelady Cemetery.

7e. **Cora Bell (I).** Born 1 Jan. 1863 (or 30 Nov. 1864) in White Co., TN. Married David J. Snodgrass on 27 May 1884 in White Co. (he was born 20 Nov. 1860, and died 12 Nov. 1928), and had children: *Daughter* (born and died 4 Feb. 1885, buried with her parents); *John Vass* (born 5 May 1887, married Chloria Enzena Mason [she was born 16 Feb. 1897], and died 31 May 1969, having had children: Cora Dasy Joyce [married David Luther Simpson {he was born 24 July 1924}, and had children: Mary Joyce {born 31 Oct. 1946, married Peter B. Carlson on 31 Oct. 1975}; Donna Sue {born 6 Nov. 1950, married John Michael Massa on 13 Dec. 1969, and had children: Carrie Kathrine <born 23 Nov. 1973>; Erica Jane}; David Luther Jr. {born 16 Sept. 1954, married Sandra Sue Davis on 3 Jan. 1974, and had children: David Mason <born 18 July 1975>}; John Cameron {born 12 Jan. 1956}; Lillian Anne {born 27 Sept. 1958}; James Allen {born 27 Mar. 1961}]; John Vass Jr. [born 18 Oct. 1927, married Phyllis Martin on 18 June 1949 {she was born 26 May 1931}]). Cora Snodgrass died in childbirth on 5 May 1887 in White Co., and is buried in the Cherry Creek Presbyterian Church Cemetery.

7f. **Emilia Florence "Amy."** Born 27 Mar. 1866 in White Co., TN. Married William J. Whittaker on 4 Jan. 1883 in White Co. (he was born 21 Aug. 1861, and died 18 Apr. 1943), and had children: *Alva* (born 19 July 1886, married Lena Elizabeth Denton [she was born 1 Aug. 1886], and died 21 Feb. 1954, having had children: Raymond W. [born Mar. 1907, married Dorothy Naylor]; Willie Alma [born Sept. 1909, married Kelly Currie]); *Bascom* (born 1 Sept. 1887, married Susie Cordelia Sims [she was born 15 Mar. 1886], and died 18 Nov. 1957, having had children: Juanita [born 26 Nov. 1921, married J. F. Gamble]; Florence [born 31 May 1923, married Walter Falk]; Benton [born 24 Sept. 1924, married Kitty Rogers]); *Nellie* (born 15 Jan. 1889, married John Bate Byars on 5 May 1909 [he was born 30 Jan. 1884, and died 29 Feb. 1960], and had children: Amy Jo [born 4 Oct. 1910, married Kai Grisson, and had children: Kai Jr.]; Etta Nell; Albert [born 28 Apr. 1912, married Gladys Barnes, and died 4 Nov. 1975 at Lake Station, IN, having had children: Clyde {born 30 Sept. 1941 in IN, and died Jan. 1993 at McMinnville, TN}; Carl {born 24 May 1944 in IN, and died Aug. 1976}]; *Nellie* married secondly Ernest Brown, and had children: Mary Frances [born 1 Dec. 1914, married John Roy Griffith, and died Dec. 1978 at Lebanon, TN, having had children: Marilyn Roy {born 14 Jan. 1936}; Mary Frances married secondly Carney Rudolph Trougher Jr., and had children: Charles Nicholas {born 8 Nov. 1943, married Jessica Lynn White}; Penelope Ann {born 17 June 1946}]; Flora Edna [born 22 Nov. 1922, married William Stephen Alderson]); *Henry C.* (born 20 Dec. 1890, married Pricilla Paul on 1 Feb. 1916, and had children: Henry C. Jr. [born 12 June 1918, married Virginia Smith]; Nancy Paulene [married Stanley Mefford]); *Combs Gerry* (born 14 Oct. 1895, married Susie Potter on 24 Sept. 1916, and died 25 Feb. 1950). Amy Whittaker died on 14 June 1939 at Lebanon, Wilson Co., TN.

7g. **Adelia Anne.** Her name is spelled "Adlia" in her obituary. Born 25 Apr. 1868 in White Co., TN. Married Jesse Vincent Terry on 31 Dec. 1885 in White Co. (he was born 8 Dec. 1859 [or 1857], son of Elijah Washington Terry and Sarah Anderson [or Angelina Denton], and brother of Sarah Emily Terry [who married her cousin, Thomas Alonzo Burgess], and died 25 Sept. 1897), and had children: *Prietta C.* (born 26 Dec. 1888, married Barlow P. Smith, and died 22 Jan. 1989 at Cookeville, TN, aged 100 years); *F. Willie* (born 3 July 1891, married Sam Hollerman, had children: William A. "Billy" [married Peggy Masters], and died about 1980); *Clara Bell* (born 19 Jan. 1893, married Jay Mitchell [he was born 19 Nov. 1892], and died Jan. 1983, having had children: Mildred Terry [born 23 Oct. 1916, married Joe Randall Adams, and died 8 Feb. 1976, having had children: (Joe) Randall II {born 12 Feb. 1956, married Debora Lee Ellis on 28 Dec. 1976, and had children: Terry Elizabeth}]). Adelia Terry married secondly Amos Broils about 1906, and died on 26 May 1911 at Sparta, TN, being buried with her first husband in the Cherry Creek Presbyterian Church Cemetery.

7h. **Ursula Olga.** Born 12 May 1870 in White Co., TN. Married John Franklin Wilhite on 3 Oct. 1894 in White Co. (he was born 30 Mar. 1868), and had children: *Annie Mae* (born 24 Aug. 1895, married Comer Sims Knowles on 13 May 1941 [he was born 31 Oct. 1890, and died May 1970 at Sparta], and was living at Sparta, TN in 1983). Ursula Wilhite died on 8 Nov. 1967 in White Co., aged 97 years, and is buried in the Highland Cemetery, Sparta, TN.

7i. **Prietta Zee.** Born 2 Feb. 1872 in White Co., TN; died there on 20 Aug. 1893, and is buried in the Cherry Creek Presbyterian Church Cemetery.

7j. **(Lycurgus) Combs.** Born 26 Jan. 1874 in White Co., TN. Married Maggie Cooper on 28 Feb. 1893 in White Co.; married secondly Ida Holsapple on 14 Nov. 1897 in White Co. (she was born 12 Oct. 1872, and died 1 Mar. 1952). Listed in the 1918 draft register and the 1900-20 censuses for White Co., TN. He lived briefly at Dinuba, Tulare Co., CA in 1909-10. Combs Burgess was a farmer, dairyman, and hotel worker in White Co. He died there on 12 June 1960, and is buried in the Highland Cemetery, Sparta, TN.

8a. **Lurley Lee.** Born 10 June 1898 in White Co., TN. Married Ernest Lee Ponder on 2 Sept. 1922 in White Co. Lurley Ponder died on 2 Mar. 1941 in White Co., and is buried in the Highland Cemetery, Sparta, TN.

8b. **Bonnie Arno.** Her name is listed in the 1900 census as Ethel M. Burgess. Born 9 Feb. 1900 in White Co., TN. She may have married Jess Stevens (as Ethel Burgess) on 14 Mar. 1919 in White Co., but if so, she soon reverted to her maiden name. Bonnie Burgess died childless on 12 July 1986 at Crossville, TN, and is buried in the Highland Cemetery, White Co.

THE OBITUARY OF ADELIA BURGESS TERRY

"Adlia Burgess Terry Broils departed this life May 26, 1911. She was the daughter of James and Caroline Burgess, born and reared in White County near Cherry Creek. She obeyed the gospel at Old Smyrna Church in Putnam County many years ago, and lived a Christian life until death. She was married to Mr. Jess Terry of Putnam County when quite a young lady. They lived together for several years; three girls were born unto them, when Terry died and left her to rear the little girls, which she did. She was never a very strong woman, and her health came very near giving away in Terry's lifetime. About five years ago she was united in marriage to Mr. Amos Broils of near Sparta. Her health gave way again last Fall or Winter, from which she never recovered. She was such a sweet little woman, and such a beautiful corpse. She always had a smile on her face while living, and it still remained when she was dead. She was the only corpse that I ever saw. I always believed she was my friend, and I loved her as dearly as anyone I ever knew, except my loved ones at home. Of course she had faults, as other people do, but I failed to recognize many of them. She was one of God's noble women who, with all her gentleness, sweetness, and sunshine, has gone from this world of sorrow to be with the Lord and rest forevermore."—*Putnam County Herald*, 20 July 1911.

[William (I)[1], Edward (I)[2], Reuben (I)[3], Thomas (I)[4], Charles Hunter[5]]

CHARLES LAFAYETTE BURGESS
(1843-1915)

OF PUTNAM COUNTY, TENNESSEE

6i. **Charles Lafayette** *[son of Charles Hunter].* Born 27 Sept. 1843 in White (later Putnam) Co., TN. Married America Deering about 1875 (she was born 7 July 1853, and died 17 Sept. 1904). Enlisted on 25 July 1861 at Tullahoma, TN in Co. E, 25th Tennessee Infantry, Confederate Army, during the Civil War, serving as a private, and was discharged on 23 Sept. 1862 for disability. On 15 Mar. 1864 he enlisted as a private in Co. B, 1st Tennessee Mounted Infantry, Union Army, an elite guerrilla unit operating behind Confederate lines. He was the only Burgess to serve in both the Confederate and Union Armies; he later drew a pension for his Union service. Listed in the 1880-1910 censuses for the 16th Civil District, Putnam Co., TN. Charles L. Burgess was a farmer in Putnam and White Cos., TN. He died there on 17 May 1915, and is buried with his wife in the Howard Cemetery.

The Children of Charles L. Burgess:

7a. **Zenith Bloomington.** Born 5 Feb. 1876 in Putnam Co., TN; died there on 24 Feb. 1876, and is buried with his parents.

7b. **(Ammon) Lafayette.** Born 2 Oct. 1878 in Putnam Co., TN. See below for full entry.

7c. **Sarah Margaret "Sally."** Born 15 May 1880 in White Co., TN; died there unmarried on 29 Oct. 1901, and is buried in the Howard Cemetery.

7d. **(Pretteman) Payne.** Born 11 Oct. 1882 in White Co., TN. See below for full entry.

7e. **Mayhue Blaine.** Born 4 June 1884 in White Co., TN. Listed in the 1918 draft register of Putnam Co., and with his brother, Payne Burgess, in the 1920 census. Mayhue Burgess was a farmer in Putnam Co., TN. He died there unmarried on 3 Dec. 1955, and is buried in the Howard Cemetery.

7f. **(Dorendia Susan) Della.** Born 17 Apr. 1886 in White Co., TN. Married Erastus Slagle on 8 Oct. 1905 in White Co. (he was born 13 Feb. 1884, and died 10 June 1958), and had children: *Morelle* (born 1 Mar. 1909, married Jimmie Moore, secondly ___ Miller, and thirdly ___ Webb, and died on 12 June 1971). Della Slagle died in White Co. on 30 Apr. 1966, and is buried with her first husband in the Howard Cemetery, White Co.

7g. **Delia Iantha.** Her name was also written Dellia and Dealia. Born 2 Aug. 1889 in White Co., TN. Married Howard M. Slagle on 31 Mar. 1906 in White Co. (he was born 1 Sept. 1885, and died 19 Sept. 1966), and had children:

***Mallie* SLAGLE.** Born 2 Apr. 1907, married Jimmie Miller (he was born 25 June 1893, and died 17 Aug. 1970), and had children: *James Lynn* (born 12 Mar. 1924, married Dorothy Wilson, and had children: Albert [born 25 Feb. 1948, married Linda A. Suddath and secondly Teresa M. Damata]); *Raymond* (born 14 Mar. 1928, married Helen McCormick, and had children: Sandra [born 11 Jan. 1949, married Larry Daniel]; *Raymond* married secondly Hazel Jones); *Henry Howard* (born 4 Feb. 1930, died 1 Nov. 1932); *Betty* (born 26 Dec. 1933, married Richard Noms [he was born 9 July 1926], and had children: Larry [born 26 Feb. 1949]; Brenda [born 8 May 1955]; Cathy [born 18 Aug. 1957]; Ricky [born 10 Apr. 1959?; dec.]); *Freeman* (born 21 Dec. 1936, may have married Aline Haley); *Richard Harold* (born 15 Jan. 1940, married Clara Hall [she was born 8 Mar. 1940], and had children: Cynthia Jean [born 19 Nov. 1956, married Michael R. Woodruff {he was born 1 Mar. 1950}]; Teresa Lynn [born 1 June 1959]); *Linda Helen* (born 1 Feb. 1942, married Roy Rippy, and had children: Roy Jr. [born 10 Feb. 1958]; Thevena [born 19 May 1959]; Becky [born 2 June 1960]; Rhonda [born 31 Jan. 1963]; Jerry Lynn [born and died 15 Jan. 1967]; *Linda* married secondly Glenn Butler); *Robert Tommie* (born 4 Jan. 1944).

***Monnie* SLAGLE.** Born 14 Nov. 1908, and died 8 Sept. 1909.

***Allie Florence* SLAGLE.** Born 13 Apr. 1910, married George R. Graham (he was born 21 Apr. 1907), and had children: *Lucille* (born 30 Mar. 1928, married Robert L. Demps, and had children: Larry D. [born 16 Sept. 1949]; Danny L. [born 15 June 1952]); *Joyce* (born 18 Dec. 1938, married Buddy T. Henry [he was born 1 Mar. 1941], and had children: Derrick [born 20 Dec. 1962]; Darryl [born 15 Sept. 1963]).

Child SLAGLE. Born 24 Dec. 1914, died 7 Jan. 1915, buried with its parents.

Charlie Lynn SLAGLE. Born 13 May 1916, married (Mary) Irene Gribble (she was born 26 May 1916), and had children: *Dean* (married Marie Ann Burgess on 12 May 1955, and had children: Rose Marie [born 22 Feb. 1956]; Karen Sue [born 27 Mar. 1957]; Mary Elizabeth [born 27 June 1959]; Connie Lynn [born 19 Aug. 1960]; Charles Howard [born 29 Oct. 1961]; *Dean* married secondly Media F. Ramsey on 1 June 1973). ***Charlie SLAGLE*** died on 16 Dec. 1952, and is buried with his wife in the Saylor Cemetery.

Elmer T. SLAGLE. Born 6 May 1922, married Bonnie ___ (she was born 1 Feb. 1925), and had children: *John* (born 27 Nov. 1946, married Barbara J. Govdaker [she was born 15 Sept. 1949], and had children: Lisa Marie [born 31 May 1966]; Tricia Michelle [born 9 Sept. 1970]; John Jason [born 24 Dec. 1974]); *Reed* (born 2 Feb. 194_, married Laurie ___ [she was born 29 Apr. 1954], and had children: Michelle Lynn [born 2 Aug. 1971]; Malissa Ann [born 8 Dec. 1974]); *Michael* (born 12 Mar. 1954). ***Elmer SLAGLE*** died in Feb. 1978 at Milan, MI.

Howard Keith SLAGLE. Born 28 Feb. 1927, married Nellie Stevens on 28 May 1946 (she was born 8 Sept. 1928), and had children: *Connie Jean* (born 13 Dec. 1948, married Lawrence E. Webb Jr. on 20 Mar. 1971 [he was born 23 Feb. 1948], and had children: Brandon Keith [born 6 Apr. 1975]).

Delia SLAGLE died on 5 Sept. 1969, and is buried in the Howard Cemetery.

7h. **Viana Artelia.** Born 5 July 1894 in White Co., TN; died there on 6 Jan. 1895, and is buried with her parents.

7i. **Richard Herbert (I).** Born 17 Oct. 1895 in Putnam Co., TN. See below for full entry.

FATE BURGESS OF PUTNAM CO., TENNESSEE

[Charles Lafayette[6]]

7b. **(Ammon) Lafayette "Fate"** *[son of Charles Lafayette].* Born 2 Oct. 1878 in Putnam Co., TN. Married Elizabeth "Lizzie" White on 26 Dec. 1909 in Putnam Co., TN (she was born 14 June 1890, and died 9 Feb. 1969). Listed in the 1918 draft register and the 1910-20 censuses for Putnam Co. Lafayette Burgess was a farmer in Putnam Co. He died there on 10 Dec. 1934, and is buried with his wife in the Howard Cemetery.

8a. **Shelia Taft.** Born 29 Nov. 1910 in Putnam Co., TN. See below for full entry.

8b. **Martha America "Amy."** Born 12 May 1912 in Putnam Co., TN. Married Willie Thurlow Buck on 25 Sept. 1943 at Napoleon, OH (he was born 12 Mar. 1899, and died 20 Dec. 1973), and had children: *Billie Jean* (born 17 July 1934 in Putnam Co., married Ralph Lyle Hagar [he was born 20 June 1925], and had children: Ralph Lyle Jr. [born 13 May 1961, married Martha Elizabeth Ray {she was born 24 Oct. 1965}]; *Billie Jean* married secondly Glenn E. Cain Jr.); *Peggy Sue* (born 10 Aug. 1947 at Detroit, MI, married Larry William Littleson on 14 May 1966 [he was born 22 Jan. 1946], and had children: Kristi Ann [born 27 Oct. 1966 at Warren, MI]; Marc William [born 30 Dec. 1968 at Warren, MI]; Courtney Beth [born 30 Apr. 1974 at Warren, MI]). **Amy** married secondly Bruce Allen Bell on 24 Oct. 1987 at Anchorage, AK. Amy Bell was a secretary and caterer at Wasilla, AK.

8c. **(Charles) Hooper.** Born 2 Oct. 1913 in Putnam Co., TN. See below for full entry.

8d. **Howard Lafayette.** Born 2 Sept. 1917 (or 1915) in Putnam Co., TN. Married Bettye Jewel Lance on 27 Sept. 1960 in Putnam Co. Howard Burgess was a teacher and a worker in an electronics parts assembly plant. He died childless on 22 Oct. 1961 at Cookeville, TN, and is buried in the Howard Cemetery.

8e. **William McKinley.** Born 24 Dec. 1919 in Putnam Co., TN. See below for full entry.

8f. **Zebbie D.** (nmn). Born 3 Mar. 1923 in Putnam Co., TN. See below for full entry.

SHELIA BURGESS OF PUTNAM CO., TENNESSEE

[Charles Lafayette[6], Ammon Lafayette[7]]

8a. **Shelia Taft** *[son of Ammon Lafayette].* Born 29 Nov. 1910 in Putnam Co., TN. Married Nathalie Cornelia Goolsby on 2 July 1947 at Rossville, GA (she was born 30 May 1926). Shelia Burgess worked for the Tennessee Valley Authority during much of his life; after moving to GA, he was a chicken farmer. He died on 11 Nov. 1963 at Murfreesboro, TN, and is buried in the National Cemetery, Marietta, GA. Nathalie Burgess lives at Auburn, GA.

9a. **Parker Dale.** Born 17 May 1948 at Duluth, GA. Married Glenda Ruth LaFever on 29 Aug. 1968 in Putnam Co., TN (she was born 10 May 1951). Rev. Parker Burgess is a minister for a Baptist Church in Marble, NC; he also owns his own landscape design and planning business.

10a. **Shellie Clint.** Born 15 May 1969 in De Kalb Co., GA.
10b. **Joshua Taft.** Born 6 Feb. 1976 in De Kalb Co., GA.

9b. **Hilda Joan.** Born 7 Nov. 1950 in Putnam Co., TN. Married Raymond Tumlin on 29 May 1969 at Doraville, GA (he was born 19 Jan. 1947), and had children: *Tonia Dawn* (born 26 Aug. 1973); *Miranda Brooke* (born 2 Sept. 1978). Hilda Tumlin currently lives at Auburn, GA.

HOOPER BURGESS OF PUTNAM CO., TENNESSEE
[Charles Lafayette[6], Ammon Lafayette[7]]

8c. **(Charles) Hooper** *[son of Ammon Lafayette].* He was also called Charley Burgess. Born 1 Oct. 1913 in Putnam Co., TN. Married Pansy Edith "Pat" Dixon about 1943 (she was born 9 June 1922). Served in the U.S. Army during World War II. Hooper Burgess was a high school teacher and farmer in Putnam Co., TN. He died there on 19 June 1975, and is buried in the Crestlawn Cemetery, Cookeville, TN. Pat Burgess lives at Cookeville, TN.

9a. **Doris Jo.** Born 24 Oct. 1943 at Cookeville, TN. Married Henry Thurman Slagle Jr. on 22 July 1969 in Putnam Co., TN, and had children: *Jamie Jo* (born 3 May 1974). Doris Slagle lives at Cookeville, TN.
9b. **Sharon Faye.** Born 19 Jan. 1949 at Cookeville, TN. Married Kenneth Edwin Spurlock on 11 Oct. 1967 in Putnam Co., and had children: *Shane Edwin* (born 6 May 1971). Sharon Spurlock works at Universal Plastics, Cookeville, TN.
9c. **(Sandra) Kay (II).** Born 24 July 1951 at Cookeville, TN. Married Roger Lee Holt on 12 Feb. 1972 in Putnam Co. (he was born 2 Oct. 1949), and had children: *(Roger) Lee II* (born 3 July 1973). Kay Holt works as an accounting clerk for Universal Plastics, Cookeville, TN.
9d. **Danny Charles (II).** Born 3 Sept. 1952 at Cookeville, TN. Married Sandra Gay Goff on 16 Dec. 1972 in Putnam Co. (div.); married secondly Beverly Diane Smith on 17 Sept. 1975 in Putnam Co. (she was the daughter of James Ralph Smith and Essie Dee Holloway). Danny Burgess is an electrician at Cookeville, TN.

10a. **Heather Danielle.** Born 21 Dec. 1976 at Cookeville, TN.
10b. **Brandon Charles.** Born 11 July 1980 at Cookeville, TN.

9e. **Deborah Ray.** Born 9 Apr. 1954 at Cookeville, TN. Married Earl Dillard Stover on 4 Mar. 1972 in Putnam Co. (div.), and had children: *Tammie Lea* (born 20 Sept. 1972). **Deborah** married secondly Floyd Nash (div.), thirdly Lewis Gooding in 1982 (div.), and fourthly Donnie Duncan. Deborah Duncan works in the Packaging Department at Universal Plastics, Cookeville, TN.

KIN BURGESS OF PUTNAM CO., TENNESSEE
[Charles Lafayette[6], Ammon Lafayette[7]]

8e. **William McKinley "Kin"** *[son of Ammon Lafayette].* His name is listed as "Don" in the 1920 census. Born 24 Dec. 1919 in Putnam Co., TN. Married Ella Mae Maxwell about 1945 (she was born 12 Mar. 1926). Kin Burgess worked as a tool and die setter in a stamping plant in Detroit, MI before retiring. He died 11 Mar. 1989 at Cookeville, TN, and is buried in the Howard Cemetery.

9a. **Ronald McKinley.** Born 23 July 1946 at Detroit, MI. Married Teresa Booth on 20 Aug. 1966 at Madison Heights, MI (she was born 22 July 1948). Ron Burgess works for the Internal Revenue Service at Cookeville, TN.

10a. **Aaron McKinley.** Born 19 May 1973 at Knoxville, TN.

9b. **Phyllis Diane.** Born 10 Oct. 1948 at Detroit, MI. Married Jack Lloyd Payne on 14 Dec. 1968 in Oakland Co., MI (he was born 10 Dec. 1945), and had children: *Jack Lloyd II* (born 5 Mar. 1970 in Germany); *Elizabeth Ann* (born 12 Dec. 1974 at Warren, MI). Phyllis Payne is a secretary for the Public Schools System at Cookeville, TN. She has contributed greatly to this book.

9c. **Patricia Ellen "Trish."** Born 29 May 1954 at Detroit, MI. Married Clinton Ammon Bowen III on 26 Aug. 1972 in Oakland Co., MI (he was born 24 Apr. 1952), and had children: *Tara McKenzie* (born 8 July 1981 in Putnam Co., TN); *Clinton Ammon IV* (born 6 Apr. 1984 in Putnam Co., TN). Trish Bowen works for the U.S. Postal Service at Cookeville, TN.

ZEBBIE D. BURGESS OF WAYNE CO., MICHIGAN

[Charles Lafayette[6], Ammon Lafayette[7]]

8f. **Zebbie D.** (nmn) *[son of Ammon Lafayette].* Born 3 Mar. 1923 in Putnam Co., TN. Married Arlene Rose Huebner (she was born 2 Nov. 1930). Zeb Burgess currently works for Fisher Body Co. at Detroit, MI.

9a. **Gertrude Elizabeth.** Born 14 Nov. 1961 at Detroit, MI.
9b. **Linda Sue (IV).** Born 1 Nov. 1962 at Detroit, MI.
9c. **Shirley Ann (VI).** Born 22 Jan. 1964 at Detroit, MI.
9d. **Sharon Rose.** Born 17 Dec. 1965 at Detroit, MI.

PAYNE BURGESS OF PUTNAM CO., TENNESSEE

[Charles Lafayette[6]]

7d. **(Pretteman) Payne "Paynie"** *[son of Charles Lafayette].* Born 11 Oct. 1882 (or 1883, according to his draft record) in White Co., TN. Married his first cousin, once removed, Mertie M. Carr on 21 Nov. 1900 in White Co. (she was born 26 Aug. 1884, daughter of Margaret Susanne Massa and James J. Carr, and granddaughter of Andrew R. Massa and Betsy Burgess, and died 19 Sept. 1960). Mertie is listed as head of the family in the 1910 census for Cumberland Co.; Payne is listed in the 1918 draft register (as "Purtyman" Burgess) and in the 1920 census for Putnam Co., TN. Payne Burgess was a federal revenue officer and farmer in Putnam Co., TN. He died there on 21 Jan. 1944, and is buried with his wife in the Howard Cemetery, White Co., TN.

8a. **Ridley A.** Born 23 Sept. 1901 in Putnam Co., TN. See below for full entry.
8b. **Child.** Born and died 1903, buried with its parents.
8c. **(Linnie) Sibol.** Her name is spelled Syble in the 1920 census. Born 25 Jan. 1905 in Putnam Co., TN. Married Thomas Alexander Brumbalow Sr. on 7 Aug. 1921 (he was born 18 Jan. 1895, and died 1 Aug. 1935), and had children:

Margaret Elouise **BRUMBALOW**. Born 2 Sept. 1922, married Rudolph Graham on 3 Mar. 1944 (he was born 10 July 1924), and had children: *Lee* (twin; born 21 Sept. 1949, married Bob Covington, and had children: Brent); *Dee* (twin; born 21 Sept. 1949).

Dimple Pauline **BRUMBALOW**. Born 27 Apr. 1924, married Hugh Johnson on 8 Sept. 1941 (he was born 4 Oct. 1916, and died 30 July 1990), had children: *Brenda* (born 16 June 1943, married William Ledbetter on 29 June 1962 [he was born 20 Apr. 1937], and had children: Denise [born 25 Oct. 1963, married Tommy Duren on 25 June 1982 {he was born 25 Dec. 1963}, and had children: Justin {born 26 May 1986}; Jeremy {twin; born 22 Mar. 1990}; Jessica {twin; born 22 Mar. 1990}]; Douglas [born 22 June 1965]); *Danny* (born 2 Feb. 1949, married Debbie Streetman on 1 Jan. 1971 [she was born 13 Apr. 1951], and had children: Kimberly [born 5 Feb. 1974]; Kevin [born 2 Dec. 1975]). Dimple Johnson currently lives at Duluth, GA.

Thomas Alexander **BRUMBALOW** *Jr.* Born 20 July 1927, married Betty Griffin on 10 Dec. 1954 (she was born 15 Nov. 1933), and had children: *Kenneth Bradford* (born 29 Mar. 1956, married Donna Beard on 1 Dec. 1979 [she was born 7 Oct. 1958], and had children: Michelle [born 8 Mar. 1982]); *Teresa Joy* (born 7 June 1960, married Billy Jones on 15 Sept. 1979 [he was born 3 Mar. 1959], and had children: David [born 9 Dec. 1981]; Dana [born 30 June 1986]).

Sibol BRUMBALOW currently lives at Duluth, GA.

8d. **Eula Ann.** Her name is spelled Ula in the 1920 census. Born 18 Aug. 1907 in Putnam Co., TN. Married Wilburn "Buck" Breeding on 13 Mar. 1932 in White Co. (he was born 25 Aug. 1906, and died 27 Dec. 1973), and had children: *Lillian Sybol* (born 20 Sept. 1932, married Perry Graham on 13 Jan. 1951 [he was born 27 Nov. 1928], and had children: Michael [married Gail ___, and had children: David; Billy]; Denise [married Chuck Owens, and had children: Demerice Rodney; Sarah]). Eula Breeding died on 3 Dec. 1975, and is buried with her husband in the Howard Cemetery, White Co, TN.

RIDLEY BURGESS OF PUTNAM CO., TENNESSEE

[Charles Lafayette[6], Pretteman Payne[7]]

8a. **Ridley A.** *[son of Pretteman Payne].* His middle initial is given as "A." in the 1910 census (possibly "Andrew" for his great-grandfather, or "Apple" for Ridley Apple). Born 23 Sept. 1901 in Putnam Co., TN. Married Velma Lee Randolph on 27 Apr. 1919 in Putnam Co., TN (she was born 7 Sept. 1904, daughter of Alonzo Randolph and Lois Ethel Bray, remarried Irvin Deck and thirdly V. Kuykendall, and died Sept. 1983 at Dumas, TX). Listed with his father in the 1920 census. Ridley Burgess was a deputy sheriff and farmer in Putnam Co. He was shot and killed by bootleggers on 3 Nov. 1932 in Putnam Co., TN, and is buried in the Howard Cemetery.

9a. **Bonnie Louise.** Born 18 Feb. 1920 in Putnam Co., TN. Married Herman Robert Packebush on 25 May 1935 (he was born 24 Aug. 1915, and died 14 June 1974), and had children: *Richard Dean* (born 30 Jan. 1936, married Louella Ferguson on 12 July 1959, and had children: (Tombers) Kay [born 24 Oct. 1959, married Daryl Dickey on 17 Oct. 1975]; Tammy Dean [born 26 Mar. 196_]; Robert Samuel [born 28 July 1965]; Sarah Jane [born 6 Oct. 196_]; Lisa Dianna [born 8 Sept. 1970]); *Sarah Lee* (born 30 June 1937, married Joe Pat Mowery on 19 May 1955 [he was born 17 Jan. 1935], and had children: Kelly Dawn [born 12 June 1957]; Karla Joe [born 3 May 1960]). Bonnie Packebush currently lives at Dumas, TX.

9b. **Leonard Carlos.** Born 17 July 1923 at Hooker, OK. Married Dona Blanche Cooper on 28 July 1942 (she was born 24 Nov. 1922). Leonard Burgess died Jan. 1984 at Dumas, Moore Co., TX.

10a. **Suzanne** (nmn). Born 23 Oct. 1948 at Borger, TX. Married Randy Eugene Green on 25 May 1967 (he was born 22 Oct. 1944), and had children: *Misty Dawn* (born 28 June 1968); *Randy Eugene II* (born 1 Oct. 1970).

10b. **(Mary) Mahana.** Born 25 Dec. 1953 at Borger, TX. Married Robert Andrews on 22 May 1976, and had two children.

9c. **Minnie Ethel.** Born 10 July 1928 at Nashville, TN. Married Arley Lloyd Stafford (he was born 8 Oct. 1928), and had children: *Michael Lloyd* (born 25 Sept. 1959). Minnie Stafford currently lives at Dumas, TX.

RICHARD H. BURGESS Sr. OF PALM BEACH CO., FLORIDA

[Charles Lafayette[6]]

7i. **Richard Herbert (I) "Tom"** *[son of Charles Lafayette].* Born 17 Oct. 1895 in Putnam Co., TN. Married Dorothy Mae Little on 11 Aug. 1925 in Putnam Co. (she was born 17 Apr. 1906 at Star Point, TN, daughter of William Jarvis Little and Linnie Leotha Young). Listed in the 1910 census living with his father, and in 1920 as "Thomas Burgess," with his cousin Payne Burgess. Served in the U.S. Navy during World War I. Tom Burgess was a barber, policeman, and construction worker. He joined the U.S. Prohibition Service (later the Alcohol Tax Unit of the Treasury Department) about 1928 in Tennessee, before retiring in 1950 to West Palm Beach, FL. He died of a heart attack on 31 May 1967 at Lantana, FL, and is buried in the Hillcrest Memorial Cemetery, West Palm Beach. Dorothy Burgess is an artist and seamstress; she currently lives at Lantana, FL.

8a. **Richard Herbert (II).** Born 5 Dec. 1926 at Sparta, TN. See below for full entry.

8b. **Charles Jarvis.** Born 7 Sept. 1928 at Sparta, TN. See below for full entry.

8c. **James Zebedee (I).** Born 28 July 1930 at Nashville, TN. See below for full entry.

8d. **William Howard (I).** Born 19 Aug. 1932 at Lawrenceburg, Lawrence Co., TN. See below for full entry.

8e. **Thomas Edward (I).** Born 7 Apr. 1936 at Lawrenceburg, Lawrence Co., TN. See below for full entry.

8f. **Margaret Ann (II) "Peggy."** Born 9 June 1938 at Crestview, Lawrence Co., TN. Married John Frederick Franz Jr. on 7 Sept. 1957 (div.; he was born 1 Dec. 1935, son of John Frederick Franz and Margaret Morgan Turrentine, and married secondly Shelia Jane Thorington on 30 Apr. 1983 [she was born 5 June 1936 at Chincoteague, VA, married firstly Michael F. Tenace {he was born 24 Feb. 1934, and died 10 Nov. 1978}]), and had children: *John Frederick III* (born 18 July 1958 at Quantico, VA); *Elizabeth Ann* (born 27 Mar. 1961 at San Diego, CA); *Gray Turrentine* (born 18 Oct. 1962 at West Palm Beach, FL, married Beth Grove on 10 Mar. 1990); Peggy married secondly Mike Markham. Peggy Markham lives at Ft. Lauderdale, FL.

8g. **Dorothy Elizabeth "Dottie."** Born 21 Dec. 1939 at Crestview, Lawrence Co., TN. Married Bobby Gene Ball Sr. on 30 June 1962 (div.; he was born 11 June 1940 at Pahokee, FL, son of Robert Alton and Virginia "Virgie" Ball), and had children: *Deborah Lyn* (born and died 9 Jan. 1963 at West Palm Beach, FL); *Bobby Gene Jr.* (born 19 Dec. 1963 at West Palm Beach, FL); *(Suzette) Lyn* (born 9 Jan. 1965 at West Palm Beach, FL). **Dorothy** married secondly Frederic William Horet. Dorothy Horet lives at Atlanta, GA.

8h. **John Franklin (II).** Born 18 Aug. 1941 at Crestview, Lawrence Co., TN. See below for full entry.

RICHARD H. BURGESS Jr. OF FORSYTH CO., GEORGIA

[Charles Lafayette[6], Richard Herbert (I)[7]]

8a. **Richard Herbert (II) "Dick"** *[son of Richard Herbert (I)].* Born 5 Dec. 1926 at Sparta, TN. Married Lenore Ann "Lee" Peters on 5 Mar. 1950 at West Palm Beach, FL (she was born 6 Oct. 1930 at Oak Park, IL, daughter of Arnold John Peters and Myrtle Ann Becher). Served in the U.S. Navy in World War II. Dick Burgess Jr. is a real estate developer at Cumming, GA.

9a. **Richard Herbert III "Rick."** Born 31 Dec. 1950 at Ft. Lauderdale, FL. Married Margaret Louise "Peggy" Shiver on 23 June 1973 at Atlanta, GA (she was born 18 Sept. 1950). Rick Burgess is a civil engineer and project manager for Hardin International, Atlanta, GA.

10a. **Elizabeth Leigh "Beth."** Born 8 Nov. 1977 at Jacksonville, FL.
10b. **Genevieve Louise "Ginny."** Born 3 May 1981 at Jacksonville, FL.
10c. **Margaret Ann (IV).** Born 29 Sept. 1985 at Atlanta, GA.

9b. **David Arnold.** Born 16 Dec. 1954 at West Palm Beach, FL. Married (Mary) Marguerite "Margie" Waldron on 20 Oct. 1979 at Macon, GA. Dr. David A. Burgess, a former Major in the U.S. Air Force, is an orthopedic surgeon at Waynesboro, VA.

10a. **Kristen Lynn.** Born 25 Nov. 1983 at Atlanta, GA.
10b. **Lauren Marguerite.** Born 10 May 1986 at Clark Air Force Base, The Philippines.

CHARLES J. BURGESS OF OKEECHOBEE CO., FLORIDA

[Charles Lafayette[6], Richard Herbert (I)[7]]

8b. **Charles Jarvis** *[son of Richard Herbert (I)].* Born 7 Sept. 1928 at Sparta, TN. Married Elise Collins on 22 Sept. 1953 (div.; she was born 26 Jan. 1935, daughter of Hobart and Celia Collins, and died on 23 May 1965 of injuries suffered in a plane crash at Beloit, WI); married secondly Pat Mathes on 26 Jan. 1966 (div.; she was born 26 Oct. 1927); married thirdly Jo Kribbs on 15 Dec. 1978 (she was born 7 Sept. 1937, daughter of Philip Kribbs and Wilavene Gray). Served in the U.S. Navy. Charles Burgess is a real estate salesman at Okeechobee, FL. He also is an avid fisherman and musician.

9a. **Charlene Elise** (twin). Born 11 Feb. 1955 at West Palm Beach, FL. She died on 1 Apr. 1965 at Beloit, WI in the light plane crash that killed her mother.
9b. **Cheryl Lynn (I)** (twin). Born 11 Feb. 1955 at West Palm Beach, FL. Married Dan Fitzgerald on 26 Sept. 1974 (div.). Cheryl Fitzgerald currently lives at Jupiter, FL.

JAMES Z. BURGESS Sr. OF PUTNAM CO., TENNESSEE

[Charles Lafayette[6], Richard Herbert (I)[7]]

8c. **James Zebedee (I)** *[son of Richard Herbert (I)].* Born 28 July 1930 at Nashville, TN. Married Bona Jean Marie "Bonnie" Stoltz on 6 Sept. 1956 at Bainbridge, GA (she was born 14 May 1934 at Harlan, IA, daughter of Bernard Nicholas "Barney" Stoltz and Anna Marie Engel). Jim Burgess operates his own title searching company at Cookeville, TN. In 1977 he published and edited *Burgess History: The Tennessee Pioneer*, a massive, well-illustrated history of the Putnam Co., Tennessee Burgess families; he also helped organize the Burgess reunions held every five years at Burgess Falls State Park. He is a major contributor to this new book.

9a. **James Zebedee (II) "Jimmie."** Born 21 Nov. 1958 at Stuart, FL. Married Amy Fulger on 24 Nov. 1990. Jimmie Burgess is a produce broker for C. H. Robinson Co., Atlanta, GA.

10a. **Erika Rae**. Born 16 Oct. 1992 at Atlanta, GA.

9b. **Michael Anthony.** Born 18 Jan. 1960 at Stuart, FL. Married Marda Janelle Dugger on 7 Oct. 1989 at Conyers, GA. Mike Burgess is a computer programmer for National Data Corporation at Atlanta, GA.

10a. **Austin Michael**. Born 24 May 1993 at Atlanta, GA.

9c. **Rochelle Lynn.** Born 23 Dec. 1963 at Stuart, FL. Married Charles Eugene Roulette on 14 Mar. 1990 at Cookeville, Putnam Co., TN (he was born 25 Feb. 1953). Rochelle Roulette works with handicapped and retarded children at Greenville, SC. She has also written two books: *The Stoltz Family History* (1986) and *The Engel Family History* (1986).

9d. **Carol Anne.** Born 11 Apr. 1973 at Atlanta, GA. Married Mark Clay Farris II on 14 Nov. 1992 at Cookeville, Putnam Co., TN. Carol Farris lives at Cookeville, TN.

WILLIAM H. BURGESS Sr. OF PERRY CO., TENNESSEE

[Charles Lafayette[6], Richard Herbert (I)[7]]

8d. **William Howard (I) "Bill"** *[son of Richard Herbert (I)]*. Born 19 Aug. 1932 at Lawrenceburg, Lawrence Co., TN. Married Lucy Andrews on 3 June 1951 (she was born 4 Aug. 1936 in NJ, daughter of Ed and Myrtle Andrews). Bill Burgess is a farmer and lumber mill operator at Lobelville, TN.

9a. **Billie Lou.** Born 26 Jan. 1953 at Palm Beach, FL. Married Terry Jones (div.; he was born 22 Apr. 1948); married secondly Bruce Reinert in 1976 (he was born 13 Apr. 1947), and had children: *Christina Mia* (born 2 Aug. 1979); *Matthew Cooper* (born 1 Oct. 1982); *Andrew Howard* (born 11 Nov. 1984); *Spencer Thomas* (born 7 Jan. 1990).

9b. **(William) Howard (III) "Howie."** Born 20 Aug. 1957 at Palm Beach, FL. Married Joyce Koponka on 23 Oct. 1982 (she was born 21 Dec. 1960). Howie Burgess is a logger at Columbia, TN.

10a. **William Howard III (IV) "Billy."** Born 9 May 1983 at Columbia, TN.

10b. **Jessica Nicole "Jessi."** Born 8 Nov. 1984 at Columbia, TN.

THOMAS E. BURGESS Sr. OF DE KALB CO., GEORGIA

[Charles Lafayette[6], Richard Herbert (I)[7]]

8e. **Thomas Edward (I)** *[son of Richard Herbert (I)]*. Born 7 Apr. 1936 at Lawrenceburg, Lawrence Co., TN. Married Marilyn Louise Hardwick on 3 Sept. 1954 (she was born 8 Nov. 1935 at West Palm Beach, FL, the daughter of Thomas Merrill Hardwick and Helen Louise Frantz). Tom Burgess owns and operates Sewing Sales & Service Co., Doraville, GA.

9a. **Thomas Edward (II).** Born 24 Apr. 1955 at West Palm Beach, FL. Married Christy Valeria Bellew on 10 July 1976 (she was born 9 Nov. 1955, the daughter of William Bellew and Bennie Southern). Tom Burgess lives at Cornelia, GA.

10a. **Craig Matthew** (ad.). Born 28 Aug. 1971 in De Kalb Co., GA.

10b. **Joshua Thomas** (triplet). Born 17 Aug. 1977 in De Kalb Co., GA; died on 16 Feb. 1979 at Renton, WA.

10c. **Joseph Christopher** (triplet). Born 17 Aug. 1977 in De Kalb Co., GA.

10d. **Jacob William** (triplet). Born 17 Aug. 1977 in De Kalb Co., GA.

10e. **Thomas Edward III "Tommy."** Born 7 June 1981 at Lobelville, TN.

10f. **Nathan Andrew.** Born 28 Mar. 1984 at Douglasville, GA.

9b. **Robert Steven "Bobby."** Born 6 Dec. 1956 at West Palm Beach, FL. Married Lori Pinkonsky on 9 Sept. 1990.

9c. **Donald Scott.** Born 21 May 1958 at West Palm Beach, FL. Married Gloria Elaine Long on 14 Feb. 1980. Don Burgess is a driver for United Parcel Service.

10a. **Robert Lloyd "Bobby"** (ad.). Born 25 Apr. 1975.

10b. **(Kevin) Brent.** Born 26 Apr. 1981 in Chattooga Co., GA.

10c. **Brian Joseph.** Born 4 Jan. 1983 in Chattooga Co., GA.

10d. **Brandi Louise.** Born 19 Apr. 1984 in Chattooga Co., GA.

9d. **Mark Timothy (II).** Born 5 Mar. 1960 at West Palm Beach, FL. Married Donna Lynn Williams on 30 Oct. 1993 at Dunwoody, GA (she was born 16 Feb. 1963 at Arlington, VA, daughter of Dwight Nelson Williams and Janice Irene Ohman).

9e. **Ellen Louise.** Born 5 Oct. 1961 at Winter Park, FL. Married Michael Anthony DeLuise Sr. on 19 June 1982 at Atlanta, GA (he was born 7 Mar. 1956, son of John Anthony DeLuise and Dorothy Ray Kennedy), and had children: *Michael Anthony Jr.* (born 16 June 1984 at Atlanta, GA); *Kathryn Louise* (born 1 Mar. 1986 at Atlanta, GA). Ellen DeLuise is a court reporter at Atlanta, GA.

9f. **Lori Lynn.** Born 30 June 1964 at Winter Park, FL. Married David Anthony Petroni on 4 Apr. 1987, and had children: *Maria Louise* (born 20 July 1990 at Cary, NC).

9g. **Glen Alan.** Born 28 Feb. 1970 in De Kalb Co., GA. Married Emily Lillian Burnside on 12 Jan. 1991 at Atlanta, GA (she was born 18 May 1969 at Atlanta, GA, daughter of James Eugene Burnside and Dale Elizabeth Welch).

JOHN F. BURGESS Sr. OF COLLIER CO., FLORIDA

[Charles Lafayette[6], Richard Herbert (I)[7]]

8h. **John Franklin (II)** *[son of Richard Herbert (I)].* Born 18 Aug. 1941 at Crestview, Lawrence Co., TN. Married Linda Kathleen Laraway on 6 Oct. 1960 at Laraway, FL (she was born 13 Mar. 1940, the daughter of Hart Massey Laraway and Estelle Ellen Wisner). John Burgess is a real estate title searcher at Marco, FL.

9a. **Karen Lee (II).** Born 21 May 1961 at Lakeworth, FL. Married Steven Young on 19 Feb. 1983 (div.); married secondly Greg Griffen on 21 May 1987 (he was born 3 Feb. 1960), and had children: *Lance* (born 29 June 1988).

9b. **John Franklin (III) "J. B."** Born 14 July 1962 at Lakeworth, FL.

9c. **Christopher Thomas "Chris."** Born 7 July 1964 at West Palm Beach, FL. Currently serving in the U.S. Navy.

[William (I)[1], Edward (I)[2], Reuben (I)[3], Thomas (I)[4], Charles Hunter[5]]

VANCE DEKALB BURGESS
(1845-1932)

OF PUTNAM COUNTY, TENNESSEE

6j. **Vance Dekalb** *[son of Charles Hunter].* Born 17 (or 21, according to his tombstone) Oct. 1845 in White Co., TN. Married Susan Florilla Deering about 1864 (she was born 17 Oct. 1845, daughter of Zebedee P. Deering and Sarah Yount, and died 25 Apr. 1921). Listed in the 1870-1900 censuses for Putnam Co., TN (in 1870 in the 1st Civil District, in 1880 in the 16th District), in 1910 in Cumberland Co., TN, and in 1920 in Putnam Co., TN. Vance Burgess was a farmer in Putnam Co. He died there on 19 (or 18) June 1932, and is buried with his wife in the Allison Cemetery, Putnam Co.

The Children of Vance D. Burgess:

7a. **(Nancy) Caroline.** Born about 1865 in Putnam Co., TN; died there before 1880.
7b. **Sarah Ann (III).** Born about 1866 in Putnam Co., TN; died there before 1880.
7c. **John A. "Johnny."** Born about 1867 in Putnam Co., TN; died there before 1880.
7d. **(Harriet) Jane.** Born 4 Nov. 1868 in Putnam Co., TN. Married John Bailey Dixon "Bird" Sliger about 1887 (he was born 29 Feb. 1868, son of Samuel Sliger, remarried Mary Cleveland Mitchell on 4 July 1920, and died 8 Dec. 1935), and had children:

Mary Flora SLIGER. Born 23 Oct. 1888, married Jimmy Rogers, and died 10 Aug. 1963, having had children: *Lillie* (married ___ Maxwell); *Lizzie* (married ___ Maxwell).

(John) Hershal SLIGER. Born 28 Dec. 1889, died 6 Dec. 1900, buried with his parents.

Vance Dow SLIGER. Born 22 Dec. 1891, married Gertrude Gentry, and died 28 June 1942 in OK, having had children: *Veler Gladys* (married ___ Minor); *Vallie* (married ___ Voyles); *John Thurman.*

Cora Belle SLIGER. Born 5 Oct. 1893, married Ridley Pendergrass, and died 24 Dec. 1975 at Ada, OK, having had children: *Pauline*; *Ila* (married ___ Penahouse); *Elowene* (married ___ Penahouse).

John Bailey Dixon SLIGER Jr. Born and died 22 Mar. 1895, buried with his parents.

Andrew Robert SLIGER. Born 1 Sept. 1896, married Roshie (or Rocie) Roberts (she died 10 Oct. 1970), and died 26 May 1963, having had children: *Verlie Marie* (married ___ Flowers); *Willard*; *Robert*; *J. B.*; *Edith* (married ___ Flowers); *Avana*; *Vera* (married ___ Deaton); *Jane* (married ___ York); *Royce*; *June* (married ___ McCalley); *Myra* (married ___ Nichols); *Aevilda.*

Dora Anna SLIGER. Born 6 Jan. 1899, married Melvin Franklin, and died 6 July 1919, having had children: *Dorlene* (born 28 June 1919, and died 3 Aug. 1919).

Nora Avo SLIGER. Born 15 July 1901, married William Arthur Austin, and died 9 June 1976, having had children: *William Arthur Jr.*; *Johnny L.*; *Flora J.* (married ___ Young); *Riba M.* (married ___ Gentry); *Clayton D.*; *Billy T.*

Charles McTeer SLIGER. Born 6 July 1903, married (Mary) Ann "Annie" Thompson, and had children: *Kebie T.* (married ___ Bennett).

John Bailey Dixon SLIGER III. Born and died 22 Feb. 1905, buried with his parents.

Ora Peek SLIGER. Born 12 Nov. 1907, and died 14 Sept. 1910, buried with his parents.

Samuel L. SLIGER. Born 2 Sept. 1910, married Boda Jarrett, and died July 1987 at Ada, OK, having had children: *Samuel L. Jr.*; *Rosemary D.* (married ___ Chatham); *Dwindle S.* (married ___ Steel).

Zora America SLIGER. Born 13 Sept. 1912, married Ernest Haskell Austin, and secondly Willis B. Dyer (he was born 24 Dec. 1897), and had children: *Elizabeth Carlene* (married ___ Robertson).

Jane SLIGER died on 15 Nov. 1918 in Putnam Co., and is buried with her husband in the Allison Cemetery.

7e. **(Dorinda) America "Merky."** Born 25 Aug. 1870 in Putnam Co., TN. Married as his third wife William Campbell Patton on 19 May 1895 (he was born 7 May 1862 in Putnam Co., son of Samuel Patton and Malinda Byers, married firstly Parthena Jane Haggard in June 1883, and had children: *Mary Frances* [born 30 Sept. 1884, and died 1898]; married secondly Sarah Texas Pharris in 1888, and had children: *Eliza Jane* [born 8 Dec. 1893, married Chaston Ellis, and died 17 Oct. 1966], worked as a veterinarian and farmer, and died 8 June 1937). America and William had children:

Lily May PATTON. Born and died 2 May 1896 in Putnam Co., TN, buried Maxwell Cemetery.

(William) Hobart PATTON. Born 18 Sept. 1897 in Putnam Co., TN, married as her second husband Lassie Odell Watts on 18 Aug. 1918 in Putnam Co. (she was born 2 Nov. 1902 in Putnam Co., daughter of Wesley Harvie Watts and Mary King Traywick, and died 16 Oct. 1973 in Putnam Co.), worked as a farmer, and died 3 Feb. 1986 at Baxter, TN, being buried with his wife in the Maxwell Cemetery. They had children: *Carlos D.* (born 19 Apr. 1920 in Putnam Co., died 1 May 1920, buried Maxwell Cemetery); *Ruby Elizabeth* (born 10 Feb. 1922, died 1 Dec. 1926, buried Maxwell Cemetery); *Azilee* (born 23 June 1923, married Alvis Clyde Wilkerson on 2 Sept. 1939 [he was the son of Benton Cisro Wilkerson and Cora Etta Gentry]; *Ralph Glen* (born 8 Sept. 1928, married Ellen Louise Denton on 23 Dec. 1950 [daughter of Jeseph Denton and Nannie Franks], and had children: Glenda Faye [born 27 Sept. 1951, married Roy Mack Edwards in Aug. 1969 {div.}, and had children: Tammy {born 5 Apr. 1972}]; Rita Louise [born 18 June 1955, married Steve Scofield {div.}]; Donna Marie [born 29 Dec. 1962 at Tampa, FL]); *Robert Denton* (born 1 July 1931, married (Patricia) Kathleen Griffin on 2 May 1952 [daughter of Rance Griffin and Edna Caldwell], and had children: Delila Sue [born 14 Sept. 1953, married Andy Libby Jr. on 12 Oct. 1974, and had children: Maurene {born 26 Oct. 1982}]; (Robert) Samson [born 21 Dec. 1955, married Patricia Chapman on 9 Aug. 1975 at Tampa, FL, and had children: Patricia Kathleen {born 1 Oct. 1978}; Robert Lelan {born 28 Sept. 1982}; married secondly Teresa Viner in 1984]; Ruby Magdalean [born 13 Oct. 1956, and had children: Patrick {born 29 Dec. 1973 at Miami, FL}; Tommy {born 12 June 1979}]; Joseph Randall [born 3 Apr. 1959 at Tampa, FL, died 16 Apr. 1959, buried Crestlawn Cemetery, Cookeville, TN]; Timothy Darnell [born 21 Feb. 1961 at Tampa, FL]).

(Joseph) Colby PATTON. Born 14 Dec. 1898 in Putnam Co., TN, married Irene Mertis Alden in 1926, and had children: *Genevieve* (born 18 July 1926 at Houston, TX); *(Joseph) Arnold* (born 5 July 1929). ***Colby*** married secondly Alma Martens on 23 June 1933, had children: *Carleann*. ***Colby*** died 6 July 1979 at Tomball, TX.

(Enoch) Roosevelt PATTON. Born 30 Mar. 1900 in Putnam Co., TN, married Alice Cullen (she was born 28 Apr. 1904, died July 1973, buried Springfield, IL), had children: *(Mary) Alice* (born 1930, married J. Raymond Plummer, and had children: Alice; Julia; Elizabeth); *Janie* (born 1931, married Richard L. Schoenberger, and had children: Mary; Elizabeth Cullen; Katie; Susan; Richie); *(William) Cullen* (born 1936, married Beverly Conger Smith, and had children: Will; George; Eyderie); *Margaret Ann "Peggy"* (born 1941, married Robert S. O'Shea, and had children: Robert W. Theodore "Ted"; Suzanne Alice), and died 1969 at Springfield, IL.

America PATTON was a midwife in Putnam Co., TN, and a member of the Methodist Church. She died there on 16 Dec. 1946, and is buried with her husband in the Maxwell Cemetery. Azilee Wilkerson has contributed greatly to this book; she currently lives at Cookeville, TN.

7f. **Charles Zebedee.** Born 3 Apr. 1873 in Putnam Co., TN. See below for full entry.

7g. **(Robert) Winfield.** Born 1 Oct. 1875 in Putnam Co., TN. See below for full entry.

7h. **Vance Andrew.** Born 22 May 1878 in Putnam Co., TN. See below for full entry.

7i. **(Susan) Bell.** Her name is listed as Belle on her marriage certificate. Born 1880 in Putnam Co., TN. Married J. Frank Chaffin on 12 Jan. 1902 in Putnam Co. (he may have been born 2 May 1871, and died 12 Oct. 1925, buried Rash Cemetery, Jackson Co.), and had children: *Lewis E.* (born 23 June 1906 in Jackson Co., TN, married Lyda Anderson [she was born 29 Jan. 1911], and died 4 Sept. 1987, having had children: Davis [born 29 June 1935, married Sue Swan, and had children: Sherry; Jeffrey]; Donald Wayne [born 4 July 1938, married Judy Swan, and had children: Donna; Jimmy]; Joy [born 10 Nov. 1942, married Joe Dennis, and had children: Juanita; Freddie; Diane]). **Bell** married secondly Dave Fox after 1920. Listed with her father in the 1920 census (as Bell Chaffin). Bell Fox died after 1920 of cancer.

7j. **(Amandá) Avo.** Her name is listed as Ivor on her marriage certificate. Born 5 May 1883 in Putnam Co., TN. Married Hiram Washington Cole on 24 June 1906 in Putnam Co. (he was born 29 Nov. 1870, and died 17 Nov. 1944), and had children:

(Ernest) Harlan COLE. Born 20 July 1907, married Estella Vieres (who died young), and died Dec. 1973, having had children: *Dewanda Mae* (born 12 Sept. 1935).

***(Thelma) Pauline* COLE**. Born 20 June 1909, married Russell Vernon Barrow, and had children: *Charles Freeman.*

***Bonnie Blue Eyes* COLE**. Born 12 Apr. 1911, married Paul Reynolds, and had children: *Paul Jr.*; *Thelma L.* (married ___ Reeves); *Shirley J.* (married ___ Stephens); *Virginia* (married ___ Richesson); *Richard D.*; *Marilyn T.* (married ___ Evans); *Robert V.*; *Rosemarie* (married ___ Keller); *Peggy A.* (married ___ Thornton).

***Lawrence Hooper* COLE** (twin). Born 22 Feb. 1913, married Mae ___, and had children: *Donald*; married secondly Anna Bunton.

***Clarence Cooper* COLE** (twin). Born 22 Feb. 1913, died young.

***Daughter* COLE** (twin). Born and died 12 Dec. 1919.

***(Dillard) Vance* COLE** (twin). Born 12 Dec. 1919, married Margaret Cardwell (she was born 26 Aug. 1921), and had children: *Margaret Helen* (married ___ Bacon); *Carolyn Diane* (married ___ Ellington); *Kenneth Vance.*

***(Susan) Beatrice* COLE**. Born 10 July 1921, married Bernard Bruley (he was born 1916, and died 1984), and had children: *Robert Ernest* [born 22 June 1963); *Steven* (born 2 Apr. 1965, married Carla Gaforfki on 22 Aug. 1987); ***Beatrice* COLE** married secondly Alva O'Brien on 14 Dec. 1985 (he was born 23 Aug. 1915).

***(Ruby) Willene* COLE**. Born 23 July 1923, married Thomas Rudolph, and had children: *Gerald Thomas*; *William Cole*; *Cynthia Mae.*

***(Emma) Jean* COLE**. Born 1925, married Samuel Guy Jones, and had children: *Nancy Marie* (married ___ Hay).

(Virginia) Estine* COLE**. Born 7 Mar. 1927, married Francis Leon Allen, and had children: *Michael David* (born Apr. 1949); *Susan Darlene* (born 11 July 1950, married Henri Julien Giraud on 5 Dec. 1969, and had children: Tracy Lynn [born 19 Nov. 1971]). ***Estine married secondly Carl Glaser, and had children: *Carla Ann* (born 8 Feb. 1955, married William McLaughlin on 11 Oct. 1973, and had children: Tara Elizabeth [born Jan. 1975]; William Edward [born 3 Aug. 1976]; Kelly Leanne [born 22 Aug. 1981]); *Edward Glenn* (born 11 June 1963).

Avo COLE died on 10 June 1957 at Detroit MI, and is buried in the Roseland Cemetery, Berkley, MI. Susan Giraud and Carla McLaughlin both live at Rockwood, MI.

7k. **Thomas Peek.** Born 24 Feb. 1885 (or 1884) in Putnam Co., TN. See below for full entry.

7l. **Margaret (IX).** Born about 1887 in Putnam Co., TN, and is believed to have died young. Order and dates uncertain.

7m. **Ollie Frances.** Born 4 Jan. 1889 in Putnam Co., TN. Married Monroe "Roe" Gentry on 31 Mar. 1907 in Putnam Co. (he was born 18 Nov. 1884, son of John Whitley Gentry and Laura Josephine Maxwell, and died 28 Nov. 1956), and died on 17 July 1969 at Baxter, TN. Ollie and Roe Gentry had children:

***Una Avannah* GENTRY**. Born 25 Jan. 1908, married Olney Boyd Gentry on 8 Feb. 1931 (he was born 12 Aug. 1907, son of Emmett Clifton Gentry and Lillie G. Johnston, and died on 23 Oct. 1979), and had children: *Olney Boyd Jr.* (born 22 Dec. 1931, died 24 Dec. 1931 at Tribune, KS). ***Una* GENTRY** lives at Cookeville, TN.

***Dow Snowden* GENTRY**. Born 6 Jan. 1910, married Esther Jackson (div.), married secondly Lassie McDonald about 1944 (she was born 3 May 1915, daughter of Rev. E. M. McDonald and Maude Lou Johnson), and had children: *Dow Snowden Jr.* (born 22 July 1945, married Kathy Owens on 12 Sept. 1969, and had children: Catherine Ann [born 16 July 1970]; Dow Snowden III [born 12 Aug. 1971]; Frances Leona [born 8 Nov. 1974]); *Myron C.* (born 13 Jan. 1947, married Linda Durocher, and had children: Juli Thiline [born 9 June 1975]; Kenneth DeWayne [born 14 Nov. 1976]); *Frances Ann* (born 16 Oct. 1948, died 10 Sept. 1951 when she was hit by an automobile); *Dehugh Mack* (born 2 Feb. 1951, married Patricia Jennings on 21 June 1981); *Paul Thomas* (born 21 Sept. 1953, married Donna Jo Alexander on 12 June 1976, and had children: Brandi Renee [born 12 Nov. 1979]; (Thomas) Alexander [born 12 July 1982]); *James Edward* (born 19 Nov. 1955, married Shirley Faye Nabors [div.], and had one daughter; married secondly Debbie Campbell on 24 Aug. 1984, and had children: Stephanie Arlene [born 4 Feb. 1979]). ***Dow Snowden* GENTRY** died on 27 July 1971 at Baxter, TN, and is buried with his wife in the Maxwell Cemetery.

***Elbert Gray* GENTRY**. Born 6 Aug. 1912, married Rubye Mae Tallant on 21 May 1938 (she was born 28 Oct. 1907, daughter of Enoch Asberry Tallant and Margaret Hughes), and died 9 July 1980 at Baxter, TN, having had children: *Elbert Blaine* (born 2 Dec. 1939, married Glenda Petty [she was born 25 Nov. 1949], and had children: Ronald Gray [born 1 Aug. 1970, married Glenda Webb, and had children: Dustin Dwain]); *Lewis Neal* (born 16 Mar. 1941, married Joyce Travathan, and lives at Memphis, TN); *Betty Ann* (born 1 June 1943, married Willie G. Kohrs, and had children: Daniel Brian [born 25 Dec. 1977]); *Robert Floyd* (born 3 Nov. 1944, married Janet Bridger [she was born 26 Sept. 1949], and had children: Laurel Leigh [born 8 Aug. 1969]; Robert Floyd Jr. [born 4 Apr. 1973, died of leukemia in 1980]); *Norman Monroe* (born 10 Aug. 1946, married Patricia Kowalski [she was born 1 June 1949], and had children: Jacqueline Grace [born 29 Aug. 1979]); *Enoch Andrew* (born 23 Oct. 1948, married Camille Gurley, and had children: Enoch Andrew Jr. [born 29 Dec. 1980]; Amanda [born 22 July 1982]); *Carol Marie* (twin; born 14 Nov. 1950, married Richard McGee, and had children: Bethany Kay [ad.]); *Connie Lee* (twin; born 14 Nov. 1950, died 4 July 1951); *Edward Davis* (born 26 July 1952, married Teresa Langford [she was born 16 Sept. 1953], and had children: Edward Davis Jr. [born 28 Oct. 1976]; Lewis Wynn [born 11 Aug. 1980]); *Ruby Kay* (born 25 May 1954, married George Womack, and had children: Rachel; Victoria).

Alma Lee GENTRY. Born 21 Dec. 1914, married Allen Sneed Neville on 16 July 1933 in Putnam Co. (he was born 25 Feb. 1907, son of James Franklin Neville and Lela Mae Allen, and died 5 July 1977). They had children:

Dow Donnell NEVILLE (born 6 Sept. 1934, married Louellen Tucker [div.], and had children: (Larry) Gordon [born 27 May 1955, married Jan Blanton in 1976, and had children: Shannon {born 1 Sept. 1977}; Jeremy James {born 2 Aug. 1978}; Joshua Tucker {born 15 June 1981}; Andrew Gordon {born 28 Oct. 1982}]; Julie [born 21 Sept. 1956, married Edward Holland, and had children: Jennifer Brea {born Sept. 1977}; Allison {born 1981}]; *Dow NEVILLE* married secondly Geneva Pistole [she was born 28 Nov. 1921, and died 18 Jan. 1986], and thirdly Shirley Armistead, and lives at Mount Juliet, TN).

(Helen) Joy NEVILLE (born 26 June 1936, married Amil Doyce Mask on 10 June 1958 in NC [he was born 14 Jan. 1931], and had children: Russell Paul [born 2 Oct. 1960, married Viola Yeyen Salvio on 18 July 1987 at Manila, Philippines {she was born 7 May 1958}, and had children: Caleb Salvio {born 29 June 1988}; Elizabeth Joy {born 21 June 1990}]; James Davis "Jim" [born 23 Sept. 1963, married Kimberly Keeffe on 7 May 1988 {she was born 29 Jan. 1959}, and had children: Timothy Isaac {born 28 June 1993}]; Judy Lynn [born 8 Feb. 1965]; *Joy* and Amil Mask live at Amarillo, TX).

Evelyn Jean NEVILLE (born 24 May 1938, married Billie Ray Lowe on 26 Nov. 1958 [he was born 1 Jan. 1933], and had children: Ray Stuart [born 8 Oct. 1960, married Robin Elaine Quesenberry on 14 Feb. 1993 at Mocks Corner, SC]; Regina Fay [born 9 Sept. 1962, married Donald Ricky Beasley on 21 Mar. 1980 at Nashville, TN, and had children: Kristy Michelle {born 26 Jan. 1980}; Eric Michael {born 31 Oct. 1981}; Shawn Patrick {born 7 May 1986}]; Ricky Dale [born 22 Sept. 1967, married Myrtie Lyn Kay on 9 June 1990 in NH, and had children: Ashley Marie {born 27 Dec. 1990}]; Rachel Ann [born 21 Apr. 1969]; *Evelyn* and Bill live at Nashville, TN).

(Lois) Faye NEVILLE (born 25 Jan. 1941, married (Denton) Eugene "Gene" Gentry on 16 Sept. 1966 [he was born 2 July 1939], and had children: Denton Eugene Jr. [born 4 June 1970]; Gene and *Faye* Gentry live at Grandview, MO).

Patsy Lee NEVILLE (born 17 Aug. 1946, married James Lee Milom on 16 Aug. 1969 [he was born 2 Sept. 1941; by his first wife he had children: Leigh Ann {born 11 Oct. 1963, married Andy Ward, and had children: Nikki <born 4 June 1990>}], and had children: (Theresa) Lynn [born 28 Aug. 1970, married (Michael) Scott Demonbreum on 10 Mar. 1990 at Henrietta, TN {div.}, and had children: Elizabeth Lynn {born 14 Jan. 1992}]; Kimberly Michelle [born 24 Oct. 1973]; *Patsy* and Jim live at Ashland City, TN).

Allen Sneed NEVILLE Jr. (born 9 Feb. 1949, married Koidula Korgermagi on 23 Mar. 1981 [she was born 3 May 1948], and had children: Jacob Karl [born 18 Jan. 1984]; Indrek [born 18 May 1989]; *Allen* and Koidula live at Dhahran, Saudi Arabia).

Alma NEVILLE died on 30 May 1992 at Nashville, TN, and is buried there with her husband in the Spring Hill Cemetery.

John Vance GENTRY. Born 13 Aug. 1918, married Lillian "Pat" Bailey, and had children: *Gordon Andrew* (ad.; born 23 May 1942); *Carol Rosalla* (ad.; born 11 June 1944, married James E. Gatton, and had children: Lori Marie [born 27 Dec. 1966]; Marie Nannette [born 3 July 1969]; Jamie Carol [born 30 Apr. 1972]); *Una Elizabeth* (born 28 Feb. 1947, married Doyle LaFeuer on 5 July 1964, and had children: Christopher Doyle [born 20 Nov. 1973]; James Lee [born 1 Dec. 1976]); *Pearl Marie* (born 8 June 1949, married Eddy Dean Hargis on 17 July 1974, and had children: Rodger Dean [born 17 July 1974]; Michael David [born Apr. 1977]); *John Vance Jr.* (born 1 Mar. 1953, married his distant cousin, Eulah Jean Burgess, and had children [see her entry]; *John* is City Manager of Cookeville, TN). ***John Vance GENTRY Sr.*** married secondly Mary Abel.

(William) Harding GENTRY. Born 12 Dec. 1920 at Baxter, TN, married Janette Alderman on 4 Apr. 1942 at Fort Polk, LA (she was born 27 Oct. 1922 at Chipley, FL, daughter of William Shepherd Alderman and Edna Mae Taylor), and had children: *(William) Harding Jr. "Sonny"* (born 13 Oct. 1946 at Albany, GA, married secondly Leeanne Pate on 10 Oct. 1986 at Memphis, TN); *(Dora) Jan* (born 25 Mar. 1950 at Albany, GA, married James Paul "Jim" Mayer on 19 Aug. 1968 at Brownsville, TN, and had children: Thomas Stanton; Marcie Roxanne); *(Patricia) Jill* (born 13 Oct. 1952 at Albany, GA, married John Shipp II in June 1974 at Brownsville, TN, and had children: Laura

Becca; John Harding; Kevin Christopher); *Lauren Mae "Laurie"* (born 25 Apr. 1957 at Albany, GA, married James "Jim" Duffey on 3 July 1983 at Brownsville, TN). Harding Gentry lives at Brownsville, TN.

Calvin Beecher GENTRY. Born 14 Oct. 1923, married (Arlie) Gylma Johnson on 10 Aug. 1947 (she was born 26 Jan. 1926, and died 13 Dec. 1990 at Memphis, TN), and had children: *Debbie Frances* (married Mark Hamilton, and had children: Chelsey).

Claude Thomas GENTRY. Born 23 June 1928, married Billie Jo Stewart (she was born 19 May 1932), and had children: *(Claude) Douglas* (born 19 Apr. 1947, married Alice Jean Halfacre, and had children: Tracy Lorraine [born 1 May 1970, married William Michael Austin on 9 Jan. 1993]; *Douglas* married secondly Beverly Hagan, and had children: Thomas Claude); *Donald Thomas* (born 14 June 1952, married Jo Ann Elmore, and had children: Jason; Charles William; *Donald* married secondly Nancy Hickey). Claude Gentry owns and operates Genco Stamping and Manufacturing Co. at Cookeville, TN.

CHARLES Z. BURGESS OF PUTNAM CO., TENNESSEE

[Vance Dekalb[6]]

7f. **Charles Zebedee** *[son of Vance Dekalb].* Born 3 Apr. 1873 in Putnam Co., TN. Married Emiline Frances "Emma" Gentry about 1893 (she died on 20 Sept. 1902); married secondly Ada Beulah Grant about 1904 (she was born 4 Feb. 1875, and died 25 May 1947 [or 1948]). Listed in the 1918 draft register and the 1900-20 censuses for Putnam Co., TN. Charles Z. Burgess was a farmer and sawmill owner in Putnam Co. He died on 24 Mar. 1956 at Cookeville, TN.

8a. **William Vance (III).** Born Dec. 1894 in Putnam Co., TN. William Burgess was accidentally killed about 1906 when he fell off a tram car.

8b. **(Mary) Ida (II).** Born 30 Sept. 1895 in Putnam Co., TN. Married John Hall on 7 Nov. 1911 in Putnam Co., and had children: *J. T.*; *A. P.*; *James*. Ida Hall died in Oct. 1980 at South Pittsburg, Marion Co., TN.

8c. **Settie Inellie Jane.** Born 26 Feb. 1897 in Putnam Co., TN. Married Lyge Tollett about 1914, and had children:

Waymon TOLLETT. Born about 1914, died at age one about 1915.

SETTIE BURGESS TOLLETT married secondly (John) Haskell Nabors on 19 Apr. 1915 in Putnam Co. (he was born 3 Feb. 1891, son of James Frank Nabors and Sarah Frances Haynes, and died 4 Aug. 1944, buried Judd Cemetery), and had children:

Harvey Edward NABORS. Born 6 June 1916, married Laura Sullivan on 5 Nov. 1933 (she was born 1919), served as a minister, and had children: *Charles Edward "Chuck"* (born 26 Sept. 1941, married Barbara Fisher, and had children: Karen; Charles Edward Jr.); *Terry Wayne* (born 17 May 1945, married Linda Judd, and had children: Mitzi; Chad); *James* (had one daughter).

Comer William NABORS. Born 17 Apr. 1918, married Ida Emery on 26 July 1936 in Putnam Co. (she was the daughter of Robert Luther Emery and Margaret Ann Baker), died in a fire on 6 June 1969, and had children: *Betty Jean* (born 16 Mar. 1938, married Thomas Griffith Jr., and had children: Ruthie Ann; Shelia Dianne); *Margie Sue* (born 11 June 1939, married Eldon Elwood Martin, and had children: Michael; Carol Sue); *Ruby Alene* (born 28 Sept. 1940, married Charles Whitmore, and had children: Teresa Jean; Kay; Junior; Vicki; Brenda); *Billy Joe* (born 1941, died young); *Wilma Ruth* (born 8 Sept. 1942, died unmarried with her father in a fire on 6 June 1969 at the Spring Street Market, Cookeville, TN, leaving children: Michelle Renee Nabors [married Michael Allen, and had children: Brandon Edgar {born 23 Dec. 1983}]); *Jimmy Lee* (born 8 Dec. 1945, married Betty Jane Braddom, and had children: Deborah Alene; Treva Jane; Tracy Lee); *Patricia Ann* (born 27 Feb. 1957, married DeWayne Tayes, and had children: Christi Michelle; Joshua DeWayne); *Shirley Faye* (born Apr. 1959, married Jimmy Gentry [div.], and had children: Stephanie Arlene); *Comer William Jr. "Billy"* (born Dec. 1961, married Carolyn Sue Globe).

Vida B. NABORS. Born 28 May 1920, died 23 Jan. 1944, buried Judd Cemetery.

Mary Emma NABORS. Born 6 Sept. 1922, married Jessie Gaw, and had children: *Wanda Rose* (born 30 Mar. 1941); *Jessie Ronald "Buddy"* (born 8 Dec. 1942); *Ridley Wayne*.

Vola NABORS. Born 25 Aug. 1924, married O. H. McAlpin.

Ruby NABORS. Born 2 Apr. 1925, married Ellis Stone, and had four children.

Lloyd NABORS. Born 25 Dec. 1927?, married Viola Stewart, and had seven children.

James R. NABORS. Born 5 Dec. 1928, married Juanita Ray Alcorn on 19 Nov. 1950, and had children: *Mitchell Wayne* (born 7 June 1955, married Janice Kimbrell on 1 Feb. 1974); *Anthony Ray* (born 25 Mar. 1962).

Bonnell D. NABORS. Born 26 Sept. 1930, married Doris LaFever, died 28 Aug. 1976, and had children: *Patricia*; *Barbara*; *Cathy*.

Novella NABORS. Born 9 Mar. 1933, married Coyle Roberson, and had five children.

Jo Ann W. NABORS. Born 21 July 1940, married Ralph James, and had children: *Dennis*; *Debra*.

SETTIE BURGESS NABORS married thirdly Virgle Enoch (he was born 30 Sept. 1911, and died Nov. 1980 at Carthage, TN, buried Brush Creek Memorial Gardens). She died on 13 Dec. 1992 at Cookeville, TN, aged 95 years.

8d. **Betty Frances.** Her name is listed as Bettie on her marriage certificate. Born 28 Feb. 1899 in Putnam Co., TN. Listed with her father in the 1920 census. Married Willie Gragg on 20 June 1920 in Putnam Co., and had children: *Cecil B.*; *Lilly B.* (married ___ Putty); *Francis*. Betty Gragg died about 1979 at Nashville, TN.

8e. **Ambrose Casswell.** Born 14 Mar. 1901 in Putnam Co., TN. See below for full entry.

8f. **Beulah Lee.** Born 20 May 1906 in Putnam Co., TN. Married Simon Elihu Thomas on 29 Dec. 1925 in Putnam Co. (he was born 6 Oct. 1905, and died 28 Jan. 1977), and had children: *(William) Carmel* (born 21 Nov. 1926, married Dean Ward, died 4 Feb. 1986); *Grace* (born 29 Oct. 1930, married [Cecil] Ray Presley); *Carl Burr* (born 26 Sept. 1936, married Dorothy Burchett). Beulah Thomas died on 2 Dec. 1983 at Cookeville, TN, and is buried in the Crest Lawn Cemetery.

8g. **Charles Peek.** Born 13 Nov. 1908 in Putnam Co., TN. See below for full entry.

8h. **Ollie Mae.** Born 23 June 1911 in Putnam Co., TN. Married Denton Livesay (he was born 5 Dec. 1908, and died Aug. 1975 at Dayton, OH), and had children: *Ronnie*; *Arnold*; *Darel*. Ollie Livesay died on 15 Mar. 1991 at Dayton, OH.

8i. **Joda Grant (I).** Born 10 Jan. 1914 in Putnam Co., TN. See below for full entry.

8j. **(Dorinda) Pearl.** Born 13 July 1916 in Putnam Co., TN. Married Charles Ransell, and had children: *Carol Ann*; *Tony Ray*. Pearl Ransell died on 24 July 1961.

8k. **John Henry (II).** Born 16 Nov. 1918 in Putnam Co., TN. See below for full entry.

AMBROSE C. BURGESS OF PUTNAM CO., TN

[Vance Dekalb[6], Charles Zebedee[7]]

8e. **Ambrose Casswell** *[son of Charles Zebedee].* Born 14 Mar. 1901 in Putnam Co., TN. Married (Ethel) Mae Henry; married secondly Nona Lynn Herron (she was born 5 Jan. 1910 at Bridgeport, AL). Listed with his father in the 1920 census (as Amhurst Burgess). Ambrose Burgess worked for the Tennessee Valley Authority. He died on 8 July 1955 at South Pittsburg, Marion Co., TN, and is buried in the Pleasant Grove Cemetery, Jasper, TN.

9a. **Jerry John** (ad.). Born 28 Feb. 1933 in Marion Co., TN. Jerry Burgess enlisted in the U.S. Army in the 1950s, was accidentally shot during a training exercise, and retired on disability. He currently lives at South Pittsburg, TN.

9b. **Bonnie Juanita** (ad.). Born 2 Jan. 1935 in Marion Co., TN. Married Rich Allen Burkhalter, and had children: *Jerry Lynn* (born 7 Sept. 1959); *Michael Alvin* (born 30 Dec. 1960). Bonnie Burkhalter died on 19 Aug. 1972 at Stevenson, AL.

9c. **(Wilma) Gail.** Born 4 July 1941 at South Pittsburg, TN. Married Martin Luther Ellis, and had children: *Martin Duyane*. **Gail** married secondly Earl Worley. Gail Worley currently lives at South Pittsburg, TN.

CHARLES P. BURGESS OF MONTGOMERY CO., OHIO

[Vance Dekalb[6], Charles Zebedee[7]]

8g. **Charles Peek** *[son of Charles Zebedee].* Born 13 Nov. 1908 in Putnam Co., TN. Married Jessie May Whitefield on 9 Feb. 1930 in Putnam Co. (she was born 14 Sept. 1911). Charles P. Burgess worked at the Frigidaire Plant in Dayton, OH. He died there on 17 May 1982.

9a. **Joyce Fay (I).** Born 19 June 1930 in Putnam Co., TN; died 4 Sept. 1938 at Dayton, OH.

9b. **Anna Kay.** Born 10 Apr. 1932 in Putnam Co., TN. Married Robert H. Davis, and had children: *Leslie Ann*; *Vanessa Jean*; *Dianna Lynn*.

9c. **(Glynna) Leoda.** Born 4 Nov. 1933 in Putnam Co., TN. Married Ronald D. Hartman, and had children: *Cathy L.*; *David L.*

9d. **Billie Jean.** Born 11 Apr. 1935 at Smithville, TN. Married Ronald F. Sandlin, and had children: *Jeffrey C.*; *Kimberly J.*; *Laura J.*; *Mark T.*

JODA G. BURGESS Sr. OF PUTNAM CO., TENNESSEE
[Vance Dekalb[6], Charles Zebedee[7]]

8i. **Joda Grant (I)** *[son of Charles Zebedee].* Born 10 Jan. 1914 in Putnam Co., TN. Married his distant cousin, Zola May Roberts (she was born 22 May 1915, daughter of William Mansfield Roberts and Ulah Solona Lindsey, and great-granddaughter of Elizabeth Burgess and Leonidas Lindsey). Joda G. Burgess was a tool and die maker at Dayton, OH before retiring. He died on 4 Dec. 1984 at Baxter, TN, but is buried in Dayton, OH.

9a. **Rosalie** (nmn). Born 19 Mar. 1935 in Putnam Co., TN. Married Virgil Click, and had children: *Vernon* (born 3 Nov. 1954); *Lois* (born 3 Oct. 1955). Rosalie Click lives at Dayton, OH.

9b. **Joda Grant (II) "Junior."** Born 4 July 1939 at Dayton, OH. Married Norma McFarland. Joda Burgess Jr. is a tool and die maker at Dayton, OH.

10a. **Lisa Marie.** Born 19 Feb. 1961 at Dayton, OH. Married Bradley Harrison (div.).

10b. **Pamla Jean.** Born 3 Nov. 1964 at Dayton, OH.

10c. **Brian Travis.** Born 9 Nov. 1967 at Dayton, OH.

9c. **Pattie Sue.** Born 24 Apr. 1941 in Putnam Co., TN. Married Leonard Brooks, and had children: *Linda* (born 5 May 1960); *Deanna* (born 16 Nov. 1961); *Cheryl Ann* (born 3 May 1963); *Kimberly* (born 4 Nov. 1964); *Jennifer* (born 4 Jan. 1973). Pat Brooks lives at Dayton, OH.

9d. **Joan (II)** (nmn). Born 9 Feb. 1943 in Putnam Co., TN. Married William Joseph "Bill" Wehrley on 21 June 1958 in Putnam Co., and had children: *Cindy Lou* (born 16 Dec. 1961); *Janet Kay* (born 7 Sept. 1963); *Robert Michael* (born 31 July 1970). Joan Wehrley lives at Dayton, OH.

9e. **(Rita) Faye.** Born 7 Nov. 1944 at Dayton, OH. Married David Gehron, and had children: *Richard* (born 28 Dec. 1960); *Robert Eugene* (born 23 May 1964); *Jason* (born 3 Feb. 1966); married secondly John Sebring. Faye Sebring lives at Dayton, OH.

9f. **William Owen (I) "Billy."** Born 4 Feb. 1954 at Dayton, OH. Married June Dillman. Billie Burgess works for General Motors at Dayton, OH.

10a. **Stacey Catherine.** Born 6 June 1981 at Dayton, OH.

JOHN H. BURGESS OF PUTNAM CO., TENNESSEE
[Vance Dekalb[6], Charles Zebedee[7]]

8k. **John Henry (II)** *[son of Charles Zebedee].* Born 16 Nov. 1918 in Putnam Co., TN. Married Clara Mae Lee on 13 Jan. 1940 in Putnam Co. Johnny Burgess was a machine operator for Dayton Walther Corporation, Dayton, OH before retiring. He currently lives at Baxter, TN.

9a. **Shirley Ann (III).** Born 5 Dec. 1941 at Dayton, OH. Married Tom Calloway, and had children: *Christie*; *Jeff.*

9b. **Linda Carolyn.** Born 10 Oct. 1947 at Dayton, OH. Married Bill Burton.

9c. **Larry Alan.** Born 18 Mar. 1951 at Dayton, OH. Married Kathy Carol. Larry A. Burgess is a cable splicer for Bell Telephone Co. at Huntsville, AL.

10a. **John Alan.** Born 7 Nov. 1978 at Huntsville, AL.

10b. **Ada Catherine.** Born 30 June 1985 at Huntsville, AL.

WINFIELD BURGESS OF PUTNAM CO., TENNESSEE
[Vance Dekalb[6]]

7g. **(Robert) Winfield** *[son of Vance Dekalb].* Born 1 Oct. 1875 in Putnam Co., TN. Married Martha Tennessee Franklin about 1896 (she was born 24 Apr. 1878, daughter of David E. Franklin and Laura Ann Stewart, and died 21 June 1958). Listed in the 1918 draft register and the 1900-20 censuses for Putnam Co., TN. Winfield Burgess was a farmer in Putnam Co. He died there on 9 June 1952, and is buried with his wife in the Stewart Cemetery.

8a. **Velma.** Born about 1897 in Putnam Co., TN; died there before 1900, and is buried in the Stewart Cemetery. Order and dates uncertain.

8b. **(Maggie) Alma.** Born Nov. 1899 in Putnam Co., TN; listed with her father in 1900, but died young before 1910, and is buried in the Stewart Cemetery.

8c. **(Avanah) Lee.** Born about 1901 in Putnam Co., TN; died young, and is buried in the Stewart Cemetery. Order and dates uncertain.

8d. **David Isaac.** Born 23 Sept. 1903 in Putnam Co., TN. See below for full entry.

8e. **(Hallie) Cleo.** Born 7 Apr. 1906 in Putnam Co., TN. Married Jimmie Whittaker on 12 Jan. 1929 (he was born 19 June 1903, and died 5 May 1932), and had children: *Doyle J.* (born 16 Mar. 1932, married Juanita Grammer). Living in 1989.

8f. **Haskell Peek.** Born 30 Jan. 1908 in Putnam Co., TN. See below for full entry.

8g. **Ernest Paskell.** Born 7 July 1910 in Putnam Co., TN. See below for full entry.

8h. **Burnist Love.** Born 3 Jan. 1912 in Putnam Co., TN. See below for full entry.

8i. **Carless Odell.** Born 8 Oct. 1915 in Putnam Co., TN. See below for full entry.

8j. **Arvil Vance.** Born 19 Nov. 1919 in Putnam Co., TN. See below for full entry.

DAVID I. BURGESS OF PUTNAM CO., TENNESSEE

[Vance Dekalb[6], Robert Winfield[7]]

8d. **David Isaac** *[son of Robert Winfield].* Born 23 Sept. 1903 in Putnam Co., TN. Married Lela Dora Gennetta Hicks on 27 Nov. 1924 at Baxter, Putnam Co. (she was born 4 Nov. 1902 in Putnam Co., daughter of Haywood Hicks and (Pearlie) Bell Webb, and died on 5 Mar. 1965). Dave Burgess was a farmer, carpenter, and construction worker in Putnam Co. and Detroit, MI. He died on 29 Dec. 1974 in Putnam Co., and is buried with his wife in the Stewart Cemetery.

9a. **Waulene Lela.** Born 25 Mar. 1926 in Putnam Co., TN; died there of pneumonia on 18 Dec. 1935, and is buried in the Stewart Cemetery. According to her brother, Paul, she was "a very intelligent and concerned girl liked by everyone."

9b. **Paul David (II).** Born 17 Jan. 1928 in Putnam Co., TN. Married Anna Lois Milligan on 18 Apr. 1948 in Putnam Co. Dr. Paul D. Burgess earned his bachelor's degree from Tennessee Technological University, his master's from the University of Missouri, and his Ph.D. from the University of Chicago in 1971. He was Assistant Director of Cooperative Extension and Professor of Extension Education at the University of Missouri, Columbia. He retired from that position in 1982, and now lives at Baxter, TN. He has contributed greatly to this book.

10a. **(Anna) Paulette.** Born 9 Apr. 1949 at Cookeville, TN. Married Duane Roger Farnham on 11 Nov. 1973 at Columbia, MO, and had children: *Duane Roger Jr.* (born 27 Nov. 1976 at Columbia, MO); *Tammara Lynn* (born 8 July 1982 at Muskegon, MI). Paulette Farnham is a registered nurse at Nashville, TN.

10b. **Carol Jean (II).** Born 5 Sept. 1950 at Cookeville, TN; died 17 May 1951 of a negative RH factor at Vienna, MO, and is buried in the Bohannon Cemetery, Putnam Co., TN.

10c. **Debora Kay.** Born 27 Jan. 1953 at St. Louis, MO. Debora Burgess earned her B.S. in Journalism from the University of Missouri in 1975. She works as an editor and writer at Washington University, St. Louis, MO.

10d. **Karen Elaine.** Born 1 Dec. 1955 at Rolla, MO. Married James Louis Burger on 30 Apr. 1977 at Columbia, MO, and had children: *Michael David* (born 23 Apr. 1979 at Columbia, MO); *Bryan Joseph* (born 16 Dec. 1982 at Columbia, MO); *Stephanie Ann* (born 2 Mar. 1986 at Columbia, MO). Karen Burger received her B.S. degree in Elementary Education from the University of Missouri in 1982. She currently teaches sixth grade at Columbia, MO.

10e. **Mark Douglas.** Born 16 Aug. 1963 at Columbia, MO. Married (Kimberly) Jan Murr on 7 May 1988. Mark Burgess graduated from the University of Tennessee. He works as Sports Editor for the Blount County Bureau of the *Knoxville News-Sentinel*, Maryville, TN.

11a. **Brandon Paul.** Born 12 Feb. 1993 in TN.

9c. **Martha Pearl.** Born 13 Aug. 1930 in Putnam Co., TN. Married Charles Aaron Cobb on 22 July 1955 (he was born 23 Oct. 1927), and had children: *Joe David* (born 5 Nov. 1964 at Knoxville, TN, married Gena M. Wilson on 17 Sept. 1988 [she was born 9 Sept. 1965]; Joe and Gena both earned bachelor's degrees from the University of Tennessee). Martha Cobb earned her B.S. from Maryville College, and a master's degree from the University of Tennessee. She has worked as a social sciences teacher at Alcoa High School, Alcoa, TN, and has also taught classes at Maryville College. She currently lives at Maryville, TN.

9d. **Roy** (nmn). He is listed with the middle name Freeman in James Z. Burgess's history. Born 30 Aug. 1933 in Putnam Co., TN. Married Jacqueline "Jackie" Tullis on 14 Sept. 1954 (she was born 15 Mar. 1935, and lives at Mayfield, KY). Roy Burgess earned his master's degree from the University of Tennessee. He worked as an extension economist for the Tennessee Valley Authority and the University of Kentucky. He died on 26 Sept. 1979 at Cookeville, TN, and is buried in the Stewart Cemetery.

10a. **Jo Ann (IV).** Born 10 Jan. 1957 at Lockport, NY. Married Curran S. Howle on 29 July 1977 in Graves Co., KY, and had children: *Elizabeth Erin* (born 24 Feb. 1981 at Paducah, KY); *Curran Jared* (born 20 July 1985 at Mayfield, KY). Jo Ann Howle earned her A.A. degree in specialized business in July 1988. She currently works at a physician's clinic at Mayfield, KY.

10b. **Sherian** (nmn). Born 12 July 1958 at Cookeville, TN. Married Gary Lynn Adams on 5 Dec. 1981 in Graves Co., KY, and had children: *Jennifer Lynn* (born 25 Jan. 1985 at Murray, KY). Sherian Adams attended Murray State University for paralegal studies, and obtained her real estate license. Gary and Sherian Adams currently own and operate Adams Heating and Air Conditioning.

10c. **David Roy.** Born 25 Oct. 1961 at Knoxville, TN. Married Mary Regan on 11 Apr. 1992. Served in the U.S. Army. David Burgess received his degree as an accredited Harley Davidson technician, and is now employed with the Regency Harley-Davidson dealership, Jacksonville, FL.

9e. **Carolyn Ruth.** Her name is given as Carol on her tombstone. Born 3 Oct. 1935 in Putnam Co., TN; died there of diphtheria on 27 Oct. 1937, and is buried in the Stewart Cemetery.

9f. **Ted Samuel.** Born 12 Feb. 1938 in Putnam Co., TN. Married Linda Sue Wallace on 18 Apr. 1964 in Putnam Co. (she was born 12 Mar. 1944, daughter of Earl Wallace and Mildred Waddell). Ted Burgess was a construction supervisor before retiring; he now lives at Silver Point, TN.

10a. **Steven Bruce (II).** Born 3 May 1966 at Cookeville, TN. Married Susan Hughes on 5 Nov. 1988. Steve Burgess lives at Silver Point, TN.

10b. **Annette Lin.** Born 16 July 1968 at Cookeville, TN. Married Kevin Maynard on 1 Oct. 1992. Annette Maynard lives at Silver Point, TN.

9g. **Dorothy Ann.** Born and died 29 Feb. 1940 in Putnam Co., TN, and is buried in the Stewart Cemetery.

9h. **Fred Harold.** Born 16 Apr. 1941 in Putnam Co., TN. Married Michele Brann on 21 May 1966 at Indianapolis, IN (she was born 8 Mar. 1944). Fred Burgess was a computer supervisor for Bell Telephone. He now lives retired at Indianapolis, IN.

10a. **Timothy Hampton.** Born 4 Dec. 1967 at Cookeville, TN. Married Susie Lantzy on 1 June 1990 at Annapolis, MD (she was born 14 Aug. 1968). Tim Burgess graduated on 30 May 1990 from the U.S. Naval Academy, Annapolis, MD. He is currently a senior medical student at Indiana University, and an Ensign in the U.S. Naval Reserve.

11a. **Kimberly Sue.** Born 20 Sept. 1992 at Bloomington, IN.

10b. **Michael Joseph.** Born 19 July 1970 at Indianapolis, IN. Mike Burgess works for the Heritage Corp., Indianapolis, IN.

10c. **Daniel Allen.** Born 25 Mar. 1973 at Indianapolis, IN. Dan Burgess works as a cast member for Disney World, Orlando, FL.

9i. **Bettie Sue.** Born 15 Dec. 1944 in Putnam Co., TN. Married (Kenneth) Gordon Presley on 29 Aug. 1964 at Gainesboro, TN (he was born 30 Mar. 1942), and had children: *Terry Dale* (born 14 Aug. 1965, died 16 Aug. 1965 at Cookeville, TN); *Genetta Sue* (born 29 Nov. 1968 at Cookeville, TN, married Paul B. Moore on 14 Jan. 1989 [he was born 11 Feb. 1966]; she earned her B.S. degree at Tennessee Technological University in 1990, and is currently a special education teacher at Chattanooga, TN). Bettie Presley works as a production supervisor for Jutco Corp., Cookeville, TN.

HASKELL BURGESS OF PUTNAM CO., TENNESSEE
[Vance Dekalb[6], Robert Winfield[7]]

8f. **Haskell Peek "Hack"** *[son of Robert Winfield].* Born 30 Jan. 1908 in Putnam Co., TN. Married Avo Lilly Herren on 19 May 1927 in Putnam Co. (she was born 23 July 1908 at Baxter, TN). Hack Burgess was a farmer near Baxter, TN before retiring. He now lives at Cookeville, TN.

9a. **Doris Helen.** Born 4 Feb. 1932 at Baxter, TN. Married Armon Reece Nash Sr. on 16 Dec. 1950 in Putnam Co. (he was born 23 Aug. 1930, son of Carl Nash and Maggie Wyatt), and had children: *Camilla June* (born 20 Apr. 1953, married James Hollis Brown on 29 Mar. 1982 [he was born 13 Jan. 1938]); *(Armon) Reece Jr.* (born 17 Nov. 1956, married Freda Magaha on 8 June 1976 [she was born 21 Sept. 1958], and had children: Christina Ann [born 25 Oct. 1978]; Kimberly Dale [born 3 Aug. 1980]; Carl Reece [born 13 Apr. 1984]). Doris Nash lives at Baxter, TN. She and her family operate the Cookeville Boat Dock concession at Center Hill Lake in the Burgess Falls Recreation Area; their establishment includes a floating restaurant specializing in freshly farmed and cooked catfish (which the author of this book heartily recommends!).

9b. **Donnie V.** (nmn). Born 8 Nov. 1937 at Baxter, TN. Married Helen June Thomas on 18 Feb. 1956 in Putnam Co. (she was born 12 Sept. 1938, daughter of Chester J. Thomas and Hattie Maloy Allison). Don Burgess was a tool and die maker in Louisiana. He now lives retired at Cookeville, TN.

10a. **Don Terry.** Born 12 Oct. 1956 at Baxter, TN. Married Deborah Kay Willis on 27 Aug. 1977. Rev. Don T. Burgess is a minister for the Church of Christ at Baxter, TN.

11a. **Don Willis.** Born 2 Sept. 1978 at Cookeville, TN.

11b. **John Thomas (IV).** Born 24 July 1980 at Cookeville, TN.

10b. **Freddie Dean.** Born 13 June 1958 at Baxter, TN. Fred Burgess is a truck driver for Putnam County.

10c. **Timothy Mandel.** Born 15 Aug. 1974 at Cookeville, TN.

ERNEST P. BURGESS OF PUTNAM CO., TENNESSEE
[Vance Dekalb[6], Robert Winfield[7]]

8g. **Ernest Paskell** *[son of Robert Winfield].* Born 7 July 1910 in Putnam Co., TN. Married (Erma) Ocia Rice on 31 Dec. 1933 in Putnam Co. (she was born 14 Mar. 1910, daughter of Jess Rice and Ollie Martin, and died 4 Aug. 1986 at Baxter, TN). Ernie Burgess was a carpenter and farmer. He died on 18 Aug. 1986 at Baxter, TN, a few days after his wife, and is buried with her in the Stewart Cemetery.

9a. **(Willie) Dillon.** Born 18 Sept. 1934 in Putnam Co., TN. Married Marie Sumner on 29 Nov. 1962 at Burnham, IL (she was born 15 Feb. 1942). Dillon Burgess was a crane operator at Dyer, IN before retiring. He now lives at Silver Point, TN.

10a. **Barbara Jean.** Born 15 Aug. 1962 at Evergreen Park, IL. She married Christopher Bonner on 1 June 1985 at Dyer, IN, and had children: *Steven Edward* (born 8 Nov. 1985 at Munster, IN). Barbara Bonner works for the Indiana Department of Motor Vehicles, Dyer, IN.

10b. **Robert Dale (II)** (twin). Born 28 June 1965 at Evergreen Park, IL. Married Loretta Ivey on 21 Aug. 1992 at Covington, GA. Robert Burgess lives at Covington, GA.

10c. **Roberta Marie** (twin). Born 28 June 1965 at Evergreen Park, IL. Roberta Burgess earned her bachelor's degree in accounting at Purdue University. She works for Horsehead Resource at Chicago, IL, and lives at Dyer, IN.

10d. **Pamela Sue.** Born 12 Apr. 1968 at Evergreen Park, IL. Married Christian Kozlowski on 16 Dec. 1988 at El Paso, TX, and had children: *Jamie Ryan* (born 22 Nov. 1989 at East Chicago, IN); *Michael Damian* (born 16 Nov. 1990 at East Chicago, IN). Pamela Kozlowski is a homemaker at Whiting, IN.

9b. **Ruby Helen.** Her marriage certificate spells her name Rubye. Born 21 Dec. 1936 in Putnam Co., TN. Married Olen Helms on 30 Mar. 1959 in Putnam Co. (he was born 22 May 1930, and died 3 May 1992 at Cookeville, TN), and had children: *Deborah Diane* (born 30 Nov. 1961 at Chattanooga, TN); *Patricia Lynn* (born 24 Dec. 1963 at Morristown, TN); *David Wayne* (born 13 June 1972 at Anniston, AL). Ruby Helms lives at Cookeville, TN.

9c. **(Lyda) Ruth Lee.** Born 10 Apr. 1938 in Putnam Co., TN. Married Alton Eugene Boyd on 30 Dec. 1961 in Putnam Co. (he was born 2 Oct. 1930). She was living at Cookeville, TN in 1986.

9d. **Reba Joyce.** Born 22 Sept. 1941 (or 1940) in Putnam Co., TN. Married Charles Edward Gentry on 6 Feb. 1958 in Putnam Co. (div.; he was born 6 Feb. 1938), and had children: *Phyllis Ann* (born 22 July 1964); married secondly James Flatt. Reba Flatt lives at Cookeville, TN.

9e. **(Lela) Cleo.** Born 30 Sept. 1943 in Putnam Co., TN. Married (Wendell) Thurston Cole on 23 Dec. 1961 in Putnam Co. (he was born 16 Dec. 1932; dec.), and had children: *(Robert) Stanley* (born 2 Aug. 1962 at Dalton, GA); *Gregory* (born 16 Sept. 1967 at Cookeville, TN). Cleo Cole lives at Cookeville, TN.

9f. **Robert Dale (I).** Born and died about 1945 in Putnam Co., TN, aged three months.

9g. **(Lloyd Ray) Dean.** Born 7 Aug. 1947 in Putnam Co., TN. Married (Ruby) Jewell Birdwell on 25 Mar. 1967 (div.). Dean Burgess worked for the Tennessee State Parks System in Jackson Co., TN before being injured in a car accident. He currently lives retired in Cookeville, TN.

9h. **(Paskell) Wayne.** Born 3 Feb. 1950 in Putnam Co., TN. Married (Mary) Helen Masters on 17 July 1971 in Putnam Co. (div.). Wayne Burgess is a construction worker in Alabama, but makes his permanent home at Cookeville, TN.

10a. **Amy Denise.** Born 6 July 1973 at Cookeville, TN. Married and had one child.

BURNIST BURGESS OF PUTNAM CO., TENNESSEE

[Vance Dekalb[6], Robert Winfield[7]]

8h. **Burnist Love "Burn"** *[son of Robert Winfield].* His name is spelled Burnest on his Social Security record and in the 1920 census. Born 3 Jan. 1912 in Putnam Co., TN. Married Ivey Dell Whitehead on 23 Dec. 1934 in Putnam Co. (dec.); married secondly Betty Sullins about 1954. Burn Burgess worked for Chrysler Corp. at Detroit, MI before retiring to Boma, TN. He died on 19 Mar. 1989 in Putnam Co., and is buried in the Smellage Memorial Gardens.

9a. **(Burnist) Denton.** Born 14 Dec. 1935 in Putnam Co., TN. Married Mary Flora Maxwell on 1 Sept. 1962 (she was born 12 Sept. 1938, daughter of Horace Vestle Maxwell and Lillie Jane Rodgers). Denton Burgess lives and works at Baxter, TN.

10a. **Michael Dewayne.** Born 13 Sept. 1963 in Putnam Co., TN.

10b. **Bobby Edward.** Born 19 Jan. 1965 in Putnam Co., TN.

9b. **James Winfield (II).** Born 12 Dec. 1937 in Putnam Co., TN. Jim Burgess worked as a laborer in various parts of the country. He died unmarried in a car accident on 11 July 1970 in Putnam Co., and is buried in the Richardson Cemetery.

9c. **Mary Frances (IV).** Born 23 Sept. 1939 in Putnam Co., TN. Married Harold Vinson; married secondly George Green. Mary Green currently lives in Louisiana.

9d. **Lonnie Love.** Born 8 Mar. 1955 in Smith Co., TN. Married Sharon Goodrich on 2 July 1977; married secondly Suzanne Callahan on 29 June 1985 in Putnam Co. (she was born on 9 Sept. 1956). Lonnie Burgess is a carpenter in Putnam Co.

10a. **Heather Love.** Born 4 Jan. 1979 in Smith Co., TN.

9e. **Dwight (II)** (nmn). Born 9 Nov. 1957 in Smith Co., TN. Married Cindy Hartzer on 24 Sept. 1977. Dwight Burgess is a foreman for a construction company in Peru, IN.

10a. **Amanda Elaine.** Born 27 Nov. 1978 at Wabash, IN.

9f. **Susan Annette.** Born 16 Mar. 1958 in Smith Co., TN. Married Wayne D. Brown on 26 June 1973. Susan Brown lives at Cookeville, TN.

9g. **Doyle Edward.** Born 27 June 1959 in Smith Co., TN. Doyle Burgess works for a television cable company at Orlando, FL.

9h. **J. D.** (no given names). Born 25 Aug. 1960 in Smith Co., TN. Married Michelle Ann Liggett on 31 Mar. 1987 in Putnam Co., TN (she was born 20 July 1964). J. D. Burgess is a construction worker at Dallas, TX.

9i. **Lesa Ann.** Her name is spelled Lisa on her marriage record. Born 11 Dec. 1963 in Smith Co., TN. Married (James) Ricky Anderson on 27 Apr. 1985 in Putnam Co.

9j. **Penny Denise.** Her middle name is spelled Denice on her marriage certificate. Born 27 Mar. 1966 in Smith Co., TN. Married Richard Evans Brown on 31 Dec. 1986 in Putnam Co., TN (he was born 8 Nov. 1959).

9k. **Patty Diann.** Born 7 Mar. 1968 in Smith Co., TN; died there on 9 July 1968, and is buried in the Boyd-Russell Cemetery, on the Shanks Farm.

CARL BURGESS OF PUTNAM CO., TENNESSEE
[Vance Dekalb^6, Robert Winfield^7]

8i. **Carless Odell "Carl"** *[son of Robert Winfield].* Born 8 Oct. 1915 in Putnam Co., TN. Married Kate Marie Essex on 15 Apr. 1939 at Livingstone, Overton Co., TN (she was born 2 Nov. 1917, the daughter of Hilary Essex and [Martha] Clyde Kendall). Carl Burgess was a farmer and sheet metal worker before retiring. He and his wife currently live at Cookeville, TN.

9a. **(Dorothy) Nell.** Born 21 Nov. 1940 in Putnam Co., TN. Married James Hunter on 12 Dec. 1959 in Putnam Co., TN (he was born 22 June 1932), and had children: *Katrina Helene* (born 26 July 1960); *Doyle Lynn* (born 11 Oct. 1962); *Sonja Gay* (born 22 Apr. 1964); *Carl Bryon* (born 25 Aug. 1971).

9b. **Carl Glenn.** Born 25 June 1943 in Putnam Co., TN. Married Mamie Dell Bean at Gainesboro, TN. Carl Burgess was a Deputy Sheriff for Jackson Co., TN before retiring. He lives at Gainesboro, TN.

10a. **Cathy Dale.** Her middle name is given as Dell on her marriage certificate. Born 18 Aug. 1967 in Putnam Co., TN. Married Ricky Dell Taylor on 15 Apr. 1988 in Putnam Co., TN (he was born 7 June 1963).

10b. **(Carl) Winfield.** Born 19 Nov. 1972 in Putnam Co., TN.

10c. **Katie Lynn.** Born 17 May 1979 in Putnam Co., TN.

9c. **Jerry Lee (II).** Born 2 Aug. 1945 in Putnam Co., TN. Married (Marion) Kay Henley on 29 Apr. 1967 in Putnam Co. (div.; she was born 9 Mar. 1947). Jerry Burgess was County Attorney for Putnam Co. between 1978-86. He currently operates a private practice, the Law Office of the Upper Cumberland, at Cookeville, TN.

10a. **LeAnn LeMar.** Born 30 Oct. 1971 at Cookeville, TN. Attends Motlow State College.

10b. **(Essex) Kare** (dau.). Born 27 Dec. 1978 at Cookeville, TN.

10c. **Hilary Carl.** Born about 1988.

9d. **Judy Gail.** Born 24 June 1947 in Putnam Co., TN. Married Gary Paul McCrary on 30 Oct. 1971 in Putnam Co. (he was born July 1949), and had children: *Scott Paul* (born 13 Dec. 1972). Judy McCrary is a nurse for a clinic at Cookeville, TN.

9e. **Dennis Lynn.** Born 22 Sept. 1950 in Putnam Co., TN. Married Deborah Faye Dilldene on 29 Apr. 1972 in Putnam Co.; married secondly Anna Faye Allison on 24 Mar. 1978 in Putnam Co. (she was the daughter of Ernest Haywood Allison and Lorene Ashburn). Dennis Burgess is a brick mason at Cookeville, TN.

10a. **Elizabeth Ann (III).** Born 17 Sept. 1980 at Cookeville, TN.

9f. **Sandra Faye.** Born 10 Apr. 1958 in Putnam Co., TN. Married Frank Edward Rigg on 12 Oct. 1973 in Putnam Co. (he was born 30 May 1952), and had children: *(Karen) Michelle* (born 16 Oct. 1977); *Martha Carol* (born 16 Oct. 1983). Sandra Rigg is a secretary at Tennessee Technological University, Cookeville, TN.

ARVIL BURGESS OF PUTNAM CO., TENNESSEE
[Vance Dekalb^6, Robert Winfield^7]

8j. **Arvil Vance** *[son of Robert Winfield].* Born 19 (or 8) Nov. 1919 in Putnam Co., TN. Married Gennie Frances Oaks on 28 Dec. 1940 (she was born 6 June 1920, daughter of Earl Oaks and Fronie Roberts, and died 4 May 1985 at Nashville). Arvil Burgess was a farmer and caterpillar tractor driver before retiring. He died on 24 Apr. 1983, and is buried in the Smellage Cemetery.

9a. **Jimmy Vance.** Born 5 Oct. 1941 in Putnam Co., TN. Married his distant cousin, Flossie Marie Randolph, on 18 Mar. 1960 in Putnam Co. (she was born 20 Nov. 1945 in Putnam Co., TN, daughter of Preston Cleo Randolph and Nota Pansy Bumbalough, who was the daughter of Nancy Burgess Bumbalough); married secondly (Gay) Opaline Randolph on 21 Sept. 1976 in Putnam Co. Jimmy Burgess works for McCords Company in Cookeville, TN.

10a. **(Connie) Darlene.** Born 22 June 1962 in Putnam Co., TN. Married Ricky Dale Gibson on 8 Aug. 1980 in Putnam Co., and had one son.

10b. **Teresa Lynn.** Born 7 Oct. 1964 in Putnam Co., TN.

9b. **Ruby Jo.** Born 2 Jan. 1943 in Putnam Co., TN. Married Thomas Maynard on 18 Dec. 1965, and had children: *Linda* (born Apr. 1960); *Brenda Carol* (born 12 Apr. 1963); *Tammy* (born 8 Nov. 1965); *Phyllis June* (born 21 June 1967). Ruby Jo Maynard lives at Silver Point, TN.

9c. **Roger Dale.** Born and died 30 Aug. 1944 in Putnam Co., TN.

9d. **Richard Leon.** Born 17 Aug. 1945 in Putnam Co., TN. Married Mural L. Moles on 8 July 1973 in Putnam Co. (div.); married secondly Carol Jean Smith on 30 July 1978 in Putnam Co. (div.). Richard Burgess was a police officer at Baxter, TN. He died there on 17 Apr. 1992.

9e. **Douglas Allen.** Born 25 Sept. 1949 in Putnam Co., TN. Married (Sara) Joan Tucker on 12 Feb. 1979 in Putnam Co. Doug Burgess is a Deputy Sheriff for Putnam Co., TN. He currently lives at Cookeville, TN.

10a. **Jennifer Lynn (I).** Born 2 Mar. 1979 in Putnam Co., TN.

9f. **Eris Ann.** Born 5 May 1954 in Putnam Co., TN. Married Carson Bryant on 14 Jan. 1972, and had children: *Christopher Wayne*; *Shawn Carson*; *Julie Ann*. Eris Bryant lives at Baster, TN.

9g. **Eulah Jean.** Born 1 Aug. 1955 in Putnam Co., TN. Married her cousin, John Vance Gentry Jr., on 3 Aug. 1973 in Putnam Co. (he was born 1 Mar. 1953, son of John Vance Gentry and Lillian "Pat" Bailey), and had children: *John Vance III* (born 5 Apr. 1978); *Thomas Andrew* (born 17 Apr. 1981). John Gentry serves as county executive of Putnam Co., TN; they live at Baxter, TN.

9h. **Donny Ray.** Born 9 Oct. 1959 in Putnam Co., TN. Married Paula Dean Leftwich on 1 June 1979 in Putnam Co. Donny Burgess is a pipe layer in Putnam Co., TN.

9i. **Tony Lynn.** Born 26 Jan. 1962 in Putnam Co., TN. Married Cynthia Carol Gaw on 6 Dec. 1982 in Putnam Co. (not recorded); married secondly Shelia Dawn Anderson on 1 Apr. 1984 in Putnam Co.

VANCE ANDREW BURGESS OF PUTNAM CO., TENNESSEE

[Vance Dekalb[6]]

7h. **(Vance) Andrew** *[son of Vance Dekalb]*. Born 22 May 1878 in Putnam Co., TN. Married Margaret Ellen Gentry on 7 Aug. 1897 (she was born 24 Apr. 1881, daughter of Silas Pittman Gentry and Mary Amanda Frances Taylor, and died 4 Feb. 1961). Listed in the 1918 draft register and the 1900-20 censuses for Putnam Co., TN. Andrew Burgess was a carpenter and farmer in Putnam Co. He died there on 12 June 1969, aged 91 years, and is buried with his wife in the Allison Cemetery.

8a. **Bedie Cleo.** Born 12 Oct. 1898 in Putnam Co., TN. Married Homer Hale on 3 Jan. 1915 in Putnam Co. (he was born 21 Oct. 1891, and died 21 Apr. 1943), and had children: *Silas*; *Gladys*; *Juanita*; *James H.* **Bedie** married secondly Jack Leaver, and had children: *Lucille*; *Rosie*; *Russel*; *Reba F.*; *Wiley*. Bedie Leaver died on 20 Apr. 1943 in Putnam Co., TN.

8b. **Bedford Augustus.** Born 28 Apr. 1901 in Putnam Co., TN. See below for full entry.

8c. **(Veda) Jewell.** Born 12 Oct. 1902 in Putnam Co., TN. Married Richard Nelson Fox on 11 Dec. 1921 in Putnam Co., TN (he was born 7 Jan. 1902, and died Oct. 1977 at Battle Creek, MI), and had children: *Nancy Ellen* (born 5 Oct. 1922 at Baxter, TN, married Villard William Williams on 26 June 1938 in Putnam Co. [he was born 1915], and had children: Nellie Margaret [born 23 Apr. 1939]; (William) Edward [born 8 Mar. 1944]; Gerald Dale [born 17 Jan. 1950]; Nancy Williams lives at Battle Creek, MI); *Richard Nelson Jr.* (born 19 Mar. 1939, married, and had children: Kimberly Ann; Christine). Jewell Fox died on 26 Sept. 1969 near Detroit, MI, and is buried in the Bellevue Cemetery, Bellevue, MI.

8d. **Thomas Claud.** Born 14 June 1905 in Putnam Co., TN. See below for full entry.

8e. **(Ally) Edna Leona.** Born 18 Nov. 1907 in Putnam Co., TN. Married Russell William Berkley, and had children: *Harold Clifton*; *Ronald William*. Edna Berkley died on 13 May 1973 at Hazel Park, MI.

8f. **Clyde Andrew.** Born 13 May 1909 in Putnam Co., TN. See below for full entry.

8g. **Prentiss Clifton.** Born 6 Jan. 1911 in Putnam Co., TN. See below for full entry.
8h. **Foy Sylvester.** Born 19 Apr. 1913 in Putnam Co., TN. He was killed on 27 July 1934 at Detroit, MI, but is buried in the Allison Cemetery, Putnam Co., TN.
8i. **(Seigel) Keith.** Born 31 July 1915 in Putnam Co., TN. See below for full entry.
8j. **Erma Enod.** Born 14 Apr. 1917 in Putnam Co., TN. Married Hildred Beadles on 1 Jan. 1939 (he was born 1 Nov. 1917, and died 12 Sept. 1975), and had children: *Gerald* (born 20 Nov. 1939, married Mary Selbey); *Nealy Vance* (born 26 June 1941, married Georgia Humphreys). Erma Beadles lives at Poway, CA.
8k. **Edith.** Born 10 May 1919 in Putnam Co., TN. Married Fred Alonzo Mansfield (he was born 5 Oct. 1916, and died May 1977 at Baxter, TN). Edith Mansfield died on 26 July 1986 at Cookeville, TN.
8l. **Silas Henry.** Born 31 Mar. 1924 in Putnam Co., TN. See below for full entry.

BEDFORD BURGESS OF MACOMB CO., MICHIGAN
[Vance Dekalb[6], Vance Andrew[7]]

8b. **Bedford Augustus** *[son of Vance Andrew].* He may have been named for Bedford Johnson, who died in Putnam Co. in 1905. Born 28 Apr. 1901 in Putnam Co., TN. Married Helen Butzin; married secondly Minnie Butzin, Helen's sister. Bedford Burgess was a factory worker at Warren, MI. He died there on 28 Aug. 1981, and is buried in the Parkview Memorial Cemetery.

9a. **Norman Joseph (I)** (ad.). Born 21 Jan. 1917 at Detroit, MI. Married Eva Eleanor Korvenpaa. Norman Burgess was a factory worker in Michigan. He died in Oct. 1986 at Sterling Heights, MI.

10a. **Patsy Ann (II).** Born 26 Feb. 1942 at Detroit, MI. Married Dominic Opal.
10b. **Linda Sue (I).** Born 18 Jan. 1944 at Detroit, MI. Married Gerald Stewart.
10c. **Charles Bedford.** Born 4 Apr. 1947 at Detroit, MI. Married Sherry Cochran. Charles Burgess is a foreman for a tire retread company at Warren, MI.

11a. **Andy Kevin.** Born 27 Oct. 1973 at Mt. Clemens, MI.

10d. **Norman Joseph (II).** Born 29 Jan. 1949 at Detroit, MI. Married Joyce Kaltz. Norman Burgess Jr. is a service manager for a truck tire retread company in Michigan.

11a. **Andrea Renee.** Born 20 Sept. 1972 at Mt. Clemens, MI.
11b. **Jeremy Michael.** Born 17 Aug. 1975 at Mt. Clemens, MI.

10e. **Harvey Emil** (twin). Born 6 May 1954 at Detroit, MI. Harvey Burgess is a foreman for Detroit Tire Co.
10f. **Helen Elaine** (twin). Born 6 May 1954 at Detroit, MI. Married David Warbois.

9b. **Edna Julia.** Born 18 Feb. 1919 at Detroit, MI. Married Chester Nowacki.

THOMAS C. BURGESS OF MACOMB CO., MICHIGAN
[Vance Dekalb[6], Vance Andrew[7]]

8d. **Thomas Claud** *[son of Vance Andrew].* His name is given as Leland Burgess in the 1920 census. Born 14 June 1905 in Putnam Co., TN. Married Mary Elizabeth Austin (she was born 26 Nov. 1907, and died 1 Jan. 1932, buried Allison Cemetery); married secondly Genevieve Brovage about 1935 (she remarried William Berkley, and lives at Hazel Park, MI). Tom Burgess was a foreman for L. A. Young Spring and Wire Co. at Center Line, MI. He died there in Apr. 1978, and is buried in the Cadillac Memorial Cemetery.

9a. **Thomas Virgil.** Born 30 Nov. 1927 at Detroit, MI. Married Merla June Spring. Thomas V. Burgess is an oil line maintenance and repairman for Ford Motor Co. at Sterling Heights, MI.

10a. **Diane Nadine.** Born 8 Aug. 1949 at Pontiac, MI. Married Lawrence Swansey.
10b. **Thomas Vance.** Born 1 July 1951 at Pontiac, MI. Married Vicki Scott. Thomas V. Burgess is a machine repairman at Roseville, MI.

11a. **Shauna Marie.** Born 7 Aug. 1977 at Roseville, MI.
11b. **Melanie Anne.** Born 4 Mar. 1981 at Roseville, MI.

10c. **Chris Dee.** Born 24 July 1953 at Pontiac, MI. Married Deborah ___; married secondly Bonnie Miller. Chris D. Burgess is a supervisor for Fiberglass Co., at Portland, MI.

11a. **Nicole Nadine.** Born 20 Feb. 1974 at Sarasota, FL.
11b. **Eric James.** Born 18 Jan. 1977 at Covington, LA.

9b. **(Margaret) Claudine.** Born 13 Sept. 1929 at Detroit, MI; died on there 15 June 1938, and is buried in the Allison Cemetery, Putnam Co., TN.
9c. **James Vance.** Born 29 Nov. 1936 at Detroit, MI. Jim Burgess works for Rollins, Burdick, Hunter, a commercial insurance agency, at San Francisco, CA.
9d. **Jo Ann (II).** Born 1 Apr. 1944 at Detroit, MI. Married Gary Gray, and secondly Lloyd Buck. Jo Ann Buck lives at New Concord, OH.
9e. **Carol Elaine.** Born 21 June 1949 at Detroit, MI. Married Lawrence Vutci, and secondly Louis Martinelli.

CLYDE BURGESS OF WAYNE CO., MICHIGAN
[Vance Dekalb^6, Vance Andrew^7]

8f. **Clyde Andrew** *[son of Vance Andrew].* Born 13 May 1909 in Putnam Co., TN. Married Myrtle Rich. Clyde Burgess worked for General Motors at Detroit, MI. He died there on 11 Nov. 1988.

9a. **Betty Catherine.** Born 20 June 1937 at Detroit, MI. Married Ron Coleman.

PRENTISS BURGESS OF PUTNAM CO., TENNESSEE
[Vance Dekalb^6, Vance Andrew^7]

8g. **Prentiss Clifton** *[son of Vance Andrew].* His name is spelled Printess in Social Security records. Born 6 Jan. 1911 in Putnam Co., TN. Married Reba Jones (who remarried). Prentiss Burgess was an office worker for Burroughs Corp. at Detroit, MI. He died in Sept. 1976 at White Pine, TN, or Tarpon Springs, FL.

9a. **Jay Randall.** Married Sally ___. Jay Burgess lives at Royal Oak, MI.
9b. **Dwight (I).** Last known living in Oklahoma.

KEITH BURGESS OF WAYNE CO., MICHIGAN
[Vance Dekalb^6, Vance Andrew^7]

8i. **(Seigel) Keith** *[son of Vance Andrew].* Born 31 July 1915 in Putnam Co., TN. Married Beatrice Lee (she was born 12 Sept. 1918); married secondly Margaret Cooker. Keith Burgess died in Oct. 1976 (within a week of Prentiss Burgess) at Allen Park, MI.

9a. **(Ruth) Eleanor.** Born 27 Jan. 1939 at Detroit, MI. Married Rudy Grigsby, and had children: *Laura* (born 10 Aug. 1959); *Samuel* (born 17 July 1961); *Rudy Jr.*; *David*; *Timothy* (born 1 June 1970).

SILAS BURGESS OF MACOMB CO., MICHIGAN
[Vance Dekalb^6, Vance Andrew^7]

8l. **Silas Henry** *[son of Vance Andrew].* Born 31 Mar. 1924 in Putnam Co., TN. Married Louise Denardi. Silas Burgess was a truck driver at Roseville, MI. He died there on 1 Apr. 1988.

9a. **Deborah Ann.** Born 7 June 1951 at Detroit, MI. Married Tom Groin.
9b. **Sandra Lynn.** Born 25 May 1953 at Detroit, MI. Married Gary Miller.

THOMAS PEEK BURGESS OF PUTNAM CO., TENNESSEE
[Vance Dekalb^6]

7k. **Thomas Peek** *[son of Vance Dekalb].* Born 24 Feb. 1885 (or 1884, according to his tombstone) in Putnam Co., TN. Married Cordia Ethel Whitehead about 1919 (she was born 5 Apr. 1901, daughter of James Whitehead and Mary Richardson, and died 13 Apr. 1985). Listed in the 1918 draft and the 1920 census for Putnam Co., TN. Thomas Burgess was a farmer in Tennessee and Arkansas. He died 26 June 1957 in Arkansas, but is buried with his wife in the Allison Cemetery, Putnam Co., TN.

8a. **Mary Arminta.** Born 31 July 1920 in Putnam Co., TN. Married Clyde Carr, and had children: *Fred* (born 30 May 1944, married Lydia Iglehart). Mary married secondly Garvis Lick, and had children: *Brenda* (who married Reyes Garcia); *Vallerie Gail* (born 23 Nov. 1951). Mary Lick lives at Baxter, TN.

8b. **(William) Lawrence.** Born 18 Feb. 1923 in Putnam Co., TN. Married (Kor) Catherine Boyd. William L. Burgess served in World War II. After returning home, he worked for the Microfilm Division of Bell & Howell. He died childless on 20 Aug. 1969 at Dallas, TX, but is buried in the Allison Cemetery, Putnam Co., TN.

8c. **Alma Ree.** Born and died 25 June 1925 in Putnam Co., TN, and is buried in the Allison Cemetery.

8d. **Lillian Frances.** Born 13 May 1928 in Putnam Co., TN. Married John H. Slaughter, and had children: *Tommie Lee* (born 10 June 1945, married Patricia Boston, and died 27 June 1971). Lillian Slaughter lives at Battle Creek, MI.

8e. **(Roscha) Annabelle.** Born 21 Jan. 1932 in Putnam Co., TN. Married Walter Lick. Annabelle Lick lives at Battle Creek, MI.

8f. **Thomas Howard.** Born 14 Mar. 1935 in Putnam Co., TN. Married Mamie Ruth Love. Rev. Thomas H. Burgess was a minister, a former mayor of Algood, TN, and a school teacher in New Mexico. He died on 24 June 1989 at Baxter, TN, and is buried in the Allison Cemetery.

9a. **Deanna Lynne.** Born 26 Apr. 1960 in Putnam Co., TN. Married Charles Franklin Carter Jr. on 11 June 1983 in Putnam Co.

9b. **Lauren Lee.** Her marriage record spells her middle name Lea. Born 1 June 1965 in Putnam Co., TN. Married Timmy Lynn Anderson on 9 Apr. 1983 in Putnam Co.

8g. **Johnny Duaine.** Born 13 Feb. 1937 at Manila, AR. Married Mary Woodward; married secondly Rebecca Allison (she was born 27 Aug. 1946, daughter of Julius F. Allison and Nettie K. Pritchard). John Burgess works for Ralston Purina Co. at Battle Creek, MI.

9a. **Debra Lynn** (ad.). Born 13 Aug. 1954.

9b. **Michael Duaine.** Born 7 July 1960 at Battle Creek, MI. Married Darlene Lois Dean.

10a. **Seth Michael.** Born 28 Jan. 1991.

10b. **Rebecca Danielle.** Born 29 Jan. 1993.

9c. **Michelle Rene.** Born 19 Nov. 1966 at Battle Creek, MI. Married Jeffery Leon Ayers, and had children: *Joshua Michael* (born 21 Mar. 1988); *Alexander John* (born 29 Jan. 1990); *Nickalas Jeffery* (born 21 Mar. 1991); *Rachel Michelle* (born 26 Feb. 1993).

9d. **Martin Ross.** Born 24 May 1969 at Battle Creek, MI.

Winfield Scott Burgess (1852-1905)

[William (I)[1], Edward (I)[2], Reuben (I)[3], Thomas (I)[4], Charles Hunter[5]]

WINFIELD SCOTT BURGESS
(1852-1905)

OF PUTNAM COUNTY, TENNESSEE

6m. **Winfield Scott** *[son of Charles Hunter].* Born 25 Feb. 1852 in White Co., TN. Married Sarah Jane Barnes about 1870 (she was born 26 Feb. 1846 in NC, and died 25 June 1910). Listed in the 1870 census with his father, and in 1880 in the 2nd Civil District, Putnam Co.; Sarah appears as head of the family in 1900. Winfield Burgess was a farmer and water mill operator in Putnam Co., TN; with his brother, Simpson Burgess, he owned Burgess Falls on the Falling Water River, and built a water-powered mill there. He died 2 May 1905 at Greenpond, TN, and is buried with his wife in the Howard Cemetery.

The Children of Winfield Burgess:

7a. **Margaret Alice "Maggie."** Born 5 Sept. 1871 in Putnam Co., TN. Married as his second wife Daniel Winburn Ray on 15 Sept. 1895 in Putnam Co., TN (he was born 5 May 1866 in Putnam Co., TN, son of William Larkin Ray and Celia Margaret West, and brother of J. Robinson Ray [who married Maggie's sister Ann]; Daniel married firstly Harriet Ellen Burgess, daughter of Joel Burgess I [see her entry for their children], married thirdly Susan Marie Bockman on 22 Dec. 1901 in Putnam Co. [she was born 29 Dec. 1866, and died 30 Aug. 1939], married fourthly Mrs. ___ Bean, and died 7 Mar. 1942 in Putnam Co., buried West Cemetery), and had children:

Minnie Ann RAY. Born 13 Nov. 1896 in Putnam Co., TN, married Ridley Lester Williams on 20 Sept. 1914 (he was born 23 Dec. 1894, and died 30 June 1973), and had children: *Estelle Marie* (born 30 June 1916; she lives at Nashville, TN); *Lemon Daniel* (born 21 Dec. 1922, married Lois Louise Ashford on 26 Apr. 1947 [born 30 Nov. 1927, and died 14 Jan. 1960]; married secondly Barbara Chaires on 16 June 1962 [born 7 Sept. 1936], and had children: Diane Marie [born 21 June 1963, married Tracey Allen Ford on 28 May 1988]; Lemon Williams lives at Franklin, TN). ***Minnie WILLIAMS*** died on 29 May 1986, and is buried in the Crestlawn Cemetery, Putnam Co., TN.

Ridley RAY. Born 4 Oct. 1898 in Putnam Co., TN. Married his third cousin, Margaret "Maggie" Farris (she was the daughter of Daniel Boone Farris and Ellen Belle Dyer, and granddaughter of Emily T. Burgess Farris, and died 9 Mar. 1921, buried West Cemetery), and had children: *(Margaret) Alline* (born 17 Jan. 1921, married Robert Maddux in Jan. 1957 [he was the son of Ernest Maddux and Moncie Leftwich], and had children: Cindy Lou [born Oct. 1958, married Terry Clayton on 10 June 1979 {he was the son of Thomas Clayton}]).

Ridley RAY married secondly Emily Jane Sayre on 2 July 1925 (she was born 2 Feb. 1904 in WV, and died 10 Sept. 1990, buried Crestlawn Cemetery, Cookeville, TN), and had children: *Emma Jean* (born 22 Sept. 1926 at Akron, OH, married Fred Howard Maynard on 22 Dec. 1946 [he died 20 Feb. 1986, buried Crestlawn Cemetery], and had children: Fred Howard Jr. [born 13 Dec. 1947 at Cookeville, TN, married Sue Smith, and had children: Melissa {born 1980}; Brian {born 1983}]; Ronald Ray [born 26 Dec. 1952 at Cookeville, TN, married Joyce Harris, and had children: Ronald Ray Jr. {born 1975}; Anthony Lee {born 1979}]); *Ridley Winburn* (born 6 June 1928 at Akron, OH, married Evelyn Bernice Hull on 8 Apr. 1950 [she was born 7 Sept. 1929 in Clay Co., TN, daughter of Hiram Edgar Hull and Minta Francis Bilbrey], died 24 Feb. 1993 at Oak Ridge, TN, buried Crestlawn Cemetery, Cookeville, TN, and had children: Mary Sue [born 7 Nov. 1956 at Cookville, TN, married Mark Randall Taylor on 13 Jan. 1990 in Davidson Co., TN]); *Charles Everett* (born 14 Mar. 1939, married (Virginia) Lois Ragland on 29 July 1965, and had children: Son [born and died Jan. 1968]; Susan [born 25 Mar. 1970]; Daniel [born 25 Sept. 1971]; Saundra [born 21 July 1976]); *Gwendolyn* (born 22 Aug. 1946). ***Ridley RAY*** died on 20 Nov. 1967.

Margaret Alice "Maggie" RAY died on 23 Aug. 1899 in Putnam Co., and is buried in the West Cemetery. Daniel Ray is listed as a widower in the 1900 census for Putnam Co., TN.

7b. **(Sarah) Ann (IV).** Born 13 Mar. 1875 in Putnam Co., TN. Married (Joseph) Robinson Ray on 22 Dec. 1898 in Putnam Co. (he was born 18 Apr. 1872, son of William Larkin Ray and Celia West, and brother of Daniel Ray [who married Ann's sister, Maggie Burgess], and died 13 Nov. 1935), and had children: *Dimple* (born 15 May 1901, married her cousin, Clay Evans Barr, on 1 May 1930 [he was born 17 Jan. 1893, and died 3 Feb. 1970], and died 25 Feb. 1976); *Hallie Allene* (born 5 July 1904, married Angus Campbell on 4 Aug. 1934 [he was born 10 July 1899, and died 17 Feb. 1972]); *Burgess Robinson* (born 9 Apr. 1913, married Ruby Carol Mott on 30 Dec. 1944, and died 10 Apr. 1967, having had children: Sarah Ann [born 27 Sept. 1946, died 1 Oct. 1946]; Ruby Carol [born 22 Mar. 1949]; William B. [born 13 Apr. 1954]); *Willadean* (born 29 Sept. 1918, married Clare M. Smartt on 12 Dec. 1941, and had children: William McClain [born 19 Nov. 1942, married Angela Tenny on 5 Oct. 1975]; Catherine Ann [married Robert Granger, and secondly Sandy Strauss]). Ann RAY died on 25 Aug. 1943, and is buried in the West Cemetery.

7c. **Almedia Lois.** Born 2 May 1877 in Putnam Co., TN. Married Daniel Morgan Howard on 16 Dec. 1895 in White Co. (he was born 29 Dec. 1872, and died 21 Dec. 1947), and had children: *Burgess Morgan* (born 20 Mar. 1896, married ___ Sparks, and had children: Delores; Ted; *Burgess HOWARD* died on 22 July 1989 at Inglewood, CA, aged 93 years); *Margaret Alice "Maggie"* (born 1898, married H. Dawson Morgan (he was born 4 Nov. 1898, and died Jan. 1984), and had children: Betty Flo [born 29 Sept. 1929, married Kaul Fincher, and had children: Kaul Morgan {dau.; born 2 Dec. 1952, married ___ Williams}; Margaret Alice {born 8 Feb. 1954}; Henry {born 3 Apr. 1969}]); *Beulah Mabel* (married Charles W. Gentry, and had children: Lois [married ___ Warden]; Charles W. Jr. [married ___ King]; Margaret [married ___ Bic]); *Demps Southard* (married Myrle Medley). Almedia Howard died on 25 June 1965, and is buried with her husband in the Howard Cemetery. Maggie Morgan raised champion walking horses at Cookeville, TN; she has contributed greatly to this book.

7d. **James Peter.** Born 14 June 1879 in Putnam Co., TN. Married (Margarette) Cordelia Farley on 10 Oct. 1906 in Putnam Co. (she was born 3 Feb. 1880, daughter of Major Jesse Farley and Elizabeth "Betsy" Allison, and died 13 Oct. 1953). Listed in the 1910 census and 1918 draft register for Putnam Co.; his wife is listed as head of the family in 1920. James P. Burgess was a real estate broker in Putnam Co., TN. He died there on 18 (or 24) Oct. 1918, and is buried with his wife in the Howard Cemetery.

8a. **Holla Otto.** Born 30 Sept. 1909 in Putnam Co., TN. Married Teola Kell (who lives at Cookeville). Holla Burgess was Superintendent of the Water and Sewer Dept. for Cookeville, TN between 1947-74, when he retired. He died at Cookeville on 19 Sept. 1979, buried in the Crestlawn Cemetery.

9a. **Gary Kell.** Born 29 Oct. 1945 at Guntersville, AL. Married Judy Faye Buckner on 4 Apr. 1970 in Putnam Co. (div.; she was born 18 Apr. 1947). Gary Burgess owns a landscaping company at Cookeville, TN.

7e. **John Martin.** Born 2 Feb. 1881 (or 14 Feb. 1882, according to his draft record) in Putnam Co., TN. Married Opal Bullock about 1905 (she was born 26 Sept. 1886, daughter of James Thomas Bullock and Mary Lou Bohannon, and brother of Harvey Bullock [who married his sister, Alice Burgess], and died 25 Nov. 1910 [or 1962], buried Howard Cemetery). Listed in the 1910 census for Cumberland Co. and 1918 draft register for White Co. John M. Burgess was a mill owner in Tennessee; he later worked for B. F. Goodrich Co., Akron, OH. He died on 21 Feb. 1958, and is buried in Michigan.

8a. **Child.** Died an infant, buried in the Howard Cemetery.
8b. **Child.** Died an infant, buried in the Howard Cemetery.
8c. **(James) Winfield (I).** Born 9 Sept. 1908 in Putnam Co., TN. Listed in the 1920 census living with Jim Bullock, his grandfather. Winfield Burgess was the manager of an A&P Store at Akron, OH. He was hit by a car on 15 Oct. 1939, and died there unmarried on 1 Nov. 1939, buried Memorial Park Cemetery.
8d. **Louise (III)** (nmn). Born 17 Sept. 1909 in Putnam Co., TN. Married John C. Bailey (he was born 16 Oct. 1907), and had children: *Eloise* (born 4 Nov. 1930, married Nevin S. Carpenter [he was born 1 Nov. 1930]); *Robert Ivan* (born 7 Nov. 1934, married Ruby Carolyn Donegin [she was born 17 Nov. 1940], and lives at Akron, OH); *John Thomas* (born 23 Jan. 1938, married Janet Habos [she was born 18 Jan. 1941], and lives at Akron, OH). Louise Bailey died on 25 (or 21, according to her Social Security record) Oct. 1988 at Akron, OH.

7f. **Alice Ola.** Born 24 Apr. 1884 in Putnam Co., TN. Married Harvey R. Bullock on 19 Oct. 1902 in Putnam Co. (he was born 6 Nov. 1882, son of James Thomas Bullock and Mary Lou Bohannon, and brother of Opal Bullock [who married John Burgess], remarried Lyda Bandy, and died 23 Jan. 1962). Alice Bullock died childless on 2 June 1928, and is buried with her husband in the Stone Cemetery.

[William (I)[1], Edward (I)[2], Reuben (I)[3], Thomas (I)[4]]

ANDERSON BURGESS
(1808-1899)

OF WARREN COUNTY, MISSOURI

5e. **Anderson** *[son of Thomas (I)].* Born 24 Apr. 1808 in Rowan (later Davie) Co., NC. Married Elizabeth Whittaker on 4 July 1830 in TN (she was born 24 Oct. 1810 in TN, daughter of William Whittaker and Ann Wiser, and died 11 Feb. 1897). Listed in the 1840-60 and 1880 censuses for Charrette Township, Warren Co., MO, but has not been found in 1870 (he is *not* the Anderson Burgess listed in the 1870 census for Monroe Co., MO). A year after his marriage, Anderson Burgess moved to Franklin Co., MO, but by 1832 had settled on Smith's Creek, near Marthasville, Charrette Township, Warren Co., MO. The published histories of his family in *A Pioneer History of the Families of Missouri*, by William S. Bryan and Robert Rose (St. Louis: Bryan, Brand & Co., 1876, p. 206), and in *History of St. Charles, Montgomery, and Warren Counties, Missouri* (St. Louis: National Historical Co., 1885, p. 1035), provide essential material on Anderson, his brothers and sisters, his father and grandfather (see below). He died in Warren Co. on 22 Mar. 1899, aged 90 years, and was buried there with his wife in the small Burgess Cemetery, across the road from St. Paul's United Church of Christ. His will (*Warren Co. Will Book #E*, p. 232-233, dated 28 Jan. 1896, probated 1 May 1899) mentions surviving sons Valentine and Dudley, deceased son Wayman, and most of his daughters.

The Children of Anderson Burgess:

6a. **Wayman L(ollar?).** Born 15 Feb. 1831 in Franklin Co., MO. See below for full entry.

6b. **Malissa Jane.** Born 6 Feb. 1833 in Warren Co., MO. Married John W. Fourt (or Fuort or Fort) on 12 Nov. 1851 in Warren Co., MO, and moved to AR. Mentioned in her father's will in 1896 and in the 1901 settlement (as Fourt), but has not been found in the 1880-1900 Missouri soundexes. She died on 6 Aug. 1909, according to Valentine Burgess's surviving Bible record.

6c. **Martha Ann (I) "Polly Ann."** Born 18 Mar. 1835 in Warren Co., MO. Married Napoleon Christopher Tice on 12 Apr. 1860 in Warren Co. (he was born 12 Oct. 1835 in Warren Co.), and had children (all mentioned in Anderson Burgess's will as beneficiaries): *William D.* (born 1861 in MO, married Fannie L. McBee on 31 Oct. 1886 in Lafayette Co.); *Julia A.* (born 1863 in MO, and died 26 Sept. 1881, buried Waverly Cemetery); *Adolphus A.* (born 1868 in MO); *Verline Elizabeth* (born 1872 in MO); *Anna C.* (born 1876 in MO, and was living unmarried in 1926 in Kansas City, MO., when she wrote a letter to the County Clerk of Lafayette Co. inquiring about her grandfather's will). Listed in the 1860 and 1880 censuses for Warren Co., but is living in 1882 in Lafayette Co., MO. Mentioned as deceased in her father's will (1896). Polly Tice died on 17 Aug. 1886, according to Valentine Burgess's surviving Bible record.

6d. **(Margaret) Clemensa.** Born 4 Mar. 1837 in Warren Co., MO. Married Preston Sullens (or Sullins) on 2 Dec. 1858 in Warren Co. (he was born 14 Feb. 1823, and died 7 Sept. 1891), and had children: *Edgar* (born 1 July 1869, died 21 May 1894, buried with his parents). Mentioned in her father's will (1896) and settlement (1901). Clemensa Sullens died on 18 Aug. 1910 in Lafayette Co., MO, and is buried in the Bates City Cemetery.

6e. **(Virlena) Elizabeth.** Her name is also spelled Verlena. Born 13 Feb. 1839 in Warren Co., MO. Listed with her father in 1860. Married Bolivar D. Bryan on 5 Apr. 1864 in Warren Co., MO. Mentioned in her father's will (1896) and 1901 settlement, but has not been found in the 1900 MO soundex. She died on 5 Mar. 1909, according to Valentine Burgess's surviving Bible record.

6f. **Dudley H(unter?).** He was probably named for Dudley Hunter, son of William and Sarah Hunter, relatives of Charles Hunter of Rowan (later Davie) Co., NC. His name is listed as William H. Burgess in the 1850 census. Born 13 May 1841 in Warren Co., MO. Married Anna E. Jones on 14 Oct. 1902 in Warren Co. (she was born 1858 in MO, daughter of Dr. Paul M. Jones and great-great-granddaughter of Daniel Boone, and died 14 Sept. 1916, buried Dundee, MO). Listed in the 1850-80 censuses with his father, in 1900 as a single man in Charrette Township, Warren Co., MO living with Jerry Murphy, and in 1910 with his wife. He is said to have gone West in his later years. He probably died childless, possibly on 23 Feb. 1921 in Warren Co., leaving a wife, Melvina A. "Maud."

6g. **Valentine "Squire."** He was probably named for Valentine Hunter, his great-uncle. Born 10 Nov. 1843 in Warren Co., MO. Married Frankie Loe Wyatt on 2 Oct. 1879 in Warren Co. (she was born 20 Apr. 1855 in MO, daughter of Francis and Annie Wyatt). Listed with his father in the 1880 census, in the 1900 census for Washington Co., AR, and in 1910 in New Florence, Montgomery Co., MO. Census records indicate the couple were childless. Squire Burgess was successively Deputy Constable, Constable, and Justice of the Peace (so indicated in the 1880 census) for Charrette Township, Warren Co., MO. He died childless on 7 Feb. 1926 in Lafayette Co., MO, and is buried in the Waverly Cemetery.

6h. **Sarah Kathryn.** Born 16 Sept. 1847 in Warren Co., MO. Married John Frederick Wilkinson on 4 Sept. 1868 in Warren Co., MO (he was born 9 Dec. 1834 in Charlotte Co., VA, and died 3 Mar. 1898), and had at least the following children: *Alice* (born Nov. 1878); *Marvin* (born Aug. 1887); *Virginia* (died young on 3 Mar. 1898, buried with her parents). Mentioned in her father's will (1896) and settlement (1901). Moved to Centralia, Boone Co., MO, where she appears in the 1880-1900 censuses (in 1900 as head of the family). Sarah Wilkinson died there on 10 Aug. 1926, and is buried in the Columbia Cemetery.

6i. **Adolphus A(nderson?).** Born 16 Nov. 1853 in Warren Co., MO. Adolphus Burgess was a farmhand for his father. He died unmarried on 2 July 1879 in Warren Co. (so noted in the second of his father's personal histories).

THE HISTORY OF ANDERSON BURGESS (1876)

Thomas Burgess, son of Reuben Burgess of North Carolina, moved to Tennessee with his family in 1814. In 1830 he was drowned in the Cumberland River, and left a widow and eleven children, Viz.: Elizabeth, George W., Charles, Anderson, Margaret, Joel, Thomas, William, Polly, Hiram, and Nellie. Two of these, Anderson and Thomas, settled in Missouri. The latter was in Nathan Boone's Company of Rangers during the Indian War, and also served in the Black Hawk War. He subsequently removed to Arkansas. Anderson married Elizabeth Whittaker, daughter of William Whittaker and Ann Wiser, and settled in Warren County in 1831. The Children were: Wayman L., Malissa J., Polly Ann, Clemensa, Virlena E., Dudley H., Valentine, Sarah C., Adolphus A.

THE HISTORY OF ANDERSON BURGESS (1885)

(Farmer, Post Office, Marthasville). This old and respected citizen of Warren County is a native of North Carolina, born in Rowan County, April 24, 1808. His father, Thomas Burgess, was from Virginia, but his Mother, whose maiden name was Polly Hunter, was born and reared in North Carolina. Anderson Burgess, after he grew up in Rowan County, was married, across in Tennessee, July 4, 1830, to Elizabeth Whittaker, a daughter of William Whittaker, formerly of North Carolina. The year after his marriage Mr. Burgess removed to Missouri, and located first in Franklin County, but shortly afterwards on Smith's creek, in what is now Warren County. Barring one or two short absences he has been a resident of Warren County ever since, for a period of over half a century, or since before the county was formed. He removed to his present place in 1855, where he has a good homestead, comfortably improved. Mr. & Mrs. Burgess have had nine children; Wayman L. (deceased), Malissa J., wife of John Fuort, a farmer in Arkansas; Polly A., wife of N. C. Tice; Clemensa, wife of P. Sulling; Virlena, wife of B. D. Bryan; Dudley H., Valentine, Sarah, wife of John Wilkerson; Adolphus A. (deceased July 2, 1879). Mr. Burgess has retired from active work himself, and rents his farm out. He is comfortably situated. His two sons are at home. Valentine is married and is now a justice of the peace of Charrette Township. He was born November 10, 1843, and was married October 2, 1879 to Miss Frankie L., a daughter of Francis and Annie Wyatt of this county. Squire Burgess makes a very capable and upright magistrate, and his courts command the respect and confidence of litigants no less than the community at large. He is a worthy member of the A.F. & A.M.

THE WILL OF ANDERSON BURGESS

Marthasville, January 28th, 1896

I Anderson Burgess of the County of Warren, in the State of Missouri, do make and publish this my last will and testament.

1st I give and bequeath to Melissa Jane my oldest daughter five hundred Dollars ($500.00)
2nd I give to the ears [sic] of my daughter Poly Ann, dec., Wm Tice, the oldest son of Poly Ann fifty Dollars ($50.00)

3rd Adolphus Tice the sum of fifty Dollars ($50.00)
4th Berline Tice the sum of fifty Dollars ($50.00)
5th Anne Tice the sum of fifty Dollars ($50.00)
6th Charley Burgess my grand children the sum of one Dollar $1.00
7th Clara Burgess the sum of one Dollar ($1.00), the too [sic] last mentioned are children are children [sic] of my son Waman dec.
8th Marget Clemence five hundred Dollars ($500.00)
9th Berline Elisabeth five hundred Dollars ($500.00)
10th Sara Kathrin five hundred Dollars ($500.00)
11th Valentine Burges has allredy received his full share
12th And lastly as to all the rest and remainder of my personal and real estate I give to my son Dudly after the deth of myselve and my wife Elisabeth Burgess, and after the payment of all my just depts [sic] and burial expenses.

In witness whereof, I have hereonto set my hand this 28th Jan. 1896.

Anderson Burgess

Signed and declared by the above Anderson Burgess to be his last will and Testemant [sic], in the presence of us who at his request, and in his presence, have subscribed our names in witness thereto.

Julius Muench
William Peters

A LETTER OF ANDERSON BURGESS TO HIS BROTHER CHARLES, 1843

"State of Missouri, Warren County, February the 22nd, 1843. Dear brother and sister, I take my pen in hand to inform you that my self and family are well at present, hoping these lines may find you all enjoying the same blessings of health. You must excuse me for not writing sooner, but I have bin [__] mooving position for some time and unsettled. I sold my land about the first of September 1842 [sic; probably 1841] and in the spring following I moved to the upper countyes of this state and stayed thare all summer and did not like [it] & move[d] back to the same settlement last fall, and bought 160 acres of land [in] January the land I sold out and feel better and enjoy [?] than I ever have bin since I have bin in the state. I gave $750 dollars, thare is a good dwelling house and stable barns and other outhouses and about thirty acres of cleared land. Your note to me in Joel Burgesses letter that you wished to by [sic] my interest in the land provided I wode [sic] take the same that the other hires [sic] had taken which you said you had got for twenty dollars each. If you will send me the twenty dollars I will take it for my parte of the land. I want you to send it to me the sum you offer twenty. I live 12 miles south of Warrington [i.e., Warrenton, MO], and eff [sic] it is not convenient for the person whome you send it by to come to my house they can leave it in Warrington with Stout (?) and Harper parteners in a safe specie in the currency of this country. I have not heard anything of Thomas sens [sic] I received Joels letter. I did hear that William was in the reglar servic but don't know for certain. I shold [sic] be much gratified to see you all but the oppertunity does not offer at the present. I want you to give my respects to mother and all inquiring frends [sic]. I want you to rit [sic] to me as soon as you get this letter. And finally (?) I am now at present and last remain your loving brother and sister til death, Anderson Burgess, Elizabeth Burgess. To Charles Burgess and Margaret Burgess."

[William (I)[1], Edward (I)[2], Reuben (I)[3], Thomas (I)[4], Anderson[5]]

WAYMAN L. BURGESS
(1831-1878)
OF WARREN COUNTY, MISSOURI

6a. **Wayman L(ollar?)** *[son of Anderson].* Born 15 Feb. 1831 in Franklin Co., MO. Married as her second husband Catharine Patton on 19 Aug. 1862 in Warren Co., MO (she was born Sept. 1844 [or 1841] in MO, daughter of Margis Patton, married firstly Henry C. Kuntze on 22 Mar. 1860 in Warren Co., and had children: *(Sarah) Elizabeth "Lizzie"* [born July 1861 in Warren Co., listed as Sarah Burgess in the 1870 census with her stepfather, married John H. Wessel on 2 July 1879 in Warren Co. {he was born Jan. 1857 in MO, and died 1923}, settled at Waverly, Lafayette Co., MO about 1884, and died 1924, buried with her husband in the Waverly Cemetery, having had at least the following children: Louise E. {born 27 Jan. 1884, married ___ Trent}; William H. {born Oct. 1886}; Benjamin {born Dec. 1888}]; Catharine married thirdly Reuben J. Smith on 8 Sept. 1880 in Warren Co. [he was born Feb. 1851 in TN], Valentine Burgess conducting the marriage as Justice of the Peace, and is listed with him in the 1900 census for Calloway Co., MO [three of five children then survive]). Listed with his father in 1860, and in the 1870 census for Charrette Township, Warren Co., MO; Catharine is listed as head of the family in 1880. Wayman Burgess was a farmer in Warren Co., MO. He died there on 6 Oct. 1878, according to Valentine Burgess's family Bible record (or 14 Oct. 1878, according to a contemporaneous family letter surviving in Tennessee; see the entry of Margaret Burgess Bradford for the text).

The Children of Wayman Burgess:

7a. **Clara (I).** She is called Catharine in a surviving family portrait. Born about 1864 in Warren Co., MO. Married Wayman W. Smith on 25 Mar. 1883 in Calloway Co., MO (he was born June 1865 in MO, and married secondly Gillie Love on 22 Sept. 1891 in Calloway Co.), and had children: *Sadie* (born Feb. 1884 in MO); *Violet* (born Apr. 1887 in MO); *William* (born Feb. 1890 in MO). Not listed with her mother in the 1880 census, but is mentioned in her grandfather's will (1896). She either died or divorced her husband about 1890.

7b. **John (VIII) "Johnnie."** Born about 1867 in Warren Co., MO. John Burgess died unmarried about 1887: "My father said that Johnnie was struck in the back by his stepfather for failing to properly saddle a horse, and died of his injuries. My father then fled to his uncle Valentine's place in Lafayette Co., MO, and never returned home. He was about seventeen years old when Johnnie died."—Charles E. Burgess, 1993.

7c. **Charles Dudley.** Born 16 June 1870 in Warren Co., MO. See below for full entry.

CHARLES D. BURGESS OF LAFAYETTE CO., MISSOURI
[Wayman Lollar[6]]

7c. **Charles Dudley** *[son of Wayman Lollar].* His name is listed in the 1870 census as Adolphus. Born 16 June 1870 in Warren Co., MO. Married Georgia Ann Morris on 27 Sept. 1894 in Lafayette Co., MO (she was born 3 July 1874, and died 12 July 1948). He moved to Lafayette Co. about 1887 to escape his stepfather's brutality. Mentioned in his grandfather's will in 1896. Listed in the 1900-10 censuses for Middleton Township, Lafayette Co., MO (and in 1910 also in Waverly). Charles D. Burgess was a horticulturist near Waverly, MO, where he managed the orchards of the Wessel family. He was also an amateur violinist, having been given an instrument by his grandfather, Anderson Burgess. He died on 27 June 1940 at Waverly, MO, and is buried in the Waverly Cemetery.

8a. **Raymond Irenus.** Born 13 Sept. 1895 at Waverly, MO. Married Margaret Virginia Fletcher on 18 Oct. 1925 in Lafayette Co., MO (she was born 29 Oct. 1895, and died 15 June 1971). Served in World War I. Raymond Burgess worked as the manager of a grain elevator, as a bank teller, and as the owner of his own grocery store. He died on 27 Jan. 1970 at Waverly, MO, and is buried there in the Waverly Cemetery.

9a. **(Virginia) June**. Born 8 Nov. 1933 at Waverly, MO. Married John Fred Hinz on 12 Oct. 1952 in Lafayette Co., MO, and had children: *Bradley Burgess* (born 1 Nov. 1964, married Melissa Susanne "Missy" Riley on 29 Aug. 1987 [she was born 4 Mar. 1969], and had children: Elizabeth Ginelle [born 14 Oct. 1989]). June Hinz owns her own grocery store at Waverly, MO. Bradley Burgess Hinz has contributed greatly to this book.

9b. **David Dowd.** Born 7 Feb. 1938 at Waverly, MO. Married Noreen Smith on 14 July 1952. David Burgess works for Transworld Airlines. He lives at Lenexa, Johnson Co., KS, near Kansas City.

10a. **Jeffrey Scott (II).** Born 23 July 1963 at Kansas City, KS. Graduated from the University of Kansas. Jeff Burgess works for Federal Express.

10b. **Chad Alan.** Born 25 Oct. 1969 at Kansas City, KS. Chad Burgess works for Hen House Grocery.

11a. **Hunter David.** Born 3 June 1991 at Overland Park, KS.

10c. **Jason Dowd.** Born 14 Apr. 1971 at Kansas City, KS. Jason Burgess is a student at Emporia State University, Emporia, KS.

10d. **Kyle Ray.** Born 15 May 1972 at Kansas City, KS. Kyle Burgess works as a landscaper.

8b. **Gladys Marie (I).** Born 7 Sept. 1898 at Waverly, MO. Married John Adrain Weedin on 14 Feb. 1918 in Lafayette Co., MO (he was born 8 July 1895, and died 13 Feb. 1986 at Waverly, MO, aged 90 years). Gladys died on 11 Sept. 1984 at Waverly, MO. Their children included:

Charles Douglas WEEDIN. Born 28 Sept. 1919, married Louise James on 2 Apr. 1939, and had children: *James Douglas* (born 14 Feb. 1940); *Mary Jane* (born 2 Aug. 1945); *Teri Lavon* (born 10 Sept. 1955). Charles Weedin works as an irrigator.

Kenneth Adron WEEDIN. Born 13 Nov. 1922, married Lois Kneuppel on 18 Oct. 1952, and had children: *John Gregory* (born 1 May 1955); *Sharon Kay* (born 3 Dec. 1957); *Mark Duane* (born 15 Dec. 1961). Kenneth Weedin worked as a chemist. He died on 11 Jan. 1985.

Frances Ann WEEDIN. Born 11 June 1929, married A. J. Hilbrenner on 23 Nov. 1949, and had children: *Dwight Jay* (born 14 Nov. 1950, married Brenda Pierson on 13 July 1972, works with his father in the coin machine business); *Jo Ann* (born 17 May 1955, married Mark Schreiman on 14 Feb. 1976); *Kevin Lee* (born 27 June 1957, married Harriet Schreiman on 30 July 1976 [div.], and works in the coin machine business).

Norman Burgess WEEDIN. Born 11 Jan. 1932, married Marie Stark on 14 Aug. 1952, works as a construction superintendent, and had children: *Diane* (born 19 Feb. 1960, married David Niederjohn on 30 July 1983 [he died 18 Aug. 1989]).

Glenn Eugene WEEDIN. Born 12 May 1937, married Odetta Danford on 14 Mar. 1964, and had children: *Elizabeth Annette* (born 22 Apr. 1958); *Ruth Diane* (born 6 Jan. 1960); *Keith Duane* (born 8 May 1961); *Glenn Eugene Jr.* (born 7 Feb. 1967). Glenn Weedin works as an inspector for the U.S. Navy.

Morris Hudson WEEDIN. Born 12 Jan. 1939, married Betty Myerson on 15 Sept. 1962, and had children: *Eric Hudson* (born 29 Aug. 1967); *Russell Paul* (born 31 Dec. 1974). Morris Weedin worked for General Motors (now retired).

8c. **Leonard Wessel.** Born 9 Nov. 1904 at Waverly, MO. Married Josie Helen "Jo" Coad on 10 Oct. 1931 in Lafayette Co., MO (she was born 10 Aug. 1907, and died 3 Mar. 1981). Leonard Burgess was a horticulturist in Lafayette Co., MO. He died there on 29 July 1970.

9a. **Donna Jo.** Born 11 Oct. 1932. Married Gilbert Louis Lefholz on 8 Aug. 1954 in Lafayette Co., MO, and had children: *Kimberly Jo* (born 2 May 1958; Dr. Kimberly Lefholz is an OB/GYN physician at Kansas City, MO). Donna Lefholz retired from the DuPont/Olin Corporations in 1993; Gilbert Lefholz retired from TWA in 1992; they currently live at Kansas City, MO.

9b. **Leonard Wayne.** Born 19 Sept. 1934. Married Barbara Ann McKnight on 5 May 1957 in Lafayette Co. Leonard Burgess is self-employed. He lives at Springfield, MO.

10a. **Lori Ann.** Born 14 July 1958. Married Jon Mark Knight on 26 Sept. 1980 (div.), and had children: *Jon Christopher* (born 12 June 1983); *Chelsa Ann* (born 11 Oct. 1987); **Lori** married secondly Jeffrey Marsh on 6 May 1993. Lori Marsh works for the Missouri Highway Department at Springfield, MO.

10b. **Pamela Jo (I).** Born 3 Apr. 1960. Pamela Burgess is a hospital administrator at Dallas, TX.

10c. **Todd McKnight.** Born 16 Nov. 1967. Married Stephanie Jo Williams on 29 July 1989. Todd Burgess is a management trainee for a corporation at Joplin, MO; they live at Webb City, MO.

11a. **Tyler McKnight.** Born 30 Mar. 1993.

10d. **Amy Beth.** Born 16 July 1974. Amy Burgess is a college student.

9c. **Sandra Sue (I).** Born 16 Mar. 1938. Married Travis Sanders on 21 July 1956 in Lafayette Co., MO, and had children: *Robin Reigh* (born 22 Aug. 1957, married David Hamilton [div.] in 1976, and had children: David Leonard [born 7 Aug. 1977]; married secondly Russell Scrutchfield on 16 Jan. 1982, and had children: Megan Rose [born 31 May 1988]; Hannah Jo [born 20 Oct. 1990]; Robin and Russell Scrutchfield are self-employed and live at Lone Jack, MO); *Charles Burgess* (born 8 Mar. 1959, and died 15 July 1981); *Ronda Susan* (born 28 Dec. 1963, married Michael Westerheid on 17 Apr. 1988; Ronda Westerheid is a registered nurse and Michael is an architect at Cincinnati, OH). Travis Sanders works for the gas company at Independence, MO.

9d. **Linda Lue (II).** Born 3 Dec. 1940. Married Charles White (div.); married secondly Paul Whitney on 10 Aug. 1981. Linda and Paul Whitney work for TWA at Kansas City, MO, and live at Platt City, MO.

8d. **Charles Elmer (II) "Carl."** Born 28 July 1907 at Waverly, MO. Married Virginia Ann Oliver on 8 Nov. 1930 at Lexington, Lafayette Co., MO (she was born 10 Aug. 1905 in Saline Co., MO). Carl Burgess worked for the U.S. Army Corps of Engineers for many years, and helped build a Army helicopter base and many other airbase facilities. He currently lives retired at Warrensburg, MO, and has contributed greatly to this book.

9a. **Barbara Jane (I).** Born 7 Feb. 1934 at St. Joseph, MO. Married Stanley Small on 21 Nov. 1956 at Warrensburg, Johnson Co., MO (he works as district manager for Modern Curriculum Press, publishers of educational books), and had children: *Gregory Niel* (born 14 Sept. 1957, married Ruthane Parsons at Warrensburg, MO, and had children: Bradley Niel [born 16 Feb. 1982]; Ryan Benjamin [born 9 Sept. 1985]; Casey Anderson [born 10 Oct. 1987]; Greg Small works as a counselor at Crest Ridge High School in Johnson Co.); *Christopher Alan* (born 4 Aug. 1965, married Kelli Murphy on 3 June 1989; Chris Small works as a principal at LaMont High School, LaMont, Missouri).

9b. **Charles Oliver.** Born 25 Mar. 1944 at Leavenworth, KS. Married Cynthia Booke on 14 June 1975 at St. Louis, MO. Charles Burgess works for the U.S. General Accounting Office at St. Louis, MO, and lives at Eureka, MO.

(front)
Georgia Ann Morris Burgess
Charles Dudley Burgess

(back)
Raymond Irenus Burgess
Leonard Wessel Burgess
Gladys Marie Burgess
Charles Elmer Burgess

Mother's Day, 14 May 1939

[William (I)[1], Edward (I)[2], Reuben (I)[3], Thomas (I)[4]]

JOEL BURGESS I
(1812-1880)
OF PUTNAM COUNTY, TENNESSEE

5g. **Joel (I)** *[son of Thomas (I)].* He is called Joseph in the 1880 mortality census and in some early tax records; however, he is *not* the father of Joseph (or Joe) Burgess of Jackson Co., TN (whose parents came from South Carolina). Born 17 Apr. 1812 in Rowan (later Davie) Co., NC. Married Ruth(a) Allison about 1832 (she was born 29 Aug. 1810 in White Co., TN, daughter of John Allison Jr. [a Revolutionary War soldier] and Sarah Toler, and died 17 Dec. [or Mar.] 1867); married secondly Lucinda "Lou" or "Synda" S. Pullen(d) about 1868 (she was born 31 Aug 1833 in VA, possibly the daughter of Thomas and Sarah J. Pullen, and died 19 May 1911). Listed in the 1840 census for White (later Putnam) Co., TN (with one son aged 5-10, two sons 0-5, and one daughter 0-5), and in 1860-70 in the 2nd Civil District, Putnam Co., TN; has not been found in 1850. He signed (as "Joseph Burgess") the 11 Feb. 1854 petition to the Tennessee State Legislature requesting that Putnam Co. be established. Joel Burgess was a farmer in Putnam Co. He died there on 16 May 1880, and is buried with both his wives in the Brown's Mill Cemetery. Lou Burgess appears as head of the family in the 1880-1900 censuses for the 2nd District, Putnam Co. (two of three children then survive); she is living with her daughter, Dee, in 1910.

The Children of Joel Burgess:

6a. **John Ross.** Born 25 July 1833 in White (later Putnam) Co., TN. See below for full entry.

6b. **Pernina.** Born 18 Aug. 1835 in White (later Putnam) Co., TN. Married Calvin Phy about 1860 (he was born 17 May 1829, son of Josiah Phy and Nancy Phillips), and had children:

Joel Kent PHY. Born 9 Feb. 1861, was raised by his grandparents, married Ruth Quarles about 1890 (she was born 23 Dec. 1868, and died 3 Sept. 1954), and died 11 Feb. 1922, buried Phillips Cemetery, having had children: *Pernina May* (born 22 Dec. 1891, married W. Bennie Whiteaker on 21 Dec. 1915 in Putnam Co. [he was the son of William Nathan "Wib" Whiteaker and Frances Ford, and died 4 Jan. 1957], and died Feb. 1974 at Cookeville, TN, having had children: William Donal [born 9 Aug. 1917, married Elizabeth Lucille O'Hara, lives at Ontario, CA, and had children: William Donal Jr. {married and had children: Rob Scott; Christopher Lee}]; Irma Hazel [born 22 Dec. 1918, married Arthur Wilson Montgomery {he was born 7 Dec. 1918, son of Gilmer Montgomery and Cora Pippin}, and had children: Arthur Wilson Jr. {born 10 Sept. 1947, married Elayne Louise Farley <she was the daughter of Ralph Douglas Farley and Vada Lou Maxwell>, and had children: Lora Lynn <born 11 Nov. 1974>; Callie Marie <born 21 May 1979>}]; Govy Joel [born 5 Nov. 1921, married Mable Bowman, and died Jan. 1967, having had children: Kenneth Joel; Sharon W. {married Randy Ingram, and had children: Rachel Elaine <born 25 May 1982>}]).

Calvin and Pernina PHY are listed in the 1860 census for Putnam Co., TN. Pernina Phy died on 25 Feb. 1861.

6c. **William (XI).** Born 1837 in White (later Putnam) Co., TN. Listed with his father in the 1840-60 censuses, but has not been found thereafter.

6d. **James Marion (I).** Born 23 Aug. 1839 in White (later Putnam) Co., TN. See below for full entry.

6e. **Thomas (IV).** Born 1841 in White (later Putnam) Co., TN. Listed with his father in the 1850-60 censuses, but has not been found thereafter.

6f. **Sarah (IX) "Sallie."** Born Nov. 1843 in White (later Putnam) Co., TN. Married James T. Sliger about 1868 (he was born 20 Oct. 1848 in TN, son of John C. Sliger and Lucinda Wilhite [who was the daughter of Reuben Wilhite and Mary Yeager], and brother of Samuel Sliger [who married Sallie's sister, Polly], and worked as a carpenter, furniture maker, and coffin maker), and had children: *Mack* (born Dec. 1869, married Ann Terry [she was born 11 Apr. 1871, daughter of William Jasper "Jass" Terry and Mary Pointer, and died 17 Mar. 1951], and died childless, buried in the Mt. Zion Cemetery, Jackson Co.). Listed in the 1870 census for the 2nd Civil District, Putnam Co., TN next to her father, in 1880 in

Putnam Co., TN, and in 1900 in Jackson Co., TN. An article in the *Putnam County Herald* on 1 Sept. 1910 says that "J. T." Sliger had gone to Texas. Sallie may have died at Ada, OK.

6g. **Emily T.** Born 26 (or 24) Nov. 1845 in White (later Putnam) Co., TN. Married Thomas Farris on 7 Sept. 1868 (he was born 13 Sept. 1842, son of Joseph Farris and Peggy Mills, and died 30 June 1914), and had children:

Richard "Dick" FARRIS. Born 1869, reputedly settled in Oregon.

Daniel Boone "Danke" FARRIS. Born 13 Oct. 1871, married Ellen Belle Dyer on 29 Oct. 1893 in Putnam Co. (she was born 28 Sept. 1870, daughter of William and Sarah Dyer, and died 24 Aug. 1934, buried with her husband in the West Cemetery), and died on 4 July 1938, having had children:

Myrtle FARRIS (born 5 Sept. 1894 in Putnam Co., married James Thomas Rowland "Roll" Bullock on 29 Dec. 1915 [he was born 14 Apr. 1889, son of David Harrison Bullock and (Sophia) Elizabeth "Betty" Terry, and died 21 Mar. 1936, buried in the Salem Cemetery], and died on 19 Oct. 1984, aged 90 years, having had children: Child [born and died 10 Oct. 1916]; Ruby Alice [born 14 Jan. 1917, died 4 Dec. 1919]; Terry Dyer [born 24 Jan. 1918, married Lillie Howell on 15 Mar. 1943 {she was the daughter of Robert G. Howell and Mary Lou Carter}, and had children: Brenda {born 1949, married Letcher Dishman, and had children: Jonathan Blake <born 1 Aug. 1982>}; Terry Lynn {born 1953, married Loretta Bowman}]; Fate [born 1921, married Mavis Cunningham, and had children: Heather; Barry; Bryan]; Will Thomas "Billy" [born 5 Feb. 1923, married Elizabeth Raines on 23 Nov. 1960 {she was the daughter of Estes Raines and Gladys Stover}, and died 24 Mar. 1985, buried Salem Cemetery, having had children: Tommie Dawn {born 8 Aug. 1970}]; Donald Howard [born 19 Mar. 1927, married Kathleen Bohannon on 4 Sept. 1948 {she was the daughter of Willis Bohannon and Elizabeth Wooten}, and had children: Wanda Ann {born 13 July 1957, married Michael Steven Pippin on 31 Aug. 1980 <he was a physician, the son of Vestle and Reba Pippin>}]).

Pleas FARRIS (born 1 Dec. 1895, and died 20 Oct. 1918 in the great flu epidemic, buried in the West Cemetery).

Young FARRIS (born 27 Apr. 1897 in Putnam Co., married Virgie Lou Jackson on 30 Jan. 1932 [she was born 16 June 1910, daughter of Ephraim W. Jackson and Jeanetta Phy, and died 4 Mar. 1987, buried with her husband in the West Cemetery], and died on 1 May 1976, having had children: Holmes Dyer [born 28 May 1933, married Ann Cummings, and had one adopted child]; Bobby Draper [born 28 Dec. 1935, married Linda Johnson on 11 June 1960 in Jackson Co. {she was the daughter of Herman and Rose Johnson}, and had children: Christopher Mack {born 14 May 1965}; Timothy Dow {born 18 Nov. 1968}]; Sharon Aline [born 1 Jan. 1946, married Charles Howard on 20 Nov. 1965 in Putnam Co. {he was a son of Clifford Howard and Dimple Huddleston}, and had children: Sonia Annette {born 24 Oct. 1966}; Charles Trevor Farris {born 13 Dec. 1977}]).

Lemon FARRIS (born 27 July 1899 in Putnam Co., married Nancy Belle Cunningham on 19 June 1921 [she was born 26 Sept. 1903, daughter of William Sidney Cunningham and Mary Lou Hampton], and died 11 Oct. 1969, buried Cunningham Cemetery, having had children):

William Clay *FARRIS* (born 17 Feb. 1922, married Lena Mae Wright [she was born 7 Feb. 1925, daughter of Estel Wright and Gladys Fitzpatrick], and had children: Linda Faye [born 9 Apr. 1947, married Terry Farmer, and had children: Matthew Justin {born 21 Mar. 1968}; Virginia Lee {born 16 July 1969}]; Myra Ann [born 9 Aug. 1949, married Bobby Kernea, and had children: Tyrus Clay {born 4 Feb. 1968}; Elaine {born 1 Feb. 1972}]; Mark Clay [born 17 July 1953, married Mary Alice Montgomery, and had children: Mark Clay Jr. {born 22 May 1972}; Patrick {born 7 Apr. 1975}]; Constance Rozelle [born 17 June 1956, married Osteen Wallace, and had children: Joseph {born 25 May 1973}; Sarah {born 16 Apr. 1979}; Amanda {born 28 Aug. 1980}]).

Guy Dibrell *FARRIS* (born 5 July 1923, married Geneva Gilliam [she was the daughter of Hartford Gilliam and Della Wilhite], and had children: Gary Dibrell [born 5 May 1947, married Patricia Ann Randolph {she was born 1952, daughter of Burdette Randolph}, and had children: Gary Ray {born 5 June 1971}]; Glenda Nyoka [born 14 Apr. 1948, married Donnie Julian, and had children: Donnie Shawn {born 28 Jan. 1968}; Gregory Steven {born 14 Aug. 1969}; Stacey Dale {born 12 June 1971}]; Michael Dewayne [born 20 Nov. 1949, married Deborah Gail Marlow, and had children: Michelle Dione {born 27 Feb. 1970}; Tricia Marie {born 27 May 1972}; Julie]; Phillip Dale [born 6 Dec. 1956, married Debbie Simcox]).

Lemon Fred *FARRIS* (born 7 July 1925, married Maudie Pippin, and had children: Royce Wayne [born 19 Oct. 1947, married Carol Pullman, and had children: Royce Wayne Jr. {born 22 Mar. 1967}; Jacoby]; Floyd Dennis [born 17 Nov. 1949, married Diane ___]).

Mary Ellen *FARRIS* (born and died 25 Dec. 1926).

Margaret Lou *FARRIS* (born 27 May 1928, married James B. Maxwell [he was born 11 May 1923, son of Solon James Maxwell and Ruth Harris], and had children: James Donald [born 28 Apr. 1948, married Evon ___ {div.}, and had children: Kimberly {born Jan. 1968}; Jimmie {born

Feb. 1969}; Tracy {born Mar. 1970}; Dennis {born 1973}]; Marilyn Ann [born Oct. 1949, married Leonard Breeze, and died on 22 Dec. 1971, having had children: Jeffrey Wayne {born Aug. 1968}; Marcia Lee]).

Charlie Daniel *FARRIS* (born 6 June 1931, married Rozelle Buckner on 15 May 1950, and had adopted children: Craig Jeffrey [born 31 Jan. 1957, married Theresa Carter {div.}, and had children: Jennifer {born 1977}]; Robin Saundra [born 7 Jan. 1959, married Andy Stewart {div.}]).

George Edward *FARRIS* (born 16 Oct. 1933, married Mary Edd McCormick on 6 Mar. 1954, and had children: Ronald Edward [born 17 Oct. 1955, married Theresa Ann Fowler on 15 Sept. 1978 {she was born 7 May 1957 at Norwich, England, daughter of Bobby Gene Fowler and Pat Padden}]; Larry Dan [born 20 Dec. 1957, married Jackie ___]; Sherry Lynn [born 1 Dec. 1960, married Tony Selby]; Patricia Ann [born 18 May 1966]).

Harvey Eugene *FARRIS* (born 29 Apr. 1936, married Peggy Sue Midgett on 1 Jan. 1955 [dec.], and had children: Peggy Sue Jr. [born 17 Jan. 1957, married Dale Delaney {div.}, and had children: Tiffany Lynn {born 5 Apr. 1974}; Peggy married secondly Carson Maynard {who died 7 Aug. 1987}]; Nancy Jo [born and died 2 Dec. 1960]; Teresa [ad.; born 4 Dec. 1965]).

Myrtle Irene *FARRIS* (born 16 Sept. 1938, married Don Agee, and had children: Nancy Denise [born Dec. 1962, married Ronald Glenn Davidson on 8 June 1985 {he was born 1964, son of Robert Davidson and Rhoda Flatt}]).

Robert Paul *FARRIS* (born 28 Oct. 1943, married Frances Beatrice "Bee" Davis, and had children: Robert Shane [born 7 Jan. 1964]; Jeffery Todd [born 9 Oct. 1966]; Vicky Leigh [born 19 Feb. 1971, died 21 Feb. 1971]; Lori Brook).

Margaret "Maggie" FARRIS (born 17 Jan. 1903 in Putnam Co., TN, married her cousin, Ridley Ray, on 28 Mar. 1920, and died 9 Mar. 1921; see his entry for her children).

Willie Holmes "Bill" FARRIS (born 28 July 1908 in Putnam Co., married Estelle Riddle on 16 Aug. 1930 [she was born 17 Feb. 1912, daughter of Wash Riddle and Rebecca Abston], and died 30 June 1980, buried Shipley Cemetery, having had children: Kenneth Lee [born 25 Dec. 1930, married Venia Hedley on 3 July 1954, and had children: Steven Lee {born 15 May 1957, married Pamela Jean Randolph <she was born 18 Apr. 1958, daughter of Kenneth Haskell Randolph and Ruth Braswell>}; Susan Elaine {born 5 May 1960, married Rick Swafford}; Sandra Michelle {born 20 July 1966}]; Rebecca June [born 22 Apr. 1937, married George Thomas on 30 June 1958, and had children: Tammy Jo {born 21 July 1959}; Vicki Renee {born 12 May 1964}]; Jackie Dale [born 12 June 1941, married Helen Goodwin on 17 Sept. 1965 {div.}, and had children: William Edward {born 10 Mar. 1964}; Jackie married secondly Carolyn Frazier on 1 June 1974, and had children: Christopher Dale {born 6 Sept. 1976}]; Helen Hazel [born 17 Feb. 1945, married Rellon Allen on 27 Mar. 1963, and had children: Rebecca Lynn {born 28 Feb. 1969}; Kelli Lee {twin; born 15 Mar. 1977}; Carrie Anna {twin; born 15 Mar. 1977}]. *Willie FARRIS* lived on the original farm of Joel Burgess I).

Joseph "Joe" FARRIS. Born 1875, married Amanda Odom on 7 Oct. 1894 in Putnam Co. (she was born 1877, daughter of Lewis Odom and Mary Rippetoe), and had children: *Jennie Miller* (born 13 Sept. 1905, married Dave Bullock Whitson on 26 Oct. 1922 [div.; he was born 1904, son of Mansfield E. Whitson and May Ann Bullock]); *Dimple May* (born 1909, married John Ensor Gaw on 30 Dec. 1938 [he was born 1909], and had children: Judy [married Gary Richardson, and had an adopted child: Jennifer Lynn]; Clarence Ensor [born 14 Sept. 1936, married Loretta Burchett {she was the daughter of John Burchett}, and had children: Randall Jeffrey {had children: Randall Tyler}; Michael]); *Tom Jeff* (born 28 Sept. 1911, married Jessie Ann Taylor on 2 Dec. 1933 [she was born 25 Mar. 1902, daughter of (Silas) Matthew Harvey Taylor and Frances Peek, and died 2 Nov. 1938, buried West Cemetery], and had children: Donald; Tommy Jean; Geraldine [born Oct. 1938, was adopted by Robert and Gertrude (Riddle) King, married William C. Sessions on 5 Sept. 1959 {he was born 24 Jan. 1924}, and had children: William C. Jr. {born 26 Aug. 1961}; Helen Elizabeth {born 27 Oct. 1964}; Rebecca Ann {born 3 Apr. 1969}]. *Tom Jeff FARRIS* married secondly Libbie Mildred Sulc on 25 Feb. 1949).

Wade Winfield FARRIS. Born 3 Feb. 1888, married Ella Shipley on 12 Sept. 1908 (she was born 22 Jan. 1890, daughter of Eli Shipley, and died 19 June 1941), and had children:

Birdie FARRIS (born 8 Oct. 1910, died unmarried on 18 June 1938, buried West Cemetery).

Troy FARRIS (born 8 Dec. 1912, married Marie Riddle on 6 July 1936 in Putnam Co. [she was born 1920, daughter of Hollis Riddle and Lois Harriett Pippin], and had children: Rellon Eugene [born 1 Jan. 1937, married Eula Sue Dubree on 12 Mar. 1955 {she was the daughter of Francis E. Dubree and Loree Smith}, and had children: Patricia Gail {born 6 Feb. 1957, married Sherman Cox}; Sandra Denise {born 20 Feb. 1961, married Carl Mitchell <div.>}]; Lola Fay [born 23 Dec. 1939, married Clifton Mayberry on 29 June 1957, and had children: Wayne Albert {born 28 July 1959}]; Glenn Edward [born 29 Oct. 1942, married Yi Morning Sun "Syvile" Lee on 7 Dec. 1965 {she was born 15 May 1942 in Korea}, and had children: Glenn Edward Jr. {born 9 Mar. 1967}]; Roy Lee [born 8 June 1945, married Margie Allen on 27 Dec. 1962 {she was born 24 Feb. 1941}, and had children: Regina Kay {born 30 Nov. 1963}; Linda Faye {born 19 June 1965}; Anital Shearl {born 27 Apr. 1966}; Darrell DeWayne {born 10 Jan. 1969}; Roy Lee married secondly Mary Ann ___, and had children: Edward Eugene {born 8 Apr. 1971}; Kenny {born 25 Aug. 1973}; Danny Allen {born 23 Jan. 1976}]; Stacy Truman [born 22 July 1949, married Patricia Young on 7 June 1975, and had children: Brandon Wade {born 13 Apr. 1982}]; Wanda Aline [born 11 Jan. 1954, married Mike Judd on 26 Aug. 1970, and had children: Eashia {born 17 July 1973}; Catherine Marie "Katie" {born 1 Sept. 1979}]).

Lotus FARRIS (born 31 May 1914, never married).

Mary Etta FARRIS (born 28 Oct. 1916, married Frank B. Harris [he was born 1 Dec. 1916, son of Benton Harris and Claudia Jones, and died 1 Aug. 1968, buried West Cemetery], and had children: Cecil Ray [born 9 May 1942, married Rose Roberts]; Wanda Rose [born 2 May 1946, married Joe Sadler, and had children: Steve; married secondly Bill Bandy, and had children: Becky]; Cathy Lou [born 3 Apr. 1950, married Jack Stewart, and had children: Rachel]).

C. B. "Snook" FARRIS (born 25 Jan. 1919, married Verta Randolph on 15 Apr. 1939 [she was born Oct. 1920, daughter of Alfred W. Randolph and Malecia "Lecie" Bumbalough], and had children: Barbara [born 30 Apr. 1940, married Norman Zubas, and had children: Michael; Sonia]; Anna Jean [born 16 Oct. 1942, married Carl Holden {dec.}, and had children: Mark; Karen]; Linnon Clay [born 5 June 1945, married Pat Yager, and had children: Lisa; Jennifer]; Patsy Geraldean [born 24 Apr. 1948, married Mike Ouston, and had children: Brian]; Judith Lee [born 12 Feb. 1952, married Phil Cawale]; Charlene [born 21 Aug. 1954, married Thomas Lobaito]; Donnie Alford [born 10 Feb. 1957, married Jean Funky]; Sonia Yvonne [born 1 Oct. 1961]; Hope Sherrie [born 1 Apr. 1964]).

Clara FARRIS (born 4 Aug. 1922, married Dover Scarlett [son of Russ Scarlett], and died 17 Oct. 1939, buried West Cemetery, having had children: Mary Ellen [born July 1939, died Aug. 1939, buried West Cemetery]).

Reba FARRIS (born 12 Dec. 1925, married Richard M. Brady, and had children: Susan Lynn [born 13 Dec. 1957, married John Alan Jones]).

Thelma R. FARRIS (twin; born 1 Mar. 1928, married Noble Stoops, and had children: Connie [born 23 Apr. 1952, married James Blair, and had children: Chad]; Jeanna [born 9 Jan. 1957]; *Thelma* married secondly Roy Julian).

Velma M. FARRIS (twin; born 1 Mar. 1928, married Robert Baker, and had children: Wayne E. [born 24 Nov. 1946, married Mureen Frost, and had children: Paula; John]; Ella [born 23 June 1949, married Joseph M. Bulach, and had children: Brenda]; David [born 25 Mar. 1951, married Becky House, and had children: Amy; Bridget]; Debbie [born 2 Aug. 1953, married Won Cheong Im, and had children: Laura Sue; Jennifer]; Donna [born 14 June 1955, married Ronald Burton, and had children: Michelle]; Sherrie [born 23 Oct. 1957]).

Hershel "Jim" FARRIS (born 19 Apr. 1931, and died unmarried on 13 Mar. 1982, being buried in the West Cemetery).

Norman Howard FARRIS (born 9 Mar. 1933, married Betty Minnear [she was the daughter of Carl and Ethel Minnear], and had children: Tony [born 17 Nov. 1962]; Mark [born 1 Aug. 1966]).

Wade FARRIS married secondly Mrs. Edna (Messinger) Price (who survived him), and died on 25 Oct. 1963, being buried in the West Cemetery.

Emily and Tom FARRIS are listed in the 1870-1910 censuses for the Second District, Putnam Co., TN. Emily Farris died on 4 Apr. 1923 in Putnam Co., and is buried with her husband in the West Cemetery.

6h. **Mary C. "Polly."** Born about 1848 in White (later Putnam) Co., TN. Married Samuel Sliger about 1869 (he was born 25 Jan. 1851 in TN, son of John C. Sliger and Lucinda Wilhite, and brother of James T. Sliger [who married Polly's sister, Sallie], married secondly Fannie Bush, and died 9 Sept. 1924, buried Sliger Cemetery), and had at least the following children: *Caroline "Carrie"* (born Jan. 1870, married W. J. "Bill" Lewis, and lived at Murfreesboro, TN); *Ollie* (born 1877, married Haskell Crabtree on 2 Oct. 1910 in Putnam Co., TN, and had children: Zeb [born 19 July 1911, died Sept. 1986 at Cookeville, TN]). Listed in the 1870-80 censuses for Cummins Mill, Jackson Co., TN.

6i. **Hiram T(homas?).** Born 3 Aug. 1852 in White (later Putnam) Co., TN. See below for full entry.

6j. **Elizabeth (XVIII) "Bettie."** Born 26 Sept. 1869 in Putnam Co., TN. Married as his second wife Zebedee Payne Huddleston about 1890 (he was born 17 Dec. 1860 in TN, married firstly Dora ___ [she was born 14 Oct. 1867, and died 23 Feb. 1888], and died 11 May 1935), and had children: *Thurman* (born June 1895). Listed in the 1900 census for Putnam Co., TN. Bettie Huddleston died on 20 Apr. 1942, and is buried in the Salem M.E. Church Cemetery.

6k. **(Lona) Dee (II).** Born 29 Dec. 1870 (or 1871) in Putnam Co., TN. Married Jesse Sherrell. Living with her mother in 1900. Dee Sherrell died on 27 July 1922, and is buried in the Brown's Mill Cemetery.

6l. **Harriet Ellen (II) "Hattie."** Born about 1873 in Putnam Co., TN. Married Daniel Winburn Ray about 1893 (he was born 5 May 1866 in Putnam Co., TN, son of William Larkin Ray and Celia Margaret West, remarried her cousin, Margaret Alice Burgess, daughter of Winfield Scott Burgess, on 15 Sept. 1895, and thirdly Susan Bockman on 22 Dec. 1901, and and fourthly Mrs. ___ Bean, and died 7 Mar. 1942), and had children: *Mamie* (born 10 Mar. 1894, married Hurshal Z. Davis on 8 Sept. 1911 [he was born 5 Aug. 1886, and died 3 Nov. 1961], and had children: Shipley Ray [died childless in 1939]; Ralph H(urshal?) [born 29 Oct. 1918, married Florence ___, and died childless on 1 Feb. 1968]; Nancy Ellen [born 18 Mar. 1925, and died unmarried and childless on 3 Feb. 1978]; *Mamie* died 12 Dec. 1980, and is buried with her children in the West Cemetery). Hattie Ray died on 22 May 1894 in Putnam Co., TN, possibly in childbirth. Daniel Ray is listed as a widower in the 1900 census for Putnam Co., TN; for his children by Margaret Alice Burgess, see her entry.

THE FAMILY OF WAYMAN L. BURGESS

(from left) John Burgess, Wayman L. Burgess, (Sarah) Elizabeth Kuntze, Charles Dudley Burgess, Catharine Patton Kuntze Burgess, Clara Burgess
(see page 523)

[William (I)[1], Edward (I)[2], Reuben (I)[3], Thomas (I)[4], Joel (I)[5]]

JOHN ROSS BURGESS
(1833-1916)

OF PUTNAM COUNTY, TENNESSEE

6a. **John Ross** *[son of Joel (I)].* Born 25 July 1833 in White Co., TN. Married Margaret "Peggy" Phy on 3 Feb. 1852 in White Co., TN (div.; she was born 20 Mar. 1829 in TN, daughter of John F. Phy and Mary "Polly" Bradford, and died 11 Aug. 1913); married secondly as her second husband Vixey "Vice" Roberson (she was born 6 Jan. 1841 in TN, daughter of William Roberson [or Rolerson], and died 6 Jan. 1920, buried Johnson Cemetery). Listed in the 1860 census for Putnam Co., TN, in 1870-80 in Cumberland Co., TN, and in 1900-10 in Putnam Co. (two children of Vixey by another marriage survive in 1900); Vixie is listed in 1920 in Putnam Co. with her son-in-law, James McCormick. John Burgess was a farmer in Tennessee, his land being located near the Cumberland Co. line, just west of Mayland. He died on 22 May 1916 in Putnam Co., and is buried in the Smith Chapel Cemetery. Peggy Burgess is living with her son James in 1900-10; seven of nine children survive in 1900, and five of nine in 1910.

The Children of John R. Burgess:

7a. **(Charles) Whitley**. Born 22 Sept. 1852 in White (later Putnam) Co., TN. See below for full entry.

7b. **Mary (XI)**. Born about 1854 in White (later Putnam) Co., TN. Listed with her father in the 1860 census, but not in 1870, and in any case died before 1900.

7c. **Rutha "Ruth."** Born about 1856 in Putnam Co., TN. Listed with her father in the 1870 census. Said to have married ___ DuBois about 1872. She died there before 1900.

7d. **(Oma) Penina "Pinna."** Her names are also spelled Omah and Perlina. Born 13 June 1858 in Putnam Co., TN. Married Samuel H. Bohannon on 8 June 1895 in White Co. (he was born Nov. 1861 in TN, and died 26 May 1919), and had one son (who survived her). Listed in the 1900 census for Cumberland Co., TN. Pinna Bohannon died of flu and dysentery on 26 Apr. 1928 in White Co., TN, and is buried in the Smith Chapel Cemetery.

7e. **Sarah E. (II)**. Born 19 Apr. 1861 (or 1860) in Putnam Co., TN. Married (William) Henry Seegraves on 1 Oct. 1877 in White Co., TN (he was born 5 Mar. 1857 in GA, son of Milzie Seegraves and Jane Gaines, and brother of Cordelia Seegraves [who married Sarah's brother, Charles Whitley Burgess], and died 16 May 1948), and had ten children, including: *George T.* (born 10 Sept. 1885, died Oct. 1973 at Sparta, TN); *Mattie Elizabeth* (born 10 Jan. 1888, married Henry Page, and died 14 Feb. 1965); *Wesley* (born Dec. 1889, died before his mother); *Margaret J.* (born Sept. 1892); *(James) Walter* (born 27 Dec. 1895, and died Mar. 1977 at Crossville, TN); *Waymon* (born 24 June 1900, died Dec. 1978 at Sparta, TN); *Lou* (born about 1902, married ___ Cunningham, and secondly ___ Bertram). Listed in the 1880-1910 censuses for Cumberland Co. (six of ten children survive in 1910). Sarah Seegraves was a member of the Baptist Church. She died on 29 Jan. 1943 in Cumberland Co., TN, and is buried in the Smith Chapel Cemetery.

7f. **Joel (II)**. Born 14 June 1862 in Putnam or Cumberland Cos., TN. See below for full entry.

7g. **Lou Rana.** She is called "Lulu" in her husband's obituary. Born 14 June 1865 (or 1864) in Putnam or Cumberland Cos., TN. Married James F. DuBois on 24 Apr. 1892 in Cumberland Co. (he was born 5 June 1866, son of John and Mary DuBois, and brother of Alice DuBois [who married Lou's brother, Joel Burgess II], and died 23 Mar. 1932), and had at least the following children: *Gertrude* (born 26 May 1893, married Fred Lappin, died Apr. 1977 in IN); *Ivor* (born Feb. 1895, married Weaver M. Carroll on 28 Aug. 1920); *(James) Lucius* (born Apr. 1899, married Edna Treadway on 23 May 1921, died 21 Feb. 1962). Listed in the 1900-10 censuses for Putnam Co., TN. Lou DuBois died on 6 Aug. 1953 in Cumberland Co., TN, and is buried in the Smith Chapel Cemetery.

7h. **(John) James**. Born 22 Feb. 1867 in White Co., TN. See below for full entry.

7i. **Nancy (V)**. Born 2 July 1870 in Cumberland Co., TN. Listed in the 1900-10 censuses for White Co., TN. Married Daniel Riley Bumbalough about 1885 (he was born Dec. 1868, son of William C. "Bill"

Bumbalough and Lucinda Broyles, and died 17 Nov. 1936), and died on 12 Dec. 1927, buried with her husband in the West Cemetery, having had children:

***Paralou* BUMBALOUGH.** Born Sept. 1889, married Dillard Finley on 1 Oct. 1905 in Putnam Co., TN (he was the son of Rufus Finley and Isabell Henry), and had children: *Minnie Belle* (born 1907, married as his second wife Andy Hood [he was born 1890, son of Isaac Hood and Martha Short, and died 5 Feb. 1969 at Board Valley, TN], and had children: James Kenneth [born 31 May 1935]; Minerva Lee [born 15 Sept. 1937, married Doug Baker {son of Landon Baker}, and had children: Charles; Linda]; Mary Magdalene [born 14 Sept. 1940, married Alva Robinson, and had children: Maggie; Roger]; Bobby Gene [born 14 July 1942, married Dorothy Paris]); *Nancy Lucinda "Nannie"* (born 11 Nov. 1908, married William M. "Billy" Randolph on 2 Feb. 1935 [he was born 18 Mar. 1885, son of John Maxwell Randolph and Amy Jane Conley, and died childless in the 1950s]); *Dan* (married Adelle Mulligan); *Wiley* (married Oshia Hood, daughter of Andy Hood and Myrtie Hamilton); *Cordell* (died an infant).

***Minnie Ethel* BUMBALOUGH.** Born May 1891, married Oscar Henry (he was the son of Jim Henry and Nancy Elizabeth Golden), and had children: *Evvie Cecil*; *Veta*; *Nota*; *A. P.*; *J. D.*

***Melvina "Vina"* BUMBALOUGH.** Born 17 Feb. 1892, married Samuel Randolph on 5 June 1910 (he was born 1 Jan. 1890, and died 18 May 1980, aged 90 years), and died 8 Aug. 1976, buried West Cemetery, having had children:

Lula Mae RANDOLPH (born 2 June 1911, married Lonnie Edward Brewington on 19 Feb. 1927 [he was born 25 Feb. 1909, son of Daniel Brewington and Cora Sparks, and died Sept. 1986, buried West Cemetery], and died 13 Feb. 1963, having had children: Dimple Odell [born 7 Dec. 1927, married Dennis Coffey in 1946, and had children: Yvonne {born 7 Nov. 1948, married Jack Olmstead, and had children: Sybil; Audrey; Amanda}; Denise {born 22 Nov. 1952}; Dale {born 11 Dec. 1953, married Martha Rector, and had children: Travis}]; Riley Edward [born 19 Feb. 1932, married Glenda Holcomb, and had children: Sherry {born 13 Mar. 1958, married Charlie Hardee, and had children: Ravia Lynn <born 1982>; Tania}; Stuart Lee {born 18 Dec. 1960}]; J. D. [born 7 Dec. 1933, married Hazel Steward {daughter of Hubert "Bill" and Savilla Steward}, and had children: Debbie {married Donald Bilbrey, and had children: Kyle}; Lisa]; Byrdie Mae [born 1 Sept. 1936, married Johnny Steward {he was the son of Thurman Steward and Dimple LaFever}, and had children: Larry {married Carol ___, and had children: Larry Jr.}; Becky {married Ricky Taylor}; Alan; Gary]; Venita Rose "Tootsie" [born 16 Jan. 1939, married Ralph Dunn on 23 Dec. 1958 {son of Enlo Dunn}, and had children: Ralph Jr. {born and died 2 Dec. 1962, buried Boiling Springs Cemetery}; Cynthia Denise {born 31 Aug. 1966}; Jennifer Lynn {born 5 Jan. 1969}]; Willene [twin; born 5 Nov. 1942, married Harold Jackson {son of Woodrow Jackson}, and had children: Jeffrey Harold; Renee; Mark; Kimberley]; Eulene [twin; born 5 Nov. 1942, married Merle Jackson {son of Herman Jackson and Maudie Jones}, and had children: Luwanna {married Glenn Hargrove, and had children: Nikki}; Tammy {married Richard Alverson, and had children: Kimberly Michelle <born 18 Feb. 1982>}; Eulene married secondly ___ Moss, and had children: Dana; Tricia; Shannon; Alecia; Eulene married thirdly ___ Holmes]; Judy [born 3 July 1947, married James Hoskins, and had children: Donald Ray; Jacquetta Carol; Valerie Jean; Beverly Sue]; Jimmy [born 30 Jan. 1955, married Pam Graves, and had children: Melissa Kay]).

Alfred Vasco RANDOLPH (born 12 Mar. 1913, married Lina Elizabeth Brewington on 10 Sept. 1933 [she was born 25 Sept. 1911, daughter of Daniel Brewington and Cora Sparks], and had children: James Vasco [born 14 Aug. 1933, married Virginia Modell Holloway on 21 May 1959 {she was born 6 Nov. 1940}, and had children: James Eric {born 22 Feb. 1960, married Rhonda Jean Eldridge}; Darrell Wayne {born 5 Apr. 1964}; Mark Randall {born 2 Mar. 1966}; Warren Kyle {born 4 Nov. 1969}]; Emmitt Eugene "Nick" [born 7 Sept. 1935, married Anna Sue West on 15 Jan. 1956 {she was born 12 Sept. 1940}, and had children: Teresa {born 13 Nov. 1957, married Jimmy Keesling, and had children: Nickie}; Vicky Marie {born 10 May 1961}]; Polly Aline [born 24 Jan. 1937, married Garland Ray Durrin on 7 July 1956 {he was born 20 Jan. 1926}, and had children: Alfred Ray {born 16 May 1957, married Rita Hensley}; Sherry Lynn {born 19 Oct. 1962, married Tommy Wilmoth, and had children: Crystal}; Sandra Faye {born 15 Sept. 1966}]; David L. V. [born 19 Oct. 1938, married Jeaneal Philpot on 4 June 1966, and had children: Lea Ann {born 20 May 1967}; William David {born 16 Dec. 1970}]; Betty Sue [born 15 Apr. 1940, married Johnny L. Whiteaker on 17 Dec. 1960 {he was born 20 Sept. 1941}, and had children: Deborah Sue {born 22 Dec. 1961}; Johnny W. {born 14 Sept. 1964}]; Jackie Ray [born 9 Oct. 1941, married Nina Murdock on 17 Dec. 1960, and had children: Allan Ray {born 4 Oct. 1961}; Jackie Lea {born 29 July 1964}]; Mabel Evelyn [born 30 May 1943, married Jimmy Waylon Tabors on 3 July 1958 {he was born 18 May 1940, son of Paul Tabors and Pearl Elizabeth Nabors}, and had children: Jimmy Michael {born 11 May 1959, married Sherry Matthews on 1 Sept. 1982}; Carolyn Ann {born 3 Mar. 1963, married David Howard}]; Wanda Faye [born 25 July 1945, married Freelin Harold Robinson on 7 Aug. 1961 {he was born 23 Nov. 1943, son of Freelin Simpson Robinson and Allie Jane Nabors}, and had three children]; Sammy Russell [born 19 Apr. 1948, married Doris Ann Bennett on 18 Aug. 1966 {she was born 24 July 1948}, and had children: Tammy Marie {born 13 June 1968}; Charles Russell {born 18 June 1969}]).

Brasky Lee RANDOLPH (born 5 Aug. 1914, married Beulah Lee Brewington on 10 Sept. 1933 [she was born 30 July 1916, daughter of Daniel Brewington and Cora Sparks], and had children: Dennis Lee [born 8 Apr. 1942, married Dinah Pearl Scott on 3 Jan. 1961 {she was born 10 Aug. 1944, daughter of Herman Scott and Amanda Belle Nash}, and had children: Steven Dennis {born 11 Apr. 1968}]).

Haskell Dee RANDOLPH (born 1916, married Ina Mae Dunn [she was born 28 Feb. 1919, daughter of Roscoe Dunn and Amanda T. Sliger], and had children: Dollie Sue [born 29 Dec. 1941, married Ray Smith {he was the son of Jim Smith and Stella Robinson}, and had children: Mickey {married Connie ___}; Cathy {married Larry Ealey}; Kimberly; Raymon]; Jackie Dee [born 6 Aug. 1943, married Donnie Ruth Bennett on 2 July 1966, and had children: Scotty Dee {born 21 Sept. 1966}; Angela Veronnie {born 16 Jan. 1975}]; Jeremiah "Jere" [born 24 Jan. 1945, married Mary Ruth Simpson {she was born 31 Jan. 1946}, and had children: Tammy Evone {born 6 June 1966}; Tracy Leanne {born 6 Nov. 1970}; Timothy Robert {born 16 Nov. 1981}]; Shirley [married Dale Morgan {div.}, and had children: Travis]).

Pina RANDOLPH (born about 1920, married Otis Luke [son of Fred Luke], and had children: Mary Etta [born 7 Sept. 1935]; Joyce; Raymond; Janice; Kay).

Ina Louoma RANDOLPH (born 16 Apr. 1923, married Arvel LaFever [he was born 13 Oct. 1922, son of Beecher LaFever and Bertha Bray], and had children: Dorothy [born 26 May 1940, married Milton Heath {he was born 1 Sept. 1935}, and had children: Steven {born 2 July 1959 at Milwaukee, WI, married Terry Ann Hall <she was born 9 Aug. 1958>, and had children: Tiffany Suzanne <born 24 July 1980 at Flint, MI>; Angela Marie <born 21 Sept. 1981 at Flint, MI>}; Terry Wayne {born 17 June 1961 at Flint, MI, married Larrie Ayers on 11 Dec. 1981 at Flint}]; Gary C. [born 26 May 1944, married Evelyn Mayhew {she was born 28 July 1943}, and had children: Gary C. Jr. {born 6 Dec. 1963}; Scotty Allen {born 22 May 1967}]; Patricia Aline [born 20 June 1948, married Jack Bledsoe, and had children: Nathan {born 19 Feb. 1971 at Flint, MI}]; Glen Allen [born 13 Jan. 1961, married Vickie Lynn Hall {she was born 2 June 1962}, and had children: Matthew Allen {born 3 Feb. 1979 at Flint, MI}; Katrina Lynn {born 16 Jan. 1982 at Flint, MI}]).

C. J. RANDOLPH (born 1927, married Gladys Virginia Collier on 22 Apr. 1944 [she was born 1927, daughter of Harvey Collier and Nancy Minnear, and died about 1980], and had children: Billy C. [born 2 May 1945, married Sharon Ann Pelfree on 5 Dec. 1964 {she was born 2 Oct. 1946}, and had children: Melissa Joann {born 2 Aug. 1971}; Jennifer Lynn {born 14 Mar. 1976}]; Brenda Carolyn [born 25 Oct. 1946, married Robert Wayne Kemp on 9 Oct. 1965 {he was born 20 July 1946}, and had children: Catherine Virginia {born 8 Dec. 1967}; Tricia Ann {born 4 Apr. 1971}; Susan Marie {born 15 Apr. 1975}]; Phyllis Ann [born 24 Apr. 1948, married Richard Dale Johns on 19 July 1968 {he was born 11 Dec. 1948}, and had children: Jillena Dale {born 15 Dec. 1971}; Anita Ruth {born 17 Oct. 1974}]; David Lewis [born 31 May 1952, married Dianne Rebecca Gagnon on 11 Aug. 1971 {she was born 20 Apr. 1953}, and had children: Kirt Leslie {born 24 June 1972}; Krista Nichole {born 20 May 1975}]; Mylinda Kay [born 19 Feb. 1954, married William Clarence Kemp on 31 Dec. 1970 {he was born 27 July 1949}, and had children: Samuel Meridith {born 17 Feb. 1971}; Shannon Kay {born 23 Jan. 1974}]; Stephen Leslie [born 26 Oct. 1956]; Helen Sue [born 12 Aug. 1960, married Roger Lee Shumard on 12 Sept. 1981 {he was born 14 Feb. 1957}]).

Daisy E. RANDOLPH (born 31 Oct. 1929, married Ernest Slagle on 26 Dec. 1947 [he was the son of Lester Slagle and Bertie Clinton], and had children: Bernice [born 31 Oct. 1948, married David Moss, and had children: Marianne {born 30 June 1971}; Alan {born 1 July 1974}]).

Clodus Raymond RANDOLPH (born 23 Nov. 1931, married Clata Lee Collier on 14 Apr. 1951 [she was born 13 Apr. 1933, daughter of Harvey Collier and Nancy Minnear], and had children: Duane [born 1952, married Connie Nash {she was born Aug. 1951, daughter of John Henry Nash and Beulah Judd}, and had children: Michael {born 19 Jan. 1972}; Tammy; David]; Sandra [born 10 May 1953, married Jackie McCloud, and had children: Tony; Randy; Timmy]; Raymond [born 16 Sept. 1957, married Sue Ellen Allison in 1986 {she was born 21 Sept. 1957, daughter of Abner Wallace Allison and Berchie Pauline Allison}]. *Clodus* married secondly Thelma Lou Duke [she was born 25 Feb. 1928, daughter of Blanchard Edward Duke and Ruth Burton]).

Child RANDOLPH (born and died 22 Sept. 1934, buried West Cemetery).

Fannie Myrtle BUMBALOUGH. Born 10 May 1894, married Staley T. Clouse [sic] on 16 Sept. 1923 (he was born 10 June 1906, son of Charlie W. Clouse and Nancy Holmes, and remarried Geneva L. Lesley on 1 May 1954), and died on 5 Dec. 1953, having had children:

Ellen CLOUSE (born about 1924, married R. D. Williams, and had children: Clara [born 8 Apr. 1941, married Carl Gentry on 16 Feb. 1957 {he was born 3 Mar. 1932, son of Clarence and Veda Gentry}, and had children: Peggy {born 22 July 1958, married Kenneth Key on 29 Oct. 1977 <he was born 16 July 1953>}; Karen {born 9 Aug. 1960, married Robert Parrish on 6 Nov. 1977 <he was born 24 Feb. 1960>}; Steven {born 29 Oct. 1962, married Elsie ___ on 4 July 1982, and had children: Steven Jr. <born 6 Sept. 1985>}; Dwayne {born 6 May 1965, married Tammy ___ on 4 June 1982, and had children: Jessica <born 30 Mar. 1986>}]; Reba Nell [born 16 Apr. 1942, married Roy Franklin Goolsby in 1959, and died 10 Dec. 1978, having had children: Lisa Gale {born 1 July 1962}; Patricia J. {born 15 June 1963, married Lloyd Ray Randolph on 20 Oct. 1981 <he was born 14 Oct. 1961>, and had children: Angela Denise <born 15 Oct. 1982>}; Lori Ann {born 29 Mar. 1966, married Joe David Hawkins on 5 Aug. 1982 <he was born 30 Jan. 1965>, and had children: David Dewayne <born 17 Sept. 1982>; Alica Ann <born 2 Sept. 1985>}; Bradley Franklin {born and died 15 Aug. 1969}; Linda Lou {born 19 Feb. 1971}]; Treva Jean [born 21 Jan. 1947, married Larry Joe Manus on 17 Mar. 1971 {he was born 12 Apr. 1951, son of Andrew Jackson Manus}, and had children: Danny Ray {born 13 Aug. 1973}; Tonya Lorine {born 27 Nov. 1973}; Rebecca Dains {born 8 June 1976}]; Annie Lou [born 24 Mar. 1949, married Jerry Wayon Miller on 4 Aug. 1965 {he was born 3 Mar. 1947, son of Edward Gain Miller and Estella Taylor}, and had children: Son {born and died Apr. 1967}; Sonda Marie {born 7 Mar. 1968}; Brenda Lou {born 15 Mar. 1970}; Jerry Wayon Jr. {born 31 July 1972}; Michael Dan {born 8 June 1973, died 10 June 1973}]; Carl Thomas [born 11 July 1957, married Reba Elizabeth Jones on 13 Dec. 1977 {she was born 21 Nov. 1957, daughter of Bailey Lee Jones and Ocia Bell Ford}, and had children: Treva Elizabeth {born 17 Nov. 1978}; Katy Michelle {born 12 Apr. 1986}]).

Jesse B. CLOUSE (born 9 July 1928, married Christine Loraine Whiteaker on 8 July 1948 [she was born 2 Feb. 1931, daughter of Mell David Whiteaker and Rhoda Ann Weaver], and works as a watchmaker).

Thurman CLOUSE (born 5 Sept. 1931, married Gladys Christine Harley on 20 Oct. 1951 at Anderson, IN [she was born 19 Mar. 1933, daughter of Hiriam Harley and Lucille Thomas], and died 8 Dec. 1980 at Anderson, IN, buried Blountsville Cemetery, having had children: Gloria Christine [born 17 Sept. 1952 at Sparta, TN, married Jan. Aug. May on 29 Aug. 1969 {he was born 17 Jan. 1952}, and had children: Jan. Aug. Jr. {born 10 Jan. 1970 at Muncie, IN}; Jessica Amber {born 10 Aug. 1978 at Indianapolis, IN}]; Glenda Lynn [born 21 June 1954 at Sparta, TN, married Roy William Herrmann on 21 May 1971 {he was born 11 July 1953}, and had children: Jason William {born 9 June 1974 at Bloomington, IN}; Andrew Christian {born 11 May 1976 at Bloomington, IN}; Angela Lynn {born 7 Feb. 1978 at Anderson, IN}]; Barry Thurman [born 26 Mar. 1961 at Anderson, IN, married Deanna Haston on 20 Oct. 1983 at Pendleton, IN, and had children: Jennifer Nicole {born 16 July 1982 at Sioux City, IA}; Kristi Lynn {born 13 Nov. 1985 at Anderson, IN}]; Wanda Yvonne [born 18 May 1963 at Anderson, IN, married Roger Keith Trueblood on 6 June 1981, and had children: Jeremy Tyler {born 10 May 1983 at Anderson, IN}]; Catherine Ann [born 8 Feb. 1967 at Anderson, IN]).

Ella V. CLOUSE (married Raymond Eugene Hahn, and had children: Deborah Sue [married Gerald Helms]).

***Dallas* BUMBALOUGH.** Born 22 Mar. 1896, married ___ Roberts, and had one child; married secondly Elizabeth "Lizzie" Randolph on 21 Aug. 1921 (she was born Dec. 1895, daughter of William James "Pinky Jim" Randolph and Victoria Bumbalough), and died Jan. 1976 at Sparta, TN.

***Nora* BUMBALOUGH.** Born Apr. 1898, married Thomas Rice (he was born about 1892, son of Bill Alex Rice), and had children: *Myrtie*; *Gertie*; *Dollie*; *Erby*.

***Leslie* BUMBALOUGH.** Born 4 Mar. 1900, married Maggie M. Bagwell (she was born about 1902, daughter of Harvey D. and Rhoda Bagwell), and died June 1974 at Columbus, IN.

***Esley* BUMBALOUGH.** Born 1902, married Ethel Rice (she was born about 1903, daughter of Bill Alex Rice), and died in Virginia.

***Lester* BUMBALOUGH.** Born 1904, married Lennie M. Brewington on 1 July 1923 in Putnam Co., TN (she was born 19 May 1907, daughter of Daniel Brewington and Cora Sparks, and died 17 June 1977, buried with her husband in the West Cemetery), and died 1941, having had children: *John Daniel* (born 17 Dec. 1923, married Mae Grogan, and died in Michigan, having had children: Kenneth; Rosemary; Marilyn); *Vewey Lee "Ted"* (born 28 July 1926, married Velma Rice about 1944 [she was the daughter of Henry Rice and Ovalla "Vallie" Campbell, and died in 1984 in MI], and had children: Linda [born 1945]; Lois Elaine; Dianne); *Marie* (born 22 Feb. 1928, married Robert Cecil Bryant, and had children: Robert Taylor [born 23 Dec. 1944]; Debbie; Donna); *Marlin "Bill"* (born Aug. 1929, married Betty Brownfield, and had children: Susie; Nancy; Barbara; David; Billy; Kimberly); *Annelle* (married Richard Davis, and had children: Brenda; Peggy Sue; Teresa; Pam).

Nota Pansy BUMBALOUGH. Born 5 Sept. 1906, married Preston Cleo Randolph on 22 Sept. 1923 (he was born 11 Dec. 1908, son of Doc Issaiah Randolph and Elizabeth "Lizzie" Worley, and died 15 Dec. 1986, buried with his wife in the West Cemetery), and died 14 Jan. 1966, having had children:

J. T. RANDOLPH (born 30 June 1924, and died unmarried on 4 Nov. 1984, buried in the West Cemetery).

Willie Daniel RANDOLPH (born 4 Mar. 1927, married Clara Lee Brown on 20 Nov. 1948 [she was born 30 May 1931, daughter of Shelia Brown and Hallie Brock], and had children: Willie Keith [born 25 Aug. 1949, married Linda Thomas {div.; she was the daughter of Bacom Thomas}, and had children: Data Michelle {born 3 Nov. 1967}; Willie married secondly Barbara Wheeler {she was born 14 May 1947, daughter of Bob Wheeler and Lucille Harness}, and had children: Keith Waylon {born 14 Jan. 1977}]; Curtiss Lee [born 30 Mar. 1951, married Linda Winnett {div.; she was the daughter of Thomas Winnett and Gladys Parrish}, and had children: Christopher Lee {born 23 Mar. 1977}; Misty Dawn {born 20 Nov. 1979}]; Juanita Gail [born 2 Oct. 1952, married Roger Dale Raines {he was the son of Clarence Raines and Bertha Harper, and died on 7 Feb. 1978}, and had children: Melissa Gail {born 27 May 1972}; Roger Dale II {born 26 Aug. 1973}; Juanita married secondly Raymon Allen]; Regina Gay [born 8 July 1955, married Jerry Helms {he was the son of Napoleon Helms and Beulah Sliger, and died 12 Oct. 1977}, and had children: Valerie Elaine {born 16 Dec. 1971}; Richard Ivan {born 11 Aug. 1974}; Regina married secondly Billy McCloud {he was the son of Lawrence McCloud and Beulah Blaylock}]; Ricky Eugene [born 2 Oct. 1956]; Janie Elaine [born 30 Mar. 1961, married Billy Thomas Dunn {he was the son of Reed Dunn and Irene Hedgecough}, and had children: Erik Thomas {born 27 Nov. 1979}]).

Hughy V. RANDOLPH (born 30 May 1929, married Dona Golden [she was born 12 Mar. 1931, daughter of Dan and Nora Golden], and died 21 Feb. 1985, buried West Cemetery).

Luther Charles RANDOLPH (born 30 May 1932, married Tina Harris [div.; she was the daughter of Benton Harris and Claudia Jones], and had children: Charles; *Luther* married secondly Susan Rice [she was born 19 June 1944], and died on 24 Mar. 1974, buried West Cemetery, having had children: Lloyd; Rose Ann; Brenda).

Shelia James RANDOLPH (born 13 May 1934, married Cathy Rigsby [she was the daughter of Lewis Rigsby and Ethel Cole], and had children: Dianna Sue [born 12 May 1957, married Ricky Gentry {div.; he was the son of Eskle Gentry and Kate White}, and had children: Greg Ine {born 25 Oct. 1974}; Christopher Ryan {born 14 June 1979}; Dianna married secondly Gary Clemons]; Lewis James [born 1960, married Debra Burton]).

Bluford Carl RANDOLPH (born 17 Mar. 1936, married Opal Long [div.], and had children: Penny Darlene [born 8 July 1957]; Marceen [born 18 Mar. 1961]; Tammy).

L. V. RANDOLPH (born 27 Oct. 1939, married Emiko Kawana [she was the daughter of Isamu Kawana, and died on 10 Mar. 1981, buried West Cemetery], and had children: Sabina Mieko [born 18 May 1966 in Japan]; Reina Emiko [born 1 Jan. 1968 in Japan]).

Flossie Marie RANDOLPH (born 20 Nov. 1945, married her cousin, Jimmy Vance Burgess, on 18 Mar. 1960; see his entry for their children).

WHITLEY BURGESS OF CUMBERLAND CO., TENNESSEE
[John Ross^6]

7a. **(Charles) Whitley** *[son of John Ross].* Born 22 Sept. 1852 in Putnam Co, TN. Married (Martha) Cordelia "Delia" Seegraves about 1876 (she was born 11 Dec. 1858 [or 1859, according to her death certificate] in Cherokee Co., GA, daughter of Milzie Seegraves and Jane Gaines, and sister of Henry Seegraves [who married Whitley's sister, Sarah], and died 27 Oct. 1934 at Smith Chapel). Living with his father in 1870; listed in the 1880-1900 censuses for Cumberland Co., TN; Delia appears as head of the family in 1910 (four of seven children survive in both 1900 and 1910). Whit Burgess was a logger in Putnam and Cumberland Cos. He was killed in an accident on 8 Nov. 1902, when a logging wagon overturned and a poplar log rolled over onto him, and is buried with his wife in the Smith Chapel Cemetery.

8a. **Cora Bell (II).** Born 15 Jan. 1878 in Cumberland Co., TN. Married William H. Page on 21 Dec. 1894 in White Co. (he was born 6 Sept. 1867 in KY, and died 11 June 1944), and had at least the following children: *Minnie L.* (born Apr. 1896); *Natie B.* (born Mar. 1898); *William* (born June 1899); *Mamie* (married ___ Able, and was living at Baker, FL in 1968); *Rhoda* (born 26 Apr. 1908, married Claude Webb, and died July 1991 at Crossville, TN); *Jay* (born 13 Oct. 1910, died Sept. 1984 at Sparta, TN); *Josephine* (born 19 Oct. 1917, married ___ Nash, and died Aug. 1985 at Jacksonville, FL). Listed in the 1900 census for Cumberland Co., TN. Cora Page died on 12 Apr. 1968 at Pleasant Hill, TN, aged 90 years, and is buried in the Smith Chapel Cemetery.

8b. **Victoria.** Born July 1879 in Cumberland Co., TN. Living with her father in the 1880 census, but died before 1900.

8c. **Mollie.** She may be the same as the Victoria Burgess listed in the 1880 census. Born 6 July 1880 (or 1879) in Cumberland Co., TN. Married John England on 3 Jan. 1897 in White Co. (he was born 22 Feb. 1876, remarried Mollie's cousin, Ivor Burgess, and died 24 Jan. 1967), and had children: *Isom* (born 6 Apr. 1898, died Apr. 1970 at Jackson, OH); *Lige* (died 16 Oct. 1936); *Fred*; *Nathan* (born 9 July 1905, married his cousin, Roxie Lee Burgess, and died Jan. 1987 at Crossville, TN); *Riley* (born 9 July 1911, died Apr. 1975 at Sparta, TN); *Clarence*; *Virgil*; *John*; *Pearl*; *Lillie*. Listed in the 1900 census for White Co., TN. Mollie England died on 5 July 1932 in Cumberland Co., and is buried in the Smith Chapel Cemetery.

8d. **Dora Ann (II).** Born 16 Jan. 1882 in Cumberland Co., TN. Married Pleasant Carel Chastain on 25 May 1899 in White Co. (he was born 21 May 1874 in TN, and died 15 July 1919), and had at least the following children: *Lovonia* (born 1901); *Mary Lee* (born 1903); *Martha* (born 1905); *Alvin* (born 29 Oct. 1908, died June 1978 at Sparta, TN); *Ethel* (born 1912); *Marie* (born 1915). Listed in the 1900 census for Cumberland Co. with her parents and husband; she and her husband are living with her mother in 1920. Dora Chastain died on 18 May 1955 in Cumberland Co., and is buried in the Smith Chapel Cemetery.

8e. **Parezetta "Parza."** Her name is written Barzette in the 1900 census. Born 11 Oct. 1884 in Cumberland Co., TN. Living with her mother in 1910. Married Alex Page on 16 July 1912 in White Co. (he was the son of William and Mary Ann Page). Parza Page died on 20 Jan. 1960 in White Co., TN, and is buried in the Smith Chapel Cemetery.

9a. **Ethel (III).** Born about 1901 in TN. Mentioned in the *Crossville Chronicle* as living with her grandmother in 1913.

ACCIDENTAL DEATH OF WHITLEY BURGESS

"While Whit Burgess was hauling logs Saturday from the farm of Joel Burgess, his brother, a few miles from Pleasant Hill, the wagon turned over and caught him under the log, crushing him in the hips. He was so badly injured that he died about six o'clock Saturday night, five hours after the accident. He was hauling logs to the mill of William Lyles on Back Creek, White County. The deceased was fifty-one years of age, and leaves a wife and four children, three of whom are married. The remains were interred at Smith's Chapel, Sunday at four P.M. He was an energetic and useful citizen whose death was deeply regretted, and was well-known here."—*Crossville Chronicle*, 12 Nov. 1902.

JOEL BURGESS II OF CUMBERLAND CO., TENNESSEE

[John Ross[6]]

7f. **Joel (II)** *[son of John Ross]*. Born 14 June 1862 (or 1863) in Putnam Co., TN. Married Alice Ephamie "Alcie" DuBois on 2 Apr. 1889 in White Co. (she was born 6 Dec. 1867 in Putnam Co., daughter of John and Mary DuBois, and sister of James F. DuBois [who married Joel's sister, Lou Rana Burgess], and died 3 Feb. 1936). Living with his brother Whit in the 1880 census; listed in the 1900 census for Cumberland Co., TN; his widow appears as head of the family in 1910 (four of four children survive in 1910). Joel Burgess was a farmer in Cumberland Co., and also served as the elected Constable of Pleasant Hill, TN, in the 1890s. He died there on 21 Nov. 1907, and is buried with his wife in the Smith Chapel Cemetery.

8a. **John Wesley (IV).** Born 6 May 1889 in White Co., TN. See below for full entry.

8b. **Mary Alice (II).** Born 11 Aug. 1890 in White Co., TN. Married (Jake) Lee Bennett on 18 Oct. 1908 in Cumberland Co. Mary Bennett died on 19 July 1928, and is buried in the Smith Chapel Cemetery.

8c. **James Luther.** Born 10 Jan. 1892 in White Co., TN. See below for full entry.

8d. **Mertie Irene.** Born 20 Jan. 1899 in Cumberland Co., TN. Married Ezra M. Bilbrey on 19 July 1923 (he was born 8 Apr. 1894, and died 2 May 1974). Mertie Bilbrey died on 30 Apr. 1966 in Cumberland Co., and is buried with her husband in the Smith Chapel Cemetery.

JOHN WESLEY BURGESS OF CUMBERLAND CO., TENNESSEE

[John Ross[6], Joel (II)[7]]

8a. **John Wesley (IV)** *[son of Joel (II)].* Born 6 May 1889 in White Co., TN. Married Myrtle Lou "Mertie" Treadway on 4 Feb. 1906 in White Co. (she was born 9 June 1891, daughter of [Peter {or Perkins}] Mancefield Treadway and Louisa M. Clouse, and sister of Gertie Treadway [who married John's brother, James Luther Burgess], and died 28 Aug. 1981, aged 90 years). Listed in the 1910-20 censuses for Cumberland Co., TN (one of one children survive in 1910), and in the 1917 draft list of Cumberland Co. John Burgess was a farmer and bus driver in Cumberland Co., and also served as Deputy Sheriff in the 1920s. He died there on 23 Apr. 1940, and is buried with his wife in the Smith Chapel Cemetery.

9a. **Horace Elvin.** His name is listed as Hardee Burgess in the 1940 draft list. Born 12 Oct. 1907 in Cumberland Co., TN. Married his second cousin, Eva Page, on 24 Feb. 1929 in Cumberland Co. (she was the daughter of Henry Page and Mattie Elizabeth Seegraves, and granddaughter of Sarah Burgess Seegraves). Horace Burgess was a grocery store owner at Pleasant Hill, TN. He died there on 12 June 1971, and is buried in the Smith Chapel Cemetery. Eva Burgess lives at Pleasant Hill, TN.

10a. **(Jeanne) Maxine.** Her name is listed as Gene Maxene in a newspaper announcement of her birth. Born 28 Feb. 1930 in Cumberland Co., TN. Married Jack W. Gregory on 20 Feb. 1960, and had children: *Jennifer* (born 1 Jan. 1961, married Tyron Throop on 30 June 1984, and had children: Kathleen Damarus [born 19 Feb. 1988]; Steven Gregory [born 7 Feb. 1990]). Maxine Gregory lives at Arlington, VA.

10b. **Sandra Josette.** Born 15 Aug. 1938 in Cumberland Co., TN. Married C. T. Mathes Jr. in 1956, and had children: *Joy Jeanne* (born 15 Dec. 1954, married Rick Ward in Dec. 1958); *Melody Joyce* (born 7 Mar. 1963, married Chuck Wyatt [div.], married secondly Dean Stalling in 1987, and had children: Mathes Cade [born 21 June 1990]). Living at Pleasant Hill, TN, in 1971.

9b. **Hollis Samuel "Simon."** Born 3 Feb. 1911 in Cumberland Co., TN. Married Sela Dayton in KY (she was born 21 June 1923 at Crossville, TN, and died 21 Dec. 1967 at North Eaton, OH, buried Butternut Ridge Cemetery); married secondly Nora Louise Treadway on 12 June 1971 in Cumberland Co. Listed in the 1940 draft list of Cumberland Co. Hollis Burgess was a farmer in TN and a factory worker in Ohio before retiring. He died in Nov. 1991 at Grafton, OH.

10a. **(Samuel) Wayne.** Born 3 Feb. 1942 at Pleasant Hill, TN. Married Sue Rock about 1962 (div.); married secondly Connie Hines. Wayne Burgess works in the meat and cooling business at Grafton, OH.

11a. **Christine Lynne.** Born 4 Aug. 1963 at Elyria, OH. Married ___ Methany, and had children: *Sam*; *Shane*; *Steve*.

11b. **Kelly Ann (I).** Born 18 Mar. 1965 at Elyria, OH.

11c. **Kirk Wayne.** Born 7 Dec. 1966 at Elyria, OH. Married Carolyn Cox.

12a. **Courtney.**

12b. **Zackary.**

10b. **Gary Leon (I).** Born 2 Sept. 1943 at Brea, OH. Married Sheryl Szczepanski. Gary L. Burgess works for Fisher Guide, a division of General Motors, at Grafton, OH.

11a. **Wendy Lane.** Born 15 Mar. 1966 at Elyria, OH. Married Michael Patterson on 16 Aug. 1980 (div.).

11b. **Robin Renee.** Born 7 Apr. 1967 at Elyria, OH. Married Mark Kiser, and had children: *Amanda* (born 25 Jan. 1990 at Elyria, OH); *Mark* (born 1991 at Elyria, OH).

11c. **Eric Gary.** Born 16 Feb. 1969 at Elyria, OH.

10c. **Brenda Kay (I).** Born 19 May 1950 at Brea, OH. Married Albert Goldsmith (div.), and had children: *Michael Vincent* (born 25 Sept. 1967); married secondly Ray Salisbury about 1977, and had children: *Holly Kay* (born 16 Mar. 1978 at Brea, OH).

9c. **(Gracie) Laurine.** Born 28 Feb. 1914 in Cumberland Co., TN. Married Willis White on 15 Apr. 1938, and had children: *(Edith) Zee* (born 1 Jan. 1941 at Newport News, VA, married John Thomas Reynolds on 28 Mar. 1964 [div.], and had children: John Willis [born 17 June 1965 at Newport News, VA]; Robin Laurine [born 18 Aug. 1967 at Newport News, VA]). Laurine White is a retired school teacher at Newport News, VA. She has contributed greatly to this book.

9d. **(Loyd) Leon.** Born 13 Feb. 1920 in Cumberland Co., TN. Married Selma Gibson (div.); married secondly Elsie Seymour. Served in World War II as a Staff Sergeant, and was wounded in Italy. Leon Burgess worked for General Motors and Terrxs Co. before retiring. He died on 8 Feb. 1991 at Sandyville, OH, and was buried there in the Green Lawn Cemetery.

10a. **Danny Charles (I)** (ad.). His surname was originally Butler. Born 1 May 1951 at Clay, WV. Married Elizabeth Hankins. Danny Burgess works for Ford Motor Co. at Elyria, OH.

11a. **Michael (III).**

10b. **Barry Allen** (ad.). His surname was originally Butler. Born 21 Oct. 1952 at Clay, WV. Married Sheryl Jones. Barry Burgess is a computer technician at Amherst, OH.

11a. **Lauren Julia**. Born 10 Jan. 1987.

10c. **Shawn Wesley.** Born 12 Nov. 1963 at Medina, OH. Married Linda Slack on 10 Feb. 1989. Served in the U.S. Army for three years.

11a. **Heather Renee.** Born 21 Aug. 1990.
11b. **Kevin Loyd.** Born 22 Apr. 1993.

9e. **Edith Lorene.** Born 11 May 1923 (or 1922, according to her death certificate) in Cumberland Co., TN; died there on 20 Dec. 1929, and is buried in the Smith Chapel Cemetery.

9f. **Johnia Mildred.** Her name is listed as "Johnie" in her first marriage record. Born 19 Nov. 1925 in Cumberland Co., TN. Married John England on 26 Dec. 1941 in GA (div.; he was the son of Beecher England); married secondly Fate Parker on 24 Dec. 1945 at Rossville, GA (he was born 1899, and died 24 Dec. 1989, aged 90 years, buried Monterey, TN), and had children: *Linda Lou* (born 9 Jan. 1945, married Jerry Sproles, and had children: Shelia Johnene [born 28 Apr. 1965 at Crossville, TN, married Sam Halloway, and had children: Jessica La Nay {born 23 Nov. 1988 at Crossville, TN}; Brittany La Shay {born 10 June 1992 at Crossville, TN}]; James Bradly [born 19 Mar. 1976 at Cookeville, TN]); *Alan Gail* (born 19 Apr. 1950 at Monterey, TN, married Marsha Jean Walker on 29 May 1969, and had children: Jason Alan [born 8 Feb. 1973 at Crossville, TN, married Angie Walker, and had children: Elizabeth Ann {born 25 Oct. 1990}; Sabrina Lyn {born 15 June 1992}]; Jamie Brian [born 8 Feb. 1973 at Cookeville, TN, married Misty Phillips]; Olivia Gail [born 13 Dec. 1976 at Cookeville, TN]); *Michael Dean* (born 2 Oct. 1958, married Wanda Jean Jarmen, and had children: Anthony Edward [born 5 June 1982 at Crossville, TN]); *Stephen Andrew* (born 27 June 1962, married Melissa Kathleen Tays, and had children: Heather Nicole [born 5 Aug. 1985]; Tabitha Danielle [born 4 Oct. 1987]; Seth Andrew [born 25 Jan. 1992]). Johnia Parker has contributed greatly to this book; she currently lives at Monterey, TN.

JAMES LUTHER BURGESS OF WHITE CO., TENNESSEE

[John Ross[6], Joel (II)[7]]

8c. **James Luther** *[son of Joel (II)].* Born 10 Jan. 1892 in White Co., TN. Married Gertie Treadway on 10 Mar. 1910 in White Co. (she was born 17 May 1894 [or 1893], daughter of [Peter {or Perkins}] Mancefield Treadway and Louisa M. "Lize" Clouse, and sister of Myrtle Treadway [who married James's brother, John Burgess], and died 29 Sept. 1978). Listed with his mother in the 1910 census, in the 1918 draft register of White Co., and in the 1920 census at Ravenscroft, White Co., TN. James L. Burgess was a coal miner at Ravenscroft, TN, and also managed restaurants in Monterey and Harriman, TN, worked at Oak Ridge during the construction of the Tennessee Valley Authority, and worked in a factory in Detroit. He retired to Sparta, TN, where he purchased the old Treadway home. He died there on 6 Apr. 1978, and is buried in the Smith Chapel Cemetery.

9a. **(Ephamie) Louise.** Her name was pronounced Lo-ize, and was spelled Louiza in the 1920 census. Born 5 Mar. 1911 in Cumberland Co., TN. Married Earl Davenport (div.), and had children:

Jimmy Earl (born 8 Sept. 1940); *Carnella G.* (born 19 Oct. 1945); *Child* (born and died 27 Feb. 1950). Louise Davenport died on 21 Nov. 1988 at Dayton, OH.

9b. **Son.** Born and died 19 Oct. 1913 in Cumberland Co., TN.

9c. **(James) Carl (I).** Born 13 Oct. 1915 in White Co., TN. See below for full entry.

9d. **Joel Mancefield.** Born 5 May 1918 in Cumberland Co., TN. See below for full entry.

9e. **Robert Manning.** Born 15 Jan. 1921 in Cumberland Co., TN. See below for full entry.

9f. **Aubrey Darce "Red."** Born 9 Jan. 1923 in Cumberland Co., TN. Married three times. Served in the Navy during World War II. Red Burgess was a construction worker at Dayton, OH until a back injury forced early retirement. He currently lives at Lafollette, TN.

9g. **(Odis) Eugene.** Born 19 Nov. 1925 in Cumberland Co., TN. See below for full entry.

9h. **Jackie Hubert.** Born 18 Mar. 1929 in Cumberland Co., TN. Jack Burgess was a laborer in White Co., TN before retiring. He died unmarried on 11 Aug. 1992 at Sparta, TN.

9i. **Aubrey Inez.** Her name is also listed as Audrey Imogene. Born and died 14 June 1933 (or 1932) in White Co., TN, and is buried in the Smith Chapel Cemetery.

CARL BURGESS OF CUMBERLAND CO., TENNESSEE

[John Ross[6], Joel (II)[7], James Luther[8]]

9c. **(James) Carl (I)** *[son of James Luther].* Born 13 Oct. 1915 in White Co., TN. Married as her second husband (Winnie) Pearl Davis England on 14 Apr. 1944 at Detroit, MI (she was born 18 July 1917, daughter of Allen and Sarah Davis, married firstly ___ England, and had children: *Harold* [born 19 Dec. 1935, married Marcy Young on 12 Aug. 1967, had three children, and died 3 May 1984]). Served in the U.S. Army during World War II. Carl Burgess worked for the General Motors Frigidaire plant at Dayton Ohio for 23 years, before retiring to Smith Chapel, TN. He was a member of the Smith Chapel Freewill Baptist Church. He and his wife both contributed greatly to this book. Carl Burgess died on 26 Oct. 1988 at Knoxville, TN, and was buried in the Smith Chapel Cemetery. Pearl Burgess currently lives in Ohio.

10a. **Carlene** (nmn). Born 9 Nov. 1939 at Detroit, MI. Married Maurice "Moe" Appleton, and had children: *Terry*; *Chip*; *Child*. Carlene Appleton is a computer operator at Dayton, OH.

10b. **James Anthony (I).** Born 15 Jan. 1943 at Detroit, MI. Married Sandy Bogard in 1967. James A. Burgess works for an aluminum siding company at Dayton, OH. He lives at Tipp City, OH.

11a. **Sheri** (nmn) (ad.). Born 8 Aug. 1964 at Dayton, OH. Married Ron McLain.

11b. **James Carl (II).** Born 13 Aug. 1970 at Dayton, OH.

11c. **Luke Anthony.** Born 29 Nov. 1976 at Dayton, OH.

JOEL M. BURGESS OF LOS ANGELES CO., CALIFORNIA

[John Ross[6], Joel (II)[7], James Luther[8]]

9d. **Joel Mancefield** *[son of James Luther].* He was named for his two grandfathers, Joel Burgess and Mancefield Treadway. Born 5 May 1918 in Cumberland Co., TN. Married Virginia Stimson on 8 June 1940 (she was born 30 Aug. 1920, and died 19 Sept. 1987 at Duarte, CA). Joel M. Burgess was a fireman for the Detroit City Fire Dept. for eight years, before moving to California in 1951. There he owned and operated Bob & Joe's Janitorial Service for 26 years, and, after retiring in 1976, worked as an apartment manager in Duarte, CA. He now lives at Dayton, OH.

10a. **Joel David.** Born 13 Feb. 1942 at Detroit, MI. Married Donna E. Hiestand on 6 Aug. 1960 in San Diego Co., CA; married secondly Kathleen J. Fitzroy on 17 Jan. 1964 in Los Angeles Co., CA; married thirdly Sheri Bergman on 23 Feb. 1974 in Los Angeles Co., CA; married fourthly Ronnie L. Delautre on 15 Apr. 1978 in Los Angeles Co., CA; married fifthly Elizabeth M. "Betty" Lindsey on 27 Nov. 1983 in Clark Co., NV. Joel D. Burgess worked for California Tool Co. for fifteen years; he now works as an assistant parts manager for an auto dealer at Baldwin Park, CA.

11a. **David Robert (II).** Born 15 Aug. 1964 at Los Angeles, CA. Married Julie Ann Barker on 15 June 1985 in Los Angeles Co., CA.

12a. **Tiffany Nicole.** Born 17 Nov. 1986 at West Covina, CA.

11b. **Sheri Denise.** Born 28 Sept. 1967 at Los Angeles, CA.

10b. **Donald Mancefield.** Born 28 July 1954 at Escondido, CA. Married Terri Hofreiter on 30 Dec. 1972 in San Diego Co., CA; married secondly Fawzalet ___; married thirdly Corrine Janice Redlowske on 20 Oct. 1979 in Clark Co., NV; married fourthly Jill ___; married fifthly Tatiana Perez about 1984; married sixthly Betina Paladian on 19 Sept. 1987. Donald Burgess served for nearly eight years in the U.S. Army as an M.P., then worked as a security patrol officer, and as a desk dispatcher for Purolator Co., Downey, CA. He died suddenly of a heart attack on 28 Sept. 1987 at Los Angeles, ten days after his mother, and nine days after his last marriage.

11a. **Taina Vanessa.** Born 2 Oct. 1984 at Los Angeles, CA.
11b. **Calais Lis.** Born 7 Jan. 1988 at Northridge, CA.

10c. **Cindy Sue.** Born 26 Oct. 1957 at Oceanside, CA. Married Duane Patrick Curry (an Air Force officer) on 5 May 1979 at Oceanside, CA, and had children: *Kimberly Ann* (born 16 Sept. 1980); *Christopher Kid* (born 8 July 1985). She now lives in West Germany.

ROBERT M. BURGESS OF WEBER CO., UTAH

[John Ross^{6}, Joel (II)^{7}, James Luther^{8}]

9e. **Robert Manning** *[son of James Luther].* Born 15 Jan. 1921 in White Co., TN. Married (Ethelyn) Geraldine "Gerry" Swicegood on 6 June 1941 at Urbana, OH (div.). Served as a bombardier in the U.S. Navy during World War II. Bob Burgess worked as a lens grinder for an optical company, and later as a toolmaker for the Fram Corp., at Roy, Utah. He died there on 7 Apr. 1979, and is buried in the Roy City Cemetery. Gerry Burgess currently lives at Roy, UT.

10a. **(Robert) David (II).** Born 24 Mar. 1943 in Cumberland Co., TN. Married Corliss Neuber. David Burgess is a civilian employee of the U.S. Air Force at Ogden, UT.

11a. **Wendy Geraldine.** Born 18 July 1963 at Ogden, UT. Wendy Burgess is a computer operator at Ogden, UT.

GENE BURGESS OF MONTGOMERY CO., OHIO

[John Ross^{6}, Joel (II)^{7}, James Luther^{8}]

9g. **(Odis) Eugene (I)** *[son of James Luther].* His name is also spelled Otis. Born 19 Nov. 1925 in Cumberland Co., TN. Married Inez Harris by 1945 (div.; she remarried ___ Carmen); married secondly ___ about 1964. Served in the U.S. Navy during World War II. Gene Burgess works as a home siding installer at Dayton, OH.

10a. **Judy Aynn.** Born 25 July 1946 at Detroit, MI. Married Bob Metzger.
10b. **Gary Eugene (I) "Butch."** Born 15 Mar. 1948 at Detroit, MI. Married Mary Ellen Hahn on 1 Jan. 1967 in San Diego Co. (div.); married secondly Carol L. Hinderliter on 13 Mar. 1976 in San Diego Co. Gary Burgess is a Fire Control Technician—Guns in the U.S. Navy, now stationed at Coronado, CA.

11a. **Carri Elaine.** Born 12 July 1967 at Oceanside, CA.
11b. **Gary Eugene II.** Born 22 Aug. 1969 at North Chicago, IL.
11c. **John Robert (II).** Born 22 Sept. 1978 at Honolulu, HI.
11d. **Andrew Jarrett.** Born 29 June 1980 at Agana, GU.

10c. **Maxina Louise "Kitten."** Born 27 Feb. 1950 at Detroit, MI; died there on 9 June 1956, when she was hit by a car, and is buried in the Smith Chapel Cemetery, Cumberland Co., TN.
10d. **Verna Lynn.** Born 25 Mar. 1965 at Pontiac, MI. Married Darine Williams.
10e. **Odis Eugene (II) "Junior."** Born 17 July 1966 at Pontiac, MI.
10f. **Debra LuJean.** Born 7 Oct. 1968 at Dayton, OH.

"BIG" JIM BURGESS OF WHITE CO., TENNESSEE
[John Ross[6]]

7h. **(John) James (I) "Big Jim"** *[son of John Ross].* Born 27 Feb. 1867 in White Co., TN. Married Mattie Ellen "Matt" Pays on 18 Aug. 1905 (or 10 Nov. 1905) in Cumberland Co. (she was born 5 Jan. 1882, and died 22 July 1967). Living with his mother in 1900; she is living with him in the 1910 census for Cumberland Co., TN (two of two children survive in 1910); listed in the 1920 census for Cumberland Co., TN. "Big Jim" Burgess was a farmer and salt mill worker in Cumberland and White Cos., TN. He died of nephritis on 31 Aug. 1938 in White Co., and is buried with his wife in the Smith Chapel Cemetery.

8a. **Eva (I)** (nmn). Her name is listed as Evor in the 1920 census. Born 15 Oct. 1906 in Cumberland Co., TN. Married Marsh Coburn. Eva Coburn died in Nov. 1986 at Oliver Springs, Anderson Co., TN.

8b. **Ivor** (nmn). Her name is listed as Ivory is some early newspaper accounts, including her mother's obituary. Born 8 Nov. 1908 in Cumberland Co., TN. Married (as his second wife) John England, widower of her cousin, Mollie Burgess, on 30 Mar. 1934 (he was born 22 Feb. 1876, and died 24 Jan. 1967); married secondly ___ Morris. Ivor Morris died on 3 Feb. 1991 at Sparta, TN.

8c. **(James) Thomas (III) "Tom."** Born 1 Mar. 1911 in Cumberland Co., TN. Married Ada Belle ___. Served in the U.S. Army during World War II. Tom Burgess was a ceramics worker in Chattanooga. He died there childless in Mar. 1976.

James Winfield BURGESS
(1908-1939)
Louise BURGESS BAILEY
(1909-1988)
Robert Ivan BAILEY
(1934-)
John Thomas BAILEY
(1938-)
(see page 519)

[William (I)[1], Edward (I)[2], Reuben (I)[3], Thomas (I)[4], Joel (I)[5]]

JAMES MARION BURGESS
(1839-1917)

OF PUTNAM COUNTY, TENNESSEE

6d. **James Marion (I)** *[son of Joel (I)].* Born 23 Aug. 1839 in White (later Putnam) Co., TN. Married Nancy W. Huddleston about 1861 (she was born 12 June 1841 [or 17 Dec. 1839] in TN, daughter of John L. Huddleston and Rebecca Moore, and died 15 June 1879 [or 16 Oct. 1891]); married secondly Rebecca Ann "Becky" ___ on 27 Sept. 1884 (she was born Aug. 1854 in TN). He claimed to have served in the 8th Tennessee Cavalry, Confederate Army, during the Civil War; both he and his widow received pensions based on his service, although he could provide no documentation; he may actually have served in Co. I, 5th (McKenzie's) Tennessee Cavalry, enlisting 21 Oct. 1862 and 14 Jan. 1863. Listed in the 1870-1910 censuses for the 2nd Civil District, Putnam Co., TN. James M. Burgess was a farmer in Putnam Co. He died there on 9 Feb. 1917, and is buried with his first wife in the Salem M.E. Church Cemetery.

The Children of James M. Burgess:

7a. **(Lona) Dee (I).** Born 12 Feb. 1862 in Putnam Co., TN. Married George W. Bohannon on 16 Nov. 1878 in Putnam Co. (he was born Dec. 24, 1860, son of Sheriff Campbell Bohannon and Rosa Henry, and died Oct. 4, 1923), and had children:

Mike Bohannon. Born Dec. 1879, married Minnie Hudgens on 5 Jan. 1902 in Putnam Co., TN (she was born 8 Aug. 1880, and died 2 Nov. 1960), and died 8 May 1960, buried Salem Cemetery, having had children: *Mamie* (born 17 Oct. 1902, died unmarried on 27 Oct. 1979); *Mattie Dee* (born 1907, married Frank Coatney Pennington [he was born 1906, son of Bob Pennington and Minnie Sims], and had children: Minnie Geneva [born 9 Apr. 1938, married Doyle Roberts, and had children: Melissa Gale {born 23 Feb. 1962}]; Glenn Dale [born 27 Aug. 1942, married Virginia Sue Allison {she was the daughter of James T. Allison}, and died 1985, having had children: Clyde Dale {born 1971}]; Bunola [born 1913, married Albert Walker, and had children: Anna Faye]).

Haskell B. Bohannon. Born 27 Aug. 1881 [or 1887], married Sarah Verna Sliger on 3 Jan. 1909 [she was born 28 May 1888, daughter of David Hampton Sliger and Margaret Peek], and had children: *Dovie* (born 13 Oct. 1911, married Franklin Earl Huddleston on 25 Jan. 1930 at Albany, KY [he was born 13 Apr. 1910, son of Beverage Huddleston and Nettie Smith], and died 4 Nov. 1973, having had children: George William [born 3 Jan. 1931, married Faye Gentry on 20 June 1959 {she was born 17 May 1936, daughter of Charles Gentry and Pearl Phy}, and had children: Heather D. {born 3 Apr. 1964}]); *Margaret Dee* (born 11 Oct. 1927, married Jennings Neal on 15 Mar. 1945 in Putnam Co. [he was born 3 Apr. 1925, son of Shirley Neal and Susie Handy, and died in a truck accident on 1 Dec. 1970], and had children: Jennings Franklin [born 3 Apr. 1946]; Susan Dee [born 31 July 1961, married Ricky Qualls in 1979]).

THE BOHANNONS are listed in the 1880-1900 censuses for the 1st District, Putnam Co., TN. Dee Bohannon died of tuberculosis on 20 June 1924 in Putnam Co., and is buried with her husband in the Salem M.E. Church Cemetery.

7b. **(Codera) Dora.** She is also called Codora in some records; Dora may have been a nickname. Born 13 Nov. 1865 in Putnam Co., TN. Married Greene B. Wilhite (or Willhait) on 19 Feb. 1882 (he was born Aug. 1864 in TN, son of Solomon Robinson "Dock" Wilhite and Harriett E. Huddleston, and died at Ada, OK), and had at least the following children: *Pearl Leslie* (born Aug. 1883, married Roy Pinkston on 25 Dec. 1904 in Putnam Co. in a double wedding with her sister [he was born Nov. 1882, son of Samuel Pinkston and Mary Jane Carter]); *Maggie D.* (born 18 May 1887, married Jesse Charles Sliger on 25 Dec. 1904 in Putnam Co. in a double wedding with her sister [he was born 3 Sept. 1874, son of Andrew Robinson Sliger and Harriett Saylors], and died 10 Mar. 1912, buried Sliger Cemetery, having had children: Bessie Dee [born 11 June 1908 in Putnam Co., married Ferdinand Petzoldt in

1926, and had children: Robert Eugene {born 5 Aug. 1929, married Lorene Clark, and died 15 Nov. 1986 at McMinnville, TN, having had children: Sandra Dee <born 21 Dec. 1964>; Terry Lynn <born 1 Feb. 1967>}]); *Rush* (born Mar. 1891, married Mollie Austin, and died childless); *Hattie J.* (born Apr. 1894, married Bill Goodwin); *Carrie B.* (born Apr. 1897, married ___ Duck); *Bertha M.* (born Sept. 1899, married ___ Harris); *Mollie* (born 1903); *Floro* (son; born 3 July 1906, and died 8 Mar. 1988 at Ada, OK). Listed in the 1900 census for Putnam Co., TN, and in 1910 in White Co. Dora Wilhite died on 4 Oct. 1954 at Ada, Pontotoc Co., OK, and is buried there in the Rosedale Cemetery.

Four Burgess Sisters and Their Husbands

(top photo, from left) Elizabeth Ann Burgess, (Arennia) Bell Burgess (back), Martha Alice Burgess (front), (Mary) Emma Burgess; (bottom photo, from left) John W. Sammons (husband of Martha), Newton J. Sammons (back, husband of Elizabeth), (Luther) Bruce Trowbridge (front, husband of Bell), Andrew Jackson Lindbloom (husband of Emma) [see pages 245-249]

[William (I)[1], Edward (I)[2], Reuben (I)[3], Thomas (I)[4], Joel (I)[5]]

HITE BURGESS
(1852-1898)
OF JACKSON COUNTY, TENNESSEE

6i. **Hiram T(homas?) "Hite"** *[son of Joel (I)].* Born 3 Aug. 1852 in Cumberland Co., TN. Married (Sarah) Augusta Sliger about 1876 (she was born 26 May 1857, daughter of Elias Sliger [who was the brother of James T. and Samuel Sliger] and Mary Ann Welch, and died 30 May 1887); married secondly Mary West about 1891 (she was born July 1870 in TN, possibly the daughter of Martin West). Living with his father in 1870, and is listed in the 1880 census for the Tenth District, Jackson Co., TN; his widow appears as head of the family in 1900, but has not been found in 1910. Hite Burgess died in Jackson Co. on 1 Apr. 1898, and is buried with his first wife in the Cummins Cemetery. Mary may be the same Mary Burgess who is mentioned in the *Crossville Chronicle* as having moved to Missouri on 11 May 1903 to live with her mother, Mrs. Martin West.

The Children of Hite Burgess:

7a. **Della (I).** Her name is listed in the 1880 census as Florence Burgess. Born Feb. 1877 in Jackson Co., TN. Living in 1900 with her stepmother.

7b. **Dow B(ell?).** Born 9 Mar. 1879 in Jackson Co., TN. Married (Delia) Belle Netherton on 27 Oct. 1916 in Jackson Co. (she was born 8 Jan. 1898, remarried Wade Washington Petty on 6 Feb. 1963 [he was born 16 June 1901, and died 24 Feb. 1967], and died 4 July 19__). Listed in the 1918 draft register for Jackson Co., TN. Dow Burgess died childless on 16 Mar. 1962 in Jackson Co., TN, and is buried in the Cummins Cemetery.

7c. **Bell.** Born 28 Oct. 1882 in Jackson Co., TN. Living with her stepmother in 1900. Bell Burgess died unmarried on 4 July 1905, and is buried in the Cummins Cemetery.

7d. **Lou Ann (I).** Her name is spelled Lue on her marriage record. Born 1 Apr. 1886 in Jackson Co., TN. Married Archie "Arch" Garrison on 7 Aug. 1910 in Putnam Co. (he was born 21 Sept. 1885, son of John Henry Garrison and Vesta Morris, and died 8 June 1964), and had children: *Gillie Mae* (born 26 June 1912 in Jackson Co., lives unmarried on the old homestead at Cummins Falls, Jackson Co., TN); *(James) Walter "Hague"* (born 2 Mar. 1914 in Jackson Co., died unmarried on 27 Oct. 1983 at Crossville, TN); *(John) Henry* (born 9 Mar. 1916 in Jackson Co., married Johnnie Montgomery, and had children: Linda; Karen); *Hite Burgess* (born 18 Feb. 1918 in Jackson Co., married Nellie Dyer on 23 Dec. 1940 in Putnam Co., and had children: Roy; Doyle; Anita); *Effie Mae* (born 7 Feb. 1920 in Jackson Co., married Pascal Allen [he was the son of Bill Allen and Cindy Pryor]); *Lucy Lee* (born 12 May 1922, died 17 May 1922 in Jackson Co., buried Cummins Cemetery); *Haney Thompson* (born 11 Nov. 1923 in Jackson Co., married Martha Lou Allen on 31 Oct. 1964, and had children: Michael); *Cletis Emogene "Toot"* (born 7 June 1925 in Jackson Co., and had children: Shirley Darlene [born 29 June 1956 in Jackson Co., married David Meyer in 1976, and works as a nurse]). Lou Garrison died on 19 June 1978 at Algood, Putnam Co., TN, aged 92 years, and is buried with her husband in the Smyrna Cemetery.

7e. **Florence (IV).** Born Feb. 1892 in Jackson Co., TN. She or her half-sister, Della, may have married James Robinson, and had children: *Lem.* Said to have moved to (Ada?), Oklahoma, and to have had other children. A Mrs. James Robinson is mentioned in the *Crossville Chronicle* in June 1904; this cannot be Florence, but it could be Della.

7f. **Ruth (I).** Born Apr. 1895 in Jackson Co., TN. No further record.

7g. **Effie.** Born Aug. 1897 in Jackson Co., TN. No further record.

[William (I)[1], Edward (I)[2], Reuben (I)[3], Thomas (I)[4]]

THOMAS BURGESS, JR.
(1815-1900)

OF WASHINGTON COUNTY, ARKANSAS

5h. **Thomas (II)** *[son of Thomas (I)].* He is called Thomas Henry by Onie Odle. Born 15 May 1815 (or 1814) in Rowan (later Davie) Co., NC, or on the way west. Married Nancy Alburty (or Alberty) on 11 June 1840 at Evansville, AR (she was born 20 June 1820 in Indiana or North Carolina, and died 10 Apr. 1878 in Washington Co.). According to Anderson Burgess's 1878 history, Thomas Burgess served in Nathan Boone's Company, U.S. Rangers during the Indian Wars of 1832-33, participating in the Black Hawk War (however, his pension record states that he served in Roberts Company, 1st Tennessee Mounted Infantry). He moved to Missouri with his brother, and then to a farm near Evansville, Vineyard Township, Washington Co., AR, on the border between Arkansas and Indian Territory (later Oklahoma). Listed in the 1837 tax list of Washington Co., AR, and in the censuses there from 1840-80; his pension record stated that he was living in Hunt Co., TX in 1893. Tom Burgess was a farmer in Arkansas. He died on 20 Apr. 1900 in Washington Co., and is buried there with his wife in the Vineyard Cemetery.

The Children of Thomas Burgess, Jr.:

6a. **(George) Washington (VII).** His surname is spelled Burges on his tombstone and in the 1880 census. Born 24 May 1841 in Washington Co., AR. Listed with his father in the 1860 census working as a teamster. Married Frances Marie ___ (she was born about 1845 in AR, died about 1895, aged 50 years, 20 months, 3 days, and is buried in the Social Hill Cemetery, Lane Creek Township, Hot Spring Co., AR). Wash Burgess is believed to have served as a corporal in Co. C, 18th Arkansas Infantry, Confederate Army, enlisting in 1862; he was captured on 9 July 1863 at Port Hudson, LA, then released on parole on 12 July. Listed in the 1870 census for Union Township, Hot Spring Co., AR working as a miller, and in 1880 in Wood Co., TX. He died, apparently childless, on 18 Apr. 1893 in Hunt Co., TX, and is buried there in the Brigham Cemetery.

6b. **Thomas (Henry?) (I).** Born about 1843 in Washington Co., AR. Listed with his father in the 1860 census. According to Onie Odle, he was killed in the Civil War; he may be the T. H. Burgess who served in the 18th Cherokee Mounted Volunteers, Confederate Army. Has not been found in the 1870-80 census indexes for TN or TX.

6c. **John Wesley (II).** Born 3 Nov. 1844 in Washington Co., AR. See below for full entry.

6d. **William A(nderson?) (I).** Born Sept. 1846 in Washington Co., AR. Listed with his father through the 1880 censuses, and in the 1900 census for Washington Co., AR with his brother, Jack. William Burgess was a farmer on his father's lands near Evansville, AR. He died there unmarried in 1904.

6e. **(Mary) Molly.** Born 20 May 1850 in Washington Co., AR. Married M. J. Bryant on 30 Aug. 1877 in Washington Co., AR (he is probably the Matthew C. Bryant who remarried her sister, Ellen). Molly Bryant died there on 19 Mar. 1878, and is buried in the Vineyard Cemetery.

6f. **(Andrew) Jackson (I) "Jack."** Born Apr. 1853 in Washington Co., AR. Listed in the 1880 census with his father (but is not there in 1870), in 1900 with his brother, William, and in 1910 in Oklahoma with his nephew, Thomas H. Burgess. Jack Burgess was a farmer in Arkansas and Oklahoma. He died unmarried about 1923 at the home of his brother, Robert, and is buried in an unmarked grave in the Bryan's Chapel Cemetery.

6g. **Robert Thornsberry.** Born 30 Apr. 1858 in Washington Co., AR. See below for full entry.

6h. **(Mary) Ellen (IV).** Born June 1861 in Washington Co., AR. Married Matthew C. Bryant (probably the same person who married her sister, Molly) on 1 Aug. 1878 in Washington Co. (he was born Oct. 1839 in TN), and had at least the following children: *Matthew* (born Dec. 1879); *Culins* (born Aug. 1882); *Ellen* (born Jan. 1884); *Oliver* (born Aug. 1891); *Fannie* (born Sept. 1894). Listed in the 1880-1900 censuses for Washington Co., AR. Ellen Bryant died about 1930 at Morris, OK.

[William (I)[1], Edward (I)[2], Reuben (I)[3], Thomas (I)[4], Thomas (II)[5]]

JOHN WESLEY BURGESS
(1844-1909)
OF DALLAS COUNTY, TEXAS

6c. **John Wesley (II)** *[son of Thomas (II)].* Born 3 Nov. 1844 in Washington Co., AR. Married Laura Catherine Futrelle about 1872 (she was born 9 June 1851 in MS, and died 19 Sept. 1940 at Dallas). Listed in the 1880-1900 censuses for Dallas Co., TX; his widow appears as head of the family in 1910. John W. Burgess was a farmer in Washington Co., AR; he came to Texas in 1872, and bought a farm in the Five Mile Creek area of Dallas Co., TX in 1874, where his old house still stands. Listed in the 1880/81 rural Directory of Dallas Co. living near Jimtown, TX, fives miles west of Dallas. He died at Dallas on 12 Dec. 1909, and is buried with his wife and several of their children in the Oak Cliff Cemetery.

The Children of John W. Burgess:

7a. **John M. (II).** Born 4 June 1873 in Washington Co., AR. John Burgess lost an arm to a mill accident early in life. Several years later, while on a family picnic at the Record Crossing of the Trinity River, he drowned while swimming. He died unmarried on 16 May 1891, and is buried in Five Mile Cemetery.

7b. **Flora Belle.** Born 9 July 1875 in Dallas Co., TX. Married David Lee Wilson by 1910 (div. 1928; he was born 1877 in MO). Living with her parents in 1900-10. Flora Wilson worked at the Titche-Goettinger Co. department store in Dallas for 35 years, became wealthy, and traveled extensively throughout the U.S. and Europe. She died childless on 21 Dec. 1936 at Dallas, and is buried in the Oak Cliff Cemetery.

7c. **Thomas Dickerson (I).** His middle name is also spelled Dickinson. Born 6 Sept. 1876 in Dallas Co., TX. Living with his mother in 1910. Married Allie ___ (she was born about 1868 in MS); married secondly Stella E. Green after 1920 (she was born 6 Sept. 1895, and died Oct. 1989 at Rice, TX, aged 94 years). Listed with his father in the 1900 census, in the 1915-48 Dallas City Directories, and in the 1920 census for Dallas Co., TX (with no children). In early life Thomas Burgess worked as a ladderman for a fire company, but later became a guard at the Federal Reserve Bank in Dallas. After his retirement, he worked as a cattle trader. He died on 19 Mar. 1951 at Dallas, TX, and is buried in the Laurel Land Cemetery.

8a. **Charles Wesley (II).** Born about 1925 at Dallas, TX. Married Mary E. ___; married secondly Louise ___. Listed in the 1947+ directories of Dallas, TX. Charles Burgess owned and operated Burgess-McGlasson Auto Parts.

8b. **Thomas Dickerson (II).** Born 12 Dec. 1927 at Dallas, TX. Married Lois ___. Listed in many of the city directories of Dallas, TX. Thomas D. Burgess died at Dallas in Apr. 1985.

8c. **Ruth (II).** Born about 1929 at Dallas, TX.

7d. **Nancy Ellen.** Born 1877 in Dallas Co., TX. Married Warren Hipps (he died in the great flu epidemic of 1918), and had children: *Roy Warren* (he was born 12 Dec. 1904, and died unmarried in Feb. 1973 at Dallas, TX). Nancy Hipps died in 1960 at Dallas, TX, and is buried in the Laurel Land Cemetery.

7e. **Mary Jane (IV).** Born 11 Feb. 1879 in Dallas Co., TX; died there on 24 Feb. 1879, and is buried in Five Mile Cemetery.

7f. **William Robert.** Born 9 May 1880 in Dallas Co., TX. Living with his mother in 1910, and is listed in the Dallas City Directories for 1905-16. William Burgess was a policeman in early life, but later worked as a guard at the Federal Reserve Bank in Dallas. He died there unmarried on 26 Dec. 1918 in the great flu epidemic, and is buried in the Oak Cliff Cemetery.

7g. **George Givens "G. G."** Born 9 July 1883 in Dallas Co., TX. Married (Eva) Pearl Gardner (div. by 1920; she was born about 1885 in TX; she may be the Eva Burgess who was born 22 Dec. 1892 and died Sept. 1972 at Killeen, TX). Listed in the 1910 census for Dallas Co. G. G. Burgess was a road contractor in New Mexico and East Texas between 1919-24; in 1922 he bought a farm near Iowa Park, Wichita Co., TX. He died there childless on 4 Apr. 1935, and is buried in the Oak Cliff Cemetery.

7h. **James Peyton.** Born 8 Aug. 1884 in Dallas Co., TX. Married Callie Jane Ritton [or Britton] about 1908 (she was born about 1886 in TX, and died 21 Apr. 1963). Listed in the 1910-20 censuses for Dallas Co., and in the 1915-50 city directories of Dallas, TX. His widow is listed as head of the family from 1951-64. Jim Burgess owned the Oak Cliff Sand and Gravel Co., and founded the first concrete block plant company in Dallas. He died on 15 June 1950 at Dallas, TX, and is buried in the Laurel Land Cemetery.

8a. **(Edith) Renalda.** Born 26 Jan. 1909 in Dallas Co., TX. Married ___ Copeland. Renalda Copeland owned an answering service at South Pasadena, CA. She died on 4 May 1985 at Pasadena, Los Angeles Co., CA, and is buried in the Live Oak Memorial Park, Monrovia, CA.

8b. **Dorothy Louise.** Born 20 Sept. 1915 in Dallas Co., TX. May have married ___ Reilly, and had children: *Patti J.* (born 1952, married Gary A. Striker on 13 Dec. 1980 in Los Angeles Co., CA, and was living at La Crescenta, CA in 1985; she was the informant on her aunt's death certificate). Deceased.

7i. **Anna Maud.** Born 2 July 1886 in Dallas Co., TX. Listed as a clerk in the 1905 City Directory of Dallas. Married Thomas Barnett Chandler on 25 June 1908 (he was born 2 Sept. 1883 in Grimes Co., TX, worked as a fireman [with the rank of Lieutenant] for the Dallas Fire Dept., and was killed on 7 Feb. 1917 at Dallas, TX, when his fire truck overturned on the way to a call), and had children: *John Lewis "Jack"* (born 14 Apr. 1909 at Dallas, TX, married Audrey Iva Poston on 12 Jan. 1929 at Dallas, and had children: John Lewis Jr. [born 18 Apr. 1931, married Tressie Brannin on 13 Jan. 1956]; Robert Wayne [born 11 May 1939, married Willman Joe Mock on 18 Mar. 1961, and had children: Mary Beth {born 12 Jan. 1962}; Robert Barnett {born 12 Jan. 1965}; John David {born 31 July 1970}]); *Katheryn Willene* (born 15 July 1911 at Dallas, TX, married Dr. Harold Van Haltern in 1935 at Dallas, and had children: Carolyn [born 23 Sept. 1936]; Eleanor [born 9 Sept 1938, married John Garrison, and had one daughter]). After her husband's untimely death, she worked at the Harris Dept. Store and at Titche-Goettinger Co. for 27 years. Anna Chandler died on 12 Sept. 1976 at Dallas, TX, aged 90 years, and is buried in the Grove Hill Cemetery. John L. Chandler has contributed greatly to this book, and currently lives at Dallas.

7j. **Charles Wesley (I).** Born 8 May 1888 in Dallas Co., TX. Married Ina Atrey about 1917 (div.; she was born about 1892 in GA); married secondly Pauline Skaggs. Listed in the 1915-24 City Directories of Dallas, and in the 1920 census for Dallas, Dallas Co., TX. Charles Burgess was a road contractor most of his life in New Mexico and East Texas. He moved to New Boston, TX in 1924, and built the new road to Texarkana. In 1933 he moved to Kilgore, TX, where he built the first streets there during the height of the oil boom, and also built the road from Longview to Kilgore, TX. He later settled in Texarkana, on the Texas-Arkansas line, where he owned the bus line that ran to the Red River Arsenal at Hicks, TX. He died on 13 Sept. 1962, and is buried in the Restland Cemetery. Not in the Texas death index.

8a. **Margery "Margie."** Born May 1918 at Dallas, TX. She moved to Boston with her mother after the separation of her parents.

[William (I)[1], Edward (I)[2], Reuben (I)[3], Thomas (I)[4], Thomas (II)[5]]

ROBERT T. BURGESS
(1856-1931)

OF MAYES COUNTY, OKLAHOMA

6g. **Robert Thorn(s)berry** *[son of Thomas (II)].* Born 30 Apr. 1858 in Washington Co., AR (or at Van Buren, Crawford Co., AR). Married Sarah Ann "Sallie" Pesterfield on 26 Oct. 1879 in Crawford Co., AR (she was born 28 Jan. 1862 in Wise Co., TX, daughter of Henry Pesterfield, and died 9 Mar. 1941). Listed with his father in the 1880 census, in the 1900 census for the Cherokee Nation, IT, and in 1920 in Mayes Co., OK. He settled in Mayes Co., IT (later OK) about 1886, where he owned a farm. He died there on 9 Oct. 1931, and is buried with his wife in the Bryan's Chapel (now Boatman) Cemetery.

The Children of Robert T. Burgess:

7a. **Thomas Henry (III).** Born 26 Sept. 1880 in Washington Co., AR. See below for full entry.

7b. **(Daniel) Jackson (I).** Born Dec. 1882 in Washington Co., AR. Listed with his father in the 1900 census. Jack Burgess died unmarried about 1906 in Mayes Co., OK, after being struck by lightning.

7c. **(Nancy) Josephine.** Born July 1884 in Washington Co., AR. Married L. Renda (or Lorenda) Jones on 1 Oct. 1908 in Mayes Co., OK (he was born 1884 in AL), and had at least the following children: *Jessie* (born 1920 in OK); *Burgess B.* (born 1922?, and died at Guymon, OK). Listed in the 1920 census for Bluejacket, Craig Co., OK. Josephine Jones died there about 1923.

7d. **Robert Washington.** Born 27 Feb. 1886 in Washington Co., AR. See below for full entry.

7e. **(Mary) Ellen (VII) "Ella."** Born 23 Mar. 1888 in Mayes Co., IT (later OK). Married William O. Mitchell on 15 Feb. 1909 in Mayes Co. (he was born 1886). Ella Mitchell died Jan. 1969 at Pryor, OK.

7f. **Anna May "Annie."** Born 24 Apr. 1890 in Mayes Co., IT (later OK). Listed with her father in the 1920 census. Married Ben Wells on 2 Jan. 1922 in Mayes Co. (he was born 23 Feb. 1882, and died Jan. 1965 in CA). Annie Wells died in Aug. 1975 at Fredonia, KS.

7g. **John William (II).** Born 28 Aug. 1892 in Mayes Co., IT (later OK). See below for full entry.

7h. **Laura P.** Born May 1895 in Mayes Co., IT (later OK); died there about 1901, and is buried in the Bryan's Chapel Cemetery.

7i. **(Samuel) Marvin.** Born 21 Oct. 1897 in Mayes Co., IT (later OK). See below for full entry.

7j. **Leona Agnes (II) "Onie."** Born 7 Oct. 1901 in Mayes Co., IT (later OK). Married Clyde Odle in May 1916 (he was born 17 Mar. 1897, son of Bob Odle, and died 28 Feb. 1978 at Colcord, OK), and had children: *Clarence* (born in Neosho Co., KS, married Hazel Lowery [died about 1967], and was killed in a train car wreck in 1965, having had children: Barbara; Charles; Clarence and Hazel Odle are buried in Bryan's Chapel Cemetery); *Ervin Lee* (born in Neosho Co., KS, married Betty Leach, had children: Sharon; Donnie, and works as a carpenter at Tulsa, OK); *Jackie Wayne* (died at eleven days, buried Bryan's Chapel Cemetery); *(Thomas) Eugene* (born 15 Dec. 1923 at Locust Grove, OK, married Gayle Heckart, was a farmer, and currently lives retired at Kansas, OK); *William Marvin "W. M."* (born 15 Dec. 1926 at Locust Grove, OK, married Beverly Dudley, and had children: Joann, and works as a tile setter); *Patricia Mae* (born 30 Dec. 1931 at Kenwood, OK, married Bob Duncan [a farmer], and had children: Deborah; Leon; Susan); *Jane Ann* (born 29 Nov. 1934 at Kenwood, OK, married Tom Judkins, and had children: Carol; Brenda; Thomas Clyde; Jane Judkins works as a secretary); *J. P.* (born 7 Aug. 1937 at Kenwood, OK, married Betty Stepp, and had children: Steve; Philip; Rodney, and works as a rancher); *John Paul* (born 31 Oct. 1939 at Kenwood, OK, married Sue Johnson, and had children: Paula Sue; Janette, and works as a high school principal). **Onie Odle** lives at West Siloam Springs, OK. Onie Odle contributed greatly to this work through her memories and the autobiographical account published below.

7k. **Jesse (II).** Born about 1904 in Mayes Co., IT (later OK); died there about 1905, and is buried in Bryan's Chapel Cemetery.

Onie Odle wrote in 1979: "Grandfather Thomas Henry Burgess owned a team of mules and a wagon when the government was resettling the Indians. Grandfather helped move the Indians from Georgia to Arkansas and Oklahoma. Grandfather and his friend, Mr. Gibson, bought up some river bottom land as partners. Mr. Gibson was married and had a large family; Grandfather was single. While he was in Missouri to visit his fiancée, the bushwackers came in and killed Mr. Gibson and his children. Mrs. Gibson was in bed with a five-day-old baby, and she managed to get out with the baby and hide in the wheat field. The enemy set fire to the wheat and oat field, and Mrs. Gibson went on into the corn field and got away.

"Grandfather and Mr. Gibson were helping supply the Army with barrels of flour, meat, and lard. The bushwackers stole all their supplies, leaving them only land. Grandfather had planned to marry his fiancée that Fall. After he lost everything, he just couldn't tell his fiancée he couldn't marry her. Her parents were wealthy. Grandfather gave most of what was left to Mrs. Gibson, and he resettled in Arkansas on forty acres of land on top of Boston Mountain, twelve miles from Van Buren. The land had to be cleared.

"He met my grandmother, Nancy Alburty; they fell in love and married. They built a log cabin close to a spring of water, and Grandfather put part of it in an orchard of apple and peach trees. He bought more land, and grew corn, wheat, and oats. He bought an apple dryer, and dried apples, and sold them in Van Buren and Fort Smith. Grandfather and Grandmother had seven children, five boys and two girls. My father, the youngest, was born April 30, 1859. Grandfather named him Robert Thornsberry for a Methodist circuit-riding preacher.

"My father was a strong man. Grandfather always had so many apples to sell, he would have my father load a wagon full of apples and go from house to house selling apples. Sometimes he would go as far as Independence, Kansas. One day Father stopped at a farmer's house to buy some oats and fodder to feed his team of horses, and that is how my father met my mother. She came out to tell him where to get the feed and collect the money. Father asked her if he could come calling on her the next Sunday afternoon, and she told him he could. They courted for a year, and then married. Mother was Sarah Pesterfield, born Jan. 28, 1862. They were married Oct. 26, 1879. Mother's father was Henry Pesterfield, he owned a little farm between Cedarvale and Dutch Mills, Arkansas. Father and Mother lived in the house with Grandfather Burgess and two of Father's bachelor brothers, Uncle Jack and Uncle Charlie. Grandmother Burgess died when Father was just a young boy. Grandfather had built a big house with a large basement under it to store apples.

"My parents raised a large family of eleven children, six boys and five girls. I am the youngest and the only one living. My parents moved from Salem, Arkansas to Indian Territory, where I was born Oct. 7, 1901, at Adair, Oklahoma. My father was a farmer. He planted oats, wheat, corn, and cotton. His special crop was sorghum cane. He had a sorghum mill, and made sorghum nearly every year. I grew up in Oklahoma, in Mayes County, near Salina.

"My husband's father, Bob Odle, and brother-in-law, Perry Hester, put in a general merchandise store in Salina. Mr. Hester decided he would rather farm, Mr. Odle bought his part of the store. We lived three miles from Salina, and my parents did their training in Mr. Odle's store. Mr. Odle also had a gristmill, where farmers took their corn to have it ground into cornmeal. We courted for a year and married. We lived around Salina and Locust Grove a few years, then we moved from Mayes County to Delaware County in 1928. I have lived in Delaware County fifty years.

"I have had lots of happiness in my life, I have also had sorrow. My husband had been married five months when his father passed away. My husband had two brothers and five sisters. They grew up being very close to each other. My husband was a farmer who worked very hard. My father and mother operated a café in Kansas in 1928. Father's health failed, so they gave the café up.

"We moved to Kenwood, Oklahoma, in 1928, where we lived for five years, then we moved seven miles east of Kenwood and lived there eight years. Our children went to school at Steely, then we moved over north of Twin Oaks, and lived there thirty-eight years. I am the mother of nine children, seven boys and two girls."

THOMAS H. BURGESS, Sr., OF MAYES CO., OKLAHOMA
[Robert Thornsberry[6]]

7a. **Thomas Henry (III)** *[son of Robert Thornsberry]*. Born 26 Sept. 1880 in Washington Co., AR. Married Mary Ann Gwartney about 1906 in Mayes Co. (she was born 10 Dec. 1887 in IT, and died 25 Jan. 1976). Listed in the 1910-20 censuses for Mayes Co., OK. Thomas H. Burgess was a farmer in Mayes Co. near Boatman, OK. He died on 15 Sept. 1958 at Pryor, OK, and is buried in the Bryan's Chapel Cemetery.

8a. **Howard H.** Born 1907 in Mayes Co., OK; died there about 1913, and is buried in the Bryan's Chapel Cemetery.

8b. **Bryant Leon.** Born 14 Mar. 1908 in Mayes Co., OK. See below for full entry.
8c. **Lucille Alma.** Born 15 Jan. 1910 in Mayes Co., OK. Married Roy Sigmund (dec.); married secondly Sam Hawkins. Lucille Hawkins died on 9 Jan. 1984 at Tulsa, OK.
8d. **Thomas Henry (IV).** Born 17 Sept. 1911 at Pryor, OK. See below for full entry.
8e. **(Daniel) Jackson (II).** Born 19 Nov. 1915 in Mayes Co., OK. See below for full entry.
8f. **Leonard Glen.** Born 17 June 1920 in Mayes Co., OK. See below for full entry.

BRYANT BURGESS OF LOS ANGELES CO., CALIFORNIA

[Robert Thornsberry[6], Thomas Henry (III)[7]]

8b. **Bryant Leon** *[son of Thomas Henry (III)].* Born 14 Mar. 1908 in Mayes Co., OK. Married Vada Lamont. Bryant Burgess was a hod carrier in the Los Angeles area, moving there about 1946. He died on 16 June 1966 at Los Angeles, CA, and is buried in the Green Hills Cemetery, Wilmington, CA. Vada Burgess was last known living at Wilmington, CA.

9a. **Shirley Ann (I).** Born 1 Dec. 1936 at Pryor, OK. Married Jerry Juhl.
9b. **Sandra Joyce.** Born 3 May 1940 at Pryor, OK. Married Odvar Connestad (dec.).
9c. **Gerri Leon.** Born 11 Jan. 1942 at Pryor, OK. Married Kaye Smittle. Gerri Burgess is a contractor in the Los Angeles area.

10a. **Mary Ann (XIII).**
10b. **Renee Lanette.** Born 15 Dec. 1963 in Los Angeles Co.

9d. **Bryant** (twin). Born and died July 1945 at Pryor, OK.
9e. **Byron** (twin). Born and died July 1945 at Pryor, OK.
9f. **Larry Bryant.** Born 5 Oct. 1947 at Torrance, CA. Married Diana Karp. Larry Burgess is an aerospace worker at El Segundo, CA.

10a. **Kimberly Marie.**
10b. **Bryant Michael.**

9g. **Starlene Lucille.** Born 19 Aug. 1950 at Torrance, CA. Married Terry L. Rowland on 15 Aug. 1969 in Los Angeles Co., CA (div.).
9h. **Sherrie Gale.** Born 25 Dec. 1954 at Torrance, CA. Married David Crockett Lawson on 19 Oct. 1985 in Clark Co., NV.
9i. **Barry Wayne.** Born 19 June 1958 at Torrance, CA. Barry Burgess works for Hughes Aircraft in the Los Angeles, CA area.

THOMAS H. BURGESS, Jr., OF MAYES CO., OKLAHOMA

[Robert Thornsberry[6], Thomas Henry (III)[7]]

8d. **Thomas Henry (IV)** *[son of Thomas Henry (III)].* Born 17 Sept. 1911 at Pryor, OK. Married (Donna) Verna Plumlee on 7 Apr. 1931 in Mayes Co. (she was born 5 Mar. 1912, and died Sept. 1990). Tom Burgess was a truck driver in California, before retiring to Pryor, OK in 1975. He died there on 9 Feb. 1985, and is buried in the Bryan's Chapel Cemetery.

9a. **(Sara) Jane** (twin). Born 9 May 1932 at Kenwood, OK. Married Marvin Garrett. Jane Garrett currently lives at Choctaw, OK.
9b. **Jackie Wayne** (twin). Born 9 May 1932 at Kenwood, OK. Married JoAnn Bonner. Jack Burgess is a maintenance man for the Riverside, CA school district. He lives at Sunnymead, CA.

10a. **Gary Leon (II).** Born 15 Jan. 1958 at Riverside, CA.
10b. **Sarah Marie.** Born 2 Feb. 1961 in Placer Co., CA. Married.
10c. **Sherry Gale.** Born 5 Feb. 1962 in Placer Co., CA. Married.
10d. **Thomas Henry (V).** Born 8 Sept. 1967 at Los Angeles, CA.

9c. **(Charles) Phillip.** Born 19 Nov. 1934 at Kenwood, OK. Married Marleen Hilbert in 1957 (div. 1980; she was born 1939). Last known living (1975) at Lameda and Torrance, CA.

10a. **Phillip Everett.** Born 21 June 1957 in Sacramento Co., CA.
10b. **Ronda Ann.** Born 10 Dec. 1962 at Los Angeles, CA. Last known living at Harbor City, CA.

10c. **Jefferey Lloyd.** Born 18 Jan. 1964 at Los Angeles, CA.
10d. **Linda Lou.** Born 21 June 1967 in Shasta Co., CA.

JACK BURGESS OF COLLIN CO., TEXAS

[Robert Thornsberry[6], Thomas Henry (III)[7]]

8e. **(Daniel) Jackson (II)** *[son of Thomas Henry (III)].* Born 19 Nov. 1915 in Mayes Co., OK. Married Cloma Mann. Jack Burgess worked for a chemical company in Houston, TX before retiring. He now lives at Wylie, TX.

9a. **Linda Lue (I).**
9b. **Sidney Ray.** He lives in New York.

8f. **Leonard Glen.** Born 17 June 1920 in Mayes Co., OK. Married Velma Coppedge on 3 June 1940 in Mayes Co. Leonard Burgess worked at the Whittaker State Home at Pryor, OK before retiring. He now lives at Kansas, OK.

9a. **Glenda Lucille.** Born 20 July 1941 at Pryor, OK. Married Tom Cantwell. Glenda Cantwell lives at Salina, OK.
9b. **James Leonard "Jimmy."** Born 2 Aug. 1945 at Pryor, OK. Married Janeen Tye. Jimmy Burgess is the Superintendent of the School District at Kansas, OK.

10a. **Tamera Len "Tammy."** Born 17 July 1969 at Siloam Springs, AR.
10b. **Treasa Ann.** Born 8 Oct. 1970 at Siloam Springs, AR.

9c. **Thomas Earl.** Born 2 Jan. 1947 at Pryor, OK. Married Jeanne Plumlee, a cousin of Verna Plumlee, wife of his uncle, Thomas H. Burgess. Tom Burgess is a bricklayer at Tulsa, OK.

10a. **James Earl.** Born 25 Aug. 1969 at Pryor, OK.
10b. **Christopher Paul.** Born 11 Jan. 1972 at Pryor, OK.
10c. **Thomas Barry.** Born 9 Feb. 1974 at Pryor, OK.

ROBERT W. BURGESS OF MAYES CO., OKLAHOMA

[Robert Thornsberry[6]]

7d. **Robert Washington** *[son of Robert Thornsberry].* Born 27 Feb. 1886 in Washington Co., AR. Married Ida Estelle Purdy on 29 Dec. 1910 at Pryor Creek, Mayes Co., OK (she was born on 26 Jan. 1889 at Augusta, GA, daughter of Thomas and Rebecca Purdy, and died 11 Oct. 1962). Listed in the 1920 census for Mayes Co., OK. Robert Burgess was a farmer at Boatman, OK until 1920, and then at Locust Grove. He later settled at Pryor in 1934, where he operated a produce store, and also was head of maintenance at the Whittaker State Home. He died on 3 Oct. 1945 at Pryor, OK, and is buried in the Pryor Cemetery.

8a. **Margaret Leona.** Born 17 Nov. 1911 at Pryor, OK. Married Watie Patillo in 1941 (he was born 6 Jan. 1899, and died 7 Feb. 1972 at Muskogee, OK), and had children: *Carolyn Sue* (born 14 Feb. 1947 at Muskogee, OK, married John William Hanson [div.], and had children: (Caroline) Nichole "Nikki" [born 3 May 1973, attends Oklahoma State University-Southwestern, Weatherford, OK, majoring in pre-pharmacy]; Margaret Ann [born 14 Oct. 1974, was a 1993 National Merit Scholar, graduated from the Oklahoma School of Science and Mathematics in 1993, and currently attends Oklahoma State University, majoring in biochemistry and pre-veterinary medicine]). Margaret Patillo lives at Miami, OK. Carolyn Hanson has been a special education instructor; she now works as a school teacher at Broken Arrow, OK.
8b. **(Robert) Newton.** Born 8 June 1913 at Boatman, OK; died there on 6 July 1922, and is buried in the Pryor Cemetery.
8c. **Doyle Eugene (I).** Born 8 Oct. 1914 at Boatman, OK. See below for full entry.
8d. **Mary Belle (II).** Born 26 Mar. 1916 at Boatman, OK. Married Ernest West on 27 May 1964 (he died 2 July 1977); married secondly Fred Coulter on 7 Jan. 1989. Mary Coulter lives at Conrad, IA.
8e. **Nannie Mae "Nan."** Born 3 Oct. 1917 at Boatman, OK. Married John C. Ford on 4 Nov. 1943 at Muskogee, OK, and had children: *John William* (born 14 Apr. 1945 at Guymon, OK, married Harriett Barnett on 19 Aug. 1966, works as a pharmacist, and had children: (Stephanie) Johnnell [born 12 June 1972 at McAlester, OK, married Darin Christopher Ramlow on 3 Nov. 1990 in Illinois];

Danae Lynn [born 30 June 1975 at McAlester, OK]). Nan Ford worked for the Southwestern Bell Telephone Co. from 1952 at McAlester, OK until her retirement. Nannie Ford, John W. Ford, and family currently live at Rockford, IL.

8f. **Irene Demoie.** Born 1 Dec. 1920 at Boatman, OK. Married Wheeler Worten on 6 Oct. 1946 (div. 1951; he may have been born 18 Aug. 1897, and died Dec. 1979 at Tulsa, OK), and had children: *Linda Lou* (born 31 July 1947 at Muskogee, OK, married Justo García Escribano on 1 Apr. 1971 [div. 1974], is employed as a social worker, and had children: Aimee [born 22 Dec. 1972]; *Linda* married secondly Jim Davies on 5 Jan. 1980, and had children: Laura Beth [born 10 Apr. 1981]; Jennifer Irene [born 1 Dec. 1983]; *Linda DAVIES* lives at Tahlequah, OK); *Karen Sue* (born 8 Dec. 1949 at Muskogee, OK, married ___ Edwards, works as a school teacher, and had children: Anthony Douglas [born 28 Apr. 1971]; *Karen* married secondly ___ Garrison, and had children: Rebecca Renée [born 19 Mar. 1976]; Robert William [born 20 Aug. 1977]; *Karen* married thirdly Frank Judkins on 16 June 1983, and lives at Broken Arrow, OK). Irene Worten worked for the Oklahoma Department of Institutions, Social and Rehabilitative Services. She currently lives at Muskogee, OK, and has contributed greatly to this book.

DOYLE E. BURGESS Sr. OF SHELBY CO., TENNESSEE

[Robert Thornsberry[6], Robert Washington[7]]

8c. **Doyle Eugene (I)** *[son of Robert Washington].* Born 8 Oct. 1914 at Boatman, OK. Married Mildred Sparks (she remarried James Hammill). Doyle Burgess Sr. was a registered pharmacist; he owned and operated the Burgess Pharmacy, part of the Rexall Drugstore chain, at Memphis, TN from 1936-64. He died there on 11 Sept. 1977, and is buried in the Memorial Park Cemetery.

9a. **(Doyle) Eugene (II).** Born 24 Oct. 1939 at Memphis, TN. Married Heather Ann Reed on 12 June 1965 at Toronto, ON, Canada (she was born 31 Mar. 1941 at Toronto, ON, daughter of Francis G. Reed and Ann Elizabeth "Lillian" Robinson; she earned a master's degree in 1985 from the Assemblies of God Seminary). Rev. Gene Burgess earned his doctorate in pharmacy in 1962 at the University of Tennessee, Memphis, TN, and his master's degree in communications in 1980 from the Assemblies of God Seminary, Springfield, MO. He was a missionary in the Philippines and Thailand for twenty years for the Assemblies of God. He now serves as pastor for the First Assembly of God Church, Munford, TN.

10a. **Deborah Michelle.** Born 29 Dec. 1969 at Memphis, TN. Married Lt. Scott Truelove on 14 Sept. 1993 at Munford, TN. Deborah Truelove earned a bachelor's degree in education and psychology from Memphis State University in 1993.

10b. **Doyle Eugene III "Som."** His nickname derives from the word for "third" in the Thai language. Born 1 Mar. 1973 at Bangkok, Thailand. Som Burgess is currently attending Memphis State University.

9b. **(Robert) Ronald (II).** Born 2 Dec. 1943 at Memphis, TN. Married (Beverly) Suzanne Strong. Ronald Burgess was Coordinator of Religious Affairs at Memphis State University; he serves as the Head of Executive Recruiting for the Promus Companies, Memphis, TN. His biography appears in *Who's Who in the South and Southwest.*

10a. **Mary Weldon.** Born 20 Dec. 1986 at Memphis, TN.

9c. **Philip Perry.** Born 4 Dec. 1946 at Memphis, TN. Philip Burgess is Head of Pharmacy Operations, Walgreen Pharmacies, Chicago, IL.

JOHN W. BURGESS OF LOS ANGELES CO., CALIFORNIA

[Robert Thornsberry[6]]

7g. **John William (II)** *[son of Robert Thornsberry].* Born 28 Aug. 1892 in Mayes Co., IT (later OK). Married Gladys Parsons on 28 Aug. 1913 in Mayes Co. (she was born 1898 in IA); married secondly Eva Hess. Listed in the 1920 census for Neodesha, Wilson Co., KS. John W. Burgess worked for the Frisco Railroad at Neodesha, KS before moving to Flint, MI, where he worked in a Chevrolet plant; after retiring, he managed the Cover Motel in Southern California. He died on 21 Apr. 1975 at Lakewood, CA, and is buried in the Green Hills Memorial Park.

8a. **Child.** Born and died about 1914.

8b. **Child.** Born and died about 1916.
8c. **(John) Basil.** Born 27 Feb. 1918 at Neodesha, KS. See below for full entry.
8d. **Charles (III).** Born 1920 at Neodesha, KS; died about 1929 at Fredonia, KS, but is buried in Neodesha, KS.
8e. **Victor Vane (I).** Born 16 Feb. 1922 at Neodesha, KS. See below for full entry.

BASIL BURGESS OF ALCORN CO., MISSISSIPPI
[Robert Thornsberry[6], John William (II)[7]]

8b. **(John) Basil** *[son of John William (II)].* Born 27 Feb. 1918 at Neodesha, KS. Married Viola R. Rolph (div.; she lives at Wichita, KS); married secondly Genie Bradbury in 1988. Listed in the 1946 city directory of Wichita, KS. Basil Burgess was a railroad engineer for the Frisco Railroad. He now lives retired at Corinth, MS.

9a. **John James (II).** Born 9 May 1944 at Festus, MO. Married Sue Scott. John Burgess is a computer programmer at Chattanooga, TN.

10a. **(John) Victor.**
10b. **James Scott.**

9b. **Sharon Ruth.** Born 2 Dec. 1948 at Wichita, KS. Married ____ Kimble. Sharon Kimble currently lives at Madison, OH.
9c. **Janice Kay.** Born 17 Jan. 1950 at Wichita, KS. Married Walter E. Miller.
9d. **Ginger Ann.** Born 6 Oct. 1952 at Wichita, KS. Married Larry Tice. Ginger Tice currently lives at Corinth, MS.

VICTOR BURGESS OF HYDABURG, ALASKA
[Robert Thornsberry[6], John William (II)[7]]

8e. **Victor Vane (I)** *[son of John William (II)].* Born 16 Feb. 1922 at Neodesha, KS. Married Lois Douglas; married secondly Viola Newman about 1976. Served in the U.S. Army Air Force during World War II. Victor Burgess moved to Hydaburg, AK, on Prince of Wales Island, in 1949, where he works as a commercial salmon fisherman.

9a. **Brian Vane (I)** (twin). Born 14 Feb. 1951 at Long Beach, CA. His common-law wife, Helen Clark, lives at Clarks Point, AK. Brian Burgess was a salmon fisherman in Bristol Bay, AK, living at Dillingham on the southwest Alaskan coast. He died on 4 July 1979 at Hydaburg, AK.

10a. **Vaughn Brian.** Born 13 Jan. 1975 in Alaska.
10b. **Brian Vane (II).** Born Mar. 1980 at Dillingham, AK.

9b. **Vicki Arlene** (twin). Born 14 Feb. 1951 at Long Beach, CA. Married Adrian Le Cornu, and had children: *Adrian Brian* (born 16 Aug. 1979); *Glen Edward* (born 18 Nov. 1981); *Jacinthe Yvone* (born 13 Sept. 1983); *Sequoia Douglas* (born 22 Oct. 1985); *Janessa Marguerite* (born 29 Oct. 1987). Vicki Le Cornu is an artist at Hydaburg, AK.
9c. **Margaret Elaine (II).** Born 7 Feb. 1954 at Hydaburg, AK. Married ___, and had children: *Victor Tumulak* (born 16 Oct. 1971); Margaret married secondly Shawn O'Neill, and had children: *Iris Jayann* (born 31 July 1978); *Valerie Katherine* (born 13 Sept. 1979); *John Galean* (born 30 May 1983). Margaret O'Neill is a social worker at Hydaburg, AK.
9d. **(Douglas) Jan.** Born 27 Feb. 1955 at Hydaburg, AK. Married Nancy Smith on 28 Jan. 1991. Jan Burgess is a commercial salmon fisherman at Hydaburg, AK.

10a. **Sara Jennifer.** Born 26 July 1992 at Hydaburg, AK.

9e. **Victor Vane (II) "Jay."** Born 21 Apr. 1956 at Hydaburg, AK. His common-law wife, Cathy Moses, lives at Fairbanks, AK. Jay Burgess was a commercial salmon fisherman on Prince of Wales Island, AK. He died there in a boating accident on 6 May 1978.

10a. **(Genevieve) Star.** Born 7 Feb. 1978 at Hydaburg, AK.

MARVIN BURGESS OF ORANGE CO., CALIFORNIA
[Robert Thornsberry[6]]

7i. **(Samuel) Marvin** *[son of Robert Thornsberry].* Born 21 Oct. 1897 in Mayes Co., IT (later OK). Married Jessie Neva Satterfield in 1919 (she was born 25 Apr. 1899, and currently lives at Palm Springs). Listed in the 1920 census in Mayes Co., OK. Marvin Burgess was a contractor at Banning and Santa Ana, CA. He died on 15 June 1969 in Orange Co., CA, and is buried in the Sunnyside Cemetery, Banning, CA.

8a. **June Marvine "Peggy."** Born 17 May 1920 at Locust Grove, OK. Married Wesley Charles Morrison in 1941 (he was born 15 Aug. 1916, and died July 1981 at Hydaburg, AK), and had children: *Shirley Jean* (born 27 Nov. 1942 at San Diego, CA, married Mansour Fazilat, and had children: Curtis Comron [born 25 July 1963]; Rodney Cambiz [born 13 June 1966]; Anthony Kavon [born 18 Feb. 1971]); *Wesley Charles Jr.* (born 4 June 1946 at Ketchikan, AK, married Barbara ___, and had children: Richard Gary [born 21 Jan. 1966]; Kimberly June [born 1 June 1969]; Amanda [born 4 Feb. 1979]); *(Neva) Marvelle* (born 20 June 1948 at Ketchican, AK, married Patrick Edward Lahmeyer on 27 May 1972 at Ketchican, and had children: Tonia Jean [born 20 Oct. 1969 at Seattle, WA, married ___ Riley, and had children: Zachary James {born 5 May 1991 at Ketchikan}]; Patrick Earl [born 25 Sept. 1979 at Ketchikan]; Jacob Wesley [born 7 May 1984 at Ketchikan]; *Marvelle* lives at Ward Cove, AK). Peggy Morrison lives with her daughter, Shirley, at Duluth, GA.

8b. **Sara Elizabeth.** Born 19 Oct. 1921 at Locust Grove, OK. Married Rupert Hinkle, and had children: *Thomas* (uses the name Hoffman); married secondly Sam Hoffman, and thirdly Jack V. Winner on 24 Feb. 1962 in Imperial Co., CA. Sara Winner currently lives at Palm Springs, CA.

8c. **(Samuel) Eugene (I).** Born 30 Mar. 1923 at Locust Grove, OK. Married Patricia H. (Saint) Roberts on 8 Oct. 1950 in Los Angeles Co., CA. (she was the daughter of George and Dorothy Saint of Yreka, CA). Gene Burgess worked as a contractor at Yreka, CA, Hawaii, and Manhattan Beach, CA. He currently lives retired at Palm Springs, CA.

9a. **Holly Sue.** Born 1955. Married Matthew C. O'Donnell on 6 Feb. 1981 in Contra Costa Co., CA (div.). Holly Burgess works as an attorney in the Los Angeles area.

9b. **Lori Jean.** Born 30 Sept. 1957 at Fullerton, Orange Co., CA. Lori Burgess is a law clerk in Ventura Co.

9c. **Samuel Eugene (II).** Born 15 May 1959 at Fullerton, Orange Co., CA. Sam Burgess was a construction worker for his father, moving to Hawaii in 1979. He died unmarried (killed) on 6 July 1980 at South Kona, HI, but is buried in the Evergreen Cemetery, Yreka, CA.

9d. **Paul C.** Born 28 Sept. 1960 at Yreka, CA. Living at Manhattan Beach, CA in the 1980s.

8d. **Bobby Mae.** Born 11 Feb. 1926 at Locust Grove, OK. Married Michael Pike, and had children: *Nancy Ann*; *Michael Jr.* Married secondly Walter Samson.

8e. **(Harriet) Joan.** Born 2 June 1932 at Locust Grove, OK. Married Judd Gregory, and had children: *Robert*; *Katherine Ann*; *David*. Joan lives at Santa Barbara, CA.

8f. **Jerry Lee (I).** Born 15 Aug. 1934 at Locust Grove, OK. Married ___, by whom he had his son. Married second Audrey ___. Jerry Burgess lives at Yakima, WA.

9a. **Marvin Wayne.** Born about 1956. Married.

10a. **Jeremy.**

10b. **Daughter.**

[William (I)[1], Edward (I)[2], Reuben (I)[3], Thomas (I)[4]]

HIRAM BURGESS
(1820-1910)
OF CUMBERLAND COUNTY, TENNESSEE

5k. **(King) Hiram (I)** *[son of Thomas (I)].* Born 6 June 1820 near Bunker Hill, White (later Putnam) Co., TN. According to oral tradition said to have married an Indian woman about 1837 (no record); married secondly Nancy Grace Campbell on 24 May 1838 in White Co., TN, with Rev. Levi Perkins performing the ceremony (she was born 8 Jan. 1822 [or 8 Feb. 1822, according to the Bible record of Richard Lafayette Burgess] in TN, daughter of Daniel Campbell and Martha "Patsy" Allison, who was a sister of Ruth Allison [who married Hiram's brother, Joel Burgess], and died on 4 May 1897). Listed in the 1840 census for the 12th District, Jackson Co., TN (next to his brother, Washington Burgess, with one son under the age of five), in 1850 in Bledsoe Co., TN (the section that became Cumberland Co. in 1856), and from 1860-80 in Cumberland Co. (in 1860 at Bee Creek; in 1870 Grace's mother Martha Campbell is living with them); living with his daughter, Emily Scarborough, at Bonair, White Co., TN in 1900.

Hiram is said to have enlisted in the U.S. Army about 1837 to help move the Cherokee Indians out of Georgia, but returned home after receiving a plea from his mother. Hiram Burgess settled near Winesap, just east of the point where the boundaries of Cumberland, Putnam, and White Cos. now intersect, about 1847. With his brothers he signed the 11 Feb. 1854 petition to the Tennessee State Legislature to erect the new county of Putnam. A lengthy biography in the 3 Feb. 1897 issue of the *Crossville Chronicle* (see below) gives his full name and date of birth, and provides many details about his life; eleven of fourteen children survived at this time (but are not mentioned by name). He was a member of the Free-Will Baptist Church from 1846. Hiram Burgess, patriarch of the largest single (and most junior) branch of the Burgess family, died on 8 Feb. 1910 at Crossville, TN, just short of his 90th birthday, and three days before his last sister, Mary, and is buried with his wife and some of his descendants in the Old Burgess Cemetery, now located on a hill overlooking the farm of his great-great-granddaughter, Mrs. Oma Hubbard. No stone remains on his tomb.

The Children of Hiram Burgess:

6a. **(Joseph) Daniel.** Born Mar. 1839 in White (later Putnam) Co., TN. See below for full entry.

6b. **(Martha) Emiline "Emily."** Born 26 Mar. 1841 in White (later Putnam) Co., TN. Married Alexander Russell (or Richard) "Alex" Scarbrough about 1855 (he was born 14 Feb. 1834 in TN, son of William Scarbrough and Susannah Bumbalough, and died 3 Sept. 1897), and had children:

(James) Hiram SCARBROUGH. Born 1856 at Pomona, TN. "He and Mr. Dugger were out coon hunting, and the dogs treed a coon in a hollow tree, so they built in the tree, laid down and went to sleep. The tree burned off, fell on Hiram, and killed him. My grandfather Ves said he was eighteen years old at his death, and the first person buried in the Thomas Springs Cemetery."—J. Fred Scarbrough.

(John) Milton SCARBROUGH. Born 24 Apr. 1859 at Pomona, TN, married Sarah Dennise Russell, and died 13 Mar. 1920, buried Stringtown Cemetery.

(Isaac) Sylvester "Ves" SCARBROUGH. Born 14 Feb. 1861 at Bon Air, TN, married Catherine Jane Houlette on 29 June 1888, and died 7 Dec. 1941 at Summitville, Coffee Co., TN, having had at least the following children: *(John) Frederick "Fred"* (born 7 Nov. 1890 at Clifty, TN, married Maggie Jaretha Tucker on 17 Apr. 1917 at Lewisburg, TN [she was born 22 Jan. 1891 at Summitville, Coffee Co., TN, daughter of Jason Pearson Tucker and Sarah Elizabeth Fletcher, and died on 30 July 1975 at Murfreesboro, TN, and is buried in the Lone Oak Cemetery, Lewisburg, TN], and had children: (John) Frederick Jr. "Fred" [born 14 June 1918 at Ravescroft, White Co., TN, married Pearl Clark McBroom on 23 Nov. 1938 at Lynchburg, Moore Co., TN {she was born 9 Jan. 1921 at Readyville, Cannon Co., TN, daughter of Claude Lee McBroom and Mary Frances Todd, and was an elementary school teacher}, and had children: John Frederick III {born 13 Aug. 1941 at Murfreesboro, TN, married Martha Faye

Wiser, a mathematics professor, on 15 June 1967 <she was born 3 Feb. 1952, daughter of Horace and Bessie Wiser>, earned his doctoral degree in education from Middle Tennessee State University, and is a college professor at Motlow College, teaching history, psychology, and archaeology}; Martha Claudia {born 3 Feb. 1952 at Murfreesboro, TN, married (Timothy) Wayne Musselwhite on 14 Aug. 1971 <he was born 23 Oct. 1949 at Chattanooga, TN, son of Robert Clayton Musselwhite and Dorothy Jean Haun>, and works as a senior negotiator for the Jet Propulsion Laboratory at Pasadena, CA}; Wilma Jean [born 25 Mar. 1920 at Manchester, Coffee Co., TN, and died of leukemia on 21 Oct. 1929 at Elora, Lincoln Co., TN]; Katherine Elizabeth [born 27 Apr. 1923 at Elora, TN, and died of uremic poisoning on 10 May 1923 at Elora]; Theodore Sylvester [born 9 Aug. 1924 at Elora, TN, married Jane Neeley on 25 Dec. 1947, and died 4 Feb. 1993 at Belfast, Marshall Co., TN]; James Robert [born 2 Aug. 1926 at Summitville, TN, married Lurah Faye Ingle on 11 Oct. 1947]; William Henry [born 3 Feb. 1929 at Elora, TN, married Myrtle Dell Wright on 24 Jan. 1956]. Fred Scarbrough was a telegraph operator and depot agent for the North Carolina and St. Louis Railway for fifty years, and a member of the Church of Christ. Margaret Jaretha Scarbrough was a school teacher and rate clerk for the Railway Express Agency. Fred Scarbrough Jr. earned his B.S. from Middle Tennessee State College and his master's degree from the University of Tennessee. He has been a teacher of agriculture and a work unit conservationist for the Soil Conservation Service of the U.S. Department of Agriculture.

William Franklin SCARBROUGH. Born 13 Jan. 1864 at Solon, TN, married Mary Francis Russell, and died 15 May 1926 at Swan Pond, Roane Co., TN.

Gilbert L. SCARBROUGH. Born 1865 at Solon, TN, died 1884 of appendicitis, buried Thomas Springs Cemetery.

(Annie) Belzora "Bell" SCARBROUGH. Born 25 Dec. 1867 at Solon, TN, married John Bennett in 1887, married secondly John West, married thirdly William Payton, and died 3 Jan. 1909, buried Stringtown Cemetery.

Richard P. SCARBROUGH. Born 1869 at Solon, died 1879, buried Thomas Springs Cemetery.

Lewis SCARBROUGH. Born 1870 at Solon, TN, married ___ Brewer. "He was supposed to have killed a man and family, left Tennessee, and we have not had any contact since about 1910."—J. Fred Scarbrough.

(Sarah) Elizabeth "Lizzie" SCARBROUGH. Born 7 Mar. 1872 at Clifty, TN, married Hill J. Cannon, and died 1 Jan. 1950 at Harriman, Roane Co., TN.

(George) Monroe "Mon" SCARBROUGH. Born 1874 at Clifty, TN, married Margaret "Maggie" Page, and died 1939 at Smith Chapel, TN.

Nancy "Nan" SCARBROUGH. Born 11 July 1876 at Clifty, TN, married Robert Lee "Bob" Page on 5 Aug. 1892, and died 3 Dec. 1965 at Clifty, TN.

Martha Jane "Mattie" SCARBROUGH. Born 30 Sept. 1878 at Clifty, TN, married Charles Passons, married secondly Noble Clark White, and died 30 Jan. 1968 at Pulaski, Giles Co., TN.

Ethel Dorena SCARBROUGH. Born 30 Sept. 1879 at Clifty, TN, married Frank Monroe Driver on 15 Dec. 1895, and died 8 Oct. 1943 when she was hit by a train in West Virginia, and is buried in the Stringtown Cemetery. "The train was coasting, she was hard of hearing and wearing a bonnet, and did not hear the train."—J. Fred Scarbrough.

Bertha Agnes SCARBROUGH. Born 10 Sept. 1881 at Clifty, TN, married Joe Eans Little on 26 June 1899, and died 28 June 1968 at Palatka, Putnam Co., FL.

Mary Zettie SCARBROUGH. Born 1 May 1884 at Clifty, TN, married Thomas Christopher Parks, and died 6 Apr. 1923 at Lost Creek, TN.

Martha Emaline SCARBROUGH is listed with her husband in the 1860-80 censuses for the 2nd District, Cumberland Co., and in 1900 at Bonair, White Co., TN (her father is recorded with her in this census). She died on 2 Mar. 1909 at Clifty, White Co., TN, aged 71 (or 67) years, 4 months, and 21 days, and is buried with her husband in the Stringtown Cemetery, White Co., TN. Her great-grandson (the grandson of Isaac Sylvester Scarbrough), (John) Frederick Scarbrough Jr., lives at Murfreesboro, TN, and has contributed greatly to this book.

6c. **Mary A(deline?).** Born about 1843 in White (later Putnam) Co., TN. She may have married Jasper L. M(o)yers about 1862 (he was born 1843 in TN, son of Alexander and Catharine Moyers), and may be listed with him in the 1870-80 censuses for the 2nd District, Cumberland Co. with children: *Willie Th.* (he is called Wiley in the 1880 census; born 1863); *Dorthula A.* (born 1865); *(James) Dillard* (born 1867); *Helan M. "Adlia"* (born 1869). By inference she is living in 1897, but died before 1937.

6d. **John Anderson (II).** Born 10 Apr. 1846 in White (later Putnam) Co., TN. See below for full entry.

6e. **Child.** Born and died about 1848 in Bledsoe (later Cumberland) Co.

6f. **(Elizabeth) Jane (II).** Born 28 Mar. 1850 in Bledsoe (later Cumberland) Co., TN. Listed with her father in the 1870 census. According to Oma Hubbard and Lottie Brewer, Jane Burgess had her arm torn off in a mill accident, and died there unmarried on 14 Mar. 1871. She is said to have been buried in the Old Burgess Cemetery, but has no headstone.

6g. **Child.** Born and died about 1851 in Bledsoe (later Cumberland) Co., TN.

6h. **Isabell C.** Born about 1853 in Bledsoe (later Cumberland) Co., TN. She is believed to have married (Martin) Lafayette Stone about 1868 (she is not with her father in the 1870 census; he was born 1846 in GA, son of Ephraim and Catherine Stone), and may be listed with him in the 1870-80 censuses for Cumberland Co., TN, with the following children: *Nancy A. C.* (born 1869); *Elizabeth* (born 1871); *Dilley* (born 1874); *Tillie* (born 1876); *America* (born 1878); *Steffen* (born Feb. 1880). By inference she is living in 1897, but dead by 1937.

6i. **William Kimsy.** Born 27 Aug. 1855 in Bledsoe (later Cumberland) Co., TN. See below for full entry.

6j. **Rutha Campbell M(oyers?) "Ruth."** Born Oct. 1858 in Cumberland Co., TN. Married her first cousin, John Wyatt Campbell, about 1878 (he was born 17 Nov. 1856, the son of Joseph D. Campbell and Elizabeth A. Allison, and brother of Washington Columbus and James E. Campbell, and died 1942; Joseph D. Campbell was the son of Daniel Campbell and brother of Nancy Grace Campbell, who married Rutha's father), and had children:

Eva CAMPBELL. Born 1879, died before 1900.

Leonard A. CAMPBELL. Born 20 Aug. 1881, married Josie Mae Davis on 7 Aug. 1910 in Cumberland Co. [she was born 21 Mar. 1891, and died 2 June 1969], and died 14 Feb. 1970, buried Davis Cemetery.

Bishop CAMPBELL. Born Mar. 1886, married Vinnie Moyers on 17 Feb. 1910 in Cumberland Co.

Amy CAMPBELL. Her name is listed as Annie in her marriage record. Born Aug. 1888, married Posey Wilson on 10 Dec. 1905 in Cumberland Co.

Lovada "Vatia" CAMPBELL. Born Jan. 1896, married Thomas Webb on 22 Dec. 1912 in Cumberland Co.

Ruth CAMPBELL is listed in the 1880-1910 censuses for Cumberland Co., TN; four of five children survive in 1900-10. Her husband was accused and convicted of murdering his brother-in-law, Charlie Burgess, but was not popularly believed to have done so. Ruth Campbell died 1939 in Cumberland Co., TN, and is buried with her husband in the Newton Cemetery.

6k. **(Jasper) Patrick Dillard "Pee."** Born 28 Dec. 1860 in Cumberland Co., TN. See below for full entry.

6l. **Charles William (I).** Born 10 Feb. 1863 in Cumberland Co., TN. See below for full entry.

6m. **(Tressa) Malissa Ann.** Born May 1865 in Cumberland Co., TN. Married as his second wife Patrick Henry Norris about 1882 (he was born 1858 in TN, son of Abner Norris and Elizabeth Queenie Lowe, married firstly Elizabeth ___, and died about 1885), and had children:

Gracie NORRIS. Born Apr. 1883, married ___ Owensby.

Malissa NORRIS married secondly her first cousin, John Henry Campbell, about 1887 (he was born Apr. 1871 in TN, son of Washington Columbus and Eliza Campbell, and may have died 23 Aug. 1916, buried in the Clifty Cemetery; Washington Columbus Campbell was the son of Daniel Campbell and brother of Nancy Grace Campbell, who married Malissa's father), and had children:

J. Victory CAMPBELL. Listed as Victor Campbell in the 1900 census. Born Dec. 1887, married Louise Thomas on 23 Feb. 1906 in Cumberland Co., and had children: *Irl* (born 1908); *Eldia* (born 1909). Listed in the 1910 census for Cumberland Co.

Vena CAMPBELL. Listed as Xena in the 1900 census. Born July 1891, married, and moved to Arkansas; her body was returned to Cumberland Co. for burial.

Lester CAMPBELL. Born Feb. 1895.

Cleo CAMPBELL. Born about 1902.

Malissa and John CAMPBELL are listed in the 1900 census for Cumberland Co., TN (four of six children then survive), but have not been found in 1910. She is mentioned in the 19 Nov. 1931 issue of the *Crossville Chronicle* (column dated 29 Oct.), but died by Feb. 1937, when William Kimsy Burgess's obituary fails to mention her. The Campbells may have moved to Arkansas.

6n. **Richard Lafayette "Fate."** Born 12 July 1867 in Cumberland Co., TN. See below for full entry.

"UNCLE" HIRAM BURGESS

"The subject of this sketch was born near Bunker's Hill, in White (now Putnam) County, June 6, 1820. At the age of seventeen he enlisted as a soldier under Grand Staff to assist in removing the Cherokee Indians from this part of the country, but, at the urgent request of his parents, he was excused. When he lacked of being eighteen years of age, he was married to Miss Nancy Campbell. They moved to the place where they now live, near Winesap, fifty years ago.

"This old couple have passed their Golden Wedding Anniversary by eight years, keeping house and living together as lovingly and agreeably as they did when they became one over fifty-eight years ago. How few there are who can show such a record! Fourteen children were born to them, eleven of whom still survive and live on adjoining farms. Grandchildren and great-grandchildren are almost innumerable.

"As his name implies, King Hiram Burgess is verily the king of his own kingdom. 'Uncle' Hiram delights in telling of the bygone days; of his conduct and mode of living. He was never drunk in his life; never used profane language; was never seriously sick; never had a fight or any difficulty; never had a lawsuit; and has been a member of the Free-Will Baptist Church for fifty-one years.

"When he came to the Plateau, fifty years ago, there were no roads here, he says—only hog paths, no saw mills, no postoffices, no mail routes, no school or church houses, no stores nearer than Sparta, no mill except the famous "Scarberry" Mill on the Caney Fork River; and no nails. When they wanted to floor their houses, they were compelled to split and hew puncheon, and then pin them down with wooden pins in lieu of nails. He invited the writer's attention to the floor he had laid in that way fifty years ago, and the proof was conclusive.

"Their neighbors were the Moyers, Lewis, and Wyatts, with a few more distant. They had no turning plows nor mowing machines, wagons, or buggies, for they did not need them. Their living was in the woods. What few cattle and sheep they had lived all winter without feed. 'Uncle' Hiram says he remembers well of feeding his horse only thirty-five small binds of fodder during the whole winter, and he kept fat on it. The hogs ran wild, and grew fat on the mast, which never failed in those days. The woods were full of wild game, such as deer and turkeys, and it was no trouble to kill as many as wanted any day. It was their money, their bread, and their all.

"'Uncle' Hiram is now nearly seventy-seven years of age, is as spry as a boy, and can walk twenty miles in half a day easily. He still sticks to his first love—hunting—but on account of the scarcity of game compared with his boyhood days, he mourns his lost opportunities. To the writer of this sketch, he said: 'Oh, how I wish it was like it used to be here. I would give anything if I could make it like it was when I first came here!' He still possesses the old gun with which he brought all his revenue from the woods. He has refused seventy-five dollars for it at different times, nor can it be bought today for that amount.

"No one knows 'Uncle' Hiram but to love and respect him. He always greets you with a smile and an outstretched hand. He owes no man—in short, he is one of the 'noblest works of God'—an honest man."—M.S.J., *Crossville Chronicle*, 3 Feb. 1897.

(back) Victor Campbell, Gracie Norris, Malissa Burgess Campbell
(front) King Hiram Burgess, Nancy Grace Campbell Burgess, John Henry Campbell, Vena Campbell, circa 1895

[William (I)[1], Edward (I)[2], Reuben (I)[3], Thomas (I)[4], King Hiram (I)[5]]

JOSEPH DANIEL BURGESS
(1839-1913)

OF CUMBERLAND COUNTY, TENNESSEE

6a. **(Joseph) Daniel** *[son of King Hiram (I)].* Born Mar. 1839 in White (later Putnam) Co. TN. Married (Mary) Elizabeth Blaylock about 1855 (she was born 4 Nov. 1837 [or 1838], daughter of William Blaylock and Nancy Neely, and died 3 May 1926). Listed in the 1860-1910 censuses for Cumberland Co., TN; eight of twelve children survive in 1900-10; Elizabeth Burgess is living with her son, Owen, in 1920. Daniel Burgess was a farmer in Cumberland Co., at one time owning over 1000 acres of land there. He died on 7 Jan. 1913 at Winesap, and is buried with his wife in the Burgess Cemetery. His obituary states that he was survived by his wife and seven sons.

The Children of Daniel Burgess:

7a. **William L(ester?) (I).** Born Apr. 1856 in Cumberland Co., TN. See below for full entry.
7b. **(Hiram) Simpson.** Born 8 Feb. 1859 in Cumberland Co., TN. See below for full entry.
7c. **(John) Willis.** Born 25 Mar. 1861 in Cumberland Co., TN. See below for full entry.
7d. **Thomas Anderson.** Born 17 Feb. 1863 in Cumberland Co., TN. See below for full entry.
7e. **Richard M(oyers?).** Born June 1865 in Cumberland Co., TN. See below for full entry.
7f. **Mary Isabel.** Born June 1867 in Cumberland Co., TN. Married Ezra Stonecipher about 1888 (he was born June 1847 TN), and had children: *Effie* (born May 1889 in MO); *Orlando* (born May 1891 in MO); *Bertha E.* (born Sept. 1893 in MO); *Josie M.* (born June 1898 in MO). Listed in the 1900 census for Webster Co., MO, but has not been found in 1910. She appears to have died before her father (1913). Several of her children were still living in Missouri as late as the 1950s, when they were visited by their cousin, (Fronia) Alice Scott.
7g. **Daniel M(anning?).** He may have been named for Daniel Manning, "cattle king of the plateau." Born Oct. 1869 in Cumberland Co., TN. Said to have died there unmarried of pneumonia about 1890.
7h. **Joseph Mansfield.** Born 28 Mar. 1872 in Cumberland Co., TN. See below for full entry.
7i. **(Isaac) Jacob.** Born 8 Dec. 1873 in Cumberland Co., TN. See below for full entry.
7j. **George (III).** Born about 1876 in Cumberland Co., TN; died young between 1880-1900.
7k. **(James) Andrew.** Born about 1878 in Cumberland Co., TN; died young between 1880-1900.
7l. **Owen Washington.** Born 10 Jan. 1881 in Cumberland Co., TN. See below for full entry.

[William (I)[1], Edward (I)[2], Reuben (I)[3], Thomas (I)[4], King Hiram (I)[5], Joseph Daniel[6]]

WILLIAM L. BURGESS
(1856-1940)

OF CUMBERLAND COUNTY, TENNESSEE

7a. **William L(ester?) (I) "Level-Headed Bill"** *[son of Joseph Daniel].* His middle initial is given as "T" in the 1860 census, but is listed consistently as "L" in all other records. Born Apr. 1856 in Cumberland Co., TN. Married Mary E. Bolin about 1874 (she was born June 1858 in TN, daughter of Samuel and Mar]garet J. Bolin, and died 2 July 1939 at Taylors Chapel, TN, aged 80 years). Listed in the 1880-1920 censuses for Cumberland Co., TN (in 1920 aged 62); ten of eleven children survive in 1900, ten of twelve in 1910. Bill Burgess was a farmer and carpenter in Cumberland Co.; he was also elected Constable of the Fifth District of Cumberland Co. on 7 Aug. 1918. He died there on 9 Mar. 1940, and is buried with his wife in the Bolin Cemetery.

8a. **(Catherine) Rose.** She is called Rosie in the 1900 census. Born Mar. 1875 (or 1876) in Cumberland Co., TN. Married Jiles (or Giles or Charles) M. Blaylock about 1895 (he was born Mar. 1856 [or 1858] in TN, son of Michael and Mary J. Blaylock, and brother of Martha E.; by another wife he had children: *Mary* [born Oct. 1885]; *Davie* [born June 1886]; *Andy* [born Feb. 1888]), and had children: *Allice* (born June 1898). Listed in the 1900 census for White Co. with her husband. Said to have died in Colorado, by inference before 1964.

8b. **(Carl?) Howard.** Listed as Caralberd in the 1880 census. Born about 1878 in Cumberland Co., TN; died there about 1887.

8c. **Elizabeth (XIX).** Born Jan. 1880 in Cumberland Co., TN. Married ___ VanWinkle, and may appear there with her brother-in-law, John VanWinkle, in the 1900 census. She is said to have died shortly thereafter (but in any case by 1964), and is buried in the Thomas Springs Cemetery. She or her sister Rose died before 1910, according to her mother's 1910 census record.

8d. **(William) Vance (II).** Born 9 Apr. 1882 in Cumberland Co., TN. See below for full entry.

8e. **(General) Marion.** Born 29 Mar. 1885 in Cumberland Co., TN. See below for full entry.

8f. **German Samuel.** Born 26 Apr. 1886 in Cumberland Co., TN. See below for full entry.

8g. **Virgil Harrison.** Born 26 Mar. 1888 in Cumberland Co., TN. See below for full entry.

8h. **Sarah (XIII).** Born Oct. 1889 in Cumberland Co., TN. Married (Charles) Maxwell "Mack" Randolph on 31 Dec. 1906 in Cumberland Co. (he may have been born 14 Sept. 1887 in TN, son of William Madison "Matt" Randolph and Sarah Ann Rice, and died June 1969 at Frankfort, Clinton Co., IN; he was the brother of Bertha Randolph, who married Sarah's brother, Vance Burgess, and is mentioned as living in Indiana in 1964), and had fourteen children, including: *Lena B.* (born 1910 in TN); *Lela* (born 1913 in TN); *Margie M.* (born 1915 in TN); *Ivy* (born 1916 in TN); *Casto* (born 1917 in TN). Listed in the 1920 census for Cumberland Co., TN. Sarah Randolph died before 1964 in Indiana.

8i. **Flora A.** Born 8 Aug. 1893 in Cumberland Co., TN. Married Willie Hyder on 17 Sept. 1911 in Cumberland Co. Flora Hyder died on 19 Jan. 1923 in White Co., TN, and is buried in the Eastland Cemetery.

8j. **Josie E.** Born May 1895 in Cumberland Co., TN. Listed in the 1920 census for White Co., TN, working as a servant for Florence Bumgarner. Married Everett Smith on 12 Mar. 1920 in White Co. By inference she died before 1964.

8k. **Myrtle L. "Mertie."** Her name is listed as Merta in the 1900 census. Born 24 May 1898 in Cumberland Co., TN. Listed in the 1920 census for White Co., TN. Living at Detroit, MI in 1940, and at Jacksonville, FL in 1965. She died in May 1972, apparently unmarried, at Venice, Sarasota Co., FL.

8l. **Ernest Thomas.** Born 1901 in Cumberland Co., TN. See below for full entry.

VANCE BURGESS OF WHITE CO., TENNESSEE

[William Lester (I)^7]

8d. **(William) Vance (II)** *[son of William Lester (I)].* Born 9 Apr. 1882 (or 1881, according to his obituary and draft record) in Cumberland Co., TN. Married Bertha May Randolph on 25 Oct. 1902 in Cumberland Co. (she was born 3 May 1890 [or 1889], daughter of William Madison Randolph and Sarah Ann Rice, and sister of Mack Randolph, who married Vance's sister, Sarah Burgess, and died 16 Sept. 1964). Listed in the 1910 census for Cumberland Co., and in the 1918 draft register and 1920 of Ravenscroft, White Co., TN. Rev. Vance Burgess was a coal mine elevator operator in Cumberland Co., and also a minister for the Church of Christ from 1910-58, serving twenty-two churches in five counties. He died there on 28 Mar. 1964, and is buried with his wife in the Never Fail Cemetery. His obituary mentions as surviving siblings only his brothers German and Virgil and his sister Myrtle.

9a. **Louella** (nmn). Born 3 June 1904 in Cumberland Co., TN. Married Charles Smith on 4 Mar. 1920 in White Co. Louella Smith lives at Oak Ridge, TN.

9b. **Roxie Lee.** Born 10 (or 19) Aug. 1906 in Cumberland Co., TN. Married her distant cousin, Nathan England (he was born 9 July 1905, daughter of John England and Mollie Burgess, and died Jan. 1987 at Crossville, TN), and had at least the following children: *Nathan H.*; *Bill*; *Gennevie* (married ___ Hamill). Roxie England died on 12 Dec. 1971 at Logan (or Monaville), WV, but is buried in the Never Fail Cemetery, Cumberland Co., TN.

9c. **(William) Lester (II).** Born 15 Aug. 1908 in Cumberland Co., TN. Les Burgess was a shoe repairman in Cumberland co. He died there unmarried in a house fire on 11 Jan. 1977, and is buried in the Never Fail Cemetery.

9d. **Sada Mae "Sadie."** Born 30 Sept. 1910 in Cumberland Co., TN. Married Oscar Boyd on 10 Aug. 1925 in White Co.; married secondly (Joel) Charles Perry on 16 Aug. 1927 in White Co., and had children: *Jack*; *Dick*; *Darwin*; *Joe*. Sadie Perry lives at Fairborn, OH.

9e. **Dallas Franklin.** Born 18 Sept. 1912 in Cumberland Co., TN. See below for full entry.

9f. **Clara Bell.** Her middle name is given as Belle in her marriage record. Born 18 Aug. 1914 in Cumberland Co., TN. Married Ed Ross Coleman on 8 Dec. 1928 in White Co. (he was born 2 Feb. 1909, and died Apr. 1975 at Crossville, TN), and had children: *Bobby Joe* (dec.); *Mary Frances* (married Kenneth Bache, and lived at Washington, DC); married secondly Kenneth Rhea Dunbar on 11 July 1952 in Cumberland Co. (dec.); married thirdly Bill Buska. Clara Buska lives at New Port Richey, FL.

9g. **Leo** (nmn). Born 7 Nov. 1916 in Cumberland Co., TN; died there in Feb. 1917, and is buried in the Never Fail Cemetery.

9h. **Mary Ann (IX).** Her name is given as Mary Anna in the 1920 census. Born 6 Nov. 1917 in Putnam Co., TN. Married Cornell C. Cobb on 19 May 1934 in Cumberland Co. (he died on 3 July 1976 at Crossville, TN), and had children: *Betty Jean* (born 21 Jan. 1936, married William Ealey); *Patty Ann* (born 18 Feb. 1938, married Austin Ealey); *James R. "Jimmy"* (born 19 Feb. 1940, married Willadean Barnes); *Lou Nell* (born 17 June 1941, married Perry Bartlett); *Charles* (born 28 Dec. 1942, married Phyllis Whiteaker, and had children: Julie Ann [born 2 Jan. 1969 in Putnam Co., TN]; David Charles [born 27 Aug. 1971 in Putnam Co., TN]); *Ronald Eugene* (born 12 Nov. 1945, married Patricia Lea); *Joanna* (born 25 Aug. 1948, married Dale Allen); *Nancy Jane* (born 12 Feb. 1954, married Randy Thompson); *Mary Linda* (born 17 Dec. 1959). Mary Cobb lives near Crossville, TN.

9i. **James Edward (V).** Born 5 June 1920 in Putnam Co., TN. See below for full entry.

9j. **Kenneth Vance (I).** Born 31 Oct. 1922 in White Co., TN. See below for full entry.

9k. **(Lillian) Anthanette "Antha."** Born 23 Jan. 1924 in Putnam Co., TN. Married Frank Hargis Jr. Anthanette Hargis lives at Chattanooga, TN.

9l. **(Ila) Jean.** Born 27 Apr. 1927 in Putnam Co., TN. Married Reece Pickett on 8 Feb. 1947 at Rossville, GA. Jean Pickett died on 5 Sept. 1990 at Chattanooga, TN.

DALLAS F. BURGESS OF WILLIAMSON CO., TENNESSEE

[William Lester (I)^7, William Vance (II)^8]

9e. **Dallas Franklin** *[son of William Vance (II)].* Born 18 Sept. 1912 in Cumberland Co., TN. Married Verda "Versie" Selby on 8 Dec. 1928 in White Co., TN (she was born 9 Dec. 1911, and died May 1979 at Franklin, TN); married secondly Viola Collier. Dallas Burgess worked for Chrysler Corp. in Michigan for 32 years before retiring. He now lives at Franklin, TN.

10a. **Son.** Born 23 Aug. 1930 in White Co., TN; died there on 30 Aug. 1930, and is buried in the Lower Board Valley Cemetery, White Co., TN.

10b. **Billie Franklin.** Born 11 Oct. 1932 in White Co., TN. Married Joyce Evans. The Rev. Bill Burgess is a Minister for the Church of Christ, at Oscoda, MI.

11a. **Peggy Ann.** Born 31 Aug. 1957 at Plattsburgh, NY. Married Randall Reberg (div.). Peggy Reberg lives at Muskegon, MI.

11b. **Larry Franklin (II).** Born 27 Feb. 1959 at Plattsburgh, NY. Married Teresa Smith. Larry Burgess is Director of Information Systems, Jersey Shore Medical Center, at Neptune, NJ, and lives at Manalapan, NJ.

12a. **Meredith Leigh.** Born 18 Jan. 1984 at Dallas, TX.

11c. **Susan Lee (II).** Born 1 Nov. 1964 at Dearborn, MI. Married Michael Ray on 20 Aug. 1988. Susan Ray is a school teacher in Ohio.

11d. **Sandra Kay (IV).** Born 17 June 1971 at Midland, MI.

10c. **Jennings Bryan "Bud."** Born 27 Dec. 1936 in Scott Co., TN. Married Linda Reynolds. A certified public accountant, Bud Burgess is Controller of Thompson & Green, at La Vergne, TN. He currently lives at Brentwood, TN.

11a. **Rita Kay.** Born 25 Nov. 1959 at Nashville, TN. Married David Lyle Solomon. Rita Solomon lives at Nashville, TN.

11b. **Terry Allen (II).** Born 2 May 1962 at Nashville, TN. Married. Dr. Terry Burgess is a dentist at Russellville, AL.

12a. **Allen (II)** (twin). Born 7 Sept. 1987.

12b. **Will** (twin). Born 7 Sept. 1987.

11c. **Stephen Paul.** Born 26 Feb. 1965 at Nashville, TN. Married Michelle ___. Steve Burgess attended Tennessee Technological University, Cookeville, TN.

10d. **Carol Ann (I).** Born 3 Aug. 1945 at Detroit, MI. Married Bernie Wagers. Carol Wagers is a school teacher at Milford, MI.

JAMES E. BURGESS OF HAMILTON CO., TENNESSEE

[William Lester (I)[7], William Vance (II)[8]]

9i. **James Edward (V)** *[son of William Vance (II)].* Born 5 June 1920 in Putnam Co., TN. Married Lenora Markham (div.; she married secondly Lewis Allen, and lives at Atlanta, GA); married secondly Julia Ruth King. James E. Burgess was a coal miner in WV, and also worked as a chef in TN. He died on 28 July 1980 at Chattanooga, TN.

10a. **Judith Kay.** Born 21 Dec. 1946 at Oneida, TN. Married Leslie Allen Holaday on 29 June 1968 in Cumberland Co. (div.). Judith Holaday lives at Nashville, TN.

10b. **Lynda Cheryl.** Born 29 Oct. 1948 at Oneida, TN. Married Larry Thomas Green on 21 June 1969 in Cumberland Co. (dec.), and had two children.

10c. **(James) Richard (VI) "Rick."** Born 15 Aug. 1952 at Montgomery, WV. Married Patty ___. Rick Burgess works for the gas company at Akron, OH.

11a. **Julia Leigh.** Born 15 May 1982 at Akron, OH.

10d. **Royce Edward.** Born 13 May 1954 at Montgomery, WV. Married Janie Lou Threet. Royce Burgess is a property appraiser for the State of Tennessee, at Crossville, TN.

11a. **(Royce) Eric.** Born 27 Dec. 1974 at Crossville, TN.

11b. **Tessa.**

10e. **Melissa Anne "Missi."** Her middle name is listed as Dane on her marriage record. Born 29 July 1956 at Montgomery, WV. Married (Robert) Patrick Caudle on 6 Aug. 1977 in Cumberland Co.

10f. **Cynthia Jean "Cindy."** Born 28 Oct. 1957 at Montgomery, WV. Cindy Burgess is a nurse.
10g. **Robin Elizabeth.** Born 27 Dec. 1959 at Montgomery, WV. Married Kenneth Cox.
10h. **Charles William (II) "Chuck."** Born 20 Nov. 1963 at Crossville, TN.
10i. **Lisa Renee.** Born 27 Sept. 1966 at Crossville, TN.

KENNETH V. BURGESS OF MONTGOMERY CO., OHIO
[William Lester (I)[7], William Vance (II)[8]]

9j. **Kenneth Vance (I)** *[son of William Vance (II)].* Born 31 Oct. 1922 in White Co., TN. Married Martha Kuenle. Kenneth Burgess was an office worker and bookkeeper at Dayton, OH. He died there on 21 Mar. 1984, and is buried in the Calvary Cemetery. Martha lives at Dayton, OH.

10a. **Ann Marie.** Born 12 May 1945 at Dayton, OH. Married John H. Goebel.
10b. **Diane Louise.** Born 30 Jan. 1948 at Dayton, OH. Married Joseph S. DiGrazia.
10c. **Kenneth Vance II.** Born 18 May 1951 at Dayton, OH. Married Katherine Zwiesler. Kenneth Burgess II owns a chain of video stores at Dayton, OH.

11a. **Sarah Katherine.** Born 3 June 1976 at Dayton, OH.
11b. **Megan Clair.** Born 26 Sept. 1980 at Dayton, OH.
11c. **David Kenneth (II).** Born 26 Nov. 1981 at Dayton, OH.

MARION BURGESS OF WHITE CO., TENNESSEE
[William Lester (I)[7]]

8e. **(General) Marion** *[son of William Lester (I)].* Born 29 (or 15) Mar. 1884 in Cumberland Co., TN. Married Cora Belle Bartlett on 4 Oct. 1907 in White Co. (she was born about 1889, and died 7 Feb. 1964, aged 74 years, buried Smith Chapel Cemetery). Listed in the 1910 census for Cumberland Co., TN, and in the 1918 draft register and 1920 census at Clifty, White Co., TN. The Rev. Marion Burgess was a Baptist minister in White Co., and also worked as a coal miner. He died there of heart failure on 9 Jan. 1933, and is buried in the Bolin Cemetery.

9a. **Lillie B.** (nmn). Born 25 Mar. 1910 in Cumberland Co., TN. Married Rufus Smith on 22 Oct. 1937 in Cumberland Co. Lillie Smith lives at Smith Chapel, near Sparta, White Co., TN.
9b. **Mary Lee.** Her name is given as Mary Lu in 1920. Born about 1912 in Cumberland Co., TN. Married Marvin W. VanWinkle on 16 Apr. 1933 in Cumberland Co. (he was the son of Alvin VanWinkle and Mary Elizabeth Evans); married secondly ___ Atkinson. Mary Atkinson lives at Eureka Springs, Carroll Co., AR (or in Georgia).
9c. **Richard Ray (I).** Born 5 Feb. 1916 in Cumberland Co., TN. Married Christine Davis on 29 Jan. 1940 in White Co.; married secondly Ellen Kimbrough (by her first husband, ___ Kimbrough, she had children: *Mary*; *Eva* [married ___ Morgan]; *Richard*; *Robert*; *Gene*; *Thomas*, all of whom were living at Dayton, OH in 1985). Listed in the 1940 draft list for Cumberland Co., and served in World War II; also listed in the 1984 city directory for Dayton, OH. Richard Burgess was a plumber for Plumbers Supply Co. at Dayton. He died there on 5 Mar. 1985, and is buried in the Memorial Park Cemetery.

10a. **Judy.** Married ___ Zandt, and was living at Milwaukee, WI in 1985.
10b. **(Richard) Ray (III).** Living in Utah in 1985.
10c. **Ann(a) (IV).** Married ___ Kimball, and was living at Milwaukee in 1985.

9d. **Effie Novella.** Born about 1918 in Cumberland Co., TN. Married Vaughn Dodson. Effie Dodson lives at Clifty, TN.

GERMAN S. BURGESS OF WHITE CO., TENNESSEE
[William Lester (I)[7]]

8f. **German Samuel** *[son of William Lester (I)].* Born 26 Apr. 1885 (or 1886 or 1884, according to his Social Security record) in Cumberland Co., TN. Married Julia E. Gracie on 25 Apr. 1907 in White Co. (she was born 20 Oct. 1890, and died on 26 June 1945). Listed in the 1910 census for Cumberland Co., and in the 1918 draft register and 1920 census at Clifty, White Co., TN. German Burgess was a coal miner in Cumberland, Bledsoe, and White Cos., TN. He died on 23 Oct. 1970 at Trenton, MI, and is buried in the Old Pleasant Hill Cemetery.

9a. **Dora Rhea.** Born 12 Dec. 1907 in Cumberland Co., TN. Married William F. Saylors on 18 May 1926 in Cumberland Co., TN. Dora Saylors lives at Lincoln Park, MI.

9b. **Beatrice (I)** (nmn). Born 26 Aug. 1910 at Pikeville, TN. Married Fred Alan Bickford on 3 Apr. 1927 in Cumberland Co. Bea Bickford lives at Spencer, TN.

9c. **(Ellis) Harold.** Born 6 May 1913 in TN. Married Lillie Tabor on 17 Aug. 1930 in Cumberland Co. (she lives in CO). Harold Burgess was a coal miner in Colorado and Kentucky. He died on 23 Apr. 1968 at Harlan, Harlan Co., KY.

10a. **Kathleen.** Born about 1932. Lives in Cumberland Co., TN.

10b. **Harold.** Born about 1934. His name may be Ellis Harold Burgess Jr. May have married Carol Darrow on 9 Jan. 1960 at Portland, OR, and is said to have lived at Portland, OR.

10c. **William Ray.** Born about 1936.

9d. **Alva** (dau.). Born 7 Mar. 1915 at Clifty, TN; died there on 29 Mar. 1915, and is buried in the Clifty Cemetery, White Co.

9e. **Kinnia Claine** (son). He is also called Kenna Clane. Born 13 Apr. 1916 in Cumberland Co., TN; died there on 29 July 1916, and is buried in the Clifty Cemetery.

9f. **Hilda.** Born 19 Aug. 1917 in Cumberland Co., TN; died there on 19 Jan. 1918, and is buried in the Clifty Cemetery.

9g. **Mary K.** Born 4 Jan. 1920 in Cumberland Co., TN; died there on 30 Apr. 1920, and is buried in the Clifty Cemetery.

9h. **G. S.** (no given names). Born 11 June 1921 in TN; he died on 26 Nov. 1939 at Isoline, TN, and is buried in the Old Pleasant Hill Cemetery.

9i. **Jean Arlis.** Her name is given as Jene Orles on her death certificate. Born 30 Dec. 1923 in TN; died there of tuberculosis on 26 Dec. 1928, and is buried in the Old Pleasant Hill Cemetery.

9j. **Child.** Born about 1925 in TN; died young.

9k. **Arlen (II) "Buddy"** (nmn). Born 5 Mar. 1927 in Cumberland Co., TN. Married Gladys Coover. Buddy Burgess is a truck driver for the power company at Pikeville, TN.

10a. **(Evelyn) Marie.** Born 9 Jan. 1948 at Crossville, TN. Married Allen Mills on 14 Dec. 1968 in Bledsoe Co., TN (he was born 5 Aug. 1949); married secondly Johnnie Sapp.

10b. **Randall Wayne.** Born 7 July 1950 at Crossville, TN. Married Brenda Morgan on 20 Sept. 1969 in Bledsoe Co., TN (she was born 23 May 1950). Randy Burgess works for a concrete company at Dunlap, TN.

11a. **James Randall.** Born 9 July 1972 at Nashville, TN.

11b. **Jeremy Wayne.** Born 7 Apr. 1973 at Nashville, TN.

9l. **Loyd Dillon.** Born 14 Apr. 1930 in Cumberland Co., TN. Married Martha Apostle. Loyd Burgess was a Chief Warrant Officer in the U.S. Army. He now lives retired at Savannah, GA.

9m. **(Evelyn) Burnell.** Born about 1932 in Cumberland Co., TN. Married R. J. McDowell (div.). Last known living at Columbia, SC in 1972.

VIRGIL H. BURGESS OF CUMBERLAND CO., TENNESSEE

[William Lester (I)[7]]

8g. **Virgil Harrison** *[son of William Lester (I)].* Born 26 Mar. 1888 in Cumberland Co., TN. Married Louvena L. "Venie" Norris on 14 Apr. 1912 in White Co. (she was born 6 Mar. 1893, and died 22 Jan. 1923); married secondly Ollie Jane Page on 28 July 1923 in White Co. (she was born 4 Sept. 1884, and died Mar. 1967). Listed in the 1918 draft register and 1920 census for Ravenscroft, White Co., TN. Virgil Burgess was a coal miner in Cumberland Co. He died there of leukemia on 11 Jan. 1965, and is buried with his first wife in the Never Fail Cemetery.

9a. **Flossie Marie.** Born 15 Jan. 1913 in Cumberland Co., TN. Married Kenneth Adams. Flossie Adams died in Nov. 1985 at Whitefish, MT.

9b. **Jessie Sanford.** Born 18 Feb. 1915 in Cumberland Co., TN. See below for full entry.

9c. **Dalton Denton.** Born 3 Oct. 1916 in Cumberland Co., TN. See below for full entry.

9d. **(Lillie) Oara.** Born 14 June 1919 in Cumberland Co., TN; died there on 16 Jan. 1920, and is buried in the Never Fail Cemetery.

9e. **(Earl) Dee.** Born 18 Aug. 1921 in Cumberland Co., TN. See below for full entry.

9f. **(Anita) Lorene.** Born 29 Jan. 1924 in Cumberland Co., TN. Married Joe Rittenberry on 7 Feb. 1937 in White Co. Lorene Rittenberry currently lives at Sparta, TN.

9g. **Harrison.** His name may have been Virgil Harrison Jr. Born 21 May 1930 in Cumberland Co., TN; died there on 3 July 1930.

JESSIE S. BURGESS OF CUMBERLAND CO., TENNESSEE
[William Lester (I)[7], Virgil Harrison[8]]

9b. **Jessie Sanford "Red"** *[son of Virgil Harrison].* Born 18 Feb. 1915 in White Co., TN. Married Nellie Margarette Turner on 4 Feb. 1938 in Cumberland Co. (she was born 16 Oct. 1918, daughter of William Ervin Turner and Alice May "Allie" Dayton), and may have died Apr. 1978). Listed in the 1940 draft list of Cumberland Co. Red Burgess worked for a wrecking company in Cumberland Co. before retiring. He currently lives at Crossville, TN.

10a. **(Sanford) Elmo (I).** Born 12 Aug. 1938 at Crossville, TN. Married Georgia Mae Woody on 29 July 1957 (she was the daughter of Millard Woody and Ola B. McCormick). Elmo Burgess is President of Burgess Construction Co., Sterling Heights, MI.

11a. **Sanford Elmo (II).** Born 3 Jan. 1958 at Crossville, TN. Married Annette Mazzoia. Sanford Burgess is Vice President of Burgess Construction Co., Sterling Heights, MI.

12a. **Anthony Sanford.** Born 11 Apr. 1979 at Mt. Clemens, MI.
12b. **Christie Fay.**

11b. **Starla Fay(e).** Born 8 Aug. 1962 at Crossville, TN.

10b. **Verble Bruce.** Born 19 Apr. 1942 in Cumberland Co., TN. Married (Cora) Ruth Elmore on 11 Mar. 1961 in Cumberland Co. Verble Burgess is a shipping foreman at Chattanooga, TN.

11a. **Tammy Jean.** Born 29 Jan. 1963 at Crossville, TN. Married Lawrence Lee Howard on 4 Sept. 1982 at Chattanooga, TN.
11b. **Jeffrey Bruce.** Born 9 Jan. 1970 at Chattanooga, TN.

10c. **(William Roger) Gerald "Jerry."** Born 30 July 1945 in Cumberland Co., TN. Married Myra Gale Longley on 8 June 1974 at Apison, TN. Jerry Burgess is an auditor for the State Comptroller's Office in Tennessee. He lives at Murfreesboro, TN.

DALTON BURGESS OF BAKER CO., OREGON
[William Lester (I)[7], Virgil Harrison[8]]

9c. **Dalton Denton** *[son of Virgil Harrison].* Born 3 Oct. 1916 in Cumberland Co., TN. Married Alice Lapray. Living in Idaho in 1941. Dalton Burgess worked for Oregon Portland Cement Co. at Huntington, OR before retiring. He died on 28 Apr. 1992 at Fruitland, ID.

10d. **Sandra Elaine.** Born 30 Apr. 1946 in Cumberland Co., TN; died on 11 Aug. 1946 at Nashville, TN, and is buried in the Never Fail Cemetery.
10b. **Larry Dalton (I).** Born 18 May 1947 at Memphis, TN. Married Penny Cragmile. Larry Burgess works for a molding company at Fruitland, ID.

11a. **Larry Dalton (II).** Born 22 Feb. 1972 at Ontario, OR.
11b. **Michelle Lee.** Born 30 Sept. 1975 at Ontario, OR.

10c. **Steven Kelly.** Born 1 Sept. 1952 at Weiser, ID. Steve Burgess works for a fruit company at Ontario, OR.

DEE BURGESS OF BAKER CO., OREGON
[William Lester (I)[7], Virgil Harrison[8]]

9e. **(Earl) Dee** *[son of Virgil Harrison].* Born 18 Mar. 1921 in Cumberland Co., TN. Married Betty Lou Davenport on 19 Sept. 1949 in Cumberland Co. (she remarried Lloyd Haskell Lewis on 21 Mar. 1966 in Cumberland Co., and lives at Crossville, TN). Dee Burgess was a school custodian at

Huntington, OR. He was injured in a fire caused by the explosion of a can of varnish remover, while trying to save several of his fellow employees, and died of his injuries on 17 June 1958 at Ontario, OR.

10a. **(Betty) Regina.** Born about 1950. Married ___ Wilson, and lives at Crossville, TN.
10b. **Ethel Louise (III).** Born about 1952. Married. In 1975 Ethel Burgess was a Sergeant in the U.S. Air Force, working as an air operations specialist. Last known living at St. Louis, MO.
10c. **Ricky Nile.** Born 24 Jan. 1954. Serving in the U.S. Merchant Marine.

ERNEST T. BURGESS OF CUMBERLAND CO., TENNESSEE

[William Lester (I)[7]]

8l. **Ernest Thomas** *[son of William Lester (I)].* Born 1901 in Cumberland Co., TN. Married (Nancy) Belle Lowe on 16 Aug. 1920 in Cumberland Co. (div.; she may have born 4 Sept. 1901, and died 11 Sept. 1977, buried Bolin Cemetery). Listed with his father in the 1920 census. Ernest Burgess was a miner in Tennessee and the midwest. He may have died in Oklahoma.

9a. **Clarence Reed "Jack."** Born 23 July 1921 in Cumberland Co., TN. Married Charlotte Gist on 29 June 1942 in Cumberland Co. (she was born 14 Apr. 1925 in Grassy Cove, TN). Served in the U.S. Army during World War II in France and Germany. Jack Burgess was an electronics technician for the Federal Aviation Administration before retiring. He currently lives at Crossville, TN.

10a. **Clarence Charles "Jack."** Born 11 Mar. 1943 at Crossville, TN. Married Donna Elaine McCain (she was born 7 Aug. 1947 at Lawrenceburg, TN). Served as an E-5 Petty Officer, Second Class in the U.S. Navy. Jack Burgess is Senior Vice President of First Alabama Bank, Hartselle, AL, where he also resides.

11a. **(Charles) Michael.** Born 25 Jan. 1967 at Huntsville, AL. Mike Burgess works as a machinist and an air frame and power plant technician.
11b. **Douglas Scott (II).** Born 4 June 1970 at Decatur, AL. Doug Burgess graduated from Auburn College with a degree in aerospace engineering.

9b. **Kenneth Winfield.** Born 3 June 1923 in Cumberland Co., TN. Married Edythe Behring; married secondly ___. Served in the Navy in World War II. Kenneth Burgess was an electrician and construction worker; he moved to Mansfield, OH about 1962. He died there childless in a power pole accident in May 1971.

(from left) Walter Kerley, Canza Well Burgess, Walter Herbert Kerley

[William (I)[1], Edward (I)[2], Reuben (I)[3], Thomas (I)[4], King Hiram (I)[5], Joseph Daniel[6]]

HIRAM SIMPSON BURGESS
(1859-1896)

OF CUMBERLAND COUNTY, TENNESSEE

7b. **(Hiram) Simpson** *[son of Joseph Daniel].* Born 8 Feb. 1859 in Cumberland Co., TN. Married Mary Emily Wyatt on 31 Jan. 1878 (she was born 10 Jan. 1859, daughter of John Wyatt and Martha Ann Matilda Moyers, remarried Isham Hale on 10 Nov. 1910, and died 19 Mar. 1944). Listed in the 1880 census for Cumberland Co., TN. Mary is listed as head of the family in the 1900-10 censuses for Cumberland Co.; nine of nine children survive in 1900-10. Simpson Burgess was a farmer in Cumberland Co. He died of a fever on 11 July 1896, and is buried in the Thomas Cemetery, Bledsoe Co.

8a. **Canza Well.** Born 12 Nov. 1878 in Cumberland Co., TN. See below for full entry.
8b. **Irvin Franklin.** Born 29 Sept. 1880 in Cumberland Co., TN. See below for full entry.
8c. **Harvey.** Born 10 Mar. 1883 in Cumberland Co., TN. Harvey Burgess was a farmhand. He died unmarried of heart failure on 5 June 1930, and is buried in the Thomas Cemetery, Bledsoe Co., TN.
8d. **Simon Peter.** Born 4 Feb. 1885 in Cumberland Co., TN. Married Dorothy G. Harritt on 29 May 1932 at Caldwell, ID. Simon Burgess was a school teacher in Oklahoma from 1908-10. He returned to Tennessee, became a Baptist minister, and later lived in both Oregon and Idaho. He died childless on 19 Apr. 1978 at Caldwell, ID, aged 93 years, and is buried in the Canyon Hill Cemetery.
8e. **(John) Linville.** Born 15 Apr. 1887 in Cumberland Co., TN. See below for full entry.
8f. **Fancy Hill.** Born 24 Oct. 1889 in Cumberland Co., TN. See below for full entry.
8g. **Martha Jane (II).** Born 12 Jan. 1892 in Cumberland Co., TN. Married DeWitt Williams on 29 June 1913 (he died 1 Mar. 1923), and had children: *Robert* (born 5 Oct. 1914); *Donald* (born 24 Sept. 1918, married Betty Nelson on 8 June 1941, and had children: Donna K. [had children: Anthony; Alexander]; Timothy D. [had children: Micky; Scott]; Michael Paul; Evelyn Ruth [had children: Katie; Susie; Heidi; Betty]; Rodney; Phillip [had children: Jennie; Annie]; Rebecca; Jonathan Douglas); *Fay E.* (born 21 Apr. 1920, married Royal Gardner on 21 May 1945, and had children: Richard Everett [born 23 Sept. 1947, married, and had children: Shawn Brian {born 11 Dec. 1977}; Jared Richard {born 7 Feb. 1978}]; Mary Louise [born 10 Nov. 1949]; Marceil Lenore [born 27 Dec. 1951, married ___ Whitney]; Fay lives at Molalla, OR). Martha married secondly James Foss in June 1925, and had children: *Marjorie* [born 25 Feb. 1927]; *(James) Arthur* [born 19 Nov. 1928]. Martha Foss died on 25 Dec. 1982 at Terrebonne, OR, aged 90 years.
8h. **George Anderson.** Born 6 Jan. 1894 in Cumberland Co., TN. See below for full entry.
8i. **Mary Ann (VIII).** Born 2 Mar. 1896 in Cumberland Co., TN. Married Fred Hubbard on 19 Apr. 1916 in Cumberland Co. (he was born 1894, and died 1959). Mary Hubbard died on 26 Nov. 1948 in Cumberland Co., TN, and is buried in the Lantana Cemetery.

CANZA WELL BURGESS OF CUMBERLAND CO., TENNESSEE
[Hiram Simpson[7]]

8a. **Canza Well** *[son of Hiram Simpson].* His name is spelled Canzy in the 1880 census, and Kanza in 1900. Born 12 Nov. 1878 in Cumberland Co., TN. Married Anna Marie Walker (or Shephard) on 12 Nov. 1899 (she was born 30 Nov. 1882 in TN, and died there on 11 Oct. 1945). Listed in the 1900-20 censuses for Cumberland Co.; five of six children survive in 1910. Canza Burgess was a farmer and sawmill worker in TN before moving to Ohio, where he worked in a rubber plant. After retiring, he returned to TN, and ran a country store in Cumberland Co. He died there on 23 June 1967, and is buried in the Lantana Cemetery.

9a. **Mary Belle (I).** Born 22 Sept. 1900 in Cumberland Co., TN. Married Sam Parks on 9 Oct. 1918 in Cumberland Co. (dec.), and had children: *Jeff*; *Maggie*; *Alice*; married secondly Tine Green, and had children: *Junior*; married thirdly ___ Johnson. Living at Akron, OH in 1967. Mary Johnson may have died in May 1984 at Akron.

9b. **Walter Nicholas.** Born 16 Dec. 1901 in Cumberland Co., TN.; died there on 20 May 1903, buried Hale's Chapel Cemetery.

9c. **Posey Lee.** Born 26 Dec. 1903 in Cumberland Co., TN. See below for full entry.

9d. **Zona Edith.** Born 2 June 1905 in Cumberland Co., TN. Married Walter Kerley on 13 July 1924 in Cumberland Co. (he was born 11 Jan. 1902, and died 12 Oct. 1990 at Crossville, TN), and had children: *Ruby Jewel* (married Marshall Tabor, and had children: Anthony Harold [married Elsie Wyatt, and had children: Ronnie; Jeff]; Larry [married Connie Reed, and had children: Dewey; Chad]; (Walter) Timothy [married Shartey Smith, and had children: Rena; Kristi; Robbin; Summer]; Zona Carolina [married Dale Eldgers, and had children: Jason; Tony]; Connie [married Phil Bridges, and had children: Steve; Bryan]; Sondra Kay [married John Johnson, and had children: Derek; Caleb]); *Herbert Lee* (married Rita Himes); *Walter Herbert* (married Margie Lee, and had children: Walter Herbert Jr.; Sharri; married secondly Kori ___, and had children: Keith; Kemley). Zona Kerley lives near Crossville, TN.

9e. **(Sidney) Edward.** Born 18 Mar. 1907 in Cumberland Co., TN. See below for full entry.

9f. **Dollie Jane.** Born 22 Oct. 1909 in Cumberland Co., TN. Married Claude Mooneyham on 31 Oct. 1926 in Cumberland Co. (he was born 4 Mar. 1902, and died Dec. 1965); married secondly Byron DeKalb "Barns" Blaylock on 20 Dec. 1979 in White Co. (he was born 29 May 1903). Living at Elyria, OH in 1967. Dollie Blaylock died childless in Nov. 1982 at Spencer, TN.

9g. **(Lue) Violet.** Born 9 Feb. 1911 in Cumberland Co., TN. Married Roy Hyder on 27 Oct. 1927 in Cumberland Co., and had children: *Wyatt*; *Earl*; *Harold*. Violet Hyder currently lives at Tacoma, WA.

9h. **Ben Ray.** Born 3 Oct. 1912 in Cumberland Co., TN. See below for full entry.

9i. **Gus Stavious.** Born 11 Apr. 1914 in Cumberland Co., TN. See below for full entry.

9j. **Chester Lee.** Born 3 Dec. 1916 in Cumberland Co., TN. See below for full entry.

9k. **Thornton Theodore White.** He is called Dick Isham Burgess in a birth announcement in the *Crossville Chronicle*, but is listed as Thornton Burgess in the 1920 census. Born 23 Dec. 1918 in Cumberland Co., TN. Married Lucy ___. Living in Ohio in 1967. Thornton Burgess was a steam fitter before retiring. He lives at Wattsburg, TN.

9l. **Paul Amos.** Born 13 Oct. 1920 in Cumberland Co., TN. See below for full entry.

9m. **Grace Belle Zora.** Her name is also written Belzora. Born 28 Dec. 1922 in Cumberland Co., TN. Married James Hemela (he was born 29 July 1920, and died Mar. 1987 at Atwater), and had six children. Grace Hemela died 2 Nov. 1962 at Atwater, OH, and is buried in the Atwater Cemetery.

9n. **Geneva Genetta "Jean."** Born 2 Aug. 1927 in Cumberland Co., TN. Married Benjamin A. "Bennie" Watley about 1946 (he was born 24 June 1923 at Crossville, TN, son of Arthur and Maude Watley, worked as a tool and die setter for Modern Tool and Die Co., Brook Park, OH, and died on 8 Feb. 1989 at Cleveland, OH, buried Brookdale Cemetery, Elyria), and had children: *Linda* (married Robert Bokor, lives at Elyria, OH); *Sharron* (married Timothy Lloyd, lives at Elyria, OH); *Deborah* (married Ralph Mullins, lives LaGrange, OH). Jean Watley lives at Elyria.

POSEY BURGESS OF SUMMIT CO., OHIO

[Hiram Simpson[7], Canza Well[8]]

9c. **Posey Lee** *[son of Canza Well]*. Born 26 Dec. 1903 in Cumberland Co., TN. Married Effie Garrett on 22 June 1924 in Cumberland Co. (she died on 11 June 1981). Posey Burgess worked for a rubber plant, and has also been a farmer, timberman, carpenter, and gardener. He now lives retired at Barberton, OH.

10a. **Essie Mae.** Born 1 Nov. 1925 at Barberton, OH. Married Robert M. Harris on 13 July 1942 (dec.). Essie Harris died in May 1986 at Barberton, OH.

10b. **Donald** (nmn). Born and died 22 Feb. 1927 at Barberton, OH.

10c. **Harry (II)** (nmn). Born 9 Feb. 1928 at Barberton, OH; died there in Jan. 1929.

10d. **Norman Lee.** Born 2 Dec. 1929 at Barberton, OH. Married Betty Kyer on 3 July 1954. Norman Burgess works for Wright Tool Co. at Barberton, OH.

11a. **Deborah Lynn (I).** Born 8 June 1955 at Barberton, OH. Married Michael Smith.

11b. **Sharon Kaye (I).** Born 20 May 1956 at Barberton, OH. Married Dennis Webber.

EDWARD BURGESS OF STARK CO., OHIO
[Hiram Simpson^7, Canza Well^8]

9e. **(Sidney) Edward (I)** *[son of Canza Well].* Born 18 Mar. 1907 in Cumberland Co., TN. Married Ruth Estevani on 25 Jan. 1931 in Stark Co., OH (div.); married secondly Audrey Mae Brown on 3 May 1941 in Stark Co. (div.); married thirdly Marjorie Ruth Williams on 7 June 1948 in Stark Co. (div.); married fourthly Geraldine L. Henderson on 29 Oct. 1960 in Stark Co. Listed in the 1952 directory for Canton, OH. Ed Burgess was a locomotive engineer for the Republican Steel Co. in Canton, and later operated Sidney Tower Painting. He died there of a heart attack on 6 Aug. 1968, and is buried in the Greenlawn Cemetery, Barberton, OH.

10a. **Harry (III).** His name may be Edward Harry Burgess. Last known living at Canton, OH.
10b. **Mildred (II).**
10c. **Deloris.**
10d. **Linda (I).**
10e. **Sidney Edward (II).**

BEN BURGESS OF CUMBERLAND CO., TENNESSEE
[Hiram Simpson^7, Canza Well^8]

9h. **Ben Ray** *[son of Canza Well].* Born 3 Oct. 1912 in Cumberland Co., TN. Married Glynden (or Glenden) Carpenter on 10 Feb. 1934 in Cumberland Co. (div.); married secondly Lucille Norris on 22 Nov. 1940 in Cumberland Co. (she was born 30 July 1922). Listed in the 1940 draft list of Cumberland Co. Ben Ray Burgess was a farmer and sawmill worker in Cumberland Co., TN. He died on 22 Mar. 1980 at Crossville, TN, and is buried in the Lantana Cemetery.

10a. **Roberta Lehia.** She is called Letitia Roberta on her marriage record. Born 16 Nov. 1934 in Cumberland Co., TN. Married Bobbie Walden Thomas on 29 Nov. 1954 in Cumberland Co.
10b. **Louise Virginia (II).** Born 28 Apr. 1942 in Cumberland Co., TN. Married Ronald Sopko. Louise Sopko lives in Ohio.
10c. **Willie Ray.** Born 14 Feb. 1944 in Cumberland Co., TN; died there in 1951, and is buried in the Lantana Cemetery.
10d. **Hossie** (nmn). Born 16 Dec. 1947 in Cumberland Co., TN. Married Gladys Marle Evans on 9 Jan. 1971 in Cumberland Co. Hossie Burgess works for a funeral home at Crossville, TN.
10e. **Verbie Lee.** Born 16 Jan. 1949 in Cumberland Co., TN; died there in 1951, and is buried in the Lantana Cemetery.
10f. **Anna Mae (II).** Born 11 Sept. 1952 in Cumberland Co., TN. Married Bluford Waldo on 9 Aug. 1975 in Cumberland Co.
10g. **Possie** (nmn). Born 30 May 1954 in Cumberland Co., TN.
10h. **Donnie Ray.** Born 24 Nov. 1966 in Cumberland Co., TN. Married Tammy Lynn Bertram on 14 Sept. 1990 in Cumberland Co.

GUS BURGESS OF SUMMIT CO., OHIO
[Hiram Simpson^7, Canza Well^8]

9i. **Gus Stavious** *[son of Canza Well].* Born 11 Apr. 1914 in Cumberland Co., TN. Married Carrie Nichols (or Nickols) on 10 June 1933 in Kentucky (she was born 27 Sept. 1917, and died 7 Feb. 1988 in OH). Gus Burgess was a farmer and timber worker in TN, before moving to Barberton, OH about 1941. He worked there for PPG Industries (industrial chemicals), and for a greenhouse. He died at Barberton on 22 Feb. 1981, and is buried in the Greenlawn Cemetery.

10a. **Lloyd Edwin.** Born 7 May 1934 at Vandever, TN. Married Wanda Britenstine. Lloyd Burgess works for PPG Industries at Barberton, OH.

11a. **Cheryl Lynn (II).** Born 22 Jan. 1956 at Barberton, OH. Married Barry Allworth.
11b. **David Michael.** Born 30 July 1957 at Barberton, OH. David is a welder for Tire Mold Co. at Akron, OH.
11c. **Joanna Marie (I).** Born 12 Jan. 1959 at Barberton, OH. Married Kenneth Mitchell.
11d. **Melinda Joy.** Born 24 Apr. 1966 at Barberton, OH.

10b. **Hollis Lee.** Born 11 Aug. 1936 at Vandever, TN. Married Carmelita Niece. Hollis is a civilian manager for 2852nd Security Police Squadron, McClellan Air Force Base, Sacramento, CA.

11a. **Carrie Alene.** Born 6 Mar. 1961 at Sacramento, CA.
11b. **Jo-Etta Lynn.** Born 19 June 1963 at Fairfield, CA.

10c. **Harold Gene.** Born 24 Dec. 1938 at Vandever, TN. Married secondly Marianne Trew about 1965. Harold Burgess worked for a water treatment plant at Barberton, OH. He died there on 10 July 1975.

11a. **Connie (II).** Born about 1959 at Barberton, OH. She lives at Little Rock, AR.
11b. **Karen (II).** Born about 1961 at Barberton, OH. She lives at Little Rock, AR.
11c. **Randall David "Randy."** Born 14 Nov. 1966 at Barberton, OH.
11d. **Charles Allen.** Born 27 Sept. 1970 at Barberton, OH. He was adopted out of the family.

10d. **Raymond Wallace.** Born 7 Feb. 1940 at Vandever, TN. Married Joyce Smith. Raymond Burgess works for Babcock & Wilcox at Barberton, OH.

11a. **Barbara Jo.** Born Jan. 1961 at Barberton, OH. Married David Greathouse.
11b. **Raymond Allen.** Born 11 Aug. 1964 at Barberton, OH.

10e. **Deborah Darlene.** Born 13 Dec. 1951 at Barberton, OH. Married Jack Johnson. Deborah Johnson lives at Mogadore, OH.
10f. **Kenneth Leon.** Born 2 Feb. 1953 at Barberton, OH. Kenneth Burgess is a roofer at Barberton, OH.

CHESTER BURGESS OF CUMBERLAND CO., TENNESSEE

[Hiram Simpson^7, Canza Well^8]

9j. **Chester Lee** *[son of Canza Well].* Born 3 Dec. 1916 in Cumberland Co., TN. Married Carrie Stone on 29 June 1935 in Cumberland Co. Chester Burgess was a heavy equipment operator in Cumberland Co. before retiring.

10a. **Billie Joe.** Born 13 July 1936 in Cumberland Co., TN. Married Charlotte Ann Metcalf on 13 July 1959 in Cumberland Co.; married secondly Betty Burriss about 1966; married thirdly Gail Seay on 1 Aug. 1987 in Cumberland Co. (she was born 3 Aug. 1945). Billie Burgess is a truck driver for a bakery at Crossville, TN.

11a. **Steven Craig.** Born 17 Feb. 1967 in OH.
11b. **Nicole Renee "Nikki."** Born 29 June 1977 at Crossville, TN.

10b. **Charlotte Lee.** Born 2 Aug. 1944 in Cumberland Co., TN. Married Carl Kilby, and had children: *Connie*; *Cindy*.
10c. **Keith (I)** (nmn). Born 22 Mar. 1950 in Cumberland Co., TN. Married Glynda Kaye Scarbrough on 12 Sept. 1966 in Cumberland Co. Keith Burgess was a truck driver at Morristown, TN. He died there in May 1984.

11a. **Keith (II)** (nmn). Born 12 Dec. 1969 at Crossville, TN. Married Natalie Ann Palmer on 23 July 1988 in Cumberland Co. (she was born 30 Sept. 1970).

12a. **Keith III.** Born 22 Apr. 1989 at Crossville, TN.
12b. **Kyle Andrew.** Born 8 Aug. 1991 at Crossville, TN.

11b. **Kevin Meade.** Born 7 Mar. 1971 at Crossville, TN.

PAUL BURGESS OF SUMMIT CO., OHIO

[Hiram Simpson^7, Canza Well^8]

9l. **Paul Amos** *[son of Canza Well].* Born 13 Oct. 1920 in Cumberland Co., TN. Married Dolores Friend. Paul Burgess worked at the B&W Boiler Plant, Barberton, OH. He died there on 15 Aug. 1989, and is buried there in the Greenlawn Cemetery.

10a. **Dona Kay.** Born 22 May 1950 at Barberton, OH. Married Dennis W. Renninger.
10b. **Barbara Ann (II).** Born 25 Mar. 1954 at Barberton, OH. Married George Coldwell.
10c. **Joyce Fay (II).** Born 7 Jan. 1958 at Barberton, OH. Married Ward Renninger.

IRVIN F. BURGESS OF CUMBERLAND CO., TENNESSEE
[Hiram Simpson[7]]

8b. **Irvin(g) Franklin** *[son of Hiram Simpson].* Most newspaper accounts spell his name Ervin, but his family Bible record gives his name as Irvin. Born 29 Sept. 1880 in Cumberland Co., TN. Married (Mary) Lou Arnett on 2 Feb. 1902 (she was born 20 May 1884, remarried ___ Hyder, and died 21 Apr. 1961, buried Burgess Cemetery). Listed in the 1910 census for Cumberland Co., TN (five of five children then survive); Lou appears as head of the family in 1920. Irvin Burgess was a farmer in TN. He is said to have moved to Lakeland, Polk Co., FL in the 1920s, and to have changed his surname to Burns, but has not been found under either name in the Florida death index through 1969.

9a. **Pearl Elizabeth.** Born 2 Dec. 1902 in Cumberland Co., TN. Married Alvin Smith Hamby on 21 June 1922 in Cumberland Co. (he was born 30 Oct. 1882, and died 19 Mar. 1965 at Crossville, TN). Pearl Hamby died on 3 Oct. 1992 at Crossville, TN.
9b. **Laura Ann.** Born 13 Mar. 1904 in Cumberland Co., TN. Married (Henry) Napoleon "Poley" King on 25 Aug. 1921 in White Co. (he was born 21 Jan. 1902, and died 23 Sept. 1949), and had children: *James Dewey* (born 18 July 1922, killed in World War II); *(Lillie) Mae* (born 29 Feb. 1924, married her cousin, Allen Newman Burgess, and had children [see his entry]); *Zola Maxine* [born 5 June 1925); *William Henry* (born 14 Apr. 1928); *Leslie Eugene* (born 23 Oct. 1930); *Milton* (twin; born 31 Mar. 1933); *Mildred* (twin; born 31 Mar. 1933); *Bethel* (born 21 Nov. 1934); *Thelma Lou* (born 2 July 1939). Laura King died Mar. 1982 in Cumberland Co.
9c. **(Rutha) Arlena Frances "Lena."** Born 1 Feb. 1906 in Cumberland Co., TN. Married Hayden Ford (he was born 19 Mar. 1891, and died Jan. 1960). Lena Ford lives near Crossville, TN.
9d. **(Willie) Martin (I).** Born 1 Dec. 1907 in Cumberland Co., TN. See below for full entry.
9e. **(Jay) Beecher.** Born 16 July 1909 in Cumberland Co., TN. See below for full entry.
9f. **Eva (II)** (nmn). Born 11 July 1911 in Cumberland Co., TN. Married Prince Albert Epperson (he was born 9 Dec. 1912, and died 10 Aug. 1980 at Hixson, TN), and had children: *Charles Kenneth* (born 23 Sept. 1935, married Faith Lyle about 1957 [div.], and had children: (Rebecca) Lynne [born 17 Oct. 1958 at Chattanooga, TN, works at Oak Ridge Associated Universities]; Theresa Gayle [born 11 June 1961 at Chattanooga, TN]). Eva Epperson lives at Chattanooga.
9g. **Rose** (nmn) **"Rosie."** Her name is given as Rosa in her birth record, several newspaper accounts, and in the 1920 census. Born 15 Mar. 1913 in Cumberland Co., TN. Married Thomas L. Dyer on 10 May 1931 in Cumberland Co., and had children: *Neal*; *(Thomas) Harold* (married Wanda ___, and lives in Cumberland Co.); *Carroll*; *(Robert) Douglas*; *Norman*; *Janice* (married ___ Turner); *Lou* (married ___ Wyatt); *Sue* (married ___ Owens). Rosie Dyer worked as a seamstress at Crossville, TN, and was a member of the Baptist Church. She died on 8 Oct. 1990 at Midway, TN, and is buried in the Burgess Cemetery.
9h. **(Isaac) Linville (II).** Born 19 Feb. 1915 in Cumberland Co., TN. See below for full entry.
9i. **(Luther) Simpson.** Born 6 Feb. 1917 in Cumberland Co., TN. See below for full entry.
9j. **Beulah Benford.** Her name is spelled Bulah in some newspaper accounts. Born 17 Apr. 1923 in Cumberland Co., TN. Married Paul Rogers (or Rodgers) on 22 Feb. 1946 at Rossville, GA. Beulah Rogers lives at Chattanooga, TN.

MARTIN BURGESS OF CUMBERLAND CO., TENNESSEE
[Hiram Simpson[7], Irvin Franklin[8]]

9d. **(Willie) Martin (I)** *[son of Irvin Franklin].* Born 1 Dec. 1907 in Cumberland Co., TN. Married Eliza Elizabeth Swafford on 1 Oct. 1931 in Bledsoe Co. (she was born 6 June 1913). Listed in the 1940 draft list of Cumberland Co. Martin Burgess was a farmer near Crossville, TN. He died there on 15 Sept. 1980.

10a. **Lola Malinda.** Born 19 July 1933 in Cumberland Co., TN. Married Onus R. Redwine on 28 Apr. 1954 in Cumberland Co.; married secondly (William) Hoyt Campbell on 5 May 1956 in Cumberland Co. Lola Campbell lives near Crossville, and has contributed greatly to this book.
10b. **(Bailey) Cogan.** Born 18 Feb. 1935 in Cumberland Co., TN; died there on 30 Apr. 1945, and is buried in the Burgess Cemetery.

10c. **Willie Martin (II) "Bill."** Born 29 Sept. 1937 in Bledsoe Co., TN. Married Christine Presley. Bill Burgess is a carpenter in Cumberland Co., TN.

11a. **Marsha Rose.** Born 19 July 1962 at Crossville, TN.
11b. **Karen Kaye.** Born 14 May 1965 at Crossville, TN. Married William Henry Norris on 22 Dec. 1992 in Cumberland Co., TN.
11c. **(William) Scott.** Born 12 Nov. 1968 at Crossville, TN. Married Julie Darlene Matthews on 18 Feb. 1990 in Cumberland Co. (she was born 17 July 1972).

12a. **Emily Marie.** Born 15 Sept. 1990 at Crossville, TN.

11d. **Brian Gregory.** Born 12 Apr. 1973 at Crossville, TN.

10d. **Perry Walter.** Born 6 Aug. 1939 in Cumberland Co., TN. Married Bonnie Lawson about 1960 (div.; she remarried George Brewer, and lives in Cumberland Co., TN); married secondly Creola Warner about 1964 (div.; she was born 14 Dec. 1942, remarried Waymond Mitchell McCloud on 7 Jan. 1983 in Cumberland Co., and died on 6 Apr. 1987, buried Burgess Cemetery); married thirdly Donna ___. Perry Burgess is a carpenter in Florida.

11a. **Loretta Orlene.** Born 27 Oct. 1961. Married Ray Glenn VanWinkle on 26 Oct. 1979 in Cumberland Co. (div.), and had children: *Darryll Glenn* (born 25 Feb. 1982); married secondly Charles Clay Young on 8 Aug. 1983 in White Co., TN (div.; he was born 1 July 1943), and had children: *Misty Charlene* (born 15 May 1984); married thirdly Robert Lewis. Loretta Lewis lives in Cumberland Co., TN.
11b. **(Perry) Donathan "Donnie."** Born 20 Oct. 1965. He was killed unmarried in an automobile accident on 18 Feb. 1988 at Jonesboro, AR, and is buried in the Burgess Cemetery.
11c. **Michael Lyndon.** Born 6 Oct. 1967 in Cumberland Co., TN. Michael L. Burgess served in the U.S. Army.
11d. **(Melinda) Elizabeth.** Born 22 Mar. 1969 in Cumberland Co., TN.
11e. **James Martin.** Born 16 July 1977.

10e. **(Wayne) Windell.** Born 4 Dec. 1940 in Cumberland Co., TN. Windell Burgess is a carpenter at Dorton, TN.
10f. **Katherine** (nmn). Born 5 Dec. 1942 in Cumberland Co., TN. Married three times. She lives at Soddy-Daisy, TN.
10g. **(Dean) Nelson.** Born 1 Nov. 1944 in Cumberland Co., TN. Married Edna Lorene Smith on 24 Dec. 1963 in Bledsoe Co., TN (she was born 5 Aug. 1945, remarried Charles Anton Iles on 25 Dec. 1966, and lives near Crossville). Nelson Burgess was a carpenter at Crossville, TN. He died there in an accidental shooting on 11 June 1966, and is buried in the Burgess Cemetery.

11a. **Cathy Caroline.** Born 19 Dec. 1964 at Crossville, TN. Married Michael Glenn Young on 2 May 1983 in Cumberland Co.
11b. **Mitchell Dean.** Born 6 Feb. 1966 at Crossville, TN. Married Charlene Kay Norris on 13 May 1984 in Cumberland Co. (div.; she was born 8 May 1968); married secondly Kristie Lee Davis on 17 Feb. 1989 in Cumberland Co. (she was born 4 Oct. 1970).

12a. **Megan Jo.** Born 30 Aug. 1990 (?) at Crossville, TN.

10h. **Leta Sue.** Born 26 Sept. 1946 in Cumberland Co., TN. Married Robert Clyde Gore (or Jordan) on 30 Mar. 1968 in Cumberland Co.
10i. **James Lloyd (I).** Born and died 13 Nov. 1948 in Cumberland Co., TN, and is buried in the Burgess Cemetery.
10j. **Randall Steven "Randy."** His birth record gives his middle name as Stevens. Born 17 Mar. 1950 in Cumberland Co., TN. Randy Burgess works in a rubber plant in Cumberland Co.
10k. **Eldon Carson.** Born 12 Aug. 1952 in Cumberland Co., TN. Married Katherine Faye "Kathy" Hyder on 6 July 1973 in Cumberland Co. Eldon Burgess owns Eldon Burgess Plumbing Service at Crossville, TN.

11a. **Tammy Michelle.** Born 7 Aug. 1975 at Crossville, TN.
11b. **Tina Renee.** Born 18 Jan. 1978 at Crossville, TN.

BEECHER BURGESS OF CUMBERLAND CO., TENNESSEE

[Hiram Simpson[7], Irvin Franklin[8]]

9e. **(Jay) Beecher** *[son of Irvin Franklin].* Born 16 July 1909 in Cumberland Co., TN. Married (Mary) Corrine Morgan in 1932; married secondly Beatrice Wilson in 1946; married thirdly Hattie Pearl (Neely) Burgess on 2 Sept. 1970 at Lafayette, GA (she was born 16 Feb. 1917 in Fenriss Co., TN, daughter of William Andrew Neely and Virginia Hall, and former wife of Wilkie Burgess, his cousin). Listed in the 1940 draft list of Cumberland Co. Beecher Burgess worked for thirty years for U.S. Pipe Co. at Chattanooga, TN before retiring to the Crossville, TN area in 1974. He died there on 10 Nov. 1985, and is buried in the Burgess Cemetery. Hattie Burgess lives near Crossville, TN, and has contributed greatly to this book.

10a. **Clyde** (nmn). Born 4 Jan. 1933 at South Pittsburg, TN. Married Phyllis Carol Crawford on 14 Feb. 1955 at Mattydale, NY (div.; she was born 15 May 1937 at Syracuse, NY). Clyde Burgess was a career enlisted man in the U.S. Air Force, retiring in 1970 with the rank of Chief Master Sergeant. He retired from United Postal Service at Clay, NY in 1994.

11a. **Kurt Douglas.** Born 2 Feb. 1959 at Chateauroux, France. Married Frankie Lavern McMahon (she was a Sergeant in the Air Force). Kurt Burgess is a Master Sergeant in the U.S. Air Force, currently stationed in Florida.

12a. **Andrew Garrett**. Born 26 Mar. 1984 at Portsmouth, NH.
12b. **Joshua Liam**. Born 6 July 1990 at Portsmouth, NH.

11b. **Garrett Cameron "Gary."** Born 14 June 1962 at Syracuse, NY. Married Verna Jane ___. Gary Burgess served in the Marine Corps. He now works for the U.S. Postal Service at Lookout Mountain, TN.

12a. **Colleen Amara**. Born 23 July 1987 at Syracuse, NY.
12b. **Sean Cameron**. Born 16 Mar. 1989 at Syracuse, NY.

10b. **(Norma) Jean.** Born 22 Feb. 1935 in Marion Co., TN. Married James Vaughn. Jean Vaughn lives at Chattanooga, TN.

10c. **(Mary) Joyce.** Born 30 Aug. 1937 in Cumberland Co., TN. Married Bobby Combs on 20 Jan. 1955, and had children: *Robin Gene* (born 1 May 1956 at Chattanooga, TN; he was adopted by his stepfather, and uses the surname Haynes; married Norma Lee Welden on 19 Dec. 1976 [div.], and had children: Brandon Heath [born 2 Mar. 1980 at Scottsdale, AL]; Mathew Wesley [born 20 Dec. 1982 at Scottsdale, AL]; Eric Daniel [born 22 Aug. 1986 at Scottsdale, AL]; *Robin Gene* married secondly Kathleen Flaherty on 21 July 1992, and had children: Emma Kaitlin [born 17 May 1993 at Portland, OR]; *Robin HAYNES* lives at Washougal, WA). **Joyce COMBS** married secondly Daniel Ervin Haynes on 1 Dec. 1956, and had children: *Lisa Karen* (born 4 Apr. 1958 at Scottsboro, AL, married Jerry Deckard Gregory on 1 July 1979 [div.], and had children: Jeremy Daniel [born 23 Nov. 1981 at Scottsboro, AL]; Jarrod Dewayne [born 6 Jan. 1984 at Scottsboro, AL]); *James Scott* (born 4 Apr. 1959 at Scottsboro, AL, married Sandra Carol Bradford on 30 Sept. 1978, and had children: James Scott Jr. [born 31 Mar. 1979 at Scottsboro, AL]; Heather Joyce [born 22 Mar. 1982 at Scottsboro, AL]); *Mark Daniel* (born 18 July 1961 at Scottsboro, AL, married Maria Charlene Knight on 23 Dec. 1983, and had children: Christina Marie [born 1 Oct. 1989 at Scottsboro, AL]; Markie Danielle [born 17 Mar. 1993 at Scottsboro, AL]). Joyce Haynes lives at Section, AL.

10d. **Judith Ella "Judy"** (ad.). Born 28 Mar. 1941 at Chattanooga, TN. Judy Burgess is a teacher at Chattanooga, TN.

10e. **Gary Robert.** Born 1 July 1947 at Chattanooga, TN. Married Sheila Webb. Gary Burgess is an electrical engineer for the Tennessee Valley Authority at Signal Mountain, Chattanooga, TN.

11a. **Anthony Leon "Tony."** Born 29 Aug. 1969 at Chattanooga, TN.
11b. **Shannon Beatrice.** Born 29 Oct. 1976 at Chattanooga, TN.

10f. **Dean Warren.** Born 18 Feb. 1950 at Chattanooga, TN. Married Brenda Bonine. Dean Burgess is a computer service technician at Atlanta, GA.

11a. **Steven Warren.** Born 18 May 1975.

IKE BURGESS OF HAMILTON CO., TENNESSEE
[Hiram Simpson[7], Irvin Franklin[8]]

9h. **Isaac Linville (II) "Ike"** *[son of Irvin Franklin].* Born 19 Feb. 1915 in Cumberland Co., TN. Married Aletha "Letha" Miller. Ike Burgess was a welder for Combustion Engineering at Chattanooga, TN. He died on 19 Feb. 1968 at Trenton, GA, and is buried in the Greenwood Cemetery.

10a. **Dennis Franklin.** Born 29 Nov. 1934 in Dade Co., GA. Married Mildred Crowe. Dennis Burgess is a Chief Master Sergeant in the U.S. Air Force, now stationed at Scott Air Force Base, Mascoutah, IL.

11a. **Darla Maria.** Born 28 Feb. 1962 at Clinton, IN. Married Dennis Bante.
11b. **Mark Anthony.** Born 25 Dec. 1962 at Clinton, IN.
11c. **Sheri Lynn.** Born 24 Jan. 1964 at Clinton, IN.

10b. **Max Dorton.** Born 8 Aug. 1938 in Walker Co., GA. Married Shirley Ruth Debter. Rev. Max Burgess is a Minister for the Church of God at Oakdale, GA, near Atlanta.

11a. **Matthew Dorton.** Born 15 May 1961 at Chattanooga, TN. Married Edie McCord. Rev. Matthew Burgess is a Minister for the Church of God, at Atlanta, GA.
11b. **Janice Anita.** Born 14 Oct. 1969 at Chattanooga, TN.

SIMP BURGESS OF CUMBERLAND CO., TENNESSEE
[Hiram Simpson[7], Irvin Franklin[8]]

9i. **(Luther) Simpson** *[son of Irvin Franklin].* Born 6 Feb. 1917 in Cumberland Co., TN. Married Nellie Eller on 19 Sept. 1937 in Cumberland Co. (dec.); married secondly Ida Miller on 1 Sept. 1978 in White Co., TN (she was born 15 Apr. 1924). Listed in the 1940 draft list for Cumberland Co. Simp Burgess is a retired construction worker, currently living at Crossville, TN.

10a. **Carl Gilbert.** Born 14 June 1938 in Cumberland Co., TN. Married Stephanie Virginia Wyatt on 25 Nov. 1962 in Cumberland Co. Carl Burgess was a tool and die maker at Oak Ridge, TN. He died on 20 Mar. 1982 at Spring City, TN.

11a. **Dana Michelle.** Her middle name is spelled Michele in one newspaper account. Born 27 Sept. 1963 at Ft. Campbell, KY. Married Michael Dean Sharp on 29 Sept. 1986, and had children: *Carl Alexander* (born 23 Aug. 1992). Dana Sharp lives at Spring City, TN.
11b. **Jeffrey Allen (I).** Born 22 Sept. 1964 at Dayton, OH. Jeff Burgess is a diesel mechanic at Jackson, TN.
11c. **Robert Lynn.** Born 30 Jan. 1969 at Dayton, OH. Married Angie Lester in Mar. 1993. Bob Burgess works at Belks Department Store.

10b. **Charles Richard.** Born 29 Mar. 1940 in Cumberland Co., TN. Married (Mary) Lucille "Lucy" England on 4 July 1979. Obtained an M.S. degree in animal husbandry from the University of Tennessee. Charles Burgess worked for the Shell Chemical Co. at Kansas, City, MO through 1974, and later as the Regional Manager for North American Plant Breeders, at Memphis, TN. He currently the owner and operator of Wholesale Country Meats, Crossville, TN.

11a. **Tiffany Ember.** Born 20 Sept. 1981 at Athens, GA.
11b. **Chism Mason.** Born 13 Sept. 1983 at Memphis, TN.

10c. **Margie Eloise.** Born 3 Nov. 1942 at Elyria, OH. Married Jerry Winton Lewis on 4 Feb. 1963 in Cumberland Co., and had children: *Hila Diane* (born 3 Apr. 1977 at Kettering, OH). Margie Lewis lives at Crossville, TN.

10d. **Monte Lynn.** Born 28 Jan. 1953 in Cumberland Co., TN. Married Phyllis Ann Randolph on 22 Apr. 1973 in Cumberland Co. Monte Burgess has been a professional photographer, rock quarrier, and a minister for the Assembly of God. He currently works as an NC machinist for George A. Mitchell Manufacturing Co., Cookeville, TN, and as a guard for the Cumberland

County Highway Department. Phyllis Burgess is a graphic designer, having once worked for the *Crossville Chronicle*. They live at Crossville, TN.

11a. **Shiloh Lynn.** Born 24 Feb. 1980 at Crossville, TN.
11b. **Lynell Renee.** Born 21 Apr. 1983 at Crossville, TN.

LINVILLE BURGESS OF TWIN FALLS CO., IDAHO
[Hiram Simpson^7]

8e. **(John) Linville** *[son of Hiram Simpson].* Born 15 Apr. 1887 in Cumberland Co., TN. Married (Melinda) Emeline Edmonds on 11 Oct. 1908 in Cumberland Co. (she was born 1892, and died 12 Feb. 1953). Listed in the 1910 census for Cumberland Co. (one of one children then survives), in the 20 June 1917 draft list of Cumberland Co., and in the 1920 census in Bledsoe Co. Linville was a farmer at Buhl, ID. He died there on 5 Feb. 1954.

9a. **Clarence Lee.** Born 2 Sept. 1909 in Cumberland Co., TN; died there on 6 Aug. 1917, and is buried in the McDowell Cemetery.
9b. **Lillie Ann.** Born 26 Sept. 1912 at Nine Mile, TN. Married Claude Bybee; married secondly William Kibby.
9c. **(Amon) Edgar.** Born 2 Mar. 1917 at Nine Mile, TN. See below for full entry.
9d. **Dollie Esther.** Born 2 Mar. 1920 at Nine Mile, TN. Married Cecil Bowyer. Dollie Bowyer died on 21 July 1988 at Twin Falls, ID.
9e. **Mary Ellen (X).** Born 11 Jan. 1923 at Nine Mile, TN. Married Alvis Partin on 22 Apr. 1939 at Buhl, ID, and had children: *William John* (ad.); *Barbara Ann* (ad., married ___ Ebbs); *Diane* (ad., married ___ Boswell). Mary Partin currently lives at Twin Falls, ID.
9f. **Walter Edward.** Born 8 Jan. 1926 at Castleford, ID. See below for full entry.
9g. **(John) Eldon (I).** Born 30 Mar. 1930 at Buhl, ID. See below for full entry.

EDGAR BURGESS OF TWIN FALLS CO., IDAHO
[Hiram Simpson^7, John Linville^8]

9c. **(Amon) Edgar** *[son of John Linville].* Born 2 Mar. 1917 at Nine Mile, TN. Married Lilas Larae Kirkbride on 21 May 1937 at Castleford, ID (she was born 7 July 1920 at Nine Mile, TN, and died on 5 Oct. 1992 at Buhl, ID). Edgar Burgess was a farmer, highway worker, and a miner at the Ruth Copper Pit, NV before retiring. He now lives at Buhl, ID.

10a. **Barbara Joan.** Born 22 June 1939 at Buhl, ID; died there on 10 Nov. 1939.
10b. **Luella Jo.** Born 13 May 1940 at Buhl, ID. Married Max Vigil. Luella Vigil lives at Ely, NV.
10c. **Dwayne Allen.** Born 19 Apr. 1941 at Buhl, ID. Married Dawna Bradley on 19 Sept. 1970 at Elmo, NV and again on 22 July 1979 at Ely, NV. Dwayne Burgess is a civilian investigator at the U.S. Naval Station, Fallon, NV.

11a. **Anthony Ray.** Born 26 Apr. 1964 at Ely, NV. Attended the University of Nevada, Reno. Married Tamaron Jyl Wright on 3 Mar. 1984 at Carson City, Douglas Co., NV; married secondly Christy Ann Lee on 22 July 1989 at Yerington, Lyon Co., NV.
11b. **(Milton) Brian.** Born 19 Jan. 1967 at Ely, NV. Married Grace Beth King on 11 June 1986 at Fallon, Churchill Co., NV.
11c. **Aubry Denholm.** Born 29 Apr. 1975 at Ely, NV.

10d. **Lavaun Edward.** Born 29 Dec. 1942 at Buhl, ID. Married secondly Mary Sue Dankworth on 6 July 1970 in White Pine Co., NV. Lavaun Burgess was an oil fields driller and tool pusher. He died July 1992 at Farmington, MN.

11a. **Larry Lavaun.** He was adopted by his stepfather, and now uses the surname Trueblood. Born 3 June 1962 at Ely, NV. Currently serving in the U.S. Navy.
11b. **Steven Wade.** He was adopted by his stepfather, and now uses the surname Trueblood. Born 8 Nov. 1963 at Twin Falls, ID.
11c. **Danielle Sue** (ad.). Born 27 Oct. 1964 at Albuquerque, NM.
11d. **Samuel Edgar.** Born 6 Jan. 1966 at Ely, NV.
11e. **Phillip David** (ad.). Born 26 Nov. 1966 at Albuquerque, NM.
11f. **Jeffrey Scott (III).** Born 6 Apr. 1971 at Ely, NV.

10e. **Leroy David.** Born 21 Feb. 1944 at Buhl, ID. Married Ellen Toedtempier. Leroy Burgess works at a steel mill in Portland, OR.

11a. **Darron Lee.** Born 3 Dec. 1965 at Carlin, NV.
11b. **Charmell LaRae.** Born 22 June 1967 at Portland, OR.
11c. **Stacy Sue.** Born 15 Mar. 1969 at Seattle, WA.
11d. **Westly David.** Born 16 May 1981 at Portland, OR.

WALT BURGESS OF TWIN FALLS CO., IDAHO

[Hiram Simpson[7], John Linville[8]]

9f. **Walter Edward** *[son of John Linville].* Born 8 Jan. 1926 at Castleford, ID. Married Lila Stombaugh in 1943; married secondly Deanne Brown. Walt Burgess owns Walt's Safety Shop, specializing in automobile front end alignments, at Buhl, ID.

10a. **Jerry Edward.** Born 16 Aug. 1943 at Twin Falls, ID. Married Etsuko Kiyan. Jerry Burgess works for Pet Milk Co. at Buhl, ID.

11a. **Allen Lee.** Born 23 Nov. 1967 at Renton, WA.
11b. **Brian David (II).** Born 30 Apr. 1973 at Twin Falls, ID.
11c. **Mark Edward (III).** Born 24 Mar. 1978 at Twin Falls, ID.

10b. **Ronnie Lee (I).** Born 7 July 1947 at Twin Falls, ID. Married Diane Nielson (div.); married secondly Mary ___. Ron Burgess is an automobile paint and body repairman at Twin Falls, ID.

11a. **Tina Marie.** Born 18 Feb. 1968 at Renton, WA.
11b. **Abbey.** Born 1984 at Twin Falls, ID.

ELDON BURGESS OF WHITE PINE CO., NEVADA

[Hiram Simpson[7], John Linville[8]]

9g. **(John) Eldon (I)** *[son of John Linville].* Born 30 Mar. 1930 at Buhl, ID. Married Betty Smith. Eldon Burgess is a machinist for the Nevada Northern Railroad at Ely, NV.

10a. **Rickey Lee.** Born 31 Aug. 1950 at Twin Falls, ID. Married Theresa Nancy Thomason on 12 July 1969 in White Pine Co., NV; married secondly Carlene Wilcox. Rickey Burgess is a Staff Sergeant (communications) in the U.S. Air Force, at MacDill Air Force Base, FL.

11a. **Paul Lee.** Born 25 Feb. 1970 at Phoenix, AZ.
11b. **Charity Lee Marie.** Born 23 Sept. 1974 at Ely, NV.
11c. **Charmin Raylene.** Born 7 Oct. 1976 at Warner Robins, GA.

10b. **Jimmey Eric.** Born 31 Aug. 1952 at Twin Falls, ID. Married Darnell Crawford on 9 July 1973 at Ely, White Pine Co., NV. Jim Burgess works at Ely, NV.
10c. **Beverley Marie.** Born 2 June 1954 at Twin Falls, ID. Married Robert James Trehune on 17 July 1972 in Eureka Co., NV. Beverley Trehune lives at Ely, NV.
10d. **Martin Grant.** Born 12 Sept. 1956 at Ely, NV. Martin Burgess is a maintenance supervisor for White Pine Co., NV.
10e. **Raylene Ann.** Born 7 Oct. 1961 at Ely, NV. Married Roland James Bloom. Raylene Bloom lives at Colorado Springs, CO.

FANCY HILL BURGESS OF CUMBERLAND CO., TENNESSEE

[Hiram Simpson[7]]

8f. **Fancy Hill** *[son of Hiram Simpson].* Born 24 Oct. 1889 in Cumberland Co., TN. Married Recie Jane Croft on 27 Sept. 1908 (she was born 17 Aug. 1892, and died 22 Dec. 1980). Listed in the 1910-20 censuses for Cumberland Co., TN (one of one children survives in 1910), and in the 20 June 1917 draft register for Cumberland Co. Fancy Burgess was a farmer in rural Cumberland Co. He died there on 19 Aug. 1972, and is buried with his wife in the Lantana Cemetery.

9a. **Rose Lee**. She is called Rosalee or Rosa Lee in some records. Born 18 Aug. 1909 in Cumberland Co., TN. Married Brown Lowe VanWinkle on 6 Dec. 1925 in Cumberland Co. (he was born 19 June 1899, son of Thomas Reuben VanWinkle and Martha Lou Bryant, and brother of Jonas Van-Winkle [who married Rose's sister, Bertha Burgess], and died 1 Dec. 1971 in Van Buren Co.), and had children: *Lonas Marlon* (born 13 Aug. 1926, died 1 Jan. 1936, buried Lone Wood Cemetery, Van Buren Co., TN); *Robert* (tax assessor of Van Buren Co. in 1982); *Calvin*; *Earl*; *Floyd*; *Thurman*; *Mamie* (married ___ Guy, and lives at Sparta, TN); *Cecil*. Rose VanWinkle died on 3 Aug. 1989 at Algood, Van Buren Co., TN, and is buried in the Lone Wood Baptist Church Cemetery.

9b. **Ross Rawlan (I)**. Born 23 Nov. 1910 in Cumberland Co., TN. See below for full entry.

9c. **Bertha May**. Born 3 Sept. 1912 in Cumberland Co., TN. Married Jonah Lee VanWinkle on 23 July 1927 in Cumberland Co. (he was born 29 Oct. 1904, son of Thomas Reuben VanWinkle and Martha Lou Bryant, and brother of Brown VanWinkle [who married Bertha's sister, Rose Burgess]), and had children: *Norene* (born 11 Jan. 1928; married Steve Hankins, and had children: Johnny Howard; Hilda; Fay [twin]; Kay [twin]; married secondly Marion Land); *Clayton* (born 14 June 1930, died [drowned] unmarried on 19 Aug. 1952 while rescuing several of his fellow soldiers in the Chip-Ori Valley, Korea); *Lincoln* (born 9 Sept. 1932, married Cassie Blaylock, and had children: Debbie); *Billy Lee* (born 17 July 1935, married Juanita Thomas, died 2 Dec. 1980, buried Lone Wood Cemetery, and had children: Rita [married ___ Rhodes, and lives at Memphis, TN]; Billy Rip; Rhonda). Bertha VanWinkle died on 17 Apr. 1975 at Crossville, TN, and is buried in the Lone Wood Cemetery.

9d. **Ralph (III)** (nmn). Born 1 May 1914 in Cumberland Co., TN; died there on 13 May 1916, and is buried in the Newton Cemetery.

9e. **Semp Daniel**. Born 1 May 1916 in Cumberland Co., TN. See below for full entry.

9f. **Otto Alex (I)**. Born 8 Jan. 1918 in Cumberland Co., TN. See below for full entry.

9g. **Ollie May**. Born 6 Dec. 1919 in Cumberland Co., TN. Married Carrol Parker, and had children: *David*; *Dorothy* (married ___ Shuford). Ollie Parker lives at Chattanooga, TN.

9h. **(Ola) Geneva "Jean."** Born 6 Aug. 1921 in Cumberland Co., TN. Married Litton Thomas on 24 Sept. 1937 in Cumberland Co., and had children: *Dennis* (killed in a racing car accident); married secondly Fred Ross, and had children: *Michael*; *Richard*. Jean Ross lives at Braddenton, NJ.

9i. **(Frank) Foster**. Born 13 Feb. 1923 in Cumberland Co., TN. See below for full entry.

9j. **Arlen (I)** (nmn). Born 22 Nov. 1925 in Cumberland Co., TN. See below for full entry.

9k. **Kent Kenard.** Born 17 Jan. 1927 in Cumberland Co., TN. See below for full entry.

9l. **Carl Marlo (I)**. Born 8 Nov. 1928 in Cumberland Co., TN. See below for full entry.

9m. **(Floyd) Dallas.** Born 6 Dec. 1930 in Cumberland Co., TN. See below for full entry.

9n. **Lue Ella.** Born and died 9 Dec. 1932 in Cumberland Co., TN.

ROSS BURGESS Sr. of CUMBERLAND CO., TENNESSEE

[Hiram Simpson[7], Fancy Hill[8]]

9b. **Ross Rawlan (I)** *[son of Fancy Hill]*. Born 23 Nov. 1910 in Cumberland Co., TN. Married Lena Wyatt on 20 Sept. 1929 in Cumberland Co. (she was born 24 Feb. 1911, daughter of Jake Wyatt and Daisy Thomas). Listed in the 1940 draft list of Cumberland Co., and served in the U.S. Navy during World War II. Ross Burgess worked as a rock quarrier, stave miller, and a carpenter before retiring. He currently lives at Crossville, TN.

10a. **James Lee (I)**. Born 26 Sept. 1930 in Cumberland Co., TN. Married Augusta Frances Simpson on 19 Apr. 1953. Jim Burgess is a slitter operator at Amherst, OH.

11a. **(James) Eugene.** Born 19 July 1954 at Amherst, OH. Married Hilda Christine Koenig on 24 Apr. 1982. Gene Burgess is a motorcycle mechanic at Parma, OH.

12a. **Geoffrey Eugene.** Born 11 Nov. 1982 at Parma, OH.

11b. **Terry Lee (II)**. Born 15 Apr. 1958 at Amherst, OH. Married Christine Marie Lovas on 21 June 1980. Terry Burgess is a sheet metal worker at Amherst, OH.

10b. **Lou Vella.** Born 3 Dec. 1931 in Cumberland Co., TN. Married John Robert Parker on 24 Sept. 1951 in Cumberland Co. (he was born 28 Feb. 1929, and died 10 Feb. 1976), and had children: *Robert Allen* (born 25 Nov. 1954, married Cynthia Baer [she was born 19 Nov. 1955], and had children: Gretchin [born 28 Oct. 1975]; John Carey [born 8 Nov. 1979]; Natlie Elizabeth [born 8 July 1981]). Lou Parker is a waitress.

10c. **Antha Mae.** Born 22 Oct. 1933 in Cumberland Co., TN. Married James Leonard Hodge on 5 July 1952 in Cumberland Co. (he was born 14 Sept. 1925, and died 11 Sept. 1982), and had children: *Danny Joe* (born about 1953, married Margret Ann Mayfield on 20 Apr. 1973 [she was born 18 Apr. 1953]); *Eddie Dean* (born 29 Nov. 1955, married Sharon Kay Wheeler on 13 Aug. 1973 [she was born 17 Dec. 1954], and had children: Edward Dewayne [born 3 July 1978]); *Donna Kay* (born 2 Mar. 1959 at Spencer, TN, married Terry Wilburn Dadson on 6 July 1977 [he was born 6 July 1956]). Antha Hodge is a machine operator at Spencer, TN.

10d. **Claude Lester.** Born 15 Feb. 1936 in Cumberland Co., TN. Married Shirley Gangle on 17 Mar. 1956 (she was born 28 Feb. 1938 at Lodi, OH). Claude Burgess works for Ford Motor Co. at Amherst, OH.

11a. **Debra Faye.** Born 8 Oct. 1956 at Amherst, OH. Married Jerry Cleo Meeks on 1 Jan. 1974 in Florida (he was born 30 Sept. 1955 at Frostproof, FL), and had children: *Stacy Joan* (born 14 Jan. 1976 at Bartow, FL); *Jerry Kevin* (born 14 Apr. 1978 at Haines City, FL).

11b. **Sherry Ann (II).** Born 21 Aug. 1959 at Amherst, OH. Married Fred Chester Stephens (div.; he was born 13 Sept. 1956 at Amherst, OH), and had children: *Jason Lester* (born 7 Nov. 1978 at Elyria, OH); married secondly Scott Alan Rankin on 9 Apr. 1982 at Lorain, OH (he was born 14 Apr. 1959 at Amherst), and had children: *Timothy George* (born 5 June 1982).

11c. **Pamela Lynn.** Born 31 Mar. 1961 at Amherst, OH. Married David Allen Aaron on 17 Nov. 1979 at Amherst, OH (he was born 29 July 1960 at Cleveland, OH).

10e. **Charles Raimon.** The official birth record gives his name as Charles Ramscoe Burgess. Born 5 Feb. 1938 in Cumberland Co., TN. Married Bertie Lee Davis (div.). Charles Burgess died in Aug. 1984 at Crossville, TN.

11a. **Reba Kay.** Born 8 May 1965 in Cumberland Co., TN. Married David ___.

11b. **Thomas Roger.** Born 29 Sept. 1966 in Cumberland Co., TN. Married Betty Gean Floyd on 18 Apr. 1988 in Cumberland Co., TN (she was born 5 Oct. 1971).

12a. **Matthew Charles.** Born 12 June 1989 at Crossville, TN.

12b. **Jessica Jean.** Born 4 Nov. 1993 at Crossville, TN.

11c. **Tony Quinn.** He was adopted by David and Fern Smith, and uses the surname Smith. Born 5 May 1968 in Cumberland Co., TN.

11d. **Rachel Pauline.** Born 16 Nov. 1969 in Cumberland Co., TN.

10f. **Travis Windell.** Born 21 Dec. 1940 in Cumberland Co., TN; died there on 7 Jan. 1941.

10g. **Winford Stanton.** Born 28 June 1942 in Cumberland Co., TN. Married Cleo Marie VanWinkle on 20 Oct. 1962 in Cumberland Co. Winford Burgess is a taxidermist and carpenter at Crossville, TN.

11a. **Chester Lynn.** Born 14 Mar. 1963 in Cumberland Co., TN; died there on 16 Mar. 1963, and is buried in the Newton Cemetery.

11b. **Rockie Dean.** Born 13 Oct. 1967 in Cumberland Co., TN. Married Sandra Diane Seals on 21 Dec. 1986 in Cumberland Co., TN (she was born 14 Mar. 1970).

10h. **Marjorie Louise "Margie."** Born 8 Feb. 1946 in Cumberland Co., TN. Married her distant cousin, (Franklin) Douglas Wyatt, on 10 Oct. 1964 in Cumberland Co. (he was born 12 Sept. 1945 at Elyria, OH), and had children: *(Franklin) Keith* (born 28 May 1965 in Cumberland Co., TN, married his distant cousin, Lisa Diane Burgess, on 19 Nov. 1985, and had children: Franklin Aaron Craig [born 7 May 1986 in Cumberland Co.]; Dusty Charmian [born 1 June 1987 in Cumberland Co.]; Brent Allen [born 22 Nov. 1989 in Cumberland Co.]); *Karen Denise* (born 22 Nov. 1968 in Cumberland Co., married Teddy Cornell Loden on 9 Aug. 1986 at Grandview, TN [he was born 15 May 1968], and had children: Whitney Danielle [born 11 Jan. 1987 in Cumberland Co.]; Colby Grant [born 18 Oct. 1990 in Cumberland Co.]); *Kimberly Dolores "Kim"* (born 11 Nov. 1972 in Cumberland Co., married Daniel Moses Dixon on 7 Mar. 1992 in Cumberland Co. [he was born 2 Mar. 1973]). Margie Wyatt has contributed greatly to this book. She and her husband live near Crossville, TN.

10i. **Ronald Eugene.** Born 12 Sept. 1948 in Cumberland Co., TN. Married Edna Marilyn Blaylock on 23 Nov. 1970 in Cumberland Co. (div.). Ron Burgess works for the State of Tennessee at Fall Creek Falls State Park, Pikeville, TN.

11a. **Mahala Lindsey.** Born 19 Sept. 1980 in Cumberland Co., TN.

10j. **Ross Rawlan (II) "Junior."** Born 26 June 1953 in Cumberland Co., TN. He died there on 24 May 1965 in an accidental shooting, and is buried in the Newton Cemetery.

SEMP BURGESS OF CUMBERLAND CO., TENNESSEE

[Hiram Simpson^7, Fancy Hill^8]

9e. **Semp Daniel** *[son of Fancy Hill].* Born 1 May 1916 in Cumberland Co., TN. Married (W.) Pauline Wyatt on 5 Nov. 1937 in Cumberland Co. (she was born 17 Jan. 1920, daughter of William West Wyatt). Semp Burgess was a farmer and sawmill worker in Cumberland Co. He now lives retired near Crossville, TN. He and his wife have contributed greatly to this book.

10a. **Kenneth Semp.** Born 29 Aug. 1938 at Crossville, TN. Married Judy Lynn Stultz on 14 May 1960 in Cumberland Co. Kenneth Burgess is an electrical engineer for Arnold Engineering, Manchester, TN.

11a. **Michael Steven.** Born 16 May 1961 at Knoxville, TN. Married Sibbieann Cooper. Mike Burgess works for Bates Casket Co.

12a. **Brooke Sibbielynn.** Born 11 June 1990 at Manchester, TN.

11b. **Sharon Lynn.** Born 15 Feb. 1963 at Manchester, TN. Married John David "J. D." Rottero, and had children: *Dustin Matthew* (born 26 Nov. 1986); *Mindy Lynn* (born 5 May 1988).

10b. **(Lois) Ann.** Born 4 Aug. 1942 in Roane Co., TN. Married David Turner Taylor on 28 Dec. 1963 in Cumberland Co., and had children: *Jay David*; *Christopher Daniel*; *Timothy James.* Ann Taylor is a teacher at Huntsville, AL.

10c. **Carolyn Sue.** Born 30 Oct. 1943 at Crossville, TN. Married Donald Ray Morrow on 29 Aug. 1964 in Cumberland Co., and had children: *Craig Andrew*; *Drew Burgess.* Carolyn Morrow is a registered nurse at Cleveland State Community College, Cleveland, TN.

OTTO BURGESS OF CUMBERLAND CO., TENNESSEE

[Hiram Simpson^7, Fancy Hill^8]

9f. **Otto Alex (I)** *[son of Fancy Hill].* His middle name is given as Elic or Alec in some records. Born 8 Jan. 1918 in Cumberland Co., TN. Married Joreece "Jody" Hayden Wyatt on 19 July 1937 in Cumberland Co. (div.; she was born 12 Dec. 1923, and remarried Donald Patterson, and lives at Mar Vista, CA); married secondly Sally Cable about 1957. Listed in the 1940 draft list of Cumberland Co. Otto Burgess was a farmer and laborer in Cumberland Co. and Dayton, OH before retiring. He currently lives at Crossville, TN.

10a. **(Robert) Donald (I).** Born 2 Apr. 1938 in Cumberland Co., TN. Married Virginia Hensley. Don Burgess was a taxi cab dispatcher at Dayton, OH and an airport porter at Las Vegas, NV. He died of diabetes and heart failure on 22 Apr. 1987 at Dayton, OH.

11a. **Clifford Wayne.** Born 1 Apr. 1963 at Knoxville, TN. Married Michelle Marie Anthony. Clifford Burgess currently lives at Dayton, OH.

12a. **Phillip Paul.** Born 7 Aug. 1985 at Dayton, OH.
12b. **Robert Daniel (II).** Born 29 Apr. 1988 at Dayton, OH.

11b. **Wade Alan.** Born 23 Dec. 1964 at Dayton, OH. Wade Burgess lives in Ohio.

11c. **Kathryn Denise "Kathy."** Born 12 Jan. 1969 at Dayton, OH. Kathy Burgess currently lives at Ocala, FL.

11d. **Sally Ann (II).** Born 14 Aug. 1970 at Dayton, OH. Married Cleroy Autry Jr., and had children: *Virginia Joyce* (born 15 Dec. 1988 at Ocala, FL); *Shanna Rosa Lateiyiea* (born 26 Aug. 1991 at Ocala, FL). Sally and Cleroy Autry currently live at Ocala, FL.

10b. **Vivian Irene (II).** Born 4 Jan. 1940 in Cumberland Co., TN. Married Jewell Frank Houston in Apr. 1958 (div.), and had children: *Vicke Lynn* (born 1 Mar. 1958 at Dayton OH, married

Robert Allen Thrower on 12 Dec. 1987, and had children: Leanne Irene [born 28 May 1988 at Long Beach, CA]; Lindsey Grace [born 29 Mar. 1990 at Los Alamitos, CA]); *Beth Anne* (born 10 Aug. 1959 at Dayton, OH, married Stephan Michael Spencer in May 1977 [div.]; and secondly Michael Robert Welch in Nov. 1981 [div.], and had children: Michael Robert II [born 16 Nov. 1982 at Los Alamitos, CA]; Erin Lynn [born 21 July 1985 at Bellflower, CA]; *Beth Anne* married thirdly Craig Eldon Diettert on 4 Aug. 1990, and currently lives at Buena Park, CA).

Vivian Irene HOUSTON married secondly Benjamin Dean "Bennie" Cook on 24 June 1965 at Las Vegas, NV (he worked for the Los Angeles City Dept. of Water and Power, before retiring, and now owns an automobile body shop), and had children: *Benjamin Dean Jr.* (born 31 Jan. 1966 at Santa Monica, CA, married Marina Federiconi on 5 July 1992, and had children: Gina Noel [born 21 Dec. 1989 at Whittier, CA]; Child [due Feb. 1994]; *Benjamin Cook Jr.* currently lives at Monrovia, CA); *Harley Boyd* (born 28 Mar. 1967 at Los Angeles, CA, and had children: Asia Rae [born 20 Jan. 1993 at Glendora, CA]); *Geraldine Yvonne* (born 27 Jan. 1969 at Sierra Madre, CA, married Ray C. Conrad on 25 Oct. 1986, and had children: Anthony Ray [born 15 Aug. 1986 at Bellflower, CA]; Cathryn Mae [born 23 May 1989 at Glendora, CA]; Jennifer Yvonne [born 21 Feb. 1991 at Glendora, CA]; *Geraldine* currently lives at Pahrump, NV); *Raymond Michael* (born 26 May 1971 at Sierra Madre, CA, married, and works with his father in the family business).

Vivian Irene COOK is a substitute teacher at Pahrump, NV.

10c. **(Boyd) Douglas (I).** Born 7 Oct. 1942 in Cumberland Co., TN. Married (Charlotte) Diane Noah. Doug Burgess was in the ironworks business at Huntington Beach, CA. He died of diabetes on 8 Dec. 1992 at Tucson, AZ.

11a. **Christina Diane.** Born 10 Mar. 1967 at Huntington Beach, CA. Married and had two children.

11b. **Boyd Douglas II** (twin). Born 30 Oct. 1970 at Huntington Beach, CA; he died there on 20 Aug. 1974, when he fell from a second story window to the patio below, and was buried in the Good Shepherd Cemetery.

11c. **(Otto) Dwayne** (twin). Born 30 Oct. 1970 at Huntington Beach, CA.

10d. **Grace Luella.** Born 3 Mar. 1944 in Cumberland Co., TN. Married Clifford Shumaker on 24 Feb. 1962 at Dayton, OH (div.); married secondly Ernest Smothers on 25 Nov. 1969 at Chicago, IL (div.); married thirdly Lawrence Shearn on 1 Dec. 1973 at Honolulu, HI (he was born 21 Apr. 1939, and died Apr. 1980 at Honolulu, HI); married fourthly Edward "Duke" Tilton on 1 Jan. 1989 at Honolulu, HI (he is a retired petty officer in the U.S. Navy). Grace Tilton worked for the Chief Petty Officers Club at Pearl Harbor, HI, where she managed the Marina Restaurant. She currently lives at Oak Harbor, WA.

10e. **Frances Charalene.** Born 2 Oct. 1945 at Dayton, OH. Married Francisco Alarcón "Frank" Ramirez II on 6 June 1964 at Las Vegas, NV (he works as a licensed contractor and landscaper), and had children: *Francisco Alarcón III* (born 29 Dec. 1964, married Joyce ___, had children: Child [due Mar. 1994], and works as a certified public accountant at Playa Del Rey, CA); *Carmelita* (born 24 Aug. 1966, married Paul Saucedo, had children: Paul Jr. [born 10 June 1993 at Santa Monica, CA], and works as an accounts specialist at Century Cable, Santa Monica); *Lucille* (born 15 July 1968, and works as an accounts receivable manager at Koontz Hardware, Beverly Hills, CA); *Natalie Ann* (born 18 Dec. 1970, married David Ray Hoskins on 7 June 1991, had children: Erick Angel David [born 13 Feb. 1991 at Culver City, CA), works as a medical assistant for a Santa Monica hospital, and lives at Mar Vista, CA); *Elizabeth Irene* (born 23 Nov. 1974 at Santa Monica, CA, and works as a secretary while simultaneously attending college); *Mariano José* (born 26 July 1976 at Santa Monica, CA, currently attending St. Monica's High School). Frances Ramirez lives at Culver City, CA.

10f. **Susan Diane.** Born 2 Nov. 1947 at Dayton, OH. Married Robert Martin on 6 Nov. 1963 (dec.), and had children: *Joreeca Lynn* (born 27 Mar. 1964 at Los Angeles, CA, married Joseph Mullins [div.], and had children: Alex Otto [born 28 Apr. 1985 at Los Angeles, CA, died there on 8 Sept. 1985]; Adam Alexander [born 25 Oct. 1986 at Crossville, TN]); *Robert Lee* (born 5 Mar. 1965 at Los Angeles, CA, married Mary Ann ___, and had children: Amber Jean [born 28 July 1991 at Salt Lake City, UT]); *Martha Sue* (born 8 Mar. 1966 at Los Angeles, CA, and had children: Michael [born 10 July 1992 at Salt Lake City, UT]); *Tina Renée EARLY* (born 16 Apr. 1971 at Los Angeles, CA, married Nathan Morris, and had children: Jonathan Nathaniel [born 14 Jan. 1988 at Crossville, TN]; Amber Diane [born 14 Oct. 1989 at Crossville, TN]). *Susan Diane* married secondly Charles Hopkins on 26 June 1986 at Crossville, TN (he died on 26 Jan. 1987 at Crossville in a car accident), and thirdly Michael Demuth on 9 Sept. 1989 at

Los Angeles, CA. *Susan DEMUTH* works as a newspaper distributor for *The Tennessean*, and lives at Crossville, TN. She has contributed greatly to this book.

10g. **Otto Alex (II).** Born 20 Dec. 1958 at Dayton, OH. Married Karen ___. Otto Burgess lives at Dayton, OH.

FOSTER BURGESS OF WALTON CO., FLORIDA

[Hiram Simpson[7], Fancy Hill[8]]

9i. **(Frank) Foster** *[son of Fancy Hill]*. Born 13 Feb. 1923 in Cumberland Co., TN. Married Ruby Duff; married secondly Dean ___; married thirdly Rebecca Porter. Dr. Foster Burgess worked as a civilian physicist for the U.S. Air Force for 24 years; he currently owns and operates Alaqua Vineyards Winery, Freeport, FL. His biography has appeared in *American Men and Women of Science*.

10a. **Sharon Sue.** Born 9 Sept. 1951 at Dayton, OH. Married Paul Troxell. Sharon Burgess-Troxell earned her M.S. at Florida State University in 1976. She currently is an Assistant Professor of Physical Education at Ball State University, Muncie, IN.

10b. **Jeanne Marlene.** Born 30 May 1953 at Dayton, OH. Jeanne Burgess is a winemaker at Lakeridge Winery and Vineyards, Clermont, FL.

10c. **Kathleen Lynn.** Born 15 June 1956 at Valparaiso, FL. Kathleen Burgess is a bank auditor.

ARLEN BURGESS OF CUMBERLAND CO., TENNESSEE

[Hiram Simpson[7], Fancy Hill[8]]

9j. **Arlen (I)** (nmn) *[son of Fancy Hill]*. His name is listed as James Arlen in his father's family Bible record, but was misrecorded. Born 22 Nov. 1925 in Cumberland Co., TN. Married Ardella Perry about 1943 (div.); married secondly Helen I. ___ about 1947 (div.; she remarried George Pound on 13 Mar. 1954); married thirdly Sheila ___ about 1960; married fourthly Patricia Miller. Arlen Burgess was a plaster construction worker at Los Angeles, CA before retiring. He now lives at Crossville, TN.

10a. **Gerald Arley.** Born 2 Apr. 1944 at Cleveland, OH. Gerald Burgess was a dishwasher at Tucson, AZ. He died there unmarried on 14 Mar. 1985.

10b. **Leslie Robert (I).** His given name was originally Arlen Jr. (III). Born 23 July 1945 at Cleveland, OH. Married Mary Scalf. Les Burgess is a bus driver at Tucson, AZ.

11a. **(Leslie) Robert (II).** Born 24 Sept. 1967 at Tucson, AZ. Married Gladys Emilia Rodríguez on 13 Nov. 1987. Robert Burgess works as an auto mechanic.

11b. **Christine Ann.** Born 27 May 1969 at Tucson, AZ. Married Michael Struppa on 17 Jan. 1992, and had children: *Kaylene Mary* (born 27 Aug. 1991 at Tucson, AZ); *Son* (born 12 Aug. 1992 at Portland, OR). Christine Struppa lives at Troutdale, OR.

12a. **Michael Ryan.** Born 20 Aug. 1985 at Tucson, AZ.

11c. **Arlen Edmund.** Born 10 Nov. 1980 at Tucson, AZ.

10c. **Edward Arnold.** He was raised by his stepfather, and uses the surname Pound. Born 21 Feb. 1948 at Pasadena, CA. Married (Barbara) Jeanie Hays. Edward Pound works for the Southern Pacific Railroad at Redding, CA.

11a. **Samuel Edward (I).** Born 11 Oct. 1972 at Watsonville, CA. He was accidentally killed when run over by a truck on 27 July 1979 at Salem, Marion Co. OR.

11b. **Wayland Christopher John.** He was adopted by George and Helen Pound. Born 30 June 1975 at Grants Pass, OR.

11c. **Roy Everett (II)** (ad.). Born 24 Jan. 1976 at Redding, CA.

11d. **Benjamin John (I).** Born 7 Feb. 1982 at Redding, CA.

10d. **Carol Ann (II).** Born 24 Apr. 1949 at Pasadena, CA.

10e. **Arlene Susan.** Born 1961. Married Terry Pierce, and lives at Panama, OK.

10f. **Amber Marie** (ad.). Born 8 July 1981 at Crossville, TN. She was the granddaughter of Patricia Miller Burgess by a previous marriage (her mother drowned in summer of 1982).

KENT BURGESS OF DAVIDSON CO., TENNESSEE
[Hiram Simpson^7, Fancy Hill^8]

9k. **Kent Kenard** *[son of Fancy Hill].* Born 17 Jan. 1927 in Cumberland Co., TN. Married Billie Hill. Served in World War II. Kent Burgess was the manager of a convenience market before retiring. He currently lives at Antioch, TN.

10a. **Therese Ann.** Born 6 Dec. 1952 at Searcy, AR. Married Kerry Lynn McClurg.
10b. **Philip Dan.** Born 23 Nov. 1954 at Hot Springs, AR. Philip Burgess is a student at MPSU.
10c. **Patrick Michael.** Born 17 Mar. 1956 at Hot Springs, AR. Married Stephanie Lee. Patrick Burgess is a computer programmer for Computer Dynamics, Houston, TX.

11a. **Michelle Pamela** (ad.). Born 1 Mar. 1978 at Corpus Christi, TX.
11b. **Joanna Marie (II)** (ad.). Born 22 Sept. 1979 at Nashville, TN.
11c. **Daniel Michael.** Born 22 Feb. 1981 at Houston, TX.

CARL BURGESS OF MONTGOMERY CO., OHIO
[Hiram Simpson^7, Fancy Hill^8]

9l. **Carl Marlo (I)** *[son of Fancy Hill].* Born 8 Nov. 1928 in Cumberland Co., TN. Married Jean Elizabeth Tawney (div.). Served in the Army in 1951. Carl Burgess was a job setter at Delco Moraine in Dayton, OH before retiring. He now lives at Germantown, OH.

10a. **(Linda) Diane.** Born 5 Nov. 1953 at Dayton, OH. Married Glen Harris.
10b. **Rebecca Kay.** Born 6 Feb. 1955 at Dayton, OH.
10c. **(Carl) Marlo (II).** Born 27 July 1956 at Dayton, OH. Marlo Burgess works for C & M Products at Dayton.
10d. **Lisa Gail.** Born 26 Oct. 1957 at Dayton, OH. Married Douglas Ray Poston (he was born 14 Feb. 1957 at Dayton, OH, son of Gradis Arnold Poston and Margaret Pearl Clouse).
10e. **Gary Lee (II).** Born 4 June 1959 at Dayton, OH. Served in the U.S. Army. Gary Burgess works as a clerk.
10f. **Pamela Jean (I).** Born 12 Oct. 1960 at Dayton, OH.

DALLAS BURGESS OF MONTGOMERY CO., OHIO
[Hiram Simpson^7, Fancy Hill^8]

9m. **(Floyd) Dallas** *[son of Fancy Hill].* Born 6 Dec. 1930 in Cumberland Co., TN. Married Inez ___; married fourthly Clara Louise Frank on 18 Mar. 1973 in Cumberland Co.; married fifthly Patricia Jean Woods. Dallas Burgess was a delivery man for a tool company before retiring. He now lives at Dayton, OH.

10a. **Larry Earl.** Child of first wife. Born 1954 at Dayton, OH. Last known living at Orlando, FL.
10b. **Renetta Lynn.** Child of second wife. Born 14 Apr. 1963 at Dayton, OH. Married Paul Holland.

GEORGE A. BURGESS OF STANISLAUS CO., CALIFORNIA
[Hiram Simpson^7]

8h. **George Anderson** *[son of Hiram Simpson].* Born 6 Jan. 1894 in Cumberland Co., Tenn. Married Stella Louise Lewis on 29 Mar. 1916 in Cumberland Co. (div.; she died about 1964); married secondly Bessie H. Catterlin (she lives at Modesto, CA). Listed on the 20 June 1917 draft list for Cumberland Co., TN. George Burgess was a laborer in Idaho, Oregon, and California. He died on 3 Feb. 1981 at Modesto, CA, and is buried in the Ceres Cemetery. His obituary mentions that he had been a resident of Modesto for 45 years.

9a. **Ruby Marie.** Born 9 Nov. 1918 in Cumberland Co., TN; died there on 18 Nov. 1918, and is buried in the Bolin Cemetery.
9b. **Geneva.** Born about 1920 in Cumberland Co., TN. Married S. W. McKenzie. Geneva McKenzie lives at Sequim, WA.

9c. **Calvin Lee.** Born 5 Dec. 1923 in Cumberland Co., TN. Married Cathryn Bean; married secondly Margaret Ellen Breland on 4 June 1971 at Port Angeles, Clallam Co., WA. Listed in the city directories of Port Angeles, WA, from 1950. Calvin Burgess owns and operates Cal's Home Repair Service at Port Angeles, WA.

10a. **Gary Lee (I).** Born 5 Nov. 1948 at Port Angeles, WA. Married Suzanne Marie Bulewicki on 8 Aug. 1971 at Port Angeles, Clallam Co., WA (div.; she remarried Robert James Jones on 23 Feb. 1976 in Clallam Co.); married secondly Julie Ann Watkins on 4 Aug. 1983 at Port Angeles, WA. Gary Burgess lives at Port Angeles, WA.

11a. **Randall Jeffrey.**
11b. **Christina.**

10b. **Janice Lynn.** Born 12 Sept. 1950 at Port Angeles, WA. Married George Mathews on 10 Dec. 1966 at Port Angeles, Clallam Co., WA; married secondly Jack Clark. Janice Clark works as a resident adviser for the developmentally disabled at Port Angeles, WA.

10c. **Michael Terry.** Born 8 Mar. 1954 at Port Angeles, WA. Married Diane Marie van der Waal on 5 Aug. 1974 at Port Angeles, Clallam Co., WA (div.; she remarried Gary Lee Armstrong on 29 June 1978 in Clallam Co.); married secondly Sandy Sue Jeffries on 26 May 1989 in Port Angeles, WA. Mike Burgess lives in Montana.

11a. **Brent.**

10c. **(Harold) Guy.** Born 31 Mar. 1955 at Port Angeles, WA. Married Bonnie Lyn Wright on 23 July 1981 in Port Angeles, Clallam Co., WA. Guy Burgess lives at Port Angeles.

11a. **Child.**

9d. **Cecile.** Born about 1925. Married Roy Stockton. Cecile Stockton lives at Phelan, San Bernardino Co., CA.

9e. **Carl Vernon.** Born 18 Dec. 1927 at Buhl, ID. Married (Mary) Rose Lecky (born 10 Apr. 1921 at Miscouche, PE, Canada, daughter of Kenneth Lecky and Anna MacDonald). Carl Burgess was a pipefitter at Port Angeles, WA, and then worked for the naval shipyard in Bremerton, WA; he moved to Merced, CA in 1975 on his retirement, and died there on 22 Sept. 1981. Rose Burgess currently lives at Merced.

10a. **Gloria Ann.** Born 26 June 1949 at Wendell, ID. Married Edward Sumpter on 4 Feb. 1978 (div.), and has children: *Angela Dawn* (born 8 Aug. 1979 at Chula Vista, CA). Gloria Sumpter is a secretary for the school district at Chula Vista, CA.

10b. **Gerald Duane.** Born 26 Nov. 1952 at Port Angeles, WA. Gerald Burgess lives at Merced, CA.

9f. **Warren Douglas (I).** Born 9 Oct. 1935 at Buhl, ID. Married Barbara Wulf. Warren Burgess was a truck driver before retiring. He now lives at Sequim, WA.

10a. **Deborah Lynn (II).** Born 21 Dec. 1961 at Fullerton, CA. Married Donald Ellis McBride on 11 Jan. 1982 at Port Angeles, Clallam Co., WA.

10b. **Bridget Dee.** Born 30 June 1963 at Fullerton, CA. Married Kurt E. Van Dusen on 15 Aug. 1981 at Port Angeles, Clallam Co., WA.

10c. **Warren Douglas (II).** Born 27 June 1969 at Fullerton, CA.

[William (I)[1], Edward (I)[2], Reuben (I)[3], Thomas (I)[4], King Hiram (I)[5], Joseph Daniel[6]]

JOHN WILLIS BURGESS
(1861-1949)

OF CUMBERLAND COUNTY, TENNESSEE

7c. **(John) Willis** *[son of Joseph Daniel].* Born 25 Mar. 1861 in Cumberland Co., TN. Married Frances Elizabeth Daniel about 1884 (she was born 9 May 1869 in TN, and died in Cumberland Co. on 9 Jan. 1967, aged 97 years). Listed in the 1870-1920 censuses for Cumberland Co., TN, but was living in Dallas Co., MO on 23 Sept. 1890; four of four children survive in 1900, six of six in 1910. Willis Burgess was a farmer in Cumberland Co. He died there on 15 Nov. 1949, and is buried with his wife in the Burgess Cemetery.

8a. **Victoria Elizabeth.** Born 3 Feb. 1886 in Cumberland Co., TN. Married James W. H. Warner on 6 May 1901 in White Co., TN (he was born 1 Jan. 1881, and died 25 Feb. 1973), and had six children, among them: *Rena* (married Cecil Bolin). Listed in the 1910 census for Cumberland Co. (two of five children are then living). Victoria Warner died on 13 Mar. 1982 in Cumberland Co., aged 96 years, and is buried in the Burgess Cemetery.

8b. **(Josie) Alice.** Born 20 Sept. 1887 in Cumberland Co., TN. Married John Frazier, and had at least the following children: *Eva* (married George Smith). Alice Frazier died on 24 May 1933.

8c. **Verta Vera.** Born 1 Oct. 1889 in Cumberland Co., TN. Married Arba R. "Arby" Bolin on 24 Oct. 1909 in Cumberland Co. (he was born 10 Jan. 1886 at Crossville, TN, son of Nathaniel S. Bolin and Martha Coffey, worked as a coal mine manager, and died 28 Mar. 1944 at Crossville), by whom she had the children listed below; married secondly Joe H. Hodgin, and died on 20 Dec. 1969 in Cumberland Co., buried in the Thomas Springs Cemetery.

Lillian Lorie BOLIN. Born 8 May 1910 at Crossville, TN, married Franklin Monroe Sapp on 3 Dec. 1923 in Cumberland Co. (he was born 6 May 1902, son of Joseph Hill Sapp and Jennie Dodson), and had children: *Robert Lee "R. L."* (born 25 Nov. 1925 at Crossville, married and had children: Kathy; *R. L.* married secondly Pauline Hartzel); *Iva Bell* (born 22 Mar. 1928); *Virginia Catherine* (born 1 Aug. 1930, died 1969 at Crossville, TN, buried Burgess Cemetery); *Leamon Boyo* (born 24 July 1932); *Freda Helen* (born 21 June 1934, married William Wendel Cassel on 22 June 1958, and secondly Darrell E. Taylor on 14 Feb. 1987 at Las Vegas, NV); *Illa Nyle* (born 22 Oct. 1936); *Mildred Leanor* (born 12 Oct. 1938); *Della Elanor* (born 19 Sept. 1940); *Opal* (born 15 May 1942, married William Baxter McCoy on 25 Mar. 1961, and had children: William Keith; Gregory Lynn; Lisa Gail); *Nathaniel Monroe* (born 1 Sept. 1944); *Davied Leisle* (born 25 Oct. 1946); *James Vaughn* (born 21 Feb. 1949); *Connie Ineze* (born 27 Feb. 1952).

Virgie BOLIN. Born 28 Sept. 1911 at Crossville, TN, married Frank Scarbrough, and had children: *Betty* (born 19 June 1926, married Bethel Flynn [he was born 24 Nov. 1920], and had children: Delmus [born 24 Apr. 1944]; Barbara [born 19 June 1948]; Martha [born 28 Sept. 1951]; Kenneth [born 21 Feb. 1953]; Evelyn [born 9 Mar. 1954]; Dennis [born 28 Feb. 1955, died 25 Nov. 1979, buried Flynn's Cove Cemetery]; Wayne [born 5 Nov. 1958]; Kathy [born 28 Jan. 1961]; Roni [born about 1963]; Karen "Sandy" [born 26 Sept. 1966]); *Gladys Marie* (born 28 Apr. 1930, married Robert Eugene Miller on 27 Dec. 1947 [he was born 19 Mar. 1922, son of Lawrence Miller and Ester Cummins, and died 22 Oct. 1987 at Melbourne, FL], and had children: Robert Eugene II); *Carlyle* (born about 1933, died 1944 at Crossville, TN); *Maurice* (born 3 Feb. 1936, married Helen Scott in 1954, and had children: Richard; Mike; Cindy [who married Henry Hunnicutt in 1985]; Linda; Tim [born 11 May 1964]; Terresa; David [born 15 May 1969, married Samantha Pendergrass]; *Maurice* married secondly Frances Pugh on 3 Dec. 1971 [she was born 21 Sept. 1950, daughter of Floyd Pugh and Lela Barnwell], and had children: Gary [born 25 Feb. 1969, married Tonya Withrow on 14 Apr. 1989 in Cumberland Co.]; Curt [born 22 Oct. 1975]). ***Virgie SCARBROUGH*** married secondly Eloch Stone.

(Edna) Celeste BOLIN. Born 29 Dec. 1915 at Crossville, TN, married Truman Sherrill in Sept. 1929 (div. 1936), and had children: *Carl* (born 18 Sept. 1932); *Nina* (born 24 June 1933). ***Celeste SHERRILL*** married secondly Roy Hyder in 1939 (he was born 19 May 1901, and died May 1942), and had children: *Frankie Jane* (born 1 July 1942, married Lyle Harrison, and had children: Kevin [born 1 July 1965]; Christopher [married Sherri Agnew]; Jonathon). ***Celeste HYDER*** married thirdly Jack Roberts on 27 Aug. 1947 (he was born 15 Sept. 1913, and died 6 Nov. 1969), and had children: *Jackie* (born 10 June 1949, married Bobby B. Dixon on 20 Dec. 1969 at Pulaski, VA [he was born 25 Nov. 1947 at Greenville, TN, son of Benjamin Dixon and Lillian Gregg], and had children: Terra Suzann [born 31 Aug. 1974]; Thomas Kress [born 2 June 1979]). ***Celeste ROBERTS*** married fourthly Herman "Nick" Nickolson on 25 June 1986 (he was born 1926).

Dorothy Jennice BOLIN. Born 27 July 1919 at Crossville, TN, married Clarence Carl "Red" Neely (he was born 15 Nov. 1914, son of (William) Andrew Neely and Virginia Hall, and brother of Willie Arthur Neely, who married Dorothy's sister, Irene), and died in childbirth on 12 Dec. 1951 at Crossville, TN, buried Burgess Cemetery, having had children: *Mary Jane* (born and died 25 July 1935 at Crossville, TN, buried Thomas Springs Cemetery); *Jerry* (born 12 Feb. 1937 at Crossville, TN); *Robert* (born 27 Mar. 1939 at Crossville, TN, died there on 26 June 1964); *Velma* (born 29 Dec. 1940 at Crossville, TN); *Roberta* (born 30 Sept. 1943 at Crossville, TN, married William Dean Henry on 12 Feb. 1960, and had children: William Dean Jr.; Tonia Diann; Carl Bryant [born 1 Aug. 1973]); *Edna* (born 31 Oct. 1945 at Crossville, TN); *Clarence Carl Jr.* (born 21 Aug. 1948 at Crossville, TN, married Judy Hood on 4 Dec. 1966 [she was born 6 June 1949, daughter of Dewey and Emma Hood], and secondly Doris Faye Adams on 4 Jan. 1949 [she was born 11 July 1957, daughter of Stanley Adams and Pauline Russell], and had children: April Dawn [born 19 Apr. 1981]; Christopher Lee [born 3 Dec. 1985]; *Clarence* married thirdly Tommie Jean Wynacht on 26 Dec. 1990 [she was born 1 Apr. 1951, daughter of Elmer Wynacht and Elease Lewis]); *Sammuel Stevens* (born 12 Dec. 1951 at Crossville, TN, married Ruth Kerley on 9 Jan. 1971 [she was born 20 Aug. 1952, daughter of John B. Kerley and Violet Brown], and had children: Sammuel Stevens II "J. R." [born 13 Nov. 1972]; Jonathan Robert "Jody" [born 24 Sept. 1976]).

(Nannie) Irene BOLIN. Born 13 Mar. 1922 at Crossville, TN, married Willie Arthur "Bill" Neely (he was the son of William Andrew Neely and Virginia Hall, and brother of Clarence Carl Neely, who married Irene's sister, Dorothy), and had children: *Wilma* (born 26 Dec. 1942 at Crossville, TN, married Dale Roberts, and had children: Derek; Jason); *Marietta N.* (born 3 July 1944, married James Lee, and worked as a nurse); *Douglas Arba* (born 20 May 1946 at Crossville, TN, married Vivian Dale Nevils [she was born 13 Mar. 1949 at Pleasant Hill, TN, daughter of Roy Sneed Nevils Sr. and Marthe Brown Allen], and had children: Adam [born 8 June 1971]; Paul [born 16 Aug. 1974]; Rebecca [born 4 Aug. 1977]); *Dean* (born about 1948, married Debra Farmer, and had children: Bradley); *Donna* (born about 1952, married Donald Loveday, and had children: Jennifer Lynn; Mathew); *Pamela* (born 2 Aug. 1958 at Crossville, TN, married John Stobart [he was born 13 Oct. 1954 at Chicago, IL, son of Edwin Stobart and Emilie Stalliones], and had children: Alexandra Emilie [born 1 Nov. 1990 at Sacramento, CA]).

Dallas Elmo BOLIN. Born 13 Oct. 1923 at Crossville, TN, married Alice Wyatt (she was born 14 Jan. 1925 at Pea, TN, daughter of Robert F. Wyatt and Francis "Fannie" Croft), worked as a truck driver, and had children: *Philip* (born 22 June 1942 at Crossville, TN, married Mildred Wyatt on 16 Jan. 1959 [div.], and had children: Timothy; Michael L. [born 24 Jan. 1966, died {drowned} on 20 June 1983 in Santa Clara Co., CA]; Brian; *Philip* married secondly Carol Ormandy on 5 Dec. 1980); *Harold* (born 15 Feb. 1945 at Crossville, TN, married Carol Wood [she was born 13 May 1947], and had children: Kevin [born 27 Nov. 1968]; Robin [born 15 Oct. 1972]; *Harold* married secondly Nina Golden in July 1987); *Edward* (born 18 Sept. 1948 at Crossville, TN, married Clara Lewis in Sept. 1966 [div.], and had children: Wendy [born 17 Jan. 1968]; Dennis [born 7 Oct. 1970]; Jeffery [born 10 June 1974?]; *Edward* married secondly Linda Osborne on 8 Aug. 1982, and had children: Kenneth [born 6 Feb. 1983]); *Wayne* (born 29 Sept. 1952, married Carolyn ___, and had children: Amber [born 1 Apr. 1982]; Heather); *Barbara* (born 5 Oct. 1954 at Crossville, TN, married secondly David Ashburn, and had children: Eric; Christopher); *Arba* (born 5 Jan. 1957 at Crossville, TN, married Mary ___, and secondly Mary Hildreth on 30 Aug. 1980 at Oak Ridge, TN [she was born 12 Aug. 1959? at Oak Ridge, daughter of W. H. Hildreth and Gladys Miriam Breland], and had children: Dustin R. [born 7 Oct. 1982]; Joy M. [born 15 Mar. 1984]).

Earl BOLIN. Born 26 Dec. 1925, and died Sept. 1973 at Crossville, TN.

Veronica Ann "Roni" BOLIN. Born 18 Aug. 1932 at Crossville, TN, married Richard Duffy in 1948 at Dayton, OH (div.; he was born 10 Sept. 1924 at Dayton, OH, son of James Francis Duffy and Catherine Spellause, and died Apr. 1968 at Dayton. ***Roni*** married secondly Donald Lee Huber on 25 July 1964 at Dayton, OH (he was born 20 Sept. 1932 at Dayton, OH, son of Herbert Christ Huber and Edna Bertha Staehlin), and had children: *Kimberly Lynn* (born 6 Dec. 1968 at

Dayton, OH); *Julia Jane* (born 4 May 1971 at Dayton, OH). Roni and Donald Huber live at Dayton, OH; they have contributed greatly to this book.

8d. **Allen Newman.** Born 12 June 1898 in Cumberland Co., TN. See below for full entry.

8e. **Nolan** (nmn). Born 8 Mar. 1904 in Cumberland Co., TN. See below for full entry.

8f. **Lelan** (nmn). Born 29 May 1909 in Cumberland Co., TN. Listed in the 1940 draft list of Cumberland Co. Lelan Burgess worked as a farmer with his brother Allen. He died unmarried on 25 Nov. 1987 in Cumberland Co., TN, and is buried in the Burgess Cemetery.

ALLEN BURGESS OF CUMBERLAND CO., TENNESSEE
[John Willis[7]]

8d. **Allen Newman** *[son of John Willis].* Born 12 June 1898 in Cumberland Co., TN. Married Myrtle Brewer on 25 Dec. 1919 in Cumberland Co. (div. 1933; she was born 26 Aug. 1902, sister of Maude Brewer); married secondly his cousin, Susie Brewer, on 23 Sept. 1933 in Putnam Co. (she died Feb. 1969); married thirdly his cousin, (Lillie) Mae King, on 1 Apr. 1942 in Cumberland Co. (she was born 29 Feb. 1924, daughter of Laura Ann Burgess and Henry Napoleon King). Allen Burgess was a farmer in rural Cumberland Co., TN. He died there on 30 May 1992, aged 93 years, and is buried in the new Allen Burgess Cemetery.

9a. **Gladys Omalee.** Born 24 Oct. 1920 in Cumberland Co., TN. Married C. Lynell Williams, and had children: *Charlotte*; *Micheal*; *Connie*. Gladys Williams currently lives at Chattanooga, TN.

9b. **Roy Everett (I).** Born 25 Mar. 1924 (or 1925) in Cumberland Co., TN. Married Wilma J. Glasscock in West Virginia. Served in World War II. Roy Burgess is a job setter for Ridge Tool Co., at Elyria, OH. He lives at North Ridgeville, OH.

10a. **Vernon Dale (II).** Born 21 June 1950 at Mannington, WV. Married Carol Eckhart. Vernon Burgess an upgrade utility man for Ford Motor Co., at Elyria, OH.

11a. **Gregory Dale.** Born 5 Oct. 1978 at Elyria, OH.

11b. **Matthew Dale.** Born 25 Oct. 1980 at Elyria, OH.

10b. **Everett Merle.** Born 5 Nov. 1951 at Elyria, OH. Married Beverly Searles. Everett Burgess works for Ridge Tool Co., at Elyria, OH.

11a. **Bryan Leighty.** Born 10 May 1979 at Overland, OH.

11b. **Raymond Wesley.** Born 18 Dec. 1982 at Overland, OH.

10c. **Renee Yvonne.** Born 12 Feb. 1953 at Elyria, OH. Married Dennis Ross, and had children: *Dustin*; *Derek*.

10d. **Bonita Gail.** Born 30 Oct. 1954 at Elyria, OH. Married Dennis Gold, and had children: *DeAnna*.

10e. **Randy Nyle.** Born 18 Mar. 1956 at Elyria, OH. Married Michelle LeVon. Randy Burgess works in a machine shop at Kalt Manufacturing Co., and lives at Lorain, OH.

11a. **Jeffery Ryan.** Born 18 June 1983 at Elyria, OH.

11b. **Joshua David.** Born 8 Apr. 1984 at Elyria, OH.

9c. **(Cleo) Marie** (twin). Born 3 Dec. 1926 in Cumberland Co., TN. Married Melvin Wyatt, and had children: *Teresa*; *Terry*. Marie Wyatt lives at Crossville, TN.

9d. **(Leslie) Burl** (twin). Born 3 Dec. 1926 in Cumberland Co., TN. Served in World War II. Burl Burgess died unmarried on 10 Jan. 1958 (or 2 Apr. 1947) at Chattanooga, TN, but is buried in the Davis Cemetery, Cumberland Co. He was a member of the Baptist Church.

9e. **Dollie Juno.** Born 10 Feb. 1935 in Cumberland Co., TN. Married Ray Cordell, and had children: *Pat*; *Kenny*. Dollie Cordell lives at Crossville, TN.

9f. **(Mary) Alma.** Born about 1940 in Cumberland Co., TN. Married Rubell Downs. Alma Downs lives at Crossville, TN.

9g. **Joyce Anita.** Born 24 Jan. 1943 in Cumberland Co., TN. Married Lester Croft; married secondly Clinton Ward. Joyce Ward lives at Elyria, OH.

9h. **Roger Dean.** Born 13 Apr. 1944 in Cumberland Co., TN. Married Joanne (or JoAnn) Parham on 6 May 1963. Roger Burgess is an electrician and plumber at Crossville, TN.

10a. **Pamela Marie.** Her middle name is given as Maria in her marriage certificate. Born 12 Jan. 1964 at Crossville, TN. Married (Willis) Franklin Brown on 30 Mar. 1990 in Cumberland Co., TN (he was born 27 Aug. 1947).

10b. **(Stephen) Eugene.** Born 26 Sept. (or June) 1971 at Crossville, TN. Married Daphne Mae Farris on 11 May 1990 in Cumberland Co., TN (she was born 21 Jan. 1971).

10c. **Larry Dean (II).** Born 27 Aug. 1975 at Crossville, TN.

9i. **Carley Gene.** Born 17 May 1945 in Cumberland Co., TN; died there on 18 May 1945, and is buried in the Burgess Cemetery.

9j. **Marvin Allen** (twin). Born 14 May 1947 in Cumberland Co., TN. Married (Velma) Diane Lewis on 19 Mar. 1966 in Cumberland Co. (she was born 14 Dec. 1948). Marvin Burgess is a carpenter at Vandever, TN.

10a. **Lisa Diane.** Born 22 Sept. 1967 in Cumberland Co., TN. Married her distant cousin, (Franklin) Keith Wyatt, on 29 Nov. 1985 in Cumberland Co., TN (he was born 28 May 1965). See Keith Wyatt's entry for her children.

10b. **Derek Heath.** Born 29 Jan. 1971 in Cumberland Co., TN. Married Theresa Dion Ward on 2 Sept. 1989 in Cumberland Co., TN (she was born 29 Aug. 1960). Derek Burgess works for Flowers Bakery, Crossville, TN.

11a. **Angelica Beth.** Born 28 Nov. 1990 in Cumberland Co., TN.

9k. **Mamie Ellen** (twin). Born 14 May 1947 in Cumberland Co., TN. Married (James) Glenn Cole on 20 Mar. 1964 in Cumberland Co. (he was born 24 June 1940), and had children: *Cynthia* (born 11 Aug. 1967); *Jimmy* (born 18 June 1972); *Crystal* (born 25 Nov. 1977). Mamie Cole currently lives in Cumberland Co., TN.

9l. **Darlene Faye.** Born 4 July 1949 in Cumberland Co., TN. Married David William Bell Sr. on 16 July 1966 in Cumberland Co., and had children: *David William Jr.* (born 6 Oct. 1967); *Monica* (born 1 Jan. 1969); *Rachelle* (born 2 June 1975). Darlene Bell lives at Crossville, TN.

9m. **Doyle Wayne.** Born 30 Oct. 1950 in Cumberland Co., TN. Married Phyllis Webb on 18 Mar. 1972. Doyle Burgess is a carpenter in Cumberland Co., TN.

10a. **Brady Wayne.** Born 23 Apr. 1976 in Cumberland Co., TN.

10b. **Darby Ann.** Born 15 Apr. 1979 in Cumberland Co., TN.

9n. **Delmer Kaye.** Born 9 Dec. 1951 in Cumberland Co., TN. Married Janice Initha Campbell on 9 Oct. 1970 in Bledsoe Co., TN (she was born 2 Sept. 1953, daughter of Creel Wilburn Campbell and Betty Jean Haston). Delmer Burgess owns a sawmill with his brother, Aster, in Cumberland Co., TN.

10a. **(Delmer) Dewayne.** Born 10 Sept. 1971 in Cumberland Co, TN. Married Theresa Erlene Walling on 5 May 1992 in Cumberland Co., TN.

10b. **Charlotte Anne.** Born 24 Sept. 1975 in Cumberland Co., TN. Married Johnny Douglas Marr Jr. on 22 Jan. 1994 in Cumberland Co. (he was the son of Johnny Douglas Marr and Ethel Houston), and had children: *Child* (due Sept. 1994).

9o. **Diane** (nmn). Born 7 Sept. 1953 in Cumberland Co., TN. Married Milton Leon Walker on 16 June 1968 in Cumberland Co., and had children: *Lynn* (born 12 Dec. 1968); *Avery* (born 6 Nov. 1969). Diane Walker lives at Crossville, TN.

9p. **(Laura) Frances.** Born 17 Feb. 1955 in Cumberland Co., TN. Married Charles Wilson James on 29 May 1971 in Cumberland Co., and had children: *Robert* (born 5 Apr. 1972); *Angela* (born 21 June 1974); *Sharon* (born 19 Sept. 1977). Frances James lives at Crossville, TN.

9q. **Willis Henry.** Born 29 Sept. 1956 in Cumberland Co., TN. Married Debbie Jane Myers on 26 Dec. 1975 in Cumberland Co. Willis Burgess works as a landscaper at Crossville, TN.

10a. **David Kenneth (I).** Born 22 Mar. 1979 in Cumberland Co., TN.

9r. **Treva Deloris.** Born 22 Dec. 1958 in Cumberland Co., TN. Married Richard DeWayne Lawson on 30 Nov. 1976 in Cumberland Co. (he was born 19 Nov. 1955, and died May 1985 at Sparta, TN), and had children: *Erick* (born 27 Nov. 1974); *Jennifer* (born 30 Nov. 1977); married secondly ___ McKinney. Treva McKinney lives at Crossville, TN.

9s. **(William) Aster.** Born 30 Mar. 1961 in Cumberland Co., TN. Married Fannie Louise Sherrill on 3 Sept. 1985 in Cumberland Co., TN (she was born 5 May 1963). Aster Burgess owns a sawmill with his brother, Delmer, in Cumberland Co., TN.

10a. **Chantilly Leah.** Born 19 Apr. 1983 at Crossville, TN.
10b. **(Dewey) Joshua.** Born 7 June 1984 at Crossville, TN.

NOLAN BURGESS OF CUMBERLAND CO., TENNESSEE
[John Willis[7]]

8e. **Nolan** (nmn) *[son of John Willis].* Born 8 Mar. 1904 in Cumberland Co., TN. Married Sarah Bell VanWinkle on 5 Apr. 1925 in Cumberland Co. (she was the daughter of William Tell VanWinkle and Stella Mae Evans, and sister of Henry Franklin VanWinkle [who married Nolan's cousin, Lillie Burgess]). Nolan Burgess worked as a lumberman and farmer in his youth. He later worked for the Ridge Tool Manufacturing Co., Elyria, OH. He now lives retired near Crossville, TN.

9a. **(Hubert) Leon.** Born 17 Mar. 1926 in Cumberland Co., TN. Married Faye Duke. Leon Burgess works as a lumberman at Leggett, CA.

10a. **Dennis Lee (I).** Born 19 Jan. 1947 at Stockton, CA. Married Mary Ann Gray on 11 July 1970 (div.). Dennis Burgess works in iron salvage at Palo Alto, CA.
10b. **Linda Fay (II).** Born 13 Sept. 1949 near Stockton, CA. Married Ernest "Scooter" Hulsey on 17 June 1967 (div.).
10c. **(Jeanette) Elaine.** Born 14 Sept. 1952 at Elyria, OH. Married Richard C. Rand on 18 Dec. 1971; married secondly Ron Conama (div.). Elaine Conama lives at Leggett, CA.

9b. **Arnold Ottis.** Born 6 Aug. 1927 in Cumberland Co., TN. Married Gloria Jean Tuttle on 27 Aug. 1949 (she was born 2 Oct. 1932). Arnold Burgess works for Ridge Tool Manufacturing Co., Elyria, OH. He lives at North Ridgeville, OH.

10a. **Cheryl Louise "Cherry."** Born 5 Dec. 1950 at Elyria, OH.
10b. **(Arnold) Michael.** Born 3 Apr. 1952 at Elyria, OH.

11a. **Daughter.**
11b. **Daughter.**

10c. **(Douglas) Patrick.** Born 15 Feb. 1955 at Elyria, OH. Pat Burgess was a police officer in Ohio (now retired).
10d. **Brian Scott (I).** Born 15 Apr. 1961 at Elyria, OH.

9c. **(Myron) Cordell.** Born 18 Dec. 1929 in Cumberland Co., TN. Married Betty Smith. Cordell Burgess works for Ridge Tool Co., Elyria, OH. He lives at North Ridgeville, OH.

10a. **Katherine Jane.** Born 20 Sept. 1950 at Elyria, OH.
10b. **Bonnie Lou (II).** Born 23 Sept. 1952 at Elyria, OH. Married Larry Ray.

9d. **Stanley Carl.** Born 26 Aug. 1931 in Cumberland Co., TN; died there on 7 May 1936, and is buried in the Thomas Springs Cemetery. His death certificate gives his date of birth as 20 July 1931, and date of death as 8 May 1936.
9e. **Venus Enlow.** His given names were originally Herbert Eugene (II). Born 23 June 1934 in Cumberland Co., TN. Married Wanda Sawyers. Venus Burgess works for Ridge Tool Manufacturing Co. at Elyria, OH. He lives at North Ridgeville, OH.

10a. **Marvin Eugene.** Born 4 Dec. 1956 at Elyria, OH. Married Anita Smith. Marvin Burgess works for Ridge Tool Co., Elyria, OH.

11a. **Wendy Dawn.** Born 27 Oct. 1974 at Elyria, OH.
11b. **Adam Eugene.** Born 6 Oct. 1978 at Elyria, OH.

10b. **Douglas Stanley.** Born 11 Nov. 1958 at Elyria, OH. Married Maureen Bachlor. Doug Burgess works at Ridge Tool Co.

11a. **Stacey Renae.** Born 17 Apr. 1980 at Elyria, OH.

10c. **Annette Marie.** Born 3 Apr. 1960 at Elyria, OH. Married Dennis Canfield, and had children: *Shawn Philip* (born 30 Nov. 1980); *Joshua Lewis* (born 14 Dec. 1983).
10d. **Timothy Wallace.** Born 14 Mar. 1962 at Elyria, OH.
10e. **Mark Steven (I).** Born and died 14 Sept. 1964 at Elyria, OH.

9f. **Mildred Pauline.** Born 10 Oct. 1935 in Cumberland Co., TN. Married Dwight Felton.
9g. **Ellis Murrell.** Born 25 Aug. 1937 in Cumberland Co., TN. Married Jean McBane. Ellis Burgess is a carpenter at Drury, MO.

10a. **Debra Jean.** Born 14 Feb. 1957 at Antioch, CA. Married James Miller.
10b. **Donna Sheryl.** Born 8 Aug. 1958 at Garberville, CA. Married Tom O'Herin.
10c. **Keith Murrell.** Born 17 Jan. 1960 at Elyria, OH. Married Tonya Melvin. Keith Burgess is a truck driver and carpenter at Mansfield, MO.

11a. **Charity Joy.** Born 8 Nov. 1979 at Cadillac, MI.
11b. **(Benjamin) Luke.** Born 27 Nov. 1980 at Mansfield, MO.

10d. **(Nolan) Shane.** His name is given as Noland in his birth announcement. Born 16 Dec. 1968 at Crossville, TN.

9h. **(Mary) Elinor.** Her name is spelled Eleanor on her marriage record, and in a Cumberland Co. directory. Born 14 May 1939 in Cumberland Co., TN. Married Floyd Allen Boring on 11 June 1955 in Cumberland Co., and had five children. Elinor Boring lives in Cumberland Co.
9i. **Gearl Dean "Jerry."** Born 13 May 1942 in Cumberland Co., TN. Married Eileen Sinkinson. Jerry Burgess works for The Ridge Tool Co., Elyria, OH.

10a. **Kelly Ann (II).** Born 8 June 1965 at Elyria, OH. Married James L. Tompkins, and had children: *Eric James* (born 8 Mar. 1992).
10b. **Scott Alan (II).** Born 15 May 1967 at Elyria, OH.
10c. **Tracy Michele.** Born 10 Feb. 1968 at Elyria, OH. Married Paul Gindlesperger, and had children: *Kara Marie*; *Brie Alexandra.*

9j. **Bobby Lee.** Born 3 Dec. 1943 in Cumberland Co., TN. Married Diana Rader. Bobby Burgess is a pharmacist at the Grafton Pharmacy, Grafton, OH.

10a. **Kevin Lee.** Born 8 June 1968 at Elyria, OH.
10b. **Tammi Lynn.** Born 29 Jan. 1971 at Elyria, OH.

9k. **Linda Sue (III).** Born 7 Nov. 1946 in Cumberland Co., TN. Married Butch Rowe (div.), and had two sons. Linda Burgess worked for Ridge Tool Co., Elyria, OH, before returning to Tennessee. She now works as a beautician at Crossville, TN.

[William (I)[1], Edward (I)[2], Reuben (I)[3], Thomas (I)[4], King Hiram (I)[5], Joseph Daniel[6]]

THOMAS A. BURGESS
(1863-1927)

OF CUMBERLAND COUNTY, TENNESSEE

7d. **Thomas Anderson "Red"** *[son of Joseph Daniel].* Born 17 Feb. 1863 (or 1864, according to his death certificate) in Cumberland Co., TN. Married Martha Elizabeth Blaylock on 10 Apr. 1881 in Cumberland Co. (she was born 5 Mar. 1869, daughter of Michael and Mary J. Blaylock, and sister of Giles M. Blaylock [who married Tom's cousin, Catherine Rose Burgess], and died 14 Feb. 1943). Listed in the 1900-20 censuses for Cumberland Co.; six of six children survive in 1900, nine of ten in 1910. Red Burgess was a farmer in Cumberland Co. He died there on 11 Dec. 1927, and is buried in the Burgess Cemetery.

8a. **Noah (I)** (nmn). Born and died 1882 in Cumberland Co., TN.

8b. **(Effie) May Mary.** Her name is given as Effie Mae Burgess in her birth record. Born 28 Aug. 1884 in Cumberland Co., TN. Married John G. Lewis on 10 Jan. 1907 in Cumberland Co. (he died about 1909), and three children, including: *Casto S.* (born 1907); after his death, she was listed with her parents in the 1910 census. May Lewis married secondly Jim Sampson about 1912, and had children: *David* (born about 1914); *Bessie* (born June 1916); *Daniel* (born 6 Feb. 1923). May Sampson died on 25 Apr. 1923 in Bledsoe Co., TN.

8c. **(Willis) Ezra.** Born 4 Oct. 1886 in Cumberland Co., TN. See below for full entry.

8d. **Lawson** (nmn). Born 20 Mar. 1890 in Cumberland Co., TN. Married Lucy Caroline Croft on 16 July 1911 in Cumberland Co. (she was born 12 Nov. 1895, and died 12 Feb. 1912 at Newton, TN); married secondly his first cousin once removed, Louise Amanda Burgess, on 6 June 1914 in Cumberland Co. (she was born 12 May 1897, and died 16 Sept. 1988). Listed in the 20 June 1917 draft list for Cumberland Co. Lawson Burgess was a farmer and rock quarryman in Cumberland Co. He died there childless on 2 Oct. 1973, and is buried in the Burgess Cemetery.

8e. **(Branch) Henderson.** Born 27 Mar. 1893 in Cumberland Co., TN. See below for full entry.

8f. **Samuel (III).** Born 30 Oct. 1895 in Cumberland Co., TN. See below for full entry.

8g. **(Mary) Elizabeth (IV) "Lizzie."** Born 21 Feb. 1898 in Cumberland Co., TN. Married her cousin, (Joseph) Gaither Campbell, on 18 July 1915 in Cumberland Co. (he was born 19 Aug. 1889, son of Daniel Jasper Lavander Campbell and Vestina Cathrine Amy Jane "Tina" Hale, remarried Rittie Stull on 24 June 1936, and died 21 June 1955), and had children: *Stacy* (married Bethel Brewer); *Will Hugh* (married Hester Lucille "Lucy" Neely on 7 Feb. 1946 in Cumberland Co.); *Everett Lee* (married Ola Brown); *Lucile*; *Dallas J.* (born 20 Feb. 1931, served in the U.S. Army, and was killed in a service accident on 30 June 1957, buried Burgess Cemetery); *Gladys* (married Ransom Hunt). Lizzie Campbell died on 3 May (or 7 May, according to her tombstone) 1935 at Knoxville, TN, and is buried with her husband in the Burgess Cemetery.

8h. **Daisy Dillie.** Born 12 Dec. 1900 in Cumberland Co., TN. Married Bates William Bertram on 12 Jan. 1921 in Cumberland Co. (he was born 10 Jan. 1880, and died 12 Sept. 1953), and had children: *Bill*; *Carlos*; *Dallas*; *Erma*; *Effie Jane* (married ___ Crawford); *Mary* (married Ed Lewis); *Ethel*. Daisy Bertram died on 9 May 1987 in Cumberland Co., TN, and is buried with her husband in the Burgess Cemetery.

8i. **Leona (II) "Lee"** (nmn). Born 25 Jan. 1902 in Cumberland Co., TN. Married Jim Hale. Lee Hale died about 1965 in Ohio, but is buried in McMinnville, TN.

8j. **(Eliza) Jane.** Born 27 Jan. 1905 in Cumberland Co., TN. Married William Jefferson Buckner on 17 Dec. 1922 in Cumberland Co. (he was born 12 Dec. 1896, and died 12 Feb. 1982). Jane Buckner died on 28 Dec. 1990 at Monterey, Cumberland Co., TN.

8k. **Lillie Ado.** Her middle name is also given as Ida. Born 27 Apr. 1907 in Cumberland Co., TN. Married (Henry) Franklin VanWinkle on 3 July 1923 in Cumberland Co. (div.; he was born 18 May 1904, son of William Tell VanWinkle and Stella Mae Evans, and brother of Sarah Bell VanWinkle [who married his cousin, Nolan Burgess], and died 25 May 1978), and had children: *Dollie* (born 26

Sept. 1924, married ___ Pippin, and died 14 July 1977, buried Thomas Springs Cemetery); *Hassie* (born 28 Aug. 1926); *Arlin F.* (born 3 Sept. 1929); *Martha* (born 12 Nov. 1931); *Daisy Pauline* (born 29 Apr. 1936); married secondly Fred Lawson on 22 Feb. 1941 in Cumberland Co. Lillie Lawson died 1987 in Cumberland Co., TN.

EZRA BURGESS OF CUMBERLAND CO., TENNESSEE
[Thomas Anderson[7]]

8c. **(Willis) Ezra** *[son of Thomas Anderson].* Born 4 Oct. 1886 in Cumberland Co., TN. Married Effie Mae Crofts on 29 Aug. 1908 in White Co. (she was born 15 Dec. 1893, and died 24 Feb. 1984). Listed in the 1910-20 censuses for Cumberland Co. (one of one children survives in 1910), and in the 20 June 1917 draft register of Cumberland Co. Elected Constable of the Fifth District of Cumberland Co. in 1948. Ezra Burgess was a farmer in Cumberland Co. He died there on 31 July 1969, and is buried in the Burgess Cemetery.

9a. **(Jay) Eston.** His name is given as J. Eston in the 1920 census. Born 25 Sept. 1909 in Cumberland Co., TN. Listed in the 1940 draft list of Cumberland Co. Eston Burgess was a farmer in Cumberland Co., TN. He died unmarried (murdered) on 25 May 1942 at Cleveland, OH, but is buried in the Burgess Cemetery.

9b. **Lottie Belle.** Her name is given as Lotta in the 1920 census. Born 19 June 1911 in Cumberland Co., TN. Married Jesse Brewer on 12 Jan. 1935 in Cumberland Co. (he was born on 1 Nov. 1908, and died on 7 Feb. 1968 at Elyria, OH). Lottie Brewer died on 11 Nov. 1991 at Crossville, TN. Her memories have provided much background material for her branch of the family.

10a. **Betty Virginia.** She was adopted by Jesse Brewer, and used that surname until her marriage. Born 22 July 1931 in Cumberland Co., TN. Married Brown Warner; married secondly Donald Behrens. Betty Behrens lives at Ocala, FL.

9c. **Wilkie Anderson.** His name is given as Anderson W. Burgess in the 1920 census. Born 21 Sept. 1912 in Cumberland Co., TN. Married Hattie Neely in 1933 in Albany, KY (div.; she remarried his cousin, Beecher Burgess); married fifthly (?) Myrtle Dixon on 22 July 1978 in Cumberland Co. (she was born 9 Feb. 1926). Listed in the 1940 draft list of Cumberland Co. Wilkie Burgess moved to Ohio in 1943, where he worked as an auto worker before retiring. He now lives at Crossville, TN. He has his mother's Burgess scrapbook.

10a. **(Effie) Juanita.** Her name is given as Junnet on her death certificate. Born 8 (or 5, according to her death certificate) May 1934 in Cumberland Co., TN; died there of diphtheria on 2 Dec. 1938, and is buried in the Burgess Cemetery.

10b. **Verna Virginia "Vernie."** Born 3 Oct. 1935 in Cumberland Co., TN. Married (James) Norman Dyer Sr. on 10 May 1955 in Cumberland Co. (he was born on 29 Jan. 1934), and had children: *James Norman Jr.* (born 7 Aug. 1958); *Dale Justin* (born 6 Jan. 1961); *Bonnie Lou* (born 2 July 1971). Verna Dyer works for Moen, Inc., Elyria, OH.

10c. **Betty (III)** (nmn) (twin). Born and died 5 Aug. 1937 in Cumberland Co., TN, and is buried in the Burgess Cemetery.

10d. **Bonnie** (nmn) (twin). Born 5 Aug. 1937 in Cumberland Co., TN; died there on 13 Aug. 1937, and is buried in the Burgess Cemetery.

10e. **Willie James.** Born 21 July 1938 in Cumberland Co., TN. Married Catherine Wright (she was born 5 Feb. 1926); married secondly Sharon K. Buchanan. Willie Burgess worked for Ford Motor Co. at Avon, OH before retiring. He currently lives at Crossville, TN.

11a. **Cathy Pearl.** Born 1 Aug. 1961 at Elyria, OH. Married Geoffrey Diederich about 1980 (div.), and had children: *Catherine Marie* (born 6 June 1981); *Virginia Allison* (born 31 May 1982); *Lauren Nicole* (born 3 May 1988).

12a. **Misty Autumn.** Born 12 Mar. 1978.

11b. **Virginia Lucille "Ginny."** Born 11 July 1964 at Elyria, OH. Ginny Burgess currently works at the Elyria Savings and Trust National Bank, Elyria, OH.

9d. **Johnie Lawson.** Born 20 Mar. 1914 in Cumberland Co., TN. Married Dorothy Essra; married secondly Ellen Strader about 1950; married thirdly Nellie Dyer about 1963. Listed on the 1940 draft list of Cumberland Co., and served in the U.S. Army in World War II. Johnie Burgess was a taxi driver at Crossville, TN. He died there on 26 Mar. 1986, and is buried in the Burgess Cemetery.

10a. **Nancy (VIII).** Born 4 Dec. 1949 at Crossville, TN. Married Frank Sygulla. Nancy Sygulla lives in Illinois.
10b. **Brenda Gail.** Born about 1950 at Crossville, TN. Married Marvin Claude Lee on 17 June 1966 in Cumberland Co. Brenda Lee lives at Ozone, TN.
10c. **Wayne.** He uses the surname Kerley. Married Dillie ___.
10d. **Tommy Ellis (II).** Born about 1955 at Crossville, TN. Married Alva Gail Redwine on 30 Aug. 1976 in Cumberland Co. (div.; she was born 1958, and remarried Harold Thomas Nelson on 1 Nov. 1988 in Cumberland Co.). Tommy Burgess lives at Ozone, TN.

11a. **Eugenia.** Born about 1977 in Cumberland Co., TN.

10d. **Sheila (I).** Married ___ Walker.
10e. **Bobbie.** He uses the surname Dyer. Born about 1964 in Cumberland Co.
10f. **Debbie (III).** She uses the surname Dyer. Born about 1966 in Cumberland Co., TN. Married ___ Sutton.
10g. **Charlotte Joan.** She uses the surname Dyer. Born 19 May 1969 in Cumberland Co., TN.
10h. **Sammie Lane.** He uses the surname Dyer. Born 22 Jan. 1970 in Cumberland Co., TN.

9e. **Lona Dell.** Born 21 May 1916 in Cumberland Co., TN. Married Chester Campbell in Kentucky in Aug. 1932, and had children: *(Josie) Elizabeth* (born Mar. 1933); *Jennings.* **Lona** married secondly Albert Pugh, and had children: *Orvis*; *Samuel "Bud"*; *Barbara.* **Lona** married thirdly Willie T. Smith (he was born 23 Oct. 1909, and died 16 June 1981). Lona Smith died on 30 Aug. 1978, and is buried in the Burgess Cemetery.
9f. **Oma Frances.** Born 16 Mar. 1919 in Cumberland Co., TN. Married Ross Thomas Hubbard on 30 Dec. 1933 in Cumberland Co. (he was born 23 May 1912), and had children: *(Thomas) Albert* (born 25 Oct. 1934, married Mary Blaylock); *Levonn Henry* (Superintendent of Schools at Harriman, TN; he was born 17 Dec. 1943, and married his distant cousin, Frances Lee Burgess [she was born 29 May 1952, daughter of (Charles) Franklin Burgess and Mamye Lee Lewis; see her entry for their children]); *Dennis Howard* (born 30 Aug. 1956, married Gail Crabtree). Oma Hubbard is a midwife and farmer in Cumberland Co.; her property encompasses the oldest Burgess settlement and cemetery in Cumberland Co. She has contributed greatly to this book.
9g. **Viola Gusta "Ola."** Born 29 Dec. 1920 in Cumberland Co., TN. Married Shirley Brewer. Ola Brewer lives at Pikeville, TN.
9h. **Alice Y.** (twin). Born 28 Apr. 1923 in Cumberland Co., TN; died there on 30 Apr. 1923, and is buried in the Burgess Cemetery.
9i. **Elcie** (nmn) (twin). Born 28 Apr. 1923 in Cumberland Co., TN; died there on 30 Apr. 1923, and is buried in the Burgess Cemetery.
9j. **Thomas Lee "Tommy."** Born 10 Aug. 1924 in Cumberland Co., TN. Married Lois Beasley. Listed in the 1940 draft list of Cumberland Co., and served in Battery B, 153rd Field Artillery, U.S. Army, during World War II. He later worked for the Tennessee Valley Authority, and in a factory at Chicago, IL. Tommy Burgess lived at Chicago Heights, IL, but died on 29 Sept. 1967 at Hammond, IN, and is buried in the Burgess Cemetery, Cumberland Co., TN. Lois Burgess lives in Cumberland Co.

10a. **Linda Mae.** Born 20 Sept. 1948 in Cumberland Co., TN. Married Henry E. Richardson Jr. on 21 May 1968 in Bledsoe Co., TN (he was born 19 May 1937); married four other times, including ___ Magnusen.
10b. **Ronald Lee (I) "Ronnie."** Born 7 Apr. 1952 in Cumberland Co., TN. Married Vicki Whitehead (who died 8 June 1973 in a car accident in FL). Ronnie Burgess lives in North Carolina.

11a. **Richard Lee "Rick."** Born 25 Nov. 1969 in Florida. He was raised by his grandmother, Lois Burgess. Married Tonya Dee Bradford in Sept. 1993 in Cumberland Co.

10c. **Sandra Jane.** Born 21 June 1954 in Cumberland Co., TN. Married ___ Lund, and lives in Florida.

9k. **Dossie Lloyd.** Born 8 July 1927 in Cumberland Co., TN. Married Mozella Brewer; married secondly Irene Turner about 1964 (she was born 14 Oct. 1930). Dossie was an auto mechanic at

Belleview, FL. He died there on 23 Aug. 1986, and is buried in the Burgess Cemetery, Cumberland Co., TN.

10a. **Lloyd Lee.** Born 15 Nov. 1946 in Cumberland Co., TN. Married Linda Carpenter. Lloyd Burgess owns Burgess Insulation at Ft. Oglethorpe, GA.

11a. **Carol Lee.** Born 4 Aug. 1971 at Elyria, OH.
11b. **Stephen Edward.** Born 9 Aug. 1974 at Elyria, OH.

10b: **(Eva) Jean.** Born 23 Nov. 1949 in Cumberland Co., TN. Married Gene Cillo. Jean Cillo lives at Jersey Shore, PA.
10c. **Edward James (I).** Born 7 Jan. 1951 in Cumberland Co., TN. Married Brenda Anderson. Edward Burgess is a Staff Sgt. in the U.S. Air Force, currently stationed in West Germany.

11a. **Brent Edward.** Born 25 Dec. 1975 at Landstuhl, West Germany.
11b. **Natalie Michelle.** Born 8 Dec. 1980 at Lompoc, CA.

10d. **Bobby Joe (II).** Born 15 Mar. 1953 in Cumberland Co., TN. Married Cindy Pugh; married secondly Louise Kilgore. Bobby sells heavy-duty truck scales at Dalton, GA.

11a. **Edward Allen (II).** Born and died 1975 in Cumberland Co., TN, and is buried there in the Burgess Cemetery.
11b. **Christy Lynn.** Born 16 Jan. 1978 in Georgia.
11c. **Paula Louise** (ad.). Born 6 Dec. 1981 in Georgia.

10e. **James Allen.** Born 10 Apr. 1965 (or 1959) in Cumberland Co., TN. Jim Burgess lives at Belleview, FL.

9l. **Macie Mae.** Her name is given as Macy May in her death certificate. Born and died 30 Dec. 1928 in Cumberland Co., TN, and is buried in the Burgess Cemetery.
9m. **Garlon Cecil.** His name is given as William Garlon in the contemporaneous newspaper announcement of his birth. Born 19 Mar. 1930 in Cumberland Co., TN. Married Sarah Elizabeth Beaty on 18 June 1955 in Cumberland Co. Garlon Burgess was a refrigeration worker and mechanic for Goodwill Industries in Florida. He died of a stroke on 21 Mar. 1970 at Elyria, OH, and is buried in the Burgess Cemetery, Cumberland Co., TN.

10a. **Larry Eston.** Born 14 Jan. 1955 in Cumberland Co., TN. Married Susan Lynn Fisher. Lives in Georgia.

11a. **Jason Matthew.** Born 28 Aug. 1975 in Georgia.

10b. **Cathy Sue.** Born 18 Sept. 1957 in Cumberland Co., TN. Married Frank Overton. Cathy Overton lives at Harlem, GA.
10c. **Juell Arenia.** Born and died 4 Feb. 1961 in Cumberland Co., TN, and is buried in the Burgess Cemetery (her aunt, Oma Hubbard, prepared her for burial).

9n. **Irma Jane.** Born 4 Jan. 1936 in Cumberland Co., TN. Married Hershell Theodore Wyatt on 6 Mar. 1961 in Cumberland Co., and had children: *Danny*; *Lynn*; *Ross*. Erma Wyatt lives in Cumberland Co.

HENDERSON BURGESS OF CUMBERLAND CO., TENNESSEE
[Thomas Anderson[7]]

8e. **(Branch) Henderson** *[son of Thomas Anderson].* Born 27 Mar. 1893 in Cumberland Co., TN. Married Ida Mary Elizabeth Wyatt on 5 Sept. 1920 in Cumberland Co. (she was born 21 Apr. 1900, daughter of Jim Wyatt and Betsey Jane Davis, and sister of Flora Wyatt [who married Henderson's cousin, James Mike Burgess], and now lives with her daughter, Duane Turner). Listed in the 20 June 1917 draft list for Cumberland Co., and in the 1920 census with his father. Henderson was a sawmill worker in Cumberland Co. He died there on 23 Aug. 1967, and is buried in the Burgess Cemetery.

9a. **Lennis Marie.** Born 4 July 1921 in Cumberland Co., TN. Married Robert Evans. Lennis Evans lives at Clarksville, TN.
9b. **Etta Mae.** Born 4 Dec. 1923 in Cumberland Co., TN. Married Clinton Threet (he was born 11 Mar. 1920 at Davison, TN). Etta Threet lives at Crossville, TN.
9c. **Alice Mabel.** Born 16 Mar. 1926 in Cumberland Co., TN. Married Hulon Masters.
9d. **Thelma Louise.** Born 12 Aug. 1929 in Cumberland Co., TN. Married Beecher Wyatt. They live near Crossville.
9e. **Lois Elizabeth.** Born 21 Dec. 1932 Cumberland Co., TN. Married Boyd Melton; married secondly Tony Ebach.
9f. **(James) Emerson.** Born 10 Aug. 1935 in Cumberland Co., TN. Married Wilma Evans; married secondly Trilby Perry on 7 June 1969 in Pontiac, MI. Emerson Burgess works in the General Motors Truck and Coach Division at Pontiac, MI.

10a. **James Lloyd (II).** Born 29 Aug. 1954 at Pontiac, MI. Married Susan Mae Harrown. James Burgess is a factory worker in Michigan.

11a. **Christopher James.** Born 9 Apr. 1979 at Pontiac, MI.
11b. **Jason Daniel.** Born 7 Feb. 1985 at Pontiac, MI.

10b. **Dallas Emerson.** Born 6 Oct. 1958 at Pontiac, MI.

11a. **Starr Marie.** Born 26 Dec. 1979 at Pontiac, MI.

10c. **Travis Lynn (I).** Born 26 July 1959 at Pontiac, MI.

11a. **Travis Lynn (II).** Born 12 May 1980 at Pontiac, MI.

10d. **Tracie Diane.** Born 24 Feb. 1970 at Pontiac, MI.

9g. **(Margaret) Christine.** Born 18 Dec. 1937 in Cumberland Co., TN. Married Charles Luther Turner on 5 Aug. 1953 in Cumberland Co.
9h. **(Wynell) Duane.** Born 24 Sept. 1942 in Cumberland Co., TN. Married John Edgar Turner on 5 June 1959 in Cumberland Co. Duane Turner lives near Crossville, TN. She has contributed greatly to this book.

SAMUEL BURGESS OF MADISON CO., ALABAMA
[Thomas Anderson[7]]

8f. **Samuel (III)** (nmn) *[son of Thomas Anderson].* Born 30 Oct. 1895 in Cumberland Co., TN. Married Viola Norris on 6 Sept. 1918 (and 27 June 1920) in Cumberland Co. (she died in May 1984, buried Brookdale Cemetery, Elyria, OH); married secondly Willie Mae Lamb. Served in the U.S. Army in World War I. Listed in the 1920 census with his father. Sam Burgess built post offices for the U.S. government; he settled near Huntsville, AL, and also lived at Albuquerque, NM. He died there on 13 Mar. 1962.

9a. **Emett.** Born 5 Jan. 1919 in Cumberland Co., TN; died there on 17 Jan. 1919, and is buried in an unmarked grave in the Burgess Cemetery.
9b. **Euris Lee.** His name is given as Ures on his death certificate. Born 3 Aug. 1921 in Cumberland Co., TN; died there on 11 Nov. 1927, and is buried in an unmarked grave in the Thomas Springs Cemetery.
9c. **Homer Gordon.** Born 1923 in Cumberland Co., TN; died there about 1924, and is buried in an unmarked grave in the Burgess Cemetery.
9d. **(Millie) Lorraine.** Born 22 Aug. 1924 in Cumberland Co., TN. Married John Pleasant on 5 Nov. 1939 in Cumberland Co. (div.), and had children: *Margaret* (married and had eight children); *Walter* (married, had one daughter, and lives at Crossville, TN); married secondly Hubert McDonald in 1957 at Houston, TX, and had children: *Hubert Jr.* (married); married thirdly Sam Kuhn. By ___ Ayala she also had a daughter: *Loretta* (born 1947 at Texas City, TX, married, and had six children). Lorraine Kuhn worked for the nursing department of Elyria Memorial Hospital, Elyria, OH. She now lives there retired.

[William (I)[1], Edward (I)[2], Reuben (I)[3], Thomas (I)[4], King Hiram (I)[5], Joseph Daniel[6]]

RICHARD M. BURGESS
(1865-1921)

OF CUMBERLAND COUNTY, TENNESSEE

7e. **Richard M(oyers?) "Dick"** *[son of Joseph Daniel].* Born June 1865 in Cumberland Co., TN. Married Ida M. Campbell in Mar. 1887 (div.; she was born Oct. 1872 in TN, daughter of Washington Columbus and Eliza Campbell, and sister of Laura and John Henry Campbell [who married Burgess cousins], and died in 1927 at Turner, KS); married secondly Bertha Lee "Bertie" (also called "Shorty") Seals on 20 Dec. 1916 in Bledsoe Co., TN (she remarried Alex G. Crofts on 14 Mar. 1922 in Bledsoe Co., and thirdly Ed Davis). Listed in the 1900-20 censuses for Cumberland Co.; the children of his brother, Joseph Burgess, are living with him in 1900; five of seven children survive in 1900, nine of twelve in 1910; Ida Burgess is listed in the 1920 census for Bledsoe Co., TN. "Uncle" Dick Burgess was a farmer in Cumberland and Bledsoe Cos. He died in Cumberland Co. about 15 June 1921, when his death was mentioned in passing in the 22 June 1921 issue of *Crossville Chronicle* (the note was dated 20 June), and is buried in an unmarked grave in the Burgess Cemetery.

8a. **Amos Washington.** Born Aug. 1888 in Cumberland Co., TN. See below for full entry.
8b. **Arthur H.** Born Nov. 1889 in Cumberland Co., TN. He was stricken with polio on 10 Apr. 1912. Listed in the 20 June 1917 draft record of Cumberland Co., TN. Said to have died unmarried in Bledsoe Co. (not listed with his mother in the 1920 census).
8c. **Child.** Born 1891 in Cumberland Co., TN; died young.
8d. **Child.** Born 1893 in Cumberland Co., TN; died young.
8e. **Mayhew Blaine.** Born 8 May 1895 in Cumberland Co., TN. See below for full entry.
8f. **Burton.** Born 5 Aug. 1897 in Cumberland Co., TN; died unmarried in Bledsoe Co. of typhoid fever on 3 Sept. 1915, and is buried in the Beach Cemetery.
8g. **(Charles) Walter.** Born 19 Dec. 1899 in Cumberland Co., TN; died unmarried in Bledsoe Co. of typhoid fever on 19 Oct. 1915, and is buried in the Beach Cemetery.
8h. **Minerva Elizabeth Amy Jane.** Born 9 Mar. 1901 in Cumberland Co., TN. Listed with her mother in the 1920 census. Married Andrew Jackson Mercer, and had children: *Genevieve* (married ___ McQuestion); *Luella* (married Earl Lawson, had children: Jimmy, and secondly ___ Akens, and lived at Dayton, TN). Minerva Mercer lived at Goodlettsville, TN, but died in 1992 at Nashville, TN.
8i. **Luella Frances.** Born 26 May 1904 in Cumberland Co., TN. Married (Aulty) Litton Walker on 2 July 1923 in Bledsoe Co., TN (he was born 14 Nov. 1903, and died 8 Sept. 1992 at Pikeville, TN), and had at least the following children: *Georgia* (married ___ Littlefield, and lives at Kansas City, KS); married secondly ___ Gray. Luella Gray died in 1984 at Kansas City, KS.
8j. **(Luther) Everett.** Born 27 Aug. 1906 in Cumberland Co., TN. See below for full entry.
8k. **Emet.** Born 18 Dec. 1908 in Cumberland Co., TN; died 15 May 1909 at Newton, TN.
8l. **Donald Lee (I).** Born 12 Feb. 1910 in Cumberland Co., TN. See below for full entry.
8m. **Trina Belle.** Born 28 May 1912 in Cumberland Co., TN. Married Joe Maher. Trina Maher died Feb. 1980 at Kansas City, KS.

AMOS W. BURGESS OF WYANDOTTE CO., KANSAS
[Richard Moyers[7]]

8a. **Amos Washington** *[son of Richard Moyers].* Born Aug. 1888 in Cumberland Co., TN. Married Emma Edmonds about 1908 (she was born 25 June 1888 at Pikeville, TN, daughter of ___ Edmonds and Nancy Sullivan, and died 23 Mar. 1963 at Kansas City, KS). Listed in the 1910 census for Bledsoe Co., TN, and in 1920 in Wyandotte Co., KS. Amos Burgess was a river barge worker in Kansas. He died (electrocuted in a boat accident) in Aug. 1927 near Turner, KS.

9a. **Herman Franklin.** Born 3 Mar. 1909 in Bledsoe Co., TN. See below for full entry.

9b. **Oma Lee.** Born 29 Jan. 1911 in Bledsoe Co., TN. Married Kenneth Holloway (dec.), and had children: *Robert*; *James*; married secondly William F. Cooper. Oma Cooper lives at Kansas City, MO.

9c. **(Daisy) Elizabeth "Betty."** Born 25 Feb. 1913 at Pikeville, Bledsoe Co., TN. Married Edward Budrin in 1932 at San Francisco, CA (he died 1933), and had children: *Edwina Lee* (born 22 Feb. 1934 [posthumously] at San Francisco, CA, married Wayne Carlton Gage on 11 Jan. 1953 at Las Vegas, NV [div. 1957; he was born 18 July 1925, and died 21 Feb. 1990 at Oroville, CA], and had children: Gary Wayne [born 11 Dec. 1953 at San Luis Obispo, CA, married Dolores McOmber on 4 Feb. 1972 at Oroville, CA {div. 1989}, and had children: Christopher Micheal {born 12 May 1972 at Oroville, CA, married Nicole Shelly on 4 Jan. 1993 at Bonner, CA, and had children: Felicia Ashley <born 1 Feb. 1993 at Seattle, WA>; Christopher Gage lives at Bonners Ferry, ID}; Scott Wayne {born Jan. 1974 at Oroville, CA, married Vanessa Claire, and lives at Lake Chelan, WA}; Jonathan Ashley {born 24 Jan. 1981 at Oroville, CA}; Gary married secondly Kay Marie Eby on 6 Mar. 1993 at Bonners Ferry, ID]; Micheal D. [born 21 July 1956 at San Luis Obispo, CA, married Cindy ___ in 1973, and had children: Christy Lee, and lives at Sacramento, CA]; *Edwina* married secondly Ruben Story in 1959 [div. 1970]; married thirdly Glen Gammon in 1981 [he was born 19 Dec. 1934, and died 22 Feb. 1993 at San Luis Obispo, CA]; *Edwina* lives at Pismo Beach, CA). **Betty BUDRIN** married secondly John O. Goostree on 14 July 1951 (he was born 18 Mar. 1913 (?) at Bomarton, TX). Betty Goostree lives at San Luis Obispo, CA.

9d. **Mattie Angeline "Bobbie."** Born 21 Feb. 1915 in Bledsoe Co., TN. Married Claude Hayes about 1935 (he was killed in action during World War II); married secondly Everett Munkers (div.; he was born 5 Oct. 1914, and died May 1986 at Kansas City, MO). Bobbie Munkers died on 3 Nov. 1992.

9e. **John V. "Jay"** (twin). Born 14 Apr. 1917 in Bledsoe Co., TN. Jay Burgess was born crippled. He died unmarried in Missouri about 1943.

9f. **Son** (twin). Born and died 14 Apr. 1917 in Bledsoe Co., TN.

9g. **Nora Belle.** Born 23 Feb. 1920 at Turner, KS. Married Dick McKee about 1942 (div.), and had children: *Nancy Lynn* (born 10 Nov. 1943, and had children: Kimberly Kathryn); married secondly Jeremiah "Jerry" Persian (he was born 22 Aug. 1909, and died on 29 Mar. 1980 at Morro Bay, CA). Nora Persian died on 9 Feb. 1985 at Paso Robles, San Luis Obispo Co., CA.

9h. **Vesta Theo.** Born 24 Jan. 1922 at Turner, KS. Married Edward Simmer in 1940 (div.), and had children: *David Lewis* (born 10 Jan. 1942, married Patty ___ [div.], and had children: David Lewis II [born Mar. 1966]; John Patrick [born 13 Oct. 1969]); *Edward Jr.* (born 12 Jan. 1944, married Donna ___ [div.], and had children: Jeffrey Edward [born Oct. 1974]; Randy Christopher [born 30 Mar. 1976]); *Tomas Richard* (born 16 Jan. 1946, married Sharon Volney in 1967, and had children: Diana Marie [born 12 Sept. 1967, married John Hammerlund in 1987, and had children: Breanna Marie {born 20 May 1988}; Sabrina Leigh {born 7 July 1990}; Child {due Feb. 1994}]; Tina Renée [born 11 Dec. 1969, married Brandon Gingg in 1992]; Richard Anthony [born 30 Apr. 1976]; Linda Lee [born 12 June 1980]). **Vesta SIMMER** married secondly Bob Cram about 1952. Vesta Cram currently lives at San Luis Obispo, CA.

9i. **(Lora) Virginia.** Born 5 Feb. 1924 at Turner, KS. Married Earl Moore. Virginia Moore died on 31 Dec. 1991 at Atascadero, San Luis Obispo Co., CA.

9j. **Dorothy Helen.** Born about 1926 at Turner, KS; died there an infant.

9k. **Shirley Imagene.** Born 8 May 1927 at Turner, KS. Married Bill Sheetz, and had children: *Elaina*. **Shirley** married secondly Ernest Rogers, and had children: *Jody*. Shirley Rogers died on 20 Sept. 1986 at La Verne, CA.

HERMAN BURGESS OF WYANDOTTE CO., KANSAS

[Richard Moyers[7], Amos Washington[8]]

9a. **Herman Franklin** *[son of Amos Washington].* Born 3 Mar. 1909 in Bledsoe Co., TN. Married Juanita Mignon Tush about 1932 (she was born 25 Nov. 1913, daughter of Luther B. Tush and Iva Della Miller, and died 27 Nov. 1985 at Kansas City, KS). Herman Burgess worked as a pipefitter for Proctor and Gamble Co., near Kansas City, KS. He died there on 27 Sept. 1983.

10a. **Jerry Ronald (I).** Born 4 June 1933 at Kansas City, KS. Married Eileen Wilcox. Jerry Burgess worked for General Motors Corp. before retiring. He now lives at Edwardsville, KS.

11a. **Deborah Eileen.** Born 8 Apr. 1955 at Kansas City, KS. Married Phil Harvison (div.).

11b. **Jerry Ronald II.** Born 31 Dec. 1957 at Kansas City, KS. Married Marsha McGuire. Jerry Burgess lives at Kansas City, KS.

12a. **Blair Elizabeth.** Born 21 Oct. 1990 at Kansas City, KS.

10b. **(Geraldine) Yvonne.** Born 2 Feb. 1935 at Kansas City, KS. Married William Brent, and had children: *Larry William* (born 15 Apr. 1959 at Frankfort, West Germany, married Nancy Ann Plumberg at Shawnee Mission, KS, and had children: Tigh William [born 24 Oct. 1983 at Shawnee, KS]; Natalie Marie [born 22 Feb. 1985 at Shawnee, KS]; Larry Brent lives at Olathe, KS); *Gregory Alan* (born 11 Aug. 1962 at Kansas City, MO, married Kara Sue Larson at Shawnee, KS, and lives at Roeland Park, KS). Yvonne Brent currently lives at Shawnee, KS.

10c. **Judith Marie.** Born 24 Apr. 1938 at Kansas City, KS. Married Robert Leroy Potter on 13 June 1958 at Kansas City, KS, and had children: *Robert Alan* (born 3 Nov. 1959 at Kansas City, KS, married Tami Wolnick, and had children: Joel Richard [born 8 Apr. 1988]; Zachary Philip [born 1 Mar. 1990]; Gabriel Robert [born 14 Oct. 1993]; Robert Potter lives at Topeka, KS); *Kimberly Ann* (born 16 Mar. 1961 at Kansas City, KS, married Philip Rudolph [he was born 3 July 1960, and died 3 Mar. 1989 at Overland Park, KS], married secondly Jim Banner, and has children: Adam Philip [born 30 Mar. 1991]; Kimberly Banner lives at Kansas City, MO). Judith is Media Director for Patterson Advertising, Topeka, KS, and is a contributor to this book.

10d. **Larry Franklin (I).** Born 31 Mar. 1942 at Kansas City, KS. Married Judy Kay Pringle. Larry Burgess works for Kansas City Power and Light Co., Kansas City, KS.

11a. **Jeffery Alan.** Born 28 May 1964 at Kansas City, KS. Married Sheila Becker.

11b. **Larry Christopher.** Born 20 Nov. 1967 at Kansas City, KS.

11c. **Jonathan Lee.** Born 16 Dec. 1969 at Kansas City, KS.

10e. **Linda Sue (II).** Born 27 Mar. 1944 at Kansas City, KS. Married Warner Smith (div.), and had children: *Stephanie Lynn* (born 14 Jan. 1967 at Kansas City, KS, and had children: Travis Warner [born 2 Sept. 1985]); Linda married secondly Bill Nichols (he died Sept. 1987), and had children: *Tracie Yvonne* (born 23 Aug. 1976). Linda Nichols lives at Kennewick, WA.

10f. **Sharon Kay.** Born 1 July 1947 at Kansas City, KS. Married Clifford Kent, and had children: *Craig Clifford* (born 1 Aug. 1968); *Sean Scott* (born 3 Apr. 1971); *Heather Yvette* (born 12 July 1975).

WILLIAM MATTHEW BURGESS OF BLEDSOE CO., TENNESSEE

[Richard Moyers[7]]

8e. **William Matthew** *[son of Richard Moyers].* He was originally named Mayhew Blaine Burgess, and his name is given as William Mayhew on his tombstone inscription. Born 8 May 1895 (or 1890) in Cumberland Co., TN. Married Julia Price (as Mayhew Burgess) on 17 Sept. 1920 in Bledsoe Co., TN (she was born 8 May 1905, and remarried Ollie V. Knight on 12 May 1962 in Bledsoe Co.); married secondly Gemie Bell Lawson about 1939; married thirdly (Julie) Iola Brock (as Matthew Burgess) on 27 July 1940 in Bledsoe Co. (she was born 14 Oct. 1907, and died 26 Jan. 1991 at Pikeville, TN, buried Humble Cemetery); married fourthly Mary ___; married fifthly Poinsettia Davis on 30 Oct. 1951 in White Co. (she was born 14 Sept. 1931). Served in Co. D., 2nd Tennessee Infantry, U.S. Army, during World War I. Mayhew Burgess was a lumberjack in Bledsoe Co., TN; he also worked for the TVA. He was living at Berea, OH in 1951. He died on 12 June 1961 in Bledsoe Co., and is buried in the McDowell Cemetery.

9a. **Nora Lee (I).** Born about 1921. Mentioned in her father's obituary (1961) as living at Pikeville. Deceased.

9b. **Everette.** Born and died 31 Aug. 1923 in Bledsoe Co., TN, and is buried in the McDowell Cemetery.

9c. **Dolly.** Born about 1925. Mentioned in her father's obituary (1961) as living at Pikeville. Deceased.

9d. **Mary Helen (II).** Born 21 July 1940. Married Cleady Brock on 9 Sept. 1958 in Bledsoe Co., TN (he was born 24 Feb. 1936), and had children: *Donald*; *Edward*; *Marshall* (born 1978). Mary Brock lives at Pikeville, TN.

9e. **Clarence Paul.** Born 28 May 1943 in Bledsoe Co., TN. Married Brenda Lee Brown on 23 Dec. 1966 in Bledsoe Co. (she was born 20 May 1948 at Elyria, OH, daughter of Norman Brown and Thelma Holloway). Clarence Burgess is a truck driver in Bledsoe Co.; Brenda Burgess is a teacher. Both have contributed greatly to this book.

10a. **Frankie Orvella.** Born 19 Oct. 1967 in Bledsoe Co., TN. Married Darrell Franklin Cate on 1 Aug. 1984 (he was born 7 May 1961 in Bradley Co., TN), and had children: *Candice Michelle* (born 25 July 1987 in Bradley Co., TN); *Tiffany Danielle* (born 19 Jan. 1991 in Bradley Co., TN).

10b. **Kevin Stacey (I).** Born 11 Oct. 1971 in Bledsoe Co., TN. Married Christie Lynn Bice on 10 Feb. 1989 in Bledsoe Co., TN (she was born 22 Aug. 1972). Kevin Burgess currently lives at Pikeville, TN.

11a. **Kevin Stacey II.** Born 31 July 1989 at Pikeville, TN.

11b. **Joshua Tyler.** Born 18 Aug. 1990 at Crossville, TN.

9f. **Henrietta (III).** Born Aug. 1950 at Berea, OH. Married Kenneth Coldwell, and had children: *Yulonna* (born 1979). Henrietta Coldwell currently lives at Rock Island, TN.

EVERETT BURGESS OF SHAWNEE CO., KANSAS

[Richard Moyers[7]]

8j. **(Luther) Everett** *[son of Richard Moyers].* Born 27 Aug. 1906 in Cumberland Co., TN. Married Vera ___. Luther Burgess was a railroad worker in Kansas. He died in Aug. 1967 at Topeka, KS.

9a. **Virginia (II) "Ginger."** Said to have lived in Oklahoma.

DONALD L. BURGESS OF BAJA CALIFORNIA NORTE, MÉXICO

[Richard Moyers[7]]

8l. **Donald Lee (I)** *[son of Richard Moyers].* He was originally named Abraham Lincoln Burgess. Born 12 Feb. 1910 in Cumberland Co., TN. Married Ethel L. Williamson about 1929 (she died 1940); married secondly Esther Waller about 1941 (by her first husband she had children: *JoAnn*; *Virginia "Ginger"*; *Teddy*); he may have married thirdly Lois C. Heiman on 11 Nov. 1950. Served in the U.S. Army during World War II. Don Burgess Sr. was a mechanic. He died about 1965 at Tijuana, Baja California Norte, México.

9a. **Donald Lee (II).** Born 16 May 1930 at Topeka, KS. Married Wanda Williamson. Don Burgess Jr. is a heavy equipment operator and mechanic at Ramona, CA.

10a. **Kendra Denise.** Born 4 Mar. 1952 at Seattle, WA. Married Steven N. Cassell on 27 Apr. 1969.

10b. **Donna Carol.** Born 8 Nov. 1953 at La Jolla, CA. Married Raymond Stoffel on 24 May 1970 (div.).

10c. **Mari Ann.** Born 24 Mar. 1955 at La Jolla, CA. Married Roy Jackson on 11 Nov. 1972 (div.).

10d. **Ronnie Lee (IV).** Born 25 May 1959 at La Jolla, CA; died on 27 Nov. 1964 at Oceanside, CA, and is buried in the Oceanside Cemetery.

10e. **Sharene Marie.** Born 15 Jan. 1964 at San Diego, CA. Married Steve Matteson.

9b. **Kathleen Wilma.** Born 8 Sept. 1932 at Kansas City, KS. Married Robert Melvin Gordon in 1953 in Anne Arundel Co., MD, and had children: *Leah Kay* (born 30 May 1954); *(Robert) Michael* (born 4 Aug. 1956, and had children: Rachel); *Ned E.* (nmn; born 22 Jan. 1963); *Gwen* (born 10 Apr. 1965, died July 1965). Kathleen Gordon works for the Volusia County government at Daytona Beach, FL.

9c. **Robert Eugene (II).** Born 7 Sept. 1935 at Pikeville, TN. Married Jackie Dickson on 29 Dec. 1979 in Coos Co., OR. Served in the U.S. Army for thirteen years, including three years in Vietnam. Bob Burgess owned his own garage worked at Bandon, OR; he later worked as a Federal Civil Service employee for the Oregon Army National Guard at Bandon, OR, and was also motor Sergeant for an infantry batallion on weekend drills. He now lives retired at Roseburg, OR.

9d. **James Ray (II).** Born about 1942 at Pikeville, TN. Jim Burgess is a truck driver in Oregon.

10a. **Jimmy John.**

10b. **Sarah (XIV).**

9e. **Carl Wayne.** Born about 1944. Carl Burgess works for the Escondido Irrigation District, Escondido, CA. Unmarried.

9f. **Son.** Born about 1955-60 at Tijuana, Baja California Norte, México.

[William (I)[1], Edward (I)[2], Reuben (I)[3], Thomas (I)[4], King Hiram (I)[5], Joseph Daniel[6]]

JOSEPH M. BURGESS
(1872-1950)

OF BLEDSOE COUNTY, TENNESSEE

7h. **Joseph Mansfield "Joe"** *[son of Joseph Daniel].* Born 28 Mar. 1872 in Cumberland Co., TN. Married Laura Campbell about 1890 (she was born about 1874, daughter of Washington Columbus and Elizabeth Campbell, and sister of Ida and John Henry Campbell [who married Burgess cousins], and died about 1900); married secondly Sarah Frances VanWinkle about 1900 (she was born 23 Feb. 1881, daughter of Benjamin VanWinkle, and died 1 May 1939). Listed in the 1910 census for Cumberland Co. (four of five children of Sarah then survive), and in 1920 in Bledsoe Co., TN; has not been found in 1900 (shortly after his first wife's death), when his children are listed with his brother, Dick Burgess. Joseph Burgess was a farmer in Bledsoe Co., TN. He died on 1 Feb. 1950 at Summer City, TN, and is buried in the McDowell Cemetery, Bledsoe Co.

8a. **Celia Ann (II).** Born 8 Sept. 1891 in Cumberland Co., TN. Married Harrison Edmons (or Edmonds) on 3 Dec. 1908 in Cumberland Co. (he may be the John Edmons born 24 Nov. 1888 who died Oct. 1981 at Buhl, ID), and had at least the following children: *Isaac* (born 1910). Listed in the 1910 census for Cumberland Co., TN. Celia Edmonds died about 1965 at Buhl, ID.

8b. **(George) Frank Monroe (I).** Born 2 Nov. 1893 in Cumberland Co., TN. See below for full entry.

8c. **Dellor** (son). Born 4 Jan. 1896 in Cumberland Co., TN; died there before 1900.

8d. **Ollie B.** Born 3 Dec. 1897 in Cumberland Co., TN. May have married T. Arthur Miller on 27 June 1915 in Bledsoe Co., TN (he was born 1 Aug. 1890, and died 19 May 1977), and had children: *Kermit*; *Stanley*; *Clifford*; *Barton*; *Juanita*; *Melba* (born 22 Jan. 1931, died 24 Mar. 1931, buried with her parents). Ollie Miller died on 10 Aug. 1938, and is buried with her husband in the McDowell Cemetery.

8e. **Alanzo.** Born 2 Jan. 1900 in Cumberland Co., TN. Not listed with his father in the 1920 census. Alanzo Burgess was reportedly killed by a runaway horse on 8 Mar. 1920 in Bledsoe Co., and is buried with his family in the McDowell Cemetery.

8f. **Oma Dell "Omie."** Her middle name is also given as Bell. Born 7 Sept. 1901 in Bledsoe Co., TN. Married John Fields on 12 Jan. 1919 in Bledsoe Co., TN, and had children: *Lois* (who married Charlie Hale, and had children: Evelyn [married ___ Smith, and lives at Pikeville, TN]; Carolyn [married ___ Limes, and lives at Pikeville, TN]; Jimmie [lives at Detroit, MI]; Charlene [married ___ West, and lives at Cookeville, TN]; Landon [lives at Detroit, MI]); *Robert*; *Frances*; *Mary*; *Martha*; *Joe*. Omie married secondly Earl Walker by 1950; married thirdly ___ Willis. Living at Pikeville, TN in 1957. Omie Willis died in 1976, and is buried in the McDowell Cemetery.

8g. **Loutisha "Tish"** (nmn). Her name is given in the 1910 census as Lutitia, as Lutisha on her marriage certificate, and as Loutish on her gravestone and in her obituary. Born 18 June 1905 in Cumberland Co., TN. Married Billie E. "Bum" Walker on 3 Dec. 1920 in Bledsoe Co., TN (he was born 21 Jan. 1900, and died 12 July 1979), and had children: *Carl Burton*; *Hollis*; *Harold*; *Angie Lee* (married ___ Smith); *Janice*. Tish Walker died on 17 Sept. 1984 at Pikeville, TN, and is buried in rural Bledsoe Co. in the Brushy Cemetery.

8h. **Gaston.** Born 13 June 1907 in Cumberland Co., TN. See below for full entry.

8i. **(Myrtle) Cleo.** Born 25 Apr. 1909 in Cumberland Co., TN. Married Mark Price on 9 Oct. 1925 in Bledsoe Co. (he remarried Josie Watson on 20 Jan. 1927 in Bledsoe Co.), and had children: *Walter* (born 18 Aug. 1926, died Feb. 1984 at Chattanooga, TN). Cleo Price died on 26 Aug. 1926, and is buried in the McDowell Cemetery.

8j. **(Charles) Jay.** Born 17 Feb. 1912 in Cumberland Co., TN. Jay Burgess was shot and killed unmarried on 15 Nov. 1931 in Bledsoe Co., and is buried with his family in the McDowell Cemetery.

8k. **Harrison Benjamin.** Born 23 Mar. 1914 in Cumberland Co., TN. See below for full entry.

8l. **Garland West.** Born 24 July 1916 in Cumberland Co., TN. See below for full entry.

8m. **(Fronia) Alice.** Born 10 Oct. 1918 in Bledsoe Co., TN. Married Archie B. Holland in 1941 (he was born 1913, and died Sept. 1982); married secondly James Scott in Nov. 1983. Alice Scott died on 16 July 1989 at Pikeville, TN. Her daughter has the family Bible of Joseph M. Burgess.

8n. **Minnie (III)** (nmn). Her middle name is listed as Rose in Joseph Burgess's family Bible record, but her birth certificate just gives the one name. Born 15 Mar. 1921 in Bledsoe Co., TN. Married Arthur K. Smith on 11 Feb. 1939 in Georgia, and had children: *Joseph Harland* (born 16 Sept. 1941 at Whitwell, TN, and lives at Chicago, IL); *Gwendolyn Laurette* (born 14 Apr. 1946 at Dunlap, TN, and lives at San Francisco, CA); married secondly Amos Leonard Dolby in Feb. 1973 (dec.). Minnie Smith worked in a factory and grocery store, and owned a restaurant at Brookville, PA. She now lives retired at Huntsville, AL.

FRANK BURGESS OF BLEDSOE CO., TENNESSEE

[Joseph Mansfield[7]]

8b. **(George) Frank Monroe (I)** *[son of Joseph Mansfield].* Born 2 Nov. 1893 in Cumberland Co., TN. Married Marcia Croft on 6 Dec. 1914 in Cumberland Co. (she was born 2 May 1899, and died 20 Apr. 1980, buried in the Big Lick Cemetery). Listed in the 1920 census for Bledsoe Co., TN. Frank Burgess Sr. was a lumberman, sheriff, and farmer in Bledsoe Co., TN. He died there on 31 Mar. 1980, and is buried in the McDowell Cemetery.

9a. **Lena Elizabeth.** Born 8 Oct. 1915 at Pikeville, TN. Married Lee Davis on 11 May 1937 in Cumberland Co. Lena Davis lives at Crossville, TN.

9b. **Lora Florence.** Born 30 June 1918 at Pikeville, TN. Married Robert L. Stevens. Lora Stevens died in 1991 at Crossville, TN.

9c. **Geneva Annora.** Born 26 June 1920 at Pikeville, TN. Married Robert Brown on 25 Nov. 1939 in Cumberland Co., and had children: *James*; *Joyce* (married Leon Nichols). Geneva Brown died on 14 Dec. 1982 at Pikeville, TN, and was buried in the Seals Cemetery.

9d. **Floyd Oscar (I).** Born 24 Sept. 1922 at Pikeville, TN. See below for full entry.

9e. **(Lillie) Frances.** Born 7 Sept. 1925 at Pikeville, TN. Married Wilson Rose.

9f. **(Thomas) Roy.** Born 3 Apr. 1928 at Pikeville, TN. See below for full entry.

9g. **(Paul) Calvin.** Born 13 Apr. 1930 at Pikeville, TN. See below for full entry.

9h. **(Joseph) Everett.** Born 28 May 1933 at Pikeville, TN. See below for full entry.

9i. **Zella Marie.** Born 29 Dec. 1935 at Pikeville, TN. Married Donald Reynolds. Zella Reynolds operates a Diet Center franchise outlet at Anaheim, CA.

9j. **(George) Frank Monroe (II).** Born 21 Apr. 1938 at Pikeville, TN. See below for full entry.

9k. **(Chester) Howard.** Born 6 July 1942 at Pikeville, TN. See below for full entry.

FLOYD BURGESS OF BLEDSOE CO., TENNESSEE

[Joseph Mansfield[7], George Frank Monroe (I)[8]]

9d. **Floyd Oscar (I)** *[son of George Frank Monroe (I)].* Born 24 Sept. 1922 at Pikeville, TN. Married Zeta A. ___ about 1942; married fourthly Charlotte Everett about 1959. Floyd Burgess was a career soldier in the U.S. Army, retiring with the rank of Master Sergeant. He and his wife now live at Pikeville, TN.

10a. **(Floyd) Oscar (II).** Born 9 Nov. 1943 in Bledsoe Co., TN. Married Donna Viles. Oscar Burgess works for General Motors at Dayton, OH. He and his wife live at Englewood, OH.

11a. **Jill Ann.** Born 12 Aug. 1964 at Dayton, OH.

11b. **Shari Kay.** Born 22 Nov. 1966 at Dayton, OH.

11c. **Tammy Sue.** Born 20 July 1970 at Dayton, OH.

10b. **Dale Elmer.** Born 23 Dec. 1946 in Bledsoe Co., TN. Married Deborah Reagan on 2 Apr. 1966 in Bledsoe Co., TN (she was born 8 Apr. 1948). Dale Burgess works for a feed company in Bledsoe Co., TN, and also owns his own livestock farm.

11a. **Sybil Danette.** Born 22 Dec. 1966 at Pikeville, TN.

11b. **Bridget Marcella.** Born 9 Mar. 1970 at Pikeville, TN.

11c. **Brandon Dale.** Born 12 Apr. 1972 at Pikeville, TN.

10c. **(Franklin) Norman.** Born about 1952. Last known living in Oregon.

10d. **Raynard Avery "Ray."** Born 20 June 1960 at Ft. Hood, TX. Ray Burgess served four years in the Air Force.
10e. **Charlene Azalea.** Born 1 Oct. 1962 at Neubrucke, West Germany. Married Danny Earl Swafford on 20 June 1980 in Bledsoe Co., TN (he was born 2 Aug. 1960).
10f. **Patricia Dowlene "Peedee."** Born 2 Oct. 1964 at Ft. Hood, TX.
10g. **Ronald Lee (III).** Born 19 Mar. 1967 at Ft. Hood, TX. Married Wanda Fay Narramore on 14 Nov. 1987 in Bledsoe Co., TN (she was born 28 July 1968).

ROY BURGESS OF WHITFIELD CO., GEORGIA

[Joseph Mansfield[7], George Frank Monroe (I)[8]]

9f. **(Thomas) Roy** *[son of George Frank Monroe (I)].* Born 3 Apr. 1928 at Pikeville, TN. Married Mary Lee Sapp. Roy Burgess is a foreman at a book bindery in Dalton, GA.

10a. **(Robert) Dexter.** Born 6 July 1951 at Dearborn, MI. Married Linda Joyce Moffitt on 6 Mar. 1970 in Bledsoe Co., TN (she was born 18 July 1949). Dexter Burgess works for Dupont Co. at Dunlap, TN.

11a. **Gabriel Dexter.** Born 6 June 1971 at Dunlap, TN; died there on 12 Mar. 1974.
11b. **(Mary) Elizabeth (IX) "Beth."** Born 12 Oct. 1977 at Dunlap, TN.
11c. **Matthew Garrett.** Born 9 Feb. 1979 at Dunlap, TN.

10b. **Donald Neal.** His middle name is written Neil in his marriage record. Born 29 Sept. 1952 at Dearborn, MI. Married Patsy Jane Hankins on 9 Apr. 1972 in Bledsoe Co., TN (she was born 5 Mar. 1953); married secondly Elsie Etherton. Don Burgess works for Lazy Boy Recliners, making reclining chairs, at Chattanooga, TN.

11a. **Amanda Dawn.** Born 29 Apr. 1974 at Pikeville, TN.
11b. **Deserae Dawn.** Born 13 Oct. 1982 at Chattanooga, TN.

10c. **Douglas Leroy.** Born 24 Feb. 1957 at Ferndale, MI. Married Sandra Kay Thurman on 8 May 1976 in Bledsoe Co., TN (she was born 11 Feb. 1958). Doug Burgess is an upholsterer at Pikeville, TN.

11a. **Joshua Wayne.** Born 12 Sept. 1977 at Crossville, TN.
11b. **Jeremiah Justin.** Born 17 Aug. 1980 at Crossville, TN.

CALVIN BURGESS OF CUMBERLAND CO., TENNESSEE

[Joseph Mansfield[7], George Frank Monroe (I)[8]]

9g. **(Paul) Calvin** *[son of George Frank Monroe (I)].* Born 13 Apr. 1930 at Pikeville, TN. Married Helen Simmons. Calvin Burgess owns a timber business and general store, the Burgess Store, on Route 101 in southern Cumberland Co., TN.

10a. **Cecil Calvin.** Born 1 Feb. 1966 at Dearborn, MI. Married Lisa Ann Cunningham on 23 Feb. 1986 in Cumberland Co. (she was born 5 Oct. 1967). Cecil Burgess works for Townsend Textron at Spencer, TN; he lives at Crossville, TN.

11a. **Abbigail Lisa "Abby."** Born 26 Sept. 1986 in Cumberland Co., TN.
11b. **Dustin Cecil.** Born 12 Dec. 1989 in Cumberland Co. TN.
11c. **Bailey Kayellie.** Born 17 Nov. 1991 in Cumberland Co., TN.

10b. **Penny Ethel.** Born 29 Feb. 1968 at Detroit, MI. Penny Burgess is a student at the University of Tennessee, Knoxville.
10c. **Casey Lynn.** Born 1 Mar. 1970 in Cumberland Co., TN. Married Brenda L. Welch on 13 Aug. 1988 in Cumberland Co. (she was born 11 Apr. 1966).

11a. **Kayla Leann.** Born 22 June 1989 at Crossville, TN.

EVERETT BURGESS OF CUMBERLAND CO., TENNESSEE

[Joseph Mansfield[7], George Frank Monroe (I)[8]]

9h. **(Joseph) Everett** *[son of George Frank Monroe (I)].* Born 28 May 1933 at Pikeville, TN. Married Myrtle ___ about 1957; married secondly Rosie Brant on 23 Dec. 1976 in Bledsoe Co., TN (she was born 17 Feb. 1954); married thirdly Jane Faye Carr on 14 Mar. 1986 in White Co., TN (she was born 30 May 1945). Everett Burgess is a factory worker at Cookeville, TN.

10a. **Brenda Kay (II).** Born 29 Sept. 1957 at Elyria, OH. Married Donald Eugene Evans on 14 June 1975 in Bledsoe Co., TN (he was born 6 Dec. 1954).
10b. **Barbara Faye.** Born 6 Sept. 1961 at Crossville, TN. Married James Edward Walker on 8 Oct. 1980 in Bledsoe Co. (he was born 6 Dec. 1959).
10c. **(Larry) Joe.** Born 4 Dec. 1967 at Crossville, TN. Married Deonna Jean Griffin on 5 July 1987 in Bledsoe Co., TN (she was born 22 Jan. 1967).

FRANK BURGESS Jr. OF SNOHOMISH CO., WASHINGTON

[Joseph Mansfield[7], George Frank Monroe (I)[8]]

9j. **(George) Frank Monroe (II)** *[son of George Frank Monroe (I)].* Born 21 Apr. 1938 at Pikeville, TN. Married Sarah Hansen. Frank Burgess is a stone salesman at Edmonds, WA.

10a. **Karen Ruth.** Born 14 June 1965 at Seattle, WA.
10b. **Kathleen Elizabeth.** Born 14 Sept. 1967 at Edmonds, WA.
10c. **Colleen Marsha.** Born 24 May 1975 at Edmonds, WA.

HOWARD BURGESS OF MONROE CO., TENNESSEE

[Joseph Mansfield[7], George Frank Monroe (I)[8]]

9k. **(Chester) Howard** *[son of George Frank Monroe (I)].* Born 6 July 1942 at Pikeville, TN. Married Peggy Dillard on 21 Nov. 1962 in Bledsoe Co., TN (she was born 26 Sept. 1945). Howard Burgess is a wholesale salesman of restaurant and hospital supplies at Sweetwater, TN.

10a. **Andrea Colleen.** Born 14 May 1971 at Athens, TN.

GASTON BURGESS OF CUMBERLAND CO., TENNESSEE

[Joseph Mansfield[7]]

8h. **Gaston.** His name is spelled Gastin on his marriage certificate. Born 13 June 1907 in Cumberland Co., TN. Married (Lou) Vena Moore on 22 May 1926 in Bledsoe Co. Gaston Burgess was a timber worker in Cumberland Co. He was killed there on 7 Oct. 1935, and is buried in the McDowell Cemetery. Vena Burgess lives in Missouri.

9a. **Myrtle Rose.** Born 2 Nov. 1927 in Bledsoe Co., TN. Last known living in Kansas City, MO.
9b. **Mary Ruth (II).** Born about 1930 in Bledsoe Co., TN. Last known living in Kansas City, MO.

HARRISON BURGESS OF WAYNE CO., MICHIGAN

[Joseph Mansfield[7]]

8k. **Harrison Benjamin.** Born 23 Mar. 1914 in Cumberland Co., TN. Married Mamie ___; married secondly Ruth ___. Harrison Burgess worked for Ford Motor Co. at Detroit, MI. He died there on 19 Nov. 1972.

9a. **Betty (II).** Last known living at Detroit, MI.
9b. **Billy (I).** Last known living at Corona, CA.

GARLAND BURGESS OF WAYNE CO., MICHIGAN
[Joseph Mansfield[7]]

8l. **Garland West** *[son of Joseph Mansfield]*. Born 24 July 1916 in Cumberland Co., TN. Married Susie Davis. Garland Burgess worked in a machine shop in Detroit before retiring. He died on 27 May 1991 at Berkley, MI. Susie Burgess currently lives at Berkley, MI.

9a. **(Clara) Joyce.** Born 27 Feb. 1942 in Cumberland Co., TN. Married William Mammen.
9b. **Gary Edward.** Born 19 Apr. 1944 at Detroit, MI. Married Debbie Dalrick. Gary Burgess works for United Parcel Service at Walled Lake, MI.

10a. **Betsy Ann.** Born 21 Apr. 1978 at Pontiac, MI.
10b. **Jeffrey Scott (IV).** Born 9 Nov. 1980 at Pontiac, MI.
10c. **Kristin.** Born 29 Jan. 1983 in Michigan.

9c. **Mary Ruth (III).** Born 31 July 1948 in Cumberland Co., TN. Married Robert McDade.
9d. **Sharon Ann.** Born 10 June 1953 at Detroit, MI. Married Rolf Weeks.
9e. **Terry Lynn.** Born 27 Dec. 1954 at Detroit, MI. Terry Burgess is a civilian worker for the U.S. Air Force.

Burton Burgess
(1897-1915)
[see page 595]

[William (I)[1], Edward (I)[2], Reuben (I)[3], Thomas (I)[4], King Hiram (I)[5], Joseph Daniel[6]]

REV. JAKE BURGESS
(1875-1940)

OF TWIN FALLS COUNTY, IDAHO

7i. **(Isaac) Jacob "Jake"** *[son of Joseph Daniel].* Born 8 Dec. 1873 in Cumberland Co., TN. Married Cora Fair M(o)yers on 18 Feb. 1895 (she was born 27 Nov. 1880 in TN, daughter of Emilla Catharine Wyatt [daughter of John Wyatt and Martha Ann Matilda Moyers], and died 23 Feb. 1972, aged 91 years). Listed in the 1900-20 censuses for Cumberland Co., TN, in 1900 as a boarder with Thomas Brawley; three of three children survive in 1900, six of six in 1910. The Rev. Jake Burgess was a Baptist minister and farmer in Tennessee and Idaho, moving to Castleford, ID, in 1927. He died there on 4 Apr. 1940, and is buried with his wife at the Buhl Cemetery, Buhl, ID.

8a. **Vinnie Jane.** Born 24 Jan. 1896 in Cumberland Co., TN. Married William Jasper Wyatt on 1 Jan. 1911 (he was born 13 Feb. 1875, son of John Wyatt and Martha Ann Matilda Moyers, and died on 14 Feb. 1964), and had children:

Fred WYATT. Born 18 Nov. 1911, married Leah H. Tate on 14 Feb. 1938, and had children: *Roland Fred* (born 14 Nov. 1938).

Nellie Elizabeth WYATT. Born 14 May 1913, married Cornelis Hoogland on 15 June 1932 (he was born 22 Feb. 1910, and died 27 Feb. 1980 at Buhl), and had children: *Jacob William* (born 1 June 1934, married Jan ___, and had children: Jeff; Kay; Jeri; Joni); *Jane Leveling Nellie* (born 6 Jan. 1935, married Bob Seelig). Nellie Hoogland died in childbirth on 6 Jan. 1935.

Ella Rose WYATT. Born 1 Nov. 1916, married Irvin Roy Sowers on 11 Oct. 1936 (he was born 4 Sept. 1915), and had children: *Harold Irvin* (born 4 Feb. 1939, married Margaret "Midge" O'Neil on 30 Sept. 1961, and had children: Karen [born 19 Oct. 1962, married Richard Jozefiak, and had children: Katherine Marie "Katie" {born 2 Nov. 1988}; Susan Marilyn {twin; born 6 Apr. 1991}; Jennifer Margaret {twin; born 6 Apr. 1991}]; Gregory [born 21 Apr. 1965); *Gloria Jean* (born 16 July 1941, married Norl Reagan on 8 Aug. 1959, and had children: Shawn Timothy [born 4 Aug. 1965]; Stacy Lynn [born 15 June 1968]); *Rosemary* (born 24 Apr. 1944, married Dennis Wellonen on 31 Aug. 1963, and had children: Jason [born 17 Nov. 1969]; Cher [born 24 Mar. 1972]); *James Arthur* (born 26 July 1946, married Helen Lange on 8 Aug. 1968, and had children: Jeffrey [born 8 Apr. 1969, married Jennifer ___, and had children: Nicole Justine "Nickle" {born 10 Nov. 1991}]; Chris [born 13 Aug. 1971]). Ella Sowers currently lives at Grants Pass, OR; she has contributed greatly to this book.

Vinnie Jane WYATT died on 29 Dec. 1916.

8b. **Della Ann Elizabeth.** Born 17 June 1898 in Cumberland Co., TN. Married Floyd Thomas Wheeler on 19 May 1922 (he was born 22 Feb. 1898, and died June 1985), and had children:

(Virginia) Lenore WHEELER. Born 3 Mar. 1923, married Wilbur Frederick Boehlke (he was born 21 May 1914, and died Sept. 1966), and had children: *Jane Elizabeth* (born 1 Jan. 1946, married Timothy Joe Griswold [he was born 17 Jan. 1944], and had children: Brian Jon [born 1 July 1965]; Teri Jane [born 2 Mar. 1967]); *David Frederick* (born 14 Dec. 1946); *Mary Ann* (born 21 June 1949, married Dennis Howard McMillin [he was born 21 June 1948], and had children: Karen Ann [born 10 May 1971]; Ryan Howard [born 14 June 1975]); *Ronald Curtis* (born 17 Nov. 1952); *Gary Richard* (born 13 Dec. 1953, married Karen Bessie Johnson on 22 June 1987 [by her first marriage, she had children: Amanda JOHNSON {born 17 Dec. 1979}], and had children: Erica Nicole [born 15 Mar. 1988]; Brandon Richard); *Jon William* (born 29 Dec. 1954, married Melody Dawn Arent [she was born 5 Sept. 1959], and had children: Jonathan David [born 26 May 1983]; Jeremy Christian [born 24 July 1987]; Jacob Robert [born 31 Aug. 1992]). ***Lenore BOEHLKE*** was an elementary school teacher for thirty years, teaching in public and parochial schools, retiring in 1987. She currently lives at Nampa, ID.

***Thomas Vernon* WHEELER.** Born 14 Dec. 1924, married Loretta Fern Barnett (she was born 17 July 1932), and had children: *Carolyn Marie* (born 11 Mar. 1948, married John Allen Jones, and had children: Serena Marie [born 4 Nov. 1967]; Eilene Lynn [born 19 Mar. 1969]); *Dennis Eugene* (born 13 Aug. 1950, married Vicki Inchausti, and had children: Tyson Vernon [born 23 July 1980]); *Debra Laverne* (born 13 July 1954, married Richard Lee Svancara, and had children: Dana Kathlene [born 28 Apr. 1978]; Jennifer [born 7 Mar. 1985]); *Christine Lynn* (born 30 Oct. 1964, married John Douglas Marcom [he was born 4 May 1959]). ***Thomas* WHEELER** currently lives at Buhl, ID.

***Leona Fair* WHEELER.** Born 8 July 1926, married William Luther Parnell (he was born 8 Aug. 1923), and had children: *Thomas Alfred* (born 22 Feb. 1947, married Joan Lynette Arford [she was born 1 Apr. 1947], and had children: Mistilyn [born 24 July 1973]; Robert Shawn [born 29 Nov. 1975]); *William Luther Jr.* (born 10 Mar. 1956, married Sharon Kaye Tappen [she was born 26 Oct. 1955], and had children: David James [born 17 Mar. 1981]; Eric William [born 29 Jan. 1983]; Chase [born 29 Nov. 1984]; Alex Charles [born 29 July 1991]); *Kevin Timothy* (born 16 Aug. 1957, married Shawn Marie Slaughenhaupt [div. 1989; she was born 30 Nov. 1957], and had children: Timothy John [born 4 Apr. 1983]; Jacklyn Rene [born 19 Nov. 1986]); *Susan Christine* (born 9 June 1960, married Jerry Craig Shafer [div. 1985; he was born 29 Sept. 1956], and had children: Krista Marie [born 30 May 1982]; Jeremy; *Susan* married secondly Michael George Vierstra on 31 July 1988, and had children: Cassie Leona [born 17 Mar. 1989]; Katie Lynn [born 11 June 1991]; Jessie Michael [born 4 Oct. 1992]). ***Leona* PARNELL** contributed greatly to this book. She died in Mar. 1985 in an automobile accident at Buhl, ID.

***(Bessie) Bonita "Bonnie"* WHEELER.** Born 2 Mar. 1928, married Raymond Louis Barsness (he was born 23 June 1924), and had children: *Daniel Raymond* (born 28 Feb. 1950, married Carol Jean Tverdy [she was born 19 Jan. 1949], and had children: Sarah Elizabeth [born 26 Apr. 1979]; Amanda Emily [born 2 June 1981]; Raymond Daniel [born 24 Mar. 1991]); *Karen Ann* (born 14 Apr. 1953, married Michael Kenneth Reid [he was born 6 Feb. 1952], and had children: Amy Heather [born 17 Jan. 1975]; Brian Michael [born 2 May 1976]; Lisa Bonita [born 26 July 1981]); *John Mark* (born 3 June 1960, married Stella Jean Hall [she was born 22 May 1960], and had children: Megan [born 3 Nov. 1983]; Andrew John [born 8 Sept. 1992]); *Rebecca Ann* (born 4 June 1962, married Michael Hazel [he was born 1 Jan. 1963], and had children: Aubree [born 9 Sept. 1982]; Aaron [born 2 July 1985]). ***Bonnie* BARSNESS** currently lives at Twin Falls, ID.

***James Alexander "Jim"* WHEELER.** Born 14 Jan. 1930, married Vivian Virginia Casebeer (she was born 6 Dec. 1933), and had children: *Nancy Carol* (born 5 June 1954, married Rick Mesaros [he was born 26 Aug. 1952], and had children: Jamie Marie [born 6 Aug. 1980]; Nicole Michele [born 26 May 1983]); *Janet Ann* (born 6 Feb. 1958, married Terryl Roy Haley [he was born 15 Nov. 1951], and had children: Carly Virginia [born 17 Jan. 1983]; Holly Ann [born 29 June 1986]). ***Jim* WHEELER** currently lives at Castleford, ID; he has contributed greatly to this book.

Alma June* WHEELER.** Born 6 Mar. 1932, married William Dwight Pitman (he was born 7 Dec. 1927; dec.), and had children: *Linda Carol* (born 21 Feb. 1953, married Douglas Martin Freeborg [he was born 22 Feb. 1953], and had children: David Douglas [born 28 July 1974]; Lisa Carol [born 1 June 1978]; Eric Michael [born 9 Oct. 1979]; Angela June [born 27 Jan. 1981]); *William Chris* (born 23 July 1954); *Michael Dwight* (born 22 Oct. 1955). ***Alma June married secondly Rawl Hursh, and currently lives at Nampa, ID.

***Floyd Edward* WHEELER.** Born 15 Nov. 1934, married Anna Lee Clifford (she was born 19 Nov. 1936), and had children: *Bruce Edward* (born 22 Mar. 1957, married A. Patrica "Patti" Villaseñor Estrada [born 28 Jan. 1964; by her first marriage, she had children: Jean {born 4 Jan. 1983}], and had children: Floyd Lee [born 29 Feb. 1988]; Jayson James [born 5 Nov. 1991]); *Jeffrey Lee* (born 31 Mar. 1959, married Wanda ___, and had children: Brandy Lee [born 29 Feb. 1988]; Brent Allen [born 26 Sept. 1992]); *Kay Renee* (born 15 June 1967, married Jimmy Weighall [he was born 27 Feb. 1966], and had children: Tara Ann [born 4 Dec. 1989]; Tyler [born 13 Jan. 1992]). ***Floyd* WHEELER** currently lives at Castleford, ID.

***Frank Allen* WHEELER.** Born 6 Nov. 1936. Frank Wheeler currently lives at Twin Falls, ID.

Della WHEELER currently lives at Castleford, ID; at age 95 she is currently one of the oldest living members of the Burgess family.

8c. **John Simpson.** Born 21 Dec. 1899 in Cumberland Co., TN. See below for full entry.

8d. **William Edward (II).** Born 29 Aug. 1903 in Cumberland Co., TN. William Burgess operated a pool hall at Castleford, ID during the early 1930s. He died unmarried of diabetes and tuberculosis on 14 Oct. 1935 at Nashville, TN, and is probably buried there.

8e. **(Jacob) Guy.** Born 15 Nov. 1906 in Cumberland Co., TN. See below for full entry.

8f. **Jerry Daniel (I).** Born 27 June 1909 in Cumberland Co., TN. See below for full entry.

8g. **(James) Ray (I).** Born 24 June 1911 in Cumberland Co., TN. See below for full entry.

8h. **Bessie Ella.** Born 27 Aug. 1913 in Cumberland Co., TN. Married Dale Rodies on 10 Nov. 1932 (dec.), and had children: *Betty Lou* (born 24 Mar. 1934, married Ted Johnson [he was born 5 Apr. 1933], and had children: Trace [born 5 Sept. 1954]; Linda [born 12 Feb. 1957]; Lauri [born 28 Oct. 1960]; married secondly Robert Bubak).

Bessie RODIES married secondly Vining Gillett (he was born 31 Mar. 1908), and had children: *David Robert* (born 25 July 1941, married Chung Hee, and had children: Trena; married secondly Carol ___ and had children: David]; **Bessie** GILLETT married thirdly Clarence Green (dec.). **Bessie** GREEN lives near Twin Falls, ID.

8i. **Son.** Born and died 17 May 1916 in Cumberland Co., TN.

8j. **Herbert Eugene (I)** (twin). Born 21 June 1917 in Cumberland Co., TN. See below for full entry.

8k. **Robert Carl** (twin). Born 21 June 1917 in Cumberland Co., TN. See below for full entry.

8l. **Tomie.** Born and died 12 July 1920 in Cumberland Co., TN, and is buried in the Winesap Cemetery.

JOHNNIE S. BURGESS OF CUMBERLAND CO., TENNESSEE

[Isaac Jacob[7]]

8c. **John Simpson "Johnnie"** *[son of Isaac Jacob].* Born 21 Dec. 1899 in Cumberland Co., TN. Married Clara Jane Thomas on 23 Aug. 1921 at Winesap, Cumberland Co., TN (she was born 26 May 1905 in Cumberland Co., daughter of Sam Thomas and Sadie Hyder, and died 26 June 1989 in Cumberland Co.). Johnnie Burgess was a farmer and sawmill worker in Cumberland Co. He died at Crossville on 6 June 1980, and is buried with his wife in the Akins Cemetery.

9a. **Kenneth (II)** (nmn). Born 21 June 1922 in Cumberland Co., TN; died within a few days.

9b. **(Velma) Lucille.** Born 19 Aug. 1923 in Cumberland Co., TN. Married Howard Selby on 21 Dec. 1940 at Albany, KY (he was born 27 June 1919, and died 16 Oct. 1984, buried Akins Cemetery, Winesap, TN), and had children:

Betty June *SELBY.* Born 10 May 1942. Married Bill Baxter (he was born 24 Jan. 1928), and had children: *Michael* (born 3 Sept. 1965, married Sherry ___ on 15 Aug. 1987).

Linda Joyce *SELBY.* Born 24 July 1944. Married Lloyd Miller on 6 June 1964 (he was born 25 May 1942), and had children: *Laura Ann* (born 13 Sept. 1967, married Emmett ___); *Tracy* (born 4 Oct. 1969, married Scott Kohler, and had children: Cody Lloyd [born 11 Feb. 1991]; Crysta Leigh [born 16 Sept. 1993]); *Tony* (born 8 Oct. 1979).

Dexter Brent *SELBY.* Born 27 Oct. 1946. Married Stella Elaine Hale on 17 Jan. 1966 (she was born 13 June 1949 in Bledsoe Co., TN), and had children: *Dirk Brian* (born 23 Jan. 1968); *Kimberly Denise* (born 18 Mar. 1969); *Dasley Bart* (born 16 Sept. 1970, married Sherrill Luchea Treadway on 18 Sept. 1993 [she was born 4 Oct. 1973], and had children: Jessica Toniqua [born 19 Apr. 1993]); *Kelly Deane* (born 17 Sept. 1971, married Luther Dalen Myres on 17 July 1993).

Anita Rose *SELBY.* Born 17 Aug. 1954. Married Rex Smith on 5 Aug. 1971 (div.), and had children: *Daphne Michelle* (born 3 Apr. 1975).

Lucille Burgess SELBY currently lives at Crossville, TN.

9c. **Arnold Curtis.** Born 1 Mar. 1926 in Cumberland Co., TN. Married (Bernice) Lou Houston on 9 Dec. 1949 at Newport, KY (she was born 1 Sept. 1930). Arnold Burgess worked for Ridge Tool Co. before retiring in 1988. He currently lives at Elyria, OH.

10a. **Charlotte Helen.** Born 3 Jan. 1966 at Elyria, OH. Married Mark S. Wolfrom (div.), and had children: *Tonya G.* (born 13 Dec. 1983); *Adam M.* (born 22 Aug. 1985); *Kimberly T.* (born 16 Oct. 1988); **Charlotte** married secondly Willis Barido in 1993.

10b. **Daniel Curtis.** Born 1 June 1969 at Elyria, OH. Married Tina Lacky on 8 Aug. 1987 at Avon, OH. Dan Burgess lives at Nashville, TN.

11a. **Jonathan D(aniel?).** Born 19 Sept. 1987 at Elyria, OH.

11b. **David A(rnold?).** Born 27 Apr. 1989 at Elyria, OH.

11c. **Kaitlyn R.** Born 21 Sept. 1993 at Nashville, TN.

9d. **James Canton.** Born 21 July 1928 in Cumberland Co., TN. Married Helen Houston (she was born 4 Oct. 1933, the sister of Lou Houston). James Burgess is a television repairman at Columbia Station, OH; he lives at Elyria, OH.

10a. **(James) Steven (II).** Born 1 Feb. 1955 at Berea, OH. Married Terry L. Flurry on 8 Feb. 1973 in Tenn. Steve Burgess is a foreman in a factory in Elyria, OH.

11a. **Benjamin James.** Born 18 Dec. 1973 at Elyria, OH.
11b. **Craig Steven.** Born 5 Nov. 1974 at Elyria, OH.
11c. **Samantha Dawn.** Born 15 Feb. 1979 at Elyria, OH.

10b. **Ricky Eugene.** Born 17 Aug. 1960 at Berea, OH. Ricky Burgess was engaged to be married to Cary White when he accidentally drowned on 20 June 1979 at his uncle's home, Elyria, OH. He was buried in the Butternut Ridge Cemetery, Elyria, OH.

11a. **Ricky Brad.** Born 29 Jan. 1980 at Elyria, OH; died there on 9 Apr. 1980, and is buried with his father.

9e. **Lewis Dale.** Born 8 Nov. 1930 in Cumberland Co., TN; died there within a few weeks.
9f. **Eula Mae.** Born 7 June 1932 in Cumberland Co., TN. Married Carlos Lee Pugh (div.), and had children: *James Lee "Jimmy"* (born 15 Mar. 195_); *Deborah* (born 17 June 195_); *John*; married secondly Frank August at Chico, CA. Eula August lives at Chico, CA.
9g. **Eugene Ray.** Born 22 Mar. 1935 in Cumberland Co., TN. Married Rachel Ward. Gene Burgess owns Burgess Appliance Service at Crossville, TN.

10a. **David Lynn.** Born 7 Feb. 1961 at Crossville, TN. Married Ronda Jean Adams on 21 May 1982 in Cumberland Co. David Burgess is manager of the Bread Box Store, Crossville, TN.

11a. **Samantha Rose.** Born 22 Mar. 1980 at Crossville, TN.
11b. **Child.**

10b. **Timothy Allen (I).** Born 1 Aug. 1964 at Crossville, TN. Married Karen ___ by 1986. Tim Burgess was the president of the Crossroads Art League, Crossville, TN, and is a well-known local artist in Cumberland Co.

11a. **Justin Wade.** Born 26 Apr. 1989 at Crossville, TN.
11b. **Eric Ryan.** Born 8 Sept. 1990 at Crossville, TN.
11c. **Child.**

9h. **Lloyd Vaughn.** Born 12 Dec. 1938 in Bledsoe Co., TN. Married Alma Lee Mooneyham on 25 June 1960 at Spenser, TN (she was born 27 Apr. 1943 at Spenser, TN). Lloyd Burgess works for Townsend Engineered Products, Spenser, TN, and lives at Crossville, TN.

10a. **(Kimberly) Vanessa.** Born 20 July 1961 at Berea, OH. Married James William Sullivan Jr. on 25 May 1990 in Cumberland Co., TN (he was born 19 July 1955), and had children: *Adam Wade* (born 7 June 1984).
10b. **Karen Yvonne.** Born 27 Nov. 1962 at Berea, OH. Married Randy Holderman on 6 Mar. 1983 in Cumberland Co. (div.), and had children: *Jessie Tyler Simpson* (born 5 Dec. 1981); married secondly David Cagle on 15 Oct. 1989, and had children: *Brandy Davron* (born 15 Mar. 1989).
10c. **Darrell LaVaughn.** Born 18 June 1964 at Berea, OH. Married Lydia R. Silcox on 14 Nov. 1987 at Crossville, TN. Darrell Burgess works for Townsend Engineered Products, Spenser, TN.

11a. **Jonathan Bryant.** Born 7 Oct. 1988 at Crossville, TN.
11b. **Jared Brand.** Born 18 June 1990 at Crossville, TN.
11c. **Jacob Bradley.** Born 15 Aug. 1993 at Crossville, TN.

9i. **Aaron Lee.** Born 14 Aug. 1942 in Cumberland Co., TN. Married Helen Ann Boston on 24 Sept. 1976 in Cumberland Co. (she was born 3 Aug. 1936, daughter of Harrison Boston and Bessie Davis, and died 5 Sept. 1990, buried Crossville City Cemetery); married secondly Wilma Brent on 22 Mar. 1991 at Crossville, TN. Aaron Burgess works for the Turner-Day Handles Mill at Crossville, TN.
9j. **(Edward) Wayne.** Born 31 Jan. 1946 in Cumberland Co., TN. Married Margaret Ann Davidson on 2 Mar. 1968 in Cumberland Co. Wayne Burgess is an auctioneer at Crossville, TN.

10a. **Pamela Jo (II).** Born 17 Aug. 1969 in Cobb Co., GA. Married Keith Allen Griffith on 15 Nov. 1987 in Cumberland Co. (div.; he was born 29 Aug. 1967).

10b. **Rebecca Ann "Becky."** Born 17 May 1971 at Crossville, TN. Married Richard George Hanselman on 19 Oct. 1990 in Germany (div. 1993), and had children: *Macey Jenise* (born 5 Dec. 1991 in Cumberland Co., *North Carolina*). Becky Burgess enlisted in 1990 in the U.S. Air Force.

GUY BURGESS OF LOS ANGELES CO., CALIFORNIA

[Isaac Jacob[7]]

8e. **(Jacob) Guy** *[son of Isaac Jacob].* Born 15 Nov. 1906 in Cumberland Co., TN. Married Alice Jo Nixon. Guy Burgess was a painter in Idaho and California. He died at Los Angeles, CA, on 24 Feb. 1978.

9a. **Alice Darlene.** Born 29 Jan. 1942 at Spokane, WA.

JERRY D. BURGESS OF SONOMA CO., CALIFORNIA

[Isaac Jacob[7]]

8f. **Jerry Daniel (I)** *[son of Isaac Jacob].* Born 27 June 1909 in Cumberland Co., TN. Married Nellie Marie Canfield (she was born 8 May 1912); married secondly Ruby Temple. Jerry Burgess owned a service station and grocery store, worked for a fire department and as a painter, and raised chickens for ten years for a government experimental station at the University of Nebraska. He now lives retired at Redding, CA.

9a. **Dorothy Elaine.** Born 19 July 1928 at Lincoln, NE. Married Charles Wolff, and had children: *Robert* (born 4 July 1949). Dorothy married secondly Ronald K. Minor on 29 Sept. 1962 (he was born 10 Mar. 1940).

9b. **Gene Ray**. He legally changed his name from Raymond Eugene Burgess. Born 29 Dec. 1929 at Lincoln, NE. Married Margerie Ruth Recknagle on 18 Sept. 1953 at Portland, OR (div.; she lives at Portland, OR); married secondly Jeanne Palmer in Oct. 1972 at Denver, CO. Gene Burgess was Chief of Police at Tillamook, Tillamook Co., OR for twenty years, and served as Director of the Oregon Humane Society, Portland, OR and as an elected member (and sometime President) of the Tualatin City Council. He now owns and operates Burgess Enterprises, which provides legal and investigative services, at Tualatin, OR.

10a. **Sandra Ruth "Sandy."** Born 16 May 1954 at Tillamook, OR. Married William Botten on 19 May 1973 in Washington Co., OR (div.), and had children: *Michael Aaron* (born 18 Feb. 1974); *Matthew Eric* (born 9 May 1977). **Sandy** married secondly Kelly Dean in July 1986 (he was born 5 July 1960), and had children: *Tracy Elizabeth* (born 23 Nov. 1987). Sandy Dean operates a day care service at Portland, OR.

10b. **Sheila Anne.** Born 9 July 1957 at Tillamook, OR. Married Kirk St. Clair on 9 Aug. 1975 in Washington Co., OR (he was born 3 Jan. 1955), and had children: *Jennifer Lynn* (born 14 Feb. 1976); *Laura Jean* (born 28 Aug. 1978); *Brenda Anne* (born 22 Aug. 1980). Sheila St. Clair lives at Tigard, OR.

10c. **Jerry Daniel II.** Born 11 Oct. 1958 at Tillamook, OR. Married Katherine Diane "Katy" Graham on 7 Aug. 1987 at Beaverton, Washington Co., OR (she was born 5 May 1962 at New Britain, CT, daughter of Michael Graham and Ruth Ann Shanor). Jerry Burgess is a landscaper for the Tualatin Hills Park and Recreation District. He has contributed greatly to this book.

11a. **Kimberly Nicole.** Born 24 Oct. 1988 at Portland, OR.

11b. **Kelsey Elizabeth.** Born 16 Mar. 1990 at Portland, OR.

10d. **Gary Richard.** Born 19 Jan. 1966 at Tillamook, OR. Married Trisha Schroeder (div.); married secondly Angela Rae Eby on 14 Aug. 1993 at Portland, OR (she was born 8 Sept. 1964). Gary Burgess is Head of Maintenance for an apartment complex at Beaverton, OR.

11a. **Shereena Sahara "Sheeny."** Born 25 Sept. 1987 at Portland, OR.

10e. **Shawn Ray** (ad.). Born 19 Apr. 1969 at Portland, OR.

9c. **Barbara Mae.** Born 30 May 1931 at Lincoln, NE. Married (Arthur) William "Bill" Kissire at Portland, OR. Barbara Kissire died childless on 29 June 1952 at Metzger, Washington Co., OR, and is buried in the Crescent View Cemetery.

JAMES RAY BURGESS OF BLEDSOE CO., TENNESSEE

[Isaac Jacob[7]]

8g. **(James) Ray (I)** *[son of Isaac Jacob].* Born 24 June 1911 in Cumberland Co., TN. Married Eleanor Gail "Nell" Gillett (she was born 21 May 1912); married secondly Leona Kennewell. Ray Burgess worked in the Oregon shipyards during World War II, and later operated a road grader in the Pacific Northwest. He also farmed and worked as an auto mechanic. He died on 10 Dec. 1981 at Pikeville, TN, but is buried in Crossville. Leona Burgess lives at Crossville, TN.

9a. **Marjorie Eleanor.** Born 24 Jan. 1929 at Chicago, IL. Married Roger Kennewell. Marjorie Kennewell lives at Portland, OR.

9b. **Virginia Louise.** Born 25 Nov. 1931 in Utah. Married Bob Lindstrom, and had children: *Stephen*; *Connie*; *Vickie*; *Terri*. **Virginia** married secondly Dick Coates. Virginia Coates lives at Eugene, OR.

9c. **Don Ray.** Born 21 June 1938 at Twin Falls, ID. Married Carol Ann Rimington on 20 Sept. 1958 at Portland, OR (she was born 3 May 1942); married secondly Kathleen Mary Drell on 1 Mar. 1980 in Washington Co., OR. Don Burgess is a carpenter and commercial construction worker at Portland, OR.

10a. **Jeffrey Scott (I).** Born 14 Aug. 1959 at Portland, OR. Married Laura Anderson on 5 Sept. 1981 in Washington Co., OR (div.); married secondly Sherril Anne Taylor on 23 Mar. 1990 (she was born 12 May 1962). Jeff Burgess is an insurance agent at Denver, CO.

11a. **Brittney Victoria.** Born 8 July 1992 at Denver, CO.

10b. **Jerome Scott "Jerry."** Born 25 Aug. 1960 at Portland, OR. Married Risa Jean Eickhoff on 27 Oct. 1979 in Washington Co., OR (she was born 16 Feb. 1962). Jerry Burgess has his own carpentry business at Tigard, OR.

11a. **Jason Mychal.** Born 18 Oct. 1980 at Portland, OR.
11b. **Jonathan David.** Born 19 Mar. 1982 at Portland, OR.
11c. **Jacob Allen.** Born 31 May 1986 at Portland, OR.

10c. **Julie Renée.** Born 23 Jan. 1962 at Portland, OR. Married Thorson Andreas Wentzek on 19 June 1980 (he was born 11 Nov. 1961), and had children: *Jessica Renée* (born 12 Jan. 1981); *Adrienne Renée* (born 22 Mar. 1983). Julie Wentzek lives at North Plains, OR.

10d. **James Ray (III).** Born 26 Aug. 1967 at Portland, OR. Married Jennifer Shipley on 26 Apr. 1989 (she was born 16 June 1972). James Burgess lives at Filer, ID.

11a. **Jocelyn Ann.** Born 11 Dec. 1988 at Portland, OR.
11b. **Joshua Cody.** Born 19 June 1990 at Portland, OR.
11c. **Jacquelyn Lee Marie.** Born 14 Feb. 1994 at Twin Falls, ID.

10e. **Jesse Ray.** Born 8 June 1969 at Portland, OR. Married Tabitha Jean Brusseau on 31 July 1991 (she was born 4 Jan. 1972). Jesse Burgess lives at Beaverton, OR.

10f. **Jillian Renée.** Born 28 Mar. 1977 at Portland, OR.

HERBERT E. BURGESS OF TWIN FALLS CO., IDAHO

[Isaac Jacob[7]]

8j. **Herbert Eugene (I)** (twin) *[son of Isaac Jacob].* Born 21 June 1917 in Cumberland Co, TN. Married Ada Augusta Dougherty (she was born 23 Apr. 1922). Dr. Herbert Burgess received a B.A. degree from Eastern Washington University in 1942, served as a gunnery officer in the U.S. Navy during World War II, and received his D.D.S. degree from the University of Washington about 1949 (in the first class graduated from the School of Dentistry there). He worked as a dentist at Twin Falls, ID. He now lives there retired.

9a. **Carol Ann (III).** Born 9 Jan. 1951 at Seattle, WA.

9b. **Michael Alan.** Born 15 Dec. 1952 at Renton, WA. Married Deidra Coats (she was born 13 Oct. 195_). Mike Burgess is a state police officer at Filer, ID.

10a. **(Michael) Jared.** Born 16 Oct. 1975 at Twin Falls, ID.

10b. **Jaime Danette.** Born 25 Nov. 1979 at Twin Falls, ID.

ROBERT CARL BURGESS OF KING CO., WASHINGTON

[Isaac Jacob[7]]

8k. **Robert Carl** (twin) *[son of Isaac Jacob].* Born 21 June 1917 in Cumberland Co., TN. Married Irene Wegner on 7 Feb. 1942 (she was born 9 Feb. 1923, daughter of Hugo and Lillie Wegner). Robert C. Burgess attended Albion State Normal School for two years, then began teaching; he received a B.A. degree in 1942 from Eastern Washington University, and an M.Ed. degree from the University of Washington in 1952. He taught for eight years, and was a school administrator for thirty years, the last fifteen as Assistant Superintendent in Charge of Personnel and Special Services, Highline School District, near Seattle, WA. He now lives there retired.

9a. **Richard Ray (II) "Dick."** Born 8 Sept. 1942 at Mt. Vernon, WA. Married Ann Baker on 16 June 1967 (she was born 20 Sept. 1942 at Madison, WI, daughter of John Gordon Baker and Elizabeth Nelson). Dr. Richard Burgess received his B.S. degree in chemistry from California Institute of Technology in 1964, his Ph.D. in biochemistry and molecular biology from Harvard University in 1969, and did post-doctoral work as a Helen Hay Whitney fellow at the Institute of Molecular Biology, Genève, Switzerland, 1969-71. He joined the McArdle Laboratory for Cancer Research, University of Wisconsin, Madison, in 1971, was promoted to full professor in 1982, and has been Director of the Biotechnology Center since 1984.

He received the Pfizer Award from the American Chemical Society in 1982, was a Guggenheim Fellow in 1983-84, and has earned research grants from the National Science Foundation, National Institute of Health, and the National Cancer Institute, among others. He has also authored numerous articles for the professional journals, and edited the book, *Protein Purification: Micro to Macro: Proceedings of a Cetus-UCLA Symposium Held at Frisco, Colorado, March 29-April 4, 1987* (New York: A. R. Liss, 1987). His biography has appeared in multiple volumes of *American Men and Women of Science*, *Who's Who in Technology*, and *Who's Who in America.* Ann Burgess earned her Ph.D. in biochemistry and molecular biology from Harvard University in 1969, and is currently Director of Biology Core Curriculum at the University of Wisconsin, Madison; her biography has appeared in *Who's Who of American Women.*

10a. **Kristin Mary.** Born 30 Nov. 1974 at Madison, WI.

10b. **Andreas Baker.** Born 25 May 1979 at Madison, WI.

9b. **Linda Irene.** Born 19 Feb. 1947 at Seattle, WA. Married David Cook (he was born 21 Oct. 1947), and had children: *Michael David* (born 3 Feb. 1974); *Christopher John* (born 2 Apr. 1977); *Megan Lynn* (born 9 Apr. 1980). Linda and David Cook received B.A. degrees from Western Washington University, and taught several years. Linda Cook now works as a bookkeeper and David as a computer specialist at Bellevue, WA.

9c. **Mary Louise (IV).** Born 3 Oct. 1950 at Renton, WA. Married Malcolm Klug (born 4 Nov. 1950), and had children: *Alan Robert* (born 17 Nov. 1980; *Kathryn Louise* (born 1 July 1984). Mary and Malcolm Klug both graduated from Stanford University in 1973, she with a B.A. degree in psychology, and he with an M.A. degree in engineering. The Klugs currently live at Bellevue, WA.

[William (I)[1], Edward (I)[2], Reuben (I)[3], Thomas (I)[4], King Hiram (I)[5], Joseph Daniel[6]]

OWEN W. BURGESS
(1881-1970)

OF CUMBERLAND COUNTY, TENNESSEE

7l. **Owen Washington** *[son of Joseph Daniel].* Born 10 Jan. 1881 in Cumberland Co., TN. Married (Sarah) Alice "Allie" Meda Wilson in 1903 (she was born 5 May 1881, daughter of Sage [or Logan] Wilson and Mary Mitchell, and died 19 May 1922, buried Thomas Springs Cemetery); married secondly as her second husband Louise Wyatt Dixon on 14 Feb. 1929 in Cumberland Co. (she was born on 7 Jan. 1895, daughter of (Joseph) Riley and Nancy Wyatt, and died 13 June 1965, buried in the Hale's Chapel Cemetery; by her first husband she had children: *(Payton) Wilburn DIXON*; *Ruby DIXON* [married Charles Reece, and died before 1988]). Living with his parents in 1900; listed in the 1910-20 censuses for Cumberland Co.; four of four children survive in 1910. Elected Justice of the Peace for Cumberland Co. in 1936. Owen Burgess was a farmer in Cumberland Co., TN. He died there on 19 (or 28) Oct. 1970, and is buried in the Burgess Cemetery.

8a. **Cora Bell (III).** Born 2 Nov. 1903 in Cumberland Co., TN. Married Wade Tucker (he was born 1 Jan. 1897, and died Nov. 1984 at Pleasant Hill, TN), and had children: *Bill* (a teacher; married Anna Ruth Dodson); *Freda* (a teacher). Cora Tucker taught school for 30 years in Cumberland Co., and another 17 years at Orlando, FL. She died in June 1987 at Pleasant Hill, TN, or Orlando, FL. She contributed greatly to this book.

8b. **Amy Dell (I).** Her name is also spelled Amie, and her middle name is given in one record as Dee. Born 23 May 1905 in Cumberland Co., TN. Married Virgil Swallows (he was born 10 Sept. 1903, and died Aug. 1974 at Lake Helen, FL), and adopted one son: *Oliver Charles*, the son of her brother, Lavern (see below for his children). Amy Swallows lived at St. Cloud, FL for twenty-six years, and at Kissimmee, FL for the last twelve years of her life. She died there on 15 Oct. 1963.

8c. **Maggie Eden.** Born 24 Apr. 1907 in Cumberland Co., TN. Married Wed C. Hassler on 13 July 1924 in Cumberland Co., and had children: *Gene* (married Pearl Webb); *Marie* (married Ray Stone); *Betty* (married A. G. Taylor); *Olaf Wayne*. Maggie Hassler lives near Crossville, TN.

8d. **(Joseph) Lavern (I).** Born 30 Jan. 1910 in Cumberland Co., TN. See below for full entry.

8e. **Clifford Lincoln.** Born 30 Jan. 1912 in Cumberland Co., TN. See below for full entry.

8f. **Mary Elizabeth (V).** Born 8 Mar. 1914 in Cumberland Co., TN. Married Virgil Stone, and had children: *Elbert*. Mary Stone lives at Crossville, TN.

8g. **Daniel Logan.** Born 21 Feb. 1917 in Cumberland Co., TN. Married (Audrey) Merle Bell (she was born about 1924, and remarried George Phillip Keck on 6 May 1990 in Cumberland Co.). Listed in the 1940 draft list of Cumberland Co., and later served in World War II, where he was severely wounded. Daniel Burgess worked for a clothing mill for many years. He was a member of Baptist Tabernacle. He died childless on 30 Jan. 1989 at Crossville, TN, and is buried in the Clifty Cemetery.

8h. **(William) Boyd.** Born 4 Dec. 1929 in Cumberland Co., TN. See below for full entry.

8i. **Wilma Evelyn.** Her middle name is given as Evelyne on her death certificate. Born 30 May 1931 in Cumberland Co., TN; died there on 31 May 1931 (or born and died on 19 May 1931, according to her death certificate).

8j. **Sibyl Ann.** Born 8 (or 25) Mar. 1934 in Cumberland Co., TN. Married (Herman) Ellis Bell on 20 July 1949 in Cumberland Co., and had children: *Bobby*. **Sybil** married secondly (George) William "Bill" Rogers, and had children: *James* (lives Collinsville, AL); *(William) Thomas* (married Claudine C. ___); *Gary L.* (married Vera ___); *Larry* (lives at Valdosta, GA); *Kathy L.* (married Alan Patton); *Deborah A.* (married Harvey L. Patton); *Tammie Kay*. Sibyl Rogers was a machine operator at Homestead Manufacturing, and a member of Calvary Temple Church. She died on 5 Sept. 1988 at Midway, TN, and is buried in the Hale's Chapel Cemetery.

LAVERN BURGESS OF KENTON CO., KENTUCKY
[Owen Washington[7]]

8d. **(Joseph) Lavern (I)** *[son of Owen Washington].* His name is also spelled Laverne in some records, and is given as Vernon in the 1920 census. Born 30 Jan. 1910 in Cumberland Co., TN. Married Anna Bell about 1927, and secondly Virginia Evans about 1929 (she was born about 1913 in TN), and thirdly Lucille Belt, and fourthly Gladys Onkst. Vern Burgess worked for Baldwin Piano Co. of Cincinnati for many years, residing at Covington, KY. He now lives with his son, Norman Burgess, at Gonzalez, LA.

9a. **Oliver Charles (I).** He was adopted by his aunt, Amy Burgess Swallows, and uses the surname Swallows. Born 13 June 1928 at Cincinnati, OH. Married Hisako Mochida. Oliver Swallows was a career Army enlisted man, serving 22 years before retiring; he has also worked as a Deputy Sheriff. He currently lives at Kissimmee, FL.

10a. **(Oliver) Charles (II).** Born 10 June 1949 at Yokahama, Japan. Married Kathy Baker. Charles Swallows works for an environmental firm in Florida.

11a. **Kristen Annabelle.** Born 23 Nov. 1973 at Jacksonville, FL.
11b. **Shannon Kathy.** Born 25 Aug. 1977 at Gainesville, FL.

10b. **Amy Dell (II).** Her middle name is also given as Dee. Born 29 July 1953 at Ft. Leonard Wood, MO.

9b. **Joseph Lavern (II) "Junior."** Born 5 Feb. 1930 at Cincinnati, OH. Married. Served in the U.S. Air Force. Joe Burgess was a professional jockey and boxer (flyweight class). He now lives retired at Lexington, KY.

10a. **Danny.** Lives Versailles, KY. He may be the Danny Burgess listed in a recent Lexington directory, with wife Toni R.
10b. **David.** Lives at Lexington, KY.
10c. **Anthony (I) "Tony."** Born about 1958. Tony Burgess holds a yellow belt rank in the sport of Tae-Kwon-Do; he participated in the American Martial Association Championship at Bowling Green, KY in 1991, and lives at Versailles, KY.

11a. **Anthony (II).** Born about 1984. Anthony Burgess holds a yellow belt rank in the sport of Tae-Kwon-Do; with his father, he participated in American Martial Association Championship at Bowling Green, KY in 1991, winning two seconds and a third in his age class.

10d. **Linda (II).**
10e. **Debbie (II).**

9c. **Norman Cecil "Buck."** Born 20 Oct. 1931 at Cincinnati, OH. Married Miyoshi Saito in Apr. 1954; married secondly Esther Lula Jones on 1 May 1964; married thirdly Lillie Margaret Milburn on 14 June 1980. Served in the Korean War. Norman Burgess is a land surveyor and construction engineer for the Army Corps of Engineers; he also serves in the Louisiana National Guard. He currently lives at St. Amant, LA.

10a. **Steven Patrick (II).** Born 21 June 1954 at Tokyo, Japan. Steve Burgess is a Chief Petty Officer (nuclear power plant operator) in the U.S. Navy.
10b. **Mark Timothy (I).** Born 16 Apr. 1957 at Clay Center, KS. Married Richelle Johnson. Mark Burgess is a store manager at Louisville, KY.

11a. **Matthew Christopher.** Born 19 Nov. 1977 at Louisville, KY.

10c. **Nicholas Arthur.** Born 13 Apr. 1958 at Clay Center, KS. Married Sharon Thompson, daughter of Lillie Milburn. Nick Burgess is a Sergeant (satellite communications) in the U.S. Army, currently stationed in Hawaii.

11a. **Stacy Ann.** Born 2 Nov. 1978 at Ft. Riley, KS.

10d. **Michael Shell.** Born 6 Feb. 1963 at Louisville, KY. Mike Burgess is a survey crewman in Louisiana.

10e. **Brian Mitchell.** Born 16 Mar. 1964 at Louisville, KY. Brian Burgess is a rod chainman on a survey team.

9d. **Thomas Charles.** Born 20 Nov. 1945 at Cincinnati, OH; died there on 1 Jan. 1946.

9e. **JoAnn (II)** (nmn). Born 26 Apr. 1947 at Cincinnati, OH. Married Robert Filipovic. JoAnn Filipovic lives at Cincinnati, OH.

CLIFFORD L. BURGESS OF OSCEOLA CO., FLORIDA
[Owen Washington[7]]

8e. **Clifford Lincoln.** Born 30 Jan. 1912 in Cumberland Co., TN. Married Betty Pauls. Listed in the 1940 draft list for Cumberland Co., and served in World War II. Clifford Burgess worked for General Telephone Co. for many years; he was also a farmer. He died in May 1985 at Kissimmee, FL, but is buried in the Thomas Springs Cemetery, Cumberland Co., TN.

9a. **Daughter**.

BOYD BURGESS OF KENTON CO., KENTUCKY
[Owen Washington[7]]

8h. **(William) Boyd** *[son of Owen Washington].* Born 4 Dec. 1929 in Cumberland Co., TN. Married secondly Ella Mae Stone. Boyd Burgess works for the Ford Motor Co., Sharonville, OH. He currently lives at Covington, KY.

9a. **(Boyd) Eugene.** Born 27 Dec. 1949 in Cumberland Co., TN. Married Marsha Andrews. Gene Burgess is a truck driver at Renton, WA.

9b. **Dennis Lee (II).** Born 6 Dec. 1951 at Vancouver, WA. Married Sandy Frye. Dennis Burgess works at a machine shop at Portland, OR.

10a. **Novina Marie.** Born 11 Mar. 1971 at Vancouver, WA. She was adopted out of the family.

9c. **Jane Ann.** Born 26 Feb. 1959 at Covington, KY. Jane Burgess works for Holiday Inn at Austin, TX.

9d. **Dwayne Bryan.** Born 20 June 1964 at Covington, KY.

[William (I)[1], Edward (I)[2], Reuben (I)[3], Thomas (I)[4], King Hiram (I)[5]]

JOHN ANDERSON BURGESS
(1846-1929)
OF CUMBERLAND COUNTY, TENNESSEE

6d. **John Anderson (II)** *[son of King Hiram (I)].* Born 10 Apr. 1846 in Bledsoe (later Cumberland) Co., TN. Married Katherine Jane (or Myrtle Catherine) Norris about 1868 (she was born 8 Apr. 1847 in TN, daughter of Abner Norris and Elizabeth "Queenie" Lowe, and died 6 June 1897); married secondly as her second husband Bell Zary (or Belzora) Walker about 1904 (she was born about 1855, daughter of Minerva Walker, and was previously married to David Walker, whom she divorced in 1887; Bell Walker had five children, three of which survived in 1910, including: *Anna Marie WALKER*, who married Canza Well Burgess). Has not been found in the 1870 census; listed in the 1880-1920 censuses for Cumberland Co. John Burgess was a farmer in Cumberland Co. He died there on 7 (or 8, according to his death certificate) Dec. 1929, and is buried in the Big Lick Cemetery.

The Children of John A. Burgess:

7a. **(Nancy) Zenia.** Her name is also spelled Zena in some records. Born 10 Sept. 1869 in Cumberland Co., TN. Married (George) Edward "Edd" Blaylock on 15 Nov. 1888 (he was born 10 Feb. 1869, son of Anderson Blaylock and Harriett M. Bolin, and died 19 Nov. 1957), and had children: *(Josie) Elizabeth "Lizzie"* (born 11 Sept. 1889, and died 13 July 1970); *(John) Anderson* (born 3 Oct. 1891, married Vadie Kerley, and died 27 Dec. 1963); *Lavenia Katherine* (born 22 Aug. 1893, married Clay Kerley, and died 3 Sept. 1978); *Ernest Martin* (born 21 Nov. 1895, married Viola Cobble, and was living at Knoxville in 1989); *Isaac Thomas "Ike"* (born 1 Mar. 1898, married Mary Hyder on 17 Dec. 1924, and died 3 May 1937); *Sidney Becher* (born 5 May 1900, married Reevie Kerley, and died 29 Jan. 1982 at Pikeville, TN); *(Anora) Belle* (born 27 Jan. 1903 in Cumberland Co., married Alvin Kerley, and had children: Thelma [married ___ Greenlee, and lives at Sherman Oaks, CA]; Lee [married ___ Leib, had children: Linda {dec.}, and lives at Sonoma, CA]; Jean [married ___ Carpenter, and lives at Mount Juliet, TN]; Helen [married ___ Balogh, and lives at Crossville, TN]; Carmon [lives at Houston, TX]; Billy [lives at Logensport, LA]; David [lives at Springfield, TN]; Belle Kerley died on 15 Aug. 1989, and is buried in the Hillcrest Cemetery, Big Lick, TN); *Frank* (born 27 Feb. 1906, married Lillie Brewer, and died 30 May 1988 at Crossville, TN); *Verda "Verdie"* (born 1 May 1908, married Lester Matthews on 28 Aug. 1927, and lives at Dayton, TN); *(Zora) Mable* (born 30 Oct. 1910, married Ralph Hamilton, and lives at Big Lick, TN); *(Martha) Ermon* (born 27 Oct 1914, married Ross Matthews, and died 1 Sept. 1932). Listed in the 1900 census for White Co., TN, and in 1910 in Cumberland Co. Zenia Blaylock was a well-known midwife in Cumberland Co. She died there on 12 Mar. 1945 in Cumberland Co., and is buried in the Big Lick Cemetery. Her obituary in the 22 Mar. 1945 issue of the *Crossville Chronicle* includes this passage:

"Some few years ago she had a stroke and was then compelled to give up her work as midwife. It would be hard to find a family in Big Lick or surrounding neighborhoods who have not had help from Aunt Zena. Many babies' lives have been saved by the administration of home remedies given by her before a doctor could arrive. She was always ready, rain or shine, cold or hot, or day or night, to go when called, and it may well be said of her, 'She hath done what she could.'"

7b. **(Mary) Elizabeth (II).** Listed as Queen M. E. in the 1900 census, and M. E. Queen in 1910. Born 3 Mar. 1871 in Cumberland Co., TN. Married (Simon) Atlas Tucker about 1885 (he was born 30 Apr. 1865, son of Elijah G. and Caroline Tucker, and died 28 Feb. 1952), and had children: *May* (born Mar. 1886, married probably P. W. Bell, and had children: Merle); *James* (born Apr. 1888); *John* (born Apr. 1890); *Lottie* (born Aug. 1893, probably married Charles Owensby [he may have been born

2 Jan. 1887, and died Sept. 1978 at Winter Haven, FL], and had children: Betty); *Mark* (born 31 Aug. 1899, died June 1978 at Crossville, TN); *Clinton*. Listed in the 1900-10 censuses for Cumberland Co., TN (six of seven children survive in 1910). Elizabeth Tucker died of pneumonia on 21 Feb. 1939 in Cumberland Co., and is buried in the Thomas Springs Cemetery.

7c. **(Jessie) Thomas (I).** Born 6 Mar. 1873 in Cumberland Co., TN. See below for full entry.

7d. **Isaac Linville (I).** Born 14 May 1878 in Cumberland Co., TN. See below for full entry.

7e. **Eliza Ann.** Born May 1880 in Cumberland Co., TN; died unmarried on 9 Feb. 1896 at Winesap, TN.

7f. **(Ara) Bell.** Born May 1883 in Cumberland Co., TN. Married (James) Franklin Scarbrough (he died on 6 Aug. 1961 at Grover City, CA), and had children: *Vera* (married ___ Payne); *Maudie* (married ___ Price); *Bernice* (married ___ Platt); *Robert*; *Virgil*; *Columbus*. Bell Scarbrough moved with her husband to Fresno, Fresno Co., CA about 1938. She died there on 5 Feb. 1958, and is buried in the Belmont Memorial Park.

7g. **John (X).** Born about 1885 in Cumberland Co., TN; died young. Order and dates uncertain.

7h. **Dora (II).** Born about 1887 in Cumberland Co., TN; died there before 1900. Exact order and dates unknown.

TOM BURGESS KILLED

"Tom Burgess of O'Connor, White County, was shot down at his home Monday night. Someone went to the home of Burgess, called him out, and without speaking a word emptied a load of buckshot into his breast. The party is unknown, and no cause whatever is assigned. Burgess was a private detective, and was related to the Burgesses of the Third District."—*Crossville Chronicle*, 5 Nov. 1902.

THOMAS BURGESS OF WHITE CO., TENNESSEE

[John Anderson (II)[6]]

7c. **(Jessie) Thomas (I)** *[son of John Anderson (II)].* Born 6 Mar. 1873 in Cumberland Co., TN. Married as a common-law wife (Rebecca) Jane Brewer about 1895 (she was born 14 Sept. 1877 in TN, daughter of William Benjamin Brewer and Rebecca Jane Webb, and sister of Ira Brewer [who died in infancy], and remarried Thomas A. Moyers about 1905, by whom she had children: *Clyde* [born 1906, died 1952]; *Clyo* [born 1908, married Clyde Hassler and died 23 May 1966, buried in the Crossville City Cemetery]; *Earl*; *Reavis*). Listed with his father in the 1900 census; Rebecca and son are listed in the 1900 census for Cumberland Co. with her parents, and in 1910 with her second husband. Tom Burgess was a detective at O'Conor, White Co., TN. He was shot and killed from ambush there on 1 Nov. 1902, and is buried in the Anderson Cemetery. His relationship with Rebecca and Ira is confirmed both by oral family tradition (particularly from Bessie Burgess Orme), and from the biography of Jane's father in *Memorial and Biographical Record: An Illustrated Compendium of Biography of Cumberland Region of Tennessee* (Chicago: G. A. Odle, 1898, p. 330-331), which mentions Jane as the "widow of Thomas Burgess."

URIOUS I. BURGESS

"Urious I. Burgess, Private First Class, serial number 1,315,949, was born in Cumberland County, Tennessee, near Winesap, and at the time of his death in France was twenty-two years of age. He had always resided in said county, and at the time he volunteered his service to his Country he was engaged in farming with his father. The writer hereof was not acquainted with him until he became a member of the Volunteer Company organized at Crossville, and consequently knows very little about his private life before entry into the service. He enlisted in the National Guard, Crossville Company, 2nd Tenn. Inf., which later merged with 2nd N.C., and became a part of that famous Thirtieth Division, Co. G, which had few if any equal, both defensively and offensively. Urious I. did not get to take part in the breaking of the Hindenburg Line, he having been removed from our ranks at the Battle of Ypres, Belgium, by a piece of shrapnel that passed completely through his body, said wounds being received on the 4th day of September, 1918, from which he died the following day at the hospital in Bregnes, France. He was buried in the cemetery Croix Rouge, Bregnes, France, by the side of many other comrades who made the Supreme Sacrifice during said battle. On November 12, 1920 his body was transported to the United States and re-interred at Winesap, Tenn. He was the son of Tom and Jane Brewer Burgess. His father died when he was four years old, and his mother, who survives, lives in Crossville. Three half-brothers, Clyde and Earl Myers of Crossville, Revis Myers in the Navy and now in China, and Mrs. Clyo Hassler, Crossville, survive."

8a. **Urious Ira.** His name is also given as Ira Urious on the 1917 draft list, and Ulysses Burgess in the 1900 census. Born May 1896 in Cumberland Co., TN. Listed with his mother in the 1900-1910 censuses of Cumberland Co., and in the 20 June 1917 draft register of Cumberland Co. Ira Burgess enlisted in Co. G, 119th Tennessee Infantry, U.S. Army, in 1918. He was sent to France, where he participated in a series of front-line battles, being wounded at the Battle of Ypres (Belgium) on 4 Sept. 1918. He died of his wounds on 5 Sept. 1918 at Bregnes, France, and was buried at the Croix Rouge Cemetery there. His body was returned home on 12 Nov. 1920 for reburial at Winesap, in an unmarked grave in the Burgess Cemetery. A lengthy memorial to Urious appears in the 12 Sept. 1935 issue of the *Crossville Chronicle*, and his name is inscribed on a monument dedicated to local soldiers who died for their country in downtown Crossville, TN.

IKE BURGESS OF CUMBERLAND CO., TENNESSEE
[John Anderson (II)[6]]

7d. **Isaac Linville (I) "I.L." or "Ike"** *[son of John Anderson (II)].* Born 14 May 1878 in Cumberland Co., TN. Married Ollie Mae Campbell on 4 Jan. 1903 (or 1902, according to her tombstone; she was born 4 Sept. 1885 [or 1887], daughter of Mary Jane and James E. Campbell [brother of Washington Columbus Campbell], and died on 24 Mar. 1967). Listed in the 1900 census for Cumberland Co. boarding with Thomas Brawley, and in 1910-20 with his family; three of four children survive in 1910. Ike was a farmer and land dealer in Cumberland Co. He was also elected to a six-year term on the Cumberland Co. Board of Education in 1921, and consistently reelected for many terms thereafter (as late as 1950). He died there on 18 May 1959, and is buried in the Big Lick Cemetery.

8a. **Matty** (nmn). Born Jan. 1904 in Cumberland Co., TN; died there on 30 Mar. 1904, and is buried in the Burgess Cemetery.

8b. **Bessie Jane.** Born 15 Jan. 1905 in Cumberland Co., TN. Married (Fred) Hobart Orme on 17 July 1921 in Cumberland Co., and had children: *Thomas Nickolas* (born 23 Feb. 1926, and died 18 July 1986, buried Parham Cemetery); *Robert*; *Charlie T.*; *Violet* (married ___ Kohanam [or Bohannon]); *Mary* (married ___ Coats); *Floyd*. Bessie Orme currently lives at Pikeville, TN. Her memories of the Burgess family have contributed much to this history.

8c. **Myrtie Mae.** Her name is also listed as Myrtle or Mertie in some records. Born 7 Jan. 1907 in Cumberland Co., TN. Married Roy Nail on 18 Jan. 1925 in Cumberland Co., and had children: *Arraleon*; *Arna*; *J. N.*; *Roy Jr.*; *Frankie*. Myrtie Nail lives at Crossville, TN.

8d. **(Jessie) Thomas (II).** Listed in the 1910 census as James T., and in 1920 as Tommy; he later called himself Tommy L. Burgess. Born 26 Feb. 1909 in Cumberland Co., TN. Married Maude Brewer on 3 Nov. 1928 (dec.). Tom Burgess was a laborer in Cumberland Co. He died there on 27 June 1974, and is buried in the Big Lick Cemetery.

9a. **(Syble) Ruth.** Born 22 Nov. 1928 in Cumberland Co., TN. Married Roe Sisk, and had children: *Charles*. Ruth Sisk was living at Chattanooga, TN in 1974.

8e. **Cora Belle.** Born 21 June 1911 in Cumberland Co., TN. Married Oscar Kerley on 25 Sept. 1927 in Cumberland Co., and had children: *Christine*; *Sybil*; *Vaughn*; *Harold*; *Oliver*; *Bennie*; *Bonnie*; *Velma*; *Anna Ruth*; *Gary*. Cora Kerley was named a "Mother of the Year" in 1971 by the *Crossville Chronicle*. She currently lives near Crossville, TN.

8f. **(Charles) Franklin "Frank."** Born 15 Nov. 1913 in Cumberland Co., TN. Married Abbie Nail (she was born 17 Mar. 1912, daughter of Floyd Nail, and died 5 Dec. 1946 at Nashville) on 25 Dec. 1936 in Cumberland Co.; married secondly Mamye Lee Lewis in 1948. Living at Red Dragon, WV in 1941. Frank Burgess was a mail carrier in Cumberland Co., TN. He died there on 12 Mar. 1976, and is buried in the Big Lick Cemetery.

9a. **Willana Marie.** Born 15 Feb. 1939 in Cumberland Co., TN. Married Hollis Edward Hale on 26 Sept. 1955 in Cumberland Co. (he died 3 July 1982), and had children: *Vicki Sue* (married Marvin Rector, and had children: Jodi Marie [married Ritchie Fields on 19 Dec. 1992]; Darrell Edward; *Vicki* married secondly Robert Wesley Rhea); *Connie Irene* (married Greg Mullinax, and had children: Amber Nicole); *Abbie Darlene* (married Randall Keck, and had children: Whitney Lynne [born 1988]; Lori Beth [twin; born 1992]; Kelli LeAnne [twin; born 1992]). Willana Hale married secondly Roy T. Hall on 13 Feb. 1988. She currently lives at Big Lick, TN.

9b. **(Eunice) Evelyn.** Born 23 Sept. 1940 at Eunice, WV. Married Elmo Cox on 2 Feb. 1957 in Bledsoe Co. Evelyn Cox lives in Cumberland Co.

9c. **Geneva Jane (II).** Born 28 July 1946 in Cumberland Co., TN. Married (Calvin) Carl Wyatt. Geneva Wyatt lives at Maryville, TN.

9d. **Ollie Jo.** Born 26 May 1949 in Cumberland Co., TN. Married Bill Gorham. Ollie Gorham is a stewardess for United Air Lines at Alexandria, VA.

9e. **Frances Lee.** Born 29 May 1952 in Cumberland Co., TN. Married her distant cousin, Levonn Henry Hubbard, on 6 June 1970 in Cumberland Co. (he was born 17 Dec. 1943 in Cumberland Co., son of Ross Thomas Hubbard and Oma Frances Burgess; he works as a Superintendent of Schools at Harriman, TN). Frances Hubbard is a school teacher at Harriman, TN.

8g. **Amanda Alice "Mandy."** Born 22 May 1916 in Cumberland Co., TN. Married Burkett Swafford on 19 June 1936 in Cumberland Co. (he was born 26 June 1910 in Bledsoe Co., son of Aaron Swafford and Nancy Alice Patton, was a maintenance worker for the U.S. Postal Service, and died 31 May 1992, buried Big Lick Cemetery), and had children: *June* (married Willard Hamby); *Jane* (married ___ Whiteaker); *(Aaron) Clay*; *Phyllis* (married ___ Underwood); *Irene* (married Ted Swafford); *Jerry* (married Debbie ___, and had children: Brandi; Marshall). Mandy Swafford lives at Big Lick, TN. She has contributed greatly to this book.

8h. **(Ann Syble) Lorene.** Born 10 May 1920 in Cumberland Co., TN. Married George Walker by 1940, and had children: *Dixie*; *Richard*; *Donald*; *Dwight*; *Carol*; married secondly Bill Stanley after 1974. Lorene Stanley lives at Elyria, OH.

8i. **Willie Eugene "Bill."** Born 6 Nov. 1923 in Cumberland Co., TN. Married Noble Sims on 5 Aug. 1944 at Rossville, GA. Served in World War II with the Seebees. Bill Burgess worked for the Frigidaire Co. at Dayton, OH. He now lives there retired.

9a. **Jean Marie.** She is called Emma Jean in a *Crossville Chronicle* column on 14 Feb. 1946. Born 13 Jan. 1945 at Dayton, OH. Married Joe Hayden.

8j. **Evelyn Louise.** Born 1 July 1925 in Cumberland Co., TN; died there on 13 June 1927, and is buried in the Big Lick Cemetery.

8k. **Nellie Christine.** Born 4 Nov. 1927 in Cumberland Co., TN. Married Marshall Houston, and had children: *Marshall Jr.*; *Ronnie*. Nellie Houston lives at Elyria, OH.

8l. **Fanny Ruth.** Her name is spelled Fannie on her marriage record. Born 24 Nov. 1931 in Cumberland Co., TN. Married Richard Dale Waldron on 28 May 1952 in Cumberland Co., and had children: *Timothy*. Fanny Waldron lives at Elyria, OH.

Robert Otis Burgess (right)
Walker Francis Quisenberry, his brother-in-law, in "Fra Diavolo" (left)

[William (I)[1], Edward (I)[2], Reuben (I)[3], Thomas (I)[4], King Hiram (I)[5]]

WILLIAM KIMSY BURGESS
(1855-1937)
OF CUMBERLAND COUNTY, TENNESSEE

6i. **William Kimsy "Stingy Bill"** *[son of King Hiram (I)].* He was also called "Uncle" Billie Burgess in later years. Born 27 Aug. 1855 (or 12 Aug., according to his death certificate) in Bledsoe (later Cumberland) Co., TN. Married Elizabeth Ann "Lizzie" Hall on or about 4 Sept. 1876 (when his father deeded him land, clearly at the time of his marriage; Elizabeth was born 3 Aug. 1858, daughter of Thomas Hall and Sarah Ann Hale, and died 20 Nov. 1927, buried Hall [or Hale] Cemetery; she was survived by five children). Listed in the 1880-1920 censuses for Cumberland Co.; six of nine children survive in 1900, five of nine in 1910. William K. Burgess was a farmer in Cumberland Co., TN. He died there of pneumonia on 24 Feb. 1937, and is buried in the Hale's Chapel Cemetery. His obituary mentions five surviving children, three daughters and two sons, and two surviving siblings, P. D. Burgess and Mrs. John Campbell.

BIGLICK FATHER AND SON PASS AWAY RECENTLY

"The serious illness and sudden death of W. K. Burgess, 'Uncle Billie' as he was known to his many friends, came as a shock to his family and friends. He was laid to rest at Hales Chapel Cemetery, February 25, 1937. Funeral services were conducted by the Rev. Eugene Smathers. Mr. Burgess was 82 years of age, and is survived by three daughters, Mrs. Sarah Cole of Sparta; Mrs. Alice Swafford, Biglick; Mrs. Anna Mooneyham, Pikeville; two sons, Henry Burgess of Winesap; and W. V. Burgess, Biglick. 'Uncle Billie' was a successful farmer and had lived many years in Burgesstown, and was a member of the Baptist Church. He also has one sister, Mrs. John Campbell, one brother, P. D. Burgess; twenty-three grandchildren and three great-grandchildren, and a host of friends who will miss him."

"W. Vance Burgess, born October 23, 1881, died March 9, 1937, at his home at Biglick. All that loved ones and friends could do were done, with Dr. Buttram in attendance. He had been in poor health for some time, but did not seem in serious condition, and was able to be with his father, W. K. Burgess, before he died, and was at his father's funeral. He was stricken with pneumonia and also suffered from stomach ulcers. He was an active member of the Presbyterian Church, becoming a member October 23, 1921, being one of the original members upon its organization here, being first a deacon and four years later, July 5, 1925, he was elected and ordained an elder, the highest office and honor which our church can bestow. For many years he has been church treasurer, giving of his zest to the work which he loved. For many years he was superintendent of our Sunday school. His services in our church and Sunday school will be sadly missed. He was married on April 7, 1907 to Miss Amy Sevier, and to this union were born six children: Violet, Estelle, Eucle, Alberta, Letha, and Marvin, all of whom survive. He also leaves three sisters and one brother: Mrs. Sarah Cole, Sparta; Mrs. Alice Swafford, Biglick; Mrs. Anna Mooneyham, Pikeville; and Henry Burgess, Winesap. Active pallbearers were: A. H. Hall, J. H. Tollett, I. L. Burgess, Ernest Blaylock, L. Selby, T. V. Hale. Honorary pallbearers were: T. L. Hale, Ed Blaylock, J. A. Kerley, Boge Hall. Funeral services were conducted by the Rev. Eugene Smathers at the church, with R. G. Putnam of Pikeville in charge. The many beautiful flowers which were sent showed the respect which all have had toward our much-loved friend and neighbor. Our deepest and heartfelt sympathy goes out to his wife, children, and loved ones."—*Crossville Chronicle*, 18 Mar. 1937.

The Children of William K. Burgess:

7a. **Sarah Ann (V).** Born 6 Oct. 1876 in Cumberland Co., TN. Married William G. Cole in Feb. 1897 (he died before 1900), and had children: *Casto* (born 25 Aug. 1898, died July 1981); married secondly

John Cole on 26 Feb. 1903 in White Co., TN (he was born Feb. 1856 in TN, the brother or uncle of her first husband), and had children: *Maud* (born 10 June 1904, married Beecher Wallace, and died 16 Mar. 1989 at Sparta, TN; Beecher Wallace currently lives at Sparta, TN); *Elizabeth* (dec.; married Casto Wallace, who lives at Sparta, TN). Listed in the 1900 census for White Co., TN living with John Cole. Sarah Cole died on 15 Aug. 1963 at Sparta, TN, and is buried in the Lost Creek Cemetery.

7b. **(Patrick) Henry.** His name is also given as Henry Patrick. Born 26 Jan. 1878 in Cumberland Co., TN. Married Minnie Chastain on 13 Apr. 1919 in Cumberland Co. (div.; she was born 14 July 1884, daughter of John Chastain, became a school teacher, and died 12 Jan. 1976, aged 91 years, buried Smith Chapel Cemetery). Listed in the 1920 census for Cumberland Co., TN. Henry Burgess was a farmer in Cumberland Co. He died childless on 23 May 1969, aged 91 years, and is buried in the Hale Cemetery.

7c. **Nancy Jane (III) "Nannie."** Born Apr. 1880 in Cumberland Co., TN. Listed with her father in the 1900 census. Married (James) Emmett Parham after 1900 (he was born 1869, and died 1944), and is mentioned in a history of the Parham family published in the 6 Sept. 1928 issue of the *Crossville Chronicle* (p. 5). Nancy Parham died in 1907, and is buried in the Parham Cemetery.

7d. **(William) Vance (I).** Born 23 Nov. 1881 in Cumberland Co., TN. See below for full entry.

7e. **Lotty M.** Born 28 Sept. 1883 in Cumberland Co., TN; died there on 29 July 1892, and is buried in the Hale Cemetery.

7f. **(Mary) Alice (I).** Born 5 Sept. 1886 in Cumberland Co., TN. Married Ell G. Kerley on 20 Nov. 1905 in Cumberland Co. (he was born 1 May 1877, and died 4 Apr. 1916, buried Wilson Cemetery), and had children: *Oscar* (born about 1906, lives at Crystal Lake, FL); *Leslie Arnold* (born 19 Dec. 1907 in Cumberland Co., married Laura Bradley, was a factory worker, had children: Gwen [married ___ Norris, had children: Lachelle {married ___ Hall, and lives at Louisville, TN}; Laura Elizabeth {married ___ Guinn, and lives at Cookeville, TN}, and lives at Crossville], and died 8 Sept. 1989 at Crossville, TN, buried Big Lick Cemetery); *Garland*; a fourth child, name unknown, who died young in a fire.

Mary Alice KERLEY married secondly W. E. "Dick" Swafford about 1917 (he was born 30 Oct. 1864, and died 1 Jan. 1940), and had children: *Archie "Tom"* (lives at Crossville); *(Willard) Alton* (lives at Crossville); *Casto A.* (born 20 June 1922, and died 20 Apr. 1945 while serving in Italy); *Vance* (lives at Crossville); *Ernestine* (married Forrest Caldwell, and lives at Elyria, OH). The then-oldest member of the Burgess family celebrated her 100th birthday on 5 Sept. 1986 at Crossville, TN. She died several months later, on 8 Feb. 1987, and was buried in the Big Lick Cemetery.

7g. **Mattie A.** Born 13 Sept. 1888 in Cumberland Co., TN; died there of diphtheria on 15 Dec. 1892, and is buried in the Hale Cemetery.

7h. **(Lou) Anna.** Listed as Annie in the 1900 census. Born 30 Dec. 1893 in Cumberland Co., TN. Married Charles Litton "Charley" Wyatt on 9 June 1913 in Cumberland Co. (he was born 1 June 1893, and died of tuberculosis on 16 Mar. 1914 at the home of his father-in-law, buried Hale Cemetery), and had children:

Charlie Winfred WYATT. Born 2 June 1914 (posthumously) in Cumberland Co., TN, married Annie Mae Fields on 31 Mar. 1935 (she was born 13 Dec. 1914), worked as an auto mechanic, and died 11 Oct. 1989 (buried Cumberland Co., TN). They had children:

Helen Ruth WYATT (born 21 Mar. 1936, married Frank Holladay [he was born 19 Feb. 1934], and worked as a nurse and a painter).

Earl Lester WYATT (born 13 Apr. 1938, married Daisy Evans [div.], and had children: Joan [born 17 June 1961]; married secondly Brenda Kaye Flynn on 11 Nov. 1963 [div.], and had children: Teresa Kaye [born 4 May 1963, married Chris Mackgum on 14 Apr. 1982]; Melissa Ann [born 19 Nov. 1964, and had children: Tiffany {born 3 June 1981}; married James Poore, and had children: Vanessa Ann {born 7 Mar. 1988}]).

Charlie Marvin WYATT (born 10 July 1941, married Joann Brown on 23 Dec. 1961 [she was born 19 Mar. 1942], and had children: Pamela Renee [born 11 July 1963, married Freddie Darnell on 6 Nov. 1981, and had children: Alex; Kristen]; Kevin Todd [born 13 Jan. 1969]; Jason Eric [born 2 Nov. 1975]).

(Franklin) Douglas WYATT (born 12 Sept. 1945 at Elyria, OH, married his distant cousin, Marjorie Louise "Margie" Burgess, on 10 Oct. 1964 [she was born 8 Feb. 1946, daughter of Ross Rawlan Burgess Sr. and Lena Wyatt], and had children: (Franklin) Keith [born 28 May 1965, married Lisa Diane Burgess on 19 Nov. 1985 {she was born 22 Sept. 1967, daughter of Marvin Allen Burgess and Velma Diane Lewis}, and had children: Franklin Aaron Craig {born 7 May 1986}; Dusty; Brent]; Karen [born about 1967, married Teddy Loden on 9 Aug. 1986, and had children: Whitney Danielle {born 11 Jan. 1987}; Colby Grant {born 18 Oct. 1989}]; Kimberly Dolores [born 11 Nov. 1972, married Daniel Dixon]).

Bobby Wayne WYATT (born 21 Mar. 1950, married Wanda Pearl Sapp on 14 Sept. 1968 [she was born 8 Dec. 1949], and had children: Jeffrey Wayne [born 26 Jan. 1971, married Tonya Carruthers {born 23 Feb. 1971}, and had children: Megan Denise {born 19 June 1989}; Trevor Wayne {born 16 Aug. 1993}]; Charlie Addison [born 25 Feb. 1979]; Brandi Michele [born 15 Mar. 1981]).

Anna Burgess WYATT married secondly (Walter) Edward "Edd" Mooneyham on 13 Oct. 1916 in Cumberland Co., TN (he died 26 Oct. 1956), and had children:

***Everett* MOONEYHAM** (nmn). Born 9 May 1918 in Cumberland Co., TN, married Clara Bess Simmons on 11 Feb. 1939 (she was born 6 Dec. 1920), and had children: *Carolyn Faye* (born 29 Oct. 1939, married John Royce Bichard on 15 Nov. 1959 [div.; he was born 9 Nov. 1934], and had children: Barry Curtis [born 29 May 1968, married Michele ___ on 23 June 1990 {born 27 May 1967}, and had children: Zachary {born 3 Sept. 1992}]; Brian Todd [born 11 Nov. 1970]; *Carolyn Bichard* is a furniture store manager); *Linda Jean* (born 21 Aug. 1950, married Jimmie Baxter Hill on 29 June 1973, and had children: Julie Hester Renée Adjuah [born 7 Jan. 1985]; Jimmie is a preacher and missionary, and lived and worked in Africa and Samoa for five years; Jimmie and Linda now live at Orlando, FL). Everett Mooneyham was a construction superintendent in Florida; he died there on 8 Apr. 1986, and is buried in the Woodlawn Memorial Cemetery, Orlando, FL.

***Clyde* MOONEYHAM** (nmn). Born 6 Sept. 1922 in Cumberland Co., TN, married Willa Frank Ferguson on 21 Feb. 1947 (she was born 18 July 1928), and had children: *Jerry Alan* (born 4 Jan. 1948, married Fran ___, and had children: John [born 11 Apr. 1979]; Crystal; Scott; Jerry Mooneyham died on 26 Sept. 1991 at Orlando, FL); *Edward Dale* (born 12 Nov. 1954, married Peggy ___ [div.], and secondly Joann ___ [div.]; Edward builds and repairs airplanes); *Judith Kaye* (born 25 Oct. 1956; Judith Mooneyham works with her brother, Edward, in the structural rebuilding of airplanes). Clyde Mooneyham is a retired gas station owner. He currently lives at Tucson, AZ.

***Ruby* MOONEYHAM** (nmn). Born 10 Apr. 1926 in Cumberland Co., TN, married Johnny Howard Brown on 22 Aug. 1948 (he was born 31 Dec. 1920, and serves as the Superintendent of Schools in Sequatchie Co., TN), and had children: *Gary Ray* (born 22 July 1949, married Carolyn Austin on 15 Sept. 1970, and had children: Casey Ray [born 30 July 1971]; Anita Louise [born 1 Mar. 1976]; Gary Brown works as a school teacher at Dunlap, TN). Ruby Brown currently lives at Dunlap, TN.

***Jewell* MOONEYHAM** (nmn). Born 21 Aug. 1928 in Cumberland Co., TN, married Wiley Woodrow Agee on 12 Jan. 1952 (he was born 19 May 1924, and died 10 Apr. 1988), and had children: *Rhonda Sue* (born and died 21 July 1953); *Donna Kay* (born and died 24 Aug. 1954); *Peggy Louise* (born 5 Nov. 1955, married James Preston Swafford on 10 June 1973 [div.]; married secondly Thomas Paul Roberts on 14 Sept. 1981 [he was born 14 Apr. 1958], and had children: April Dyan [born 19 Dec. 1984]; Peggy Roberts works as a vocational school secretary at Pikeville, TN); *Ronald Steven* (born 30 Aug. 1958, and died 6 May 1961, accidentally drowned); *John Edward* (born 15 Dec. 1966, married Kimberly Beth Mains on 12 Aug. 1989 [she was born 2 Sept. 1968]; John Agee is a civil engineer, and Kimberly works as a wildlife and fisheries biologist).

Anna MOONEYHAM died on 3 Aug. 1979 at Dunlap, TN, and is buried with her second husband in the Seals Cemetery, Bledsoe Co., TN. Linda Hill has contributed greatly to this book.

7i. **Son.** Born 8 May 1897 in Cumberland Co., TN; died there on 11 May 1897, and is buried in the Hale Cemetery.

Linda Hill wrote in 1993: "Lou Anna Mooneyham was a tiny woman. She stood under five feet tall and weighed less than one hundred pounds as an adult. She loved flowers and gardening and did a lot of sewing. She also enjoyed carpentry work and made many items, including a bedroom closet. Anna played the piano, organ, accordion, and guitar, and enjoyed singing. Edd Mooneyham was a farmer and general store shopkeeper. He had to have both legs amputated in 1950 and 1952 due to sugar diabetes. Each of their children was given one name only, because Edd disliked the idea of more than one name. He operated a post office in his store, and said it was confusing to get mail addressed in a variety of ways to one individual. After his death, Anna lived with her daughters, alternating between their homes in Dunlap and Pikeville."

VANCE BURGESS OF CUMBERLAND CO., TENNESSEE
[William Kimsey[6]]

7d. **(William) Vance (I)** *[son of William Kimsy].* Born 23 Nov. 1881 in Cumberland Co., TN. Married (Mary) Amy Siever (or Sevier) on 7 Apr. 1907 in Cumberland Co. (she was born 6 June 1886, and died 19 Apr. 1958). Listed in the 1920 census for Cumberland Co., TN. Vance Burgess was elected an Elder of the Presbyterian Church on 5 July 1925; he also farmed in Cumberland Co., TN. He died there of pneumonia on 9 Mar. 1937, a few days after his father (their obituaries were published simultaneously in the *Crossville Chronicle*), and is buried in the Big Lick Cemetery.

8a. **(La) Violet.** Born 28 May 1908 in Cumberland Co., TN. Married Glenn R. Wood on 7 July 1941 in Cumberland Co. (he was born 3 July 1908, and died May 1990 at Crossville, TN). Violet Wood was a school teacher at Dayton, OH. She died on 13 Aug. 1980 in Cumberland Co., and is buried in the Big Lick Cemetery.

8b. **(Oliver) Estille.** Born 7 Mar. 1913 in Cumberland Co., TN. See below for full entry.

8c. **Eucle (I)** (nmn). Born 28 Apr. 1916 in Cumberland Co., TN. See below for full entry.

8d. **Alberta Nina.** Born 18 Dec. 1918 in Cumberland Co., TN. Married Everett Louis Gibson on 6 July 1940 at Big Lick, Cumberland Co. Alberta Gibson lives near Crossville, TN.

8e. **Letha Amanda.** She is called Althea in a 1932 newspaper clipping. Born 17 July 1925 in Cumberland Co., TN. Married Hershell Matthews on 11 May 1946 in Cumberland Co. (he was the son of Mahlon Matthews, and died Sept. 1993). Letha Matthews lives at Louisville, KY.

8f. **Marvin Kimsy.** Born 13 May 1928 in Cumberland Co., TN. See below for full entry.

ESTILLE BURGESS OF CUMBERLAND CO., TENNESSEE

[William Kimsey[6], William Vance (I)[7]]

8b. **(Oliver) Estille** *[son of William Vance (I)]*. His name is spelled Estel in the 1920 census. Born 7 Mar. 1913 in Cumberland Co., TN. Married Dora Bradley on 8 Apr. 1934 in Cumberland Co. (she was a school teacher, the daughter of James H. Bradley and Margaret Elizabeth Houlette, and sister of Mae Bradley [who married Estille's cousin, Steve Burgess]). Listed in the 1940 draft list of Cumberland Co.; elected Supervisor of the Second District of Cumberland Co. in 1937; elected to the Board of Education for Cumberland Co. in 1943. Estille Burgess was Transportation Supervisor for the Cumberland Co. School System before retiring. He currently lives near Crossville, TN.

9a. **Billie Lee (II).** Born 22 Mar. 1936 in Cumberland Co., TN; died there on 23 Mar. 1936, and is buried in the Big Lick Cemetery.

9b. **Wayne Lincoln** (ad.). He uses the surname Bradley, but is also called Wayne Bradley Burgess in some newspaper accounts. Born 12 Feb. 1942 in Cumberland Co., TN. Married Faye Allred. Wayne Bradley works for the Tennessee State Dept. of Weights and Measures in Cumberland Co.

10a. **Larry Wayne (II).** Born 11 Jan. 1963 at Big Lick, TN. Larry Bradley works for Ford Motor Co. in Florida.

10b. **Sheila Diane.** Born 28 Feb. 1964 at Big Lick, TN. Sheila Bradley is a nurse at Nashville, TN.

9c. **(Jessie) Carolyn.** Her marriage record spells her name Caroline. Born 22 Jan. 1945 in Cumberland Co., TN. Married Johnny Eldridge Barker on 2 Oct. 1965 in Cumberland Co.

EUCLE BURGESS Sr. OF CUMBERLAND CO., TENNESSEE

[William Kimsey[6], William Vance (I)[7]]

8c. **Eucle (I)** (nmn) *[son of William Vance (I)]*. Born 28 Apr. 1916 in Cumberland Co., TN. Married Cora Wilbanks, daughter of Eston Wilbanks, on 25 June 1938 in Cumberland Co. (she was appointed in 1975 to the Cumberland Farmers Home Administration County Committee). Listed in the 1940 draft list of Cumberland Co. Elected Chair of the Cumberland County Production and Marketing Administration (later the Agricultural Stabilization and Conservation Committee) on 10 Nov. 1949, and re-elected in 1951 and 1955. Eucle Burgess worked for the U.S. Dept. of Agriculture as District Director of the allotment and soil conservation program for the state of Tennessee, with his headquarters located in Nashville. He died at Knoxville on 5 July 1986, and is buried in the Big Lick Cemetery. Cora Burgess currently lives near Crossville, TN.

9a. **Sherry Ann (I).** Her name is spelled Sherrie in early newspaper accounts. Born 5 Jan. 1940 in Cumberland Co., TN. Married (Malcolm) Bruce Treadway on 20 Apr. 1957 in Cumberland Co. (he was born 1938, the son of Malcolm Mansfield Treadway, and died 7 Dec. 1964 in Cumberland Co. in a trucking accident), and had children: *Michael Bruce*; *Mitchell Lynn*; *Mack Jonathan*; *Martin Shan* (married Elizabeth ___, and had children: Everett Bruce [born 24 Nov. 1988 at Crossville, TN]); Sherry Burgess married secondly Daryl Smith.

9b. **Linda Gail (I).** Her middle name is spelled Gale in her birth announcement. Born 6 Mar. 1944 in Cumberland Co., TN. Married Jim L. Milam on 4 July 1970 in Cumberland Co.

9c. **Eucle (II) "Butch"** (nmn). Born 27 Aug. 1950 in Cumberland Co., TN. Married Judy Ann Brown on 14 Apr. 1976 in Cumberland Co. (div.); married secondly Catherine Jean "Cathy" McCoy on 10 Mar. 1979 in Cumberland Co. (div.); married thirdly Vickie Ann Hinch on 8 Oct. 1984 in Cumberland Co. (she was born 22 June 1946). Butch Burgess is Director of the Boys' Club at Crossville, TN.

10a. **(Eucle) Chad.** Born 13 Jan. 1981 at Crossville, TN.
10b. **Lynn McDaniel.** Born 13 Apr. 1986 at Crossville, TN.

MARVIN BURGESS OF LEXINGTON CO., SOUTH CAROLINA

[William Kimsey[6], William Vance (I)[7]]

8f. **Marvin Kimsy.** Born 13 May 1928 in Cumberland Co., TN. Married Dorothy Yowell on 7 Apr. 1951. Enlisted in the U.S. Army in 1950, and served as a sergeant in Co. E, 31st Infantry Regiment, 7th Division during the Korean War. Marvin Burgess joined the U.S. Soil Conservation Service in 1952 at Nashville, TN, and served with that agency in Tennessee, New Hampshire, and South Carolina. He retired from the SCS in May 1985; at the time he was State Resource Conservationist, headquartered at Columbia, SC. He currently lives at Columbia, SC.

9a. **Kimsy Vance.** Born 2 July 1953 in Lincoln Co., TN. Married Barbara Jane Bryant. Kim Burgess teaches at the Christian School, Chalcedon Presbyterian Church, Roswell, GA.

10a. **Justin Bryant.** Born 3 May 1986 at Roswell, GA.
10b. **Lindsay Elizabeth.** Born 24 June 1989 at Roswell, GA.

9b. **Steven Wayne.** Born 29 Sept. 1954 in Humphreys Co., TN. Married Teresa Davis. Steve Burgess is a construction manager at Atlanta, GA.

10a. **Amanda Michelle.** Born 14 Jan. 1983 at Atlanta, GA.
10b. **Ryan Davis.** Born 19 Sept. 1987 at Atlanta, GA.

9c. **Brent Douglas.** Born 16 June 1957 in Williamson Co., TN. Married Deborah Todd. Brent Burgess is a plant manager at Atlanta, GA.

10a. **Brittany Anne.** Born 20 Nov. 1984 at Carrollton, GA.
10b. **Brandon Micah.** Born 5 Aug. 1986 at Carrollton, GA.

9d. **Cynthia Kay.** Born 12 Mar. 1960 in Williamson Co., TN. Married Joseph Baron McGougan. Cynthia McGougan lives at Rockford, IL.

Silvester BURGESS (1911-1985)

[William (I)[1], Edward (I)[2], Reuben (I)[3], Thomas (I)[4], King Hiram (I)[5]]

"P." BURGESS
(1860-1939)

OF CUMBERLAND COUNTY, TENNESSEE

6k. **(Jasper) Patrick Dillard "P." or "P.D."** *[son of King Hiram (I)]*. His name is spelled Patrige on his death certificate, and Pea in the 1920 census. Born 28 Dec. 1860 in Cumberland Co., TN. Married Rhoda Ann Hale about 1884 (she was born 10 Mar. 1869 in TN, daughter of Michael and Suzannah Hale). Listed in the 1900-20 censuses for Cumberland Co.; six of six children survive in 1900, nine of nine in 1910. Pea Burgess was a farmer in Cumberland Co., TN. He died on 17 Jan. 1939 at Vandever, TN.

The Children of "P." Burgess:

7a. **(Anna) Viola.** Born 5 Nov. 1885 (or 1879, according to her tombstone) in Cumberland Co., TN. Married Dardies (or Dardier) Hedgecoth about 1900 (he was born 1 Apr. 1867 [or 1871], and died 4 July 1944), and had at least the following children: *Martha Jane* (married Frank Webb); *Nathan*; *Daily*; *Stella* (married ___ Brown); *Ava Lee* (married ___ Mooneyham); *Charles* (born 10 Dec. 1917, died Feb. 1982 at Crossville, TN); *Garland*; two infants. Viola Hedgecoth died on 12 Dec. 1952 in Cumberland Co., and is buried in the Lantana Cemetery. Her daughter, Martha Webb, lives near Crossville.

7b. **(Mary) Ellen (VI).** Born 10 Aug. 1887 in Cumberland Co., TN. Married Perry Earnest Beyer (or Byers) on 2 Jan. 1910 in Cumberland Co. (he was born 1881, and died 1956, buried Lantana Cemetery), and had children: *Zona* (dec.; she may have been born 8 June 1928, and died Mar. 1974); *Gracie* (dec.); *Lola* (dec.); *Arzonia* (dec.); *Otto* (dec.); *Casto* (who lives near Chattanooga). Ellen Beyer died in Jan. 1977 at Pikeville, TN.

7c. **Emma Jane.** Born 7 Apr. 1889 in Cumberland Co., TN. Married Henry Hyder on 4 July 1915 in Cumberland Co. (he died or was divorced by 1920), and had children: *Ulish* (born 1 Apr. 1916, died Mar. 1993 at Crossville); *Lillie* (born 1917); *Pearl* (married ___ Summerfield). Listed in the 1920 census with her father. Married secondly Brown Webb. Emma Webb died on 29 May 1969 in Cumberland Co., and is buried in the Hale Cemetery.

7d. **(William) Lemuel.** Born 12 Dec. 1891 in Cumberland Co., TN. See below for full entry.

7e. **(James) Mike.** Born 1 Sept. 1893 in Cumberland Co., TN. See below for full entry.

7f. **King Hiram (II).** Born 12 Sept. 1896 in Cumberland Co., TN. See below for full entry.

7g. **Susie Eveline.** Born 6 May 1901 in Cumberland Co., TN. Married Steve Harrison Brewer on 25 Mar. 1917 in Cumberland Co., and had at least the following children: *Nellie* (married ___ VanWinkle); *Elvert*. Susie Brewer died on 30 Jan. 1969 in Cumberland Co., and is buried in the Hale Cemetery.

7h. **(George) Clay.** Born 5 May 1906 in Cumberland Co., TN. Married Gladys Hyder; married secondly Carrie Bessie (Herman) Brown on 18 Nov. 1964 in Cumberland Co. (she died 26 Mar. 1967). Listed in the 1940 draft list of Cumberland Co. Clay Burgess was a farmer in Cumberland Co. He died there childless on 9 Nov. 1975, and is buried in the Hale Cemetery.

7i. **Oscar Uless.** Listed as Ulas O. in the 1910 census. Born 23 Feb. 1910 in Cumberland Co., TN. Listed in the 1940 draft list of Cumberland Co. (as Oscar Uliah Burgess). Oscar Burgess was a farmer in Cumberland Co. He now lives there retired. Never married.

LEMUEL BURGESS OF CUMBERLAND CO., TENNESSEE
[Jasper Patrick Dillard[6]]

7d. **(William) Lemuel** *[son of Jasper Patrick Dillard]*. Born 12 Dec. 1891 in Cumberland Co., TN. Married (Donna [or Donia] Gertie Sherrill on 19 Apr. 1914 in Cumberland Co. (she was born 9 Dec. 1896, daughter of Jessee Sherrill and Emma Walker, and granddaughter of Mrs. Bell Zary Burgess [second wife of John Anderson Burgess], and died on 21 Dec. 1960). Listed in the 1920 census for Cumberland Co., TN, and in the 20 June 1917 draft register. Lem Burgess worked for the Cumberland County Road Commission; he was accidentally killed on 11 July 1958, and is buried in the Hale's Chapel Cemetery.

EMPLOYEE OF COUNTY 2ND '58 FATALITY

"Lem Burgess, age 66, employee of the county highway department, died at the Medical Center here Friday, July 11, as a result of injuries when a road watering truck crushed him. According to reports from the County Road Commission, Burgess slipped and fell under the rear wheels of the heavy truck as he got out of the cab to close a water valve. The driver of the truck was bringing the truck to a stop when the accident occurred. The rear wheels of the heavy truck passed over the lower part of Mr. Burgess' body....Funeral services were held Sunday, July 13, at Hale's Chapel Church, where burial followed. William Lemuel Burgess was born December 12, 1891, and died July 11, 1958, being 66 years and seven months of age. He is survived by his wife, Mrs. Gertie Sherrill Burgess; their son, Jessie, who lives here; their daughter, Mrs. Ethel Neely, of North Olmsted, Ohio; eight grandchildren, four great-grandchildren; four brothers, King, Mike, Clay, and Oscar, all of whom live in this county; three sisters, Susie Brewer, Emma Jane Webb, who lives here, and Ellen Byers, of Pikeville. Many other relatives and friends will mourn his passing. 'Lem,' as he was affectionately known, will be greatly missed by all who knew him. He had been a friend to many people during his lifetime."—*Crossville Chronicle*, 17 July 1958.

8a. **Ethel D.** Born Oct. 1915 in Bledsoe Co., TN. Married John Allen Neely on 25 May 1933 in Cumberland Co. (he died on 2 Oct. 1993 at Crossville, TN, and is buried in the Burgess Cemetery, Cumberland Co., TN). Ethel Neely currently lives at Crossville, TN.

9a. **Richard (II).** Born 8 Jan. 1932 in Cumberland Co., TN.

8b. **Jessie Patrick.** Born 25 Mar. 1918 (or 1917, according to Social Security records) in Cumberland Co., TN. Married Dovie M. Boring on 28 Sept. 1946 in Cumberland Co. (she was born 11 Nov. 1926, and remarried Arthur Farmer). Listed in the 1940 draft list of Cumberland Co. (as Jessie Patric). Jessie Burgess was a farmer in Cumberland Co. He died there on 18 Dec. 1973, and is buried in the Hale's Chapel Cemetery.

9a. **Barbara Jane (II).** Born 13 Sept. 1947 in Cumberland Co., TN. Married Jerry Bruce McDonald on 21 Sept. 1963 (dec.), and had children: *Angela Faye* (born 20 July 1964 at Crossville, TN, married Donald Edward Gibson Jr. on 17 July 1982 [he was born 14 Nov. 1962 at Melbourne, FL], and had children: Donald Ryan [born 3 Feb. 1988 at Crossville, TN]; Adam Kyle [born 11 July 1993 at Crossville, TN]); married secondly George Davis; married thirdly Larry Haston (he was born 2 June 1950). Barbara Haston currently lives at Dalton, GA.

9b. **Horace Lawson.** Born 11 Dec. 1950 in Cumberland Co, TN. Married Vickie Dyer; married secondly Deborrah Kay Myers on 31 Oct. 1988 in Cumberland Co. (she was born 10 Sept. 1952, daughter of Hazel Horn of Frankfort, IN); married thirdly Julia Leigh Dunaway on 13 Apr. 1990 in Cumberland Co. (she was born 21 Oct. 1959). Horace Burgess is a maintenance man at Homestead School, Crossville, TN.

10a. **Kevin Scott.** Born 31 Aug. 1970 at Crossville, TN.

9c. **Johnny Clyde.** His name is spelled Johnnie and Jonnie on his marriage records. Born 23 Sept. 1953 in Cumberland Co., TN. Married Sue Elaine Sherrill on 30 Dec. 1972 in Cumberland Co.; married secondly Janet Lynn Baisley on 14 Feb. 1981 and 24 Mar. 1984 in Cumberland Co. (she was born 4 Apr. 1957); married thirdly Beverly King on 12 May 1989 (she was born 1 Apr. 1954 in Cumberland Co.). Johnny Burgess is a bus driver and painter at Crossville, TN.

10a. **Andrew Patrick.** Born 20 Mar. 1975 at Crossville, TN.

9d. **Jackie Lee.** Born 2 Apr. 1958 in Cumberland Co., TN. Married Linda Gail Hargis on 29 July 1976 in Cumberland Co. Jack Burgess works for the Cumberland Co. Farmers' Co-op at Crossville, TN.

10a. **Matthew Lee (II).** Born 4 July 1977 at Crossville, TN.
10b. **Rebecca Jane.** Born 4 Jan. 1979 at Crossville, TN.

9e. **Jerry Lynn.** Born 23 Mar. 1961 in Cumberland Co., TN. Married Tena Louise Hubbard on 4 July 1983 in Cumberland Co.; married secondly Robin Renee Davis on 5 Jan. 1987 in Cumberland Co. (she was born 23 May 1968).

10a. **Jessica Marie.** Born 9 Feb. 1984 in Cumberland Co., TN.
10b. **Nicholas.**
10c. **Levi Chad.** Born 2 Oct. 1989 in Cumberland Co., TN.

9f. **Jessie Truman "J. T."** Born 16 Apr. 1965 in Cumberland Co., TN. Married Christie Smith on 1 Aug. 1987 in Bledsoe Co., TN (she was born 23 Dec. 1969). J. T. Burgess was a welder at Pikeville, TN. He died there on 14 Oct. 1988, and is buried in the Hale's Chapel Cemetery.

10a. **Clarissa Lee.** Born 8 July 1987 in Cumberland Co., TN.

MIKE BURGESS OF CUMBERLAND CO., TENNESSEE
[Jasper Patrick Dillard[6]]

7e. **(James) Mike** *[son of Jasper Patrick Dillard].* Born 1 Sept. 1893 (or 1892, according to his obituary) in Cumberland Co., TN. Married Flora Mae Wyatt on 24 June 1920 in Cumberland Co. (she was born 9 July 1898, daughter of Jim Wyatt and Betsey Jane Davis, and sister of Ida Wyatt [who married Mike's cousin, Branch Henderson Burgess], and died 20 Mar. 1971). Listed in the 1920 census with his father, and on the 20 June 1917 draft list of Cumberland Co. Served in Co. G, 119th Tennessee Infantry, during World War I. Mike Burgess was a farmer in Cumberland Co. He died there on 13 July 1975, and is buried in the Davis Cemetery.

8a. **Trena Bell.** Born 21 Apr. 1921 in Cumberland Co., TN. Married Junior Thompson on 30 Jan. 1943 in Cumberland Co. Trena Thompson died there in Apr. 1979.
8b. **(Willie) Clarence.** Born 16 Sept. 1923 in Cumberland Co., TN. Married Betty Ozell Reagan. Clarence Burgess is a farmer in Cumberland Co., TN.

9a. **James Richard (V).** Born Oct. 1951 in Cumberland Co., TN. Married Beatrize Macias. James Burgess is a government accountant at Huntsville, AL.

10a. **Darren Lee** (twin). Born 3 Dec. 1971 in AZ.
10b. **Darlene** (nmn) (twin). Born 3 Dec. 1971 in AZ.

9b. **Shirley Ann (V).** Born 18 Sept. 1953 in Cumberland Co., TN. Married Jackie Lee Simmons on 4 Feb. 1972 in Cumberland Co. (he was born 9 May 1958); married secondly Timothy Ross Sherrill on 24 Mar. 1984 in Cumberland Co.

8c. **Della Marie.** Born 20 Nov. 1924 in Cumberland Co., TN. Married Clarence Dunbar. Della Dunbar works on the staff of the Cumberland Medical Center, Crossville, TN.
8d. **Rhoda Jane.** Born 14 June 1933 in Cumberland Co., TN. Married William O'Neill Arnold Fin(d)ley on 6 June 1952 in Cumberland Co.

KING HIRAM BURGESS II OF CUMBERLAND CO., TENNESSEE
[Jasper Patrick Dillard[6]]

7f. **King Hiram (II)** *[son of Jasper Patrick Dillard].* Born 12 Sept. 1896 in Cumberland Co., TN. Married Matilda May "Tildy" Campbell on 28 May 1916 in Cumberland Co. (she was born 18 Feb. 1896, daughter of Daniel Jasper Lavander Campbell and Vestina Cathrine Amy Jane "Tina" Hale, and a niece of Washington Columbus Campbell, and lives at Crossville). Listed in the 1920 census for Cumberland Co., TN. King Burgess was a farmer in Cumberland Co. He died there on 27 Dec. 1980, and is buried in the Burgess Cemetery.

8a. **Lula Mae** (twin). Born 19 Nov. 1916 in Cumberland Co., TN. Married Baxter Hale, and had children: *Dallas Roy* (twin); *Alice Joy* (twin; died at age three); *Bettie Katherine*. Living in Philadelphia in 1941. Lula Hale currently lives at Crossville, TN.
8b. **Lola Belle** (twin). Born 19 Nov. 1916 in Cumberland Co., TN; died there on 6 Feb. 1917, and is buried in the Thomas Springs Cemetery.

8c. **(Jay) Lee.** He is usually called J. Lee Burgess in early newspaper accounts. Born 19 May 1919 in Cumberland Co., TN. Married (Mary) Elizabeth Brewer on 9 Aug. 1938 in Cumberland Co. (she was born 16 Oct. 1922, sister of Mozella Brewer, and died 12 Mar. 1984). Listed in the 1940 draft list of Cumberland Co. Jay Lee Burgess worked as a quality control inspector for the Ford Motor Co. at Elyria, OH. He drowned there when his car went off the road into the Black River, on 13 (or 12) June 1971. He and his wife are buried in the Akins Cemetery, Cumberland Co., TN.

9a. **JoAnn (I)** (nmn). Her name is also spelled Joann. Born 14 July 1939 in Cumberland Co., OH. Married (David) Neal Dyer on 16 Oct. 1954 in Cumberland Co.; married secondly Farrell Mustard. JoAnn Mustard lives at Vanceburg, Lewis Co., KY.

9b. **Wanda Jean.** Born 19 June 1941 in Cumberland Co., OH. Married David Coward. Wanda Coward lives in Lorain Co., OH.

9c. **Joyce** (nmn). Born 3 July 1942 in Cumberland Co., TN; died there on 28 July 1942, and is buried in the Akins Cemetery.

9d. **Bonnie Lee.** Born 12 Aug. 1944 in Cumberland Co., TN. Married Robert "Bob" Koviak (or Kovack). Bonnie Koviak lives in Lorain Co., OH.

9e. **(James) Richard (III) "Rickie."** Born 20 Jan. 1947 in Cumberland Co., TN. Rickie Burgess has been a sawmill worker, air conditioner repairman, construction worker, and welder. He currently lives in Cumberland Co., TN.

10a. **Rickie.** Born about 1970 in Cumberland Co., TN.

10b. **Sheila (II).** Born about 1973 in Cumberland Co., TN.

9f. **Dexter Paul.** Born 14 Jan. 1953 in Cumberland Co., TN. Married Sheryl Jalowick. Dexter Burgess is a screw machine operator at Elyria, Lorain Co., OH.

10a. **Michael Paul.** Born 9 Aug. 1977 at Elyria, OH.

10b. **Tracey Ann.** Born 6 June 1980 at Elyria, OH.

8d. **(James) Wesley (I).** Born 18 Mar. 1921 in Cumberland Co., TN. Married Zella Anne C___ about 1946 (div.); married secondly Oda Byrd. Served in World War II. Wesley Burgess is a carpenter in Cumberland Co., TN.

9a. **Shirley Ann (IV).** Born 12 Feb. 1946 at Manchester, KY. Married Everett Lee "Junior" Bowen Jr. on 7 Nov. 1964 in Cumberland Co.

9b. **Ronnie Lee (II).** Born 28 Apr. 1948 at Dayton, OH. Married Barbara ___. Served in the U.S. Army. Ronnie Burgess is a stucco plastering contractor at Stuart, Martin Co., FL.

9c. **Wilma Jean.** Born 8 Jan. 1950 in Cumberland Co., TN. Married Gary Alton Beaty on 29 Aug. 1970 in Cumberland Co.

9d. **Carrol** (nmn). Her marriage record spells her name Carol. Born 11 Nov. 1952 in Cumberland Co., TN. Married James Edward Hyder on 22 Dec. 1970 in Cumberland Co.; married secondly Tom Hurley.

8e. **(Ruby) Imagene "Jean."** Her name is often spelled Imogene in early records. Born 18 June 1924 in Cumberland Co., TN. Married Tony Basso, and had children: *Jimmy*; *Joseph "Joey"* (drowned at age 22 in Florida). Jean Basso died Nov. 1976 at Warren, Trumbull Co., OH.

[William (I)[1], Edward (I)[2], Reuben (I)[3], Thomas (I)[4], King Hiram (I)[5]]

CHARLES WILLIAM BURGESS
(1863-1910)

OF CUMBERLAND COUNTY, TENNESSEE

6l. **Charles William (I) "Charlie"** *[son of King Hiram (I)].* Born 10 Feb. 1863 in Cumberland Co., TN. Married (Martha) Ann Hale about 1884 (she was born 23 Sept. 1867 in TN, daughter of Isham Hale and Mary [Fryer or Norris?], remarried Bigah DeBo[a]rd on 24 Sept. 1916 in Bledsoe Co., and died 12 Feb. 1945 at Crossville). Listed in the 1900 census for Cumberland Co. Charlie Burgess was a farmer in Cumberland Co. He was shot and killed on 23 Feb. 1910, allegedly by his brother-in-law, John Wyatt Campbell (who, although convicted, was not popularly believed to have committed the act), and is buried in the Old Burgess Cemetery. Martha is listed as head of the family in the 1910 census for Cumberland Co.; five of six children survive in 1900, nine of ten in 1910. The dates of birth of their children are taken from the surviving family Bible record.

CHARLES BURGESS MURDERED

"Last Saturday afternoon our little town was thrown into a great state of excitement by the report that the body of Charles Burgess of the 3rd District, who had been missing from home since Wednesday, had been found, and that all indications pointed toward murder. The coroner immediately responded, and he, with a number of other citizens, went to the place of the supposed crime. On arrival there a jury of inquest had already taken charge of the body, and were examining witnesses. Dr. E. W. Mitchell, assisted by Dr. F. J. Upham, made an examination of the body, which showed that the deceased had been shot twice, once in the back just above the right hip bone, the ball coming out in front; the other ball entered the back of the head, and came out about one and one-half inches from where it entered. The jury were of the opinion that the last named ball was the one which was fired last, and which did not go through the skull, but struck it with such force that it broke both plates of the skull and doubtless caused instant death, since no signs of struggle were visible. After a long and tedious examination of witnesses, the jury agreed on a verdict, and on the strength of that verdict John Campbell was placed under arrest. The preliminary hearing was had on Tuesday, Esq. Harry Martin presiding. The evidence showed that on the day Burgess disappeared Campbell was seen to go in the same direction the deceased had gone, only a short time before, that two shots were heard in that direction early in the morning, that Campbell and Burgess had had some unpleasantness the Monday previous, in which they were both more or less to blame, and that so far as the witnesses examined knew, no other person in that vicinity had any ill will toward the deceased. Esquire Martin held that it was evident to his mind that crime had been committed, that the chain of circumstantial evidence which the State had attempted to make, was broken, but that he felt Mr. Campbell should be held to wait the action of the Grand Jury, and fixed the amount of his bond at $5,000. Mr. Campbell and Mr. Burgess, the deceased, were brothers-in-law, and farmers, who lived near one another, and the evidence failed to show any threats ever made by Mr. Campbell against the life of the deceased."—*Crossville Chronicle*, 4 Mar. 1910.

The Children of Charlie Burgess:

7a. **Riley Lynville.** Born 31 May 1885 in Cumberland Co., TN. Married Nettie Gentry. Riley Burgess was a farmer near Crossville, TN. He died there childless on 2 Jan. (or Feb.) 1962, and is buried in the Old Burgess Cemetery, believed to be the last person interred there.

7b. **Eva Levenia.** Born 13 Jan. 1887 in Cumberland Co., TN. Married James Hall about 1902 (he was born 4 July 1880, and died 24 Jan. 1955), and had children:

Arthur HALL. Born 31 July 1903, married Alice Wright (dec.).

Ethel Berniece HALL. Born 4 Oct. 1907, married (William) Elvie Hamby on 25 Dec. 1935 (he was born 25 June 1907, and died 29 Oct. 1979), and had children: *Sybil Irene* (born 11 Jan.

1937, married Carl E. Taylor, and had children: Julie Anita [born 28 Apr. 1959; she currently works as a registered nurse at Tampa, FL]; (Eva) Lynn [born 12 Jan. 1961, married (John) Mark Roberts {he was born 11 Oct. 1962}, and had children: Jackson Cody {born 3 Oct. 1991}; they live at Lake Tansi, Cumberland Co., TN]; Charlotte Carlene [born 22 Jan. 1971, currently a student at Tennessee Technological University]; Sybil Taylor lives at Crossville, TN); *Betty Ruth* (born 23 Apr. 1939, married Glen Richard Williams on 20 Apr. 1957 [he was born 26 Oct. 1931], and had children: Linda Melissa [born 26 Sept. 1964, married Brett Masters {he was born 9 July 1962}, and had children: Jacob Corey {born 21 Jan. 1987}; Kaitlea Taylor {born 22 Oct. 1990}]; Betty Williams lives at Cookeville, TN).

***Annie* HALL.** Born 16 Apr. 1910, died about 1912 at age two when she accidentally drowned.

***Roy* HALL.** Born 11 July 1915, married Ethel ___, and died 13 June 1949, buried Crossville City Cemetery.

***Homer Henry* HALL.** Born 27 Jan. 1919, married Aileen Garrett, and had five children. Homer Hall died on 31 July 1993, and is buried in the Crossville City Cemetery.

Eva HALL died on 8 Mar. 1974 in Cumberland Co., and is buried in the Crossville City Cemetery.

7c. **Myrtle Lilly.** Born 13 Oct. 1888 in Cumberland Co., TN. Married Charles Monroe Wells on 31 Jan. 1906 in Cumberland Co. (he was born 16 Apr. 1873, brother of Noah Wells [who married her sister, Chloe], and died on 31 Dec. 1928), and had children:

***Willie David* WELLS.** Born 4 Aug. 1907, married Carrie Dodson (dec.), and had children: *Lula Faye* (married Kenneth Carey; dec.); *(Luther) William "Bill"* (born 18 Aug. 1939, married Linda Moseley [she was born 20 Oct. 1949], and had children: Vanessa [born 20 Dec. 1969, married Bobby Allred {he was born 4 Jan. 1966}]); *Bobby Joe*. ***Willie* WELLS** died on 15 Aug. 1985.

***Laura Frances* WELLS.** Born 11 Apr. 1909 at Crossville, TN, married Carrie Dine Caudill on 4 Apr. 1926 at Crossville, TN (he was born 23 Apr. 1904 at Cedar Bluff, Tazewell Co., VA, and died on 5 Feb. 1975 at Sheffield, Colbert Co., AL), and died on 20 Jan. 1978 at Cookeville, TN, being buried with her husband in the Barton Cemetery, Barton, AL. They had children:

James Leon CAUDILL (born 12 Feb. 1927 at Crossville, TN, married Billie Rachle Turnage on 1 Sept. 1956 at Meridian, MS [she was born 16 Oct. 1929 at Chunky, MS], and had children: James Leon Jr. [born 19 Nov. 1957 at Huntsville, AL]; Leland Curtis [born 3 Oct. 1959 at Huntsville, AL, married Teresa Louise Kriedman on 16 June 1979 at Meridian, MS {born 4 Feb. 1959 at Fort Atkinson, WI}, and had children: Terry Lou {born 15 Dec. 1980 at Meridian, MS}; Rita Marie {born 11 Aug. 1983 at Meridian, MS}]; Rachle Ann [born 9 Dec. 1961 at Meridian, MS, married Gary Don Williams on 1 Sept. 1987 at Meridian {born 3 May 1961 at Amarillo, TX}]; John Allen [born 19 Oct. 1964 at Meridian, MS]).

Walter Ray CAUDILL (born 23 Nov. 1930 at Crossville, TN, married Doris Celestine Johnson on 31 Aug. 1951 at Iuka, MS [she was born 17 Oct. 1933 at Florence, AL], and had children: Brent Allen [twin; born 17 Apr. 1966 at South Bend, IN]; Kent Ray [twin; born 17 Apr. 1966 at South Bend, IN]. Walter Caudill died on 26 Mar. 1991 at South Bend, IN, and is buried at Florence, AL).

Floyd Donald CAUDILL (born 17 Feb. 1933 at Crossville, TN, died 10 June 1933).

Barbara Aliene CAUDILL (born 21 Aug. 1934 at Crossville, TN, married Robert Edward Bullion Jr. [he was born 7 Apr. 1935 at Sheffield, AL], and had children: Ronald Edward [twin; born 31 May 1954 at Sheffield, AL, married Judith Lynn Goins on 1 Sept. 1973 at Tuscumbia, AL {div.}, and had children: Brentley Jay {born 7 June 1977 at Sheffield, AL}; married secondly Sandy ___]; Donald Ray [twin; born 31 May 1954 at Sheffield, AL, married Janet Leigh Kimbrough on 21 Aug. 1972, and had children: Tonya Michelle {born 23 Aug. 1974 at Sheffield, AL, and had children: Brianna Leigh <born 23 Aug. 1990>}; Heather Rochelle {born 16 July 1976 at Sheffield, AL}; married secondly Kay ___ on 27 Mar. 1991]; Sharon Darlene [born 8 Aug. 1956 at Sheffield, AL, married Kenith Michael Vaden on 24 Jan. 1975 at Sheffield, AL {born 10 Feb. 1952 at Florence, AL}, and had children: Kenith Michael Jr. {born 9 Sept. 1976 at Sheffield, AL}; Christopher James {born 20 May 1980 at Florence, AL}]).

Luther Wallace "Buster" CAUDILL (born 12 Nov. 1935 at Crossville, TN).

Billy Norman CAUDILL (born 3 Apr. 1939 at Pleasant Hill, TN, married Bobbie Cornett on 13 Sept. 1963 at Sheffield, AL [she was born 9 Dec. 1938 at Atmore, AL], and had children: Bethany Carol [born 13 Feb. 1965 at Florence, AL, married Danny Ray Ridgeway on 30 Sept. 1989 at Sheffield, AL {born 19 Feb. 1963 at Sheffield}, and had children: Madelyn Grace {born 11 Oct. 1991 at Florence, AL}]; Norman Shea [born 22 Sept. 1968 at Florence, AL]; Wesley Brad [born 30 Aug. 1970 at Florence, AL]).

Richard Lee ALSBROOK (he uses the surname Alsbrook; born 22 Oct. 1941 at Tuscumbia, AL, married Patricia Perry on 11 Nov. 1962 at Tuscumbia, AL [born 22 Oct. 1941 at Tuscumbia], and had children: Ral Dion [born 14 Dec. 1963 at Russellville, AL, married Kimberly Diane Lamb on 6 June 1986 at Morristown, TN {born 28 Sept. 1965}, and had children: Jeremiah Riley {born 24 Apr. 1989 at Morristown, TN}; Jordan Dion {born 21 Dec. 1991 at Morristown, TN}]; Richard married secondly Virginia Ellen Waits on 15 May 1971 at Rockmart, GA [she was born 10 May 1939 at Taylorsville, GA], and had children: Teresena Leigh [born 16 Feb. 1972 at Rockmart, GA, married Mark Keith Collier on 15 Aug. 1992 at Rockmart {born 16 July 1971}]; Scotty Dewayne [born 27 Oct. 1982 at Rockmart, GA]).

Roger Keith CAUDILL (born 16 June 1954 at Tuscumbia, AL).

Thomas Warren WELLS. Born 14 Feb. 1911, married Verla Mae Bowen (she was born 5 Feb. 1921), and had children: *Shirley Ann* (born 12 Nov. 1951, married Floyd Welch). ***Thomas WELLS*** died on 14 May 1988.

Charles Edward WELLS. Born 6 July 1913, died unmarried on 5 May 1993.

Martha Rebecca WELLS. Born 27 Feb. 1915, married Andrew John Ciprian (he was born 11 Dec. 1917, and died 21 June 1966), and had children: *Gloria* (lives in California); *Joseph.*

Robert Lee WELLS. Born 22 Sept. 1917, married Edith Barns (she was born 11 July 1920), and had children: *Roger*; *Gordon*; *Milburn* (born 16 May 1941). ***Robert WELLS*** died on 1 Dec. 1980 in Florida.

Mary Elizabeth WELLS. Born 17 Oct. 1919, married Ernest Harper (he died 18 Aug. 1981), and had children: *Margie Lee*; *William Mitchell.* Mary died on 25 Dec. 1989.

Edna Lucille WELLS. Born 24 Apr. 1923, married A. B. "Alvin" Atkins Jr. (he was born 22 Apr. 1921), and had children: *Lawrence Alvin* (born 24 Sept. 1947, married Cathy Franz, and had children: Stephen Lawrence [born 10 June 1985]; Lauren Elizabeth [born 21 Nov. 1988]); *Ronald Edward* (born 9 Jan. 1950, married Sandra Hyder, had children: Kimberly Ann [born 2 Jan. 1974], and died 1 Mar. 1983). ***Edna ATKINS*** currently lives at Cookeville, TN.

Nathaniel WELLS. Born and died 12 Jan. 1925.

George Gideon WELLS. Born 24 Dec. 1926, married Maude Gist (she died 9 July 1991), and had children: *Steven* (lives at Knoxville, TN); *Kim* (son); *Connie* (married Danny Morgan, and had children: Kevin).

Myrtle WELLS died on 8 Jan. 1930 in Cumberland Co., and is buried in the Crossville City Cemetery.

7d. **Chloe Blanche.** Born 3 Sept. 1891 (or 1890) in Cumberland Co., TN. Married Noah Wells on 13 Feb. 1909 in Cumberland Co. (he was born 12 Oct. 1875, brother of Charles M. Wells [who married her sister Myrtle], and died 4 Dec. 1958), and had children:

(Lola) Evelyn "Eva" WELLS. Born 2 Feb. 1910, married Paul B. Turner on 23 June 1929 (he was born 19 Nov. 1907), and had children: *Marie* (married Dexter Phillips, and had children: Lorina; Calvin; Paul David); *Lloyd* (married Ellen Norris, and had children: Barbara); *Elene* (married William Brown, and had children: Linda Carroll [born 17 Jan. 1963, married ___ Reppert, and had children: Marlana Diana {born 19 Oct. 1989}; Stacy Renee {born 10 Dec. 1991}]); *Florence Rebecca* (born 21 Dec. 1936, married Frank D. Sevier, and had children: Kimberly [born 4 Jan. 1977]; Christopher); *Jean* (born 10 Jan. 1938, married John H. Jestice [born 5 May 1937], and had children: Betty Jean [born 26 June 1958, married (Ancil) Clay Sitton {born 4 Aug. 1959}, and had children: Jonathan Marshall {born 27 Sept. 1976}; Benjamin Adam {born 5 Oct. 1977}]; John H. Jr. [born 21 July 1961, married Joann ___ {born 17 June 1964}, and had children: Katrisha {born 23 Sept. 1982}; Olyvia {twin; born 29 Dec. 1983}; Tanya {twin; born 29 Dec. 1983}]); *Lou Ella* (born 9 Sept. 1941, married Robert C. Kemmer, and had children: Jill [born 15 Aug. 1975]; Robert Allen [born 1 July 1986]; Mary Beth [born 18 Jan. 1988]); *Katherine* (born 11 Aug. 1943, married Donald Myers, and had two daughters); *Noah Ervin* (married Margie Howard, and had children: Noah Ervin Jr.; two daughters); *Roy*; *Vivian.* ***Eva TURNER*** died on 26 Oct. 1968, and is buried in the Turner Cemetery.

Nannie Elizabeth WELLS. Born 16 Nov. 1911, married (Ernest) Hatton Gentry on 11 May 1930, and had children: *Elmer* (born 28 Aug. 1935, married Daisy Smith, and had children: Angela); *James* (married Elizabeth Tabor, and had children: Debbie; Juanetta; Donald); *Ernest* (born 28 Aug. 1943, died 4 Feb. 1961, buried with his parents); *Linda* (married Raymond Smith, and had children: Tressa [ad., buried Never Fail Cemetery]; Daniel C.; Darlene). ***Nannie GENTRY*** died on 19 Feb. 1982 at Crossville, TN, buried Tolletts Chapel Cemetery.

Allen Eugene WELLS. Born 24 May 1914, married Mary Ellen Pace on 29 Apr. 1939 (she was born 4 Apr. 1918), and had children: *Joyce Anita* (born 10 Mar. 1940, married David Willis Chadwell on 9 June 1961 at Crossville, TN [he was born 3 June 1940, began his ministry at the age of fourteen, spent four years as a missionary in Africa, and currently is a minister for the Church of Christ at Oxford, MS], works as a school and Bible teacher, and had children: John Willis [born 24 Mar. 1963 at Tallahassee, FL, married Sherri Chapman {she was born 30 June 1963 in AR}, works as a minister for the Church of Christ, and had children: Calli {born 18 June 1985 at Searcy, AR}; Jordan Allen {born 29 Apr. 1987 at Myrtle, MS}]; Kevin Lynn [born 26 Sept. 1965 at Senatobia, MS, married Linda Elizabeth Collins on 6 June 1987 {she was born 29 May 1964 at Memphis, TN}, and had children: Caroline Elizabeth {twin; born 31 Dec. 1993}; Taylor Kevin {twin; born 31 Dec. 1993}; Kevin Chadwell works as a CPA with Ernest and Young Associates; Linda is a school teacher at Memphis, TN]; Anita Kay [born 2 July 1968 at Senatobia, MS, married Mark Stephen Beshire on 3 Aug. 1990 at Senatobia, MS {born 5 July 1968}; Anita manages a printing company and Mark is a musician at Little Rock, AR]); *Jerry Eugene* (born 12 Oct. 1942, married Thelma Denise ___ on 18 May 1968 [born 29 July 1943]), and serves as president of Glenwood Convalescent Hospital at Oxnard, CA; Thelma works as a real estate broker). ***Allen WELLS*** was a salesman for L. P. Shanks Wholesale Grocery, before retiring from that company after forty-six years. He currently lives at Crossville, TN.

Cordell WELLS. Born 13 Apr. 1917, died 3 Mar. 1923.

Dorthy WELLS. Born 3 Sept. 1919, died 8 Oct. 1919.

Ernest Hatton WELLS. Born 1 Aug. 1921, married Signa Faye Stinnett on 15 Dec. 1954 at Arlington, VA, and had children: *David Allen* (born and died at Huntsville, AL, buried Crossville City Cemetery); *William Ernest* (born 23 June 1958, and lives at Maryville, TN); *Ronald Eston* (born 4 June 1959, married Muriel Kirkpatrick [born 18 June 1962], and had children: Eric [born 9 Sept. 1980]; Lindsey [born 15 Apr. 1981]); *Laurence R.* (born 29 Jan. 1966, lives at Maryville, TN). ***Ernest WELLS*** had a long and successful career as an electronics engineer with NASA, including project engineer on several of the early Redstone rocket firings, before retiring. He currently lives at Huntsville, AL.

Paul Faxon WELLS. Born 8 Mar. 1924, died 27 Apr. 1925.

(Helen) Louise WELLS. Born 23 Aug. 1926, married Lynn Eugene Carson on 16 Dec. 1950 (he was born 4 Mar. 1921), and had children: *Linda Lou* (born 11 Jan. 1955, married Larry Conatser [div.], and had children: Bryan [born 19 Sept. 1974]; Carola [born 4 Apr. 1976]; Linda married secondly Larry Mondy [he was born 18 Feb. 1943]); *Lynn Eugene Jr.* (born 27 July 1956, married Darlene Pugh [born 24 Oct. 1959], and had children: Jeremy [born 16 July 1978]; Destiny [born 5 June 1982]); *Laura Ann* (born 20 Mar. 1959, married Bobby Allen Brooks [born 13 May 1943], and had children: Michael Allen). ***Louise and Lynn CARSON*** are both retired from the Cumberland County school system.

Moses WELLS (nmn). Born 13 June 1931, married Ruby O. Kerley on 7 Nov. 1955, and had children: *Randall Lee* (born 8 June 1956, married Darlene Massengill [born 2 May 1959], and lives at Knoxville, TN); *Danny Joe* (born 20 Aug. 1959, married Nancy Woody [born 4 Sept. 1961], and had children: Philip Allen [born 10 Sept. 1990]; Jessica Ruth [born 31 July 1993]); *Gary* (born 23 Oct. 1963, married Jodi Stoner). ***Moses WELLS*** died on 14 June 1977.

Margaret Alice WELLS. Born 19 Feb. 1934, died 12 May 1936, buried Crossville City Cemetery.

Chloe WELLS died on 23 Feb. 1973 in Cumberland Co., and is buried in the Crossville City Cemetery. Her son, ***Allen WELLS***, currently lives in Cumberland Co., and has contributed greatly to this book.

7e. **Steve Henry.** Born 17 Aug. 1893 in Cumberland Co., TN. See below for full entry.

7f. **Venis** (son). Born 15 Mar. (or May) 1895 in Cumberland Co., TN; he drowned there (murdered) on 19 Aug. 1897, and is buried in the Burgess Cemetery.

7g. **(Louise) Amanda "Mandy."** Born 12 May 1897 in Cumberland Co., TN. Married her first cousin, once removed, Lawson Burgess, on 6 June 1914 in Cumberland Co. (he was born 20 Mar. 1890, and died 2 Oct. 1973). Mandy Burgess was a member of the Baptist Church. She died childless on 16 Sept. 1988, aged 91 years, at Crossville, TN, and is buried in the Burgess Cemetery. Clyde Burgess recalled (1994) that Mandy took him hunting for game birds when he was a young boy in the woods in rural Cumberland Co.

7h. **Canzada** (nmn). Born 8 Nov. 1900 in Cumberland Co., TN. Married James Elliott Reece on 24 Sept. 1916 in Cumberland Co. (he was born 4 Feb. 1887, son of Henry and Elizabeth Reece, and died 16 Apr. 1974), and had children: *Ina Macie* (born 15 July 1919, died 20 Dec. 1920); *Charles Henry* (born 15 Apr. 1921, died May 1991); *James Venable "Bud"* (born 23 July 1923, married Ruby Hitchcock, and secondly Ila Ree Sherrell, and died Oct. 1992); *Mattie Mae* (born 14 Aug. 1926, married James Richard Miller); *Gladys Novella* (born 10 Apr. 1930, married Dan Marvin Hale on 17 Aug. 1976 at Marietta, GA, and lives at Crossville); *Daisy Arleva* (born 24 Sept. 1934, married George Fellowes, and lives in Wisconsin); *Evelyn Bernice* (born 21 Dec. 1936, married Howard Litchford, and lives at Knoxville, TN). Canzada Reece died on 17 June 1980, and is buried in the Thomas Springs Cemetery.

7i. **(James) Ernest.** His name was also spelled Earnest. Born 31 July 1903 in Cumberland Co., TN. Married Lula Mae Stuhl (she was born 1922). Earnest Burgess was a farmer at Vandever, TN. He died there childless on 9 Apr. 1965, and is buried in the Burgess Cemetery. Lula Burgess lives at Athens, FL.

STEVE BURGESS OF SULLIVAN CO., TENNESSEE
[Charles William (I)[6]]

7e. **Steve Henry** *[son of Charles William (I)]*. Born 17 Aug. 1893 in Cumberland Co., TN. Married Mae Bradley on 28 Mar. 1914 in Cumberland Co. (she was the daughter of James H. Bradley and Margaret Elizabeth Houlette, and sister of Dora Bradley [who married Steve's cousin, Oliver Estille Burgess]). Listed in the 20 June 1917 draft list of Cumberland Co. Steve Burgess was a miner, farmer, logger, and dairyman in Cumberland and Sullivan Cos., TN before retiring. He died on 18 Aug. 1991 at Kingsport, TN, aged 98 years, the oldest Burgess male in the direct line, and was buried in the Holston View Cemetery. Mae Burgess lives at Kingsport, TN.

8a. **Son.** Born and died about 1915 in Cumberland Co., TN.
8b. **(James) Dalton.** Born 29 Jan. 1916 in Cumberland Co., TN. Married Pansy Culbertson. Dalton Burgess was a truck driver for the State of Virginia. He died on 29 Nov. 1988 at Gate City, VA.

9a. **Bobby Joe (I).** Born 17 Jan. 1936 (or 1937, according to Social Security records) at Kingsport, TN. Married Betty Jo Kimball; married secondly Eleanor Lockhart. Bobby Burgess was a construction worker at Gate City, VA. He died there in a car accident on 13 June 1974.

10a. **Bobby Joe (III).** Born 9 June 1955 at Kingsport, TN. Married Martha Patricia Coley. Bobby Burgess lives at Kingsport, TN.

11a. **Holly Lynn.** Born 17 Apr. 1982 at Kingsport, TN.
11b. **Twin.**
11c. **Twin.**

10b. **(Juanita) Jan.** Born 27 Oct. 1958 at Indianapolis, IN. Married Joe Lawson.

9b. **Judy Annette.** Born 12 Aug. 1940 at Gate City, VA. Married Harry Lee Oliver.
9c. **(Peggy) Jean.** Born 9 Aug. 1941 at Kingsport, TN. Franklin D. Fraley. Jean Fraley lives at Cicero, IN.

8c. **(Cecile) Marie.** Born 19 Feb. 1918 in Cumberland Co., TN. Married Willie L. Dougherty. Marie Dougherty lives at Nicholsville, VA.
8d. **Marjory Kathleen.** Born 16 July 1920 in Cumberland Co., TN. Married J. M. Covertson. Marjory Covertson lives at Yuma, VA.
8e. **Hillis Lee.** Born 5 Dec. 1922 in Cumberland Co., TN. Married Flora Drucilla Stapleton. Hillis Burgess was a book and periodical binder for the California State Printing Office, Sacramento, CA, and the Government Printing Office, Washington, DC. He died 1 Oct. 1983 at Kingsport, TN, and is buried in the Holtston View Cemetery, Gate City, VA. Flora Burgess lives at Kingsport, TN.

9a. **Randall Lee.** Born 15 Mar. 1956 at Kingsport, TN. Married Jennie Masalini. Randy Burgess works for the U.S. Forest Service at Mt. Gilead, NC.

8f. **Beecher Ernest.** Born 9 May 1925 in Cumberland Co., TN. Married Lou Suite. Beecher Burgess works for a paper mill at Kingsport, TN.

9a. **Linda Carol.** Born and died 27 Apr. 1947 at Kingsport, TN.

8g. **Robert Earl.** Born 23 Feb. 1927 in Cumberland Co., TN; died there in Apr. 1927.
8h. **Billie Jack.** Born Mar. 1931 in Cumberland Co., TN; died there in July 1931.

[William (I)[1], Edward (I)[2], Reuben (I)[3], Thomas (I)[4], King Hiram (I)[5]]

FATE BURGESS
(1867-1928)
OF CUMBERLAND COUNTY, TENNESSEE

6n. **(Richard) Lafayette "Fate"** *[son of King Hiram (I)].* Born 12 July 1867 (or 1865, according to his death certificate) in Cumberland Co., TN. Married Martha Ann Katherine Moyers (or Myers) on 19 July 1888 (or 1887, according to his Bible record; however, the former date is confirmed from a contemporaneous newspaper account) at her parents' home in Bledsoe Co. (she was born 19 Nov. 1872 in TN, daughter of George A. and [Suzannah] Arena Moyers, remarried Ebb Davis, and died 23 [or 22] Nov. 1964, aged 92 years, buried Davis Cemetery; her obituary states: "She was a midwife for many years, and the weather was never too bad for her to ride a mule or walk several miles to help the sick or deliver a new baby. She was also known for her beautiful handmade quilts. No one was ever turned away from her table at mealtime or put out in the cold when night came."). Listed in the 1900-20 censuses for Cumberland Co.; three of four children survive in 1900, four of five in 1910. Fate Burgess was a farmer in Cumberland Co., TN. He died there of pneumonia on 26 Jan. 1928 (his family Bible record states 1927, but the newspaper obituary appeared in 1928), and is buried in the Old Burgess Cemetery.

The Children of Fate Burgess:

7a. **James Harrison.** Born 11 July 1889 in Cumberland Co., TN. See below for full entry.
7b. **(Nancy Ann) Arrena "Ronnie."** Her name is also spelled Arriena. Born 24 Dec. 1892 in Cumberland Co., TN; died there on 16 Aug. 1897, and is buried in the Old Burgess Cemetery.
7c. **Fred McKinley.** Born 30 Sept. 1896 in Cumberland Co., TN. See below for full entry.
7d. **Lula Winnie.** Born 30 Apr. 1899 in Cumberland Co., TN. Married Dossie Harris Suggs on 22 Dec. 1917 in Cumberland Co. (he was born 10 Nov. 1895, and died 18 Mar. 1959), and had children: *Ruth Ann* (born 20 Mar. 1920); *Ruby* (born 18 July 1922); *Thomas Jefferson* (born 13 Sept. 1926, married Patricia Ann Robbins [she was born 1 Nov. 1945 at Chattanooga, TN, daughter of Vola Robbins, and died 17 Dec. 1989 at Crossville, TN, buried Lantana Cemetery], and had children: Kevin; Alvin); *Richard* (born 30 Oct. 1930, was killed in a plane crash on 26 Jan. 1950 while on active service in the Army); *Betty J.* Lula Suggs died on 1 Jan. 1980 in Cumberland Co., and is buried in the Lantana Cemetery.
7e. **Mennia Dell "Minnie."** Born 15 (or 4) Mar. 1902 in Cumberland Co., TN. Married Sam Wright on 14 Mar. 1930 in Cumberland Co. (he was born 22 Nov. 1894, and died 7 Aug. 1960), and had children: *Alma* (married Oliver Stone); *Burness* (married ___ Tollett); *Ruby*; *Dollie*; *Judy*. Minnie Wright died on 15 Sept. 1983 in Ohio, and is buried in the Davis Cemetery.
7f. **Martin Hiram Revis.** Born 9 Dec. 1912 in Cumberland Co., TN. See below for full entry.
7g. **(George) Alva.** Born 8 July 1914 in Cumberland Co., TN. See below for full entry.

JAMES H. BURGESS OF CUMBERLAND CO., TENNESSEE
[Richard Lafayette[6]]

7a. **James Harrison** *[son of Richard Lafayette].* Born 11 July 1889 (or 1888, according to his family Bible record) in Cumberland Co., TN. Married Lou Davis on 20 Mar. 1910 in Cumberland Co. (div.; she was born 17 Dec. 1886, daughter of C. D. Davis and Phronia Music, and died 19 Dec. 1967, buried Big Lick Cemetery); married secondly Willie Marie Owensby after 1930. Listed in the 20 June 1917 draft list of Cumberland Co., and in the 1910 census there. Jim Burgess was a farmer in Cumberland Co. He died on 7 Dec. 1960 at his home near Vandever, TN, and is buried in the Davis Cemetery. In addition to the children listed below, James and Lou Burgess had five unnamed infants who died young, and are buried together at the Music Cemetery, Big Lick, TN.

8a. **Silvester "Vester"** (nmn). Born 8 Jan. 1911 in Cumberland Co., TN. See below for full entry.
8b. **(James) Alfred.** Born 2 July 1912 in Cumberland Co., TN. See below for full entry.
8c. **(Hiram) Ell.** Born 21 Dec. 1914 in Cumberland Co., TN. See below for full entry.
8d. **Dora Elizabeth.** Born 15 June 1918 in Cumberland Co., TN. Married Ruben Davis on 3 May 1940 in Cumberland Co., and had children: *Tellas Clancy* (born 9 Mar. 1941, died 18 Nov. 1942); *David Edward* (born 3 May 1942, died Aug. 1942); *Marcella Louvena* (born 1 Feb. 1946, and had children: Sherie Marlene DAVIS [born 27 Oct. 1980]); *Mona Angelina* (born 17 Dec. 1948, married ___ Burke, and had children: Jason Roy [born 13 Aug. 1966]; Chester Jerome [born 18 May 1968]; Angela Edith [born 15 Nov. 1969]); *Melinda Elizabeth* (born and died 1951?); *Mollie Maxine* (born 1953?, and had children: Tasha Shandora DAVIS [born 8 Oct. 1981]); *Rodney Ruben* (born 29 May 1958). Dora Davis lives at Crossville, TN. She has contributed greatly to this book.
8e. **Uless "Dick"** (nmn). He is called Ulysses in his draft and other early records. Born 14 Apr. 1921 in Cumberland Co., TN. Listed in the 1940 draft list of Cumberland Co., and served in World War II. Uless Burgess was a farmer in Cumberland Co. He re-enlisted in Battalion A, 764th Field Artillery, U.S. Army, and was killed on 20 Aug. 1950 in a trucking accident at Dayton, Rhea Co., TN. He died unmarried, and is buried in the Big Lick Cemetery.
8f. **Ethel (IV)** (nmn). Born 3 Dec. 1923 in Cumberland Co., TN. Married William E. "Billy" Moles on 11 June 1949 at Dayton, OH (he was born 18 May 1926, and died Apr. 1975), and had children: *Karen* (married Michael Lakey [div.], and had children: Kristy; Brian; married secondly Mick Evans, and had children: Joey; Marc; Karen Evans lives at Dayton, OH). Ethel Moles lives at Dayton, OH.
8g. **Cora** (nmn). Born 29 Nov. 1928 in Cumberland Co., TN. Married Albert Edward Campbell on 12 June 1944 (he was born 24 June 1921, served in World War II, and was a construction worker before retiring), and had children:

Buster Lee CAMPBELL. Born 1 Feb. 1946 at Pleasant Hill, TN, married Olia Margaret "Molly" Martin on 23 Sept. 1967 (she was born 6 Feb. 1947 at Rockwood, TN), and had children: *Amy LeAnn* (born 17 Nov. 1970 at Nashville, TN); *Ivy LyNel* (born 11 June 1972 at Nashville, TN). Buster Campbell owns and operates the Short Stop Market at Crossville, TN, and also builds and sells homes in Cumberland Co.

Marvin Edward CAMPBELL. Born 16 Apr. 1954 at Crossville, TN, married Barbara Jean Dishman on 30 June 1979 (she was born 13 Aug. 1952 at Crossville, TN], and had children: *Marci Jean* (born 25 June 1984 at Crossville, TN); *Michael Edward* (born 16 Oct. 1987 at Crossville, TN). Marvin Campbell works as a rural letter carrier for the U.S. Postal Service in Cumberland Co., TN.

(Wilma) Jean CAMPBELL. Born 2 July 1955 at Crossville, TN, married James Allen Fitzgerald Jr. on 7 Apr. 1979 (he was born 30 Aug. 1954 at Memphis, TN, and works as a certified public accountant for Hospital Corporation of America), and had children: *William James III* (born 22 Apr. 1987 at Dunedin, FL); *Ian James* (born 18 Sept. 1991 at Nashville, TN). Jean Fitzgerald works as an audit supervisor for HCA, and lives at Franklin, TN.

Paul Dean CAMPBELL. Born 29 Nov. 1960 at Crossville, TN. Married Pamela Annell Bartlett on 30 Dec. 1990 (she was born 30 Apr. 1962 at Cookeville, TN), and had children: *Jacob Coby* (born 5 Sept. 1992). Pam Campbell is a nurse at Cookeville; Paul works as a manager for Atlantic Soft Drink Co., Cookeville, TN.

Carl David CAMPBELL. Born 9 Sept. 1962 at Crossville, TN, and works in construction at Columbus, OH.

Cora Burgess CAMPBELL lives at Crossville, TN; she has contributed greatly to this book.

VESTER BURGESS OF CUMBERLAND CO., TENNESSEE

[Richard Lafayette[6], James Harrison[7]]

8a. **Silvester "Vester"** (nmn) *[son of James Harrison].* Born 8 Jan. 1911 in Cumberland Co., TN. Married Rowena Brown on 1 Aug. 1942 in Cumberland Co. (she was born 2 June 1921 in Cumberland Co.). Vester Burgess was a farmer in Cumberland Co. He died on 4 Oct. 1985 at Crossville, TN, and is buried in the Big Lick Cemetery.

9a. **Hubert** (nmn). Born 28 Dec. 1934 in Cumberland Co., TN; died there on 10 Jan. 1936, and is buried in the Big Lick Cemetery.
9b. **Frances (IV)** (nmn). Born 30 Apr. 1943 in Cumberland Co., TN. Married Dorman Elmore, and had children: *(Frances) Darlene*; *Dorman Jr. "Junior"*; *Donna Sue*; *James Paul.*

9c. **Marvin** (nmn). Born 23 May 1945 in Cumberland Co., TN; died there on 24 June 1954, and is buried in the Big Lick Cemetery.

9d. **Betty (IV)** (nmn). Born 15 Nov. 1952 in Cumberland Co., TN. Married Earl Boyd Underwood on 11 Oct. 1972 (div. 1988; he was born 23 Feb. 195_], and had children: *Wallace Earl* (born 15 Jan. 1973 at Crossville, TN, married Stacy Ramsburg); *Elizabeth Ann* (born 30 Dec. 1974 at Crossville, married Greg Scott Walker on 13 Apr. 1991, and had children: Kayla LeAnn [born 30 Apr. 1991]; Kelsie Nicole [born 23 Oct. 1992]); *James Patrick* (born 27 Dec. 1975 at Crossville); *Kristy Lynn* (born 20 Feb. 1982 at Crossville); *Linda Gail* (born 19 Nov. 1984 at Crossville); *Michael Shane* (born 31 Dec. 1986 at Crossville). **Betty Burgess Underwood** married secondly Donny Lee Lawson on 13 Apr. 1991 in Bledsoe Co., TN, on the same day that her daughter was married (he was born 3 Feb. 1965 in Cumberland Co.). Betty Lawson currently lives in rural Cumberland Co., TN.

9e. **Toy** (nmn). Born 17 Apr. 1957 in Cumberland Co., TN. Married Elaine Lafollette Canning. Toy Burgess works in a lumber mill near Crossville, TN.

10a. **Toy Branson.** Born 11 Nov. 1981 in Cumberland Co., TN.
10b. **Kleya Shelaine.** Born 18 Aug. 1983 in Cumberland Co., TN.
10c. **Taylor Grant.** Born 12 Dec. 1985 in Cumberland Co., TN.

9f. **Ida (III)** (nmn). Born 14 Apr. 1959 in Cumberland Co., TN. Married Lake Thomas Angel on 14 Sept. 1980 in Bledsoe Co., TN (div.; he was the son of Gilbert and Mary Rose Angel), and had children: *Melissa Rose* (born 10 Feb. 1981); *Blake Thomas* (born 7 Mar. 1987). Ida Angel lives at Murfreesboro, TN.

ALFRED BURGESS OF MARION CO., TENNESSEE

[Richard Lafayette[6], James Harrison[7]]

8b. **(James) Alfred** *[son of James Harrison].* Born 2 July 1912 in Cumberland Co., TN. Married Lillie Mo Jane Dodson on 17 Feb. 1933 at Albany, KY (div. 1963; she was born 12 Sept. 1915 in Pickett Co., TN, and died 27 May 1986, buried Red Hill Cemetery, Whitwell, TN); married secondly Ruby Hale about 1965 (she was born 3 Nov. 1924, and died 12 Oct. 1982). Served in the U.S. Navy during World War II. Alfred Burgess worked as a molder for U.S. Pipe Co. at Chattanooga and Whitwell, TN, until retiring in 1973. He died of cancer on 11 Oct. 1975 at Nashville, TN, but is buried in the National Veterans Cemetery, Chattanooga, TN.

9a. **(James) Richard (II).** Born 8 July 1934 at Chattanooga, TN. Married Ruth Evelyn Gholston on 15 Mar. 1958 (she was born 1 Jan. 1940). Richard Burgess was a printer and carpenter before retiring. He currently lives at Ringgold, GA.

10a. **Cynthia Darlene "Cindy."** Born 2 Apr. 1961 at Chattanooga, TN. Married Craig Steven Fettinger (div.), and had children: *Stephen Richard* (born 29 Dec. 1977); married secondly Daniel "Danny" Land on 21 Mar. 1986.

10b. **Cherie Denise.** Born 7 Apr. 1965 at Chattanooga, TN. Married Calvin Land on 8 May 1987, and had children: *Alesia Nicole* (born 17 Mar. 1988). Cherie Land currently lives at Ringgold, GA.

9b. **Joseph Roscoe "Joe."** Born 18 Mar. 1940 at Chattanooga, TN. Married Shirley Lois White on 30 June 1961 (she was born 13 May 1941). Served in the U.S. Air Force. Joe Burgess currently works as a machinist for U.S. Pipe Co. at Chattanooga, TN. He resides at Whitwell, TN.

10a. **Debora Diana "Debbie."** Born 15 Nov. 1962 at Atwater, CA. Married Gary Miller in July 1982 (div.); married secondly Michael Allen Whitamore on 8 Apr. 1989 (he was born 10 Sept. 1963), and had children: *Michael Allen II* (born 10 Mar. 1994 at Chattanooga, TN).

10b. **David Duane.** Born 7 Dec. 1964 at Whitwell, TN. Married (Gloria) Ann Rheal on 14 Feb. 1988 (she was born 30 Nov. 1964). David Burgess works for the Wheland Co. at Chattanooga, TN; he lives at Whitwell, TN on the original homestead of his grandfather.

10c. **Joseph Keith "Joey."** Born 28 Jan. 1970 at Whitwell, TN.

9c. **Roy Franklin.** Born 10 Nov. 1941 at Chattanooga, TN. Married Betty Reynolds on 16 Nov. 1968 (div.); married secondly Joyce Ann Garnett Fletcher on 18 Dec. 1985 (she was born 17 Feb. 1945). Roy Burgess works as a crane operator for Agrico at Plant City, FL; they live at Lakeland, FL, and also have a home at Whitwell, TN.

10a. **Pricilla Anne "Prissy."** Born 27 Mar. 1970 at Lakeland, FL. Married Daniel Brice LaLonde on 25 Oct. 1986 (he was born 20 Jan. 1969), and had children: *Daniel Brice Jr.* (born 29 Jan. 1987 at Bartow, FL); *Bethany Anne* (born 2 Apr. 1989 at Lakeland, FL); *Katie Danielle* (born 15 Feb. 1994 at Lakeland, FL). Daniel LaLonde works as an electrician at Publix Warehouse, Lakeland, FL; they currently live at Lakeland, FL.

10b. **Mary Jane (VII).** Born 2 Jan. 1972 at Lakeland, FL. Married Michael Reid "Mike" Traviss on 16 May 1992 (he was born May 1966). Mary Traviss works in medical records at Watson Clinic, and Mike works at Shakespearin Car Detail, Winter Haven, FL.

9d. **Geneva Jane (I).** Born 26 July 1944 at Chattanooga, TN. Married (Thomas) Ras Cooley on 6 Jan. 1967 (he was born 29 Aug. 1945), and had children: *Janet Meshelle* (born 16 Nov. 1975 at Dunlap, TN); *Rachael Gail* (born 18 Dec. 1977 at Dunlap, TN). Geneva Cooley works in the Deli Department at Hales Supermarket, and Ras is a welder at Combustion Engineering Co., Chattanooga, TN. They currently live at Whitwell, TN on the original family plot.

9e. **(Wanda) Faye.** Born 10 Feb. 1947 at Whitwell, TN. Married Wiley Lou Ross Jr. on 16 May 1964, and had children: *Kurt Dwayne* (born 24 Feb. 1965, married Billie Marie Smith on 16 June 1984, and works as a truck mechanic); *Sandra Lynn* (born 14 May 1966, married Nick Shelton on 4 Oct. 1986, and had children: Child [due June 1994]; Sandra works as a medical assistant; Nick is a dentist and truck driver); *Kelly Deon* (born 18 May 1970, and works as a truck driver); *Kiff Djames* (born and died 7 Oct. 1978). Faye Ross is a secretary for a construction company at Jasper, TN. She currently lives at Victoria, TN. Faye Ross has contributed greatly to this book.

9f. **Lou Alice.** Born 11 Dec. 1949 at Whitwell, TN. Married Robert Carlton "Bobby" Renegar Jr. on 12 Sept. 1967 (he was born 8 Jan. 1948), and had children: *Daniel Brian* (born 3 Dec. 1972 at Miami, FL, currently attending college). Lou Renegar is a home child care provider, and Bobby is a police sergeant at the Cleveland, TN Police Department; they live at McDonald, TN.

9g. **Dorthy Juanita.** Born 23 Oct. 1951 at Whitwell, TN. Married Gene Roberts on 5 Apr. 1986. Dorthy Roberts was a secretary for twenty-one years at Central Soya Co., Chattanooga, TN before becoming a licensed practical nurse; Gene Roberts is an electrician. They currently live at Chattanooga, TN.

9h. **June Marie.** Born 27 Apr. 1960 at Whitwell, TN. Married Howard Alan Nicholas on 6 Apr. 1991 at Atlanta, GA (he was born 16 July 1969 at Bellville, IL), and had children: *Breanna Diane* (born 14 Feb. 1992 at Atlanta, GA); *Quinn Alan* (born 14 Aug. 1993 at Atlanta, GA). Howard Nicholas is a research specialist for Innotrac, with Bell South Mobility and Compass Research. June Burgess-Nicholas is an accountant, human resources director, and gospel singer; she has contributed greatly to this book. She currently lives at Stone Mountain, GA.

ELL BURGESS OF CUMBERLAND CO., TENNESSEE

[Richard Lafayette[6], James Harrison[7]]

8c. **(Hiram) Ell** *[son of James Harrison].* His name is also listed as "L." in some records; some family members state that "Ell" was his only name. Born 21 Dec. 1914 in Cumberland Co., TN. Married Irene Phyllis Bohannan (she was born 24 May 1929, and lives at Mayland, TN). Listed in the 1940 draft list of Cumberland Co. Ell Burgess was a coal miner and construction worker in Cumberland Co., TN. He died on 13 May 1976 at Crossville, TN, and is buried in the Big Lick Cemetery.

9a. **Pamela Elizabeth.** Born 26 Sept. 1953 at Crossville, TN. Married David Lee Fish on 22 Mar. 1969 in Cumberland Co. (he was born 26 Mar. 1949, and works as a plumber), and had children: *Tammy Darlene* (born 25 Feb. 1970 in Cumberland Co., married Greg Phillips); *David Lee Jr.* (born 6 Aug. 1971 in Cumberland Co.); *Kimberly* (born 1 Jan. 1974 in Cumberland Co.).

9b. **Billy Ray.** Born 26 Jan. 1956 at Crossville, TN. Married Shelia Kaye Durham on 14 Nov. 1973 in Cumberland Co. Billy Burgess works for Russell Stovers Candies at Cookeville, TN.

9c. **Kenneth Lynn.** Born 30 Oct. 1958 at Crossville, TN. Married (Dimple) Darlene Lance on 9 June 1983 in Cumberland Co. Kenneth Burgess was a construction worker in Cumberland Co. He was injured in an automobile accident on 12 June 1988, and now lives retired at Mayland, TN.

FRED McK. BURGESS OF CUMBERLAND CO., TENNESSEE

[Richard Lafayette[6]]

7c. **Fred McKinley** *[son of Richard Lafayette].* Born 30 Sept. 1896 in Cumberland Co., TN. Married Eliza Hamilton on 25 Aug. 1924 in Cumberland Co. (she was born 29 Apr. 1908, daughter of Robert Hamilton and Mary Lou Parks, and died of tuberculosis on 13 May 1937 in Bledsoe Co., buried Swafford Cemetery); married secondly Rosa Goad on 13 May 1944 in Cumberland Co. (div.; she remarried Webster A. Landers on 22 Sept. 1949). Fred Burgess was a laborer at Vandever, TN. He died there on 4 Nov. 1977, and is buried in the Davis Cemetery.

8a. **(Mary) Ruth (I).** Born about 1926 in Cumberland Co., TN. Married (Emerson) Bruce Brewer on 30 Mar. 1942 in Cumberland Co. Ruth Brewer lives at Cincinnati, OH.

8b. **Brown Lee.** He was named for Tennessee Senator J. Brown Lee; his birth record gives his name as Owen Lee Burgess. Born 1 Jan. 1928 (or 10 Jan., according to his birth record, or 10 Feb., according to the newspaper announcement of his birth) in Cumberland Co., TN. Brown Burgess is a rubber worker and farmer at Clifty, TN.

8c. **(Arnel) Willard.** He also used the name Willard Oliver Burgess. Born 9 Apr. 1931 in Cumberland Co., TN. Married Doris Jean Leach on 14 Aug. 1954 in Cumberland Co. (div.); married secondly Wanda Lewis; married thirdly Inez Inetha Crawford Haston on 28 Feb. 1976 in Cumberland Co. Willard Burgess worked for the Crossville Rubber Co. He died on 23 July 1988 at Crossville, TN, and is buried in the Davis Cemetery.

9a. **James Oliver.** Born May 1956 in Cumberland Co., TN. Married Jean Leachwelder (a registered nurse). James Burgess is a missionary in Honduras.

10a. **Donna** (ad.). Born about 1970 in TN.

10b. **William Benjamin.** Born 1 Jan. 1974 at Crossville, TN. Relationship not verified.

10c. **Christopher David.** Born 6 Oct. 1975 in Cumberland Co., TN.

9b. **Angela Kay.** Born 23 Oct. 1959 in Cumberland Co., TN. Married Phillip Richard Crumley on 26 Dec. 1987 in Cumberland Co. (he was born 22 May 1954). Angela Crumley lives at Crossville, TN.

9c. **Keith Arnel.** Born 20 Aug. 1966 in Cumberland Co., TN. Married Penny ___. Keith Burgess lives at Rickman, TN.

10a. **Joshua Keith.** Born 4 Nov. 1988 in Cumberland Co., TN.

9d. **Christopher Ray.** Born 30 Dec. 1971 at Crossville, TN. Chris Burgess lives at Cookeville, TN.

8d. **(Mauda) Mae.** Born 2 Jan. 1934 in Cumberland Co., TN. She was raised by Helen Wehrie and Zena Walker. Married Don Magelitz. Mae Magelitz lives at Manassas, VA.

MARK BURGESS OF CUMBERLAND CO., TENNESSEE

[Richard Lafayette^{6}]

7f. **Martin Hiram Revis "Mark"** *[son of Richard Lafayette].* Born 9 Dec. 1912 in Cumberland Co., TN. Married Lucille Walker on 6 Jan. 1935 in Cumberland Co. (she was born 28 Mar. 1919 in Cumberland Co.). Listed in the 1940 draft list of Cumberland Co. as Mark Armrevis. Mark Burgess was a farmer all of his life near Crossville. He now lives there retired.

8a. **(Earven) Buster.** Born 30 Nov. 1935 in Cumberland Co., TN; died there on 14 Dec. 1935, and is buried in the Davis Cemetery.

8b. **Carlos Franklin.** Born 2 Dec. 1936 in Cumberland Co., TN. Married Dortha Hale (she was born 28 May 1943). Carlos Burgess is a truck driver for Flowers Bakery. He lives at Vandever, TN.

9a. **(Carlos) Martin "Marty."** Born 8 Dec. 1967 at Vandever, TN. Marty Burgess died unmarried on 29 July 1986 in Cumberland Co., when his all-terrain vehicle crashed into a tree. He is buried in the Davis Cemetery.

9b. **Peggy Michelle.** Born 2 July 1972 at Vandever, TN. Peggy Burgess is a student at the University of Tennessee, Knoxville, TN.

8c. **(James) Hershell.** Born 3 Nov. 1938 in Cumberland Co., TN. Served in U.S. Army for two years. Married Donna Cox on 12 May 1990 in Bledsoe Co., TN (she was born 9 Apr. 1950). Hershell Burgess works for the Tennessee Valley Authority, at the Watts Bar Nuclear Power Plant, Spring City, TN.

9a. **Chelle.**

9b. **James Mark.** Born 3 May 1989 at Crossville, TN. He may be the last Burgess born of the ninth generation.

8d. **Floyd Stanley.** Born 10 Oct. 1940 in Cumberland Co., TN. Married Kathleen Christian on 16 Oct. 1964 (she was born 14 Sept. 1945). Served in the U.S. Air Force for four and one-half years. Floyd Burgess is a foreman for the Tennessee Valley Authority Central Shop, at Spring City, TN. He lives at Vandever, TN. Kathleen Burgess has contributed greatly to this book.

9a. **Charles Floyd "Chuck."** Born 10 Aug. 1967 at Vandever, TN. Married Kimberley Raye Stone on 14 June 1986 (div. 1988; she was born 22 Feb. 1969). Chuck Burgess earned a B.S. degree in civil engineering from Tennessee Technological University, Cookeville, TN. He now works as the Solid Waste Director for the Cumberland Co. government, and also serves in the Tennessee National Guard.

9b. **Lynn Dwayne.** Born 17 Sept. 1969 at Vandever, TN. Married Shannon Dawn Gentry on 7 Sept. 1992. Lynn Burgess served for four years with the 82nd Airborne Division, U.S. Army. He now works for the Dana Corp. at Crossville, TN.

10a. **Katilyn Michelle.** Born 8 Mar. 1993 at Crossville, TN.

9c. **LeAnn Tonia.** Born 5 June 1972 at Vandever, TN. Married Richard H. "Ricky" Bilbrey on 2 Dec. 1989, and had children: *Ashley Nicole* (born 2 May 1990).

8e. **Wilma Shirle(y).** Born 26 July 1948 at Vandever, TN; died there 23 Mar. 1949, and is buried in the Davis Cemetery.

ALVA BURGESS OF CUMBERLAND CO., TENNESSEE
[Richard Lafayette[6]]

7g. **(George) Alva** *[son of Richard Lafayette].* Born 8 July 1914 in Cumberland Co., TN. Married Minnie Alice Wyatt on 12 Nov. 1932 at Monticello, KY (div.; she was born 23 Oct. 1913, remarried Odell Dixon, and died 23 Dec. 1958 in Bledsoe Co., TN, buried Wyatt Cemetery); married secondly Katherine Burns about 1951 (she was born 1929). Listed in the 1940 draft register of Cumberland Co. Alva Burgess was a carpenter in Cumberland Co. He died there on 17 Nov. 1980, and is buried in the Green Acres Cemetery.

8a. **Bonzella "Bonnie"** (nmn). Born 20 (or 19) Feb. 1934 in Cumberland Co., TN. Married Robert Cook. Bonnie Cook is a registered nurse and nurse instructor at the Cumberland Medical Center, Crossville, TN.

8b. **David Lee (II).** Born 13 Aug. 1944 in Cumberland Co., TN. Married Barbara Lou Ogle on 7 Oct. 1963. David is a heavy equipment operator for United Turf at Powells Point, Currituck Co., NC.

9a. **Teresa Dianne.** Born 5 Apr. 1965 in Cumberland Co., TN. Twice married, and had children: *Brandon Leigh* (born 17 Dec. 1985 at Ft. Stewart, GA). Teresa is an administrative assistant at Coastland Realty, Currituck, NC.

8c. **Daniel Bruce.** Born 24 Apr. 1952 in Cumberland Co., TN. Married Phyllis Ralph. Dan Burgess is a maintenance man for the Pasquotank Co. School System, Elizabeth City, NC.

9a. **Scott Bruce.** Born about 1974 at Elizabeth City, NC.
9b. **Shelly Alice.** Born about 1977 at Elizabeth City, NC.
9c. **Stacy Dolores.** Born about 1980 at Elizabeth City, NC.

Burgess Marble Monument, Georgetown Cemetery, Georgetown, KY

UNRELATED BURGESSES

SLAVES

SURNAMES UNKNOWN

SPOUSES AND OTHERS

www.ingramcontent.com/pod-product-compliance
Lightning Source LLC
Chambersburg PA
CBHW080809280326
41926CB00091B/4110
* 9 7 8 0 8 9 3 7 0 4 7 9 7 *